Chinese Scholars on Inner Asia

Indiana University Uralic and Altaic Series
Edward J. Lazzerini, Editor
Volume 174

CHINESE SCHOLARS ON INNER ASIA

LUO Xin 羅新 Editor

Roger Covey Translation Editor

Indiana University

Sinor Research Institute for Inner Asian Studies

Bloomington, Indiana

2012

Library of Congress Control Number:
ISBN: 9780933070585

Printed in the United States of America

Dedicated to the memory of
Professor Denis Sinor (1916–2011)

CONTENTS

INTRODUCTION

Luo Xin 羅新

This collection of fifteen essays has been selected from a great many works by Chinese scholars who have researched the history of Inner Asia. Even so, we must first stress that although our selection took as its basis recommendations from a great many specialists, nonetheless this selection could not possibly avoid possessing a certain arbitrariness. And it also must be said that it is impossible to consider that these essays are the most brilliant and the most successful out of all of the research on Inner Asia by Chinese scholars. In reality, because of the limitations of our process and the limitations of our personal capabilities, we were not able to include much important research, either because the texts were too long (for example, many of the works of Yekemingghadai Irinchin 亦鄰真), or because our own understanding was insufficient – and therefore many essays were surely omitted by mistake. This is why we once again stress that it is impossible to use this selection to generalize about the entirety of research on Inner Asia by Chinese scholars.

However, the authors of these essays are certainly representative of Chinese historians researching Inner Asia. So, just as in the Chinese adage "by seeing one part one may know the whole," this selection of essays certainly, within limits, represents important points of interest, approaches, and achievements of Chinese scholars relative to research on Inner Asia. By reading this book's broad selection of essays, researchers in this same field in the English-speaking world who are not able to read Chinese may have their interest piqued, and may be inspired to go a step further in understanding Chinese work in this field. If so, this meets exactly the primary objective of the selectors and translators of this collection of essays.

As everyone knows, the most important sources for the history of Inner Asia are written in only a few languages, among which, even if Chinese is not the single most important, it is among the most important. For example, the Xiongnu 匈奴, the Wuhuan 烏桓, the Xianbei 鮮卑, and the Rouran 柔然 groups played a key role in the early historic period in Inner Asia. But, except for a limited amount of archeological information, for researching them we are only able to rely on the Chinese-language historical materials. Following the fifth century CE, historical materials begin to break through the limitation of solely being Chinese, and we have written materials in Sogdian, Turkish, Uyghur, Tibetan, Tangut, Nuzhen (Jurchen), Arabic, Persian, Mongolian, and Manchu, and well as Latin, Greek, French, and other Western languages. But, at the same time, even if we lay aside consideration of the quality of the historical materials, we still must note that the quantity of Chinese historical material is without a doubt the largest. Yet, the quality of Chinese historical material, in the end, strictly speaking, does not at all depend on these historical materials themselves, but rather, it depends on the users and interpreters of these Chinese sources. And continuously down to the present, the most important of those relatively well-able to use and interpret these Chinese historical materials are Chinese and Japanese researchers.

Western researchers often do not understand the quantity of Chinese historical materials available on Inner Asian history. Even Denis Sinor once asserted, in his famous book *Inner Asia: History, Civilization, Languages; A Syllabus*, "The entire Chinese material that deals with the Turks, who formed one of the most important empires of Central Eurasia and who were for some two hundred years the most dangerous enemies of the ruling dynasty, would not amount to more than two hundred and fifty printed pages, if it were put into western book form."[1] The basis for this conclusion was, perhaps, material from the translation of Liu Mau-tsai's 劉茂纔 book *Die chinesischen Nachrichten zur Geschichte der Ost-Türken (T'u-küe)*, which has been widely quoted in the West.[2] However, Liu Mao-tsai's collection was completely sloppy and arbitrary, and it mainly relied on the official histories. Many important historical materials, such as the *Comprehensive Mirror for Aid in Government* 資治通鑒 and others, were all neglected, and he further overlooked valuable material hidden in various kinds of collectanea and encyclopedias. In addition, many decades of work have unearthed a large amount of historical material in the form of stone carvings, which have provided precious information on the Turks. The Chinese scholar Wu Yugui 吴玉貴, in his book published not long ago, *Chinese-language Historical Materials on the Second Turkish Qaghanate Chronologically Compiled and Researched* 突厥第二汗國漢文史料編年輯考, gathers and arranges Chinese-

[1] Denis Sinor, *Inner Asia: History, Civilization, Languages; A Syllabus*, Uralic and Altaic Series, vol. 96 (Bloomington, Indiana, 1969), p. 51.

[2] Liu Mau-tsai, *Die Chinesischen Nachrichten zur Geschichte der Ost-Türken (T'u-küe)* (Wiesbaden: Otto Harrassowitz, 1958).

language historical materials pertaining to the Eastern Turk 東突厥 (or Kök Turk 藍突厥) second Qaghanate (the later Qaghanate), and it fills three large volumes.[3] One can imagine that if historical materials pertaining to the Western Turks and to the first Qaghanate were added, that the quantity would certainly surpass ten large volumes. And if published in a Western language, then this would be even larger.

Chinese scholars feel abashed that even though Chinese-language historical materials on Inner Asia are so numerous, this has not led Chinese researchers in the Inner Asian field to win prestige commensurate with those materials. Although it is not possible to say that Inner Asian research in China is a new science, yet because modern Chinese scholarship arose very much later than that in the West, it encountered many setbacks due to rising nationalism in Japan and other countries. As the modern academic branch of Inner Asian research in China started relatively late, its development was sluggish, and it was constrained by non-academic factors. However, it is worthwhile to note that despite the numerous difficulties, many generations of Inner Asian researchers in China nonetheless made great efforts in their work amidst these difficulties, and they achieved sure successes of which we can be proud. Knowledge of the history of Inner Asia accumulated and expanded as Inner Asian research in the academic world in China strove for and arrived at a sure position and influence. Among the authors of the essays in this book, two of them (Han Rulin 韓儒林 and Yekemingghadai Irinchin 亦邻真) have already passed away. Not only does their personal research stand out from among their peers, but they also set an example for the younger generation in their training of researchers into Inner Asian history. Moreover, Cai Meibiao 蔡美彪, Chen Dezhi 陳得芝, Zhou Qingshu 周清澍, and Zhang Guangda 張廣達 are all researchers of the older generation, and all are representative of the difficulties of working under the terrible conditions of Chinese academia at that time. It must be stressed that even now they are still extremely active researchers, and their work directly influences the new generation of scholars. The other authors all have

[3] Wu Yugui, ed., *Chinese-language Historical Materials on the Second Turkish Qaghanate Chronologically Compiled and Researched* 《突厥第二汗國漢文史料編年輯考》 (Shanghai: Zhonghua Book Company, 2009). [On Professor Luo Xin's point, note that the list of "Chinese-language Primary Sources Cited" in this book alone runs to more than ten pages. Translator's note.]

emerged within the last thirty years, after conditions for academic research in China comparatively improved. They grew up as newcomers, and their research represents new directions and new efforts.

Han Rulin was of the generation of Chinese scholars who received the influence of Paul Pelliot and other Western scholars. Yekemingghadai Irinchin and Zhang Guangda were of the generation that came of age in the early period, and so they received a relatively large influence from Soviet scholars. However, the new generation of scholars who have grown up over the past 30 years, in addition to receiving the direct influence of their Chinese teachers, have also had extensive contact with the previous 60 years of research by Western scholars. And at the same time, the same as with Inner Asian research in the West, they have also accepted the influence of the social sciences. Despite the many languages of Inner Asian research, the characteristic of internationalization is embodied in many of the selected research topics and accomplishments of Chinese researchers. However, a relatively distinctive point is that Chinese scholars' work is even more outstanding in its thorough unearthing of historical information in Chinese-language sources. If we were to say that their research success in the world of international research on Inner Asia is unique and has value, the most important reason would be that they better utilize Chinese historical materials. The fifteen essays included in this book all possess this merit.

The fifteen essays in this book, according to their research objectives, include two essays researching Tang Dynasty Sogdians and Sogdian culture, one researching the Western Turks, one researching the early stages of the Arabic subjugation of Persia and relations between the Tang Dynasty and Persia, three researching the Khitan (Qidan), six researching the Mongols and the Yuan Dynasty, one researching the Xiongnu, and one researching the Manchus. The summaries of these essays below will serve as an extremely brief introduction.

Wu Yugui's 吴玉貴 essay *Turks in the Gaochang Provisioning Texts* and Jiang Boqin's 姜伯勤 essay *The Chinese Persia Expeditionary Force as Referenced in the Turfan Documents* both utilize Turfan documents to reveal the existence of the Tang Dynasty Chinese government and military in Central Asia. The former essay researches the Western Turks, and the latter researches how the remnants of Sasanian Persian power resisted the Arab forces after the Arabic conquest with the support of the Tang Dynasty. Turfan and Dunhuang documents, the Han Chinese bamboo documents from Hexi 河西, and other similar newly unearthed historical materials have all led, over the last one hundred years, to these new Chinese-language historical materials becoming the focus of attention for Inner Asian research, and have given a great impetus to the development of modern Chinese scholarship. Because these new historical materials have to a very great degree made up for the shortcomings of traditional Chinese sources, therefore their appearance has caused Chinese researchers to take up new ways of looking at things in the examination of ancient documents. So Chinese researchers have gained a great many new topics and new avenues of approach.

Zhang Guangda's 張廣達 essay *The Nine Zhaowu Surnames (Sogdians) in the Six Hu Prefectures and Other Places in the Tang Dynasty* and Rong Xinjiang's 榮新江 essay *The Religious Background to the An Lushan Rebellion* both research Tang Dynasty Sogdians and Sogdian culture. Zhang Guangda's essay was written early, and he took the lead in research on Sogdians of the Six Hu Prefectures, which shows that he had almost a premonition about the great quantity of amazing Sogdian cultural remains later unearthed in China. Rong Xinjiang's essay is founded on Edwin G. Pulleyblank's book *The Background of the Rebellion of An Lu-Shan.*[4] It utilizes Rong's deep understanding of Chinese historical materials as well as the new achievements of Chinese scholars in Tang Dynasty Sogdian research, and it successfully pushes the field forward.

Wang Xiaofu's 王小甫 essay *The Establishment of the Khitan State and Uyghur Culture*, Liu Pujiang 劉浦江 and Kang Peng's 康鵬 essay *The Forenames and Courtesy Names of the Khitans: The Father-Son Name Linkage System from the Perspective of Cultural Anthropology*, and Cai Meibiao's 蔡美彪 essay *Khitan Tribal Organization and the Birth of the Khitan State* all research Khitan history. Wang Xiaofu's essay reveals that Uyghur cultural elements played an important role in the abrupt rise of the Khitans, and it stresses that in Inner Asian history there were close connections and interactions between different political entities. Liu Pujiang and Kang Peng's essay uses the methods of cultural anthropology to deal with historical materials on unearthed stone carvings, stressing the deep cultural connections between Khitan society and the even vaster area

[4] Edwin G. Pulleyblank, *The Background of the Rebellion of An Lu-Shan* (London: Oxford University Press, 1955).

of the various original ethnic group societies. Cai Meibiao's essay takes the concept and theory of historical materialism as its frame, and does its best to use the principles of concrete evidence in historical science to explore major threads in Khitan history, and similarly achieves a success to be admired by posterity.

The six essays researching the Mongols and the Yuan Dynasty each have their own particular emphasis. Yekemingghadai Irinchin's 亦邻真 essay *Regarding the Mongol Bo'ol in the 11th and 12th Centuries* uses its very short length to deal with exceedingly important problems in Mongolian history, and it displays the author's broad field of vision, deep reserve of knowledge, and incisive intellectual capabilities. In his not numerous, but very important, essays, Irinchin has established an especially long-standing and sparkling example for the new generation of Chinese researchers on Inner Asia. Zhou Qingshu's 周清澍 essay *A Critical Examination of the Year of Birth of Chinggis Khan* is the most important contribution from a Chinese scholar on this dispute-filled issue. Han Rulin's 韓儒林 essay *The Kirghiz and Neighboring Tribes in the Yuan Dynasty* is a thorough examination of the history of the Turkic peoples on the Yuan Dynasty Mongol steppe. Chen Dezhi's 陳得芝 essay *The Kerait Kingdom up to the Thirteenth Century* is an important revelation of middle Mongolian history prior to the arising of Chinggis Khan, and it shows a deep understanding of research into historical trends on the Mongol steppe. Liu Yingsheng's 劉迎胜 essay *A Study of Küšän Tarim in the Yuan Dynasty* utilizes material in many languages to conduct interesting research on the history of southern Xinjiang during the Mongol Yuan Dynasty. Luo Feng's 羅豐 essay *Liquor Still and Milk-Wine Distilling Technology in the Mongol-Yuan Period* is the only essay in this book written by an archaeologist, and it reflects how a Chinese archaeologist utilizes newly unearthed material data to resolve issues in Inner Asian history that can not be resolved by using traditional documents.

The basis for Luo Xin's 羅新 essay *Reflections on the Appellations of Xiongnu Shanyu Titles* is his new analytic method towards traditional research on ancient Inner Asian political titularity. That is, he conducts a differential analysis on the structure and function of a group of political titularities, and from this achieves a new understanding of Inner Asian titles. By using this method of analyzing the historical materials on

Xiongnu Shanyu 單于 titles, it is possible to discover that in the past these titles were regarded as surnames of the Shanyu. In fact, these titles were their newly received appellations taken after receiving the Shanyu position, not their original names. The success of this analytic method to a very large degree is due to the fact that the syntactic sequence of modifiers and modified is completely the same in the Altaic languages and in Chinese. Apart from some archaeological discoveries, one can say that research on the Xiongnu in the historical sources has hardly any room for expansion. Because of this, progress in historical research on the Xiongnu can only be hoped for by new analytic methods and new understandings of Inner Asian traditions.

The final essay is Yao Dali's 姚大力 *From Tribal Confederacy to Ethnic Community: On Historical Changes in Manchu Identity before the Mid-Qing*, which is an important achievement of recent years in Chinese scholars' research into Manchu identity. The author explores a very difficult-to-grasp type of balance between the political reconstruction and ethnic origins of Manchu identity. The essay reveals the author's brilliant theoretical attainments and capabilities for deciphering documents. It is worthwhile to stress that in addition to Chinese-language historical materials, this essay utilizes a large quantity of Manchu-language archives. It should be noted that the majority of these Manchu archives were put in order by Japanese scholars, which reflects the important contributions of Japanese scholars to this field.

These essays were all published earlier in Chinese, but for many of them the authors have made revisions for this translation, and therefore many of the essays are different from their original Chinese versions. We hope that these translations will lead Westerners in the same field to have an interest in paying close attention to the work of the Chinese. Indeed, in this way the above-mentioned Chinese adage "by seeing one part one may know the whole" truly does express our aspirations.

Finally, I must explain that for the publication of this book I am first of all grateful to the suggestion of the late Professor Denis Sinor. It was he who first proposed this matter to Roger Covey, and further, by his attention and help Professor Sinor facilitated this project's ultimate completion. I also am grateful to all of those who participated in creating this book, all of my friends who did translation and editing work; working together with them was a truly unforgettable and happy experience.

A NOTE ON THE TRANSLATIONS

Roger Covey

It is axiomatic that any translation satisfies few who know the original, and this must be true for the material in this book, the subject matter of which covers such a great diversity of domains and time periods. Nonetheless, this editor believes it worthwhile to explain how a consideration of the two main target audiences for this book determined the translation standards that were used.

One audience is scholars of Inner Asia who do not read modern and classical Chinese. For their sake items have been translated that are usually left transliterated. This includes titles of classical Chinese texts, titles of Chinese journal articles and Chinese scholarly publications, personal titles and positions (where we almost always follow Charles O. Hucker, *A Dictionary of Official Titles in Imperial China*[1]), and many place names. Reign period names, however, have been left in pinyin. Otherwise the use of pinyin has been almost entirely eliminated in the text and footnotes. Full pinyin transcriptions will be found in the bibliography and in the list of Chinese-language primary sources, which, however, is alphabetized by translated title. For the more important Chinese-language primary sources, the pinyin titles are cross-referenced to the translated titles in the index. The pre-computer era method of referencing classical Chinese texts with strings of capital letters has been avoided. Contrary to the customary Chinese academic practice, citations in classical Chinese have been fully translated throughout.

A second audience is those scholars who read modern and classical Chinese, but who will be reading outside of their specialty. For them, we have included complex Chinese characters everywhere in the text, the footnotes, and the scholarly apparatus, so that these translations may more readily serve them as a platform for extending their knowledge. Even those scholars reading inside their specialty, who of course will have already read the Chinese originals, will find new, interesting nuggets of information and analysis. Many of these essays were revised or enlarged by their authors especially for this translation, in some cases very substantially.

---

1 Charles O. Hucker, *A Dictionary of Official Titles in Imperial China* (Stanford: Stanford University Press, 1985).

Japanese scripts have been retained, and titles of Japanese journal articles and books have been translated throughout. Quotations in Western European languages have been translated where they occur in the main body text, but usually not when they appear in the footnotes. Russian sources have been left in Cyrillic, though Russian authors' names have been transliterated by a modified Library of Congress system, and titles of books and articles have been translated.

For more common Mongolian names, places, and terms we have followed Christopher Atwood's *Encyclopedia of Mongolia and the Mongol Empire*[2] (so "Chinggis Khan"); and following Atwood we use Qaghan for earlier periods, but Khan for later periods. For other Mongolian names and terms we usually follow Mostaert-Vladimirtsov system transliterations, though there are some exceptions. Transliterations from Turkish follow primarily Talât Tekin, *A Grammar of Orkhon Turkic*.[3] We have retained the traditional Kirghiz, instead of Qïrghïz, and we use Khitan, not Qidan. However, in all cases, fidelity to the Chinese scholars' essays means that transcriptions and transliterations appearing in those original Chinese-language essays have almost always been retained.

Because both of the audiences for this book are in the scholarly community, this editor has pushed the translations hard toward the precise and literal, and away from the interpretive and idiomatic. As Edward Schafer memorably wrote more than half a century ago: "the responsibility of the translator is to convey the *linguistic content* of the text."[4] Thus these translations capture the rich flavor of the best Chinese scholarship. And absolutely no editorial license has been taken – this is what the Chinese scholars wrote. Only a very few explanatory notes have been added, which everywhere are indicated by square brackets […]. Very rarely a translator's footnote has been added, which is always indicated by a symbol, instead of a number.

---

2 Christopher P. Atwood, *Encyclopedia of Mongolia and the Mongol Empire* (Facts on File, 2004). For Professor Atwood's explanation of his transcription conventions see page ix of the introduction.

3 Talât Tekin, *A Grammar of Orkhon Turkic* (Bloomington: Indiana University Uralic and Altaic Series 69, 1969), pp. 23-4.

4 Edward H. Schafer, "Non-Translation and Functional Translation – Two Sinological Maladies," *The Far Eastern Quarterly*, vol. 13, no. 3 (May, 1954), p. 254.

The original versions of these essays were first published in China as follows:

Wu Yugui 吴玉貴. "Turks in the Gaochang Provisioning Texts" 《高昌供食文書中的突厥》. *Northwest Journal of Ethnology* 《西北民族研究》, 1991, no. 1.

Jiang Boqin 姜伯勤. "The Chinese Persia Expeditionary Force as Referenced in the Turfan Documents"《吐鲁番文書所見的"波斯軍"》. *Journal of Chinese Historical Studies*《中國史研究》, 1986, no. 1.

Zhang Guangda 张廣達. "The Nine Zhaowu Surnames (Sogdians) in the Six Hu Prefectures and Other Places in the Tang Dynasty"《唐代六胡州等地的昭武九姓》. *Journal of Peking University* 《北京大學學報》, 1986, no. 2.

Rong Xinjiang 榮新江. "The Religious Background to the An Lushan Rebellion"《安祿山的种族与宗教信仰》, first published as "An Lushan's Ethnicity and Religious Beliefs"《安祿山的種族与宗教信仰》. In *Collected Essays from the Third Annual China Tang Dynasty Culture Academic Research Symposium* 《第三屆中國唐代文化學術研討會論文集》. Taipei: 中國唐代學會編輯委員會, 1997; but see footnote one in Rong Xinjiang's essay.

Wang Xiaofu 王小甫. "The Establishment of the Khitan State and Uyghur Culture"《契丹建國与回鶻文化》. *Social Sciences in China* 《中國社會科學》, 2004, no. 4.

Liu Pujiang 劉浦江 and Kang Peng 康鵬. "The Forenames and Courtesy Names of the Khitans: The Father-Son Name Linkage System from the Perspective of Cultural Anthropology" 《契丹名、字初釋——文化人類學視野下的父子連名制》. *Literature and History*《文史》, 2005, no. 3.

Cai Meibiao 蔡美彪. "Khitan Tribal Organization and the Birth of the Khitan State" 《契丹的部落組織和國家的產生》. *Historical Research* 《歷史研究》, 1964, nos. 5-6.

Yekemingghadai Irinchin 亦鄰真. "Regarding the Mongol *Bo'ol* in the 11th and 12th Centuries." In *Collected Essays on Yuan History* 《元史論叢》, vol. 3. Beijing: Zhonghua Book Company, 1986.

Zhou Qingshu 周清澍. "A Critical Examination of the Year of Birth of Chinggis Khan" 《成吉思汗生年考》. *Literature and History* 《文史》, vol. 1 (1962).

Han Rulin 韓儒林. "The Kirghiz and the Neighboring Tribes in the Yuan Dynasty" 《元代的吉利吉思及其鄰近諸部》. *Journal of Research on Yuan History and Northern Nationalities History* 《元史及北方民族史研究輯刊》, vol. 5 (1981).

Chen Dezhi 陳得芝. "The Kerait Kingdom up to the Thirteenth Century" 《十三世紀以前的克烈王國》. In *Collected Essays on Yuan History* 《元史論叢》, vol. 3. Beijing: Zhonghua Book Company, 1986.

Liu Yingsheng 劉迎胜. "A Study of Küšän Tarim in the Yuan Dynasty" 《元代曲先塔林考》. *Journal of Central Asian Studies* 《中亞學刊》, vol. 1 (1983).

Luo Feng 羅豐. "Liquor Still and Milk-Wine Distilling Technology in the Mongol-Yuan Period" 《蒙元時期的釀酒鍋與蒸餾乳酒技術》, *Archaeology* 《考古》, 2008, no. 5.

Yao Dali 姚大力. "From Tribal Confederacy to Ethnic Community: On Historical Changes in Manchu Identity before the Mid-Qing" 《"满洲"如何演變为民族—論清中葉前"满洲"認同的歷史變遷》. *Social Sciences* 《社會科學》, 2006, no. 7.

The reader of Chinese is again cautioned that the majority of these essays have been revised, in some cases very substantially, since their original publication.

This editor was solely responsible for the translations of the essays by Rong Xinjiang and Zhang Guangda, and for translating Professor Luo Xin's introduction. For the other essays, draft translations were received from a number of scholars, as follows:

Dr. Sally Church, for whose yeoman work this editor is grateful: the essays by Han Rulin, Chen Dezhi, and Liu Yingsheng;
Yin Hong 殷宏: the essay by Liu Pujiang and Kang Peng;
Lin Ying 林英: the essay by Jiang Boqin;
Zhou Yongjia 周咏笳: the essay by Zhou Qingshu;
Chao Gejin 朝戈金 and Zhu Gang 朱剛: the essay by Yekemingghadai Irinchin;

Ding Xiaolei 丁晓雷: the essay by Luo Feng;
And Dr. Chih Lo 羅芝, with the assistance of others: the essays by Wu Yugui, Wang Xiaofu, Cai Meibiao, Luo Xin, and Yao Dali.

However, all of these translations (excepting the excellent translation of Yao Dali's essay, in which that author participated, and Yin Hong's excellent translation of Liu Pujiang and Kang Peng's essay) were either extensively revised or rewritten by this editor, so he bears sole responsibility for any errors and infelicities which remain. Valuable comments on many of the translations were received from Professor Andrew Eisenberg.

This editor was also responsible for the bibliography, the list of Chinese-language primary sources, and the index. In addition to the usual analytic material, the index contains entries for the more important primary sources in any language, including footnoted material; so, for example, one may easily find all of the citations from the *Hudūd al-'Ālam*. The index also contains entries for every scholar or author cited in the main body text, again including footnoted material; so, for instance, one may easily find all the citations from the publications of Paul Pelliot.

Finally, this editor is grateful to the legendary Denis Sinor, to whom this book is dedicated, for suggesting this project and for encouraging it over the many years it took to bring it to completion.

TURKS IN THE GAOCHANG PROVISIONING TEXTS

Wu Yugui 吴玉貴

Six of the nine provisioning texts excavated from the number 307, 329, and 517 Qu 麹 family Gaochang 高昌 era tombs in Astana 阿斯塔那 Turfan had content related to the Turks. The people to whom who provisions were provided included Turkic emissaries of Abo Kehan 阿博珂寒 (Apa Qaghan 阿波可汗), Tanhan Kehan 貪旱珂寒 (Tanhan Qaghan 貪汗可汗), Shuluo Kehan 恕羅珂寒 (Chuluo Qaghan 處羅可汗), Nanxiang Kehan 南厢珂寒 (the Qaghan of the Southern Wing), and Beixiang Kehan 北厢珂寒 (the Qaghan of the Northern Wing). A "nephew" is also mentioned, along with the names of iron and gold masters of the Turkic Qaghan. Such records in these texts are not without value to the study of Turkic history and the relationship between Gaochang and the Turks. This paper aims at making preliminary explanations of issues related to the Turks found in these texts.[1]

I

In the second, third, and fourth volumes of *Documents Unearthed in Turfan* 吐魯番出土文書 there are over twenty texts whose contents are related to provisioning,[2] but there are great differences amongst those being provisioned, the contents of the provisioning, and the record-keeping formats. As many parts of the texts are missing, a clear categorization cannot be made. According to my preliminary investigations, the provisioning texts can be divided into two general categories. The first category of those being provisioned is complex, and, apart from guest emissaries, it includes those being provided with "shangxian" 上現 [meaning unknown], those provided with "material for constructing steles," those provided with "garrison troops," etc. Many kinds of food were provided, and, apart from the staples of wheat flour, common millet, broomcorn millet, and wheat bran, the texts also include foods such as meat, meat from animals not slaughtered, liver, lungs,

---

[1] See Wang Su 王素, "'Documents Unearthed in Turfan,' Evaluation of the First Three Books" 《〈吐魯番出土文書〉前三冊評介》 in *The Study of Chinese History* 《中國史研究》, 1983, no. 2.

[2] *Documents Unearthed in Turfan* 《吐魯番出土文書》 (Beijing, 1981).

sheep's heads, dates, and liquor, and even include records of everyday items such as drawn hemp, hair, camel fur, sheepskin, boots, and skirts. The second category of those being provisioned is rather uniform: the vast majority were guest emissaries and a few were refugees. The food provided was also basically limited to wheat flour, common millet, broomcorn millet, and wheat bran. These types of texts are rather detailed on the matter of recording the food that was provided and usually divide the guest emissaries in attendance based on their status into three ranks (upper, middle, and lower).[3] I believe that the second type of provisioning text may have been the provisioning record from a Gaochang guesthouse that received foreign emissaries. The content of the six texts related to the Turks that I discuss in this paper all belong to the second category of texts.

None of the six texts give their year. Tomb number 517 is a group burial tomb, and in it was found the *Gaochang 31st Year of Yanchang (591) Zhang Yi's Wife Meng Gravestone* 高昌延昌三十一年(591)張毅妻孟氏墓表 and the *Gaochang 37th Year of Yanchang (597) Zhang Yi Epitaph* 高昌延昌三十七年(597)張毅墓志. The *Gaochang 31st Year of Yanchang (unknown name) Burial Clothing and Objects Record* 高昌延昌三十一年缺名隨葬衣物疏 was found by the female corpse, and the *Gaochang 37th Year of Yanchang Wude Burial Clothing and Objects Record* 高昌延昌三十七年武德隨葬衣物疏 was found by the male corpse, and the years of the "clothing and objects records" and the epitaphs are the same.[4] Tombs 307 and 329 did not include epitaphs, and the texts they contained did not state their year. Based on the tomb shapes, the unearthed texts, and the characteristics of the unearthed relics, the time of these two tombs can be

---

[3] For reference, Wu Yugui's 吳玉貴 "Two Gaochang Provisioning Texts" 《兩件高昌供食文書》 (in *The Study of Chinese History* 《中國史研究》, 1990, no. 1) discusses the *Gaochang Zhufotu Provisioning Record* 《高昌竺佛圖等傳供食帳》 and the *Gaochang □shan Provisioning Record* 《高昌□善等傳供食帳》 from tomb number 307 in a preliminary investigation of the second type of text and problems related to the semi-monthly provisioning records. [□ represents a missing or illegible character.]

[4] Five Tang texts, including the text "The report to the civil service of Xizhou Commander-in-chief from Puchang County of Xizhou regarding some remount stations' budgets for rebuilding station walls in the second year of the Kaiyuan reign period (682) of the Tang Dynasty" 《唐開耀二年（682）西州蒲昌縣上西州都督府戶曹牒為某驛修造驛牆用單功事》 were found in tomb number 517, and the explanatory notes believe that these five texts were later introduced by grave robbers and are unrelated to the original year of the tomb, so they will not be discussed here.

determined as the late Qu family Gaochang period. Furthermore, the *Firewood Cart Text Fragment* 調薪車殘文書 was excavated from tomb number 307, and based on the phrase "the start of the eighth month of the leap year," it can be determined to be the ninth year of the Qu family Gaochang Yanshou 延壽 reign period (632). Of the texts and objects from the three tombs, the earliest specific date is the 31st year of the Yanchang 延昌 reign period (591), and the latest is the ninth year of the Yanshou reign period (632) – slightly later than the activities of the Turkic Qaghans mentioned in the provisioning texts. For reference, the following are a table of the number of times each Turkic Qaghan appears in these texts (table one) and a table comparing the years in which the Turkic Qaghans were active and the years given in the texts and objects excavated from the tombs (table two).[5]

Table 1:

Tomb	Text	Abo (Apa) Qaghan	Tanhan Qaghan	Shuluo (Chuluo) Qaghan	Nanxiang Qaghan	Beixiang Qaghan	Qaghan
TAM307	Zhufotu 竺佛圖	1			1		1
	□shan □善	1	1		3		3
	Linghu令狐		1				
	Duzi 都子				1		
TAM329	Yuanzhi 元治			1		1	2
TAM517	Duzi 都子		2				

[5] The "Qaghan" column in table one represents Qaghans whose names are not given in the texts. For the "dates given in historical records" in table two, see section two of this paper.

Table 2:

Qaghan	Dates from the tomb texts (objects)	Dates given in the historical records	Difference in years
Abo (Apa) Qaghan	591-632?	583-587	4-45
Shuluo (Chuluo) Qaghan	Late Qu family Gaochang era	604-611	
Tanhan Qaghan	591-632?	583	8-49
Nanxiang Qaghan	591-632?	Missing	
Beixiang Qaghan	Late Qu family Gaochang era	Missing	

One problem that requires explanation is that there are no specific dates on the texts from tomb number 307, and the "explanatory notes" in *Documents Unearthed in Turfan* date the *Firewood Cart Text Fragment* to the ninth year of the Yanshou period [632], but according to the people that appear in the texts from tomb number 307, this tomb should date from roughly the same year as tomb number 517. There are three pieces of evidence for this:

First, Abo (Apa) Qaghan and Tanhan Qaghan are both seen in the *Gaochang □shan Provisioning Record* 高昌□善等傳供食帳 from tomb number 307, and Tanhan Qaghan is also seen in the *Gaochang Duzi Provisioning Record* 高昌都子等傳供食帳 from tomb number 517.

Second, line three from the *Gaochang Huya Duzi Provisioning Record* 高昌虎牙都子等傳供食帳 from tomb number 307 says "□ Huya Duzi provided fifteen jin 斤" [a *jin* was a measure of weight, in the Tang dynasty equal to about 1.3 pounds], and the seventh line of the first section of the *Gaochang □shan Provisioning Record* says "Next Huya Duzi provided." The second line of the first section of *Gaochang Duzi Provisioning Record* from tomb number 517 says "□□Duzi provided one *hu* 斛 four *dou* 斗" [a *hu* was a measure of capacity equal to about 1.7 bushels and was comprised of ten *dou*]. This "□□Duzi" should be the "Huya Duzi" from tomb number 307, and the missing text before this "Duzi" should be "Huya" – the two are the same person.

Third, the sixth line of the second section of the *Gaochang Zhufotu Provisioning Record* from tomb number 307 mentions an individual called Mingwei 明威 Fonu 佛奴, and the third line of the first section of the *Gaochang Duzi Provisioning Record* from tomb number 517 says "□□Fonu." The missing text before Fonu here should be Mingwei, and this should be the same person as the Mingwei Fonu of the tomb number 307 text.

As Tanhan Qaghan, Huya Duzi, and Mingwei Fonu appear at the same time in the texts from tombs number 307 and 517, we have dated both tombs as belonging to the same period.

As can be seen from the above tables, the dates on the excavated texts and objects from the tombs are four to 49 years later than those given in historical materials. If we ignore the dating to the ninth year of the Yanshou reign period by the text's editors and only look at the epitaphs (or records of clothing and objects), then the dates of the Turkic Qaghan activities mentioned in the texts are only four to fourteen years earlier than those of epitaphs. The tomb texts belonged to the tomb occupants before they died, so it should be reasonable that they give earlier dates.

2

Abo (Apa) Qaghan appears twice in the texts, Tanhan Qaghan appears four times, and Shuluo (Chuluo) Qaghan appears once. These three Qaghans can all be found in Chinese historical records and are important figures in Turkic history. The following is an explanation of these figures.

Records of Apa Qaghan can mainly be found in the *History of the Sui: Account of the Turks* 隋書・突厥傳. Apa was also called Daluobian 大邏便, and was the son of the great Turkic Qaghan of the Eastern Turks, Muqan 木杆 Qaghan (553-572). In 572 Muqan Qaghan died, and was succeeded by his younger brother, Taspar 佗鉢 Qaghan. In 581 Taspar Qaghan died, and the four sons of Eastern Turkic Qaghans (Yixiji 乙息紀 Qaghan's son Shetu 攝圖 who became Shabolüe 沙鉢略 Qaghan; Muqan Qaghan's son Daluobian who became Apa Qaghan; Taspar Qaghan's son Anluo 庵邏; and Rudan 褥但 Qaghan's son Buli 步離) began to contest for the throne. In the end Yixiji's son Shetu won out, and was named Shabolüe Qaghan. As a conciliatory gesture, Shabolüe Qaghan made Muqan's son, Daluobian, Apa Qaghan.

In 582 Shabolüe Qaghan led the Turkic army in a split invasion of the Sui Dynasty, and Apa Qaghan led the forces through Liangzhou 涼州. The next year the Sui army led an eight-pronged counterattack, and Apa met the Sui Marshal 元帥 Dou Rongding 竇榮定 in Liangzhou. Dou Rongding's Deputy General 偏將 Zhangsun Sheng 長孫晟 took advantage of the conflict between Apa and Shabolüe, and he convinced Apa to side with the emperor and unite with Tardu 達頭 to increase his strength. Apa agreed and sent an emissary to the court. Shabolüe Qaghan was subsequently defeated at the White Pass 白道. After his defeat, he focused his anger on Apa for his duplicity and attacked Apa Qaghan in the Northern Capital 北牙, thereby "completely subjugating his people and killing his mother." Apa had nowhere to return to, so he fled west to Tardu Qaghan, son of the Western Turk Istämi 室點密.[6]

Once Apa Qaghan had fled to the Western Turks, the Turkic Qaghanate was struck by an internal struggle for leadership among the lesser Qaghans of the Tumen 土門 line, and a war broke out between the Eastern (Tumen) and Western (Istämi) Turks. Thereafter, under the support of the Western Turk Tardu Qaghan, Apa Qaghan "attacked Shetu in the east, and regained his old land."[7] He held it until the seventh year of the Kaihuang 開皇 reign period (587), when he was captured alive by Shabolüe Qaghan's successor, Bagha (Mohe)莫何 Qaghan (Chuluohou 處羅侯). The split between Apa Qaghan and Shabolüe Qaghan split the Eastern Turks into two, and this was a turning point in forming the long-term strife between the Eastern and Western Turks that was critical to their history. The third generation Apa Qaghan Chuluo 處羅 took advantage of Tardu's loss north of the Gobi Desert, and, in what once was the area most of the Western Turks occupied, he forced Istämi's descendant Shekui 射匱 Qaghan to submit to him, which is why the *History of the Sui* calls the Apa line of Turks the "Western Turks." But it is worth pointing out that Apa Qaghan and Nili 泥利 Qaghan of the Apa line were both under Tardu Qaghan and should have resided to the northwest of the leadership of the Turkic Qaghanate, which was an area roughly between Ötüken Mountains and the Altai Mountains.[8] The period in which Apa Qaghan dispatched emissaries to Gaochang in the texts should be the third year of the Kaihuang reign period (583) to the seventh year (587), and, as we have seen from the above, this period conforms to the period of the epitaphs.

---

[6] See *History of the Sui* 《隋書》, ch. 84, "Account of the Turks" 《突厥傳》; ch. 51, "Biography of Zhangsun Sheng" 《長孫晟傳》; ch. 39, "Biography of Dou Rongding" 《竇榮定傳》; and ch. 44, "Biography of Yang Shuang" 《楊爽傳》.

[7] *History of the Sui*, "Biography of Zhangsun Sheng."

[8] See Duan Lianqin's 段連勤 "Several Problems Concerning the Early History of the Western Turks and the Western Turk Empire" 《關於西突厥與西突厥汗國早期歷史的幾個問題》 in *Xinjiang Social Sciences* 《新疆社會科學》, 1984, no. 3.

"Tanhan Qaghan" is written in two different ways in the *Gaochang Duzi Provisioning Record*, and both names refer to the same person. Two different characters for "han" (literally meaning "drought" 旱 [written in the Gaochang texts as 水+旱] and "sweat" 汗) are often used interchangeably in Turfan texts, such as the line "one set of inner garments and undershirt" in the *Gaochang Yihe Fourth Year (unknown name) Burial Clothing and Objects Record* 高昌義和四年缺名隨葬衣物疏,[9] in which the "drought" version is used, and the second line of the *Gaochang Xia Village Family Person's Wheat Field Contract* 高昌某人夏鎮家麥田券 that reads "if there is a drought," in which the "sweat" version is used.[10] This means that this Tanhan Qaghan 貪旱珂寒 should be the same as the Tanhan Qaghan 貪汗可汗 found in historical materials.

Tanhan Qaghan lived during the same period as Apa Qaghan. In 583 Apa Qaghan split with Shabolüe Qaghan, and because Tanhan Qaghan had a close relationship with Apa, he was expelled by Shabolüe, and he threw his lot in with Tardu Qaghan of the Western Turks. *History of the Sui: Account of the Turks*: "There also was Tanhan Qaghan, who had always gotten along well with Apa, and as Shabolüe took his people and expelled him, he fled in defeat to Tardu." This is the only time Tanhan Qaghan appears in historical materials.

Tanhan Qaghan and Apa Qaghan lived in the western region of the Eastern Turks, and the name Tanhan is related to the Tanhan Mountain north of Gaochang. *History of the Sui: Account of Gaochang* describes the Gaochang geography as: "To the north of (Gaochang) is a red stone mountain, and seventy *li* north of this mountain is Tanhan Mountain, which is covered in snow in the summer. To the north of this mountain is the region of the Tiele 鐵勒." Tanhan Mountain is the present-day Bogda 博格達 Mountain located in the eastern part of the Tianshan 天山 Mountains in Xinjiang. The "Tiele region" refers to the Tiele tribe's occupancy of Tanhan Mountain in the first year of the Daye 大業 reign period (605). Before the Daye reign period this region was controlled by the Turks. Tanhan Mountain may have received its name for being the

[9] See *Documents Unearthed in Turfan*, vol. 3, "Gaochang Yihe Fourth Year (unknown name) Burial Clothing and Objects Record" 《高昌義和四年缺名隨葬衣物疏》 (Cultural Relics Press, 1981), p. 61.

[10] See Ibid., "Gaochang Xia Village Family Person's Wheat Field Contract" 《高昌某人夏鎮家麥田券》, p. 191.

grazing land of Tanhan Qaghan.[11] Tanhan Mountain connects with Gaochang, and is easily accessible from there, so Tanhan Qaghan had close relationships with emissaries from Gaochang.

In the historical materials, Tanhan 貪汗 is used in connection with names – apart from Tanhan Qaghan, there is also Yili 移力 Tanhan. Matsuda Toshio says, "In the *History of the Sui: Account of the Turks*, we have Tanhan Qaghan, and in the *Old Tang History: Account of the Turks* 舊唐書・突厥傳 there is a person named Yili Tanhan. The latter Tanhan likely stands for the official title *tarqan* (dagan 達干), and we cannot say with certainty that the former was the same character."[12]

Note that *tarqan* is a Turkic official title, and can be seen in the Turkic stele *Tonyukuk Inscription* 暾欲谷碑, *Kül Tegin Inscription* 闕特勤碑, *Bilgä Qaghan Inscription* 毗伽可汗碑, and *Ongin Inscription* 翁金碑.[13] The word *tarqan* has a long history amongst the northern nomadic tribes; it was widely used, and its use varied greatly throughout time. The Rouran's 柔然 tahan 撻寒, the Turk and Uyghur dagan 達干, and the Mongolian darqan 答剌罕 are all different translations of *tarqan*.[14]

---

[11] Tanhan Mountain is referred to as Tanwu 貪污山 Mountain in the *History of the Sui*. This was changed to Tanhan Mountain in the Zhonghua Book Company 中華書局 punctuated edition. The "Collators' Record" 《校勘紀》 says, "'Han' 汗 was originally 'Wu' 污 according to the 'Account of the Turks,' the *History of the Northern Dynasties: Account of Gaochang* 《北史・高昌傳》, and the *Encyclopaedic History of Institutions* 《通典》, ch. 191, and has therefore been changed." Matsuda Toshio 松田寿男 believes that "Tanwu Mountain" was correct – see *Research on the History and Geography of Ancient Tianshan* 《古代天山歷史地理學研究》, part 3, "A Discussion of the Topography of Tianshan as Reported in Sui and Tang Historical Documents" 《論隋唐史籍所載天山形勢》, paper 1, "A History of the Rise of the Turks" 《突厥勃興史論》, Chen Junmou 陳俊謀, Chinese translation (China Nationalities Academy Press 中央民族學院出版社, 1987). As all of these books have "Tanhan Mountain," "Wu" appears to be an error for "Han," so I do not agree with Matsuda here.

[12] See Matsuda Toshio's *Research on the History and Geography of Ancient Tianshan* 《古代天山歷史地理學研究》, p. 278.

[13] The Turkic stele inscriptions referred to in this paper are all taken from Geng Shimin's 耿世民 translated version; see Lin Gan's 林幹 *History of the Turks* 《突厥史》 (Inner Mongolia People's Press, 1988), appendix, "Turkish Language Stele Inscriptions Translated (Geng Shimin, translator)" 《突厥文碑铭譯文（耿世民譯）》. Hereafter this will not be noted.

[14] See Han Rulin 韓儒林 "A Study of the Mongolian Dalahan" 《蒙古答剌罕考》 and

During the Tang Dynasty, apart from dagan 達干, there were translations such as daguan 達官,[15] duogan 鐸干, and dagan 達乾.[16] Based on the opinion of China's Turkic language expert Geng Shimin 耿世民, the word tanhan 貪汗 should be the translation of the Turkic word tamghan, and not *tarqan*, such as with the Turkic "išbara tamghan čur" and "bilgä išbara tamghan tarqan," which Geng Shimin translates as "Shiboluo Tanhan Chuo" 始波羅貪汗啜 and "Pijia Shiboluo Tanhan Dagan" 毗伽始波羅貪汗達干.[17] This problem still awaits further study.

The word "Tanhan" (both variants) is mostly used as a Turkic name in Turfan texts, such as Tanhan Qaghan 貪旱珂寒, Tanhan Tiqin 貪旱提懃, Tubie Tanhan 吐別貪旱, Zhiju Tanhan 知[here 口+知]舉貪旱, Gugen Tanhan 孤艮貪旱,[18] Tanhan Daguan 貪旱達官,[19] and Tanhan 貪旱.[20] In Chinese histories Turkic people are often called by their official title, and while we still cannot determine the meaning of the word "tanhan," it is almost certain that it was an official Turkic title.

Shuluo Qaghan is the Qaghan Chuluo, the third generation of the Abo (Apa) lineage of the historical records. Chuluo Qaghan's full name was

---

"A Philological Study of Turkish Official Position Titles" 《突厥官號考釋》 in *Collection from the Yurt* [Han Rulin's papers] 《穹廬集》 (Shanghai People's Press, 1982).

[15] In the *Encyclopaedic History of Institutions*, ch. 199, "Turks" last part, apart from "Mohe Dagan" 莫賀達干 being written as "Mohe Dayu" 莫賀達于, all "Dagan" 達干 are written as "Daguan" 達官, and *Biography of the Tripitaka Dharma-Master of the Great Compassion Monastery* 《大慈恩寺三藏法師傳》, ch. 2 also has "Daguan." Also, the *Encyclopaedic History of Institutions*, chs. 197 and 198 mostly mistakes "Dagan" for "Dayu."

[16] See Cen Zhongmian 岑仲勉, "Annotation and Translation of Turkish Stele Inscriptions"《突厥文碑注釋》in *Collected Histories of the Turks* 《突厥集史》, vol. 2 (Zhonghua Book Company, 1958), p. 867.

[17] *Ongin Inscription* face, rows 4 and 5.

[18] The above names are all included in the six provisioning texts cited in this paper.

[19] See *Documents Unearthed in Turfan*, vol. 4 (Cultural Relics Press, 1983), p. 132, "Notice for Sending Someone from the Military Bureau to Safeguard the Foreign Emissary at the Guesthouse in the 14th Year of the Yanshou Reign Period (637) in Gaochang Kingdom" 《高昌延壽十四年（637）兵部差人看額館客使文書》 and "The Memorandum for Money and Grain of Jiabi Tanhan and Others in an Unknown Year in Gaochang Kingdom"《高昌年次未詳迦匕貪旱等錢谷備忘》.

[20] *Documents Unearthed in Turfan*, vol. 4, appendix, p. 29, "Record of Yuanli and Others from Gaochang County Regarding their Provisioning in Turn" 《高昌元禮等傳供食帳》.

Nijue Chuluo Qaghan 泥撅處羅可汗; he was named Daman 達漫, and his mother (Lady Xiang 向) was Han Chinese.

In the seventh year of the Kaihuang reign period (587), Apa Qaghan was defeated north of the Gobi Desert, and his countrymen established Yangsuteqin's 鞅素特勤 son as Nili Qaghan 泥利可汗. In the third year of the Renshou 仁壽 reign period (603), the Tiele tribes raised their armies against the Turks and defeated Nili Qaghan. The next year Nili Qaghan's son Chuluo Qaghan succeeded him. *History of the Sui: Account of the Western Turks* 隋書・西突厥傳 systematically describes the affairs of Chuluo Qaghan; however it seems to be in error concerning the events surrounding Chuluo's succession. The record is as follows:

> Daluobian [Apa Qaghan] was captured by Chuluohou, and the state established Yangsuteqin's son as Nili Qaghan. Apa died and was succeeded by his son Daman, named Nijue Chuluo Qaghan. His mother (Lady Xiang) was Han Chinese. She gave birth to Daman and Nili died, then remarried Nili's younger brother, Poshiteqin 婆實特勤. At the end of the Kaihuang reign period Poshi and Lady Xiang went to the court and were caught in the Tardu rebellion. They stayed in the capital, residing in Honglu 鴻臚 temple.

This passage has two suspicious places. The first is that from analyzing the context, "She gave birth to Daman and Nili died" stresses that her giving birth to Daman and Nili's death happened during a short span of time. The year of Nili's death is not specified in the histories. *History of the Sui: Account of the Turks* says, "In this year Nili Qaghan and Yabghu 葉護 were defeated by the Tiele. Not long after the tribes led by Bujia 步迦 rebelled, and Bujia fled to the Tuyuhun 吐谷渾." Bujia is Tardu Qaghan. The *History of the Sui* here goes from the first year of the Renshou reign period to the third year of the Daye reign period, so, from the content of the history, "this year" should be the first year of the Renshou reign period. However, the *History of the Sui*, chapter 51, *Biography of Zhangsun Sheng* 長孫晟傳 says:

> In the first year of the Renshou reign period…Yang Su 楊素 was commissioned to be the Commander-in-chief of the army 軍元

> 帥, Sheng 晟 was the emissary to those who had surrendered, and Ran'gan 染干 was sent to attack the North. In the second year the army once again attacked north of the river, and many of the commanders such as Sili Sijin 思力俟斤 refused to fight. Sheng and the Chief General Liang 梁 ambushed them causing them to flee for over sixty *li*, and most of the enemy surrendered. Sheng then had Ran'gan dispatch emissaries to the Tiele and other tribes in the North to win them over. In the third year more than ten tribes including the Tiele 鐵勒, Sijie 思結, Fuliju 伏利具, Hun 渾, Husa 斛薩, Aba 阿拔, and Pugu 僕骨 all betrayed Tardu and surrendered. Tardu's people scattered, fleeing west to the Tuyuhun.

The date in the *Comprehensive Mirror for Aid in Government* 資治通鑒, chapter 179, is the same as that in "Biography of Zhangsun Sheng." Clearly, the Tiele tribe's betrayal, and the defeat of Nili and Tardu occurred in the third year of the Renshou reign period. In the above quoted "Account of the Turks" and in the *History of the Sui*, chapter 48, "Biography of Yang Su," Yang Su was ordered to march in the first year of the Renshou reign period (601), so this can be dated to the first year of the Renshou reign period. In the third year of the Renshou reign period Nili was defeated. One year later, his successor Chuluo Qaghan was defeated by the Tiele and fled. *History of the Sui: Account of the Tiele* 隋書・鐵勒傳:

> In the first year of the Daye reign period [605], the Turk Chuluo Qaghan attacked the Tiele and other tribes, exacting heavy taxes and taking their possessions. He was suspicious that the Xueyantuo 薛延陀 tribe would betray him, so he gathered all of their commanders and had them all killed.

At the latest, Chuluo Qaghan's succession took place before the first year of the Daye reign period. In other words, Nili Qaghan's death and Chuluo Qaghan's succession should have taken place between the third and fourth years of the Renshou reign period (603-604). The "birth of Daman" and "death of Nili" took place at different times.

Second, and more importantly, "Account of the Western Turks" says that Nili died, and "then Xiang remarried his younger brother, Poshiteqin.

At the end of the Kaihuang reign period Poshi and Lady Xiang went to the court." The *Encyclopaedic History of Institutions* 通典, chapter 199, "Turks, last part" also says, "she gave birth to Daman and Nili died, and Lady Xiang remarried his younger brother Poshitele(qin). At the end of the Kaihuang reign period, Poshi and Lady Xiang went to Chang'an." The *Comprehensive Mirror for Aid in Government*, chapter 180, continues the above two records, saying, "Nili died, and was succeeded by Daman, named Chuluo Qaghan. His mother, Lady Xiang, was originally Han Chinese, and remarried Nili's younger brother Poshitele(qin). At the end of the Kaihuang reign period, Poshi and Lady Xiang went to the court."

There were twenty years in the Kaihuang reign period, which ran from 581 to 600 and was succeeded by the Renshou reign period (601-604). According to the above conclusion, Nili died sometime between the third and fourth years of the Renshou reign period, and Lady Xiang remarried after Nili died. Therefore, the earliest date of her remarriage was after the fourth year of the Renshou reign period, and they must have entered the court at an even later date and not in the last year of the Kaihuang reign period while Nili was still in power.

Chuluo Qaghan ascended the throne in the fourth year of the Renshou reign period and in the first year of the Daye reign period was defeated by the Tiele and forced to flee westward. After moving west, Chuluo momentarily had great power, and Shekui Qaghan once served as a vassal of Chuluo's. However, in the sixth year of the Daye reign period, Shekui Qaghan attacked and defeated Chuluo. The next year, Chuluo was forced to lead his people in submission to the Sui, and the Sui court enfeoffed him as Hesana 曷薩那 Qaghan,[21] and he married the Sui Xinyi 信義

[21] *History of the Sui: Biography of Pei Ju* 《隋書•裴矩傳》, *Account of the Western Turks* 《西突厥傳》, *New Tang History: Account of the Western Turks* 《新唐書•西突厥傳》, and the *Old Tang History: Account of the Western Turks* 《舊唐書•西突厥傳》 all have "Hesana" 曷薩那, while *History of the Sui: Annals of Yangdi* 《隋書•煬帝紀》, *Important Documents of the Tang* 《唐會要》, ch. 94, "The Western Turks," and the *Old Tang History*, ch. 55, "Biography of Li Gui" 《李軌傳》 all have "Hepona" 曷婆那. Both Hesana and Heshana are different translations of the same name. *Comprehensive Mirror for Aid in Government* 《資治通鑒》, ch. 181, "Eighth Year of Daye" "大業八年" has "Hepona." *Textual Analysis of the 22 Histories* 《廿二史考異》 [Qian Daxin 錢大昕, 1728-1804] says: "The *Biography of Tang Li Gui* has 'Heshana Qaghan,' and today we follow the *History of the Sui*." *Extensive Notes on the Comprehensive Mirror for Aid in Government* 《資治通鑒廣注》 [by Hu Sanxing 胡三省, 1230-1302] says: "today's *History of the Sui* has Hesana." Note that the *History of the Sui* that Sima Guang 司馬光 and Hu

princess. After the fall of the Sui, he once again submitted to the Tang in the first year of the Wude reign period and was enfeoffed as the Prince of Guiyi 歸義.[22] The next year he was killed by an Eastern Turkish emissary. Chuluo Qaghan was active in the western regions for eight years (604-611), and of the three Apa Qaghans his reign was the longest.

Tomb number 329, in the text in which Shuluo Qaghan appears, does not have a specific date, but based on Chuluo Qaghan, we can firmly date it to the period 604-611, which by and large coincides with the dating to the late Qu family Gaochang period by the "explanatory notes" in *Documents Unearthed in Turfan.*

3

In the provisioning texts, the Nanxiang 南厢 Qaghan (the Qaghan of the Southern Wing) appears during the same period (583-587) as Apa Qaghan and Tanhan Qaghan. The Beixiang 北厢 Qaghan (the Qaghan of the Northern Wing) appears during the same period (604-611) as Chuluo Qaghan, slightly later than Nanxiang Qaghan. Regarding the Nanxiang and Beixiang Qaghans, neither one of them could exist without the other. Even though the Nanxiang and Beixiang Qaghans are recorded in sequence in the texts, I believe that they appeared at the same time, just as the Western Turks divided into Dongxiang 東厢 (Eastern Wing) and Xixiang 西厢 (Western Wing) during the Zhenguan reign period. That is to say that the Nanxiang and Beixiang Qaghans from the texts should have ruled during the period from 583 to 611.

There are no records of the Nanxiang and Beixiang Qaghans in the Chinese histories, but the histories do mention the Southern and Northern Courts of the Western Turks. The earliest record of the Southern and Northern Courts can be found in Du You's 杜佑 *Encyclopaedic History of Institutions*, chapter 199, "Turks, last part":

Sanxing speak of is *History of the Sui: Account of the Western Turks*. I suspect "Hepona" is a mistake for "Heshana," and "Hesana" was later revised based on other sources. Also, the same goes for *Comprehensive Mirror for Aid in Government*, ch. 186, "The First Year of Wude" 《武德元年》 which has "Heshana."

[22] *Important Documents of the Tang*, ch. 94; *Comprehensive Mirror for Aid in Government*, ch. 186; and *Outstanding Models from the Storehouse of Literature* 《冊府元龜》, ch. 964 all have "Prince of Guiyi" 歸義王, and the *Old Tang History: Account of the Western Turks* has "Prince of Guiyijun" 歸義郡王.

> The Western Turk Daluobian 大邏便 (Muqan 木杆 Qaghan's son – Du You's note): At first, Muqan split with Shabolüe Qaghan into two (Daluobian is Apa Qaghan – Du You's note).[23] His state was in the old lands of the Wusun 烏孫 and reached in the east to the Turkic state, in the west to the Leizhu (Aral) Sea 雷翥海, in the south to Shule 疏勒 (Kashgar), and in the north to Hanhai 瀚海, and was 7,000 *li* northwest of the capital. It took seven days of travel northwest of the state of Yanqi 焉耆 (Karashahr) to reach the Southern Court and eight days of travel due north from the Southern Court to reach the Northern Court. The Tiele, Qiuci 龜茲 (Kuchā), and the states of the Western regions all belonged to him. His people included the various tribes of the Dulu 都陸, Nushibi 弩失畢, Kirghiz 曷羅祿, Chuyue 處月, Chumi 處密, and Yiwu 伊吾.

In this passage, "His state was in the old lands of the Wusun" to "the states of the Western regions all belonged to him" is all territory of the Istämi-lineage Western Turkic Qaghanate. This is undisputed in the academic world. Later, the *Old Tang History: Account of the Western Turks* and the *New Tang History: Account of the Western Turks* generally continue from the *Encyclopaedic History of Institutions* in documenting the Southern and Northern Courts of the Western Turks. The line "eight days of travel due north from the Southern Court" is "travelled straight north for eight days" in the *Old Tang History* and "travelled north for eight days" in the *New Tang History*, and of all the records the *Encyclopaedic History of Institutions* is the clearest.

Edouard Chavannes' *Documents sur les Tou-Kiue (Turcs) occidentaux*[24] quotes Greek historical records: In 568 the Eastern Roman Empire sent Zemarkhos as an emissary to the Turks, where he met the Turkic Qaghan Dizaboul (Istämi) at Ektag Mountain. In 576 Valentin was sent as an emissary to the Turks to revise the agreement that Zemarkhos had made with Dizaboul. When he arrived Dizaboul had died, so he met Tardou (Tardu) Qaghan at Ektel Mountain. Chavannes believed that Ektel

---

[23] "Muqan" should be "Daluobian" or "Abo Qaghan"; The *Encyclopaedic History of Institutions* is in error here.

[24] Édouard Chavannes, *Documents sur les Tou-Kiue (Turcs) occidentaux*, Chinese translation 《西突厥史料》 by Feng Chengjun 馮承鈞 (Zhonghua Book Company, 1958). The following quotes from Chavannes all come from this translation.

is Ektag, and Ektag is a variant of Ak-tag. Ak-tag means "white mountain." Chinese historical records mention a "white mountain" north of Kuchā as a literal translation, and mention "Ajietian 阿羯田 Mountain" and "Ajie 阿羯 Mountain" as transliterations. Chavannes and Matsuda Toshio 松田寿男 both believe that the place where Istämi and Tardu twice met the emissaries of the Eastern Roman Empire was the same place as the "Southern Court" mentioned in the preface to the "Account of the Western Turks" of the various works. However, the two scholars have different views on the specific location of the Southern Court.

In Chavannes's notes to the *Account of the Western Turks* he believes, based on the *Gazetteer of the Western Regions* 西域圖志, that the Southern Court lay along the bank of the Konggesi River. Later, when discussing Menander's record of the Turkic Qaghan court at Ektag Mountain, he says, "the Western Turkic Qaghan's Southern Court was located in today's Tekesi River region near the northern mountain of Kuchā." Matsuda Toshio has studied the Southern Court in depth, and denies the theory of the Tekesi River. He believes the Southern Court was in the Yulduz valley. Of the two theories, Matsuda's is likely the correct one.[25]

Chavannes believes that the Northern Court may have been in one of two locations: one is near present-day Ili City, and the other is near Lake Ebi 額畢 (present-day Lake Aibi). Matsuda Toshio believes that "the Northern Court mentioned here lay approximately within the Beshbalïq area if we take into consideration that the later Duhu Superior Prefecture 都護府 located east of Urumqi in modern Jimsar County was called the Northern Court."[26] Note that Matsuda's argument here neglects the fact that he placed the Southern Court in the Yulduz valley, and the so-called Beshbalïq lies to the northeast of the Yulduz valley, which is quite far from the location given in the histories. Matsuda's error came from misinterpreting the original historical texts. Matsuda quotes the *Old Tang History: Account of the Turks*, and as this work aimed at conciseness, it deleted the three words "from the Southern Court," to say, "it took seven days of travel northwest of the state of Karashahr to reach the Southern Court, and eight days of travel due north to reach the Northern Court." Even though this passage has been edited, the meaning is clear that the

---

[25] Matsuda Toshio 松田寿男, *Research on the History and Geography of Ancient Tianshan* 《古代天山歷史地理學研究》, p. 326.

[26] Ibid., p. 321.

Northern Court was eight days journey due north of the Southern Court. However, Matsuda stresses that the Southern and Northern Courts took Karashahr as their reference point. In other words, Matsuda understood "and eight days of travel due north" as "and eight days of travel due north from Karashahr," so he placed the northern court in Beshbalïq. This section of the *Old Tang History* came from the *Encyclopaedic History of Institutions*, which clearly says, "and eight days' of travel due north from the Southern Court to reach the Northern Court." The reference point for the Northern Court is the Southern Court, and not the Northern Court, so Matsuda is clearly in error here.

Geographically speaking, we agree with Chavannes's second explanation that the Northern Court was near Lake Ebi. This not only matches the geography of the histories, but also, as this location has plentiful grasslands and water, it would be ideal for grazing. In the Yonghui 永徽 reign period (650-655) of Tang emperor Gaozong 高宗, after the Western Turk Išbara Qaghan (Ashina Helu 阿史那賀魯) betrayed the Tang, "there were several counties in the western region, and he established the court at the Shuang River 双河 and Thousand Springs 千泉. He called himself Shaboluo 沙鉢羅 Qaghan, and ruled over the ten clans 姓 of the Duolu 咄陸 and Nushibi 弩失畢."[27] Thousand Springs is a literal translation of Bing-yul and is located between Baishui City 白水城 and the Talas River. The *Gazetteer of the Western Regions* 西域圖志 takes the Shuang River to be the Borotala River region,[28] but Tao Baolian 陶保廉 believes it lay between the Jing 精 and Borotala Rivers.[29] The Jing River is near Borotala County. This generally coincides with the various histories that say "and eight days of travel due north from the Southern Court" (in the Yulduz River valley). We can see that Lake Ebi is where the Turks established their administration, and it is reasonable to take this as being where the Western Turks held their Northern Court.

The above mentioned Southern and Northern Courts appear in the prefaces to the "Account of the Western Turks" of various works, and when cited they are taken to be from the early period of the Western Turks. However, in actuality, the *Encyclopaedic History of Institutions* confuses the Istämi-lineage Western Turks with the Apa-lineage Turks that split off

---

27 *Old Tang History: Account of the Western Turks.*

28 *Gazetteer of the Western Regions* 《西域圖志》, ch. 22.

29 Tao Baolian 陶保廉, *Travel Diary of the Xinmao Year* (1891) 《辛卯侍行記》, ch. 6.

from the Eastern Turks as recorded in *History of the Sui: Account of the Western Turks*. The two *Tang Histories* carried over this error from the *Encyclopaedic History of Institutions*.[30] As for the excerpt from the *Encyclopaedic History of Institutions* preface quoted above, the location it mentions is undoubtedly that of the Istämi-lineage Western Turks. However, the remaining portion is unrelated to the Istämi-lineage Western Turks. The beginning, from "The Western Turk Daluobian" to "split…into two" is copied from the *History of the Sui*, and describes the origins of the Apa-lineage Turks – it is completely unrelated to the origin of the Istämi-lineage Western Turks. The meaning of the sentence "His people included the various tribes of the Dulu, Nushibi, Kirghiz, Chuyue, Chumi, and Yiwu" (this is the same as in the *Old Tang History: Account of the Western Turks*) is to say that the "Western Turks," apart from their fundamental composition, also include elements of the Dulu, Nushibi, Kirghiz, Chuyue, and Chumi. The *New Tang History: Account of the Western Turks* is even clearer in its record: "It took seven days of travel northwest of the state of Yanqi [Karashahr] to reach the Southern Court, and eight days of travel north to reach the Northern Court, with the various tribes of the Dulu, Nushibi, Kirghiz, Chuyue, Chumi, and Yiwu." This "Dulu" 都陸 is the same as "Duolu" 咄陸 above, and this "Nushibi" 弩矢畢 is the same as the other "Nushibi" 弩失畢. This clearly eliminates the Duolu and the Nushibi from the fundamental composition of the "Western Turks" and lists them along with other tribes like the Kirghiz. But we know that the five Duolu surnames [clans] and the five Nushibi surnames [clans] were fundamental components of the Istämi-lineage Western Turks. This record is clearly about the *History of the Sui* Apa-lineage Turks and not about the Istämi-lineage Western Turks. From the first to the sixth years of the Daye reign period of the Sui Dynasty, Chuluo Qaghan of the Apa lineage occupied a large area of land belonging to the Istämi-lineage Western Turks and forced Shekui Qaghan of the Istämi lineage to serve him. "The various tribes of Dulu and Nushibi" is referring to this situation. Since the *Encyclopaedic History of Institutions* and the two *Tang Histories* confuse these two different Turkic lineages, it is difficult for us to date the founding of the Southern and Northern Courts to the early Western Turkic period based solely on the prefaces of these

[30] See Wu Yugui 吳玉貴, "A New Study of the Western Turks" 《西突厥新考》, *Northwest Journal of Ethnology* 《西北民族研究》, 1988, no. 1.

texts.

Matsuda Toshio has discussed the date of the founding of the Southern and Northern Courts, and believes that "the appearance of the names for the Southern and Northern Courts among the Western Turks occurred after the mid-Tang Dynasty Zhenguan reign period when the state began to split, and the internal struggles started to increase in intensity." But the Western Turkic Southern and Northern Courts Matsuda speaks of refer to the Northern Court established by Duolu Qaghan to the west of Zuhe 鏃曷 Mountain and the Southern Court established by Shabolüe Qaghan to the north of the Suihe River 睢合水. These are completely different from the Southern and Northern Courts in the "Account of the Western Turks" in the prefaces of the different texts that Matsuda discusses. Therefore Matsuda later said that confusing the Northern and Southern Courts from the mid-Zhenguan reign period and from the prefaces was his own mistake. The Northern and Southern Courts of the prefaces "seem to have been extracted from records of the early Tang that are easily distinguished from the records of the Northern and Southern Courts of the mid-Zhenguan reign period and later, and there are no later records of their type."[31]

In looking through records in these books about the Western Turks, apart from the prefaces, from the reemergence of Shekui Qaghan during the late Sui Dynasty to the split of the Western Turks during the Tang Dynasty Zhenguan reign period, there are no records of the Southern and Northern Courts. Matsuda's dating of the Southern and Northern Courts to the early Zhenguan reign period seems to be baseless. The appearance of the Nanxiang and Beixiang Qaghans in the Turfan texts provides very valuable clues to studying the period in which the Southern and Northern Courts of the Western Turks were established.

I believe that the Nanxiang and Beixiang Qaghans of the texts should be the names of the Turkic Qaghans stationed at the Southern and Northern Courts, respectively. Above we have seen that the Nanxiang and Beixiang Qaghans reigned from 583 to 611, which by and large coincides with the reigns of the Western Turkic Tardu Qaghan (576-603) and Shekui Qaghan (605-616). If this is the case, then at the latest the Western Turks had the Nanxiang and Beixiang Qaghans by the middle of the Western

---

[31] Ma Yong 馬雍 "A Study of the Establishment of Diplomatic Relations between the Turks and the Gaochang Qu Family Dynasty" 《突厥與高昌麴氏王朝始建交考》 in *A Collection of Essays in Commemoration of Mr. Xiang Da* 《向達先生紀念論文集》 (Xinjiang People's Press, 1986), p. 56, n. 2.

Turk Tardu Qaghan's reign. It would make sense if the Nanxiang and Beixiang Qaghans came to power at the same time as the founding of the Southern and Northern Courts, or slightly later. If this conclusion is correct, then the founding of the Western Turk Southern and Northern Courts can be dated back to the period from 583 to 587, the same period that "Abo (Apa) Qaghan" appears in the texts.

From 583 to 587 the Eastern Turks split, and Apa Qaghan, Tanhan Qaghan, and Diqincha 地勤察 successively fled to the Western Turk Tardu Qaghan, forming an alliance headed by Tardu against the great Turkic Qaghan Shabolüe. Tardu took advantage of the split within the Eastern Turks and sent his army north of the Gobi Desert, seizing the title of Great Qaghan and establishing himself north of the Gobi Desert in the 20th year of the Kaihuang reign period as Bujia Qaghan, thereby becoming the Great Turkic Qaghan. It is then reasonable that during this period Tardu Qaghan established Lesser Qaghans in the Western Turkic Southern and Northern Courts.

Here I should stress that after the third year of the Renshou reign period (603) great changes happened in the government of the Western Turks. Along with the rebellion of the Tiele and other tribes, the Tardu alliance completely collapsed. Nili Qaghan of the Apa lineage was defeated by the Tiele, and the Great Qaghan Tardu faced rebellion north of the Gobi Desert and fled westward to the Tuyuhun. His fate is unknown. In this way the Apa-lineage Turks and the Istämi-lineage Western Turks lost their leaders. After Chuluo Qaghan of the Apa lineage succeeded the throne, the Tiele submitted to him. Not long after, however, the Tiele and other tribes, headed by the Xueyantuo, rebelled again, taking a large portion of present-day eastern Xinjiang.[32] Chuluo Qaghan was forced to flee westward, taking most of the land belonging to the Istämi-lineage Western Turks. Shekui Qaghan of the Istämi lineage then moved west to the Syr Darya region, and submitted himself as a vassal to Chuluo Qaghan. *History of the Sui: Account of the Western Turks*: "Chuluo Qaghan did not have a stable residence and stayed mostly in the ancient lands of the Wusun. Two Lesser Qaghans were re-established, who controlled their separate regions. One was to the north of the state of Chach 石國, who governed the barbarian states, and the other was to the north of Qiuci 龜兹 (Kuchā) in a place named Yingsuo 應娑." Yingsuo is the Yulduz valley and

---

[32] *History of the Sui: Account of the Tiele* 《隋書・鐵勒傳》.

was originally the place where Istämi and Tardu Qaghans of the Western Turkic Istämi lineage ruled, and it was also the location of the Southern Court mentioned in the various records. However, the Lesser Qaghan established by Chuluo to the north of the state of Chach 石國 was not in the same location of the Northern Court established in the Lake Ebi region by Tardu. We still have no way of determining whether the "Beixiang Qaghan" that appears in the records next to "Chuluo Qaghan" was located to the north of the state of Chach or in the Lake Ebi region. From the "Beixiang Qaghan" in the Turfan texts we know that after Chuluo Qaghan of the Apa lineage occupied most of the Western Turkic lands, he also continued the Nanxiang and Beixiang Qaghan system of the Western Turks. If the two Lesser Qaghans recorded in the *History of the Sui* are the Nanxiang and Beixiang Qaghans under Chuluo Qaghan, then during the reign of Chuluo Qaghan the location of Nanxiang Qaghan's residence did not change, and the Beixiang Qaghan moved from the Lake Ebi region to north of the state of Chach.

4

Section one, line two of the *Gaochang □shan Provisioning Record* from tomb number 307 says, "…*dou* 斗, supplying nephew Tiqin 提秦 Keduqian 珂都虔 forty-five people…" Section two, line nine of the same text says, "…six *dou*, supplying nephew (Tiqin) (Kedu)qian forty-five people, ended on the thirtieth day, together…" These two passages clearly record the same event. Tiqin of the text is a different translation of *tegin* 特勤 and is a Turkic official position. Keduqian is a name, and "nephew" is written in a variant form: waisheng'er 外生兒 for waisheng 外甥. There are examples of such a variation in historical texts. The *History of the Song: Account of Gaochang* 宋史・高昌傳 record of the Xizhou 西州 Uyghurs says, "In the sixth year of the Taiping Xingguo 太平興國 reign period [981], the king was first called the Nephew 外生 Master King Arslan 阿厮蘭漢." Here Arslan literally means "lion king" 師子王. From the *History of the Song: Biography of Huigu* 宋史・回鶻傳 we know that "nephew" is meant here. The text reads, "At first the Tang princess married below her status, and the Uyghurs called the Chinese court 'elder uncle,' and whenever the Chinese court replied they would say nephew 外甥. After the Five Dynasties this custom was followed." The *New History of the Five Dynasties: Biography of Huigu* 新五代史・回鶻傳 says as well, "At the borders of the Five Dynasties were those living in Ganzhou 甘洲 and Xizhou 西州. They often came to China, and when the Ganzhou Uyghur people came on their many visits they called the Chinese people 'elder uncle,' and the Chinese responded by calling them nephew 甥."[33] Clearly the two words for nephew are interchangeable, and from the Turfan texts and the *History of the Song: Account of Gaochang* we can see that from the Sui Dynasty to the Song Dynasty nephew was written as "waisheng" 外生 in the Gaochang area. The Xizhou Uyghurs calling themselves "waisheng" is different from the "waisheng'er" 外生兒 of the Turfan texts. The former had already changed into a name for government relations, and the latter showed that "Tiqin Keduqian" was the nephew of the Gaochang king.

This nephew appeared at the same time as Apa Qaghan, from roughly the third to the seventh years of the Kaihuang reign period of the Sui Dynasty, which corresponds to the 23rd to 27th years of the Gaochang King Qu Qiangu's 麴乾固 Yanchang reign period. From their names we know that Tiqin Keduqian was the son of the Gaochang princess and nephew of Qu Qiangu. Also, from his office of *tiqin* (*tegin*) we know that he was definitely a Turk. In other words, one of Qu Qiangu's sisters married a Turk. Tiqin Keduqian led an emissary group of up to 45 people, and as this was the largest of all the emissary groups, this shows that he did not just have an ordinary relationship with Gaochang. The appearance of this nephew provides new materials for the study of the relationship between Gaochang and the Turks.

Political marriage was a common foreign relations strategy used by the Turks. Continuously from when Tumen Qaghan unsuccessfully sought the hand of a Rouran in marriage and raised an army to establish the Turkish Qaghanate, up until the fall of the Turks in the early Tang Dynasty, there are records in all of the histories of Turk marriages with foreigners, and the Eastern and Western Turks are no exception. In order to control the merchant routes the Western Turks adopted a type of "loose reins" 羈縻 method of governing the oases states of the Silk Road. They bestowed the official position of Eltäbär 頡利發 (Xielifa) upon the kings of these western states and sent a Tudun 吐屯 [a Turk Governor resident in an area]

---

[33] See the *Old History of the Five Dynasties* 《舊五代史》, ch. 138, "Biography of Huigu" 《回鶻傳》.

to supervise the collection of taxes from them.[34] At the same time, through foreign marriages they strengthened their relations with the states of the western regions, thereby strengthening their influence over the region. For example, the daughters of both Western Turk Tardu Qaghan and Yabghu Qaghan were married in succession to the king of the kingdom of Samarkand.[35] The Shule (Kashgar) king also took a daughter of the Western Turks as his wife.[36] The younger brother of Qulichuo 屈利啜, an important vassal of the Western Turks, once married the daughter of the Karashahr king.[37] As Gaochang lay along important traveling routes, it had especially close relations with the Turks, and each successive king after Gaochang's sixth generation king Qu Baomao 麴寶茂 had marriage alliances with them.

After Gaochang's eighth generation king Qu Boya 麴伯雅 ascended the throne, the Turks forced him to follow the Turkic custom of marrying his grandmother, the daughter of the Turkic Qaghan. The *History of the Sui: Account of Gaochang*: "(Qu) Jian 麴堅 died and his son Boya succeeded him. His "damu" 大母 was the daughter of a Turkic Qaghan, and, when his father died, the Turks ordered him to follow their custom. Boya resisted for a long time, but he was forced, and he had no other choice but to concede." Note that Boya's father should be Qiangu, and the reference to his father as Qu Jian is an error.[38] According to Ma Yong 馬雍, "damu" means grandmother. This daughter of the Turks was probably the daughter of Istämi Qaghan of the Western Turks and the same person

---

[34] *Old Tang History: Account of the Western Turks*.

[35] For Tardu Qaghan's daughter see *History of the Sui: Account of the Kingdom of Kang* 《隋書・康國傳》, and for Yabghu Qaghan's daughter see the *Old Tang History: Account of the Kingdom of Kang* 《舊唐書・康國傳》.

[36] *Old Tang History: Account of Shule* 《舊唐書・疏勒傳》.

[37] *Old Tang History: Account of Karashahr* (Yanqi) 《舊唐書・焉耆傳》.

[38] Huang Wenbi 黄文弼 says, "The 'Account of Gaochang' in the *History of the Northern Dynasties* and the *History of the Sui* both say that Jia 嘉 died and his son Jian 堅 succeeded him; Jian died and his son Boya 伯雅 succeeded him. However, now we have evidence that after Jian died he was succeeded by the generations of Xuanxi 玄喜 and Baomao 寶茂, so to say that Boya succeeded Jian is erroneous, and we should be suspicious of the claim that Jian succeeded Jia as well." See Huang Wenbi's "Chronological Record of the Qu Family of Gaochang" 《高昌麴氏紀年》 in *Northwest Science Field Study Group Series* 《西北科學考察團叢刊》 2, *Archaeology* 《考古學》, vol. 1, "Gaochang" part 1 (1930).

seen in the *Qu Family Temple Construction Stele* 麹氏造寺碑 who was married to the sixth generation Gaochang king Qu Baomao. In 555 Istämi married his daughter to Qu Baomao; after Baomao died, his son Qiangu succeeded him, and when Qiangu died the Turks forced his son Boya to marry Istämi's daughter. Conventionally speaking, Istämi's daughter was Boya's grandmother, but as his father also married her, she became Boya's step-mother. The Turks forced Boya to marry her, and since he was taking over from his father, it was not seen as a grandson marrying his grandmother.[39]

From the Turfan texts we know that not only did the sixth generation Gaochang king Qu Baomao marry the daughter of a Turkic Qaghan, but he also married his own daughter to the Turks. Baomao's grandson Keduqian held the Turkic post of *tegin* (*tiqin*). The *Encyclopaedic History of Institutions*, chapter 197, says that the Turkic "Qaghans, like the ancient Shanyu 单于, were called Tele [*tegin*] by their sons and brothers." Also, the *Encyclopaedic History of Institutions*, chapter 199, says the Western Turks "had the offices of *yabghu* 葉護, *šad* 設, and *tegin* 特勒, which were often held by the sons and younger brothers of the Qaghans, or by a member of their clan."[40] We know from this passage that Keduqian held the office of *tegin*, and the husband of Qu Baomao's daughter must have been a Turkic Qaghan or a member of their clan.

The eighth generation Gaochang king Boya also married his daughter to Tardu Šad 怛[here 口+旦]度設, the eldest son of the Western Turk Tong Yabghu Qaghan 統葉護可汗, and she became Katun (Qadun) 可賀敦 [wife of a chief] and gave birth to a son. *Biography of the Tripitaka Dharma-Master of the Great Compassion Monastery* 大慈恩寺三藏法師傳, chapter two:

> From here [Tiemen 鐵門] he traveled several hundred *li* and forded the Fuchu River 縛芻河, reaching the Kingdom of Huo 活國. This was where Yabghu Qaghan's eldest son Tardu Šad resided, who was also the brother-in-law of the Gaochang king. The Gaochang king had him [Xuanzang 玄奘, the Dharma-Master]

[39] Ma Yong 馬雍 "A Study of the Establishment of Diplomatic Relations between the Turks and the Gaochang Qu Family Dynasty" 《突厥與高昌麴氏王朝始建交考》.

[40] *Old Tang History: Account of the Western Turks* does not have the characters "有設" ("have the office of *šad*").

> bring a letter to Tardu Šad. When the Dharma-Master arrived, the princess Katun had already died, and Tardu Šad had taken ill. When he heard that the Dharma-Master had come from Gaochang and saw the letter from the Gaochang king, Tardu Šad and his sons and daughters cried without stopping....After Tardu Šad died, as the Gaochang princess' son was still young, Tardu Šad's son from a former wife Tegin usurped the title of *šad* and married his step-mother.

The Fuchu River is the Amu Darya. The Kingdom of Huo is Warwāliz or Valvlij[41] and is located at the convergence of the Dashi and Tālaqān Rivers near the present-day Qunduz River [in northern Afghanistan].[42] According to the *Great Tang Dynasty Record of the Western Regions* 大唐西域記, chapter 16, the Kingdom of Huo's "king was a Turk who governed the Tiemen 鐵門 [literally, "Iron Gate"] and smaller states to the south, who were always on the move, never settling for long in one place." Tong Yabghu sent his eldest son to live in the Kingdom of Huo to manage the lands to the south of Tiemen, to the north of the Hindu Kush, to the west of the Pamirs, and the smaller states to the east of Persia.[43] At this time the Gaochang king was the seventh generation king Qu Wentai 麴文泰, and Tardu Šad was the Gaochang king's brother-in-law, as his wife was the daughter of Qu Boya. According to the "Account of the Turks" in the *History of the Zhou* 周書, the *Encyclopaedic History of Institutions*, and the *Old Tang History*, the Turkic Qaghan "called his wife Katun, like

[41] "Ehuan City" 遏換城 in the *Old Tang History: Gazetteer*《舊唐書•地理志》 and "Ahuan City" 阿緩城 in the *New Tang History*.

[42] See Ji Xianlin 季羡林, *Collated and Annotated Edition of the Great Tang Dynasty Record of the Western Regions* 《大唐西域記校注》 (Zhonghua Book Company, 1985), p. 963, note to "Huoguo" 《活國》.

[43] *Great Tang Dynasty Record of the Western Regions* 《大唐西域記》, ch. 1, "The Ancient Land of Tukhāra (Tokharia)" 《睹貨邏國故地》 says, "From Tiemen to the ancient lands of Tukhāra is over 1,000 *li* from south to north and over 3,000 *li* from east to west. In the east are the Pamirs and to the west is Persia; in the south are the great snow mountains [the Hindu Kush], in the north is Tiemen, and through the center runs the great Fuchu River [today's Amu Darya]. In the several hundred years since the king's line died out, the tribal leaders fought one another and split into 27 states. Even though each state was different, they all belonged to the Turks." This was the land under Tardu Šad's control.

Yanzhi 閼氏 [wife of a chief] of old.[44] Clearly Katun is the name for the Turkic Qaghan's wife. Even though Qu Boya's daughter was the wife of Tardu Šad, she was also called Katun, and we can see that the Gaochang princess had quite high status among the Turks. This passage also clearly states that after Tardu Šad died, because the Gaochang princess' son was too young, the position of *šad* was usurped by the former son Tele 特勒. This proves that the Gaochang princess' son was the legal successor of Tardu Šad, which must have been directly related to the princess' status. It can also prove that the Turks highly valued their relationship with Gaochang.

In summary, the following is a family tree showing the marriage relations between Gaochang and the Turks (double lines represent marriage):

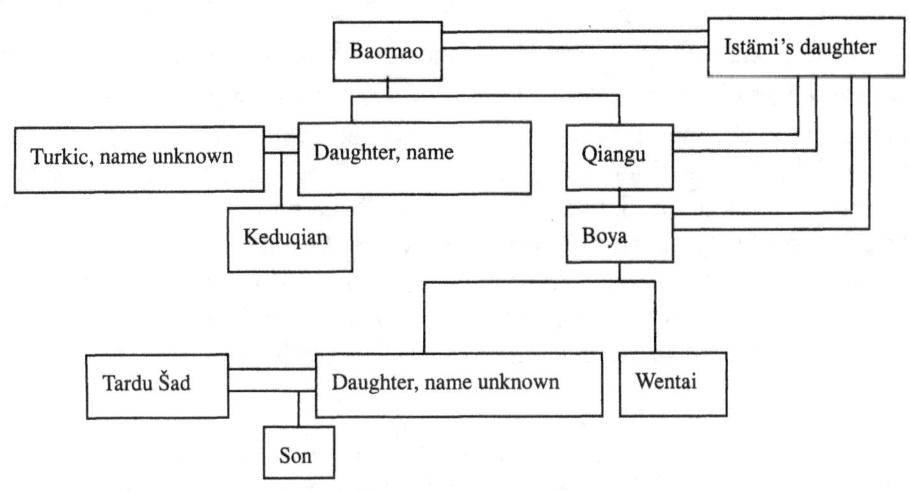

[44] Kehedun 可賀敦 is Kedun 可敦 in the *New Tang History: Account of the Turks*, and the variant "Kedun" 珂頓 in the text "Record of Zhongbao and Others from Gaochang County Regarding their Provisioning in Turn" 《高昌衆保等傳供糧食帳》 from *Documents Unearthed in Turfan*, vol. 2 (Cultural Relics Press, 1981).

5

The banquet texts also mention Turkic "iron masters" and "gold masters." Section one, line three of the *Gaochang □shan Provisioning Record* reads: "(Tian)ashan 田阿善 provided, five *dou* [a measure of capacity equal to about .17 bushels] of wheat flour, supplying Abo (Apa) Qaghan iron master Juzhi 居織…"[45] Section one, line six of the *Gaochang Linghu Provisioning Record* 高昌令狐等傳供食帳 says, "… three *sheng* 升 [1/10 of a *dou*] of broomcorn millet, supplying Tanhan (Qaghan) gold master Mopantuo 莫畔陀, one upper-ranked (person)…" This "iron master" and "gold master" were sent by the Turkic Apa Qaghan and Tanhan Qaghan, respectively.

Apart from iron and gold masters, Turfan texts mention painting masters,[46] archery masters,[47] paper masters,[48] painting craftsmen, leather working craftsmen, leather tanning craftsmen, carpenter craftsmen, oil craftsmen, and pig slaughtering craftsmen.[49] We have discovered that in the Turfan texts, all instances of "X master 師" appear in texts from the Gaochang Kingdom era, and instances of "X craftsmen 匠" are only seen in Tang texts. On the other hand, those engaged in handicrafts were called "masters" in the Gaochang Kingdom era and called "craftsmen" during the Tang. In the texts the Turks "Juzhi" and "Mopantuo" are named "iron master" and "gold master," respectively, as Gaochang used the local custom for names of Turkic occupations, and we do not know what the Turks called such occupations themselves. As the name implies, an "iron master" is a blacksmith, and a "gold master" is a goldsmith.

---

[45] The original line reads, "…shan provided, five *dou* of wheat flour, supplying Apa Qaghan iron master Ju…" This line was modified based on section two, line ten of the same text. For more details see the texts at the end of this paper.

[46] *Documents Unearthed in Turfan*, vol. 2, p. 333, "Register of Painting Masters, Master Gluers, and Other Workers Sent from Gaochang County" 《高昌入作人畫師、主膠人等名籍》.

[47] Ibid., vol. 4, p. 172, "Order from the Capital Administration Office to the Adjutant of Shichang County for Sending Master Bow-Maker Hou Weixiang and Others to the Court in the Second Year of the Yihe Reign Period (615) in Gaochang Kingdom" 《高昌義和二年（615）都官下始昌縣司馬主者符為遣弓師侯尾相等詣府事》.

[48] Ibid., vol. 4, p. 188, "Register of the Escapee Shi Yanming and Others in Gaochang County" 《高昌逋人史延明等名籍》.

[49] Ibid. vol. 4, p. 15, "Register of the Craftsman He Haoren and Others of the Tang Dynasty" 《唐何好忍等匠人名籍》.

Throughout history the Turkic peoples have been intimately familiar with gold working. *History of the Zhou: Account of the Turks* 周書・突厥傳 records that before the founding of the Turkic state, "they were vassals to the Ruru 茹茹 and lived on the south side of Gold Mountain as blacksmiths for the Ruru," and the Ruru saw the Turks as "smithing slaves." *History of the Sui: Account of the Turks* also mentions that the Turks "lived on Gold Mountain and worked as blacksmiths." When the Roman emissary Zemarkhos visited the Turks in 568, he travelled through Samarkand, where a Turkic person tried to sell him iron. Menander believes that the Turks wanted the Roman emissary to know that their state was rich in iron ore. Iron was also an important item they collected from their vassal lands. The *New Tang History: Biography of Huigu* appendix "Account of the Yenisei Kirghiz (Xiajiasi)" 黠戛斯傳 says that they "had gold, iron, and tin, and every time it rains they found a type of iron called "jiasha" 迦沙; weapons made of this iron were extremely sharp, and they often were presented to the Turks." *History of the Sui: Account of Shule* (Kashgar) says that the kingdom of Shule "is abundant in rice, millet, hemp, wheat, copper, iron, brocade, and orpiment, and each year these were offered to the Turks."[50] Furthermore, regarding Bogda 博格 Mountain and the Altai 阿爾泰 Mountains, which were so closely related with the origins of the Turks, the former is still famous for being rich in iron ore, and the latter is well-known for producing nonferrous metals such as gold and copper. The importance of iron to the Turks has been known throughout history, but historical records of this importance are limited to just a few passages with similar content. The Turkic "iron masters" from the Turfan texts supply us with new materials for studying Turkic handicraft industries, and these few fragments are of great value.

As we know from historical materials, Turkic gold and silver products were finely crafted. When the Roman emissaries met with the Western Turkic Istämi Qaghan in the great tent, "they saw him seated upon a

---

[50] The "Collation Notes" to the Zhonghua Book Company punctuated edition of the *History of the Sui* read, "'brocade' is 'tin' in the *History of the Northern Dynasties: Account of Shule*, and it is 'silver' in the *Taiping Imperial Encyclopedia* 《太平御覽》 number 793." Note that the *Encyclopaedic History of Institutions*, ch. 192, "Shule" reads: "The land is abundant in rice, chestnuts, sugarcane (this should be an error for 'hemp'), wheat, copper, iron, cotton brocade, and orpiment." Perhaps the *History of the Sui* "brocade" 錦 is an abbreviation of "cotton brocade" 綿錦, and "silver" 銀 and "tin" 錫 are mistaken characters for "brocade."

golden throne with two wheels, which was pulled by a horse." "The Qaghan received the Roman emissaries in two rooms, one of which had a portrait showing the Qaghan lying on a golden bed surrounded by golden vases and jars, and the other had wooden pillars decorated in gold and one golden bed held up by four golden peacocks. In the doorway was a cart full of silver plates and silver animal figures." Clearly these gold and silver products were quite exquisitely crafted, making a deep impression on the Roman emissaries, which is why they were described in such detail. This was not an isolated incident – in the first year of the Zhenguan reign period Xuanzang also recorded the gold and emerald splendour of the Western Turkic Tong Yabghu Qaghan's tent: "the Qaghan lived in a great tent that was extravagantly decorated, and dazzled the eye."[51] Clearly gold and silver were commonly used in the daily lives of the Turkic nobility.

Historical materials clearly record that Turkic people worked iron, but do not mention whether they were good at making gold and silver objects. The histories only say that the Turkic people used a great number of gold and silver objects, but we cannot say with certainty that these were produced by the Turks themselves. The Turkic "gold master" in the Turfan texts proves that the Turks not only "worked iron" and had "iron masters," but also had "gold masters," indicating professional gold and silver workers. It is entirely possible that the gold and silver objects that appeared amongst the Turks were created by themselves. In addition to silk, grains, and people, gold and silver were important objects of Turkish trade and plundering. *Kül Tegin Inscription* (S4-5): "A land better than the Ötüken Mountains does not exist at all! The place from which the tribes can be (best) controlled is the Ötüken Mountains. Having stayed in this place, I came to an amicable agreement with the Chinese people. They (i.e., the Chinese) give (us) gold, silver, and silk in abundance." (N12): "From the Chinese emperor, Ísiyi Likäŋ came. He brought an immeasurable quantity of treasures, gold, and silver in abundance." *Bilgä Khagan Inscription* (S11): "They brought scent…gold and silver in abundance." (N11): "For the benefit of my Turks and my people I won and acquired their yellow gold and white silver…" *Tonyukuk Inscription* (S2-4): "The Turkish people had never before reached the Iron Gate and the mountain

---

[51] Hui Li 慧立 and Yan Cong 彥悰, *Biography of the Tripitaka Dharma-Master of the Great Compassion Monastery* 《大慈恩寺三藏法師傳》, ch. 2 (Zhonghua Book Company, 1983).

which is called 'Son of Heaven.' Now, since I caused (the Turkish armies) to reach as far as these lands, they brought home the yellow gold and the white silver, girls and women, and crooked camels in great abundance."[52] Almost all of the received items surely included gold and silver. Apart from being used as coins to be exchanged, a considerable portion of the large amount of gold and silver that the Turks traded for or plundered was certainly used to make gold and silver products. The Turks' love for gold and silver was related to the development of their gold and silver working industry.

The goal of the Turkic iron and gold masters who acted as emissaries in coming to Gaochang was related to the iron and gold trade. In the provisioning texts already published, foreign emissaries were divided into three ranks (upper, middle, and lower) for the provisioning, and these ranks were related to the status of the emissaries. As the texts are missing some parts, we do not know the rank of the "iron master Juzhi." As "gold master Mopantuo" was placed within the upper rank, we can infer that the iron master was also given this rank. The iron and gold masters from the texts not only represented the Turkic Qaghans in their roles as foreign emissaries and enjoyed the best treatment their hosts had to offer, they also had a type of official position within the iron and gold working industry of the Turkic Qaghanate. Overall, from looking at the ranks of the iron and gold masters at the banquets, as compared with the traditional recognition within the feudal Chinese society of farmers of "planting and study first, trading and business second, and craftsmanship third," handicrafts had a higher status in the economic lives of the Turkic peoples.

6

The following are six provisioning text records relating to the Turks.[53] The records are based on *Documents Unearthed in Turfan*, and the original vertical alignment has been changed to horizontal alignment here. I have made notes when traditional characters and variants have been simplified and when an extra row of characters has been included. I have changed some of the original markings. Also, those words that I have added are

---

[52] Talât Tekin, *A Grammar of Orkhon Turkic* (Indiana University, 1968), pp. 261, 271-2, 279, 281, and 289, slightly modified.

[53] Texts A, B, C, D, and E are recorded in *Documents Unearthed in Turfan*, vol. 3, p. 250, 255, 259, 260, and 542, respectively; Text F is recorded in the vol. 4 appendix, p. 24. [The punctuation in the translations follows Yu Wugui's Chinese. Translator's note.]

marked with "( )", and a brief explanation is given at the end of each text for characters added or changed. For clarifications see the scan of the original.

A. *Gaochang Zhufotu Provisioning Record* 《高昌竺佛圖等傳供食帳》

(1)

(Beginning missing)

1. … people, ended on the fifteenth day, thirteen *hu* 斛 [one Tang Dynasty *hu* equals about 1.7 bushels] and two *dou* 斗 [1/10 of a *hu*] of common-use wheat flour, broomcorn millet

2. … *sheng* 升 [1/10 of a *dou*]. Next Zhufotu provided, five *hu* and six *dou* of wheat flour, nine *sheng* of broomcorn millet, supplying Pohu Tudun Niuerhan 婆瓠吐敦牛爾旱, two upper-ranked people, three middle-ranked people [one *hu* equals ten *dou*, and one *dou* equals ten *sheng*, editor]

3. (ended on) the thirteenth day. Five *hu* and six *dou* of common-use wheat flour, nine *dou* of broomcorn millet. Next Lüsengzhong 吕僧忠 provided, six *dou* of wheat flour, one *dou* two *sheng* of broomcorn millet, supplying Jibiling 雞弊零

4. Sulijiege's 蘇利結個 wife, four middle-ranked people, two lower-ranked people, ended on the fifteenth day, seven *hu* two *dou* of common-use flour, one *hu* four *dou* four *sheng* of broomcorn millet, next on the sixth day, Linghu 令狐

5. □monk provided, three *dou* six *sheng* of wheat flour, three *sheng* of broomcorn millet, supplying Wuhunmohexian's 烏渾摩河先 emissary Hegan 河干, two upper-ranked people, one middle-ranked person, ended on the tenth day, common-use (wheat flour one *hu* eight *dou*, one *dou* five *sheng* of broomcorn millet).

(End missing)

60TAM307:5/3(a)

Based on the format of the provisioning records, line three should have a character for "ended on" before "the thirteenth day." Also, in line five on the sixth day of a certain month the food amounted to three *dou* six *sheng* of wheat flour and three *sheng* of broomcorn millet, and on the tenth day the food should then be "one *hu* eight *dou* of wheat flour and one *dou* five *sheng* of broomcorn millet."

(2)

(Beginning missing)

1. …ten two *hu* six *dou*, broomcorn millet three *hu* seven *dou*…er 儿 provided, two *dou* three *sheng* of (wheat flour), broomcorn millet three (*sheng*, supplying)…

2. …Enhe 恩紇, one upper-ranked person, one middle-ranked person, ended on the fifteenth day, (common-use wheat flour three) *hu* four and a half *dou*, four and a half *dou* of broomcorn millet. Next Hu 虎…

3. …two *sheng*. Next provided one *dou* of common millet, and one *dou* of wheat bran,…han's 寒 emissary Zhiju 知[here 口+知]舉 Tanhan 貪旱[here and throughout 水+旱], four upper-ranked people…

4. …*hu* one *dou* two *sheng*, six *dou* of common millet, wheat bran six…three *dou* three *sheng*, supplying Nanxiang 南厢 Qaghan…

5. One upper-ranked person, two lower-ranked persons, ended on the fifteenth day, common…(four *hu*) nine and a half *dou*. Next provided two *dou* of wheat flour, supplying…

6. …han's 旱, sons and brothers, two lower-ranked people, ended on the thirteenth day, common … one (two) *hu* six *dou*. Next Mingwei 明威 Fonu 佛奴 provided, wheat flour…

7. …Qinwuluohun 勤烏羅渾, fifty one people, ended on ten□□, sixty one *hu* two *dou* of common-use flour. Next Huya 虎牙…

8. …provided, one *dou* of broomcorn millet, one *dou* of wheat bran, supplying Zhantou 棧頭□□ high official, eighteen upper-ranked people, ended on the fourteenth day (and a half)…

9. …one *hu* and four and a half *dou* of common millet, one *hu* and four and a half dou of wheat bran. Next provided one *hu* five *dou* and two *sheng* of wheat flour, broomcorn …

10. four upper-ranked people, ten middle-ranked people, ended on the fourteenth day and a half, twenty-two *hu* four *sheng* of common-use flour, broomcorn millet four…

11. …nine *sheng*, supplying Zhantou 棧頭 Andouzhemohexian 案豆遮摩訶先, two upper-ranked people…

12. …*hu* eight and a half *dou*. Next provided one *hu* one *dou* of wheat flour, three *dou* of broomcorn millet, supplying…

13. …four *hu* five *dou*, broomcorn millet four *hu* three…

14. …people, ended on…

(End missing)

60TAM307:5/2(a)

This text is the provisioning record for the first day of a certain month (for more details see Wu Yugui's *Two Gaochang Provisioning Texts* 兩件高昌供食文書; the following deals with the days in the record, which will not be mentioned again). "two *dou* three *sheng*" of line one is missing the type of food. The texts usually couple "wheat flour" with "broomcorn millet," so "wheat flour" has been added. With a daily food amount of two *dou* three *sheng* of wheat flour, the first to the fifteenth day should amount to three *hu* four and a half *dou* of wheat flour, so "common-use wheat flour three" has been added to line two. Also, as the provisioning in line two is four and a half *dou* of broomcorn millet, the "broomcorn millet three" missing text in line one should be "*sheng*."

In line five the daily food is three *dou* three *sheng*, and the first to the fifteenth day should amount to four *hu* nine and a half *dou*, so "four *hu*" can be added to "nine and a half *dou*."

In line six the daily food is two *dou*, and the first to the thirteenth day should be two *hu* six *dou*, so the original "one *hu* six *dou*" seems to be a mistake.

In line eight the daily food is two *dou* each of common millet and wheat bran, and as one *hu* four and a half *dou* of each were provided, clearly the word "and a half" is missing after "ended on the fourteenth day." It seems to be an error that the original ended the sentence after "fourteenth day."

(3)

(Beginning missing)

1. Xian 先, three upper-ranked people, three middle-ranked people, three hundred and fifteen *jin* 斤 [one Tang Dynasty *jin* equals about 1.3 pounds] of common-use. Next provided nine *jin*, supplying Tanhan Tiqin's 貪旱提懃 emissary…

2. (ended on the) twenty-second day and a half, sixty-seven and a half *jin* of common-use. Next provided fourteen *jin*, supplying Zhantou high official's emissary Yanpantuo 炎畔陀, seven middle-ranked people, ended on ended on [*sic*] the seventeenth day, twenty-eight *jin* of common-use, (next)

3. provided eight, supplying Zhantou high official's emissary Pipo 脾婆, four middle-ranked people, ended on the twenty-second day, fifty-six

jin of common-use. Next provided seven *jin*, supplying Abo Qaghan's emissary □

4. Zhenkelizhen 振珂離振, one upper-ranked person, one middle-ranked person, ended on

(End missing)

60TAM307:5/4

Based on the context, the characters which were missing at the start of line two before "twenty-second day and a half" should be "ended on." In the same line the note in the original record on "ended on ended on" says "there is an extra character for 'ended on'." This is correct. In the same line the "next" character at the end was originally "□", and it was added based on the context.

(4)

(Beginning missing)

1. …one *dou* three *sheng* of wheat flour, supplying Pohugushi 婆瓠孤時…

2. …*dou* seven *sheng*…

(End missing)

60TAM307:5/2(a)

B. *Gaochang Huya Duzi Provisioning Record*
《高昌虎牙都子等傳供食帳》

(Beginning missing)

1. …food…

2. □□ two *jin*, supplying Xianketiqian 現珂提虔 one person, and his sons and brothers twenty-two people.

3. (Next) Huya Duzi 虎牙豆子 provided, fifteen *jin*, supplying Nanxiang Qaghan's emissary Zhi 知[here 口+知]

4. Ju Tanhan 舉貪旱, one upper-ranked person, two accompanying upper-ranked persons, ended on □ half. Next Caoziyue 曹子岳

5. □ *jin* supplying Aduhexijin's 阿都紇希瑾 emissary Pantuo's 畔陀 sons and brothers, three middle-ranked people

6. …rewarded food…

(End missing)

60TAM307:4/2(a)

"Next" in line three was originally "□", and was added based on the context.

In line four, according to the notes to the original record, there is a character for "younger brothers" 弟 below "Caozi," which was crossed out.

There is an additional line between lines four and five; to the right of "Aduhe" 阿都紇 is "rewarded food to thirteen people."

C. *Gaochang □shan Provisioning Record*
《高昌□善等傳供食帳》

(1)

1. …Tuo 陀, ten middle-ranked people, ten lower-ranked people, ended on the thirtieth day…

2. …*dou*, supplying nephew Tiqin 提秦 Keduqian 珂都虔 forty-five people, (ended on the thirtieth day, with)…

3. …(Tian)ashan (田)阿善 provided, five *dou* of wheat flour, supplying Abo Qaghan iron master Ju(zhi)居(織)…

4. …seven *hu* five *dou* of.…Ciqishaohe 此畦少何 provided, five *dou* of wheat flower, supplying Zhantou high official…

5. …three people of lower rank, ended on the thirtieth day, (seven) *hu* five *dou* of common-use wheat flour. Next Kang Shide 康師得…

6. …Qaghan Taspar 佗鉢 high official □□, six upper-ranked people, four middle-ranked people, ended on the thirtieth (day)…

7. …Next Huya Duzi provided, …of wheat flour, two *dou* of common millet, supplying Nan(xiang) Ke 南(厢)珂…

8. …son and younger brother, six upper-ranked people, ended on the thirtieth (day), …three *hu* of common millet. Next on the seventeenth day…

9. …*dou*, supplying Yisangye's 移桑拽 emissary Fu 浮…ended on the thirtieth day, common-use wheat flour …

10. …(Kang) Shide (康)師得 provided, three *dou* of wheat flour, supplying…han's 寒 emissary Hudiankuhezhen 呼典枯合振…

11. …wheat flour…Next provided…

60TAM307:5/1(a)

There is an extra line between the first and second lines; to the right of "Tiqin Keduqian" is "Fuli 浮利, four middle-ranked people, four lower-ranked people, that was all." Between the eighth and ninth lines, to the right of "Yisangye's emissary Fu..." is "...four people."

In line two, "ended on the thirtieth day, with" is added based on the second part of line nine of this text (just below).

In line three, "Tian'a" and "zhi" are added based on line ten of part two of this text. Based on this, this original title of this text, "Gaochang □ shan Provisioning Record" should be "Gaochang Tian'ashan Provisioning Record." There are two characters missing before the character "shan," which was initially mistaken for one character.

In line five, "seven" was originally "□", but as this text is a record for the sixteenth day of a certain month, and the "Zhantou high official" emissary group eats five *dou* daily, so from the sixteenth to the thirtieth would be "seven *hu* five *dou*."

"Day" of lines six and eight and "xiang" of line seven have been added based on the context.

(2)

(Beginning missing)

1. ...one *dou* of wheat flour, supplying ...

2. ...one *hu* four *dou* of wheat flour, next on the eighteenth (day)...

3. ...emissary Zhiju Tanhan, Ji (?) [薊?], two upper-ranked people, ended on ...

4. ...*dou*, supplying Nanxiang (K)han's emissary Zhiju Tanhan, upper ...

5. ...provided, two *dou* of wheat flour, supplying Zhantouzhewugen 棧頭折無艮, one middle-ranked person, one lower...

6. ...day, Zhengjiazi 鄭伽子 provided √√√ *dou*, supplying by Jibiling marched on...

7. ...*dou*. Next the twenty-first day, Zhufotu provided, √√√ *dou*, supplying Hunlingju's 渾零居 Bi 弊...

8. ...Ji (?) [薊?], two upper-ranked people, ended on the thirtieth day, common-use √√√ *hu*, three *hu* of common millet. Next Mingwei (Fonu)...

9. ...six *dou*, supplying nephew (Tiqin) (Kedu)qian, forty-five people, ended on the thirtieth day, together...

10. ...Tian'ashan provided, (five *dou*) of wheat flour, (supplying Abo) Qaghan's iron master Juzhi...

11. ...seven *hu* (five) *dou* of wheat flour, (next Qishaohe 畦少何 provided,) five *dou* of wheat flour, supplying Zhantou high (official)...

12. …people, two middle-ranked people (three lower-ranked people, ended on the thirtieth day,) seven *hu* five *dou* of (common-use) wheat flour. Next Kang Shide …

(End missing)

60TAM307:4/4(a)

"Day" in line two and "Ke" [thus "qaghan"] in line four were added based on the context.

"Fonu" in line eight was added based on "Mingwei Fonu" of text A, part two, line six.

Additions to lines nine to twelve were based on lines two to five of the first part of this text.

(3)

(Beginning missing)

1. …Moke 摩珂…ten middle-ranked…

2. …millet six *sheng*, supplying Wumohu 烏莫胡…zhi 至, middle-ranked…

3. …millet one *dou*, supplying Tanhan Qaghan…people, ended…

4. …three *dou* three *sheng* of wheat flour, six *sheng* of broomcorn millet, (supplying) Tanhan…

5. …Huya Duzi provided,…three *sheng*, supplying Nanxiang Qaghan…

6. …sons and brothers, one upper-ranked person, two lower-ranked people, ended on…(Ming)wei Fonu provided, wheat flour…

7. Wuluo[gen?] 烏羅[火+艮] fifty-three people, ended on…(Lü)sengzhong (呂)僧忠 provided, wheat flour one…*

8. …nine *sheng*, supplying Zhantou Moke…people, thirteen middle-ranked people, ended on…

9. …*sheng*, six *sheng* of broomcorn millet, supplying Zhantou…ended on the twenty-first day…

10. …millet one *dou* two *sheng*, supplying Zhantou Fu…ended on…

(End missing)

60TAM307:4/3(a)

There is an additional line between lines six and seven; to the right of "fifty-three people" is "two people on the twenty-second day," and to the

* The character [火+艮] does not exist in Chinese dictionaries, and was probably a local Turfan variation; its pronunciation should have been "gen," but could also have been "ghan" or "qan." The name 烏羅[火+艮] may be the same as Wuluohun 烏羅渾 from the historical records of that era. Translator's note.

right of "thirteen people" between lines seven and eight is "twenty-first day…"

"Supplying" in line four was added based on the context.

"Ming" of line six was added based on text A, part two, line six.

"Lü" of line seven was added based on "Lüsengzhong" of text A, part one, line three.

D. Gaochang Linghu Provisioning Record
《高昌令狐等傳供食帳》

(1)
(Beginning missing)

1. …one *sheng*, two *dou* four *sheng* of broomcorn millet…

2. …Lun 倫 high official, seven upper-ranked persons, eight middle-ranked persons, fourteen lower-ranked persons…

3. …one *hu* six *dou* eight *sheng* of wheat flour. Next common millet…

4. …(Wu)luo[gen?] (烏)羅[火+艮], six upper-ranked persons, five middle-ranked persons, fourteen lower-ranked persons,…

5. …three *dou* of broomcorn millet, supplying refugees A 阿□, seven people, that was all. Next Yanseng 嚴僧…

6. …three *sheng* of broomcorn millet, supplying Tanhan (Qaghan) gold master Mopantuo, one upper-ranked (person)…

7. …Zhang Rongzhen 張容真 provided, □□□*sheng* of wheat flour, one *dou* two *sheng* of broomcorn miller, supplying …

8. …one upper-ranked person, four middle-ranked persons, that was all.…Tijia 提伽 provided, one *hu* eight *dou* of wheat flour…

9. …three *sheng*, supplying Xijinmo 希槿摩…six upper-ranked persons, eleven middle-ranked persons, that was all.…

10. …Zhongseng 衆僧 provided, one hu…of wheat flour, two *dou* seven *sheng* of…millet, supplying Yin 垔…

(End missing)

60TAM307:5/2(b)

"Wu" of line four has been added based on "Wuluo[gen?]" from text C, section three, line seven.

"Ke" and "person" in line six have been added based on the context.

(2)

(Beginning missing)

1. …sixteenth day of the twelfth month, Li Chen 李琛 provided, four *dou* of wheat flour, one *dou* of common millet, supplying Shiyu 侍御

2. Shida 仕達, four people, that was all. Next Xiaoji Mianqiong 校即麵瓊 provided, three *dou* of wheat flour, supplying Shilongai 石隆愛

3. …Yue 岳, three people, that was all. Next Kang Gousao 康苟掃 provided, one *dou* of wheat flour, supplying Yuanfuda 員浮達

(End missing)

60TAM307:5/3(b)

As for "Mianqiong" of line two, the notes to the original record say that "Mian" 麵 is thought to be a mistake for "Qu" 麴.

E. Gaochang Huya Yuanzhi Provisioning Record
《高昌虎牙元治等傳供食帳》

(1)

(Beginning missing)

1. …Qaghan emissaries…

2. …next Huya Can 虎牙参…

3. …person. Next Hu 虎…

4. …provided, one and a half *dou*, supplying…Qian 虔 high official, one upper-ranked person…

5. …next Yan 顏…and a half *dou*, supplying Tutunye…吐屯抴

6. …high official, four upper-ranked persons, one middle-ranked person, that was all. Next Huya Yuanzhi provided,…

7. …Poyan 婆演 high official Biehui 別迴, that was all. Next…

8. …supplying Shuluo Qaghan Wudulun 烏都倫 high official…

9. …next Huya Yuanzhi provided,…

10. …that was all. Next…

11. …Buliuduo 不六多 married wives. Next Kang Yuanxiang 康元相

12. …supplying Beixiang Qaghan's emissary Tubie Tanhan, one upper-ranked person, that was all.

13. …provided, two *dou*, supplying Beishiyifugu's 卑失移浮孤 emissary Wuyuyanyili 烏庾延伊利

14. …next one upper-ranked person, two middle-ranked

persons.…five *dou*, supplying She'ni 射尼

15. …Qaghan's emissary Tutun…four persons, that was all.

16. …Tutun high official Bie 别

17. …nine *sheng*, supplying Tan 貪

18. …person, that was all.

19. …Alai 阿賴□

(End missing)

60TAM329:23/1,23/2

(2)

(Beginning missing)

1. …that was all.…four *hu*, supplying Shu Tanhan 屬貪旱…

2. Next Kang Zhaogou 康趙苟 provided,…Beimian 卑面 two persons took medicine.

3. …Na 那…Barbarian tailor Alaizi's 阿賴姿 son, lower

4. …next Hu 虎…supplying Tubie Tanhan …

(End missing)

(3)

(Beginning missing)

1. …provided, one *hu*…Ni 尼…

2. Next Huya Zhongda 仲達 provided, one *hu*, supplying…

3. Next Huya Canyue 参悦 provided, four *hu*, supplying…Jianchuhuan 見出桓

4. …Princess. Changshi Boyue 常侍伯悅…De□德

(End missing)

60TAM329:23/4

F. Gaochang Duzi Provisioning Record
《高昌都子等傳供食帳》

(1)

(Beginning missing)

1. …Luo 羅…

2. …(Huya) Duzi provided, one *hu* four *dou*, supplying…

3. …(Mingwei) Fonu provided, two *hu* two *sheng*, supplying Wai 外…

4. …provided, three and a half *dou*, (supplying) Jibishi 雞弊世…

(End missing)

73TAM517:04/8-4

"Huya" in line three is added based on "Huya Duzi" from text B, line three and from text C line, one.

"Mingwei" in line three is added based on "Mingwei Fonu" of text A, part two, line six.

"Supplying" of line four is added based on the meaning of the context.

(2)

(Beginning missing)

1. …provided, two *hu*…

2. …welcomed Tanhan Qaghan's emissaries.

3. …provided, five *sheng*, supplying Zhu'ayou 朱阿祐. Next provided, two *dou* one *sheng*, carpenter Yin 陰…

4. …Tanhan Qaghan Gugen 孤艮 Tanhan, five upper-ranked persons, in all twenty…

5. …supplying Tan 貪…

(End missing)

73TAM517:40/8-3

(3)

(Beginning missing)

1. …sixteen people, in all…

(End missing)

73TAM517:04/10(a)

To the lower right of the character "jin" 盡 ("in all") is an extra line that reads "twenty-fourth day."

THE CHINESE PERSIA EXPEDITIONARY FORCE AS REFERENCED IN THE TURFAN DOCUMENTS

Jiang Boqin 姜伯勤

The year 651 CE saw the escape to Merv of the Sasanian Emperor Yazdgerd (Yazdegerd) III (reigned 632-651), the last emperor of the Sasanian Empire. According to the Zoroastrian *Bundahishn*, in the 20th year of his reign the Arabs commenced a large scale invasion of Persia. Yazdgerd III failed in the war and escaped into Khorasan and then Turkistan. He looked for military assistance there, but was killed by locals.[1] The death of Yazdgerd III proclaimed the end of the Sasanian Dynasty.

Ten years later, in 661 CE, the Tang Dynasty appointed Peroz III, the son of Yazdgerd III, as the Governor (Commander-in-chief 都督) of Persia. His seat was Jiling City 疾陵城 (Zarang, the capital of the Persian province Sīstān).[2] In the spring of the next year he was appointed King of Persia by the Tang emperor.[3] Peroz III visited the Tang court in 674.[4] In 679 Narses (Narsieh), the son of Peroz III, succeeded to the crown of his father, and he was appointed King of Persia. He was sent to Sūyāb (Suiye 碎葉, near modern Tokmak) and then to Tukhāra 吐火羅 (Tokharia), where he stayed for 20 years.[5]

Notably, the record of Sasanian royal descendents after Peroz III, all of whom at one time stayed in China, is mainly in Chinese. In recent years references to the "Chinese Persia Expeditionary Force" 波斯軍 (literally and hereafter the "Persia Army") and to "Escorting the King of Persia" 送波斯王 have been found in Turfan documents. The phrase "Persia Army" especially deserves our attention. But what was the nature of this term?

---

1 Itō Gikyō 伊藤義教, *An Introductory Study of Persian Culture* (*Perusha bunka torai kō: Shirukurodo kara Asuka e*) 『波斯文化渡来考』 (Tokyo: 1980), pp. 12-3.

2 Zhang Xinglang 張星烺, *Collection of Records on Sino-Western Relations* 《中西交通史料滙編》, vol. 3 (Beijing: Zhonghua Book Company 中華書局, 1978), p. 109.

3 *Outstanding Models from the Storehouse of Literature* 《冊府元龜》, ch. 964. [These appointments were, of course, unrelated to actual control of Persia. Translator's note.]

4 *New Tang History: Annals of Emperor Gaozong* 《新唐書・高宗紀》.

5 *New Tang History: Account of Persia* 《新唐書・波斯傳》.

I. The Persia Army 波斯軍 *and the Commander of the Persia Army* 波斯軍使

The following Chinese document, number Ast-III-4-093, was found by Aurel Stein during his third expedition in Central Asia:

The part before the following is missing.
1 …long time…
2 …Ji 岌 now takes the imperial edict, and claims before the Grand Army 大軍 that □
3 all the Han and foreign 蕃 soldiers should be led by strong men. If the record keepers 要籍 and the attendants 傔人 that will march into the territory of the enemy
4 are sent from the imperial capital, there will be many Assault Resisting Garrison Commanders 折衝, Militia Garrison Commanders 果毅, attendants, and translators. It will create more trouble for the post stations along the road
5 □ (so) the military affair will be delayed. Now that most of them are already in the West, the military force in the prefectures of Yizhou 伊州, Tingzhou 庭州, and Xizhou 西州
6 should be under the command of Huaiji 懷岌, and it is very reasonable for him to take with him the aforementioned people as well.
7 It is also a timely move to settle the military emergency. We hope that His Highness 殿下 will kindly approve this plea. Together
8 with Huaiji, who is about to go, he should have the authority to temporarily appoint Acting Militia Garrison Commanders 檢校果（毅）who should be dispatched to make arrangements for those who will enter the enemy territory.
9 □ If Huaiji's request is kindly approved, these people should receive rewards *en route* 行賜, and attendants and others
10 □ We also hope that His Highness will kindly issue a special edict regarding the Persia Army. According to the special edict, the Acting Militia Garrison Commanders, attendants, and translators
11 □ are to be dispatched from wherever it is convenient. After the expedition those who deserve official titles 得官

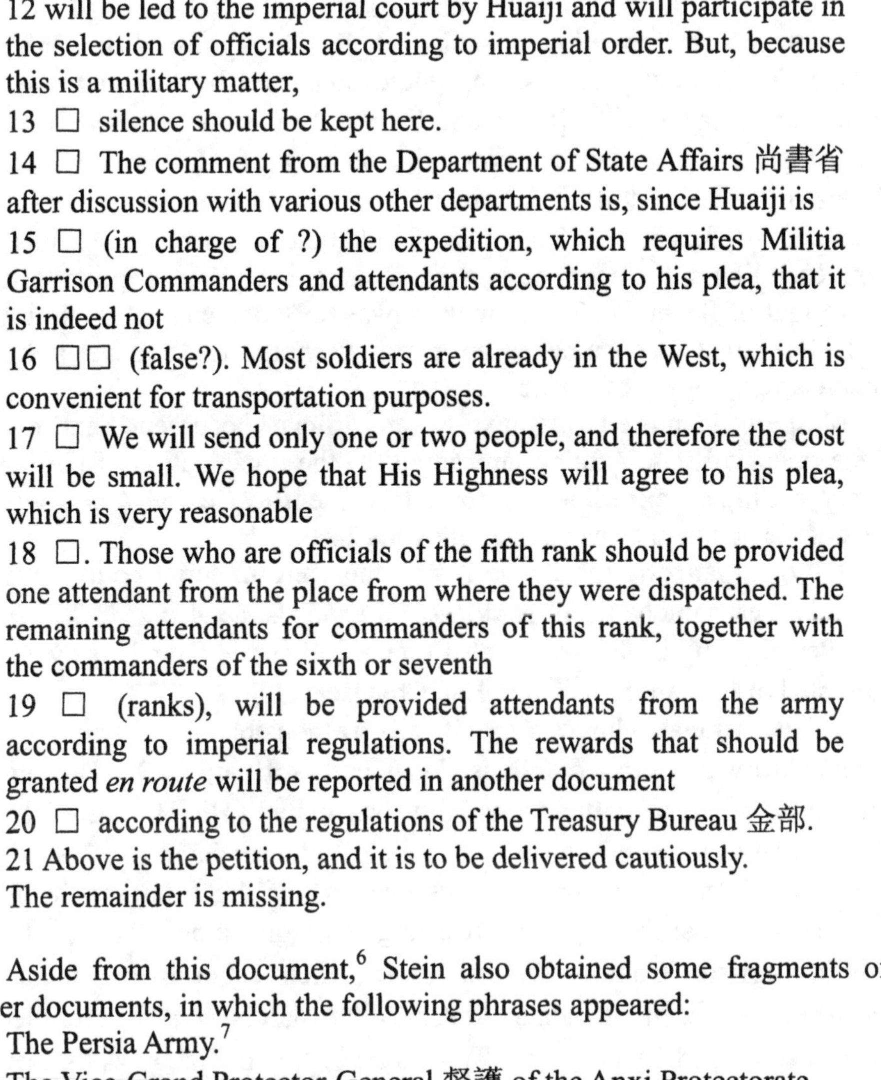

12 will be led to the imperial court by Huaiji and will participate in the selection of officials according to imperial order. But, because this is a military matter,
13 □ silence should be kept here.
14 □ The comment from the Department of State Affairs 尚書省 after discussion with various other departments is, since Huaiji is
15 □ (in charge of ?) the expedition, which requires Militia Garrison Commanders and attendants according to his plea, that it is indeed not
16 □□ (false?). Most soldiers are already in the West, which is convenient for transportation purposes.
17 □ We will send only one or two people, and therefore the cost will be small. We hope that His Highness will agree to his plea, which is very reasonable
18 □. Those who are officials of the fifth rank should be provided one attendant from the place from where they were dispatched. The remaining attendants for commanders of this rank, together with the commanders of the sixth or seventh
19 □ (ranks), will be provided attendants from the army according to imperial regulations. The rewards that should be granted *en route* will be reported in another document
20 □ according to the regulations of the Treasury Bureau 金部.
21 Above is the petition, and it is to be delivered cautiously.
The remainder is missing.

Aside from this document,[6] Stein also obtained some fragments of other documents, in which the following phrases appeared:

The Persia Army.[7]

The Vice-Grand Protector-General 督護 of the Anxi Protectorate.

The (loading) of donkeys for Persia.[8]

However, we have no way to know the lost contents of these documents, of which we have only fragments. Maspero gave a Chinese

---

[6] Henri Maspero, *Les documents chinois de la troisième expedition de Sir Aurel Stein en Asie Centrale* (London, 1953), no. 264, Ast-III-4-093, plate 15.

[7] *Treasures of Dunhuang* 《敦煌寶藏》, book 55, fragments of document number 012 (Taipei 臺北: Xin Wen Feng Publishing Company 新文豐出版公司, 1985).

[8] *Treasures of Dunhuang*, fragments of document number 027.

transcription of the document number Ast-III-4-093 (above) in his book. The author's transcription in this article is slightly different from Maspero's. However, because the photo consulted by the author is not clear, the character "權" [translated here as "have the authority"] in the second part of line eight follows the reading of Maspero. Moreover, Professor Ikeda On 池田温 has kindly pointed out that since the size of the document is 23.2cm × 39.2cm, there should be only one character missing from each line in the upper part of the document. My transcription follows the format of Ikeda On. To know there was only one character missing in each line of the document can certainly help us to have a better understanding of the complete text.

Maspero identified this text as an official document sent to the Department of State Affairs inquiring as to the organization of the Persia Army, a Chinese expeditionary force to be sent to Central Asia. A close look at the document reveals the following facts:

1. For organizing the Persia Army, the Tang imperial court issued a special edict, namely, the *Special Edict for the Persia Army* 波斯軍別敕. The Persia Army in this text is also referred to as the Grand Army, and it consisted of both foreign 蕃 and Han Chinese soldiers.

2. The official who was specifically responsible for organizing this Grand Army is recorded in this document as Huaiji 懷岌. The higher official who had overall responsibility was called "His Highness" 殿下. Possibly he was a prince during the reign of Emperor Gaozong 高宗.

3. Huaiji suggested that the commanders of the foreigners and the Chinese troops, such as Assault Resisting Garrison Commanders 折衝 and Militia Garrison Commanders 果毅, and their subordinates, including record keepers 要籍, attendants 傔人, and translators 譯語, be recruited in the prefectures of Yizhou 伊州, Tingzhou 庭州, and Xizhou 西州, instead of being directly dispatched from the imperial capital, due to the inconvenience of transport.

4. Huaiji asked that he should be granted the authority to temporarily appoint 權檢校 commanding officers (Acting Militia Garrison Commanders 檢校果毅) for the militia. These commanders and military attendants, who would be recruited from Yizhou, Tingzhou, and Xizhou, should receive rewards *en route*. After the conclusion of the punitive expedition, they would receive official rank by appointment of the court.

5. After the report of Huaiji came the advice from the Department of

State Affairs. It considered that Huaiji was responsible for the expedition, and the cost according to his proposal was quite economical. Therefore, they hoped that the higher official (His Highness) would approve Huaiji's proposal. A further suggestion from the Department of State Affairs was that officials of the fifth rank should be given an attendant from where they were dispatched, but the remainder should be selected from the Persia Army. The attendants for the sixth-rank and seventh-rank officials should also be provided by the Grand Army, i.e. the Persia Army. On the other hand, the rewards *en route* for these recruits should be granted according to the regulations of the Treasury Bureau.

In summary, this document actually is an official dispatch from Huaiji, the person responsible for organizing the Persia Army's attack, to His Highness, the highest supervisor of expeditionary military action. The proposal from Huaiji comprises the first part of the document, while the second part contains the further suggestions made by a certain commission in the Department of State Affairs after receiving Huaiji's report. Finally, the two parts were submitted together to higher officials for approval.

As everyone knows, the Persia Army (also called the Grand Army) mentioned in this document was an expeditionary force that was organized by the Tang government in the Western Regions 西域 from 677 to 681. The "Monograph on the Army" in the *New Tang History* 新唐書・兵志 says:

> The officials in charge of the army, towns, frontier defense commands 鎮, and defense detachments 守捉 were named Commissioners 使. The official in charge of the Circuit 道 [a kind of frontier military jurisdiction, in this case fictitiously under the control of the Chinese, encompassing several armies] was named Area Commander-in-Chief 大總管, which later was changed to Great Commander-in-Chief 大都督. Down to the reign of Emperor Taizong, those who participated in military expeditions were called Area Commanders-in-Chief, whereas those stayed in their own provinces were called Great Commanders-in-Chief.

The *Encyclopaedic History of Institutions* 通典, chapter 32, "Official Positions" 职官 in the entry for Commander-in-Chief 都督 has the following: "Moreover, there is the Expeditionary Commander-in-Chief 行軍大總管, who is in charge of a punitive expedition, and is responsible for military affairs in the Circuit where his army is going to march."

Tang Zhangru 唐長孺 in his *Annotations to the Monograph on the Army in the Tang Histories* 唐書兵志箋正 says:

> The Area Commander-in-Chief or Great Commander-in-Chief are commanders in charge of prefectures. Only the title of Expeditionary Commander-in-Chief is connected with a Circuit 道.[9]

Regarding the differences between Tang Dynasty "frontier defense command armies" 鎮軍 and "expeditionary armies" 行軍, expeditionary armies meant those which on a certain occasion set out on a punitive expedition in a certain Circuit or formed part of a military campaign. See the essay by Kikuchi Hideo 菊池英夫, "The Development of the 'Army' prior to the Establishment of the Military Commissioner" 『節度使確立以前における「軍」制度の展開』.[10] The Persia Army in the Turfan documents was an expeditionary force which was going to attack the Persian Circuit. The "Persian Circuit" referred to the route to the city of Zarang, provincial capital of Sīstān in Persia, although the expedition did not in fact reach that destination. According to the "Account of Persia" in the *Old Tang History* 舊唐書・波斯傳, "the expedition was unable to enter (Persia), and the land of Persia was gradually encroached upon by the Arabs 大食."

According to the relevant historical records, for conducting the "Expeditionary Army" of the Persia Army, there was established a commander entitled Commander of the Persia Army 波斯軍使. The "Spirit Way Stele for Lord Wang from Taiyuan, the Commander-in-Chief of Tang

---

[9] See Tang Zhangru 唐長孺, *Annotations to the Monograph on the Army in the Tang Histories* 《唐書兵志箋正》 (Beijing: Science Press 科學出版社, 1957), pp. 75-6, 80.

[10] Kikuchi Hideo 菊池英夫, "Setsudoshisei kakuritsuizenniokeru 'gun'seido no tenkai" 「節度使制確立以前における「軍」制度の展開」 (The Development of the 'Army' prior to the Establishment of the Military Commissioner), in *Tōyō Gakuhō* (*Journal of Oriental Studies*) 『東洋学報』, vol. 44, no. 2 (1961).

Dynasty Xiazhou" 唐故夏州都督太原王公神道碑, in chapter six of the *Collected Works of Zhang Yue* 張說之集 records:

> Pei 裴, of the Ministry of Personnel 吏部, apparently set up the Persia Army to attack Persia, but in fact his objective was to oppose the Turkish chieftain Li Zhefu 李遮匐. Lord Wei 偉公 took the position of Vice-Commander of the Persia Army and Protector-General 都護 of the Anxi Protectorate. Du Huaibao 杜懷寶, the former Protector-General of the Anxi Protectorate, was appointed the Prefect 刺史 of Tingzhou 庭州. Lord Wang 王公 was stationed at Sūyāb...After a short time, the Emperor appointed Lord Wang Prefect of Tingzhou, commander of Persia, and Protector-General of the Jinshan 金山 Area Command 都督府. Du Huaibao, the former commander, again took the office of Protector-General of the Anxi Protectorate and was stationed at Sūyāb. Initially the imperial court thought that the system of military frontier defense commands could not keep the peace in the principalities under Tang suzerainty, therefore Lord Wang took the position of Du Huaibao. Later, the court did not want to lose control of the military frontier defense commands, so Du Huaibao was restored to his former position.

Pei, of the Ministry of Personnel, in the stele text, refers to Pei Xingjian 裴行儉, Vice-Director of the Ministry of Personnel. According to the biography of Pei Xingjian in the *New Tang History*, in the second year of the Yifeng 儀鳳 reign period (677) Ashina Fuyan Duzhi 阿史那匐延都支, the Qaghan of the Western Turks, and Li Zhefu 李遮匐 attacked the Anxi Protectorate. Pei Xingjian gave this advice: "The Persian King has died, and his son Narses (Narsieh) 泥涅師師 resides in the capital as a hostage prince. I hope that our court can send him to Persia to restore his reign. The prince and the accompanying expedition will pass by the territory of the two revolting tribes. We can definitely have military success if we act in accordance with these circumstances." The Emperor Gaozong accepted Pei Xingjian's advice. According to the textual research and criticism of Cen Zhongmian 岑仲勉, it should have been in the summer of the first year of the Tiaolu 調露 reign period (679) when Pei

Xingjian captured Ashina Fuyan Duzhi.[11] So the events in the above quoted stele inscription must have taken place at that time. The stele inscription recorded that there were two people serving as commanders of the Persia Army:

1) The first Persia Army Commander. According to the stele inscription, the first commander of the Persia Army ("波斯使" in the inscription, meaning "波斯軍使") was Du Huaibao, the Protector-General of Jinshan, whose term of office as commander ended in the summer of the first year of Tiaolu reign period (679). At the same time, Du Huaibao also assumed the position of Protector-General of Jinshan and became the Prefect of Tingzhou.[12] In the inscription, Du Huaibao is called "former commander," because Wang Fangyi 王方翼 (the Lord Wang in the inscription) later assumed Du Huaibao's position. During the term of office of Du Huaibao, Wang Fangyi was the Vice-Commander of the Persia Army and the Protector-General of the Anxi Protectorate.

2) The second Persia Army Commander. According to the stele inscription and the research of Cen Zhongmian, Huang Huixian 黄慧賢, and others, at the time of the Yonglong 永隆 and Kaiyao 開耀 reign periods (680-681), the second commander of the Persia Army was Wang Fangyi, who was the Prefect of Tingzhou and also acted as the Protector-General of Jinshan. During this time, Du Huaibao was appointed as the Protector-General of the Anxi Area Command and was stationed at Sūyāb.

The Commander and Vice-Commander were the senior commanding officers in charge of the Persia Army expeditionary force; in the previously cited document number Ast-III-4-093, Huaiji was the person responsible for organizing the Persia Army's attack. However, because of the scarcity of historical materials, it is difficult to infer or prove the relationship between Huaiji and the Persia Army Commander Du Huaibao. But, it is possible to be certain that according to the approximate schedule for preparation of the expedition, one can infer that the document number

---

[11] Cen Zhongmian 岑仲勉, *Supplementary Documents on the Western Turks and Related Textual Criticism* 《西突厥史料補闕及考證》 (Beijing: Zhonghua Book Company 中華書局, 1958), p. 58.

[12] Huang Huixian 黄惠賢, "The Change in the Political Situation in the Western Region during the Chuigong Reign Period according to the Military Name List of Gaochang County, Xizhou" 《從西州高昌縣徵鎮名籍看垂拱年間西域政局之變化》, in *Preliminary Exploration of the Dunhuang and Turfan Documents* 《敦煌吐魯番文書初探》 (Wuhan University Press 武漢大學出版社, 1983), pp. 418-23.

Ast-III-4-093 should be dated in the period from 677 to 679, during the term of office of Du Huaibao as Persia Army Commander, or a little earlier.

The terms "His Highness" 殿下 [lines 7, 10, and 17], "deserve official titles" 得官 [line 11], "provide attendants" 給傔 [lines 18 and 19], and "rewards *en route*" 行賜 [line 9] in the document number Ast-III-4-093 deserve further discussion.

First, the term "His Highness." The eighteenth entry in the "Law of Etiquette" 儀制令第十八 in the *Collected Vestiges of the Tang Statutes* 唐令拾遺 records: "The cabinet ministers and officials in the Eastern Palace 東宮 [the palace of the crown prince] should call the royal prince His Highness, which should also be used in petitions, whereas the officials should use only their names."[13] This record is also seen in the *Ritual Regulations Written in the Kaiyuan Reign Period: Miscellaneous Regulations* 開元禮・雜制, the *Compendium of Administrative Law of the Six Divisions of the Tang Bureaucracy: Ministry of Rites, Bureau Director and Vice-Director* 唐六典・禮部郎中員外郎, and the *Important Documents of the Tang: List of Petition Types* 唐會要・牋表類. In the previously cited document, the commander Huaiji used his name in accordance with the law. "His Highness" was certainly a prince in charge of the military affairs in the Western regions. The "Annals of Emperor Gaozong" in the *Old Tang History* says:

> (In the third month of the third year of the Shangyuan reign period, 676), the Tibetans invaded the four prefectures of Shan 鄯, Kuo 廓, He 河, and Fang 芳. On the yiyou 乙酉 day, Li Xian 李顯, Prince of Zhou 周王, and the Metropolitan Governor 牧 of Luozhou 洛州, assumed the office of Commander-in-Chief of the Taozhou Circuit 洮州道, leading twelve commanders 總管, including Liu Shenli 劉審禮, the Minister of Works 工部尚書. Li Lun 李輪, the Prince of Xiang 相王, assumed the office of Commander-in-Chief of the Liangzhou Circuit 涼州道, leading Left Guard General 左衛

---

13 Niida Noboru 仁井田陞, *Collected Vestiges of the Tang Statutes* (*Tōrei shui*) 『唐令拾遺』 (Tōhō Bunka Gakuin Kenkyūjo 東方文化学院東京研究所, 1933), p. 417. This reference was kindly pointed out to the author by Professor Deng Wenkuan 鄧文寬.

將軍 Qibi Heli 契苾何力 to make a punitive expedition against the Tibetans.

Emperor Gaozong's military campaigns in Hexi 河西 during the Shangyuan and Yifeng reign periods (674-679) were aimed at the Tibetans and the Western Turks. For example, the famous memorial *Discussing the Ten Tribes* [the Western Turks] *and the Four Frontier Defense Commands* [the Anxi Protectorate] 論十姓四鎮疏 by Guo Yuanzhen 郭元振 discussed how to dissolve the alliance between the Turks and the Tibetans. The strategic goal of the establishment of the "Persia Army" was to, under the pretence of sending back the Persian King, eliminate Li Zhefu's Western Turk tribes. Possibly, the "His Highness" in this Turfan document referred to Li Lun 李輪, the Prince of Xiang, who later changed his name to Li Dan 李旦 and then became Emperor Ruizong 睿宗.[14] In the document, Huaiji hopes that "His Highness" will grant him the power of dispatching Acting Militia Garrison Commanders, attendants, and translators, from wherever it is convenient. Clearly, "His Highness" possessed the highest administrative power over the Persia Army, and his status rightly accorded with the title of Prince of Xiang, the Commander-in-Chief of the Liangzhou Circuit (frontier military district). Besides, the appointment of Prince Xiang took place at the same time, though he did not join the army personally. But this identification is only hypothetical and awaits further verification.

Second, the term "deserve official titles." The commander of the Persia Army needed to appoint certain number of Assault Resisting Garrison Commanders and Militia Garrison Commanders. However, there was not enough time to grant official certification, due to the urgency of the military situation, and so Huaiji asked for "authority to temporarily appoint." Therefore, as pointed out by Professor Cen Zhongmian, as there was not enough time to receive government instructions, the word "acting" 檢校 had to be added before the granted titles in order to signify this difference.[15] In the Turfan document, these Garrison Commanders were

[14] The "His Highness" may be Li Xian 李顯. See Sun Jimin 孫繼民, "Identification and Explanation of the Document Fragment Unearthed at Turfan *Official Document of the Tang Department of State Affairs*" 《吐魯番所出〈唐尚書省牒〉殘卷考釋》, *Dunhuang Research* 《敦煌研究》, 1990, no. 1.

[15] Cen Zhongmian 岑仲勉, *Sui and Tang History* 《隋唐史》 (Zhonghua Book Company,

called Acting Militia Garrison Commanders 檢校果毅, pending the completion of the punitive expedition, after which these commanders would be received at the imperial court with Huaiji and their formal official certification would then be granted.

Third, the term "provide attendants." These so-called attendants (傔 or 傔人) were the retinue of the commanders.[16] According to the biography of Feng Changqing 封常清傳 in the *New Tang History*, it is recorded that Gao Xianzhi 高仙芝, who took the position of Supreme Commander 都知兵馬使, had a retinue of over 30 attendants. The *Compendium of Administrative Law of the Six Divisions of the Tang Bureaucracy*, chapter five, in the regulation in the entry "Director of the Bureau of Military Appointments" 兵部郎中 says:

> Every Commander-in-Chief and Vice-Commander-in-Chief of a Frontier Defense Command should have attendants 傔人 and special memorialists 别奏, whose duties are to wait on the commanders....Great Commanders 大使 of the third rank or above should have 25 attendants and ten special memorialists. Commanders of the fourth rank should have 20 attendants, and the fifth, 15 attendants....All attendants and special memorialists are to be selected by the commanders themselves.

According to this regulation, commanders of the fifth rank are allowed 15 attendants and can select them themselves. However, according to the document number Ast-III-4-093, commanders of the fifth rank in the Persia Army were only allowed to take one attendant from the place where they were dispatched. The remaining 14 would be chosen from the army. This probably was due to urgency of the military situation and to avoid having to send them from long distance, and so to settle the matter on the spot in Tingzhou, Xizhou, and Yizhou by using a flexible method.

Further, the document refers to the local recruitment of a kind of record keeper 要籍, who were also a kind of "attendant" 親從 for the

---

1982), p. 533.

[16] Yan Gengwang 嚴耕望, "A Study of the Aides and Staff of Commanders of Military Provinces in the Tang Period" 《唐代方鎮使府僚佐考》 in *Collected Manuscripts on Tang History Research* 《唐史研究叢稿》 (Hong Kong, 1969), pp. 207-8.

commanders.[17] The term for locally recruited translators *yiyu* 譯語 is equivalent to the term *yiyuren* 譯語人, which makes frequent appearances in newly discovered Turfan documents. Both terms denote translators who are well-versed in their national language.

Finally, the term "rewards *en route*" can be seen in an imperial edict in the sixth month of the fourteenth year of Kaiyuan reign period (726), from chapter 135 of the *Outstanding Models from the Storehouse of Literature* 冊府元龜. It is related to issues concerning "recruitment" 兵募 or "impressment" 差兵. For explaining this issue, we intend to take a step forward in the discussion below: the Persia Army was endowed with the characteristics of an "expeditionary army" and had a certain relationship with recruitment or impressment.

II. The Persia Circuit Expeditionary Army 波斯道行軍 *and Impressment* 差兵

The relationship between the Persia Circuit Expeditionary Army and impressment is to be found in the document unearthed in Turfan in recent years, number 64 TAM35: 19 (a). The document is entitled *Record of the Contraction of an Illness by the Soldier Sun Haizang of the Tang Dynasty from Xizhou, Gaochang County, Taiping Township* 唐西州高昌縣下太平鄉符為檢兵孫海藏患狀事, and it reads:

1. Gaochang County 高昌縣

2. Sun Haizang 孫海藏 has contracted the diseases *fengxian* 風癇 and *lenglou* 冷漏 and should be treated as handicapped.

3. The chief of Taiping Township 太平鄉 reports: he has received a plea. The above mentioned person who sent in the plea says that in the beginning (he) contracted the disease *fengxian*. Later the illness

4. became more severe and turned into *lenglou*. Yesterday (he) was recruited to join the Persia Circuit march. When the army arrived at Puchang 蒲昌, his disease recurred several times. The medical examination

5. proved that he was not able to proceed. By the benefaction

[17] Ibid., pp. 203-4.

of the Encampment Office 營司 (he) was sent to Liuzhong County 柳中縣 for recuperation

6. and given a pass 公驗. Later, the commander sent *jianzhong* 建忠 [a fifth rank military title] Qu Sengseng 鞠僧僧 an order that if his illness has been cured,

7. (he) must be ordered to go and catch up with the army. When he arrived at Jiaohe 交河, and his disease was not yet

8. cured. The checkup in Jiaohe again confirmed that he was unable to proceed. Then he was settled in Jiaohe,

9. and a petition was delivered to the Grand Army to inform them of this situation; now the Grand Army had ordered that the description of his disease should be sent to the prefectural government, and then that the prefecture should

10. order the county to receive (the soldier). Now a *shoushi* 手實 [self-submitted household registration] should be made and delivered by a patrol. It should be submitted together with the pass 公驗 given by the Encampment Office 營司.

11. Also the order from the Grand Army should be checked and the description of the disease should be checked as well to determine whether the classification of handicapped is appropriate.

12. The order from the Encampment Office was thus checked and the description of the disease matched that of Sun [Hai]zang 孫(海)藏.

13. Also in the order from the Adjutant 軍司 of the Persia Circuit Army, the petition from Gao Tongda 高通達 was mentioned as saying: "I am informed that the aforementioned

14. person has the diseases *lenglou* and *fengxian* and can not move forward, and was kept in Jiaohe County of Xizhou for recuperation,

15. and I am willing to secure replacements for Sun's duties. According to the report from Jiaohe County, the description of the disease

16. matches that of Sun." The Vice-Director of the Secretariat 侍郎 thus ordered that the petition be approved, and [the official in] the township was asked to provide

17. …warrantors Zhang Choushi 张醜是 and other four persons, the village head 里正, Doctor Du Dinghu 杜定護

18. …the illnesses *fengxian* and *lenglou* for years.[18]
The following part is missing.

Professor Yang Debing 楊德炳 has given a clear explanation of this document in his *A Preliminary Exploration of the Treatment of Soldier-Patients and the Provisions for their Return Journey Home.*[19] Now, based on the foundation of Yang Debing's research, the author wants to add more notes on the two terms "Persia Circuit Adjutant" 波斯道軍司 and "impressment on the Persia Circuit march" 差波斯道行.

First, the Persia Circuit Adjutant. The term "Grand Army" in line nine "and a petition was delivered to the Grand Army to inform them of this situation; now the Grand Army had ordered…" and in line eleven "Also the order from the Grand Army should be checked…" is the same as the term in line two of document number Ast-III-4-093. In that line "now takes the imperial edict, and claims before the Grand Army," the "Grand Army" refers to the Persia Army. Line 13 of the *Record of the Contraction of an Illness* [just above] "Also in the order from the Adjutant of the Persia Circuit Army…" refers to an official dispatch from the Persia Army command structure. We know from the document that the Persia Army had an Adjutant 軍司 and an Encampment Office 營司, which indicates a two-rank command structure in the organization. The sixth line has "Later, the commander sent *jianzhong* 建忠 Qu Sengseng 鞠僧僧 an order…" The same word *jianzhong* appears in the document unearthed at Turfan number 72TAM78:5, *Order from Tuyou Battalion to Jianzhong Zhao Wuna for the Arrest of Zhang Shixuan, a Soldier from Jiaohe County in the 18th Year of the Tang Kaiyuan Reign Period* (740) 唐開元二十八年土右營下建忠趙伍那牒為訪捉配交河兵張式玄事, in the phrase "*jianzhong* in charge of the right encampment 右營."[20] As already pointed out by Yang Debing, the term Vice-Director (侍郎 in the phrase "侍郎判") in line 16 refers to Pei Xingjian, whose official title was Vice-Director of the Ministry of Personnel 吏部侍郎. Pei Xingjian was actually the highest commander of

[18] *Documents Unearthed in Turfan* 《吐魯番出土文書》, vol. 7, pp. 394-5.

[19] Yang Debing 楊德炳, "A Preliminary Exploration of the Treatment of Soldier-Patients and the Provisions for their Return Journey Home" 《關於唐代對患病士兵的處理與程糧等問題的初步探索》, in *Preliminary Exploration of the Dunhuang and Turfan Documents* 《敦煌吐魯番文書初探》, pp. 486-7.

[20] *Documents Unearthed in Turfan*, vol. 8, p. 385.

the Persia Army who, around the time of the summer of 679, acted in concert with the Adjutant of the Persia Army with the alleged goal of returning the Persian king and pacifying the Arabs.

Second, "impressment on the Persia Circuit march." The so-called Persia Circuit (see lines four and thirteen) indicates the Persia Army's route of march. By combining this document with other related historical materials, we can know that the route was from Xizhou Puchang County to Xizhou Jiaohe County to Sūyāb. In essence, the ultimate goal of this expeditionary army was to capture Ashina Fuyan Duzhi and to station troops in Sūyāb. From Sūyāb the Persian King Narses would continue his travel to Tukhāra (where he would stay in exile) accompanied by only a small group of soldiers, without the action of a punitive expedition. Therefore, the ostensible rationale for the Persia Circuit was to escort back the Persian king to Tukhāra. But the real rationale was a military campaign from Xizhou to Sūyāb to settle the rebellion of the Western Turks Ten Tribes Qaghan Ashina Fuyan Duzhi.

This document of Sun Haizang from Gaochang County, Taiping Township by its words "impressment on the Persia Circuit march," accurately reflects the recruitment of soldiers in Xizhou by Pei Xinjiang in July, 679. According to the biography of Pei Xingjian in the *Old Tang History*: "When he arrived at Xizhou, the local people and officials went to the suburban area to welcome him. He recruited thousands of sons and younger brothers from prestigious local families to accompany him to the west…at that time, almost 10,000 foreign young men and sons of tribal chieftains enlisted in the army." This record reflects the fact that Pei Xinjiang recruited soldiers from the local people. Other documents of the same period, for instance the documents concerning the impressment of soldiers during the Tang Dynasty in the *Treasures Remaining in the Shifting Sands* 流沙遺珍, record that "in the jurisdiction of Xizhou 1,200 soldiers were impressed."[21] The document *Fan Deda's Official Certificate* 氾德達告身, from the first year of the Yongchun 永淳 reign period (682), says that the soldier Fan Deda was recruited from Xizhou. This clearly illustrates that the recruitment of soldiers took place widely in Xizhou.[22]

---

[21] Jin Zutong 金祖同, compiler, *Treasures Remaining in the Shifting Sands* 《流沙遺珍》 (1940).

[22] Tang Zhangru 唐長孺, "Notes on Turfan Documents Concerning the Impressment of Soldiers" 《唐西州差兵文書跋》, in *Preliminary Exploration of the Dunhuang and Turfan Documents* 《敦煌吐魯番文書初探》, p. 439.

And in the previously cited document *A Record of the Contraction of an Illness* the person Sun Haizang impressed on the Persia Circuit march was no doubt such a recruited (impressed) soldier. According to Tang law, "when impressment is conducted in the prefectures, soldiers should be selected from families that are wealthy and have comparatively more male adults."[23] The recruited and impressed soldiers would be given rewards from the court *en route*. For instance, the imperial order in the sixth month of the 14th year of the Kaiyuan period (726) as recorded in chapter 135 of *Outstanding Models from the Storehouse of Literature* says:

> Regarding recruited soldiers, the court will take more care. Rewards *en route* will be granted when they leave their homes, and provisions for the journey 程糧 will be granted for their travel home.

The connection with the phrases in the previously mentioned document number Ast-III-4-093 "these people should receive rewards *en route*" (line nine) and "The rewards that should be granted *en route* will be reported in another document □ according to the regulations of the Treasury Bureau" (in lines 19 and 20) proves that in the Persia Army from its inception there existed widespread impressment. In the Tang government Department of State Affairs 尚書省 under the Ministry of Revenue 戶部 there was the Treasury Bureau 金部 Director 郎中 and Vice-Director 員外郎, whose responsibilities included "awards to all officialdom, frontier defense commands, and foreigners" 百官，軍鎮，蕃客之賜. So awards in the Persia Army for government troops must have depended upon the management procedures of the Treasury Bureau. Therefore, the wide-spread existence of impressed soldiers in the Persia Army reflected one facet of the military system of the early Tang period.

III. "Escorting the Persian King" 送波斯王 *and "Pacifying the Arabs"* 安抚大食

According to the conventional view in Chinese historical materials, the objective of the formation of Pei Xingjian's Persia Army was to capture

[23] *Compendium of Administrative Law of the Six Divisions of the Tang Bureaucracy* 《唐六典》, ch. 5, "The Military System" 《兵部》.

Ashina Fuyan Duzhi, the Qaghan of the Ten Tribes of the Western Turks, and another tribal leader Li Zhefu. Specifically, the "Spirit Way Stele for Lord Wang from Taiyuan, the Commander-in-Chief of Tang Dynasty Xiazhou" 唐故夏州都督太原王公神道碑 contained in the previously cited *Collected Works of Zhang Yue* says: "Pei, of the Ministry of Personnel, apparently set up the Persia Army to attack Persia, but in fact his objective was to oppose the Turkish chieftain Li Zhefu." After examining the Arabic sources, Professor Wang Xiaofu 王小甫 pointed out that Pei Xingjian's activity had nothing to do with the conquest of the Arabs, even though he bore the title of "Envoy for Pacifying the Arabs." However, Pei Xingjian's actions had influence on the future of the Persian king and his offspring in Tukhāra. The "Account of Persia" section of the *New Tang History* says:

> In the first year of the Tiaolu reign period (679), the Emperor ordered Pei Xingjian to command an army and sent him off. He was to restore Narses' crown and lands. When they arrived at Sūyāb in the Anxi Protectorate, Pei Xingjian returned to the capital because the route was so long. Narses thus stayed in Tukhāra for twenty years.

In the ninth month of the first year of the Tiaolu reign period (679), Pei Xingjian returned to Chang'an. From that year to the next, namely the first year of the Yonglong reign period (680), the Persian King Narses was sent to Tukhāra escorted by some soldiers of the Persia Army. The document *Order in the First Year of the Yonglong Reign Period* (680) *from the Army Office for Recording the Yangren of Guardsmen on March and in Garrison, as well as Meritorious Service Conferees, Augerers, and Others* 唐永隆元年軍團牒為記注所屬衛士徵鎮様人及勳官議符諸色事 unearthed from Astana 阿斯塔那 tomb number 191 has the following record:

> Bai Huanjin 白歡進, 41 years old, escorted the Persian king. His *yangren* 様人 was Kang (Wen?)yi 康□義. He was promoted to the Light Chariots 上輕軍 [a merit title] and has gone to the government office to sign the certificate.
>
> Zhao Lixiang 趙力相, 35 years old, escorted the Persian king.

His *yangren* was Kang Tanzhu 康曇住.[24]

□Bitou 俾頭, 49 years old, escorted the Persian (king). His *yangren* was Fan Dui 氾塠□.[25]

...41 years old, escorted the Persian king. His *yangren* was Zhang 张...[26]

The fragment on the back part of this document says: "*yangren*, meritorious service conferees, augerers, and all others have been recorded as above, cautiously submitted." There are the signatures of the brigade deputy chief, the brigade chief, the brigade commander, and in total twelve people. The date was recorded as "the tenth month of first year of the Yonglong reign period (680)." In this document, field soldiers whose tasks were itemized as "to escort the Persian king," "to go to Tingzhou as a garrison," and "to guard prisoners in this prefecture," have under their names the names of their y*angren* recorded. Concerning this, a document unearthed at Turfan, *Record of the Facial Features of Zhao Xuzhang and Others* 唐趙須章等貌定簿, says:

> Zhao Xuzhang 趙須章, 22 years old, male adult, □□looks like Zhao Yong 趙永□, first class; □ (middle), of a third-grade household.
>
> □□Dui 塠, 27 years old, male adult, went westward, looks like Niu Ying 牛應. His father is aged, and a nephew will reach adulthood next year, of third-grade household.[27]

But what does *yangren* 様人 mean? An account of the Song Dynasty (960-1279) military system gives us a clue. In the era before photography was invented, the name of a soldier in the lists was attached to the name of another person who looked similar to them, in order to prevent escape.

To summarize, the documents considered here demonstrate that Narses was still *en route* back home in 680 CE and was accompanied by a Tang military force. Afterwards he arrived in Tukhāra.

---

[24] *Documents Unearthed in Turfan*, vol. 6, p. 547.

[25] *Ibid.*, p. 553.

[26] *Ibid.*, p. 555.

[27] *Ibid.*, p. 446.

THE NINE ZHAOWU SURNAMES (SOGDIANS) IN THE SIX HU PREFECTURES AND OTHER PLACES IN THE TANG DYNASTY

Zhang Guangda 張廣達

The so-called Nine Zhaowu Surnames 昭武九姓 refer to the Sogdians of Central Asia.[1] In ancient times the Sogdians were well known for being excellent at trade and being full of initiative – they went wherever there was opportunity for profit. For a long period they controlled international trade passing through many hands on the Silk Road, leaving their footprints across the Eurasian heartland. During the course of several hundred years of trading they accumulated enormous experience and

---

[1] Sogdia, or Sute 粟特, was Sugda- or Suguda- in ancient Persian. It is written as Suγδa- (Vd. I, 4) and Suxδa- (Yt. X, 14) in the ancient Iranian Zoroastrian *Avesta*. The Greeks called the area Sogdiana and its people Sogdianoi, and it was called Sogdoi in Herodotus' *The Histories*. In Sogdian documents it is recorded as swγδ-, suγδ-, sγwδ-, and sγuδ-. See W. B. Henning, "Argi and the 'Tokharians'," in *Bulletin of the School of Oriental Studies*, vol. 9, no. 3, 1938, p. 548; W. B. Henning, *Selected Papers I, Acta Iranica 14,* second series, vol. 5 (Leiden: Brill, 1977), p. 576; I. Gershevitch, *A Grammar of Manichean Sogdian* (Oxford, 1954, second edition 1961), item 421. In Chinese historical documents, it is recorded as Suyi 粟弋 in the "Account of the Western Regions" 《西域傳》 section of the *History of the Later Han* 《后漢書》; Shuyao 屬繇 in chapter 30 《魏略・西戎傳》 of the *Record of the History of the Three Kingdoms* 《三國志》; Sute 粟特 in the "Account of the Western Regions" section of the *History of the Northern Dynasties* 《北史・西域傳》. In Chinese Buddhist documents, it is called Suli 窣利 in chapter one of Xuan Zang's 玄奘 *Great Tang Dynasty Record of the Western Regions* 《大唐西域記》; Suli 速利 in the Tang Dynasty Yi Jing's 義淨 *Tales of the Hierarchs Searching for Buddhist Scriptures in the Western Regions during the Tang Dynasty* 《大唐西域求法高僧傳 •玄照傳》; Sunlin 孫鄰 in Yi Jing's *One Thousand Character Sanskrit Glossary* 《梵語千字文》; and Suli 蘇哩 in a footnote for the item for Hu 胡 in the Tang Dynasty Li Yan's 利言 *A Miscellaneous Collection of Sanskrit Terms* 《梵語雜名》. Regarding later translations of the term "Suli," Josef Marquart thought it was a transliteration of the Pahlavi term Sūlik, see Marquart, *Die Chronologie des Alttürkischen Inschriften* (Leipzig, 1898), p. 56. H. W. Bailey examined a manuscript numbered Ch. 00269, taken away by Aurel Stein, and proposed that the word Sūlya in line 78 should be a transliteration of the Tibetan word Sulig 疏勒, and later this was proven to a transliteration of Suli 窣利. See H. W. Bailey, "Ttaugara," *Bulletin of the School of Oriental and African Studies*, vol. 8, no. 4 (1937), p. 883, n. 3, and p. 918. In ancient Turkic, Sute is Soγd(ï)q, see Annemarie von Gabain, *Alttürkische Grammatik* (Leipzig, 1950), p. 334.

formed specialized organizations,[2] becoming international businessmen for the ancient Eurasian heartland and the countries bordering it. Today, based on documents and records and on certain cultural remains from the Silk Road, we know that they not only performed a key function in the development of East-West trade, but they also played an important role in cultural diffusion and in the promotion of political contacts between many countries. In terms of cultural diffusion, it is well known that the Chinese technology of papermaking passed through the Sogdian political center of the Kingdom of Kang 康國 (the predecessor to the city of Samarkand in Uzbekistan) and then to the West; and that Buddhism, Zoroastrianism, Manichaeism, and Nestorianism to a large extent were disseminated to the East through the Sogdians. In addition, it is very well known that music, dance, and other forms of Chinese arts from the Northern Wei (368-534) to the Sui and Tang periods (581-907) were deeply influenced by the Sogdians. The political power of the Qaghanates established by the Turks, Uyghurs, and other nomadic peoples depended on Sogdians to administer records, and the Qaghanates adopted the Sogdian alphabetic script, which thus had a direct influence on the formation of the written forms of Mongolian and Manchu. With regard to political aspects, the Sogdians served as political advisors to the Turkish, Uyghur, and many other Qaghanates of nomadic steppe peoples. And they acted as military leaders and diplomatic envoys between countries east and west, north and south.

In Central Asia, the Sogdians settled along the Niumishui 忸密水 valley (Nāmīk, or the modern Zeravshan River) and along the Dumoshui 獨莫水 valley (probably the modern Kashka River), an area between the Oxus 烏滸水 (i.e. the Amu Darya) and the Jaxartes 藥殺水 (i.e. the Syr Darya). Along the over 650 kilometers east-to-west course of the Zeravshan there were a number of fertile districts, and in these large and small fertile districts scattered peoples spoke Sogdian (one of the East Iranian languages), and they founded many city-states and kingdoms. For example, Samarkand 撒馬爾干, called the Kingdom of Kang or

---

[2] In 1907, Aurel Stein discovered in watch tower TXIIa, west of Dunhuang, nine letters written in ancient Sogdian, among which were several letters sent from either Guzang 姑臧 (Liangzhou 涼州) or Dunhuang to Samarkand and Bukhara reporting on the business situation and business difficulties. See H. Reichelt, *Die Soghdischen Handschriftenreste des Britischen Museums*, vol. 2 (Heidelberg: Carl Winter, 1931), pp. 1-56; J. Harmatta, "A New Document in the History of the Silk Road," in *Jahrbüch für Wissenschaftsgeschichte*, no. 11 (1971).

Samojian (薩末鞬 or 颯秣建) in the Chinese documents, developed from the cities of Maracanda and Afrasiāb. Bukhara 布哈拉, called the Kingdom of An 安國 or Buhe 捕喝/布豁 in the Chinese documents, developed from the cities of Varākhsha 瓦拉赫沙 and Rāmīthān 阿濫謐. It is worth noting that the frequent contact between the Sogdians and China proper also made the Chinese names of the Kingdom of Kang and the Kingdom of An well known in Central Asia, so that the Sogdians were called Kang 康 (γ'n=Xān'), after the Kingdom of Kang, and An 安 (''n=Ān), after the Kingdom of An.[3] Other famous city-states in Sogdian territory included Sutrūshana (or Ushrūsanā) 蘇對沙那 (in Chinese also known as 率都沙那, 蘇都識匿, 蘇都沙那, and 窣堵利瑟那), which was known in the Tang Dynasty as the Eastern Cao Kingdom 東曹國; Kapūtānā 劫布呾那 (or Kebud, also known in Chinese as Jiabudan 伽不單) , which known in the Sui Dynasty as the Cao Kingdom 曹國 and in the Tang Dynasty as the Western Cao Kingdom 西曹國 (Ishitikhan); Māymurgh 弭秣賀 (also transliterated as Mimo 彌末), which was known in the Tang Dynasty as the Mi Kingdom 米國; Kushānīka 屈霜你迦國 (Kushāniyya, or 貴霜匿), which was known in the Tang Dynasty as the He Kingdom 何國; Kāshāna 羯霜那 (Kesh, Kashsh, or Kishsh), which was known in the Tang Dynasty as the Kingdom of Shi 史國; and Chach 赭時 (also in Chinese 者舌, 赭支, or 柘支), which was known in the Tang Dynasty as the Shi Kingdom 石國. These city-states each preserved a certain independence, and usually accepted the Kingdom of Kang as the head of all the kingdoms.

A record that appears repeatedly in Chinese documents is that the chiefs of the Sogdian city-states all had Zhaowu 昭武 as their surname. For example, the entry in the "Account of the Western Regions" 西域傳 for the Kingdom of Kang in the *History of the Northern Dynasties* 北史 says: "Originally surnamed Wen 溫, the King was of the Yuezhi 月氏 people and used to live in the city of Zhaowu to the north of the Qilian Mountains 祁連山. Because they were invaded by the Xiongnu 匈奴, Zhaowu was

[3] W. B. Henning, "The Sogdian Texts in Paris," *Bulletin of the School of Oriental and African Studies*, vol. 2, no. 4, 1946, p. 736; and "The Date of the Sogdian Ancient Letters," *Bulletin of the School of Oriental and African Studies,* vol. 12, no. 3-4 (1948), p. 603, n. 2. See also W. B. Henning, *Selected Papers II, Acta Iranica 15* (Leiden: Brill, 1977), pp. 254 and 317.

moved westward to the Pamirs and developed into a kingdom. Relatives of a collateral branch of the King's family later founded their own kingdom affiliated to the Kingdom of Kang, and they all adopted the surname Zhaowu to demonstrate their loyalty."[4] It says further, that "the Mi Kingdom (Māymurgh) 米國, the Kingdom of Shi (Kāshāna) 史國, the Cao Kingdom (Kapūtānā) 曹國, the He Kingdom (Kushānīka) 何國, the Lesser An Kingdom 小安國, the Nasebo Kingdom 那色波國, the Wunahe Kingdom 烏那曷國, and the Mu Kingdom 穆國 are all affiliated."[5] The entry for the Kingdom of Kang in the "Account of the Western Regions" in the *New Tang History* 新唐書 has a similar record, except that the affiliated kingdoms are different: the Kingdom of An, the Cao Kingdom, the Shi Kingdom (Chach) 石國, the Mi Kingdom, the He Kingdom, the Huoxun Kingdom 火尋國, the Wudi Kingdom 戊地國, and the Kingdom of Shi (Kāshāna) 史國. It also indicates explicitly that all the above nine kingdoms are the "So-Called Nine Surnames." The Tang Dynasty term "the Nine Zhaowu Surnames" originated here.[6] Moreover, it is necessary to point out that although the names of the Nine Zhaowu Surname kingdoms differed in Chinese documents (excepting the Kingdom of Kang, the An Kingdom, the He Kingdom, the Mi Kingdom, the Kingdom of Shi 史國, the Cao Kingdom and the Shi Kingdom 石國), the different names do not hinder our understanding of the commonality of the Nine Zhaowu Surnames.

In the Tang Dynasty the business activities of the Sogdians reached their period of highest prosperity, and the forms of Sogdians reappear to us in the large number of excavated pottery figurines leading camels and horses. A large number of Sogdian immigrants resided in Chang'an 長安, Luoyang 洛陽, and in a great many wards of other large Tang cities. The contribution of Sogdians to the development of Tang Dynasty economy, culture, and art is very familiar due to the outstanding research of scholars such as Kuwabara Jitsuzō 桑原隲藏, Ishida Mikinosuke 石田幹之助, Xiang Da 向達, and others.[7] It should be noted that Sogdians also

---

4 *History of the Northern Dynasties* 《北史》, Zhonghua Book Company block printing edition, ch. 97, p. 3233.

5 Ibid., p. 3234.

6 *New Tang History*《新唐書》, ch. 221b, p. 6243.

7 Kuwabara Jitsuzō 桑原隲藏, "On the People from the Western Regions who Came to Live in China during the Sui and Tang Periods"「隋唐時代に支那に來住した西域人に

established very many immigrant settlements along the main routes from Sogdiana east to China and in the steppe. Chinese documents of the Tang Dynasty, especially the manuscripts from Dunhuang and Turfan, as well as some Islamic documents, demonstrate to us certain aspects of some of the activities in the immigrant settlements established by the Sogdians, and they assist our progress in understanding the important functions of Sogdians in the political incidents and social life of the Tang Dynasty.

I.

Among the settlements established by the Sogdian immigrants, the Six Hu Prefectures 六胡州 should be considered as having the most influence on the political life of the Tang Dynasty. In April 1981, the joint-burial tomb of An Pu 安菩, the Great Chief of the Six Hu Prefectures, and his wife was discovered in a southern suburb of Luoyang, and this event again aroused interest in the Six Hu Prefectures.

The joint-burial tomb of An Pu and his wife is located on the northeastern side of the Longmen 龍門 Mountains, 13 kilometers south of Luoyang. Approximately 140 relics were unearthed, including large delicate pottery figurines.[8] In the tomb was a stone epitaph with an epitaph cover having nine characters written in *kaishu* 楷書 script, "Epitaph of the Tang General of Dingyuan, Lord An" 大唐定遠將軍安君誌. The epitaph itself is entitled "Epitaph of Lord An, the Great Chief of the Tang Six Hu Prefectures" 唐故六胡州大首領安君墓誌 and has in total 458 Chinese characters. Regarding the man in the tomb, his given name was Pu 菩 and his courtesy name 字 was Sa 薩. According to the inscription, An Pu was born in 600 and died in 664. It says, "In the past,

---

就いて」, in *Festschrift of Articles on Sinology in Honor of Dr. Naitō's 61st Birthday* 『内藤博士還暦祝賀支那學論叢』 (Kyoto: 1934), pp. 277-424; see also Kuwabara Jitsuzō 桑原隲藏, *The Collected Works of Kuwabara Jitsuzō*, vol. 2 (Iwanami Shoten 岩波書店, 1968); Ishida Mikinosuke 石田幹之助, *Spring in Chang'an* 『長安の春』 (Sōgensha 創元社, 1941); Xiang Da 向達, *Tang Dynasty Chang'an and the Civilization of the Western Regions* 《唐代長安與西域文明》 (Sanlian Press 三聯書店, 1957), pp. 1-116.

[8] For reference, see the preliminary excavation report on the An Pu tomb, Zhao Zhenhua 趙振華 and Zhu Liang 朱亮, "A Preliminary Study of the An Pu Tomb Inscription" 《安菩墓誌初探》, *Cultural Relics of the Central Plains* 《中原文物》, 1982, no. 2, pp. 21-6 and 37-40.

the Grand Chief of the An Kingdom defeated the Xiongnu 匈奴, and he later surrendered to the Tang with all of the conquered property and people. In return there was conferred on him an official Tang rank, equivalent to the fifth rank of a capital official, and the military title of General of Dingyuan 定遠將軍. His chiefdom was preserved as before. His great-grandfather was named Bo Tarqan 鉢達干, and his grandfather Ji Li 系利. At that time the Northern Di 北狄 invaded southward into the Tang (and the Grand Chief) was dispatched to fight against them." Due to his bravery on the battlefield, one fighting as if he were ten, he successfully captured "their property and people, and presented their left ears at the western capital [the Tang court]." In the inscription, however, it is unclear what "in the past" means. It might refer to either the early years of An Pu or to his predecessors. Based on the context, I think it may refer to his predecessors, probably his father, because both his great-grandfather and grandfather are mentioned in the following part, and only his father's name is not seen there. According to the epitaph, it was because the Tang had defeated the Turks (in the epitaph it is literally the Xiongnu, but in the Tang Dynasty the terms Xiongnu 匈奴 or Xianyun 獫狁 were often used to refer to the Turks) that the Grand Chief of the An Kingdom surrendered his property and people to the Tang. The chief was given an official rank equivalent to the fifth rank of a court official and was entitled General of Dingyuan. All these accounts are identical to the records in the *Essentials of Government of the Zhenguan Era* 貞觀政要 and the *Encyclopaedic History of Institutions* 通典. According to chapter 197, "Border Protection" 邊防, in the *Encyclopaedic History of Institutions*, "the defeat of Jieli 頡利 [Illig Qaghan]…induced many people to surrender. Titles of General and official ranks above the fifth rank were conferred on more than one hundred chiefs. The number was about half of all the officials. However, only the comitatus 柘羯 refused to surrender…"[9] The entry

[9] *Encyclopaedic History of Institutions*《通典》, ch. 197, "Border Protection 《邊防》 13" (Zhejiang Book Company 浙江書局 edition), pp. 18b-9a. The Chinese word "comitatus" 柘羯 is a transliteration from the Sogdian word čakir, meaning warrior, military bodyguard, or personal attendant. The Mongol historian B. Ia. Vladimirtsov (Б. Я. Владимирцов) of the former Soviet Union argues that the Mongolian name Chahaerbu 察哈爾部 is derived from this word. See B. Ia. Vladimirtsov, "Mongolica I" in *Proceedings of the Eastern Department of the Russian Archaeological Society* (*Записки. Восточного отделения Российского Археологического общества*), 1925,

"Stability of the Frontier" 安邊 in the *Essentials of Government of the Zhenguan Era* contains a similar record with one more specific sentence, "All chiefs who surrendered were granted titles of General or Commandant 中郎將."[10] The title "General of Dingyuan" mentioned in An Pu's epitaph must be the same as one of the conferred titles mentioned in the records above. The *Compendium of Administrative Law of the Six Divisions of the Tang Bureaucracy* 大唐六典 contains an explanation of the title "General of Dingyuan," which was then a title in the upper fifth rank; during the Liang 梁 Dynasty, Dingyuan was at the twelfth rank and "was given exclusively to foreigners."[11] During the Tang Dynasty, it was a Military Prestige Title 武散官, probably similar to those given to foreign chiefs who had surrendered.

According to the epitaph, the wife of An Pu, surnamed He 何 (622-704), was "the eldest daughter of General-in-Chief He from Chang'an, entitled Madame Jinshanjun 金山郡." According to their surnames, both An Pu and his wife were Sogdians. The epitaph also records the name of their son, An Jinzang 安金藏. Both the *New Tang History* 新唐書 and the *Old Tang History* 舊唐書 contain biographies of An Jinzang.[12] According to the biographies, An Jinzang's mother died in the early years of the Shenlong 神龍 reign period (705-707). From the clues provided by the epitaph, it can be confirmed that his mother died in the first month of the fourth year of the Chang'an 長安 reign period (704). The biographies also state that An Jinzang buried his mother to the north of Nan Quekou 南闕口, building a stone tomb. From this we can know that at that time the area south of An Pu and his wife's tomb was called

---

pp. 326-7. For more details on "comitatus" see A. M. Mandel'shtam (A. M. Манделъштам), "Towards the Question of the Meaning of the Term 'čakir'" ("К вопросу о значении термина 'чакир'"), *Bulletin of the Department of Social Sciences of the Academy of Sciences of the Tajik Soviet Socialist Republic* (*Известия Отделения общественных наук Академии наук Таджикской ССР*), vol. 5 (1954), pp. 103-8.

[10] Wu Jing 吳兢, *Essentials of Government of the Zhenguan Era* 《貞觀政要》 (Shanghai Classics Publishing House 上海古籍出版社, 1987), p. 275.

[11] *Compendium of Administrative Law of the Six Divisions of the Tang Bureaucracy* 《大唐六典》 (Tokyo: Hiroike Gakuen 廣池學園, 1973), p. 115.

[12] *Old Tang History* 《舊唐書》, ch. 187a, pp. 4885-6; *New Tang History* 《新唐書》, ch. 191, pp. 5506-7.

Quekou 闕口.[13] The tomb and funeral objects of An Pu and his wife are very impressive, which may be due to the fact that their son An Jinzang's loyalty to the emperor was well recognized and rewarded. During the Zaichu 載初 reign period (689-690) of the Empress Wu Zetian 武則天, Ruizong 睿宗 was chosen as imperial heir and granted the surname Wu. However, his activities were under extremely strict surveillance. At that time An Jinzang served under the registrar at the Court of Imperial Sacrifices 太常 and so was in close attendance to the heir. In the second year of the Changshou 長壽 reign period (693), the heir was accused of conspiracy to usurp the throne. The Empress ordered Lai Junchen 來俊臣 to investigate the people around the heir by use of torture. Many could not bear the cruel inquisition and wanted to plead guilty, despite their innocence. Only An Jinzang acted proactively, using his waist sword to commit hara-kiri, showing his loyalty and proving that there was no plot against the throne. An Jinzang's action greatly surprised Wu Zetian, who finally pardoned Ruizong.[14] An Jinzang's loyalty to Ruizong, as demonstrated by his suicide, received much praise from Emperor Xuanzong 玄宗 and many following Tang monarchs, down to the Zhonghe 中和 reign period of Emperor Xizong 僖宗 (881-885), when a descendant of An Jinzang named An Jingze 安敬則 received an official rank because of his ancestor's honorable deeds.[15] From this we can know that since immigrating from the Turkic Qaghanate into China in the early Tang, the family of the leader of the An Kingdom had a rather long and continuous history.

What interests us, however, is the record about the Great Chief of the An Kingdom and the Six Hu Prefectures. The Japanese scholar Onogawa Hidemi 小野川秀美 and the Canadian scholar Edwin Pulleyblank have done careful studies of the history of the Six Hu Prefectures.[16] Previous studies were all based on the following entry in the *New Tang History*:

---

[13] *Old Tang History*, ch. 187a, p. 4885.

[14] *Old Tang History*, ch. 187a, pp. 4885-6; *New Tang History*, ch. 191, pp. 5506-7. See also the *Comprehensive Mirror for Aid in Government* 《資治通鑒》, "The first month of the second year of the Changshou reign period of Empress Wu Zetian," ch. 205, p. 6490.

[15] *New Tang History*, ch. 191, p. 5507.

[16] Onogawa Hidemi 小野川秀美, "The Evolution of the Six Hu Prefectures of the Ordos Loop" 「河曲六州胡の沿革」, *Journal of East Asian Humanities* 『東亞人文学報』, vol. 1, no. 4, 1942, pp. 193 (957)-226 (990); Edwin Pulleyblank, "A Sogdian Colony in Inner Mongolia," *T'oung Pao*, vol. 41 (1952), pp. 317-56.

In the first year of the Tiaolu 調露 reign period (679) the Tang court relocated the conquered Turks to the southern perimeter of Lingzhou 靈州 and Xiazhou 夏州, and founded Luzhou 魯州, Lizhou 麗州, Hanzhou 含州, Saizhou 塞州, Yizhou 依州, and Qizhou 契州 – the so-called Six Hu Prefectures – and Chinese officials were appointed as Prefects 刺史 of these prefectures. In the fourth year of the Chang'an reign period (704) these were amalgamated to form Kuangzhou 匡州 and Changzhou 長州. In the third year of the Shenlong reign period (707) the Lanchi 蘭池 Area Command 都督府 was re-established and the Six Prefectures under it were reclassified as six counties 縣. In the tenth year of the Kaiyuan 開元 reign period (722), Luzhou, Lizhou, Qizhou, and Saizhou were re-established. In that same tenth year Kang Daibin's 康待賓 uprising was defeated and his people were moved to Henan 河南 and the Yangtze River and Huai River 淮河 regions. In the eighteenth year of the Kaiyuan reign period (730) Kuangzhou and Changzhou were re-established. In the twenty-sixth year of the Kaiyuan reign period (738) many Sogdians were moved to Youzhou 宥州 and counties such as Yan'en 延恩, and they were later organized into the Jinglüe 經略 (take charge and put in order) Army. In the second year of the Zhide 至德 reign period (757) the commandery was renamed Huaide 懷德. In the first year of the Qianyuan 乾元 reign period (758) the original name was restored. In the Baoying 寶應 reign period (762-763) it was changed back. In the ninth year of the Yuanhe 元和 reign period (814) the Jinglüe Army was reconstituted in a place about 300 kilometers northeast of the original prefectures.[17]

However, the record in the entry "New Youzhou" 新宥州 in the *Maps and Gazetteer of the Provinces and Counties in the Yuanhe Period* 元和郡縣圖志 tells a different story. According to this entry, in the first year of the Tiaolu reign period (679) the Six Prefectures were located in the south of Lingzhou.[18] It cites a petition of Li Jifu 李吉甫 that "The court had

---

[17] *New Tang History*, ch. 37, "Monograph on Geography" 《地理志》, pp. 974-5.

[18] Li Jifu 李吉甫, *Maps and Gazetteer of the Provinces and Counties in the Yuanhe Period* 《元和郡縣圖志》 (Zhonghua Book Company punctuated edition, 1983), first book, p. 106.

originally founded the Six Prefectures within the territory of Lingzhou."[19] This quotation is also found in the *Outstanding Models from the Storehouse of Literature* 冊府元龜. The Lingzhou mentioned in the *Maps and Gazetteer of the Provinces and Counties in the Yuanhe Period* was recorded as both Lingzhou and Yanzhou 鹽州 in the *Outstanding Models from the Storehouse of Literature.*[20] In addition, two poems of Li Yi 李益, a poet of the mid-eighth to early ninth centuries, also show that the Six Hu Prefectures were distributed in the territories of both Lingzhou and the southern part of Xiazhou.[21] It is incorrect to say the Six Hu Prefectures were exclusively in the southern part of Lingzhou.

It is recorded that An Pu (mentioned above), the Great Chief of the Kingdom of An, brought his property and people to surrender to the Tang, and then was granted the official title of Great Chief 大首領 of the Six Hu Prefectures. Studies have proven that An Pu died in 664, which shows that the Six Hu Prefectures were in fact founded earlier than the first year of the Tiaolu reign period (679) indicated in the historical record. In the twentieth year of the Zhenguan 貞觀 reign period (646) Emperor Taizong 太宗 defeated the Xueyantuo 薛延陀 and decided to go to Lingzhou for a tour of inspection. He arrived in Jingyang 涇陽 in the eighth month, and tribes of the Tiele 鐵勒 sent ambassadors to meet with him. Taizong received them with a banquet in the provincial imperial residence, entertained the envoys, and conferred separately on many of them prestige titles such as Commandant 郎將 and Commandant of Zhaowu 昭武校尉.[22] Taizong also wrote a letter to the chiefs of the Tiele and dispatched with it an ambassador named An Yongshou 安永壽, a Commandant of the Metropolitan Guard on the Right 右領軍中郎將, who was originally a member of the Nine Surnames of Zhaowu.[23] According to these records,

---

[19] Ibid., p. 106.

[20] *Models from the Storehouse of Literature* 《冊府元龜》, chapter 993, "Officials in Local Administration, Defensive Preparations, 6"《外臣部備禦六》 (Zhonghua Book Company, 1960), pp. 2667-8.

[21] *Complete Tang Poems*《全唐詩》, ch. 282 (Zhonghua Book Company punctuated edition, 1960), p. 3211.

[22] *Important Documents of the Tang*《唐會要》, Sinology Fundamental Texts edition 國學基本叢書本, ch. 96, "Tiele"《鐵勒》(Shanghai: The Commercial Press 商務印書館), last book, p. 1725.

[23] *Comprehensive Mirror for Aid in Government*, "The eighth month of the 28th year of the Zhenguan reign period," ch. 198, p. 6239.

we can conclude that Chinese prestige titles could be bestowed on ambassadors of the Tiele, and it is reasonable that after their surrender to Tang, their chiefs could be appointed as Commander-in-Chiefs 都督 or Prefects 刺史 of the Protected ("loose rein") Prefectures 羈縻州, and the chiefs of the Sogdians could remain in their leadership positions as before.

As is well known, there was turmoil at the end of the Sui Dynasty. Zhengdao 政道, the posthumous son of Jian 暕 the prince of Qi 齊王 and grandson of the Sui emperor Yangdi 隋煬帝, followed Empress Xiao 蕭后 to the Turks. Chuluo (Chula) 處羅 Qaghan of the Eastern Turks (made supreme Qaghan in 619) granted titles to the Sui royalty, and "the Chinese who fled to the northern foreigners were organized into tribes and settled in the town of Dingxiang 定襄."[24] If the Han Chinese in the Qaghanate were organized into tribes, then, similarly, settlements of the Nine Zhaowu Surnames in the area should have existed in the same way. In the eleventh year of the Daye 大業 reign period of the Sui emperor Yangdi (615), Pei Ju 裴矩 worked out a stratagem to lure Shishu Huxi 史蜀胡悉, a trusted advisor to Tujieli Shibi 始畢 Qaghan (Ashina Duojishi) of the Eastern Turks (609-619), to come to Mayi 馬邑 for trade. "Without announcing his departure and plans," Shishu Huxi "led his tribes, driving their domestic animals, and hurriedly galloped into battle."[25] In 619, Illig Qaghan (Jieli) 頡利 (Qaghan 621-630) commissioned Yan Tuo Šad 延陀設, Bu Li Šad 步利設, Tong Tegin 統特勤, and Hu Tegin 斛特勤 to administer the [Xue]yantuo [薛]延陀, Xi 霫, Hu 胡, and Huxue 斛薛 tribes.[26] All these records prove that the Sogdians were organized into tribes within the Qaghanate.

The Sogdians resettled in the territory of Qaghanate by tribes, so that in the fourth year of the Zhenguan reign period, when Illig Qaghan (Jieli) was defeated, they came to surrender to Tang by tribe as well. How to relocate the surrendered Turkic people prompted a fierce argument in the Tang court. Emperor Taizong finally adopted Wen Yanbo's 溫彥博 proposal to act in accordance with Emperor Guangwu 光武 of the Eastern Han, who had resettled the surrendered Xiongnu to the area of the Ordos

---

[24] *History of the Sui* 《隋書》, ch. 59, "Biographies of Emperor Yangdi's Three Sons" 《煬帝三子傳》, p. 1444.

[25] Ibid., ch. 67, "Biography of Pei Ju" 《裴矩傳》, p. 1582.

[26] *New Tang History*, ch. 215a, "Account of the Turks" 《突厥傳》, p. 6038.

Loop [literally, Wuyuansai 五原塞], and so Taizong established prefectures including Shun 順, Beifu 北撫, Beikai 北開, Beining 北寧 and Bei'an 北安 between Youzhou 幽州 and Lingzhou in order to relocate the surrendered Turkic tribes. In the sixth month of the same year, Commandant 中郎將 Shi Shanying 史善應 was appointed Supervisor-in-Chief of Beifu Prefecture; Kang Sumi 康蘇密, a Sogdian chief who had sent the Empress Xiao and the grandson of the Sui emperor Yangdi to the Tang in the first month of that year, was appointed the Supervisor-in-Chief of Bei'an Prefecture. So, in the five Protected Prefectures 羈縻州 two of the supervisors were Sogdian. An Pu would have moved to the Ordos Loop area at about the same time or earlier. According to historical records, An Feihan 安朏汗, another chief of the Sogdians, also came to surrender at about the same time. An Feihan "led about five thousand of his clan to surrender to Tang. They were relocated to Weizhou 維州. An Feihan was appointed Prefect 刺史 and entitled General of the Left Militant Guard 左武衛將軍."[27] Later An Fuguo 安附國, son of An Feihan, took over his father's position as Prefect of Weizhou. An Fuguo's second son An Sigong 安思恭 was appointed the Prefect of Luzhou 魯州.[28] There is no doubt that the Luzhou mentioned here is the one belonging to the Six Hu Prefectures.

Based on the above discussion we can conclude that in the fourth year of the Zhenguan reign period there were quite a number of people who followed the Eastern Turks southward to surrender to the Tang. An Feihan brought in about five thousand people and was appointed the Prefect of Weizhou. An Pu remained the Great Chief of the Six Hu Prefectures. He was conferred the prestige title of General for Pacifying Faraway Lands 定遠將軍, equivalent to the fifth rank of a court official, however he "remained a chief as before." All of this proves that the Nine Zhaowu Surnames came to surrender according to their tribes, and their senior official positions 長官 were undertaken by their chiefs as before.

---

[27] Li Zhiyuan 李至遠, "Spirit Way Stele for the Marquis An, the Prefect of Weizhou" 《唐維州刺史安侯神道碑》, in *Complete Prose Literature of the Tang* 《全唐文》, ch. 435 (Zhonghua Book Company, 1983), p. 4435, last column. This Weizhou has no connection with the similarly named Weizhou of Wei River Commandery 維川郡 in Jiannan Circuit 劍南道.

[28] Ibid.

According to the *New Tang History*, in the first year of the Tiaolu reign period (679), the Six Hu Prefectures were established and the Prefects were all Chinese. This record, however, does not mean that the Six Hu Prefectures were established in 679. Instead, this refers to the year when Chinese officials replaced the chiefs of the Sogdians as Prefects. The change was apparently the result of a revolt of two tribes of the Ashina 阿史那 – the Wenfu 溫傅 and the Fengzhi 奉職 – which caused disturbances among the other 24 Protected Prefectures.[29] The Tang court had no choice but to reinforce their control over the Six Hu Prefectures.

The revolt of the two tribes, the Wenfu and the Fengzhi, demonstrated the revival of the Eastern Turks and became the prelude for the restoration of the Turkish Qaghanate. The Turks increased the strength of their forces and their raiding activity. In the second year of the Kaiyao 開耀 reign period of Emperor Gaozong 高宗 (681), the Sogdian An Yuanshou 安元壽, the Commissioner of Herds 羣牧使 for Xiazhou, presented a memo to the court saying, "since the first year of the Tiaolu reign period (679) we have lost about 180,000 horses, and more than 800 people have been killed by the Turks."[30] In 682, Ilterish (Guduolu) 骨咄祿 of the Ashina 阿史那 clan came into power and became Qaghan. His brother Qapaghan Qaghan (in Chinese Mochuo 默啜, Bäg-čur or Bug-chor in Tibetan, reigned 691-716) allied with Tibet and frequently attacked the areas under the control of Empress Wu Zetian. Tibet demanded from Empress Wu the Four Garrison Commands of Anxi 安西四鎮 (the Anxi Protectorate) and the people of the Ten Surnames of the Western Turks (On Oq) 西突厥十姓. Bäg-čur demanded from Empress Wu the Six Hu Prefectures and the subjugated Turks who had been relocated to the Hexi 河西 region. In the first year of the Shengong 神功 reign period (697) Bäg-čur once again demanded the Six Hu Prefectures and the territory of the Shanyu Protectorate 單于都護府, as well as seed-grain, silk, farming implements, and iron. Upon the petition of the court officials Yao Shou 姚壽 and Yang Zaisi 楊再思, the Empress "gave several thousand households of the Six Hu Prefectures to Bäg-čur, and 40,000 *hu* 斛 of seed-grain [about 800,000 liters], 50,000

---

[29] Onogawa Hidemi 小野川秀美, "The Evolution of the Six Hu Prefectures of the Ordos Loop," p. 197 (961).

[30] *Comprehensive Mirror for Aid in Government*, ch. 202, "The seventh month of the first year of the Kaiyao reign period of Emperor Gaozong," p. 6402.

duan 段 of various kinds of colored silk [about 460,000 meters], 3,000 pieces of farming equipment, 40,000 *jin* 斤 of iron [about 9,600 kilograms], as well as an imperial marriage."[31] Soon after that, Bäg-čur again attacked the Tang. In 701-02, Bäg-čur dispatched two of his nephews, the later Bilgä Qaghan 毗伽可汗 and his brother Kül Tegin 闕特勤, and attacked the Six Hu Prefectures. This event is recorded in the inscriptions on the Orkhon Turkic stone steles erected on the Mongolian steppe[32] – the monuments for Bilgä Qaghan and Kül Tegin.[33]

The *Bilgä Qaghan Inscription* 毗伽可汗碑 says, "(24th line)…when I was eighteen I led an army to attack the Six Hu Prefectures (altï čub soγdaq) and (25th line) defeated them there. The Tang Prince Commander-in-Chief 都督 (Ong *tutuq*) led an army of 50,000. We fought against each other in ïduq-bashe, where I defeated this army…"

The *Kül Tegin Inscription* 闕特勤碑 says, "(31st line)…At the age of sixteen, he performed the following military exploits to expand the territory and power of my uncle Qaghan [Bäg-čur]: we attacked the Six Hu Prefectures and conquered them. We fought against an army of 50,000 led by the Tang Prince Commander-in-Chief. (33rd line) Kül Tegin

31 Ibid., ch. 206, "The third month of the first year of the Shengong reign period of Empress Wu Zetian," p. 6516. *Encyclopaedic History of Institutions* 《通典》, ch. 198. *Old Tang History* 《舊唐書》, ch. 194. According to the *Old Tang History*, ch. 185, p. 4794, in the entry "Biography of Tian Renhui's son Tian Guidao" 《田仁會子田歸道傳》, the Empress Wu Zetian did not agree to Bäg-čur's demand. For the question of whether what Bäg-čur asked for was the territory of Hexi (or Ordos) Six Hu Prefectures or the households of the Six Prefectures in the Hexi region, see Cen Zhongmian 岑仲勉, "Surrendered Households of the Six Prefectures" 《六州降戶》 in *Questions on Records of the Sui and Tang in the Comprehensive Mirror for Aid in Government* 《通鑑隋唐紀比事質疑》 (Zhonghua Book Company, 1964), pp. 123-4.

32 For an introduction to the circumstances of the two steles, see Cen Zhongmian 岑仲勉, *Collected Histories of the Turks* 《突厥集史》, vol. 2 (Zhonghua Book Company, 1958), pp. 887-9 and 917-8.

33 On the Kül Tegin stele, the inscription of 40 lines on the east face supplemented by 13 lines on the right side is known as the "big inscription"; The Bilgä Qaghan stele was broken into two parts, the 41 lines on the front face supplemented by 15 lines on the left side are known as the "big inscription," the 15 lines on the right side are known as the "small inscription." The Kül Tegin big inscription lines 1-30 and the Bilgä Qaghan big inscription lines 3-23 have the same fundamental content. See S. G. Kliashtornyĭ (С. Г. Кляшторный), *Ancient Turkish Runic Monuments as Sources for the History of Central Asia* (*Древнетюркские рунические памятники. как источник по истории Средней Азии*) (Moscow, 1964), pp. 59-60.

attacked on foot and caught the jorič [brother-in-law] of the Prince Commander-in-Chief with his armor on and submitted the jorič and his armor to the Qaghan. There we annihilated that army."[34]

The German scholar Josef Marquart's explanation of the above two passages is well accepted. Based on the Persian historian al-Tabarī, who recorded an attack of the Turks on Nasaf in the Islamic calendar year 82, or 701 CE, Marquart argued that the battle mentioned in the inscriptions is the war of 701 as recorded in the Muslim documents. Marquart also argued that the Tang Commander-in-Chief was Prince Dan 相王旦, the Metropolitan Governor 牧 of Bingzhou 并州 and the Anbei Commander-in-Chief 安北大都督 (a Japanese scholar later corrected this, that it should be either the Grand Protector of Anbei 安北大都護 or the Grand Marshal of the Army of Anbei Circuit 安北道行軍大元帥; see *Comprehensive Mirror for Aid in Government* 資治通鑒, ch. 207), who later became the Emperor Ruizong. As far as the phrase "altï čub soγdaq" (Sogdian) is concerned, Marquart believed that the word čub referred to Zhaowu 昭武.[35] Many famous scholars such as Édouard Chavannes have agreed with this argument. The phrase "altï čub soγdaq" is often translated as "the six tribes of the Sogdians." Yet there remain in scholarly circles many different opinions about this explanation. Is "altï čub soγdaq" one word or two? And to what place does it refer?[36] In 1961, the Soviet Turkologist, S. G. Kliashtornyĭ (С. Г. Кляшторный), proposed a new argument regarding "altï čub soγdaq" and the Six Hu Prefectures:[37]

> 1) As to what Marquart has pointed out, the inscription speaks about the battle with the Tang Prince Commander-in-Chief immediately after the mention of the expedition to altï čub soγdaq in 701. The former refers to the battle between the Turks and

---

[34] The translation is based on S. G. Kliashtornyĭ (С. Г. Кляшторный), "Sogdians in Central Asia" ("Согдийцы в Центральной Азии") in *Epigraphy of the East* (*Эпиграфика Востока*), vol. 14 (1961), pp. 29-31. A French version of the article was published in *Ural-Altaische Jahrbücher*, vol. 33, nos. 1-2 (1961), pp. 95-7.

[35] Josef Marquart, *Die Chronologie des Alttürkischen Inschriften* (Leipzig, 1898), pp. 68-72.

[36] S. G. Kliashtornyĭ (С. Г. Кляшторный), *Ancient Turkish Runic Monuments as Sources for the History of Central Asia*, pp. 78-80.

[37] The translation is based on S. G. Kliashtornyĭ, "Sogdians in Central Asia," pp. 29-31. In the French version, pp. 95-7.

Prince Dan in 702 recorded in Tang documents. So the attack on altï čub soγdaq in 701 and the battle against the Chinese Commander-in-Chief Prince Dan in the spring of 702 are in reality connected together as two consecutive battles in one great military campaign. The time of the two battles having been in succession precludes the possibility that the battle in altï čub soγdaq took place in the Sogdian area of Central Asia.

2) Altï means "six" in Turkic. Soγdaq was customarily translated as Hu 胡 during the Tang Dynasty. Therefore, if čub is a transliteration of "prefecture" 州,[38] then there is no problem in concluding that altï čub soγdaq is a transliteration and translation of "Six Hu Prefectures."

Kliashtornyĭ's (Кляшторный) arguments are reasonable and convincing, and they did away with a long-standing perplexity. Bäg-čur's demand for and conquering of the Six Hu Prefectures in fact indicates clearly that in the contest between the Turks and the Tang the position of the Six Hu Prefectures was quite important. In the fourth year of the Chang'an reign period of Empress Wu Zetian (704), the Six Hu Prefectures were amalgamated to form Kuangzhou and Changzhou. In the third year of the Shenlong reign period of Emperor Zhongzong 中宗 (707), the Tang court re-established the Lanchi 蘭池 Area Command 都督府, the seat of which was "eighty *li* north of Baichi County 白池縣 in Yanzhou, and each of the former Six Prefectures became six counties."[39] The frequent institutional changes were a result of numerous raids at that time in all areas by the Tibetans and the Turks, which forced many minority tribes such as the Tiele 鐵勒 and the Dangxiang 党项 to move to this area

[38] Based on the criteria of the pronunciation of ancient Turkic, the Chinese character *zhou* 州 could have had two types of transliteration: 1) t'sšəu＞čiu＞či, see the Hungarian scholar B. Csongor, "Chinese in the Uighur Script of the T'ang-period", in *Acta Orientalia Hungarica*, vol. 2, 1952, p. 116; and 2) t'sšəu＞ubč or čuw, because Chinese characters ending with a labial often change to the Turkic bilabial consonant *b*. See S. G. Kliashtornyĭ, *Ancient Turkish Runic Monuments as Sources for the History of Central Asia* (Moscow, 1964), p. 94, footnote 75; and S. G. Kliashtornyĭ, "Sogdians in Central Asia" in *Epigraphy of the East,* p. 31, footnote; and in the French version, p. 97, footnote 4.

[39] *Maps and Gazetteer of the Provinces and Counties in the Yuanhe Period* 《元和郡縣圖志》, ch. 4, p. 106.

in order to avoid the chaos. For example, one purpose in establishing the Lanchi Area Command was the assignment of restraining the Dangxiang.[40] To defend against the increasing attacks of the Turks, the Tang court strengthened their defensive measures. In the second year of the Shenlong reign period (708), the Tang Commander-in-Chief 大總管 of the Shuofang Circuit 朔方道 (a frontier military jurisdiction), Zhang Renyuan 張仁愿, took advantage of the Turks making a westward expedition and thus there being relative peace north of the Gobi Desert, and built three cities on the north, east, and west of the Ordos Loop to resettle the surrendered tribes, which strengthened the Tang court's ability to defend Longyou 隴右 and Shuofang 朔方 [the Ordos Loop area]. These were the territories for the Tang pastured herds and their base for obtaining horses, and so they were the target of Turkish raids for horses.[41] In the ninth month of the second year of the Kaiyuan reign period of Emperor Xuanzong (714) "Jiang Hui 姜晦, Vice Minister of the Court of Imperial Sacrifices 太常少卿, submitted a petition to take people without any official rank to go to the Six Hu Prefectures to purchase horses, requesting that the prestige title of Mobile Corps Commander 遊擊將軍 be awarded to each person who could obtain thirty horses."[42] At that time, about three hundred people without official rank came to the Six Hu Prefectures to buy horses, so that if the mission had been completed successfully, the Tang would have obtained 9,000 horses, and there would have been in the Six Hu Prefectures about 300 people entitled to prestige titles above the fifth rank, such as Military Service Prestige Officer 武散官 and Mobile Corps Commander.

Between 713 and 721, under the attacks of the Turks, the Nine Surnames of the Tiele tribes such as the Uyghurs, the Tongra 同羅, the Hun 渾, the Pugu 僕固 (Bókú, Barghut), and the Jiadie [足+夾, a Chinese character not in Unicode]跌 decided to move into China proper. They were successively resettled in Lingzhou, in the area of the three resettlement cities mentioned above, and in Daizhou 代州. The resettlement of different

---

[40] *Old Tang History*, ch. 43b, "Monograph on Geography" 《地理志》, the entry "Lanchi Area Command" 《蘭池都督府》, p. 1123.

[41] Zhang Yue 張說, *Stele Praising the Supervision of the Longyou Herds in the Thirteenth Year of the Kaiyuan Reign Period of the Great Tang Dynasty* 《大唐開元十三年隴右監牧頌德碑》, in *Complete Prose Literature of the Tang* 《全唐文》, ch. 226, pp. 2282-3.

[42] *Important Documents of the Tang*, ch. 72, "Horses" 《馬》, p. 1302.

nationalities together aggravated the conflicts between them. Wang Jun 王晙, Administrator 長史 of Bingzhou, suggested that the surrendered households be relocated to the interior, which caused some tribes such as the Jiadie to surrender to the Turks. Shanyu Vice Protector-General 單于副都護 Zhang Zhiyun 張知運 confiscated weapons from the surrendered households causing made many people to become enraged and rebel. "The Sogdians of Lanchi have been organized for a long time, they are all obedient people, similar to the people of the Tang."[43] However, inappropriate administration by the Tang officials and oppression of the Sogdians of Lanchi finally caused, during the fourth to the sixth months of the ninth year of the Kaiyuan reign period (721), Kang Daibin 康待賓, An Murong 安慕容, Duo Lansha (šad) 多覽殺, He Heinu 何黑奴, Shi Shennu 石神奴, Kang Tietou 康鐵頭, and others to lead the surrendered tribes in a widespread rebellion. These leaders of the rebellion usually held Turkic official ranks such as *yabghu* 葉護, as well as Tang prestige military titles such as General-in-Chief 大將軍 and General. The rebelling territory of the "Nine Hu of the Six Prefectures" was in "a strategic location to meet the bandits" [i.e., between the Turks and Tang]. About 70,000 people rebelled and attacked and captured the Six Hu Prefectures, due to their having numerous horses and powerful weapons. This rebellion, however, was defeated by an alliance composed of the Commander-in-Chief 大總管 of the Shuofang Circuit (frontier command), Wang Jun; the Military Commissioner 節度使 of Longyou, Guo Zhiyun 郭知運; the Defense and Reprisal Commissioner-in-Chief 防禦討擊大使 of Shuofang Circuit, Wang Maozhong 王毛仲; the Military Commissioner-in-Chief 節度大使 of the Heavenly Soldiers Army 天兵軍, Zhang Yue 張說; and the Vice Military Commissioner-in-Chief 節度副大使 of Shuofang Circuit, Lun Gongren 論弓仁; who were in the company of the Lingzhou Sogdian Kang Zhi 康植,[44] the Tuyuhun 吐谷渾 of Hexi 河西,[45] and tribes of the

---

[43] *Outstanding Models from the Storehouse of Literature*《冊府元龜》, ch. 986, p. 11584.

[44] *New Tang History*, ch. 148, "Biography of Kang Rizhi" 《康日知傳》, p. 4772.

[45] Xia Nai 夏鼐, "Epitaph of the Wuwei Tang Dynasty Tuyuhun Murong"《武威唐代吐谷渾慕容氏墓誌》, originally published in *Collected Essays of the Institute of History and Philology, Academia Sinica* 《中央研究院歷史語言研究所集刊》, vol. 20 (1948), republished in *Collected Essays on Archaeology*《考古學論文集》 (Science Press, 1961), pp. 103-5.

Tiele of Hedong 河東. In the eighth and ninth months of the same year, Kang Yuanzi 康愿子 of Lanchi 蘭池 again revolted and proclaimed himself Qaghan, planning to loot horses and trek westwards across the Yellow River to a place of safety. Zhang Yue dispatched an army to track down and engage the rebel army, and again a rebellion of the Nine Surnames of Zhaowu was suppressed. As a consequence, the Tang Court decided to relocate "the remaining 50,000 people of the Ordos Loop Six Hu Prefectures to prefectures (in the flood ravaged regions of the Yangtze and Huai 淮河 Rivers) such as Xu 許, Ru 汝, Tang 唐, Deng 鄧, Xian 仙, and Yu 豫. An area over 1,000 *li* in the Ordos south of the river and the Shuofang region became empty."[46] However, the relocated Sogdians loved their homeland 戀本 and desired to go back 懷歸, and began to gradually return to all their prefectures within the pass [i.e., on the frontier]. In the eighteenth year of the Kaiyuan reign period (730) Kuangzhou and Changzhou were re-established. At about the same time, Emperor Xuanzong dispatched Niu Xianke 牛仙客 to go to these prefectures to have the Sogdians settle down in peace 安輯 by "choosing a land of fertile fields within places such as Yanzhou 鹽州 and Xiazhou 夏州 in order to establish a new prefecture, and depending on the measurement of the households the number of counties would be established."[47] They recruited deserters and traitors, those Sogdians who had not yet returned to the Six Prefectures, originally from Lingzhou, Qingzhou 慶州, and others who belonged to prefectures south of the Huai River. In this manner, during the Kaiyuan reign period, nine or ten years after the rebellion, the Nine Surnames of Zhaowu resettled again in the Lingzhou and Yanzhou regions. This probably explains why in the twenty-sixth year of the Kaiyuan reign period (738) the Tang court established Youzhou 宥州 and the three counties of Yan'en 延恩, Huaide 懷德, and Guiren 歸仁 to resettle previous residents, and afterwards founded the Jinglüe 經略 "take charge

[46] *Old Tang History*, ch. 8, *Basic Annals of Xuanzong*《玄宗本紀》, p. 184. *Comprehensive Mirror for Aid in Government*, ch. 22, "The eighth month of the tenth year of the Kaiyuan reign period of Emperor Xuanzong," p. 6752. *Important Documents of the Tang*, ch. 73, "Lingzhou Area Command" 《靈州都督府》, last book, p. 1316.

[47] "Imperial Decree Dispatching Niu Xianke to Inside the Pass for Settling Down in Peace the Sogdians of the Six Prefectures" 《遣牛仙客往關内諸州安輯六州胡敕》 in *Collected Edicts of the Tang* 《唐大詔令集》, ch. 128 (Commercial Press, 1959), p. 690.

and put in order" Army.[48] In the early years of the Tianbao reign period, according to a petition of Wang Zhongsi 王忠嗣, the Military Commissioner of the Shuofang Circuit, the Jinglüe Army was moved to the town of Yuduole 榆多勒, located three hundred *li* northwest of Xiazhou.

During the An Lushan rebellion period (755-763), Sogdians of the Six Prefectures in the Ordos region also had activities worthy of attention.

In 756 (in the sixth month of the fifteenth year of the Tianbao reign period) An Lushan 安祿山 dispatched his General Sun Xiaozhe 孫孝哲 to occupy Chang'an 長安 and had the Sogdian An Zhongshun 安忠順 station his troops in Chang'an Yuanzhong 苑中 to garrison the capital region 關中. At that time some of An Lushan's followers, Tongra and Turks, were also stationed in Chang'an Yuanzhong. In the seventh month the chieftain of the Turks, Ashina Congli 阿史那從禮, led five thousand of cavalry, "stole two thousand horses, fled to the north, and schemed with other Sogdians to seize border territory."[49] In the ninth month, Ashina "Congli enticed tens of thousands of Nine Surname Six Prefecture Sogdians to assemble north of the Jinglüe Army"[50] and prepare to march on Lingzhou, where Emperor Suzong 肅宗 recently had succeeded to the throne, and to take the military initiative. Suzong, relying on the army of Pugu Huai'en 僕固懷恩, defeated the conspirators and finally swept away the impediments to the plan to have the Tang Shuofang [Jinglüe] Army coordinate with the Uyghurs that month to recapture the western capital Chang'an.

According to the extant historical records, the Tang Dynasty used to requisition military force from time to time from the Six Hu Prefectures. As early as the summer of the first year of the Wansui Dengfeng 萬歲登封 reign period (696), when Empress Wu Zetian was enthroned, the Khitan 契丹 of Yingzhou rebelled against the Tang, captured Yingzhou, and besieged Tanzhou 檀州. Empress Wu Zetian promptly freed slaves and reviewed the cases of prisoners, and "dispatched against the foreigners

---

[48] *New Tang History*, ch. 37, "Monograph on Geography" 《地理志》, p. 975. [The Jinglüe Armies were under the direct command of the Military Commissioner of each Circuit (frontier military command). Translator's note.]

[49] *Comprehensive Mirror for Aid in Government*, ch. 218, "The fifth month of the first year of the Zhide reign period of Emperor Suzong," p. 6986.

[50] Ibid., "The ninth month of the first year of the Zhide reign period of Emperor Suzong," p. 6997.

elite troops from Hedong Circuit and the Six Hu Prefectures, as well as those from prefectures such as Sui 綏, Yan 延, Dan 丹, and Xi 隰, all of whom went to Yingzhou."[51] As for the An Lushan rebellion, both An Lushan and Shi Siming 史思明 were mixed-race foreigners from Yingzhou, and there were very many Sogdians from the Six Prefectures in their army. For example, An Qingxu 安慶緒, the son of An Lushan, fled northward from Luoyang in early 758: his General Li Guiren 李歸仁 and elite soldiers of the *yeluohe* 曳落河,[52] the Tongra, and tens of thousands from the Six Prefectures were routed and returned to Fanyang 范陽. Shi Siming dispatched an envoy to offer amnesty and enlist the rebels, the Tongra returned to their homeland, and the *yeluohe* and the Sogdians from the Six Prefectures surrendered to Shi Siming.[53]

In the mid-eighth century, the contest between the Tang and Tibet intensified in the areas of Yanzhou and Xiazhou, most probably due to pressure from Tibet. In the twelfth month of the second year of the Zhenyuan 貞元 reign period of Emperor Dezong 德宗 (early 787), the Sogdians in the Six Hu Prefectures moved eastward to Shizhou 石州 (Lishi 離石 in modern Shanxi 山西 Province) and surrendered to Ma Sui 馬燧, the Military Commissioner 節度使 of Hedong. From then on, these Sogdians of the Six Prefectures resettled in areas between Yunzhou 雲州 (Datong 大同 in modern Shanxi Province) and Shuozhou 朔州 (Shuo County 朔縣 in modern Shanxi Province).[54] In 814 (the ninth year of the Yuanhe 元和 reign period) the Tang court once again re-established Youzhou 宥州 in the area that had previously belonged to the Six Hu Prefectures. This was because of an attack of the Uyghurs in the previous

---

[51] Chen Zi'ang 陳子昂, "Report to the Court on Classified and Important Military and State Issues" 《上軍國機要事》, in *Complete Prose Literature of the Tang* 《全唐文》, ch. 218, p. 2135, last column.

[52] *Yeluohe* was probably a transcription of the Arabic word raqiq's irregular plural ariqqä. In identity and function they were similar to the Central Asian Sogdian comitatus 柘羯. See Maejima Shinji 前嶋信次, "Some Central Asian Words of the Time of the An Lu-shan and Shih Ssu-ming Rebellion" 「安史之亂時的幾個中亞語詞」 in *Memoirs of the Toyo Bunko* 『東洋文庫研究部歐文紀要』, no. 35 (1977), pp. 111-2.

[53] *Comprehensive Mirror for Aid in Government*, ch. 220, "The twelfth month of the second year of the Zhide reign period of Suzong," p. 7047.

[54] Ibid., ch. 232, "The twelfth month of the second year of the Zhenyuan reign period of Emperor Dezong," p. 7477.

winter coming south of the desert, which had caused panic within the Tang court. Li Jifu 李吉甫 therefore suggested the establishment of a new Youzhou in the north of Yanzhou and Xiazhou, as well as the re-establishment of three counties including Yan'en 延恩. New Youzhou was set up in the town of the Jinglüe Army 經略軍城, and 9,000 soldiers and their families under Commander Zheng Gao 鄭杲 were allocated to there from the Shence 神策 Army field headquarters at Fucheng 鄜城. "On the day of the establishment of the New Youzhou, while constructing the walls, there were dug up 254 cauldrons, all of which could be used for cooking."[55] It seems that these cauldrons were buried by previous residents, who had hoped to move back some day. New Youzhou and the Jinglüe Army had the same names as their predecessors, but their functions were different. Because people of the previous Six Hu Prefectures had been relocated to Yunzhou and Shuozhou, the purpose of the army was to defend against the Uyghurs and the Dangxiang, rather than against the Turks.

In the twenty or so years after the people of the Six Hu Prefectures had moved to Yunzhou and Shuozhou, the Shatuo 沙陀 Turkish tribe moved eastward to live together with the Sogdians in order to avoid the attacks of the Tibetans. The Shatuo originally were one of the tribes of the Western Turks and had lived in the area east of Pulei 蒲類 (modern Barköl 巴里坤 in northern Xinjiang Province). In 789-790 (the fifth and sixth years of the Zhenyuan reign period) when the Uyghurs and the Tibetans fought for Beiting 北庭 (Beshbalïq), which surrendered to the Tibetans, the Shatuo, who were well known for bravery among foreigners, were resettled in Ganzhou 甘州. In 808 (the third year of the Yuanhe reign period), because of their suspicion of the Tibetans, the Shatuo turned to Fan Xichao 范希朝, the Military Commissioner of Yanzhou and Lingzhou. In the next year, Fan Xichao was appointed the Military Commissioner of Hedong, and the Shatuo followed him to Hedong, and they later became the frontier guard army called the Xingbei Shatuo 陘北沙陀. During the reign of Emperor Wenzong 文宗 (reigned 827-840), the Xingbei Shatuo, because they were brave and good at fighting, were feared by the Sogdians of the Six Hu

---

[55] *Maps and Gazetteer of the Provinces and Counties in the Yuanhe Period* 《元和郡縣圖志》, ch. 4, p. 107.

Prefectures,[56] so the Tang court commissioned Zhuye Zhiyi 朱邪執宜, the chief of the Shatuo, to administer eleven abandoned frontier garrisons of Yunzhou and Shuozhou and to control the Six Hu Prefectures, as well as to defend against the Uyghurs of the Nine Surnames north of the Gobi Desert. After the death of Zhuye Zhiyi, his son Zhuye Chixin 朱邪赤心 continued fighting against the Uyghurs for the Tang, attacked Liuzhen 劉稹 in Zelu 澤潞 Province, beat back the Tuyuhun 吐(谷)渾, and successfully suppressed the rebellion of Pang Xun 龐勳, for which the Tang court bestowed on him the Chinese name Li Guochang 李國昌. During the era of Li Guochang and his son Li Keyong 李克用, the Shatuo established a close relationship with the Sogdians from the Six Prefectures who had moved to Yunzhou and Shuozhou.[57] In 874, in the eleventh month of the first year of the Qianfu 乾符 reign period of Emperor Xizong 僖宗, Li Jun 李鈞, because of the good relationship between his father Li Ye 李業, the Military Commissioner of Taiyuan 太原, and the Shatuo, was appointed as the Military Commissioner of Lingwu 靈武 and the Pacification Commissioner 宣慰使 to the Three Tribes and the Six Prefectures of the Shatuo.[58] In the *New History of Five Dynasties*, Xu Wudang 徐無黨 noted this, saying: "There are no other names found elsewhere for the so-called Three Tribes and Six Prefectures of the Shatuo, and according to the *Tang History* it is only in these words."[59] This note shows that Xu Wudang did not know what the Six Prefectures and Three Tribes referred to. In fact, the Six Prefectures referred to the Sogdians who moved from Lingzhou and Yanzhou to Yunzhou and Shuozhou, and lived together with the Shatuo.[60] The Three Tribes referred to the Shatuo, the Sage 薩葛, and the Anqing 安慶, because, as is clear in the following records, the Three Tribes were usually listed together. This is not by chance: in 877 (in the tenth month of the fourth year of the Qianfu reign period) Li Jun together with the tribes

---

[56] *New Tang History*, ch. 218, "Account of the Shatuo" 《沙陀傳》, p. 107.

[57] Kuwabara Jitsuzō 桑原隲蔵, "On the People from the Western Regions," pp. 378-9. Ishida Mikinosuke 小野川秀美, *Spring in Chang'an*, p. 213 (977). Pulleyblank, "A Sogdian Colony in Inner Mongolia," *T'oung Pao*, vol. 41 (1952), p. 343.

[58] *Old Tang History*, ch. 19b, "Basic Annals of Yizong" 《僖宗本紀》, p. 692.

[59] *New History of the Five Dynasties* 《新五代史》, ch. 4, "Basic Annals of Zhuangzong of the Later Tang" 《後唐莊宗本紀》, p. 32.

[60] Pulleyblank, "A Sogdian Colony in Inner Mongolia," p. 343.

Shatuo, Xuege 薛葛 (Sage), and Anqing fought against Li Guochang and his son;[61] in 880 (in the sixth month of the first year of the Guangming 廣明 reign period of Emperor Xizong) Li Zhuo 李琢, the Bandit Suppression Commissioner 招討使 of Weizhou, Shazhou 沙州, and other prefectures, and the Tuyuhun fought against the chief of the Shatuo Li Youjin 李友金, the Commander-in- Chief 都督 of the Sage Mi Haiwan 米海萬, and the Commander-in-Chief of the Anqing Shi Jingcun 史敬存;[62] in 881 (in the second month of the first year of the Zhonghe 中和 reign period of Emperor Xizong), Chen Jingsi 陳景思, the Daizhou 代州 Northern Mobile Brigade Commander 行營都押, led the three tribes of Shatuo, Sage, and Anqing, and 30,000 people of the Tuyuhun to go and support the capital region 關中.[63] It is worth noting that name of the Commander-in-Chief of the Sage, Mi Haiwan, was evidently one of the Zhaowu Surnames, and that Sage and Xuege have been proven by scholars to be two different transliterations of the same word, Sogdian.[64] The *New History of the Five Dynasties*, in the biography of An Congjin 安從進, says that he was from the Suoge 索葛 tribe of Zhenwu 振武.[65] His surname, An, was without doubt one of the Zhaowu Surnames. And Shi Wenming 史文明 has pointed out that An Congjin was from the Suoge tribe, which once again is strong circumstantial evidence that Sage, Xuege, and Suoge are different transliterations of the same word, Sogdian. As to the Anqing tribe where Shi Jingcun became the Commander-in-Chief, it is possible that the surname Shi also originated from the Nine Zhaowu Surnames of the Six Prefectures.

The close relationship between Shatuo and the Sogdians at the end of the Tang Dynasty had an important influence on the history of the following Five Dynasties period.[66] People have noticed that there were

---

61 *Old Tang History*, ch. 19b, *Basic Annals of Yizong* 《僖宗本紀》, p. 700.

62 Ibid., p. 707.

63 Ibid., p. 710.

64 Pulleyblank, "A Sogdian Colony in Inner Mongolia," pp. 343-4.

65 *New History of Five Dynasties* 《新五代史》, ch. 51, "Biography of An Congjin" 《安從進傳》, p. 586.

66 For example, Kuwabara Jitsuzō 桑原隲藏 in the above mentioned essay listed a number of followers of the famous Shatuo General Li Keyong 李克用, including Mi Haiwan 米海萬, Kang Junli 康君立, An Jinquan 安金全, An Quanjun 安全俊, An Jingzhong 安敬忠, An Yuanxin 安元信, Shi Jingsi 史敬思, Shi Jiantang 史建瑭, and Shi

quite a number of figures surnamed Kang 康, An 安, Shi 史, Shi 石, and He 何 active on the stage of history during the Five Dynasties. In the Later Tang 後唐, Later Jin 後晉, and Later Han 後漢 Dynasties, all founded by the Shatuo, there were imperial concubines named Lady An, Lady Mi, Lady He, and Lady Cao 曹. Fundamental studies tracing this to its source have shown that this situation evolved from the era of An Pu [mentioned above] or an even earlier period of the Six Hu Prefectures. The Tang Dynasty Six Hu Prefectures provide us with rare concrete examples for studying Sogdians in the political history of the Tang Dynasty.

II.

The migration of the Sogdians into China, however, did not begin in the Tang Dynasty. For example, even the region of the Six Hu Prefectures discussed above did not originate in the Zhenguan era of the early Tang when the Sogdians came to surrender to the Tang. In 426-427, Tuoba Tao 拓跋燾, the Emperor Taiwu of the Northern Wei Dynasty 北魏太武帝, attacked the Great Xia Kingdom 大夏國 (407-431), which had been founded by the Tuge 屠各 tribe of the Xiongnu. He destroyed Helian Chang 赫連昌, the ruler of Great Xia, and then received Sogdian (Hu 胡) households, moving their residence into Hu Town 胡(地)城.[67] Afterwards, in the first year of the Renshou 仁壽 reign period of the Sui emperor Wendi 文帝 (601), it was renamed as Lingwu County 靈武縣, and immigrants settled down in this Sogdian (Hu) town. From this it can be seen that the Lingwu County of the Tang Dynasty originated from Sogdian households who had immigrated to Hu Town to establish it. Although there are no solid historical records indicating who these Sogdian households were, they were definitely, without a doubt, not the indigenous commonly seen tribes such as the Tuge or the Buluoji 步落稽.

The activities of the Nine Zhaowu Surnames in East Asia can be traced back to as early as the Western Han and Eastern Han Dynasties, and forward to as late as the era of Qubilai Khan in the Yuan Dynasty, where they appear at Tiande Base (Tenduc) 天德軍 and at the Xuanhua Garrison

---

Junhe 石君和. They were all Sogdians. See Kuwabara Jitsuzō 桑原隲蔵, "On the People from the Western Regions," pp. 378-9.

[67] Li Jifu 李吉甫, *Maps and Gazetteer of the Provinces and Counties in the Yuanhe Period* 《元和郡縣圖志》, ch. 4, "Lingzhou, Lingwu County" 《靈州靈武縣》, p. 94.

宣化府 in Xuanmalin 宣麻林.[68] The word *guhu* 賈胡[69] (meaning traders from foreign countries) appears many times in the historical documents of the Eastern Han, and the term must have included Sogdian traders. Accompanying the development of their business activities, the *guhu* built stables for camel caravans and founded specific organizations for protection, which was a necessity for ensuring the safety of their business. The *guhu* developed gradually from temporarily present travelers into permanent residents, and they resettled along the places where the camel stables had been built, which gradually became settlements. The Sogdians originally founded kingdoms in the fertile areas of Central Asia. They focused primarily on trade, but also attended to agriculture and animal

---

[68] Rashīd al-Dīn, *Jāmi' al-Tawārīkh* (*Compendium of Chronicles*), vol. 2, Blochet edition, p. 463. There is a record of three routes from Khanbalïq 大都 to Shangdu (Xanadu) 上都 (Kaiping 開平, about 240 kilometers northwest of modern Beijing) during the era of Qubilai Khan. The second route was via a city called J̌oĭu. A city nearby was called Sīmāli, whose residents were mostly from Samarkand, and who had many farms similar to those of Samarkand. See the *History of the Yuan* 《元史》, ch. 122, "Biography of Hasannei" 《哈散納傳》: "Until the era of Emperor Taizong, there were three thousand households of Uyghur craftsmen stationed in Xuanmalin 蕁麻林 and an army of the Argun 阿爾渾 supervised these various craftsmen." Here Xuanmalin refers to Sīmāli. Marco Polo went to Xuanhua Garrison from Tiande Base (Tenduc) 天德軍 through Xuanmalin. He met people from Central Asia in both places. The difference with the Tang Dynasty, however, was that the people from Central Asia who resided there in the Yuan Dynasty were mostly forced to migrate there by the Mongols.

[69] In the *History of the Later Han* 《後漢書》, chapter 24, the biography of General Ma Yuan 《馬援傳》 records that at the time of expedition against the five barbarian tribes of Wuling 武陵, Geng Shu 耿舒 mocked Ma Yuan's use of soldiers to take action against various Western Regions *guhu* 賈胡 as going to a place of wheel ruts and stopping. Chapter five, the biography of Li Xun 李恂, says that Ma Yuan was conferred the prestige title of Vice-Commandant of the Western Regions, and that hostage sons, envoys, and *guhu* from various countries often presented him reliable slaves and concubines, horses from Yuan 宛, gold and silver, and incense and carpets of various types. According to chapter 34, the biography of Liang Ji 梁冀 appended to the biography of Liang Tong 《梁統附梁冀傳》, Liang Ji started a rabbit farm tens of *li* in extent, where he raised rabbits, and marked their fur. If someone killed a rabbit, the punishment for the guilty was death. Once there was a Western Regions *guhu* who did not know about this taboo and killed a rabbit, and as a result of the investigation more than ten people were sentenced to death. In addition, the *Han Records of the Eastern Pavilion* 《東觀漢記》 in chapter 61 records that at the death of Emperor Guangwu 光武帝, the Western Regions *guhu* of Chang'an set up a tent to hold the memorial ceremony (Saoye Publishing House 掃葉山房 block printing edition, ch. 16, page 22a).

husbandry. They had mastered a relatively high level of irrigation technology, and this high level gave the Sogdian immigrants the ability to base themselves along the Silk Road in the oases amid the sandy arid regions. Their religions, such as Zoroastrianism, as well as music, dance, entertainment, and marriage and funerary customs inevitably followed along their routes to more and more places, including agricultural regions and nomadic grassland regions. By the early fourth century at the latest there were about one hundred offspring of the nobility of the Kingdom of Kang 康國 in Dunhuang. In the research of the famous scholar of Ancient Iranian, W. B. Henning, he deduces that the number of noble offspring of the Kingdom of Kang and their families and servants had reached about 1,000.[70] These Sogdian businessmen established their own society in Dunhuang. During the era of the Sixteen Kingdoms, Liangzhou 涼州 was not only the political center of the five Liang Kingdoms and the cultural center of the Hexi Corridor, but also was the residential area for many nationalities. In addition, perhaps since the time that the Xiongnu had established there the town of Guzang 姑臧 (written Kc"n=Kucān in the Sogdian ancient letters), this area was also a center of international trade and transportation, and impressive numbers of Sogdian businessmen lived there. In 439, when Tuoba Tao, Emperor Taiwu of Northern Wei, led a large army and attacked the Northern Liang 北涼 and took Guzang, all of the Sogdians doing business in Northern Liang territory became captives. More than ten years later, shortly after the enthronement of Emperor Wencheng 文成 of the Northern Wei (425-467), a historical record says, "the King of the Sogdiana dispatched an envoy to ransom [the captives], and [the emperor] granted the request."[71] This record is the best evidence proving the activities of Sogdian businessmen in Liangzhou.

Judging from various historical records, the Sogdians came eastward along the Talas River 怛邏斯河 and the Chu River 楚河. In the late 620s and the 630s, the eminent Tang monk Xuanzang 玄奘 (600-664) went to India seeking sutras. When he returned, having recorded throughout his journey the situation in all the countries through which he traveled, not only did he call the territories of all the Nine Zhaowu Surname kingdoms

---

[70] W. B. Henning "The Date of the Sogdian Ancient Letters," *Bulletin of the School of Oriental and African Studies,* vol. 12, no. 3-4 (1948), p. 606, n. 9.

[71] *History of the Northern Dynasties* 《北史》, ch. 97, "Account of the Western Regions" 《西域傳》, p. 3221.

between the Oxus (Amu Darya) and the Jaxartes (Syr Darya) as Suli 窣利 (or Sogdiana 粟特), he also called the areas from Kāshāna (史國 the Kingdom of Shi, 羯霜那 in Xuanzang's text) stretching to Sūyāb 碎葉城 Suli as well. This was precisely because he had seen a string of Sogdian settlements dispersed along the valleys of the Chu and Talas Rivers to the west of Sūyāb, and consequently this was the reason he incorporated these areas into Sogdiana. The Song Dynasty author Shi Zanning 釋贊寧 compiled the *Biographies of Eminent Monks Compiled in Song Dynasty* 宋高僧傳 and in the biography of Shi Sengjia 釋僧伽 wrote: "Shi Sengjia was born in Kushānīka (the He Kingdom 何國), north of the Pamirs, and he said that his secular family name was He 何, but just as a monk originally from Samarkand (the Kangju Kingdom 康居國), he easily took a name as a Kang monk.…He explained that Kushānīka was located in the northeast of Sūyāb, and was subordinate only to Sūyāb."[72] In Xuanzang's *Great Tang Record of the Western Regions* 大唐西域記, Kushānīka was recorded as Qushuangnijia 屈霜你伽, and was also transliterated as Guishuangni 貴霜匿. According to the tenth-century Persian geographer al-Istakhrī, Guishuangni "is the most civilized city in Sogdiana, it is the heart of all Sogdian cities." Another tenth-century Islamic geographer Ibn Hawqal said that Qayy or Qayyi was a Sogdian region, "the heart of the Sogdians," and that although the two names were different, they referred to one place. Marquart consequently concluded that the Chinese classical records of the He Kingdom (ra': in Chinese historical phonology the *guo* rime group 果攝, the *ge* rime 歌韻, the *xia* initial 匣母) must have been namely Qayy or Qayyi, which equaled Guishuangni in Chinese.[73] But Guishuangni was located to the west of the Kingdom of Kang, and the He Kingdom north of the Pamirs where the Monk Sengjia was born was located in the northeast of Sūyāb and was subordinate to Sūyāb. Based on this clarification, we can conclude that this He Kingdom certainly was founded by immigrants from another He Kingdom located west of the Kingdom of Kang. Mahmūd al-Kāshgharī, an eleventh-century scholar from Shule 疏勒 (modern Kashgar), also confirmed that the Sogdians had

[72] Shi Zanning 釋贊寧, *Biographies of Eminent Monks Compiled in the Song Dynasty* 《宋高僧傳》, ch. 18, "Biography of the Monks at the Tang Dynasty Sizhou King of Universal Light Temple" 《唐泗州普光王寺僧伽傳》.

[73] J. Marquart, *Die Chronologie des Alttürkischen Inschriften* (Leipzig, 1898), p. 60.

great influence in the above-mentioned regions. The place that al-Kāshgharī called arγu included the region from Balasaγun near Sūyāb to the Talas River, or from Balasaγun to Baishui City 白水城. One of the special features of the ancient arγu region was that the people there spoke an Iranian language (speaking concretely, this must have been Sogdian) or a dialect of Iranian mixed together with some Turkic (tat).[74]

In the Tang Dynasty, Sogdian immigrants had already established many settlements east of the Pamirs. Today we know that all of the following regions, and others, had Sogdian settlements: Lake Puchang 蒲昌海 (modern Lop Nor), Boxian Garrison 播仙鎮 (modern Qiemo 且末), Xizhou 西州 (modern Turfan), Yizhou 伊州 (modern Qumul or Hami 哈密), Dunhuang, Suzhou 肅州 (modern Jiuquan 酒泉), Ganzhou 甘州 (modern Zhangye 張掖), Liangzhou (modern Wuwei 武威), Chang'an 長安, Lantian 藍田, Luoyang 洛陽, Lingzhou 靈州, Yanzhou 鹽州, Xiazhou 夏州, and later Yunzhou and Shuozhou, as well as Fanyang 范陽 (modern Beijing) and Liucheng 柳城 in Yingzhou. Below is a brief discussion of several of these Sogdian settlements.

In the region of Lake Puchang, Sogdian settlements were founded during the Zhenguan reign period (627-649). "During the Zhenguan reign period, Kang Yandian 康艶典, the supreme leader of the Kingdom of Kang, came eastward to settle in the town (Shicheng Garrison 石城鎮); he was followed by other Sogdian tribes, and they settled together in a place later called Dianhe Town 典合城."[75] Shicheng Garrison was located 300 *li* south of Lop Nor and 240 *li* east of Xincheng (New Town) 新城, also called Nuzhicheng 弩支(之)城 (Nuj-Kant). Shicheng Garrison was located four *li* south of Putaocheng (Grape Town) 蒲桃城 and 480 *li* northwest of Sapicheng (Sapi Town) 薩毗城, which was near the Sapi Marshes (Sapicheng is also called Canpi 璨毗 or Canwei 璨[here 王+祭]微 in Dunhuang documents, and is called Tshal-byi and mtshal-byi in Tibetan language documents). The above-mentioned four cities were all built by Kang Yandian. In the second year of the Tianshou 天授 reign period of Empress Wu Zetian (691), Kang Fudanyan 康拂躭延 was

---

[74] Mahmūd al-Kāshgharī, *Dīwān lughāt al-Turk* (*Compendium of the Languages of the Turks*), Bessim Atalay, ed. (Ankara: Alâeddin Kiral Basimevi , 1939-1943), vol. 1, p. 454.

[75] *Gazetteer of Shazhou and Yizhou* 《沙州伊州地志》 [Dunhuang text S. 367], first year of the Guangqi reign period (885), lines 11-2, line 55, and lines 35-7.

appointed Garrison Commander 鎮將安頓 and Commander-General 統領 of the Sogdians of the Nine Zhaowu Surnames.

In Boxian Garrison there was already, during the reign of Emperor Gaozong, a certain He Fudiyan 何伏帝延 as the leader of the Sogdian settlements. In a title-list of foreign leaders attributed to the monuments for Emperor Gaozong and Empress Wu, the Song Dynasty historian You Shixiong 游師雄 recorded that at the Qianling 乾陵 Mausoleum of Emperor Gaozong and Empress Wu, on the stone statues of foreign kings and leaders with their full names and official titles, was the inscription "He Fudiyan of ... Boxian Town" 播仙城口河伏帝延. Professor Chen Guocan 陳國燦 of Wuhan University absolutely correctly points out that the gap in this text should be filled with the character *zhu* 主 (leader), and the character He 河 should be corrected to He 何.[76] The name Boxian Town is also seen in the *New Tang History* in the biography of Guo Yuanzhen 郭元振.[77] Dunhuang manuscript S. 367, the incomplete *Gazetteer of Shazhou and Yizhou* 沙州伊州地志 scroll from the first year of the Guangqi 光啟 reign period (885), and the *New Tang History* in the "Geography" section, both quote Jia Dan 賈耽 [the Tang Dynasty geographer] that the journey from the Chinese frontier commandery into the four barbarian tribes on the border passed through Boxian Garrison. The former noted that "it previously had been called Qiemo Town 且末城" and was renamed in the third year of the Shangyuan 上元 reign period of Emperor Gaozong (676). Since Fudiyan 伏帝延 was a common name among the Sogdians, it was also transliterated in Chinese documents as Fudanyan 拂耽延 and in other ways. In the past, scholars usually took the term *fudanyan* to be a designation for Manichean monks, the same as furaštadān, meaning "the person who understands the doctrine."[78] In modern times, W. B. Henning, based on the few known Sogdian language

---

[76] Chen Guocan 陳國燦, "Research on the Stone Statues and their Name and Title Lists at the Tang Dynasty Qianling Mausoleum" 《唐乾陵石人像及其銜名的研究》, in *Collected Works of Cultural Relics* 《文物集刊》, vol. 2 (1980), pp. 189-203. Relevant is the entry "The Boxian Town Leader He Fudiyan" 播仙城主何伏帝延, see p. 197.

[77] *New Tang History*, ch. 122, "Biography of Guo Yuanzhen" 《郭元振傳》, p. 4363.

[78] Haneda Tōru 羽田亨, "The Region North of the Gobi Desert and the People from Samarkand" 「漠北之地和康國人」, in *Collected Historical Articles of Doctor Haneda* (*Haneda hakushi shigaku ronbunshū*) 『羽田博士史學論文集』, vol. 1 (1957), pp. 401-2.

names, examined ’prtmy’n and concluded that it was the Sogdian language word partam-yā, meaning “the first gift,” referring in particular to “the first son.”[79] In passing it can be mentioned that for a long time many scholars have been working to verify the name of the strategist and general of the Eastern Turkic revival in the second half of the seventh century Ashina Yuanzhen 阿史那元珍, and they believe that this person must have been the one named Tonyukuk 暾欲谷, as recorded on the Orkhon Turkic Tonyukuk stele. Recently, some scholars have concluded that Tonyukuk is semantically consistent with the Chinese word *yuanzhen* 元珍. The word *ton* 暾 (tun), meaning “the first son” in Turkic, could be an extension of the meaning of the Chinese word *yuan* 元 [meaning original or primary]; and the word *yukuk* 欲谷 originated from the Turkish verb yoq, meaning “to treasure” or “to preserve,” could be an extension of the meaning of the Chinese word *zhen* 珍 [meaning precious].[80] As to whether or not it is possible to conclude this there remain pros and cons, but Tonyukuk does also have the meaning of “first born son,” and we can deduce that Tonyukuk and Fudiyan are nearly semantically the same name. No matter how the name Fudiyan is interpreted, he undoubtedly was a Sogdian; he acted as the leader of Boxian Town and stood side-by-side with the other leaders of foreigners. This proves that in the early Tang period there also was an important settlement of Sogdian immigrants in the modern Qiemo district of Xinjiang Province.

In Xizhou, not later than after the mid-sixth century, Sogdians began to settle down in Gaochang 高昌, engaged in agriculture and viniculture, and developed extremely brisk trade activities under the name of “non-Chinese (Hu) merchants” 興生胡.[81] According to the tenth-century anonymous writer of the Persian text *Hudūd al-‘Ālam* (*The Regions of the World*), “in the area of present-day Turfan there are five villages belonging to Sogdians, among which reside Christians, Zoroastrians, and Sapi 薩毗.”[82]

---

[79] This is a suggestion that W. B. Henning made to Pulleyblank. See Pulleyblank, “A Sogdian Colony in Inner Mongolia,” *T’oung Pao*, vol. 41 (1952), p. 333, n. 1.

[80] S. G. Kliashtornyĭ, *Ancient Turkish Runic Monuments as Sources for the History of Central Asia* (Moscow, 1964), p. 31.

[81] Jiang Boqin 姜伯勤, “The Sogdians in Dunhuang, Turfan, and on the Silk Road” 「敦煌·吐魯番とシルクロード上のソグド人」, *East and West Quarterly*『季刊東西交渉』, vol. 5, nos. 1-3 (1986).

[82] V. Minorsky, trans., *Hudūd al-‘Ālam* (*The Regions of the World*) (London, 1937), p. 95.

The Yiwu 伊吾 region had a settlement of Sogdians from Chach 石國 (the Shi Kingdom), and in 610 (the sixth year of the Daye 大業 reign period of the Sui emperor Yangdi) Xue Shixiong 薛世雄 conquered Yiwu, and the Sui bought land to the east and established Yiwu Commandery. In the turmoil at the end of the Sui Dynasty Yiwu came again under the control of the Sogdians. In 630 (the fourth year of the Zhenguan reign period) the leader of Yiwu, Shi Wannian 石萬年, led seven cities in surrendering to the Tang.[83]

Dunhuang was one of the most important places of settlement for the Sogdians. After 750, but before Shazhou 沙州 (Dunhuang) was taken by Tibet, most of the Sogdians lived in Conghua 從化 township [literally, the Surrender to the Transformation (Sinicization) township] , one *li* 里 east of the city. The township of Conghua was one of the thirteen townships of Shazhou, but few Sogdians lived in the other townships. According to the third fragment of Dunhuang manuscript P. 3559 (the *Selective Imposition Register* 差科簿 from around 750 of Dunhuang Commandery, Dunhuang County), there were three village headmen 里正 in Conghua, which implies that there lived there about 300 households of the Nine Zhaowu Surnames, for a population of about 1,400 – 1,500 people. Among them the majority were surnamed Kang 康, An 安, He 何, Cao 曹, Shi 石, Shi 史, Mi 米, and Luo 羅 from Tukhāra 吐火羅; they lived together with Chinese, provided selective labor services (corvée), and served in the garrison. According to the selective imposition name register, there were about one hundred Nine Zhaowu Surname people who kept their Sogdian surnames. About half of the younger generation adopted Chinese surnames, which displays the profundity of their Sinicization.[84] In addition, according to the Dunhuang manuscript containing the *Poem on the Zoroastrian Temple in Ancheng* 安城祆詠, Ancheng Zoroastrian incantations, and other material, there existed in Dunhuang an "An town" (Ancheng 安城) built of wooden planks. During the period of Tibetan control of Dunhuang, the

---

[83] *Gazetteer of Shazhou and Yizhou* 《沙州伊州地志》, first year of the Guangqi reign period (885), lines 11-2, line 55, and lines 35-7.

[84] Regarding the situation of the Sogdian settlements in Dunhuang County, Ikeda On has done exhaustive research. See Ikeda On 池田溫,「8 世紀中葉における敦煌のソグド人聚落」 (The Sogdian Settlements in Dunhuang in the Mid-Eighth Century), in *Eurasian Cultural Studies* (*Yurashia Bunka-kenkyū*) 『歐亞大陸文化研究』, no. 1 (1965), pp. 49-92.

Tibetans levied taxes on products and squeezed out commerce, and Sogdians who were skilled at business absolutely were suppressed. They were probably also organized into tribes. For example, Kang Zairong 康再榮 was appointed the Commissioner of the Great Tibet Uyghur tribe in Shazhou 沙州大蕃紇骨薩部落使.[85] In 848, the second year of the Dazhong 大中 reign period of Emperor Xuanzong, Zhang Yichao 張議潮 of Shazhou led an insurrection to expel the Tibetan rulers, and turned away from Tibet and returned to the Tang. Raising revolt in common with Zhang Yichao were the Sogdian An Jingmin 安景旻 and the Tribal Commissioner 部落使 Yan Yingda 閻英達.[86] Clearly An Jingmin was a Sogdian or a sinicized descendant of someone from the An Kingdom.

During the chaos at the end of the Sui Dynasty, He Panren 何潘仁[87] of Sizhuyuan 司竹園 in Zhouzhihehu County 周至和戶縣, and Kang Laohe 康老和[88] of Zhangye, and other Sogdians or their descendants one after another raised troops in revolt. However, among the Sogdians participating in the uprising, the most powerful force was in Liangzhou in the Hexi Corridor. In 617 (the thirteenth year of the Daye reign period of the Sui emperor Yangdi) Garrison Commander 軍府官 Xue Ju 薛舉 led an uprising in Jincheng 金城, and Li Gui 李軌 Adjutant 司馬 of Yingyang Garrison 鷹揚府 from Guzang 姑臧 (modern Wuwei) in the Hexi Corridor, along with Guan Jin 關謹 and Liang Zan 梁贊, who were both from the same commandery, as well as the Sogdians Cao Zhen 曹珍 and An Xiuren 安修仁 and others, collaborated in plans for the insurrection. Cao Zhen and others suggested that Li Gui be the leader, and Li Gui ordered An Xiuren to lead the Sogdians into the city at night, where they raised a banner and shouted loudly, proclaiming Li Gui to be the Prince of Great Liang in Hexi 河西大梁王. Soon afterwards they had all of the five

[85] Xiang Da 向達, *Tang Dynasty Chang'an and the Civilization of the Western Regions* 《唐代長安與西域文明》 (Sanlian Press 三聯書店, 1957), p. 30, n. 31.

[86] *Comprehensive Mirror for Aid in Government*, ch. 249, "The first month of the fifth year of the Dazhong reign period of Emperor Xuanzong," textual analysis 考異 citing the veritable records 實錄, p. 8049.

[87] *Old Tang History*, ch. 58, "Biography of Chai Shao" 《柴紹傳》, p. 3215; *Outstanding Models from the Storehouse of Literature*, ch. 345, "Generals, Assistants for Imperial Affairs, 6" 《將帥部・佐命六》, p. 4090, last column.

[88] *History of the Sui*, ch. 5, "Annals of Emperor Gong" 《恭帝紀》, p. 100.

commanderies in the Hexi Corridor including Zhangye, Dunhuang, Xiping 西平, and Fuhan 枹罕. The chief strategist [of Li Gui's] named Liang Shuo 梁碩 "noticed the flourishing of all the various Sogdian tribes and so secretly advised that Li Gui increase his precautions and surveillance, which raised the suspicions of the revenue minister 戶部尚書 An Xiuren."[89] An Xiuren's elder brother An Xinggui 安興貴 was then in Chang'an, and he and An Xiuren secretly proposed to gather the foreigners (hu 胡) and rise against the rebels, and they then captured Li Gui and returned him to the Tang, which pacified the Hexi Corridor. From this it can be seen that the return of the Hexi Corridor to the Tang mainly depended upon power of the Sogdians. Due to this the brothers of An Xiuren enjoyed the best treatment at the Tang court: in 616 (the ninth year of the Wude 武德 reign period) An Xinggui and An Xiuren each were appointed to receive the tax revenue of six hundred households (in the early Zhenguan reign period Meritorious Minister 勳臣 Li Jing 李靖 only received that of five hundred households);[90] in 684 (the first year of the Guangzhai 光宅 reign period) An Yuanshou 安元壽, the son of An Xinggui and General of the Awesome Guard on the Right 右威衛將軍, was buried in the Emperor Taizong's mausoleum area Zhaoling 昭陵;[91] in 706, the second year of the Shenlong reign period, an imperial edict was issued granting the same tax revenue as they had before been given to the 25 meritorious founders of the nation, among which was included An Xiuren.[92] During the An Shi Rebellion, a Sogdian merchant from Wuwei, An Menwu 安門物, and Gai Tinglun 蓋庭倫, the Military Commissioner 節度使 of the Hexi Corridor, and others murdered Military Commissioner Zhou Mi 周泌, then gathered 60,000 people, and the Sogdians occupied five of the seven small fortresses within the Wuwei city walls.[93] During

---

[89] *Old Tang History*, ch. 55, "Biography of Li Gui" 《李軌傳》, p. 2249.

[90] *Important Documents of the Tang*, ch. 90, "Those Conferred with Grain" 《食實封數》, last book, p. 1647.

[91] Bureau for the Administration of Cultural Relics at Zhaoling 昭陵文物管理所, *Record of the Investigation of Companion Burials at Zhaoling* 《昭陵陪葬墓調查記》, *Cultural Relics* 《文物》, 1977, no. 10, pp. 34, 36.

[92] *Important Documents of the Tang*, ch. 90, the entry "Miscellaneous Notes on Reasons for Conferments" 《緣封雜記》, last book, p. 1647.

[93] *Comprehensive Mirror for Aid in Government*, ch. 219, "The first month of the second year of the Zhide reign period of Emperor Suzong," p. 7015.

the era of Emperor Daizong 代宗, Li Baoyu 李抱玉, an Assistant General under General Li Guangbi 李光弼, submitted a memorial stating that his native place was Liangzhou, and that his surname by birth was An (so a descendant of An Xinggui), but because he was ashamed of having the same surname as An Lushan, he changed his surname to Li.[94] This record shows that Li Baoyu and his cousin Li Baozhen 李抱真 were both from the An family of Liangzhou. How did the An family of Liangzhou become so powerful? As early as the Three Kingdoms period there were already the so-called "three types of Hu" in Wuwei.[95] During the Northern Wei Dynasty there were An-surnamed foreigners living in the Liang area. The *Compilation of Surnames in the Era of Yuanhe* 元和姓纂 in the An family article in chapter four says, "[the An families] of Guzang Liangzhou came from the An Kingdom; in the Han Dynasty they sent a son as hostage to the imperial court, and he was allowed to reside in Liangzhou. From An Nantuo 安難陀 of the Northern Wei until his grandson Pan Poduo 盤婆多, the generations lived in Liangzhou and were Sabao 薩寶 [the administrative leader of a Sogdian community appointed by the Chinese]. Pan Poduo had a son named Xinggui 興貴, who later captured Li Gui and sent him to the capital, and for his meritorious service he was conferred the titles of Great General of the Militant Guard on the Right 右武衛(or 位)大將軍 and Duke of the Reverted Country 歸國公 (or Duke of Liang)."[96] From this it can be seen that the An family had already become powerful and respected in Liangzhou and held the position of Sabao for generations, which was the reason they attracted nobles and commoners of foreign lands to become affiliated to them.

The Sogdian settlements extended eastward reaching Youzhou 幽州 and Yingzhou 營州. The Youzhou Area Command 都督府 had a district subordinate to Huzhou 胡州 named Linzhou 凜州, established during the early years of Tianbao reign period (742-755), which was used as the seat

---

[94] *Old Tang History*, ch. 131, "Biography of Li Baoyu" 《李抱玉傳》, p. 3646.

[95] *The Record of the History of the Three Kingdoms* 《三國志》, ch. 16, "Biography of Su Ze" 《蘇則傳》, p. 492.

[96] Lin Bao 林寶, *Compilation of Surnames in the Era of Yuanhe* 《元和姓纂》, ch. 4, sixth year of the Guangxu 光緒 Emperor (1880), Jinling Book Company edition 金陵書局, p. 16a. Cen Zhongmian 岑仲勉, *Four Annotated Records of the Compilation of Surnames in the Era of Yuanhe* 《元和姓纂四校記》 (Shanghai Commercial Press, 1948), pp. 371-2.

of government for the territory of Fanyang.[97] In 742, the first year of Tianbao reign period, Ayi Kül Tarqan 阿義屈達干, a noble of the Kang 康 family from among the twelve families of northern foreigners, surrendered to the Tang. His grandfather and father both were Commanders-in-Chief of their tribe during the Turkish period, and when Ayi Kül Tarqan brought his clan to the Tang he still served as tribal Commander-in-Chief, commanding other tribes.[98] Pulleyblank noticed that Ayi Kül Tarqan's father was only a Guard Officer 衛衙 under Qapaghan (Bögü, in Chinese Mochuo 默啜), the Turk Qaghan, and held no office under his brother Kutluk (Qutlugh) 骨咄祿. This perhaps explains why, in 698, at the request of Qapaghan, Ayi Kül Tarqan's father came into the Turkish region from the Six Hu Prefectures within Lingzhou and Yanzhou.[99] In 717, the fifth year of the Kaiyuan reign period, Song Qingli 宋慶禮, the Fiscal Commissioner of Agriculture 支度營田使 for Hebei 河北, founded the city of Yingzhou in Liucheng (Chaoyang 朝陽 in modern Liaoning 遼寧 Province). As Song Qingli was the acting Supervisor-in-Chief 檢校都督 of Yingzhou, "he established about eighty station garrisons for growing food 屯田 [military colonies]," and "recruited Sogdian traders for setting up markets," and "in a few years many foreigners (*fan* 蕃) came to settle there."[100] From this can be seen that the region where An Lushan, Shi Siming, and other Yingzhou foreigners (called the Zhaowu Nine Surname traders 商) from early years had activities was a place where many Sogdians lived.

In short, during the Tang Dynasty, the Sogdians (the Nine Zhaowu Surnames) resided not only in the Six Hu Prefectures, but also still lived in a certain number of important regions in the northwest, as well as some places in the northeast. Due to the limitations of length, this article could only make a superficial and far from complete introduction to the Tang Dynasty settlements of the Nine Zhaowu Surnames: their scattering, their

---

97 *New Tang History*, ch. 43, *Monograph on Geography* 《地理志》, 7b, p. 1128.

98 Yan Zhenqing 顏真卿, "Spirit Way Stele for the Honorable Kang (Ayi Kül Tarqan), Acting Left Guard of the Imperial Insignia, General-in-Chief, and Xiazhou Commander-in-Chief" 《行在(左)金吾衛大將軍夏州都督康公神道碑》 in *Complete Prose Literature of the Tang* 《全唐文》, ch. 342, pp. 3474-5.

99 Pulleyblank, "A Sogdian Colony in Inner Mongolia," p. 340.

100 *Old Tang History*, ch. 185b, "Biography of Song Qingli" 《宋慶禮傳》, p. 4814. *New Tang History*, ch. 130, "Biography of Song Qingli" 《宋慶禮傳》, p. 4494.

migrations, and their continuing situation. It provides some historical background material concerning the Nine Zhaowu Surnames, with the objective of assisting the understanding of Tang Dynasty political incidents, relationships between ethnic groups, the development of trade, as well as providing an understanding of the necessary social background for cultural exchange. As for the role that the Nine Zhaowu Surnames played in Tang Dynasty political life, as well as in the cultural of the central plains [China proper], in art, and in religion, they had a deep and far-reaching influence on many aspects of these. But that is a task for another time and for discussion in other articles.

The Religious Background to the An Lushan Rebellion

Rong Xinjiang 榮新江

The An Shi Rebellion 安史之亂 (also called the An Lushan Rebellion 安祿山之亂) was a great event in Chinese history, the influence of which was deep and far-reaching. It was, one could say, the most important transformational divide in Chinese history.[1] In the early 20th century the Japanese scholar Naitō Konan 内藤湖南 proposed the "Tang-Song transformation theory" 唐宋變革論, in which he considered the Tang-Song boundary to be the point in Chinese history where "ancient times" moved towards "modern times." But at that time Naitō did not have a full and firm grasp of the details of Tang-Song history. Later his pupils ceaselessly enriched the "Tang-Song transformation theory" and remedied its oversights, but such a transformational phenomenon proposes that basically everything can be traced back to the middle Tang period. Yet, according to the very deep research and thinking into ancient Chinese

---

[1] The initial draft of this essay was submitted as a paper to the November 1996 conference in Taipei "The Third Annual China Tang Dynasty Culture Academic Research Symposium" 第三屆中國唐代文化學術研討會. That draft of this essay was completed during a period of giving lectures in August of that year at the Freie Universität Berlin, but at that time I suffered from not having research materials, so the discussion in the paper was not sufficiently full. The essay was published in *Collected Essays from the Third Annual China Tang Dynasty Culture Academic Research Symposium* 《第三屆中國唐代文化學術研討會論文集》, which was an informal publication. Moreover the essay was not proof-read, and it had very many mistaken characters, so I again had it published in *Selected Works of the 100th Anniversary of Peking University China Studies: History Volume* 《北京大學百年國學文粹・史學卷》 (Beijing: Peking University Press, 1998), and it was also included in the work edited by me *Medieval China and Foreign Civilizations* 《中古中國與外來文明》 (Beijing: Sanlian Press 三聯書店, 2001). In the more than ten years since, the author's viewpoint has not changed, but there has been a sharp increase in related discussion and data from relevant excavations of the tombs of Sogdians who entered China and their tomb epitaphs. Now, on the foundation of the original draft, utilizing the new data, I have rewritten the essay, at the same time responding to problems raised by related books of research, and going one solid step further, the author proposes the view that An Lushan utilized Zoroastrianism to launch the insurrection. The length of this essay has doubled, which is the reason for publishing it again here, and so instruct the learned.

history of the famous Chinese scholar Chen Yinke 陳寅恪, it was the An Shi Rebellion that actually was the watershed in ancient Chinese history. Chen Yinke's point of view can be termed the "Tianbao transformation theory" 天寶變革論, and scholars researching the conclusions of the "Tang-Song transformation theory" have more and more supported the "Tianbao transformation theory." This author is an endorser of the "Tianbao transformation theory," and for this reason he is concerned about the problems of the An Shi Rebellion from the perspective of the history of Sino-foreign relations, feeling that there are still a great many related problems that have not been discussed.

Since the middle Tang, historians have brought forward many viewpoints regarding the government and military background to the An Lushan insurrection. However, the majority of past historians researching the period of the An Shi Rebellion have relied on traditional historical materials which severely criticized An Lushan and Shi Siming 史思明 as traitors. They completely adopted the evaluation of the imperial government sources, including that An Lushan and Shi Siming were considered "foreigners" 胡人, and even that the Han literati considered them to be "mixed-race foreigners" 雜種胡. The reality was, just as we will show below, that An Lushan and Shi Siming both were typical foreigners. We research this type of foreigner, which must be contrasted with those scattered across Inner Asia. The character of these foreigners should be analyzed from the perspective of Inner Asian history; in this way we at last will pierce through the traditional historical materials and will see that these traditional historians unintentionally have left us a highly valuable record.

Previously no one has paid attention to the religious background of the An Lushan insurrection, but in fact there are unequivocal accounts written in the traditional historical materials. This essay starts out with a discussion of the ethnic background of An Lushan, Shi Siming, and the other rebellion leaders. It utilizes the great progress and results in recent years of research into the Sogdians, and based on the Sogdian residential areas and religious environment in which An Lushan, Shi Siming, and others grew up, reveals hints in the historical materials to show that Zoroastrian religious appeal was utilized during the time of the An Lushan insurrection.

It is worthwhile to go a step further in an inquiry into the question of the origin of An Lushan's ethnicity. Since the 1950s and 1960s scholars, based on research into Chinese and Iranian documents from Dunhuang and Turfan (including those in medieval Persian, Parthian, Sogdian, Khotanese, etc.), have provided rich materials for this discussion, and have made us capable of providing new interpretations of already known historical materials. In recent years some graves of Sogdian leaders, Sabao 薩保, have been discovered in the central plains region of China, which have provided images and data for our understanding of the social life and religious culture of Sogdians who had come to China. This has enabled us to get an even clearer understanding of the ethnic group characteristics of An Lushan and others.

I. The Ethnic Group Characteristics of An Lushan

In order to explain the religious background of An Lushan, Shi Siming, and others in the insurrection, first one should at least be clear about their ethnic group origins and their environment growing up, and even the situation in the settlements where Sogdian foreigners made their lives.

Regarding An Lushan's ethnicity, as early as 1925 Kuwabara Jitsuzō 桑原隲藏, relying on Yao Runeng's 姚汝能 *Factual Traces of An Lushan* 安祿山事跡, believed that he was a Sogdian born in the Kingdom of Kang (Samarkand) 康國 in Transoxiana.[2] Xiang Da 向達 affirmed this view.[3] Chen Yinke pointed out a further advance: during the so-called An Shi Rebellion period, the people called "mixed-race foreigners" 雜種胡 by the Tang Chinese were for the most part Sogdians of the Nine Surnames 九姓粟特胡人.[4] In 1955 Edwin G. Pulleyblank, based on An Lushan's

---

[2] Kuwabara Jitsuzō 桑原隲藏, "On the People from the Western Regions who Came to Live in China during the Sui and Tang Periods" (Zui-Tō jidai ni Shina ni raijūshita Seiikijin ni tsuite) 「隋唐時代に支那に來住した西域人に就いて」, in *Festschrift of Articles on Sinology in Honor of Dr. Naitō's 61st Birthday* 『内藤博士還暦祝賀支那學論叢』 (Kyoto, 1926), pp. 624-6.

[3] Xiang Da 向達, "Tang Dynasty Chang'an and the Civilization of the Western Regions" 《唐代長安與西域文明》, originally in *Yenching Journal of Chinese Studies* 《燕京學報》, monograph series number 2, Beijing, 1933, p. 14, p. 30 footnote 36; included in Xiang Da, *Tang Dynasty Chang'an and the Civilization of the Western Regions* (Beijing: Sanlian Press, 1957), p. 14, p. 30 footnote 36.

[4] Chen Yinke 陳寅恪, *Manuscript of Discussions on the Political History of the Tang Dynasty* 《唐代政治史述論稿》 (Shanghai: The Commercial Press 商務印書館, 1947), pp. 21-3.

surname and other sources, argued conclusively in detail that he was a Sogdian living in the interior of the Turkish Qaghanate north of the Gobi Desert and was the son of An Yanyan 安延偃. Pulleyblank did not agree with the view that An Lushan's original surname was Kang 康, emphasizing that he was probably a Sogdian of the group who immigrated to north of the Gobi Desert from the Six Hu Prefectures 六胡州. Early in the Kaiyuan 開元 reign period (713-741) there was rebellion among the Turks, An Lushan's father died, and he fled to Tang China with his uncle An Bozhu 安波注 and his two sons.[5] Therefore it is an almost foregone conclusion that An Lushan was a Sogdian. Forty years later Antonio Forte refuted Pulleyblank's view, believing that contemporaries of An Lushan had no doubt that his surname was Kang, but he also believed that An Bozhu and An Yanyan both were Turks, and that after seeking refuge with An Zhenjie 安貞節 they then took the surname An.[6]

When An Lushan followed his mother to An Yanyan's clan, it was precisely then that his cultural attributes and value system took shape, and in this way he in the end finally became a Sogdian, but still a Turk; this was a very important phase. Because of this, the experience of An Lushan's early years and the question of which ethnicity he belonged to must still be investigated.

Concerning An Lushan's origin, the account of the mid-Tang author Yao Runeng in the first chapter of *Factual Traces of An Lushan* is still the most detailed:

> An Lushan was a 'mixed-race foreigner' from Yingzhou 營州. His childhood name was Yaluoshan 軋犖山. His mother, from the Ashide 阿史德 clan, was a Turkish maga [female magus 巫] . She had no son and so prayed to the god Yaluoshan, who responded and a son was born. On that night a red light shone beside him, and the wild animals in all directions howled. Astrologers saw the radiant beam of an evil star fall upon his yurt. There were who knows how many strange portents and omens. His mother thought

[5] E. G. Pulleyblank, *The Background of the Rebellion of An Lu-Shan* (London: Oxford University Press, 1955), pp. 7-23, footnotes pp. 104-21. The entry written by Pulleyblank on "An Lu-Shan" in *Encyclopaedia Iranica* (London: 1985) has this view without change.

[6] Antonino Forte, *The Hostage An Shigao and his Offspring* (Kyoto: Istituto Italiano di Cultura Scuola di Studi sull' Asia Orientale, 1995), pp. 100-7.

he was divine, and so named him 'Yaluoshan' (original footnote: the Turks called their god of battle Yaluoshan). He was orphaned in his youth, and followed his mother to the Turks. His mother afterwards married An Yanyan, the younger brother of the foreign general An Bozhu.

In the early years of the Kaiyuan reign period, An Yanyan's clan settlement was ruined. Xiaojie 孝節, the son of the foreign general An Daomai 安道買, together with the sons of An Bozhu, Sishun 思順 and Wenzhen 文貞, fled completely from among the Turks. An Daomai's second son Zhenjie 貞節, who was the chief administrative aide 别駕 to the head of Lanzhou 嵐州, took them in. An Lushan was more than ten years old, and since Zhenjie had come along with his brother Xiaojie, he became blood-brothers with An Lushan and Sishun. Therefore An Lushan took the surname An (original footnote: the memorial of the Prince of Fenyang 汾陽 *Requesting the Rehabilitation of An Sishun* 請雪安思順表 says 'his original surname was Kang,' but does not provide any details) and took the given name 'Lushan.'[7]

To the Tang court An Lushan was a rebellious traitor, but in the Hebei 河北 region he indeed was a short-lived emperor and continuously venerated as a sage.[8] Just as for an historical emperor or sage, An Lushan's birth was endowed with a layer of mythological color, but by penetrating through this myth we can still see some historical reality.

Factual Traces of An Lushan calls An Lushan's mother a member of the Ashide clan and a Turkish maga. Among the Turkish Qaghanate, the name Ashide was second only to the Qaghan clan name Ashina 阿史那, and the historical Qaghans took many wives with this surname as

---

[7] See Robert des Rotours, translator, *Histoire de Ngan lou-chan* (Ngan lou-chan che tsi) (Paris, 1962) [a translation into French of Yao Runeng's *Factual Traces of An Lushan*], p. 2; Pulleyblank, *The Background of the Rebellion of An Lu-Shan*, p. 7; and *Factual Traces of An Lushan* 《安祿山事跡》, first chapter, the punctuated edition (Shanghai Classics Publishing House 上海古籍出版社, 1983), p. 1, but in this punctuated Chinese text the character 神 should go with the preceding phrase. Accordingly "軋犖山" is not the name of a mountain, but the name of a god, as discussed below.

[8] *New Tang History* 《新唐書》, ch. 127, "Biography of Zhang Hongjing" 《張弘靖傳》 (Beijing: Zhonghua Book Company 中華書局, 1975), p. 4448.

empresses (Kedun 可敦). We are uncertain as to whether or not An Lushan's Turkish mother was really from the Ashide clan, and it is possible that the creator of the mythology had to find some royal lineage for An Lushan, and for this reason his mother was agreed to be a member of the Ashide clan. A member of the Turkish clan Ashide and a certain Sogdian with the surname Kang, together gave birth to this child, who afterwards received the name "Yaluoshan" (ancient pronunciation *·at-låk-san). In the *Comprehensive Mirror for Aid in Government* 資治通鑒 it is written as "Aluoshan" 阿犖山 (ancient pronunciation *·â-låk-ṣan). According to W. B. Henning's philological research, the Chinese when transliterating "r" in the initial position from foreign vocabulary often added a vowel in front of the "r," and therefore this absolutely is a transliteration of the Sogdian word *roχšan* (*rwxšn* light, *rwγšn* bright). After the Sogdians entered the China plains they employed the characters "lu shan" 祿山 (ancient pronunciation *luk-ṣan) for the words "light" and "bright." This original language was also the same as Sogdian, but in order to conform with the Chinese two character given name system they omitted the initial Chinese character.[9] Therefore, it must be that An

[9] Henning cites Pulleyblank, *The Background of the Rebellion of An Lu-Shan*, pp. 15-6. Wang Xiaofu 王小甫 believes that "Yaluoshan" is a transliteration of the Zoroastrian spirit Verethraghna (Warahrān/Bahrām), namely a god of war, and further, that "Lushan" is a transcription of the Iranian word roshān, indicating a spirit of divine light; see Wang Xiaofu 王小甫, "The Cult of Fire and the Rise and Decline of the Turks: A Case Study of the Ancient Turkic God of War" 《拜火教與突厥興衰——以古代突厥鬥戰神研究爲中心》, *Historical Research* 《歷史研究》, 2007, no.1, pp. 24-40. An image of the Sogdian god of war has been discovered in the Sogdian homeland at Panjikant, where he has the form of Śiva, with three heads and a hand grasping a three-pronged halberd. But this is not at all the same as the so-called god of war form of a high priest with a bird's body discovered on the face of a stone slab at the grave of Kül Tegin (a general of the second Turkish Qaghanate). Below the wall painting of the god at Panjikant is the Sogdian language inscription wšpr(kr), namely the Zoroastrian god Weshparkar, which can not be the same as Yaluoshan. For a drawing and the inscription, see A. M. Belenitskii and B. I. Marshak, "The Paintings of Sogdiana," in *Sogdian Painting, The Pictorial Epic in Oriental Art*, by G. Azarpay (Berkeley: University of California Press, 1981), pp. 29-30, fig. 5. Seemingly, from the perspective of Yao Runeng saying "Yaluoshan was the Turkish war god," one can conclude that the term "Yaluoshan" should be accepted as a Turkish word and not Iranian. Zhong Han 鍾焓, prior to Wang Xiaofu, had already understood this point, but he was unable to deny Henning's point of view concerning the transcription of "Yaluoshan" and roχšan. He believed that the Sogdian word roχšan changed its meaning after entering Turkish, indicating a war god;

Lushan's Sogdian mother gave him an authentic Sogdian language given name, not a Turkish language given name. This type of view is identical to where Yao Runeng's notes refer to Shao Yue's 邵說 *Memorial on Behalf of Guo, Duke of Ling* 代郭令公請雪安思順表, which says that An Lushan's "original surname was Kang" 本實姓康. Antonino Forte's view that An Lushan's biological father was a Sogdian surnamed Kang is praiseworthy, so that An Lushan was of mixed Sogdian and Turkish lineage, which in the eyes of the Chinese would be a "mixed-race foreigner." In the seventh year of the Tianbao 天寶 reign period (748) *The Inscription of the Great Tang Boling Commandery Dedicated at North Peak Antianwang Temple on Heng Mountain* 大唐博陵郡北嶽恒山封安天王之銘 was set up, in which An Lushan is considered to be from an important family in "Changle" 常樂. Changle was located in western part of the Hexi Corridor 河西走廊, adjoining Dunhuang, and this definitely was a place where Sogdian immigrants to China with the surname Kang settled down to live.[10] But according to the understanding of the author of *Factual Traces of An Lushan*, Yao Runeng, An Lushan's given name came from his Turkish mother, and "Yaluoshan" was the name of a Turkish war god.

---

see his "The Inner Asian Cultural Background of An Lushan and Other Mixed-Race Foreigners" 《安祿山等雜胡的內亞文化背景》, *The Study of Chinese History* 《中國史研究》, 2005, no. 1, pp. 68-9. But, based on *Factual Traces of An Lushan* as already related, "Yaluoshan" and "Lushan" were derived from the same origin, and there is absolutely no language transformation problem. In addition, Zhong Han himself has already pointed out that among the Dunhuang and Turfan documents roχšan is transliterated as "Lushan" and as "Yaluoshan." Even though he emphasized the majority view of earlier translations, we nonetheless can not dismiss the existence of the minority view; moreover, many Sogdians recorded in the Dunhuang and Turfan documents were Sogdians living in the Tang Dynasty prefectures and counties and most of them, of course, used the Chinese flavored "Lushan." Therefore, up to now, concerning Yao Runeng's sentence "Yaluoshan was the Turkish war god," there still is no satisfactory explanation. This author on this topic does not dare pretend to be knowledgeable, here he only replies to criticism from scholars of this essay's first draft.

[10] Rong Xinjiang 榮新江, "The Migrations and Settlements of the Sogdians in the Northern Dynasties, Sui and Tang" 《北朝隋唐粟特人之遷徙及其聚落》, in Center for the Study of Traditional Chinese Culture Peking University 北京大學中國傳統文化研究中心, editors, *Studies in Sinology* 《國學研究》, vol. 6 (1999), pp. 40-2; translated and edited by Bruce Doar in *China Archaeology and Art Digest*, vol. 4, Zoroastrianism in China (Dec. 2000), pp. 130-1.

In any case, from the perspective of ethnicity, it can be said that An Lushan was of mixed lineage. But from the perspective of the mythology of An Lushan's birth and especially from his Sogdian language given name, he had other, more Sogdian, ethnic group characteristics.

In the view of the contemporary upper class of Tang Dynasty society, the Turkish Ashide clan obviously had a higher position than that of the Foreigners of the Nine Surnames 九姓胡 (Sogdians), therefore An Lushan himself made use of the fact that his own mother was ethnic Turkish, and became friendly with the important Chinese military governor of Turkish descent Geshu Han (Qosu Qaghan) 哥舒翰. *Factual Traces of An Lushan*, chapter one, says:

> (Geshu) Han's mother was of the Yuchi 尉遲 clan, a woman from Khotan 于闐....(An Lushan) said to Han: 'My father was a foreigner, my mother was a Turk. Your father was a Turk, your mother was a foreigner, I am of quite the same race as you, why can't we become blood brothers?'[11]

We know that Geshu Han was a Türgiş 突騎施 Turk subordinate to the Geshu tribe, and his father Geshu Dao Yuan 哥舒道元 once assumed the Tang Dynasty post of Anxi 安西 Vice-Protector General 副都護 garrisoned at Khotan, and took a Khotanese princess as his spouse. Therefore Geshu Han's mother was a member of the Khotanese royal house of the Yuchi clan.[12] An Lushan's origin probably was as a Kang-surnamed Sogdian from the Hexi Corridor Changle Commandery (Guazhou 瓜州), from which he moved away to the Turkish area, his father taking a Turkish Ashide clan woman as his wife, who gave birth to An Lushan. Obviously, in the eyes of An Lushan himself, Khotanese and

---

[11] *Factual Traces of An Lushan*, first chapter, p. 14. Compare Pulleyblank, *The Background of the Rebellion of An Lu-Shan*, p. 11, and Robert des Rotours, *Histoire de Ngan lou-chan*, p. 120.

[12] *Old Tang History* 《舊唐書》, ch. 104, "Biography of Geshu Han" 《哥舒翰傳》 (Beijing: Zhonghua Book Company, 1975), p. 3211; *New Tang History* 《新唐書》, ch. 135, "Biography of Geshu Han" 《哥舒翰傳》, p. 4569. Regarding the situation of Geshu Dao Yuan in Khotan, see Rong Xinjiang, "Regarding Several Problems of the Influence of Tang-Song Period Central Plains Culture on Khotan" 《關於唐宋時期中原文化對于闐影響的幾個問題》, *Studies in Sinology* 《國學研究》, vol. 1 (1993), p. 416.

Sogdians both were "foreigners" (胡 hu), but Turks were not the same kind of "foreigners," and even though foreigners and Turkish ethnic types were "quite similar," nonetheless they after all were not the same. An Lushan himself, as a "mixed-race foreigner from Yingzhou" 營州雜種胡, after all belonged to the "foreigners" 胡, and using the perspective of today's ethnic identification, this was An Lushan's "ethnic self." Since the early twentieth century, Khotanese and Sogdian language documents have been excavated at Dunhuang and in some areas of Central Asia making clear that both languages belong to the Indo-European language family, Iranian group (Middle Iranian), Eastern Iranian branch, and because of this it is possible to prove that An Lushan was a Sogdian of Iranian extraction. In one document excavated at Dunhuang (P.t.1263), a Chinese-Tibetan 蕃 language lexicon, the character for "foreigner" (胡 hu) corresponding to Sog (the Tibetan "Sogdian") also completely confirms this point.[13] In addition to the above mentioned Chen Yinke reference to "mixed-race foreigner" as being Sogdian, Edward H. Schafer has pointed out that in the broad sense foreigner (胡人 huren) indicated people from the northern and western areas outside of China, and in the narrow sense it mainly indicated Iranian foreigners.[14] In Moriyasu Takao's 森安孝夫 recently published essay *The Hu (Sogdians) during the Tang Dynasty and Buddhist World Geography*, which relies on *A Miscellaneous Collection of Sanskrit Terms* 梵語雜名 and materials held in Japan in Chinese and Tibetan, and which compares names on maps of the Western Regions 西域, he stresses that "foreigner" (胡 hu) indicated Sogdians, and that "foreign women" (胡姬 huji) were young Sogdian women.[15]

---

[13] Paul Pelliot, *Histoire ancienne du Tibet* (Paris, 1961), p. 143; A. Spanien and Y. Imaeda (eds.), *Choix de documents tibétains, II*, (Paris, 1979), pl. 525; Moriyasu Takao 森安孝夫, "The Northern Peoples DRU-GU and HOR in Tibetan Sources" 「チベット語史料中に現すれる北方民族——DRU-GU と HOR」, *Journal of African and Asian Studies*『アジア.アフリカ言語文化研究』, no. 14 (Dec. 1977), p. 39; Rong Xinjiang, "A Study of the Longjias"《龍家考》, *Journal of Central Asia*《中亞學刊》, Peking University Press, vol. 4 (1995), p. 147.

[14] Edward H. Schafer, *The Golden Peaches of Samarkand. A Study of T'ang Exotics* (Berkeley: 1963), pp. 4-5

[15] Moriyasu Takao 森安孝夫, "The Hu (Sogdians) during the Tang Dynasty and Buddhist World Geography" 「唐代における胡と仏教的世界地理」, *The Journal of Oriental Research*『東洋史研究』, vol. 66, no. 3 (2007), pp. 1-33.

Returning again to the above cited *Factual Traces of An Lushan*, after his mother married the foreigner An Yanyan and after the Yanyan clan was ruined and scattered, Yaluoshan together with the sons of the foreign general An Daomai and the sons of An Bozhu entered Tang China. Yaluoshan "took the surname An and took the given name 'Lushan.'" Regardless of who An Lushan's actual parents were, from the passages cited above we can know that he from infancy entered An Yanyan's clan settlement, and that the leader of this "clan settlement" 族落 was the foreign general An Bozhu's elder brother An Yanyan. From the historical sources I am unable to see whether or not this clan settlement was similar to what Antonino Forte calls the Turkish clan settlement; it in reality was just a "foreigner clan" (胡部 hubu) of independent character that was part of the Turkish Qaghanate north of the Gobi Desert.[16] Henceforth, for An Lushan's entire life among the Sogdian community, he acknowledged An Yanyan as his father, and, of course, his language and culture were Sogdian. If, from the point of view of culture, we differentiate ethnicity based on a person's language, then even more should we say that An Lushan was a Sogdian. Just after he accompanied his other brothers surnamed An into Tang ruled territory, and the same as with other Sogdians who entered China, he received a Chinese style given name. Therefore, to fit with the surname An, he changed the "Yaluoshan" 軋犖山 to the much better "Lushan" 祿山, giving the same pronunciation, but with Chinese characters. I believe that among the Sogdians, they still called him *roχšan*.

According to the account in *Factual Traces of An Lushan* below, An Lushan gradually grew into an adult:

> He grew into a treacherous thief, savage and cruel; he knew many stratagems, was able to judge well men's hearts, understood nine foreign languages 蕃語, and served all kinds of foreigners (蕃 fan) in the frontier markets as a middleman 互市牙郎.[17]

---

[16] Mori Masao 護雅夫, "Sogdian Clan Settlements in the East Turkish Qaghanate" 「東突厥汗國内的粟特人部落」, in *Historical Studies of the Ancient Turkic Peoples* 『古代トルコ民族史研究』, I (Tokyo: Yamakawa Publishing 山川出版社, 1975), pp. 61-93.

[17] *Factual Traces of An Lushan*, first chapter, p. 1; see Robert des Rotours, *Histoire de Ngan lou-chan*, p. 11.

Sogdians originally were an ethnic group engaged in trade, and their traces are spread everywhere over the ancient Eurasian trade routes. From the Wei and Jin Dynasties through the Sui and Tang Dynasties, a large number of Sogdians came to the east, prospered, and returned. They shuttled back and forth, coming and going between the Sogdian homeland, the city-states, fertile areas, and countries of the western regions, and between the steppe nomad Qaghanates and the imperial court of the central plain [China proper].[18] This was precisely because they had the ability, passed from generation to generation, to conduct relations between every ethnic group, and therefore the Sogdians, for the most part, thoroughly understood many types of languages. The so-called "nine foreign languages," or what is called in the *Old Tang History* 舊唐書 and the *New Tang History* 新唐書 the "six foreign languages," both express the meaning of multiplicity. Because the Sogdians had this kind of capability, the Sogdian language became at that time the *lingua franca* on the Silk Road, used for contact between dissimilar ethnic groups. The

[18] Rong Xinjiang, "A Study of Sogdian Migrations and Settlements in the Western Regions" 《西域粟特移民聚落考》, in *Investigations and Research into the Western Regions* 《西域考察與研究》, Ma Dazheng 馬大正 and Yang Qian 楊鐮, eds., (Urumqi: Xinjiang People's Press, 1994), pp. 157-72; Rong Xinjiang, "The Migrations and Settlements of the Sogdians in the Northern Dynasties, Sui, and Tang Periods" 《北朝隋唐粟特人之遷徙及其聚落》, *Studies in Sinology* 《國學研究》, vol. 6 (1999), pp. 27-85; Rong Xinjiang, "Supplement to a Study of Sogdian Migrations and Settlements in the Western Regions" 《西域粟特移民聚落補》, *Studies of the Western Regions* 《西域研究》, 2005, no. 2, pp. 1-11; Rong Xinjiang, "Supplement to a Study of Migrations and Settlements of the Sogdians in the Northern Dynasties, Sui, and Tang Periods" 《北朝隋唐粟特人之遷徙及其聚落補考》, *Eurasian Studies* 《歐亞研究》, vol. 6 (2007), pp. 165-78; Rong Xinjiang, "The Migrations and Settlements of the Sogdians in the Northern Dynasties, Sui, and Tang," pp. 117-63; Rong Xinjiang, "Sogdians around the Ancient Tarim Basin," in *Ērān ud Anērān, Studies Presented to Boris Il'ič Maršak on the Occasion of his 70th Birthday*, ed. M. Compareti, P. Raffetta and G. Scarcia (Venezia: Libreria Editrice Cafoscarina, 2006), pp. 513-24; Rong Xinjiang, "Further Remarks on Sogdians in the Western Regions," in *Exegisti Monumenta. Festschrift in Honour of Nicholas Sims-Williams* (Iranica 17), ed. Werner Sundermann, Almut Hintze, and François de Blois (Wiesbaden: Harrassowitz Verlag, 2009), pp. 399-416. For the latest summary see É. de la Vaissiere, *Sogdian Traders. A History*, tr. by J. Ward, Handbook of Oriental Studies, Section 8: Central Asia, vol. 10, (Leiden and Boston: Brill, 2005); Moriyasu Takao 森安孝夫, "The Chinese Silk Road and the Tang Empire" 「シルクロードと唐帝国」, *What is Human History?* , no. 5 『興亡の世界史 5』 (Tokyo: Kodansha 講談社, 2007).

Tang imperial government understood this point early on, and therefore regardless of the fact that the Tang central authorities dwelt in two capitals, there was still frequent border town trade in prefectural capitals, all using Sogdians as translators. The *Important Documents of the Tang* 唐會要 in chapter 61 in the item on impeachments says: "On the 24th day of the eleventh month of the first year of the Yonghui 永徽 reign period (650) the Secretariat Director 中書令 Chu Suiliang 褚遂良 forced the sale [at a below market price] of Secretariat translator Shi Hedan's 史訶擔 residence, and the Investigating Censor 監察御史 Wei Renyao 韋仁約 exposed this misdeed." Shi Hedan's family background was Kāshāna (Kesh, the Kingdom of Shi) 史國 Sogdian, his name was also written as Shi Hedan 史訶耽, and his grave has been discovered in Guyuan 固原.[19] Documents discovered in Turfan prove that a translator from Xizhou 西州 also was of the Nine Zhaowu Surnames (a Sogdian).[20]

Being engaged in trade was the ability that Sogdians were best at, and the Tang imperial government also attached importance to this point. There has been discovered at Dunhuang a selective imposition register 差科簿 of the tenth year of the Tianbao reign period (751) for Dunhuang Commandery in Dunhuang Prefecture that makes clear that a market administrator 市壁師 of the same type (Sogdian) managed the marketplace commerce for special corvée duties 色役, and this case was due to a Sogdian of Conghua 從化 township assuming the office.[21] In the trade at border markets among ethnic groups outside the borders of China, Sogdians relied on their language superiority. Further, they were performers of an important function. A trade document unearthed at Turfan, concerning horses from a Tang Xizhou 西州 administrative center, between three people, either Qarluq 葛邏祿 (a Turkish tribe) or Türgiş (a Turkish tribe), indicates that the Xizhou frontier market also was

---

[19] Luo Feng 羅豐, *Sui and Tang Tombs in the Southern Suburbs of Guyuan* 《固原南郊隋唐墓地》 (Beijing: Cultural Relics Press 文物出版社, 1996), pp. 55-77, 206-11.

[20] Li Fang 李方, "Translators in the Turfan Documents" 《吐魯番文書中的譯語人》, *Cultural Relics* 《文物》, 1994, no. 2, pp. 45-51.

[21] Ikeda On 池田温, "The Sogdian Settlements in Dunhuang in the Mid-Eighth Century" 「8世紀中葉における敦煌のソグド人聚落」, *Studies in Eurasian Culture* 『ユーラシア文化研究』, no. 1 (1965), pp. 49-92.

intermediated by Sogdians.[22] Similarly, An Lushan at the Tang Dynasty border town of Yingzhou 營州 acted as a "frontier market middleman" 互市牙郎, which was the best reflection of his Sogdian nature. Moreover, An Lushan "did the foreigner's whirling dance, and was as fast as the wind" 作胡旋舞，其疾如風.[23] The foreigner's whirling dance and the foreigner's leaping dance 胡騰舞 were a special skill of the Sogdians. Historical records and Tang poems and prose have many descriptions of this, and in recent years the tombs of Yu Hong 虞弘, An Jia 安伽, Shi Jun 史君, and others have been discovered with images having these figures displayed.[24]

If we rely on Chen Yinke's point of view that "the differences between ethnic groups are mostly tied to the culture that men receive, and are not carried by lineage" 種族之分，多繫於其人所受之文化，而不在其所承之血統 in order to judge An Lushan, then he without doubt was a genuine Sogdian.

II. From the Liucheng 柳城 Foreigner Settlement to the Youzhou 幽州 Military Group

The beginning of *Factual Traces of An Lushan* states: "An Lushan was a mixed-race foreigner from Yingzhou" 安祿山，營州雜種胡也. The

---

[22] Jiang Boqin 姜伯勤, *Dunhuang and Turfan Documents and the Silk Road* 《敦煌吐魯番文書與絲綢之路》 (Bẹijing: Wenwu Press, 1994), p. 116; Dong Guodong 凍國棟, *The Tang Dynasty Commercial Economy and Business Management* 《唐代的商品經濟與經營管理》 (Wuchang 武昌: Wuhan University Press 武漢大學出版社, 1990), pp. 172-83.

[23] *Factual Traces of An Lushan*, first chapter, p. 6.

[24] See Ishida Mikinosuke 石田幹之助, "A Note on the 'Foreigner's Whirling Dance'" 「"胡旋舞"小考」, in *Spring in Chang'an* 『長安の春』 (Tokyo: Heibonsha, 1967), pp. 25-43. Chen Haitao 陳海濤, "The Foreigner's Whirling Dance, the Foreigner's Leaping Dance, and the Cudrania Branch Dance – A Small Analysis of the Dances Belonging to the An Jia Tomb and the Yu Hong Tomb" 《胡旋舞、胡騰舞與柘枝舞——對安伽墓與虞弘墓中舞蹈歸屬的淺析》, *Archaeology and Cultural Relics* 《考古與文物》, 2003, no. 3, pp. 56-60, 91. Zhang Qingjie 張慶捷, "The Sogdian 'Foreigner's Leaping Dance' in the Northern Dynasties, Sui, and Tang" 《北朝隋唐粟特的"胡騰舞"》, Rong Xinjiang, ed., *Sogdians in China – New Explorations in History, Archaeology, and Language* 《粟特人在中國——歷史、考古、語言的新探索》 (Beijing: Zhonghua Book Company, 2005), pp. 390-401.

New Tang History biography calls him a "Yingzhou Liucheng foreigner" 營州柳城胡也. Although An Lushan was "orphaned when young," and he was moved away from the An surnamed Sogdians, nevertheless, there were many Sogdian foreigners at Liucheng. Although the handed-down historical material recording this border town is sparse, we still have the capability to find at least four more instances.

1) Regarding the rebellion and Shi Siming, who was as equally famous as An Lushan, *Factual Traces of An Lushan*, chapter two, in an original footnote says:

> Shi Siming was a mixed-race foreigner from Yingzhou. His original given name was "Sugan" 窣干, which Emperor Xuanzong 玄宗 changed to "Siming" 思明. He was thin and small, with a small mustache and beard, had deep eyes and hawk-like shoulders, with a strong but impatient personality. He was born in the same township as An Lushan, but one day before him. Siming was born on the last day of the year, Lushan on the first day. While growing up they were very fond of each other, and they both as cavalrymen had a reputation for bravery. He understood six foreign languages 蕃語, and the same as (An Lushan) was a middleman.[25]

The An Shi Rebellion's other leading role was played by Shi Siming, who also was a mixed-raced foreigner from Yingzhou. The so-called "same township" was a Tang Dynasty way of saying Sogdians after the Tang government had registered them and had classified them by their home village. If this occurred during the period of the Turkish Qaghanate north of the Gobi Desert, then their home village was just the same as their tribe. Shi Siming's original given name "Sugan" should be the same as "Yaluoshan," a transcription from the Sogdian language, the meaning of which perhaps was what Emperor Xuanzong changed his name to: "thinking deeply on brightness" (Siming 思明).[26] Shi Siming from his

---

[25] *Factual Traces of An Lushan*, last ch., p. 42; Pulleyblank, *The Background of the Rebellion of An Lu-shan*, pp. 16-7; Robert des Rotours, *Histoire de Ngan lou-chan* , pp. 321-2.

[26] Pulleyblank proposes that the ancient pronunciation of "Sugan" "窣干" was *suet-kan, see Pulleyblank, *The Background of the Rebellion of An Lu-shan*, p. 111, n. 40. In a Manichaean manuscript discovered at Turfan of the *Šābuhragān* 《沙卜拉干》, written in old Persian , the incomplete text (M506、M7981) has the word Swc'gyn, meaning

birth to adulthood had everything in common with An Lushan, "he understood six foreign languages, and the same as (An Lushan) was a middleman," meaning that he was an authentic Sogdian, and not, as the *Old Tang History* biography says, that he was a "Turkish mixed-race foreigner" 突厥雜種胡.[27]

2) The An Shi Rebellion's other important person was Li Huaixian 李懷仙. The *Old Tang History*, chapter 143, "The Biography of Li Huaixian" says:

> Li Huaixian was a foreigner from Liucheng. His family served the Khitan 契丹 for many generations, and he was a general who surrendered to the Tang and afterwards was governor 守 of Yingzhou. When An Lushan revolted, Li Huaixian joined him and served as an Assistant General 裨將, following him into Luoyang

---

"burning, shining" (see M. Hutter, *Manis kosmogonische Sābuhragān-Texte*, Wiesbaden, 1992, pp. 61, 63, 65, 162). Very probably this is the original word behind "Sugan." In the summer of 1996 the author during an interview in Paris asked the view on just this question of Sogdian script expert Professor Werner Sundermann, and essentially received his confirmation.

[27] The argument of Zhong Han's 鍾焓 article cited above (footnote nine) directed against the first draft of this essay considers that Shi Siming identified himself as a Turk, and under his character traits emphasizes that "from the point of view of Shi Siming's appearance, it is rather that he resembled more an Inner Asian than a Sogdian, and this naturally was the result of his clan's long-term intermarrying with Turks" (Zhong Han, "The Inner Asian Cultural Background of An Lushan and Other Mixed-Race Foreigners," pp. 76-8). This argument is not without rational composition, but historical texts do not have any record of Shi Siming's "clan's long-term intermarrying with Turks." Regarding Shi Siming's identity, the earliest record is "mixed-race foreigner from Yingzhou" 營州雜種胡 in *Factual Traces of An Lushan*. Afterwards there is the *Old Tang History's* "Yingzhou Ningyizhou Turkish mixed-race foreigner" 營州寧夷州突厥雜種胡人, and finally the *New Tang History's* "Ningyizhou Turkish" 寧夷州突厥種. Based on Shi Siming's given name and cultural characteristics, I still firmly believe that he was a Sogdian. However, I previously have never denied that An Lushan, Shi Siming, and other mixed-race foreigners themselves had Turkish cultural characteristics. Sogdians actually were immigrants, and when they entered Han Chinese lands, at the time of the Turks and even the northeastern Xi 奚, Khitan 契丹, and other strong ethnic groups' areas of influence, they all frequently identified with these strong ethnic groups. The Sogdians claimed that they were Han Chinese, Turkish, Xi, or Khitan, and after they entered into another strong ethnic group's area of influence, they again changed their own ethnic identity. For this reason we can not easily believe the specific analysis undertaken of Sogdian peoples ethnic identification recorded in the old histories.

> 洛陽. After An Qingxu's 安慶緒 failure and death, Li Huaixian served under Shi Siming. Li Huaixian was a very good rider and archer, and was clever and talented. During Shi Chaoyi's 史朝義 rule of the rebel territory (761-763), Li Huaixian was appointed as Regent Guard 留守 of Yanjing 燕京 and Administrator (satrap 尹) of Fanyang 范陽. In the first year of the Baoying 寶應 reign period (762), when Marshall 元帥 Yong Wang 雍王 of the Tang led the Uyghur army to recapture the eastern capital [Luoyang], Shi Chaoyi crossed the Yellow River and fled north. Then Yong Wang ordered Vice-Marshal 副元帥 Pugu Huai'en 僕固懷恩 to lead the army and pursue Shi Chaoyi. Since at that time the fierce throng (the rebel army) was disintegrating, and the Tang was regaining its power and restoring order in the land, when the bandit cohorts heard that Pugu Huai'en was coming, they were so impressed by his reputation that they surrendered and pledged their allegiance to the Tang. When Shi Chaoyi fled to Fanyang with his few thousand remaining evildoers, Li Huaixian lured him into a trap and captured him, then cut off his head and presented it to the Tang court.[28]

Since Li Huaixian was a foreigner, his surname "Li" 李 must have been taken from the surname of the Tang Dynasty imperial house. However, he probably changed his surname relatively early, and therefore historians did not get material concerning his original surname. Because "Liucheng foreigner" 柳城胡 in the Tang Dynasty had nearly become an An Lushan specialization, therefore we can infer that Li Huaixian was a Sogdian foreigner, and this must be a tenable argument. Historical materials say that he "served the Khitan for generations" 世事契丹, which means that his family's ethnic group was not Khitan.

3) Another example illustrative of the issue is Kang Ayi Kül Tarqan 康阿義屈達干. In the *Collected Works of Yan Lugong* (Yan Zhenqing 顏真卿) 顏魯公文集, chapter six has the *Spirit Way Stele for the Honorable Kang, Lord Specially Advanced, Acting Left Guard of the Imperial Insignia, General-in-Chief, Supreme Pillar of the State, Qinghe*

---

[28] *Old Tang History*, ch. 143, p. 3895; *New Tang History*, ch. 212, pp. 5967-8 is about the same.

Commandery Dynasty-Founding Duke, Posthumous Commander Unequalled in Honor, and Xiazhou Commander-in-Chief 特進行左金吾衛大將軍上柱國清河郡開國公贈開府儀同三司兼夏州都督康公神道碑 and the text says:

> His given names were Ayi Kül Tarqan, and his family name was Kang, and his hometown was Liucheng. His ancestors were of noble birth in the Northern Foreigners of the Twelve Surnames 北蕃十二姓. His great grandfather was Illig Qaghan 頡利, who was a Commander-in-Chief 都督 (*tutuq*). His grandfather was Ran 染, who was the son-in-law of the Qaghan, and bore the title Supreme Commander of the Army 都知兵馬使. His father was Eltäbär 頡利發, who was a Chief Guardian 衛衙官 of Qapaghan Qaghan (Mochuo 默啜), and presided as a Tribal Commander-in-Chief 部落都督. All of them had great exploits and achievements, and were famous on the northern frontier….In the first year of the Tianbao reign period (742) he surrendered to the Tang, and the Military Commissioner 節度使 of Shuofang 朔方 (a frontier defense command), Wang Husi 王斛斯, reported this to the Tang court….At that time the Military Commissioner of Fanyang, An Lushan, had been working on his malicious plan, and desired that Kang would take his side, so he secretly reported to the court that he had appointed Kang as Tribal Commander-in-Chief 部落都督, and Kang served under him as Commissioner of the Vanguard 先鋒使.[29]

The last part of the stele text records that after the An Lushan revolt, Kang Ayi Kül Tarqan led his four sons back to serve the Chinese court.

Judging by the surname Kang, Kang Ayi Kül Tarqan was a Sogdian from the Kingdom of Kang (Samarkand) 康國, who had come to the north of the Gobi Desert. Although he was of noble birth in the Northern Foreigners of the Twelve Surnames, the names, beginning from his great-grandfather who had a pure Turkish name "Illig" (Chinese: Xieli or Jieli

---

[29] *Four Branches of Literature Collection* 《四部叢刊》edition，pp. 1b-2b；*Complete Prose Literature of the Tang* 《全唐文》, ch. 342 (Zhonghua Book Company facsimile edition, 1983), p. 3474.

頡利), continuously down to his own given name "Kül Tarqan" 屈達干, all indicate a deep Turkish influence. But, because these many generations of ancestors continuously served as "Tribal Commander-in-Chief," therefore this tribal pattern still preserved original aspects of the Sogdians. "Ayi" 阿義 was his given name, which certainly was derived from some Sogdian given name. Before the time of Kang Ayi, this Sogdian tribe was continuously among the northern foreigners (蕃 fan), namely among the Turkish Qaghanate north of the Gobi Desert, where they were called "Liucheng People" 柳城人, indicating that Kang Ayi after returning to court was registered at Liucheng. This was probably arranged by An Lushan, so that Kang would collaborate with An Lushan's Liucheng foreigner power base, and thus be useful to him. It is worthwhile noting that after Kang Ayi entered Tang China, he was still considered a "Tribal Commander-in-Chief," indicating that in the Liucheng territory it was taken for granted that part of the Sogdians lived among his tribe. This also was a reason that we say that An Lushan and Shi Siming's village was actually the same tribe.

In addition, the *Spirit Way Stele for the Honorable Kang* records that Kang Ayi's wife's surname was Shi 石, and her father's name was Shi Sannu (Stone Three Slaves) 石三奴. W. B. Henning established through textual research that the name "Sannu" was a free translation of the ancient Persian Sēbuχt, meaning "saved by the three (viz. divinities)."[30]

---

[30] See E. G. Pulleyblank, "A Sogdian Colony in Inner Mongolia", *T'oung Pao*, vol. 41 (1952), p. 340, n. 2. Henning points out that "three divinities" 三神 indicates the Christian god, and that "three divinities" are the trinity found in Manichaean texts. However, most Manichaean religious doctrine originated from Zoroastrianism. This evidence concerning this view of "three divinities" received its inspiration from Zhang Guangda's 張廣達 lecture in autumn 1996 at the Freie Universität Berlin "Tang Dynasty Manichaeism" 《唐代的摩尼教》. In 2004 Zhang Guangda 張廣達 in "On the Chinese Manichaean Fragmentary Texts of the Tang Dynasty" 《唐代漢譯摩尼教殘卷》 considered that the character "chang" 常 in "san chang" 三常 could be a borrowing of the connotation of the same character "chang" in the Confucian phrase "moral obligations" 綱常, but more probable is that it came from the same character in the Buddhist saying "the Buddha nature means Buddhata" 佛性即常, where "chang" indicates the Buddhata (the Buddha nature intrinsic to all sentient beings), but there is no explanation for the origin of the combined term "san chang" 三常. The essay was first printed in *The Journal of Oriental Studies* 《東方學報》, vol. 77 (2004), then in *The Transmission of Text, Image, and Culture* (*The Collected Works of Zhang Guangda*, vol. 3) 《文本、圖像與文

This interpretation, that Shi Sannu came from the Sogdian kingdom of Chach 石國 (the Shi Kingdom), provides conclusive proof. Sogdians intermarried and this was one of the best methods for preserving their own tribal patterns. An Lushan's first wife was from the Kang clan and also was a Sogdian who came from the Kingdom of Kang (Samarkand).

4) On December 9, 1998, a Tang grave with two people was discovered inside the grounds of the Beijing Yanjing Automotive Factory 燕京汽車製造廠. The archaeological report has still not been published, but based on what is recorded in the epitaph, the man in this joint burial grave was surnamed He 何, with the given name Shu 數 and the courtesy name 字 Yanben 延本. He was a Liucheng man and died in the ninth year of the Kaiyuan reign period (721) at Fanyang 范陽. The woman was Lady Kang 康氏, and she died in the first year of the Shuntian 順天 reign period of Shi Siming (759), and in that same year her son He Lingzhang 何令璋 requested the joint burial.[31] From this can be seen that within the An Lushan and Shi Siming Youzhou 幽州 Military Group there were many Sogdian foreigners from Liucheng. This person He Shu and his wife Lady Kang were typical Liucheng Sogdian foreigners.

Without a doubt, Yingzhou or Liucheng around the Kaiyuan and Tianbao reign periods had a quite extensive Sogdian settlement. It is known from Dunhuang and Turfan documents that Sogdians in Shazhou 沙州 and Xizhou 西州 were all recruited into villages by the Tang court – into Shazhou as Conghua 從化 township and into Xizhou as Chonghua 崇化 township.[32] However, the Yingzhou Liucheng Sogdian settlement was

---

化流傳（張廣達文集 3）》 (Guilin: Guangxi Normal University Press, 2008), pp. 337-8.

[31] For the report at the time of the discovery see *Beijing Youth Daily* 《北京青年報》 12/13/1998. I am indebted to Zhao Fusheng 趙福生 of the Beijing Cultural Relics Research Institute 北京市文物研究所 for showing me the contents of the epitaph, and I sincerely thank him.

[32] See Ikeda On 池田温, "The Sogdian Settlements in Dunhuang in the Mid-Eighth Century" 「8世紀中葉における敦煌のソグド人聚落」, *Studies in Eurasian Culture* 『ユーラシア文化研究』, no. 1 (1965), pp. 49-92 and Jiang Boqin 姜伯勤, *Dunhuang and Turfan Documents and the Silk Road* 《敦煌吐魯番文書與絲綢之路》 (Beijing: Wenwu Press, 1994), p. 173. [The Chinese names of these townships mean, literally, "Surrender to the Transformation (Sinicization)" and "Venerate the Transformation." Translator's note.]

somewhat different. At that time the Tang court had a low level of control there, and because of this very many Sogdians must have lived in this Sogdian settlement.

The origin of Liucheng Sogdian foreigners is first seen in the summer of the first year of the Wansui Dengfeng 萬歲登封 reign period of Wu Zhou 武周 [Empress Wu Zetian 武則天] (696). Since the Khitan 契丹 stormed and captured Yingzhou, the Empress Wu Zetian "strongly urged that the soldiers of the Hedong Circuit 河東道 and the Six Sogdian Prefectures, and those of the Buluoji people of Suizhou, Yanzhou, Xizhou and other prefectures, should all go to Yingzhou 大發河東道及六胡州、綏、延、丹、隰等州稽、胡精兵，悉赴營州,"[33] meaning that a large number of Sogdians of the Six Hu Prefectures went to the region of Yingzhou. Later, early in the Kaiyuan reign period (after 713), An Lushan and others took a roundabout course to arrive in Liucheng. In the first year of the Tianbao reign period (742) Kang Ayi led his tribe and arrived there. Gao Shi's 高適 poem *Song of Yingzhou* 營州歌 chants of the general idea of the situation at this time:

> The youths of Yingzhou are brimming with the steppe,
> Wearing a disorderly mess of fox fur robes they hunt below the city walls.
> A thousand cups of "prisoner's brew" can not make them drunk,
> Those foreign boys can ride horses by the age of ten.
>
> 營州少年滿原野，狐裘蒙茸獵城下。
> 虜酒千鐘不醉人，胡兒十歲能騎馬。[34]

The situation of the Liucheng Sogdian settlement was different from that of Shazhou and Xizhou, in that the settlement was formed by many

---

[33] Chen Zi'ang 陳子昂, "Report to the Court of Eight Items on Classified and Important Military and State Issues" 《上軍國機要事八條》, *The Collected Works of Chen Boyu* 《陳伯玉文集》, ch. 8, in the *Four Branches of Literature Collection* 《四部叢刊》 edition, p.12a; Dong Gao 董誥 and others, editors, *Complete Prose Literature of the Tang* 《全唐文》, ch. 211, p. 2135.

[34] *Complete Poems of the Tang* 《全唐詩》, ch. 214 (Beijing: Zhonghua Book Company, 1960), book 6, p. 2242.

immigrations of relatively large groups of Sogdians. In addition, all of them who had moved from inside the Eastern Turkish Qaghanate to come there were skilled in riding and shooting, and had combat capability. From the point of view of the Tang court, Yingzhou faced the Khitan 契丹 and Xi 奚, two strong northeastern tribes, both of which conducted unceasing hostilities, so the Tang court wanted to use these martial Sogdians to deal with these two foreign tribes. For this reason the Tang court during this period did not disperse the Sogdian settlements, so that they could utilize these foreign (蕃 fan) soldiers and generals to defend against invasion from the Xi and Khitan. In reality, this also meant that An Lushan and Shi Siming and others grew up under conditions of warfare with these two northeastern foreign tribes.

The methods of the Tang court actually provided strength to An Lushan's rebellion. During the An Shi Rebellion, without a doubt the revolting armies had great numbers of Sogdians in them,[35] and historical records record that many of the An Shi army generals were also Sogdians by family background. Facts concerning these people are delineated as follows:

An Qingxu 安慶緒, An Lushan's second son, who in the eleventh year of the Tianbao reign period (752) assumed the posts of Military Vice Commissioner 節度副使 for Fanyang 范陽, Chief Minister of the Court for Diplomatic Relations 鴻臚卿, and simultaneously the Governor of Guangyang 廣陽 Commandery; in the second year of the Zhide 至德 reign period (757) he killed An Lushan, and made himself Emperor of the Great Yan 大燕, with the reign period name Tianhe 天和.[36]

An Lushan had eleven sons, among which was Qingzong 慶宗, who climbed socially by marrying the Rongyi 榮義 Princess, and who worked for his father at the capital by acting as Lushan's eyes and ears.[37] The others also must have served in An Lushan's retinue as high-ranking military officers.

An Zhongchen 安忠臣, who was an adopted son of An Lushan.[38]

---

[35] Chen Yinke 陳寅恪, *Manuscript of Discussions on the Political History of the Tang Dynasty* 《唐代政治史述論稿》, pp. 29-33, already discussed in detail.

[36] *Factual Traces of An Lushan*, first ch., p. 14; last ch., pp. 38-40.

[37] Ibid., middle ch., p. 21.

[38] Ibid., first ch., p. 10.

An Zhongshun 安忠順, who later changed his name to Shouzhong 守忠, who in the tenth year of the Tianbao reign period (751) took a leading place among An Lushan's generals; after Lushan attacked and occupied Chang'an 長安, he ordered An Shouzhong 安守忠 to assemble his troops and garrison the Western Capital (Chang'an).[39]

He Qiannian 何千年, who in the tenth year of the Tianbao reign period (751) became one of An Lushan's generals; in the 14th year (755) he became An Lushan's Vice-General, and An Lushan memorialized the throne to have 32 foreign 蕃 (fan) generals replace Han Chinese generals. After Lushan had raised troops, he first ordered He Qiannian to lead several thousand warriors in an ambush at Heyang 河陽 bridge.[40]

He Side 何思德, a senior general under the leadership of An Lushan whose appearance was similar to An Lushan's. In the autumn of the tenth year of the Tianbao reign period (751) he was in the vanguard of the punitive expedition against the Khitan.[41]

Shi Dingfang 史定方, Military Commissioner 節度使 of Pinglu 平盧, who served as a cavalry general under An Lushan, and who in the tenth year of the Tianbao reign period (751) rescued Lushan from encirclement by the Khitan.[42]

An Siyi 安思義, one of An Lushan's military officers, who was stationed at Zhending 真定 and afterwards surrendered to the Tang general Li Guangbi 李光弼.[43]

An Dai 安岱, An Lushan's trusted follower posted to the capital, who in the fifth month of the 14th year of the Tianbao reign period (755) was arrested and killed by Yang Guozhong 楊國忠 of the Tang.[44]

Kang Jie 康傑, who wrote the calligraphy for the *Inscription of the Great Tang Boling Commandery Dedicated at North Peak Antianwang*

---

[39] *Comprehensive Mirror for Aid in Government* 《資治通鑒》, ch. 216, pp. 6980, 7008; *Factual Traces of An Lushan*, first ch., p. 12, last ch., p. 37.

[40] *Factual Traces of An Lushan*, first ch., p. 12, middle ch., pp. 19, 24. [The Heyang bridge was a key military location northeast of Luoyang 洛陽. Translator's note.]

[41] Ibid., first ch., p. 13.

[42] Ibid.

[43] *New Tang* History, ch. 225, "Biography of An Lushan" 《安祿山傳》, p. 6419; *Comprehensive Mirror for Aid in* Government, ch. 217, p. 6954.

[44] *Factual Traces of An Lushan*, middle ch., p. 21.

Temple on Heng Mountain 大唐博陵郡北嶽恒山封安天王之銘, erected in the seventh year of the Tianbao reign period (748).

Kang Ayi Kül Tarqan 康阿義屈達干, who was attached to An Lushan's vanguard. In the fourth year of the Tianbao reign period (745) he received the post of Fanyang Vice Military Commissioner 經略副使. In the fifth year he became Regional Military Vice-Commissioner 節度副使.[45]

Kang Jie 康節, who was Prefect 刺史 of Xingzhou 邢州 under An Lushan.[46]

Cao Runguo 曹閏國, who was a military officer under An Lushan and Shi Siming, General of the Cloud-like Flags 雲麾將軍 and acting General-in-Chief of the Imperial Insignia Guard 守左金吾衛大將軍, and who afterwards surrendered to the Tang court.[47]

He Yuanchan 何元辿, who in the second month of the 13th year of the Tianbao reign period (754) was appointed to the Shanggu Commandery 上谷郡 Reform the Government Assault Resisting Garrison 修政府折衝, and who made for An Lushan the *Perfection of Wisdom Sutra, Mahāprajñāpāramitāsūtra* 大般若波羅密多經.[48]

An Shenwei 安神威, who together with Sun Xiaozhe 孫孝哲 served An Lushan and were ordered west to attack Chang'an.[49]

An Taiqing 安太清, who was originally one of An Lushan's subordinate commanders 部將;[50] he later assisted Shi Siming in killing An Qingxu, and served under Shi Siming as an important General-in-chief in

---

[45] *Collected Works of Yan Lugong* (Yan Zhenqing 顏真卿) 《顏魯公文集》, ch. 6, in the *Four Branches of Literature Collection* 《四部叢刊》 edition, pp. 1b-2b; *Complete Prose Literature of the Tang* 《全唐文》, ch. 342, p. 3474.

[46] *Collected Works of Yan Lugong*, ch. 6.

[47] "Epitaph of Cao Runguo" 《曹閏國墓誌》 in Zhou Shaoliang 周紹良 editor-in-chief, *Collected Tang Dynasty Epitaphs* 《唐代墓誌彙編》 (Shanghai: Shanghai Classics Publishing House 上海古籍出版社, 1992), pp. 1787-8.

[48] Beijing Library Epigraphy Group and China Buddhist Texts Library Stone Sutra Group 北京圖書館金石組, 中國佛教圖書文物館石經組, editors, *Collected Fangshan Stone Sutra Inscriptions* 《房山石經題記彙編》 (Beijing: Bibliography and Document Publishing House 書目文獻出版社, 1987), pp. 96, 99-100.

[49] *New Tang History*, ch. 225, "Biography of An Lushan," p. 6419.

[50] Ibid., p. 6414.

the garrison of Huaizhou 懷州, and afterwards was captured alive by Li Guangbi 李光弼.[51]

An Wuchen 安武臣, one of An Qingxu's subordinate commanders 部將, who in the seventh month of the second year of the Zhide reign period (757) led the troops that stormed and captured Shan Commandery 陝郡.[52]

An Xiongjun 安雄俊, one of An Qingxu's subordinate commanders 部將, who with Cai Xide 蔡希德, An Taiqing, and others stormed and captured Hebei 河北.[53]

Shi Siming 史思明, who was a mixed-race foreigner from Yingzhou, from the same township as An Lushan, able to speak six foreign languages, and a market middleman the same as An Lushan. Later, again with An Lushan, he served under the Commissioner 節度使 of Fanyang, Zhang Shougui 張守珪, as a reconnaissance officer 捉生將 [literally, officer who seizes those alive]. After An Lushan raised troops, he was given the post of Prefect 刺史 of Pingzhou 平州. After An Qingxu killed An Lushan, he granted Shi Siming the surname An 安 and the given name Rongguo 榮國, and conferred on him the title Prince of Guichuan 嬀川. In the second year of the Qianyuan 乾元 reign period (759), Shi Siming at Weizhou 魏州 declared himself the Prince of Yan 燕王, with the reign period Shuntian 順天. He was asked to rescue Xiangzhou 相州 [Yecheng 鄴城, where An Qingxu was besieged by Tang loyalist forces], and he defeated the nine Tang Military Commissioners 節度 surrounding it, killed An Qingxu and his brothers, and established himself as emperor.[54]

Shi Chaoyi 史朝義, Shi Siming's eldest son, made Prince of Huai 懷王, who in the second year of the Shangyuan 上元 reign period (761) killed Shi Siming and established himself as emperor, with the reign period name Xiansheng 顯聖.[55]

Kang Meiyebo 康沒野波, a subordinate officer of Shi Siming, who as the vanguard attacked Pingyuan Commandery 平原郡, so that Yan

---

51 *Factual Traces of An Lushan*, last ch., p. 41; *Comprehensive Mirror for Aid in Government* , ch. 221, pp. 7071-2, 7099.

52 *Comprehensive Mirror for Aid in Government*, ch. 219, p. 7028.

53 *New Tang History*, ch. 225, "Biography of An Lushan," p. 6422.

54 *Factual Traces of An Lushan*, last ch., pp. 40, 42; *Comprehensive Mirror for Aid in Government*, ch. 219, p. 7008.

55 *Factual Traces of An Lushan*, last ch., pp. 42-4.

Zhenqing 顏真卿 abandoned the commandery, crossed the river, and fled south.[56]

Kang Wenjing 康文景, who was a subordinate officer of Shi Siming.[57]

General Cao 曹將軍, a closely attached trusted subordinate of Shi Siming, who later, under the orders of Shi Chaoyi and others, participated in the killing of Shi Siming, who cursed him saying "this foreigner is killing me" 此胡殺我, knowing that he was a foreigner.[58]

He Shu 何數, who during Shi Siming's time served as the Beiping Lulong Garrison 北平盧龍府 Adjunct Commandant 别將.

He Lingzhang 何令璋, a son of He Shu, who during Shi Siming's time served as a Mobile Corp Commander 遊擊將軍, and acted as the Right Guard Shanggu Commandery Suicheng Garrison Adjunct Commandant 右衛商孤郡遂城府别將, Commandant of Light Chariots 輕車都尉 [a merit title], and Administrative Assistant to the Military Officer in Charge of Capitulators 都知降戶使判官.[59]

Shi Diting 石帝廷, who was a subordinate officer under An Lushan and Shi Siming.[60]

Kang Xiaozhong 康孝忠, who was Minister of the Ministry of Revenue 戶部尚書 for Shi Chaoyi.[61]

Kang (unknown given name) 康, son-in-law of the Protector-General 都護 of Annan 安南 Kang Qian 康謙, who while in the An Shi rebel army implicated Kang Qian and was killed.[62]

The Tang Dynasty historiographers in the records of meritorious military service in the Tang army only occasionally mention the high-ranking military officers of the An Shi armies, and therefore the above are all only some of the members of the rebel armies. These Youzhou generals

---

[56] *Comprehensive Mirror for Aid in Government*, ch. 219, p. 7005; *Old Tang History*, chapter 200, p. 5377.

[57] *New Tang History*, chapter 207, "Biography of Yu Chaoen" 《魚朝恩傳》, p. 5863.

[58] *Factual Traces of An Lushan*, last ch., pp. 43-4.

[59] For the above two items see the *Epitaph of He Shu* 《何數墓誌》, which was shown to me by Zhao Fusheng 趙福生.

[60] *New Tang History*, ch. 224, "Biography of Li Zhongchen" 《李忠臣傳》, p. 6387.

[61] *Comprehensive Mirror for Aid in Government*, ch. 222, "the third month of the second year of the Shangyuan reign period of the Emperor Suzong" 《肅宗上元二年三月》, pp. 7109-10.

[62] *New Tang History*, ch. 225, "Biography of An Lushan," p. 6425.

were not necessarily all born in Liucheng. However, based on the movements of Shi Siming and others, particularly from the point of view that their supreme leader An Lushan came from Liucheng, among them must have been many who came from Liucheng. Members of the Liucheng Sogdian settlement must have been the main force of the Youzhou Military Group, and must have been the principal military power relied on by the An Lushan Rebellion. Some people emphasize that among the An Lushan rebel army the chief conspirators all were Han Chinese. We can see the general perspective of people of that time regarding the high-ranking military leadership of An Shi armies: in the twelfth month of first year of the Deyuan 德元 reign period of Emperor Suzong 肅宗 (756), "the Emperor asked Limi 李泌: 'The enemy are so strong, when will be able to bring everything under control?' Li Mi responded: 'What I have noticed is that the traitors have transported everything that they captured, such as young women, children, gold, silver, and other treasure, all back to Fanyang. Based on this, how could he have any great ambition for establishing hegemony! At present only captured generals will serve him. The Chinese, except for Gao Shang 高尚 and very few others, have become his subjects only because they were forced to do so. In my opinion, in less than two years all under heaven will be free of the bandits.' The Emperor asked: 'Why do you say so?' Li Mi replied: 'The traitors have very few valiant generals besides Shi Siming, An Shouzhong 安守忠, Tian Qianzhen 田乾真, Zhang Zhongzhi 張忠志, and Ashina Chengqing 阿史那承慶.'"[63] From this we can see that the most important military leaders serving under An Lushan must have been Sogdians, and this must be an accurate observation.

As for the soldiers serving under An Lushan and Shi Siming, the proportion of those that were foreigners (hu 胡) was also quite large. In the second month of the first year of the Deyuan reign period (756), Li Guangbi 李光弼 arrived at Changshan 常山, where the local militia 團練 of 3,000 men had been killing foreign soldiers, in order to carry out the surrender of An Siyi 安思義. Li Guangbi asked how these Tang troops were able to resist Shi Siming's relief army, and An Siyi said in answer: "Although the fighting spirit of the foreign cavalry is good, they are not able to be prudent, and carelessness does not gain victory, so they became

---

[63] *Comprehensive Mirror for Aid in Government*, ch. 219, p. 7008.

discouraged and left" 胡騎雖銳，不能持重，苟不獲利，氣沮心離.[64] This description of the An Shi rebel army by a Sogdian foreign military leader shows that a special characteristic of the foreigners was that they were adept at horsemanship and archery in waging war, and that in their origin as traders they had the special characteristic of pursing material gain. Both characteristics are concisely depicted, so that we are able to learn about the fundamental situation of these foreigners in arms serving under An Lushan and Shi Siming.

III. An Lushan's Religious Beliefs and their Cohesive Force

Earlier scholars have not been careful enough concerning the question of An Lushan's religious beliefs. Since An Lushan was a foreigner, he of course must have been the same as other foreigners, and have had his own religious beliefs. Because the beliefs of most Sogdians arose from Persia, they practiced Zoroastrianism with Sogdian special characteristics, which in China was called Xianjiao 祆教. Therefore I believe that An Lushan also was a Xianjiao believer. In addition, in fact it is clear that An Lushan fully utilized this type of religious belief to unite a large number of foreign peoples.

Although this is the case, I do not deny that An Lushan acted as an agent of the government and at the same time utilized other religious forces. In the 14th year of the Tianbao reign period (755) An Lushan built a pagoda in Youzhou in the southeast corner of the Great Temple to Mourn the Loyal 大憫忠寺, the "spotless pure bright treasure pagoda" 無垢淨光寶塔.[65] His title inscription still survives engraved in the stone classics at Fangshan 房山.[66] On the 25th day of the fifth month in the

---

[64] Ibid., ch. 217, p. 6954.

[65] *General Gazetteer of the Unity of the Yuan* 《元一統志》 ch. 1, "Secretariat of Tongshan East and West, Locations in Hebei" 《中書省統山東西河北之地》 (Beijing: Zhonghua Book Company, 1966), p. 25; *Collected Gazetteer Records of Xijin: Ancient Traces* chapter《析津志輯佚·古迹》 (Beijing: Beijing Classics Press, 1983), p. 119.

[66] Lu Zengxiang 陸增祥, preparer, "The Eight Jades Hall Bronze and Stone Inscriptions Supplement and Correction" 《八瓊室金石補正》, ch. 58, included in *A New Collection of Stone Carved Materials* 《石刻史料新編》 part 1, book 7 (Taipei: Xin Wen Feng Publishing Company 新文豐出版公司, 1977), p. 4938; *Collected Fangshan Stone Classics Inscriptions* 《房山石經題記彙編》 first section, "Steles and Inscriptions (Tang to Republican Era)" 《碑和題記（唐至民國）》, p. 15.

seventh year of the Tianbao reign period (748) An Lushan erected the *Inscription of the Great Tang Boling Commandery Dedicated at North Peak Antianwang Temple on Heng Mountain* 大唐博陵郡北嶽恒山封安天王之銘, and this maneuver had a strong Daoist flavor.[67] Shi Siming's situation was fundamentally similar.[68]

According to my analysis and research on Dunhuang and Turfan documents and related historical materials, and my systematic investigation of Sogdians' migrations and settlements, I discovered that in most cases, at the location of Sogdian settlements and in amongst the settlements, they had a Zoroastrian temple 祆舍, namely, a place where foreigners could offer sacrifices to Zoroastrian gods and spirits. I can cite the following examples in proof.

At the ancient city of Gaochang 高昌 in the Turfan basin, according to what is recorded in the second chapter of the *Golden Light Sutra* (*Suvarṇaprabhāsa*) 金光明經 unearthed in Turfan at Anle 安樂 city in the Spread Buddhism pagoda 發佛塔, in the gengwu 庚午 year (430) there was in the eastern part of Gaochang a Zoroastrian temple for worshipping a Zoroastrian god 胡天神.[69] This temple must have been on the periphery of the Sogdian settlement. Recently the grave of a Sogdian was discovered at Badamu 巴達木 and a document was unearthed in Turfan, both having records of Sogdians arriving in Gaochang at the time of the Gaochang Kingdom.[70] They both include the existence of a Sogdian settlement leader

---

[67] Lei Wen 雷聞, "The Five Peaks Immortals Temple and Tang Dynasty National Sacrificial Ceremonies" 《五嶽真君祠與唐代國家祭祀》, in *Excluding the Jiaomiao Sacrifices – Sui Tang National Sacrificial Ceremonies and Religion* 《郊廟之外——隋唐國家祭祀與宗教》 (Beijing: Sanlian Publishers, 2009), p. 188.

[68] See You Li 尤李, "A Philological Study of 'The Ode of the Treasure Pagoda of the Temple to Mourn the Loyal,' Also Discussing the Multi-Valent Nature of An Lushan's and Shi Siming's Religious Beliefs" 《〈憫忠寺寶塔頌〉考釋——兼論安祿山、史思明宗教信仰的多樣性》, *Literature and History* 《文史》, 2009, no. 4.

[69] Regarding this discussion and the results of the latest research, see Rong Xinjiang, "The Golden Light Sutra Unearthed at Turfan, the Manuscript Text and Issues of When Zoroastrianism First Spread to Gaochang" 《吐魯番出土〈金光明經〉寫本題記與祆教初傳高昌問題》 in Zhu Yuqi 朱玉麒, general editor, *Literature and History of the Western Regions* 《西域文史》, vol. 2 (Science Press，2007), pp. 1-13 and plate 1.

[70] See Rong Xinjiang, "Sogdians Seen in New Documents from Turfan" 《新出吐魯番文書所見的粟特人》, *Turfan Studies* 《吐魯番學研究》, 2007, no. 1, pp. 28-35.

with the title "sabao" 薩薄(簿) (namely the Sabao 薩保),[71] and so reciprocally confirm each other.

In the late Sui Dynasty and early Tang Dynasty, Yizhou 伊州, on the eastern side of Turfan, was occupied by Sogdians, and because of this had quite an extensive Sogdian settlement. In the fourth year of the Zhenguan 貞觀 reign period (630), because the Eastern Turks had been eliminated by the Tang Empire, the Yizhou leader Shi Wannian 石萬年, originally subordinate to the Turkish Qaghanate, commanded his people to submit to the Tang. According to the remains of a document unearthed at Dunhuang, *Gazetteer of Shazhou and Yizhou* 沙州伊州地志, at the Yiwu 伊吾 County seat below the Yizhou city walls there was a Zoroastrian temple with a priest 祆主 named Di Pantuo 翟槃陀. There was also another temple with the worshipped deity named "Alan" 阿攬.[72] Turfan documents have many names of Sogdians which include the expression "Alan."[73] The explanation is that this was a deity worshipped by the Sogdians.[74]

Because of the quantity of documents discovered at the Dunhuang Library Cave, we have a relatively thorough understanding of the Shazhou

---

[71] Tang Zhangru 唐長孺, ed., *Documents Unearthed at Turfan* 《吐魯番出土文書》, vol. 1 (Beijing: Cultural Relics Press, 1992), p. 136.

[72] Lionel Giles, "A Chinese Geographical Text of the Ninth Century," *Bulletin of the School of Oriental Studies*, vol. 6, no. 4 (1932), pp. 825-46; Haneda Toru 羽田亨, "The Tang First Year of the Guangqi Reign Period Manuscript Remnant of the Gazetteer of Shazhou and Yizhou" 「唐光啟元年寫本沙州伊州地志殘卷」, in *Collected Essays on History and Geography Commemorating Doctor Ogawa* 『小川博士還曆記念史學地理學論叢』 (Tokyo, 1930), pp. 131-52; Arthur Waley, "Some References to Iranian Temples in the Tun-huang Region," *Bulletin of the Institute of History and Philology, Academia Sinica,* vol. 28, part 1 (1956), p. 125.

[73] "Names Recorded at Gaochang: Cao, Mu, Men, Tuo, and Others" 《高昌曹莫門陀等名籍》 has "Cao Alan" 曹阿攬 and "Cao Alanyan" 曹阿攬延, *Documents Unearthed in Turfan* 《吐魯番出土文書》, vol. 1, p. 359.

[74] See D. Weber, "Zur sogdischen Personennamengebung," *Indogermanische Forschungen*, vol. 77, 1972, p. 202 ; Cai Hongsheng 蔡鴻生, "Collected Studies of the Customs of Tang Dynasty Foreigners of the Nine Surnames" 《唐代九姓胡禮俗叢考》, *Literature and History* 《文史》, vol. 35 (1992), pp. 121-2; Cai Hongsheng 蔡鴻生, *Tang Dynasty Foreigners of the Nine Surnames and Turkish Culture* 《唐代九姓胡與突厥文化》 (Beijing: Zhonghua Book Company, 1998), p. 41; Y. Yoshida, "Review of N. Sims-Williams, Sogdian and other Iranian Inscriptions of the Upper Indus II," *Bulletin of the School of Oriental and African Studies*, vol. 57, no. 2 (1994), p. 392

region Sogdian settlement located at Dunhuang. One *li* 里 to the east of Shazhou City was the location of one of the 13 townships 鄉 of Dunhuang established by Sogdian immigrants, Conghua 從化. This originally was a Sogdian settlement 聚落, but after it became part of Tang China it became an official township. However, it still served as a Sogdian residential district. According to what is recorded in the third chapter of the Dunhuang manuscript the *Topographical Classic of Shazhou* 沙州圖經, one *li* east of the city was a Zoroastrian temple, and this Zoroastrian temple, which was located inside Conghua township, was a center of spiritual belief for the Sogdian people.[75]

In the early seventh century, during a period of civil strife in the central plains, the Shanshan 鄯善 region, south of Lop Nor 羅布泊, became a government vacuum. In the early years of the Zhenguan reign period (from 627), the supreme leader of the Kingdom of Kang, Kang Yandian 康豔典, led his people from Samarkand to the east, occupied this place, and founded Tuncheng 屯城, Xincheng 新城, Putaocheng (Grape Town) 蒲桃城, Sapicheng (Sapi Town) 薩毗城, and other Sogdian settlements. In the second year of the Shangyuan reign period of the Emperor Gaozong 高宗 (675), Shanshan Town 鄯善城 became Shicheng Garrison 石城鎮 and was made administratively subordinate to Shazhou. However, at this place a member of the Kang clan still assumed the post of garrison commander 鎮將: in the second year of the Tianshou 天授 reign period of the Empress Wu Zetian (691), the Shicheng Garrison commander was Kang Fudanyan 康拂耽延.[76] Earlier scholars absolutely did not understand that here there also was a Zoroastrian temple, even to the point that, because they misread the name "Fudanyan" 拂耽延 as the Manichaean "Fuduoyan" 拂多誕 they thought that Manichaeism had

---

[75] Regarding the Dunhuang Sogdian settlement and records of the Zoroastrian temple and a detailed analysis, see Ikeda On 池田温, "The Sogdian Settlements in Dunhuang in the Mid-Eighth Century" 「8 世紀中葉における敦煌のソグド人聚落」, pp. 49-92. Cf. Arthur Waley, "Some References to Iranian Temples in the Tunhuang Region," pp. 123, 124-25.

[76] Paul Pelliot, "Le 'Cha tcheou tou tou fou t'ou king' et la colonie sogdienne de la région du Lob nor," *Journal Asiatique*, série 2, vol. 7 (1916), pp. 111-23; Ikeda On 池田温, "A Concise Study of the Topographical Classic of Shazhou" 「沙州圖經略考」 in *A Festschrift of Articles on East Asian History on the Occasion of Dr. Enoki's 61st Birthday* 『榎博士還曆記念東洋史論叢』 (Tokyo, 1975), pp. 91-3.

spread there.[77] However, due to the discovery of the record "one Zoroastrian temple" 一所祆舍 in the fifth chapter of the *Topographical Classic of Shazhou*,[78] it is known that adjunct to this Sogdian foreigner settlement there was a Zoroastrian building.

Liangzhou 涼州 was a large place inhabited by Sogdians, and as early as the early years of the fourth century the ancient Sogdian letters record that this place was an important stopover for Sogdian merchant groups. These quite large merchant groups mostly came from Samarkand.[79] In addition to the Tang Dynasty genealogical work the *Compilation of Surnames in the Era of Yuanhe* 元和姓纂, and the *New Tang History*, and other historical materials recording the Northern Wei to Tang Dynasty Liangzhou Sabaos from the An clan 安氏 of Wuwei 武威 [another name for Liangzhou], there has also in recent years been discovered at Xi'an 西安 a tomb of a Liangzhou Sabao named Shi Jun 石郡 from the end of the Northern Zhou 北周 Dynasty.[80] The Tongzhou 同州 Sabao An Qie 安伽, whose original birthplace was also Liangzhou/Wuwei, was buried on the outskirts of Northern Zhou Chang'an in almost the same place.[81] Here

---

[77] Regarding the original Sogdian text of Fudanyan, see E. G. Pulleyblank, "A Sogdian Colony in Inner Mongolia," p. 333, n. 1; D. Weber, "Zur sogdischen Personennamengebung," p. 300; Yoshida Yutaka 吉田豊, "Notes on the Sogdian Language" 「ソグド語雑録」, part 2, *Orient* 『オリエント』, vol. 31, no. 2 (1989), pp. 172-3.

[78] Regarding the Zoroastrian temple, see Ikeda On 池田温, "A Concise Study of the Topographical Classic of Shazhou" 《沙州圖經略考》, p. 97.

[79] N. Sims-Williams, "The Sogdian Ancient Letter II", in *Philologica et Linguistica: Historia, Pluralitas, Universitas. Festschrift für Helmut Humbach zum 80. Geburtstag am 4. Dezember 2001*, M. G. Schmidt and W. Bisang, eds. (Trier: Wissenschaftlicher Verlag, 2001), pp. 267-80; F. Grenet, N. Sims-Williams, and É. de la Vaissière, "The Sogdian Ancient Letter V," *Bulletin of the Asia Institute*, new series, vol. 12 (2001), pp. 91-104.

[80] Xi'an City Cultural Relics Preservation and Archaeology Institute 西安市文物保護考古所, "A Brief Archaeological Report on the Excavation in Xi'an of the Tomb of the Northern Zhou Dynasty Liangzhou Sabao Shi Jun" 《西安北周涼州薩保史君墓發掘簡報》附錄, *Cultural Relics* 《文物》, 2005, no. 3, pp. 31-2.

[81] Rong Xinjiang, "A Few Issues Concerning the Tomb of the Northern Zhou Tongzhou Sabao An Qie" 《有關北周同州薩保安伽墓的幾個問題》 in *Northern China and the Eurasian Continent in the Fourth through Sixth Centuries* 《4～6世紀的北中國與歐亞大陸》, Zhang Qingjie 張慶捷 and others, editors (Beijing: Science Press, 2006), pp. 129-31. For the official archaeological report see Shaanxi Provincial Archaeological

there was without doubt in the Northern Dynasties through the Sui/Tang period the largest region of foreigners assembled in Hexi 河西, but Sogdian settlements did not end there. According to what was written by Zhang Zhuo 张鷟 of the Tang Dynasty in chapter three of *Complete Stories of the Court and the People* 朝野僉載, this place had a Zoroastrian temple.[82]

An even greater number of Sogdian foreigners were assembled in the capital of the Sui and Tang Empires, Chang'an. These included merchants, those who had entered service to the Sui and Tang government at different levels as civil and military staff, dancers, musicians, barmaids of all kinds, and others.[83] Of them a great many resided in the wards in the vicinity of the Western Market, convenient for foreign traders to conduct business and for coming and going to the west. The areas around Buzheng 布政 ward, Liquan 醴泉 ward, and Chonghua 崇化 ward, the three wards where these Sogdians resided, all had Zoroastrian temples, places where the Sogdian foreigners entrusted their spirit.[84]

The situation in the eastern capital Luoyang 洛陽 during the Sui and Tang Dynasties was similar to that in Chang'an, and there was a large foreigners' residential district, which flourished particularly during the Wu Zetian era. The center of Luoyang's business activities was the South Market, and this was also a center of Sogdian people's activities, therefore

Research Institute 陕西省考古研究所, *The Northern Zhou Tomb in Xi'an of An Qie* 《西安北周安伽墓》 (Beijing: Cultural Relics Press, 2003).

[82] *Complete Stories of the Court and the People* 《朝野僉載》 (Beijing: Zhonghua Book Company, 1979), p. 65.

[83] Xiang Da 向達, "Tang Dynasty Chang'an and the Civilization of the Western Regions" 《唐代長安與西域文明》 pp. 4-40; Rong Xinjiang, "The Migrations and Settlements of the Sogdians in the Northern Dynasties, Sui, and Tang" 《北朝隋唐粟特人之遷徙及其聚落》, pp. 56-8; in the translated and edited version, pp. 137-42.

[84] Xiang Da 向達, "Tang Dynasty Chang'an and the Civilization of the Western Regions" 《唐代長安與西域文明》, pp. 89-92; Xie Haiping 謝海平, *A Study and Review of the Life of Foreigners Staying in Tang Dynasty China* 《唐代留華外國人生活考述》 (Taipei: The Taiwan Commercial Bookstore 臺灣商務印書館, 1978), pp. 29-33; Lin Wushu 林悟殊, *Persian Fire Worship and Ancient China* 《波斯拜火教與古代中國》 (Taipei: Xin Wen Feng Publishing Company 新文豐出版公司, 1995), pp. 139-49; Li Jianchao 李健超, *A Revised and Expanded Study of Wards of the Two Tang Capital Cities* 《增訂唐兩京城坊考》 (Xi'an: San Qin Press 三秦出版社, 1996), pp. 149, 182, 207, 219, 227.

the neighboring Huijie 會節 and Fushan 福善 wards both had Zoroastrian temples.[85]

The Zoroastrian temples mentioned above all were from the Wei, Jin, Northern and Southern Dynasties, Sui, and Tang periods, and along with the establishment of Sogdian settlements, temples were ceaselessly built. It is worth noting that despite the great distance between the original Sogdian land and the Tang Dynasty Hebei Circuit 河北道, those arriving late, after the An Shi Rebellion, still constructed Zoroastrian temples. As the Song Dynasty Wang Guan's 王瓘 *Corrected Records of the Northern Routes* 北道刊誤志 says: "Ying 瀛 Prefecture Yueshou 樂壽 County also has a Zoroastrian temple, erected in the third year of the Tang Dynasty Changqing 長慶 reign period (823), originally titled Heavenly God."[86] I believe that this was because after the An Shi Rebellion, foreigners within Tang China's original territory received biased treatment, due to the large number of immigrants who had arrived at the three garrison areas in Hebei which were under the control of the generals of An Lushan and Shi Siming. Along with the large number of foreigners arriving, it was inevitable that they would construct new Zoroastrian temples.[87]

Now I return to my consideration of the situation of An Lushan and Shi Siming as Sogdian foreigners residing in Liucheng. Regarding the religious beliefs there, the historical materials have no unequivocal records; however, it is not difficult to explore this subject. From information about Kang Ayi contained in the *Spirit Way Stele for the Honorable Kang* composed by Yan Zhenqing 顏真卿 [referenced above], it can be seen that he and foreigners with a family background in Liucheng had much contact. For composing this stele, Yan Zhenqing must at least have seen

---

[85] Xie Haiping 謝海平, A Study and Review of the Life of Foreigners Staying in Tang Dynasty China 《唐代留華外國人生活考述》, pp. 46-7; Rong Xinjiang, "The Migrations and Settlements of the Sogdians in the Northern Dynasties, Sui, and Tang" 《北朝隋唐粟特人之遷徙及其聚落》, pp. 24-55; in the translated and edited version, pp. 142-4.

[86] See Wen Tingshi 文廷式, *The Digressions of Chunchangzi* [Wen Tingshi] 《純常子枝語》, ch. 8; and Kanda Kiichirō 神田喜一郎, "Notes on Zoroastrianism" 「祆教瑣記」, *Historical Review* 『史林』, vol. 18, no. 1 (1933), p. 16.

[87] Rong Xinjiang, "Sogdian Foreigners Movements after the An Shi Rebellion" 《安史之亂後粟特胡人的動向》, Ji Zongan 紀宗安 and Tang Kaijian 湯開建, editors-in-chief, *Ji'nan University Historical Studies* 《暨南史學》, vol. 2 (Guangzhou: Ji'nan University Press 暨南大學出版社, 2003), pp. 102-23.

their genealogies, or heard them telling even more stories than are recorded on the *Spirit Way Stele for the Honorable Kang*. Yan Zhenqing [here Lugong 魯公] as he was growing up received the childhood name "Muhu" 穆護. "Muhu" actually is a Zoroastrian clerical name: Yao Kuan 姚寬 in the first chapter of *A Thicket of Words by the Western Stream* 西溪叢語 says: "In the fifth year of the Tang Dynasty Zhenguan reign period (631), in order to pass on doctrines to disciples, the Zoroastrian missionary Muhu Helu went to the imperial residence to memorialize the throne about Zoroastrianism, and then an imperial edict ordered the erection of a Zoroastrian temple in the Chonghua ward of Chang'an 唐貞觀五年，有傳法穆護何祿將祆教詣闕聞奏，敕令長安崇化坊立祆寺." This is the clear proof that was needed.[88] This indicates that Yan Zhenqing probably had definite knowledge of Zoroastrianism from the Kang family.[89] Because of this it is not difficult to imagine that there was a connection between the Kang Ayi family and Zoroastrianism.

More important evidence exists in the deeds of An Lushan himself. The first chapter of *The Factual Traces of An Lushan* says:

> [An Lushan] hid among foreign (胡 hu) merchants in all the circuits 道 in which they did business. Each year he would convey from foreign lands precious treasures worth millions. Whenever merchants came to him An Lushan would sit on a large couch wearing foreign clothes, and he would burn incense and set out precious treasures, and command 100 foreigners to serve him on his left and right. The assembled foreigners surrounding him bowed down to him and supplicated themselves asking for blessings from heaven. An Lushan grandly set out livestock for sacrifice, and all the magi would beat drums, sing, and dance, which went on until dusk when all dispersed.[90]

---

[88] For details see Rao Zongyi 饒宗頤, "A Study of the Song Muhu" 《穆護歌考》, *Collected Works of Xuantang* (Rao Zongyi)*: Works on History* 《選堂集林·史林》, middle ch. (Hong Kong: Zhonghua Book Company 中華書局, 1982), pp. 472-509.

[89] Xiang Da 向達 in his "Tang Dynasty Chang'an and the Civilization of the Western Regions" 《唐代長安與西域文明》 on page 15 had already seen this type of connection, but precisely because he considered "Muhu" to be a Manichaean monk's name he was mistaken.

[90] *Factual Traces of An Lushan*, first ch., p. 12; R. des Rotours, *Histoire de Ngan lou-*

The final sentence in the "Biography of An Lushan" in the *New Tang History* reads: "[An Lushan] would grant an interview to a crowd of merchants, set out animals for sacrifice, and the magae 女巫 would beat drums and dance in front of him, believing he was deified." The activities of this ceremony from the beginning to the end were attended entirely by foreigners. In addition, An Lushan especially wore foreign clothing, indicating even more that what was engaged in here was a ceremonial activity of foreigners themselves.[91] Such a group of foreigners offering sacrifices to "heaven" 天 were, after all, sacrificing to which gods? "Heaven" actually means "xian" 祆 [the first character in the Chinese word for Zoroastrianism], and the "heaven" to which foreigners offered sacrifices was just the foreigner's heaven, that is to say the Zoroastrian gods. Prior to the Tang Dynasty, in the Chinese language there was no way to designate the character for the Zoroastrian spirit "xian" 祆, and ordinarily everyone used the character "heaven" 天 to express "xian" 祆, and the characters for "heavenly god" 天神 to express "Zoroastrian god" 祆神.[92] After entering Tang China, because they had the character "xian" 祆, people did not pay much attention to the fact that "heaven" 天 represented the meaning of "xian" 祆. Due to this, scholars have not paid attention to the fact that this sacrificial ceremony must have been Zoroastrian. Of course, merely from this passage, one can not easily consider the sacrificial ceremony of An Lushan and others to be Zoroastrian. However, we can compare it to the following from the third chapter of *Complete Stories of the Court and the People* 朝野僉載 recording the completely identical Zoroastrian activities of this type of

---

chan, pp. 108-9

[91] Cai Hongsheng 蔡鴻生 on page 37 of *Tang Dynasty Foreigners of the Nine Surnames and Turkish Culture* 《唐代九姓胡與突厥文化》 considers that this was a customary display of lavish one-upmanship among foreigners.

[92] See Chen Yuan 陳垣, "A Study of the Entry of Zoroastrianism in to China" 《火祆教入中國考》, *Journal of Sinological Studies* 《國學季刊》, vol. 1, no. 1 (1923); here I have relied on the author's 1934 corrected edition published in *Collected Academic Essays of Chen Yuan* 《陳垣學術論文集》, vol. 1 (Beijing: Zhonghua Book Company, 1980), pp. 303-28; Rong Xinjiang, "A Study of When Zoroastrianism was First Introduced to China" 《祆教初傳中國年代考》, in *Medieval China and Foreign Civilizations* 《中古中國與外來文明》, pp. 294-300.

foreign merchant in the Zoroastrian temple within Luoyang. This is clear at a glance:

> "In Lide 立德 ward and on the west side of South Market 南市 ward the Henan regional government has Zoroastrian temples, and each year foreign merchants pray for good fortune, cook pigs and sheep, play the pipa 琵琶, the drums, and the flute 笛, drink freely, sing songs, and dance drunkenly.[93]

Comparing these two passages, "each year foreign merchants" with "foreign merchants....Each year"; "cook pigs and sheep" with "set out livestock for sacrifice"; and "play the pipa, the drums, and the flute, drink freely, sing songs, and dance drunkenly" with "beat drums, sing, and dance" we see that both passages are cut from the same cloth. This proves that An Lushan was the kind of person that burned incense and worshipped, and this must be to a Zoroastrian deity; the places for these activities must be a Zoroastrian temple. The same situation can also be seen recorded in the "Monograph on Rituals" 禮儀志 section in the seventh chapter of the *History of the Sui* 隋書: "In the final years of the Houzhu 後主 reign period (565-576) of the Northern Qi 後齊 Dynasty, they did not worship the spirits of their dead, they arrived to personally beat drums and dance in order to serve the foreign gods, and in the Kingdom of Wei 鄴中 (220-265) many did not follow the correct rites, and these customs have continued without interruption down to the present day."[94] This indicates that these types of Zoroastrian religious ceremonial activities were of quite old origin.

The *New Tang History* records the sentence: "The magae would beat drums and dance in front of him, believing he was deified," which can not but make us think of the statement regarding An Lushan: "His mother, from the Ashide clan, was a Turkish maga. She had no son and so prayed to Yaluoshan, who responded and a son was born." This mythological story of course was told by An Lushan to be heard by his contemporaries. He himself was named as an incarnation of prayers being answered by the god Yaluoshan, either being called "Yaluoshan" or "Lushan," also having

---

[93] *Complete Stories of the Court and the People* 《朝野僉載》 (Beijing: Zhonghua Book Company facsimile edition, 1979), p. 64.

[94] *History of the Sui* 《隋書》, ch. 7 (Beijing: Zhonghua Book Company, 1973), p. 149.

this religious meaning. The fundamental religious doctrine of Zoroastrian worship of Ahura Mazdā, the source of light, stressed that Ahura Mazdā was the vanquisher of darkness (Angra Mainyu). W. B. Henning has already indicated that "Yaluoshan" or "Lushan" came from the Sogdian language *roχšan*, meaning "light, bright," and such a "Yaluoshan god" is exactly a "god of light," and as followers of Zoroastrianism worship a god of light,[95] this is a general term for deity or Zoroastrian god. In reality, among foreigners, An Lushan was without doubt an incarnation of the Zoroastrian "God of Light" and received people's worship. After his death Shi Siming posthumously conferred on Lushan the title "Emperor of Brightness" 光烈皇帝,[96] similarly getting the meaning "light" 光明. Shi Siming's given name "Sugan" 窣干, having the meaning in the Sogdian language of "shine" or "burn," was for this reason changed to "thinking deeply on brightness" 思明 (Siming). This similarly has a Zoroastrian flavor, and because of this Shi Siming also fully understood the reality underneath the surface of An Lushan's given name.

Further, it is worth paying attention to the fact that An Lushan's mother was a "Turkish maga" 突厥巫 and "prayed to the god Yaluoshan" 禱軋犖山神. Previous scholars seeing the character "magus/maga" 巫 (wu) in the historical materials of ethnic groups in the north of China called it shamanism, but this actually is a mistaken and indiscriminate copying of a Western anthropological concept. One must look at the context of the character "magus/maga" in historical materials for a concrete analysis. In reality the praying of the Ashide clan was that of Sogdian people introducing the Zoroastrian "God of Light" to the north of the Gobi Desert.[97] Based on the Bugut 布古特 stele inscription, Zoroastrian beliefs

[95] This god is also mistaken for a Manichaean deity. The introduction to the *Compendium of the Doctrines and Styles of the Teaching of Mani, the Buddha of Light* 《摩尼光佛教法儀略》 says: "Frēstag-rōšan 佛夷瑟德烏盧詵者, in translation the Apostle of Light, is also called the King of Law (dharamrāja) 法王 of perfect wisdom, and again Mani, the Buddha of Light. These are different designations of the response, transformation, and Dharma bodies 應化法身 of our unsurpassable, bright, and all-wise Healing King 醫王." The *Taisho Tripitaka* 《大正新修大藏經》, ch. 54, p. 1279, last column. Cf. Pulleyblank, *The Background of the Rebellion of An Lu-shan*, p. 111, note 37.

[96] *Factual Traces of An Lushan*, last ch., p. 41

[97] Wang Xiaofu 王小甫 in his essay cited above in footnote nine says: "When the Turkish magi prayed to Iranian gods it is clear beyond doubt that they acted as Zoroastrian high priests" (p. 37). The objects of prayer were regarded as Iranian gods, and the fundamental

spread early to the Turkish Qaghanate north of the Gobi Desert.[98] This maga of the Ashide clan must have been a Turkish maga and Zoroastrian high priest rolled into one. She was different from a pure Zoroastrian high priest, all of whom were male, but females also served in the role of high priests in a certain kinds of religions. The *New Tang History* records An Lushan and other people's activities as Zoroastrian high priests where "the maga would beat drums and dance in front of him, believing he was deified." Perhaps this was also the result of receiving the influence of Turkized Zoroastrian beliefs. An Lushan and Shi Siming were both warriors and did not have a high level of culture. They both conducted the activities of Zoroastrian high priests with a great flavor of sorcery, which can be completely understood.

---

view of the original draft of this essay is identical. Zhong Han 鍾焓 in his essay cited above in footnote nine says "In the Sogdian Zoroastrian Pantheon itself it was absolutely not the case that there was a name roχšan that could be a literal translation for the deity 'the God of Light.' Therefore is it possible to propose that the An family utilized this propitious portent at his birth to reach the conclusion that he was deified as the Zoroastrian 'God of Light'? This point is still not without doubt." However, in the notes he again says: "The Zoroastrian god Miθra (Mithra) to a certain extent possessed the qualities of a 'God of Light'" (pp. 69-70). The author believes that the "God of Light" in the An Lushan mythology must be a general term for the Zoroastrian great god, because the important thing facing An Lushan was the differing cultural knowledge of the people or soldiers, so it was not absolutely necessary to clarify the knowledge of which specific deities were involved.

[98] This point has been made even more certain by the discovery of the Bugut 布古特 stele, see S. G. Kljaštornyj and V. A. Livšic, "The Sogdian Inscription of Bugut Revised," *Acta Orientalia Hungaricae*, vol. 26, fasc. 1 (1972), pp. 69-102; L. Bazin, "Turc et Sogdien," in *Mélanges linguistiques offerts à Émile Benveniste* (Paris, 1975), pp. 37-45. Yoshida Yutaka 吉田豊, based on the latest on-the-spot inspection and textual research on the original stele text, for what earlier scholars read as the sentence "建立新的僧伽藍" (nwh snk' 'wst), he newly reads as "樹立教法之石" (nwm snk' 'wst), making a connection between this stele text and Zoroastrianism. See Moriyasu Takao 森安孝夫, ed., *Provisional Report of Researches on Historical Sites and Inscriptions in Mongolia from 1996 to 1998* 『モンゴル国現存遺迹·碑文調查研究報告』 (Toyonaka-shi 豊中市: Chūō Yūrashiagaku Kenkyūkai 中央ユーラシア学研究会, 1999), pp. 122-3. Gong Fangzhen 龔方震 and Yan Kejia 晏可佳, also based on the Zoroastrian terminology in the Bugut Sogdian language Turkish stele inscription, judge that the Turkish Tapar Qaghan 陀鉢可汗 had earlier once believed in Zoroastrianism; see those authors' *History of Zoroastrianism* 《祆教史》 (Shanghai Academy of Social Sciences Press 上海社會科學院出版社, 1998), p. 230.

For quite a long time in their life in their own settlements, Zoroastrianism was an important bond for uniting the Sogdians who had entered Tang China. Zoroastrian temples were a center for the religious activities of foreigner Zoroastrian high priests and played the role of solidifying foreigners' spirits.[99] An Lushan, when he played the part of the "God of Light," utilized the Zoroastrian beliefs of the Sogdian people to unite them. He did not merely unite the members of the foreign settlements from Liucheng to Youzhou, he also utilized the Sogdians' excellence at foreign trade, and united Sogdians from various scattered localities. He utilized Zoroastrian mystical preaching, using the title "God of Light" to appeal for support among the people and raise troops. This can give us an understanding of why so many people followed him into armed rebellion.

IV. Conclusion

Regarding the background of the An Lushan Rebellion, the academic world already has many research results, which is not necessary to repeat. Through the above investigation I only want to indicate the following points:

1) The main force of An Lushan's army was foreign 蕃 (fan) troops and foreign generals, and the important military leaders as a group by family background were of the Nine Zhaowu Surnames (Sogdians). Of these military leaders, some had led tribes commanded for many generations by their ancestors and descendants, and in these tribes had lineage relationships formed through marriage alliances. This type of tribal soldier, unified and good at fighting, was the main pillar of the An Shi Rebellion army.

2) An Lushan's family background was as a Sogdian, widely known for being good merchants. He was very familiar with prosperous merchant trade, and he had a deep knowledge of the principles of amassing wealth through commerce. Prior to raising an army, An Lushan dispatched Sogdian foreign traders to utilize the trade network that Sogdian

---

[99] Rong Xinjiang, "Foreigner Settlement Religious Beliefs and Social Function of Zoroastrian Temples in the Northern Dynasties, Sui, and Tang" 《北朝隋唐胡人聚落的宗教信仰與祆祠的社會功能》 in Rong Xinjiang, ed., *Tang Dynasty Religious Beliefs and Society* 《唐代宗教信仰與社會》 (Shanghai: Shanghai Lexicographical Publishing House 上海辭書出版社, 2003), pp. 385-412.

businessmen had built within the boundaries of the Tang Empire. They went to all areas engaging in business and trade, attracted foreign businessmen from all areas, and transported rare and precious treasures from foreign countries to the You 幽 and Yan 燕 regions in northeastern China. *Factual Traces of An Lushan* records that An Lushan many times gave tribute to Emperor Xuanzong 玄宗 of gold and silver plates and other items, and that Xuanzong granted him items in return, the value of which was not any less. This commerce and trade of accumulating wealth and offering and being granted objects in return constituted the economic basis of the An Lushan Rebellion.

3) An Lushan, by calling himself the incarnation of the "God of Light," and by personally taking charge of the activities of Zoroastrian high priests among groups of foreigners in the Sogdian settlements, made himself into the religious leader of the ordinary people of foreign tribes. He utilized religious power to unite Sogdians and foreign peoples within and outside of China's borders, and he utilized his identity as "God of Light" to appeal for support among the people. Regarding the large number of foreign 蕃 (fan) soldiers and generals who followed An Lushan in rising in rebellion, we can not but consider that the "God of Light" inspired their spirit and strength. I emphasize the religious background of why An Lushan rebelled and why he had the capability for rebellion: this is precisely the object of this essay.

This essay unhesitatingly stresses that Sogdian foreigners were a special aspect of the An Shi rebel army, and especially stresses the religious background for An Lushan's utilization of Zoroastrianism to launch the rebellion. However, this is only to make up for earlier scholars' insufficiencies in research regarding the An Shi Rebellion, and not at all to deny that the An Shi rebel army had an overall character consisting of many types of nationalities and many religions. Precisely because the An Shi Rebellion was not a single ethnic uprising, we can not regard the war between the Tang court and the An Shi rebel army as a struggle between nationalities.

But the leaders who initiated this rebellion, An Lushan and Shi Siming, after all were by family background Sogdian foreigners, and because of this, after the An Shi Rebellion, inside the borders of Tang China arose an attack on foreigners and a rejection of foreignization. There especially was a negative repercussion against foreignization in mid-Tang dynasty thinkers' circles, which evolved into the Renew Antiquity 復古 movement initiated by Han Yu 韓愈 and others. For Chinese classical culture this acted blindly as a high-level ideological trend, and it ultimately brought about the Song Dynasty introversion and weakness. If we consider the Tang-Song era changes from an even more macroscopic point of view, then we can not but trace these back to the An Shi Rebellion; in addition, we should also trace these changes back to the great background of the even more vast migratory movements of Asian continental peoples and the mutual influences of religious thought.

THE ESTABLISHMENT OF THE KHITAN STATE AND UYGHUR CULTURE

Wang Xiaofu 王小甫

Much excellent, systematic research has been done on the status and effect of the Uyghurs within the Khitan state and society.[1] However, very few scholars have mentioned the influence of the Uyghur culture of Manichaeism, characterized by its worship of light, on the development of Khitan society,[2] which is the purpose of my paper. Your criticisms and corrections are welcome.

1. *The problem of Abaoji's* 阿保機 *ascension to the throne and the myth of his birth*

The *History of the Liao* 遼史, "Annals of Taizu (the first part)" 太祖記上: "In the 12th month (of the third year of the Tianyou 天佑 reign period of the Tang Dynasty, 906 CE) Hendeji [written as 痕德堇 Hendejin] Qaghan passed away, and his ministers followed his will in establishing Taizu. Helu 曷魯 and others urged him to accept. Taizu thrice declined, then finally accepted." From the "Biography of Yelü Helu" 耶魯曷魯 in the same book: "When the Yaonian 遙輦 clan Hendeji Qaghan passed away, his ministers followed his will in establishing Taizu. Taizu declined,

---

[1] See Wang Riwei 王日蔚 "Research on Connections Between the Khitan and the Uyghurs" 《契丹與回鶻關係考》, *Journal of Historical Geography* 《禹貢》,vol. 4, no. 8 (Dec. 1935); Li Futong李符桐 "Connections Between the Uyghurs and the Foundation of the Liao Dynasty State"《回鶻與遼朝建國之關係》 (Taipei: Wen Feng Press 文風出版社, 1968), later included in Li Futong's essay collection *The Complete Collected Essays of Li Futong* 《李符桐論著全集》, vol. 2 (Taipei: Student Book Company, 1992), pp. 263-405; Wang Minxin 王民信 "The Formation of the Community of Khitan Royal Relatives on the Distaff Side" 《契丹外戚集團的形成》 in *Commemorative Essays on Khitan History* 《契丹史論叢》 (Taipei: Xue Hai Press 學海出版社, 1973), pp. 73-87.

[2] On the worship of light as the main characteristic of Manichaeism and the Uyghur adoption of Manichaeism, see Lin Wushu 林悟殊 "Questioning When Manichaeism Entered China" 《摩尼教入華年代質疑》 and "The Social Historical Origins of Uyghur Belief in Manichaeism" 《回鶻奉摩尼教的社會歷史根源》 in Lin Wushu 林悟殊, *Manichaeism and its Spread Eastward* 《摩尼教及其東漸》 (Zhonghua Book Company, 1987), p. 58 and pp. 87-99.

saying, 'Formerly our ancestor Yilijin 夷離董 Yali 雅里 declined the throne, so how could I now do what you say?' Helu said to him, 'Our former ancestor declined when there was no will and no auspicious sign and was urged by his compatriots to accept. Now you have the support of your predecessor, and both Heaven and Earth are in accord, as if their orders matched. Heaven cannot be disregarded, men cannot be brushed aside, and our lords cannot be disobeyed.' Taizu said, 'The will is as it is, but how do you know the way of Heaven?' Helu said, 'I have heard about your birth, where a Heavenly aura appeared and extraordinary fragrances filled the room. [Your mother] dreamt of a spirit guiding her and a dragon that gave her golden ornaments. The way of Heaven is known, and its virtue must be followed. Our country is weak, and we have been ravaged by our neighbors for a long time, which is why a saint was born to revive us. The Qaghan knew the will of Heaven, which is why he gave his order. The nine encampments of the Yaonian are close together and must have a leader; the lesser and greater ministers are all followers of yours, which is the will of Heaven. Your uncle Shilu 釋魯 once said, "I am like a snake, and my nephew is like a dragon. The will of Heaven and men cannot be disregarded." The next day the emperor ascended the throne, and ordered Helu to be in charge of civil and military affairs.' We can see that to carry out the revolution by a new surname, it was not enough to just have the will of his predecessor and the support of the ministers, but also auspicious signs of the 'way of Heaven' 天道 must appear to appease the hearts of the people."

In that case, where did these auspicious signs that Helu mentions come from? What was this "way of Heaven" that could produce saints and surpass worldly customs? I believe it was Manichaeism, the religion of light worship. Let us first take a look at the birth myth of Yelü Abaoji 耶律阿保機. Apart from the above section from the "Biography of Yelü Helu," the *History of the Liao* also has an account in the "Annals of Taizu": "He was born in the thirteenth year of the Xiantong 咸通 reign period of the Tang Dynasty. Previously his mother had dreamt that the sun fell down to rest in her breast, and she was with child. When she gave birth there was a magical light and a strange fragrance in the room. The baby had the body of a three-year-old and could immediately crawl. His grandmother the Jianxian 簡献 Empress thought this strange and bowed to him as her son. She often disguised him in other tents, or painted his face so that others would not know him. At three months he could walk; at one year could speak and foresaw events that had not occurred yet. He said himself it was as if he had gods guarding him on both sides." I have found that these myths of Abaoji's birth must have been mostly imitations of Manichaean birth and enlightenment myths.

Chapter one of *The Compendium of the Doctrines and Styles of the Teaching of Mani, the Buddha of Light* 摩尼光佛教法儀略 [hereafter, *The Compendium of the Doctrines*], "On (His) incarnation and native country, (His) names and titles, and (His) peculiar tenets" 託化國主名號宗教, excavated from Dunhuang says, "When he was about to be born, two spiritual lights [i.e. the Sun and the Moon] descended and split into three bodies of light: the one who received the teachings of tranquility from the Venerable Light 明尊 and was reborn was therefore called the Messenger of Light; the one with a sharp mind full of wisdom was called the Wise Dharma King; the one with a saintly soul and penetrating perception was called the Manichaean Buddha of Light. The light penetrated all within and without, the great wisdom reached the Heavens, and they reached the highest positions of veneration. Laozi caused a pregnancy and filled it with the light of the Sun. Sakyamuni received the fetus, and the sun combined with its image. Of nature and soul, what made the three saints special?…The Manichaean Buddha of Light was born in Persia in the palace of emperor Ba 跋, where Manyan 满艳, the wife of Jinsajianzhong 金薩健種, gave him birth….He was born from the chest and lived a special life. His spirit passed the nine tests of the sage, there were five auspicious Heavenly signs, and his life was not an ordinary one….The *Mahāmāyāsūtra* 觀佛三昧海經 says, 'When the Manichaean Buddha of Light was born, lights were often seen and taken to be Buddhist happenings.' The *Laozi Converts the Buddhists Sutra* 老子化佛經 says…'I rode the natural air of the light, flew to Persia in the jade land of Xinuo 西挪 and was seen as a prince. I abandoned my family for the Way and was called Mani.'"[3] It was said that "When he was 12 Mani had his

[3] *Manichaeism and its Spread Eastward*, appendix, "*The Compendium of the Doctrines and Styles of the Teaching of Mani, the Buddha of Light* annotated" 《〈摩尼光佛教法儀略〉釋文》, pp. 230-1. [Note the differences throughout this essay with the older English translation: G. Haloun and W. B. Henning, "The Compendium of the Doctrines and Styles of the Teaching of Mani, the Buddha of Light," *Asia Major*, new series, vol. 3 (1953), pp.189-92. Also, the *Laozi Converts the Buddhists Sutra* 《老子化佛經》 appears as the *Laozi Converts the Foreigners Sutra* 《老子化胡經》. Translator's note.]

first great vision, his second when he was 24."[4] When Mani began preaching, "Besides the broad front of those who rejected him were those who were inclined to recognize him as a true prophet. They said, 'Has a voice perhaps spoken to him in secret, and is he saying what has been revealed to him?…Has a face appeared to him in a dream and is he telling what he has seen?'"[5] It is not difficult to see that the main events of Abaoji's birth myth, such as "dreamt that the sun fell down to rest in her breast" ("when he was about to be born, two spiritual lights descended" and "born from the chest"), "a Heavenly aura" ("Messenger of Light," "light penetrated all within and without," and "when born, lights were often seen"), "at one year he could speak and foresaw events that had not occurred yet" ("a sharp mind full of wisdom" and "a saintly soul and penetrating perception"), and "dreamt of a spirit guiding her" all find their origins in the myth of Mani's birth and revelation.

A few other events concerning the birth myth of Abaoji can be found in Manichaean teachings. For example, "extraordinary fragrances filled the room" must have been a metaphor for the first of the five great spirits revered in Manichaeism, pure air.[6] The five great spirits are the bright universal elements of air, wind, light, water, and fire, all of which are the objects of worship in Manichaeism. The Manichaean Chinese hymnscroll *Hymns for the Lower Section* [i.e., believers] 下部贊 excavated from Dunhuang has the following "Eulogy of the Light World" 嘆明界文: "The trunk, branches, and leaves of the precious tree are covered in sweet

---

[4] Hans-Joachim Klimkeit, *Manichaean Art and Calligraphy* (Leiden: Brill, 1982), p. 4. In Chinese translation [德]克林凯特, *Ancient Manichaean Art* 《古代摩尼教藝術》, Lin Wushu 林悟殊, trans. (Sun Yat-sen University Press, 1989), pp. 22 and 24.

[5] "Cologne Mani Codex" 《科隆摩尼古卷》 86, 10-16, from Hans-Joachim Klimkeit, *Manichaean Art and Calligraphy* (Leiden: Brill, 1982), p. 5.

[6] This refers to the "five bright elements" of Manichaeism, i.e. pure air, brilliant wind, bright power, brilliant water, and brilliant fire. See the above mentioned *Manichaeism and its Spread Eastward*, p. 15. Klimkeit, on page nine of *Manichaean Art and Calligraphy* says, "In many texts he [the Father of Light] is also surrounded by five magnitudes, or five bright cosmological elements—ether, air, light, water, and fire. This pentad is correlated with five anthropological categories, the concepts of reason, mind, intelligence, thought and understanding" (p. 32 in the Chinese translation *Ancient Manichaean Art*). Clearly these five bright elements are the basic objects of worship in Manichaeism, so their names are mostly the same and have no differences of a fundamental nature.

dew, a fragrant air fills the world, and the precious flowers are colored red and white. The gardens of that state are expansive and silent, filled with extraordinary fragrances; there is nothing of ruins, brambles, and dirty grasses in this place"; "A fragrant aura fills the world, a single sea of unity, flowing everywhere unimpeded, in it the saints swim in the very finest fragrance."[7]

"Dragon that gave her golden ornaments" is a metaphor for the second of the five great spirits, brilliant wind. The difference between wind and air is that one can be heard, and the other can be smelled. *Hymns for the Lower Section* "Eulogy of the Light World" says: "The brilliant wind blows by and all are joyous, it blows freely in all directions, lightly brushing the treasured towers and houses, precious bells and chimes made everlasting sound"; "The brilliant sound of the eulogy pleases all, its clear, beautiful sound causes all to fall silent, all above and below tremble at the marvelous sounds, the elements of Sangharama could not lie still. The sound was quite extraordinary, the reverberating sounds telling of glorious virtue. All of the saints were pleased in the end, in a state of everlasting peace without tiring."[8] "As if he had gods guarding him on both sides" refers to the light messengers in Manichaeism, one form of the spirits of salvation. Studies have shown that in Manichaeism, "Jesus, the Virgin of Light, and Vahman formed a trinity that was often prayed to."[9] Jesus was just one identity of the Third Envoy; the Virgin of Light 惠明使 was often portrayed as a woman; and Vahman (大智甲 or 瓦孟) was the so-called guide of souls.[10]

A ninth century illustrated Manichaean scripture was excavated in the ancient city of Gaochang 高昌 at Turfan: "The black lines to the left of the pictures, however, contain the Middle Persian words *pdkr'i whman*, 'The Picture of Vahman'. From Central Asian hymns we know that Vahman had a close and special connection with the Manichaean church, which he indeed represented, being personified by the Manichaean *Archegos*, the highest representative of the church. We shall certainly not be wrong in assuming that it is this highest clerical dignitary that is here depicted (or at

---

7 *Manichaeism and its Spread Eastward*, appendix, "'Hymns for the Lower Section' annotated" 《〈下部讚〉釋文》, p. 256.

8 Ibid., pp. 256 and 258.

9 *Ancient Manichaean Art*, p. 97.

10 See ibid., pp. 35-6, 41, 78-9, 91-2, and 97-8.

least a senior bishop), the king kneeling in full armour before him. King and cleric grasp one another's right hand, which in the complex framework of Manichaean symbolism may be a reference to salvation." "But the soul resting on the bishop is *Vahman*, the personified spirit of the church...invoked as conductor of souls...he conducts the soul before the judge, who is God himself, here manifest in four-fold form." This "Picture of Vahman," or "image of the king" as it is called by scholars, is very helpful to us in understanding the "as if he had gods guarding him on both sides" part of Abaoji's birth myth. This is because "in Manichaean origin myths that are often brought up, even though the meaning of each section of text may be different, they can be explained by the same illustration"; and "The judging deity (called King of Pingdeng 平等王 in Chinese Manichaean scriptures – Wang Xiaofu) can also be interpreted as a person's own good deeds. A typically East Asian trait of Manichaeism is thus brought to light. The eschatological events at the end of time, judgment and eternal life, are now already coming to pass, are already taking place. The end events are partly de-eschatologized, psychologized, internalized. The adoption by the king of the holy religion marks him as now already justified, submitting to judgment."[11] Clearly, Abaoji was taken to be the trinity spirit of salvation, because of this spirit's deed of saving the king in Uyghur Manichaeism,[12] and this image suggests that Abaoji was the king who was saved. In other words, this spiritual deed was equivalent to declaring that Abaoji was born to be the king.

To summarize, almost all of the elements of Abaoji's birth myth can be traced to Manichaean myths and religion. Furthermore, we can find traces of Manichaean influence in some of Abaoji's more important measures and even in some Khitan customs.

We have already seen that after Yelü Helu finishes telling the myth of Abaoji's birth, he continues by saying, "The way of Heaven is known, and its virtue must be followed. Our country is weak, and we have been ravaged by our neighbours for a long time, which is why a saint was born to revive us." Under the background of the above birth myth, the so-called

---

[11] Hans-Joachim Klimkeit, *Manichaean Art and Calligraphy* (Leiden: Brill, 1982), pp. 35-6; in Chinese translation *Ancient Manichaean Art*, pp. 78-9, 42, and 79.

[12] Klimkeit believes: "Maybe either Bögü Khan is portrayed who embraced the 'religion of light' in 762, or another king who like him adopted Manichaeism with his retinue." Hans-Joachim Klimkeit, *Manichaean Art and Calligraphy* (Leiden: Brill, 1982), p. 35; in Chinese translation *Ancient Manichaean Art*, p. 78.

"saint" very likely is a metaphor for the third of the five great spirits in Manichaeism, bright power. The Manichaean *Hymns for the Lower Section* "Eulogy of the Light World" says, "The golden, hardened, precious Earth is exquisite, with innumerable brilliant colors shining around, the saints live there in peace unimpeded, forever free of restraint and worries. The images of the saints are quite extraordinary, their bodies full of collected light, the light of millions of Suns and Moons cannot match that of one fibre of their hair. Within and without there is not a shadow, their marvellous bodies in millions of variations, they travel around the golden Earth, with no weight in the slightest."[13] From this we can see that the Manichaean spirits and messengers are often called saints.[14] Taking a look at the *History of the Liao* we find that Abaoji is called a "saint" in many places. For example, in "Annals of Taizu (the first part)" for the first year of the Shence 神册 reign period (916) his honorific title is "Great Saintly Great Bright Heavenly Emperor" 大聖大明天皇帝, and the place where he was invested as emperor is called the "Saintly Forest of Investiture" 册聖林. The "Biography of Nichen Yelü Xiadi" 逆臣耶律轄底傳 says: "Taizu was about to ascend the throne, when he offered it to Xiadi 轄底. Xiadi said, 'The emperor is a saint appointed by heaven. How could your servant dare to take it!'" "Annals of Taizu (the last part)" says that in the sixth month of the third year of the Tianzan 天贊 reign period (924) Yelü Abaoji publicly predicted his own end and mentioned that "the bright king of saints will only be met once in ten thousand years," and "his brilliant schemes and saintly luck match that of those in Heaven." Abaoji's posthumous title at first was the Risen to Heaven Emperor 升天皇帝, and in the 26th year of the Tonghe 統和 reign period (1008) it became the Saintly First Emperor 聖元皇帝, and in the 21st year of the Zhongxi 重熙 reign period (1055) it once again changed to Great Saintly Great Bright Spirit Fierce Heavenly Emperor 大聖大明神烈天皇帝.[15]

---

[13] *Manichaeism and its Spread Eastward*, appendix, "'Hymns for the Lower Section' annotated", p. 254.

[14] This type of wording is common in Manichaean scriptures – see the appendix to *Manichaeism and its Spread Eastward.*

[15] See Liu Fengzhu 劉鳳翥 "A Study of Liao Taizu's Imperial Honorific Title and Posthumous Honorary Title" 《遼太祖尊號謚號考辨》 in *Social Sciences Journal* 《社會科學輯刊》, 1979, no. 1; included in Sun Jinyi 孫進已, et al., eds. *Compilation of*

It is worth noting that along with "Great Saintly," Abaoji was called "Great Bright," and even the words "Spirit Fierce" were used. The honorific title of Abaoji's Uyghur empress Shulü 述律 was "Responding to Heaven Great Bright Earthly Empress" 應天大明地皇后. This strengthens the Manichaean sense of light worship in these titles. The worship of light was at the center of the Manichaean faith, and its highest deity was called the "Venerable Light" or "Great Venerable Light." Its ideal world was called the "Bright Land," "Light Land," "Light Kingdom," or "Light Paradise." The Manichaean *Hymns for the Lower Section* "A Gāthā in Praise of the Unsurpassed Venerable Lord of Light" 嘆無上明尊偈 says, "Our long-lived Venerable Light father stays secluded in a peaceful place of great brightness. Higher than men or the Heavens, he stays steadfast without interfering with the state. For his own nature he opens the gate of wisdom, laying open the path to Nirvana. He shows us the sea of our nature and is the ancestor of the light world above and dark world below." "Eulogy of the Light World" of the same work says, "The Buddhas and Messengers of Light live there, which is where the Venerable Light lives. Light shines throughout and all is quiet, and there is long-lasting happiness without making sacrifices; they are pleased without aggravation, and bitterness is nowhere to be found"; "In the highest world of light the saints reside. With all the worlds as its territory, it sends down light to the golden, precious earth; time passes endlessly, nothing is ever shaken."[16]

Given this, we can believe that the "Bright King Tower" 明王樓 built in the second year after Abaoji ascended the throne could also have been a Manichaean place of worship within the palace. It is interesting that the first internal rebellion after Abaoji ascended the throne was related to this tower. Originally, even though Abaoji introduced the relatively developed Uyghur Manichaean culture, thereby justifying his replacement of the Yaonian clan, Khitan society was still on its way to developing a high level of cultural attainment. Abaoji's effort to mythologize his own method of replacing the Qaghan lineage with an imperial one was detrimental to the interests of the traditions of the nobility, which first led to the rebellion of Lage 剌葛 and others. This rebellion was raised and put

---

Works on Khitan History 《契丹史論著彙編》, first part (Liaoning Province Social Sciences Academy History Research Institute, 1988), pp. 235-6.

16 *Manichaeism and its Spread Eastward*, appendix, pp. 250-1, 253, 254, and 257-8.

down three times over the course of two years and included the following developments: "Lage led his people to the lake of the Yishijin 乙室堇, and as he had the imperial flags and banners he planned to crown himself. The empress dowager secretly sent someone telling him to flee…the emperor sent an army after him. Lage sent his ally Yindishi 寅底石 to march on the imperial residence, and they burned the army equipment and tents, setting their army loose on a killing spree. The empress hurriedly sent Shugulu 蜀古鲁 to the rescue, but he only could capture the imperial flags and drums. Lage's ally rushed to the western towers and burned the Bright King Tower. The emperor went to the Tu River 土河 [the modern Laoha River 老哈河]…and pursued Lage to the north…and ordered the prime minister of the north Diligu 迪里古 to lead the attack…Lage fled in defeat, and left the spirit tent 神帳 he captured along the road. The emperor saw it and paid his respects." The previous generation of scholars have pointed out that in this historical passage, "we can see that the spirit tent was with the Khitan tribes, and they likely were quite faithful people."[17] What exactly the spirit tent was we do not know, but the process of its gain and loss shows us that it was likely a construction of a religious nature as the Bright King Tower was. The Lage faction's burning of the Bright King Tower shows that at the time the cultural battles were very closely linked with the struggle for power. After one year Abaoji built the Kaihuang palace 開皇殿 on the foundation of the Bright King Tower,[18] and a year after that he was given an honorific title and established the Shence reign period, thereby formally establishing a state with an imperial lineage.

---

[17] See Chen Shu 陳述, *Khitan Government Historical Manuscripts* 《契丹政治史稿》 (People's Publishing House 人民出版社, 1986), p. 68.

[18] *History of the Liao: Annals of Taizu (the first part)* 《遼史・太祖紀上》. As for the meaning in Chinese history of titles like Kaihuang 開皇, Shihuang 始皇, and Huangshi 皇始, please see *Comprehensive Mirror for Aid in Government* 《資治通鑒》, ch. 7, 26th year of Qin Shihuang 秦始皇 (221 BCE) entry; and ch. 108, 21st year of the Taiyuan reign period of Jin Emperor Xiao Wudi 晉孝武帝泰元 (396 CE) notes to the entry "The Officials of the Northern Wei Urge their King Gui to Claim the Emperorship" 《魏群臣勸魏王珪稱尊號》. For related studies see Tian Yuqing 田餘慶 "The Formation and Development of the Inner Palace Institution of the 'Mandatory Suicide of the Birth Mother of the Crown Prince' after the Northern Wei" 《北魏後宮子貴母死之制的形成和演變》 in *Studies in Sinology* 《國學研究》, vol. 5 (1998), pp. 389 and 402-3 n. 81.

To add one more thought to this section, just as others have noticed, "dreamt of the sun entering her bosom" or "felt the sun and was with child" were myths of the birth of heroes common to China's northern and northeastern peoples.[19] My research at least shows that if the Khitan had this kind of traditional myth, then by Abaoji's time it already conformed with Uyghur Manichaean culture, something that cannot be said about similar myths of other ethnicities.

2. The location of Muye 木業 *Mountain and the "Black Ox and White Horse"* 青牛白馬 *legend*

There are other important Khitan customs which show the influence of Uyghur Manichaean culture, such as the so-called Muye Mountain sacrifice. The *History of the Liao: Monograph on Geography (1)* 遼史・地理志一 Supreme Capital Circuit 上京道 Yongzhou 永州 entry says, "[Yongzhou] was established by the Heavenly Empress Dowager, and this is where Taizu built the southern tower…the Huang River 黃水 [the modern Shira Muren/Mürin] in the east and Tu River in the south flow together here, which is why it is called Yongzhou[20]….It contains Muye Mountain on which were built Khitan ancestral temples. Qishou 奇首 Qaghan is in the southern temple, and Kedun 可敦 is in the northern one. They contain paintings and statues of the two saints and their eight sons. It is said that a divine man rode a white horse from Mayu 馬盂 Mountain eastward floating along the Tu River. A heavenly woman rode a black oxcart from the flat pine forest floating along the Huang River. At Muye Mountain the two rivers met, and the two became a couple, giving birth to eight sons. Their descendants gradually prospered, dividing into eight tribes. Whenever they send out their army or when spring and autumn arrives, they use a white horse and black ox, signifying that they have not forgotten their origin." This is the most important entry on the Muye Mountain sacrifice and the so-called Khitan ancestors. Furthermore, recent research has shown that for many reasons there still has not been an

---

[19] For example, long before the Khitan, Koguryŏ 高句麗 had the legend that the ancestor's mother felt the sun and became pregnant – see *History of the Wei: Account of Koguryŏ* 《魏書・高句麗傳》.

[20] The Chinese character "yong" 永 consists of other two characters, one of which means "two" and the other of which means "river".

adequate explanation of the meaning and pronunciation of Qishou Qaghan and the location of Muye Mountain, and the tale of the joining of the white horse spirit and black ox heavenly maiden is still shrouded in mystery.[21] Actually, it has long been thought that the myth of the Black Ox and White Horse cannot be traced to actual events, but that after Abaoji replaced the Yaonian clan and ascended the throne, "he created the story of the Spirit and the Heavenly Maiden to instil fear in those tribes who would not submit, and to show that the cooperation between the Diela 迭剌 clan and the Uyghurs was completely in line with the affairs of heaven and earth, or in other words, that it was all arranged by the Heavenly Emperor."[22] Recently, others have pointed out that "the Khitan origin legend was borrowed from the Uyghurs."[23] These views may not give us all of the answers, but provide useful points of view for helping to decipher this mystery.

I am not interested in denying that the Khitans had their own ancestral legend and totemic worship, but just want to say that the above legend from the *History of the Liao: Monograph on Geography* is not necessarily the original version and may have been the result of integration with Uyghur Manichaean culture during Abaoji's time.

First, Muye Mountain was not the birthplace of the Khitan ancestor Qishou Qaghan, and the divine man and heavenly woman did not give birth to the Khitan ancestor, but rather the eight sons whose numbers multiplied. The *History of the Liao: Monograph on Geography (1)* Supreme Capital Circuit "Longhua Prefecture" 龍化州 entry says, "[Longhua Prefecture] was originally Anping County 安平縣 of northern

---

[21] See Liu Pujiang 劉浦江, "The Historical Memory of the Khitan People—Taking the 'Black Ox and White Horse' Legend as its Center" 《契丹族的歷史記憶——以"青牛白馬"說為中心》 (hereafter "The Historical Memory of the Khitan People") in *Collection of Commemorative Essays for Mr. Qi Xia* 《漆俠先生紀念文集》 (Hebei University Press, 2002), pp. 157, 160, and 164-5. Here I would like to thank Mr. Liu's masterful work with its abundance of materials that have helped me immensely.

[22] Wang Minxin 王民信, "The Relationship between the Ancient Eight Tribes of the Khitan and the Dahe, Yaonian, and Diela Clans" 《契丹古八部與大賀遥輦迭剌的關係》 in *Commemorative Essays on Khitan History* 《契丹史論叢》, p. 47.

[23] Yang Fuxue 楊富學, "A Discussion of the Origin Myth of the Khitan People Borrowed from the Uyghurs" 《契丹族源傳説借自回鶻論》 in *Essays on the Historical Culture of Chinese Northern Nationalities* 《中國北方民族歷史文化論稿》 (Gansu People's Press, 2001), pp. 144-55.

China. The Khitan ancestor Qishou Qaghan resided here, and it was called Longting 龍庭 (dragon hall). Taizu built here the eastern tower…in the first year of the Tianyou reign period (904) he built the eastern city, which was quite magnificent to behold. In the 13th year, at Jinlinggang 金鈴岡 east of the city Taizu received the honorific title of Great Saintly Great Bright Heavenly Emperor and founded the Shence reign period." "Annals of Taizu (the first part)" states that three years before Yelü Abaoji became emperor and founded his state (913) he once "climbed Du'an 都庵(菴) Mountain carrying the historical remains of his ancestor Qishou Qaghan and wandered about casting glances and sighing." Apparently Longhua Prefecture and Du'an Mountain were more or less in the same place.[24] Therefore, "Annals of Taizu" eulogizes, "Qishou was born on Du'an Mountain and moved to the shores of the Huang River." Clearly, the achievements of the true Khitan ancestor must have been constructed in his place of residence, the dragon hall, and moving the sacrificial shrine to Muye Mountain of Yongzhou on the shores of the Huang River was only done in response to the needs of Abaoji to become emperor and found his state. Therefore, the sacrificial temple of Muye Mountain was really for another sacrifice, and the Black Ox and White Horse referred to someone other than Qishou Qaghan.

Second, the important names related to Muye Mountain reflect the same geographical characteristics. The *History of the Liao: Explication of the National Language* 遼史・國語解 says, "Yongzhou lies between the Huang and Tu Rivers, so it was called Yongzhou, as the character 'Yong' stands for 'two' and 'water.'" Even though the above mentioned section of *History of the Liao: Monograph on Geography* says that Yongzhou was built in the Liao Dynasty during the reign of Emperor Shengzong 聖宗 by the Chengtian 承天 Dowager Empress, it received its name rather late, and the local geographical characteristics would have formed long before that. I believe that the name "Qishou" 奇首 of the so-called Khitan ancestor can be understood further from the local geographical characteristics. We still do not fully understand the meaning of the word "Qishou" in the Khitan language. But looking from another point of view, "Qishou" may have been a transliteration of the Uyghur "eki sub / ekki süw,"[25] which

[24] See Liu Pujiang 劉浦江, "The Historical Memory of the Khitan People," p. 160.

[25] The former is found in an eighth-century Turkic stele; see Talât Tekin, *A Grammar of Orkhon Turkic*, chapter 4 "Vocabulary List" (Indiana University Press, 1968), pp. 330

meant two waters or two rivers. This type of Uyghur reading can be explained by following the path of transmission of Manichaeism. As is widely known, the central Asian Sogdian merchants were mainly responsible for the transmission of Manichaeism within the Uyghur tribes, and the breaking off of the initial vowel is a characteristic of the Sogdian language. The most famous example is the chief Zoroastrian god Ahura Mazda, whose name became Xurmazta in the Sogdian language, and once it was again transmitted to the grasslands it became the great deity Hormusda, who is still part of the traditional faith of Mongols and northeastern ethnic groups of China today.[26] Therefore, the Khitan ancestor's name of Qishou Qaghan must have been given after they moved to the shores of the Huang River, or in other words, it was given based on the Uyghur Manichaeism teachings of Abaoji's time.

Another related place name is the so-called Yelü clan's prefecture 郡 of origin, Qishui 漆水 (Qi River). Liu Pujiang 劉浦江 has done a great deal of work on geography in his paper "The Historical Memory of the Khitan People," and even though he cannot solve this mystery, he puts forth a useful hypothesis: "'Qishui,' which was seen by the Khitan as the Yelü clan's prefecture of origin, should be looked for within the area of early Khitan activity. I believe that the reason Qishui Prefecture was named thus may have been similar to the Jinyuan 金源 Prefecture of origin of the Jurchen Wanyan 完顏 clan. The Jin Dynasty did not have an administrative area called Jinyuan Prefecture; rather, it originated in the Jurchen area of origin, the Anchuhu River 按出虎水, and similarly, Qishui must have been a river as well. We can make a courageous guess that Qishui may have been another name for the Huang or Tu Rivers, or for one of their branches." By using Liu's guess we are nearly at our goal, we just need to take Qishui to be a transliteration of a Uyghur word and the mystery can be solved. I believe that Qishui is like Qishou in that both are transliterations of the Uyghur words "eki sub / ekki süw" and were simply two different spellings used in different situations. Their meaning is "two

---

and 369. The latter is found in an 11th century dictionary, see Mahmūd al-Kāshgharī, *Compendium of the Turkic Dialects*, vol. 3 (Duxbury, Mass.:Tekin, 1985), pp. 21 and 169 [an edition of *Dīwān lughāt al-Turk* (*Compendium of the Languages of the Turks*)].

[26] See Wang Xiaofu 王小甫, *The History of Political Relations between the Tang, Tibet, and the Arabs in Central Asia (634-792 A.D.)* 《唐、吐蕃、大食政治關係史》 (Peking University Press, 1995), pp. 243-4 and 247.

waters" or "two rivers," and they were located around the ancestral temples or Muye Mountain in the area later named Yongzhou. With the series of works from Abaoji's time we are justified in saying that this was the Yelü clan's prefecture of origin.

Finally, we can take the same point of view in looking at the name Muye Mountain itself. The *New History of the Five Dynasties* 新五代史 in the "Account of the Khitan in the Supplementary Record of the Four Barbarian Tribes" 四夷附錄契丹 says, "They lived in a place called Xiaoluoge 梟羅個 Moli 没里. Moli means 'river.'" I believe that the word "Muye" 木業 may also have been a transliteration of the Khitan word for "river." We can compare these two transliterations: from the pronunciations in the *Extended Rhymes* 廣韵 rime book we can take the pronunciation of "Moli" to be *muətlĭə and the pronunciation of "Muye" to be *mukjɛĭp.[27] Jia Jingyan 賈敬顔 says, "'Moli' is the Mongolian word 'mure[n].'" [28] Comparing these two transliterations with the pronunciations of the original words, only the pronunciation of the character "ye" 業 and the initial "yu" 余 are slightly different, but not so different as to be incompatible. For example, Guo Xiliang's 郭錫良 *Handbook of Ancient Pronunciation of Chinese Characters* 漢字古音手冊 takes the ancient pronunciation of the initial "'yu' 餘 to have changed to a different 'yu' 余, and Wang Li 王力 has recently changed his reconstruction of this pronunciation to ɫ, a lateral sound corresponding to the nj position."[29] "nj" is the initial consonant of the Chinese word "ri" 日. The "shetouyin" 舌頭音 (tip of the tongue) "linniu" 鄰紐 category of initials in Old Chinese were *duan* 端 (t), *tou* 透 (t'), *yu* 余 (ɫ), *ding* 定 (d), *ni* 泥 (n), and *lai* 來 (l), and the "zhunshuangsheng" 准双声 (similar initials) were *ni* 泥 (n) and *ri* 日 (nj), and all could have undergone shifts

[27] See Guo Xiliang 郭錫良, *Handbook of Ancient Pronunciation of Chinese Characters* 《漢字古音手冊》 (Peking University Press, 1986), pp. 26, 36, 83, and 107.

[28] See Jia Jingyan 賈敬顔, *Collected Studies of Ancient Northeastern Nationalities Ancient Geography* 《東北古代民族古代地理叢考》 (China Social Sciences Press, 1994), p. 13.

[29] See Wang Li 王力, "Introductory Remarks" 《例言》 in *China Social Sciences* 《中國社會科學》, 2004, no. 4, pp. 4-5.

in pronunciation.[30] Even though this is the case for Old Chinese, this situation also could occur between different ethnic languages. For example, the Mongolian word for "river" was transliterated as "munian" 木輦 in early Yuan Dynasty texts,[31] and the Geography section of the *Translated Words Written in the Zhiyuan Reign Period* 至元譯語・地理門 [the earliest Sino-Mongol glossary] compiled in the early Yuan has the transliteration "mulian" 木連.[32] Therefore, it is possible that Muye was a transliteration from Mongolian into the Khitan "muren/ mürin" or "river." The Khitan language is generally recognized as an older form of ancient Mongolian,[33] and in Mongolian "the category of countable nouns when they do not have additional plural elements is uncertain, they can be both singular and plural."[34] Therefore, Muye may have meant two rivers or many rivers in the Khitan language, with the same meaning as the Uyghur transliterations Qishou and Qishui, like the implied meaning of the Chinese Yongzhou.

From this we can see that the name Muye Mountain refers to its geographical location, which was undoubtedly where the above quoted *History of the Liao: Monograph on Geography* clearly states: "where the Huang River in the east and the Tu River in the south meet." This lasted through to the Liao Dynasty Emperor Xingzong 興宗 era, when there was

---

30 See Wang Li 王力, *Dictionary of Cognate Words* 《同源字典》 (Beijing: Commercial Press, 1982), pp. 79-80.

31 E.g. Liu Yu's 劉郁 *Record of an Embassy to the West* 《西使記》; see Wang Guowei 王國維, *Four Ancient Travel Diaries* 《古行記四種》, p. 8 in *Posthumous Papers of Wang Guowei* 《王國維遺書》, vol. 13 (Shanghai Ancient Books Book Company 上海古籍書店). Also see Tan Qixiang 譚其驤, ed., *The Historical Atlas of China* 《中國歷史地圖集》, vol. 7, pp. 36-7.

32 See Jia Jingyan 賈敬顏, Zhu Feng 朱鳳, co-editors, *Compilation of the Mongol Translated Words and the Nüzhen* (Jurchen) *Translated Words* 《蒙古譯語、女真譯語彙編》 (Tianjin Ancient Books Press 天津古籍出版社, 1990), p. 2. [*Mongol Translated Words* 《蒙古譯語》 is another name for *Translated Words Written in the Zhiyuan Reign Period* 《至元譯語》, translator's note.]

33 Jia Jingyan 賈敬顏 believes that, "it should be believable that the Khitan spoke an older form of ancient Mongolian with a heavy palatal pronunciation." See his "Khitan Script" 《契丹文》 in *Ancient Scripts of Chinese Nationalities* 《中國民族古文字》 (China Nationalities Ancient Scripts Research Committee, 1982), pp. 106-7.

34 Dao Bu 道布, ed., *A Brief Survey of the Mongolian Language* 《蒙古語簡誌》 (Beijing: Nationalities Press 民族出版社, 1983), p. 22.

even the saying "Muye Mountain Liao river spirit" in the *History of the Liao: Monograph on Ritual (1)*. The problem is that there is no mountain (Chinese "shan" 山) in this location,[35] so I believe this character "shan" should be explained in another way. I have noticed that the *History of the Liao: Monograph on Ritual* first lists the "mountain sacrifice ceremony" 祭山儀, which is the so-called Muye Mountain sacrifice, and in this entry no mountains are mentioned. According to the *History of the Liao: Monograph on Ritual* there are four main parts to the so-called mountain sacrifice ceremony: sacrifice to the spirit tablets of the Deities of Heaven and Earth, traveling around and going through the heavenly gate trees, sacrifice to the East (worshiping the Sun, see below), and once again a sacrifice to the spirit tablets of the Deities of Heaven and Earth. The entire sacrificial activity begins and ends with the Deities of Heaven and Earth, so we can be sure that it is a sacrifice to heaven and has nothing to do with mountains and is not carried out on a mountain. Considering that the traditional rites begin with the rites of the sacrifice to heaven, I would like to make a bold proposal: the "mountain sacrifice ceremony" is a ceremony of sacrifice to heaven with Khitan characteristics, and the so-called "shan" 山 (mountain) is a character mistakenly taken to be the pronunciation of the Chinese character "tian" 天 (Heaven). Muye Mountain (Shan) is actually Muye Tian, i.e. sacrifice to heaven at the two rivers. The method of eliciting the location from the contents of the sacrificial ceremony is the same as that seen in early materials that call the location of the sacrifice to the Zoroastrian god (Hutianshen 胡天神) Hutian 胡天.[36] In the early Khitan state there were few cultural objects, and many names of systems were borrowed from the Chinese, and errors in pronunciation occurred,

---

[35] See Liu Pujiang 劉浦江, "The Historical Memory of the Khitan People," p. 164.

[36] *History of the Jin: Shi Jilong Chronological Records, Last Part* 《晉書・石季龍載記下》: "Sun Fudu 孫伏都 and Liu Zhu 劉銖 of Longxiang 龍驤 gathered three thousand Jie 羯 warriors and hid them in Hutian 胡天 in hopes of killing [Ran] 冉 Min 閔." *Comprehensive Mirror for Aid in Government*, ch. 98, fifth year of the Yonghe 永和 reign period of Emperor Mu 穆 of the Jin 晉 Dynasty (349) entry "The Zhao emperor [Shi] Jian commanded the Leping King [Shi] Bao)" 《趙主鑒使樂平王苞》 records this event, and the note reads, "Hutian is the name of the forbidden residence of the Shi 石 clan." See Tang Zhangru 唐長孺, "A Study of Mixed Foreigners in the Wei and Jin" 《魏晉雜胡考》 in *Commemorative Essays on Wei, Jin, and Northern and Southern Dynasties History* 《魏晉南北朝史論叢》 (Sanlian Press, 1978), pp. 416-7.

such as "changwen" 敞穩 or "changgun" 常衮 for "jiangjun" 將軍, "xiangwen" 詳穩 for "xianggong" 相公, "lingwen" 令穩 for "linggong" 令公, "changshi" 敞史 for "zhangshi" 长史, and "dashi" 大石 for "taishi" 太師.[37] I believe the name of the mountain sacrifice ceremony was created in this way, and Muye Shan was simply an error in pronunciation. Using database software to search the *History of the Liao*, I found that there are no descriptions of mountainous terrain in the passages relating to Muye Shan, so we can see that it was not a mountain at all, and it only became a mountain when later scholars made the textual association with a mountain.

I also suspect that the mountain sacrifice ceremony of Muye Shan was really a type of Manichaean religious ceremony that integrated old Khitan customs of sacrificing to Heaven. For example, the *History of the Liao: Monograph on Ritual (1)* says that during the ceremony they must "plant two trees to be the spirit gate;" and "Manichaeism often employs the concept of planting two trees to represent the two worlds, one is called the Bright Tree of Life and the other the Dark Tree of Death."[38] Also, from the *History of the Liao: Monograph on Ritual* we can see that the mountain sacrifice ceremony is filled with a strong consciousness of worshiping the Sun and the East, which may have been a reflection of the Manichaean teachings that in the end souls pass through the Sun Palace on their way to the Heaven of Light. Then the deity to which they sacrificed may have likely been similar to the one referred to by the name "Muye Shan," the Heavenly spirit of water, which alludes to the fourth of the five Manichaean spirits, brilliant water. Here the geographical characteristics are most suitable for showing worship of water. The Manichaean *Hymns for the Lower Section* "Eulogy of the Light World" says, "The hundred lakes, streams, rivers, and source of the spring are all pure, fragrant, and exquisite; if you enter them you will not float or sink, and there is no violent water that will do you harm"; "There are countless types of precious mountains in that land, as well as innumerable types of fragrant smokes; within and without light purifies the body, in an endless sea of sweet dew. The clear spring flows unending, the sweet dew is free from bitterness; the saints have all they could ever need, as this place is never

---

37 See Jia Jingyan 賈敬顏, "Khitan Script," op. cit., p. 99.

38 *Manichaeism and its Spread Eastward* 《摩尼教及其東漸》, p. 14. See *Ancient Manichaean Art* 《古代摩尼教藝術》, pp. 71-2.

lacking."[39] This revered spirit was Qishou Qaghan, the ancestor Abaoji tried so hard to introduce and mythologize. Of course, the purpose for which Abaoji mythologized his ancestor was simply to mythologize himself.

One sacrifice to both Heaven and Earth may have been an old custom of the Khitan, but evidence for the counterparts of the juxtaposed Deities of Heaven and Earth can be found in Manichaean mythology. As mentioned above, in Manichaeism, Jesus, the Virgin of Light, and Vahman formed a trinity that was often prayed to. However, Jesus was just a split phase of the Third Envoy, the Virgin of Light was often portrayed as a woman, and Vahman was the guide of souls, who could also be considered as a metaphor for a king who has attained salvation. This myth could solve the problem surrounding the fact that the Deities of Heaven and Earth appear in the mountain sacrifice ceremony as two phases of one deity, as well as the problem of Qishou Qaghan and Kedun's pairing as heterosexual figures in the ancestral legend. Even more amazingly, coupled with the birth myth of Abaoji ("As if he had gods guarding him on both sides"), it further strengthened the form and status of Abaoji's spiritual and legal legitimacy.

The key to understanding the Black Ox and White Horse of the Khitan ancestral myth is that Qishou Qaghan and the eight sons of the Divine Man and Heavenly Maiden mythologized by Abaoji belong on two completely different categorical levels. Abaoji's ancestor was a Heavenly deity, and the eight sons who symbolized the ancestors of the eight tribes of the Khitan were ordinary men.[40] I believe the Black Ox and White Horse were not the Deities of Heaven and Earth for the following primary reasons:

---

[39] *Manichaeism and its Spread Eastward*, pp. 255 and 256.

[40] The Khitan did not have only eight tribes. See Yang Zhijiu 楊志玖, "A Study of Abaoji's Ascent to the Throne" 《阿保機即位考辨》 in *Bulletin of the Institute of History and Philology Academia Sinica* 《中央研究院歷史語言研究所集刊》, vol. 17 (April 1948). Therefore, the eight tribes have only a passed-down symbolic meaning, and it is difficult to conduct thorough historical research on them. Or, this can be understood as just a forced comparison resulting from the influence of the eight Xianbei 鮮卑 tribes. For related materials see *History of the Liao: Monograph on Imperial Guards, Middle Section: Tribes, First Part* 《遼史·營衛志中·部族上》. For the most recent material see Liu Pujiang's 劉浦江 "The Historical Memory of the Khitan People," pp. 160-2.

1. According to the *Record of the Lands North of Yan* 燕北錄 by Wang Yi 王易 of the Song Dynasty, "The Red Maiden is called 'Lüehu'ao' 掠胡奥 in the barbarian language. Legend has it that she was found in the stream of the Huang River by the seven riders of Yinshan 陰山, and she gave birth to their people. Her likeness was made into a wooden statue painted with color that is often found in the temple of Muye Shan. Each time the leader of the barbarians holds the Firewood Investiture Ceremony 柴册禮, this statue is taken from the temple and returned three days afterwards."[41] Just as Liu Pujiang says in his "The Historical Memory of the Khitan People," "This so-called Red Maiden is clearly the Heavenly Maiden who floated down the Huang River on the Black Oxcart." At the same time, the Muye Shan temple contains the likenesses of Qishou Qaghan and Kedun, so the Black Ox Heavenly Maiden could not be the Deity of Earth. In *History of the Liao: Monograph on Ritual (1)* the notes to the Khitan "Firewood Investiture Ceremony" 柴册儀 mention "placing it in the room for searching for the reborn empress mother," and at first this is the only idol of the ceremony. This must be the Red Maiden and signifies that the invested Qaghan has been reborn in this world.

2. The *History of the Liao: Biography of Taizu Chunqin Empress Shulü* (note: Yelü Abaoji's Uyghur empress, see section four below) 遼史・太祖淳欽皇后述律氏傳 says: "The Empress was firm and resolute and made ingenious plans. Once she went to the meeting place of the Liao and Tu Rivers, where there was a maiden riding a cart pulled by a black ox. The maiden hastily made way and soon disappeared. Not long after there was a folk tale that went, 'The Black Ox Maid once made way.' The saying goes that the Black Ox Maid is the Deity of Earth. After Taizu became emperor, his servants gave her the honorific title of Earth Empress." Clearly, this folk tale is a prophecy that the empress Shulü 述律 was Kedun from the legend and the Deity of Earth from the mountain sacrifice ceremony. Even the Black Ox Maid (or Red Maiden) made way for her, thereby implying the Earth Empress was sent by Heaven. Even if the Black Ox Maid was the Deity of Earth, why would she make way for empress Shulü, and what deity would that make Shulü? We can see that

41 This is the same Huang River mentioned above that refers to the Xar Moron (Shira Muren) River in eastern Inner Mongolia. Luo Bingliang 羅炳良, ed., *An Unofficial History of China: Liao, Xia, Jin, and Yuan Dynasties* vol. 《中華野史・遼夏金元卷》 (Taishan Press, 2000), p. 10.

the phrase, "the saying goes that the Black Ox Maid is the Deity of Earth," was later added unnecessarily out of ignorance and an effort to force an explanation. Incidentally, according to one study the empress was called "Telijian" 忒里蹇 in the Khitan language, with the honorific name of "Nouwome" 耨斡麼, but "Kedun" was a Turkic and Uyghur name.[42] This serves as supplementary evidence for the argument that the titles Qishou Qaghan and Kedun came from the era when Yelü Abaoji married a Uyghur (a Manichaean).

3. The hardest part to understand is why the Khitan often sacrificed a black ox and white horse.[43] For example, the above section from the *History of the Liao: Monograph on Geography (1)* says, "Whenever they send out their army or when spring and autumn arrive, they use a white horse and black ox, signifying that they have not forgotten their origin." The Taiwanese scholar Wang Minxin 王民信 has pointed out that, "It was irrational for them to sacrifice a black ox and white horse. The black ox and white horse helped to found the Khitan people, so why did they have to be killed in order to 'signify that they have not forgotten their origin'? The Turkic people 'came from wolves,' so they 'put golden wolf heads on their flags…as they came from wolves, and to signify that they had not forgotten their origin.' The Turks did not sacrifice wolves in their ceremonies. The Manchu ancestors were said to have been saved by a magpie, and they did not shoot down magpies in a sacrifice to Heaven, showing that they had not forgotten their origin. Not only does it go against common sense for the Khitan to kill a black ox and white horse to sacrifice to Heaven, but such action is not recorded in the *Encyclopaedic History of Institutions* 通典 or in either version of the *Tang History*."[44] Even though there are instances of the ancient northern and northeastern

[42] See Wang Minxin 王民信, "The Relationship between the Ancient Eight Tribes of the Khitan and the Dahe, Yaonian, and Diela Clans" 《契丹古八部與大賀遥輦迭剌的關係》 in *Commemorative Essays on Khitan History* 《契丹史論叢》, p. 45.

[43] Feng Jiasheng 馮家昇 has detailed statistics on this, see his "The Relationship between Khitan Conventions of Worship and other Religious Mythological Customs" 《契丹祀天之俗與其宗教神話風俗之關係》 in *A Compilation of the Best Works of Feng Jiasheng* 《馮家昇論著輯粹》 (Zhonghua Book Company, 1987), pp. 51-7.

[44] Wang Minxin 王民信, "The Relationship between the Ancient Eight Tribes of the Khitan and the Dahe, Yaonian, and Diela Clans," p. 46.

peoples of China sacrificing white horses,[45] this was not done because they were totems signifying their ancestors, nor was it because they represented heavenly spirits. The purpose of sacrifice was to curry favor with the objects of the sacrifice, so what was the reason for sacrificing the representative or signifier of the sacrificial object?

Overall, this type of phenomenon that lay between the secular and the religious worlds and was both related to tribal origins and required the use of sacrifice was not commonly seen. As a black ox was sacrificed along with the white horse, we must consider other cultural elements of the entire tradition. Feng Jiasheng 馮家昇 has pointed out that, "are not the man and woman mentioned like Adam and Eve?"[46] Unfortunately Feng did not elaborate on this point. Actually, considering cultural factors of Uyghur Manichaeism, taking the divine man and heavenly maiden to be Adam and Eve is the most suitable explanation.

Studies have shown that Manicheans believed that in order to stop elements of light from attaining salvation, the Prince of Darkness created a pair of devils to swallow other animals in order to collect and imprison the light in their bodies. These devils mated and gave birth to two bodies, the origin of the human race, Adam and Eve. Even though the bodies of Adam and Eve were made of dark material, their souls were formed from elements of light. Manicheans believed that the human body was a small

---

[45] See Feng Jiasheng 馮家昇, "The Relationship between Khitan Conventions of Worship and other Religious Mythological Customs," in *A Compilation of the Best Works of Feng Jiasheng* 《馮家昇論著輯粹》, pp. 68-9. Also, when Tang Taizong 唐太宗 first ascended the throne, he killed a white horse and swore allegiance with Illig (Jieli 頡利) Qaghan at Bian Bridge 便橋 (both *Tang Histories: Account of the Turks* 《唐書・突厥傳》); when Su Dingfang 蘇定方 attacked Baiji 百濟, he sacrificed a white horse along the bank of the river (*Survey of the Geography of the Eastern State* (Korea), *Revised and Augmented* 《(新增)東國輿地勝覽》, vol. 18, "The Historical Sites of Chungcheongnam-do, Gongju Jin, and Buyeo Hyun" 《忠清右道公州鎮扶餘縣古迹》). Evgeniia Ivanova Derevianko's (Евгения Иванова Деревянко) *Amur Tribes of the First Millennium A.D.* (*Племена Приамурья. I тысячелетие нашей эры*, original in Russian, translated into Chinese as [俄]E・I・傑烈維揚科, *Tribes Along the Banks of the Heilongjiang* 《黑龍江沿岸的部落》) also mentions several similar examples from ancient nationalities (Lin Shushan 林樹山 and Yao Feng 姚鳳, trans.), p. 294.

[46] "An Interpretation of the Black Ox and White Horse as Khitan Worship" 《契丹祀天以青牛白馬之解釋》 in *A Compilation of the Best Works of Feng Jiasheng* 《馮家昇論著輯粹》, p. 63.

world which contained both elements of light and dark materials. The dark materials were primarily greed and desire, which promoted the promulgation of the human race in order to ensure that the elements of light would be imprisoned in humans' bodies without attaining salvation for generation after generation. No matter what, the human race began with Adam and Eve, causing the light to continually be trapped within the bodies of humans. The Prince of Darkness did this so that it would be harder and more complicated to save and restore the light, and the Great Venerable Light had to send even more Heavenly messengers of light to do the work of salvation. Because humans were the descendants of dark devils, and their souls were made of elements of light, this led to a problem of the process of saving human souls. The spirits of salvation first sent human souls to the Moon Palace for refinement, then purified souls were sent to the Sun Palace, and finally they returned to the Kingdom of Light.[47]

Clearly, in this type of religion it is most suitable for the black ox and white horse to be the symbols of the tribal ancestors and to be used in a sacrifice to Heavenly spirits and for prayers of salvation from original sin and for human souls. If we consider that the spirit of salvation appealed to was really an allegory for Abaoji's ancestors and even Abaoji himself, then this religious reformation of the ancestral legend is even more interesting: the father-son relationship of the legend becomes a spiritual relationship, and the problem of ruling the secular world becomes the problem of religious salvation. Between this type of Manichaean doctrine and the explanation of the black ox and white horse being the Deities of Heaven and Earth as well as the Qaghan and all Khitans being descendants of that divine tribe, which would Yelü Abaoji choose as he plotted to gain the throne? I think the answer should be evident.

In the final part of this section I would like to provide another piece of evidence that the Black Ox and White Horse were Adam and Eve. The above mentioned *Record of the Lands North of Yan* by Wang Yi of the Song Dynasty says, "The Red Maiden is called 'Lüe'hu'ao' 掠胡奥 in the barbarian language. Legend has it that she was found in the stream of the Huang River by the seven riders of Yinshan, and she gave birth to their people." Liu Pujiang has already shown that the Red Maiden was the Heavenly Maiden of the Black Ox, an argument that I will not recount

[47] This paragraph recounts the account of Manichaeism given in *Ancient Manichaean Art*, pp. 36-7 and 43-4 and *Manichaeism and its Spread Eastward*, pp. 17-8.

here. "Lüe'hu'ao" was the name of the ancestor in the legend, and I suspect that the first character "lüe" 掠 was mistaken for the similar character "liang" 椋, and "Liang Hu'ao" 椋胡奧 was the contemporary transliteration for Adam and Hawwah (Eve). As mentioned above, Manichaeism was transmitted by the Sogdian people through central Asia to the Uyghurs, and the breaking off of the initial vowel is a characteristic of the Sogdian language. In Old Chinese "d" and "l" were of the same "linniu" 鄰紐 category (similar position, but slightly different method of pronunciation), and a shift in pronunciation may have occurred. As the transliteration was from a foreign word, [A]dam Hawwah was heard as "Liang Hu'ao," and recorded as such. Therefore, Liang Hu'ao may have been the earliest translation of the names Adam and Eve in ancient China. This also indirectly proves that the Khitan ancestors Black Ox and White Horse in the historical records had already been integrated into Uyghur Manichaeism during Abaoji's time.

3. *Burning firewood, the sacrifice to the East, and others*

The Khitan had the so-called Firewood Investiture Ceremony 柴冊儀, as recorded in *History of the Liao: Explication of the National Language*: "The Firewood Investiture was the name of a ceremonial rite. Firewood was piled up to form an altar, which received the jade certificate of investiture submitted by the vassals. When the rites concluded, the firewood was ignited as a sacrifice to heaven. The ceremony was created by Zuwu 阻午 Qaghan." This was an old Khitan custom equivalent to the Chinese "Imperial Investiture Ceremony" 皇帝受册儀. I believe that the activity of burning firewood here is worth looking into. The firewood is burnt to send a message to Heaven, similar to the Firewood Burning Ceremony ("fanliao" 燔燎) in Tang China. The problem is that the Khitan often held the ceremony on its own, unlike the Tang ceremony, which was just one part of a greater ceremony. For example, the Taiwanese scholar Wang Minxin has pointed out that, "in the sixth year of Emperor Taizu, due to the rebellion of the Diela 迭剌, Yindishi 寅底石, Anduan 安端, and other tribes, Taizu led his army south to Shiqi [17] Lake 十七泺, where he burned firewood. The next year the rebellion was quelled, and he burned firewood again. In the third year of the Huitong 會同 reign period of Emperor Taizong he led his officers to pay respects to the Taizu palace.

On the third day he burned firewood and upon conclusion of the ceremony made another sacrifice at the spirit tent. These firewood burnings seem to be unrelated to the 'burning firewood to signal to Heaven' of the Firewood Investiture Ceremony, as he was not given an honorific title and did not ascend the throne, but it is true these ceremonies must have been very important (I suspect that the firewood burning was a ceremony of sacrifice to Heaven and was purely a celebratory event)."[48] Therefore, this behavior of burning firewood is clearly a kind of fire worship.

According to *History of the Liao: Monograph on Ritual (1)*, the Khitan ceremonies that include fire worship were all auspicious ceremonies, such as the Burning Festival Ceremony 爇節儀: "...when the emperor passed away, his family would place the national repository and his money and grain in a yurt in a small felt palace. Gold statues of the emperor and his empress and consorts were also placed within. At festivals, anniversaries of deaths, or the first and fifteenth of each month they would make a sacrifice before the yurt. They also made a platform of earth about one *zhang* 丈 high and on it placed a large dish, which held sacrificial wine and food. It was burned in a custom they called the Burning Festival 爇節." Research has shown that the Burning Festival is the same as the commonly-called "shaofan" 燒飯, a tradition of burning the remaining sacrificial food of the Liao, Jin, and Yuan Dynasties.[49] Clearly, the Burning Festival, or food burning is one kind of fire worship that may very likely have originated in the earlier custom of fire sacrifice, which had already evolved into a full-fledged ceremonial rite. We can be sure that the worship of fire was not done in order to worship the dead, but mainly was related to a wish for the advancement of the soul. One study points out that in the traditional ways of thinking of some of the north Asian peoples the spirits of fire and death are in clear opposition to one another, as the spirit of fire symbolizes or represents life and is the enemy of death.[50]

---

[48] Wang Minxin 王民信, "The Khitan Firewood Investiture Ceremony and the Rebirth Ceremony" 《契丹的柴册儀與再生儀》 in *Commemorative Essays on Khitan History* 《契丹史論叢》, p. 95.

[49] See Chen Shu 陳述, *Khitan Government Historical Manuscripts*, p. 45.

[50] See Evgeniia Ivanova Derevianko, *Amur Tribes of the First Millennium A.D.*, Chinese translation, p. 146.

The Khitan also had a fire spirit: *History of the Liao: Monograph on Ritual (1)* says, "Year Parting Ceremony 歲除儀: On the first night they came with the Tribal Judges 夷離畢 and all the ministers to the front of the palace, where they burned salt and lamb fat. The magus 巫 (wu) and Great Magus 大巫 each congratulated the fire spirit, and at the gate had the emperor face the flames and bow (note: the earlier emperors bowed themselves, but later Emperor Daozong 道宗 began having the Tribal Judges bow)." These fire worshiping activities that entered the national rites and were conducted with the emperor present were no longer traditional folk customs, but were sacrifices that showed systematic religious concepts. Considering the historical and cultural background of the founding of the Khitan state, I believe that the Khitan's fire spirit is the same as the Uyghur Manichaean fire spirit Brilliant Fire, one of the five great Manichaean spirits. The Manichaean *Hymns for the Lower Section* "A Hymn of Universal Petition and Praise" 普启贊文 says, "Then came again five Buddhas of Light, water, fire, bright power, and brilliant wind, with pure air that was soft in nature, they are the power behind the Venerable Light's power." The *Hymns for the Lower Section* "Eulogy of the Light World" says, "Bright brilliant fire is peerless, its brilliant color is clear and dazzling, its heat will never be extinguished, and its extraordinary brightness is difficult to match. The body of flames is clear and empty without scorching, when you enter them they do not burn, they do not emit smoke or ashes, and burn nothing."[51]

From the record in the *History of the Liao: Monograph on Ritual* we see that many of the Khitan national ceremonies have a magus or great magus present; for example, in the mountain sacrifice ceremony "the Great Magus offered a libation of wine"; in the sacrifice to the East "the magus wore white clothes, while the *tiyin* 惕隐 [a Khitan office] bowed with a white scarf and wore it. The magus spoke three times, and each time the emperor, empress, and everyone in attendance bowed"; in the Prayer for Rain and Archery Ceremony, "the magus offered a libation and grains and planted a willow, offering congratulations"; in the Tomb Prayer Ceremony, "the magus offered congratulations and burned the sacrificial meat and clothing, then offered a libation and sacrifice"; and in the Funeral Ceremony, "the magi removed their aprons. The next morning they were led to the place of sacrifice and five made funerary offerings.

[51] *Manichaeism and its Spread Eastward* 《摩尼教及其東漸》, pp. 243, 256-7.

The Great Magus led the prayer." These magi and great magi clearly became councilors to these highly religious ceremonies because they were intimately familiar with the proceedings, which is why I believe that they may have been Manichaean priests. The reason they were called magi 巫 was either because they were formerly magi and were converted to Manichaeism, or because their behavior was seen by later historians as similar to that of magi.

White clothing is also a characteristic of Manichaeism. Research has shown that "worshipping white is a characteristic of Manichaeism. *The Compendium of the Doctrines* says that Mani 'wore a white robe' and 'sat on a white seat' and stipulates that Manicheans of the highest four ranks must wear white clothes and caps. The Manichaean priest found on the wall painting at Gaochang (near Turfan in Xinjiang) was also wearing white clothing and a white cap. Song texts mention that Manichaean adherents at the time wore white clothing, and were called 'of the white clothed way' or 'white clothed masters.' Manichaean followers in the Arab Abbasid period (750-1258) wore white 'brimless hats.' As Manicheans from China, Gaochang, and the Arab states all revered white, this did not become a custom only after it came to China, but was a characteristic that had continually been passed down."[52] Therefore *History of the Liao: Annals of Taizu (the first part)* says that in the first month of spring of the seventh year "his younger brother Lage begged to surrender, and the Emperor wore white clothing while riding a reddish white horse" to receive it, which can be seen as evidence of Abaoji's belief in Manichaeism. The Khitan also revered white and especially liked white horses, as they were herders. Apart from the white horse that was mentioned above as being sacrificed along with a black ox, there was a white horse spirit that was the object of sacrifice.[53] There are also many place names that use the words "white horse" in their title, such as White Horse Pot 白馬埚, White Horse Pond 白馬淀, White Horse Lake 白馬濼, and White Horse Mountain 白馬山. *Monograph on Geography (1)* says that Muye Shan of Yongzhou had "a Xingwang 興王 temple with an image of Guanyin in white clothing. Taizong 太宗 led Shijin 石晉, who would rule China; on the way back from Luzhou 潞州 Taizong entered Youzhou 幽州 and visited the Dabei 大悲 temple, where he pointed at this statue and

[52] *Manichaeism and its Spread Eastward*, p. 56.

[53] See Liu Pujiang 劉浦江, "Memories of the Khitan," p. 160.

said, 'I dreamt a spirit ordered that the youth Shi 石 become emperor of China, and this is he.' Therefore it was moved to Muye Shan, where a temple was built and annual sacrifices were made, and he was revered as a spirit of health." It is very hard to say that it is just a coincidence that this situation resembles the many Manichaean images of female messengers and *Electae* (priests)[54] that are wearing white clothing.[55] We can say that by Abaoji's time the traditional Khitan psychology of revering white had taken on aspects of Manichaeism.

We know that these Khitan who revered white also had an important custom of praying to Black Mountain. The *History of the Liao: Monograph on Ritual (6)* "Miscellaneous Etiquette for the Seasons" 歲時雜儀 entry says, "At the winter solstice it is the national custom to slaughter a white sheep, white horse, and white goose. Blood is taken from them, and along with wine the Son of Heaven prays to Black Mountain. Black Mountain is at the northern edge of the territory, and it is said the souls of the people are served by its spirit, like China's Tai 岱 Mountain (Taishan). Each year on this day, the five capitals send thousands of paper troops, which were burnt in a sacrifice to the mountain. The custom is very solemn, and without making a sacrifice they do not dare approach the mountain." The Japanese scholar Torii Ryūzō 鳥居龍藏 refuted the saying that it was "like China's Tai Mountain," and believed the Khitan faith in Black Mountain was like the earlier faith of the Wuhuan in Red Mountain, as they both were part of the traditions of the Donghu 東胡 ethnic group and were expressions of the thought of returning to the Land of the Yellow Spring.[56] Actually, even though it was the custom of the northern peoples to use color words in common toponomy,[57] the word "Qara" that is

---

[54] Manichaean adherents are called "Hearers," and the priests are called "Electae/Electi," and they have different status within the religion. See Hans-Joachim Klimkeit, *Manichaean Art and Calligraphy*, p. 12, in Chinese translation *Ancient Manichaean Art*, pp. 43-4.

[55] See *Ancient Manichaean Art*, pp. 56, 70, 86, 93, and 94-5.

[56] See Torii Ryūzō 鳥居龍藏, "A Study of the Khitan Black Mountain and Black Range" 《契丹黑山黑嶺考》 in *Yenching Journal of Chinese Studies* 《燕京學報》, vol. 28 (Dec. 1930), included in Sun Jinyi 孫進已, et al., ed., *Compilation of Works on Khitan History* 《契丹史論著彙編》, pp. 1101-5.

[57] See E. M. Murzaev (Э. М. Мурзаев), *Схема физико-географического районирования Средней Азии* (*A Schema of the Physical-Geographic Division into*

directly translated into Chinese as "hei" 黑 (black), still had a special meaning in their culture. The new edition of the *Encyclopedia of Islam* "Black Khan Dynasty" 黑汗王朝 (Ilek Khanids or Qarakhanids) entry cites the German Oriental scholar Omeljan Pritsak's explanation in *Qara, Studie zur türkischen Rechtssymbolik*: "Qara literally means 'black,' but was also used in early Turkish to designate the prime compass point of the north, hence it acquired the meaning 'principal' or 'chief.'"[58] From this we can see that the word "black" used in proper nouns is "Qara" (transliteration "hala" 哈剌 or "kala" 喀喇), which often does not mean the color, nor does it show a reverence for the color black. It is simply used as a qualifier, using a traditional method to show the primary status, grand nature, and imagery of worship of the central word. For example, "Kala Kunlun" means "Great Kunlun," "Hala Qidan" means "Grand Khitan," and "Amuer" means "big river."[59] Therefore, when the histories say, "Black Mountain is in the north; it is commonly said the souls of the nation are served by the spirit," it is worth taking special notice.

Torii Ryūzō has made on-site investigations of these places and believes that Black Mountain and the Black Range (the Da Xing'an 大興安 range between present-day Inner Mongolia's Balinyou Banner 巴林右旗 and Xiwuzhumuqin Banner 西烏珠穆新旗) really was at the far northern edge of Khitan territory.[60] However, he believes "it is commonly said the souls of the nation are served by its spirit" (the cited *Record of an Embassy to the Liao* 使遼錄 has "when barbarians die their souls return to this mountain") refers to the Land of the Yellow Spring, which is difficult to accept. The key problem is that he did not understand that if it was the

---

Regions of Central Asia), in Russian, translated into Chinese as 穆爾札也夫, 《中亞細亞（自然地理概要）》 by Yu Hao 郁浩 (Commercial Press 商務印書館, 1959), p. 49, table 3.

58 Omeljan Pritsak, "Qara, Studie zur türkischen Rechtssymbolik" in *Zeki Velidi Togan'a Armağan* (Istanbul, 1955), pp. 239–63; see *Encyclopedia of Islam*, new edition, vol. 3 (Leiden: Brill, 1971), p. 1113.

59 See Liu Fengzhu 劉鳳翥, "Remarks on the Source of the 'Amuer' and the Khitan Language 'Black River'" 《"阿穆爾"源於契丹語的"黑水"說》 in *Collected Writings on Heilongjiang Cultural Relics* 《黑龍江文物叢刊》, 1984, no. 1, in Sun Jinyi 孫進已, et al., eds., *Compilation of Works on Khitan History*, last part, p. 744.

60 See Torii Ryūzō 鳥居龍藏, "A Study of the Khitan Black Mountain and Black Range," p. 1113.

destination for returning souls in the Khitan spiritual world, why did it have to be in the North? One explanation may be that the change from the Wuhuan Red Mountain to the Khitan Black Mountain in the legend of the Donghu ethnic group was not just a change in color, but also a change in the direction and nature of worship. Heaven is in the North, which is a concept the Khitan adopted from Uyghur Manichaeism. "Manichaeism often used two types of trees to express the concept of two worlds. One was called the Bright Tree of Life, and the second was called the Dark Tree of Death...according to the Manichaean wall painting discovered at Bezeklik, we know the shape of the Manichaean tree of life, of its plentiful leaves and fruit, and its three trunks, which represent the three directions of the kingdom of light."[61] These three directions are North, East, and West. "According to the basic myth the primeval and eternal Paradise of Light extends to the north, east, and west. Only to the south is it bounded by the Kingdom of Darkness. The Kingdom of Light is ruled by the 'Father of Greatness' and is inhabited by divine beings which have issued from the Father and live in close union with him."[62] According to Manichaean teachings, the kingdom of light is also the final resting place of good souls.[63] Therefore, the Khitan worship of Black Mountain was

---

[61] *Manichaeism and its Spread Eastward*, p. 14. See *Ancient Manichaean Art*, pp. 71-2. Notes to the Khitan "Rebirth Ceremony" 再生儀: "in the southeast of the room of rebirth three different trees were planted in reverse order" (*History of the Liao: Monograph on Ritual (6)*). These three different trees may have been the three trees symbolizing the kingdom of light in Manichaeism, and they were planted in reverse order, because the directions of rebirth and the afterlife are different. Many Khitan wall paintings have been discovered in China, so it should be possible to recognize these three trees.

[62] Hans-Joachim Klimkeit, *Manichaean Art and Calligraphy* (Leiden: Brill, 1982), p. 9; in Chinese translation, *Ancient Manichaean Art*, p. 32. Also see the Manichaean *The Book of Giants* 《大力士經》 on p. 71 of the translation.

[63] See *Ancient Manichaean Art*, pp. 38, 41-2, and 44; *Manichaeism and its Spread Eastward*, p. 18. According to the traditional Persian religion, Zoroastrianism, the devils reside in the North (see Wang Xiaofu 王小甫, *A History of Relations between the Tang, the Tibetans, and the Arabs,* p. 26). Manichaeism is just the opposite, perhaps because of heterodox practices. But Indian religions also believe that that Shambhala, the ideal kingdom, is in the North; see the *Gexi Quzha Tibetan Dictionary (appendix of explanatory notes on Chinese)* 《格西曲札藏文辭典（附漢文註釋）》 (Chinese translation of the Tibetan *Chos kyi grags pa*; Beijing: 1990), p. 877. This very likely reflects the cultural branches that formed when the early Indians and Iranian peoples moved out of central Asia and split apart (see Wang Xiaofu, p. 243). It is said that the

really using a traditional method ("black" is equivalent to "north," "primary," and "first") to express the direction in which souls of the dead traveled to reach the highest Heavenly kingdom and was not an expression of grief towards those returning to the Yellow Spring.

Closely related to this is the Khitan sacrifice to the East, or the custom of worshipping the Sun and the East. As mentioned above, the Khitan mountain sacrifice ceremony was infused with a strong consciousness of worshipping the Sun and the East, and I believe that this very likely may be a reflection of the Manichaean teaching that the soul in its final journey goes from the Sun palace to the Heavenly Kingdom of Light. The following will provide further analysis of this conclusion. The *History of the Liao: Explication of the National Language* says, "Sacrifice to the East: a national custom, all sacrifices are made facing east, so they are called Sacrifices to the East." *History of the Liao: Monograph on Ritual (1)* also especially points out, "Sun Worship Ceremony: the emperor ascends an open stage, lays down a pad, bows to the Sun twice, and offers incense. The gate attendants allow him to pass, then the ministers and officers stand on both sides of the palace steps, and they bow again. The emperor takes a seat on his throne. The public register is read, and the northern row rises then sits, and at this time the prime minister comes down and is bowed to again and does not leave the row. The 'ten thousand blessings to the saintly bow' 聖躬萬福 is called out, and they bow again, everyone waits respectfully, as does the Master of Court Etiquette 宣徽 with the horizontal rows. All of the officers, gate attendants, and northern row announce their affairs first, and the rest follow. The music officers and others follow." Scholars have studied the Khitan custom of worshipping the Sun and the East, and there are two main problems: one is the reason why they do this, and the other is whether or not the Khitan made sacrifices and bowed to both the Sun and the Moon.

As for the first problem, Feng Jiasheng 馮家昇 once pointed out that, "It was not only the Khitan who worshipped the Sun and the East, nearly all of the northern peoples did it. Their environments were the same, so their customs and habits were largely similar. The weather to the north of

Western word Shangri-La arose from the Sanskrit word Shambhala. Tibetan Buddhism also used this legend. No matter what, the fundamental meaning of this legend is to point believers to the north and not in any other direction, which is a point that researchers should especially keep in mind.

the Great Wall is cold, as everyone knows. When the sun rose it brought warmth, and when it set it brought cold. There was little time that was warm each year.…As this was the case, the people took advantage of the geography and the rising and setting of the sun to determine the direction in which their houses faced…streets faced the sun, and especially archways were made to open eastward towards the sun."[64] Furthermore, as those who have lived in the north know, in order to bring warmth into the home, the doors and windows must face south. They cannot face East, as in the winter, when sunlight is most needed, the sun can hardly be seen all day. Therefore, worshipping the Sun and the East is not related to solar heating. Actually, Feng Jiasheng has already found that the ancient ethnic groups of the Turks and Uyghurs had the custom of worshipping the Sun, but unfortunately, because he is stuck in old ways of thinking he believes that "the Khitan already worshipped the Sun and the East, and were not necessarily influenced by Turkic customs"[65] and cannot deeply investigate the path of transmission. I believe that the Khitan custom of worshipping the Sun was not necessarily influenced by the Turks, but it was entirely possible that it was influenced by the Uyghurs. The Turkic Qaghanate had long since died out, and its Zoroastrian custom of "worshipping the Sun and fire" emphasized fire rather than the sun.[66] The Uyghur national religion was the Manichaean worship of light, and, as stated above, based on Manichaean teachings the stages of salvation for human souls were as follows: the spirit of salvation first brought the human soul to the Moon Palace for refinement, then the purified soul was sent to the Sun Palace, and finally it returned to the Kingdom of Light.[67] This must have been the origin of the Khitan sacrifice to the East and prayer to the Sun, and even of the formation of the custom of worshipping the Sun and the East.

As for the second problem, the *History of the Liao* clearly mentions the Khitan making sacrifices to the Sun and the Moon in two places; see "Annals of Shengzong 聖宗 (1)": twelfth month of the first year of the

---

64 Feng Jiasheng 馮家昇, "A Philological Study of the Sun and the Khitan" 《太陽契丹考釋》 in *A Compilation of the Best Works of Feng Jiasheng* , pp. 44-5.

65 See ibid., pp. 47-8.

66 See Wang Xiaofu 王小甫, *A History of Relations between the Tang, the Tibetans, and the Arabs*, appendices 1 and 2, pp. 224-56.

67 See *Ancient Manichaean Art*, pp. 38, 41-2, and 44; *Manichaeism and its Spread Eastward*, p. 18.

Tonghe reign period, "on the wushen 戊申 day, the emperor's birthday, sacrifices were made to the Sun and Moon. When the ceremony ended the officials offered their congratulations"; "Annals of Shengzong (2)": eleventh month of the fourth year of the Tonghe reign period, "on the guiwei 癸未 day sacrifices were made to the Sun and Moon, and a blessing was made for the imperial son-in-law Commander (Xiao) 蕭 Qinde 勤德." Only one place mentions clearly that the Moon was not prayed to; the "Monograph on the Army (first part)" 兵衛志上 "Military System" 兵制 entry: "When an army was raised, the emperor led Han and non-Han military and civil officials in a sacrifice of a black ox and white horse for Heaven and Earth and the Sun spirit. The Moon was not prayed to. Nearby officials were ordered to inform Taizu's tomb and the lesser tombs, as well as the spirit of Muye Shan, and the armies were readied to march." Raising an army was a special case and cannot be said to be the norm, but it is suspicious that the "Monograph on Ritual" has a Sun prayer ceremony, but does not have a specific Moon prayer ceremony. *History of the Liao: Monograph on Ritual: Exegesis* 考證 after the above "Military System" entry mentions, "the Sun prayer ceremony varies: sometimes they pray to the Sun alone, and at other times they pray to the Sun and the Moon. Even though the Moon prayer ceremony is not recorded, it should be equivalent to the Sun prayer ceremony."[68] Feng Jiasheng believes that, "The Moon prayer ceremony is not of great importance, so the monograph does not mention it. The difference in importance between the worship of the Sun and Moon is clear, so why say that praying to the Moon is the same as to the Sun?"[69] But in the *History of the Liao* there are many instances in which the Sun and Moon are mentioned together for the Khitan, such as "on the dingyou 丁酉 day of the eighth month of the fifth year of the Tianzan 天贊 reign period of Emperor Taizong, as the banquet and sleeping chambers of the Great Saintly Emperor and Empress were called the Sun and Moon Palace, the Sun and Moon Stele was erected"; and "on the guisi 癸巳 day of the sixth month of the first year of the Huitong reign period, the Hall of the Four Seasons, Sun, and Moon was ordered built, and the names of the ancient emperors and kings were painted in its two corridors." In the first year of the Baoda 保大 reign period, "the Jin 金

---

[68] From Feng Jiasheng 馮家昇, "A Philological Study of the Sun and the Khitan," p. 41.

[69] Ibid., p. 42.

armies saw the banners of the Sun and Moon and knew the Emperor Tianzuo 天祚 was under it." It is evident that we are correct in saying the Khitan prayed to both the Sun and the Moon. But Feng Jiasheng's conclusion that there is a difference in importance between the two may have been true. According to Manichaeism, "the reason the Moon is not bright for fifteen days is that human souls are there being refined, and the impure dark elements among them cause this darkness. When the souls have been purified, they are sent to the Sun Palace, and the Moon Palace is once again empty and pure and becomes light. This is what takes place every month for fifteen days."[70] This was likely the reason that when the Khitan prayed to both the Sun and Moon, "worshipping the Sun was more important than worshipping the Moon."

This reminds me of Yelü Abaoji's public prediction of his death in the *History of the Liao: Annals of Taizu (the last part)* sixth month of the third year of the Tianzan reign period (924), where his closing words were, "the Sun and Moon are not far away, and we should make guarding preparations soon." *History of the Liao: Monograph on Geography (1)* says, in the Zuzhou 祖州 "inner city, the palace was called 'two lights' and it contained the portrait of the emperor's grandfather and father; 'two worlds' which had a silver statue of Taizu; 'black dragon'; 'Qingmi' 清秘...which was Taizu's tomb carved from a mountain, and it was called the 'bright palace' 明殿....the gate was called 'black dragon.'"[71] The content of these passages may have been related to Manichaeism. The *Manichaean Sutra Fragment Number One* 摩尼教殘經一 excavated at Dunhuang says, "Aimlessly wandering the City of the Heart I knew the Light Palace of the Sun and Moon the master had happily spoken of, its spiritual power changing, full of might; in the religion, only faith is taught"; *Hymns for the Lower Section*: "Towards the Palaces of the Sun and Moon and the two Palaces of Light, each of the three kind fathers offers high praise."[72] According to Manichaean teachings, for the soul (light elements) on the path to salvation, "In the sun, the Third Messenger, the Mother of Life and the Living Spirit reside, in the moon Jesus the

---

70 *Manichaeism and its Spread Eastward*》, p. 18.

71 The "Bright Palace" 明殿 was the name of Abaoji's resting place; for related studies see Chen Shu, *Khitan Government Historical Manuscripts*, pp. 45-6.

72 *Manichaeism and its Spread Eastward*, pp. 221 and 263.

Splendour, the Maiden of Light and First Man [original will] have their place."[73]

The Khitan had the Junji Taiyi 君基太一 deity, as recorded in *History of the Liao: Explication of the National Language*: "Junji Taiyi was the name of a deity. Whichever nation his spirit approached would be built successfully by its leader, confidence would be enjoyed through the upper and lower stratums, the people would be governed peacefully and would share in the prosperity." In the ninth year of the Taizu 太祖 reign period (915), "this year Junji Taiyi was seen several times, and his portrait was ordered painted." The phrase "nation…would be built successfully" was clearly added later by historians who did not understand the situation. What kind of deity was this Junji Taiyi? I believe that he originated in the Uyghur Manichaean spirit of light. Studies have shown that "Jesus, the lord of salvation, lived in the Moon Palace, and in Turkic texts he was in essence equivalent to the Moon Palace. The spirits of the Sun and Moon ("Kün-ai-táńgri" in Uyghur) were spirits of salvation that were widely worshipped in central Asian Manichaeism." Junji Taiyi clearly was an intentionally stylized transliteration of the Uyghur "Kün-ai-táńgri," whose original meaning was the heavenly spirits of the Sun and Moon. We often see this kind of embedded title in Qaghan honorific titles from the Uyghur Qaghanate period.[74] Here I will also mention that in the later Song Dynasty patronage of Daoism, the *History of the Song: Monograph on Ritual (6)* 宋史・禮志六 mentions ten Taiyi spirits, among which include the names Junji Taiyi, Chenji 臣基 Taiyi, and Minji 民基 Taiyi, which make me suspect that they came from copying Junji Taiyi of the Khitan. If so, this is a typical case of the transmission and integration of traditional culture.

Finally, I would like to briefly discuss Khitan funerary customs. The *History of the Northern Dynasties: Account of the Khitan* 北史・契丹傳 says: "It was not considered manly to cry in grief after one's father and mother died. Their bodies were simply placed in trees on a mountain, and after three years their bones were collected and burned." We can see that the early funerary system of the Khitan was in the form of a Heavenly

---

[73] Hans-Joachim Klimkeit, *Manichaean Art and Calligraphy* (Leiden: Brill, 1982), p. 11; in Chinese translation *Ancient Manichaean Art*, p. 35, also see p. 75 of the same work.

[74] See *Ancient Manichaean Art*, pp. 74, 82, and 96.

burial and a fire burial.[75] Furthermore, the *New Tang History: Account of the Northern Di Khitan* 新唐書・北狄契丹傳 says: "Their customs are mostly the same as the Turks. They do not bury their dead, but take the corpse by horse and cart to a mountain and place it in a tree. When sons and grandsons die the parents cry for a day; when parents die they do not cry and do not have a mourning period." Clearly, Tang Dynasty Khitan were influenced by the Turkic worship of the Sun and fire, and abandoned the custom of fire burial. However, Ouyang Xiu 歐陽修, the author of the *New Tang History* also wrote in the *New History of the Five Dynasties: Account of the Khitan in the Supplementary Record of the Four Barbarian Tribes* 新五代史・四夷福錄契丹, "when their fathers and mothers died it was not considered brave to cry. Their corpses were taken deep into the mountains and placed in great trees, and after three years they were taken and their bones were burned." At first this looks to be the same version as the *History of the Northern Dynasties: Account of the Khitan*, but in comparison with the *Tang History* version, we know that in the Five Dynasties the Khitan funerary customs were no longer influenced by the Turks, and further, fire burials were conducted at a corresponding level.[76]

Fire burials were seldom seen among the Khitan nobility, but there are two points worth noting: one is that funeral beds or platforms were used, and that coffins were seldom used,[77] so this may have been a type of naked burial; the second is that it was very rare to use objects of the living world in the funeral. For example, the *History of the Liao: Monograph on Geography (1)* says that in the palaces within the inner city of Zuzhou 祖州, "the weapons, clothing, and furs worn by Taizu before investiture were kept to show to his descendants so that they would not forget their origin"; *History of the Liao: Monograph on Ritual (2)* says, "Funeral Ceremony:

---

[75] See Jia Zhoujie 賈洲傑, "Research on the Khitan Funerary System" 《契丹喪葬制度研究》 in *Journal of Inner Mongolia University* 《内蒙古大學學報》, 1978, vol. 2, included in Sun Jinyi 孫進已, et al., ed., *Compilation of Works on Khitan History*, last part, p. 589.

[76] See ibid., pp. 592-3. Some believe that the reason for the Khitan fire burials was the flourishing of Buddhism, but that happened after the Liao Emperor Shengzong 聖宗 (982-1031) – see Feng Jiasheng 馮家昇, "The Relationship between Khitan Conventions of Worship and other Religious Mythological Customs," pp. 58-62.

[77] See Jia Zhoujie 賈洲傑, "Research on the Khitan Funerary System" 《契丹喪葬制度研究》, pp. 591-2.

Shengzong passed away…the Great Magus prayed. The imperial clan, relatives of the empress, great ministers, and officials of the capital took turns offering sacrifices. They took clothing, bows and arrows, saddles and bridles, paintings, horses and camels, and ceremonial flags and burned them. They went to the tombs in the mountains, and when the funeral ended offered their eulogies." I suspect that this was all influenced by Manichaeism. Regarding a fragment of Manichaean scripture excavated from Dunhuang, Chen Yuan 陳垣 said, "one line of the fragments says, 'usually when there is a corpse, if it was covered this would be blasphemous' which shows us they used naked burials, which was the Manichaean way." He also quotes: "Liao Gang 廖剛, *Collected Works of Gaofeng* 高峰文集, volume two, "Report to the Court Asking for the Forbiddance of Cults and Heresy" 乞禁妖教扎子 says: '…(the fasting worshipping Mani) died, then people burned the body with firewood and did not use any coffins or burial clothes and did not hold another funeral or sacrifice…' This does not explicitly point out that it was Manichaean, but such a method of reducing a person can only mean that it was Manichaeism."[78]

However, before the founding of their state the Khitan had their own customs, and after the period of Emperor Shengzong Buddhism became popular, and there were many types of funerary forms. Some scholars have pointed out that regarding the Khitan funerary system, "if it was created before the founding of the Liao Dynasty, it had a clear break in the middle. Does this mean that in the late Tang that Khitan society experienced a brief, but large change that was not recorded in the histories? Even though there may be no textual evidence, why is it hard to find evidence for this change in archaeological findings?"[79] Perhaps the reason was that during this time the Khitan converted to Manichaeism, and naked burials, simple burials, and fire burials were popular. The answer to this question awaits further detailed investigation.

---

[78] Chen Yuan 陳垣, "A Study of the Entry of Manichaeism into China" 《摩尼教入中國考》, in his *Collected Academic Essays of Chen Yuan* 《陳垣學術論文集》, vol. 1 (Zhonghua Book Company, 1980), pp. 359 and 372.

[79] Jia Zhoujie 賈洲傑, "Research on the Khitan Funerary System," p. 592.

4. *On Empress Shulü* 述律

To put it concisely, Yelü Abaoji's Uyghur empress Shulü was an important figure in helping to propel him to the throne and was a Uyghur representative that participated in the founding of the Khitan state. Studies have shown that before the founding of the state the Khitan tribes had continually upheld a system of intermarriage.[80] Before Abaoji the Yelü clan of the Diela tribe had never married with a Uyghur,[81] but Abaoji broke with his clan's tradition and married a Uyghur woman.[82] Under the fierce traditional background of political marriage, this action was useful in the plan to use the great power of the Uyghur tribes.[83] Others have systematically studied the important effect of Uyghurs on Khitan society and political activities, and here I simply aim to discuss the effect the Shulü clan had from a cultural perspective.

---

[80] See Liu Pujiang 劉浦江, "The Historical Memory of the Khitan People," p. 160-2.

[81] *History of the Liao*, ch. 32, *Monograph on Imperial Guards, Middle Section: Tribes, First Part* 《營衛志中・部族上》: "Nieli 涅里, as leader of Zuwu 阻午 Qaghan, split the three Yelü 耶律 into seven parts and the two Shenmi 审密 into five parts, so with the former eight tribes they were twenty tribes in all. The three Yelü were called the Dahe 大賀, Yaonian 遥辇, and Shili 世里, and were the imperial tribe. The two Shenmi were called the Yishiyi 乙室已 and the Bali 拔里, and were the maternal uncles of the state." We can see that no matter how the Khitan tribes were divided, from the period of the Yaonian tribal confederation, the Yelü clan did not marry with the Uyghur Shulü clan. For related studies see Jin Yufu's 金毓黻 *A Study of the Liao Tribes* 《遼部族考》 and Wang Minxin's 王民信 "The Formation of the Community of Khitan Royal Relatives on the Female Side," pp. 74-5.

[82] Perhaps it was this that led to the regrouping of the Khitan tribes, thereby causing the Khitan marriage system to go from marrying outside of the tribe to marrying within the tribe and outside of the clan. This problem is worth a separate study and has already been discussed in Liu Pujiang, "The Historical Memory of the Khitan People," pp. 160-2.

[83] Uyghurs had important status within the political activities of the Khitan, as can be seen in the following record from the *History of the Liao*: *Annals of Taizu* "on the wuzi 戊子 day of the seventh month in the autumn of the fourth year, the (Shulü) empress' elder brother Xiao Dilu 蕭敵魯 became the Prime Minister of the Northern Superior Prefecture 北府, and this was when the empress' clan began to serve as Prime Ministers" (p. 4); "paid respects to Dilu, the Prime Minister of the Northern Prefecture and established a lineage for the office." (p. 1223)

The *History of the Liao: Biography of Taizu Chunqin Empress* 遼史・太祖淳欽皇后述律氏傳 says: "Shulü was called Ping 平 and also called Yueliduo 月里朵, and her antecessor was the Uyghur person Nuosi 糯思." I am guessing that Yueliduo is the transliteration of the Uyghur "ört,"[84] which means flames, brilliance, or radiance.[85] It is not hard to see that this name had a strong sense of Manichaean light worship. In the illustrated Manichaean scriptures found in the ancient city of Gaochang, near Turfan, regarding one painting dated to the late eighth century named "Manichaean Goddess with *Electae*" the scholar Hans-Joachim Klimkeit says, "The Manichaean savior figure accompanied by two *Electae* is female, who can only be the Maiden of Light. She is standing on a splendid, brightly colored, spreading lotus throne. She holds in her right hand an object which is perhaps to be interpreted as a lotus flower, perhaps as a votive *stupa* or reliquary, or perhaps even as a censer as Le Coq suggests." "The two *Electae* standing behind the goddess are on a large lotus throne such as one seen in Buddhist designs. It seems obvious that the *Electae* feel a special relationship with the light goddess, who is, perhaps the Virgin of Light."[86] The Virgin of Light is a Manichaean goddess of salvation, and, according to the religion's teachings, she, Jesus, and the First Man (original will) live together at the first station on the path of salvation, the Moon Palace.[87] In Manichaeism, Jesus, the Virgin of Light, and Vahman form a trinity that was often prayed to, but Jesus was just a split phase of the Third Envoy. As mentioned above, Vahman was the guider of souls and also a metaphor for the king that had gained salvation. As this deified Yelü Abaoji, it also deified his wife Shulü as the Virgin of Light.

The advantage this myth has is that it can explain the problem in the mountain sacrifice ceremony of the Deities of Heaven and Earth appearing as two images of one deity. It can also explain the problem of the heterosexual consort of Qishou Qaghan and Kedun in the ancestral legend, as well as raise and strengthen the status of the political life of Abaoji's

[84] For more on matching pronunciations, see Wang Xiaofu 王小甫, *A History of Relations between the Tang, the Tibetans, and the Arabs*, appendix 1, pp. 225-6.

[85] See Talât Tekin, *A Grammar of Orkhon Turkic*, chapter 4, vocabulary list, p. 364.

[86] Hans-Joachim Klimkeit, *Manichaean Art and Calligraphy* (Leiden: Brill, 1982), p. 47.

[87] See ibid., p. 11; in the Chinese translation *Ancient Manichaean Art* 《古代摩尼教藝術》, pp. 98, 35, and 96-7.

Uyghur empress, Shulü, within the Khitan state. I believe that this is the real meaning of the folk tale "The Black Ox Maid Once Made Way." The Manichaean *Hymns for the Lower Section:* "A Gāthā in Praise of the Unsurpassed Venerable Lord of Light" says, "The highly revered Huiming 惠明 was the king of the doctrine and could accept our parting with death and our errors. Everything is known within and without the light, making us all saints."[88] Then Abaoji became the Heavenly Emperor, and Shulü became the Empress. Abaoji "was given the honorific title of Great Saintly Great Bright Heavenly Emperor 大聖大明天皇帝, and the empress was called the Responding to Heaven Great Bright Earth Empress 應天大明地皇后. A grand pardon was pronounced, and the first year of the Shence period was proclaimed."[89]

Another matter involving Shulü is the so-called "Fuyu incident" 扶余之變, or death of Abaoji. The biggest problem with Abaoji's death is that according to *History of the Liao: Annals of Taizu (the last part)* he himself predicted his death three years before, and it was precisely three years later on the mysterious day of the "Fuyu incident" that he died. One cannot help but feel that this was a little strange. As the prophecy was publicly made, we cannot eliminate the possibility that Abaoji himself directed this performance, but no matter who was behind it, it is worth looking carefully at the cultural causes acting behind the scenes.

Let us take a look at Abaoji's prophecy in *History of the Liao: Annals of Taizu (the last part)*, in the third year of the Tianzan reign period (924): "On the yiyou 乙酉 day in the sixth month the empress, imperial prince, great general, two prime ministers, and departmental heads were summoned, and it was proclaimed that, 'Heaven has come to watch; it favors all people. The heavenly lord the bright king is seen once in ten thousand years. I have followed the will of Heaven and ruled the masses. Each time a campaign is raised Heaven's will is adhered to. Careful plans are made and used or discarded skillfully. They move upon orders from the state, and the people offer their support. Wrongs are righted, and those far and wide are not punished. It can be said to contain the great seas as well as mount Tai 泰! Since our nation was founded, it has been the parents of the people. The laws have been established, so what do our descendants have to fear? The time it rises and it falls depends upon me.

---

[88] *Manichaeism and its Spread Eastward*《摩尼教及其東漸》, p. 251.

[89] *History of the Liao: Annals of Taizu, first part* 《遼史・太祖紀上》.

Our brilliant schemes and saintly luck match that of those in Heaven. Of all the nations' kings, which of them could transform their bones? In three years on the bingxu 丙戌 day at the first of autumn I will return. How could our families bear the burden of the two unfinished things? The Sun and Moon are not far off, so we should guard for preparation soon.' All those who heard it were greatly startled, and none knew its true meaning." Apparently this prophecy was revised by historians, and the phrase "The laws have been established, so what do our descendants have to fear" is language used posthumously, and departs from the tone of the entire prophecy. No matter what, Abaoji's grand and majestic prophecy that seemed to welcome death as a return greatly startled the common people, and this type of tone was rife with religious devotion. The phrases "Heaven has come to watch; it favors all people. The heavenly lord the bright king is seen once in ten thousand years. I have followed the will of Heaven, and ruled the masses. Each time a campaign is raised Heaven's will is adhered to. Careful plans are made and used or discarded skillfully"; "The time its rise and its fall depends upon me. Our brilliant schemes and saintly luck match that of those in Heaven. Of all the nations' kings, which of them could transform their bones?"; and "The Sun and Moon are not far off, so we should guard for preparation soon" can all find their counterparts in Manichaean doctrines of the salvation of the soul. We can say that Manichaeism was Abaoji's spiritual support. The problem is who enacted his will? The only answer can be Shulü.

According to *History of the Liao: Annals of Taizu (the last part)*, in the seventh month of the first year of the Tianxian 天顯 reign period (926), Yelü Abaoji was returning from defeating the Bohai 渤海 Kingdom when, "on the jiaxu 甲戌 day he reached Fuyu Superior Prefecture 扶余府, but the emperor was displeased. That evening a great star fell in front of the tent. At dawn on the xinsi 辛巳 day a yellow dragon appeared over the inner city that was one *li* 里 long and dazzlingly radiant, which entered the imperial temporary palace. Dark purple haze covered the sky, which dispersed the next day. That day the emperor passed on at the age of fifty-five. In the third year of the Tianzan reign period the so-called 'bingxu day at the first of autumn when I will return' had arrived. On the renwu 壬午 day the empress claimed control of all military and civil affairs." The great star clearly is a celestial body, and according to Manichaeism the celestial bodies and stars were made from light elements that were polluted with darkness.[90] This was suitable for use as an allegory for a king who had attained salvation. "A Great Star fell in front of the tent" was equivalent to a Manichaean announcement of a death. "A yellow dragon appeared over the inner city that was one *li* long and dazzlingly radiant, which entered the imperial temporary palace" is related to the Manichaean myth of the "Column of Glory." According to Manichaean teachings the spirits of salvation in the third universe were the Third Envoy, the Virgin of Light, the Column of Glory, and Vahman; their head the Third Envoy lived in the Sun Palace, the Virgin of Light lived in the Moon Palace, and Vahman was the spirit of guidance and judgment for souls.[91] "Pure souls that attained salvation gathered as the Column of Glory, which we see as the Milky Way. In Manichaean teachings it is a deity, as well as the path along which souls travel to reach the Moon Palace, Sun Palace, and their final destination the Kingdom of Light."[92] We can see that Abaoji's first posthumous title was Ascending to Heaven Emperor 升天皇帝, and the "Annals of Taizu (the last part)" says, "the palace in which Taizu passed away was at the meeting of two rivers southwest of Fuyu City, and later the Ascending to Heaven Palace was built here, and Fuyu became the Huanglong 黃龍 [Yellow Dragon] Prefecture." "A dark purple haze covered the sky, which dispersed the next day" is undoubtedly a metaphor for the dark materials that are cast off after a soul ascends to Heaven.[93] Of course these myths were used to pass along information, and whether they were hyperbole or concealed the actual situation cannot be known with the historical materials available today.[94]

The *History of the Liao: Biography of Taizu Chunqin Empress* says, "Taizu passed away, and the empress was in charge and handled the military and civil affairs. At his burial she wanted to accompany him to the afterlife, but her family and the officials remonstrated with her, so she cut off her right hand and placed it in the coffin. Taizong ascended the throne and honored her as Empress Dowager." The "Monograph on Geography (1)" entry "Supreme Capital Circuit at Huang Superior

---

90 See *Ancient Manichaean Art*, p. 34; *Manichaeism and its Spread Eastward*, p. 16.

91 See *Ancient Manichaean Art*, pp. 35, 41, and 78-9.

92 *Manichaeism and its Spread Eastward*, p. 18.

93 See *Ancient Manichaean Art*, p. 37; *Manichaeism and its Spread Eastward*, p. 19.

94 See *History of the Liao: Judgment on the Annals of Taizu* 《遼史・太祖紀贊》; Chen Shu 陳述, *Khitan Government Historical Manuscripts*, pp. 70-1.

Prefecture" 上京道臨潢府 says, "Taizu passed away, and the Responding to Heaven Empress cut off her hand at the Yijie 義節 temple and placed it in Taizu's mausoleum. The temple built the Severed Wrist Tower 斷腕樓 and erected a stele there." On Shulü's cutting of her wrist, the *New History of the Five Dynasties: Supplementary Record of the Four Barbarian Tribes(2)* 新五代史·四夷福錄契丹 has a more detailed record: "Shulü was a wise and enduring person. When Abaoji died she sent for the wives of the great generals and said, 'I am now a widow, so how is it suitable that you all have husbands?' She then killed the hundred or so generals and said, 'they can go to their emperor.' Those attendants who had wronged her were sent to Muye Shan and killed in Abaoji's mausoleum. She said, 'you can go see your emperor in the underworld.' The great general Zhao Siwen 趙思温 was originally Chinese and was greatly loved by Abaoji for his ability and courage. Shulü once became angry with him and wanted him sent to Muye Shan, but Zhao Siwen was not willing to go. Shulü said, 'you were the trusted follower of the former emperor, how could you not go to see him?' Zhao Siwen replied, 'I was not as close as the empress, why does she not go herself?' Shulü said, 'I originally wanted to follow the emperor to the underworld, but as my sons are still young, and there are many problems facing our nation, I could not go. Therefore I cut off my hand and sent it to him.' Her attendants remonstrated, so she cut off his hand and did not kill Zhao Siwen." It appears that Shulü did cut off her hand. Chen Shu 陳述 thinks that, "Zhao Siwen's refusal to go and Shilü's releasing him after cutting off his hand does not seem to follow reason, and there must be another explanation for this."[95] I believe that Manichaean mythology may offer an explanation. According to its doctrines, all Manichaean deities are a part of the Great Venerable Light, but are also different from the Great Venerable Light, and their individual responsibilities are different.[96] As explained above, Jesus, the Virgin of Light ("woman" equivalent to "Empress Shulü"), and Vahman ("king attaining salvation" equivalent to "Abaoji") were a trinity (i.e. parts of a body).[97] The severing of the wrist can attest to this, and Abaoji ascended to Heaven as he was able, while Shulü's power was undiminished. Zhao Siwen was Han Chinese, and as the ignorant cannot

---

[95] Chen Shu 陳述, *Khitan Government Historical Manuscripts*, p. 70.

[96] See *Ancient Manichaean Art*, p. 33

[97] See ibid., pp. 88 and 97.

be found guilty, he was released without being killed. This added to the mystery of these events and the holiness of her person.

There are other Khitan customs and legends that can be explained by Manichaeism, such as the so-called "Wai He" 喎呵 of the first Khitan lord,[98] who very likely may have been the spirit 嗢末 Hormizd of Manichaeism. But even though Qing emperor Qianlong's explanation of "belief in spirits" was enough to be accepted by the academic world,[99] this of course does not affect our discussion, and will not be discussed in further details here.

In conclusion, considering the background of the collapse of the Manichaean Uyghur Qaghanate in 840 and the subsequent influx of Uyghurs into Khitan society, which had a great effect on history, it is hard to say that the similarities in their myths and legends are simply a coincidence. The collapse of the Uyghur Qaghanate brought new stimulating elements to traditional Khitan society: Uyghurs entered Khitan society, infusing new blood into the Khitan tribes; the Uyghur Manichaean religion was transmitted, providing new spiritual weapons for making changes in traditional Khitan society. Yelü Abaoji used the support of his Uyghur wife (very likely supported by trade activities) and mythologized himself using Manichaeism, thereby breaking with tradition and achieving revolution. He established his state, set up the imperial system, and became a folk hero of the Khitan.

---

[98] See Chen Shu 陳述, *Khitan Government Historical Manuscripts*, p. 47.

[99] See Liu Pujiang 劉浦江, "The Historical Memory of the Khitan People," p. 166.

THE FORENAMES AND COURTESY NAMES OF THE KHITANS: THE FATHER-SON NAME LINKAGE SYSTEM FROM THE PERSPECTIVE OF CULTURAL ANTHROPOLOGY *

Liu Pujiang 劉浦江　　Kang Peng 康鵬

Although historians have attached much importance to historical studies of the northern peoples of China, nevertheless, constrained by the paucity of literature and sources, and by the limitations of traditional research methods, it is yet unsafe to affirm that these studies can rival in depth those of the Chinese dynasties, which have considerable maturity. For example, the history of the Khitans, who founded the Liao 遼 Empire, which stretched well into the territories populated by the Han Chinese people, and which lasted more than two hundred years, still remains to be thoroughly surveyed. To break this impasse, it is necessary, therefore, to blaze some fresh trail, which is just what this essay attempts to do by undertaking a thorough study of the Khitan name system. This essay employs as fully as possible the sources written in the Khitan language and the theories and methods of the science of cultural anthropology, as well as familiar Chinese documents and traditional research methods. It turns out, to our great relief, that in reality there still exists much room for historical studies of the Khitans to be deepened and expanded.

Part I. The Mystery of the Khitan "Second Name"

Among the ancient peoples in the North Asia, it is the Khitan people who may presumably be justified in claiming the most complex name system, the true nature of which has not been revealed by the various investigations undertaken by earlier historians based upon the *History of the Liao* 遼史 and other Chinese documents.[1] This

---

* This article was part of the research project "A Study of the Interactions between Medieval Chinese Political Systems and the National Traditions of North Asian Peoples" undertaken by the Center for Research on Ancient Chinese History at Peking University. It was sponsored by the Supporting Program for Excellent Talents of the New Century by the Ministry of Education, PRC [Authors' note].

[1] See Du Xingzhi 都興智, "The Surnames and Forenames of the Khitans" 《契丹族的姓氏和名稱》, *Journal of Liaoning Normal University* 《遼寧師範大學學報》, 1990, no. 5; Zhang Guoqing 張國慶, "A Brief Discussions of the Naming Customs of the Khitans in

situation did not change until recent years, when the explanations put forward by Khitan linguists through their research into the stone inscriptions in Khitan small script have elucidated some of the mysteries, making possible a deep understanding of Khitan naming customs.

In brief, the Khitan name included two parts. The first part, according to Chinese literature of the Liao Dynasty, was called the forename 名 (or small forename 小名, or small courtesy name 小字). It was usually composed of one single word, but sometimes had two or three words. The second part was the courtesy name 字, which was a single word, without exception.[2] In the epitaphs written in Khitan small script, between the forename and courtesy name of the owner there always stands the word [illegible]. This word is a genitive suffix denoting the ordinal number "second," and is the crux of the Khitan name system. As to the meaning of the word in this particular context, researchers have proposed two different conjectures. Scholars such as Ji Shi 即實 and Wang Hongli 王弘力 have held that that word signifies the familial rank of the owner. However, this is contradicted by the fact that whatever the rank the owner held, this word appears nearly all the time between his names. Liu Fengzhu 劉鳳翥 would render the word as "second" and thereby construe the words coming after it casually as Guoxing 國姓, meaning the surname of the imperial family, Zongshi 宗室, meaning the imperial family members, or Hengzhang 横帳, a specific branch of the imperial house, etc. However, Liu Fengzhu did not note that the words appearing before or after [illegible] are generally components of the names of the owner. It seems now that these explanations both miss the mark.

It is only during recent years that Khitan linguists have introduced opinions worthy of notice regarding the interpretation of this word. Professor Aisin Gioro Ulhicun 愛新覺羅・烏拉熙 read it as the courtesy name of the Khitans, and she maintained that its original meaning was "of a pair," indicating that the word after it is the "large name," forming a

the Liao Dynasty" 《略談遼代契丹人的命名習俗》, *Museum Research* 《博物館研究》, 1991, no. 2; Feng Jiqin 馮繼欽, "A Study of the Khitan Surnames and Forenames in the Jin and Yuan Dynasties" 《金元時期契丹人姓名研究》, *Heilongjiang National Series* 《黑龍江民族叢刊》, 1992, no. 4.

[2] What is indicated here is the naming customs of male Khitans. It is not easy to obtain a deep understanding of the names of female Khitans due to the lack of sources. Therefore this article's object of study is confined to the names of male Khitans.

match for the small forename before it.[3] Although this theory makes a mistake in understanding the original meaning of the word, it is still quite an advance in that it links the word with the Khitan courtesy name. In his recently published article "An Examination of the Epitaph of Xiao Wuluben 蕭烏盧本 and Two Others in the Liao Dynasty" Liu Fengzhu eventually clarifies the true meaning of the word [Khitan script] – that is, when it comes to the Khitan forename and courtesy name, this word means "the second name" in relation to the forename (or small forename). This clarification makes feasible a complete translation of the forename and courtesy name inscribed in the second line of the *Epitaph of Yelü (Han) Dilie* 耶律(韓)迪烈墓誌銘:

[Khitan script]	[Khitan script]	[Khitan script]	[Khitan script]	[Khitan script]
child	name	Dilie 迪烈	second (name)	Kongning 空寧

According to Mr. Liu's explanation, the full name of the owner appearing in the title of the epitaph can be translated literally as Kongning Dilie 空寧・迪烈.[4]

The correct decipherment of the word [Khitan script] thus constitutes by far the most important breakthrough in the exploration of Khitan names and lays a solid foundation for this research. It is customary for the owner's names to be displayed in the stone inscriptions in the same manner as in the *Epitaph of Yelü Dilie*. The so-called "child name" (paraphrased as "small

---

[3] Aisin Gioro Ulhicun 愛新覺羅・烏拉熙春, "An Examination of the Genealogies of the Tomb Owners Recorded in the 'Epitaph of Yelü Dilie' and the 'Epitaph of the Deceased Ms. Yelü': with a Note about the Khitan Forenames and Courtesy Names" 「〈耶律迪烈墓誌銘〉與〈故耶律氏銘石〉所載墓主人世系考——兼論契丹人的"名"與"字"」, *Journal of East Asian Literature and History* 『東亞文史論叢』, premier issue, Festschrift in Memory of the 85th Anniversary of Mr. Jin Qicong's Birth (March 2003), pp. 79-93; also published in *Ritsumeikan Bungaku* 『立命館文學』, no. 580 (June 2003), pp. 1-16; and in Aisin Gioro Ulhicun, *History of the Liao and Jin Dynasties and the Khitan and Jurchen Scripts* 『遼金史與契丹、女真文』 (Kyoto: Research Institute for History and Culture of East Asia 東亞歷史文化研究會, 2004), pp. 69-84.

[4] Liu Fengzhu 劉鳳翥, Tang Cailan 唐彩蘭, and Gaowa 高娃, "An Examination of the Epitaph of Xiao Wuluben and Two Others in the Liao Dynasty" 《遼代蕭烏盧本等三人的墓誌銘考釋》, *Literature and History* 《文史》, 2004, no. 2. Yelü Dilie, though coming originally from the Han family of Yutian 玉田韓氏 and having the Chinese forename Chengkui 承窺, had been Khitanized, therefore his Khitan names entirely followed Khitan customs.

forename") is generally treated in the biographies in the *History of the Liao* as the forename of the biographees, while the "second name" is taken as the courtesy name. In terms of Khitan custom, their second name stood before the small forename in the full name. This is the latest academic achievement of research into the Khitan name system.

The above explanation brings with it more questions. Is the relationship between the Khitan small forename and second name akin to that between the Chinese forename and courtesy name? Why does the second name stand before small forename in a Khitan full name? What in the world does the appearance of a second name in the Khitan small script stone inscriptions denote? Entertaining these questions, we make a thorough survey of all the stone inscriptions in both Khitan large script and small script that contain Khitan names in hopes of finding answers therein.

Unexpectedly, it turns out that the crux of all these riddles lies in the second name, which, as we will discover, has some obvious characteristics, especially its suffix syllable. On the basis of an investigation of the name sources in Khitan small script, we will determine that the suffixes of all second names are composed of one of five characters: [Khitan], [Khitan], [Khitan], [Khitan] or [Khitan], in contrast with the lack of any particular suffix to the small forenames. Next we will cite instances illustrating this discovery, with a concise examination whenever doubts arise as to the type or meaning of the script.

1) Those second names with the suffix character [Khitan]

It is this character that first catches our eyes when we analyze the name sources in Khitan small script. Among all Khitan second names, those with this suffix account for roughly 60% or so. The above mentioned Yelü Dilie's second name [Khitan] is of this kind.

Another example can be taken from the *Epitaph of Yelü Zongjiao* 耶律宗教墓誌銘, which introduces the name of the owner in the second line as follows:

[Khitan]	[Khitan]	[Khitan]	[Khitan]
name	Lufen 驢糞	second (name)	Chaoyin 嘲隱

Yelü Zongjiao was the fourth son of Yelü Longqing 耶律隆慶, the younger brother of Emperor Shengzong 聖宗. According to the textual research of Yan Wanzhang 閻萬章, the words "Lufen" 驢糞 in "The List of the Imperial Princes" 皇子表 and "The List of the Members of the Imperial Family" 皇族表 in the *History of the Liao*, and "Lufen" 旅墳 in "Annals of Shengzong" 聖宗紀 and "Annals of Xingzong" 興宗紀, are all the Khitan forenames of Yelü Zongjiao.[5] The word [illegible] (name) is an incomplete form of the words [illegible] [illegible] (small forename). Although it is recorded that "The Prince's forename is Zongjiao, courtesy name Xigu 希古" in the Chinese version of the *Epitaph of Yelü Zongjiao*, nonetheless these are his Chinese names. His Khitan second name is absent from the Chinese written records. Consulting examples of the transliterations of Khitan names in the *History of the Liao*, his second name, whose suffix is [illegible], might be transliterated as Chaoyin 嘲隱.[6]

A third example comes from the *Epitaph of Yelü Zhixian* 耶律智先墓誌銘, in which his names lie in the fourth and fifth lines:

[illegible] [illegible] [illegible] [illegible] [illegible]
small name Yanliu 延留 second (name) E'liben 訛里本

The first and second words of this sentence are incorporated into a single word in the versions published by both Liu Fengzhu and Qenggeltei 清格爾泰,[7] with no explanation given. After checking the rubbing version, we contend that they are two separate words. This two-word phrase was discovered first in the eighth line of the *Epitaph of the Prince of Xu* 許王墓誌 and was misidentified in *Research on the Khitan Small Script* 契丹小

---

5 Yan Wanzhang, "An Examination of the 'Epitaph of Yelü Zongjiao' in Khitan Small Script" 《契丹小字〈耶律宗教墓誌銘〉考釋》, *Journal of Liaohai Cultural Relics* 《遼海文物學刊》, 1993, no. 2. The transcription of the epitaph is included in appendix II of "A Fifth Decipherment of the Khitan Small Script" 《契丹小字解讀五探》 by Liu Fengzhu 劉鳳翥, et al., *Chinese Studies* 《漢學研究》, vol. 13, no. 2 (1995), p. 337.

6 For instance, Yelü Hanba's 耶律韓八 courtesy name was Chaoyin 嘲隱; see chapter 91 of the *History of the Liao*.

7 Cf. Zhao Zhiwei 趙志偉 and Baoruijun 包瑞軍, "An Examination of the 'Epitaph of Yelü Zhixian'" 《契丹小字〈耶律智先墓誌銘〉考釋》, appendix I, *Minority Languages of China* 《民族語文》, 2001, no. 3, p. 38; Qenggeltei 清格爾泰, *Questions on the Decipherment of the Khitan Small Script* 《契丹小字釋讀問題》 (Tokyo: Research Institute for Languages and Cultures of Asia and Africa at the Tokyo University of Foreign Studies 東京外國語大學亞非語言文化研究所, 2002), p. 233.

字研究 as [Khitan] [Khitan].[8] This was later corrected to [Khitan] [Khitan] by Ji Shi 即實, who pointed out that its meaning is "small forename."[9] This phrase also appears also in the sixth line of the *Epitaph of Yelü Renxian* 耶律仁先墓誌 and, considering its context, it should be read as "small forename" there as well. Since the phonetic sound of the words [Khitan] and [Khitan] may be reconstructed respectively as * p' - ə[10] and * p - xəi - i, and considering that synonymic variants are common in Khitan small script, it is highly probable that the word [Khitan] is a variant of [Khitan]. That is to say, [Khitan] [Khitan] and [Khitan] [Khitan] are synonyms, both meaning "small forename." The third word in the above quotation is just the Khitan small forename of Yelü Zhixian, and, according to the phonetic values of the four characters, which are already known, it could be rendered as "Yanliu" 延留 in Chinese. The last word, which is the second name of Yelü Zhixian and was in common use among the Khitans, was generally transliterated into Chinese as "E'liben" 訛里本 or "Wuluben" 烏盧本. Similarly, the last character of the word is [Khitan].

2) Those second names with the suffix character [Khitan]

Of the various Khitan second names, those with the suffix character [Khitan] were also widely used, probably with a frequency second only to those with the suffix character [Khitan].

For example, the *Epitaph of Yelü Dilie* records the names of the owner in the fourth line as follows:

[Khitan] [Khitan] [Khitan] [Khitan]
name Dilie 迪烈 second (name) Salai 撒懶

As to the tomb owner's small forename Dilie 迪烈, there is still a

[8] Qenggeltei 清格爾泰 and Liu Fengzhu 劉鳳翥, *Research on the Khitan Small Script* 《契丹小字研究》 (Beijing: China Social Sciences Press, 1985), p. 563.

[9] Ji Shi 即實, "The Decipherment of the 'Epitaph of Sen Ne' "《〈森訥墓誌〉釋讀》, in *Seeking the Road out of the Forest of Enigmas: New Decipherments of the Khitan Small Script*《謎林問徑——契丹小字解讀新程》 (Shenyang: Liaoning Nationalities Press 遼寧民族出版社, 1996), p.142.

[10] Since the phonetic value of the character [Khitan] as reconstructed by previous scholars lacks a credible basis, this article argues that it should be pronounced ə according to the Chinese transliteration 訛里本 (E'liben) of the name [Khitan].

dispute requiring resolution. Although the word (Dilie 迪烈), commonly used by the Khitans, appears in other stone inscriptions in the distinct forms or (the first characters of both of which are homophones and thereby are interchangeable), it has been demonstrated that the word form in the quotation is just a variant,[11] with which we agree. Dissent arises when it comes to the form of the second character of the word, which Liu Fengzhu and Qenggeltei copy as ,[12] in contrast to the identification of made by Dr. Bao Lianqun 包聯群, who was prompted by this decipherment to doubt whether this word was the small forename "Dilie" 迪烈 of the owner.[13] Careful checking against the rubbing version lends us the confidence to certify that the correct form of the word is . This assertion, instead of a destabilizer of the original decipherment, is strong evidence in favor of the present reconstruction of the phonetic sound of this word. The word , whose last character is pronounced as -t, corresponds phonetically with its Chinese counterpart "迪烈," because the character "烈," reconstructed in the *fanqie* 反切 pronunciation system of *Extended Rhymes* 廣韻 with "liang xue" 良薛, is also pronounced in the entering tone ending with the consonant -t.

The second name of Yelü Dilie was in the past mistakenly read as "the Second Hengzhang" 横帳 by Liu Fengzhu. According to his analysis, this Yelü Dilie 耶律迪烈 is just that Yelü Dilie 耶律敵烈 recorded in chapter 96 of the *History of the Liao*. The latter's biography says that "Yelü Dilie 耶律敵烈 is called by the courtesy name Salai 撒懶." Based on this sentence, he transliterated the words in the title of the epitaph as Yelü Salai 耶律撒懶, and created confusion by deciphering the same word in the fourth line as "Hengzhang" 横帳. The name "撒

[11] Lu Yinghong 盧迎紅 and Zhou Feng 周峰, "An Examination of the 'Epitaph of Yelü Dilie' in Khitan Small Script" 《契丹小字〈耶律迪烈墓誌銘〉考釋》, in *Minority Languages of China* 《民族語文》, 2000, no. 1. This article reflects Liu Fengzhu's opinion, and the following citations of Mr. Liu's points come from this article.

[12] The copy by Liu Fengzhu is included in the appendix to "An Examination of the 'Epitaph of Yelü Dilie'," and that by Qenggeltei in *The Decipherment of the Khitan Small Script,* p. 224.

[13] Bao Lianqun 包聯群, "A Supplementary Examination of the 'Epitaph of the Deceased Prince of Dilie of the Great Liao in Jambudvipa [the terrestrial world]' " 《〈南贍部洲大遼國故迪烈王墓誌文〉的補充考釋》, *Journal of Inner Mongolia University* 《內蒙古大學學報》, 2002, no. 3, pp. 15-9.

懶" (Salai), used specifically as a second name by the Khitans, appears also in the first line of the *Epitaph of Shilu Taishi* 室魯太師墓誌碑: [Khitan script] [Khitan script] [Khitan script] [Khitan script], the whole sentence meaning "The small forename of Salai Taishi 撒懶太師 is Shilu 室魯."[14] The word [Khitan script] in this epitaph differs slightly from [Khitan script] in the *Epitaph of Yelü Dilie*, but it is still reasonable to claim that they are synonyms. Whatever their forms are, they both end with the character [Khitan script].

A second instance is observed in "The List of the Imperial Princes" 遼史・皇子表 in the *History of the Liao*, where it is recorded that the third son of Emperor Xuanzu 玄祖, whose forename was Shilu 釋魯 and courtesy name Shulan 述瀾, was generally known as Zhongfufang 仲父房. The *Epitaph of Yelü Renxian* in Khitan small script in the third line bore his names, which have been degraded to such an extent that only the first word can be identified as [Khitan script], with the rest impossible to decipher. Students commonly translate this sole identifiable word as "釋魯" Shilu,[15] but we hold that it should be interpreted as Shilu's second name Shulan 述瀾 for the following three reasons. First, the phonetic values of the five characters constituting the word correspond approximately with the Chinese pronunciation of Shulan. Second, the Chinese "釋魯" should be written in Khitan small script as [Khitan script], as has been indicated above. Third, judging from the context of the word, the line imparts the complete form of the owner's name "Shulan Shilu" 述瀾・釋魯, Shulan standing before incompletely written Shilu. In the final analysis, this word, which can be

---

[14] The *Epitaph of Shilu Taishi* 《室魯太師墓誌碑》 has not yet been published. The citation in this article has been transcribed from the rubbing version. The tomb owner is recorded as Salai Shilu 撒懶室魯, yet it is noted in "Biography of Yelü Shilu" in chapter 95 of the *History of the Liao* 《遼史・耶律適祿傳》 that the courtesy name of Shilu is Salai 撒懶, so the discrepancy between the two records of the year of death casts into doubt the conjecture that the two names are of the same person.

[15] See Ji Shi 即實, "The Decipherment of the 'Epitaph of Jiulin' " 《〈糺鄰墓誌〉釋讀》, in *Seeking the Road out of the Forest of Enigmas*, pp. 203-4; Liu Fengzhu 劉鳳翥, *A New Study of the Khitan Scripts* 《契丹文字新研究》, unpublished; Aisin Gioro Ulhicun, "A Comparative Study of the 'Epitaph of Yelü Renxian' and the 'Epitaph of Yelü Zhixian' " 「〈耶律仁先墓誌銘〉與〈耶律智先墓誌銘〉之比較研究」, *Ritsumeikan Bungaku* 『立命館文學』, no. 581 (Sept. 2003).

safely transliterated as the second name Shulan, also has the suffix character 出.

3) Those second names with the suffix character [Khitan]

The character [Khitan] is also a characteristic suffix of Khitan second names and has been widely discovered in the stone inscriptions.

The *Epitaph of Xiao Zhonggong* 蕭仲恭墓誌銘 in Khitan small script of the Jin 金 Dynasty can be cited as an example, the owner's name being recorded in the second line as follows:

[Khitan] [Khitan] □ [Khitan] [Khitan]

Second (name) Wuyan 兀衍 small name Shulizhe 朮里者

This sentence has been repeatedly discussed by scholars. As early as the first publication of the epitaph, Wang Jingru 王靜如 concluded that the tomb owner was Xiao Zhonggong, but scholars have long been unsure which of the above words indicated the name of the owner. Yan Wanzhang arbitrarily explained the second word [Khitan] as "surname Xiao" 蕭氏.[16] Wang Hongli maintained that the owner's name was [Khitan], which he derived from the first word in the quotation by deleting the last suffix character indicating the genitive case. Wang also maintained that the owner was the man recorded in "The Biography of Xiao Zhonggong" in the *History of the Liao* as he "whose autonym is Shulizhe 朮里者," which means "second," in accord with the word "zhong" 仲 (meaning "second" in Chinese) in his Chinese name Xiao Zhonggong 蕭仲恭.[17] In comparison Ji Shi proposed that [Khitan] is the alias of Xiao Zhonggong, and that the second word quoted in the above sentence was his autonym and the last word his forename. This answer is the closest to the truth up to now.[18] Based upon our knowledge of Khitan names, this sentence can now be unambiguously deciphered. This sentence puts the second name

---

[16] Yan Wanzhang 閻萬章, "An Examination of the Khitan Epitaph Excavated from a Tomb of the Jin Dynasty in Xinglong, Hebei Province" 《河北興隆金墓出土契丹文墓誌銘考釋》, *Archaeology and History in Northeast China* 《東北考古與歷史》, vol. 1 (Beijing: Cultural Relics Publishing House, 1982), p. 118.

[17] Wang Hongli 王弘力, "A Study of the Khitan Epitaphs in Small Script" 《契丹小字墓誌研究》, *Minority Languages of China* 《民族語文》, 1986, no. 4, pp. 56-70.

[18] Ji Shi 即實, "The Decipherment of the 'Epitaph of Geyekun' " 《〈戈也昆墓誌〉釋讀》, in *Seeking the Road out of the Forest of Enigmas*, pp. 104-5.

before the small forename, opposite to the general custom reflected in the stone inscriptions in Khitan small script. The third word, being illegible, might be read as either [Khitan script] or [Khitan script]. The last word is Xiao Zhonggong's small forename Shulizhe 朮里者. The word [Khitan script] is his second name, which, since Ji Shi's transliteration "Geyekun" 戈也昆 is far off the mark, can be transliterated as "Wuyan" 兀衍[19] according to examples of transliteration from the Liao Dynasty. It should be noted that this second name ends with the suffix [Khitan script].

"Biography of Xiao Zhonggong" in the *History of the Jin Dynasty* 金史・蕭仲恭傳 says that his son Xiao Gong 蕭拱 "is called in the Khitan language Dinian Abu 迪輦阿不." This name also appears in the twenty-eighth line of the *Epitaph of Xiao Zhonggong* as [Khitan script] [Khitan script], of which the former is the second name Dinian 迪輦, and the latter is the small forename Abu 阿不.[20] Dinian was a commonly used Khitan second name. For example, the second son of Emperor Xuanzu 玄祖, whose forename was Yanmu 岩木, had his courtesy name recorded in "The List of the Imperial Princes" in the *History of the Liao* as Dinian 敵輦. His name can be seen in its complete form in the second line of the *Epitaph of Yelü Renxian* as [Khitan script] [Khitan script]. Although the word [Khitan script] is slightly different in form from [Khitan script], which appears in the *Epitaph of Xiao Zhonggong*, as a result of the fact that the two words, whose first characters are homophones, are used interchangeably, yet they both end with the suffix [Khitan script].

4) Those second names with the suffix character [Khitan script]

Among Khitan second names, there are some, though not too many, which end with the suffix character [Khitan script].

In the *Epitaph of Yelü Hongyong* 耶律弘用墓誌銘, the owner's name appears in the second line as follows:

[Khitan script]	[Khitan script]	[Khitan script]	[Khitan script]	[Khitan script]
small	name	Weiyin 隗因	second (name)	Woluwan 斡魯宛

[19] For instance, the courtesy name of Xiao Tuyu 蕭圖玉 is Wuyan 兀衍; see chapter 93 of the *History of the Liao*.

[20] This name was first deciphered by Ji Shi; see *Seeking the Road out of the Forest of Enigmas*, p. 122.

This epitaph was first deciphered and published by Chen Naixiong 陳乃雄,[21] but he did not provide the transliteration given in the quotation, which was the work of Liu Fengzhu.[22] It is necessary to explain that the form of the fourth word [Khitan script] is slightly different from its generally recognized form [Khitan script]. This is due to the difference between their initial characters, which are ordinarily deemed as two homophonic, yet separate, characters. However, it is highly likely [Khitan script] is a variant of [Khitan script], which finds support in the existence of practical examples. The last word is the owner's second name, which, although transliterated by Liu Fengzhu as Aoluwo 敖盧斡, should be deciphered as Woluwan 斡魯宛, following the transliteration examples from the Liao Dynasty. This second name ends with the suffix [Khitan script].

Another example is the Khitan name of Yelü Xinxian 耶律信先, who was the fifth younger brother of Yelü Renxian, and whose name appears in the seventh line of the *Epitaph of Yelü Renxian* as [Khitan script] [Khitan script].[23] The latter word is his small forename in Khitan, which also appears in eleventh line of the *Epitaph of Yelü Zhixian*, and can be transliterated as "Nielugu" 涅魯古[24] according to its phonetic reconstruction. The prior word is the second name, which Ji Shi has transliterated as "Sabuwan" 撒不椀.[25]

---

[21] Chen Naixiong 陳乃雄 and Yang Jie 楊傑, "An Examination of the Khitan Epitaph in Small Script Excavated from a Tomb of the Liao Dynasty in Wurigentala" 《烏日根塔拉遼墓出土的契丹小字墓誌銘考釋》, in *Northwest Journal of Ethnology* 《西北民族研究》, 1999, no. 2, pp. 72-88, 285.

[22] Liu Fengzhu 劉鳳翥 and Qing Gele 清格勒, "An Examination of the 'Epitaph of the Princess of Song Wei Principality' and the 'Epitaph of Yelü Hongyong' in Khitan Small Script" 《契丹小字〈宋魏國妃墓誌銘〉和〈耶律弘用墓誌銘〉考釋》, in *Literature and History* 《文史》, 2003, no. 4.

[23] There have been three copies of the *Epitaph of Yelü Renxian* published in turn by Ji Shi, Liu Fengzhu, and Qenggeltei, but all three have mistakenly transcribed this name as Yelü Xinxian 耶律信先. This article has corrected their mistakes based upon Liu Fengzhu's unpublished essay *A New Study of the Khitan Scripts*.

[24] The Khitan name of Yelü Xinxian does not appear in the *History of the Liao*. The *Epitaph of Xiao Xingyan* 《蕭興言墓誌》 notes that Xiao Xingyan married his daughter to Nielugu Linya's 涅魯姑林牙 son Tabuye 撻不也, and that Gai Zhiyong 蓋之庸 held that this Nielugu is the same person as Yelü Xinxian (*A Study of the Stone Inscriptions of the Liao Dynasty in Inner Mongolia* 《內蒙古遼代石刻文研究》, Inner Mongolia University Press, 2002, p. 281), with which this article agrees.

[25] Ji Shi 即實, "The Decipherment of the 'Epitaph of Jiulin'," in *Seeking the Road out of*

This decipherment runs counter to transliteration examples from the Liao Dynasty. The Khitan names in Chinese 撒班 (Saban), 撒版 (Saban), 撒板 (Saban), 薩板 (Saban), and 撒本 (Saben), which are commonly employed in the *History of the Liao*, must be the Chinese transliterations of this word. This commonly used second name also ends with the suffix [illegible].

5) Those second names with the suffix character [illegible]

Only two cases of this suffix character are found in the stone inscriptions of Khitan small script.

The *Epitaph of Xiao Tuguci* 蕭圖古辭墓誌銘 presents the owner's name in the second line as follows:[26]

[illegible] [illegible] [illegible] [illegible]

Name Tuguci 圖古辭 second (name) Bolu'en 勃魯恩

Liu Fengzhu holds that this is Xiao Tuguci 蕭圖古辭, a governor of Huanglong Prefecture 黃龍府, who appears in the records of the third year of the Xianyong reign period in the *History of the Liao*, "Annals of Daozong" 道宗紀. The last word of the citation is the owner's second name, which can be transliterated as Bolu'en 勃魯恩[27] based upon the reconstructed phonetic sound of its characters. The fifth line of this epitaph contains the owner's full name [illegible] [illegible], transliterated as Bolu'en Tuguci 勃魯恩・圖古辭. The second name ends with the suffix [illegible].

The second case occurs in the seventh line of the *Epitaph of Yelü Dilie*, which reminisces about the owner's ancestors, where a name is referred to as:

[illegible] [illegible]

Helu'en 曷魯恩 Xiamage 匣馬葛

According to the epitaph, this man is Tiela's second son, who was also

the Forest of Enigmas, p. 210.

[26] This transcribed citation of the epitaph is taken from Liu Fengzhu's copy, which is included in the appendix to "The Excavation Report of the Liao Tomb in Sijiazi, Fuxin" 《阜新四家子遼墓發掘簡報》, by Liang Zhenjing 梁振晶, in *Collected Writings of Liaoning Archaeology*《遼寧考古文集》(Shenyang: Liaoning Nationalities Press, 2003), pp. 121-33.

[27] The name Bolu'en appears in the record of March of the second year of the Tianzan 天贊 reign period in "Annals of Taizu" 《太祖紀》 in the *History of the Liao*.

the owner Yelü Dilie's seventh generation ancestor. The latter word of the quoted name is the small forename, which has been deciphered by Aisin Gioro as Xiamage 匣馬葛.[28] The former word, which was mistakenly split into two distinct words, is the second name.[29] It may well be plausible to surmise that the Khitan names Helu'en, which appears in the record of September of the eleventh year of the Tianxian reign period 天顯 in "Annals of Taizong" 太宗紀 in the *History of the Liao*, and Heluning 曷魯寧, recognized in the records of March of the first year of the Tonghe 統和 reign period and April of the fifth year of the Kaitai 開泰 reign period in "Annals of Shengzong" 聖宗紀 in the *History of the Liao*, are both possibly its Chinese counterparts. It might be better to translate the Khitan name into Chinese as "Helu'en" 曷魯恩, based upon the present knowledge of the phonetic value of that character. This word denoting the second name also ends with the suffix character 杏.

In addition to those cases identified in the above-quoted stone inscriptions of Khitan small script, where the five characters of 伏, 出, 为, 内, 杏 are used as suffixes to designate second names, there is also found in the stone inscriptions in Khitan large script a characteristic suffix character 朩 indicating the second name. Let us cite some examples.

There exists a name in the second line of the *Epitaph of Yelü Xinie* 耶律習涅墓誌銘 in Khitan large script as follows:[30]

---

[28] Aisin Gioro Ulhicun, "An Examination of Xiamage"「匣馬葛考」, *Ritsumeikan Bungaku*, no. 582 (Sept. 2003), pp. 57-66. See also Aisin Gioro Ulhicun, *History of the Liao and Jin Dynasties and the Khitan and Jurchen Scripts* 『遼金史與契丹、女真文』 (Kyoto: Research Institute for History and Culture of East Asia 東亞歷史文化研究會, 2004), pp. 39-48. As for the confusion in the records of the *History of the Liao*, all students of Liao history since Qian Daxin 錢大昕 have regarded Tiela 帖剌, Puguzhi 蒲古只, and Xiamage 匣馬葛 to be names of the same person, while Aisin Gioro Ulhicun's examination has revealed that Puguzhi and Xiamage were, in fact, Tiela's eldest son and second son respectively.

[29] Lu Yinghong 盧迎紅 and Zhou Feng 周峰, "An Examination of the 'Epitaph of Yelü Dilie' in Khitan Small Script"; Qenggeltei 清格爾泰, *The Decipherment of the Khitan Small Scripts*, p. 224. "An Examination of Xiamage" by Aisin Gioro Ulhicun makes the same mistake.

[30] Versions of both the rubbing and a facsimile of the epitaph are published in Jin Yongtian 金永田, "An Examination of the 'Epitaph of Yelü Xinie' in Khitan Large Script"《契丹大字"耶律習涅墓誌"考釋》, in *Archaeology*《考古》, 1991, no. 4. The transcribed citations and explanations all come from *A New Study of the Khitan Scripts*

序 夵　　　伙 平
Xining 習寧　Lubugu 盧不姑

This man is Xinie's sixth generation ancestor. A Chinese version of the *Epitaph of Yelü Xinie* unearthed at the same time recorded that "the Yuyue Prince 于越王, the Grand Marshal of the Army 兵馬大元帥, called Xining 習寧 by taboo name (諱, *hui*, a reverent appellation of the forename) and Lubugu 盧不姑 by small courtesy name, is the sixth generation ancestor 六世祖 of the Revered One 公."[31] Also, it is recorded in his biography in chapter 76 of the *History of the Liao* that "The courtesy name of Yelü Lubugu 耶律魯不古 is Xinning 信寧." "魯不古" (Lubugu) is a variant of "盧不姑" (Lubugu), and "信寧" (Xinning) is a variant of "習寧" (Xining). Since the records of Khitan names in Chinese stone inscriptions of the Liao Dynasty are not as regular as those of the *History of the Liao*, it could be posited that the "small courtesy name" of Lubugu 盧不姑 in this epitaph actually refers to his small forename, and Xining indicates his second name, namely the courtesy name mentioned in the *History of the Liao*. The Khitan name custom used in large script dictates that the second name precede the small forename in writing. The second name of the large script ends with 夵.

We have another example in the fifth line of the same epitaph:

夊夵　　　臭考
Ying' en 應恩　Guanyin 觀音

This is the great-grandfather of Yelü Xinie, and the Chinese version of the epitaph records that the "Military Commissioner 節度使, called Ying'en 應恩 by taboo name and Guanyin 觀音 by small forename, is the great-grandfather of the Revered One." Chapter 79 of the *History of the Liao* says that Yelü Xianshi 耶律賢適 had a son named Guanyin, who was the same one as in this epitaph. Guanyin was his small forename and Ying'en his second name, which also ends with the character 夵.

On account of the relative paucity of stone inscriptions in Khitan large script, and of the fact that the current level of decipherment of Khitan large script is far lower than that of small script, this is, as yet, the only suffix character indicating the second name found in the Khitan large

---

(unpublished) by Liu Fengzhu.

[31] Gai Zhiyong 蓋之庸, *A Study of the Stone Inscriptions of the Liao Dynasty in Inner Mongolia*, p. 357.

script stone inscriptions. It could well be expected, in the light of the following grammatical analyses of the syllables of the suffix characters indicating second names, that there should be several additional suffix characters for second names. This remains open to further research.

To summarize, the evidence from the stone inscriptions in both Khitan small script and large script corroborates the same fact; that is, that the suffix characters of Khitan second names are a kind of appendix featuring some specific syllables. This fact was actually noticed nearly twenty years ago by scholars such as Wang Hongli, who has written penetratingly that "most of the Khitan small forenames end with the syllable *–n*."[32] Even though this statement is not entirely correct – it is in fact the Khitan courtesy names (i.e., the second names) rather than the small forenames that end with the syllable *–n* – it is still worthy of praise that Mr. Wang had been heedful of the evidence, though regrettably without follow-up. Recently, after analyzing several suffix characters of Khitan names in small script, Aisin Gioro has proposed a more explicit point of view. She believes that Khitan forenames and courtesy names are generally cognate, and that the words used as courtesy names are as a rule composed of the same words as forenames with an appendent suffix character whose phonetic sound ends with the consonant *-in* or *-n*.[33]

This rule was first discovered by Nie Hongyin 聶鴻音. He analyzed the suffix characters of Khitan courtesy names as recorded in the *History of the Liao* from the perspective of Chinese phonology. He held that the

---

[32] Wang Hongli 王弘力, "A Study of the Khitan Epitaphs in Small Script," p. 59.

[33] Aisin Gioro Ulhicun, "The Characteristics of the Khitan Names: with a Note about the Suffixes of the Derivative Adjectives in the Khitan Language" 「契丹人的命名特徵——兼論契丹語派生形容詞的後綴」, in *Studies of the Khitan Language and Scripts* 『契丹語言文字研究』(Kyoto: Research Institute for the History and Culture of East Asia 東亞歷史文化研究會, 2004), pp. 210-25. Aisin Gioro Ulhicun holds that the characters [Khitan character], [Khitan character], [Khitan character], [Khitan character], [Khitan character], [Khitan character] are all suffixes of Khitan names. However, due to a misunderstanding of the differences between the Khitan small forename and second name, she mistakes the small forenames of [Khitan characters] (謝十 Xieshi), [Khitan characters] (高十 Gaoshi), [Khitan characters] (瑰引 Guiyin) for second names and therefore reaches an incorrect conclusion. Actually, the second name of Han Xieshi 韓謝十 is [Khitan characters] (延寧 Yanning), which appears in the sixth line of the *Epitaph of Yelü (Han) Dilie* 《耶律(韓)迪烈墓誌銘》; and that of Han Gaoshi 韓高十 is [Khitan characters] (王寧 Wangning), which appears in the thirteenth line of the *Epitaph of Han Gaoshi*; and that of Yelü Guiyin is [Khitan characters] (查懶 Chalai), which appears in the fifth line of the *Epitaph of Yelü Renxian*.

Khitan courtesy names show that there are two kinds of noun appendices, i.e. -n and –in, and that they are complementary in distribution in that –n stands only after the vowels a, e, i, and o, while –in stands only after the vowel u and consonants. Thus a phenomenon deserving careful thought revealed itself to him: that between Khitan forenames and courtesy names there stood no such semantic connection as exists in Chinese names, and that in most cases the names are linked through a transformation of their suffixes. Nie Hongyin wrote that "the Khitans always used the same group of words for the denomination of forenames, whereas another group of words was used specifically to denote courtesy names, the latter seeming to be constructed out of the former by certain grammatical means."[34]

The phenomenon revealed by Mr. Nie matches nicely with the rule of Khitan second name suffixes identified in the Khitan stone inscriptions. Both of them point to the same problem. The question here is, what are the common grounds of the distinct suffixes in the Khitan second names cited above? And what are the differences separating them? To answer these questions, it is necessary to probe their phonetic values and grammatical significance.

1) The first suffix in Khitan small script: **伏**

Research on the Khitan Small Script reconstructed this character's phonetic value as [nə]. This was based upon the Khitan designation of dogs as "niehe" 揑褐 in the "Monograph on Ritual" 禮志 section of the *History of the Liao* and upon the fact that, among the twelve animals symbolizing the year in which one is born, the dog is written in Khitan small script as **伏为**. This phonetic reconstruction is evidently not quite correct, since in the "Monograph on Imperial Guards" 營衛志 section of the *History of the Liao* "filial piety" is called in Khitan "赤寔得本" (chi shi de ben), whose suffix character in Khitan small script is also **伏**. If the above reconstruction is correct, then this constitutes a paradox.

There are many instances of this character in the name sources in Khitan small script, which can be exploited to correct the phonetic reconstruction above. We have learned from the biographies in the *History*

[34] Nie Hongyin 聶鴻音, "The Substantive Suffixes of *-n and *-in in the Khitan Language" 《契丹語的名詞附加成分*-n 和 *-in》, *Minority Languages of China*, 2001, no. 2, pp. 56-60. The following citations of Nie's analysis all come from this same article and their references will be omitted.

of the Liao that the Khitans' Chinese courtesy names end mostly with the characters 隱 (yin) or 寧 (ning), whereas in Khitan small script they generally end with the suffix [Khitan]. Examples are [Khitan] (留隱 Liuyin), [Khitan] (乙辛隱 Yixinyin), [Khitan] (韓隱 Hanyin), [Khitan] (國隱 Guoyin), [Khitan] (遵甯 Zunning, or 遜寧 Xunning), and so on. According to Nie Hongyin, the suffixes of these names bear the common phonetic sound *–in*. Here are the supporting cases he cites from the *History of the Liao*: a forename 柳 (Liu) and a courtesy name 留隱 (Liuyin), in the latter case *–in* being affixed to the vowel *u*; the forenames 乙辛 (Yixin) and 翰 (Han) and the courtesy names 乙辛隱 (Yixinyin) and 韓隱 (Hanyin), again in the latter two cases *–in* being subjoined to the consonant *n*.

However, another series of second names with the [Khitan] suffix, such as [Khitan] (訛里本 E'liben) and [Khitan] (曷魯本 Heluben) seem to contradict the rule of *–in* phonetic reconstruction. It could be reasonably inferred, according to Chinese phonology in the Liao Dynasty, that the suffix [Khitan] in these second names should be reconstructed as –ən.

Possibly this confusing contradiction might be resolved by a phonetic explanation. As far as the knowledge of the phonetic rules of Khitan small script is concerned, generally the characters employed to represent consonants have an uncertain vowel, which for the definition depends upon the phonetic sound after which it is appended. In view of these factors, the phonetic range of the suffix [Khitan] can be reconstructed as *in~ən; and judging from practical examples, it is only found affixed to consonants and the vowel u. As to the grammatical role of this character, scholars such as Qenggeltei have presumed that it was a suffix of the stative words.[35]

2) The suffix in Khitan large script: [Khitan]

The Khitan large script [Khitan] was given a reconstructed phonetic value of either –in or –ən by Liu Fengzhu, who proposed that "–in or –ən could be used to transliterate either the 隱 (yin) of 留隱 (Liuyin) or the Chinese word 恩 (en)."[36] This statement requires further discussion.

---

[35] Qenggeltei and Liu Fengzhu, *Research on the Khitan Small Script,* p. 138.

[36] Liu Fengzhu 劉鳳翥 and Wang Yunlong 王雲龍, "An Examination of the 'Epitaph of Yelü Changyun' in Khitan Large Script" 《契丹大字〈耶律昌允墓誌銘〉之研究》,

Evidence has shown that this large script could be used as an alternative to the suffix [Khitan] in small script. For example, from the fact that the word [Khitan] in the fourth line of the *Epitaph of the Princess of Song Wei Principality* 宋魏國妃墓誌銘 in Khitan small script is transliterated into Chinese in the Liao Dynasty as Liuyin 留引 or Liuwen 六溫 (namely Xiao Xiaocheng 蕭孝誠),[37] while the word [Khitan] in the seventh line of the *Epitaph of Yelü Changyun* 耶律昌允墓誌銘 in Khitan large script was transliterated into Chinese as Liuyin 留隱 in "Biography of Yelü Haili" 耶律海里傳 in the 84th chapter of the *History of the Liao*, it can be deduced that [Khitan] in Khitan large script and [Khitan] in Khitan small script are the same word. That is, [Khitan] is equivalent to [Khitan], and [Khitan] is equivalent to [Khitan]. Another example is the second name [Khitan] (乙辛隱 Yixinyin), which frequently appears in the stone inscriptions in Khitan small script. It is written in the ninth line of the *Epitaph of Yelü Xinie*, which is inscribed in large script as [Khitan].[38] This shows that [Khitan] is equivalent to [Khitan] and that [Khitan] is equivalent to [Khitan]. Again, in the fourth line of the *Epitaph of the Princess of Song Wei Principality* in small script, there is the word [Khitan], which was transliterated into Chinese in the Liao Dynasty as Jieli 解里, Xieli 諧里, and Xieling 諧領 (namely 蕭和 Xiaohe).[39] Because the word [Khitan] in the sixth line of the *Epitaph of Yelü Changyun* in large script is identified as the courtesy name of Hailin 孩鄰 as recorded in "The Biography of Yelü Balide" 耶律拔里得 in chapter 76 of the *History of the Liao*, and since Hailin 孩鄰 and Xieling 諧領 are variants of the same name, it is therefore plausible to conclude

---

"Appendix I, The Table of the Reconstructed Phonetic Values of the Khitan Large Script," *Yenching Journal of Chinese Studies* 《燕京學報》, Peking University Press, new series, vol. 17 (Nov. 2004), p. 86.

[37] See the *Epitaph of the Princess of Song Wei Principality* and the *Epitaph of the Great Princess of Liang Principality* 《梁國太妃墓誌銘》, both in Chinese and unpublished.

[38] The name Yixin 乙信 in the *Epitaph of Yelü Xinie* in Chinese is an elided version of Yixinyin with the end syllable omitted.

[39] See, respectively, the *Epitaph of the Princess of Song Wei Principality*; the *Epitaph of Lady Xiao, Princess of Jin Principality and Wife of Yelü Yuan* 《耶律元妻晉國夫人蕭氏墓誌; and the *Epitaph of the Great Princess of Qin Principality* 《秦國太妃墓誌》, all in Chinese and unpublished. The former two names both have their end consonants omitted, and only Xieling 諧領 can be judged to be a relatively normative Chinese transliteration.

that the word [Khitan] in large script and the word [Khitan] in small script are the same word. That is, [Khitan] equals [Khitan] and [Khitan] equals [Khitan].[40] The above evidence shows us that the large script suffix character of second names [Khitan] was identical to the small script word [Khitan] in regards to both phonetic sound and grammatical significance.[41]

3) The second suffix in Khitan small script: [Khitan]

No consensus has been achieved thus far concerning the phonetic value of [Khitan].[42] Judging from a re-inscription in the thirty-eighth line of the *Epitaph of Xiao Zhonggong*, the word [Khitan] seems to have been changed to [Khitan], and scholars infer that [Khitan] and [Khitan] may have a common grammatical role and phonetic sound. Both of these two characters appear to be suffixes of some kind of adjectival verbs.[43]

In the above cases of second names ending with [Khitan], either [Khitan], [Khitan] (撒懶 Salai) or [Khitan] (述瀾 Shulan), the phonetic value of the suffix characters can all be reconstructed as –n. In his analysis of Khitan courtesy names, Mr. Nie also holds that the phonetic value of the suffix character of "撒懶" is –n appended to the vowel a. Qenggeltei points out that although the sounds of [Khitan] and [Khitan] still evade our confirmation, at least one respect is certain, i.e. that [Khitan] appears in most cases after the vowel ɑ, while [Khitan] appears after the vowel ə. This differential use of the two

---

[40] Two additional pieces of evidence support this verdict. The word [Khitan] in the seventh line of the *Epitaph of Yelü Changyun* in Khitan large script is transliterated in "Biography of Yelü Haili" in the *History of the Liao* 《遼史・耶律海里傳》 as Haili 海里, and the word [Khitan] in the seventh line of the *Epitaph of Yelü Xinie* in Khitan large script is transliterated in the Chinese version as Jieli 解里.

[41] Nie Hongyin holds that the suffix syllable of the names 孩鄰 (Hailin) and 海鄰 (Hailin) in the *History of the Liao* is -i appended with –n. This article disagrees, because in the case of the word [Khitan], its suffix syllable should be the consonant -r appended with –in.

[42] It is read as -ʧʊ in *Research on the Khitan Small Script*; as t~tɑ in Shen Hui's 沈彙 "An Examination of the Authors of the Stone Inscriptions in Khitan Small Script" 《契丹小字石刻撰人考》, *Archaeology and Cultural Relics* 《考古與文物》, 1982, no. 6; and as sɑ in Qenggeltei's *The Decipherment of the Khitan Small Script*. All of these reconstructions are mere conjectures.

[43] Qenggeltei and Liu Fengzhu, *Research on the Khitan Small Script*, pp. 144-5.

characters presumably relates to the law of vowel harmony.[44] This conclusion corresponds roughly with the phonetic rule for the suffixes of Khitan second names.

4) The third suffix in Khitan small script:

Scholars differ greatly with each other regarding this character's phonetic reconstruction. It is reconstructed in *Research on the Khitan Small Script* as -ʧʊ, by Shen Hui 沈彙 as -i, by Ji Shi as -kun, by Wang Hongli as - dʒə, by Qenggeltei as -sə,[45] and by Aisin Gioro as -əi.[46] All of these reconstructions are merely personal opinions, unsupported by sound foundations.

Actually the range of the phonetic values of may be fixed if we take into consideration the Chinese transliteration of Khitan second names ending with . In "Biography of Xiao Wuna" 蕭兀納傳 in the *History of the Liao* the word in the second line of the *Epitaph of Xiao Zhonggong* includes the transliterated Chinese name Temian 特免. The names Temoyan 特末衍 in "Biography of Yelü Zhangnu" 耶律章奴傳 in the *History of the Liao* and [Xiao] Temoning [蕭]特末寧 in the *Epitaph of Lady Xiao, Princess of Qin Yue Principality and Wife of the Younger Brother of the Emperor* 皇弟秦越國妃蕭氏墓誌 should both be the variants of this name. Another second name containing was , as mentioned above, which was transliterated into Chinese as 迪輦 (Dinian) or 敵輦 (Dinian). Since the name Diliening 迪烈甯 in the *Epitaph of Xiao Yi* 蕭義墓誌 has been identified by Xiang Nan 向南 to be Xiao Dilu 蕭敵魯,[47] whose courtesy name is recorded in "Biography of Xiao Dilu" 蕭敵魯傳 in the *History of the Liao* as Dinian 敵輦, it is safe to affirm that Diliening 迪烈寧 is a variant of Dinian. These Chinese transliterations suffice to define the range of the phonetic values of to be *in~ian.

---

[44] Qenggeltei, *The Decipherment of the Khitan Small Script*, pp. 83-4.

[45] For these different opinions, see Qenggeltei, *The Decipherment of the Khitan Small Script*, p. 96.

[46] Aisin Gioro Ulhicun, "The Phonetic Reconstruction of the Khitan Small Script" 「契丹小字的語音構擬」, *Ritsumeikan Bungaku*, no. 577 (Dec. 2002), pp. 42-3.

[47] Xiang Nan 向南, ed., *The Stone Inscriptions of the Liao Dynasty* 《遼代石刻文編》 (Shijiazhuang: Hebei Education Press, 1995), pp. 623, 625.

5) The fourth suffix in Khitan small script: [Khitan character]

As yet no explicit phonetic value has been reconstructed for this character. In Khitan small script there is another character [Khitan character], similar in form to [Khitan character], which served to denote the genitive attribute grammatically and appeared frequently in Chinese loanwords. Its phonetic sound has been reconstructed approximately as *-in*. Aisin Gioro has proposed an explanation for the difference between the two characters: they are two phonetic characters, which when standing at the end of a syllable indicate the consonant n, the difference being that [Khitan character] mostly stands after the wide vowels and [Khitan character] mostly after the vowel i.[48]

An incidental clarification needs to be made here. In a recently published article, Aisin Gioro holds that the character [Khitan character] is also a suffix of Khitan courtesy names. The only example she cites is the Khitan name [Khitan character], which appears in the twenty-sixth line of the *Epitaph of Yelü Nu* and in the fifth line of the *Epitaph of Yelü Renxian.*[49] This is an obvious misunderstanding arising from her confusing the small forename with the second name. She mistakes the last character of [Khitan character], which was used as a small forename and transliterated into Chinese in the Liao Dynasty as Guoyin 國隱 or Guiyin 瑰引, for a kind of suffix. Actually, this small forename is an etymon, on the basis of which was constituted the second name [Khitan character] (see the fourth line of the *Epitaph of Yelü Nu*), which can be transliterated as Guoning 國寧, and the suffix of which is [Khitan character] rather than [Khitan character].[50] In the stone inscriptions in Khitan small script unearthed thus far, there are no cases of the character [Khitan character] serving as a suffix of second names, and there is no evidence showing that the two characters could be used interchangeably.

A typical example of a second name ending with [Khitan character] is found in the seventh line of the *Epitaph of Yelü Renxian* in the word [Khitan character], which was transliterated variously in the *History of the Liao* as 撒班 (Saban), 撒版 (Saban), 撒板 (Saban), 薩板 (Saban), and 撒本 (Saben), etc. It is

[48] Aisin Gioro Ulhicun, "Notes on the Khitan and Mongolian Histories" 「契丹蒙古劄記」, the entry "The Characteristics of the Northern Peoples' Names," *Ritsumeikan Bungaku*, no. 586 (Oct. 2004), p. 13.

[49] Aisin Gioro Ulhicun, "The Characteristics of Khitan Names: with a Note about the Suffixes of the Derivative Adjectives in the Khitan Language," pp. 211-3, 219.

[50] There will be no discussion as to the identification of this forename and courtesy name, but see Part II of this article.

recorded in "Biography of Xiao Xiaozhong" 蕭孝忠傳 in the *History of the Liao* that Xiao Xiaozhong's courtesy name was 撒班 (Saban), which was written as 撒八寧 (Sabaning) in the record of the jisi 己巳 day in October of the seventh year of the Chongxi 重熙 reign period in "Annals of Xingzong" 興宗紀 in the *History of the Liao*. "Biography of Yelü Asi" 耶律阿思傳 notes Asi's courtesy name as 撒班 (Saban), which is written in the *Epitaph of Xiao Yi* as "撒巴寧" (Sabaning). It is therefore more desirable, considering these various Chinese transliterations, to reconstruct the phonetic sound of [Khitan character] as *n-in. Nie Hongyin contends that the phonetic sound of the suffix character of Saban is –*n* appended to *a*, while in second names ending with [Khitan character], [Khitan character] was commonly affixed to the character [Khitan character], whose phonetic value can be established approximately as [o].

6) The fifth suffix character in Khitan small script: [Khitan character]

The meaning of this character is ox. Liu Fengzhu has reconstructed its sound as -ni, holding that it was a loanword from Chinese and akin in sound to the Chinese word *niu* 牛 (cattle).[51] This point is not sufficiently convincing. Among the Khitan words denoting the twelve animals symbolizing the year in which one is born, only that for dragon is a loanword from Chinese – the others are all of Khitan origin. Moreover, since the ox was not strange to the Khitans (for example, the Khitans had a legend of the black ox and the white horse), for what reason would they borrow a word from Chinese? Qenggeltei has maintained that this character was sounded as -un, possibly cognate with the Mongolian word *unijə* (meaning a cow).[52] We have some sympathy for this view considering the two cases cited above of [Khitan characters] (勃魯恩 Bolu'en) in the *Epitaph of Xiao Tuguci* and [Khitan characters] (曷魯恩 Helu'enin) the *Epitaph of Yelü Dilie*. The suffix character [Khitan character] of both words presumably bears the sound of –un as an affixation to the vowel u, which has been affirmed definitively to be the reconstructed sound of the [Khitan character] standing before it.

51 Liu Fengzhu 劉鳳翥, "A Fourth Decipherment of the Khitan Small Script"《契丹小字解讀四探》, in *Proceedings of the 35th Permanent International Altaistic Conference* (Taipei: Center for Chinese Studies Materials, United Daily News Cultural Foundation, 1992).

52 Qenggeltei, *The Decipherment of the Khitan Small Script*, pp. 38-9.

This phonetic reconstruction fits well into the rule of vowel harmony.

The reconstruction and distribution of the phonetic values of the suffix characters in second names in both small script and large script discussed above can be summed up as follows:

The small script character [illegible] and the large script character [illegible] : * in ～ən, appended only to consonants or to the vowel u;

The small script character [illegible] : * -n, mostly after the vowel α;

The small script character [illegible] : * in ～ ian, mostly after the vowel ə;

The small script character [illegible] : * n ～ in, after the vowel o;

The small script character [illegible] : * -un, after the vowel u.

Cursory as these phonetic analyses are, two rules can still be seen. First, the suffix characters of all second names, either in small script or in large script, contain a common basic phonetic value –n. Second, these five kinds of suffix characters of second names are apparently complementary to each other, presumably for the sake of vowel harmony. These rules intimate that the various suffix characters of second names in the Khitan language should play the same grammatical role. Nie Hongyin had once supposed that the two suffixes –n and –in, which he had derived from an analysis of Khitan second names, might possibly be genitive suffixes, which may well be correct, according to the analyses of the suffix characters of the second names in both small script and large script. A comparison with the Mongolian and Daur languages akin to Khitan may help elucidate this point.

In the eyes of some current scholars of Mongolian studies, the Khitan language is identical with primitive Mongolian, or at least can be viewed as one of the base languages of Mongolian, therefore the comparison between Khitan and Mongolian is naturally instructive. There are three kinds of genitive suffixes in modern Mongolian: 1) -yin, used after the words ending with vowels; 2) -un, used after the words ending with all consonants except n; and 3) -u, used after the words ending with the consonant n. Since the sound -n is commonly contained in these three kinds of genitive suffixes (in the case of the third kind, the consonant n stands before the vowel), there comes into being, after a further abstraction of their grammatical roles, a kind of simplified genitive, i.e., a genitive whose suffix contains merely the sound –n. This phenomenon is currently in the process of evolution in speech, but up to now has not been registered in the written language.[53]

In addition, the Daurs are held by many historians to be of Khitan stock, thus within the Mongolian language group the Khitan language is regarded as closest to the Daur language,[54] which means that a comparison between the two may be of some use. The suffixes of Daur personal pronouns are divided into three kinds, that of the first person, that of the second person, and that of the third person, each kind being further divided into singular and plural forms, without regard for the rule of vowel harmony. All of these suffixes to the Daur personal pronouns have one thing in common – the end sound is invariably –n.[55]

Thus it is apparent that the suffixes of Khitan second names are similar to the genitive suffixes in both the Mongolian and the Daur languages in that no matter whether or not they fit into the rule of vowel harmony, their basic sounds are uniformly –n. Although it is permissible thus far to conclude that the analysis of the grammatical role of the suffix characters in various second names in both Khitan small script and large script is persuasive, new questions arise concomitantly from this conclusion. Why are genitive suffixes appended without exception to Khitan second names? What is the implication of the existence of those suffixes in Khitan full names? Therein is concealed a secret remaining as yet unknown, which will reveal an aspect of a people's culture that vanished into the depths of history long ago. The stone inscriptions in Khitan script remain crucial to the disclosure of this secret.

Part II. The Phenomenon of Father-Son Name Linkage as Seen in the Khitan Stone Inscriptions

The following discovery is a logical consequence of our preliminary knowledge of the unique Khitan full name (composed of second name and small forename) and, especially, of the successful identification of the

[53] Qenggeltei 清格爾泰, *Mongolian Grammar*《蒙古語語法》(Huhhot: Inner Mongolia People's Press, 1991), pp. 150, 152.

[54] See Liu Fengzhu 劉鳳翥, "A Concise Commentary on the Phylum Identity and Characteristics of the Khitan Language" 《略論契丹語的語系歸屬與特點》, *The Continent Magazine* 《大陸雜誌》, vol. 84, no. 5 (May 1992).

[55] Namcarai 拿木四來, "The Genitive Suffixes of the Daur Nouns" 《達斡爾語名詞的領屬附加成分》, in *Collected Studies of Minority Languages of China* 《民族語文研究文集》 (Qinghai Nationalities Press, 1982), pp. 453-7.

suffix character of second names. From the tomb owners' genealogies, as recorded in several epitaphs inscribed with the Khitan small and large scripts, an interesting rule leaps to our attention: a similar connection exists between the names of some fathers and their sons. Here follow the specific cases.

1) Yelü Hou 耶律吼 and Yelü Helubu 耶律何魯不

"The Biography of Yelü Hou" in chapter 77 of the *History of the Liao* records that "Yelü Hou, whose courtesy name is Helu 曷魯…has a son Helubu 何魯不." The accessory biography of Helubu annexed to his father's biography says that "the courtesy name of Helubu is Xiening 斜寧." The name Helubu 何魯不, also written as Helibi 曷里必 in the *History of the Liao*, appears in the records of July of the seventh year of the Baoning 保寧 reign period in "Annals of Jingzong" 景宗紀 in the *History of the Liao*. The middle of the 1990s saw the discovery of the *Epitaph of Yelü Dilie* 耶律迪烈 in Khitan small script, which had been stolen from a tomb in Zhalute Banner 扎魯特旗, Inner Mongolia. Since the owner, according to the textual analysis of Liu Fengzhu, was a fifth generation descendant of Yelü Hou 耶律吼,[56] the names of Yelü Hou and his son are recorded. The Khitan name of Yelü Hou in its full form appears in the eighth line of the epitaph as [Khitan small script] (曷魯本・吼), while his son Helubu's name appears in the tenth line as [Khitan small script] (the eldest son Xiening Helubu 斜寧・何魯不).[57] Actually, the names of Yelü Hou and his son had already been found in the fifth line of the *Epitaph of the Deceased Ms. Yelü* 故耶律氏銘石 and deciphered correctly by Ji Shi.[58] Nonetheless, we still have some doubt concerning

---

[56] "The Biography of Yelü Dilie", *History of the Liao*, chapter 96.

[57] Lu Yinghong 盧迎紅 and Zhou Feng 周峰, "An Examination of the 'Epitaph of Yelü Dilie' in Khitan Small Script," *Minority Languages of China* 《民族語文》, 2000, no. 1.

[58] Ji Shi 即實, "An Examination of the 'Epitaph of the Deceased Ms. Yelü' " 《〈銘石〉瑣解》, *Seeking the Road out of the Forest of Enigmas*, pp. 187-9. According to Aisin Gioro Ulhicun, the owners of the *Epitaph of Yelü Dilie* and the *Epitaph of the Deceased Ms. Yelü* are father and daughter, which explains the fact that both of the epitaphs feature the retrospective genealogy of Yelü Hou and his son. See her "An Examination of the Genealogies of the Tomb Owners Recorded in the 'Epitaph of Yelü Dilie' and the 'Epitaph of the Deceased Ms.Yelü': with a Note about Khitan Forenames and Courtesy Names."

the names of the father and son. The small forename of Yelü Helubu was [Khitan], written in the *History of the Liao* as Helubu 何魯不 or Helibi 曷里必; while his father's second name was [Khitan], sounding * xol - p - ən and recorded in the *History of the Liao* as Helu 曷魯. With the elided suffix's syllable restored, this should be transliterated, as Ji Shi has pointed out, as Heluben 曷魯本. In our opinion this is the most faithful transliteration. This indicates that the small forename of Yelü Helubu, [Khitan], is almost identical with his father Yelü Hou's second name [Khitan], except for the lack of suffix character. In other words, the second name of Yelü Hou is composed of the small forename of his eldest son and the genitive suffix character [Khitan]. Had there been no records in the stone inscriptions in Khitan small script, this subtle relationship between the names of the father and son could scarcely have been seen.

2) Yelü Nu 耶律奴 and Yelü Guoyin 耶律國隱

The *Epitaph of Yelü Nu* in Khitan small script records the owner's name in the fourth line as follows:

[Khitan]	[Khitan]	[Khitan]	[Khitan]	[Khitan]
child	name	Nu 奴	second (name)	Guoning 國寧

The last word [Khitan], not yet identified, was separated into two distinct words and thereby mistakenly deciphered as Guoxing 國姓 by Liu Fengzhu, who further interpreted the last two words as "Guoxing of the second class."[59] This word appears also in the title of the epitaph in the first line, and these two instances of the word in different lines can be recognized as identical after a careful comparison with the rubbing version. Current knowledge of Khitan names enables us to affirm that it is the second name of Yelü Nu, which can be transliterated as Guoning 國寧, based upon the phonetic value of the character.

Yelü Nu has no biography in the *History of the Liao*, yet his wife Xiao Yixin 蕭意辛 is recorded in "Biographies of Distinguished Women" 列女傳 in the *History of the Liao* as follows: "Ms. Xiao, the wife of Yelü Nu, is

---

[59] Shi Jinmin 石金民 and Yu Zemin 于澤民, "An Examination of the 'Epitaph of Yelü Nu' in Khitan Small Script" 《契丹小字〈耶律奴墓誌銘〉考釋》, *Minority Languages of China*, 2001, no. 2. This article reflects Liu Fengzhu's view of point. The facsimile of Qenggeltei makes the same mistake; see *The Decipherment of the Khitan Small Script*, p. 242.

called Yinxin 意辛 by small forename…Her son is named Guoyin 國隱, and so on." In the twenty-sixth line of the epitaph the son is recorded as follows:

male child two the eldest son Guoyin 國隱

Guoyin 國隱 was the small forename of the eldest son of Yelü Nu. A comparison discloses that it is the genitive suffix character that distinguishes the second name of Yelü Nu from his eldest son's small forename .

3) Yelü Guiyin 耶律瑰引 and Yelü Renxian 耶律仁先

The Chinese name of Yelü Renxian's father was Sizhong 思忠, which appears in the Chinese epitaphs of Yelü Renxian, Yelü Zhixian, and Yelü Qingsi 耶律慶嗣. His Khitan name was Guiyin 瑰引, as recorded in the "Biography of Yelü Renxian" in chapter 96 of the *History of the Liao*: "His father Guiyin, the Prime Minister of Nanfu (南府, the Southern Administration), is entitled Prince of Yan 燕王." This Khitan name is also found in the "List of the Members of the Imperial Family" and the "Biography of Yelü Xinxian" in the *History of the Liao*. His Khitan name in its full form is identified in the fifth line of the *Epitaph of Yelü Renxian* in Khitan small script:

Chalan 查懶 Guiyin 瑰引 Prime Minister 宰相

Since there has been no consensus achieved as to the form and meaning of this name, it is therefore necessary to make a further analysis. Liu Fengzhu construes the last two words as "the Prime Minister of the country" 國之宰相, with the first word untouched,[60] while Ji Shi renders the whole as "the Prime Minister Chalachu Guiyin" 查剌初瑰引宰相,[61] which is in the main acceptable, except for the decipherment of the first word. As is shown above, the name of Yelü Nu's son is recorded in the *History of the Liao* as Guoyin, which, appearing in the *Epitaph of Yelü Nu*

60 Liu Fengzhu 劉鳳翥, "A Fourth Decipherment of the Khitan Small Script," appendix I, p. 550. His latest study (unpublished), *A New Study of the Khitan Scripts,* still supports this opinion.

61 Ji Shi 即實, "The Decipherment of the 'Epitaph of Jiulin'" in *Seeking the Road out of the Forest of Enigmas*, pp. 206-7.

as , is identical in form with the small forename of Yelü Guiyin cited above. This identification justifies Ji Shi's explanation of as Guiyin 瑰引 – evidently Guiyin and Guoyin are transliterations of the same word. In addition, the name of Yelü Guiyin has been ferreted out in the eighth line of the *Epitaph of Yelü Zhixian*:

Chalai 查懶 Yan 燕 Prince Guiyin 瑰引

The first word in this line is interpreted in the facsimiles of Liu Fengzhu and Qenggeltei as , which, after comparison with the rubbing version, can be rectified as , because the last character of the word is in cursive calligraphy, rather than . The word is commonly used in the stone inscriptions in small script as a second name, while the word is never found in other stone inscriptions. The latter three words of the line cited above were interpreted by Liu Fengzhu as "the Kingdom of Yan" 燕王國,[62] showing that the small forename of Yelü Guiyin was still treated as a loanword from Chinese. Admittedly, the title interposed between the second name and the small forename may easily court misunderstanding. But in fact, the employment of such a formula as "second name + official title or honor + small forename" to designate personages is a general rule in the stone inscriptions in small script. To cite an example, Yelü Renxian in the tenth line of the *Epitaph of Yelü Zhixian* is called Jiulin Shangfu Song Wang Chalai 糺鄰尚父宋王查剌, and his son is called Hudujin Zhaotao Linggong Tabuye 胡獨堇招討令公撻不也. Altogether, the second name of Yelü Guiyin, though not appearing in Chinese literature, does appear in the stone inscriptions in Khitan small script with the normal form , which can be transliterated as Chalai 查懶.

Yelü Renxian, the eldest son of Yelü Guiyin, whose Chinese name is recorded in the *Epitaph of Yelü Renxian* in Chinese as "The prince's forename is Renxian, courtesy name Yide 一得, and surname Yelü," has his Khitan name recorded in chapter 96 of the *History of the Liao*: "Yelü Renxian, courtesy name Jiulin 糺鄰, small forename Chalai 查剌." This means that his Khitan small forename was Chalai and his second name

---

[62] Zhao Zhiwei 趙志韋 and Baoruijun 包瑞軍, "An Examination of the 'Epitaph of Yelü Zhixian'," appendix I.

was Jiulin. In the sixth line of the *Epitaph of Yelü Renxian* in small script, his name appears as:

Jiulin 糺鄰 Prince small name Chalai 查剌

His Khitan name is also found in the tenth line of the *Epitaph of Yelü Zhixian*, where it introduces the owners' brothers and sisters:

eldest (brother) Jiulin 糺鄰 shang (尚 venerable) fu (父 elder) Song 宋 Prince Chalai 查剌

The decipherment of the second name of Yelü Renxian, i.e. (糺鄰), first offered by Ji Shi, so far remains controversial. The authors have no intention of getting involved now in this controversy and will leave it until later for another article. In contrast, it is indubitable that (Chalai) is Yelü Renxian's small forename. The correct rule (that is, the father's second name and the eldest son's small forename are cognate and the difference lies only in the genitive suffix in the former) becomes evident after a comparison between Yelü Guiyin's second name and his eldest son Yelü Renxian's small forename .

4) Xiao Tabuye 蕭撻不也 and Xiao Temo 蕭特末

According to the "Biography of Xiao Zhonggong" in chapter 82 of the *History of the Jin Dynasty* 金史, Xiao Zhonggong's grandfather was Tabuye 撻不也, and his father was Temo 特末. Tabuye was also named Xiao Wuna 蕭兀納 and has a biography in chapter 98 of the *History of the Liao* which records that "Xiao Wuna is also named Tabuye, and his courtesy name is Temian 特免." In the second line of the *Epitaph of Xiao Zhonggong*, the Khitan full name of Xiao Tabuye is recorded as follows:

Grand 祖 – Father 父 Temian 特免 Tabuye 撻不也

The two sons of Xiao Tabuye, of which Xiao Temo is the eldest, are recorded in the fourth and fifth lines:

Children two the eldest son Wugulin 兀古鄰 Temo 特末

Among the names of this pair of father and son, the small forename of Xiao Tabuye, Tabuye 撻不也, has been recognized above, and the second name of Xiao Temo, Wuguli 兀古鄰, is a corrected transliteration according to the decipherment by Wang Hongli.[63] Only Temo and Temian need further clarification. The name (Xiao) Temo, as is mentioned in the *Epitaph of Yelü Qingsi* 耶律慶嗣墓誌 in Chinese, stands in the sixty-third line of the *Epitaph of Yelü Renxian* in Khitan small script as, and the latter's end character is a dative-locative suffix, and its etymon is the ur-type for Temo. Given the interchangeability of the two characters and, the above-cited can surely be affirmed as the small forename of Xiao Temo. The second name of Xiao Tabuye was written as, which, differing from (特末 Temo) only in its end character, is evidently the Khitan equivalent of the Chinese name Temian 特免, as recorded in "The Biography of Xiao Wuna" in the *History of the Liao*. This Khitan word had quite a few distinct Chinese transliterations in the Liao Dynasty. For example, in the twenty-first and twenty-fourth lines of the *Epitaph of Yelü Zongjiao* in Khitan was transliterated in the simultaneously unearthed Chinese version as Temei 特每, as Temoyan 特末衍 in "Biography of Yelü Zhangnu" 耶律章奴傳 in the *History of the Liao*, and as Temoning 特末寧 in the *Epitaph of Lady Xiao, Princess of Qin Yue Principality and Wife of the Younger Brother of the Emperor*.[64] They are presumably transliterations of the same Khitan word.

The difference between Xiao Tabuye's second name and his

---

[63] This has been transliterated in "A Study of the Khitan Epitaphs in Small Script" by Wang Hongli 王弘力 as Wuguni 兀古匿. The article holds that although it is recorded in the *History of the Liao*, it is nevertheless used as small forename. When used as second name, it has a consonant as its end, and therefore it should be transliterated as Wugulin 兀古鄰. The courtesy name 兀古鄰 Wugulin of Yelü Pode 耶律頗德, recorded in chapter 73 of the *History of the Liao* and the courtesy name 烏古鄰 Wugulin of Yelü Bage 耶律八哥 recorded in chapter 80 are distinct transliterations of the same word.

[64] See Gai Zhiyong 蓋之庸, *A Study of the Stone Inscriptions of the Liao Dynasty in Inner Mongolia*, p. 266, where Temoning 特末寧 is mistaken for Teweining 特未寧.

eldest son Xiao Temo's small forename [Khitan characters] may seem not to follow the same model of the instances cited above in that their end characters are completely distinct, and the second name is not constituted simply by affixing a character to the small forename. Nonetheless it is still evident that the two words are cognate, and the word [Khitan characters] used as the second name is actually constituted by appending a genitive suffix to the word [Khitan characters], which is used as small forename. There are some other pairs of small forename and second name similar in kind to this case in the stone inscriptions in Khitan small script. For example, the pair of small forename [Khitan characters] (撻不也 Tabuye) and second name [Khitan characters] (撻不衍 Tabuyan) fit into this model.

5) Yelü Balide 耶律拔里得 and Yelü Haili 耶律海里

It is recorded in "The Biography of Yelü Balide" in chapter 76 of the *History of the Liao* that "Yelü Balide, courtesy name Hailin 孩鄰, is the son of Gala 剌葛, younger brother of Taizu 太祖." According to the opinions of Deng Guangming 鄧廣銘 and Wang Minxin 王民信, the names Mada 麻答 (or 麻荅) and Jieli 解里, which frequently appear in the *History of the Liao* and the historical literature of the Song Dynasty, are also variants of the name Yelü Balide.[65] A survey of historical sources indicates that the two names probably come from the *Veritable Records of the Five Dynasties* 五代實錄; Jieli apparently being an obvious transliteration of Hailin, and Mada perhaps a not quite correct transliteration of Balide 拔里得.[66] In the sixth line of the recently

---

[65] Deng Guangming 鄧廣銘, "A Corrective Examination of the Two Entries of 'Yu Zhang Qin Jun' and 'Da Shou Ling Bu Zu Jun' of 'Monograph on the Army' in the *History of the Liao*" 《〈遼史・兵衛志〉"御帳親軍"、"大首領部族軍"兩事目考源辨誤》, in *Academic Works of Deng Guangming Selected by Himself* 《鄧廣銘學術論著自選集》 (Beijing: Capital Normal University Press, 1994). Wang Minxin 王民信, "Who is the Mada Recorded in the *History of the Liao*?" 《〈遼史〉裏的麻答是誰？》, in *Studies of the Liao, Jin and Western Xia Histories* 《遼金西夏史研究》 (Tianjin: Tianjin Ancient Books Publishing House, 1997).

[66] Yelü Balide conquered Bianzhou 汴州, the capital city of the Later Jin 後晉, and thereby ended the reign of the dynasty in the last year of the Huitong 會同 reign period, which explains why in the *Comprehensive Mirror for Aid in Government* 《資治通鑒》 and the *New History of the Five Dynasties* 《新五代史》 we see the frequent appearance of the names of Mada, Jieli etc. When composing the *Record of the Khitan State* 《契丹

excavated *Epitaph of Yelü Changyun* in Khitan large script, the owner of which has been determined to be a fourth generation descendant of Gala 剌葛, the younger brother of Taizu, is found the Khitan full name of Yelü Balide:[67]

戓乔　　　　主不
Hailin 孩鄰　Balide 拔里得

Yelü Balide's son was Yelü Haili, whose biography in chapter 84 of the *History of the Liao* says: "Yelü Haili, courtesy name Liuyin 留隱, is the eldest son of *lingwen* 令穩 Balide." The full name of Yelü Haili appears in the seventh line of the *Epitaph of Yelü Changyun*:

天　　　　北　　　充乔　　　戓
the eldest　son　Liuyin 留隱　Haili 海里

Yelü Haili's small forename was 戓, which, as a commonly used Khitan small forename, was sometimes transliterated in the Chinese stone inscriptions of the Liao Dynasty as Jieli 解里. The second name of his father Yelü Balide, that is 戓乔, is constituted by subjoining the genitive suffix 乔 to 戓. This second name was relatively normatively transliterated in "The Biography of Yelü Balide" as Hailin 孩鄰, while the transliteration as Jieli in the *History of the Liao* and the historical literatures of the Song Dynasty omitted the genitive suffix, only to then confuse the small forename with the second name. Nevertheless, the records of the stone inscriptions of Khitan large script indisputably disclose the connection between the forename and courtesy name of the pair of father and son, Yelü Balide and Yelü Haili.

6) Yelü Jieli 耶律解里 and Yelü Zhilugu 耶律直魯姑

The *Epitaph of Yelü Xinie* 耶律習涅墓誌銘, written in Chinese, records that "The Revered One's name is Xinie 習涅, with small forename

---

國誌》, historians in the Yuan Dynasty wrote the biography of Mada by copying materials from the *Comprehensive Mirror for Aid in Government*. It is possible that the descriptions of the deeds of Mada and Jieli in the biographies in the *History of the Liao* all come from the *Record of the Khitan State*. Since it is safe to affirm that the earliest Chinese transliterations of Mada and Jieli were made by Chinese during the Five Dynasties, phonetic corruptions were therefore hardly avoidable.

[67] See Liu Fengzhu 劉鳳翥 and Wang Yunlong 王雲龍, "An Examination of the 'Epitaph of Yelü Changyun' in Khitan Large Script"; only the name Balide is not explained in Liu and Wang's article, and therefore it has been tentatively transliterated on the basis of that article.

Paba 杷八, and he is the son of Great Hengzhang Yixin Zhilugu Langjun 大横帳乙信直魯姑郎君....Grand Marshal 太尉, called Zhilugun 直魯袞 by taboo name and Jieli 解里 by small forename, is the grandfather of the Revered One."[68] This record tells that the small forename of Yelü Xinie's grandfather was Jieli, and the so-called "Zhilugun" was actually his second name. His Khitan full name is included in the seventh line of the *Epitaph of Yelü Xinie* in Khitan large script:[69]

汁 乔　　　戓
Zhilugun 直魯袞　Jieli 解里

The full name of Yelü Xinie's father, according to the above-cited Chinese epitaph, is Yixin Zhilugu 乙信・直魯姑, which appears in the ninth line of the large script epitaph as:

弖已沓乔　　　汁
Yixin [yin]乙信［隱］　Zhilugu 直魯姑

Yelü Jieli's small forename 戓 appears as well in the *Epitaph of Yelü Changyun* mentioned above, where it is used as Yelü Haili's small forename Haili. Therefore it is clear that Jieli and Haili are distinct transliterations of the same word. Yelü Zhilugu's second name 弖已沓乔 should be transliterated normatively into Chinese as Yixinyin 乙信隱, which was written as Yixin 乙信 in the Chinese epitaph. The elision of the character "yin" 隱 arose from omitting the transliteration of the suffix character 乔. When turning to the relationship between the courtesy name of the father and the forename of the son, it is evident that the second name 汁乔 of Yelü Jieli is composed of the small forename 汁 of his son Yelü Zhilugu and a genitive suffix character 乔. Although whether or not Yelü Zhilugu is the eldest son is not mentioned, this is highly likely the case considering the various instances cited above.

The six cases above, culled from the Khitan stone inscriptions, among which four are in small script and two in large script, all prove the same rule. This rule can also be seen in Chinese literature of the Liao Dynasty, as shown by the following examples.

1) Yelü Lihu 耶律李胡 and Yelü Xiyin 耶律喜隱

"Biography of Emperor Zhangsu" 章肅皇帝傳 in chapter 72 of the

---

[68] Gai Zhiyong 蓋之庸, *A Study of the Stone Inscriptions of the Liao Dynasty in Inner Mongolia*, p. 357.

[69] See Liu Fengzhu, *A New Study of the Khitan Scripts*, unpublished.

History of the Liao records that "Emperor Zhangsu has a small forename Lihu 李胡 and another name Honggu 洪古, and his courtesy name is Xiyin 奚隱....His two sons are: Xiyin 喜隱, the Prince of Song 宋王, and Wan 宛, the Prince of Wei 衛王." An incidental biography of Yelü Xiyin follows, which notes that "Xiyin's courtesy name is Wande 完德." Lihu was the third son of Taizu, and his eldest son's small forename was Xiyin, while his own second name was Xiyin. There was evidently some relationship between the father's second name and the son's small forename. However, the transliteration of Xiyin 奚隱 was not quite accurate, because if Lihu's second name was composed of his eldest son's small forename Xiyin 喜隱 as the etymon and a genitive suffix, then it may have been better rendered as Xining 喜寧. Since this pairing of small forename and second name has not yet been identified in the Khitan stone inscriptions, it is therefore impossible to reach a firm conclusion.

2) Yelü Yaliguo 耶律牙里果 and Yelü Dilie 耶律敵烈.

As is noted in "The List of Imperial Princes" in the *History of the Liao*, Taizu's fourth son Yaliguo 牙里果 was called Dinian 敵輦 by courtesy name; and Yaliguo had two sons, the elder Dilie 敵烈 and the younger Xidi 奚底. The relationship between the father's second name and the elder son's small forename is sharply visible here. Yaliguo's second name Dinian 敵輦, written in the inscriptions in Khitan small script as [illegible], and his eldest son's small forename Dilie 敵烈, written as [illegible], are two cognate words, and the second name [illegible] is composed of the small forename [illegible] and a genitive suffix.

3) Yelü Longyou 耶律隆祐 and Yelü Hudugu 耶律胡都古

It is recounted in "The List of Imperial Princes" in the *History of the Liao* that Emperor Jingzong's 景宗 third son Longyou 隆祐 "is called Gaoqi 高七 by small forename and is also named Hudujin 胡都堇....His three sons are: Hudugu 胡都古, Helu 合祿, and Tiebu 貼不." The description of the name Yelü Longyou in this entry is rather confusing. Precisely speaking, Longyou was his Chinese forename (in addition, he should have a Chinese courtesy name, which is missing from the sources), Gaoqi was his Khitan small forename, and Hudujin was his Khitan second name. The small forename of Yelü Longyou's eldest son was Hugudu, written in Khitan small script as [illegible], while Yelü Longyou's second name

Hudujin was written in Khitan small script as [Khitan script]. The relationship between the father's courtesy name and the son's forename is evident.[70]

4) Yelü Duozhen 耶律鐸軫 and Yelü Dilie 耶律低烈

"Biography of Yelü Duozhen" 耶律鐸軫傳 in chapter 93 of the *History of the Liao* records that "Yelü Duozhen's courtesy name is Dinian 敵輦....His son is named Dilie 低烈." The relationship between the father's courtesy name and the son's forename is identical to that between the names of Yelü Yaliguo and Yelü Dilie discussed above.

A summary of the above textual analyses allows us to inductively generate the following table:

	Second name of the eldest son	Small forename of the eldest son	Second name of the father	Small forename of the father
Yelü Hou 耶律吼 and his son	[Khitan script] 斜寧 Xiening	[Khitan script] 何魯不 Helubu	[Khitan script] 曷魯本 Heluben	[Khitan script] 吼 Hou
Yelü Nu 耶律奴 and his son		[Khitan script] 國隱 Guoyin	[Khitan script] 國寧 Guoning	[Khitan script] 奴 Nu
Yelü Guiyin 耶律瑰引 and his son	[Khitan script] 糺鄰 Jiulin	[Khitan script] 查剌 Chala	[Khitan script] 查懶 Chalai	[Khitan script] 瑰引 Guiyin
Xiao Tabuye 蕭撻不也 and his son	[Khitan script] 兀古鄰 Wugulin	[Khitan script] 特末 Temo	[Khitan script] 特免 Temian	[Khitan script] 撻不也 Tabuye
Yelü Balide 耶律拔里得 and his son	[Khitan script] 留隱 Liuyin	[Khitan script] 海里 Haili	[Khitan script] 孩鄰 Hailin	[Khitan script] 拔里得 Balide
Yelü Jieli 耶律解里 and his son	[Khitan script] 乙信隱 Yixinyin	[Khitan script] 直魯姑 Zhilugu	[Khitan script] 直魯袞 Zhilugun	[Khitan script] 解里 Jieli

[70] Nie Hongyin's argues that there exists a relationship between the Khitan forenames such as Hudu (胡篤 or 胡睹) and Hudugu 胡都古 and the courtesy name Hudujin (胡篤堇, 胡都堇, 胡睹堇, 胡獨堇), in that the latter is constituted by affixing a substantive suffix –in to –quduγ (Nie Hongyin 聶鴻音, "The Substantive Suffixes of *-n and *-in in the Khitan Language"). In point of fact this describes this type of situation.

Yelü Yaliguo 耶律牙里果 and his son		敵烈 Dilie	敵輦 Dinian	牙里果 Yaliguo
Yelü Longyou 耶律隆祐 and his son		胡都古 Hudugu	胡都堇 Hudujin	高七 Gaoqi
Yelü Duozhen 耶律鐸軫 and his son		低烈 Dilie	敵輦 Dinian	鐸軫 Duozhen
Yelü Lihu 耶律李胡 and his son	完德 Wande	喜隱 Xiyin	奚隱（奚寧?）Xiyin or Xining?	李胡 Lihu

Altogether, the stone inscriptions in both Khitan large and small script and the Chinese historical sources from the Liao and Jin Dynasties all point to one affirmative conclusion: although the Khitan small forename and second name are called in the Chinese literature of the Liao Dynasty as, respectively, forename 名 and courtesy name 字, there exists no such a semantic correlation between them as is found in Chinese names. Nevertheless, it is noticeable that such a correlation is displayed between some pairs of Khitan father's second name and the eldest son's small forename. That is, the father's second name and the eldest son's small forename are cognate words, and the former is constituted by an affixation of a genitive suffix to the latter. This reminds us that there must have been some unknown kind of linkage system between the names of fathers and sons during Khitan history. In order to answer the question of what kind of name linkage system existed, it is necessary to turn to cultural anthropology.

Part III. The Decipherment of the Khitan Father-Son Name Linkage System from the Perspective of Cultural Anthropology

The name linkage system is a worldwide cultural phenomenon that exists among various peoples. It includes primarily the father-son, the mother-son, the grandfather-grandson, the maternal uncle-nephew, and the husband-wife types, among which the father-son name linkage system is the most widespread. As is well known, there is a relatively distinctive and typical father-son linkage system among the Tibeto-Burman peoples, and thus research on name linkage systems by the anthropologists in China is quite rich. The father-son name linkage system among the Tibeto-Burman peoples came to the attention of anthropologists and linguists in the middle of the 1930s, owing to the publication of *The Collected Yi Script Texts* 爨文叢刻 by Ding Wenjiang 丁文江.[71] The year 1938 saw the birth of the pioneering research into the name linkage system, Ling Chunsheng's 凌純聲 "An Examination of the Wuman 烏蠻 and the Baiman 白蠻 Peoples in Yunnan in the Tang Dynasty" 唐代雲南的烏蠻與白蠻考.[72] This work studied the father-son name linkage system among the Liuzhao 六詔 people, and revealed that this system might be a unique characteristic of the Tibeto-Burman peoples. From then on, as the publications of anthropological materials and studies on the subject accumulated, it was gradually realized that name linkage systems exists far beyond the Tibeto-Burman peoples. Yang Ximei 楊希枚 points out that this system is an important element of ethnic cultures around the world and can be found in Asia, Africa, Europe, the Near East, New Guinea, etc. It exists not only in the cultures of primitive peoples in modern times, but also existed in the cultures of civilized peoples in their ancient period. According to his research, only in the Americas have no materials concerning this phenomenon been discovered.[73]

As to the types of parent-child name linkage systems, anthropologists prior to the 1960s only knew something about the types of parent-to-child name linkage (i.e. patronymic or matronymic name linkage), hardly taking notice of any child-to-parent name linkage. In his "The Evolution from the *Congming* 從名 System [i.e. the system of designating the child with the

---

[71] In addition, in the beginning years of the 20th century Japanese scholars published anthropological field investigation reports concerning the natives of Taiwan, who Japanese scholars call "Takasago-zoku" 高砂族. Though containing quite a lot of material about name linkage systems, this research was not widely exploited for study in this field until the 1930s.

[72] Ling Chunsheng 淩純聲, "An Examination of the Wuman and the Baiman Peoples in Yunnan in the Tang Dynasty" 《唐代雲南的烏蠻與白蠻考》, in The Institute of History and Philology, Academia Sinica 中央研究院歷史語言研究所, *Anthropology Bulletin* 《人類學集刊》, vol. 1, no. 1 (Dec. 1938).

[73] Yang Ximei 楊希枚, "A Study of the Name Linkage System and the Surname and Clan Name System" 《聯名與姓氏制度的研究》, *Bulletin of the Institute of History and Philology, Academia Sinica* 《歷史語言研究所集刊》, *Festschrift in Memory of the 65th Anniversary of Mr. Hushi's (胡適) Birth*, vol. 28, part 2 (May 1957).

parent's name] to the Parent-Child Name Linkage System" published in 1961, Yang Ximei, based upon the presumptive evolution from the *congming* system to the name linkage system, drew the conclusion that there should be two types of parent-child name linkage systems, each including two subtypes, as follows:[74]

<table>
<tr><td rowspan="2">Type I. Parent-to-Child Name Linkage System (using the parent's name as part of the child's name, i.e. patronymic/matronymic name linkage)</td><td>a) parent's name linked before (son of "father's name"—"son's name")</td></tr>
<tr><td>b) parent's name linked after ("son's name"— son of "father's name")</td></tr>
<tr><td rowspan="2">Type II. Child-to-Parent Name Linkage System (using the child's name as part of the parent's name)</td><td>c) child's name linked before (father of "son's name"—"father's name")</td></tr>
<tr><td>d) child's name linked after ("father's name"— father of "son's name")</td></tr>
</table>

More detailed information about these four subtypes will be given in this article.

(1) The parent-to-child name linkage system with the parent's name linked before (type a).

The parent-to-child name linkage system is such a widespread case of the general parent-child name linkage system that many anthropologists today still hold the mistaken belief that it is the only type of parent-child name linkage system. The above model of parent-to-child name linkage consists of two subtypes: the subtype in which the parent's name is linked before the child's name, and the subtype in which the parent's name is linked after the child's name. The former exists among peoples such as the Tibeto-Burman peoples; the Liuzhao people (progenitors of the Yi people 彝族, the Bai people 白族 and the Naxi people 納西族 in contemporary China); some of the peoples speaking Hmong-Mien or Miao-Yao

---

[74] Yang Ximei 楊希枚, "The Evolution from the *Congming* System to the Parent-Child Name Linkage System" 《從名制與親子聯名制的演變關係》, *Bulletin of the Institute of History and Philology, Academia Sinica*, the fourth supplementary issue: *Festschrift in Memory of the 65th Anniversary of Mr. Dong Zuobin's Birth* 《慶祝董作賓先生六十五歲論文集》, part II (June 1961), pp. 758-76.

languages; the peoples of Huaxia 華夏族, Chu 楚人, and Yue 越人 during the Spring and Autumn Period of ancient China;[75] the peoples in India; the ancient Japanese; etc.

(2) The parent-to-child name linkage system with the parent's name linked after (type b)

This subtype is also widely found among the peoples of the world. Examples include the aboriginals in Taiwan – the Taiya people 泰雅人, the Saisiyat people (薩斯特人 or 賽夏人); the Amei people 阿美人; and the Pingpu people 平埔人; as well as the Turkish peoples; the Uyghur people of the Qarakhanid Dynasty; some members of the Miao people 苗族; European peoples; African peoples; the Arabs; the Papuans in New Guinea; etc.

(3) The child-to-parent name linkage system with the child's name linked before (type c)

Compared with the parent-to-child name linkage, the child-to-parent name linkage system is rare. Yang Ximei holds that there should exist such a type of name linkage system, which is divided into two subtypes: that of the child's name linked before and that of the child's name linked after. Yang Ximei offered merely two uncertain clues as to this type of system. First, some names in the Spring and Autumn Period, such as Gongfu Wenbo 公父文伯, Huangfu Chongshi 皇父充石, Fufu Zhongsheng 富父終甥, and Gongshu Wenzi 公叔文子, judging purely by their form, seem to be of this type. Drawing an affirmative conclusion, however, is impeded by the paucity of written sources. The second clue is the name linkage system of the Dayak people in Borneo. According to the view of Ling Chunsheng, the Dayak people have a child-to-parent name linkage system with the child's name linked before, which evolved from the system of designating the parent's name with the proposed child's name (the child-to-parent *congming* system 親從子名制). If this opinion is

[75] In the essay "A Study of the Name Linkage System and the Surname and Clan Name System" cited above, Yang Ximei argues that the so-called fact that "the courtesy name of the grandfather was used by grandsons as the clan name" 孫以王父字爲氏 in the Spring and Autumn Period, which actually includes various kinds of cases, such as sons and grandsons borrowing their fathers' and grandfathers' forenames or courtesy names as their clan names, might well be a transitional type. This type, in terms of the form, can be identified as the parent-to-child type of name linkage system with the parent's name linked before; see pp. 713-24.

accepted, then the Dayak name linkage system is just of this type.[76]

(4) The child-to-parent name linkage with the child's name linked after (type d)

Yang Ximei argued that this subtype of child-to-parent name linkage system should exist in the societies of the Moroccans, the Arabs, the English, and the Babylonians. Nevertheless, all of his evidence was based upon theoretical reasoning rather than upon solid anthropological materials.

There is no doubt that the theory of "Two Types and Four Subtypes" proposed by Yang Ximei is a breakthrough worthy of regard; yet to be honest, at the time he put forward his conception of the child-to-parent name linkage system, it remained a theoretical hypothesis. His evidence for the name linkage type with the child's name linked after was not persuasive, and that with the child's name linked before had merely two supportive clues, which can scarcely be called justification. He concluded that the parent-child name linkage system can be divided into four subtypes, but the type of the child-to-parent name linkage had as yet only the subtype of the child's name linked after confirmed by anthropological materials. Moreover, this type can not equal the parent-to-child name linkage type in its breadth of distribution.

Up until now, the above theory of two types and four subtypes of the parent-child name linkage system was still a hypothesis awaiting corroboration. However, the now available anthropological material enables us to reach a conclusion supporting this hypothesis.

The child-to-parent name linkage system with the child's name linked after will be discussed first. In fact, there are good examples of this subtype of name linkage system in anthropological materials in China. For example, in the society of the Lahu people 拉祜族 of the Tibeto-Burman peoples there exist models of both parent-to-child name linkage and child-to-parent name linkage. The formula of child-to-parent name linkage is the parent's autonym + the eldest child's small forename + pa (巴, meaning "father" in the Lahu language) or e (耶, meaning "mother" in the Lahu language). For example, if the father is named Zhatuo 扎妥, the

[76] The author contends in the same essay that the name linkage system of the Dayak people in Borneo is simply the parent-to-child type with the parent's name linked after. But he contradicts this when he agrees with Ling Chunsheng in order to provide proof for support of his supposition of the existence of the child-to-parent name linkage system with the child's name linked before.

mother named Nala 娜倮, and their eldest daughter is named Nasi 娜斯, then the full name of the father is "Zhatuo Nasipa" (扎妥娜斯巴, meaning "Zhatuo, Father of Nasi"), and the full name of the mother is "Nala Nasi'e" (娜倮娜斯耶, meaning "Nala, Mother of Nasi").[77] It is obvious that this type of name linkage system is consistent with the model put forward by Yang Ximei of child-to-parent name linkage with the child's name linked after.

The subtype of the child-to-parent name linkage with the child's name linked before will be highlighted below for its direct connection with the name linkage system of the Khitans. The most typical and persuasive kind of ethnological material concerning this subtype comes from the Wa people 佤族, whose language is one of the Mon-Khmer languages of the Austro-Asiatic language family, and whose name linkage system has special characteristics. The small forename of the Wa people is made up of rank name and autonym. Rank names vary with gender. The male rank names from the first rank to the eighth rank are rendered into Chinese as Ai 艾, Ni 尼, Shamu 沙姆, Sai 賽, Ao 奥, Luoke 洛克, Jiatc 加特, and Baite 伯特. The corresponding female rank names are rendered as Ye 葉, Yi 依, Amu 阿姆, Ouke 歐克, Yate 雅特, Fo 佛, Yipu 依普, and Wu 午. Autonyms usually come from the Heavenly Stem 天干 or the Earthly Branch 地支 of the day of birth, or sometimes from some propitious words. Take, for example, the small forename Aidao 艾刀. Ai 艾 means the eldest son, while dao 刀 denotes that he was born on a ren day (壬, the ninth of the 12 Heavenly Stems). After getting married and becoming fathers, adult males will use father-son linked names (the autonym of his eldest son plus his own autonym), and their small forenames are abandoned. For example, if the small forename of Aidao's eldest son is Aijia 艾戛, then the father-son linked name of Aidao is Jiadao 戛刀.[78]

[77] He Jiren 和即仁, "The Lahu People," in Zhang Lianfang 張聯芳, ed., *Names of the Chinese People* 《中國人的姓名》 (Beijing: China Social Sciences Press, 1992), pp. 349-50; Wang Zhenghua 王正華 and He Shaoying 和少英, *A Cultural History of the Lahu People* 《拉祜族文化史》 (Kunming: Yunnan Nationalities Press 雲南民族出版社, 1999), p. 140.

[78] Wei Deming 魏德明, *A Cultural History of the Wa People* 《佤族文化史》 (Kunming: Yunnan Nationalities Press, 2001), pp. 155-6. Li Daoyong 李道勇, "The Wa People," in Zhang Lianfang 張聯芳, ed., *Names of the Chinese People*, pp. 334-42.

The Awa Mountain region in Ximeng 西盟 Wa 佤 Autonomous County, Yunnan Province, is a center for the traditional culture of the Wa people, where the child-to-parent name linkage system has been kept quite intact. Many pedigrees of the Wa people, as recorded by ethnologists in their investigations into the society and history of minority peoples after 1949, have clearly revealed historical traces of this type of name linkage system. Here are two typical genealogical examples.

The first one is the genealogy of the Aiguai 艾怪 family with the surname Yongpulei 永鋪擂 in the village of Yuesong Zhai 岳宋寨, Ximeng County, from the primogenitor Limao 里卯 to Guaifang 怪仿, amounting to 23 generations.[79]

> Guaifang 怪仿（23）← Fangsan 仿散（22）← 散桃木（21）← 桃木行（20）← 行昂（19）← 昂賽（18）← 賽抗（17）← 抗康尼（16）← 康尼宋（15）← 宋查因（14）← 查因仅（13）← 仅鋪鹿埃（12）← 鋪鹿埃瑪特（11）← 瑪特孩因（10）← 孩因怪（9）← 怪格郎（8）← 格郎耙特（7）← 耙特標（6）← 標恩 （5）← 恩普特（4）← 普特崗（3）← 崗里（2）← Limao 里卯（1）

The investigators said that the genealogy was provided by Aiguai 艾怪, whose family had been acting as chieftains in Yuesong Zhai for generations, and that Guaifang 怪仿 is Aiguai 艾怪. This report raises some doubts. Judging from the Wa people's name linkage system, since Guaifang's father was named Fangsan 仿散, the small forename of Guaifang should be Aifang 艾仿, and Guaifang became his father-son linked name after becoming a father. Aiguai 艾怪 should be the eldest son of Guaifang 怪仿. Possibly Aiguai 艾怪 was still unmarried, thus he was called by his small forename.

The second genealogy comes from the San 散 family in the village of Zhongke Dazhai 中課大寨, Zhongke Township 中課鄉, Ximeng County, totaling 26 generations from Liweiqi 立委其 to Aicui 艾翠.[80]

---

[79] Quoted from Tian Jizhou 田繼周, et al., "A Report of the Society and Economy of the Wa People in Yuesong, Ximeng County,"《西盟縣岳宋佤族社會經濟調查》in *The Reports of Society and History of the Wa People* 《佤族社會歷史調查》, vol. II (Kunming: Yunnan People's Press, 1983), pp. 2, 35 (note 4).

[80] Quoted from Luo Zhiji 羅之基, et al., "A Report on the Surnames of the Wa People in

Aicui 艾翠 （26）← 翠朧（25）← 朧耕（24）← 耕康（23）← 康松 （22）← 松可恩（21）← 可恩夥（20）← 夥朵埃（19）← 朵埃果阿（18）← 果阿來（17）← 來散（16）← 散章（15）← 章敖（14）← 敖芬 （13）← 芬歐克 （12）← 歐克峭士（11）← 峭士克立阿（10）← 克立阿克魯恩）（9）← 克魯恩貢（8）← 貢托（7）← 托朧（6）← 朧格拉特（5）← 格拉特普依 （4）← 普依司崗 （3）← 崗立（2）← Liweiqi 立委其（1）

All the names in this genealogy are father-son linked names except the last generation Aicui, which is the small forename.

These genealogies of the Wa people are valuable sources for the name linkage system. The two genealogies transcribed above bring out the fact that the Wa people have been strictly enforcing the custom of child-to-parent name linkage. The father-son linked names recorded above all accord, without exception, with the already known Wa people's rules of name linkage. This type of name linkage can be generalized by the formula of BA—CB—DC, which corresponds in the main with the "father of 'son's name' + father's name" subtype of the child-to-parent name linkage system proposed by Yang Ximei, and which is simplified as the formula "son's name + father's name." In addition, there is yet another facet of the Wa people's name linkage system deserving our attention. In societies practicing the parent-to-child name linkage system, the genealogies adopt the downward order of arrangement, beginning with the primogenitor, whereas it is the upward order ending with the primogenitor that is assumed in the dozens of genealogies of the Wa people discovered so far. The reason for this contrary order is that this arrangement is more conducive to memorization by descendants, since the child-to-parent name linkage system requires that a senior's linked name be derived from the junior's small forename.

In addition to the Wa people, the Yao 瑤 people and the Naxi 納西 people in several areas also claim to bear witness to this subtype of name linkage system. In the small Pingcha Village 平茶村 of the Yao people, in Gundong Township 滾董鄉, Liping County 黎平縣, Guizhou 貴州 Province, there coexist two types of name linkage systems. Before

---

Ximeng County," *The Reports of Society and History of the Wa People* 《佤族社會歷史調察》, vol. 4 (Kunming: Yunnan People's Press, 1987), pp. 34-5.

marriage and fatherhood, a person's name is given by linking the names of three generations – grandfather, father, and himself – in the form of "surname + autonym + name of father + name of grandfather. For example, in the name Bu Laohe Wangbao Ying 卜老和王保英, Bu 卜 is the surname, Laohe 老和 is the autonym, Wangbao 王保 is his father's name, and Ying 英 is his grandfather's name. However, if a person gets married and becomes a father, then the child-to-parent name linkage system in the form of "surname + Bu (補, meaning 'father' in the Yao language) + small forename of the first child + autonym" replaces the practice of linking the names of three generations. For example, if the eldest child of Bu Laohe 卜老和 is a daughter named Meisheng 妹生, then the parent-child linked name of Bu Laohe will be Bu Bu Meisheng He 卜補妹生和.[81] This latter name linkage system is exactly the child-to-parent name linkage system with the child's name linked before of Yang Ximei.

Akin to the case of most of the Tibeto-Burman peoples, the parent-to-child name linkage system is generally used in the society of the Naxi people. However, in the Naxi villages of Nanxi 南溪 and Jizi 吉子, Lijiang 麗江 County, Yunnan Province, there is a particular kind of child-to-parent name linkage system which takes the form of "small forename of the eldest child + Ba (meaning 'father') + small forename of the father." For example, a person in the Jizi village is called A Guo Xing 阿國興 by small forename, and his eldest son's small forename is A Fu 阿福, and thus he is named Fu Ba Xing 福爸興 by father-son linked name.[82] This name linkage system, simple as it is at first sight, also qualifies as of the subtype of the child-to-parent name linkage system with the child's name linked before.

This kind of name linkage system appears in non-Chinese anthropological materials as well. Charles Hose, a British anthropologist, after a field investigation in Borneo together with some of his colleagues, claimed to have discovered among the indigenous Kenyah and Dayak tribes a kind of child-to-parent name linkage in the form of "Tama (meaning 'father') + small forename of the eldest son + autonym of the father." For example, the eldest son of Jau was called Obong by small

---

[81] Hu Qiwang 胡起望, "The Yao People," *Names of the Chinese People*, p. 198.

[82] He Jiren 和即仁, "The Naxi People," *Names of the Chinese People*, p. 361.

forename, thus his father-son linked name was Tama Obong Jau, usually abbreviated as Tama Obong (meaning "father of Obong").[83] The chief of the Madang tribe of the Kenyah people, whose full name was Tama Kajan Odoh, dictated his family's genealogy as follows:[84]

19. Kajan
18. Tama Kajan Odoh
17. Sigo
16. Apoi
15. Baun (♀)
14. Odoh Sinan (♀)
13. Along
12. Apoi
11. Laking
10. Laking Giling
09. Giling Sinjan
08. Sinjan Putoh
07. Putoh Ati
06. Ati Aiai
05. Jalong
04. Balari
03. Umbong Doh (♀)
02. Kusun Patu
01. Balingo

According to the investigators, this genealogy covers 19 generations in all, yet the names of the first and second generations were written together as Kusun Patu Balingo, and the fifth and the sixth generations as Ati Aiai Jalong, leaving only 17 generations remaining. The genealogy of the 19 generations listed above is the corrected version based upon the view of Ling Chunsheng.[85] According to the rules of the child-to-parent name linkage system among the Kenyah people, it is not difficult to determine the name linkage relationship between fathers and sons from the 6th to the 11th generations and from the 18th to the 19th generation. Other generations only have their autonyms recorded. Perhaps their linked names were omitted by the dictator. If the omitted linked names are restored to an intact form, then a clearer genealogy appears as follows:

83 Charles Hose and William McDougall, *The Pagan Tribes of Borneo* (London: Macmillan, 1912), vol. 1, pp. 79-82.

84 Ibid., vol. 2, pp. 11-2.

85 Ling Chunsheng 淩純聲, "The Father-Son Name Linkage System in the Southeast Asia" 《東南亞的父子連名制》, originally published in *Special Issue of the Continent Magazine*, series 1, 1952, pp. 171-220; see also his *Chinese Ethnic Minorities in the Frontier Regions and the Culture of the Pacific Rim* 《中国邊疆民族與環太平洋文化》, (Taipei: Linking Publishing Co. Ltd., 1979), p. 442.

19. Kajan
18. Tama Kajan Odoh
17. Tama Odoh Sigo
16. Tama Sigo Apoi
15. Baun (♀)
14. Odoh Sinan (♀)
13. Along
12. Tama Along Apoi
11. Tama Apoi Laking
10. Tama Laking Giling
09. Tama Giling Sinjan
08. Tama Sinjan Putoh
07. Tama Putoh Ati
06. Tama Ati Aiai
05. Tama Aiai Jalong
04. Tama Jalong Balari
03. Umbong Doh (♀)
02. Kusun Patu
01. Tama Patu Balingo

The underlined words in this genealogy have been added supplementarily according to the rules of the name linkage system among the Kenyah people. In this restored genealogy, all the names, except those of the second, third, fourteenth and fifteenth generations, are father-son linked names grounded upon the Kenyah name linkage rules. The several cases of the generations without linked names can be explained by the fact that the third, fourteenth and fifteenth generations are females whose names do not follow the name linkage rules. In a word, this genealogy shows that the name linkage system among the Kenyah people belongs to Yang Ximei's subtype of child-to-parent name linkage system with the child's name linked before.

Nevertheless, Yang Ximei himself brings forward another quite distinct explanation of the name linkage system among the Kenyah and Dayak peoples. In his view, the name Tama Obong is of the child-to-parent name linkage type, with Obong as the eldest son's autonym. Similar is the name Tama Obong Jau, with Obong Jau as the linked name of the eldest son, which means that Obong Jau is taken as Obong's father-son linked name with Jau as his father's name, and that it is thus of the type of parent-to-child name linkage with the parent's name linked after. Then Yang Ximei concludes that among the Kenyah and Dayak peoples there exists both the system of child-to-parent name linkage (with the child's name being either the autonym or the linked name) and that of parent-to-child name linkage with the parent's name linked after. With this understanding in mind, he maintains that only the name Tama Kajan Odoh in the above genealogy is of the type of child-to-parent name linkage, and that the others mostly are of the type of parent-to-child name linkage with the parent's name linked after.[86]

The above arguments are too unconvincing to win support. The following three points exemplify our doubts.

First, the knowledge we have as to the name linkage system among the Kenyah and Dayak peoples comes completely from the investigation report of Hose and his colleagues, who did not affirm the existence among the local people of the parent-to-child name linkage system with the parent's name linked after. It is therefore groundless for Yang Ximei to take Obong Jau as a linked name consisting of Obong's autonym and his father's name Jau.

Second, the investigators pointed out clearly that the linked name Tama Obong Jau is the full form of the father-son linked name constituted by adding the father's autonym Jau to the child-to-parent linked name Tama Obong. This corresponds well with the father-son name linkage system with the child's name linked before, whereas Mr. Yang understands it as a kind of compound name linkage system with a hybrid name linkage of both child-to-parent and parent-to-child types. It is true that the coexistence of both child-to-parent and parent-to-child types of name linkage systems have been found among the same people, yet such a compound kind of name linkage system as is shown by Yang Ximei has been never heard of. The father's autonym is transmitted to the son's name in order to constitute the son's linked name, and then the father's autonym combines with the son's linked name to form his own father-son linked name in the form of "father of ('son's autonym'— son of 'father's autonym')." This senseless piling up of names is really unimaginably queer.

Third, as is the case with the genealogy of the Wa people discussed above, the genealogy dictated by Tama Kajan Odoh was originally arranged in upward order, which is characteristic of the child-to-parent type of name linkage system. Going against completely the connotations of the original dictation, Yang Ximei changes it to the downward order so that he can fit it into the parent-to-child type with the parent's name linked after, which is known among Taiwan's aboriginal peoples such as the Taiya people. Even in his upside-down genealogy, there still stand quite a

[86] Yang Ximei 楊希枚, "The Evolution from the *Congming* System to the Parent-Child Name Linkage System," pp. 753-5. As is pointed out above, this was not his original idea, as shown when he seconds the opinion of Ling Chunsheng so as to support his concept of "child-to-parent name linkage with the child's name linked before."

few paradoxical cases, which mitigate against the parent-to-child type of name linkage system with the parent's name linked after. Yang Ximei employs the term "variant name" to designate these cases. For example, Doh of the third generation is deemed a possible variant name of Kusun, Jalong of the fifth generation that of Aiai, and Along of the thirteenth generation that of Sinan, etc. Such a kind of explanation can hardly avoid being blamed as slipshod.

To summarize, Yang Ximei's understanding about the above name linkage system is inadvisable. Actually, this type of name linkage system is the child-to-parent type with the child's name linked before, which he had been unable to produce evidence to substantiate.

Based upon the name linkage phenomenon of the Kenyah and Dayak peoples, Ling Chunsheng draws a conclusion that the child-to-parent name linkage system originated in the system of designating the parent with the child's name. The following example shows this process of evolution:

Tama Obong → Tama Obong Jau → Obong Jau

Mr. Ling gives more details about the process. According to him, the first stage is a period of a pure *congming* system, namely one which designates the parent with the child's name. Since it is highly probable that different persons may have the same name under the *congming* system, which is inconvenient for genealogical recording, there thus appears a second stage – a transitional type between the *congming* system and the name linkage system, a type dictating that the parent's name is indicated both by a designation with child's name and by a linkage with his own autonym. Finally, this developed into the third stage, when only the parent-son name linkage system, the authentic name linkage system, is in use and the *congming* system is discarded.[87]

In fact, cases of the *congming* system similar to Tama Obong abound in anthropological materials. Among the Yamei people, an aboriginal people in Taiwan, the birth of the eldest son in a family will change the father's name into "Shiaman (father) + the son's small forename," will change the mother's name into "Shina (mother) + the son's small forename," and will change the grandparent's name into "Shiapun (grandparent) + the grandson's small forename."[88] This can be termed the

[87] Ling Chunsheng 淩純聲, "The Father-Son Name Linkage System in the Southeast Asia," pp. 458-60.

[88] Utsugawa Nenozō 移川子之藏, *A Study of the Genealogy of the Gaosha People in*

child-to-parent *congming* system with the child's name coming after. In addition, a similar *congming* system exists among the Kam-Tai speaking peoples, including the peoples of Zhuang 壯, Dai 傣, Dong 侗, and Shui 水, and among some branches of the Yao people – mainly the Pan Yao 盤瑶 and the Baiku Yao 白褲瑶. The *congming* system among all these peoples will presumably eventually result in the name linkage system, i.e. that child-to-parent name linkage system with the child's name linked before, as practiced by the Kenyah and Dayak peoples, according to Ling Chunsheng's inference.

We can say now that we have reached the ultimate goal of the preceding discussion, which was to test the theory of "Two Types with Four Subtypes" of the parent-child name linkage system, as put forward by Yang Ximei. However, it is a pity that, up to now, the study of the father-son name linkage system by Chinese ethnologists still stands where it was prior to the 1960s, when only the parent-to-child type of name linkage system was noticed, without any recognition of the child-to-parent type. In the volume devoted to nationalities in the *Encyclopedia of China,* published in the 1980s, the father-son name linkage system is classified into three kinds: first, that of the sequential order, namely the father's name anteceding the son's name; second, that of the reverse order, namely the son's name anteceding the father's name, which is observed among the Wa people, the Miao 苗 people in Taijiang 台江 County of Guizhou Province, and the Uyghur and Kazakh peoples in Xinjiang; and third, that of adding surnames before or after the names.[89] The first kind belongs to the parent-to-child name linkage system with the parent's name linked before. The third kind is actually identical to the first kind, except for the addition of surnames. The second kind belongs to the parent-to-child name linkage system with the parent's name linked after, but the Wa people feature the child-to-parent name linkage system with the child's

---

Taiwan 『台湾高砂族系統所属の研究』, first published by the Research Institute of Folklore and Anthropology at Taipei Imperial University in 1935, reprinted in photocopies by Gaifusha 凱風社 Publishing Co. in Tokyo in 1988, vol. I, *The Text*, p. 548. The second volume of the book, *The Sources*, includes two genealogies of the Yamei people (see p. 131, the 308th and 309th genealogies), and among the 60 names, ten belong to this type of *congming* system.

[89] Zhan Chengxu 詹承緒, "The Father-Son Name Linkage System" 《父子連名制》, in *Encyclopedia of China*, *Volume of Nationalities* (Beijing: The Encyclopedia of China Publishing House, 1986), p. 124.

name linked before, so two contrary types of name linkage system are confused here. In his recently published doctoral dissertation *On the Surnames and Forenames*, Naribilige 納日碧力戈 also proposes two types of name linkage system, i.e. that of the parent's name linked before and that of the parent's name linked after. He holds that the latter exists among aboriginals in Taiwan such as the Taiya people and the Saisiyat people, the Wa people, the Miao people, European peoples, Near Eastern peoples, African peoples, and Papuan peoples.[90] It is obvious that he still mistakes the child-to-parent type of name linkage system among the Wa people for the parent-to-child type.

Attention will now be paid to the Khitan name linkage system. As has been mentioned above, it was the tradition of the Khitan names that the second name appeared before the small forename in its full form. However, the general rule of father-son name linkage demonstrated in the stone inscriptions in both large and small script is that the father's second name and his son's small forename were cognate, and that the former was constituted by adding a genitive suffix to the latter. Which kind of father-son name linkage system was it, then? There are only two alternatives: it was either the parent-to-child type with parent's name linked after, which, from the standpoint of the son's name, can be thought of as the formula "son's autonym affixed with a genitive suffix + father's name," or it was the child-to-parent type with the son's name linked before, which, from the standpoint of the father's name, can be considered as the formula "the eldest son's small forename affixed with a genitive suffix + father's autonym." In our view, it is the latter type to which the Khitan practice belonged, for the following three reasons:

(1) The appellations of "small forename" and "second name" in the epitaphs in Khitan small script indicate that the Khitan name linkage system is of the child-to-parent type.

As has been pointed out above, it is usual for certain Khitan names to be designated in the stone inscriptions as [Khitan script] or [Khitan script], which is translated as "child name" and paraphrased as "small forename" 小名, and it is customary for another name, constituted by an annexation of a genitive suffix to the eldest son's small forename, to be inscribed as [Khitan script], translated as "of the second (name)." The difference between the two

[90] Naribilige 納日碧力戈, *On the Surnames and Forenames* 《姓名論》 (Beijing: Social Sciences Academic Press, 1997), pp . 74-6.

kinds of names is thus clearly revealed: "small forename" is evidently the autonym that exists at the beginning, whereas "second name" is a derivative name due to the son-to-father name linkage. More supporting evidence for the temporal order of the two names comes from the fact that "small forename" is deemed in the *History of the Liao* to be the Khitans' forename and "second name" is deemed to be the courtesy name 字. Inasmuch as the name derived from the son's name is called the "second name," it is feasible to affirm that the Khitan name linkage system was of the child-to-parent type.

(2) This kind of name linkage between Khitan fathers and their eldest sons precludes the possibility of the downward name transmission from father to son.

In the Khitan cases of father-son name linkage discovered up to now, nearly all support the indication that the child whose name is linked to father is always the eldest son. The only two apparent exceptions are Yelü Jieli 耶律解麗 and Yelü Zhilugu 耶律直魯姑, which have no explicit delineation as to whether or not the son was the eldest son, so these may not actually be exceptions to the rule. A plausible conclusion is that the Khitan father-son name linkage system accepts only linkage between the eldest son's name and the father's name. What on earth does this conclusion mean? In our view, anthropological sources, both Chinese and foreign, show that in the case of the father-to-child type of name linkage system, the names of all children are linked to the father's name, while in the case of the child-to-parent type, only the name of the eldest child, either the son or daughter, is linked to the father's name. None but the exceptional cases of the eldest child being aborted or being captured by another tribe would enable a linkage between the second child's name and the father's name. It would be reasonable to judge that the Khitan name linkage system is of the child-to-parent type, rather than of the parent-to-child type.

(3) The form of the Khitan full name is predicated upon the child-to-parent type of name linkage system with the child's name linked before.

It has been mentioned above that the normal form of the full name of the Khitans, as reflected in the stone inscriptions in both Khitan large and small script, is "second name + small forename," that is, "the eldest son's small forename with a genitive suffix + autonym." From the analysis of this type of name linkage, this should be of the child-to-parent type with the son's name linked before, a subtype proposed by Yang Ximei.

However, this conclusion remains open to further confirmation. Strictly speaking, the form of the Khitan full name was actually represented as "son's name + father's name," which may indicate either the child-to-parent type or the parent-to-child type of name linkage. For example, it is characteristic of the father-son name linkage system among the Saisiyat people to add the genitive auxiliary word *a* after the son's name and before the father's name to explicate the parentage. As an example, the name Dawusi a Emao 達烏斯・阿・厄茂 denotes Dawusi the son of Emao.[91] Although name linkage among the Saisiyat people is identical to that among the Khitans in its exterior form, the former is of the parent-to-child type with the parent's name linked after. For what reasons do the two opposite name linkage systems exhibit the same form? The crux of this matter lies in the differences between the grammatical structures of the two peoples' languages.

This question points to the relationship between the name linkage system and language. When analyzing the patterns of name linkage systems, Yang Ximei contends that it is highly probable that the same name linkage system is used by peoples of the same language family or of similar language families. For example, the parent-child name linkage system among the Han Chinese people and the Tibeto-Burman peoples, whose languages are monosyllabic, generally has the parent's name linked before, while among Indo-European peoples, Indonesian peoples, and African peoples, whose languages are polysyllabic, the parent's name is linked after.[92] Naribilige disagrees with this opinion and holds that the type of the name linkage system has no correlation with whether the language of a people is monosyllabic or polysyllabic, and that the linkage form – linked before or after – is predicated at first mainly upon the position of the substantive attributes relative to the headwords in the language. "With the concomitant social factors excluded, in a manner of speaking, the name linkage system with the parent's name linked before is matched with those languages whose substantive genitive attributes antecede the headwords, and that with the parent's name linked after is

---

91 Yang Ximei 楊希枚, "The Personal Denomination System among the Saisiyat People in Taiwan" 《臺灣賽夏族的個人命名制》, *Bulletin of Academia Sinica* 《中央研究院院刊》, vol. 3 (1956), p. 325.

92 Yang Ximei, "The Evolution from the *Congming* System to the Parent-Child Name Linkage System," pp. 759-60.

matched with those languages whose substantive genitive attributes lie after the headwords," he argues.[93] Apparently, this explanation is more credible than that of Yang Ximei. As far as we know, the languages of the Indonesian subfamily of the Austronesian family position the headwords before the substantive genitive attributes. Therefore, the Saisiyat linkage formula "son's name + father's name" indicates the parent-son name linkage system with the parent's name linked after, and the said formula may be expressed more exactly as "autonym + genitive auxiliary word + father's name." In contrast, in the Altaic language family the substantive genitive attributes stand before the headwords, thus the Khitan formula "son's name + father's name" indicates the parent-son name linkage system with the child's name linked before, which can be expressed more exactly as "son's name + genitive suffix + autonym." Another example of the type with the parent's name linked after is currently prevalent among the Turkish people, who were influenced by Persian and Arabic after Turkish Islamization, for both the latter two are languages which postpose the substantive attributes.

A new question arises in this case. According to the above conclusion, in the Khitan formula "son's name + father's name," the preposed son's name should be the substantive genitive attribute and the postposed father's name the headword, yet it seems unreasonable to denote the father's linked name through such a hypotaxis. The crux still lies in the genitive suffix of the Khitan second name. In fact, Nie Hongyin and Aisin Gioro have identified the suffix of the Khitan "courtesy name" 字, without knowing its function. Nie Hongyin holds that there is a lack of sound historical sources for its explication, and that it is even not clear whether the Khitans made such an affixation in order to denote the genitive attribute of a noun or to create a new noun.[94] Aisin Gioro, with similar perplexity, argues that the end consonant –n in the Khitan language had the function of denoting the genitive suffix of a noun, but it remains equivocal as to whether the consonant –n appearing at the end of the name words is a suffix of word building or of case denotation.[95] In a

---

[93] Naribilige 納日碧力戈, "An Analysis of Restrictive Lingual Factors in Ethnic Names" 《民族姓名的語言制約因素析要》, *Minority Languages of China* 《民族語文》, 1990, no. 4; *On the Surnames and Forenames*, pp. 177-8.

[94] Nie Hongyin 聶鴻音, "The Substantive Suffixes of *-n and *-in in the Khitan Language."

[95] Aisin Gioro Ulhicun, "An Examination of the Genealogies of the Tomb Owners

later article, however, she inclined to the suffix's word-building function, i.e. the adjectivalization of the word stem.[96] This hypothesis leads to another question: why did the Khitans use adjectivalized words as their "courtesy names"? Now, after gaining an explicit understanding of Khitan name linkage, we can provide a convincing explanation. In the Khitan formula "second name + small forename," that is, "the eldest son's small forename with a genitive suffix + autonym," there is an omission. This omission is of the word "father" after "second name," which explains the reason why the Khitan second name is always affixed with a genitive suffix.[97] This means that there is no relationship between the son's name and the father's name such as that between the substantive attribute and the headword. What constitutes a hypotaxis with the son's name should be the omitted word "father," while the postposition of the father's autonym serves only for avoidance of the coincidence of names. Thus, the formula for the Khitan name linkage system can be expressed precisely as "(father of) 'son's name' + 'father's name'." This is the child-to-parent type of name linkage system with the child's name linked before, the same type as that among the Wa people, some branches of the Yao and Naxi peoples, and the Kenyah and Dayak peoples in Borneo. According to Yang Ximei, a system of this type may be reduced to the formula "father of 'son's name' + 'father's name'," which is very close to that of the Khitans.

A supplementary point is that the significance of the second name in the Khitan name customs, composed of an affixation of a genitive suffix to the eldest son's small forename, may not be confined to the name linkage system. In the opinion of Ling Chunsheng, the child-to-parent type of name linkage system originated from the child-to-parent *congming* system. Thus, in terms of the Khitan formula of linked name "second name + small forename," if the small forename is omitted, then it is purely the formula of the child-to-parent *congming* system. Because of the elision of the word "father," the significance for the *congming* system inherent in

---

Recorded in the 'Epitaph of Yelü Dilie' and the 'Epitaph of the Deceased Ms. Yelü': with a Note about the Khitan Forenames and Courtesy Names."

[96] Aisin Gioro Ulhicun, "The Characteristics of the Khitan Names: with a Note about the Suffixes of the Derivative Adjectives in the Khitan Language," in *Studies of the Khitan Language and Scripts*, pp. 222-3.

[97] The headwords after the restrictive attributes are often omitted in the Khitan language. For example, the word [illegible] mentioned above and meaning "second" is not followed by the headword "name."

the second name has disappeared, especially in the Chinese literature.

Although the Khitans had both a small forename and a second name, it was rare for them to be called by both names. Which name, the "forename" or the "courtesy name," did they use then for designation in their own tradition? Let us start with the historical literature. According to usage in the *History of the Liao*, it was small forename that was commonly used for identification, while in the biographies only the biographees' second name (courtesy name) appears. An exception is the Taizu Emperor of the Liao Dynasty, Yelü Abaoji 耶律阿保機, who was distinguished by the use of his second name. "Annals of Taizu" 太祖紀 in the *History of the Liao* notes that "(his) surname is Yelü, taboo name is Yi 億, courtesy name is Abaoji 阿保機, and small forename is Chuolizhi 啜里只." That is, Yelü Yi was Taizu's Chinese forename, Chuolizhi was his Khitan small forename, and Abaoji was his Khitan second name. In the *Miscellanea in the Khitan Court* 虜廷雜記 by Zhao Zhizhong 趙志忠, it is recorded that "Taizu's taboo name is Yi, and his Khitan name is Abaoji."[98] It is thus manifest that the second name "Abaoji" had its original genitive suffix elided and its exact transliteration should be Abaojin 阿保謹. The fact that Liao Taizu was marked in history with his second name can be deemed to be merely an exception.

As for the designation by small forename or by second name in the stone inscriptions of the Liao Dynasty, there seems to be no rule. Take the name Xiao Han 蕭罕 as an example. The *Epitaph of Xiao Jin* 蕭僅墓誌銘 records that "his father is named Han by taboo name," and the *Epitaph of Han Kuangsi* 韓匡嗣墓誌銘 records that his third daughter was "married to the imperial brother-in-law's younger brother Xiao Han." They both adopt the appellation by small forename. However, in the *Epitaph of Lady Xiao, Wife of Han Kuangsi* 韓匡嗣妻蕭氏墓誌銘 it is his second name Xiao Liuning 蕭流寧 that is recorded.[99] On the whole, either in the

---

[98] Quoted from *Textual Analysis* 《考異》 in the records of May, the first year of the Kaiping 開平 reign period of Emperor Taizu 太祖 of the Later Liang 後梁 Dynasty, *Comprehesive Mirror in Aid of Government* 《資治通鑒》, ch. 266.

[99] Xiang Nan 向南, ed., *The Stone Inscriptions of the Liao Dynasty*, p. 191; Liu Fengzhu 劉鳳翥 and Jin Yongtian 金永田, "An Examination of the Three Epitaphs of Han Kuangsi and His Family of the Liao Dynasty," *Journal of Chinese Studies* 《中國文化研究所學報》 (Hong Kong: Chinese University Press), new series, 2000, no. 9.

Chinese stone inscriptions or in the Khitan equivalents in both large and small script, it is more frequent to encounter the designation by second name, which stands nearly without exception, especially when the official titles and the noble titles appear with the names.

However, this explanation is more theoretical than practically serviceable for the simple reason that the Khitan names recorded with characters in literature and other sources are not necessarily those that were used in daily life. Cultural anthropology may provide proof of this. As is well-known, according to the general custom of those peoples among which the parent-child name linkage system is prevalent, it is impolite to call an adult person by his small forename, which also applied to the Khitans. It is therefore acceptable to surmise that the small forename was the appellation employed in childhood within the clan, while second name was widely used for social intercourse in adulthood. It is imaginable that the second name in the form of "(father of) 'son's name'" was qualified as an honorable appellation symbolizing status and rank. This corollary does not contradict the fact that in the *History of the Liao* the Khitans are habitually designated by their small forenames, because it is necessary for historical records and epitaphs to point out the autonym in order to avoid confusion when introducing a person.

Due to the previous ignorance of the Khitan name linkage system, it was easy for scholars to misunderstand the origin of the Khitan "courtesy name." Nie Hongyin conjectured that the Khitans were called in childhood by their "forename" and in adulthood by their "courtesy name," presumably influenced directly or indirectly by Chinese culture. According to Aisin Gioro, the Khitan courtesy name "is highly likely copied from the custom of the Han Chinese."[100] It is now clear that the Khitan courtesy name was rooted in a pure and trueborn kind of national culture. Historical sources show that the Khitan name linkage system was a national tradition with a long history. The progenitor of the Yaonian 遥輦 tribe of the Khitan people was Zuwu 阻午 Qaghan, "whose Khitan name is Dinian Zuli 迪輦俎里."[101] Dinian (written as [illegible] or [illegible] in

[100] Nie Hongyin 聶鴻音, "The Substantive Suffixes of *-n and *-in in the Khitan Language"; Aisin Gioro Ulhicun, "An Examination of the Genealogies of the Tomb Owners Recorded in the 'Epitaph of Yelü Dilie' and the 'Epitaph of the Deceased Ms. Yelü': with a Note about the Khitan Forenames and Courtesy Names."

[101] *History of the Liao: Geneological Tables* 《遼史・世表》, chapter 63.

Khitan small script) is a second name with a genitive suffix commonly used by the Khitans, which indicates that, as late as the late period of the Dahe 大賀 tribe, the child-to-parent type of name linkage system with the child's name linked before was practiced by the Khitans. Theoretically speaking, it is possible that the father-son name linkage system may have appeared among the Khitans when they evolved into the patrilineal society.[102]

As for the reason for the birth of the father-son name linkage system, there had been an explanation that the name linkage system was a kind of substitute for the surname system, but this has been disproven. Anthropological studies show that both systems often coexist within the same society. After careful research into the relationship between them, Yang Ximei holds that the name linkage system might be a potential origin of the surname system. As the case of Taiwanese aboriginals displays, he argues, there are three stages in the evolution process from the name linkage system to the surname system: the name linkage system (the proto-surname system), followed by the unstable surname system, followed by the stable surname system. The first stage is marked by alternate name linkage between parent and child, followed by the second stage in which all generations of posterity adopt a certain progenitor's name as surname. Finally comes the third stage in which the stable surname system crystallizes. In the meantime, he also acknowledges that even if the stable surname system derives from the name linkage system, the coexistence of the two may still be permissible, for they play different roles. The name linkage system is mainly used within the tribe, while the surname system is used outside of the tribe.[103]

In terms of the Khitan name linkage system, there seems to be as yet no validation of its correlation with the surname system, and no tendency for development towards the surname system. It is well known that in the entire history of the Khitans there were only two surnames, Yelü and Xiao,

---

[102] We have tried to trace the origins of the Khitan name linkage system among the ancient Altaic peoples, without, for various reasons, finding satisfactory answers. It is not yet safe, for lack of sources, to make an explicit affirmation that the name linkage system existed among the Xianbei 鮮卑 and Turkic peoples. Although the parent-child name linkage system with the parent's name linked after is found among the Uyghurs, there it is the product of Islamization and has no logical connection with the name linkage system of the Khitans. As to the Mongols, Jurchens, and Manchurians, no name linkage system has ever existed in their societies.

[103] Yang Ximei, "A Study of Name Linkage System and Surname System," pp. 698-725.

but this cannot explain the existence of the name linkage system. In the Chongxi 重熙 reign period of Emperor Xingzong 興宗, Yelü Shuzhen 耶律庶箴 "presented a petition to the emperor in order to increase the surnames of the country: 'Ever since the foundation of our dynasty, laws and institutions have been established except that only two surnames, i.e. Yelü and Xiao, are available. Initially when Emperor Taizu created the Khitan large script, he recorded the place names of all the tribes as a supplementary chapter at the end of the name book. I beg Your Majesty to popularize these names as surnames among the tribes in order to make marriages conform to ceremonies.' His Imperial Majesty rejects this petition for the reason that the established institution can not be reformed in a hurry."[104] It is manifest from this quotation that even when more surnames were in need, they were taken from the place names of the various tribes without resort to the name linkage system. Needless to say, the child-to-parent type of name linkage system was apparently unable to replace the surname system.

In regard to the function of the name linkage system, a relatively credible assumption is that, in addition to its use as an expression of genealogical identity, it was used primarily for the denotation of personal identity. Thus the historical fact of the phenomenon of homonymy and the name linkage system both appear in the same society.[105] This explanation fits the case of the Khitans, whose society witnessed the quite common phenomenon of homonymy. A simple reading of the *History of the Liao* and the Chinese stone inscriptions of the Liao Dynasty suffices to engender an impression that the Khitan words used for personal names are limited. This impression is strengthened by a study of the stone inscriptions in both Khitan large and small script, as there are in the Chinese literature and sources from the Liao Dynasty many variant transliterations of the Khitan names, which, after collation, may be reduced to merely several dozens. This circumstance entails the existence of the name linkage system.

Although name transmission from child to parent was a general rule of the Khitan name linkage system during the Liao Dynasty, some exceptions were still found. For the discussion of this it is necessary to

---

104 "Biography of Yelü Shuzhen," *History of the Liao* 《遼史 •耶律庶箴傳》, chapter 89.

105 Yang Ximei, "A Study of Name Linkage System and the Surname and Clan Name System," pp. 723-5; "The Evolution from the *Congming* System to the Parent-Child Name Linkage System," p. 776.

resort to cultural anthropology. As has been shown by the investigations of H. L. Roth, the British anthropologist, the Dayak people in Borneo practiced the child-to-parent type of name linkage system, and, according to the rule, it should be the eldest child's name that is transmitted to the parent's name. However, when a minor Dayak without children was in urgent need of a linked name, then he could link his name to that of his cousins.[106] Another case comes from the Malayan society, in which the child-to-parent type of name linkage system was also prevalent. However, it was their custom that the name of those parents who bear children be linked to the eldest child's small forename, while for those childless parents, the linkage to their brothers' names was specified.[107] Similar Khitan cases are also found. The "Biography of Yelü Dilie" in chapter 75 of the *History of the Liao* notes that "the courtesy name of Yelü Dilie is Wulizhen 兀里軫." In the subjoined biography of his younger brother Yelü Yuzhi 耶律羽之, it is recorded that "the small forename of Yuzhi is Wuli 兀里, and his courtesy name is Yindishen 寅底哂." The courtesy name of Yelü Dilie is recorded in "The Biography of Yelü Yuzhi"[108] as Wulizheng 汙里整, and in the *Outstanding Models from the Storehouse of Literature* 冊府元龜[109] as Wuzheng 污整, both forms being variant

[106] Henry Ling Roth, *The Natives of Sarawak and British North Borneo* (London, 1896), vol. 2, p. 274.

[107] James George Frazer, *Golden Bough*, the abridged edition (London: Macmillan, 1922), p. 248.

[108] Inner Mongolia Institute of Cultural and Historical Relics and Archaeology, "A Report on the Excavation of the Tomb of Yelü Yuzhi of the Liao Dynasty" 《遼耶律羽之墓發掘簡報》, *Cultural Relics* 《文物》, 1996, no. 1.

[109] It is recorded in "Subdivision of Amicable Communication, Division of Alien Subjects" 外臣部・通好門 in chapter 980 of *Outstanding Models from the Storehouse of Literature* 《冊府元龜》, that in May of the second year of the Changxing 長興 reign period (931 CE) of Emperor Mingzong 明宗 of the Later Tang 後唐 Dynasty, "the Qingzhou 青州 government reported that some peasant, who was gathering firewood and vegetables beyond Haibei 海北, brought back from the elder cousin of the King of Dongdan 東丹王 and Regent 留守 of the Southern Capital 京尹, Wuzheng 污整, a letter which inquired upon the whereabouts of Li Muhua 李幕華, with the intention of paying tribute." According to "The Biography of Yelü Dilie" in the *History of the Liao*, Dilie was appointed Governor 留守 of the Southern Capital in the second year of the Tianxian 天顯 reign period, therefore, this Wuzheng refers in point of fact to that Yelü Dilie as Governor of the Southern Capital. It is a canard of the Southern people that he was called "the elder cousin of King of Dongdan." Note also that Dongping prefecture 東平府 was

transliterations of Wulizhen 兀里軫. The records in the *History of the Liao* tell us that Yelü Dilie's second name Wulizhen should be constituted by adding a genitive suffix to the etymon Wuli, the small forename of his younger brother Yelü Yuzhi. Only two possibilities can explain this case: either Yelü Dilie bore no children,[110] or his second name was given to him before adulthood. "The Biography of Yelü Yuzhi" tells us that Yuzhi had five brothers: the eldest brother Helu 曷魯, the second elder brother Wulizheng 汙里整, and his third elder brother and two younger brothers, all three of whom died very young. So Yuzhi ranked fourth. It is thus unambiguous that among Yelü Dilie's four younger brothers, only Yelü Yuzhi came of age, which offers justification for the name linkage between the two brothers, which can be considered as a variant of the Khitan child-to-parent type name linkage system.

Judging from various evidence, after the founding of the Liao Dynasty the traditional child-to-parent type of name linkage system had to a large extent become a mere formality. Even though almost every male Khitan had a second name with a genitive suffix, and many cases of father-son name linkage can be cited, it is not difficult to find many counterexamples, i.e. cases proving that there was no correlation between the father's second name and his eldest son's small forename. This demonstrates that although the fundamental characteristics of the traditional Khitan name linkage system still remained, strict observation of the rules of the child-to-parent type name linkage system may have been relaxed by the Khitans, whose linked names might have become mere formalities. Presumably, the partial preservation of the custom can be attributed to some kind of social function, in addition to the practical need of personal identification, because the Khitan second name in the form of "(father of) son's name" was most probably a symbol of rank and status. Thus the custom was that every male had a second name, which did not necessarily

---

not elevated to the status of Southern Capital until the December of the third year of the Tianxian reign period, thus it was exactly in the fifth year, i.e. 930 CE, rather than in the second year, that the appointment occurred.

[110] There is no mention in "The Biography of Yelü Dilie" of whether Yelü Dilie had children, yet "The Biography of Yelü Hugu" 《耶律虎古》 in chapter 82 of the *History of the Liao*, notes a "Yelü Hugu, courtesy name Hailin 海鄰, grandson of Dilie, Yilijin 夷離堇 (Confederation Military Commander) of the Sixth Division 六院" [a branch of the royal clan]. Yelü Dilie had acted as Yilijin of the Diela 迭剌 tribe, so perhaps Yelü Hugu was his grandson.

take the eldest son's small forename as its etymon, and which was not influenced by being either childless or unmarried. In "The Biography of Yelü Xieniechi" 耶律斜涅赤 in chapter 73 of the *History of the Liao*, an example is given: "The courtesy name of Yelü Xieniechi is Sala 撒刺....His original courtesy name was Duowan 鐸盌. As an assistant to Emperor Taizu in the early stage of career, he was once beset by illness, which was cured by the imperial favor of a goblet of wine. Since the goblet is called 'sala' in the Khitan language, he changed his courtesy name according to the imperial edict." If by tradition a second name was formed on the basis of the eldest son's small forename, then how could it have been changed so facilely? This story indicates that, as early as the initial stages of the Liao Dynasty, the traditional child-to-parent type name linkage system was possibly experiencing the tendency towards becoming a mere formality. Perhaps many Khitans were called by their second name when they were still underage. Of course, it is possible for this kind of second name not to bear any relationship with the eldest son's small forename, nor necessary for it to form a linked name with names of full brothers or cousins. It suffices for the second name to conform to the traditional form of the name linkage system. Only under these circumstances could the second name be changed without trouble, to such an extent that Yelü Xieniechi could use a random word as his second name. Yet we have also noticed that even in the last years of the Liao Dynasty, there were still some Khitan conservatives sticking strictly to the rules of the father-son name linkage system, such as Xiao Tabuye and Xiao Temo mentioned above.

Part IV. Epilogue: Issues with Names and Differing Cultural Backgrounds

From the end of the ninth century onward, contact between Khitan and Chinese cultures became more and more frequent. Especially the annexation of the Yanyun 燕雲 sixteen prefectures to the Liao territories created an opportunity for direct communication and reciprocal fusion of the two types of national cultures. It is not difficult to imagine the effects that the special historical environment and distinct cultural backgrounds may have had on the national characteristics of name customs. On the one hand, Khitan names were unavoidably imprinted by Chinese culture; on the other hand, ample historical literature and sources show that the names of some of the Han Chinese people under the Liao government manifest an apparent inclination to Khitanization. For all the attention scholars of Liao history have given to these mutual influences, only a true understanding of the Khitan name customs can produce a correct explanation of the phenomenon of cultural fusion reflected therein.

The first problem regarding the communication between the two peoples was how to translate the Khitan names into Chinese. In other words, how did the Han Chinese people think of and understand Khitan names. Among all the extant Chinese documents concerning Liao history, it is the *History of the Liao* whose Chinese transliterations of Khitan names are the most normative in that in its biographies the Khitan small forename is generally termed "forename" 名 (or "small forename" 小名 or "small courtesy name" 小字), and the Khitan second name is generally termed "courtesy name" 字.[111] It can be deemed a proper method of translation to borrow the Chinese terms "forename" and "courtesy name" to designate the Khitan small forename and second name respectively. This is because both the Khitan small forename and the Chinese forename are autonyms, and both the Khitan second name and the Chinese courtesy name are a type of new designation obtained after reaching adulthood, with merely a difference in derivation. In as much as the present version of the *History of the Liao*, compiled officially during the Yuan Dynasty, is based mainly upon Yelü Yan's 耶律儼 *Veritable Records of the Imperial Dynasty* 皇朝實錄 and Chen Daren's 陳大任 *History of the Liao* 遼史, of which the former has claims to be the most primary source, the normative transliterations of Khitan names in it may well come from historical sources managed and processed by the official historians of the Liao Dynasty such as Yelü Yan.

In contrast, the Chinese translations of Khitan names in the stone inscriptions of the Liao Dynasty are more random than rigorous. One of the commonly used methods of translation is metaphrase, i.e. the literal translation of the full form of the Khitan name in its original order of second name standing before small forename, regardless of which is the forename and which is the courtesy name. For example, the full name of Zhongfufang Shilu 仲父房釋魯 was written as [Khitan small script characters] in Khitan small

[111] The terms "small courtesy name" and "courtesy name" in the *History of the Liao* have distinct meanings and are used differently. Owing to the lack of a basic understanding of Khitan name customs, current researchers into Liao history often confuse the two.

script, while the normative description in the *History of the Liao* is "Shilu, courtesy name Shulan."[112] "Shula Shilu" 述剌實魯 in the *Epitaph of Yelü Renxian*, "Shulie Shilu" 述烈實魯 in the "Biography of Yelü Zhixian, and "Shulie Shilu" 述列實魯 in the *Epitaph of Yelü Qingsi* are all metaphrases of a single Khitan name. As another example, there is Han Kuangsi's 韓匡嗣 great-grandson Dilu 滌魯, whose full name is written in the seventh line of the *Epitaph of Yelü Dilie* in Khitan small script as ,[113] transliterated in his biography in the *History of the Liao* as Dilu Zunning 滌魯遵寧, and metaphrased in the *Epitaph of Xiao Wuluben Niangzi* 蕭烏盧本娘子墓誌銘 as Xunning Diligu 遜寧迪里姑.[114] Even considering the simplifications these translations entail, their ignorance of the distinctions between the Khitan small forenames and second names renders difficult the explicit identification of the Khitans concerned and generates clouds of doubt as to the extent of the translators' understanding of Khitan name customs.

In addition to the metaphrasing method, and in even more cases, the Khitan small forenames and second names are rendered, respectively, following the Chinese tradition. But time and time again, whenever this method of translation is adopted, the translations in the stone inscriptions of the Liao Dynasty exhibit a real misunderstanding on the part of the translators of Khitan name customs. The *Epitaph of the Princess of Song Wei Principality* 宋魏國妃蕭氏墓誌銘 describes the tomb owner's progenitors as follows: "great-grandfather, name Jieli 解里, small forename Taowei 桃…grandfather, name Liuwen 六溫, small forename Gaojiu 高九…father, name Shishili 時時里, small forename Dilie 迪烈." Based upon the sources concerned in the *History of the Liao* and the stone inscriptions in Chinese and in Khitan script, it can be known that the great-grandfather of the Princess of Song Wei Principality was called Xiao He 蕭和 by Chinese name, Taowei 桃隈 by Khitan small forename (the *History of the Liao* transliterates it as Taogui 陶瑰), and Jieli 解里 (also Xieli 諧里 or Xieling 諧領 in some stone inscriptions) by Khitan

---

112 "The List of the Imperial Princes," *History of the Liao*, chapter 64.

113 Tang Cailan 唐彩蘭, et al., "An Examination of the 'Epitaph of Han Dilie'," 《契丹小字〈韓敵烈墓誌銘〉考釋》, appendix, *Minority Languages of China*, 2002, no. 6, p. 34.

114 Liu Fengzhu 劉鳳翥, Tang Cailan 唐彩蘭, and Gaowa 高娃, "An Examination of the Epitaph of Xiao Wuluben and Two Others in the Liao Dynasty," appendix I.

second name. Her grandfather was called Xiao Xiaocheng 蕭孝誠 by Chinese name, Gaojiu 高九 by Khitan small forename, and Liuwen (or Liuyin 留引 in some stone inscriptions) by Khitan second name. Her father was called Xiao Zhixian 蕭知玄 by Chinese name, Dilie 迪烈 by Khitan small forename, and Shishili 時時里 by Khitan second name.[115] The author of the epitaph termed their second names as "name" 名 possibly for the reason that he understood the Khitan second name as the "large name" 大名 or "formal name" 學名. What is more, some stone inscriptions of the Liao Dynasty even translate the Khitan second name as "taboo name" 諱. The *Epitaph of Yelü Xinie* 耶律習涅墓誌銘 notes that "the Yuyue Prince 于越王, the Grand Marshal of the Army 兵馬大元帥, called Xining 習寧 by taboo name and Lubugu 盧不姑 by small courtesy name, is the sixth generation ancestor of the Revered One; Shumishi 樞密使; the Prince of Xiping 西平王, called Aoguozhi 奧聒只 by taboo name and Xiansheng 賢聖 by small courtesy name, is the great-great-grandfather of the Revered One; the Military Commissioner 節度使, called Ying'en 應恩 by taboo name and Guanyin 觀音 by small courtesy name, is the great-grandfather of the Revered One; the Grand Guardian 太尉, called Zhilugun 直魯袞 by taboo name and Jieli 解里 by small courtesy name, is the grandfather of the Revered One."[116] There is a biography of Yelü Xinie's sixth generation ancestor in chapter 76 of the *History of the Liao*, which notes that "the courtesy name of Yelü Lubugu is Xinning"; and in chapter 79 his great-great-grandfather has a biography, which records that "the courtesy name of Yelü Xianshi 賢適 is Aguzhen 阿古真," and which also mentions his great-grandfather by his small forename Guanyin. In addition, the small forenames and second names of Yelü Xinie's ancestors

---

[115] Liu Fengzhu and Qing Gele, "An Examination of the 'Epitaph of the Princess of Song Wei Principality' and the 'Epitaph of Yelü Hongyong' in Khitan Small Script"; Wei Kuige 魏奎閣 and Yuan Haibo 袁海波, "Addenda of the Genealogy of the Xiao He Family, the Maternal Relatives of the Liao Emperor" 《遼外戚蕭和家族世系表新補》, *Journal of Liaoning Technical University* (Social Sciences Edition), 2003, no. 3, pp. 66-9; Aisin Gioro Ulhicun, "An Examination of the Genealogy of the Great King Gaojiu" 「高九大王世系考」, *Journal of East Asian Literature and History* (Kyoto), the premier issue (March 2003).

[116] Gai Zhiyong 蓋之庸, *A Study of the Stone Inscriptions of the Liao Dynasty in Inner Mongolia*, p. 357.

from his sixth generation ancestor, Lubugu, down to his grandfather Jieli, all appear in the *Epitaph of Yelü Xinie* in Khitan large script. These records show that the "small courtesy name" that the author of the epitaph refers to is the Khitan small forename, and that he calls the Khitan second name the "taboo name," which is indeed a great misunderstanding of Khitan names. The "taboo name" in Chinese culture is actually the autonym, thus it is still not far off the mark to call the Khitan small forename the Chinese "taboo name," but the Khitan second name can by no means be equated to the latter. All of this demonstrates that the common Han Chinese people of the Liao Dynasty still had some way to go before recognizing the essence of Khitan culture.

After the founding of the Khitan state, and especially after the Khitan occupation of the Yanyun area, Chinese culture began to become more powerful, and this inexorably injected many new elements into traditional Khitan name customs. Even in the names in the Khitan language, the subtle influences the Chinese civilization exerted upon them are remarkable, not to mention the Chinese names that the Khitans were accustomed to, which can be seen in the words used by the Khitans as personal names. The investigations undertaken by ethnologists show that the words used as personal names by different Altaic peoples have certain characteristics in common. In the early history of the ethnic minorities of the Mongolians, the Daurs, the Manchurians, and the Hezhe 赫哲 [the Nani], the words used as personal names were mostly those denoting plants and animals, or some ordinary vessels; only when contact with Chinese culture became more and more frequent did abstract words begin to be employed.[117] This ethnological finding may well be taken as a cross reference in the examination of the change of the words used by the Khitans as personal names. Although there are hardly any materials left regarding Khitan personal names in the period of the Dahe tribe and the Yaonian tribe, it can be judged, based on the then contemporary life style of fishing and hunting and on the stage of social evolution of the Khitans in that period, that the characteristics of the words used as personal names were probably similar to those in the early history of the above mentioned Altaic peoples. What then were the words used for personal names by the

---

[117] Zhang Lianfang 張聯芳, ed., *Names of the Chinese People*, pp. 90-6, 115-26, 147-51; Ling Chunsheng 淩純聲, "The Hezhe People on the Lower Reaches of the Songhua River" 《松花江下游的赫哲族》, *Bulletin of the Institute of History and Philology, Academia Sinica*, offprint edition, the first series, vol. 14, part 1 (1934), p. 213.

Khitans of the Liao Dynasty? A rough statistic analysis of Khitan names in the stone inscriptions in both Khitan large and small script and in the Chinese literatures and sources shows that 胡都古,[118] meaning felicity 福, and 乙辛,[119] meaning longevity 壽, are the two words used most frequently in Khitan names. This illustrates the influence of Chinese culture upon the Khitans, since even their names in their own language were characterized by Chinese cultural values.

Of course, the most direct influence that Chinese culture exercised upon Khitan naming customs is revealed by the Chinese names that were adopted by the Khitans. Frequent communication and cultural contact between the two peoples during the Liao Dynasty brought a large part of the Khitans to live in a bilingual, i.e. Chinese-Khitan, environment, which was often accompanied by the binominal naming system. As seen from the Chinese literature of the Liao Dynasty and the stone inscriptions, it was commonplace at that time for the Khitans to have Chinese names. Theoretically speaking, the binominal system in the strict sense should amount to the juxtaposition of two sets of names, i.e. the Khitan small forename and second name with the Chinese forename and courtesy name. The names of Yelü Hezhu 耶律合住 may serve as an example. "The Biography of Yelü Hezhu" in chapter 86 of the *History of the Liao* notes that "the courtesy name of Yelü Hezhu is Niangun 粘袞." Hezhu was his Khitan small forename, Niangun his Khitan second name, while his Chinese names are missing from the *History of the Liao*. According to the analysis of Luo Jizu 羅繼祖, Yelü Hezhu is the same person as Yelü Cong 耶律琮, who appears in such literature as *Extended Continuation of the Comprehensive Mirror for Aid in Government* 續資治通鑒長編 of the Song Dynasty.[120] His full Chinese name is found on the *Spirit Way Stele for Yelü Cong* 耶律琮神道碑: "The Revered One's taboo name is Cong, courtesy name Boyu 伯玉, and surname Yelü."[121] However, a Khitan

---

118 The second name with this word as the etymon is (胡都堇, Hudujin).

119 The second name with this word as the etymon is (乙辛隱, Yixinyin).

120 Luo Jizu 羅繼祖, *Collation Notes to the History of the Liao* 《遼史校勘記》 (Shanghai: Shanghai People's Press, 1958), p. 20.

121 Li Yiyou 李逸友, "The Stone Inscriptions from the Tomb and the Spirit Way Stele of Yelü Cong of the Liao Dynasty" 《遼耶律琮墓石刻及神道碑銘》, *Archaeology and History in Northeast China*, vol. 1 (Beijing: Cultural Relics Publishing House, 1982), p. 181.

person such as Yelü Cong, whose courtesy name and forename are both known, is not typical of the whole Khitan people, most of whom seem to have had only Chinese forenames, with courtesy names rarely seen. Although the poverty of historical sources may be adduced to some degree as an explanation, in more cases the reason may well be that, in fact, the Khitan had only a single Chinese forename.

The Chinese words chosen by the Khitans as their names deserve our study as well. Two cultural orientations are inherent in this choice of words: Confucian culture and Buddhist culture, which were evenly matched during the entire period of the Liao Dynasty. The Chinese words used by the Khitans seem to convey an impression of a subtle distinction – Confucian culture predominates in the formal names used in social life, while Buddhist culture predominates in the informal names used in family life. To put it more precisely, on the one hand, the formal Chinese forenames of the Khitans are generally characterized by a strong Confucian color. This is shown by the typical cases of the Chinese forenames of Yelü Renxian 耶律仁先 and his four brothers, i.e. Renxian (仁先 precedence of humanity), Yixian (義先 precedence of justice), Lixian (禮先 precedence of etiquette), Zhixian (智先 precedence of wisdom), and Xinxian (信先 precedence of trust),[122] and by those of Xiao Dewen 蕭德溫 and his brothers, i.e. Dewen (德溫 acquisition of moderation), Deliang (德良 acquisition of kindness), Degong (德恭 acquisition of courtesy), Dejian (德儉 acquisition of frugality), and Derang (德讓 acquisition of comity).[123] On the other hand, Chinese loanwords with Buddhist implications were often used as small forenames within many Khitan families. For example, the respective small forenames of the Shengzong Emperor 聖宗, his younger brother Longqing 隆慶, and another younger brother were Wenshunu (文殊奴 the servant of Mañjuśrī Bodhisattva), Puxiannu (普賢奴 the servant of Samantabhadra Bodhisattva), and Yaoshinu (藥師奴 the servant of Bhaiṣajyaguru Buddha) respectively. The Shengzong Emperor's queen Rende 仁德 and the Daozong Emperor's queen Xuanyi 宣懿 were called, respectively, Pusage

---

[122] "Epitaph of Yelü Renxian" 《耶律仁先墓誌》, in Xiang Nan 向南, ed., *The Stone Inscriptions of the Liao Dynasty*, p. 354.

[123] "Epitaph of Xiao Dewen" 《蕭德温墓誌》, in Xiang Nan, ed., *The Stone Inscriptions of the Liao Dynasty*, p. 372.

(菩薩哥 Bodhisattva) and Guanyin (觀音 Avalokiteśvara) by small forename. Xiao Xiaozhong 蕭孝忠 had a son called Yaoshinu by small forename and a daughter called Guanyinnu (觀音女 girl of Avalokiteśvara).[124] Finally, Yelü Yuanning 耶律元寧 had three sons whose small forenames were Guanyinnu (觀音奴 the servant of Avalokiteśvara), Cishinu (慈氏奴 the servant of Maitreya Bodhisattva), and Shijianu (釋迦奴 the servant of Śākyamuni).[125] What could such an interesting phenomenon tell us? For the Khitans, Buddhism was their religious faith, while Confucianism applied mainly to their mundane needs. The small forenames taken from Buddhist personae give one a feeling of intimacy, while those names originating from Confucian ideals seem more solemn. Furthermore, it was through Chinese culture that the Khitans accepted Buddhism, with the result that they employed Chinese loanwords even in the small forenames that had a Buddhist flavor.

This fusion of cultures during the Liao Dynasty was by no means a unidirectional trend towards Sinicization. The Khitans were not the only people who confronted the bilingual and binominal problem. In fact, there were also a large number of Han Chinese people who showed an apparent tendency toward Khitanization, of which the Han family in Yutian 玉田韓氏 is an example. From the graveyard of the Han Kuangsi 韓匡嗣 family in the Baiyinhan Mountain 白音罕山 region in Balinzuo Banner 巴林左旗, Inner Mongolia, there have been 12 epitaphs excavated in recent years. They include two epitaphs in Khitan small script, the *Epitaph of Yelü Dilie* and the *Epitaph of Han Gaoshi* 韓高十墓誌銘. It has been revealed that more epitaphs were unlawfully unearthed and stolen. The discovery of epitaphs inscribed in Khitan script in Chinese tombs is undoubtedly the most credible evidence for the existence of bilingualism. The messages provided by the two epitaphs in Khitan small script show that nearly every member of each generation in the Han family in Yutian following Han Zhigu 韓知古 had Khitan names, including both the small forename and the second name, which were no different from the naming customs of the

---

124 "Epitaph of Xiao Xiaozhong" 《蕭孝忠墓誌》, in Xiang Nan, ed., *The Stone Inscriptions of the Liao Dynasty*, p. 416.

125 "Epitaph of Yelü Yuanning" 《耶律元寧墓誌》, in Gai Zhiyong 蓋之庸, *A Study of the Stone Inscriptions of the Liao Dynasty in Inner Mongolia*, p. 21.

Khitans.[126] These sources are quite valuable specimens for the study of the cultural fusion during the Liao Dynasty.

The stone inscriptions in Chinese also indicate that children in the Khitanized Chinese families of the Liao Dynasty had names in both Chinese and Khitan. For example, the *Epitaph of Yelü Yuanzuo* 耶律元佐墓誌銘 records that he "had a five-year-old son, whose small forename is Dula 度剌 and Chinese small forename is Yaoshinu 藥師奴."[127] Yelü Yuanzuo was just that Han Xieshi 韓謝十 recorded in the *History of the Liao* who belonged to the Han family in Yutian. His son had two small forenames at the same time, Dula (the Khitan name) and Yaoshinu (the Chinese name). In addition, some other evidence indicates that children in some Khitanized Chinese families might have had only a Khitan small forename, and that their Chinese names might not have been used until adulthood. It is characteristic of the Chinese stone inscriptions of the Liao Dynasty that Chinese names are recorded in the epitaphs, but exceptions can sometimes be found. For example, in the *Epitaph of Han Dechang* 韓德昌墓誌銘 all his ancestors and brothers are designated by their Chinese names, while his children are called by Khitan names: "He had two sons, Guosan 郭三 and Jieli Abo 解里阿缽."[128] A possible explanation is that Han Dechang died at the early age of 29, when his two underage sons were too young to have Chinese names. This surmise is further

---

[126] Liu Fengzhu 劉鳳翥, "An Examination of the 'Epitaph of Han Gaoshi' in Khitan Small Script" 《契丹小字〈韓高十墓誌〉考釋》 in *A Bow to Fragrance Collection: Festschrift in Memory of the Ninetieth Anniversary of Mr. Zhang Zhenglang's Birth* 《揖芬集——張政烺先生九十華誕紀念文集》 (Beijing: China Social Sciences Press, 2002); Liu Fengzhu 劉鳳翥, Tang Cailan 唐彩蘭, and Gaowa 高娃, "An Examination of the Epitaph of Xiao Wuluben and Two Others in the Liao Dynasty." According to the statistics of Aisin Gioro Ulhicun, there are 52 people having a confirmably Khitan name among the eight generations of Han Zhigu family as recorded in the above two epitaphs; see Aisin Gioro Ulhicun, "An Overview of the Epitaphs in Khitan Small Script" 「契丹小字墓誌綜考」, in *Studies of the Khitan Language and Scripts* (Kyoto: Research Institute for History and Culture of East Asia, 2004), pp. 288-92.

[127] Jin Yongtian 金永田, "An Examination of the Epitaphs of Han Dewei and Yelü Yuanzuo" 《韓德威和耶律元佐墓誌銘考釋》, *Cultural Relics* 《文物》, 1998, no. 7, pp. 73-8.

[128] Liu Fengzhu and Qing Gele, "An Examination of the 'Epitaph of Han Dechang' and the 'Epitaph of Yelü (Han) Gaoshi' of the Liao Dynasty" 《遼代〈韓德昌墓誌銘〉和〈耶律（韓）高十墓誌銘〉考釋》, *Studies in Sinology* 《國學研究》, vol. 15 (June 2005).

corroborated by the *Epitaph of Zhao Kuangyu* 趙匡禹墓誌, which enumerates one by one the names of the tomb owner's ten sons, of whom nine adults are recorded by their Chinese names, and only the eighth son, who is recorded to have died young, is designated by Xiamai 轄麥.[129] Xiamai is a commonly used Khitan small forename, written in Khitan small script as [Khitan small script] and transliterated otherwise as Xiamaige 轄麥哥 or Xiamage 匣馬葛. It can be affirmed that Xiamai did not have a Chinese forename because he died too early in childhood. We have noticed that such situations occurred usually in those Chinese families who intermarried with the Khitans and thus led a social life in which Khitan culture predominated. It might be that the Khitan language was the first language within these families. Therefore every child had a Khitan small forename before they grew up, when association with Chinese society necessitated a Chinese name. After they died, if the epitaph was written in Chinese for the Han Chinese people, then their Chinese names would be recorded. If their epitaph was written in Khitan for the Khitans, then their Khitan names would appear. Such was the bilingual and binomial situation which faced the Khitanized Han Chinese of the Liao Dynasty.

In addition to those completely Khitanized Han Chinese, there was another group of people standing in the crevice between Chinese and Khitan cultures who should not be neglected. In the inscription *Stele of Canonizing Kindness* 崇善碑, engraved in the middle or late period of the Liao Dynasty, there appear such names as Wang Temo 王特末, Li Wutela 李烏特剌, Tian Chala 田查剌, Wang Yila 王移剌, Yang Saba 楊撒八, Dai Suwo 戴蘇斡, Gao?luwo 高□魯斡, Zhang Zhuomoli 張酌末里, Cao Dalugu 曹達魯古, and so on. Although the stele was discovered in the southern piedmont of the Han Mountain region 罕山 in Balinyou Banner, Inner Mongolia, which was the hinterland of the Khitan state, the majority of the names on it are of Chinese people. In the opinion of Su He 蘇赫, these were possibly the servile families belonging to a certain Ordo 斡魯朵 [an encampment serving as a regional capital].[130] These Han Chinese, even though they had long lived on the steppes, seem to show an obvious

---

129 Xiang Nan, ed., *The Stone Inscriptions of the Liao Dynasty*, p. 300.

130 Su He 蘇赫, "An Examination of 'The Stele Inscription of Canonizing Kindness'" 《崇善碑考述》, *Collected Essays on Liao and Jin History* 《遼金史論集》, vol. 3 (Beijing: Bibliography and Literature Press, 1987).

tendency to Khitanization. They were not integrated into Khitan society, for their names, though in the Khitan form, were still marked by Chinese culture. Judging by the transliterated pronunciations, they were all Khitan small names, which might show that these people, unlike the Khitans, did not give themselves a second name. In view of the low social status of these Chinese people, it might well be that they had all through their life only such a single Khitan-Chinese hybrid name, which was neither a Chinese name nor a genuine Khitan name. Strictly speaking, this can not claim to be a type of binominal system.

Among the ancient Altaic peoples, the Khitans had a rather complicated name system. Luckily enough, however, the Khitans have left us a large quantity of stone inscriptions that make it feasible to bring to light once more the Khitan culture which vanished long ago. We might expect that with more discoveries of sources in the Khitan language and more progress in research, the history and culture of this ancient people will stand more vividly before the world.

KHITAN TRIBAL ORGANIZATION AND THE BIRTH OF THE KHITAN STATE

Cai Meibiao 蔡美彪

The first definite records of the Khitan come from 389 CE, or the third year of the Dengguo 登國 reign period of the Northern Wei Dynasty. By this time their matriarchal society had given way to a patriarchal one, and they began to become civilized. However, 500 years elapsed from this time until the establishment of the Khitan state in 916. We have valuable materials from this period because during this time the Khitan established relations with the governments of China, and later, after the founding of the Khitan state, the Khitan began recording the history of their previous generations. Even though these scattered materials are far from complete and cannot provide us with many details, after careful collation of the facts, we can see the overall process of development of the Khitans from tribes to state.

In this paper I plan to follow chronological order in making a preliminary investigation of the development of Khitan tribal organizations into the Khitan state.

1. The early tribes and the Dahe 大賀 tribal confederation

The eight early tribes

The beginning of Khitan history can be found in the records from the third year of the Dengguo 登國 reign period, which was also the year in which the Northern Wei attacked the Khitan.[1] After this the Khitan resided south of the Huang River 潢水 (the present-day Shira Muren/Mürin, or Xilamulun 西喇木倫) and north of the Tu River 土河 (the present-day Laoha River 老哈河), and made a living by fishing, hunting, and grazing. The histories call the Khitan "mostly thieves", which shows that they had become a patriarchal society, and began to plunder other peoples.

History of the Wei: Account of the Khitan 魏書・契丹傳 also says:

---

[1] See *History of the Wei: Annals of Taizu* and *Account of the Khitan* 《魏書・太祖紀》 and 《魏書・ 契丹傳》, and *History of the Northern Dynasties: Account of the Khitan* 《北史・契丹傳》. See Chen Shu's 陳述 *Khitan Government Historical Manuscripts* 《契丹史論證稿》, chapter 2, section 2.

Since the Zhenjun 真君 period they came to make offerings at court, and presented fine horses each year. In the Xianzu 顯祖 period the emissary Mofuhe 莫弗紇 (tribal leader) Hechen 何辰 presented an offering, and was rewarded with a banquet as a member of a lesser state. He returned and told of his experience, saying how beautiful the country was, and how much he admired it. Thereupon all of the northeastern peoples heard of this, and everyone dwelled upon what they heard. The Xiwandan 悉萬丹, He 何(or A 阿)dahe 大何, Fufu 伏弗,[2] Yuyuling 郁羽陵, Rilian 日連, Pili 匹絜,[3] and Tu 吐(or Chi 叱)liuyu 六于 tribes all sent fine horses and furs to the Heavenly palace, and required this to

[2] *History of the Wei Dynasty: Account of the Khitan* originally had "Fufuyu 伏弗郁 and Yuling 羽陵 tribes." Note that the *History of the Wei: Annals of Xianzu* 《魏書・顯祖紀》 has two Khitan tribe names, namely the Jufufu 具伏弗 and Yuyuling 郁羽陵. *Outstanding Models from the Storehouse of Literature* 《冊府元龜》, ch. 969 has the same. The Yuyuling tribe is also mentioned in *History of the Wei: Account of the Wuji* 《魏書・勿吉傳》. The character "yu" 郁 of "Fufuyu" in the "Account of the Khitan" appears to be misplaced. *Encyclopaedic History of Institutions* 《通典》, ch. 200, "Border Defense Section" 《邊防典》, *History of the Northern Dynasties: Account of the Khitan*, and *History of the Liao: Monograph on Imperial Guards* 《遼史・營衛志》 all perpetuate this mistake. This error should now be corrected. Also, Fufu is the same as Jufufu, as the first syllable was removed. *History of the Wei Dynasty: Account of the Wuji* reverses the characters in "Fufu." *History of the Northern Dynasties: Account of the Wuji* 《北史・勿吉傳》 has the same mistake.

[3] *History of the Wei Dynasty: Account of the Khitan* originally had "Pijie tribe Li tribe" 匹絜部黎部. "Annals of Xianzu" and "Account of the Wuji" of the same book all have Pilier 匹黎爾. *Outstanding Models from the Storehouse of Literature*, ch. 969 has Pili, without the character "er" 爾. One version has "Yanerli" 延爾黎, which is a mistake for "Pilier." *History of the Wei Dynasty: Account of the Khitan* originally mistakes "li" 黎 as "jie" 絜, and after later corrections it was again mistaken as two tribes. This error should now be corrected. *Encyclopaedic History of Institutions: Border Defense Section* 《通典・邊防典》 takes it as one tribe, correctly calling it Pili 匹黎. *History of the Northern Dynasties: Account of the Khitan* perpetuates the mistake from *History of the Wei Dynasty: Account of the Khitan* and also changes the second character to "jie" 潔, which is even further from the correct one. The *History of the Liao: Monograph on Imperial Guards* "The Eight Ancient Tribes" 《古八部》 entry copies *History of the Wei Dynasty: Account of the Khitan*, and mistakes Pili and Li as being two tribes, with the result that the eight tribes are one number short.

become a regular practice, which was agreed to. Then the offerings became regular between Helong 和龍 and Miyun 密云.

This is a record of the seven tribes, which, together with the tribe of the leader Hechen, formerly of the Northern Wei, made eight tribes. This excerpt shows that the Khitan already had trade relationships with their neighbors. However, each of the eight tribes came on their own to make "court offerings," and each traded with the Northern Wei separately – they did not yet have a unifying organization.

The following materials can provide further information on the Khitan tribes' trade with the Northern Wei. *History of the Wei: Annals of Xianzu* 魏書・顯祖紀 records a visit to the court in the second month of the first year of the Huangxing 皇興 reign period [467], and lists just four tribes, the Jufufu 具伏弗, Yuyuling 郁羽陵, Rilian 日連, and Pilier 匹黎爾, together with the states of Khotan 于闐 (Yutian) and Persia 波斯. The same text records the fourth month of the first year in the Huangxing reign period, during which the eight Khitan tribes – the Jufufu, Yuyuling, Rilian, Pilier, Chiliuyu 叱六于 (yu 于 was originally mistaken as shou 手), Xiwandan 悉萬丹, Adahe 阿大何, and Yuzhenhou 羽真侯 – "each sent emissaries to make offerings at the court."[4] Even though they happened to all come to the court at the same time, they still each sent separate emissaries, and did not act as one. When the *History of the Wei* and *History of the Northern Dynasties: Account of the Wuji* 魏書・勿吉傳 describe the neighbors of the Wuji 勿吉, the Khitan tribes are called the Jufufu, Pilier, Ba 拔(A 阿)dahe, Yuyuling, and Yuzhenhou states. That the Khitan tribes were taken to be individual "states" reflects the fact that they did not have a common leader at the time, and that each tribe acted individually.

However, these eight Khitan tribes without a unifying organization still maintained a fraternal blood relationship amongst themselves, as is shown in an ancient Khitan legend.

---

[4] The Khitan tribes listed in *History of the Wei Dynasty: Account of the Khitan* are in fact the seven tribes other than Hechen's 何辰. The *Annals of Xianzu* entry for the fourth month of the first year of the Huangxing reign period lists the Yuzhenhou 羽真侯, and as the eight Khitan tribes originally were one number short, the Yuzhenhou must be this one. If this is the case, then Hechen was the tribal leader (Mofuhe 莫弗紇) of the Yuzhenhou. The name Yuzhenhou is also seen in *History of the Wei Dynasty: Account of the Wuji*.

This widespread and long-lived legend says that in the era before they could remember, there was a man who came along the Tu River riding a white horse, and a woman who came along the Huang River riding a black ox, and at Muye 木業 Mountain, "they met and became a couple, giving birth to eight sons. Their descendants gradually came to prosper, and divided into eight tribes."[5] This legend is clearly not as old as Khitan history, and at most reflects memories from their patriarchal period, just like the Mongolians who had moved to the sources of the three rivers recalling their ancestor Bodončar 孛端察兒. Therefore, we can assume that the legend originated from the early Northern Wei or slightly earlier.*

From an overall analysis of these historical records and legends, we can see some characteristics of the Khitan tribes of this period:

1) By this time they had long since given up their matrilineal society and moved to a patrilineal one.

2) They firmly remember that the eight tribes came from a common male ancestor, which serves as evidence of their blood kinship.

3) The eight tribes treated each other as brothers, and had not yet taken the step toward unification and organizing themselves. They each individually and separately made contact with their neighbors.

4) Each of the eight tribes had its own name: (1) Xiwandan, (2) Adahe, (3) Jufufu, (4) Yuyuling, (5) Rilian, (6) Pilier, (7) Chiliuyu, and (8) Yuzhenhou. We still do not know the meaning of their names. Based on the knowledge we have of the Khitan language, these may not have been names of revered animals, but more likely originated in the place names (including mountains, rivers, and lakes) where the tribes first lived.[6]

5) Just as the Native Americans had the custom of using animal

---

[5] Found in the *History of the Liao: Monograph on Geography* 《遼史・地理志》; also see *History of the Liao: Record of the Khitan State* 《遼史・契丹國志》; *A Brief History of the Eastern Capital Era* 《東都事略》, ch. 123; and Fan Zhen's 范鎮 [1107-1088] *Record of Events from the Eastern Study*《東齋紀事》. The *History of the Liao: Monograph on Imperial Guards*《遼史・營衛志》also says, "The Khitan's ancestor was called Qishou 奇首 Qaghan. He had eight sons whose descendants' clans prospered and later divided into eight tribes, settling between the forest and desert. Now Muye Mountain in Yongzhou 永州 has a Khitan ancestral temple with statues of Qishou Qaghan, Kedun 可敦 and the eight sons."

* For Wang Xiaofu's view on this issue, see pages 148-153. Translator's note.

[6] The *Record of the Khitan State* "Origin of the Clans" 《族姓原始》 entry provides a reference: "The Khitan tribes originally did not have any surnames or clan names, and they took their names from the places where they resided."

names, the name of the tribes' common ancestor came from the two clans or tribes that the white horse and black ox symbolized. (They kept up the tradition of praying to Heaven and Earth with the sacrifice of a white horse and black ox until after the Khitan state was founded.)

6) The eight tribes did not include their maternal clans. The tribes their maternal clans belonged to were not a part of the eight tribes.

These characteristics are also corroborated in later historical developments.

The military union of the eight tribes

Each of the Khitan tribes continued to act individually for quite a long time. It was only when the Sui court came to power that changes began to take place. *Sui History: Account of the Khitan* 隋書・契丹傳 leaves us with an important record of events:

> At the end of the Kaihuang 開皇 reign period [the Khitan] tribes eventually came together and moved north, following the water and grasslands. Two hundred *li* 里 north of Liaoxi 遼西, they lived near the Gechen River 紇臣水. Their lands spanned five hundred *li* east to west and three hundred *li* south to north. They were divided into ten tribes, the largest of which had an army of three thousand, and the smallest of which had an army of over a thousand. They moved with the seasons, following the water and grasslands as their animals grazed. When they held military campaigns their leaders met together. The armies and masses were used to conduct campaigns.

New Tang History: Account of the Khitan 新唐書・契丹傳 gives the following account, in which the events can roughly be seen as contemporary to the above excerpt:[7]

> They did not hunt or reside in one place for very long. Their leaders, the Dahe clan, had an army of 40,000, which was divided into eight tribes. When a battle was to be fought all the tribes acted collectively, whereas hunting was still conducted separately.

---

[7] *New Tang History: Account of the Khitan* 《新唐書・契丹傳》.

Both of these different accounts have omissions and discrepancies, but both clearly show how the Khitan tribes had entered a new stage of development in the late Sui and early Tang. (1) During this period the Khitan were mainly hunters and herders, and the army of the eight tribes was 40,000 strong, so their actual population was many times this size. (2) The armies of each tribe were of different sizes, which indicate that the tribes themselves were of different sizes, and some grew stronger than others. When they began to unite they already had a so-called "leader," who was the highest ranking tribal leader of all of the tribes collectively. However, (3) they did not form a long-lasting confederation among all of the tribes, and instead were only loosely and temporarily united. Hunting was still carried out by each individual tribe. It was only when they attacked outsiders that each leader of the fraternal tribes met, and they moved in unison. The power of the collective tribal leader was only limited to readying for battle and moving the armies and masses. Engels points out that at one point of development for the Native Americans, "confederations among related tribes often had to temporarily form in emergencies, and then dispersed when the need was eliminated."[8] The Khitan in the late Sui and early Tang also underwent such a process of historical development.

How did this situation arise? The historical materials do not leave us with a direct account. What we do know is that from the mid-sixth century onward the powerful Northern Qi, Turks, and Sui who surrounded the Khitan all attacked them at one point or another, dealing them heavy blows.[9] The need for defending against outside attacks was clearly an important factor in spurring them toward unity. On the other hand, as the histories say that the "Khitan attacked the borders" and "invaded and plundered," we can see that along with the development of herding and the proliferation of its clans and tribes, the Khitan, who followed the water

---

[8] Friedrich Engels, *The Origin of the Family, Private Property, and the State* 《家庭、私有制和國家的起源》 (Chinese translation of *Der Ursprung-der Familie, des Privatei genthums und des Staats*) (People's Publishing House 人民出版社, 1954), p.89.

[9] See *History of the Northern Qi Annals of Emperor Wenxuan* 《北齊書・文宣帝紀》; *History of the Zhou: Account of the Turks* 《周書・突厥傳》; *History of the Northern Dynasties: Account of the Khitan*; *Sui History: Account of the Khitan*; *Old Tang History: Biography of Wei Yunqi* 《舊唐書・韋雲起傳》; and *Outstanding Models from the Storehouse of Literature*, ch. 977.

and grasslands, were continually increasing their own territory.[10] This necessarily encouraged their unification, which helped them in driving out their neighbors.

The eight Khitan tribes did not have much difficulty in going from individual to united action, as it was usually the case that related tribes helped out one another when fighting against outsiders. Once all of the necessary requirements were in place, it was extremely natural for the tribes to select a common tribal leader to deal with outsiders. From our perspective this was just a small step in the historical development of their tribal organization, but this small improvement took place over a long period of at least two hundred years.

Nevertheless, the Khitan people did not seem to have remained very long under only temporary unification. They quickly became aware of the power of unity, and when external and internal factors necessitated such strengthening, this temporary unification quickly developed into a fixed, long-lasting confederation.

The Dahe 大賀 tribal confederation

The earliest Khitan tribal confederation was formed during the early Tang. As the tribal leader was of the Dahe clan, this period is usually called the Dahe clan period. This period lasted until 730, or the 18th year of the Kaiyuan 開元 reign period of Tang Emperor Xuanzong 玄宗. Based on investigations of related historical materials, the Dahe tribal confederation had the following characteristics:

(1) The eight tribes formed a tribal confederation with a common leader, the tribal confederation leader. The confederation leader directed the eight tribes, including their foreign relations.

Outstanding Models from the Storehouse of Literature 冊府元龜 notes that in the second year of the Tang Dynasty Zhenguan 貞觀 reign period (628), the Khitan leader Mohui 摩會 "led his tribes in surrender," so by this time the confederation had probably already formed. The next year the Tang court awarded Mohui with drums and flags, which had always been the symbol for the confederation of the northern tribes. In the 22nd year of the Zhenguan reign period (648), the Tang court established the Khitan

[10] *History of the Northern Qi: Annals of Emperor Wenxuan*, and *Old Tang History: Biography of Wei Yunqi*.

Songmo Area Command 松漠都督府, and named the Khitan leader Kuge 窟哥 as the Songmo Commander-in-chief (*tutuq*) 都督, bestowing upon him membership in the royal Li 李 clan. The eight Khitan tribes were divided into nine "zhou" 州 or prefectures (a separate Chishan 赤山 Prefecture was divided from the Pili), each tribal leader was called Prefect 刺史, and each belonged to the Songmo Area Command and fell under Kuge's leadership.[11] The nine prefectures that the eight tribes formed were actually ten when including the Songmo Area Command – this was because under the Tang system only those governments with ten prefectures could be awarded the title of Superior Area Command 大都督, and does not mean that there were new changes in the eight tribes.[12] Looking past the outer appearance of the traditional Tang political system, this shows that the eight Khitan tribes were truly under the leadership of the head of the tribal confederation.

---

[11] See *New Tang History: Account of the Khitan*; *Outstanding Models from the Storehouse of Literature*, ch. 977; and *Comprehensive Mirror for Aid in Government* 《資治通鑒》, ch. 199.

[12] The *New Tang History: Monograph on Official Posts* 《新唐書・百官志》 "Superior Area Command" 《大都督府》 entry has the original note: "At the beginning of the Wude 武德 reign period important border areas were governed by military governors who were given the title 'Commissioned with Extraordinary Powers' 使持節....In the seventh year they were named Commanders-in-chief 都督. Those with ten districts were called Superior Area Commanders 大都督. In the second year of the Zhenguan reign period the word 'Superior' was eliminated." The Tang court divided the eight tribes of Khitan into nine prefectures, with Songmo Garrison considered as the tenth prefecture. This was clearly to match the number of prefectures required to give Kuge the title "Superior Commander-in-chief" 大都督 and did not imply an increase of Khitan tribes. For a discussion of the establishment of the Songmo government, see Tamura Jitsuzō 田村実造, "Tōdai niokeru kittenzoku no kenkyū" 「唐代に於ける契丹族の研究」 ("Studies of the Khitan during the Tang Dynasty"), *Man-Mō shi ronsō* 『満蒙史論叢』 (*Collected Essays on Manchu and Mongolian History*), vol. 1; and see Atago Matsuo 愛宕松男, *Kittan kodai shi no kenkyū* 『契丹古代史の研究』 (*Studies of the Ancient History of the Khitan*) (Kyoto: The Society of Oriental Researches 東洋史研究会, 1959). Atago Matsuo compares the "original tribe" of the Songmo government with the Daizhou 帯州 Yishige 乙失革 tribe set up by the Tang. However, according to the *Old Tang History: Monograph on Geography* 《舊唐書・地理志》 the Daizhou Yishige tribe was "moved to Qingzhou 青州" in the first year of the Wansui Tongtian 萬歲通天 reign period, and it is clear that this is not the Li Jinzhong 李盡忠 tribe that rebelled that year. The Yishige tribe will be further discussed later in this paper.

In the histories of the Tang Dynasty we no longer see records of the eight tribes acting individually, as we saw from the Northern Wei. During the entire Dahe clan period the relations between the Khitan and the Tang, which included civil and military affairs as well as "tribute to the court" and "rewards," were usually managed by the Songmo Governor, i.e. the tribal confederation leader, or an "emissary" 使臣 sent by him.

(2) The tribal confederation established a tribal council, and the confederation leader was elected at the council attended by the eight tribes. This council also had the power to remove the confederation leader from office. Here we can refer to a quote from the *New History of the Five Dynasties: Account of the Khitan*:

> The leader of the tribes was called the Dahe clan. They were then divided into eight tribes.…The tribal leaders were called "Big men" 大人. They promoted one leader to be in charge of the flags and drums controlling the eight tribes. When this leader had held office for many years, or if there was a disaster or disease and the herd shrank, the eight tribes would hold council, and replace him with another leader in charge of the flags and drums. The one who was replaced knew that this was their way, and did not contest it.

The same or similar accounts can be found in the *Comprehensive Mirror for Aid in Government* 資治通鑒, *Old History of the Five Dynasties, Record of the Khitan State* 契丹國志, and *Miscellanea in the Khitan Court* 虜廷雜記.[13] This record of the system for selecting the tribal confederation leader can be trusted for the most part. The *History of the Liao: Genealogical Tables* 遼史・世表 account that Shao Gu 邵固 was "commonly elected by his people" is further proof of coming to power through election.

(3) From the above quote we know that the confederation already had the responsibility for leading the herding work of the eight tribes. Zhao Zhizhong 趙至忠, who once served as an official at the Liao court, said, "If there were no disasters, the herd was strong in number, and the people were at peace, then the king would not be replaced. If this were not the

---

[13] *Comprehensive Mirror for Aid in Government* 《資治通鑒》, *Old History of the Five Dynasties* 《舊五代史》, *Record of the Khitan State* 《契丹國志》, and *Miscellanea in the Khitan Court* 《虜廷雜記》.

case the tribal council would select a new king."[14] Together with the above quote from the *New History of the Five Dynasties*, this is a record of a system which can be seen as the tradition founded by the Dahe clan.

(4) Each of the eight tribes had a tribal leader, who was referred to by the Tang as Prefectural Governor. Their power did not seem to be very great, and they had to follow the directions of the confederation leader, but they were also members of the tribal council that could elect and remove the confederation leader from office.

(5) The power to be elected confederation leader did not lie with all of the tribal leaders, but only with those of the Dahe clan. An analysis of the relationships between the confederation leaders who held power can explain this point. Among Kuge's descendants, apart from Abugu 阿卜固, whose clan was not specified, Li Jinzhong 李盡忠 was "Kuge's grandson"; Li Shihuo 李失活 was "Jinzhong's cousin"; Suogu 娑固 was "Li Shihuo's 李失活 younger brother"; Shao Gu's 邵固 "cousin was Yuyu" 郁于; and Yuyu's younger brother was Tu(Duo)yu 吐(咄)于. The final confederation leader Suogu was "Jinzhong's younger brother," as well as "Tu[Duo]yu's younger brother."[15] Even though succession was not made directly from father to son, the confederation leaders were all closely related grandsons or brothers. Here we can already see the earliest vestiges of the system of leadership succession within the clan. However, the confederation leaders could only rise to power by being elected by the tribal confederation, and this is not evidence enough that legal succession took place without holding an election.

The histories do not clearly state where the confederation leaders, the Dahe clan, came from. Only a brief passage in *New Tang History: Account of the Khitan* provides some information:

> Kuge had two grandsons, one named Kumoli 枯莫离, who was the Left Guard General 左衛將 for the Danhan 彈汗 Prefecture Prefect 刺史; another was named Jinzhong, who was the Military

---

[14] *Miscellanea in the Khitan Court* 《虜廷雜記》, in *Comprehensive Mirror for Aid in Government, Textual Analysis* 《資治通鑒考異》.

[15] See the "Account of the Khitan" in both *Tang Histories* and the *History of the Liao: Genealogical Tables* 《遼史・世表》. In the *Old Tang History: Account of the Khitan* Suogu is "Shihuo's cousin" 失活從父弟; I have followed the *New Tang History: Account of the Khitan*.

Guard Great General 武衛大將軍 and Songmo Commander-in-chief.

Danhanzhou (彈汗州 or 殫汗州) was another name for the Adahe tribe. This passage tells us that Dahe was a clan in the Adahe tribe. But the Adahe tribe was not equivalent to the Dahe clan, and the Dahe clan, the head of the confederation, was not the head of the Adahe tribe – they just had a fraternal blood relationship. This is to say that the Adahe tribal leader was not elected as the tribal confederation leader, but rather that one clan, the Dahe, emerged from the Adahe tribe with the privilege of electing successors. Its fraternal clans still belonged to their original tribes. The division of the Adahe / Danhan and Dahe in the historical materials from the Tang Dynasty reflects the actual differences between them.

These are the few points we can make about the Dahe tribal confederation. Next I will investigate the Khitan tribes outside of the eight allied tribes.

First is the problem of the Sun 孫 clan.

During the Dahe clan period an important historical event occurred: in the first year of the Wansui Tongtian 萬歲通天 era of Empress Wu Zetian (696), the Dahe confederation leader who was given the name Li Jinzhong joined with another Khitan tribe under Sun Wanrong 孫萬榮, the Tang appointed Prefect 刺史 of Guicheng Prefecture 歸誠州, in a large-scale rebellion against the Tang.[16] Sun Wanrong had a formidable army and his

[16] Also see the "Account of the Khitan" in both *Tang Histories*. The meaning of "Guicheng Prefecture" 歸誠州 is not known. Sun Wanrong was a descendant of Sun Aocao 孫敖曹, who surrendered to the Tang in the Wude 武德 reign period and was appointed the Area Commander-in-chief 總管 of Liaozhou 遼州. During the Zhenguan reign period its name was changed to Weizhou 威州, and the title Area Commander-in-chief was abolished. According to the *New Tang History: Monograph on Geography* Weizhou became a part of Youzhou 幽州 in the first year of the Wansui Tongtian reign period, which was the year in which Sun Wanrong raised his army. Therefore, Sun Wanrong's "Guicheng Prefecture" could not have been either Weizhou or the old Liaozhou. The same record of the same book lists "Guicheng Prefecture" apart from the "seventeen prefectures 州 and one garrison 府 of the Khitan," but does not give any explanation. This very likely may have been added based on Sun Wanrong's title, but its location is unclear. Another possibility is that "Guicheng Prefecture Prefect" 歸誠州刺史 was simply a title and there really was no such prefecture. The issue awaits further study.

own "family slave," so the Sun clan must have been a powerful tribe.[17] Where did this tribe come from, and what was its relation to the Dahe clan? The following excerpts provide us with some clues:

Old Tang History: Annals of Empress Zetian 舊唐書・則天皇后紀: "The Khitan leader Li Jinzhong and his wife's elder brother Sun Wanrong, the Governor of Guichengzhou, killed the commander Zhao Wenhui 趙文翽 and raised an army in rebellion."

The *Comprehensive Mirror for Aid in Government*, chapter 205, also says, "Jinzhong was the brother-in-law of Wanrong."[18]

From this we can see that the Sun clan was related by marriage with the Dahe clan, who had been given the surname Li. When analyzing the origin of the eight tribes above, we mentioned that their maternal clan was not a member of the eight tribes. The existence of the Guichengzhou Sun clan provides proof of this. The origin of the Sun clan was likely the clan of the daughter of the "black ox rider" mentioned in the legend, and the clan's descendants may have included the Shenmi 审密 (Xiao 蕭) who had for generations married with the Yelü 耶魯 clan.[19]

One event worth mentioning is that after Li Jinzhong was defeated and died, the remnants of his confederation were once governed by Sun Wanrong. This can not be explained by the fact that they fought together;

---

[17] On the Sun Wanrong uprising the *New Tang History: Account of the Khitan* says: "[Sun] Wanrong was desperate, and was riding with his family slave to the east of the Lu River 潞河. He was very tired and lay down in a forest, and his slave cut off his head." This is the only entry related to family slaves from the Dahe clan period.

[18] The Bona 百衲 edition of the *Old Tang History: Account of the Khitan* has "Wanrong and the king's brother-in-law the Songmo commander Li Jinzhong…" Atago Matsuo has noted that mentioning "king's brother-in-law" is perplexing, and discusses this (see pp. 208-9 of his work.) In fact, "King's" 王 in the Bona edition is an error for "his" 其. The Jiandian 檢殿 edition has "his." The *Old Tang History: Annals of Empress Zetian* 《舊唐書・則天皇后紀》 and the *Encyclopaedic History of Institutions: Border Defense Section* 《通典・邊防典》 both mention Li Jinzhong "and his wife's elder brother" Sun Wanrong, so Jinzhong is Wanrong's brother-in-law, and the character "his" is correct. This record in the *Comprehensive Mirror for Aid in Government* has a basis and is not an arbitrary alteration.

[19] The Shenmi 審密 included the Bali 拔里 (one version has Shouli 收里) and Yishiji 乙室己 tribes. The Yishiji are probably identical with the Yishige 乙室革, and the Bali (Shouli) may have been descendants of the Sun clan. Atago Matsuo compares the Li clan of the Songmo Military Government with the Yishige tribe, and thus has a different focus than this paper (see chapter three of his work).

and it indicated that not only the sons of the leader's brothers, but also the sons of his sisters could take over or participate in the leadership of confederation affairs. Therefore, this Sun clan that did not belong to the eight tribes formed close ties with the confederation through marriage relations.

During the Dahe clan period, apart from the Sun clan there were a few other Khitan tribes that existed independently outside of the confederation of the eight tribes.

The *Old Tang History: Monograph on Geography* 舊唐書・地理志 Daizhou 带州 entry says: "In the 19th year of the Zhenguan reign period (645) Daizhou was established within Yingzhou 營州. This was where the Khitan Yishige 乙失革 tribe was located, and the tribe fell within the jurisdiction of the Yingzhou Commander-in-chief. In the first year of the Wansui Tongtian reign period they moved to Qingzhou 青州. At the beginning of the Shenlong 神龍 reign period it fell within the jurisdiction of the Youzhou 幽州 Area Command." The first year of the Wansui Tongtian reign period was the same year in which Li Jinzhong and Sun Wanrong united their armies, so we know that the Yishige tribe did not participate in this battle. In the 19th year of the Zhenguan reign period this tribe became a prefecture of the Tang, and as this occurred before the 22nd year of the Zhenguan reign period in which the eight tribes became prefectures, this further shows that this tribe acted independently outside of the confederation of the eight tribes. The Yishige tribe was once believed to be identical with the Yishihuo 乙室活 tribe, and the tribe to which Li Shihuo of the Dahe clan was a member. This is difficult to believe. As a confederation leader, Li Shihuo surrendered to the Tang in the fourth year of the Kaiyuan reign period, and, as was explained above, he originally was a member of the Dahe clan that split from the Adahe tribe. This was clearly unrelated to the Yishige tribe. As for the Yishihuo tribe, the *Monograph on Geography* in both *Tang Histories* clearly state that they became part of the Xinzhou 信州 under the Tang, and this is not easily confused for Daizhou. This Yishige tribe was likely the "Yishiji" 乙室己 that later was annexed to the Shenmi.

The Yishihuo was a very important tribe, and later we will see the great effect they had on history. The earliest records of this tribe are from the first year of the Wansui Tongtian reign period (696) when Sun Wanrong and Li Jinzhong rebelled. In this year the Tang court founded

Xinzhou, which they were a part of, and we can see that they were another tribe that had not participated in the battle.[20] If the Yishige truly were the later Yishiji, then the Yishihuo and Yishige were a pair of tribes outside of the Dahe and Sun clans that intermarried.

Another large tribe outside of the confederation lived in Xuanzhou 玄州, which was established by the Tang. The *New Tang History: Account of the Khitan* says, "Tang Taizong's 唐太宗 troops returned from attacking the Koreans, and Quju 曲據, the leader of the great Khitan tribe Ruhe 辱紇, led his people back to the Tang. Their home was Xuanzhou, of which Quju was appointed Prefect 刺史, and his tribe belonged to the Yingzhou Area Command 營州都督府." The Xuanzhou entry in "Monograph on Geography" in the *New Tang History* also says, "[Xuanzhou] was established in the 20th year of the Zhenguan reign period (646) for the tribe led by the [Ru]he leader Quju." "Quju" is also Li Qulü 李去閭 in the *Old Tang History: Monograph on Geography*, and this was naturally an ordinary name with the surname Li 李 bestowed by the Tang, just like Sun Wanrong was also called Li Wanrong, and should not be misunderstood as belonging to the same clan as the Dahe that were given the surname Li as well.[21] Xuanzhou was established well before the 22nd year of the Zhenguan reign period when Kuge took over the eight tribes and the prefectures were established. The *History of the Liao: Monograph on Imperial Guards* listing Xuanzhou as part of the ten prefectures of Kuge's Songmo Superior Prefecture is clearly the work of later historians wanting to make an even ten prefectures and is not reliable evidence. The "Monograph on Geography" in both *Tang Histories* list Xuanzhou separately from the Songmo Superior Prefecture, and list it under the Yingzhou Area Command. It is very clear that the tribe was not within the ten prefectures and was an independent tribe outside of the eight tribes.

Apart from this, before the eight tribes became prefectures, the Tang court already had established prefectures for other tribes, such as Weizhou 威州, established in the second year of the Wude 武德 reign period (619); Changzhou 昌州, established in the second year of the Zhenguan reign period (628); and Shizhou 師州, established in the third year of the Zhenguan reign period. These were either tribes outside of the eight-tribe

---

[20] *Old Tang History: Monograph on Geography.*

[21] See the *New Tang History: Account of the Turks* and the *Old Tang History: Monograph on Geography.*

confederation, or were scattered and separated from the eight tribes. Therefore, the *Old Tang History: Monograph on Geography* says they are "all northeastern barbarians, scattered within Youzhou 幽州 and Yingzhou, and divided into prefectures that did not belong to any others."

The existence of Khitan tribes outside of the confederation reveals this fact: the Dahe tribal confederation formed the core of the Khitan people, but this confederation by no means included all of the Khitan people.

We can therefore add two more characteristics of the Dahe tribal confederation:

(6) The Sun clan (or Shenmi) that for generations married the Dahe clan confederation leaders were not within the eight tribes of the confederation, but were related by blood to the confederation through marriage.

(7) Some Khitan tribes still existed independently outside of the confederation and were scattered about. That is to say that the tribal confederation was formed by the Khitan, but it did not develop into a unifying body.

Finally, I will discuss the issues surrounding the military leaders of the confederation during the Kaiyuan reign period of the Emperor Xuanzong.

After the Li Jinzhong and Sun Wanrong rebellion against the Tang failed, the tribes of the confederation scattered, and attached themselves to the Turks for approximately twenty years. In the third year of the Kaiyuan reign period of Emperor Xuanzong (715) "Jinzhong's cousin" Li Shihuo led his tribe in submission to the Tang. At this time a new phenomenon appeared among the Dahe tribal confederation: a new position appeared that was subordinate only to the confederation leader. Ketuyu 可突于 assumed this new office, and his tribal origin is unknown.[22] Tang Emperor

---

[22] Ketuyu is found in the two *Tang Histories: Account of the Khitan*, the *Old Tang History: Account of the Xi People* 《舊唐書 •奚傳》, the *New Tang History: Biography of Wu Chengpi* 《新唐書・烏承玭傳》, and *Outstanding Models from the Storehouse of Literature*, ch. 992. Based on the *New Tang History: Biography of Xin'an Wangyi* 《新唐書・ 信安王幃傳》 and the *Comprehensive Mirror for Aid in Government*, Matsui Hitoshi 松井等 and others in the "History of the Rise of the Khitan" 「契丹勃興史」 (in *Manchuria-Korea Geographical History Research Report* 『滿鮮地理歷史研究報告』, no. 1) took it to be "Ketugan" 可突干. (Note that Wang Mingsheng 王鳴盛 had already said this in the 18th century in his *Disputations on the 17 Histories* 《十七史商榷》.) Tamura Jitsuzō does not agree with this and takes it to be Ketuyu (see note 79 of his work). Cen Zhongmian 岑仲勉 has proven the reliability of Ketuyu by using the "Epitaph

Xuanzong continued the old practice of naming the leader of the eight Khitan tribes Prefectural Governor and named Li Shihuo as the Songmo Commander-in-Chief. They also established the Jingxi 静析 Army for the Khitan, and named Li Shihuo as the Jingxi Army Chief Official 大使, and Ketuyu as "Jingxi Army Vice Chief Official 副使."[23] Tang imperial orders and histories use their usual language, and also call Ketuyu "Headquarters Adjutant" 衙官 and "Army and Cavalry Commander" 掌兵馬.[24] Looking at Ketuyu's later activities, we have reason to believe that he was a military commander under the direction of the confederation leader.

I have not listed the military commander as a characteristic of the Dahe tribal confederation, because before Ketuyu we do not find this office, and the previous confederation leaders doubled as military commanders. The period in which Ketuyu was military commander was the same period in which the Dahe tribal confederation began to break apart. During this time the confederation no longer had one leader managing both civil and military affairs, nor did it resemble the Iroquois which had two military commanders of equal rank. Instead they had a confederation leader who dealt with confederation affairs, and also had a military commander who was second to him. This led to conflict. The confederation leaders after Li Shihuo mentioned in the histories (Suogu 娑固, Yuyu 郁于, Tu(duo)yu 吐(咄)于, and Shaogu 邵固) were either placed there by Ketuyu or killed by him.[25] It seems that he could rely on his military power to influence the confederation elections, and also could avoid circumventing the recall power of the electorate and sack a confederation leader on his own. That is to say, that after this position of

---

of Liu Yuanshang" 《劉元尚墓誌》 in chapter 90 of the *Collection of the Best Bronze and Stone Inscriptions* 《金石萃編》 (see his *Collected Histories of the Turks* 《突厥集史》, first part, pp. 429-30). Judging from the phonetic rules of vowels in the Khitan language, "yu" is also a better choice.

[23] See *New Tang History: Account of the Khitan* and *Outstanding Models from the Storehouse of Literature*, ch. 992.

[24] See *Outstanding Models from the Storehouse of Literature,* ch. 992; *Collected Works of Zhang Jiuling* 《曲江集》, ch. 5, "Imperial Decree to King Julie, Officer Ketuyu, and Other People of the Khitan" 《勅契丹王據埒可突于等書》; and the *Old Tang History: Account of the Khitan.*

[25] See the two *Tang Histories: Account of the Khitan; Old Tang History: Annals of Xuanzong*; *New Tang History: Biography of Xin'an Wangyi* 《新唐書· 信安王幃傳》; and *Outstanding Models from the Storehouse of Literature*, ch. 986.

military commander was created, Ketuyu began to erode the traditional election system and fought to take power. The result of this struggle was that in 730 Ketuyu established as leader Qulie 屈列, who came from another tribe, and he seized the exclusive power of the Dahe clan to elect the confederation leader, thereby ending the period of the Dahe tribal confederation.

2. *Ketuyu and Nieli's* 涅里 *revolution and the re-establishment of the tribal confederation*

From Ketuyu to Nieli

Ketuyu overthrew the Dahe clan, but could not completely discard the old tribal system and establish a new one in its place. Nevertheless, the Dahe tribal confederation faced a serious attack that had important implications for Khitan history. Ketuyu's "mind was not at ease," and he led his tribe to side with the Turks, which led to a series of historical events that brought about a great revolution in the Khitan tribal organization.

At the time the Tang's basic strategy towards the northern tribes was "to use the two barbarians [Khitan and Xi 奚] to control the Turks." They hoped that the Khitan would adhere to the Tang and defend against attacks from the Turks. This is why Ketuyu repeatedly dethroned the tribal leaders, but continued to obtain the approval of the Tang and did not send a punitive force against them. But when Ketuyu betrayed the Tang and allied with the Turks, this went against the Tang state's fundamental interests. The Tang then sent out several armies to attack Ketuyu.

During this period an event occurred with long-lasting ramifications: the Yishihuo tribe mentioned above rose to prominence with the support of the Tang. The *Collected Works of Zhang Jiuling* (張九齡) 曲江集 includes a draft imperial decree from Tang Emperor Xuanzong that says, "Khitan King Julie 据埒 and his officer Ketuyu, and Shuhuo 蜀活 Prefectural Governor Yujie 鬱捷."[26] "Julie" is Qulie 屈列, and "Shuhuo Prefectural Governor Yujie" is the head of the Yishihuo tribe, Li Yuzhe 李遇折.[27] This imperial decree is a fairly reliable source document. It tells

[26] *Collected Works of Zhang Jiuling* 《曲江集》, ch. 5. "Imperial Decree to King Julie, Officer Ketuyu, and Other People of the Khitan" 《勑契丹王據埒可突于等書》.

[27] Also mistakenly written as Li Guozhe 李過折. Atago Matsuo gives a thorough

us that the Yishihuo tribe which was outside of the confederation possessed power and status no less than that of Qulie and Ketuyu. The *Old Tang History: Account of the Khitan* says that Li Yuzhe "shared responsibility of the army and horses with Ketuyu"; "Biography of Zhang Shougui" 張守珪傳 of the same work says he "struggled for power with Ketuyu"; and *Outstanding Models from the Storehouse of Literature* says he was the "Khitan official of the army and horses."[28] These excerpts all attest to the fact that he had formidable military power.

Therefore, the Tang court united with the forces of the Yishihuo tribal leader Li Yuzhe in wiping out Ketuyu. In the 22nd year of the Kaiyuan reign period, the Youzhou Governor Zhang Shougui 張守珪 enticed Yuzhe into beheading Qulie, Ketuyu, "and scores of their party." The next year Yuzhe was granted the title "Prince of Beiping Commandery" 北平郡王 and "Songmo Prefecture Commander-in-chief."[29] That he was not granted the title of "Songmo Superior Prefecture Commander-in-chief" was clearly because after several battles it was difficult to restore the ten prefectures of Songmo Superior Prefecture.

In the fight to destroy Ketuyu the Yishihuo tribe further gained in strength. However, Li Yuzhe's position as "Songmo Prefecture Commander-in-chief" did not last for very long, as he was subsequently killed by Nieli. Nieli is written in different ways in *Comprehensive Mirror for Aid in Government* (where it is 涅禮) and "in Yelü Yan's 耶律儼 *History of the Liao* (where it is 涅里), and it is written as 'Yali' 雅里 in Chen Daren's 陳大任 version."[30] The *Comprehensive Mirror for Aid in Government* records this event as "the Khitan King Yuzhe was killed by his vassal Nieli,"[31] and Nieli is not associated with another tribe. We can therefore see that Nieli was a member of one of the Yishihuo (乙失活 or 乙室活) tribes. The Liao people took Nieli as the forefather of the Diela 迭剌 tribe, and the Diela tribe was originally split from the Yishi 乙室 tribe

---

discussion showing that "Yujie" 鬱捷 in *Collected Works of Zhang Jiuling* (cited above, part three, chapter four) is a different translation of Yuzhe, which I have followed here.

[28] See *Outstanding Models from the Storehouse of Literature,* ch. 964. *Comprehensive Mirror for Aid in Government,* ch. 214 has "Adjutant 中郎 official of the army and horses."

[29] *Old Tang History: Account of the Khitan*. See *Comprehensive Mirror for Aid in Government*, ch. 214 and "Textual Analysis" 《考異》 of the same section.

[30] See *History of the Liao: Geneological Tables*.

[31] *Comprehensive Mirror for Aid in Government*, ch. 214 .

(i.e. the Yishihuo 乙室活 tribe; for elaboration on this issue, see below).

After Nieli killed Yuzhe, the Tang court issued an imperial decree naming him as the "Khitan Commander-in-chief" and also said, "Since Yuzhe [originally mistaken as Guozhe] is dead, and you assume the office of Commander-in-chief, whether the people are at peace again…you deserve due reward, and this matter will be conducted presently."[32] Nieli sided with the Tang and soundly defeated the Turks, thereby obtaining the support of the Tang who called him "Songmo Commander-in-chief Right Imperial Guard Great General 松莫都督右金吾衛大將軍."[33] From the Tang's point of view, Nieli was the successor to Yuzhe and even to the Dahe clan, but, in actuality, among the Khitan Nieli was only a military commander, and was not yet able to reorganize the confederation or select a confederation leader. In the 25th year of the Kaiyuan reign period (737) the Khitan betrayed the Tang and established their independence. However, they suffered defeat at the hands of Zhang Shougui, and had to flee Songmo. It was only after this that they began to rebuild the tribal confederation. This task was actually completed by Nieli, who assumed the role of military commander of the army and cavalry, and for the position of confederation leader he selected Zuwu 阻午 of the Yaonian 遥輦 clan.

From this brief historical sketch we see that from Ketuyu to Nieli the organization of the Khitan tribal confederation underwent a complete overhaul through violent struggle. The reestablished Yaonian tribal confederation had many new characteristics compared to the Dahe tribal confederation. The materials available to us now allow us to study the new confederation in detail.

The tribal composition of the Yaonian 遥輦 tribal confederation

How did this new Yaonian tribal confederation come about?

After having endured several battles, most of the Khitan tribes had been scattered, and some of them had been wiped out in the fighting.

---

32 *Collected Works of Zhang Jiuling* 《曲江集》, ch. 5, "Imperial Decree to the Military Commander (*tutuq*) Nieli of the Khitan" 《勅契丹都督涅禮書》.

33 *Collected Works of Zhang Jiuling* has 'mo' 模, revised from the *Complete Prose Literature of the Tang* 《全唐文》. See *Collected Works of Zhang Jiuling*, ch. 5, "Imperial Decree to Songmo Commander-in-chief (*tutuq*) Nieli" 《勅松漠都督涅禮書》.

Others were taken captive or surrendered to the Tang; for example, An Lushan 安祿山 "took over eight thousand who surrendered from the Tongra 同羅, Xi 奚, and Khitan."[34] The imperial decree sent by the Tang to Zhang Shougui also mentioned "recently it has been heard that many of their [i.e. Khitan] family members had been captured by us."[35] Yet another group was clans or tribes that surrendered to the Tang and who thereafter gradually melted into Chinese society. For example, Kailuo 楷洛, the father of the famous Tang commander Li Guangbi 李光弼, was a Khitan tribal leader who led his people in surrendering to the Tang.[36] Wang Wujun 王武俊 and Zhang Xiaozhong 張孝忠 were also said to have been descendants of Khitan or Xi tribal leaders.[37] Danhanzhou, where the Dahe clan originated, was incorporated into the Tang in the fourth year of the Kaiyuan reign period (716), and its name was changed to "Guishunzhou 歸順州."[38] Later it followed the Tang system in establishing prefectures and counties, and generally speaking the remaining parts later gradually blended into Chinese society.

Therefore *History of the Liao: Monograph on Imperial Guards* says, "In the Tang Kaiyuan and Tianbao reign periods, the Dahe clan grew weak, and the Liao ancestor Nieli established Dinianzuli 迪輦俎里 as Zuwu 阻午 Qaghan. As [Sun] Wanrong was defeated, and the Khitan tribes scattered, they divided their former tribesmen into eight tribes," and also "The Yaonian clan received the remnants of the defeated and scattered tribes of [Sun] Wanrong and Ketuyu and further formed eight other tribes." What was the composition of these other eight tribes? Even though the histories do not say directly, and by analyzing the *History of the Liao: Monograph on Imperial Guards* concerning the origins of the tribes during the Liao

---

[34] *Comprehensive Mirror for Aid in Government*, ch. 216 and *New Tang History: Biography of An Lushan* 《新唐書・安祿山傳》.

[35] *Collected Works of Zhang Jiuling*, ch. 5, "Imperial Decree to the Military Commissioner of Youzhou Zhang Shougui" 《敕幽州節度張守珪書》.

[36] *Old Tang History: Biography of Li Guangbi*: "Li Guangbi was from Liucheng 柳城, Yingzhou. He was a former Khitan tribal leader, and his father was Kailuo 楷洛." *Comprehensive Mirror for Aid in Government*, ch. 215: "On the guiwei 癸未 day of the fourth month of the fifth year of the Tianbao 天寶 reign period in summer, the Khitan leader Kailuo became the Prince of Gongren 恭仁王."

[37] *Old Tang History: Biography of Wang Wujun* 《舊唐書・王武俊傳》 and *Biography of Zhang Xiaozhong* 《張孝忠傳》 of the same work.

[38] Both *Tang Histories: Monograph on Geography*.

Taizu Abaoji period, we can, without too much trouble, recreate their composition.

First, the following are excerpts of the relevant records from *History of the Liao: Monograph on Imperial Guards*:

> Wuyuan 五院 tribe: their ancestor was called Yigu 益古. Six camps. Zuwu Qaghan and his younger brother Saliben 撒里本 bestowed the leadership of this tribe and called them the Diela tribe....Four Shilie 石烈: Damiegu 大蔑孤 Shilie, Xiaomiegu 孝蔑孤 Shilie, Oukun 甌昆 Shilie, and Yixiben 乙習本 Shilie.
>
> Liuyuan 六院 tribe:...Four Shilie: Xialan 轄懶 Shilie, Asu 阿速 Shilie, Wonabo 斡納撥 Shilie, and Wona'aci 斡納阿剌 Shilie.
>
> Yishi 乙室 tribe: their ancestor was called Saliben. In the time of Zuwu Qaghan, the leadership of this tribe was bestowed upon his elder brother Yigu who divided the tribe and called it the Yishi tribe....Two Shilie: Alida 阿里答 Shilie and Yuzhu 欲主 Shilie.
>
> Pin 品 tribe: their ancestor was called Nanü 拏女, Zuwu Qaghan made their camps into a tribe....Two Shilie: North Zhelizhi 哲里只 Shilie and South Xialan 轄懶 Shilie.
>
> Chute 楮特 tribe: their ancestor was called Wa 洼. Zuwu Qaghan made their camps into a tribe....Two Shilie: North Shilie and South Shilie.
>
> Wuwei 烏隗 tribe...their ancestor was called Salibu 撒里卜, he shared a camp with his elder brother Niela 涅剌....Zuwu Qaghan divided them into two: Salibu as the Wuwei tribe and Niele 涅勒 as the Niela tribe....Two Shilie: North Shilie and South Shilie.
>
> Niela 涅剌 tribe: their ancestor was called Niele. Zuwu Qaghan made their camps into a tribe....Two Shilie: North Tali 塌里 Shilie and South Chali 察里 Shilie.
>
> Tulübu 突呂不 tribe: their ancestor was called Taguli 塔古里, he lead three camps. Zuwu Qaghan ordered one of them to become the Tuju 突舉 tribe under the leadership of his younger brother Hangwo 航斡. Taguli was still in charge of the other two, and renamed them the Tulübu tribe....Two Shilie: North Tuobu 托不 Shilie and South Xu 須 Shilie.

> Tuju 突舉 tribe: their ancestor was called Hangwo. Zuwu Qaghan made their camps into a tribe....Two Shilie: North Shilie and South Shilie.

In the above records, the Wuyuan and Liuyuan tribes were split from the Diela tribe by the Liao emperor Abaoji after the founding of the Khitan state. After restoring these tribes, the eight tribes established by the Yaonian Zuwu Qaghan were: 1. Diela, 2. Yishi, 3. Pin, 4. Chute, 5. Wuwei, 6. Niela, 7. Tulübu, and 8. Tuju.[39]

From the establishment of these eight tribes we can see some basic points about the new Yaonian tribal confederation.

(1) The Yaonian tribal confederation strictly followed the old traditions of the eight-tribe confederation, and divided the remaining clan tribes into eight tribes to match the number of former tribes. The Diela tribe was split from the Yishi tribe, the Wuwei tribe was split from the Niela tribe, and the Tuju tribe was split from the Tulübu tribe. The Pin and Chute tribes were "made from their camps." The event "Yelü Yali 耶律雅里 divided the five tribes into eight" recorded in *History of the Liao: Monograph on the Army* 遼史・兵志 did actually take place. That is to say that the Yaonian tribal confederation continued the old organizational form of the eight tribes, but it was not a simple restoration of the eight Dahe tribes, but rather a new division.

(2) The clans that made up each tribe were the so-called "camps" or "shilie" 石烈. Each clan had its own name, and each tribe had at least two clans. The status of the eight tribes was: the Yishi tribe originally had eight clans, and six were split off to form the Diela tribe. The Tulübu tribe originally had three clans, one of which was split into two to form the Tuju tribe. The Chute tribe originally only had one clan, and "its tribe was made

---

[39] The names of the eight Yaonian tribes in *New History of the Five Dynasties: Account of the Khitan in the Supplementary Record of the Four Barbarian Tribes* 《新五代史・四夷附錄契丹傳》 are Danlijie 但利皆 (the modern edition "Lijie" 利皆 is incorrect, revised from *Comprehensive Mirror for Aid in Government*, "Notes on Foreigners 胡"), Yishihuo, Shihuo 實活, Nawei 納尾, Pinmo 頻沒, Nahuiji 納會鷄, Jijie 集驛, and Xiwa 奚嗢. *Veritable Records of Han Gaozu* 《漢高祖實錄》 as quoted in *Comprehensive Mirror for Aid in Government, Textual Analysis* is roughly the same. Others have checked these against the names of the eight tribes in the *History of the Liao: Monograph on Imperial Guards* record of the eight Yaonian tribes of the Taizu tribes, but the results were not satisfactory, and this problem awaits further study.

from its camp" probably means that its old clan was split into two tribes, which is why it only had the South and North Shilie, rather than each having their own names. The Wuwei and Niela tribes were originally of the "same camp," which was likely originally one large clan or phratry that was first divided into two, and each part was again divided into two to form two tribes. Therefore, the two Shilie of the Wuwei tribe did not have their own names, and were only referred to as South and North. The "Tali" and "Chali" of the Niela tribe were possibly different transliterations of the same name, or were two clans within the same phratry. As for the Pin tribe which was "made from its camp," each of its Shilie had their own names. However, careful inspection shows that the Pin tribe Xialan Shilie has the same name as a Shilie in the Diela tribe. It is possible that the original Xialan Shilie of the Yishi tribe was split into two parts, one of which went to the Diela tribe, and another of which became the new Pin tribe. This phenomenon is plausible. Of the Native Americans, Engels said: "If the clans of one phratry die out, then to keep a balance, sometimes a few clans will be taken from another phratry to make up for the imbalance. Therefore, we can find clans with the same names within different phratries in different tribes."[40] We can see a similar phenomenon amongst the different Khitan tribes.

(3) As some of these tribes were former clans, the tribal names were the names of the original clans, and it is hard to trace the relationship between these tribes and older tribes. However, we can be sure that the eight Yaonian tribes included clans that originally were a part of the Dahe tribal confederation, and included clans from outside of the confederation. The existence of this complex composition meant that the Yaonian tribal confederation no longer resembled the Dahe clan, which had eight tribes, all with fraternal relations. *History of the Liao: Monograph on Imperial Guards* shows that the only pairs of tribes with such fraternal relations were the Yishi / Diela, the Wuwei / Niela, and the Tulübu / Tuju. Between the others there was no such relationship. Of the other two tribes, only the Xialan Shilie of the Pin and the Diela tribes had common origins. The weakness of the blood relations within the Yaonian tribal confederation was an important new characteristic that differed from the Dahe clan.

(4) I previously mentioned that Nieli, the vassal of the leader of the Yishihuo tribe Yuzhe, was a member of the Yishihuo tribe. The Liao

---

[40] Engels, *The Origin of the Family, Private Property, and the State* (Chinese translation), p. 85.

people also named Nieli as the founder of the Diela tribe. This further proves that the Yishi tribe that came from the Diela tribe could only be the Yishihuo tribe that rose to power during the decline of the Dahe clan. Among the five fundamental tribes of the eight Yaonian tribes, three of them were formed from single clans, and the Tulübu tribe had three clans, and the Yishi had as many as eight clans, which made it the strongest tribe. From the above analysis we can also see that not only the Yishi tribe and the Diela tribe split from it, but also that all of the clans within these tribes were more powerful than all of the other newly formed tribes. The *History of the Liao: Monograph on Official Posts* 遼史・百官志 calling the Diela and Yishi "large tribes" and the other six tribes "small tribes" reflects their actual status. The problem is not only how many clans belonged to each tribe, but in explaining that this newly formed Yaonian tribal confederation was centered around the Yishi and Diela tribes that grew in strength through fighting, and gathered with it a few clans that had been scattered in the fighting.[41]

Qaghan – the leader of the Yaonian tribal confederation

The new confederation was like the old one with a common confederation leader. The first confederation leader was the above mentioned Yaonian Zuwu Qaghan.

There are no direct accounts of the origins of the Yaonian clan and their relationship to the confederation tribes. During the reign of the Liao Dynasty emperor Xingzong 興宗, Xiao Hanjianu 蕭韓家奴 once submitted a report saying, "After our ancestor the Wa 洼 Qaghan of the Yaonian, the royal lineage was cut off. Until Yilijin 夷離堇 Yali 雅里 established Zuwu 阻午 [as the Qaghan], this grand title was stable."[42] From this we know that Zuwu's ancestor Wa was a famous tribal leader. He was definitely not

[41] Matsui Hitoshi 松井等 and others have argued that the Yaonian clan was an untrue legend and was not a part of actual history (See Matsui Hitoshi, "History of the Rise of the Khitan"). Atago Matsuo's disagreement with this view is reasonable (see part 3, chapter 4, section 5 of Atago Matsuo, *Studies of the Ancient History of the Khitan* 『契丹古代史の研究』). But Atago Matsuo sees the meaning of the Yaonian clan as a betrayal of the Tang and self-establishment of an "independent Khitan," and that the Yaonian inherited from the Dahe, but this overlooks a huge change within the Khitan tribal organization.

[42] *History of the Liao: Biography of Xiao Hanjianu* 《遼史・蕭韓家奴傳》.

of the Dahe clan, and was not the leader of the Yishihuo tribe. The compiler of the *History of the Liao* concluded he was Qulie, to whom Ketuyu gave the throne.[43] Even though this conclusion is plausible, there is not enough evidence to prove it.

We know very little about Zuwu Qaghan. The *History of the Liao: Genealogical Tables* comparison of him with Li Huaixiu 李懷秀 in Tang historical materials (Li Huaijie 李懷節 in *Outstanding Models from the Storehouse of Literature*, both *Tang Histories: Annals of Xuanzong*, and *Comprehensive Mirror for Aid in Government*) is clearly strained. Others have recently associated him with Qulie, but this also lacks conclusive evidence.[44] However, as a descendant of Wa, at the time he was certainly a person who was well known as being qualified for election.

From this time on the confederation leader formally assumed the title of Qaghan. This title did not have greatly significant meaning, however. As with Li Jinzhong, who once declared himself Qaghan, it signified a break with the Tang in a stand for independence, and the Khitan used the Turkic title of Qaghan to replace the Tang-awarded title of Commander-in-chief 都督. The meaning of this title was not the same as when the Turkic Qaghanate was established and the title took on the new meaning of "king" 國王, but rather kept with the original meaning of "tribal confederation leader."

As with the Dahe, the Yaonian tribal confederation leaders after Zuwu had to be elected by the eight tribes.

History of the Liao: Monograph on Ritual 遼史・禮志, which was based on the work of Yelü Yan 耶律儼, records an ancient ceremony – the Firewood Investiture Ceremony 柴冊儀. Its main contents were selecting an auspicious day, setting up the Firewood Investiture Palace, and piling up firewood. The "emperor," who "was escorted by the elders of the eight tribes," made a sacrifice to the sun and raced his horse. The horses were controlled by the "Waiwei" 外威, an elder from the maternal clan. The "emperor" lay on the ground and followers covered him with fur. Afterwards, the "emperor" climbed a tall hill and the people bowed to him, and he said, "with all of our uncles and brothers present, the sagely one should be chosen. But I am young and not virtuous, so how can I be

---

43 See *History of the Liao: Genealogical Tables.*

44 See Atago Matsuo, *Studies of the Ancient History of the Khitan* 『契丹古代史の研究』, part 3, chapter 4, section 3.

leader?" His "group of vassals" then said they would all pledge their loyalty to him. Then they "burned the firewood as a signal to Heaven," thereby ending this grand ceremony.[45]

The title "emperor" was used after the founding of the Liao, which was here clearly introduced by the compilers, and the wording has been edited by Chinese historians. We can nevertheless still clearly see that this is a traditional ceremony of a religious nature held when the eight tribes selected the confederation leader. It is said that this ceremony was established by Zuwu Qaghan, which at the very least means that the selection ceremony became more systematic and formal starting with the selection of Zuwu Qaghan. The *History of the Liao: Monograph on Imperial Guards* and *Monograph on the Army* both say that Nieli gave the throne to Zuwu. The enthronement of Yaonian Zuwu undoubtedly was supported by Nieli, but for it to be legal he had to be elected by the eight tribes first.

One element of the election of the confederation leader that was the same as with the Dahe tribal confederation was that the person selected could only be from the Yaonian clan. Therefore, it did not matter whether the Yaonian belonged to a certain tribe, since they became independent from the tribe they belonged to and became a clan with the privilege of electing the leadership.

To summarize, the new confederation leadership system was a continuation and development of the old confederation system.

1. The eight tribes of the Yaonian tribal confederation still had a confederation leader as the common leader of all tribes.
2. The confederation leader was elected by the eight tribes and held a religious ceremony.
3. The confederation leader could only be from the Yaonian clan.

Yilijin 夷離堇 *– the military commander*

According to *History of the Liao: Biography of Yelü Helu* 遼史・ 耶律曷

---

[45] *History of the Liao: Monograph on Ritual* 《遼史・禮志》"Firewood Investiture Ceremony" entry. "Burned the firewood to signal to heaven" comes from *Extended Continuation of the Comprehensive Mirror for Aid in Government* 《續資治通鑒長編》, ch. 110, quoted from *Veritable Records of Renzong* 《仁宗實錄》. See Chen Shu 陳述, *Khitan Government Historical Manuscripts* 《契丹史論證稿》, part 4, section 2. [For Wang Xiaofu's analysis see pages 161-163. Translator's note.]

魯傳, Taizu Abaoji once said, "Formerly my ancestor Yilijin Yali did not consider himself fit for office and resigned." The "did not consider himself fit for office and resigned" is not to mean he "was too modest to be ruler" as the historians portray it, but was based on at least two reasons. On the one hand, Nieli killed Yuzhe and took over the army, and even though he had once been awarded the title of "Songmo Commander-in-chief" by the Tang, he was not elected by the Khitan tribes, which was against their tradition. On the other hand, after Nieli chose the Yaonian clan to rule, he still held the title of *yilijin*, or confederation military commander, and still controlled the army and cavalry, so he had true power over the confederation.

The title *yilijin* may have first come into use at this time. But the confederation military leadership system in any event started during the time of "Jingxi Army Vice Emissary" "Headquarters Adjutant" Ketuyu. However, even though the military leadership system after Nieli largely continued the old system, it had some new characteristics.

1. Starting with Nieli, the responsibilities of the military commander expanded. *History of the Liao: Explication of the National Language* 遼史・國語解 records that "*yilijin* was a high office that commanded the army and cavalry." "Monograph on Penal Law" 刑法志 of the same work says: "Zuwu Qaghan knew that Yali of the imperial clan was competent and named him *yilijin*, who was in charge of the law." *History of the Liao: Judgment on the Annals of Taizu* 遼史・太祖紀贊 also says that he "was contracted to carve wood and dug holes as a prisoner." We should not understand these records as saying that the Khitan had established their state, but showing that as *yilijin* the tribal confederation military commander had not only power over the army and cavalry, but also power of legal judgment.

2. As military commander of the tribal confederation, the *yilijin* had to be elected by the eight tribes for the title to be legal. *History of the Liao: Biography of Yelü Xiadi* 遼史・耶律轄底傳 says, "As is the tradition, the Rebirth Ceremony 再生禮 was held for the *yilijin*. Yanguzhi 罨古只 went to the tent and changed his clothes. Xiadi 轄底 then got a red gown and sable hat and rode out on a white horse. The people were ordered to shout, 'the *yilijin* is coming out!' and everyone bowed to him. Then the Firewood Investiture Ceremony was held, and the *yilijin* then took office." This is a later account of using the election ceremony to swindle the position of

yilijin during the Yaonian tribal confederation period. But it nevertheless reflects that assuming the office of *yilijin* followed the "tradition," and also required holding the Rebirth Ceremony and the Firewood Investiture Ceremony like that of the Qaghan.[46] This "tradition" can be understood as a custom originating from Zuwu and Nieli.

3. Just like the limitation of Qaghans to the Yaonian clan, the *yilijin* of the confederation was limited to the Nieli clan of the Diela tribe. I have previously concluded that the Yaonian tribal confederation was actually the union of the Yishi tribe and several other scattered clans. Nieli also stripped the Yishi tribe down to two clans, and formed the Diela tribe by the six clans that were taken from the Yishi. Because the Diela tribe of Nieli was the foundation and the most powerful tribe in the eight-tribe confederation, and because the army and cavalry of the confederation were mainly those of the Diela tribe, it was natural that their commander *yilijin* was taken from the Nieli clan of the Diela tribe. As history shows, for the entire Yaonian clan period all of the *yilijin* were the descendants of Nieli or their brothers descendants.

3. Social changes in the late Yaonian clan period and gradual reforms in tribal organization

We have previously investigated a few new occurrences since the establishment of the Yaonian tribal confederation. If we follow the clues we should be able to see the complete course of development before the establishment of the Khitan state, but the historical records stop here. Nieli enthroned Zuwu and reestablished the confederation, then went over to the Turks. When the Turkic Empire fell into decline the confederation was under control of the Uyghur Qaghanate. In 751 (the tenth year of the Tianbao reign period) An Lushan once again fought the Khitan, where he suffered a great defeat and returned.[47] Not long after that the Tang faced the An Lushan rebellion. As recorded in *History of the Liao: Genealogical Tables*, "after the An Lushan rebellion Hebei 河北 was cut off and the roads were blocked, and there was no way of knowing the lineage." Tang

[46] The Rebirth Ceremony was a part of the Firewood Investiture Ceremony. See *History of the Liao: Monograph on Ritual.*

[47] See *Old Tang History: Account of the Khitan*, *New Tang History: Annals of Xuanzong*, both *Tang Histories: Biography of An Lushan*, and *Comprehensive Mirror for Aid in Government*, ch. 216.

historical materials have no other significant records. This situation continued up until 842 (the second year of the Huichang 會昌 reign period) when the Khitan once again became attached to the Tang.

During this period, the Khitan's relationship with the Tang was a fragile one. Even though in *Outstanding Models from the Storehouse of Literature* from 757 to 839 (from second year of the Zhide 至德 reign period to the fourth year of the Kaicheng 開成 reign period) there are records of Khitan leaders coming to the Tang court, this was obviously just a common exchange of goods, and did not represent political dependency.[48] This situation is attested in the *New Tang History: Account of the Khitan*, which also says, "The Son of Heaven detested their [i.e. Khitan] patronage of the Uyghurs, and did not bestow official titles upon the tribal leaders anymore." During this time the Khitan did not receive much benefit from their relations with the Uyghurs. *Outstanding Models from the Storehouse of Literature* records that in 813 (the eighth year of the Yuanhe 元和 reign period) a Khitan "Dagan" 達干 came to the Tang court, and the next year a tribal leader with the title of "Meiluo" 梅落 came to court as well.[49] This is the first record of these two titles of Khitan clan elders. The titles clearly did not come directly from Turkish, but from the Uyghur "Tarqan" and "Buyiruq."[50] Even though they used Uyghur titles, no large changes took place within the Khitan tribal

---

[48] See *Outstanding Models from the Storehouse of Literature,* chapters 972 and 976.

[49] *Outstanding Models from the Storehouse of Literature,* ch. 972: "In the eleventh month of the ninth year of the (Yuanhe reign period) 29 people including Kege 可葛, a Khitan Dagan 達干, came to court." "In the eleventh month of the ninth year of the (Yuanhe reign period) the great Khitan leader Meiluo Hulie 梅落鶻劣 came to court." In chapter 916 as well: "On the renchen 壬辰 day of the twelfth month of the eighth year of the (Yuanhe reign period), the Emperor received a Khitan emissary Dagan Kege and others in Linde Palace 麟德殿 and gave them different amounts of colorful brocade."

[50] *History of the Liao: Monograph on Official Posts* has "Shilie Dacigan" 石烈達剌干 which was derived from Dagan 達干, and Hong Jun 洪鈞 in *Yuan History Translated and Corrected* 《元史譯文證補》, ch. 27, middle section, correctly says: "Dagan was used in the same way by Uyghurs and Turks." Meiluo 梅落 is "Meili" 梅里 in the *History of the Liao*, and "Meili" or "Meilao" 梅老 in *Outstanding Models from the Storehouse of Literature* and both *Histories of the Five Dynasties*. Regarding these two names see Cen Zhongmian's 岑仲勉 *Collected Histories of the Turks* 《突厥集史》, last part; the Turkic *Kül Tegin Inscription* 《闕特勒碑》; the *Bilgä Qaghan Inscription* 《毗伽可汗碑》 and notes; and S. E. Malov (С. Е. Малов), *Памятники Древнетюркской Письменности* (*Ancient Turkic Stele Inscriptions*), pp. 374 and 427, glossary, and works cited.

organization. Li Deyu's 李德裕 *Stele Inscription for Meritorious Service at Youzhou* 幽州紀功碑銘 says: "At first the Xi 奚 and Khitan had barbarian (Uyghur) emissaries monitoring their countries, whose responsibility was to make annual offerings and to spy on behalf of the Chinese."[51] *Comprehensive Mirror for Aid in Government*, chapter 246 also says, "At first the Xi and Khitan were controlled by the Uyghurs, and emissaries were sent to each to observe and monitor the annual offerings made." In general, the Khitan were under enormous pressure from the Uyghurs, so their development greatly stagnated.

In 842 (the second year of the Huichang reign period) the Uyghurs died out and the Khitan's newly enthroned Quxushi 屈戍始 Qaghan also acquiesced to receiving a Tang title. For the next sixty years the Tang government continued its decline. After the Khitan broke free of Uyghur control they also lessened the pressure they faced from the Tang. In such a new environment where their neighbors were gradually losing strength, they had conditions advantageous for development. "In the Xiantong 咸通 reign period [860-873] their king Xierzhi 習爾之 [Xianzhi 鮮質] sent another emissary to court, and the tribes gradually grew in strength."[52] After the Guangqi 光启 reign period [885-887], or the Khitan Yaonian clan Hendeji 痕德菫 (Qinde 欽德) period, Khitan society saw new developments that arose from its internal fragmentation.

---

[51] *Collected Works by the Prime Minister during the Huichang Reign Period* 《會昌一品集》, ch. 2, "Stele Inscription for Meritorious Service at Youzhou" 《幽州紀功碑銘》.

[52] *New Tang History: Account of the Khitan. Outstanding Models from the Storehouse of Literature,* ch. 972 has "In the end of the Xiantong reign period of Emperor Yizong 懿宗 on the fifth day Xierzhi 習爾之 and others came to court and offered items." Note that *History of the Liao: Genealogical Table* uses the *New Tang History* error of taking "Xi'er" 習爾 for Xierzhi, and like Yaonian Bala 巴剌 Qaghan, it was added later and cannot be relied upon. *History of the Liao: Monograph on Imperial Guards* says Xianzhi 鮮質 Qaghan attacked the Xi and "took those who surrendered"; *New Tang History: Account of the Khitan* says that in the Xiantong Xierzhi period the Khitan "tribes invaded"; the *Account of the Xi* of the same work says in the Xiantong period the "Khitan were strong and the Xi did not dare resist them, and led their tribe in submission." Based on the time period, historical events and pronunciation of the translated name, Xierzhi should be the same as Xianzhi. The affairs of the nine Yaonian Qaghans should be explored in a separate paper.

The emergence of Khitan class conflicts

What new changes did Khitan society face during this time?

The fact of the matter is that during this period the Khitan increasingly plundered their neighbors and captured a large number of animals and slaves from them.

The Khitan plundering of their neighbors started with attacking the Xi 奚, who were "a different type of the same people." The *New Tang History: Account of the Xi* says, "In the ninth year of the Xiantong reign period [868] their king Tujinsu 突堇蘇 sent the great military commander Sage 薩哥 to court. After this the Khitan became strong and the Xi dared not oppose them, so all of their tribes were enslaved." *History of the Liao: Monograph on Imperial Guards* even more clearly states: "The Xi kingdom had six tribes, five tents, and their ancestor was called Shise 時瑟…who died. His younger brother Tulesi 吐勒廝 succeeded him. The Yaonian Xianzhi Qaghan attacked him and captured seven hundred households of resistors, and gathered all that surrendered. In Shise's time, the Xi were friendly with the Khitan, so they only took half of the [Xi] dependents and left the rest. From then on the Xi's power began to wane."[53] The Yaonian clan did not completely wipe out the Xi tribes, but after attacking them they captured a great many "dependents." After this, Abaoji's father Saladi 撒剌的 again "captured seven hundred Xi households" for the Yaonian *yilijin*. These captives were "sent to live by the Qing 清 River in Raole 饒樂,"[54] which means they were sent back to Khitan territory to become slaves.

Saladi's younger brother Shilu 釋魯 (also transliterated as Shulan 述瀾) started an even larger campaign to plunder the neighboring tribes. "To the north he attacked the Yujue 于厥 and Shiwei 室韋, and to the south he plundered the Yi 易, Ding 定, Xi 奚, and Xi 霫." The histories said he "first started construction, established cities and towns, then taught the people to plant mulberry trees and hemp and to weave."[55] This means that his targets not only expanded to those in the north, but also reached into Chinese agricultural areas, and a large number of farmers were taken captive. This activity continued and developed until after Hendeji Qaghan

[53] See *New Tang History: Account of the Xi*.

[54] *History of the Liao: Annals of Taizu*.

[55] *History of the Liao: Judgment on the Annals of Taizu* 《遼史・太祖紀贊》.

came to power in the Guangqi period. The *Old History of the Five Dynasties* says that during this time the Khitan "took advantage of the fact that the Central Plains were chaotic and their northern frontier was unguarded, and encroached upon their counties. The tribes of the Tatars, Xi 奚, and Shiwei were all attacked and enslaved. The tribal tents flourished, and they plundered at will."[56]

In 901 (the first year of the Tianfu 天复 reign period of the Tang Dynasty) the future Liao emperor Abaoji was made *yilijin* by Hendeji. For several years in succession after this Abaoji led Khitan troops in great campaigns to plunder the neighboring tribes. In 901 "he defeated the Shiwei, Yujue, and Xi 奚 commander Xiaci 轄刺, and captured their people in great numbers." In the seventh month of 902 he attacked Hedong 河東 and Daibei 代北, took nine counties, and "captured 95,000 slaves and countless numbers of camels, horses, oxen, and sheep." In the spring of 903 he attacked the Jurchen and "captured three hundred of their households." In the winter he attacked Jibei 薊北, and "returned after taking captives." In 904 he attacked the Heichezi 黑車子 Shiwei, and in 905 he attacked Liu Rengong 劉仁恭, "taking several prefectures and bringing all their people back with him."[57]

Several years of campaigning brought about important results. A huge number of new factors were introduced into Khitan society: people from the Xi, Shiwei, and Jurchen, as well as a large number of Han Chinese. These people were not members of any Khitan tribe or clan, but were outsider slaves and governed peoples. The clan system that revolved around blood relations did not know how to deal with outsiders, let alone slaves, and had no way of governing them effectively. As more and more outsiders came, they increasingly disturbed the old system of tribal organization and pushed the development of the tribal organization toward its conclusion.

The impetus for this was not only the influx of foreign elements, but also came from slaves within the society.

In the above discussion of the Sun Wanrong rebellion I quoted the *New Tang History: Account of the Khitan* saying Sun Wanrong was "killed by a family slave." At that time it was entirely possible that he had slaves in his

---

[56] *Old History of the Five Dynasties: Foreign Exemplary Lives: Account of the Khitan* 《舊五代史・外國列傳・契丹傳》.

[57] Also see *History of the Liao: Annals of Taizu.*

family. However, based on the materials available to us today we have no way of knowing the nature and source of the slavery with certainty.

After the Xiantong reign period, along with the development of plundering their neighbors, the Khitan slavery system was not just limited to military captures, but also began to involve the possibility of enslaving their own people. During Hendeji Qaghan's rule before Abaoji served as *yilijin*, there was already the so-called "Law of Condemnation into Slavery" 籍没之法 [literally, the "Law of Registration and Confiscation"].[58] After the attempt of the Puguzhi 蒲古只 tribes on the life of Abaoji's uncle was detected, "their families became slaves of the Wali 瓦里."[59] *History of the Liao: Explication of the National Language* says, "The Wali is a government organization which all palace tents 宫帐 have. When the imperial clansmen, the relatives of the emperor's wife and other officials committed crimes, their family members were held here."[60] The Puguzhi tribes were forgiven after the founding of the Liao Dynasty, and were made "Tent Administrators" 著帳郎官[61] – that is they were the leaders of the imperial servants. Therefore, originally thc Wali was of even lower status. The Liao emperor and empress' palace tents and mausoleums all had Wali, which provided slaves as attendants. "Condemned into the Wali" 沒入瓦里 meant that the criminal was sentenced to be a special slave to the nobility – this we know with certainty. From the record of "Condemnation as Family Dependents" 沒入家屬 we know that families with private property had long since appeared within the clans. Since it was called the "Law of Condemnation into Slavery," it was certainly not limited to just the case of the Puguzhi. The criminal's family was taken from the clan they originally belonged to and became slaves. This practice would not only have led to conflicts between clan members, but would also necessarily have led to larger and larger gaps within the clan system.

Appearing along with the slavery system was the formation of noble families and a privileged class.

---

[58] *History of the Liao: Monograph on Penal Law* 《遼史・刑法志》.

[59] *History of the Liao: Monograph on Imperial Guards* 《遼史・營衛志》.

[60] See *History of the Liao: Monograph on Official Posts*, the entry on "Tent Officials of the Northern Administration" 《遼史・百官志》，《北面著帳官》.

[61] *History of the Liao: Monograph on Official Posts*, and *Monograph on Imperial Guards* of the same work.

The tradition of Yaonian clan selection of the confederation Qaghan in effect was broken, and it became an unequivocal and exclusive privilege. Such a gradual change from an election system to a succession system can be seen in the histories of other tribes throughout the world. It was this element that necessarily gave birth to the privileged nobility, and added a new characteristic to the Yaonian clan period. Just as the Dahe and Yaonian clans had emerged from the tribal confederation, the elected Qaghan was also separated from the Yaonian clan, which led to the formation of a privileged family. Even the later generations of families of those Qaghans who had stepped down or died continually enjoyed privileged status and power. This power was maintained until after the Liao state was formed. *History of the Liao: Monograph on Official Posts* has "Great Imperial Administrator of the Nine Yaonian Tents" 遥輦九帳大常袞司, whose responsibilities were "providing supplies for the nine generations of Yaonian Qaghans, whose names were Wa 洼, Zuwu 阻午, Huci 胡剌, Su 蘇, Xianzhi 鮮質, Zhaogu 昭古, Yelan 耶瀾, Baci 巴剌, and Hendeji 痕德堇." Each Qaghan had his own palace tent, and each palace tent governed its own number of foreigners.[62] Compared with the Diela tribe *yilijin*, the Qaghan palace tents were weaker. However, the appearance of these palace tents nevertheless had great significance for the formation of a privileged class.

A more significant fact was the formation of the privileged family of the military commander, the *yilijin*.

The *yilijin* of the Diela tribe was the military commander of the confederation, and even though he had to be elected, Nieli's descendants held the privilege of succession. This also laid a foundation for a system of succession as well as for privileged nobility. From looking at the records of the *History of the Liao* from before Abaoji's time, we see that from the time of Noulisi 耨里思, four generations back from Abaoji, thirteen people held the post of *yilijin* in the Diela tribe, for a total of 24 times.[63] They

[62] *History of the Liao: Monograph on Official Posts*, the "Great Imperial Administrator of the Nine Yaonian Tents" 《遥輦九帳大常袞司》 entry has "Yaonian Jiu Xiangwen Si" 遥輦糺詳穩司. This character "jiu" 糺 should be "jiu" 乣, who are the foreign elements who were ruled over. This must be explained in a separate paper.

[63] *Yilijins* from Noulisi on seen in the *History of the Liao* are Suzu 肅祖 Noulisi 耨里思 (*Genealogical Tables* quotes the "Annals of Yelüyan" 《耶律儼紀》); Noulisi's son Qiashen 洽昚 (*List of Imperial Princes* 《皇子表》) and Yizu 懿祖 Salade's 薩剌德 son Tiela 帖剌 "being *yilijins* of the Diela tribe for nine times" (*List of Imperial Princes*);

were all fathers and sons, or brothers. After the founding of the Liao, the so-called "two courtyards and three rooms" 二院散房 nobility were their descendants. They were probably like the Qaghans, and those who became *yilijin* formed their own independent family who enjoyed permanent privileges. However, these noble families in actuality had much more power than the Qaghan palace tents. As they controlled military affairs, the military campaigns against foreigners increased their power, and enabled them to obtain much livestock and many captives. Apart from the *yilijin* military commanders, their subordinates also benefited from the military campaigns, thereby amassing wealth and slaves in varying degrees. Plundering their neighbors became their profession and objective, and they used this to become a wealthy new noble class.

Looking back at the above analysis we can see the greater picture of the Khitan tribal system on its path to extinction.

(1) The large influx of foreign elements and slaves eroded the foundations of the clan system. Just as Engels said, "the prerequisite for the existence of the clan system is that the members of one clan or tribe lived together in one place all by themselves. This type of situation has long since stopped. Clans and tribes have intermingled everywhere. Slaves, protected people and foreigners have come to live among free people."[64]

(2) The establishment of the "Law of Condemnation into Slavery" shows that people from the same tribe being enslaved was no longer an occasional event, but had become a publicly acknowledged law. This resulted in conflicts between members of the same clan or tribe. As such occurrences became increasingly common, the tribal organization that had

---

Xuanzu 玄祖 Yundeshi 匀德實 (*Monograph on Food and Money* 《食貨志》); Xuanzu's second son Yanmu 岩木 "being *yilijin* of the Diela tribe for three times" (*List of Imperial Princes*); Yanmu's three sons: Huguzhi 胡古只, Moduo 末掇, and Chubulu 楚不魯 (*Table of Imperial Kinsmen* 《皇族表》 and *Biography of Yelü Antuan* 《耶律安摶傳》); Xuanzu's oldest son Dezu Sala 德祖撒剌 (Saladi; *Judgment on the Annals of Taizu*, also see *Record of the Khitan State* and *Annals of Taizu*); Puguzhi 蒲古只 "again was *yilijin* of this tribe" (*Biography of Yelü Duozhen* 《耶律鐸臻》); Ousi 偶思 "again was *yilijin* of this tribe" (*Biography of Yelü Helu*); Yanguzhi 罨古只; and Xiadi 轄底 (*Biography of Yelü Xiadi*). Furthermore, *History of the Liao: Judgment on the Annals of Taizu* says, "Salade once fought with Huang Shiwei 黃室韋, and Yizu had several bunches of arrows." This Salade once served as the *yilijin* in charge of the military.

[64] Engels, *The Origin of the Family, Private Property, and the State* (Chinese translation), p. 161.

once regulated the affairs according to the will of clan members increasingly became an oppressive organization that governed the tribes.

(3) The tradition of the Qaghans and *yilijin* being selected from the same clan or family and the privileges enjoyed by their families led to the emergence of a nobility above the clans and tribes. Along with the benefits that plundering their neighbors brought, the military commanders and their subordinates became wealthy slave owners. This economically privileged class naturally became a politically governing class. At the same time, the old tribal organization was required to become one that robbed and pressured its neighbors, becoming an organization that protected the benefits of the privileged class and oppressed the governed class.

The contest to become yilijin and transformation of the tribal organization

The result of the appearance of the slavery system and class divisions was that the old system was undermined and societal differences became irreconcilable. *History of the Liao: Biography of Yelü Helu* says that Helu urged Abaoji, saying, "Even though in the past Yilijin Yali was supported by a great many, he resigned and established Zuwu Qaghan. After more than ten generations the vassals split apart in turmoil and their government was overthrown, and submitted and adhered to another state, like a decorated banner. Military messages were sent here and there, and the people were tired of running for their lives. The chance to become king came at this moment." "The vassals split apart in turmoil and their government was overthrown" and "military messages were sent here and there, and the people were tired of running for their lives" here are clearly literary ornaments added by Chinese court historians, but they show that on the eve of the establishment of the Khitan state, their society had already fallen into a state of turmoil. This is what Engels referred to when saying, "this type of society had already given rise to irreconcilable differences and divisions that could not be overcome."[65]

Within this turmoil, from the Xiantong reign period onward three periods of struggle for the position of *yilijin* erupted among the nobility of the Khitan Diela tribe. Since the *yilijin* could use his plundered wealth and slaves to bolster his power, the struggle for this position naturally caused a violent split within the nobility. Along with this struggle the old tribal system continued its deterioration, exclusion, and reformation.

---

65 Ibid., p. 163.

(1) The first struggle and establishment of the office of Prison Warden 決獄官.

The first struggle for the position of *yilijin* erupted during the Tang Dynasty Xiantong reign period (860-873), in the time of Yaonian Xianzhi (Xierzhi) Qaghan. *History of the Liao: Annals of Taizu* says:

> He was born in the thirteenth year of the Xiantong reign period of the Tang Dynasty. Previously his mother had dreamt that the sun fell down to rest in her belly, and she was with child. When she gave birth there was a magical light and strange fragrance in the room. The baby had the body of a three-year-old and could immediately crawl. His grandmother the Jianxian 簡献 Empress thought this strange and bowed to him as her son. She often disguised him in other tents, or painted his face so that others would not know him.

This account makes Taizu Abaoji's birth into a myth. However, the background to this myth hides important historical truths, which can be corroborated in the following excerpts:

> *History of the Liao: Account of the Empresses* 遼史・后妃傳: Xuanzu's 玄祖 [Abaoji's grandfather Yundeshi 匀德實] Jianxian Empress Xiao 蕭 was also named Yueliduo 月里朵. Xuanzu was killed by Langde 狼德, and so the Empress lived as a widow in constant fear. She ordered her four sons to go to their neighbors Yelü Taiya 台押, where they found safety. When Taizu was born, the Empress found that his look was extraordinary and feared there might be a secret plot to harm him, so she had him raised in a different tent.

History of the Liao, chapter 713, "Biography of Yelü Yuwen" 耶律欲穩傳:

> Yelü Yuwen was also named Xiacigan 轄刺干, and was of the Tulübu tribe. His ancestor Taiya was the Yeci 拽刺 of the north during the Yaonian period (Yeci means 'brave warrior' in the Khitan language, and is similar to the Mongol and Manchu word

> 'Baturu.' Here it is used as a noble title; author's note). When the Jianxian Empress and her sons were in danger, they relied upon him for security.

History of the Liao, chapter 715, "Biography of Yelü Duozhen":

> His forefather was Puguzhi. During the Yaonian clan period Puguzhi again served as that tribe's *yilijin*. Yelü Langde killed Xuanzu and went on a spree of lawlessness. Puguzhi lured his [Langde's] people with a scheme, and had them all executed.

The attack on Xuanzu Yundeshi is only covered by these few passages, but at the time it was an unprecedented event of great significance. Yundeshi was the *yilijin* and controlled the military. That he was killed and even his widow and descendants fled to the Tulübu tribe under a different tent to avoid harm shows that the Langde group must have had great power. Langde's tribe and lineage are unknown. It is very possible that after Langde killed Yundeshi, he became *yilijin* for a period of time. Even though there are no direct records of this, the histories say he "killed Xuanzu and went on a spree of lawlessness," and Puguzhi could only have his people executed by luring them with a scheme. From these excerpts we can tell that Langde must have once obtained the highest rank below that of the confederation leader, and had control of the army. Puguzhi, who eliminated Langde, was the forefather of Yundeshi's older brother Xiamage 匣馬葛. He and Yundeshi were not directly related, but were still of the same family. This is how the office of *yilijin* was taken back.

At about the same time, a position of "Prison Warden," which was held by the Shenmi (Xiao) clan, who had marriage relationship with the royal clan, appeared in the Yaonian tribal confederation. *History of the Liao: Biography of Xiao Dilu* 遼史・蕭敵魯傳 says, "the great-great-grand-father was called Humuli 胡母里, and he often acted as an emissary to the Tang during the Yaonian clan period. The Tang once kept him in Youzhou, but he broke out and fled back through the passes one night. After this he and his offspring held the position of Prison Warden." The "Prison Warden" was a new official position. Originally the tribal organization's power of legal judgment was insufficient. The establishment of this new official position reflected the irreconcilable differences between the classes, and also shows that in order to rid itself of these conflicts the tribal organization was transforming itself by strengthening functions that were against its very nature – functions of oppressing and governing the tribal people.

(2) The second struggle and the establishment of the position of *yuyue* 于越 and the *tama* 撻馬

After Puguzhi the office of *yilijin* was still held by those from the Xuanzu Yundeshi line. Other than them, only Puguzhi's descendant Ousi briefly held this position. After Abaoji's father Dezu Sala 德祖撒剌 (Saladi) served as *yilijin*, Yanguzhi, a descendant of Yundeshi's younger brother Tiela 帖剌, was elected to the post. This is when the more influential second struggle broke out.

I briefly mentioned this second contest when quoting the *History of the Liao: Biography of Yelü Xiadi* in my discussion of the election of the *yilijin*. This conflict used the election system to undermine the very same system. When Yanguzhi held the selection ceremony his step-brother Xiadi gathered his gang and forcefully held the Firewood Investiture Ceremony, thereby seizing the office of *yilijin*. Here we must point out that the reason Xiadi could so easily achieve victory was that he received the support of Dezu Sala's (Saladi's) younger brother Shilu, who had a strong reputation. *History of the Liao: Biography of Yelü Xiadi* says he "named himself *yilijin*, and ruled the state along with Yuyue Shilu." After Xiadi came to power he was still in effect controlled by Shilu.

The result of this struggle was that the tribal confederation organization once again transformed itself.

First was the establishment of the *yuyue*. *History of the Liao: Preface to the Monograph on Official Posts* 遼史・百官志序 says, "The *yuyue* sat and gave his opinion in imitation of the Chinese Chancellor"; and under the "*Yuyue* Ministry" 于越府 entry, "The Great *Yuyue* Ministry has no administrative duty, and has status above all other officials. This title is bestowed upon those who have contributed extraordinarily to the state. This is a very prestigious office of the Liao state, and is equivalent to the Three Dukes 三公 of the southern [i.e. Chinese] system." Before the founding of the Khitan state, this official who "has no administrative duty and has status above all other officials" was actually a "prestigious official" who was higher than the *yilijin* and all other confederation officials. Shilu, who orchestrated the Xiadi victory, was the first to hold the position of *yuyue*. The histories called him "Supreme Commander of

State Affairs" 總軍國事 and "Official of the State" 當國.[66] His position was second only to the confederation leader Qaghan, but he held the actual power over the military and civil government that the Qaghan did not have. The *yilijin*, who had control of the army and cavalry, also took orders from the *yuyue*.

Next was the establishment of the *tama*, or royal guard. This was an independent personal bodyguard created by Shilu. They were mostly selected from the confederation troops to form a retinue, which also formed the core of the Khitan armed forces. As Shilu's nephew and trusted follower, Abaoji was named to serve as "Tama Yueshali" 撻馬狘沙里, who was the head of the royal guards.[67] It is easy to draw connections between them and personal guards of other northern peoples, such as the Mongolian "Qiexue" 怯薛 and the ancient German comitatus. However, they differ from German guards in that they did not add to the king's power, but instead added to the power of the *yuyue* who was about to replace the Qaghan.

This is how Yuyue Shilu not only had military power surpassing that of the Qaghan, but had battle ready forces under his personal command. When he served as *yuyue* he "to the north attacked the Yujue and Shiwei, and to the south plundered the Yi 易, Ding 定, Xi 奚, and Xi 霫," and apparently he conducted extensive military campaigns against his neighbors. *History of the Liao: Annals of Taizu* says he "began to have ambition for more territory and subjects." He clearly had already laid the foundations for overthrowing the Yaonian tribal confederation.

(3) The third struggle and Abaoji's replacement of the Yaonian

Shilu had to stop upon reaching this point, however, and he could not proceed any further. His greatly increased power induced strong resistance against him from the nobility who had the privilege of being elected *yilijin*. The three tribes of the Puguzhi, who originally wiped out Langde's group, enlisted Shilu's son Huage 滑哥 and killed Shilu, and the Yilijin Xiadi fled to the Bohai 渤海 Kingdom. This was already in the Hendeji Qaghan period.

However, Shilu's opponents did not achieve their purpose either.

[66] *History of the Liao: Annals of Taizu*.

[67] *History of the Liao: Explication of the National Language*: "*Tama* was in the retinue 人從. Shali 沙里 was of the nobility. They led all of the officials." Also, "*Tama* was an official in the retinue 扈從."

Because Abaoji controlled the *tama* crack troops, he defeated the Puguzhi and two other tribes. After Xiadi fled, Abaoji was promoted from the leader of the guards to the military leader *yilijin*, and controlled all of the armed forces. For three years after 901 he further increased his power by plundering his neighbors. In 903 he became the new *yuyue* "Commander-in-Chief" and also held the position of *yilijin*. This is when he gained complete military power within the tribal confederation. His actual power and economic strength had already far surpassed that of the confederation Qaghan Hendeji. It was now just a matter of time before Abaoji replaced the Yaonian clan and established a new state dictatorship of the nobility based on his amassed wealth and slaves and his simultaneous holding of the positions of *yuyue* and *yilijin*.

Abaoji replaced the Yaonian Qaghan in the first month of 907.[68] In the three years before this he had continually attacked the Shiwei, Jurchen 女真, Xi 奚, and Xi 霫 tribes in the north, and to the south attacked the Han Chinese territory governed by Liu Rengong. The histories say he "obtained many Chinese captives."[69] During this time not only did Abaoji obtain a great number of captives, but also continued to attack Chinese villages and cities. The expansion of his territory and tribal members further undermined the clan system and furthered the birth of his state.

However, the replacement of the Yaonian by Abaoji did not yet signify the foundation of the Khitan state.

History of the Liao: Annals of Taizu says: "In the first month of spring in the first year of the [Taizu period] on the gengyin 庚寅 day, he ordered his officials to set up an altar in Ruyuwangjihuiguo 如迂王集會堝, burned firewood to signal Heaven, and became emperor." Here "Wangjihuiguo" 王集會堝 should mean the same location where the old tribal confederation selected the Qaghan, whereas "Burning firewood to signal

---

[68] *History of the Liao: Annals of Taizu* and *Biography of Yelü Helu* both say that in the 12th month of 906 "Hendeji Qaghan [Qinde] died and his vassals carried out his will of crowning Taizu." But *New History of the Five Dynasties: Account of the Khitan in the Supplementary Record of the Four Barbarian Tribes* says, "the eight tribes thought the Yaonian would not rule, and selected from amongst themselves Abaoji instead." *Outstanding Models from the Storehouse of Literature,* ch. 956 says: "King Qinde's government waned and Abaoji, leader of another tribe, was most highly regarded. The tribal tents had slowly prospered, and he replaced Qinde as king." The *New History of the Five Dynasties* and the *Outstanding Models* records seem to be the most appropriate.

[69] *New History of the Five Dynasties: Account of the Khitan in the Supplementary Record of the Four Barbarian Tribes.*

to Heaven" must refer to the traditional "Firewood Investiture Ceremony" held when electing the Qaghan. After Abaoji rose to power he declared "the imperial family [Abaoji's family] succeeded the nine Yaonian clan tents as the tenth tent."[70] Clearly he was doing his all to express to the Khitan people that just as the Yaonian clan had succeeded the Dahe clan, he was the successor to the Yaonian clan.

Abaoji's move partly came from preserving traditional customs, but mainly came from the old nobility, who were still very powerful. This can also be seen over the course of his rise to power. *History of the Liao* says that he came to the power because he was "urged on by Helu 曷魯 and others."[71] This Helu was a descendent of the Puguzhi tribe, the enemy of Abaoji, but from a young age he and Abaoji "became friends who shared furs and horses with one another"[72] and became sworn brothers. When Abaoji served as Tama Yueshali and *yilijin*, Helu was continually a great helper of his. *History of the Liao: Biography of Yelü Helu* gives a detailed account of the conversation with Abaoji when "Helu encouraged him." Looking beneath the flattering words of the Chinese historians, this at least shows that before Abaoji came to power he planned to obtain the support of the influential and powerful Helu to offset those forces which opposed him. Abaoji also obtained the approval of his uncle Xiadi who had been *yilijin* before him. After the rebellion Xiadi returned to the Khitan from the Bohai Kingdom. "Taizu was about to ascend the throne, when he offered it to Xiadi. Xiadi said, 'The emperor is a saint appointed by Heaven. How could your servant dare to take it!' Taizu then named him *yuyue*."[73] Actually, Abaoji was using the office of *yuyue* in exchange for allowing him to replace the Qaghan. Meanwhile, Xiadi's son Dielidi 迭里底 (one version has a different character "li" 栗 in Dielidi) was named *yilijin* of the Diela tribe. At this time the *yuyue* and *yilijin* naturally were not equal to the *yuyue* and *yilijin* posts held by Abaoji, because after he replaced the Qaghan he already had absolute power over military and civil affairs. However, this fact clearly shows that in this period Abaoji still had to give Xiadi and his son the highest positions of power so that he could obtain the support of the only family whose power was second only to that of his own.

70 *History of the Liao: Annals of Taizu.*
71 See ibid.
72 *History of the Liao: Biography of Yelü Helu.*
73 *History of the Liao: Biography of Yelü Xiadi.*

Because of the temporary strength of this old power, even when Abaoji had overthrown the Yaonian clan, he still could not at once fundamentally overthrow the old tribal system and establish a state with a new class system. However, after he replaced the Yaonian clan and kept a hold on his power, he used new measures to increase his own power and allow the state to continue down its path of development.

The establishment of the *tiyin* 惕隐 was the first important measure adopted by Abaoji in the second year of his rule. *Tiyin* is also transliterated as *tiliyi* 梯里已, and was a new office "in charge of the civil and religious affairs of the royal family" or "administering the tribes."[74] This post was responsible for managing the civil and religious affairs of the Diela tribal nobility. The first *tiyin* was Abaoji's younger clan brother Lage 剌葛 (i.e. Saci 撒剌). This clearly was an important office, and *History of the Liao: Monograph on Official Posts* lists it as second only to *yuyue*, which is reasonable. The establishment of this post further undermined and replaced some of the official responsibilities of the tribal organization. As the clan system already could not deal with the privileged noble families, a new post had to be formed to undertake this task. This not only reflects that the main group within this privileged class was already removing itself from the clan organization, but also shows that this group already needed a special post for managing its internal affairs, thereby maintaining the governance of the group and the entire class. Of course Abaoji needed the *tiyin* to control the noble families and to ensure their submission to him.

Another new measure was that "on the wuzi 戊子 day of the seventh month in the autumn of the fourth year [of Abaoji's rule], the (Shulü) empress' elder brother Xiao Dilu 蕭敵魯 became the Prime Minister of the Northern Superior Prefecture 北府, and this was when the empress' clan began to serve as Prime Ministers."[75]

The title "Prime Minister" may have come into use at a later time, but before Abaoji came to power there was already the division of the Northern and Southern Superior Prefectures. *History of the Liao: Monograph on the Army* attributed the establishment of the two Superior Prefectures to Nieli, which was entirely possible. This split the eight tribes

---

[74] *History of the Liao: Monograph on Official Posts* and *Explication of the National Language* of the same work.

[75] See *History of the Liao: Annals of Taizu.*

in the confederation into one group with the Diela tribe at its center, and another group with its fraternal tribe the Yishi at its center. The first group had five tribes which included the Pin, Wuwei, Niela, and Tulübu tribes, which all belonged to the Northern Superior Prefecture. The latter group had three tribes and included the Chute and Tuju tribes. The two strongest tribes, the Diela and Yishi, became the privileged tribes of the Northern and Southern Superior Prefectures. Members of their nobility served as Prime Ministers in both Superior Prefectures, and respectively managed the other member tribes within their groups. The "Prime Ministers" were not selected from the tribes, but were instead appointed by the Qaghan. In this way they not only encroached upon the power of the tribal leaders, but within the confederation they used the Southern and Northern Superior Prefectures to erode the traditional principle of equality among different tribes.

Abaoji went one step further, namely that "this was the start of the Empress' clan becoming Prime Ministers." The current Northern Superior Prefecture Prime Minister was not of the Diela tribal nobility, but the "Empress' elder brother Xiao Dilu." He and Abaoji's Chunqin 淳欽 Empress (Shulü 述律) had the same mother but different fathers, and their great-great-grand-father was the "Prison Warden" Humuli. If we say that Xiao 蕭 of the Shenmi serving as the Prison Warden can be explained as the clan system era custom of maternal clan members ruling over the affairs of the clan, then it was entirely the nobility of outside tribes who governed the five tribes of the Northern Superior Prefecture. Abaoji used the trusted nobility to strengthen his position and power, while attacking the old tribal system.

There was one more measure that greatly helped to solidify Abaoji's position, which was the strengthening of the organization of the royal personal guards. Abaoji's camp tent established a "camp guard army" 宿韋軍 or "central division" 腹心部 and "selected over two thousand of the most stalwart men to serve."[76] Leading these personal guards were his trusted supporters from his youth: Helu 曷魯, the Empress' elder brother Xiao Dilu, and Dilu's younger brother Aguzhi 阿古只. Xieniechi 斜涅赤 of the Diela tribal nobility, "was enlisted under Taizu's command early on,"[77] along with Yuwen 欲穩, who belonged to the Tulübu 突呂不 tribal

[76] *History of the Liao: Biography of Yelü Helu.*
[77] *History of the Liao: Biography of Yelü Xieniechi.*

nobility and once had protected Abaoji's grandmother and her family, participated in leading this guard organization.[78] This was clearly a band of strong and reliable crack troops. These guards were different from the *tama* royal guards from before, and resembled the German comitatus. They no longer enhanced the *yuyue's* power to usurp the throne, but rather strengthened the power of the new "Emperor" Abaoji. To use the words of Engels, they furthered the appearance of kingly power.

4. *The struggle between the old and new systems and the founding of Abaoji's state*

The clash of two powers

As proven by the history of all the world's peoples, the replacing of an old system with a new one is always met with fierce resistance. Old ways will not die out on their own without being attacked, and new ways will not take hold without a struggle. Khitan society already had increasing class conflicts and the need for state building, and the neighboring Chinese state had a huge influence on them and provided them with a contemporary role model. Nevertheless, the Khitan state had to be built upon the ruins of the clan system after undergoing a hard struggle with the old ways.

The following is a brief account of the process of this struggle.

The struggle began in the fifth year after Abaoji replaced Yaonian (911). Why did it not happen in the previous four years? Chinese historical materials have a legend that under the old Khitan system an election was held every three years, and the newly elected office-holder then replaced the older one. That Abaoji was old and was not replaced incurred rebukes from the tribes.[79] There may be some grounds for this legend. The clearer

---

[78] For those in control of governance see this account in the *History of the Liao*.

[79] See *New History of the Five Dynasties: Account of the Khitan in the Supplementary Record of the Four Barbarian Tribes* and *Comprehensive Mirror for Aid in Government*, ch. 266. On Abaoji's ascending the throne, Chinese histories say that after he reigned for nine years and was not replaced, he "raised an army at Yan Pool 鹽池" and killed the leaders of the eight tribes. See *Comprehensive Mirror for Aid in Government* and *New History of the Five Dynasties*. This legend seems to have originated in the fact that during the nine-year period when Abaoji replaced the Yaonian, he defeated the Niela 涅剌 tribe, as well as the rebellion of the brothers and the Yishi 乙室 tribe, and subsequently established an imperial state. Chinese historians are not aware of the details of this matter and gloss over the tale and make additions to it. This paper pays attention to the

fact is that after Abaoji ascended the throne, "he increasingly put pressure on the tribes."[80] He continually changed the old system in order to develop his actual power and strengthened his dictatorial authority, which eventually resulted in opposition from the old nobility.

The main opposition did not come from the descendants of the Yaonian clan. The histories say that after Abaoji replaced the Qaghan, "the old Yaonian tribe harbored resentments."[81] They were not satisfied with the disappearance of their right to be selected Qaghan, but they could only stand to the side and complain, because they had long since lost the military power to resist Abaoji. The main source of resistance also did not come from the weaker tribes in the confederation, because after the establishment of the Yaonian tribal confederation they had absolutely no power to resist. We are told by only one line in *History of the Liao: List of Imperial Princes* that after Abaoji ascended the throne he once ordered his younger brother Lage to attack the Nielie 涅烈 tribe (i.e. the Niela 涅剌 tribe).[82] This tribe may have raised some resistance, but nevertheless their resistance must have been very weak, and did not stand up to a single attack from Abaoji.

The main resistance to Abaoji did not come from the above elements, but from "right next door," which was the clan related to Abaoji that came from the Diela tribe. The leader of the resistance was Abaoji's younger brother Lage, who had just assumed office as *tiyin*, and who had defeated

---

reasonable parts of the story, and relies mostly on the Khitan historical materials of the *History of the Liao*. *New History of the Five Dynasties: Account of the Khitan in the Supplementary Record of the Four Barbarian Tribes* mentions a Chinese person telling Abaoji to not take a successor. *Textual Analysis and Criticism of the Comprehensive Mirror for Aid in Government* 《資治通鑒考異》 quotes Jia Wei 賈緯, *History of the Northern Dynasties*, which also mentions Li Keyong 李克用 telling Abaoji to "not be replaced by the clans." These legends reflect the influence the feudal states of the Tang and Later Liang 後梁 necessarily had on the Khitan, and are worth noting. However, Abaoji's founding of the state was not at all decided by casual statements, but was determined by necessary factors within the development of Khitan history.

80 From *New History of the Five Dynasties: Account of the Khitan in the Supplementary Record of the Four Barbarian Tribes*.

81 *History of the Liao: Biography of Yelü Haili*.

82 *History of the Liao: List of Imperial Princes* "Lage" entry: "When Taizu ascended the throne he was the *tiyin*. He attacked and defeated the Nielie 涅烈 tribe. He then became the *yilijin* of the Diela tribe…he had a foolish and rash nature, and was proud of his defeat of the Nielie tribe." The *Basic Annals* 《本紀》 does not record these matters. This is the only entry with information on the Niela tribe's rebellion against Abaoji.

the Niela tribe. He gathered around him his younger brothers Diela 迭剌, Yindishi 寅底石, and Anduan 安斷 who were all nobles qualified for office. In 911 Abaoji had learned of the first rebellion, so it could not commence immediately. *History of the Liao: Annals of Taizu* says: "In the fifth month of the fifth year the emperor's younger brothers Lage, Diela, Yindishi, and Anduan planned a rebellion. Anduan's wife Zhanmugu 粘睦姑 learned of it and reported it, and the report was later verified. The emperor could not bear to punish them. He and the brothers climbed a mountain, made a sacrifice and swore to Heaven and Earth, and their crime was forgiven. Lage was then driven out and became the *yilijin* of the Diela tribe." Here the *tiyin*, whose original responsibility was to strengthen rule over the tribes, became the leader of the resistance. That Abaoji did not punish them and instead climbed a mountain and made an oath suggests that the rebels had a lot of power in the society. Lage became the *yilijin* of the Diela tribe, and the *tiyin* position was then filled by Huage 滑葛, the son of the former Yuyue Shilu. Huage had once plotted against Shilu with the Puguzhi and two other tribes, and was clearly a powerful figure from the rebel faction. *History of the Liao: Biography of Huage* says that "Taizu ascended the throne…even though he knew Huage was a fierce rebel, he showed acceptance and made Huage the *tiyin*." The acceptance the emperor showed here of Huage was like his inability to punish Lage, which was a compromise he made with the old power of the rebel faction.

However, the compromise did not and could not staunch the progression of the resistance. In the seventh month of the next year the second rebellion broke out. The leaders once again were Lage, Diela, Yindishi, and Anduan, but they also gained the support and control of the *yuyue* official Xiadi. The newly appointed *tiyin*, Huage, also participated in the plot. This is how Abaoji's most important ministers, the *yuyue*, *tiyin*, and *yilijin*, formed a strong group acting against him. The formation of this group undoubtedly was a great threat to Abaoji.

The rebellion also came at an opportune time. In the autumn of 912 Abaoji personally led a campaign against the tribes in the southwest and ordered Lage to attack Pingzhou 平州. When Abaoji returned with his army in the tenth month Lage, after defeating Pingzhou, "used his army to block the road" and planned to attack Abaoji on the road. Abaoji's strategy in response is worth taking note of. He did not start a counterattack immediately, but rather avoided direct conflict and moved his army southward, and on the same day held the Firewood Burning Ceremony 燔

柴禮 to select the Qaghan. Even more important is that on the next day the rebels had no choice but to "send someone to ask for punishment."[83] This course of events clearly shows that the rebellion had openly supported the maintenance of the traditional election system. When Abaoji took this over himself they lost their reason to resist.

Of course, holding the traditional election of the Qaghan could only momentarily alleviate the conflict, and could not eliminate the resistance of the old nobility. After only a few months the third and largest armed rebellion broke out in full force.

The leaders of this rebellion were the same group as before. One new element to their group was the nobles of the Yishi 乙室 tribe, a fraternal tribe of the Diela 迭剌 tribe, who threw in their lot with the rebels. This even further added to the strength of the rebellion.

The rebellion broke out in the third month of 913. Unlike the previous time, the rebels first acted in close coordination with one another and publicly started a movement to take the Qaghan throne. Lage on the one hand dispatched Diela and Anduan to lead their armies against Abaoji, and on the other hand planned to establish his own "flags and drums of the Son of Heaven." When Abaoji discovered the plot he detained Diela and Anduan, and personally led a large force to chase down Lage. Meanwhile, another branch of Lage's army led by Yindishi went straight to attack Abaoji's Qaghan tent. At the time only the Chunqin Empress was left in Abaoji's camp tent, and she had to "arrange a defense at a strategic place." The rebel army burned the Qaghan's "military supplies and tents" and "the army was left to kill with abandon."[84] They took the flags and drums and ancestral "spirit tent" 神帳 that was symbolic of the Qaghan. The Bright King Tower that Abaoji built after coming to power was also burned down. The Chunqin Empress sent troops after them, but they only managed to recover the flags and drums.

The well-prepared, large-scale rebellion came suddenly, and Abaoji had no choice but to look to outsiders for help, so he went to the Shiwei and Tuhun 吐渾 (Tuyuhun) tribal leaders. During the pacification of the rebellion his "central guards" played a clear role. In the fourth month of that year Xiao Dilu and Aguzhi led them in attacking Lage with support from the Shiwei and Tuyuhun armies, and finally scattered Lage's army,

---

83 See *History of the Liao: Annals of Taizu*《遼史・太祖紀》.

84 See ibid.

bringing back the "spirit tent." The rebel leaders Lage and Xiadi were brought captive before Abaoji.

This contest with the rebels lasted for two months, and the scope of the battle was unprecedented. Abaoji's army even "boiled horse and pony meat and gathered wild vegetables for food," "most of their livestock died on the road" and they "abandoned their equipment and clothing in the Chuli River 楚里河 and scattered for several hundred *li* 里."[85] Later, when recounting the crimes of the rebels, Abaoji said, "The wanton actions of those officers were immoral, and they hurt those who were honest, brought disaster to the people, and took their property. The people used to have thousands of horses, but now they all go on foot. Since the establishment of our state such a thing has never happened."[86] It is evident that this was a great battle in Khitan history, and the Khitan people paid dearly for it. Only after a fierce conflict could Abaoji emerge victorious.

Studying Abaoji's handling of the rebels is also very rewarding. After the rebellion was put down, Abaoji "handed out heavy and light sentences" to "six thousand of the rebels." He first dealt with the rebel leader Xiadi, and "ordered him to throw himself off a cliff to his death." He also had the rebel Diligu of the Yishi tribe put to death. Later, in the winter of that year he "saw the elders and discussed the government," and "burned firewood at the lotus river."[87] That is to say that he once again gathered the tribal elders and held the traditional Qaghan election ceremony.

The rebel leaders from the royal family were not dealt with until 914, after the Firewood Burning Ceremony. Huage, the son of Shilu who was sentenced to death, "had his crimes confirmed by the group of elders." As for the "most evil" Lage and Diela, who were younger brothers of the emperor, they were only "beaten and released." Yindishi and Anduan were even "released from their crimes" and not punished.[88] This unusually lenient treatment did not come from Taizu's benevolence, as the histories say; but it once again shows that the "brothers' rebellion" had strong support from Khitan society, and was based on the traditional system.

What, then, was the nature of this struggle?

---

[85] See ibid.

[86] See ibid.

[87] See ibid.

[88] See ibid.

After Xiadi was defeated he said to Abaoji: "At first I did not know the grandeur of the Son of Heaven, and after your majesty ascended the throne you were well guarded – more so than ordinary folk. When I once presented a memorial to you my mind was not at ease, and I began to think of usurpation."[89] After Abaoji ascended the throne he attacked to the north and to the south, continually increasing his wealth, which clearly led to extravagant hopes of the nobility who possessed the same qualifications to usurp the throne. However, this at most explains a general reason behind the rebellion, but not the nature of the struggle. Abaoji was opposed as the largest slave owner and the reformer of the old system. He further destroyed the old tribal organization, continued to establish his dictatorship over the slave-owner nobility, and destroyed the tribal system of succession. He furthered the system of leadership succession, which by necessity conflicted with the interests of the nobility of equal rank. The rebellious nobility who plotted to take the throne naturally planned at the same time to restore and maintain the old tribal system of succession, so that they could gain the opportunity and power to be selected. In this way, no matter whether they were aware of it, they in actuality joined with the old social powers and became the upholders and representatives of the old system. The reason that the rebellion could break out on a large scale, and the reason that Abaoji again and again made use of the old system was that the power of the old Khitan clan system had become one of the main pillars supporting the rebellion. Of course, it is a law of history that even if the rebellion had been successful, the rebel leaders would have in the end gone down the path of establishing a state governing system and dictatorship of the ruling class, and would not have let the dying tribal system continue. However, when they publicly trumpeted the old system and rose up against Abaoji, the struggle between the two sides was necessarily a life and death struggle between old and new power and old and new systems within the Khitan society. In other words, this struggle was reflected most sharply and deeply within the nobility.

The founding of Abaoji's state

The Khitan state was founded in 916 after Abaoji defeated the rebellion of the old nobility. From this time until his death a decade later, Abaoji continued to campaign against the tribes in the north, moved deep into

---

[89] *History of the Liao: Biography of Yelü Xiadi.*

Chinese territory in the south, and in the east eliminated the Bohai Kingdom. At the same time he widened the plundering of his neighbors, and he wiped away the vestiges of the clan system and gradually created the new system of the Qaghan state. The following aspects of this new state are the most important ones in my view.

The first was the establishment of hereditary imperial succession. In 916 Abaoji, as the head of the Khitan slave-master system, imitated the Han Chinese imperial system in starting the Shence 神册 reign period, using the title of "Emperor" 皇帝, "calling himself the Great Saintly Great Bright Heavenly Emperor" 大聖大明天皇帝, and "making his son Bei 倍 the imperial heir apparent."[90] In this way the election system of the tribal confederation was officially terminated and hereditary imperial succession was announced. If we were to see later instances of the Firewood Investiture Ceremony for the election being held, it would signify merely that the traditions and religious customs of the clan system had been preserved.

A governing mechanism formed around the emperor. In addition to replacing the officials established since the Yaonian period, several new offices were added. In the sixth year of the Shence reign period the imperial order of "ascertaining the classes of officials" 正班爵 specified the different grades of each level of official.

The second aspect was the localized dictatorial governance of the Khitan tribes. I mentioned above that after Abaoji replaced the Yaonian he used the Xiao clan from outside the eight tribes as "the Northern Superior Prefecture Prime Minister for generations" 世為北府宰相, who governed the five tribes of the Northern Superior Prefecture. Now this was taken one step further, and the Yishi, Chute 楮特, and Tuju tribes were transformed into a group governing the Southern Prefecture. *History of the Liao: Annals of Taizu* says: "After the brothers' rebellion, the position of Southern Superior Prefecture Prime Minister was long left vacant, because many of the qualified nobility died in that disaster. The position was temporarily filled by Xiadezhiligu 轄得只里古 of the Chude 鋤得 [Chute] tribe. Many from the Superior Prefecture asked that a member from the royal family should be selected as Prime Minister, but his majesty thought the old system should not be changed at will. However, the request was repeatedly made and then his majesty, after petitioning the ancestors,

90 See *History of the Liao: Annals of Taizu.*

acceded to this request. This was the start of Southern Superior Prefecture Prime Ministers being selected from the royal family." Together with previously mentioned historical facts, this excerpt clearly shows that because many of the Yishi tribal nobility participated in the rebellion and were subsequently killed, the Chude [Chute] tribe was for a time in charge of the Southern Superior Prefecture. Now Abaoji changed the "old system" and "the emperor's younger brother Su 蘇 was made Prime Minister of the Southern Superior Prefecture," who governed this tribal group that had the Yishi tribe at its core. This further helped to destroy the old tribal system by using the nobility of the Diela tribe who were not a part of the Yishi tribe group to govern this group. The two groups of the eight Khitan tribes then were completely governed by those appointed by the emperor from either the emperor's clan or the empress' clan. At the same time the people of each tribe had fixed locations in which they resided. *History of the Liao: Monograph on Imperial Guards* and *Monograph on the Army* specified their stationed 鎮駐 areas. In this way, even though they still kept the old tribal names, in actuality they were not the same as the old tribes, and became "localized tribes." In other words, they had actually become certain levels of civil and military organization in fixed locations under the governance of the kingdom. Along with the changes, the *yilijin* of each tribe had their titles changed by Abaoji to *lingwen* 令穩 (from the Chinese word *lingyin* 令尹, "district magistrate"), and became state officials of a certain level under the direct governance of the Prime Ministers of the Southern and Northern Superior Prefectures.

The third aspect was the governance of the captured and conquered foreigners. Abaoji divided the captured and conquered northern hunting and fishing nomads into eight new tribes under the governance of the eight Khitan tribes. The 700 Xi 奚 households that were captured during the Xianzhi Qaghan period became the Diela Dieda 迭剌迭達 tribe. The Xi households that were subsequently captured were divided into the Yishi Aokui 乙室奧隗 tribe and Chute Aokui 鋤特奧隗 tribe. The captured Daluguo 達魯虢 tribe became the Pin Daluguo 品達魯虢 tribe. The two (major and minor) conquered Huang Shiwei 黃室韋 became the Tulübu Shiwei 突呂不室韋 tribe and Niela Mogu 涅剌摩古 tribe. The 6,000 captured Yuguli 于骨里 households were divided into the Wugu Niela 烏古

涅剌 tribe and Tulu 圖魯 tribe.[91] These new tribes that were formed according to the customs of the northern peoples were clearly completely different from the old tribes, and most of them were made up of foreign captives. Only the conquered Shiwei tribe may have had some blood relations within the clans, but their combination of old tribes was clearly destroyed and they were forcefully separated. These eight new tribes were given names from the eight Khitan tribes, and governed by the nobility of the eight tribes. They were in effect a type of enslaved military and civil unit. They were divided under the Northern and Southern Superior Prefectures and governed under the state Military Commissioner 節度使 and each had its own fixed "station" 鎮戍 area.

The Xi 奚, who were the same ethnicity as the Khitan, originally were a tribal confederation comprised of five tribes. After they were repeatedly plundered by the Khitan, their remaining people were completely conquered. In the Abaoji period they basically maintained their original tribal organization, but were merged with the Khitan as a "great tribe" 大部族 within the Khitan state. It was only after a period of time that they gradually changed their original organization.

As for the large numbers of Han Chinese people who were captured and relocated, Abaoji basically used the Chinese prefecture and county system to govern them. *New History of the Five Dynasties: Supplementary Account to the Four Books: Account of the Khitan* 新五代史・四書附祿・契丹傳 says, "At the time Liu Shouguang 劉守光 was vicious and cruel, and many people from Youzhou 幽州 and Zhuozhou 涿州 escaped to the Khitan. Abaoji took advantage of the moment to invade. He attacked the cities and towns and captured their people, and established cities based on the Tang prefecture and county system." Zhao Zhizhong's 趙至忠 *Miscellaneous Records at Yin Mountain* 陰山雜錄 also says, "The Liang died out and Abaoji led his army directly to Zhuozhou. At the time the Anci 安次, Lu 潞, Sanhe 三河, Yuyang 魚陽, Huairou 懷柔, and Miyun 密云 Counties of Youzhou were captured and he took their people and returned. Then he established prefectures and counties for them to reside in and did not change the Chinese place names." In this way in Khitan governed areas Abaoji successively established Linhuang 臨潢 County, Bacheng 霸城 County, Sanhe 三河 County, Yuyang 魚陽 County, Miyun

91 See *History of the Liao: Monograph on Imperial Guards.*

密云 County, and the prefectures of Huizhou 惠州, Zezhou 澤州, and Tanzhou 檀州.[92] In these counties and prefectures the captured Han Chinese peasants were governed and enslaved by the Khitan nobility, but they kept their own customs and engaged in agricultural production. It is said that a Chinese vassal, Han Yanhui 韓延徽, who had surrendered to the Khitan, was useful in this regard. *Comprehensive Mirror for Aid in Government*, chapter 269, says he "first had the Khitan establish governments, build city walls, and set up markets and neighborhoods for the Chinese people so that they could meet one another and start to work the fields. From then on the Chinese people lived in peace, and fewer and fewer people had to flee."

After Abaoji defeated the Bohai Kingdom, he basically maintained their original feudal order, and changed the name to the Dongdan 東丹 Kingdom, and named the imperial prince Bei 倍 as the king of Dongdan. As for the Bohai people who were captured, they intermixed with the captured Chinese people, and like the Chinese, they were governed under counties and prefectures.

The fourth aspect was the creation of public power for the nobility. As the Khitan army plundered its neighbors and grew, it no longer was made up of the same people as before. Even though the organization on the largest level maintained its original system, the military makeup of the clan system had completely changed, and it became a public power of the Khitan nobility that was used to attack and defend, and to oppress the slaves within the society, forcing them to submit. The central state had at its core the so-called "personal army of the imperial tent" 御帳親軍. A "prefecture and county tribal" army controlled by the nobility was set up in each area, and upon military emergencies, they "gathered upon orders." Apart from this, the king surrounded himself with the newly created "palace cavalry guard" 宮韋騎軍 who "defended at home, were a retinue 扈 abroad, and protected the royal tomb" and who were in effect special guards of the imperial nobility.[93]

Another important event was that after the founding of the Khitan state, along with the creation of a Khitan script, there began to be formulated written Khitan law, and the first "Legal Code" 法典 was compiled. The

[92] See Chen Shu 陳述, *A Study of Khitan Social and Economic History* 《契丹社會經濟史稿》 (Shanghai: Sanlian Press 三聯出版社, 1963), chapter 1, section 2.

[93] See *History of the Liao: Monograph on the Army*.

era of "carving wood as contracts and digging holes as prisons" had passed. In the fifth year of the Shence reign period Abaoji's cousins Lubugu 魯不古 and Tulübu 突呂不 created the "Khitan large script."[94] The next year Abaoji "said to his vassals: 'The affairs of the state, large and small, must be governed by laws, otherwise there will be no governance, and the officials will not know their limitations,' and ordered his vassals to create the laws to govern the Khitan and other barbarians."[95] The law was created by the same Tulübu who had created the script. *History of the Liao: Biography of Tulübu* says that in this year, "he received the order to write the criminal law." Unfortunately this criminal law has long since been lost and we have no way of knowing what it was like. Some have thought that this was a fundamental law book of the Khitan, and that the later laws of the Liao Dynasty were made based on it.[96] No matter what, we know with certainty that the creation of writing and laws reflected the need for solidifying the state governing processes, and they were used to maintain the slave-master class relationship and oppress the slaves. At the same time, the Khitan state also established a great court of law, the Tribal Judges Court 夷離畢.

The state, which upheld class oppression, was finally born upon the remnants of the Khitan clan system. During the Abaoji period Khitan society already possessed the fundamental characteristics of a state, but the state organism was still only a rough model, and was gradually built up through Abaoji's successor Yelü Deguang's 耶魯德光 reign. The formation of this state government was influenced in many ways by the Chinese feudal system. Due to outward expansion an ever increasing number of Northern and Han Chinese peoples were brought under the control of the Khitan. Complex characteristics emerged within Khitan societal relations and the state system, and along with these came internal conflicts between the systems of slavery and feudalism. All of these factors fall outside the scope of this paper and should be the subject of a separate study. However, it is undeniable that the founding of Abaoji's state was the beginning of a new historical era for the Khitan. As a class oppressing mechanism, the

---

94 *History of the Liao: Annals of Taizu* and *Biography of Tulübu*.

95 *History of the Liao: Monograph on Penal Law.*

96 Takikawa Masajirō 瀧川政次郎 and Shimada Masao 島田正郎, *Ryōritsu no kenkyū* 『遼律之研究』 (*Studies on Liao Law*) (Tokyo: Ōsaka Yagō Shoten, 1944), chapter 2, section 2.

state's establishment ended the era of the clan system for the Khitan, and ushered in a new era.

5. Conclusion

We have already discussed the Khitan tribal organization and the history of the formation of the Khitan state. Due to the lack of materials, especially economic data, we are unable to understand in detail many aspects of Khitan economic development. Here we have just made a broad sketch of the situation, and from this sketch we will now draw some simple conclusions.

We know almost nothing about the origin of the Khitan clans and their earliest formation. The materials we do have mainly record the tribal activities from the patriarchal era. Now, based on textual accounts, we can further discuss the origins and formation of some of these tribes, and the path of development for the Khitan from clans to tribes.

On Native American tribal organization Engels says the following:

> …for with the prohibition of marriage within a clan, each tribe had necessarily to consist of at least two clans in order to be capable of independent existence. As the tribe increased, each clan again subdivided into two or more clans, each of which now appears as a separate clan, while the original clan, which embraces all the daughter clans, lives on as a phratry.…Originally, indeed, no Seneca could marry within his phratry, but this prohibition has long since been lapsed and is limited only to the clan. The Senecas had a tradition that the Bear and Deer were the two original clans, of which the others were offshoots.[97]

The Khitan tribes also had a legend that the two clans that worshipped the White Horse and Black Ox were the original clans, and the other clans came from these two. They also prohibited marriage within the clan, so the generations of the two clans intermarried. These aspects are all extremely similar to or the same as those of the Seneca.

---

[97] Engels, *The Origin of the Family, Private Property, and the State* (Chinese translation), p. 85.

However, the historical records also tell us that the Khitan appear to have not become a tribe from the intermarriage between these two clans, but rather from the independent and parallel development and prospering of each. Clearly it was because of economic development and population increase that the White-Horse-worshipping clan split into several independent clans, and by the Dahe 大賀 clan period had split into eight fraternal clans. With further development each of these clans split into two or more clans. This was when the eight fraternal clans became the eight fraternal tribes. They respected the prohibition on marriage within the clan, and also prohibited marriage between clans, so they married with the descendants of the Black Ox daughter clans. As for this original daughter clan, the Sun 孫 clan or the Bali 拔里 (one version has Shouli 收里) of the Shenmi, we do not know about their internal composition and status of their development. However, we can be sure that they grew in strength independently, and existed equally with the Dahe clan, and continued the custom of marrying with the Dahe clan.

After a while the Yishihuo 乙室活 and Yishiji 乙室已 tribes appeared. At first may have been two clans that intermarried, but during the decline of the Dahe tribal confederation, the Yishihuo had already become a large tribe that included several clans. One interesting phenomenon is that with the breakup of the Dahe and reformation of the Yaonian tribal confederation, they sill followed the old principles, and combined the two pairs of intermarrying tribes. The Yishihuo tribe split into two, and joined with the remnants of the Dahe clan to form a new confederation. The Yishiji tribe, who had originally married with the Yishihuo tribe, joined with the Shenmi, who had originally married with the Dahe clan, to form the new Shenmi.[98] The imperial Yelü clan and the empress' Xiao clan of the Liao were formed in this way. However, by that time they had long since lost the nature of the original clan organization, and formed two groups of privileged nobles that originated from the intermarrying clans, but were the hereditary rulers.

In this way the development from clans to tribes was not only different from that of the Native Americans, but was also unique to the Altaic

[98] *History of the Liao: Monograph on Imperial Guards*: "Of the two Shenmi, one was called Yishiji, and the other Bali, and they were uncles to the state." See the "Office of the Great Uncles-in-Law of the Emperor" 《大國舅司》 entry of "Monograph on Official Posts" 《百官志》 in the same work, and the preface to the *Account of the Empresses* 《后妃傳》 *Table of Royal Relatives on the Distaff Side* 《外戚表》.

peoples in China. Neither the later Jurchen and Mongols, nor the much later Manchus underwent such a development.

Of course, this path of development only shows some characteristics of the origins and formation of the Khitan tribes during their patrilineal era, and proves they originated from marriages between clans. Internal and external marrying "tribes" like those described by J. F. McLennan did not exist at all here.

It is not at all strange that we do not find a prevalence of phratries within the Khitan tribal organization. This is because, as in the Native American tribes described by Engels, they "mostly lacked the intermediate link of the phratry."[99]

The following is a summary of the Khitan's different stages of development from tribes to a state: (1) The period of independent, scattered tribal activity. During this period there was already some trade with outsiders. (2) The period of the Dahe tribal confederation. The eight fraternal tribes with a common ancestor formed what was at first a temporary, but later turned into a long-lasting confederation, and established the custom of selecting the confederation leader. (3) The Yaonian tribal confederation period. The reestablished confederation resembled the old confederation in form, but in actuality it was the combination of the two strong tribes, the Yishi and Diela, along with a few smaller tribes, that formed two groups that were controlled by the Yishi and Diela tribes. The confederation military commander was selected by the Diela tribe, thereby forming the foundation for privileged nobility. (4) The late Yaonian tribal confederation period. During this time the Khitan entered a new era of rapid development. Khitan society had long nurtured the elements of a slavery system, and several years of victorious outward campaigns caused the rapid growth of the number of captured slaves, and increased the wealth and power of all of the military leaders. Conflicts between social classes clearly formed. The gap in wealth among the clans caused friction among clan members, and the addition of a large number of foreigners rapidly undermined the functioning of the tribal organization. The clan system had finally come to an end, and the state came into being at the hand of Abaoji.

---

[99] Engels, *The Origin of the Family, Private Property, and the State* (Chinese translation), p. 86.

We can see that the Khitan, who made their living by fishing, hunting, and herding, followed a path that was not entirely the same as the Athenians who lived by the Aegean Sea and engaged in trade, farming, and handicrafts. The rise and fall of their neighboring tribes affected them in many ways, adding twists and turns to the path of their development. The development of the Khitan tribal organization and formation of the state was not as simple and typical as that of Athens. However, basically speaking, the Khitans developed from scattered tribes who "did not know what a state was" into a tribal confederation, and, after having undergone its ups and downs, when conflicts between social classes formed they finally overthrew the tribal organization and built a mechanism of class oppression – the state. This is a common rule of human development that appears amidst complex historical events.

Engels wrote:

> The state is, therefore, by no means a power forced on society from without; just as little is it "the reality of the ethical idea," "the image and reality of reason," as Hegel maintains. Rather, it is a product of society at a certain stage of development; it is the admission that this society has become entangled in an insoluble contradiction with itself, that it has split into irreconcilable antagonisms which it is powerless to dispel. But in order that these antagonisms, these classes with conflicting economic interests, might not consume themselves and society in fruitless struggle, it became necessary to have a power, seemingly standing above society, that would alleviate the conflict and keep it within the bounds of "order"; and this power, arisen out of society but placing itself above it, and alienating itself more and more from it, is the state.[100]

Lenin said that Engels "in this paragraph clearly shows the use of Marxism in the history of states and the basic philosophy behind its meanings."[101] Even though the history of the Khitan has many distinct

---

[100] Ibid. p. 163.

[101] Lenin, *Nations and Revolution* 《國家與革命》, in *The Collected Works of Lenin* 《列寧全集》, ch. 25, p. 374.

characteristics, the basic process of its state formation once again proves correct the basic philosophy of Marxism, and repudiates its denouncers.

Finally, I should point out that the establishment of the Khitan state did not happen on its own, but was accompanied by a fierce conflict between the old and new systems and powers. Compared with ancient Roman history, Khitan history has the benefit of preserving the materials that allow us to specifically see the struggle that brought about end of the clan system and the establishment of the state. As explained in this paper, this conflict brought about a sharp response among the Khitan nobility, which in the end took the form of violence. Abaoji only victoriously established the Khitan state after an arduous battle through which he attacked the old power of the clan system.

The state is the result of irreconcilable class conflict. But when the conditions are ripe, this result must first undergo a process of violent struggle between new and old systems.

Marx said: "Violence is the midwife of history."[102] Lenin went on to say, "Violence is the tool and method used by social movements to open new roads and destroy hard political forms that have long since been dead."[103] In class societies, all changes in social forms, and the hand-off of a state from one class to another are like this. Khitan history shows that the establishment of their state was like this as well.

---

[102] Karl Marx, *Capital*《資本論》 (Peoples Publishing House 人民出版社), p. 949.

[103] Lenin, *The Collected Works of Lenin*, vol. 25, p. 386.

REGARDING THE MONGOL *BO'OL* IN THE 11TH AND 12TH CENTURIES

Yekemingghadai Irinchin 亦邻真

At about the time of the Liao Dynasty, an enslaved and exploited labor force called the *bo'ol* appeared on the Mongolian steppe. In general meaning, the Mongolian word bo'ol is equivalent to the Turkic word *qul,* and in both Yuan Dynasty documents and in *The Secret History of the Mongols* 元朝秘史 these two words are translated into Chinese as *nubi* 奴婢 (servant).* In modern Mongolian social science writings, bo'ol means slaves – they are slave owners' chattel without any personal freedom, merely so-called "talking tools." Modern definitions of this word prevent people from precisely understanding its historical meaning; instead, they are led to draw an equal sign between the word bo'ol of the 11th and the 12th centuries and its modern usage. Therefore, they conclude that there were slaves in Mongolian society in the 11th and the 12th centuries, and furthermore, that Mongolian society was once a slave society. How can we understand the nature of the bo'ol at that time, relying on precise analysis of relevant historical data, so as to avoid being misled by modern usage?

Researching the bo'ol has critical significance for illuminating both the form of 11th and 12th century Mongolian society and the different stages of Mongolian history. Clarifying the socio-economic position of the bo'ol has a strong connection with researching the nature of Mongolian society at that time. Naturally this is a large subject. This essay merely conducts a superficial exploration of some aspects of this problem.

1

Roughly speaking, the bo'ol appeared in the Mongol tribes at about the time when the so-called Proto-Mongolians (Shiwei-Dada 室韋達怛)

---

* Translator's note: excerpts from *The Secret History of the Mongols* are quoted from Igor de Rachewiltz, trans. and ed., *The Secret History of the Mongols* (Leiden: Brill, 2006). However, some transcriptions of more commonly known Mongolian names and terms are based upon Christopher Atwood, *Encyclopedia of Mongolia and the Mongol Empire* (see "A Note on the Translations" at the beginning of this book). Also consulted was Francis Woodmen Cleaves, trans. and ed., *The Secret History of the Mongols* (Cambridge, Massachusetts: Harvard University Press, 1982). In a few instances transcriptions of names are based upon those supplied by the author in his original essay.

migrated on a large scale to the Outer Mongolian steppe. In the ninth century the Uyghur Empire ended, Turkic tribes moved westward one after the other, and the Outer Mongolia steppe began the process of Mongolization. This kind of historical picture is probably not mistaken: the early Mongols, consisting mainly of forest hunter peoples, burst into the Turkic tribes' rangeland, plundered the livestock, and at the same time also captured the people engaged in herding. From then on, the early Mongols' primitive communal social structure began to quickly collapse. With the development of private ownership, the primitive social equality between people quickly became a past that could not be returned to. Tribal chiefs possessed large amounts of livestock, compelled the service of the poor members of the tribe, and gradually formed a steppe aristocratic class called the *noyan* 那顏. In order to plunder wealth, the steppe aristocrats ceaselessly launched wars among the tribes. The final outcome of each tribal war always was that those who were defeated suffered a disastrous decline: they not only lost their possessions, but also would lose their lives, or at least their personal liberty, and become the victors' bo'ol.

Along with the intensification of class differentiation, tribal warfare became more and more cruel. The capturing of populations became one of the most important objectives of tribal wars. This kind of war became more frequent, and the bo'ol became ever more numerous.

The defeated in these tribal wars, normally the adult males, were massacred, and the women were forced to become wives and concubines. Some of the females, together with their children, became bo'ol. This exactly was the fundamental origin of the bo'ol. In the time of Chinggis Khan's sixth generation forefather Qaidu 海都, some of the adult males of the J̌alayir (Jalayir) 札剌亦兒 clan were killed, and their women and children became Qaidu's bo'ol. In Chinggis Khan's time, the Merkit 蔑兒乞 and the Tatars 塔塔兒 suffered exactly the same fate.[1] There were specific terms in Old Mongolian used to express this kind of mass slaughter or plunder of a population: to execute adult males was called *ülitkekü* (to measure), meaning to measure the prisoners' height by linchpin (車轄, the bolt lock of a chariot axle). The majority of defeated

[1] Rashīd al-Dīn: *Jāmi' al-Tawārīkh* (*Compendium of Chronicles*), translated into Russian as Рашид-ад-Дин, *Сборник Летописей*, edited by A. A. Semenova (Семенова), vol. 1 (Москва - Ленинград: Издательство Академии Наук СССР, 1952), book 2, p. 19. *The Secret History of the Mongols*, sections 112 and 154.

tribal males taller than that part of a chariot would be executed. To plunder women was called *ebüritkü* (to harbor in one's bosom), meaning to take them as wives and concubines. To take bo'ol as plunder was called *bo'olitqu* (to be bo'ol), or *e'üten-tür oro'ulda-* (to be let through the door).[2] This indicates that to slaughter able-bodied men and to plunder women and children was already at that time a common phenomenon of war and also the basic way of obtaining bo'ol.

In conditions where a pastoral economy held the dominant position, to obtain bo'ol via trade was almost impossible to imagine. There is a story passed down in *The Secret History of the Mongols* that says that Chinggis Khan's eleventh generation forefather Dobun Mergen 朵奔蔑兒干 begged a piece of venison from someone, which he then used to trade for a little child from a poor Baya'ut 伯牙兀歹 family, who was then made his family servant. To magnify this story to try and prove one's presumption that the "slave trade" existed long ago among the Mongols simply would not be fruitful. In the *Jāmi' al-Tawārīkh* there is another version of the same story, telling how a man of the Dörben 朵儿邊 clan named Tu (Hu?) Lun Sahal 土(忽?)倫薛客勒 used a piece of venison to trade for a Baya'ut child and sent him as a gift to Dobun Mergen's wife Alan Qo'a 阿闌豁阿.[3] *The Secret History of the Mongols* and the *Jāmi' al-Tawārīkh* versions are different, indicating only that this is an old story; its historical value is that it reflects a single fact: from very early on a Baya'ut family became the Kiyan 乞顏 family's bo'ol. As for the other primitive literary story elements, they should not be taken seriously.

Bo'ol status was by nature hereditary. The natural growth of the bo'ol population of course constituted another source of bo'ol. Chinggis Khan's tenth generation forefather Bodončar 孛端察兒 plundered the Uriangqadai 兀良合歹 family, which kept its bo'ol status without interruption until Chinggis Khan's time. In Qaidu's time, a group of J̌alayir (Jalayir) 札剌亦兒 were bo'ol and their offspring were still bo'ol in Chinggis Khan's time.[4] Inheriting social status was one of the most important characteristics of Mongolian society in the 11th and the 12th centuries. And

[2] *The Secret History of the Mongols*, sections 112, 139, 154, and 214.

[3] Ibid., sections 15 and 16. *Jāmi' al-Tawārīkh*, Russian translation, vol. 1, book 2, p. 10.

[4] *The Secret History of the Mongols*, sections 39 and 97. *Jāmi' al-Tawārīkh*, Russian translation, vol. 1, book 1, p. 92.

it is not necessary to distinguish a hereditary bo'ol social stratum from any other kind of bo'ol, because there is not any historical evidence telling us of any type of bo'ol that was not hereditary. This issue will be discussed later in this paper.

The bo'ol belonged to families and to individuals. Descriptions from *The Secret History of the Mongols* provide a very vivid explanation: *e'üten-nü emčü* (to be let through the door as personal property) bo'ol and *bosoqa-yin* (within the threshold) bo'ol. Here, constrained by the need for alliteration, the prefixes *e'üten-nü*, *emčü*, and *bosoqa-yin* should be understood as adjectives of the word bo'ol; they are not labels that categorize bo'ol into different groups – they did not signify bo'ol outside of the family or not belonging to individuals. The very expression "to be let through the door" (to be bo'ol) indicates vividly the fact that a bo'ol belonged to a specific family. Every bo'ol had a certain master – noyan. For example, Sorqan Šira's 鎖兒罕失刺 noyan was Tödö'en Otčigin 脫朵延・斡惕赤斤; Badai's 巴歹 and Kišiliq's 乞失里黑 noyan was Yeke Čeren 也客扯連. J̌elme (Jelme) 者勒蔑, Muqali 木華黎, and Buqa 不合 were all designated as subjects of Chinggis Khan; J̌ebke (Jebke) 者卜客 was designated a subject of Qasar 合撒兒.[5]

It ought to be clear that in the Mongolian society of that time no clans or tribes forming the bo'ol social system were defined as one clan wholly subjected to another. There are no historical records that can prove the existence of such a system. Vladimirtsov, in his discussion of *unaghan bo'ol*, once emphasized a slave system in which one clan wholly owned another.[6] In reality, this is equivalent to raising a large issue: did nomadic helotism ever exist on the Mongolian steppe? However, the historical record runs completely counter to this point of view. The bo'ol in the historical records are described as *e'üten-nü* 家門中的, meaning bo'ol belonging to a single family, or *emčü* 梯己的, meaning bo'ol belonging to individuals. Moreover, a bo'ol from the era of Qaidu, J̌alayir by his family name, was called BaNDHi XANaDAN (*nubi* [servants] in a family, 家庭

---

5 *The Secret History of the Mongols*, sections 219, 51, 97, and 137.

6 Boris Iakovlevich Vladimirtsov (Борис Яковлевич Владимирцов), *Общественный строй монголов. Монгольский кочевой феодализм* (*The Social System of the Mongols. Mongolian Nomadic Feudalism*), translated into Chinese by Liu Rongjun 劉榮焌 as *A History of the Mongol Social System* 《蒙古社會制度史》 (China Social Sciences Press, 1980), pp. 103 and 154.

的奴婢),[7] and this is probably the earliest record seen in the *Jāmi' al-Tawārīkh*. From descriptions in *The Secret History of the Mongols* one can clearly understand that once a tribe was defeated, the population remaining after the slaughter all would be distributed among the nobles and warriors from the winning side. For example, "the rest we will enslave" 各處分 and "they distributed them among each other so that nobody went short" 任誰行也不曾缺少了，共散與了[8] became principles of customary law of Mongol society. However, the bo'ol were entirely different from helot peoples, because the former are divided among families and individuals, while the latter could keep their entity as a tribe, but would offer tribute and service to the victor.

The bo'ol had various obligations to their masters, the noyan. First, they had to provide their labor to the noyan without compensation. For example, Badai and Kišiliq herded horses for Yeke Čeren, J̌etei (Jetei) 者台 and J̌elme (Jelme) slaughtered cows for Chinggis Khan, and Sorqan Šira "used to churn their koumiss all through the night until daybreak."[9] The bo'ol also had to accompany their noyan into battle and on hunts. As a result, the bo'ol of that time can not be considered slaves or mere "talking tools." Vladimirtsov was the first scholar to formulate a scientific explanation of the characteristics of the bo'ol. This outstanding Mongolist correctly pointed out that the bo'ol (it should be "unaghan bo'ol," according to his research) were not slaves; they owned personal property, possessed a certain individual freedom, and did not have to return all of the results of their labor to their master.[10]

The bo'ol could have families. For exactly this reason, the status of bo'ol could be hereditary. Most newly-plundered bo'ol were children; they were adopted into the masters' household later as indentured servants. Based on this point, it seems that the bo'ol were similar to household slaves in patriarchal societies. However, before long the bo'ol had the opportunity to establish their own families or set up their own tents, in order to serve their masters, becoming a subject population.

The bo'ol possessed their own property. For example, Sorqan Šira had his own tent, chariots, horses, and sheep. Badai and Kišiliq had their own

---

[7] Rashīd al-Dīn: *Jāmi' al-Tawārīkh*, Russian translation, vol. 1 , book 2, p. 19.
[8] *The Secret History of the Mongols*, sections 154 and 187.
[9] Ibid., sections 219, 214, and 85.
[10] B. Ia. Vladimirtsov, *The Social System of the Mongols*, Chinese translation, p. 103.

tents and sheep as well.[11] However, it is out of the question for a slave to own any property, as the slave himself is the property of his owner.

People of that time usually considered the bo'ol as unequal or lower members of the family, that is, servants or underlings. As a result, the bo'ol could be called *de'ü* (younger brother).[12] According to historical records, bo'ol and *qaraču* (*qaraču* means common people under a noble's rule) could be placed on a par with each other, and bo'ol were seen as equal to *nökör* (companions). When J̌amuqa (Jamuqa) 札木合 was finally captured, before being killed he pointed to his five companions with his last words: "*qaraču* bo'ol have gone so far as to raise their hands against their lord."[13] A fact worth noticing here is that J̌amuqa, with great anger, termed his fellows *qaraču* bo'ol in the last moments of his life. Of course we cannot conclude accordingly that there are no clear boundaries among *nökör*, *qaraču*, and bo'ol. But they share one thing in common: they all had a subject relationship with their masters. There was no uncrossable boundary between *nökör* and bo'ol. For instance, J̌elme, Muqali, and others whose identity was bo'ol all were Chinggis Khan's most famous and reliable *nökör*. The bo'ol often produced *nökör,* and the bo'ol were an important source of *nökör* personnel.

In the Mongolian society of that time there developed layer upon layer of subordinate relationships. Relying on violence, the noyan employed *nökör* as thugs in order to control the *qaraču* (herdsman who already did not have complete personal freedom) and to use the even more deeply subjected bo'ol. An analogy is always problematic, but if it includes the already raised thoughts, then it might as well be said: the Mongolian society of the 11th and 12th centuries might be viewed as the embryo of the feudal structure which emerged later in the 17th century – noyan and *nökör* are in some respects analogous to monarch and officials, and so *qaraču* and bo'ol are precursors of *albatu* and *khamJilgh*.

"Let these sons of mine be the slaves of your threshold; if they stray from your threshold, cut off their heel tendons! Let them be the personal slaves of your door; if they abandon your door, cut out their livers and cast them away!"[14] Those lines written in *The Secret History of the Mongols* are frequently cited as irrefutable proof that the bo'ol were slaves: how

---

[11] *The Secret History of the Mongols*, sections 86, 87, and 169.
[12] Ibid., section 108.
[13] Ibid., section 200.
[14] Ibid., section 137.

could one be anything except a slave, if he would be killed for leaving his master without permission? In fact, however, those lines are merely the words by which one pledged his subject relationship. In the Mongolian society of that time it was a common phenomenon to use one's life to guarantee that one would faithfully abide by a subject relationship. Altan 阿勒坦, Qučar 忽察兒, and Seče Beki 薛扯别乞, and others all were genuine steppe nobles, but at the time they supported Chinggis as Khan they all were respectful and submissive in the same words: "In the days of war, if we disobey your commands, deprive us of *all* our goods and belongings, and our noble wives, and cast our black heads on the ground!"[15] These people made a pledge with sincere words: whether in war or in peace, if they violated Chinggis Khans' decree, then they would request that their wives be taken and their sons be scattered, their families broken up and its members dispersed, and that they be beheaded. Bo'ol used their lives to guarantee their obligations to their masters; nobles used their lives, their wives and children, and their personal property to guarantee their acknowledged allegiance and obligations to the Khan. Both bo'ol and nobles each used their lives to guarantee their respective obligations. It is incorrect to firmly believe that the bo'ol were "talking tools" simply because they would be executed if they left their masters.

The bo'ol of the 11th and 12th centuries were essentially the subjected population of the noyan, and they were the early stage of the system of serfdom in a nomadic economy. Compared to slaves, they had private property and families of their own, and even partial personal freedom. Still, when compared to members of primitive communal societies, they were a labor force under the enslavement and exploitation of the noyan social class. The personal subject relationship of the bo'ol in the 11th and 12th centuries should be understood as a system similar to serfdom.

2

Some researchers have preferred to categorize the bo'ol of ancient Mongolian society into different kinds, dividing the bo'ol into *unaghan bo'ol*, *ötögü bo'ol*, *ötöle bo'ol*, and the like. Some even claim they have discovered the types *ongqun bo'ol* and *etügen bo'ol*. In this way the issue of the bo'ol has been made more and more complicated.

Vladimirtsov quite correctly pointed out that there were great

---

[15] Ibid., section 123.

differences between the bo'ol and true slaves. But, he again raised the issue of unaghan bo'ol, and he believed them to be a type of hereditary, clan or family serf-like vassal (крепостиой вассал, translated into Chinese as 屬部). He even believed there to be a large number of unaghan bo'ol.[16] As a matter of fact, unaghan bo'ol never existed in ancient Mongolian society. Vladimirtsov's conception of unaghan bo'ol was derived from an incorrect reconstruction by I. N. Berezin (И. Н. Березин). Berezin arbitrarily misunderstood AWNKW as *unaghan* (colt) in his edition of the *Jāmi' al-Tawārīkh*, and Vladimirtsov accepted this notion unconditionally. However, from the perspective of phonology, this reconstruction can not be tenable. The transcription of Mongolian consonants in the *Jāmi' al-Tawārīkh* is very accurate; it never confuses the hard consonant "Q" with the soft consonant "K." The letter "q" in *unaghan* (as *unuqan* in ancient Mongolian) cannot be transcribed as the consonant "K." Given the word AWNKW contains the soft consonant "K," it should be a soft, front-vocalic word rather than the hard, back-vocalic word – *unuqan.* It was the sharp-eyed Paul Pelliot who first recognized this mistake made by Berezin and Vladimirtsov.[17] As can be seen from the perspective of the historical materials, there are simply no traces of the word unaghan bo'ol in any Mongolian and Chinese historical record of that time.

AWNKW is an error remaining in hand-copied manuscripts. In Persian there is little difference between the letters "N" and "T." Consequently, it is easy to mistake AWTKW as AWNKW The translation of the *Jāmi' al-Tawārīkh* into Russian used as its basis a compilation of many kinds of hand-copied manuscripts. In chapter one of book two, O. I. Smirnova (О.И. Смирнова) transcribed the word correctly as "*utegu.*" But in book one the Russian translator L. A. Khetagurov (Л. А. Хетагуров) still preserved the error *ungu.*[18] The records from book one and book two both refer to a historical fact – how the J̌alayir people became ötögü bo'ol. Obviously, one of the two transcriptions must be an error. Due to the deficient work of textual criticism in the Russian translation, they not only

---

[16] B. Ia. Vladimirtsov, *The Social System of the Mongols*, Chinese translation, pp. 103-4.

[17] Paul Pelliot and Louis Hambis, eds. and trans., *Histoire des campagnes de Gengis Khan*, vol. 1 (Leiden: E. J. Brill, 1951), p. 85.

[18] Rashīd al-Dīn: *Jāmi' al-Tawārīkh*, Russian translation, vol. 1, book 1, pp. 15 and 19; book 2, p. 93.

kept *ungu*, but also in the notes referred to Vladimirtsov's unaghan bo'ol. Thus it can be seen that the incorrect reconstruction of Berezin and Vladimirtsov has definitely had a large influence in Soviet Mongol academic circles.

There was also a Soviet scholar named E. R. Rygdylon (Э. Р. Рыгдылон) who tried to pour old wine into new bottles on the issue of AWNKW.[19] On one hand, Rygdylon interpreted AWTKW as *etügen* (the goddess of the land), saying that etügen bo'ol referred to a slave belonging to the goddess of the land; on the other hand, he interpreted AWNKW as a transliteration of *ongqun* (free). In his opinion, a bo'ol of the goddess [of the land] had the same meaning as a free bo'ol, and they both indicated "freed slave." However, E. R. Rygdylon's idea has many weak points. Instead of deciding whether AWTKW or AWNKW was actually correct, he grasped them both, and gave them both the strained interpretation "freed slave." This shows that his textual research and powers of discernment had very large deficiencies. In what follows we will see that it is impossible for AWTKW to be any "goddess of the land." As mentioned above, AWNKW could not be a word with a hard consonant, yet *ongqun* is a word with a hard consonant. Enlightened by Vladimirtsov's demonstration, E. R. Rygdylon acknowledged that the bo'ol are not slaves, but he could not escape from the convention of the modern meaning [of the word slave] to say that the bo'ol never were slaves. So he came up with a compromise formulation: they once were slaves, but had been freed. The grounds of his argument obviously are entirely weak.

AWTKW BΓWL in the *Jāmi' al-Tawārīkh* is the transcription of the Mongolian phrase ötögü bo'ol. The original Mongolian text can be seen in the *Spirit Way Stele Inscription for Jigüntei, Late Overseer of the Bureau of All Classes of Artisans, Granted by Imperial Order under the Great Yuan* 大元敕賜故諸色人匠府達魯花赤竹公神道碑銘 preserved at Boro Hota in Ongnigud Banner 翁牛特旗烏丹镇鎮. The information contained in the Jigüntei 竹溫台 epigraph, made in the fourth year of the Zhiyuan 至元 reign period of Emperor Huizong 惠宗 (1338), was published in 1951 by the American scholar Francis Woodman Cleaves. In his publication,

19 E. R. Rygdylon (Э. Р. Рыгдылон), "О монгольском термине онгу-богол" ("About the Mongolian Term *ongqun bo'ol*") in *Philology and History of the Mongolian Peoples* (*Филология и история монгольских народов. Памяти академика Б.Я. Владимирцова*) (Москва: Издательство восточной литературы, 1958), pp. 166-72.

Cleaves translated the original Mongolian text into English, transcribed the Mongolian language into the Latin alphabet, and made a very detailed annotation of the text.[20] The *Spirit Way Stele Inscription for Jigüntei* was written in Chinese by Jie Xisi 揭傒斯, while the Mongolian version was translated on the basis of the Chinese inscription. The Mongolian version refers to the fact that Jigüntei received the favor of the Emperor – "*ötögü bohod-un uruq-ača hülehü ülühü büi*"[*] (is it not more than what was done for the descendants of ötögü bo'ol?). The original Chinese text is "與元勛世臣等，不亦盛哉？"[21] *Ötögü* means "the aged" or "the elders." The offspring of ötögü bo'ol refers to the "grand meritorious ministers and hereditary officers" 元勛世臣, and this can not be misread. Without question it was incorrect for Cleaves to interpret ötögü bo'ol as "the elders and the slaves."[22] It is important that on the Jigüntei stele ötögü bo'ol is a designation used to honor those grand meritorious ministers and hereditary officers, and fundamentally it can not include oppressed and exploited laborers. The phrase ötögü bo'ol on the Jigüntei stele and what we are discussing here (bo'ol – a subject relationship among people as in serfdom) are two entirely different things in terms of social content.

Let us return to the historical record in *Jāmi' al-Tawārīkh*:

> Ötögü bo'ol refers to slaves or slaves' offspring belonging to Chinggis Khan's ancestors. Some of them had made meritorious contributions to the tribe and then became influential and powerful in the era of Chinggis Khan. This is why they are called ötögü bo'ol.[23]

As pointed out by Vladimirtsov, the notion of "slave" recorded in the *Jāmi' al-Tawārīkh* means, in the eyes of Rashīd al-Dīn "or those accustomed to the unlimited and freely exercised authority of Oriental monarchs, that all subjects are 'slaves.' His understanding of this word is

---

[20] Francis Woodman Cleaves, "The Sino-Mongolian Inscription of 1338 in Memory of Jigüntei," *Harvard Journal of Asiatic Studies*, vol. 14, no. 1-2 (June 1951), pp. 1-104.

[*] As transcribed by the author. Translator's note.

[21] *Spirit Way Stele Inscription for Jigüntei, Late Overseer of the Bureau of All Classes of Artisans, Granted by Imperial Order under the Great Yuan* 《大元敕賜故諸色人匠府達魯花赤竹公神道碑銘》; line 23 in Mongolian, line 18 in Chinese.

[22] Cleaves, "The Sino-Mongolian Inscription of 1338," p. 70.

[23] Rashīd al-Dīn: *Jāmi' al-Tawārīkh*, Russian translation, vol.1, book 2, p. 15.

quite different from ours."[24] The "slaves" in the *Jāmi' al-Tawārīkh* are what we have been focusing on – bo'ol. In this sense, we might realize that the record in the *Jāmi' al-Tawārīkh* does not actually contradict the stele of Jigüntei. There are two conditions required for one to be a ötögü bo'ol: first, he must be an offspring of Chinggis Khan's hereditary bo'ol; second, he must have made meritorious contributions and must be powerful and influential. If he was not influential and powerful, one could only be bo'ol, not ötögü bo'ol. This is the reason why the *Jāmi' al-Tawārīkh* restricts ötögü bo'ol to "certain people" of Chinggis Khan's hereditary bo'ol. As a result, in Rashīd al-Dīn's eyes almost all Mongolian officers are ötögü bo'ol. And it is not incredible that in the Muslim world of Iran, all the Mongolian nobles who came there on campaign from their homeland would be considered grand meritorious ministers and hereditary officers as a matter of course.

In fact, historical records of the Yuan Dynasty reflect clearly the social status of ötögü bo'ol. Below is material from an entry in *Comprehensive Records of the Censorate* 憲臺通紀:

> The imperial edict to promote Grand Master 大夫 Toghan 脱歡 Darqan 答剌罕 to a higher Prestige Title 散官.
>
> On the 12th day of the seventh month, the third year of the Yanyou 延祐 reign period [1316], a report was received from the Censorate 御史臺, which says: In the past when Örlüg noyan and Toquči took the offices of Censor-in-chief (御史)大夫, and when Qorči took the office of Vice Censor-in-chief (御史)中丞, Your Majesty had promoted them to higher rank in the Prestige Title 散官 system. Now Toghan Darqan has held the office of Censor-in-chief for four years. He had the status of old servant 老奴婢, and he has served the Censorate very well. According to previous formulae, should he also be promoted to a higher Prestige Title? The imperial edict says: 'He is different from others. Today I will tell the Secretariat 中書省 to give him a commission.'
>
> The commission from the Secretariat says: the emperor's edict says so, therefore here we proclaim that Censor-in-chief Toghan Darqan, who has held the Prestige Title rank of Grand Master for

[24] B. Ia. Vladimirtsov, *The Social System of the Mongols*, Chinese translation, p. 103.

Glorious Happiness 榮祿大夫, now be promoted up to the Prestige Title rank of Grand Master of the Palace with Golden Seal and Purple Ribbon 金紫光祿大夫, still with the office of Censor-in-chief.[25]

This record is crucial for the issue of ötögü bo'ol. First, "old servant" 老奴婢 here refers to ötögü bo'ol. Here we can again see a record in the Chinese sources concerning ötögü bo'ol, in addition to the original Mongolian text of the Jigüntei stele. Second, "status of old servant" 老奴婢根脚, namely ötögü bo'ol, and "He is different from others." This type of family status was, among subjects of the Yuan Dynasty, the most illustrious; they enjoyed various kinds of special privileges, and there was no other family background that could compare with theirs. Third, we can see that the notion of ötögü bo'ol by no means includes the oppressed and exploited bo'ol, and, in addition, it was not limited to the original servants 奴婢 of the Chinggis Khans. Toghan was the son of Harqasun 哈剌哈孫 and the great-great-grandson of Kišiliq. Kišiliq was not a "servant" of Chinggis Khan. Because he reported a plot instigated by Ong Khan 汪罕, he was ennobled as Darqan by Chinggis Khan: "You…*enjoy the privilege* of being freemen to the offspring of *your* offspring, allowed to carry quivers and drink the ceremonial wine! When swiftly pursuing many foes, if you get booty, what you get you shall take away. When *in a battue* you slaughter wild beasts, what you slaughter you shall take away."[26] A Darqan was a type of specially privileged noble exempt from many feudal obligations. Although the title of Darqan was hereditary in the family, in the same way as before they were still referred to as having the "status of

---

[25] *Yongle Encyclopedia*《永樂大典》, ch. 2608, pp. 17-8.

加脫歡答剌罕大夫散官

延祐三年七年十二日，本臺官奏：前先月兒魯那演、脫忽赤大夫、火你赤中丞等勾當裏行數年的其間，上位都曾添與散官來。如今答剌罕做大夫四年也。他是老奴婢根腳有；臺裏在意行來。依着先大夫的體例，他根底添與散官呵，怎生？麼道奏呵，"他不比別個的有。我對省家說則，今日便教與宣者"麼道聖旨了也。欽此。

中書省劄付：特奉聖旨：榮祿大夫、御史大夫脫歡答剌罕特加金紫光祿大夫，職事如故。欽此。

[26] *The Secret History of the Mongols*, section 187.

old servant," because this was the greatest honor. From the above we can conclude that in the Yuan Dynasty ötögü bo'ol was synonymous with grand meritorious ministers and hereditary officers. Only the high ranks of the nobility were able to have this title.

To summarize, ötögü bo'ol refers to the rising nobles of the Mongolian Khan's court.

In ancient Mongolian society, the status of bo'ol was hereditary. Given that fact, one may ask why people of that time used the special designation of ötögü bo'ol to refer to the hereditary bo'ol social class.[27] In fact, not all hereditary bo'ol could become ötögü bo'ol; only those powerful noyan who made an exceptional contribution could take this honorific title. In ancient Mongolian society, one type of enthralled class of laborer, the bo'ol social class, did not contain a special stratum for the ötögü bo'ol.

The mistake of taking the ötögü bo'ol (grand meritorious ministers) for an upper stratum of the bo'ol class became customary after it was started by Vladimirtsov. As part of his mistake, Vladimirtsov not only misunderstood ötögü bo'ol as unaghan bo'ol, but also concluded that they were of a social status higher than the ötöle bo'ol. However, once again, what are the ötöle bo'ol? As has been repeatedly shown, Vladimirtsov was misled by Berezin and used an erroneous text of *Jāmi' al-Tawārīkh.*

The *Jāmi' al-Tawārīkh* very seldom mentions AWTALW BΓWL. However, Berezin thinks this reconstruction is the Mongolian ötöle bo'ol (ordinary bo'ol), whose Russian translation is простой раб. Once again, Vladimirtsov accepted this unconditionally.[28] But, Paul Pelliot pointed out that this was still the wrong transcription of the word AWTKW.[29] This is certainly the case: the Persian letters "K" and "L" are similar in shape, and it is easy to make the mistake of transcribing "KW" as "LW."

When it comes to the description of the Uriangqadai 兀良合惕 clan's "thousand household" noyan named Udachi 玉迭赤 (Ortugchi? 斡脫赤?), the *Jāmi' al-Tawārīkh* mentions that they "are AWTALW BO'OL, so their men and women never get married." The Russian translation made an unnecessary supplement to this sentence – their women never marry other men, their men never marry other women.[30] In this way, the Uriangqadai

---

[27] Paul Pelliot also translated *ötögü bo'ol* as "hereditary slaves."

[28] B. Ia. Vladimirtsov, *The Social System of the Mongols*, Chinese translation, p. 110.

[29] Paul Pelliot and Louis Hambis, eds. and trans., *Histoire des campagnes de Gengis Khan*, vol. 1 (Leiden: E. J. Brill, 1951), p. 85.

[30] Rashīd al-Dīn: *Jāmi' al-Tawārīkh*, Russian translation, vol.1, book 2, p. 159.

people seem to have been endogamic and have had a system of consanguineous marriage. However, according to ancient Mongolian folklore, this is simply ridiculous. Therefore, "they never get married" can only be understood as they never intermarry with people coming from the Golden Family of Chinggis Khan. Not intermarrying with the family of Chinggis Khan is called a special feature of the ötögü bo'ol Muqali family. Muqali's father Gü'ün U'a 孔溫窟哇 was "a relative of the Chinggis Khans (literally, the "heavenly house"), but they would never marry into them" 親連天家，世不婚姻.[31] Hümün Hoga's family name was J̌alayir, and he had a servant-master relationship with the Mongolian Golden family Borjigin (Borjigid) 孛兒只斤. The expression "was a relative of the Chinggis Khans" was just the literati's flattering compliment, while "they would never marry into them" is exactly like Uriangqadai clan – they never intermarry with people coming from the Golden Family of Chinggis Khan. It turns out then, that the Uriangqadai clan "thousand household" noyan mentioned in the *Jāmi' al-Tawārīkh* was still known as ötögü bo'ol. In short, all the misunderstandings are derived from a manuscript clerical error – "K" was wrongly construed as "L."

Aside from considering corrupted text in a very few places in *Jāmi' al-Tawārīkh*, no trace of the words ötöle bo'ol can be found anywhere in either *The Secret History of the Mongols*, or in any historical documents of the Yuan Dynasty. Therefore, in the end, without historical proof, it can not be believed that there was an ötöle bo'ol stratum among the bo'ol social class. It must be pointed out that in *Jāmi' al-Tawārīkh*, there is no record describing the social status of AWTALW bo'ol as higher or lower than that of other people, and there is also no record describing AWTALW as "ordinary." All of the explanations about "ordinary slaves" and their social status were reconstructed and deduced by Berezin and Vladimirtsov.

The different kinds of bo'ol recognized by some, which we discussed above, such as unaghan bo'ol, ötöle bo'ol, ongqun bo'ol, and etügen bo'ol, did not exist. Among them, both *unaghan* and *ötöle* are misreadings for *ötögü,* and ötögü bo'ol refers to the rising nobles that could not have been connected to enthralled laborers. As for the ongqun bo'ol and etügen bo'ol, they are just individual subjective ideas that up to now lack support. After

---

[31] Yuan Mingshan 元明善, "Stele for Grand Councilor Dong Pingzhong Prince of Xian" 《丞相東平忠憲王碑》, in *Categorized Literature from the Yuan Period* 《元文類》, ch. 24.

deleting the various adjectives that are prefixes or mistaken inventions, all that remains is the concept of bo'ol itself.[32] Only the word bo'ol has the authority to represent the serf-like subjected population in ancient Mongolian society.

Following the emergence of the serf-like subject relationship between people, Mongolian society transitioned from a primitive communal society into a class society. The general prerequisite for the emergence of this type of personal subject relationship was the appearance and development of private property.

Compared to the economic constraints of capitalism, the class society of pre-capitalism is characterized by various degrees of personal constraints. For personal coercion of workers, the most extreme form of constraint is the system of slavery, and next is the system of serfdom and other systems with different forms of personal subject relationships. When a primitive communal society finally collapses, if a system of slavery under appropriate conditions receives very significant development, then the main production of that society will be the production by slaves, and a slave society will be formed; if what receives very significant development is another form of personal subject relationship, and personal constraints do not commonly reach their most extreme form, then, in this way, the societal form will move towards taking serfdom as its essential exploitive system. According to the point of view of Marx, the slave system and the serf system are "inevitable and certain outcomes"[33] of the evolution of a primitive communal society. Following the emergence and development of the bo'ol system, Mongolian society revealed the first page of its history as a class society and entered nomadic and militaristic patriarchal feudalism.

---

[32] Some Soviet Mongol scholars used to ignore textual research and emendation, and they have insisted on categorizing the bo'ol into multifarious kinds. For example, I. Zlatkin firmly believed that "unaghan bo'ol, ötögü bo'ol, and ötöle bo'ol" existed as different social strata. See I. Ia. Zlatkin (И. Я. Златкин), "Генезис крепостничества в средневековой Монголии" ("The Origination of the Medieval Mongolian Serf System"), *Народы Азии и Африки* (*Peoples of Asia and Africa*), vol. 1 (1977).

[33] *The Complete Works of Marx and Engels,* Chinese translation, 《馬克思恩格斯全集》, vol. 46, book 1, p. 496.

A Critical Examination of the Year of Birth of Chinggis Khan

Zhou Qingshu 周清澍

Originally in Chinese historical source documents it was recorded that Chinggis Khan died at the age of 66.[1] These documents also say that Chinggis Khan was born in 1162. The *History of the Yuan* 元史 and other various kinds of annalistic works of general history recovered by Qing Dynasty scholars all cite this point.[2] However, in Persia, Mahmud Ghazan, Khan of the Ilkhanate and a descendant the royal clan which also controlled the Yuan Dynasty, commissioned his Grand Vizier, Rashīd al-Dīn, to write the *Jāmi' al-Tawārīkh* (*Compendium of Chronicles*), which indicates that Chinggis Khan died at the age of 72, which means that he was born in 1155.[3] Since the *Jāmi' al-Tawārīkh* used information from the Mongolian language *Altan Debter* (*Golden Book*), which for the research of Mongolian history is a most important classic work, it was impossible for historians not to take it seriously. At the end of Qing Dynasty, Hong Jun 洪鈞 wrote *Yuan History Translated and Corrected* 元史譯文證補,

---

[1] *History of the Yuan* 《元史》, ch. 1, "Basic Annals of Taizu" 《太祖本紀》, p. 23; Tao Zongyi 陶宗儀, *South Village Records Compiled after Returning to the Farm* 《南村輟耕錄》, ch. 1 (Beijing: Zhonghua Book Company 中華書局, 1959); *Record of the Personal Campaigns of the Holy Warrior, Collated and Annotated* 《聖武親征錄校注》 in *Posthumous Papers of Wang Guowei* 《王忠愨公遺書》, pp. 28, 43; Sagang Sečen, *Erdeni-yin Tobči* (*Precious Summary*) 《蒙古源流箋證》, Chinese annotated edition reprint (Beijing: Zhonghua Book Company, 1962), ch. 3, p. 6, ch. 4, p. 6. *Erdeni-yin Tobči* (*Precious Summary*), Harvard-Yenching Institute, Scripta Mongolica II, part ii, pp. 64, 108; part iii, pp. 56, 95; part iv, pp. 68, 108 (Harvard University Press, 1956).

[2] Shao Yuanping 邵遠平, *History of the Yuan, Classified Compilation* 《元史類編》, ch. 1 (block printing by Sao Ye Shan Fang 掃業山房, 1795), p. 10a; Wei Yuan 魏源, *History of the Yuan, New Compilation* 《元史新編》, ch. 1 (block printing by Shen Wei Tang 慎微堂, 1905), p. 2b; Zeng Lian 曾廉, *Yuan Documents* 《元書》, ch. 1 (block printing by Cengyi Tang 層漪堂, 1911), ch. 1, p. 13a. *Continuation of the Comprehensive Mirror for Aid in Government* 《續資治通鑑》, ch. 5 (Chinese Classics Publishing 古籍出版社), fifth book, p. 4463; *Synopsis and Detail Catalog of the Continuation of the Comprehensive Mirror for Aid in Government* 《續通鑑綱目》, ch. 19 (block printing by Shandong Book Company 山東書局, 1881).

[3] Rashīd al-Dīn (Рашид-ад-дин), *Сборник Летописей* (Russian translation of the *Jāmi' al-Tawārīkh* [*Compendium of Chronicles*]), vol. 1, book 2, pp. 74, 75, 84, 107, 233, 246-7.

mostly based on the *Jāmi' al-Tawārīkh*. He also accepted the argument that Chinggis Khan was born in 1155, and wrote a special study to prove it.[4] From the time that Hong Jun introduced the *Jāmi' al-Tawārīkh* into China and added textual research, up until recent decades, the theory referred to above has held an overwhelmingly dominant position among scholars in China who research Mongolian history.[5] In the Soviet Union many authoritative scholars also supported this view.[6] In 1938, Paul Pelliot proposed the theory that Chinggis Khan was born in 1167, and a certain number of recent works by foreign scholars have adopted this view (see below). I believe that Chinggis Khan was undoubtedly born in 1162, but since the various historical records are greatly divided on this matter, it is still necessary for me to analyze and prove it.

---

[4] *Yuan History Translated and Corrected* 《元史譯文證補》 (block printing by Lu Runxiang 陸潤庠, 1897), ch. 1a, pp. 9b, 10a, ch. 1b, p. 24a; appendix "A Study of the Age of Taizu" 《太祖年壽考》, ch. 1b, pp. 35-6.

[5] Ke Shaomin 柯紹忞, *New History of the Yuan* 《新元史》, pp. 6606-9 (Kaiming Book Company 開明書局, 1936), and *Textual Research on the New History of the Yuan* 《新元史考證》, ch. 2, p. 1b, ch. 3, p. 11a; Tu Ji 屠寄, *Historical Records of the Mongols* 《蒙兀爾史記》, ch. 1, p. 18a, ch. 2, p. 1a, ch. 3, p. 31b; Feng Chengjun 馮承鈞, *Biography of Chinggis Khan* 《成吉思汗傳》, p. 24; Yu Yuan'an 余元盦, *Biography of Chinggis Khan* 《成吉思汗傳》, p. 9, and *Outline of Inner Mongolian History* 《内蒙古歷史概要》, p. 26; Tao Ketao 陶克濤, *Outline of the Development of Inner Mongolia* 《内蒙古發展概述》, p. 28.

[6] V. V. Bartol'd, *Turkestan Down to the Mongol Invasion* (London: E. J. W Gibb Memorial Trust, 1958), p. 459; Б. Я. Владимирцов (B. Ia. Vladimirtsov), *Чингис-хан* (*Chinggis Khan*), translated by Yu Yuan'an 余元盦 as 《成吉思汗傳》, pp. 20, 158. Soviet Science Academy and Mongolian People's Republic Science Committee, eds., *История Монгольской Народной Республики* (*History of the Mongolian People's Republic*) (Москва, 1954), Chinese translation 《蒙古人民共和國通史》, p. 45. *Очерки Истории СССР XI-XIII вв* (*Essays on the History of the USSR in the 11th through 13th Centuries*) (1953), p. 795, Chinese translation 《蒙古统治时期的國史略》, last vol., p. 20; *Всемирная История* (*World History*), Chinese translation 《世界通史》 ch. 3, p. 516; Б. Д. Греков and А. Ю. Якубовский (B. D. Grekov and A. Iu. Iakubovskii), *Золотая Орда и её Падение* (*The Golden Horde and its Collapse*) (Москва-Ленинград, 1950), p. 45. This book says, "Chinggis Khan was born in 1155." However, the footnote says, "The birth year is not confirmed. There is still another opinion, indicating he was born a few years later."

I. There is a Clear and Unambiguous Basis for Chinggis Khan Being Born in 1162

The *History of the Yuan* in the "Basic Annals of Taizu (Chinggis Khan)" 太祖本紀 records: "In the 22nd year (the year dinghai 丁亥, 1227) Taizu 太祖 was ill on the renwu 壬午 day of the seventh month. On the jichou 己丑 day he died in the royal encampment of Halaotu 哈老徒 in Sa'ari-ke'er 薩里川…at age 66."[7]

In the past, the evaluation of the *History of the Yuan* was negative. Because its editors were in rush to finish the book, it was "just piled up from the available materials, without any fixed method."[8] One can say that they just made a compilation of historical materials from the Yuan Dynasty, without even having the time to do editing or unified transliteration. For example, Zhang Xuecheng 章學誠 [a Qing Dynasty historian] once criticized the "Basic Annals" section, saying, "The *History of the Yuan* has altogether two hundred and three volumes, of which one hundred are annals 紀 or monographs 志. One can tell that it is not well-balanced without even reading it."[9] Gu Yanwu 顧炎武 [a Chinese philologist and geographer of the late Ming and early Qing period] said, regarding the historical records in the "Basic Annals" and the "Monograph on Astronomy" 天文志, that "there is repetition, and in the later part of the monograph it says to refer to missing records in "Basic Annals"; this is also not in a formal style."[10] Zhao Yi 趙翼 [a Qing Dynasty historian] said, "The imperial edict regarding the enthronement of Emperor Taiding 泰定…was written just like the language of a country lady, but the compilers of the *History of the Yuan* did not even polish it."[11] The

---

[7] *History of the Yuan* 《元史》, Bona edition 百衲本, ch. 1, p. 23a.

[8] Shao Jinhan 邵晉涵, *The South of the River Catalog*《南江書錄》, 42a, the entry "Yuan History" 《元史》, in Liu Shiheng 劉世珩, compiler, *Collectanea from the Studio of Accumulated Learning* 《聚學軒叢書》.

[9] "Writing at Random" 《信摭》, in *Posthumous Papers of Zhang Xuecheng, Miscellaneous Notes* 《章氏遺書外編》 (Wuxing 吳興: Liu family 劉氏 block printing).

[10] Gu Yanwu 顧炎武, *Record of Knowledge Gained Day by Day* 《日知錄》, ch. 26, the entry "History of the Yuan" 《元史》.

[11] Zhao Yi 趙翼, *Critical Notes on the 22 Histories* 《廿二史劄記》, ch. 29, the entry "Translations of Imperial Decrees during the Yuan Dynasty are Very Different: Sometimes Elegant, Sometimes Unrefined" 《元人譯詔旨雅俗不同》.

Annotated Catalog of the Imperial Library by Command 四庫全書總目提要 criticizes the *History of the Yuan* saying that books made by the people of the Yuan Dynasty "were not used to correct the histories and biographies," nor "was there careful textual research to correct the errors in the primary sources."[12] Criticisms such as "not well-balanced," "not in a formal style," the compilers "did not even polish it," nor "was there careful textual research," and others correctly demonstrate that the *History of the Yuan* was made by copying first-hand historical materials. The historical sources for the "Basic Annals" were the *Veritable Records* 實錄. According to the *History of the Yuan*, Wang E 王鶚 first compiled the *Veritable Records* in 1262, and the first draft of the Chinese edition was completed by 1286.[13] At that time there were even people still alive who had seen Chinggis Khan in person. Moreover, the *Veritable Records* were considered the most important contemporaneous record by the rulers of each dynasty, so they should be one of the most reliable sources for the birth records of the emperors.

In addition, the *South Village Records Compiled after Returning from the Farm* 南村輟耕錄 by Tao Zongyi 陶宗儀 has a record identical to the one in the *History of the Yuan*: "in the third year of the Baoqing 寶慶 reign period of the Song Dynasty, in the year dinghai 丁亥 (1227), Taizu…died on the jichou 己丑 day in the seventh month, at the age of 66."[14]

The *Records Compiled after Returning from the Farm* was printed in the last years of Yuan Dynasty prior to the compiling of the *History of the Yuan,* so it is impossible that the author got the information from the *History of the Yuan*. Tao Zongyi was an ordinary scholar, who failed in the civil service exams, therefore it is very difficult to believe that he could have had direct access to the forbidden *Veritable Records* stored at the palace. This proves that the record "Chinggis Khan died at age of 66" was not only recorded in the *Veritable Records*, prior the completion of the

---

[12] *Annotated Catalog of the Imperial Library by Command* 《四庫全書總目提要》, ch. 46, the entry "History of the Yuan" 《元史》.

[13] *History of the Yuan*, ch. 5, "Basic Annals of Shizu (Qubilai Khan)" 《世祖本紀》, the Zhongtong 中統 reign period, year three, the wusheng 戊申 day of the eighth month; ch. 14, the Zhiyuan 至元 reign period, year 23, the wuwu 戊午 day of the 12th month.

[14] Tao Zongyi, *South Village Records Compiled after Returning to the Farm*, ch. 1, the entry "The Orthodox Succession of the Emperors" 《列聖授受正統》 (Beijing: Zhonghua Book Company, 1959).

History of the Yuan, but that it was also well known to the literati of the Yuan court, especially those who attended to the state archives and so were in a position to know the most.

And further, it was also recorded in the *Record of the Personal Campaigns of the Holy Warrior* 聖武親征錄 that: "In the year guihai 癸亥 (1203)…(Chinggis) Khan conquered Ong Khan. In the winter of that year, the king hunted in the Teme'en-ke'er 帖麥該川….The khan was 42. It was the time when the Naiman 乃蠻 Khan Tayang 太陽 sent the envoy Yuehunan 月忽難 in order to ally with the Önggüd 王孤 digid-quri [chief] Ala-Qush 阿剌忽思火力, saying: 'It has been said that someone in the East claims to be the king…How can there be two rulers in the world! I hope you can help me as the right wing of the army, so that we can capture bows and arrows from them!'"[15]

According to the material in this passage, if Chinggis Khan had been 42 in the year guihai 癸亥 (1203), it would exactly conform with him "having lived 66 years" in the year dinghai 丁亥 (1227). If we compare the contents of the *Record of the Personal Campaigns of the Holy Warrior* with the *Jāmi' al-Tawārīkh*, we can easily know that the *Jāmi' al-Tawārīkh*, which depends on the *Altan Debter* (*Golden Book*), and the *Record of the Personal Campaigns of the Holy Warrior* were both based on the same source. We can say that the *Record of the Personal Campaigns of the Holy Warrior* is just a Chinese translation of the Mongolian *Altan Debter*. This record on the one hand shows that there was a source even earlier than the *Veritable Records* which confirmed that Chinggis Khan was born in 1162, and on the other hand it shows that Rashīd al-Dīn might have excluded the account that originally existed in the *Altan Debter* in order to agree with his belief that Chinggis Khan had lived for 72 years.

Besides the existing Chinese primary sources, some records in Mongolian language documents handed down in Mongolia also have completely identical information.

The first is in the well-known *Erdeni-yin Tobči* [*Precious Summary*, by Sagang Sečen, 1662], which says: "In the year renwu 壬午 (1162), Hö'elün Üjin by Yisügei Ba'atur' gave birth to a boy….His childhood nickname was the God-granted Temüjin….He died on the 12th day of

---

[15] Wang Guowei 王國維, *Record of the Personal Campaigns of the Holy Warrior, Collated and Annotated* 《聖武親征錄校注》 in *Posthumous Papers of Wang Guowei* 《王忠慤公遺書》, pp. 28b, 43.

seventh month in the year dinghai 丁亥 (1227) at the age of 66."[16]

The *Erdeni-yin Tobči* listed the seven sources it consulted, one of which is still accessible to us, the *Šir-a Tu'uji* (*Yellow Annals*). An annotated edition has been translated as *Erten-ü Mongghol-un Qad-un Ündüsün-ü Yeke Šir-a Tu'uji* (*The Great Yellow Annals of the Origin of the Ancient Mongolian Khans*). It says: "At age of 66, Chinggis Khan died on the 12th day of the seventh month of the fire and pig year (the year dinghai 丁亥, 1227) in Xixia 西夏 [the Tangut Empire]."[17]

And there is the *Altan Tobči* (*Golden Summary*), which appeared before the *Erdeni-yin Tobči*, and researchers believe that the *Erdeni-yin Tobči* referenced it. This book also says: "Chinggis Khan was born in the year renwu 壬午 (1162)."[18]

The *Altan Tobči* (Ulaanbaatar edition) of Lubsang-Danzin (Tibetan: Blo-bsang bsTan-'dzin) belongs to another type of historical document in the Mongolian language, and it has special value since it originated directly from the Mongolian language *The Secret History of the Mongols* 元朝秘史. This book also says that Chinggis Khan was born in the year renwu, and "died in the year dinghai on the 12th day of seventh month at the age of 66."[19]

Although the earliest Mongolian documents mentioned above were not written earlier than 17th century, it can not be said that they followed or had any connection with Chinese historical works after the *History of the Yuan*. The reasons for this are as follows:

1. Although the *Šir-a Tu'uji* and the *Altan Tobči* were completed at the end of the Ming Dynasty, judging by the situation of [limited]

---

[16] Sagang Sečen, *Erdeni-yin Tobči* (*Precious Summary*) 《蒙古源流箋證》, Chinese annotated edition, ch. 3, p. 6b, ch. 4, p. 6b, reprint (Beijing: Zhonghua Book Company, 1962); Sagang Sečen, *Erdeni-yin Tobči* (*Precious Summary*), Harvard-Yenching Institute, Scripta Mongolica II, part ii, pp. 64, 108; part iii, pp. 56, 95; part iv, pp. 68, 108 (Harvard University Press, 1956).

[17] Н. П. Шастина (N. P. Shastina), ed. and trans., *Шара Туджи. Монгольская Летопись XVII века* (*A Mongolian Chronicle of the 17th Century*) (Moscow - Leningrad, 1957), pp. 22, 39 of the original, pp. 128, 136 of the Russian translation.

[18] Kobayashi Takashirō 小林高四郎, *Mōko ōgonshi: Mōko minzoku no koten* 『蒙古黄金史:蒙古民族の古典』 (*The Golden Chronicle of Mongols—The Classic of Mongolian Nationality*), p. 26. Japanese translation of the *Altan Tobči* (Tokyo: Seikatsusha, 1941).

[19] *Erten-ü Qag-un Ündüsülegsen Törö Yosun-u J̌okiyal-i Tobčilan Quriyagsan Altan Tobči* (Ulaanbaatar edition, 1937), pp. 25-6, 102; *Altan Tobči*, new edition of a new Mongolian translation (Ulaanbaatar, 1957), pp. 20, 158.

China-Mongolia cultural contact during the Ming Dynasty, there is no possibility that they utilized any Chinese documents post-dating the establishment of the Ming.

2. There are no traces in the content of either the *Erdeni-yin Tobči* or any books published earlier of copying from the *History of the Yuan.*

3. The *History of the Yuan* records that Chinggis Khan died on the jichou 己丑 day of the seventh month, and there are also the records in the Mongolian historical documents showing he died on the 12th day of the seventh month. Based on the calculations of calendrical science, these two dates coincide exactly. However, given the state of calendric knowledge and discussion in the 17th century in the Mongolian region, even if the authors of these Mongolian books had been able to read the *History of the Yuan*, it would have been difficult for them to figure out that the jichou 己丑 day of the seventh month was the 12th day of the seventh month. Even the great master of textual criticism of the Qing Dynasty Qianlong and Jiaqing 乾嘉 reign periods, Qian Daxin 錢大昕, who was well-versed in calendric calculation, did not figure out which Heavenly Stem and Earthly Branch was the shuo 朔 day of the seventh month in his *Study of the Intercalary Months in the Four Histories of the Song, Liao, Jin, and Yuan Dynasties* 宋遼金元四史朔閏考.[20] This also demonstrates that consistency of the dates of Chinggis Khan's birth and death in the Mongolian historical tradition is unequivocal.

4. Mongolian language documents did refer to Tibetan historical records, but it was difficult for Tibetan records to utilize Ming Dynasty Chinese records. For example, the *Clarification of What Should Be Known* 彰所知論, which influenced the *Erdeni-yin Tobči* and other books in their "basic ideas, organization, and style," was "written for Qubilai Khan's son Jingim 真金 by the imperial teacher."[21] Therefore, even if a few Mongolian records consistent with Chinese records were introduced indirectly from Tibet, these Tibetan sources were only the works by Yuan Dynasty Lamas who then served in the central plains [China proper].

---

[20] Qian Daxin 錢大昕, *Supplement to the 25 Histories*《二十五史補編》, vol. 6, p. 8482, the third year of the Baoqing 寶慶 reign period of the Song emperor Lizong 宋理宗, the year dinghai 丁亥 (Shanghai: Kaiming Book Company 開明書局).

[21] Chen Yinke 陳寅恪, "The *Šes bya rab gsa*《彰所知論》(*Clarification of What Should Be Known*) and the *Erdeni-yin Tobči* 《蒙古源流》", *Bulletin of the Institute of History and Philology* 《歷史語言研究所集刊》, Academia Sinica, vol. 2, no. 3 (1931).

Besides the written records, the birth dates of Chinggis Khan are also to be seen in an inscription on the *Chuoketu* (*Choktu*) *Taiji Stele* 綽克圖台吉碑, which was erected in the year of wood and mouse 木鼠 (the year jiazi 甲子, 1624). At the end of the inscription it explains: "It has been 464 years since Chinggis Khan was born in the year of water and horse 水馬 (the year renwu 壬午, 1162)."[22]

From this it can be seen that Mongolian language historical records recorded the birth year of Chinggis Khan, or were directly based on remaining Yuan Dynasty historical materials, or were indirectly based on records written by Tibetan Lamas who had contact with the Yuan rulers. These records and those in the *History of the Yuan* were based on different sources, but they came to the identical conclusion.

II. Discussing Chinggis Khan Being Born in 1155

1. The Accounts of Rashīd al-Dīn are not Sufficient Evidence

Unlike the argument that Chinggis Khan was born in 1162, the birth record in the *Jāmi' al-Tawārīkh* is based on only one authority. Mongolian documents in Western regions prior to the *Jāmi' al-Tawārīkh* (such as the *Ta'rīkh-i Jahān-Gushā*) do not have this theory. And neither in later books, except for those that directly used the *Jāmi' al-Tawārīkh* as their master copy, can identical records be found. Therefore, we can say that the *Jāmi' al-Tawārīkh* is the sole evidence for this belief.

In addition, Rashīd al-Dīn admitted that his knowledge of Chinggis Khan's birth date was based on other people's oral tradition. He also admitted that a valuable source for the *Jāmi' al-Tawārīkh*, the *Altan Debter*, did not say that Chinggis Khan was born in 1155. Of course, material based on oral tradition is far from being as trustworthy as the explicitness of written records.

Moreover, the account in the *Jāmi' al-Tawārīkh*, which originated from oral legends, is unreasonable. It not only records the birth year of Chinggis Khan differently from other books, but, also, even Temüjin's age at his father's death is different than in the extremely reliable *The Secret History of the Mongols* (the *Jāmi' al-Tawārīkh* has age thirteen and *The Secret*

---

[22] Če. Damdinsürüng, *Mongγol Uran J̌okiyal-un Degeǰi J̌aγun Bilig Orusibai* (*The Essence of Mongolian Literature*), vol. 14 (Ulaanbaatar, 1959), p. 278.

History of the Mongols has age nine). It seems as if one of the reasons for this difference was the attempt Rashīd al-Dīn made to put together this argument, namely: Chinggis Khan not only died in the year of the pig (the earthly branch hai 亥 corresponds to the year of the pig), but he was born and his father died in the year of the pig. Some books later than the *Jāmi' al-Tawārīkh* even say he was crowned in the year of the pig and died in the month of the pig [the 12th month].[23] This kind of bizarre coincidence is, of course, very doubtful.

The first person to doubt the point of view of this Persian record was Joseph von Hammer-Purgstall. Later, the Japanese scholar Naka Michiyo 那珂通世 developed Hammer-Purgstall's idea. He said, "That theory is completely wrong. His birth, his death and that of his father, and his ascension to the throne were all major events in human affairs, and four of the major events for Chinggis Khan. That all of them occurred in the year of the pig, even if you called it a coincidence, would be extremely rare. Hammer-Purgstall said, 'The Persians hated Chinggis Khan, so they said that his birth, death, and enthronement all happened in the year of the pig.' All believers in Islam consider pigs as unclean, which was Hammer-Purgstall's reason for his view."[24] Recently, the Soviet scholar N. P. Shastina (Н. П. Шастина) also published the same opinion.[25]

Since the *Jāmi' al-Tawārīkh* was written on the imperial edict of Ghazan Khan, Rashīd al-Dīn would not dare to fabricate the story that "It was common knowledge among all of the Mongolian Khans, court officials (*noyan*), and ministers that he (Chinggis Khan) died at the age of 72." Perhaps at that time this story had actually already been circulating. It

---

[23] Abū al-Ghāzī Bahādur said that Chinggis Khan ascended the throne in the year of pig and died in the year of pig. See his *Šajara-yi Turk*, in French as *Histoire des Mongols et des Tartares par Aboul-Ghâzi Bèhâdour Khan*, trans. and annot. by Le Baron Desmaisons (St. Petersburg, 1874), pp. 87, 143 ; in the English translation, vol. 1, p. 146.

[24] Naka Michiyo 那珂通世, "Textual Criticism and Annotation of the Yuan Dynasty 'Record of the Personal Campaigns of the Holy Warrior'" 「校正增注元親征録」(*Kōsei zōchū Gen shinsei roku*), in *The Posthumous Works of Naka Michiyo* 『那珂通世遺書』 (Tokyo, 1915).

[25] Н. П. Шастина (N. P. Shastina), editor and translator, *Шара Туджи-Монгольская Летопись XVII века* (Russian version of the *Šir-a Tu'uji*), p. 176, annotation 21. N. P. Shastinoĭ said, "It is obvious that Rashīd al-Dīn intentionally picked an uncertain birth year in order to prove that Chinggis Khan, who died in the year of the pig (1227), was also born in the year of the pig (according to Muslim culture, pigs are low and degraded animals), and to express his negative attitudes towards Chinggis Khan, since this Persian scholar was not able to openly show his real opinion."

at first was probably started by the astrologers, who are mentioned again and again in the *Jāmi' al-Tawārīkh*. They latched on to the premise that Chinggis Khan died in the year of the pig, and consequently said that he lost his father at the age of 13 and died at the age of 72, in order to come to the conclusion that the year of his birth and his father's death both fell in the year of the pig. After the *Jāmi' al-Tawārīkh* the strained interpretation of the astrologers was further developed, consequently adding the theory that he was enthroned in the year of the pig and died in the month of the pig. From the seventh to the 13th centuries, astrology was extremely popular in the Islamic countries, and those astrologers were very similar to the ancient Chinese geomancers 陰陽家. They were accustomed to use the dates of birth, death, and other events to explain the mandate of heaven and one's personal fortune and misfortune. They arranged the major events of Chinggis Khan's life according to the times of the twelve year repeating animal cycle of the Earthly Branches, and gave it quite a mysterious flavor, even a hidden sarcastic meaning. However, from the point of view of the Mongol rulers this was, of course, after the astrologers had greatly developed and were respectfully received by the rulers, who therefore all happily believed it.

But, that time was not too far removed from the passing of Chinggis Khan, and the Mongolians in the western regions still knew the real lifespan of Chinggis Khan (which will be explained below). The dissemination of the story fabricated by the astrologers was probably due to the difference between the Islamic calendar and the solar calendar, and the unfamiliarity of the Mongols about how the calendar was constructed (the Islamic calendar is one year shorter than the solar calendar every 30 years).

The original version of the *Jāmi' al-Tawārīkh* also contains a few doubtful places.

In terms of chronology, the *Jāmi' al-Tawārīkh* starts from the year of the rabbit (1195), but the *Record of the Personal Campaigns of the Holy Warrior* starts from the year renxu 壬戌 (1202). Wang Guowei 王國維 raised doubt about this in his annotations to the *Record of the Personal Campaigns of the Holy Warrior*: "The two books had the same master copy, but they are different at this point, and it is not known whether Rashīd al-Dīn added more years in the Heavenly Stems and Earthly Branches cycle or if this book (the *Record of the Personal Campaigns of the Holy Warrior*) omitted them."[26] This is not a difficult question to answer if you compare the two accounts closely.

First of all, considering the various historical sources, the chronology of the "Taizu Annals" in the *History of the Yuan* also starts from the year renxu 壬戌 (1202), and the chronology of *The Secret History of the Mongols* starts with the year of the rooster (1201). Even though the master copy of these two books is different from the one for the *Record of the Personal Campaigns of the Holy Warrior*, they are all identical on this point – that for any event in the historical materials which transpired prior to 1202, the year is unclear. It can be seen from this that the *Record of the Personal Campaigns of the Holy Warrior* did not "omit" years, but rather the *Jāmi' al-Tawārīkh* "added more years in the Heavenly Stems and Earthly Branches cycle."

Second, there is a period in Chinggis Khan's history from the end of the year of the rabbit (1195) until the beginning of the year of the pig (1203) written up in the *Jāmi' al-Tawārīkh*. The content of this period, just like the other three books, records events that happened between the time when Ong Khan and Yisügei became blood-brothers (*anda*) to when Chinggis Khan annihilated Ong Khan. If one checks the original text of these three books, one can discover among them many sections dating from prior events, which are simply not events that happened during this period, and it is not possible to sequence each of these events into an annual chronology. This is the second proof of "adding more years in the Heavenly Stems and Earthly Branches cycle" in the *Jāmi' al-Tawārīkh*.[27]

Third, Rashīd al-Dīn said: "about the history before he was 41...the author of this history does not know the events that happened in each year, he has only sketched out the history of these 41 years. Not until the later

[26] Wang Guowei, *Record of the Personal Campaigns of the Holy Warrior, Collated and Annotated*, p. 14b.

[27] Rashīd al-Dīn (Рашид-ад-дин), *Сборник Летописей* (Russian translation of the *Jāmi' al-Tawārīkh*), vol. 1, book 2, pp. 107-35. Its contents are parallel to the *Collated and Annotated Edition of the Record of the Personal Campaigns of the Holy Warrior*, pp. 14b-42a, and the *History of the Yuan*, ch. 1, pp. 6a-13a. One can see this more clearly by comparing the *Jāmi' al-Tawārīkh* with *The Secret History of the Mongols*. The events of this period in the *Jāmi' al-Tawārīkh* are not connected with the ones in *The Secret History of the Mongols*. They are parallel to the dated events that run from section 150 to section 177 of *The Secret History of the Mongols*. These describe earlier events, such as when Chinggis Khan sent a minister to censure Ong Khan. These are entirely a reconstructed history of Chinggis Khan and should not at all have been sequenced into a chronology.

part of his life can one (at last) relate a year by year account."[28] However, the *Record of the Personal Campaigns of the Holy Warrior*, in the year guihai 癸亥 (1203) says, "At that time (he) was 42 years old." Does this not show that the historical events of Chinggis Khan of which one can "relate a year by year account" start in the year renxu (1202), which was exactly when he was 41? This cannot be a coincidence, and can only prove that Rashīd al-Dīn found the same record in the *Altan Debter* that was written in the *Record of the Personal Campaigns of the Holy Warrior*. In order to reconcile "the year by year account" of Chinggis Khan after he was 41 years old with his birth year, which Rashīd al-Dīn believed to be the year of the pig (1155), he had to move back the chronology of events by seven years, just like his birth year.

Finally and most noteworthy is that Rashīd al-Dīn in one place revealed what he had done. He wrote the history of Chinggis Khan's fourth period (1204–1210) starting exactly from the *Record of the Personal Campaigns of the Holy Warrior*: "at that time (the Khan) was 42 years old," which was also the time when the Naiman tribe sent an envoy to ally with the Önggüd to invade Mongolia.[29] However, in the title of the period before this one (1196-1203) he wrote, "In the final year (of this period), Chinggis Khan was 41."[30] This is obviously a contradiction with what he said in the previous period (1167-1194), that "in the last year of this period, Chinggis Khan was 41."[31] This type of contradiction is understandable. The latter was fabricated to change the birth year to 1155, while the former just accidentally preserved the true records from the original historical sources, which are the same as the ones in the *Record of the Personal Campaigns of the Holy Warrior*.

Because the *Jāmi' al-Tawārīkh* had "added more years in the Heavenly Stems and Earthly Branches cycle" it, as one would expect, made a mistake on the date of an historical event explicitly verifiable in the Chinese records. That is where the *Jāmi' al-Tawārīkh* states, "Chinggis Khan learned of the utter defeat of Megüjin-se'ültü of the Tatars....He went on a punitive expedition against them, and they were routed....The Grand Councilor 丞相 granted Chinggis Khan an imperial honorific title

[28] Rashīd al-Dīn (Рашид-ад-дин), *Сборник Летописей* (Russian translation of the *Jāmi' al-Tawārīkh*), vol. 1, book 2, p. 74.
[29] Ibid., p. 146.
[30] Ibid., p. 107.
[31] Ibid., p. 84.

for this achievement."[32] Since this battle was a great victory, it was mentioned several times in the "Annals" and biographical sections of the *History of the Jin Dynasty* 金史 where it is confirmed to have happened in 1196.[33] The *Jāmi' al-Tawārīkh* recorded this event in the period from when Chinggis Khan lost his father at age of 13 up until he was 40 years old. According to Rashīd al-Dīn's argument that Chinggis Khan was born in 1155, he should have been 40 years old in 1194, so this event should have happened before 1194, which is completely a contradiction to the explicit record in the *Altan Debter*. Therefore, only when we accept the theory that Chinggis Khan was 41 in the year renxu (1202), which is also the year when his life started to be recorded chronologically in the *Record of the Personal Campaigns of the Holy Warrior*, would it then be consistent for the event mentioned above to have happened before he was 40 years old.

The argument in the *Jāmi' al-Tawārīkh* did not even receive recognition in the writings on international Islamism. For example, Abū al-Ghāzī Bahādur (1603-1663), Khan of the Central Asian kingdom of Khiva, once wrote in part on Mongol history, in which he also said that

---

[32] Ibid., pp. 92-3.

[33] *History of the Jin Dynasty* 《金史》, ch. 94, "Biography of Grand Councilor Xiang" 《丞相襄傳》. See ch. 10, "Basic Annals of Shizong" 《世宗本紀》; ch. 94, "Biography of Jiagu Qingchen" 《夾谷清臣傳》 and "Biography of Wanyan Anguo" 《完顏安國傳》. Also please see the textual research in Wang Guowei 王國維, *Collected Works from the Hall of Observation* 《觀堂集林》, chs. 14 and 15, especially ch. 14, pp. 637-8 (Beijing: Zhonghua Book Company 中華書局, 1959, new photocopy edition). Ke Shaomin 柯紹忞 [1850-1933] tried to show that this event happened in 1194. He said that according to the *Record of the Great Jin State* 《大金國志》 the Tatars' victorious battle occurred in the year jiayin 甲寅 (1194), and that the *History of the Jin Dynasty* 《金史》 can not be reliably used to correct this mistake in history books written by Westerners (see Ke Shaomin 柯紹忞, *New History of the Yuan* 《新元史》, "Basic Annals of Taizu" 《太祖本紀 》, p. 6606; and Ke Shaomin 柯紹忞, *Textual Research on the New History of the Yuan* 《新元史考證》, ch. 2, p. 4a). The *Records of the Great Jin State,* ch. 19, also records "The Mongols kept invading our frontier. Aiwang 愛王 led troops to put them down and appease the people there," but this has long since been confirmed by Wang Guowei as a pseudograph. It never really happened (*Collected Works from the Hall of Observation*, ch. 15, pp. 757-63). Actually, the book only mentions "Mongols." It is hard to define them as Tatars, let alone define "Aiwang" 愛王 as Wanyan Xiang 完顏襄 [the Jin Dynasty minister].

Chinggis Khan died at the age of 65.[34] This record provides confirmation of the view in the *History of the Yuan* from historical material in Western regions. He mainly used material from the *Jāmi' al-Tawārīkh* to write his book, but even so he did not use its view that Chinggis Khan lived to age 72. The explanation of this point is that the Mongol clans still had family genealogies or other reliable data at hand, and because of this he abandoned the doubtful record in the *Jāmi' al-Tawārīkh*. Another point is that this shows that Rashīd al-Dīn's words "It was common knowledge among all of the Mongolian khans, court officials (*noyan*), and ministers that he (Chinggis Khan) died at the age of 72" are insufficient as proof.

2. *Hong Jun's* 洪鈞 *Textual Analysis on the Age of Taizu* (Chinggis Khan) 太祖年壽考異 *is not "Accurate"* 精當

Hong Jun's *Textual Analysis on the Age of Taizu* was an important essay for impelling a great many scholars to believe that Chinggis Khan was born in 1155. Some scholars have considered that this article "settled all the arguments," and they have praised its "balance and accuracy" and so on.[35] To determine whether or not it actually is "accurate," we can perform an item by item analysis.

Hong Jun's first reason is that the *Complete Report on the Mongolian Tatars* 蒙韃備錄 says that Chinggis Khan was born in the year jiaxu 甲戌 (1154), which is the year before yihai 乙亥 (1155), and these years are close to each other…if jiaxu and renwu 壬午 were nine years apart, there would not be this mistake." In order to explore this, we might as well look a little at the original words in the *Complete Report on the Mongolian Tatars* [an eye-witness report of the early Mongol Empire by Zhao Gong

34 Abū al-Ghāzī Bahādur, *Šajara-yi Turk* (*Genealogical Tree of the Turkmen*) (1659), vol. 1, pp. 63, 146. However, he still relied on the *Jāmi' al-Tawārīkh* and recorded the year of birth as the year of the pig and his year of ascending the throne as the year of the pig. The occurrence of this type of contradiction probably is because he knew with certainty that Chinggis Khan lived to age 65 (or even 66), but the argument about the year of the pig was then current, and for this reason he preserved it. In the same way C. d'Ohsson's *Histoire des Mongols, depuis Tchinguiz Khan jusqu'à Timour Bey ou Tamerlan* used the birth year from the *Jāmi' al-Tawārīkh* and the life-span from the *History of the Yuan*.

35 See Li Zhichun 李志純，*A Study of the History of the Yuan* 《元史學》, pp. 163-6; Zhang Chengpei 張承佩, *A Critical Biography of Chinggis Khan* 《成吉思汗評傳》, pp. 17-20. These two books both have separate special sections propagandizing for *Textual Analysis on the Age of Taizu* 《太祖年壽考異》.

趙珙]: "Reigning emperor Chinggis Khan was born in the year jiaxu. That culture had no calendrical system 庚甲, however, based on the records we have now, it is easy to find out his birth year. That culture counted every grass-growing season as a year. When people asked each other's age, they would say how many grass-growing seasons do you have?" In the later part of the book, it says: "They also named the years as year of the rabbit or year of the dragon, and only for the previous year did they change to using the year gengchen 庚辰."[36] From the above passage, we can tell that the Mongols at that time recorded their age only by using the "grass-growing seasons" 幾草, and did not use the Heavenly Stems and Earthly Branches. They only used the Heavenly Stems and Earthly Branches for the previous year, and based on this custom, if a Mongolian had told someone the age of Chinggis Khan, it would have been more reliable to use the number of grass-growing years. However, what Zhao Gong (1195-1246) recorded was not the number of years, but the Heavenly Stem and Earthly Branch, and one can tell from this that he must have gotten this as hearsay from people in Yan 燕 [modern Beijing, which Zhao Gong visited as an envoy from the Song court] during the Yanjing 燕京 period. This is just as Shen Zengzhi 沈曾植 said, "Meng Gong 孟珙 (Zhao Gong) said the Mongolians 'do not use the Heavenly Stems and Earthly Branches, and made the calculation of the year by using hearsay, not books,' therefore his theory is based on his guesswork, not necessarily on any evidence."[37]

Let us look now at the second argument that Hong Jun raised, this one from Yang Weizhen's 楊維楨 *Debate on Orthodoxy* 正統辨. The *Debate on Orthodoxy* is included in the third volume of Tao Zongyi's *South Village Records Compiled after Returning to the Farm*. As discussed above, Chinggis Khan's year of birth, death, and coronation are all confirmed in the first volume of *South Village Records Compiled after Returning to the Farm*. How can we ignore the official record in the first volume, but pay heed only to the obscure and unclear record in the third volume of *South Village Records Compiled after Returning to the Farm*? By analyzing the *Debate on Orthodoxy* a little it is not difficult to see the

---

36 Wang Guowei 王國維, *Complete Report on the Mongolian Tatars Annotated and Corrected* 《蒙韃備錄箋證》, pp. 2b, 3b.

37 Sagang Sečen, *Erdeni-yin Tobči* (*Precious Summary*) 《蒙古源流箋證》, Chinese annotated edition, ch. 3, p. 6b.

holes in the argument. Yang Weizhen said, "…it is recorded that Taizu 太祖 of the Song Dynasty was born in the year dinghai 丁亥 [927] and founded his empire in the year gengshen 庚申 [960], and our Taizu [Chinggis Khan] was born and founded the empire in the years of the same name…" Yang Weizhen just copied this passage from the *Essentials of Government of the Three Reigns in the Late Song* 宋季三朝政要. The original text is as follows:

> Taizu of the Song Dynasty was born in the year dinghai [927] and founded his empire in the year gengshen [960]. He ordered Cao Bin 曹彬 to conquer Jiangnan 江南 [all territory south of the Yangtze River]. The royal army crossed the river in the year jiaxu 甲戌 [974] and conquered Jiangnan in the years yihai 乙亥 [975] and bingzi 丙子 [976]….Now the Great Yuan Taizu Holy Warrior Emperor 大元太祖聖武皇帝 [Chinggis Khan] was also born in the year yihai, and ascended the throne in the year gengshen and ordered Bayan 佰顏 to conquer Jiangnan. His great army also crossed the Yangtze River and conquered Jiangnan in the years yihai and bingzi.[38]

Since this book was first printed in 1312 (the year renzi 壬子 of the Huangqing 皇慶 reign period of Emperor Renzong 仁宗), but was probably written even earlier, normally it would be taken as reliable. However, the author of this book was a surviving adherent of the old regime from the end of the Song Dynasty and had just started to serve the Yuan Dynasty. Therefore he was not familiar with the prior history of the Mongol rulers,[39] and if one carefully evaluates the above passage, then mistaken identifications can easily be discovered. Because Taizu (Chinggis Khan) did not "ascend the throne in the year gengshen," much less did he "order Bayan to conquer Jiangnan." If we insist that the words prior to "ordered Bayan…" be considered related to Chinggis Khan, then

[38] *Essentials of Government of the Three Reigns in the Late Song* 《宋季三朝政要》, ch. 6, p. 9a, in *Collected Books in the House for Regal Writings* 《宸翰樓叢書》, block printing edition of 1312, photocopied by Luo Zhenyu 羅振玉.

[39] See *Annotated Catalog of the Imperial Library by Command* 《四庫全書總目提要》, p. 1046 (ch. 47, *Essentials of Government of the Three Reigns in the Late Song* 《宋季三朝政要》) and the postscripts and main body of the text.

because the following passage is related to Shizu 世祖 [Qubilai Khan, who historically did "order Bayan…"], therefore the writing is not coherent. Since there is only one subject in this sentence and it all runs together, it is impossible that it refers to both Chinggis Khan and to Qubilai Khan. Actually, Qubilai Khan was born in the year yihai (1215) and founded the empire [i.e. ascended to the Mongol throne] in the year gengshen (1260).[40] Therefore, we can only interpret this to mean that the author here mistook Shizu for Taizu.[41]

In fact, Yang Weizhen himself did know the years when Taizu was born, died, and ascended the throne. However, in order to prove the legitimacy of the Yuan Dynasty succession to the Song, he did not hesitate to use every reason to defend his own opinion. He even ambiguously quoted the words "inferring destiny and explaining both cause and effect" 推演命數，兼陳因果 [the Mandate of Heaven theory] from the *Essentials of Government of the Three Reigns in the Late Song*. After this quote he added, "fifty years after Taizu founded the empire and seventeen years after Shizu's coronation, all under heaven [the country] was united."[42] These words obviously are a contradiction with Taizu having "founded his empire in the year gengshen [1200]," because from that year to Shizu ascending the throne had been another gengshen year [1260] – a difference of exactly 60 years. From this one can tell that Yang Weizhen's mental view at this place was to use the ascension to the throne in the year bingyin 丙寅 (1206) as the basis for his calculation, therefore he cited about "fifty years after Taizu founded the empire."

---

[40] *History of the Yuan*, ch. 4, "Basic Annals of Shizu" 《世祖本紀》, year one of the Zhongtong 中統 reign period, which was the year gengshen 庚申 (1260).

[41] The Qing Dynasty scholar Li Ciming 李慈銘 long ago discovered this error in the *Essentials of Government of the Three Reigns in the Late Song* 《宋季三朝政要》, but he thought it was a "mistake in the original block carving" 原刻誤. The full title of Chinggis Khan in this book is the "Taizu Shengwu" Emperor 太祖聖武皇帝. However, the full title of Shizu is the "Shengde Shen'gong Wenwu" Emperor 聖德神功文武皇帝. Therefore, this does not seem to be a block carving error. See Li Ciming 李慈銘, *Diary from the Studio of Unadorned Silk* 《越縵堂日紀》 (photolithographic edition, 1922), ch. 18, p. 19b. This was announced by William Hung, "The Transmission of the Book Known as 'The Secret History of the Mongols'," *Harvard Journal of Asiatic Studies*, vol. 14, no. 3/4 (Dec. 1951), see especially footnote 104, pp. 476-8, and brought to my attention by my teacher, Weng Dujian 翁獨健.

[42] Tao Zongyi, *South Village Records Compiled after Returning to the Farm*, ch. 3, p. 37, the entry "Debate on Orthodoxy" 《正統辨》.

That Taizu ascended the throne in the year bingyin 丙寅 (1206), which is included in the *Jāmi' al-Tawārīkh*, has been generally acknowledged in all kinds of historical materials. There is no lack of this kind of record in other sources written by people of the Yuan Dynasty. It was even mentioned in the works of Ouyang Xuan 歐陽玄,[43] who admired the *Debate on Orthodoxy*. Hong Jun was fully aware of this issue, so he explained:

> All the books have no dispute about gengshen [1200] as the year of establishment of the empire. However, there is detailed account in the historical sources of the Western Regions 西域 that they conquered the Tayiči'ut 泰亦赤兀 and defeated the Qatagin 合答斤 and other tribes in the year of the monkey [the year gengshen]. It was at that time that they "took power and secured their hegemony," which they called "establishment of the empire," though this was a little farfetched. However, Taizu said in his imperial edict summoning Qiu Chuji 邱處機 [the Daoist adept]: "In the space of seven years I have accomplished a great task, uniting all under heaven in all directions." It had just been seven years from the year gengshen until he ascended the throne in the year bingyin [1206]. Yang Weizhen 楊維楨 [1296-1370] says: this theory might be based on some valid source, instead of being a totally groundless inference.

As discussed above, that for events prior to 1202 the *Jāmi' al-Tawārīkh* cannot be relied on, so it is difficult to confirm what really happened in the year of the monkey [1200]. Even if these events really happened in the year of the monkey, it barely can be called "took power and secured their hegemony," let alone "establishment of the empire." In addition, Hong Jun using the "imperial edict summoning Qiu Chuji" to explain this matter is in reality a quotation taken out of context and a wild conjecture. The original words can be seen volume ten of the *South Village Records Compiled after Returning from the Farm*, in the entry "Daoist Immortal Qiu" 丘真人:

---

[43] Ouyang Xuan 歐陽玄, *Collected Works of Guizhai* 《 齋文集》, ch. 9, "Spirit Way Stele for Wen Zhengxu" 《文正許先生神 碑》.

> In the space of seven years I have accomplished a great task, uniting all under heaven in all directions. It was not because my conduct was so virtuous, but because the Jin 金 government was unstable. Because I have received the blessing and protection of heaven, I have had the honor to receive the utmost respect [i.e. become Khan]. Our territory joins to the south the Song Dynasty and to the north borders the Uyghurs; the Xia 夏 in the east and the Yi 夷 in the west have both subjected themselves to our rule.

It is very clear in this passage that the "great task" he accomplished in seven years was "uniting all under heaven," with his territory reaching "to the south the Song Dynasty." One of reasons that he was able to achieve this step was because "the Jin government was unstable." Obviously, this had no connection with the union of the Mongolian tribes in 1206. This just refers to the seven year period between 1211 when Chinggis Khan conquered the Jin until 1218 (the year wuyin 戊寅) when he invaded Xixia 西夏 and defeated Koryŏ 高麗, which was a year before he issued the edict summoning Qiu Chuji.

To summarize, both the record in the *Jāmi' al-Tawārīkh* and the collateral evidence in Hong Jun's *Textual Analysis on the Age of Taizu* are insufficient to confirm that Chinggis Khan was born in 1155. Although many scholars have had blind faith in Western writings and have blindly followed Hong Jun's opinion, the renowned researcher into Mongolian history Wang Guowei was an exception. In the chronological sections of his *Complete Report on the Mongolian Tatars Annotated and Corrected* 蒙韃備錄箋證 and his *Collated and Annotated Edition of the Record of the Personal Campaigns of the Holy Warrior* he did not make any statement referring to Chinggis Khan being born in 1155. Instead, in the *Chronological Table of the Tatars* 韃靼年表, which he compiled, he still adopted as Temüjin's birth year the second year of the Jin Dynasty Dading 大定 reign period (1162), as recorded in *The Secret History of Mongols*.[44] Another example is Naka Michiyo, the founder of Japanese research into Mongolian history. In his annotations to the *Veritable Records of Chinggis Khan* 成吉思汗實錄 he quoted at length the *Jāmi' al-Tawārīkh* and the works of Hong Jun, but never annotated that Chinggis Khan was born in 1155. Instead, he without exception relied on the *History of the Yuan* for

---

[44] Wang Guowei 王國維, *Collected Works from the Hall of Observation*, ch. 14, p. 26b.

Taizu's chronology. As mentioned above, he was actually skeptical about the records in the *Jāmi' al-Tawārīkh*. From this we can see that the serious researchers, those who are knowledgeable of the Chinese records, have taken a rather prudent attitude towards this issue.

3. Paul Pelliot's Argument that Chinggis Khan was Born in 1167

On December 9, 1938, at a meeting of the Société Asiatique, Paul Pelliot presented a report claiming that he had discovered Chinese historical material proving that Chinggis Khan was born in 1167, but this was simply Yang Weizhen's *Debate on Orthodoxy*. Because Yang Weizhen had said, "...it is recorded that Taizu of the Song Dynasty was born in the year dinghai 丁亥 [927]...and our Taizu [Chinggis Khan] was born...in the year of the same name," so calculating according to the Heavenly Stems and Earthly Branches system, dinghai was 1167. Pelliot also quoted a sentence from the *Record of the Personal Campaigns of the Holy Warrior* as collateral evidence.[45]

It is very clear to Chinese scholars that Pelliot did not "discover" any new Chinese historical material, but only made superficial changes to Hong Jun's argument in *Textual Analysis on the Age of Taizu*. But because foreign scholars were not very familiar with the Chinese texts, they therefore, one after another, accepted this Sinologist's "authoritative" theory. René Grousset of France introduced this "new success" of Pelliot in his three books on Mongolian history, especially in his *Le conquérant du monde: vie de Gengis-Khan*, where he even confirmed "the most recent research achievement of Pelliot" as a final conclusion.[46] In recent years this theory has become even more prevalent; for example, the Japanese scholar Mori Masao 護雅夫 believes, "the theory of 1167 is the most convincing so far."[47] Therefore, the English version of the *Encyclopedia of Islam*[48] and the Japanese *Dictionary of Asiatic History* 《亞細亞歷史事

---

[45] Société Asiatique, "Séance du 9 Décembre 1938," *Journal Asiatique*, vol. 231 (1939), pp. 133-4; Paul Pelliot, *Notes on Marco Polo*, vol. 1, p. 287 (Paris, 1959).

[46] René Grousset, *L'empire des steppes: Attila, Gengis-Khan, Tamerlan* (Paris, 1939); *L'Empire Mongol*, (Paris, 1941); *Le conquérant du monde: vie de Gengis-khan* (Paris, 1944).

[47] *Encyclopaedic Dictionary of the World* 『世界大百科事典』, ch.19, the entry "Chinggis Khan" (Tokyo, 1957).

[48] John A. Boyle, "Chinggis Khan" in the *Encyclopedia of Islam*, second edition, vol. 2 (Leiden: Brill, 1965). Boyle also translated *Ta'rīkh-i Jahān-Gushā* into English as *The*

典》,[49] both of which were published in 1960, in their entries on Chinggis Khan directly adopted the argument for 1167 as his birth year.*

Whether or not this result is "convincing" can be made clear by looking at the *Essentials of Government of the Three Reigns in the Late Song* 《宋季三朝政要》. Because the phrase Yang Weizhen quoted, "Taizu [Chinggis Khan] was born…in the year of the same name," is ambiguous, it is very difficult to decide whether that he was only using the Earthly Branches [a twelve year cycle] or both the Heavenly Stems and Earthly Branches [a 60 year cycle]. But the *Essentials of Government of the Three Reigns in the Late Song*, the master copy for the *Debate on Orthodoxy*, indicates clearly that "Taizu" "was born in the year yihai," and that "Taizu" was a mistake for "Shizu." Therefore Pelliot's "new discovery" shows he only knew one aspect of this issue, and therefore there are no grounds for his deduction.

Just as Pelliot's premise is not valid, his collateral evidence also has no grounds. He said a sentence in the *Record of the Personal Campaigns of the Holy Warrior* could prove his theory, because it says that in the year bingxu 丙戌 (1226) "the emperor (Chinggis Khan) was sixty already 矣 (yi)." He also strove to refute the record of the dinghai year 丁亥 (1203) that the emperor "in that year was 42." In fact, the phrase "sixty already" has been corrected by textual researchers such as He Qiutao 何秋濤, Wang Guowei, and Naka Michiyo to "sixty five." It is very likely that the character "wu" 五 (five) was miscopied as "yi" 矣 (already) due to unclearness in the original manuscript.[50] If we rely on Pelliot's theory that Chinggis Khan was born in 1167, then the text saying that in the year guihai 癸亥 (1203) he "in that year was 42" must be a mistake for 37. This type of mistake obviously is impossible.

History of the World-Conqueror (Cambridge: Harvard University Press, 1958).

[49] Murakami Masatsugu 村上正二, "Yuan Taizu" 「元太祖」, in *Historical Dictionary of Asia* 『亞細亞歷史事典』 (Tokyo: Heibonsha, 1959-1962), p. 6.

* Translator's note: This can even be seen in Herbert Franke and Denis Twitchett, eds., *The Cambridge History of China, Volume 6, Alien Regimes and Border States, 907-1368* (Cambridge University Press, 1994), p. 333, which cites Pelliot.

[50] Wang Guowei, *Record of the Personal Campaigns of the Holy Warrior, Collated and Annotated*, p. 64; Naka Michiyo, "Textual Criticism and Annotation of the Yuan Dynasty 'Record of the Personal Campaigns of the Holy Warrior'".

IV. Conclusion

As discussed above, that Chinggis Khan was born in 1162 is clearly and unambiguously proven by the most reliable historical source, the *History of the Yuan*, and other various primary sources. This is absolutely certain. Therefore, 1962 is 800th anniversary of the birth of Chinggis Khan.

January 1962 at Inner Mongolian University

This article was first published in *Literature and History* 《文史》, vol. 1, 1962. It was discussed at the Symposium in Memory of the 800th Anniversary of the Birth of Chinggis Khan in that same year. It was later revised.

THE KIRGHIZ AND NEIGHBORING TRIBES IN THE YUAN DYNASTY

Han Rulin 韓儒林

Since the Emperor Jiaqing 嘉慶 (1796-1821) and Emperor Daoguang 道光 (1821-1851) periods of the Qing Dynasty, there has been a great proliferation of studies concerning the territories of China's northwest. There is now a 150 year history behind the efforts of Chinese scholars to identify and locate the politically and economically important places occupied by the Kirghiz and neighboring tribes of the Northwest during the Yuan Dynasty period. In order to understand the contours of the struggle between the Yuan central government and the rebellious princes of the Northwest, one must distinguish the circumstances and geographical outlook of each tribe separately from those of the others, otherwise one would fall into in a thick fog and may miss the important points. Unfortunately Qing scholars were limited by times in which they lived. Lacking detailed maps and foreign source materials, they were also hindered by their deficiencies in the languages of the ethnic minorities who lived in these areas, and their studies progressed and developed in a way that was not sufficiently ideal.

The Yuan sources concerning the Kirghiz and neighboring tribes are extremely disparate, but there are three main sources that provide relatively comprehensive lists of their names: (1) section 239 of *The Secret History of the Mongols* 元朝秘史 (the abbreviated entry for the events of the wuyin 戊寅 year, in the *Record of the Personal Campaigns of the Holy Warrior* 聖武親征錄); (2) the "Appendix on the Northwest" 西北地附錄 in the "Monograph on Geography" 地理志 of the *History of the Yuan* 元史; and (3) the "Treatise on the Tribes" (literally, *Aqwām-i Atrāk* or "Turkish Tribes") in the *Jāmi' al-Tawārīkh* (*Compendium of Chronicles*) by the Persian scholar Rashīd al-Dīn (1247?-1318). This last source was unavailable to Chinese scholars until Hong Jun 洪鈞 (1840-1893) gained access to it at the end of the Qing period.

The first scholar to study the "Appendix on the Northwest" was probably Xu Song 徐松 (1781-1841). Unfortunately, according to Wei Yuan 魏源 (1794-1856) in his preface to his "Map of the Yuan Dynasty Border Regions" 元代疆域圖 (in his *Illustrated Treatise on the Maritime Kingdoms* 海國圖志, chapter three), Xu Song's "Notes to the 'Appendix on the Northwest' in the Yuan Period" 元代西北地附錄注 was never completed. In the 17th year of the Jiaqing era (1812) Xu Song was sent on official business to Ili for seven years, charged with "going out to the frontier, and writing a small handbook, mapping the windings of the mountains and rivers of every place he went." He thus had the practical experience of personally investigating the geography of Xinjiang. Therefore, his *Record of the Water Routes of the Western Regions* 西域水道記 and other works are still highly valued by scholars today, and he has become known as the individual who periodized the study of the northwestern territories. However, he did not go to the Yenisei River basin, but was influenced by the *Outline of the Waterways* 水道提綱.* Therefore, though he correctly identified the Angara 昂可剌 River, he was mistaken in his identification of rivers such as the Abakan (Apu 阿浦) and the Usa (Yuxu 玉須).

Wei Yuan, in his *Illustrated Treatise on the Maritime Kingdoms*, included one map and four studies relating to geographical research of the Northwest during the Yuan Dynasty. His map, called "A Map of the Evolution of the Northwestern Border Regions during the Yuan Period" 元代西北疆域沿革圖, was included in chapter three of this work. The four studies were parts one and two of his "A Study of Expeditions to the Western Regions in the Yuan Period" 元代征西域考 in chapter 32 of the *Illustrated Treatise on the Maritime Kingdoms*, and parts one and two of his "A Study of the Northern Border Regions in the Yuan Period" 元代北方疆域考 in chapter 56. Wei Yuan said: "The Kem 謙 (Qian) River…passes through the regions where various tribes live on its way to the Northern Ocean," and "Understanding the Kem River and the northern mountains will give you a clear conception of the geography of the five tribes (of Mongolia)." However, because he interpreted what on today's maps is the upper reaches of the Angara 安加拉 River as the Kem River of the Yuan period, the locations he assigned to the various tribes were almost all incorrect.

He Qiutao 何秋濤 (1824-1862) was the author of *Complete Historical Record of the Northern Lands* 朔方備乘. He thought that Wei Yuan's "A

* A work in 28 chapters, written by Qi Zhaonan 齊召南 (1706-1768) in 1761, describing the rivers and other bodies of water of the early Qing period, including China, Central Asia, and Tibet. Translator's note.

Study of the Northern Border Regions in the Yuan Period" was yet deficient in places, and included it in chapter 54 of his *Complete Historical Record of the Northern Lands*, supplemented by his own critical suggestions. He had seen rather detailed complete maps of Western countries and geography, and made some breakthroughs concerning the geography of the Kirghiz and other tribes. For example, he said, "The various specialists all thought that the Yenisei (written 伊聶塞) River was the ancient Kem (Qian) River" (chapter 54, page eight), and "the Kem River is probably the Yenisei River of today" (introduction chapter nine, page six). His assessment of the geography of the Kem River was correct. Its route through the various tribal territories was easy to confirm, and he did not make the error that Wei Yuan committed of placing the Qapqana (Qabqana) 撼合納 tribe south of the Onon 斡難 River in eastern Siberia.

Li Wentian 李文田 (1834-1895) made critical annotations to He Qiutao's *Yuan Record of the Personal Campaigns of the Holy Warrior Proofed and Corrected* 校正元聖武親征錄 in his *Notes on The Secret History of the Mongols* 元秘史注, but did not express any opinions on the question of the location of the Kirghiz and other tribes; he only quoted from the "Monograph on Geography" in the *History of the Yuan* and simply made mutual comparisons with it.

Chapter 28 of Hong Jun's *Yuan History Translated and Corrected* 元史譯文証補 was a "Study of the Tribes" 部族考, which was actually a Chinese translation of Rashīd al-Dīn's "Treatise of the Tribes" chapter in the *Jāmi' al-Tawārīkh*, incorporating the results of his own investigations. Unfortunately, only the table of contents [of this chapter] survives, and we do not have the work itself. A note in his "Biography of J̌oči (Jochi) 朮赤," chapter four, page one, explains that according to the sources on the Western regions, "there are eight rivers at the origin of the Kem 謙 River. The Oyirats (Oirats) 衛剌特 live nearby on the left-hand (western) side, and east of it are three tribes: the Urasut 烏拉速特, the Telengüt 帖楞郭特, and the Käšdim 客失的迷. They live west of Lake Baikal; the Oyirats and Kirghiz are their neighbors." Here he is following two passages written in the "Treatise of the Tribes" in the *Jāmi' al-Tawārīkh*, one on the Urs 兀兒速 and other such tribes, and the other on the Oyirat 斡亦剌 tribe. After Hong Jun introduced this record in the *Jāmi' al-Tawārīkh* to East Asian scholarship, Naka Michiyo 那珂通世 (1851-1908) in his "Textual

Criticism and Annotation of the Yuan Dynasty 'Record of the Personal Campaigns of the Holy Warrior'" (*Kōsei zōchū Gen shinsei roku*) 「校正増注元親征録」 (page 101, included in *The Posthumous Works of Naka Michiyo* 『那珂通世遺書』, Tokyo: 1915), Ding Qian 丁謙 (1843-1919) in his *Textual Research on the Secret History of the Mongols* 元秘史考証 (chapter 12, pages 1-2), and Tu Ji 屠寄 (1856-1921) in his *Historical Record of the Mongols* 蒙兀爾史記, chapter three (under the second year of Chinggis Khan) all adopted what Hong Jun had said. However, Hong Jun thought that the Telengüt (written 帖良兀) and the Käšdim (written 客思的迷) tribes were east of the Oyirats, which was obviously mistaken. The conditions under which Hong Jun worked were far superior to that of his predecessors; therefore, in the field of the northwest territories he was able to make huge strides in research concerning the Kirghiz.

Ding Qian followed Shi Shijie 施世傑 (the Qing Dynasty author of *A Study of the Toponyms of Mountains and Rivers in the Secret History of the Mongols* 元秘史山川地名考), Hong Jun, and Li Wentian. He was equipped with what he considered to be an indispensable "detailed map," and also had at his disposal a "double translation of national history," i.e. a copy of Hong Jun's translation of Berezin's (И. Н. Березин) Russian edition of the *Jāmi' al-Tawārīkh*. He should therefore have had good results. However, reading his notes on section 239 in *Textual Research on the Secret History of the Mongols*, one finds him still repeating what Hong Jun had said, without making any new contributions.

The third chapter of Tu Ji's *Historical Record of the Mongols* relates Ǯoči's expedition against the People of the Forest, and chapter 160, which concerns the "Appendix on the Northwest Territories" in the "Monograph on Geography" of the *History of the Yuan*, almost entirely reiterates Hong Jun's views. He not only exaggerates Hong Jun's mistakes, but also arbitrarily changes the words in the *History of the Yuan* to match his opinions. The "Monograph on Geography" in the *History of the Yuan* says that the Kem River "flows into the Angara River," but Tu Ji forces his opinion on the text, insisting that the characters were mistakenly reversed in the original, and changing it to the Angara River "converged into the Kem," in order to make it "closely agree with present-day maps." This is shocking. It is like amending the text of the "Tribute of Yu" 禹貢 chapter in the *Book of Documents* 商書, where it says "From Mount Min [Yu the Great] traced the Yangtze River which, branching off to the east, formed the Tuo River" 岷山導江, 東別為沱, and arguing that, based on modern knowledge of geography, Mount Min should be changed to Mount Tanggula 唐古拉.*

Scholars of previous generations were limited by the era in which they lived, and the magnitude of their accomplishments was various, but we admire their achievements in the face of the hardships they endured in their pioneering work. Without their trailblazing and industrious labors, and the detours they had to take along the way, we would have had to travel along those same circuitous paths ourselves.

The early Japanese specialists in Yuan history, such as Naka Michiyo, author of *Chinggis Khan's Veritable Records* (*Jingis Kan jitsuroku*) 『成吉思汗実録』, a Japanese translation of *The Secret History of the Mongols*, as well as of the work "Textual Criticism and Annotation of the Yuan Dynasty 'Record of the Personal Campaigns of the Holy Warrior'" (mentioned above); and Yanai Wataru 箭内亙, author of *A Study of the Names of the Three Guard-Stations in the Uriyangkhai Region* (*Uryōgō san'ei Meishō kō*) 『兀良哈三衛名称考』, both noted the difficulties surrounding the Kirghiz. These studies are familiar to scholars in China, so I will not discuss them in detail here.

The ancient history of Siberia attracted a lot of attention from Western scholars in the 17th and 18th centuries, due to the Dutch scholar Nicholas Witsen's *Noord en Oost Tartarye* (*Tatar Territories' North and East*) of 1692, and the Swedish scholar and prisoner of war P. J. Strahlenberg's *Das nord und östliche Theil von Europa und Asia* (*Northern and Eastern Eurasia*) of 1730. Later on, Russian scholars continued to make it the subject of their inquiries. After World War II, the Soviets engaged in large-scale investigations and excavations in the Khakas-Minusinsk basin and the Altai and Tuva regions, but unfortunately their works are not easy for us to obtain in China. As for the studies of the Kirghiz and other tribes in the Yuan period done by Western oriental scholars, we are handicapped by our lack of knowledge and experience, having seen very few of them. The most important of those that we have been able to consult are Paul Pelliot's posthumous works: *Notes sur l'histoire de la Horde d'or* (1950), *Histoire des Campagnes de Gengis Khan (Cheng-wou ts'in-tcheng lou)* with Louis Hambis (Leiden: Brill, 1951), *Notes critiques d'histoire Kalmouke* (Paris: Librarie d'Amérique et d'Orient, Adrien-Maisonneuve,

* Tanggula is in Qinghai 青海 where Yangtze River originates. Translator's note.

1960), and others. Section 239 of *The Secret History of the Mongols* lists the names of all the Kirghiz tribes, both east and west, which were conquered by Ǯoči during his expedition against the People of the Forest. Pelliot translates this section into French on page five of his *Notes critiques d'histoire Kalmouke*, and includes detailed notes on pages 56-64 (notes 34-60). His colleague Louis Hambis wrote "Notes sur Käm: Nom de L'Yénissei Supérieur," published in *Journal Asiatique* 244 (1956), pages 281-300, and "Käštim et Ges-dum," published in *Journal Asiatique* 246 (1958), pages 313-327. These two articles treat the Kirghiz and other tribes. Their linguistic studies regarding the interpretation of these tribal names, and their well-documented and extensive evidence, and detailed textual research are very stimulating for the reader. However, their original works are all extant and available for consultation; it is therefore not necessary to repeat here what is said in these essays.

After China's liberation in 1949, a large number of ancient texts were reprinted, some in punctuated editions, and these have made this work considerably easier for historians. However, most of these works are not indexed, and if scholars wish to find specific information in a certain book, they have to read the whole book from beginning to end, searching for items one at a time. Modern libraries now have digitized collections, and our view is that at this time when computer equipment is not universally available, we should create categorized indices of the important subjects in the 24 histories, the *Comprehensive Mirror for Aid in Government* 資治通鑑, and other important works, providing short quotations from the original sources, in order to save scholars' time in consulting and searching. The indices of the Liao, Jin, Yuan, and other histories that have been done in Japanese academic circles, which include short quotations from the original texts, are used universally by Chinese and foreign scholars alike when searching for things in these works. Almost all the scholars in China who study the northwestern territories have come into contact with quotations from the *History of the Yuan* in essays concerning the Kirghiz and the region of Kemkemjihud (Kem Kemji'üt, Qianqianzhou 謙謙州 or 欠欠州, the present-day Tuva Republic of Russia). However, Tamura Jitsuzō's *Collection of Vocabulary Used in the History of the Yuan* (*Genshi goi shūsei*) 『元史語匯集成』 lists these materials separately under abbreviated tribal names such as Ji 吉 and Qi 乞 (two different Chinese transcriptions of Kirghiz in Yuan sources), or Qian 謙 and Qian 欠 (two different Chinese transcriptions of Kemkemjihud in

Yuan sources), and treats the other surrounding tribes in a similar fashion, enabling one to find them at a glance, and saving scholars the labor of having to peruse through and pick out material.

I. The Locations of the Various Kirghiz Tribes

Section 239 of *The Secret History of the Mongols* says: "In the year of the hare (1207), Chinggis Khan sent J̌oči with the troops of the right wing on an expedition against the People of the Forest 林中的百姓 (called *hoiyin irgen* in *The Secret History of the Mongols*). Buqa 不合 went with him acting as a guide. Quduqa Beki 忽都合別乞 of the Oyirat came to submit ahead of the Tümen Oyirat. He came and, acting as a guide, led J̌oči to the territory of the Tümen Oyirat and made them submit at the Šiqšit 失黑失惕 River. J̌oči brought the Oyirat 斡亦剌惕, Buriyat 不里牙惕, Barqun 巴爾渾, Ursut 兀兒速惕, Qapqana 合卜合納思 (Qabqana), Qangqa 康合思, and Tubas 禿巴思 under submission. When he reached *the territory of* the Tümen Kirgisut, their leaders Yedi Inal 也迪亦納勒, Aldi Er 阿勒迪額爾, and Örebek Digin 斡列別克的斤 – came to submit….After J̌oči had subjugated the People of the Forest from the Šibir 失必爾, Kesdim (Käšdiyim, Käšdim,客思的音), Bayit 巴亦惕, Tuqas 禿合思, Tenlek (Tänläk,田列克), Tö'eles (Tö'öläs,脫額列思), Tas 塔思, and Bajiqit 巴只吉 up to this side, he came back bringing with him the commanders of ten thousand and of thousands of the Kirgisut and the leaders of the People of the Forest."*

According the record in this section of *The Secret History*, the Kirghiz can be taken as central, and the People of the Forest can be divided into eastern and western groups. Although we cannot be absolutely certain precisely where they all lived, we can specify either exactly or roughly the geographic position inhabited by most of the tribes.

1. Oyirat 斡亦剌 (Oirat)

In 1953, the archaeological team of the Science Committee of the Mongolian Peoples Republic discovered a stone inscription called the

---

* English translation taken from Igor de Rachewiltz, trans., *The Secret History of the Mongols*, vol. 1 (Leiden: Brill, 2006), p. 164, very slightly modified. Translator's note.

Stele of the Śākya Temple 釋迦院碑, which was erected in the summer of the dingsi 丁巳 year (1257) during the reign of Emperor Xianzong 憲宗 (Möngke Khan) in the Yuan period. It had been set up by the Oyirat 外剌 royal son-in-law 駙馬 Baltu 八立托 and Princess Yixiye 公主一悉葉 on the northern shore of the Delger 德勒格 River, a branch of the Selenga River in the third *bage* 巴格 of Arbulagh (Arbulag) district (*sum*) in Khövsgöl province. The inscription is written in both Chinese and Mongolian. This place must have been the Oyirats' summer palace and one of their centers of political activity.[1]

Heading upstream, northwest on the Delger River, one crosses over the watershed at the eastern end of the Tannu 唐努 Mountain range and reaches the upper source of the Kaa Kem 華克木 River, which is the Šišqit 錫什錫德 River (Shishkhid-ghool). Pelliot thought that *shishkhid* (*shishqit*) should be identified with *shikhshid*, caused by the two middle consonants, q and sh, being reversed. This is probably correct.[2] The region that the Oyirat and Tubas tribes surrendered to J̌oči was in the basin of this river.

Rashīd al-Dīn's "Treatise on the Tribes" in the *Jāmi' al-Tawārīkh* says, under the heading "The Ouriats, Yūrat": "The camp (literally, yurt) and dwelling place of this people, the Ouriat (Oyirat) is in the basin of the [eight] rivers*…and from that place, the rivers flow outward and converge into a single river, called Kem 謙 (Qian), and afterwards the Kem River flows into the Angara 昂哥剌 (Anqura in Persian) River." The Kaa Kem River, which is at the upper source of the Kem River, has many tributaries, and the so-called eight rivers should be some of its tributaries. This suggests that the major portion of the Oyirat tribe lived in the river basins of the Delger and Kaa Kem Rivers.

Sir Henry H. Howorth, in his *History of the Mongols* (London: 1876), volume one, page 682, also once conducted work on investigating the eight rivers, relying on an excerpt from Rashīd al-Dīn's description of the Oyirats that was recorded in Abū al-Ghāzī Bahādur Khān's *Šajara-yi*

[1] Х. Пэрлээ (Khodoogiĭn Pèrlèè), "К истории древних городов и поселений в Монголии" ("On Ancient Mongolian Cities and the History of their Settlements"), with a facsimile of the inscription at the Śākya temple 釋迦院, *Советская археология* (*Soviet Archaeology*), 1957, no. 3, pp. 43-53.

[2] Paul Pelliot, *Notes critiques d'histoire Kalmouke*, in *Oeuvres Posthumes de Paul Pelliot*, vol. 6 (Paris: Librairie d'Amerique et d'Orient, Adrien-Maisonneuve, 1960), p. 57.

* Kūk, Ūn, Qarā Ūsūn, SNBY Tūn, Aqra, Āg, Jūrčah, and Čaghān. Translator's note.

*Turk.** Whether or not Abū al-Ghāzī Bahādur Khān's work was correct in its transcription of the names of these eight rivers, Howorth's search for them among the tributaries of the Angara River was truly a futile endeavor. As for the relationship between the Angara and Kem Rivers, the "Appendix on the Northwestern Territories" in the "Monograph on Geography" of the *History of the Yuan* and the Kirghiz section in the *Jāmi' al-Tawārīkh* both say that the Kem flowed into the Angara. This was the Yuan Dynasty geographic conception. According to the sources that we were able to consult in Nanjing – the Berezin edition of the *Jāmi' al-Tawārīkh* (page 101), the 1958 Russian translation of the *Jāmi' al-Tawārīkh* (volume one, part one, page 112), and the *Šajara-yi Turk* (see above; our edition is in Arabic) used by Howorth – regarding the names of these eight rivers, these three books all transcribe five of them differently, with the other three being exceptions, as they are named after colors. I am afraid it is dangerous to conduct an investigation into comparative phonology relying on unconfirmable transcriptions. Hambis, in his "Notes sur Käm," once tried to locate the eight rivers among the branches of the Bii Kem 貝克木 (Biy Kem, Upper Yenisei) and Kaa Kem Rivers, but his investigative work was still not entirely satisfactory ("Notes sur Kam, nom de I'Yenissei superieur," *Journal Asiatique*, no. 244 [1956], pages 285-286).

2. Buriat 不里牙惕 (Buliyati)

These are the present-day Buriat 布里雅特 people who live on the eastern side of Lake Baikal. This tribe is not treated in the *Jāmi' al-Tawārīkh*.

3. Barqun 巴爾渾

The *Jāmi' al-Tawārīkh* has Barqūt. This tribe lived east of Lake Baikal in the Barqujin 巴爾忽津 River basin. In the Chinese province of Heilongjiang there are both new and old Barqut 巴爾虎 people, therefore Chinese scholars have for a long time identified the Barqutai 巴爾忽歹 with this tribe.

---

* Abū al-Ghāzī Bahādur Khān, 1603-1663, was sultan of Khiva and a Chaghatay historian. *Šajara-yi Turk* (*Genealogical Tree of the Turkmen*), 1665; the title in Arabic is *Shajarat al-Atrāk*. Translator's note.

4. Ursut 兀爾速惕

The *Jāmi' al-Tawārīkh* has Ūrāsūt. The "Annals of Yingzong" 英宗紀 (Suddhipala, reigned 1320-1323) in the *History of the Yuan* writes it as Wuersu 兀爾速; the "Monograph on Geography" writes it as Urs 烏斯. Hong Jun said: "On Russian maps, the Urs River is in the upper reaches of the Yenisei River, and enters it from the east. There are two villages on the banks of this river, called Upper and Lower Wusa 烏薩, whose pronunciation is similar to Urs. The *History of the Yuan* says that Urs is named after a river north of the Kem 謙 (Qian) River, which is consistent with what the other sources say" (Hong Jun, *Supplement to the Translation of the History of the Yuan Dynasty* 元史譯文証補, chapter 26b, page 12). It seems that the Urs tribe lived in the mountainous area north of the Sayan Mountain Range 薩彥嶺, where the road was very steep and precipitous. It is easy to imagine how difficult it would have been for traveling. It is understandable that the Yuan government especially established two postal stations at Ursut (Urs).[3]

5. Qapqana 撼合納

The *Jāmi' al-Tawārīkh* does not have an entry on this tribe. The "Monograph on Geography" in the *History of the Yuan* says that this tribe "is east of the Urs, at the origin of the Kem River." The southern source of the Kem River, the Kaa Kem, is the place where the Oyirat tribes lived, as noted above. The Qapqana River, which was shaped like a cloth sack, must have been in the valley of the Kem's northern source, the Bii Kem River. Hong Jun had already pointed out that this valley was due east of the Urs tribe. Pelliot drew up its name as "Qapqanas," saying that the Turkish word *qap* means "sack": "It is true that there is a clan of the Bajiqit 巴只吉惕 tribe named Qapqa, but this name, if we wish to seek its etymology, is best explained by the Turkish word *qapqan*, which means 'a trap for catching birds and foxes.' It passed into Mongolian in the form *khabkha*, and even into Russian as *kapkan*" (Pelliot, *Notes critiques d'histoire Kalmouke*, page 58).

---

[3] See Chen Dezhi 陳得芝, "A Study of the Postal Routes in Yuan Dynasty Lingbei Province" 《元嶺北行省諸驛道考》, *Collected Papers of Research on Yuan History and Northern Nationalities History* 《元史及北方民族史研究集刊》, Nanjing University 南京大學, no. 1 (1977).

6. Qangqa 康合思
Nothing is known about this tribe. The *Jāmi' al-Tawārīkh* has no entry on it.

7. Tubas 禿巴思
Tubas is the plural of Tuba. See Han Rulin, "Tang Dynasty Dubo"《唐代都波》, *Social Science Front*《社會科學戰綫》, no. 3 (1978).

8. Kirghiz 乞兒吉思
The Kirghiz entry in the "Treatise on the Tribes" of the *Jāmi' al-Tawārīkh* says, "the two regions of Kirghiz and Kemkemjihud adjoin each other, and form a single country." On the northern frontier there are not many places that could have served as political or economic centers. Considering geographical conditions, historical records, and archaeological finds, only the upper regions of the Yenisei River, the Minusinsk (Минусинск) plain, and the Tannu Uriankhai 唐努烏梁海 (Tuva, Тувя) basin could have been cultivated or used as grazing lands for animal herds, and would have qualifications as centers of political activity. Archaeological discoveries from these two regions of the upper reaches of the Yenisei River have included a Han Dynasty Li Ling Temple 李陵宮,[4] a copper mirror from the Former Han Dynasty,[5] an ancient tomb,[6] a Tang Dynasty Turkish stone inscription,[7] copper coins from the Tang Dynasty Huichang 會昌 (841-846) reign period,[8] a Yuan Dynasty city complete with agricultural tools,[9] and official tallies 符牌.[10]

---

[4] С. В. Киселев (S. V. Kiselev), *Древняя история Южной Сибири* (*The Ancient History of South Siberia*) (Москва: Академия наук СССР, 1951), pp. 479-84.

[5] Yang Liansheng, "An Inscribed Han Mirror Discovered in Siberia," *T'oung Pao*, vol. 42 (1954), pp. 330-40.

[6] С. В. Киселев (S. V. Kiselev), *Древняя история Южной Сибири* (*The Ancient History of South Siberia*) (Москва: Академия наук СССР, 1951), pp. 479-84.

[7] Wilhelm Radloff, "Die altturkischen Inschriften aus dem Flussgebiete des Jenissei," in *Die alttürkischen Inschriften der Mongolei* (1895-1899), vol. 1, pp. 299-326.

[8] Ibid.

[9] С. В. Киселев (S. V. Kiselev), et al., *Древнемонгольские города* (*Ancient Mongolian Cities*) (Москва: Академия наук СССР, 1965), pp. 59-119.

[10] "The journey from Cha-Kul (Qianqianzhou 欠欠州) to Minnusinsk (*sic*, Kirghiz) is reckoned to take from three to five days" (Douglas Carruthers, *Unknown Mongolia: A Record of Travel and Exploration in North-west Mongolia and Dzungaria*, 2nd ed. [London: Hutchinson & Co, 1914], p. 110). In the *History of the Yuan*, chapter 20, the

What is today the lower reaches of the Yenisei River is where the Angara tribe lived during the Yuan period. Hong Jun said that "the Angara, since 'the night was as short as the time it takes to roast spareribs' must have been approximately 60 degrees north, and the Kem, which flowed into it must have been between 58 and 59 degrees" (*Supplement to the Translation of the History of the Yuan Dynasty*, page 26). Therefore the Angara tribe, which was a vassal state of the Kirghiz, must have been located beyond the convergence of the two rivers in the lower reaches of the Yenisei River.

9. Šibir 失必爾

Under the heading for the Kirghiz in the "Treatise on the Tribes" of the *Jāmi' al-Tawārīkh*, it says, "The Angara River flows to the border of the territory of the Ibir Šibir 亦必爾・失必爾 tribe." This is one of the northernmost tribes of the People of the Forest. During Qaidu's 海都 rebellion in the Yuan period, Uwaš 玉哇失 with a Ba'arin 八憐 general and others once "did battle at Ibir Šibir" (see *History of the Yuan*, chapter 132).

In the first half of the 14th century al-'Umārī stated in *Masālik al-absār fī mamālik al-amsār* (*The Routes toward Insights of the Capital Kingdoms*) that the territory of Šibir was extremely cold and was covered with snow. Ibn Arab Shah (d. 1450) said that the northern part of Qïpčaq 欽察 territory is near the land of Šibir. In the 16th century, when the Tsarist Russians invaded western Siberia, they found a city called Šibir, the capital city of the Tatar Kucum Khan, on the Irtysh (Иртыш) River in the

---

fifth year of the Dade 大德 reign period, it says, "From Činqai 稱海 to the northern borders 北境, the 12 postal stations were covered with snow." The term "northern borders" probably refers to an area within the territory of the Kirghiz. Indeed there were two postal routes through Kirghiz territory, one connected to the Činqai and the other to the Oyirats. In 1846, an "Official Tablet of the Zhiyuan period" 至元國書牌 was discovered in the region of Minusinsk; see E. A. Wallis Budge's English translation, *The Monks of Kublai Khan* (London, 1928), p. 62, illustration 5; and Haneda Tōru 羽田亨, *Genchō ekiden zakkō* 『元朝駅傳雑考』 (*The Postal Stations of the Yuan Dynasty*), facsimile reproduction 11 at the end of the volume. A circular tally was unearthed in the Tobolsk region (see Haneda Tōru, *The Postal Stations of the Yuan Dynasty*, facsimile reproduction 4). This is evidence that the Yuan Dynasty postal route went to these two places.

upper reaches of the Tobolsk (Тобольск) River, 16 Russian miles from the source of the Irtysh River. In 1581 it was captured by Yermak, the leader of the Kazakh 哥薩克 people, and remains of it can still be found. Based on this we can imagine the geographic extent of Šibir during the Yuan and Ming periods.

10. Käšdiyim (Käšdim, Kesdim) 客思的音

The name of this tribe is written Käšdim 客失的迷 in the *Record of the Personal Campaigns of the Holy Warrior*. This name, KshDM, was seen early in a Tang Dynasty Turkish language cliff face inscription, the Tannu Uriankhai Kemkemjihud (Kemchik 克木池克) *Qaya Baši* (*Qaya Bashi*) *Inscription*. The cliff face inscription says: "[As] the Regional Chief of Yinanzhu 伊難珠・俱祿・剌史・匐, I am the most highly venerated one in the six tribes of Keshdim."[11] This cliff is on the right-hand (western) bank of the Kemchik River, directly across from the entrance where on the left-hand (eastern) bank the tributary Ishkem 亦失克木 River flows into the Kemchik River. According to the map in Douglas Carruthers' *Unknown Mongolia* (London: Hutchinson, 1913), this is precisely at the western end of the ancient road between the Uluq Kem 烏魯克木 and Kemchik Rivers.

Pelliot and Hambis both have done relatively detailed research on the name of this tribe. Pelliot said, "I can trace the name of the Käštäm in Chinese texts back to an account which must be dated 652."[12] On the back of one of the old Tibetan language manuscripts which he took from Dunhuang (number 1283), there is an eighth century report to the Uyghur king concerning a five-man Uyghur mission that had been ordered to investigate the rulers of the northern territories. The mission itinerary refers to thirty-five tribes (line 63 of the manuscript). In Basmil 拔悉密 territory, there was a tribe called Ges-dum, which Pelliot thought was the Kesdim. But, Pelliot passed away before he had time to publish his results.[13] Later, Hambis later wrote the article, "Käštim et Ges-dum," in

[11] Wilhelm Radloff, "Die Inschriften auf der Felswand Kemtschik-Kaja-Baschy," in *Die alttürkischen Inschriften der Mongolei* (St. Petersburg, 1897), vol. 1, p. 326.

[12] Paul Pelliot, *Notes sur l'histoire de la Horde d'or*, in *Oeuvres Posthumes de Paul Pelliot*, vol. 2 (Paris: Librairie d'Amerique et d'Orient, Adrien-Maisonneuve, 1949), p. 142.

[13] Jacques Bacot, "Reconnaissance en haute Asie septentrionale par cinq envoyés ouigours au VIIIe siècle," *Journal Asiatique*, no. 244 (1956), pp. 137-53.

which he undertook an explanation. He considered it to be Keshichan 可史襜, which had sent an envoy to pay tribute during the Yonghui 永徽 reign period of the Tang (in 652), as recorded in the "Legendary Nations (of the Northwest)" 鬼國 section of the *Encyclopaedic History of Institutions* 通典, chapter 200. This tribe lived in the Kemkemjihud River basin during the Tang Dynasty. The English translation of *Hudūd al-'Ālam* says that in 982 the tribe lived west of the Kirghiz 黠戛斯 (page 286).[14] In the Yuan Dynasty it was part of the land granted to Qorči 豁爾赤. In the Ming and Qing periods, according to John F. Baddeley's color map of the ethnic groups who lived in this region in 1673, in his *Russia, Mongolia, China: Being Some Record of the Relations Between Them from the Beginning of the 17th Century to the Death of the Tsar Alexei Mikhailovich, A.D. 1602-1676* (London: Macmillan and Company, 1919), the people who lived in the northern part of the upper reaches of the Ob River (number 43) were the Käšdim tribe (volume one, page 140), and those who lived in the southern part of it (number 25) were the Telengüt (volume one, page 139). It seems that even in modern times there is an Ach-Kestim population in this region living with members of the Telengüt (Teleut) clan mixed among them.[15] Today they are in the Gorno-Altai Autonomous Regions – see the article in the *Great Soviet Encyclopedia*, edited by A. M. Prokhorov (New York: Macmillan, 1973). It seems that this tribe lived has not significantly changed its location for the past 1,000 years.

11. Bait 巴亦惕

The *Jāmi' al-Tawārīkh* does not record this tribe. There are Bait people in Khovd 科布多 [in Western Mongolia]. In 1912, B. Ia. Vladimirtsov (Б. Я. Владимирцов) wrote *A Report on the Bait People of the Khovd Region* (*Отчет о командировке к баитам Кобдоского округа*) (St. Petersburg). Although this title refers to people of the same name, we do not know if it is the same tribe.

12. Tuqas 禿合思

The *Jāmi' al-Tawārīkh* does not record this tribe.

---

[14] Louis Hambis, "Käštim et Ges-dum," *Journal Asiatique*, no. 246 (1958), p. 315.

[15] Pelliot, *Notes critiques d'histoire Kalmouke*, p. 60.

13. Telengüt 田列克

According to the order in which the various tribes are named, compared to that in *Record of the Personal Campaigns of the Holy Warrior*, previous scholars have all specified this tribe as the Telengüt (帖良兀 Tieliangwu), but without providing a rationale. Pelliot thought that there was a phoneme out of place in the Mongolian "Tenleg," and that it should be "Teleng."[16] This is a worthwhile suggestion. The plural of Teleng is Telengüt. He also said, "the name of this tribe is already seen from the various Turkish stele inscriptions of the Orkhon 嗢昆 River."[17] However, he did not indicate the names of the steles. Friedrich Hirth says, in his *Nachwörte zur Inschrift des Tonjukuk* (page 133), "According to Gustav Schlegel's book, *Uigurischen Denkmal*, volume one, page one, 'Duolange' 多覽葛 is pronounced To-lam-kat in Cantonese, which is Telengut." The first seven pages of Schlegel's book consists of a section he wrote on Uyghur chronology, "Die Chronologischer Abriss der Geschichte der Uiguren,"[18] but this too does not indicate which stele contains the name Telengut. The academic world concurs that the so-called Orkhon River stele is one of the Tang Dynasty Turkish language Kül Tegin 闕特勤, Bilgä Qaghan 毗伽可汗, or other steles, but none of these steles record this name.

The Orkhon River Turkish inscription steles were discovered in 1889, and in 1893 they began to be decoded. Starting in 1892, the Russian Orkhon River investigation team published a set named *Reports by the Investigative Team of the Orkhon River* (*Сборникъ трудовъ Орхонской Экспедицiи*) and a set called *Catalog of the Ancient Objects of Mongolia* (*Каталог древних предметов Монголии*). On August 23rd 1900, the French scholar Édouard Chavannes published a French translation of them in his *Documents sur les T'ou-kiue (Turcs) occidentaux*, and presented it to the Imperial Academy of Sciences in St. Petersburg. In 1903 this became the sixth volume of the *Reports by the Investigative Team of the Orkhon River*, published in the Russian capital. He was absolutely no stranger to the content of the Orkhon River steles. He too used Duolange as the transliteration for "Telangoutes." However, he indeed said that "the Duolange were the Telangoutes as recorded in Rashīd al-Dīn's *Jāmi' al-*

---

[16] Pelliot, *Notes sur l'histoire de la Horde d'or*, p. 142.
[17] Pelliot, *Notes critiques d'histoire Kalmouke*, p. 73.
[18] Gustav Schlegel, *Chinesische Inschrift auf dem uigurischen Denkmal in Kara Balgassun* (Helsingfors: Société Finno-ougrienne, 1896), pp. 1-7.

Tawārīkh, who lived in the territory of the Kirghiz and Kem-Kemdjoute" (*Documents sur les T'ou-kiue (Turcs) Occidentaux*, page 369).

The place where the Telengüt tribe lived was in the present-day Gorno-Altai Autonomous Region. In 1859, Wilhelm Radloff was still able to go among the Teleut tribe in the region of the Altai Mountains to investigate Turkish dialects.[19]

14. Tö'eles 脫額列思

The "Treatise on the Tribes" in the *Jāmi' al-Tawārīkh* (Berezin edition, page 108) writes the name of this tribe as Tūlās. In footnote 55 it is written Tūālās. Pelliot said, "At least as a name, I have little doubt that it is connected to the very well-known Tölös or Töles of the Orkhon River steles."[20] Can the problem be this simple? Note that only the two forms, Tölis and Töls, appear in the Orkhon River steles.[21] From the time when all of the steles were discovered began to be decoded, scholars of each country had a different way of reading the word – Tölis, Töles, Tölös, Tölish, Tölesh, etc. In fact, the other transliterations, apart from Tölis, are all interpreted based on their subjective opinions.

Wilhelm Radloff read Tölis as Töles, and Töls as Tölös.[22] Vilhelm Thomsen at first read them all as Tölis,[23] but later as Tölish.[24] S. E. Malov

---

[19] Wilhelm Radloff, *Versuch eines Wörterbuch der Turk. Dialekte* (St. Petersburg, 1893-1911), preface.

[20] Pelliot, *Notes critiques d'histoire Kalmouke*, p. 60.

[21] Wilhelm Radloff, *Die alttürkischen Inschriften der Mongolei*, vol. 1; line 13 of the eastern side of the Kül Tegin stele has Tölis (Radloff, p. 10). It is written Töls in line 12 of the eastern side of the Bilgä Qaghan stele (Radloff, p. 48); in line 13 of the southern side, according to Сергей Ефимович Малов (Sergeĭ Efimovich Malov), in *Памятники древнетюркской письменности Монголии и Киргизии* (*Monuments of Ancient Turkish Writing of Mongolia and Kyrgyzia*) (Москва-Ленинград: Издательство Академии наук СССР, 1959), p. 15, in the carved inscription on the stone column in front of the Bilgä Qaghan tomb (Radloff, *Die alttürkischen Inschriften* , p. 243); and in line 1 of the Uyghur *Moyunčor Inscription* 《磨延啜碑》 (Malov, *Monuments of Ancient Turkish Writing of Mongolia and Kyrgyzia*, p. 30).

[22] Wilhelm Radloff, *Die alttürkischen Inschriften der Mongolei*, vol. 1 (St. Petersburg: 1894), pp. 1, 129, 426. Vilhelm Thomsen, in his *Inscriptions de l'Orkhon déchiffrées* (Helsingfors: Société de la litterature finnoise, 1896), p. 146, quotes Radloff's work *Aus Sibiren: Lose Blätter aus dem Tagebuche eines reisenden linguisten* (Leipzig: T. O. Weigel, 1884), saying, "Even now, there is still a group of people called Tölös among the tribes in the Altai Mountains." This is the reasoning behind Radloff's reading of Töls as Tölös.

read Töls as Töles.[25] Pelliot on the one hand chose Tölös or Töles as a way of writing the name, in order to show its connection with Tö'eles. However, on the other hand, he said that Töles was Tölesh (falsely read Tölös), a name that appears in the various steles from the Orkhon River. Therefore he read it as Tölesh.[26] Not only did he fail to explain why certain different versions of the name were advocated at different times, but he also did not mention whether this tribal name had been transliterated into Chinese in the Tang historical records. The content of lines one to 30 on the eastern side of the Kül Tegin stele and lines one to 23 of the Bilgä Qaghan stele are in fact identical. The Töls of the 12th line on the eastern side of the Bilgä Qaghan stele is the same as the Tölis of the 13th line on the eastern side of the Kül Tegin stele. We do not know why each had to be written differently.

As to whether Tölis had been transliterated into Chinese in the Tang sources, Radloff at first seems not to have done any investigative work. Thomsen thought it was a transliteration of Tiele 鐵勒.[27] Chavannes adopted Radloff's reading of it as Tölös, but for transliteration he held Thomsen's view.[28] Gustav Schlegel said that Chile 敕勒 and Tiele were pronounced *Tit-lik* in Guangdong pronunciation, and he expressed doubt about using these names as transliterations of either Tölös or Töles.[29] Josef Marquart, relying on the Turkish stele inscriptions and both the *Tang*

---

23 Vilhelm Thomsen, *Inscriptions de l'Orkhon déchiffrées* (1896), p. 102, the content of lines 1-30 of the eastern side of the Kül Tegin stele and lines 3-23 of the eastern side of the Bilgä Qaghan stele is identical. The Töls of the Bilgä Qaghan stele is the Tölis of the Kül Tegin stele; it should of course be read as Tölis.

24 Vilhelm Thomsen, "Alttürkische Inschriften aus der Mongolei," *Zeitschrift der Deutschen Morgenlandischen Gesellschaft*, New Series 3, cumulative vol. 78 (1924), pp. 121-75, especially p. 147.

25 С. Е. Малов (S. E. Malov), *Памятники древнетюркской письменности* (*Monuments of Ancient Turkic Writing: Texts and Research*) (Москва-Ленинград: Издательство Академии наук СССР, 1951), p. 38; S. E. Malov, *Monuments of Ancient Turkish Writing of Mongolia and Kyrgyzia*, p. 18.

26 Pelliot, *Notes sur l'histoire de la Horde d'or*, p. 142.

27 Thomsen, *Inscriptions de l'Orkhon déchiffrées*, pp. 61 and 146.

28 Édouard Chavannes, *Documents sur les T'ou-kiue (Turcs) occidentaux* (St. Petersburg, 1903), p. 71; see also Friedrich Hirth, "Nachworte zur Inschrift des Tonjukuk" (暾欲谷), included in Radloff, *Die alttürkischen Inschriften der Mongolei*, vol. 2 (St. Petersburg, 1899), pp. 1-129, especially p. 37.

29 Gustav Schlegel, *Chinesische Inschrift auf dem uigurischen Denkmal in Kara Balgassun* (Helsingfors: Société Finno-ougrienne, 1896), p. 2.

Histories, took the view that the *šad* 設 was the ruler Tarduš 達頭, and that therefore Tölis was of course under the jurisdiction of a *yabghu* 葉護.[30] Thomsen held the same view as Marquart. They thought that in both the stele inscriptions and the *Tang Histories*, the "right wing" 右廂 and "left wing" 左廂 probably corresponded to what the *Tang Histories* called, respectively, the southern and northern tribes. However, Thomsen did not agree. He thought that the Tarduš who lived on the west corresponded to the right wing, and that the Tulishi 突利施 (Töliš) who lived on the east corresponded to the left wing.[31] However, the character "tu" 突, which occurs in both Türk 突厥 and Türgiş 突騎施, is classified as belonging to the *mo* 没 rime, which included all foreign sounds ending with a –t (or other consonant), and according to Tang Dynasty rules of transliteration, it should be written as Tür. So why should the character "tu" in Tulishi be transliterated as Tö (Töliš)? This is still an open question. Given the circumstances under which the above-mentioned specialists carried out their research, we can only suggest that the Tö'eles (Tūlās, Tūālās) tribe of the Yuan Dynasty evolved from the Töliš (Tölis = Töls) tribe of the Tang Dynasty.

---

[30] Joseph Marquart, *Die Chronologie der Alttürkischen Inschriften* (Leipzig: Dieterich, 1898), p. 52. The eastern side of the Turkish Kül Tegin stele says, in lines 13-14 "[my father, the kagan] (also organized there) the Tölis (Tulishi 突利施) and the Tarduš (Datou 達頭) (peoples), and gave them a *yabghu* 葉護 and a *šad* 設. To the right (south) the Great Tang (the Chinese people)…to the left (north) Baz Khan…" [see Talât Tekin, *A Grammar of Orkhon Turkic*, Uralic and Altaic Series, vol. 69 (Bloomington: Indiana University Press, 1968), p. 265; translator's note]. The *New Tang History* 《新唐書》, chapter 217b, "Account of the Xueyantuo" 《薛延陀傳》, says, "Yinan 夷男…had 200,000 crack troops, and appointed his two sons, Tarduš 大度設 and Töliš 突利失, to command the two branches of his army, and called them the northern and southern tribes." The *Old Tang History* 《舊唐書》, chapter 194a, in the section on the "Turks" says: "Qutluq 骨咄祿…set himself up as khan, and appointed his younger brother Bak čör 默啜 as *šad* 設 and Duoxi beg 咄悉匐 as *yabghu*." *Important Documents of the Tang* 《唐會要》, chapter 94, says: "Mochuo 默啜 [Qapaghan Qaghan] set up his younger brother Duoxi Beg as *šad* of the left wing 左相察 and Qutluq's son Mek-kiu 默矩 as *šad* of the right wing 右相察. Each commanded over 20,000 troops." Marquart came to his conclusion based on the above-mentioned Chinese and Turkish sources.

[31] Vilhelm Thomsen, *Turcica: études concernant l'interprétation des inscriptions turques de la Mongolie et de la Sibérie* (Helsingfors: Société Finno-ougrienne, 1916), p. 98.

Barqut 巴爾忽惕, Tö'eles 脫額列思, and Qori 豁里 are listed together in the same section of the "Treatise on the Tribes" in the *Jāmi' al-Tawārīkh*. They were neighbors of each other and were closely related. For instance, "Ariq-Böke 阿里不哥 had a concubine…she was a Tö'eles, from the Barqut branch."[32] They lived at a place called Barqujin pass (巴爾忽真 or 巴爾忽津). However, the Tö'eles were also a tribe when Qorči was in the Altai region. For this reason, we believe that they, like the Ba'arin̩ tribe, probably joined Qorči when he moved from the east to the west.

15. The Tas tribe 塔思部

Nothing is known about them and they are not recorded in the *Jāmi' al-Tawārīkh*.

16. Bajiqit (Bajǐgit) 巴只吉惕

This name also appears in sections 262 and 270 of *The Secret History of the Mongols*. John of Plano Carpini called them "the Bascarts or great Hungary"; they were thought to be the ancient Hungarians, or Huns.[33] William of Rubruck calls them Pascatir, and also identifies them with "greater Hungary." He says: "After traveling 12 days from the Etilia (Itil, the Turkish name for the Volga), we found a great river which they call Jagac (Jayaq, the Ural), and it comes from the country of Pascatir (Bajiqit) in the north, and falls into this previously-mentioned sea (*i.e.* the Caspian Sea, the Kül Tängsi). The language of Pascatir is the same as that of the Hungarians….'Twas from this country of Pascatir that went forth the Huns, who were afterward, the Hungarians; hence it is the same as Greater Bulgaria."[34] They live in the present-day Ural Mountains. The Russian

---

[32] Rashīd al-Dīn, "Treatise on the Tribes," *Jāmi' al-Tawārīkh*, translated into Russian as Рашид-ад-Дин, *Сборник Летописей*, vol. 1, part 1 (Москва-Ленинград: Издательство Академии Наук СССР, 1952), p. 122.

[33] Giovanni da Pian del Carpine (Johann de Plano Carpini), *Geschichte der Mongolen und Reisebericht 1245-1247*, translated and annotated by Friedrich Risch (Leipzig: E. Pfeiffer, 1930), pp. 192, 230, 270; William Woodville Rockhill, trans. and annot., *The Journey of Friar John of Pian de Carpine to the Court of Kuyuk Khan, 1245-1247*, in *The Journey of William of Rubruck to the Eastern Parts of the World 1253-55, As Narrated by Himself, with Two Accounts of the Earlier Journey of John of Pian de Carpine* (London: Hakluyt Society, 1900), p. 12.

[34] Willem van Ruysbroeck, *Reise zu den Mongolen 1253-1255*, translated and annotated by Friedrich Risch (Leipzig: A. Deichertsche verlags-buchhandlung D. Werner Scholl,

chronicles call this region Ugra or Yugra. When the Hungarian people began migrating to Europe in the ninth century,[35] the Bajiqit who were left behind mixed with the Turks and the Mongols, and lost their own language. In the end, a completely new ethnic group came into being, still called Bajiqit.[36]

Chinggis Khan united the Mongols in 1206 and established political power. When he was rewarding the people who contributed to his victory, he said to Qorči: "Take the 3,000 Ba'arin 巴阿里 people already under your command, and add to them the people of Adarkin 阿答爾乞 (the Činas [Činōs] 赤那思, Tö'eles 脫斡劣思, and Telengüt 帖良古惕), governed by Taqai 塔該 and Ašiq 阿失黑, and the people of the other ethnic groups and combine them together to make up your *tümen* [a military unit of 10,000 men]. You will then be able to control, from the camp where you are located, the territory of the People of the Forest who live along the Irtysh River" (*The Secret History of the Mongols*, section 207).* Only in 1207 did J̆oči (Jochi) subdue and win the allegiance of the People of the Forest. In 1206, Chinggis Khan had conferred on Qorči one part of the territory of the People of the Forest in the Irtysh River basin, consisting of the Telengüt, Tö'eles, and other tribes. This serves to show that some tribes in this region had already been subdued by Chinggis Khan before J̆oči advanced with his troops.

So, when did Chinggis Khan subdue the Telengüt and other tribes? Which tribes were engaging in nomadic herding in the Irtysh River basin

---

1934), p. 131; William Woodville Rockhill, trans. and annot., *The Journey of William of Rubruck to the Eastern Parts of the World 1253-55, As Narrated by Himself* (London: Hakluyt Society, 1900), pp. 129-30.

35 E. Bretschneider, *Mediaeval Researches from Eastern Asiatic Sources* (London: Kegan Paul, Trench, Trübner, 1888), vol. 1, p. 327.

36 Н. П. Шастина (N. P. Shastina), *Путешествие в восточные страны Плано Карпини и Гильома Рубрука* (*Annotated Translation of Carpini's and William of Rubruck's Travels*) (Москва: Государственное издательство географической литературы, 1957), p. 211.

* The interpretation of this passage here differs from those of Frances Cleaves and Igor Rachewiltz, illustrating the importance of Han Rulin's contribution to the understanding of *The Secret History of the Mongols*. See Francis Woodman Cleaves, trans., *The Secret History of the Mongols*, Harvard-Yenching Institute (Cambridge, Mass.: Harvard University Press, 1982), pp. 147-8; and Igor de Rachewiltz, trans. and commentator, *The Secret History of the Mongols: A Mongolian Epic Chronicle of the Thirteenth Century*, 2 vols., Brill's Inner Asian Library, 7 (Leiden: Brill, 2004), p. 139. Translator's note.

at that time? What was the general situation of the location and extent of the territory granted to Qorči?

When Chinggis Khan first rose to power, the western part of Mongolia was occupied by Naiman 乃蠻 tribes. *The Secret History* and the *Jāmi' al-Tawārīkh* contain comparatively detailed records of the situation of the Naiman tribes at that time.

In the Naiman section of the "Treatise on the Tribes" in the *Jāmi' al-Tawārīkh*, it says, "One branch of the Naimans lived in the dangerous and difficult mountainous region, and the other branch lived on the steppe. They were in the Great Altai 按台 Mountains, the Qara-Qorum plain on which Ögödei 窩闊台 built the towering palace, the Alūī-Sarās 阿雷撒剌思 Mountains, and the Kök Irtysh 蘭也爾的失 River. The Irtiš mürin (muren) 也兒的失木憐 is the Irtysh River. The mountains between this river and the region inhabited by the Kirghiz people, which constitute the frontier of Naiman territory, skirt Moghulistan 蒙兀斯坦, the area inhabited by Ong Khan. Naiman territory also bordered on the adjacent Uyghuristan desert" (see Pelliot, *Histoire des Campagnes*, p. 299).

This was the territory of the Naimans in their most prosperous period. When Chinggis Khan united the Mongolian territory, the Naimans had already split into two.

Section 158 of *The Secret History of the Mongols* says: "After that (1202), when Chinggis Khan and Ong Khan led an expedition against Buyiruq 不亦魯黑, a member of the Güčügüt 古出古敦 clan of the Naiman tribe, Buyiruq was at the Saqaq River 消豁黑水[37] in the region of Uluq Tagh 兀魯黑塔黑.[38] When Chinggis Khan and Ong Khan arrived, Buyiruq could not face them in battle, so he crossed over the Altai Mountains and fled. They pursued him to the Ürünggü 兀瀧古 River[39] in

[37] The Saqaq River 消豁黑水 is now called the Soghuk 索果克 Darya and is a tributary of the Khovd 科布多 River. In the Qing period, a sentry post called Suoguokekalun 索果克卡倫 was established on this river. From Khovd to this sentry post there were nine postal inspection stations 巡查卡倫驛站.

[38] Uluq Tagh 兀魯黑塔黑 should be the Kuitun Mountains 奎屯山, which reach 4,374 meters in height, also called Friendship peak (Dosluk Čokisi) 友誼峰. It is at the watershed of the Saqaq River, a branch of the Khovd River, and the Buqturma River, a branch of the Irtysh River on its right bank.

[39] Written in Chinese as 烏倫古 (Wulungu) on modern maps.

the region of Qum Sengir[40] 忽木升吉爾…and then along the Ürünggü to Qïzïl Baši Lake 乞濕泐巴失海子,[41] where Buyiruq was killed" (see section 177).

Based on the route Buyiruq took when he fled, we know that he lived in the region of the Altai Mountains. This was exactly the branch of the Naimans that, according to the *Jāmi' al-Tawārīkh* , lived in the dangerous and difficult mountains.

In 1204, Tayang Khan 太陽汗 was defeated and died in the Naqu Qun 納忽昆 Mountains east of the Orkhon River. His son Güčülük (Küchülüg) Khan 古出魯克罕 fled along the Tamir 塔米兒 River (*The Secret History of the Mongols*, sections 195-196), and took refuge with his uncle Buyiruq. In 1205, when Buyiruq died, Güčülük retreated to the Buheiduerma 不黑都爾麻[42] area on the right-hand (western) branch of the Irtysh River to regroup and encamp his troops and horses. Chinggis Khan's long-distance expeditionary army arrived, and the Naiman people suffered a great defeat. Fleeing, they tried to cross the Irtysh River, but many fell in and died. The remainder traveled through Uyghur and Qarlu'ut 合兒魯兀惕 (Qarluq) territory (west of the present-day Ili region), and fled into Muslim territory, which was the Western Liao 西遼 (the Qara-Khitai Khanate) at the time, based in the Ču 垂 River region. Based on the situation and route taken by Güčülük when he fled in defeat, we can tell that he and his father (Tayang Khan) must have lived on the steppe on the upper reaches of the Irtysh River.

The Telengüt tribe lived in the upper reaches of the Ob River and the basin of its tributary, the Tobolsk River, which was connected to the areas

---

[40] Qum Sengir 忽木升吉爾 is also written 横相乙爾 in *History of the Yuan*, chapter 2. It is translated into Chinese as either Shajia 沙岬 (sandy cape) or Shajiao 沙角 (sandy promontory). It must be where the bend in the Buluntuo Lake 布倫托海 is, west of the point of intersection between 92 degrees east and 46 degrees north. See Paul Pelliot and Louis Hambis, translators and annotators, *Histoire des Campagnes de Gengis Khan: Cheng-wou ts'in-tcheng lou (Record of the Personal Campaigns of the Holy Warrior)* (Leiden: E. J. Brill, 1951), pp. 315-6.

[41] The Ürünggü River on modern maps, but on old maps it was Buluntuo Lake 布倫托海.

[42] The present-day Buqturma River, which has its origin on the Kuitun peak in the Altai Mountains. See footnote 38 above. Xu Song 徐松, in his *Records of Waterways of the Western Regions* 《西域水道記》, ch. 5, p. 27, translates it as the Buketuerma 布克圖爾瑪 River.

of the upper reaches of the Irtysh River and its tributary, the Buqturma, and other such places. The year in which the Telengüt were subdued was the very time that Chinggis Khan wiped out the Naimans. This is why in 1206 Chinggis Khan was able to bestow on Qorči the territory of the People of the Forest of the Irtysh River – the Telengüt, Tö'eles, and other tribes. From this we can see that Qorči's territory was part of the former Naiman territory.

The Ba'arin tribe, who lived in Qorči's territory, participated in Qaidu's rebellion. Rashīd al-Dīn records that Toq Temür 托黑帖木兒 [not the later Toq Temür, Yuan Emperor Wenzong 文宗], having set up Širgi 昔里吉 as ruler and suffering defeat at the hands of the Khan's army, plundered the Ba'arin tribe along the route of his flight,[43] eventually reaching the bank of the Irtysh River. The *History of the Yuan* records that in the first year of the Dade reign period (1297), Čonqur 床兀兒 led troops on a northern expedition, and that the various armies in his command crossed the Jin 金 Mountains (the Altai) and invaded "Ba'arin territory" 八鄰之地, which was part of Qorči's lands.[44] Qorči was a member of the Ba'arin tribe, and this tribe of 3,000 formed an important component of his tümen. This is why in the Yuan Dynasty Qorči's assigned land was called the land of the Ba'arin. However, because there were still people of the Čինas ethnic group in his tümen, the territory occupied by this tribe was also called "Činas territory" at the time; see *Categorized Literature from the Yuan Period* 元文類, chapter 26, "Yu Ji" 虞集 [the great literatus Yu Wenjing 虞文靖], "Stele Relating the Achievements of Čonqur's Family" 句容郡王世績碑. Chapter 20 of the *History of the Yuan* records that in the fifth month of the fourth year of the Dade reign period (1300), Emperor Chengzong 成宗 (Temür Khan) bestowed more than 65,000 *ding* 錠 of silver on the captured military households of Ba'arin and Tö'eles. These tribes were both subject peoples of Qorči.

After J̌oči led an expedition against the People of the Forest, Chinggis Khan said to him, "You, eldest of my sons, who only now for the first time have left home, you have been lucky. Without wounding or causing

[43] *Jāmi' al-Tawārīkh*, ch. 2; *Djami el-tévarikh: Histoire générale du monde*, Edgar Blochet, ed. (Leyden: E. J. Brill, 1911), p. 439. *Jāmi' al-Tawārīkh*, Russian translation, p. 169.

[44] *History of the Yuan*, ch. 128, "Biography of Čonqur 床兀兒."

suffering to man or gelding in the lands where you went, you came back having subjugated the fortunate People of the Forest. I shall give this people to you" (*The Secret History of the Mongols*, section 239).*

The Persian account by Rashīd al-Dīn describes J̌oči's territory in the Irtysh River region more concretely than that of 'Ala-ad-Din 'Ata-Malik Juwaīnī: "All the territory and people of the Irtysh River and Altai Mountains region, including the surrounding winter camp and summer pastureland, were all given by Chinggis Khan to J̌oči….J̌oči's camp was in the region of Irtysh River, where the capital of government was located."[45]

When Yelü Dashi 耶律大石 was resisted by the Kirghiz people, he went west to Emil 葉密立 and built a city there. The various Turkish tribes in the area submitted to him, their numbers reaching 40,000.[46] Later on this became the capital of Ögödei's territory. Almalïq 阿力麻里 near Quyas served as the regional capital of the Qarluq 哈剌魯 ruler Ozar (or Buzar) Khan. Qayalïq 海押立 was the regional capital of the Qarluq Arslan Khan 阿兒思蘭汗.[47] Later on these cities became the political centers of the Chaghatay Khanate. The area called Beiting 北庭 in the Tang period (whose Turkish name was Beshbalïq, literally "five-towns"), was the Uyghur capital during the Yuan period. Based on the above situation we can see that the capitals of Chinggis Khan's second and third sons were the former capitals of the great tribes he conquered. J̌oči's capital on the Irtysh River certainly could not have been an unnamed place. From its geographical position, I think it originally was a center of political activity for the tribal leaders of the great Naiman state in western Mongolia.

According to the biography of Qubilai Khan in the *Jāmi' al-Tawārīkh*, Sorghanghtani Beki's 唆魯禾帖尼 territory was passed on to her youngest

---

* English translation taken from Igor de Rachewiltz, trans., *The Secret History of the Mongols*, vol. 1 (Leiden: Brill, 2006), p. 164-5. Translator's note.

[45] *Jāmi' al-Tawārīkh*, ch. 2, Blochet edition, p. 131, Russian translation, p. 78. 'Ala-ad-Din 'Ata-Malik Juwaīnī, *Ta'rīkh-i Jahān-Gushā* (*The History of the World-Conqueror*), translated and edited by J. A. Boyle, with an introduction by David O. Morgan (Seattle: University of Washington Press; Manchester: Manchester University Press, 1997; Paris: UNESCO Publishing, 1997; first edition 1958), p. 42.

[46] Juwaīnī, *The History of the World-Conqueror*, Boyle translation, p. 355.

[47] *Jāmi' al-Tawārīkh*, ch. 2, Blochet edition, pp. 74, 75.

son Ariq-Böke. "His summer camp was in the Altai Mountains, and his winter camp was among the Uriyangkhai (Uriyangqai) and Kirghiz; the two were three days' journey apart."[48] The Uriyangkhai 兀良哈 mentioned here were those near the forest that was within the borders of the Kirghiz tribe. Judging from this, the political center of Sorghanghtani Beki's territory probably was the former camp of the Kirghiz tribal leaders.

In the second year of Xianzong's 憲宗 (Möngke Khan) reign (1252), Ögödei's son Malik 篾里 was sent to the Irtysh River. In the second year of the Zhiyuan 至元 reign period (1265) under Emperor Shizu 世祖 (Qubilai Khan), Junzhou 鈞州 (present-day Yu County 禹縣 in Henan 河南, whose ancient name was Yangdi 陽翟) was subordinate to Mingli 明里 (Malik). In the tenth year of the Dade reign period (1306), Haishan 海山 went to the region of the Irtysh to accept the surrender of Ögödei's fourth grandson, Tümän 禿滿, and others. The following year Tümän was enfeoffed as the Prince of Yangdi 陽翟.[49] His fief was also in the region of the Irtysh River.

Based on what has been said above concerning the geographical circumstances of the princes' territories, Qorči's allotted land was in the northwestern part of former Naiman territory, which was in the upper reaches of the Irtysh River. The area west of this adjoined J̌oči's territory, and the area northeast of it, all the way to the upper reaches of the Ob River, bordered on Sorghanghtani Beki's territory. Eastward, it did not go beyond the Altai Mountains, and westward it did not cross the Irtysh River. The territories of Qorči, J̌oči, Tümän, and the others interlocked with each other like pieces of a jigsaw puzzle.

II. The Geographical Bases of Ariq-Böke and the other Rebellious Princes

The section on "Annual Grants" 歲賜 in the "Monograph on Food and Money" 食貨志 in chapter 95 of the *History of the Yuan* says: "All of the princes and their empresses and princesses will have allotments for the production of food 食采." The various princes and empresses had this type of food production land grants both north of the Gobi Desert (i.e. Mongolia and the area to its north) and in the central plain [China proper].

---

[48] *Jāmi' al-Tawārīkh*, ch. 2, Blochet edition, pp. 560, 561; Russian translation p. 201.

[49] See *Historical Record of the Mongols* 《蒙兀爾史記》, ch. 148, p. 54.

Ariq-Böke's allotment of land north of the Gobi Desert was among the Kirghiz in Kemkemjihud, and that in the central plain was in Zhending Route 真定路. The section on "Annual Grants" says: "Prince Ariq-Böke, son of Taizu's fourth son Ruizong 睿宗 (Tölüi 拖雷, using his posthumous title) had an annual stipend of 100 *ding* 錠 of silver, 300 *pi* 匹 of brocade, and silk for five households 五戶絲. In the bingshen 丙申 year (1236) he had separate control over 分撥 eight tümens in Zhending Route." According to the Mongol custom, the youngest son inherited the wealth, so the territory in Zhending was inherited from his parents. His parents' memorial hall 影堂 was there.[50]

Ariq-Böke's territory north of the Gobi Desert, among the Kirghiz in Kemkemjihud, was also inherited from his mother, Sorghanghtani Beki, who had passed away in 1252. Rashīd al-Dīn says that "Sorghanghtani Beki's territory was handed down to Ariq-Böke."[51] After Ariq-Böke was defeated, when he set out to his elder brother Qubilai's place to implore his pardon: "He (Ariq-Böke) took all of his wives and children with him, and left his four sons (I omit their names here) in his own territory." "His

---

[50] In the "Annals of Taizong (Ögödei)" 《太宗紀》, *History of the Yuan*, ch. 2, it is recorded under the seventh month (autumn) of the eighth (bingshen 丙申) year (1236) that, "An edict was issued granting to the empress the civilian households of Zhending as her territory." This refers to Chinggis Khan's empress Börte Hüjin 孛兒台旭真. Following the Mongol custom by which the youngest son inherited a family's property, her territory was passed down to her youngest son Tölüi 拖雷 after her death. This is why the *Stele at Xuansheng Confucian Temple in Zhending Route* 《真定路宣聖廟牌》 by Bozhuluzhong 孛术魯翀 says, "When Zhending Route was first instituted in Zhenzhou 鎮州, the local people of Li Superior Prefecture 蠡府 and its five regions – Zhongshan 中山, Ji 冀, Jin 晉, Zhao 趙, and Shen 深 – were presented to Empress (Sorghanghtani Beki), whose honorific title was 'Distinguished, Virtuous, Modest, and Sage' 顯懿莊聖, and who was the empress of Emperor Ruizong 睿宗 (Tölüi, whose honorific title was 'Humane, Sage, Brilliant, and Lofty' 仁聖景襄), as hers from which to obtain food and local products" (*Categorized Literature from the Yuan Period* 《元文類》, ch. 20). In 1251, when Möngke took the Khan throne, he "ordered that Zhending's gold and silver be used…to reward those who supported him" (*History of the Yuan*, ch. 125, "Biography of Bulu Qaya" 《布魯海牙》). When Sorghanghtani Beki died, her territory was inherited by her youngest son Ariq-Böke. The Imperial Spirit (Memorial) Hall 神御殿 of Tölüi and Sorghanghtani Beki was set up in the Xiaosi Hall 孝思殿 of Yuhua temple 玉華宮, established by Qubilai Khan at Zhending "in order that sacrifices could be offered to the emperor and empress on the anniversary of their deaths."

[51] *Jāmi' al-Tawārīkh*, ch. 2, Blochet edition, p. 566; Russian translation p. 202.

summer camp was at Ulīās tū, and his winter camp was between the Uriyangkhai and Kirghiz, and these two places were three days' journey apart."[52] The original Persian text on which the Russian translation was based says that his summer camp was at Altae, clearly a mistake for Altai. His summer camp was regularly in the mountains, and his winter camp in the steppe. The transcription of Ulīās tū can not be accepted.

In 1254 (which was the year of the fish, i.e. dragon) while he was at his summer camp where he had ascended the throne, Möngke decided to advance and attack the Southern Song Emperor Zhao Kuo 趙擴. "He ordered his youngest brother Ariq-Böke to take command of the remaining Mongolian army and the various *ordos*, and entrusted his *ulus* to him."[53] Möngke led troops into Sichuan 四川, and Qubilai entered Hubei 湖北. According to Hao Jing's 郝經 *Commentary on the Return of the Army* 班師議, on the 12th day of the seventh lunar month in 1259, when Qubilai arrived at Ru'nan 汝南 on the bank of the Huai River 淮河,[54] he had already received news of Möngke's death in Hezhou 合州.

In accordance with Mongolian tradition, Qubilai and Ariq-Böke, and all of Möngke's sons, were qualified to inherit the Khan throne after Möngke's death. As for the political situation in Mongolia at the time, Ariq-Böke was in a better political position than all the others because he occupied the Mongolian base territory, and because Möngke Khan "had entrusted his *ulus* only to him."[55] Therefore at Möngke's summer abode west of Qara-Qorum 和林城, on the bank of the Altan 西按坦 River, Ariq-Böke summoned [all the princes] to a conference and ascended the throne.[56]

---

[52] *Jāmi' al-Tawārīkh*, ch. 2, Blochet edition, pp. 560-1; Russian translation p. 201.

[53] *Jāmi' al-Tawārīkh*, ch. 2, Blochet edition, p. 319; Russian translation p. 145.

[54] *Categorized Literature from the Yuan Period*, ch. 13, Hao Jing 郝經, *Commentary on the Return of the Army* 《班師議》. *Jāmi' al-Tawārīkh*, ch. 2, Blochet edition, p. 380, says that Qubilai Khan heard the news of Möngke's death when he reached "the shores of the Huai River." The *History of the Yuan* says that Möngke died on the guihai 癸亥 (21st) day of the seventh month, but this cannot be relied upon. Tu Ji said he died on the guiwei 癸未 day, but this too is mistaken.

[55] *Jāmi' al-Tawārīkh*, ch. 2, Blochet edition, p. 425; Russian translation p. 166.

[56] *Categorized Literature from the Yuan Period*, ch. 70, Ouyang Gui 歐陽圭, "Account of Family History of the Xie Clan of Gaochang" 《高昌偰氏家傳》. *History of the Yuan*, ch. 4, "Annals of Emperor Shizu (Qubilai Khan)."

Qubilai and Ariq-Böke struggled for the throne's material foundation, most importantly in the central plain [China proper]. Ariq-Böke's base was primarily north of the Gobi Desert. There was a huge difference in the strength of their forces, but Ariq-Böke and Qubilai were alike in that they adopted combined Mongol and Chinese battle lines and vigorously utilized the manpower and material goods of the central plain in their struggle to take the throne. In the eleventh month of 1259, Dorji 脱里赤* was ordered to expand his forces in the various prefectures south of the desert. In the intercalary eleventh month of the same year, the senior provincial-level official (the Overseer 行省事) was ordered to plunder the weapons of the people of Yandu 燕都 (the capital area, present-day Beijing).[57] In addition, "Alamdar 阿蘭答兒 and Quntuqai 渾都海 were (sent) to occupy the Guan-Long 關隴 region [the Ordos Loop area],"[58] and Liu Taiping 劉太平 and Qorqai 霍魯海 took care of gathering provisions and plotted taking of Qin 秦 (Shaanxi) and Shu 蜀 (Sichuan).[59] Based on the circumstances at that time, Ariq-Böke and his supporters were preparing first to seize the northwestern part of the central plain and use it as a base from which to fight for the throne. Ariq-Böke strove to get Chinese generals, but according to the historical records, he only had Liu Taiping alone, who helped him organize the weapons and military forces, and so could not possibly compete with Qubilai. He also wanted to utilize Mongolian and Chinese intellectuals to help him with his strategic planning. His mother Sorghanghtani Beki chose two scholars for him for this purpose: the teacher and famous Zhending scholar Li Pan 李槃[60] and the local Zhending intellectual Zhang Chu 張礎.[61] However, they both could clearly see that Ariq-Böke's material base was too weak, and he would not be able to contend with Qubilai, so they were firmly unwilling to attach themselves to him. Only the Mongolian civil official Bo Luhuan 孛魯歡, whose fief was also in Zhending and Shulu 束鹿, supported his activities to seize the throne.[62]

---

* One of the highest ranking officials under Ariq-Böke. Translator's note.

[57] *History of the Yuan*, ch. 4, "Biography of Emperor Shizu (Qubilai Khan)."

[58] Ibid., ch. 121, "Biography of Anjur" 《按竺邇傳》.

[59] Ibid., ch. 126, "Biography of Lian Xixian" 《廉希憲傳》.

[60] *History of the Yuan*, ch. 126, "Biography of Lian Xixian" 《廉希憲傳》.

[61] Ibid., ch. 167, "Biography of Zhang Chu" 《張礎傳》.

[62] *Jāmi' al-Tawārīkh*, ch. 2, Blochet edition, p. 425; Russian translation pp. 166-7.

After Möngke's attack on Hezhou 合州 and his death in the Diaoyu 釣魚 Mountains, his army, which he had formerly used to attack the Southern Song, moved north under the command of his son Asutai 阿速台. It was at this time that Ariq-Böke planned to occupy the Guan-Long region. His army was stationed in the Hexi 河西 corridor and Liupan 六盤 Mountains district. Ariq-Böke then ordered his subordinate general Alamdar to act as the commanding general of Asutai's branch of the army. Before long Alamdar was defeated by Qubilai's subordinate generals at Shandan 刪丹, and the remnants of this army, which had formerly attacked Sichuan, thereupon escaped in disorder to Kirghiz, Ariq-Böke's military base area.[63]

Therefore, although Ariq-Böke's political position was superior because he had possession of the Mongolian capital Qara-Qorum, he was defeated in the end, for lack of material strength, by Qubilai's general Yisüngge 移相哥, so he returned to Kirghiz.[64]

Afterwards, Qubilai encamped his troops among the Önggüd 汪吉 and cut off the Mongol supply lines. Ariq-Böke asked for assistance from the Chingissid princes of Chaghatay in Central Asia, but failed to obtain it and thereupon led his troops eastward, expecting that the various princes along the eastern route would join up with him. But failure followed upon failure, and in the end all he could do was to flee to Kirghiz, leading his hungry, exhausted army to be stationed on the banks of the Dasu River 答速河 in Kemkemjihud.[65] Because Ariq-Böke was now so far off on the distant frontier, having lost the support of the manpower and material resources of the central plain, he was left with no options; therefore he surrendered to his brother Qubilai and asked for lenience.

Ariq-Böke surrendered in 1264. In 1268 Qaidu revolted again. In 1270 Qubilai Khan sent Liu Haoli 劉好禮 of Wanzhou 完州 Baoding Route 保定路 to serve as the *daruqači* 斷事官 (Judge/Overseer) of the territory of the five tribes, including the Kirghiz region, Qapqana, Kemkemjihud, and Yilanzhou 益蘭州. Peasants and soldiers of the central plains region were then relocated in order to reclaim land for military camps and civilians, and to establish artisan bureaus 人匠局 for organizing and managing the

---

[63] *Jāmi' al-Tawārīkh*, ch. 2, Blochet edition, pp. 294-397; Russian translation p. 161.
[64] *Jāmi' al-Tawārīkh*, ch. 2, Blochet edition, p. 393, Russian translation p. 161.
[65] *Jāmi' al-Tawārīkh*, ch. 2, Blochet edition, p. 397; Russian translation p. 161.

kinds of handicraft industries that were being moved there. They were also instructed to establish official post stations 傳舍 and improve the roads and communications. It was hoped that the Kirghiz and Kemkemjihud region would become a base from which to defend against the rebel princes in the Northwest. Within a short time after this, however, the northwestern princes themselves occupied Kemkemjihud, and in 1279 they summoned Liu Haoli there. In the next year, there was nothing for Liu Haoli to do but to bribe the rebellious generals and flee back to Daidu 大都 [modern Beijing].

In 1276 Toq Temür, son of Qubilai Khan's younger brother Suiduge 歲都哥, incited Möngke's son Širgi to rebel. Širgi and the others were defeated and fled to the Irtysh River. From there Toq Temür advanced to attack Kirghiz.[66]

In the 30th year of the Zhiyuan reign period (1293), Qubilai dispatched Tutuq 土土哈 to pacify the rebellious princes. When the troops arrived at the Kem River, they gathered up the people of the five tribes to the greatest extent possible.[67]

Later, in the last year of Chengzong's (Temür Khan) reign (1307), a mission was sent to requisition hostages (translating turqaq 禿魯花 as "hostage"), horses, and falcons 鷹鶻 from the Kirghiz tribe.[68] At the beginning of Yingzong's 英宗 reign (1320-1321), there was a flood in Kirghiz: "the Ursu 烏爾速, Qapqanas 憨哈納思, and other tribes were poverty-stricken, and the revenue office 戶 issued two mares (to each household)."[69] This proves that the Kirghiz were under central government control during the Yuan period, and that tax was collected in kind and dispensed to aid people in disaster, exactly the same as with the people in the interior of China.

Yang Yu's 陽瑀 *New Tales from the Mountain Dweller* 山居新話 was written in the eighth year before the fall of the Yuan Dynasty (1360). At that time it had already been five years since Zhu Yuanzhang 朱元璋 had fought his way into Nanjing 南京 and Chen Youliang 陳友諒 had already

---

[66] *Jāmi' al-Tawārīkh*, ch. 2, Blochet edition, p. 439; Russian translation p. 169.

[67] *History of the Yuan*, ch. 128, "Biography of Tutuq" 《土土哈傳》.

[68] Ibid., ch. 22, "Annals of Wuzong" 《武宗紀》. [The term "hostage" is translated as "day-guard" by Rachewiltz; translator's note.]

[69] *History of the Yuan*, ch. 27, "Annals of Yingzong" 《英宗紀》.

proclaimed himself emperor at Dangtu 當涂 (in Anhui 安徽). Yang Yu also recorded how his two friends sent him as a present salt from the mines of Kirghiz.[70] This proves that at the end of the Yuan Dynasty, the Kirghiz still were within Yuan Dynasty territory.

III. The Establishment of the daruqači 斷事官 *(Judge/Overseer) of the Five Tribes*

The region inhabited by the Kirghiz in the Yuan period was the base of operations used by Ariq-Böke and the other rebel princes of the Northwest. After Ariq-Böke was defeated, the Yuan government, in order to develop the economy of this enormous region and consolidate its hold over the Northwest, moved a large number of soldiers, craftsmen and peasants there from the central plain, and established all kinds of administrative organizations in order to strengthen their political and military hold on the region.

In the seventh year of the Zhiyuan reign period (1270), the Yuan government appointed Liu Haoli from Wanzhou, Baoding Route, as the *daruqači* of the five tribes, including the Kirghiz. The government seat was in Yilanzhou 益蘭州.[71] Based on archaeological excavations, the *daruqači's* jurisdiction was also the so-called Dayingpan 大營盤.[72] It was located in what is now the lower reaches of the Elegest (Элегест) River, on the left bank of the Yenisei River in what is now the Tuva Republic of Russia.[73]

According to the "Monograph on Geography" in the *History of the Yuan*, the five tribes under Liu Haoli's jurisdiction were the Kirghiz, Qapqana, Kemkemjihud, Yilanzhou, and Ursu. There was also the Angara tribe, but because it belonged to the Kirghiz rather than being an independent tribe, the reference to Kirghiz on this list also includes the

---

[70] Yang Yu 楊瑀, *New Tales from the Mountain Dweller* 《山居新話》.

[71] *History of the Yuan*, ch. 167, "Biography of Liu Haoli" 《劉好禮傳》 and ch. 63, "Appendix on the Northwest" 《西北地附錄》, in the "Monograph on Geography."

[72] Yang Yu, *New Tales from the Mountain Dweller*.

[73] Л. Р. Кызласов (L. R. Kyzlasov), "Средневековые города Тувы" ("The Medieval Cities of Tuva"), *Советская археология* (*Soviet Archaeology*), 1959, no. 3; Л. Р. Кызласов (L. R. Kyzlasov), "Городище Дён-терек" ("The Hillfort of Dën-Terek") in C. B. Киселев (S. V. Kiselev), et al., *Древнемонгольские Города* (*Ancient Mongolian Cities*) (Москва-Ленинград: Академия наук СССР, 1965), pp. 60 and 117.

Angara tribe. Thus in the 30th year of the Zhiyuan reign period (1294), when Tutuq put down Qaidu's rebellion and advanced to take Kirghiz, the *History of the Yuan* says that he absorbed the people of the five tribes.[74]

For the geographical area covered by each of these five tribes, see "The Postal Route from Kirghiz to Oyirat 外剌," section four of Chen Dezhi's 陳得芝 article "A Study of the Postal Routes in Yuan Dynasty Lingbei Province" referenced in footnote three of this essay. The article points out that the Kirghiz lived in the vicinity of the upper reaches of the present-day Yenisei River, that the Qapqanas 憨合納斯 were in the present-day Bii Kem (Biy Kem, Upper Yenisei) River basin, and that the Ursut 烏爾速 were in the region of the present-day Urs River 烏斯河, a tributary of the Bii Kem River. I will not give the others here. The *History of the Yuan* says: "Kemkemjihud 謙州 (Qianzhou) was named after the river of that name. It was southeast of the Kirghiz, southwest of the Kem (Qian) River, and north of the Tanglu Mountains 唐麓嶺."[75] According to this passage, Qianzhou was in today's Kemchik River basin. The section on Kirghiz in the "Treatise on the Tribes" of the *Jāmi' al-Tawārīkh* says: "The lands of Kirghiz and Kemkemjihud were adjoined to each other, the two forming a single territory,"[76] which explains why Kemkemjihud and the Kirghiz were often mentioned together.

The Angara tribe, as a tribe subordinate to the Kirghiz, had a large and expansive territory; it was not limited to today's Angara River basin. In present-day geographical terms, the Angara River flows into the Yenisei River, and the lower reaches are still named the Yenisei River. However, in the Yuan Dynasty the Angara River meant something different from today. The "Monograph on Geography" in the *History of the Yuan* says that the Kem River "flows into the Angara River, and enters the sea in the north."[77] This means that after the two rivers converge, the area of the lower reaches was called the Angara River, not the Kem. The Kirghiz section of the *Jāmi' al-Tawārīkh* also says, "the Angara River flows

---

[74] *History of the Yuan*, ch. 128, "Biography of Tutuq."

[75] Ibid., ch. 63, "Monograph on Geography."

[76] *Jāmi' al-Tawārīkh*, ch. 1, "Treatise on the Tribes," И. Н. Березин (I. N. Berezin) edition, *Труды Восточнаго Отдѣленія Императорскаго Археологическаго Общества* (*Transactions of the Eastern Department of the Imperial Archaeological Society*), vol. 7, p. 168; *Jāmi' al-Tawārīkh*, Russian translation, p. 150.

[77] *History of the Yuan*, ch. 63, "Monograph on Geography."

directly to Ibir-Šibir territory."[78] Šibir is the northernmost tribe of the People of the Forest. Thus the territory of the Angara tribe included the lower reaches of the present-day Yenisei River, all the way up to the Arctic Ocean. That is to say, the modern Yenisei River basin was entirely under the jurisdiction Liu Haoli, the *daruqači* of the five tribes. This is why he once personally went to Angara to investigate the scenery of the farthest north, saying, "In the region of the Angara 盎吉剌 River the sun never sets; there is only a dark cloud covering the sun."[79]

We have established that the territory of the Kirghiz and the others of the five tribes was the Yuan government's defense base against the rebellious princes in the Northwest. However, this region had a backward economy, extremely lacking in food and daily necessities as well as all other materials needed to support life. Given the travel and transport conditions at that time, it was extremely difficult to send large quantities of supplies there from the central plain. This is why, after leading the expeditions against the People of the Forest, but before launching his western expeditions, Chinggis Khan moved workers and peasants in such large numbers from the central plain to the area north of the Gobi Desert – to the region inhabited by the Kirghiz, to Kemkemjihud, and to other places.[80] They were to develop the agriculture and industry of the region, and solve the problem of provisioning the army stationed there. The craftsmen, peasants, and soldiers who were resettled there were so numerous that they had to be divided into groups, and various administrative organizations had to be established to manage their industrial and agricultural production. In general it can be said that the artisan bureau 人匠局, which managed the handicraft industry, was separated into sections for military and civilian use. The most important such bureaus established in Kemkemjihud were the following:

1) "The Kemkemjihud Military Weapons Bureau, headed by a post of rank five. There was one commissioner and one vice commissioner."[81] In

[78] *Jāmi' al-Tawārīkh*, ch. 1, "Treatise on the Tribes," Berezin edition, vol. 7, p. 168; *Jāmi' al-Tawārīkh*, Russian translation, p. 150.

[79] Sheng Ruzi 盛如梓, *Collected Notes of an Aged Learner at the Commoner's Study* 《庶齋老學叢談》, first chapter.

[80] *History of the Yuan*, ch. 147, "Biography of Shi Bingzhi" 《史秉直傳》. Li Zhichang 李志常, *Record of the Journey to the West of the Daoist Monk Changchun* 《長春真人西游記》, Studies of Ancient China Library edition 國學文庫, pp. 99-100.

[81] *History of the Yuan*, ch. 90, "Monograph on Official Posts" 《百官志》.

1219, when Chinggis Khan was preparing to launch his westward expedition, Jia Taraqun 賈塔剌渾 of Jizhou 冀州 had already received orders to lead the artillery (mangonel) troops 炮軍 in an advance to Kemkemjihud.[82] In the first year of Qubilai's reign (1270) "first-class craftsmen from Kemkemjihud were moved to Songshan 松山."[83] It was inevitable that organizations for the manufacture, repair, and management of military weapons be established in Qianzhou since it was such an important strategic region for the northwestern army.

2) The inhabitants of the area were not capable of making their own crockery. Unable to build their own boats, they could only cross rivers in dugouts. The land was fertile and suitable for planting, and they produced good iron, but they could not cast their own agricultural implements. After Liu Haoli reported these backward circumstances to the court in Daidu, the government then sent artisans to instruct the inhabitants how to work with clay to make pottery, smelt metal, build boats, and other skills in order to raise the standard of living of the people of the five tribes.[84]

When Chinggis Khan was on his western expeditions, there were already 1,100 Chinese artisans in Kemkemjihud occupied in weaving fine silks, gauze, brocade, and damask.[85] Of course, it was the responsibility of these Chinese artisans to manufacture all types of military clothing and other objects. In 1269, according to the *History of the Yuan*, "impoverished Kemkemjihud artisans were sent a relief package amounting to 5,999 *dan* 石 of rice," [approximately 600,000 liters] which proves how numerous the workers in this region had become.[86]

The Abakan (阿巴干, Абакан) and Tuva (Тува) basins had abundant supplies of fish. In fact, each tributary and lake of the Bii Kem River had about ten different varieties of fish. For this reason, people were also moved here who specialized in manufacturing fishing equipment.[87]

---

[82] Ibid., ch. 51, "Biography of Jia Taraqun" 《賈塔剌渾傳》.

[83] Ibid., ch. 7, "Annals of Shizu (Qubilai Khan)."

[84] Ibid., ch. 63, "Monograph on Geography." Carruthers says, "in autumn by canoe and in winter on the ice by sleigh" (Douglas Carruthers, *Unknown Mongolia: A Record of Travel and Exploration in North-west Mongolia and Dzungaria*, p. 76).

[85] Li Zhichang 李志常, *Record of the Journey to the West of the Daoist Monk Changchun* 《長春真人西游記》, p. 100.

[86] *History of the Yuan*, ch. 6, "Annals of Shizu (Qubilai Khan)."

[87] Ibid., ch. 11, "Annals of Shizu (Qubilai Khan)."

The "Monograph on Geography" in the *History of the Yuan* says that Qianzhou (Kemkemjihud) "had fertile land suitable for growing crops. In the summer it was planted and in the autumn it was harvested, and the land was easy to work."[88] Because of the large army that was stationed there during the Yuan period, and the large numbers of artisans who had been moved there, they could not have relied on the local inhabitants to produce all the food and supplies they needed. Therefore the Yuan government utilized the advantageous local conditions to engage in the establishment of military colonies (屯墾 or 屯田). The military colonies were of two types: military settlements 軍屯 and civilian settlements 民屯. The clothes, agricultural implements, fishing equipment, and other such items for the soldiers in the military camps had to be provided by the Yuan government,[89] therefore the civilian settlements were important.

The weather and soil in the middle of the Abakan plain and the Tuva basin were quite suitable for human habitation. On the plateau they could rely on nearby rivers to draw water for irrigation. There was farmland where they could plant wheat, millet, and other agricultural products. The Chadan (Чадана) River valley was a good example of this. Remains have recently been found of complex water engineering works along the banks of the Ili-Kem River (Или-хем) [a small channel west of the Yenisei] and the Temir-usu Gol (river) (Темир-сук), and the Lan River 攔河 Dam remains containing irrigation and construction works in the Uyuk (Уюк) and Turan (Туран) River basins are almost completely intact.[90] All of this proves that at some time in the past there was a very high level of engineering technology in this region. When were these remains of water engineering works left behind? Who built them? The people who now live there all give a very simple answer: it was taught to them by Chinggis Khan.

As Carruthers noted, "Jenghis is still worshipped amongst the Uriankhai as a deity. All good things are attributed to the great Mongol chieftain; he taught them, they say, to sow wheat and to make irrigation-canals."[91] These legends can only explain the historical position occupied

---

[88] Ibid., ch. 63, "Monograph on Geography."

[89] Ibid., ch. 11, "Annals of Shizu (Qubilai Khan)."

[90] Рафаил Михайлович Кабо (Rafail Mikhaĭlovich Kabo), *Очерки истории и экономики Тувы* (*Summary of Tuva's History and Economy*), chapter 2 (Москва, 1934).

[91] Douglas Carruthers, *Unknown Mongolia: A Record of Travel and Exploration in North-west Mongolia and Dzungaria*, p. 204.

by Chinggis Khan among the northern peoples. In fact, he was not at all involved in planting agricultural products or establishing water conservancy engineering projects. Chinggis Khan was a crack shot with a bow and arrow, but taking up a hoe to plow and till the soil was something completely outside his area of expertise.

The "Annals of Shizu (Qubilai Khan)" in the *History of the Yuan* say that in the ninth year of the Zhiyuan reign period (1272), "the income from the Kirghiz military colony's rent was reduced, and numerous people from the South were sent to the North with plows to assist them in cultivating the land."[92] When the Yuan rulers built their capital in Beijing, not only were northern "Han Chinese" people sent there, but numerous people were also sent to the Yenisei River basin military colonies from the area south of the Huai River 淮河. There must have been a reason for this. The North consists almost entirely of dry land, and its water management was not well-developed at the time. Because of their familiarity with wet rice cultivation, the peasants from the south were expert in building irrigation channels. Therefore we consider that the water engineering works, whose remains can be seen in various places in Kemkemjihud, must have been built by "southerner" peasants who had been resettled there during the Yuan Dynasty.

Handicrafts such as clothing, agricultural implements, fishing equipment, porcelain, and other products needed to be stored, and the harvests of wheat, barley, and other agricultural products also needed to be stored in warehouses. This must have been why Liu Haoli built storage granaries 庫廩 to solve the problem of storage and preservation.

Kemkemjihud produced salt from mines and salt from the sea. Salt comes in two kinds, red and bluish-black. In the Jiangnan 江南 area of China [the area south of the Yangtze River] most people eat sea salt, therefore people who returned south from Kemkemjihud often carried salt from that region back with them, to present to their relatives and friends as gifts. It was described as "either square and hard, or pulverized and soft, or in large pieces that could roll around on a plate." At that time in that region, "the Dayingpan 大營盤 [of Kemkemjihud] also accepted this (salt) for taxes." The so-called Dayingpan must have been one of the organizations set up by the *daruqači* of the five tribes.* According to the

---

[92] *History of the Yuan*, ch. 7, "Annals of Shizu (Qubilai Khan)."

* As noted above, it is also the name of Tölüi's camp. Translator's note.

biography of Liu Haoli in the *History of the Yuan*, this kind of tax was once remitted under that official when he occupied the post.[93]

After Qubilai subdued Ariq-Böke, he took Kemkemjihud and the areas inhabited by the Kirghiz and the other tribal peoples – his mother's territory. Qubilai made these regions a base from which to suppress the rebellious princes of the Northwest. Whether it was to move artisans and peasants of the central plain, or to send armies to the region, it was necessary to improve the conditions of communications and transport. After the *daruqači* Liu Haoli arrived there in the seventh year of the Zhiyuan reign period (1270), he began to establish postal stations 傳舍 in order to facilitate travel. By the 28th year of the Zhiyuan reign period (1291), the Yuan government went even further and formally organized the six postal stations from Kirghiz to Oyirat. I will not go into this here in depth, and will only explain the transport situation between north and south in this region.

There was a legend in Mongol times that there was a land near the area where the Angara River flowed into the sea, and there was supposedly white silver everywhere. All of the tools and implements used by the inhabitants of this region were made of white silver. Qubilai's mother Sorghanghtani Beki's territory north of the Gobi Desert was in the Kirghiz territory and in Kemkemjihud, not far from the Arctic Ocean. Legend has it that she sent three *emir* (異密, or senior officials) by boat, in command of 1,000 people, to find this place, the white-silver land, however, they of course failed to find it and returned.[94]

Once Chinggis Khan had established his state, the northern part of Mongolia was already empty of his enemies. In order to find out the situation in the extreme North, his son Ögödei sent Heduan 和端 and others to make investigations deep into the Arctic Ocean region. They went as far as the Arctic Circle, "the land where the sun never sets," and it took several years for them to go and come back.[95] The route of Heduan's Arctic Ocean investigative team should have started from Qara-Qorum and gone through Kemkemjihud. From Kemkemjihud, following on the

[93] Yang Yu, *New Tales from the Mountain Dweller*; *History of the Yuan*, ch. 167, "Biography of Liu Haoli."

[94] *Jāmi' al-Tawārīkh*, "Treatise on the Tribes," Russian translation, p. 102. The Berezin edition does not contain this legend.

[95] Yelü Zhu 耶律鑄, *Anthology of the Drunken Hermit at the Twin Streams* 《雙溪醉隱集》, ch. 5, "The Dingling Poems Annotated" 《丁零詩注》.

route of the three *emir*, they would have followed the Kem River, the Angara River, and finally reached the Arctic Ocean.

"This whole region between the Altai Mountains and Lake Baikal, along the Russo-Chinese frontier, is a hill-country of a densely forested nature, holding a scanty population and possessing few ways of communication."[96] To go from Qara-Qorum to the extreme north under the conditions of that day, passing through Kemkemjihud was the only feasible route. Yilanzhou was located in the center of the Kemkemjihud basin, and from there, crossing rather easily through the Shabin-daba 沙賓達巴 or Kurtushi 庫爾吐石 passes, it would take no more than three or five days to reach Kirghiz, where Sorghanghtani Beki stayed in the winter (on the Abakan plain).[97] Setting out from here one could use the route taken by the three *emir* to conveniently reach the extreme north. Thus we can see that the route through Kemkemjihud basin was part of the most important communications route connecting Mongolia and Siberia, and provided supply depots for long-distance travelers.

Carruthers writes: "Between Cha-Kul Valley and the Kemchik River we found a well-built high-road, six yards in width, raised above the level of the surrounding steppe and having a ditch on either side. The surface was as smooth and well-metalled as an English high-road....It ran with Roman directness between the two points here mentioned – a distance of about fifty miles. It appeared incredible to us that any volume of trade could necessitate the building up of so formidable a route. Its object remains inexplicable. The area it crosses needs no road-building to make transport possible. The ground is hard, smooth steppe, suitable to every kind of traffic; therefore road-making seems to be a labour-wasting folly....All we can infer from its presence is that once this region must have been of greater importance, many more caravans must have been in the custom of using the route, and a greater amount of communication must have existed between Mongolia and Siberia....The greater portion of it can be used for wheeled traffic."[98]

---

[96] Douglas Carruthers, *Unknown Mongolia*, p. 73.

[97] Ibid., pp. 110 and 113.

[98] Ibid., pp. 114-5. According to the map included at the end of the volume, this ancient route arose in the west from the place where the Cha-Kul River and the Yenisei River ("Ulu Kem" in Carruthers) converge. To the west it reaches the place where the Chadan ("Chedan" in Carruthers) River and the Kemchik River come together.

Douglas Carruthers was correct in his assessment. Kemkemjihud was a very important place during the Yuan period. Yilanzhou, the seat from which the *daruqači* governed the Kirghiz and the other of the five tribes, was not only the political center of the vast Kemkemjihud-Kirghiz region in the Yuan period, with large numbers of artisans and peasants coming and going frequently, but it was also a strategic military point, especially important for the transport of army supplies. The great general Uwaš of the Yuan army once fought the rebellious prince Qaidu in Ibir-Šibir,[99] and when Tutuq's "troops arrived at the Kem River, absorbing all the Kirghiz and the people of the five tribes, he stationed his troops there to guard it."[100] If they had not had this wide, solid road on which to transport such a large quantity of goods, how could they have accomplished the mission of pacifying the rebels? This surviving 150 *li* long ancient road between Cha-Kul and Kemchik can only have been a postal route built in the Yuan Dynasty by the *daruqači* or the Bureau of Transmission 通政院 of Kemkemjihud, or the Ministry of War, under orders from the Central Secretariat 中書省. Carruthers, who did not read Chinese historical sources, relied on Howorth who, in his *History of the Mongols*, speculated that this ancient highway was part of "a winding road…for the passage from Mongolia to Siberia" built in the beginning of the Qing period (1657) by "one of the Altai khans of North-western Mongolia."[101] This is entirely mistaken.

The Yuan Dynasty astronomer Guo Shoujing's 郭守敬 most important field testing was in the 16th year of the Zhiyuan reign period (1279), after the Yuan Dynasty had united the entire country and its domain was vast and extensive, when he set up stations for using gnomons to measure solsticial shadow lengths 測景所. From south to north, beginning from the "Southern Ocean" at a latitude of 15 Chinese degrees north, he set up one of these stations every 10 degrees. The northernmost one was set up at the Arctic Ocean, which was at 65 Chinese degrees north. Each station had a director and an assistant astronomical observer 監候官 in charge of ten astrological apprentices 星曆生, who carried the astronomical instruments 天文儀器 "that were used to make measurements in the four directions,"

[99] *History of the Yuan*, ch. 132, "Biography of Uwaš" 《玉哇失傳》.
[100] Ibid., ch. 128, "Biography of Tutuq."
[101] Douglas Carruthers, *Unknown Mongolia*, p. 114.

and took observations in the open country.[102] To have a scientific measurement team of such a considerable scale without a transport route, so that they would not have to worry about running out of supplies, is utterly unimaginable. Given the transport conditions of the time, the only route they could have taken was from Daidu through Qara-Qorum to the *daruqači's* seat in Yilanzhou (from which he governed the five tribes), and then passing through a gap in the Sayan Mountain range to the region of the Kirghiz. From there it would have made most sense to follow the route to the north taken by the people who had been sent by Sorghanghtani Beki to seek white silver.

In the 24th year of the Zhiyuan reign period (1287), the Department of State Affairs 尚書省 was restored, and a Uyghur man named Sangge 桑戈 was appointed Manager of Governmental Affairs 平章政事 (*wazīr*, meaning "prime minister," in the Persian text). When Sangge held this post (from the 24th to the 28th year of the Zhiyuan reign period), Rashīd al-Dīn says, "Many Muslim merchants came to the Khan's capital (Beijing) from the Qori 火里, Barqut 巴爾忽, and Kirghiz."[103] In the 28th year of the Zhiyuan reign period (1291), postal stations were established between Kirghiz and Oyirat. The fortune-seeking merchants who traveled from the Kirghiz region to Daidu in that year must have used this newly constructed postal road.

In 1280, Liu Haoli returned to Daidu, and not long thereafter was appointed Minister of Personnel 吏部尚書. The *History of the Yuan* records that in 1283, "Liu Haoli described the customs of the Kirghiz to the emperor,"[104] but unfortunately his information has not survived. The Yuan government engaged in industrial and agricultural construction all over the area inhabited by the Kirghiz in Kemkemjihud, and, of course, many settlements and towns appeared. Based on excavations by archaeologists in recent years in the Elegest (Элегест) River basin,

---

[102] See the results given in the section entitled "Observations throughout the Empire" 《四海測驗》, in the "Monograph on Astronomy" 《天文志》 in the *History of the Yuan*, ch. 48; also *Categorized Literature from the Yuan Period* 《元文類》, ch. 50, "Biographical Sketch of Master Guo, Administrator of the Astrological Commission Bureau" 《知太史院事郭公行狀》.

[103] *Jāmi' al-Tawārīkh*, ch. 2, Blochet edition, p. 521; Russian translation, p. 190.

[104] *History of the Yuan*, ch. 20, "Annals of Shizu (Qubilai Khan)."

Shagonara (Шагонара), and other places, there are remains such as Dën-Terek (Дён-терек), and Oimak (Оймак), and others.[105]

The tenth century *Hudūd al-'Ālam* (*Regions of the World*) records the existence of only one city in Kirghiz, i.e. Kemidjkat (Kemkemjihud, Qianzhou), the home of their Khan. There were no other cities or villages, only tents. In the 11th century, Gardīzī said that the Kirghiz Khan's capital was a seven day journey north of those mountains (the Tanman 貪漫 Mountains, i.e. Kūkmān, Kögmen).[106]

At the beginning of the 14th century, however, the Persian writer Rashīd al-Dīn said that the place had many cities and villages, actually indicating the existence of the city of Qīqās near the Angara River.[107]

Putting aside the question of whether or not the geographical knowledge in the *Hūdud al-'Ālam* or Gardīzī's work is completely correct, each had its own basis. They each dated from a different time period, the settled population differed, and the number of residential areas naturally would have been different. It is understandable that Kirghiz would have had only one city, the capital, during the 10th and 11th centuries (the Liao period). However, Rashīd al-Dīn was writing in the beginning of the 14th century, and by that time the territory of the five tribes had military colonies, civilian colonies, craftsmen of all types, an artisans' bureau, garrison troops, storage facilities, postal stations, and a whole range of administrative organizations with bureaucrats to staff them.[108] It would have been almost like the cities in the central plain. Therefore Rashīd al-Dīn's description of there being many cities and villages was, of course, also an inevitable phenomenon.

IV. The Eastern Migration of the various Kirghiz Tribes

A large number of handicraft industry workers and peasants from the central plain region were resettled to the territory of the Kirghiz and

---

[105] Л. Р. Кызласов (L. R. Kyzlasov), "Средневековые города Тувы" ("The Medieval Cities of Tuva"), *Советская археология* (*Soviet Archaeology*) 1959, no. 3; Л. Р. Кызласов (L. R. Kyzlasov), "Городище Дён-терек" ("The Hillfort of Dën-Terek") in С. В. Киселев (S. V. Kiselev), et al., Древнемонгольские Города (*Ancient Mongolian Cities*) (Москва-Ленинград: Академия наук СССР, 1965).

[106] *Encyclopaedia of Islam*, vol. 2, English edition, p. 1025.

[107] *Jāmi' al-Tawārīkh*, "Treatise on the Tribes," Berezin edition, vol. 7, p. 168; Russian translation, p. 102.

[108] Yang Yu, *New Tales from the Mountain Dweller* .

Kemkemjihud during the Yuan period, and were engaged in industrial and agricultural production. In addition, quite a large number of Kirghiz people and members of other tribes migrated eastward.

Rashīd al-Dīn records: "At the time of Chinggis Khan, there was a commander of the tümen on the left flank named Ūdāchī who was from the Uriyangkhai tribe of the People of the Forest. Later on, after the time of Chinggis Khan, Ūdāchī's sons commanded their own army, and at the place known as Būrqān Qāldūn 不爾罕合勒敦 guarded and protected the great traditions (Iūsūn) of Chinggis Khan's forbidden area (Ghurūq). They did not engage in war, and continuously up to now their descendants are still sent to guard and preserve these traditions."[109]

The text continues: "This tribe, together with the descendants of Ūdāchī, led their tümen in following the law (Iāsā) and traditions (Iūsūn), and in guarding and protecting this great forbidden area in Būrqān Qāldūn."[110]

As noted above, the winter camp within Qubilai's mother's territory was located in the region of the Uriyangkhai and Kirghiz, a distance of only three days' journey from their summer camp in the Altai Mountains. These Uriyangkhai, whose lands mutually adjoined the Kirghiz and the Altai Mountains, were similar to all the other neighboring Kirghiz tribes – they were all People of the Forest. This is why the "Treatise on the Tribes" in the *Jāmi' al-Tawārīkh* places the section on the Uriyangkhai tribe within its description of the other People of the Forest, right after the Urs 烏思, Telengüt, and Käšdim. This tribe's territory was very wide and expansive, with the easternmost group living close to the Oyirats of the Barqujin 巴爾忽津 River region, the Bulqajin 不剌合臣, the Kärämüčin 客列木臣, and other tribes of adjacent border areas ("Treatise on the Tribes," *Jāmi' al-Tawārīkh*, Barqut section).

The forbidden area guarded by the Ūdāchī is called "Qiniangu" 起輦谷 (Gürelgü) in the Chinese sources. It was the imperial burial ground for the Yuan emperors in the generations after Chinggis Khan. *The Secret History of the Mongols* was completed in 1240, only 13 years after

---

[109] *Jāmi' al-Tawārīkh*, "Treatise on the Tribes," Berezin edition, pp. 117, and 191-2; Russian translation, pp. 125, and 158-9. Iūsūn is a mistake for Yasun. [The Persian text has Yūsūn. Translator's note.]

[110] *Jāmi' al-Tawārīkh*, ch. 1, "Biography of Chinggis Khan"; Russian translation, vol. 1, part 2, p. 273.

Chinggis Khan's death (1227), and it was written on a barren island in the Kerulen (Kherlen) River. In section 89, the author relates how Chinggis Khan's family had once "established a camp…on the Senggür 桑沽爾 Stream in the Gürelgü 古連勒古 Mountains, which stand before the Būrqān Qāldūn Mountains." The Senggür Stream is a left-bank tributary of the Kerulen River, at a point slightly east of 109 degrees east. It flows from north to south into the Kerulen. Būrqān Qāldūn is in the Great Kentei (Khentii) 肯特 Mountains; it cannot be very far from the Senggür River. The forbidden area guarded by the Uriyangkhai People of the Forest is called Ghurūq or Qurūq in Turkish. In Carl Brockelmann's *Mitteltürkischer Wortschatz nach Maḥmūd al-Kāšgarīs Dīvān luγāt al-Turk* (Budapest: Kőrösi Csoma-Gesellschaft, 1928), Qoriq is translated as a "forbidden region," and Qorughchī is translated as "guards" (pages 160-161). Joseph Etienne Kowalewski's *Dictionnaire Mongol-Russe-Français* (Taipei: SMC Publishing, 1993; reprint of the first edition, Kazan: 1844-1849) translates the verb *qariqu* as "close off, forbid" (page 955), and the word *qorugha* as a "sealed-off place" (page 963). *A Brief History of the Black Tatars* 黑韃事略 says, "Temüjin's 忒沒真 tomb has arrows stuck into it to make walls and a cavalry patrol 邏騎 to guard it" (this work is translated into German as *Meng-ta pei-lu und Hei-ta shih-lüeh: chinesische Gesandten-berichte über die frühen Mongolen 1221 and 1237*, by Erich Haenisch, Yao Ts'ung-wu, Peter Olbricht, and Elisabeth Pinks (Asiatische Forschungen series, 56; Wiesbaden: Otto Harrassowitz, 1980). Ye Ziqi's 葉子奇 *Master of Grasses and Trees* 草木子 (Beijing: Zhonghua Book Company, 1959) says that the coffins of the Yuan Dynasty emperors were "sent directly to this northern imperial cemetery and buried deep in the ground. Tens of thousands of horses were used to pound the earth flat with their hooves, and the restrictions would not be lifted until the grasses became green again." Although the Chinese and foreign records are not completely the same, they are all consistent in calling Chinggis Khan's burial ground a forbidden place. If we look at the forbidden area at the foot of Purple and Gold Mountain 紫金山 in Nanjing, whose circumference is 10 *li*, where filial tombs were erected in the early Ming in order to guard and protect Zhu Yuanzhang's imperial tomb, we can imagine the situation of Gürelgü.

The *Erdeni-yin Tobči* (*Precious Summary*) 蒙古源流[111] and the *Altan Tobči* (*Golden Summary*) 黄金史[112] both say that at the time when Chinggis Khan was buried "eight white chambers" were built as places for prayer and sacrifice. There are not any records of this type in any Yuan Dynasty, Chinese, or foreign source, whether in Mongolian, Chinese, Persian, or any other language. Abū al-Ghāzī Bahādur Khan's statement that Chinggis Khan was proclaimed Great Khan in "eight circles" 八個圈子 was also a Ming Dynasty legend.[113] Chapter 74 of the *History of the Yuan*, in the section on "Ancestral Temples" 宗廟 in the "Monograph on Sacrifices" 祭祀志 says: "In the first year of the Zhiyuan reign period the imperial ancestral temple 太廟 was erected, and was equipped with eight rooms. There was a chamber for each ruler: Yisügei 也速該, Chinggis Khan, Ögödei, J̌oči, Ča'adai (Chaghatai) 察合帶, Tölüi 拖雷, Güyüq 貴由, and Möngke." It is probably the case that when the Mongol rulers lost political power in the central plain and retreated north of the Gobi Desert, they were unable to take the imperial ancestral temple in Daidu with them, therefore the so-called "eight white chambers" (Nayiman Chaghan Ger, literally translated as "eight white tents"), north of the Gobi Desert must have been modeled after the eight chambers of the imperial ancestral temple in Daidu (Beijing). Or, at the end of the 15th century after Dayan Khan 達延汗 united the Mongols, it could have been moved to or reconstructed at Ordos. This is why Dayan Khan, Daraisun Küdeng Khan, and the other emperors ascended the throne in front of eight white chambers: to express reverence for their ancestors and carry forward the great Yuan emperors' line.[114] The *Erdeni-yin Tobči* and other such works, which are full of rumor and hearsay, cannot be considered historical materials. They say only that the Uriyangkhai were the ones who guarded

---

[111] Sagang Sečen, *Erdeni-yin Tobči* (*Precious Summary*) 《蒙古源流》, ch. 4, Isaac Jacob Schmidt, *Geschichte der Ost-Mongolen und ihren Fürstenhauses, verfasst von Ssanang Ssetsen, Chungtaidschi der Ordus* (St. Petersburg, 1829), annotated edition, p. 109.

[112] Charles Bawden, trans., *The Mongol Chronicle Altan Tobči* (Wiesbaden: O. Harrassowitz, 1955), p. 145. The Zhonghua Book Company edition of *The Secret History of the Mongols* 《蒙古秘史》, p. 267, quoting the *Altan Tobči*.

[113] Sagang Sečen, *Erdeni-yin Tobči*, ch. 4, Schmidt, annotated edition, p. 389.

[114] Sagang Sečen, *Erdeni-yin Tobči*, ch. 4, Schmidt, annotated edition, pp. 193 and 199.

and protected the forbidden area,[115] a legend that is still preserved without change. However, the assertion that the Uriyangkhai people were guarding "the monarchs' golden treasures"[116] just can not be believed. The banner of the Ordos Commandery Princes 郡王 has now changed its name to Yijinhuoluo 伊金霍洛, which, according to Antoine Mostaert, literally means "rulers' circle," referring to the "tents surrounded by a wall of trees."[117] He interprets this as the Mongolian word for "circle" (qoriya), corresponding to *huoluo* 霍洛, which he thinks was transmuted from the word Qurūq (forbidden area), dating from the years when the Uriyangkhai of the Forest guarded Chinggis Khan's burial place.

The fief of Chinggis Khan's younger brother, Temüge Otčigin 帖木格斡赤斤, was in the most northeastern part of Mongolia, extending to the upper reaches of the Songhua (Sungari) River 松花江, and the Nen River 嫩江 (Nonni) basin. In the 24th year of the Zhiyuan reign period (1287), Otčigin's great great grandson Naiyan 乃顏 revolted, but he was captured in less than three months. In the 28th year of the Zhiyuan reign period (1291), Naiyan and his remaining troops fled into Jurchen territory and

---

[115] Antoine Mostaert, "Ordosica," *Bulletin of the Catholic University of Peking* 《輔仁英文學志》, vol. 9 (1934), p. 38: "Today, the ones who take responsibility for guarding the dead are the Darxat (Daerhete 達爾哈特). This name is the plural form of the word Darxan. Originally it was not the name of a people, but was the way of referring to tax evaders. In the Ordus region this term was also used to refer to the Mongols who take responsibility for guarding the 'Eight Rooms,' although we say that they originally seemed to belong to many different clans." Note that the Darxat people who took up this responsibility of guarding the tombs may have also been originally descendants of the Uriyangkhai People of the Forest. According to Zhang Xiangwen 張相文 (1876-1933), in his *Collected Manuscripts from the South Garden* 《南園叢稿》, ch. 3, p. 4, these "so-called eight white rooms do not survive today"; "The households charged with looking after the imperial tombs, which numbered over 500 families…had special rights with regard to the princes and nobles of the Mongol banners: they were exempt from all taxes and corvée labor. They also sometimes went out with their books and documents asking for donations, like itinerant monks, and wherever they went the Mongol banners had to provide them generously with oxen and sheep, and did not dare be stingy with them. However, they had to take turns guarding the tombs, and usually 70 or 80 households were installed there for this purpose. They did not have houses, but lived either in tents or in makeshift willow huts."

[116] Sagang Sečen, *Erdeni-yin Tobči*, ch. 6, Schmidt, annotated edition, p. 191.

[117] Antoine Mostaert, "Ordosica," *Bulletin of the Catholic University of Peking*, vol. 9, p. 49.

formed an alliance with the Jurchen and the Water Tatars 水達達 of the area north and south of the Huntung River 混同江 (today's Songhua River). In the 30th year of the Zhiyuan reign period (1293), the Yuan government then in Naiyan's former territory established Zhaozhou 肇州 as a garrison post. "Biography of Liu Qara Ba'adur" 劉哈剌八都魯傳 in the *History of the Yuan*, chapter 169, says that Qubilai Khan issued the following instructions to Qara Ba'adur: "Abalahuzhe 阿八剌忽者, which is in Naiyan's former territory, produces fish. Today I will establish a city there so that the people from the three tribes – Urs 兀速, Qapqanas 憨哈納思, and Kirghiz – will live there. I will call the city Zhaozhou. You will go there and serve as its Pacification Commissioner 宣慰使."

Some say that Yuan Dynasty Zhaozhou was in Zhuershan 珠爾山, within the city limits of Shuangcheng 雙城 in Jilin 吉林 Province, others say that it was where the Lalin River 拉林河 enters the Songhua River. The Jilin 吉林 Museum excavated a city called Tahu 他虎 in Beishangtaizi 北上臺子 village, ten kilometers southeast of Da'an 大安 City (*Archaeology* 考古, 1964, no. 1). Judging by its geographical position, this city must have been Zhaozhou 肇州 (also written with the characters 趙州), which was on the postal route in Yuan and Ming times; see the *Yongle Encyclopedia* 永樂大典, chapter 19,422, page 12, also chapter 19,426, page two; see also *Gazetteer of Liaodong* 遼東志, chapter 9, in the section *Record of Foreign Lands* 外志, "Way-Stations of the Western Regions" 海西西陸路站. The people of the three tribes, including the Kirghiz, who had been moved to this region must have had a close relationship with the three guard-stations 衛 in the Uriyangkhai region, which had been set up in northeastern China at the beginning of the Ming.

The eastward migration of the Kirghiz and the other two tribes has been studied by He Qiutao 何秋濤, Li Wentian 李文田, Hong Jun 洪鈞, and others. The Japanese scholar Yanai Wataru's 箭内亘 *Uryōgō san'ei Meishō kō* 『烏良哈三衛名称考』 (*A Study of the Names of the Three Guard-Stations in the Uriyangkhai Region*), notes in his conclusion that the Chinese and the Mongolian names of the three guard-stations bear no resemblance to each other; but he does not discuss this. In the *Veritable Records of the August Ming* 皇明實錄 for the 22nd year of Emperor Hongwu (1389), it says, "On the xinmao 辛卯 day of the fifth month the

Military Command 指揮使司 for the three guard-stations of Taining 泰寧, Yanduo 顏朵 (*sic*), and Fuyu 福餘 were established among the Uriyangkhai…and Torqučar 脫魯忽察爾 was appointed Vice Commander 指揮同知 for the Duoyan 朵顏 (*sic*) guard-station." The names of the three guard-stations are not the same in Chinese and Mongolian. The Sino-Mongolian glossaries 譯語部分 in the *Records of Armaments and Military Provisions* 武備錄 and Wang Minghe's 王鳴鶴 *Collection of Literature on Military Issues* 登壇必究 both give the Mongolian transcriptions for all the Chinese names. For Taining they give Wangliu 往流, for Fuyu they give Wozhe 我著, and for Duoyan they give Wuliang'an 五兩案. If we compare these two types of Chinese and Mongolian names, it is not difficult to see that the Chinese names for the three guard-stations are place names, while the Mongolian names are names of tribes.

Taining 泰寧 – Wangliu 往流. According to the Yuan and Ming postal routes, Yuan Dynasty Taizhou 泰州, which is Ming Dynasty Taizhou 台州, is 140 *li* north of Talu 塔魯 (called Taoer 洮爾 in the Ming). In 1956, the Taizhou stele 泰州碑 (now in the collection of the Heilongjiang 黑龍江 Museum) was discovered in Tazicheng 塔子城, 80 *li* northwest of Tailai 泰來. The Ming Dynasty Taining guard-station seems to have been established in this location; see the *Yongle Encyclopedia* 永樂大典, chapter 19,426, "Postal Stations" 驛站 two, page two; and *Gazetteer of Liaodong* 遼東志, chapter nine, in the section "Record of Foreign Lands" 外志, "Way-Stations of the Western Regions" 海西西陸路站.

In the *Continuation of Comprehensive Investigations Based on Literary and Documentary Sources* 續文獻通考, Wangliu 往流 is called Wangliu 罔留; both were used in the *Altan Tobči* as transliterations of "Onglighut,"[118] which means "the king's people." The structure of this word is the same as "Tutuqlighut" ("the Commander-in-Chief's people" 都督的人民). In the Ming period Onglighut was written Ongnighut; it is a transliteration of the name of the present-day Ongniute 翁牛特 Banner in Inner Mongolia. Who was this "king"? We are told in chapter 21 of the *History of the Yuan*, under Emperor Chengzong (Temür Khan), in the

---

[118] Antoine Mostaert, "Ordosica," *Bulletin of the Catholic University of Peking*, vol. 9, p. 34.

seventh month of the ninth year of the Dade reign period (1305) that "Toqto'a's Kirghiz tribe was issued five months of food." Otčigin's great great grandson Toqto'a was enfeoffed as Prince of Liao 遼王, therefore this portion of the Kirghiz tribe must have belonged to him.

Fuyu 福餘 – Wozhe 我著. During the Jin 金 period, Puyulu 蒲與路 was in the present-day Wuyur 烏裕爾 River basin in Heilongjiang Province. At the beginning of the Ming, the Fuyu guard-station was probably here. During the Liao and Jin periods there was a famous tribe in the northeast called Wure 兀惹 (also written 烏惹), which in the Yuan period was called Wuzhe 吾者. Wozhe is probably the same as Wure and Wuzhe, the pronunciation, of course, having changed over time. Jin Yufu's 金毓黻 *A Comprehensive History of China's Northeast* 東北通史 on page 329 follows the *Comprehensive Investigations Based on Literary and Documentary Sources* 文獻通考 in saying that Emperor Taizong 太宗 of the Song period "issued an edict to the Prince of Yanfu 琰府, in Wushe 烏舍 City, Fuyu 浮渝 Prefecture, Bohai 渤海," taking Wushe to be Wure and Fuyu 浮渝 to be Fuyu 扶餘, and considering such a Ming Dynasty Fuyu guard-station was already, from the Liao Dynasty, where the Wozhe tribe lived.

Duoyan 朵顏 – Wuliang'an 五兩案. *A Textbook for Translation between the Chinese and Barbarian Languages* 華夷譯語 records a letter, called "Torqučar's letter" 脫爾豁察爾書, from the Vice Commander of the Military Guard 指揮使司同知 of Duoyan guard-station, but its meaning is not very clear. A note on chapter 88 of the *History of the Yuan*, in the Zhonghua Book Company punctuated edition, collates from the Mongolian text and translates it into modern Chinese as follows: "From our sovereign Chinggis Khan's generation down to today, my Urianghad People of the Forest have never left Toyan Ondur 多延溫都爾 in the area of the Shuo River 搠河." Most scholars think that Toyan Ondur refers to the Soyorji 索岳爾濟 Mountains, and that the Shuo River is the present-day Chaor River 綽爾河. In the Ming period, the last point of the western regions way-stations was at the Uriangqan River 兀良河, also called the Wuliangha 烏良哈. I think the Urianghad People of the Forest referred to here were not the guards of Chinggis Khan's tomb, but indeed were the descendants of the Kirghiz and the other two tribes who came eastward in the 30th year of the Zhiyuan reign period (1293). This is why the three guard-stations that were set up at the beginning of the Ming in the areas of Duoyan, Taining, and Fuyu were called the "three guard-stations of the Uriyangkhai." Thus we can infer that in Yuan and Ming times, the name "Uriyangkhai" was extremely broad in scope, becoming a general name for the Kirghiz and neighboring tribes.

Apart from this, there were quite a few other places in the east to which the Kirghiz, Kemkemjihud, and other tribal peoples were moved. In the last year of Qubilai's reign (1293) there were "700 Kirghiz households in the military colony of Hesihe 合思合."* Hesihe, also translated as Hasihan 哈思罕, is a place south of Liaoyang 遼陽 on the Liaodong 遼東 Peninsula, which in the Liao and Jin periods was called Hesuguan 曷蘇館. It must have been the same place as Hesihe.

In the "Monograph on Official Posts" 百官志 of the *History of the Yuan* (chapter 88), it says, "In Haixi 海西, Liaodong, Hasihan, and other places there were falconers and various artisans, and the Ger-ün köhüd 怯憐口 tümen administered 4,000 artisan households of the Hasihan, Zhaozhou, and Toyan Ondur 朵因溫都爾 (Uriyangkhai)." These places were all inhabited by people from the Kirghiz and other tribes who had moved and settled here.

In the first year of the Yuanzhen 元貞 reign period (1295), the Kirghiz and other peoples who lived in Jinshan 縉山 (Yanqing 延慶, in present-day Beijing) were moved to Shandong 山東 and were given land, oxen, and seeds. At the end of the Yuan, Yang Yu 楊瑀 said in his *New Tales from the Mountain Dweller* 山居新話, "Jianzhou 缣州 is the present-day Nancheng Jianzhou camp 南城缣州營, and these are their descendants." Viewed in this way, we can see that some of their descendants must be among present-day Chinese residents of the central plain. The Kirghiz and Kemkemjihud were desperately lacking handicraft industry workers. Therefore after Chinggis Khan subdued and won the allegiance of these regions, he immediately moved large groups of handicraft workers there from the central plain. In the second year of the Zhiyuan reign period (1265) he moved various Kemkemjihud households to Zhongdu 中都 (present-day Beijing, called Zhongdu in the first year of the Zhiyuan reign period, and Daidu in the ninth year), and in the seventh year he moved

---

* According to his biography in the *History of the Yuan* (chapter 14), for the seventh month of 30th year of the Zhiyuan reign period. Translator's note.

first-class artisans from Kemkemjihud to Songshan (south of present-day Chifeng County 赤峰縣, Inner Mongolia). In the latter move, he was probably moving Chinese artisans from Kemkemjihud back home to the central plain; it seems unlikely that he could have been moving the only remaining Kirghiz handicraft workers into the interior of China.

March 1978 in Nanjing 南京

Timeline

Date	Event
1199	Temüjin, together with the Kerait tribal leader Ong Khan, attacked the Naiman tribe. The Naimans were defeated at Qïzïl Baši 乞濕勒巴失. Their Khan, Buyiruq 杯祿, fled to Kemkemjihud (Rashīd al-Dīn, *Jāmi' al-Tawārīkh*, translated into Russian as Рашид-ад-Дин, *Сборник Летонисей*, vol. 1, part 2, p. 112).
1200	J̌aqa-gambu (Jaqa-gambu) 札紺孛 suspected that his elder brother Ong Khan would do him harm, so he fled to the Naimans (*Jāmi' al-Tawārīkh*, vol. 1, part 2, p. 118).
1202	Temüjin defeated the Naimans at Köyiten 闕亦田. The Oyirat tribal leader Quduqa-Beki 忽都花別乞 came to the aid of the Naimans (*Jāmi' al-Tawārīkh*, vol. 1, part 2, pp. 121-2; *Record of the Personal Campaigns of the Holy Warrior* begins its account with this record; *The Secret History of the Mongols*, section 143, lists it under the year of the chicken [1201]).
1203	Ong Khan attacked Temüjin. Temüjin defeated him at Qalaqaljit-elet 合蘭真沙陀 and drank the muddy water of Lake Baljuna 班朱尼. Temüjin sent an envoy to reprimand Ong Khan. Ong Khan was defeated, fled to the Naimans, and was killed (*Jāmi' al-Tawārīkh*, vol. 1, part 2, pp. 125-6; 127-9, 132-4. *Record of the Personal Campaigns of the Holy Warrior*; *The Secret History*, sections 170, 176, 185, and 188; *History of the Yuan*, ch. 1, "Annals of Taizu [Temüjin]").
1204	Temüjin led an expedition against the Naimans. Tayang Khan was defeated and died in the Nahukun Mountains. [His son] Küšlük 曲出律 fled and took refuge with his uncle Buyiruq Khan. The Oyirat tribal leader Quduqa Beki joined the united army of the Naimans and the Merkits (*Jāmi' al-Tawārīkh*, vol. 1, part 2, pp. 147-8; *The Secret History*, sections 193-6; *Record of the Personal Campaigns of the Holy Warrior*; *History of the Yuan*, ch. 1, "Annals of Taizu [Temüjin]." Because the *History of the Yuan* record is identical with that in *Record of the Personal Campaigns of the Holy Warrior*, from here on the former will not be cited.
1206 (1st year of Emperor Taizu	Temüjin was proclaimed Chinggis Khan (*Jāmi' al-Tawārīkh*, vol. 1, part 2, p. 150; *The Secret History*, section 202; *Record of the Personal Campaigns of the Holy Warrior*).

太祖)	The Khan gave Qorči 10,000 members of the Ba'arin 巴阿鄰, Činas 赤那思, Tö'eles 脫斡劣思, Telengüt 帖良古惕, and Naiman tribes, and issued orders for [him] to guard the People of the Forest along the Irtysh River (*The Secret History*, section 207). Troops were sent out on an expedition against Buyiruq Khan, who was killed on the Saqaq 莎合 River in the Uluq Tagh 兀魯黑塔黑 Mountains. Quchulü and the Merkit leader Toqto'a 脫脫 fled along the Irtysh River (*Jāmi' al-Tawārīkh*, vol. 1, part 2, pp. 150-1; *Record of the Personal Campaigns of the Holy Warrior*; *The Secret History*, listed under the year of the dog [1202], section 158).
1207 (Taizu 2)	Altan 按彈 and Bura 不兀剌 were sent as envoys to the Kirghiz (*Jāmi' al-Tawārīkh*, vol. 1, part 2, p. 151; *Record of the Personal Campaigns of the Holy Warrior*). J̌oči (Jochi) subdued the various People of the Forest (*The Secret History*, section 239. See *Jāmi' al-Tawārīkh*, vol. 1, part 2, p. 253).
1208 (Taizu 3)	During the winter, the Oyirat tribal leader Quduqa Beki surrendered; he was put in the front lines of an expedition against Toqto'a and Küšlük. They reached a place called Buqdurma 不黑都爾麻 on the Irtysh River, and Toqto'a died in battle. Küšlük fled to Qara Khitai 哈剌契丹 (*Jāmi' al-Tawārīkh*, vol. 1, part 2, pp. 151-2; *Record of the Personal Campaigns of the Holy Warrior*. *The Secret History* records this event in the year of the rat [1205], see section 198).
1209 (Taizu 4)	The Uyghurs submitted (*Jāmi' al-Tawārīkh*, vol. 1, part 2, p. 152; *Record of the Personal Campaigns of the Holy Warrior*; *History of the Yuan*, ch. 122, "Biography of Barjuq-art-tegin 巴爾术阿爾忒的斤"); Juwaīnī, *The History of the World-Conqueror*; Boyle translation (1971), p. 44.
1211 (Taizu 6)	Halalu submitted (*Jāmi' al-Tawārīkh*, vol. 1, part 2, pp. 153-4, 163; *Record of the Personal Campaigns of the Holy Warrior*).
1213 (Taizu 8)	Shi Bingzhi 史秉直, Lord of Yongqing 永清豪強, surrendered to the Mongols, and led the over 100,000 families, who had capitulated and been organized into military camps to cultivate wasteland in Bazhou 霸州, on a great migration to the north of the Gobi Desert (*History of the Yuan*, ch. 147, "Biography of Shitianni" 《史天倪傳》).
1217 (Taizu 12)	Troops were sent on another expedition against the Tumat tribe (*Jāmi' al-Tawārīkh*, vol. 1, part 2, p. 178; *Record of the Personal Campaigns of the Holy Warrior*. *The Secret History* records this event under the year of the rabbit [1207], see section 240).
1218 (Taizu 13)	Jia Taraqun 賈塔剌渾 commanded the artillery (mangonel) troops, and stationed them at Kemkemjihud (*History of the Yuan*, ch. 151, "Biography of Jia Taraqun"). The Kirghiz rebelled; J̌oči was ordered to put down the rebellion. He conquered the Ulus 烏思, Qapqanas 憾哈納思, and other tribes

	(*Jāmi' al-Tawārīkh*, vol. 1, part 2, p. 256; *Record of the Personal Campaigns of the Holy Warrior*).
1219 (Taizu 14)	Chinggis Khan discussed launching an expedition against the Western regions (*Jāmi' al-Tawārīkh*, vol. 1, part 2, p. 197).
1221 (Taizu 16)	The Taoist monk Changchun (Qiu Chuji 邱處機) received an imperial order and left on his journey to the west from Xuande 宣德 (*Record of the Journey to the West of the Daoist Monk Changchun*, ch. 1; *History of the Yuan*, ch. 202, "Biography of Qiu Chuji").
1223 (Taizu 18)	Qiu Chuji returned to the Qixia 棲霞 temple near Činqai 鎮海 City. He heard that Chinese craftsmen had been moved to Kemkemjihud (*Record of the Journey to the West of the Daoist Monk Changchun*, ch. 2).
1227 (Taizu 22)	Chinggis Khan died. The Ūdāchī of the Uriyangkhai tribe in the forests guarded the forbidden region where Chinggis Khan was buried (*Jāmi' al-Tawārīkh*, vol. 1, part 2, pp. 234-5, 273).
1241 (13th year of Emperor Taizong 太宗)	Ögödei died. He had sent Heduan and the others deeply into the Arctic to conduct investigations, and it had taken several years to go there and back. They had reached the vicinity of the Arctic Circle, the "island where the sun never sets" (Yelü Zhu 耶律鑄, note to "Two Poems on the Dingling"丁零二首, *Anthology of the Drunken Hermit at the Twin Streams* 雙溪醉隱集, ch. 5).
1248 (3rd year of Emperor Dingzong 定宗)	After Qubilai, in his residence, summoned Zhang Dehui 張德輝 north of the Gobi Desert, Zhang Dehui recommended Li Pan 李槃 and others from Zhending 真定 [Route], in the territory of Qubilai's mother, the empress Sorghanghtani Beki. [Li] Pan received the empress' order to serve as Ariq-Böke's Expositor-in-Waiting 講讀 (*History of the Yuan*, ch. 163, "Biography of Zhang Dehui"; *History of the Yuan*, ch. 126, "Biography of Lian Xixian 廉希憲").
1250 (gengxu 庚戌 year)	At this time, Gaocheng 藁城 in Zhending was given to Sorghanghtani Beki, Tölüi's wife, as her fief. Sorghanghtani Beki selected young men from her territory to go to Qara-Qorum (*History of the Yuan*, ch. 148, "Biography of Dong Wenyong" 董文用傳).
1251 (1st year of Emperor Xianzong 憲宗)	The official Möge 末哥 was sent in command of 20,000 troops to Kirghiz and Kemkemjihud (*Jāmi' al-Tawārīkh*, Boyle's English translation *The Successors of Genghis Khan* [New York, 1971], p. 214). The various princes were each moved to their own territory. Taizong's grandson Qaidu was moved to Haiyali 海押立, and Mieli 篾立 [was moved] to the Irtysh River (*History of the Yuan*, ch. 3, "Annals of Xianzong 憲宗 [Möngke Khan]"). Xianzong's mother Sorghanghtani Beki died. Kirghiz and Kemkemjihud were her territories. She had sent the three emirs, in command of 1,000 men, to go by ship and look for the legendary places in the Angara River near the sea where everywhere there was

	white silver. Failing to find such places, they returned (V. V. Bartol'd [В. В. Бартольд], *Twelve Lectures on the History of the Turks of Central Asia*, translated into German by Theodor Menzel as *Zwölf Vorlesungen über die Geschichte der Türken Mittelasiens* [Berlin: Deutsche Gesellschaft für Islamkunde, 1935], p. 186, quoting from Abū al-Ghāzī Bahādur Khān's work).
1256 (Xianzong 6)	Shi Tianlin 石天麟 was sent as an envoy to Ögödei's descendant, Prince Qaidu, and was detained (*History of the Yuan*, ch. 153, "Biography of Shi Tianlin"). Lian Xixian 廉希憲 recommended Zhang Chu 张礎, a scholar from Ariq-Böke's territory of Zhending, to serve at Qubilai's residence. Ariq-Böke held a grudge against Zhang Chu because he (Zhang Chu) would not attach himself to him (*History of the Yuan*, ch. 167, "Biography of Zhang Chu").
1257 (Xianzong 7)	Xianzong left his younger brother, Ariq-Böke, to guard Mongolia, stationed at Qara-Qorum, while he himself commanded a large army and attacked the Song (*History of the Yuan*, ch. 3, "Annals of Xianzong"; (*Jāmi' al-Tawārīkh* II, p. 224, recorded under the year of the rabbit).
1260 (1st year of the Zhongtong 中統 reign period of Emperor Shizu 世祖 [Qubilai Khan])	Ariq-Böke occupied Qara-Qorum and engaged in a struggle with Qubilai for the Khan's throne. He was defeated by Qubilai's general Yisüngge 移相哥, and retreated to Kirghiz (*Jāmi' al-Tawārīkh* II, p. 253). Ariq-Böke's tribal generals Alamdar 阿蘭答爾 and Qunduqai 渾都海 were defeated and killed at Liangzhou 涼州. The remnants of his army fled to Kirghiz, Ariq-Böke's territory (*History of the Yuan*, ch. 4, "Annals of Shizu [Qubilai Khan] 1"; *Jāmi' al-Tawārīkh* II, p. 254).
1261 (Zhongtong 2)	Ariq-Böke attacked Yisüngge and defeated him. Qubilai personally led an expedition against and defeated Ariq-Böke at Shimughultai naur 昔木土腦爾 (*Jāmi' al-Tawārīkh* II, pp. 256-7; *History of the Yuan*, ch. 4, "Annals of Shizu [Qubilai Khan] 1"). He was then in Elet 額利惕 and defeated Ariq-Böke's right wing. Ariq-Böke fled to the north. (*Jāmi' al-Tawārīkh* II, p. 257; *History of the Yuan*, ch. 4, "Annals of Shizu [Qubilai Khan] 1").
1262 (Zhongtong 3)	Ariq-Böke advanced and attacked Ča'adai's descendant Prince Alqu 阿魯忽 (Aluhu, Alughu) and defeated him. He camped for the winter at Almaliq 阿力麻里 (*Jāmi' al-Tawārīkh* II, p. 259).
1264 (1st year of the Zhiyuan 至元 reign period)	Ariq-Böke surrendered to Qubilai Khan (*Jāmi' al-Tawārīkh* II, p. 261; *History of the Yuan*, ch. 5, "Annals of Shizu [Qubilai Khan] 2"). Qubilai's influence reached Kemkemjihud. It must have been this year when he ordered Boba 伯八 to lead the troops and horses of the various tribes and set up a military colony at Kemkemjihud 欠欠州 (*History of the Yuan*, ch. 193, "Biography of Boba").
1265	An edict was issued ordering that the various kinds of craftsmen of

(Zhiyuan 2)	Činqai, Ber-balïq 百八里, and Kemkemjihud 謙謙州 move to Zhongdu 中都 (Beijing) and be given 15,000 *liang* 兩 of silver for their travel expenses (*History of the Yuan*, ch. 6, "Annals of Shizu [Qubilai Khan] 3").
1268 (Zhiyuan 5)	Qaidu raised troops and moved southward. The Yuan army met them going the other way and defeated them at Beiting 北庭 (Beshbalïq) (*History of the Yuan*, ch. 63, "Appendix on the Northwest," "Monograph on Geography," ch. 6).
1269 (Zhiyuan 6)	The poverty-stricken Kemkemjihud, craftsmen were given 5,999 *dan* 石 of rice as government relief (*History of the Yuan*, ch. 6, "Annals of Shizu [Qubilai Khan] 3").
1270 (Zhiyuan 7)	Liu Haoli 劉好禮 was appointed *daruqači* for Yilan, Kirghiz, and the others of the five tribes (*History of the Yuan*, ch. 167, "Biography of Liu Haoli"; ch. 63, "Appendix on the Northwest," "Monograph on Geography").
1271 (Zhiyuan 8)	The top craftsmen from Kemkemjihud were moved to Songshan, and provided with oxen and equipment (*History of the Yuan*, ch. 7, "Annals of Shizu [Qubilai Khan] 4"). Namoqan 那木罕 established a temporary camp at Almaliq 阿力麻里 (*History of the Yuan*, ch. 13, "Annals of Shizu [Qubilai Khan] 10").
1272 (Zhiyuan 9)	The amount of tax that had to be submitted by Kirghiz was reduced. Also, many southerners were sent there to help with the cultivation, bringing oxen and equipment with them (*History of the Yuan*, ch. 7, "Annals of Shizu [Qubilai Khan] 4").
1275 (Zhiyuan 12)	Hantum 安童, fourth generation grandson of Muqali 木華黎, was ordered to assist the prince of Beiping 北平, Namoqan, in his mission to protect Almaliq (*History of the Yuan*, ch. 126, "Biography of Hantum").
1276 (Zhiyuan 13)	The Chingissid princes Širgi 昔里吉 and Toq Temür 脫鐵木兒 rebelled, killed Boba, and put Namoqan and Hantum in fetters (*History of the Yuan*, ch. 9, "Annals of Shizu [Qubilai Khan] 6"; see *Jāmi' al-Tawārīkh* II, p. 266).
1277 (Zhiyuan 14)	Bayan 伯顏 defeated Širgi at the Orkhon River 斡魯歡河 (*History of the Yuan*, ch. 127, "Biography of Bayan"). Širgi fled to the Irtysh River. Toq Temür advanced and attacked the territory of the Kirghiz and later appointed Sarman 撒里蠻 as ruler (*Jāmi' al-Tawārīkh* II, p. 267).
1279 (Zhiyuan 16)	When the various northern princes rebelled, Liu Haoli was detained and then released. At this time Liu Haoli was again summoned to Kemkemjihud (*History of the Yuan*, ch. 167, "Biography of Liu Haoli").
1280 (Zhiyuan 17)	Liu Haoli fled back to the capital (Daidu). During the Yuan period, a city was founded at the place where the Angara and Kem Rivers converge. Its name was Kirghiz (黠戛斯, Qījās). It must have been

	established by Liu Haoli, the man who was appointed as *daruqači* for the five tribes (*Jāmi' al-Tawārīkh* , Russian translation, vol. 1, part 1, p. 102). In order to produce a new calendar, Guo Shoujing 郭守敬, with the Yuan government's support, established a station to measure solsticial shadow lengths 測景所 in the Arctic Circle, at 65 Chinese degrees north (*History of the Yuan*, ch. 164, "Biography of Guo Shoujing").
1281 (Zhiyuan 18)	Because there were 142 households of Kemkemjihud weavers who were very poor, they were given government relief in the form of grain 粟; their wives and children whom they had helped were returned to their homes by the officials (*History of the Yuan*, ch. 11, "Annals of Shizu [Qubilai Khan] 8"). The soldiers of the military colony established in Kemkemjihud were issued paper money, clothing, and other items, as well as agricultural and fishing implements (*History of the Yuan*, ch. 11, "Annals of Shizu, 8").
1283 (Zhiyuan 20)	The Minister of Personnel Liu Haoli reported to the emperor about the customs of the Kirghiz (*History of the Yuan*, ch. 12, "Annals of Shizu [Qubilai Khan], 9"). 600 oxen were lent to the poverty-stricken Kirghiz people (*History of the Yuan*, ch. 12, "Annals of Shizu [Qubilai Khan], 9").
1284 (Zhiyuan 21)	The Chingissid prince Yaqutu 牙忽都 defeated Qaidu (*History of the Yuan*, ch. 17, "Biography of Yaqutu"). Namoqan and Hantum submitted in succession (*History of the Yuan*, ch. 126, "Biography of Hantum").
1285 (Zhiyuan 22)	Du'a 都哇, Khan of the Chaghatay *ulus*, who had been put in place by Qaidu, surrounded the Uyghur capital city (*History of the Yuan*, ch. 122, "Biography of Barjuq-art-tegin," recorded under the 12th year of the Zhiyuan reign period; this is according to the investigations of Tu Ji; see *Historical Record of the Mongols*, ch. 36, "Biography of Barjuq-art-tegin").
1286 (Zhiyuan 23)	Qaidu invaded the Altai Mountains. Tutuq 土图哈 and Dorduqa 朵兒朵懷 both joined him (*History of the Yuan*, ch. 128, "Biography of Tutuq"). Sums of 56,139 silver *ding* 錠 and 13 *liang* 兩 worth of paper money were bestowed on the various craftsmen of Kemkemjihud (*History of the Yuan*, ch. 14, "Annals of Shizu [Qubilai Khan] 11").
1287 (Zhiyuan 24)	Because the imperial grandson was a military governor on the northern frontier, Tiemuer 鐵穆耳 ordered Tutuq and others to follow him (*History of the Yuan*, ch. 128, "Biography of Tutuq").
1288 (Zhiyuan 25)	Qaidu and Du'a attacked the borderlands (*History of the Yuan*, ch. 15, "Annals of Shizu [Qubilai Khan]", 12). Uwaš's defeat of Qaidu's Ba'arin general and others at Ibir-Šibir must have been during this year (*History of the Yuan*, ch. 132, "Biography of Uwaš").

1289 (Zhiyuan 26)	As for the Kirghiz military households who lived in Qara-Qorum, an investigation into the welfare of the poor people was carried out and relief was provided (*History of the Yuan*, ch. 15, "Annals of Shizu [Qubilai Khan] 12"). The Kirghiz and other tribes from the military colonies in Qara-Qorum were sent on a northern expedition (*History of the Yuan*, ch. 15, "Annals of Shizu [Qubilai Khan] 12"). Kamala 甘麻剌, Prince of Jin 晉, launched an expedition against Qaidu, and reached the Khangai Mountains 杭海嶺. Tutuq accompanied him in the military campaign (*History of the Yuan*, ch. 128, "Biography of Tutuq"). Bayan was ordered to subdue Qara-Qorum. Qaidu invaded Qara-Qorum, and Emperor Shizu [Qubilai Khan] personally launched an expedition [against him].
1291 (Zhiyuan 28)	Six postal stations were set up from Kirghiz to Oyirat 外剌 (*History of the Yuan*, ch. 16, "Annals of Shizu [Qubilai Khan] 13").
1292 (Zhiyuan 29)	Malik Temür 明里鐵木爾 rebelled in the name of Qaidu, but Bayan defeated him at the Asaqutu Mountain 阿撒忽禿嶺 (*History of the Yuan*, ch. 127, "Biography of Bayan"). An edict was issued to Tutuq to advance and take Kirghiz (*History of the Yuan*, ch. 128, "Biography of Tutuq").
1293 (Zhiyuan 30)	Tutuq's troops arrived in the Kem River 欠河 area, and absorbed all the five tribes completely. Qaidu led troops to the Kem River and inflicted another defeat on them (*History of the Yuan*, ch. 128, "Biography of Tutuq"). The people of the three tribes of Urs, Qapqanas, and Kirghiz were resettled in Naiyan's former territory, and the city of Zhaozhou 肇州 was established (*History of the Yuan*, ch. 169, "Biography of Liu Qara Ba'atur"). In the 12th month, Bayan returned to Datong 大同 from the north. Üsü-temür 玉昔帖木爾 took his place and led troops north of the Gobi Desert (*History of the Yuan*, ch. 127, "Biography of Bayan"). The 700 Kirghiz households that Jirqu 只爾忽 removed formed the basis of a military colony in Hesihe 合思合 (*History of the Yuan*, ch. 17, "Annals of Shizu [Qubilai Khan] 14").
1295 (1st year of the Yuanzhen reign period of Emperor Chengzong 成宗)	The Kirghiz and other people who lived in Jinshan 縉山 were resettled in Shandong, and were given oxen and seeds for their farms (*History of the Yuan*, ch. 18, "Annals of Chengzong [Temür Khan] 1").
1297 (1st year of the	Tutuq's son Čonqur 床兀爾 defeated Qaidu at the Daruqu 答魯忽 River south of Ba'arin 八鄰. His general, Boba 孛伯, was also defeated

Dade 大德 reign period)	at the Alei River 阿雷河 (*History of the Yuan*, ch. 128, "Biography of Čonqur").
1298 (Dade 2)	Čonqur defeated Du'a, Čičektü 徹徹禿 and others. He advanced and attacked Qočqar 火爾哈赤 (*History of the Yuan*, ch. 128, "Biography of Čonqur").
1299 (Dade 3)	The emperor's son Haishan 海山 was ordered to take the place of Kökečü 闊闊出, the Prince of Ningyuan 寧遠, and be Regional Commander 總兵 to guard the region north of the Gobi Desert (*History of the Yuan*, ch. 22, "Annals of Wuzong 1").
1300 (Dade 4)	Haishan fought against Qaidu in battle at Körebe 闊別列, and defeated him (*History of the Yuan*, ch. 22, "Annals of Wuzong 1"). Čonqur attacked the rebellious princes Tümen 禿麥 and Urus 斡魯思 at Kök 闊客 (*History of the Yuan*, ch. 128, "Biography of Čonqur").
1301 (Dade 5)	Qaidu and Du'a entered and invaded the Altai Mountain area. Haishan defeated them, and Qaidu was killed (*History of the Yuan*, ch. 22, "Annals of Wuzong 1"). Qaidu's son Čapar 察八爾 succeeded him and as a leader of his people (*History of the Yuan*, ch. 119, "Biography of Boanhu" 《博安忽傳》).
1303 (Dade 7)	The Chaghatay princc Du'a, Qaidu's son Čapar, and Malik Temür requested permission to surrender (*History of the Yuan*, ch. 21, "Annals of Chengzong [Temür Khan] 4").
1305 (Dade 9)	The Kirghiz tribe led by Prince Toqto'a 脫脫 of Liao 遼 was given a five months supply of food (*History of the Yuan*, ch. 21, "Annals of Chengzong [Temür Khan] 4").
1306 (Dade 10)	Haishan went to the territory of Irtysh 也里的失 to receive the surrender of Tümän 禿滿, Malik Temür, Arqui 阿魯灰, and the other princes. Čapar fled to Du'a's tribe and imprisoned his family in their tent (*History of the Yuan*, ch. 22, "Annals of Wuzong 1").
1307 (Dade 11)	Üljei 完澤 was sent to accompany Kirghiztai Inal 乞爾吉亦難 in an expedition against the Kirghiz and to collect hostages 禿魯花, horses, and falcons 鷹鶻 (*History of the Yuan*, ch. 22, "Annals of Wuzong 1").
1308 (1st year of the Zhida 至大 reign period of Emperor Wuzong 武宗)	Tümän was invested as Prince of Yangdi 陽翟 (*History of the Yuan*, ch. 22, "Annals of Wuzong 1").
1321 (1st year of the Zhizhi 至治 · reign period of	There was a flood in Kirghiz (*History of the Yuan*, ch. 27, "Annals of Yingzong 1"). The Ursu, Qapqanas, and other tribes were poverty-stricken, so each household was provided with two mares (*History of the Yuan*, ch.

Emperor Yingzong 英宗)	27, "Annals of Yingzong 1").
1360 (20th year of the Zhizheng 至正 reign period of the Shundi 順帝 Emperor)	Yang Yu 陽瑀 wrote in the "Postscript to the *New Tales from the Mountain Dweller*" 《山居新話後序》 that his friends gave him black rock salt produced in Kemkemjihud (Yang Yu, *New Tales from the Mountain Dweller*, p. 3).

THE KERAIT KINGDOM UP TO THE THIRTEENTH CENTURY

Chen Dezhi 陳得芝

1. Introduction

Before Chinggis Khan established his regime, there were, for the most part, five powerful tribes which contended with each other for hegemony on the Mongolian plain. These included the Tatars 塔塔兒 (or 韃靼), who occupied the vast, grassy plain surrounding Büyür na'ur 捕魚兒海 (present-day Buir Lake 貝爾湖); the Mongols 蒙古 from the Onon River, the Kerulen River, and the Burkhan Mountains 不兒罕山 (the present-day Kentei Mountains); the Merkits 篾兒乞 from the middle and lower reaches of the Selenga River; the Naimans 乃蠻 east and west of the Altai Mountains; and the Kerait 克烈, who controlled the heart of the area north of the Gobi Desert – the valleys of the Khangai Mountains 杭海山, the Orkhon River 斡兒寒河, and the Tu'ula (hereafter Tula) River 土兀剌河. Among them the Kerait tribe was the strongest and most prosperous.

Kerait 克烈 is also transliterated as Qielie 怯烈, Qielieyi 怯列亦, Qieliyi 怯里亦, Kelieyiti 客列亦惕, Kailie 凱烈, and so forth. At that time the Kerait people were at relatively high level of social development compared to the other tribes on the Mongolian plateau. Long before the Mongols had risen to power, they already held sway over all the tribes in the area north of the Gobi Desert. At the end of the 12th century, the Kerait tribal leader Ong Khan 王汗 led expeditions in all directions, attempting to annex the various tribes and unite all of the regions north of the Gobi Desert under his rule. At that time the Mongol Qiyan 乞顏 clan was still subordinate to the Kerait tribe, and Temüjin 鐵木真, the Qiyan chieftain who later became Chinggis Khan, was still only a vassal of Ong Khan. As he described himself, he was just a hawk hunting its prey on behalf of Ong Khan.[1] However, the arrogant Ong Khan, who looked down upon his

[1] See Rashīd al-Dīn, *Jāmi' al-Tawārīkh* (*Compendium of Chronicles*), translated into Russian as Рашид-ад-дин, *Сборник Летописей*, vol. 1 edited by A. A. Semenova (A. A. Семенова), part 2 (Москва - Ленинград: Издательство Академии Наук СССР, 1952), p. 129. It reads (in translation and transliteration): "again, oh khan, my father…I became a bird, like a hunting eagle, and flew towards the Chiurkhu Mountains, and over the Buir Lake, and seized the cranes with grey-black feet for you. If you ask, 'Who were they?'

rivals, was in the end defeated by Temüjin, who rose up powerfully within his ranks. As soon as the Kerait kingdom had reached its maximum size, it was suddenly and completely devoured by the newly risen Mongols. The military expeditions that had been launched under Ong Khan's banner merely paved the way for Chinggis Khan's world conquest, which leveled everything in its path.

The history of the Kerait tribe should be seen as a very important chapter in the history of the Mongolian plateau in pre-Mongol times, from the destruction of the Uyghur Qaghanate to the establishment of the Mongol nation. Both Chinese and foreign scholars have done a massive amount of work editing and annotating the sources for the history of the Kerait, investigating the origins of the various clans, and putting the historical events in order. However, there are still many issues to be resolved. This article aims to build on the foundations of the work done in the past and bring it forward through further investigation.

2. The Kerait People as an Ethnic Group within the Mongols

As to the ethnic group to which the Kerait people belonged and its origin, there are still many questions to be answered. Most scholars have been inclined to the view that they were a Turkish-speaking group, but they tend to be cautious and to reserve final judgment on the matter. Paul Pelliot said:

> None of the stories about the origin of the Mongols mentions the Kerait tribe. It is still difficult to determine whether the Kerait people were Mongols who had received heavy Turkish influence, or Turkish who had gone through the process of Mongolization. No matter which was the case, most of the Kerait rulers must have been Turkish. In this way of viewing the matter, although people say that Tuowolingle 脫斡鄰勒[2] is a Mongolian name, I would rather see it as a Turkish name.[3]

They were the Durban and Tatar tribes…" (*dīgar ei khan pedar man ba'd az ān men be-kūh Jūrqū mānand singqūr parande shodam wa Būīr nāūūr –ra be-gozāshtam wa kolangān ke pāyehāī īshān kebūd wa khākestar rang būd jehat tū be-gereftam agar tū gūyī ān kodām ast qūm Dūrbān wa Tātār and wa...*).

[2] Ong Khan's name. The *Record of the Personal Campaigns of the Holy Warrior* 《聖武親征錄》 transliterates it as Tuolian 脫憐, and the *History of the Yuan* 《元史》 writes

However, Pelliot did not provide any grounds for this view.

In an article on the origins of the Mongol tribes, Yekemingghadai Irinchin 亦鄰真 fills the gaps in Pelliot's theory. His view is that "The Kerait people do not appear to be the original Mongols. Apart from their Turkicized Syriac religious (Nestorian) names, the names of Kerait people that appear in historical sources are almost all Turkish. If they were the original Mongols, they must have been highly Turkicized." He also points out that the "Treatise on the Tribes" in the *Jāmi' al-Tawārīkh* groups the Kerait together with the Naiman, Önggüd 汪古, Tangut 唐古, Uyghur, and Kirghiz 乞兒乞思 tribes, thereby distinguishing them from the Mongol tribes – "this provides food for thought."[4] Here Irinchin points to two pieces of evidence supporting the view that the Kerait people were Turkish. One is that their names were Turkish, and the other is that the *Jāmi' al-Tawārīkh* distinguishes them from the Mongolian-speaking tribes in its classification, grouping them with tribes that are almost all Turkish – with the Tanguts as the only exception.

---

it as Tuoli 脫里. The *Jāmi' al-Tawārīkh* (*Compendium of Chronicles*) has Toghril and explains it as follows: "In Turkish and the language of the Kerait tribe, Toghril is Tunghrul. They use this word as the name of a type of bird. Although no one has ever seen this bird, it is very famous among the people and is highly praised. It is like the western '*anqa*' (the name of a magic bird in Muslim historical sources, recorded from Caucasian legends). People believe that this bird is like an eagle, its beak and claws are as hard as steel, and it can bring down and kill two or three hundred birds with a single attack in flight" (*Jāmi' al-Tawārīkh*, Russian translation, vol. 1, part 2, p. 108). The word Toγril can be found in Mahmūd al-Kāshghāri's *Dīwān lughāt al-turk* (*Compendium of the Languages of the Turks*). It is a kind of hunting eagle. This word becomes To'oril in Mongolian. See *Histoire des Campagnes de Gengis Khan* (*Cheng-wou Ts'in-Tcheng Lou*), a French version of the *Record of the Personal Campaigns of the Holy Warrior* translated and annotated by Paul Pelliot and Louis Hambis (Leiden, 1951), p. 210.

[3] "La légende des origins mongoles ne leur fait aucune place, et il est encore difficile de dire si les Kerait étaient des Mongols qui avaient fortement subi l'influence torque ou des Turcs en voie de se mongoliser; en tout cas, beaucoup de titulatures kérait étaient torques, et Togroul est plutôt un nom turc qu'un nom mongol." Paul Pelliot, *La Haute Asie* (Paris, 1931), p. 25, quoting from René Grousset, *L'empire des steppes*, 4th ed. (Paris, 1969), p. 245.

[4] Yekemingghadai Irinchin 亦鄰真, "On the Origins of the Ethnic Groups of Northern China and the Mongols," 《中國北方民族與蒙古族族源》, *Journal of Inner Mongolian University* 《内蒙古大學學報》, 1979, nos. 3-4 (joint volume).

Zhou Qingshu 周清澍, in his discussion of the origin of the Önggüd tribe, also mentions the Kerait tribe. Based on the classification of the tribes in the *Jāmi' al-Tawārīkh*, he concludes that the Kerait, Naiman, and Önggüd tribes "may have been remnants of the Turkish and Uyghur groups who ruled over the Mongolian steppe in succession before the collapse of their regimes." He also makes two more points: first, that the Kerait people, together with the Naiman and Önggüd people, had been converted to Nestorianism 景教, and second, that they intermarried with each other. He uses the latter to support the view that these three tribes may have belonged to the same ethnic group 族. However, he also expressed the view that "it is very difficult to determine whether the Kerait tribe was purely Turkish-speaking or not."[5]

The evidence mentioned above is not sufficient to determine the ethnic group to which the Kerait belonged. The tribes of the Mongolian-speaking people were dominated for a long period by the Turks and Uyghurs, and they then migrated one after another into the land that was originally Turkish. Thus it was unavoidable that they would be influenced by the Turkish economy and culture, although different tribes were influenced at different levels. It is not difficult to find examples of Turkish names in the various Mongol tribes. For example, among the Tayiči'ut 泰赤烏, Suldus 遜都思, and Negüs 捏古思 there are people named Toghroul (Toghril) in all of them.[6] Chinggis Khan had an inherited slave called Toghroul (Toghril), who rebelled and threw in his lot with Ong Khan.[7] The Mongol tribal leader Ambaqai Khan's 俺巴孩汗 father was called Senggüm-bilge 想昆必勒格, the term *senggüm* being a misreading of the Liao Dynasty official title *xiangwen* (General) 詳穩, a title derived from the Chinese *xianggong* (Grand Councilor) 相公, which was borrowed by the Khitan and granted to the main or most powerful chieftain of a subordinate tribe, and *bilge* 必勒格 being a Turkish word meaning "wise" or "intelligent."

---

[5] Zhou Qingshu 周清澍, "The Ethnic Origin of the Önggüd" 《汪古部的族源》, *Collected Papers of the Memorial Conference for the Foundation of the China Mongolian History Institute* 《中國蒙古史學會成立大會紀念集刊》 (Hohhot, 1979), pp. 199-200.

[6] *Jāmi' al-Tawārīkh*, Russian translation, vol. 1, part 1, pp. 182 (Tayiči'ut clan), 174 (Suldus clan); vol. 1, part 2, p. 276 (chiliarch Toghril from the Negüs clan).

[7] *The Secret History of the Mongols*, section 180, in the *Four Branches of Literature Collection*, third series edition, ch. 6.

The latter was taken by the Turkish Bilgä Qaghan 毗伽可汗 as his title. The J̌e'üret (Je'üret) 照烈 tribal leader's name was Ülüg-ba'atur 玉律拔都. In Turkish, *ülüg* means lucky.[8] In the Mongol Qiyan tribe, there was a person from the J̌ürki 主爾乞 (J̌ürkin, Jürkin) clan called Boli 播里 (Böri, written 不里孛闊, Büri Bökö, in *The Secret History of the Mongols*), who wounded Chinggis Khan's younger brother Belgütei 別里古台 in the shoulder at the meeting of the Mongol tribes on the Onon River 斡難河. Böri means "wolf" in Turkish, which in Mongolian is called *čino*. The Turkish name Fulin Khan 附鄰可汗, also transliterated as Buli 步利, or Fuli 附離, was the same name (Böri).[9] There was a person called Taqai-daru 塔海答魯 in the J̌e'üret tribe. In Chinggis Khan's army there was a great general from the Suldus tribe named Taqai-ba'atur 塔海拔都爾. According to Pelliot, Taqai may be the Turkish word Tarai, meaning "maternal uncle," which has the same meaning as the Mongolian word *naqaču*.[10] There are more examples of this type which could be cited, but it is clear that among Mongols the phenomenon of borrowing Turkish words to make names was not rare. However, this seems insufficient evidence to prove conclusively that the Kerait belonged to a Turkish ethnic group.

As for the language of the Kerait people, apart from their names there is no other direct evidence of it. All we have is the statement in the *Jāmi' al-Tawārīkh* that the Kerait people "have some similarities with the Mongol tribes. Their customs, habits, dialect and vocabulary are quite close to each other" (Они [кераиты] имели сходство с монгольскими племенами, и их обычаи, нравы, наречия и словарный состав [لغت] — близки друг к другу).[11] However, in 1246, the Pope's ambassador to the Mongols, John of Plano Carpini, recorded something noteworthy:

---

[8] For this character see the *Tonyukuk Inscription* 《暾欲谷碑》 in Runic Turkic.

[9] *Histoire des Campagnes de Gengis Khan*, p. 189; Han Rulin 韓儒林, "A Philological Study of Turkish Official Position Titles" 《突厥官號考釋》, in *Collection from the Yurt* [Han Rulin's papers] 《穹廬集》 (Shanghai, 1982), p. 311. Cha'adai's grandson was also called Böri 部里 (written Boli 孛里 in "Annals of Xianzong" 《憲宗紀》 in the *History of the Yuan* 《元史》).

[10] *Histoire des Campagnes de Gengis Khan*, p. 127.

[11] *Jāmi' al-Tawārīkh*, Russian translation, vol. 1, part 2, p. 108.

> In the East there is a land…which is called Mongolia. At one time there were four tribes in this land. One was the Yekamongol, which means the Great Mongols; the second was the Su-Mongol, that is to say, the Mongols of the water, but these called themselves Tartars after a certain river named the Tartur, which flows through their territory; the third was called the Merkit; and the fourth was the Mecrit. All of these tribes were alike in appearance and had the same language, although they were separate from each other, having their own provinces and rulers.[12]

Scholars are not united in their identification of the tribe that Carpini called "Mecrit." Later on, in the eighth year of Carpini's embassy to the Mongols, the French envoy William of Rubruck recorded that Ong Khan (Unc) "had under him people called Crit and Merkit, who were Nestorian Christians."[13] Armand D'Avezac thought that Rubruck's "Crit and Merkit" should be changed to "Crit and Mecrit," in order to make it consistent with Carpini's record. He thought these two names referred to a single tribe (just as with Longa and Solanga, and Chin and Machin), and that this was the Kerait tribe. However, Rockhill was suspicious of this view.[14] According to him, there was no doubt that Rubruck's Crit was Kerait, and that Merkit was just Merkit. Without a doubt, Armand D'Avezac had no grounds for forcibly changing it to Mecrit. The Merkit people were not Nestorians, nor did they fall under Ong Khan's jurisdiction. Rubruck was just repeating hearsay.

In the "Treatise on the Tribes" in the *Jāmi' al-Tawārīkh*, the section on Merkit says: "Although some groups of Mongols call the Merkit people Makrit, the two refer to the same thing (хотя некоторая часть монголов называет меркитов мекритам, [но] смысл обоих [названий] один и тот же)."[15] It thus seems that we can take Carpini's Mecrit and Merkit as referring to the same tribe. However, Carpini's travel account mentions these two names twice, clearly referring to two different tribes. So it seems

---

[12] Christopher Dawson, ed., *The Mongol Mission* (London and New York: Sheed and Ward, 1955), p. 19.

[13] Ibid., p. 122.

[14] W. W. Rockhill, trans. and ed., *The Journey of William of Rubruck to the Eastern Parts of the World*, (London: 1900), p. 111; Armand D'Avezac's above-mentioned argument (see his *Relation des Mongols ou Tartares par le frère Jean du Plan de Carpin* [Paris: 1839], p. 534) is reported by Rockhill on page 111, note 2.

[15] *Jāmi' al-Tawārīkh*, Russian translation, vol. 1, part 1, p. 114.

that we cannot conflate the two. Liu Qi 劉祁 in his *Record of the Embassy to the North* 北使記 records that in the year 1220 an envoy from the Jin 金 Dynasty named Wugusun Zhongduan 吾古孫仲端, who traveled through Mongolia and the Western regions gathering information, recorded the names of such northwestern tribes as Molixi 磨里奚, Mokeli 磨可里, Qiliqisi 紇里紇斯 (Kirghiz), Naiman, Hangli 航里, Guigu 瑰古, Tuma 途馬, Helu 合魯, and so forth. Wang Guowei 王國維 thought that Molixi was Merkit, and that Mokeli was Kerait.[16] This accords with what Carpini said. Yanai Wataru 箭内亙 also takes this view. Moreover, he thinks that Mokeli is Carpini's Mecrit.[17] Wada Sei 和田清 identifies the Mokeli and Mecrit with the Bekrin (also written Mekrin) recorded in the "Treatise on the Tribes" in the *Jāmi' al-Tawārīkh*, and he also thinks that they are the same as the Miekeli 乜克力 tribe of the Ming period.[18] However, the Bekrin tribe of the *Jāmi' al-Tawārīkh* lived in the "dangerous mountains of Uyghuristan"; it was a small tribe, being merely one thousand households in size.[19] Yet, Carpini says that the Mecrit were one of the four great Mongol tribes. Thus the geography and circumstances of the two tribes (Carpini's Mecrit and Rashīd's Bekrin) are completely different. In my humble opinion, the Mecrit tribe that Carpini spoke of was probably the Kerait tribe, because in the Mongolian territory east of the Naimans, the three tribes – Mongols, Tatars, and Merkit – stood up to each other as equals, and the Kerait tribe was not among them. Carpini's statement that these four tribes had a similar language provides a very important piece of information about the Kerait language.

In the categorization of the tribes in the *Jāmi' al-Tawārīkh*, the first category (which is the first section of the "Treatise on the Tribes") is the descendants of the Oghuz 烏古思. The other 24 similar tribes all belong to the Turkish language group, with the exception of the Yuliboli 玉里伯里

---

[16] Wang Guowei 王國維, *Corrected Records of Ancient Travel Accounts* 《古行記校錄》.

[17] Yanai Wataru 箭内亙, *Mōkoshi kenkyū* (*Research on Mongolian History*) 『蒙古史研究』 (Tokyo, 1930), p. 538.

[18] Wada Sei 和田清, "Bame koku riki kō" (A Study of the Miekeli) 「乜克力考」, in *Kuwabara hakase kanreki kinen tōyōshi ronsō* (*Collected Papers on Oriental History: A Festschrift in Honor of the 60th Birthday of Dr. Kuwabara*) 『桑原博士還暦記念東洋史論叢』 (Kyoto, 1931), pp. 337-46.

[19] *Jāmi' al-Tawārīkh*, Russian translation, vol. 1, part 1, p. 149.

clan of the Qïpčaq 欽察 tribe, a Mongol-speaking clan who moved westwards from eastern Mongolia and assimilated with the Turkish tribes.[20] The fourth category, "The Turkish tribes formerly called Mongol" (Rashīd al-Dīn called all the tribes in Mongolia Turk), includes the Derlekin (Derelegin) 迭列列斤 and Nīrū'un 尼魯溫 Mongols, both belonging to the Mongolian language group. However, it is different with the second and third categories of tribes. For example, the second category, "Turkish tribes presently called Mongol, but in ancient times having their own separate names," were not all Mongolian-speaking clans. Among them the J̌alayir (Jalayir) 札剌亦兒, Tatar, Merkit, Oyirat 斡亦剌,[21] and other tribes can probably be called Mongolian-speaking tribes, but the Telengüt 帖良古 and the Kūstimī 客思的迷 were without a doubt Turkish-speaking tribes.[22] The third category is entitled "Turkish tribes which have their own separate kings and rulers." Most of these were Turkish clans, but the Tangut people were a branch of the Tibeto-Burman language group. In this section, Rashīd al-Dīn gives another account of the three tribes: Uyghur, Qarluq, and Qïpčaq, which he had previously listed in the first section, and he narrates their history, succession of rulers, and the circumstances under which they submitted to Mongol power. It appears that the tribes in this category are distinguished by "each having had its own ruler" and by "moreover having established a separate country or kingdom" (see the preface to the *Jāmi' al-Tawārīkh*). The reason why they were grouped together was not because they belonged to the same ethnic group.[23] These probably were the reasons why the Kerait tribe was listed in this category.

---

[20] Pelliot, "Kuman" 庫蠻; see Feng Chengjun 馮承鈞, *Continued Collection of Translations and Studies on Historical Places in the Western Regions and Southern Seas* 《西域南海史地考證譯叢續編》 (Shanghai, 1933), p. 25.

[21] The *Jāmi' al-Tawārīkh* records that the Merkits "were part of the Mongol tribes" (vol. 1, part 1, p. 114), and that their language (speaking of the Oyirat tribe) "was Mongolian, but somewhat different from the language of the other Mongol tribes" (vol. 1, part 1 p. 118).

[22] See Han Rulin's 韓儒林 "Chinggis Khan's and Other Neighboring Tribes in the Yuan Dynasty" 《元代的吉利吉思及其鄰近諸部》, in *Collection from the Yurt*, pp. 343-5.

[23] Murakami Masatsugu 村上正二 thinks that geographically speaking the various tribes in the third group in the *Jāmi' al-Tawārīkh* lived in the western part of Mongolia, and that culturally speaking they were at a higher level than the other tribes, and that politically speaking they were a tribal group that was already organized on national lines. See his "Mongoru teikoku seiritsu izen ni okeru yūbokumin shobuzoku ni tsuite" 「モンゴル帝

As for the clan or ethnic group to which the Kerait people belonged, Rashīd al-Dīn says, in the entry "Kerait Tribe" (قوم کرایت) of the third section of his "Treatise on the Tribes," "[They] are an ethnic group within the Mongols (نوعی از مغول اند), and their territory is the Onon and Kerulen Rivers, which is the land of the Mongols. This region is near the boundaries of Khitan territory."[24] This description is more concrete and detailed than that of the entry on Merkits in the same work. This passage has probably been noticed by many scholars, but they may have been influenced by the categorization of the tribes in this book, while at the same time being unclear about the origin of the Kerait tribe, and this may be why they have not been easily convinced by Rashīd al-Dīn's explanation.

However, Rashīd al-Dīn's explanation is not unfounded. It reflects what was thought about the ethnicity of the Kerait people during the Yuan period. As everyone knows, Tao Zongyi's 陶宗儀 *South Village Records Compiled after Returning from the Farm* 輟耕錄, under the heading "Clans" 氏族, places the Kerait (there called the Qieliedai 怯烈歹) among the "72 Mongol peoples." The categorization of clans in the *South Village Records* is based on the principle that there were four unequal social classes of people at the time: the Mongols, the Semu people 色目人 [a social class lower than the Mongols, but above the indigenous Chinese], the Han (Chinese) people 漢人, and the Southern people 南人, and that peoples categorized as ethnic groups considered Mongol were all treated as belonging to the same class as the Mongol ruler (*guoren* 國人, person of the nation). Thus they were in an advantageous position. This category, for the most part, included Rashīd al-Dīn's fourth category of Nīrū'un and Derlekin Mongols, and also the tribes in his second category "Presently called Mongols." The categorization in the *South Village Records* has some duplications, mistakes, and chaotic characteristics. For example, among the "72 Mongol peoples," there is listed the Beteki Naiman 別帖乞

国成立以前における遊牧民諸部族について」 ("The Nomadic Tribes before the Emergence of the Mongol Empire"), *Tōyōshi kenkyū* (*Journal of Oriental Research*) 『東洋史研究』, vol. 23, no. 4 (1964).

24 *Jāmi' al-Tawārīkh*, Russian translation, vol. 1, part 1, p. 127. In the Persian original, this paragraph is نوعی ازمغول‌اند ومقام ایشان اونن وکلوران است زمین مغولستان .

乃蠻歹,[25] but the "31 Semu peoples" also include the Naiman 乃蠻歹. However, Kerait appears on the Mongol clan list only; it is not included in the Semu list, as the Naiman, Önggüd 雍古歹, Tangut 唐兀, Uyghur, and others are.

In this way, the categorization of the Kerait in the *South Village Records* is consistent with Rashīd al-Dīn's in calling the Kerait "a subgroup of the Mongols," although he has a different grouping of the tribes. I do not think that Tao Zongyi's categorization is mistaken. Cheng Jufu 程鉅夫 says in his *Stele Inscription for the Artillery Brigade Commander from the Kerait Clan* 炮手軍總管克烈君碑銘: "This gentleman's name is Xu Shidai 昻實帶 (Hüshidai); he is a Mongolian."[26] Hüshidai's (1257-1311) grandfather was called Xilijisi 昔里吉思 (Sergis), which was a religious name often seen among the Kerait Nestorians during the Yuan Dynasty. He held a hereditary official position in charge of the artillery (mangonel) troops, but he was very fond of Chinese culture. He established the Yichuan Academy 伊川書院, and he cultivated 1000 *mu* 亩 [about 170 acres] of farmland to support his studies. In his later years he devoted himself to study, never putting his books down. He associated with Chen Tianxiang 陳天祥, Yao Sui 姚燧, Lu Zhi 盧摯, and others, changed his name to Shixi 士希, adopted the courtesy name 字 of Jizhi 及之 and the nickname 號 of Xizhai 西齋, and composed over 500 poems. There is also an inscription by Huang Jin 黃溍 called the *Spirit Way Stele for Hexi Longyou Circuit Surveillance Commissioner Lord Kailie* 河西隴右道肅政廉訪使凱烈公神道碑, which says, "This man's name was Bashi 拔實, his courtesy name was Yanqing 彥卿, and he was of the

---

[25] The character *li* 里 in Bietielidai 別帖里歹 should be the character *ji* 吉 or *qi* 乞. The character *nai* 乃 has been removed from the beginning of Mandai 蠻歹 and mistakenly inserted after Waimodai 外抹歹 making it "Waimodainai 外抹歹乃." The Beteki were a sub-tribe of the Naiman tribe. See Han Rulin 韓儒林, "Notes from Reading on Mongol Clans" 《蒙古氏族劄記》, in *Collection from the Yurt*, pp. 52-3.

[26] *Collection from the Snowy Tower* 《雪樓集》, ch. 22 (facsimile of the Hongwu 洪武 edition, 1926). Qian Daxin 錢大昕 expressed the view in his "Postscript to the Imperial Edict for the Yichuan Academy Stele" 《敕賜伊川書院碑跋》 (in *Postscript to Bronze and Stone Inscriptions from the Hall of Subtle Research* 《潛研堂金石跋尾》, ch. 19) that Hüšidei 昻實帶 was a Huihui (Muslim) because he held the position of "Artillery Brigade Commander" 炮手軍總管, but this was mistaken.

Mongol Kailie 凱烈 clan."[27] Kailie is another way of writing Kerait. Bashi (1308-1350) was also a member of the Kerait clan and was highly steeped in Chinese culture. His family lived in Daidu 大都 [modern Beijing], and "He had a library full of books and studied diligently and industriously." He was very close to a number of Chinese literati, and the place where he lived had a study called the Veranda of the Four Recitations 四詠軒, to which he invited friends over to write poetry. Xu Youren 許有壬 wrote a preface to Bashi's poems entitled *Preface to Bashi's Poetry from the Veranda of the Four Recitations* 拔實彥卿四詠軒詩序 and called him a *guoren* (person of the nation, i.e. Mongol). [28] Apart from this, the biographies in the *History of the Yuan* of Shuozhituluhua 槊直腯魯華 (Čöji Turqaq, ch. 122), Süge 速哥 (ch. 124), and Yexianbuhua 也先不花 (Esen Buqa, ch. 134) all refer to these men as members of the "Mongol Kerait clan."

During the Yuan Dynasty, because ethnic inequality was imbedded in all of the various government regulations, it was not infrequent for people to pretend to be Mongols or Semu people when they were not from these groups. Ouyang Xuan 歐陽玄 of the Yuan period said, "the foundation for perfecting the system of official selection lies in the strict separation of the ethnic groups, in order to honor the *guoren* (Mongols)....Recently the Nüzhen 女真 (Jurchen) and Hexi 河西 (Tangut) mixed with the Semu people, even though there were clear regulations against this, and the Beiting 北庭 (Uyghur) people were all regarded as Mongols because of the similarities of their ethnic features. The result is that they are all rich enough to ride in well-constructed carriages pulled by beautiful horses, and they are well-connected and prominent. The people of your majestic clan are sincere by nature and are not boastful. I fear that after several hundred years, there will no longer be any trace of them, because they will be indistinguishable from the others."[29] However, those who intentionally mixed with the Mongols were for the most part trying to hide their original

---

[27] *Collected Works of Huang Jinhua* 《黃金華文集》, ch. 25, in the *Four Branches of Literature Collection*, first series edition.

[28] *Collection of the Zhizheng Reign Period* 《至正集》, ch. 35 (Henan lithographic edition 河南石印本, 1911).

[29] Ouyang Xuan 歐陽玄, "Examination on Political Questions"《策對》, *Collected Works of Guizhai* 《圭齋集》 [or 《圭齋文集》], ch. 12, in the *Four Branches of Literature Collection*, first series edition.

clan origin and just call themselves "Mongols" (there are many examples of this recorded in the *History of the Yuan*), so we should not think that this designation is true. Those who clearly indicated their clan name could not mix with others. Although the Beiting (Uyghur) people were sometimes treated as Mongols, they were definitely not called Mongol Uyghurs. Moreover, Cheng Jufu, Huang Jin, and Xu Youren (who lived in the early, middle, and late Yuan period, respectively) were all famous civil officials who held various posts throughout the royal court and in local government, and who wrote quite a number of funerary inscriptions for Mongols and Semu people. They could hardly have been unable to distinguish between the two tribes. We can see that the above-mentioned Kerait people are not examples of those of mixed race or those who looked the same as Mongols. The Kerait people were a sub-group of the Mongols, and in the Yuan Dynasty people had no doubt of this. Rashīd al-Dīn's view on this point here receives strong confirmation.

3. The Ethnic Origin of the Kerait tribe: Tatar 達靼 *and Zubu* 阻蔔

As for the origin of the name Kerait, the "Treatise on the Tribes" in the Kerait section of the *Jāmi' al-Tawārīkh*, says the following:

> These Kerait people have many sub-tribes and branches. They are all Ong Khan's officials and people.
>
> Kerait. It is said that in ancient times there was a king شادشاهی who had seven (or in one edition, eight) sons. They were all born with dark skin, and therefore they were called "Kelie" (Kerait). Later all the sons' descendants had special names for their own branch clans. Thereupon, the name "Kelie" was only used for the ruler's branch of the clan. The rest of the sons became the officials and people of the ruler's brothers.[30]

The *Jāmi' al-Tawārīkh* goes on to give the names of the five Kerait sub-tribes and the prominent individuals from those sub-tribes. However, even when Kerait was included among them, there were only six branches, not seven or eight. Among them are the names of four of these tribes, which are also seen in other historical records:

[30] *Jāmi' al-Tawārīkh*, Russian translation, vol. 1, part 1, p. 128.

J̌irgin (Jirgin, Jirqin) 只爾斤. In Persian it is written Jīrqīn. The *Record of the Personal Campaigns of the Holy Warrior* 聖武親征錄 writes it Zhulijin 朱力斤. *The Secret History of the Mongols* calls it J̌irgin. Rashīd al-Dīn says, "They are respected and heroic tribes among those of Ong Khan."

Dongqayit 董合亦惕. The 1317 Istanbul manuscript edition and the Tashkent manuscript edition write it as Qōngqāīt, and the Russian translation follows these sources. The London and Leningrad manuscript editions and the Berezin collated editions all write it Tōngqāīt Karāīt.[31] It must therefore be the Olon Dongqayit in *The Secret History of the Mongols* (*olon* means "many" in Mongolian). The *Record of the Personal Campaigns of the Holy Warrior* writes the name of the tribe Dongai 董哀.

Saqayit 撒合亦惕. This name is written Sāqīāt in the Persian collated edition. L. A. Khetagurov's (Л. А. Хетагуров) Russian translation writes it Saqait, but does not explain the evidence for transcribing it in this way. According to Juwaīnī's *Ta'rīkh-i Jahān-Gushā*, Ong Khan was the ruler of Kerait and Sāqīz.[32] Pelliot thought that the so-called Sāqīz should be amended to Sāqīt (ساقيز > ساقيت) according to the name given by Rashīd ("*Je pense que ce sont là les soi-disant Saqiz, dont je proposerais de lire le nom* ساقيت *Sāqiyat*") and that it was the same as Sāqīāt, a branch of the Kerait clan in the *Jāmi' al-Tawārīkh*. He also said that it should not be confused with the Saqayit 撒合夷 tribe, the ninth of the 13 wings of Chinggis Khan recorded in the *Record of the Personal Campaigns of the Holy Warrior*.[33] "The History of Chinggis Khan" تاريخ چينگگيزخان in the *Jāmi' al-Tawārīkh*, which lists the 13 wings, subsumes in the ninth wing those tribes led by Chinggis Khan's uncle Dāritai Otčigin 答里台斡赤斤, Nekün Taiji's 捏坤太石 son Qučar 忽察爾, and other leaders, in which there is a tribe called Saqayit, which was said to be a tribe of the Derlekin (Derelegin) Mongols.[34] However, the "Treatise on the Tribes" in the same work treats the Saqayit tribe within its section two, which is entitled "The

---

[31] *Jāmi' al-Tawārīkh*, vol. 1, part 1, Persian collated edition (Moscow, 1965), p. 257.

[32] 'Ala-al-Dīn 'Ata-Malik Juwaīnī, *Ta'rīkh-i Jahān-Gushā* (*The History of the World-Conqueror*), John Andrew Boyle's English translation (Manchester, 1958), chapter 1, p. 35; and He Gaoji's 何高濟 Chinese translation 《世界征服者史》 (Inner Mongolia People's Press 内蒙古人民出版社, 1980), vol. 1, p. 38.

[33] *Histoire des Campagnes de Gengis Khan*, p. 220.

[34] *Jāmi' al-Tawārīkh*, Russian translation, vol. 1, part 2, p. 87.

Various Tribes that are Presently Called Mongols." Now, according to the "History of Chinggis Khan" in the *Jāmi' al-Tawārīkh*, after Ong Khan attacked Chinggis Khan in the great battle at Qalaqaljit elet 合蘭真沙陀 (*elet* means 'desert' in Mongolian), Dāritai Otčigin, Qučar, and other nobles of the Mongolian tribes plotted to attack Ong Khan and set themselves up as kings, but the plot was discovered, and they were defeated by Ong Khan. "Dāritai Otčigin then, with one of the Nīrū'un tribes, the Sāqīāt sub-tribe of the Kerait, and the Nūnjīn 嫩真部 tribe, returned their allegiance to Chinggis Khan."[35] The *Record of the Personal Campaigns of the Holy Warrior* also records this event and gives the names of the three tribes that, together with Dāritai Otčigin, gave their allegiance to Chinggis Khan. These were the Ba'arin 八鄰, the Saqayit 撒合夷, and the Nünjin 嫩真. Thus the Sāqīāt sub-tribe of the Kerait tribe, recorded in the *Jāmi' al-Tawārīkh*, is the same as the Saqayit tribe recorded in the *Record of the Personal Campaigns of the Holy Warrior*, and should be amended to Sāqāīt. This was the tribe that participated in the battle of the 13 wings. Rashīd al-Dīn thought that this was one of the Derlekin tribes and placed it in section two of the "Treatise on the Tribes," but he was mistaken on both counts. In *The Secret History of the Mongols*, this tribe is called the Saqayit (see section 122).

Tübegen 土別干. In the Persian collated edition of the *Jāmi' al-Tawārīkh* it is written Tūmāūūt (the Russian translation uses this name) or, in some editions, Tūbāūūt. This must be the same as the Tümen Tübegen (*tümen* means "ten thousand") tribe of the Kerait people recorded in *The Secret History of the Mongols*. The *Record of the Personal Campaigns of the Holy Warrior* writes it Tuman Tuboyi 土滿土伯夷. The surname Tuboqielie 禿伯怯烈氏 in "Biography of Xiaonaitai" 肖乃台傳 (*History of the Yuan*, ch. 120), and the surname Tubieyan 土別燕氏 in "Biography of Wanze (Öljei)" 完澤傳 (*History of the Yuan*, ch. 130) are different ways of writing the name of this same sub-tribe of the Kerait.

Albat (?) 阿勒巴惕. The Persian collated edition writes it Albāt. There are two manuscript editions where the diacritical mark of the third character is dropped. The Leningrad and London editions both write it Alīāt. This name does not appear in any other historical records.

---

[35] Ibid., p. 132.

The origin of the name "Kelie" (Kerait) is not clear. Abū al-Ghāzī says, in his *Šajara-yi Turk* (Ebulgazi Bahadr Han and Petr. I. Desmaisons' French translation *Histoire des Mongols et des Tartars* [St. Petersburg: 1874]), that Kerait means *qarābarān* (black fleeced sheep), a logical consequence of the seven brothers being born with dark skin, and it is clearly associated with the fact that in Turco-Mongolian *qara* means "black." Pelliot suspects that this was Rashīd al-Dīn's original idea. Moreover, he thought that the popular etymology that he pointed out could be regarded as "Keri'e," which in Mongolian means "crow" and in Turkish is *qarya*. It is very possible that this originated in onomatopoeia. In Rashīd al-Dīn's view it was because the eight brothers all had dark skin (in the original language written as Siyāh-järdä), and hence the name "crow." This term in Turkish is, in its appearance, close to *qara*.[36]

According to the *Jāmi' al-Tawārīkh*, the name "Kerait" goes back a long time. However, it is strange that there is no record of it prior to the 13th century.[37] Armand D'Avezac had identified the Kerait with Chile 敕勒 (or Tiele 鐵勒).[38] Tu Ji 屠寄 made a far-fetched interpretation based on phonetic comparison, interpreting Kerait and Kangli 康里 as different transliterations of the same name and claiming that they were "originally Kangju 康居 (Sogdian) tribes in the Han period." He said, "Kangli and Kelie were originally very close in sound, and the historians thought they were western and eastern parts of the same area. Therefore they wrote them differently in order to distinguish between them." He also used "Biography of Buhumu" 不忽木傳 in the *History of the Yuan* to document

---

[36] "Mais je doute que telle soit l'idée de Rašid, et l'étymologie populaire qu'il rapporte peut viser en réalité le nom *käri'ä* (corbeau); pour lui, à cause de ces huit frères noirauds, les Kerait auraient été appelés 'les Corbeaux'. Il se trouve d'ailleurs que le nom du 'corbeau', assez probablement d'origine onomatopéique, qui est *käri'ä* en Mongol, est *qarya* en turc, et ainsi, au moins en turc se rapproche en apparence de *qara*, 'noir'." *Histoire des Campagnes de Gengis Khan*, p. 209.

[37] The thirteenth-century Syrian historian Bar-Hebraeus, author of *Chronicon Ecclesiasticum* (*Ecclesiastical Annals*), quoted a letter of 1009 sent from the Nestorian metropolitan in Merv to the Patriarch John VI in Baghdad, in which he described the baptism of the Kerait king and officials. Pelliot suspected that the original text did not necessarily mention this name and that Bar-Hebraeus may have added it. See *Histoire des Campagnes de Gengis Khan*, p. 208; René Grousset, *L'empire des steppes*, 4th ed. (Paris, 1969), p. 245.

[38] Armand D'Avezac, *Relation des Mongols ou Tartares par le frère Jean du Plan de Carpin*, p. 536.

this point, saying that Buhumu's grandfather had served Ong Khan, "so he should be known as a leading figure of the Kerait tribe for generations. However, the *History of the Yuan* says his ancestors were chieftains of the Kangli tribe. This clearly shows that Kerait and Kangli were the same ethnic group."[39] Note that the name Kangli was first seen in Mahmūd al-Kāshgharī's dictionary, *Dīwān lughāt al-Turk* (*Compendium of the Languages of the Turks*), which calls it the name of an important person from the Qïpčaq (this is probably a tribal name). This work also says the name meant "a type of two-wheeled vehicle." "Biography of Tiegehannu" 粘割韓奴 in chapter 121 of the *History of the Jin Dynasty* 金史 records that in the Dading 大定 reign period (1161-1189) the ruler of the Naiman 粘拔恩, together with the tribal leader of the Kangli named Bogu 孛古, submitted to the Jin court. This was the first time the name appeared in Chinese records. Kangli is the Turkish *qangli* (an adjectival form of *qang*), which means "vehicle." The Kangli tribe was a Turkish tribe that inhabited the area north of the Aral Sea and the Syr Darya. In the Mongol-Yuan period both eastern and western historical sources contain numerous records of this. The "Treatise on the Tribes" in the *Jāmi' al-Tawārīkh* categorizes the Kangli as subordinate to the Oghuz clan.[40] The Kerait and the Kangli were different tribes, and their names are also different phonetically. There was a branch of the Kangli people who served Ong Khan, but this still does not prove that they were the same tribe. Tu Ji's view is clearly untenable. Armand D'Avezac's opinion that Kerait and Chile 敕勒 (pronounced *tiək-lək* in ancient times) were the same not only lacks evidence, but is also wrong from the point of view of phonetics (i.e., they are not similar in sound).

Sakurai Masuo's 桜井益雄 article "A Study of the Kerait" 「怯烈考」[41] makes a relatively thorough study of the Kerait tribe's name, origin, and history. He follows what is said in the "Appendix on the Northwestern Territories" 西北地附錄 in the "Monograph on Geography" 地理志 in the *History of the Yuan*, under the section on Qianzhou 謙州: "It is said that

---

[39] Tu Ji 屠寄, *Historical Record of the Mongols* 《蒙兀爾史記》, ch. 20, "Biography of Ong Khan and J̌amuqa (Jamuqa) 《王罕・劄木合》."

[40] Pelliot has a detailed explanation of the name of the Kangli tribe. See *Histoire des Campagnes de Gengis Khan*, p. 112-6.

[41] Sakurai Masuo 桜井益雄, "Kyō retsu kō" ("A Study of the Kerait") 「怯烈考」, in *Tōhō Gakuhō* (*Journal of Oriental Studies*) 『東方学報』, vol. 7 (Tokyo, 1935).

this was where Ong Khan first lived." He is of the opinion that the Kerait tribe originated in the region south of the Kem River 謙河 (in the upper reaches of present-day Yenisei River). The Kerait tribe was made up of several tribes and took the name of the ruling Kerait clan as its general name. Its sub-tribes included the Tübegen tribe. Sakurai Masuo begins with the assumption that the Kerait people originally lived in the Kemkemjihud region (Qianzhou), and he infers that the Tübegen tribe must have been the same as the Dubo 都波 (都播) of the Tang Dynasty. This was the same group that in the middle of the ninth century followed the Kirghiz 黠戛斯 southward and attacked and destroyed the Uyghur Qaghanate and then settled in the former Uyghur territory. Later, when Kerait became the ruling clan, the entire tribe began to be called the Kerait. As for the question of whether the Kerait clan was originally the Dubo sub-tribe, or whether it had a different origin, Sakurai Masuo did not make this clear.

As for the statement in the "Monograph on Geography" in the *History of the Yuan* that "this (Qianzhou) was where Ong Khan first lived," Tu Ji had already included this in his biography of Ong Khan and J̌amuqa (Jamuqa) 王罕劄木合. However, he changed it to say, "Qianzhou was also the place where the Kerait tribe first resided," an entirely arbitrary assertion. This statement in the *History of the Yuan* is hearsay, most probably derived from a false rumor or fabrication.[42] In the *Jāmi' al-Tawārīkh* there are rather detailed records concerning the regions inhabited by the Kerait tribe (see below), but there is no mention of Qianzhou. By the time of Ong Khan's grandfather, at the very latest, they were already inhabiting the region of the Orkhon River. Therefore the story that Ong Khan first lived in Qianzhou cannot be relied upon. It is even more unjustified to conclude on the basis of this evidence that the Kerait tribe originally lived in Qianzhou. The theory that the Dubo tribe followed the Kirghiz southward and settled in the former territory of the Uyghurs and became the Kerait tribe is also conjecture, based on the supposed phonetic similarity between the names Dubo and Tübegen. If the Dubo people, after the destruction of the Uyghur Qaghanate, had lived in the former Uyghur territory and formed themselves into a large tribe, there would have been some trace of this in the historical records, especially in the records of the Liao conquests of this area. However, there is no trace

---

[42] Pelliot made this point. See *Histoire des Campagnes de Gengis Khan*, p. 209.

of it. Sakurai cites as evidence both the "Monograph on Official Posts" 百官志 in the *History of the Liao* 遼史 concerning the Office of the General of the Teman Army 特滿軍詳穩司 and the Tuoman tribe 駝滿部 in the *History of the Jin Dynasty*, but neither of these has anything to do with the Dubo.[43] Only the tribe called Tubas 秃巴思, mentioned in *The Secret History of the Mongols* as living in the region of the Kem River, can be seen as the Dubo of the Tang Dynasty (if one adds the plural suffix 's').[44] However, this is completely different from the Tübegen subgroup of the Kerait tribe.

In the middle of the ninth century, after the Uyghur Qaghanate was defeated and destroyed, there was a significant change in the makeup of the ethnic groups on the Mongolian plateau, which is reflected in the historical documents of the tenth to twelfth centuries. Many new tribes appeared, and the Kerait was one of them. In order to acquire a clear understanding of the origin of the Kerait people, we must examine the process by which this change occurred.

In the year 840 the Kirghiz attacked the capital city of the Uyghur Qaghanate, present-day Qara Balqasun 哈剌八剌哈孫 on the upper reaches of the Eerhun River 鄂爾渾河. They killed the Uyghur Qaghan, burned the generals' quarters, and the Uyghur "masses scattered." This was when Mang Tegin 龐特勤 (Pang Tigin) led the fifteen tribes in flight westward to the Qarluq 葛邏祿, and Ormudz 唱沒斯 and the others each led their tribes in surrender to the Tang. The newly elected Ögä Qaghan 烏介可汗 also led 100,000 people of the thirteen tribes who lived near his capital Ordubalïq (Ordu-Baligh) to the south, leaving the Uyghur Qaghanate court to the north of the Gobi Desert completely empty. Not long after that, the Kirghiz sent envoys to the Tang court to re-establish friendly relations, saying that "they would move to Heluochuan 合羅川 and settle in former Uyghur territory."[45] After that, they launched another

---

[43] The Teman 特滿 army must have been one of the tribal armies sent by the Liao to be stationed in the Northwest Route 西北路. They were not a local tribe. The Tuoman 駝滿 tribe was a Jurchen tribe.

[44] *The Secret History of the Mongols*, section 239; Han Rulin 韓儒林, "A New Exploration of the Tang Dynasty Dubo" 《唐代都波新探》, *Collection from the Yurt*, p. 331.

[45] *Comprehensive Mirror for Aid in Government* 《資治通鑒》, ch. 246, in the second year of the Huichang 會昌 reign period under Emperor Wuzong 武宗, in the "Annals of

eastward attack against the Shiwei 室韋 and took the last remnants of the Uyghurs, whom the Shiwei had previously captured, and then returned. In the Xiantong 咸通 reign period (860-873), they sent envoys to the court three more times, but after this the Tang historical records contain no further mention of the activities of the Kirghiz.[46] Quite a few works on history state that after destroying the Uyghurs, the Kirghiz settled in Uyghur territory and founded a country there, which lasted until the beginning of the tenth century, when the Khitan forces started oppressing the inhabitants, driving them back to the upper reaches of the Yenisei River. However, this is pure speculation. In fact, according to the *History of the Liao*, in 924 Yelü Abaoji 耶律阿保機 launched an expedition westward and took the Uyghur capital 回鶻城. He definitely did not do battle with the Kirghiz (written in the *History of the Liao* as Xiajiasi 轄戛斯), and he attacked primarily the Zubu 阻蔔 tribe. The name Zubu does not appear before the Liao period. Wang Guowei in his *Study of the Tatars* 韃靼考 summoned a large quantity of evidence to prove that the Zubu (also written Zupu 阻Related), mentioned in the *History of the Liao* and the *History of the Jin Dynasty* were the Tatars. This theory has long been accepted in the academic world, and many scholars have expounded and promoted it, so we will not comment any further on it here.

In chapter 103 of the *History of the Liao*, in "Biography of Xiao Hanjianu" 蕭韓家奴傳, it says: "The various Zubu tribes have always been there. Formerly they settled in the area north to the Luqu (Kerulen) River 臚朐河 and south to the border. Most of the people lived in a scattered manner, and no one united them. All they did was to go back and forth and raid settlements. When Emperor Taizu 太祖 on his westward expeditions reached the region of the flowing sands, the Zubu people surrendered at the sight of the oncoming force, and all the various countries of the Western regions began to send tribute (to the Liao court)." However, Yelü Abaoji's troops were attacked by the Zubu and Tatar tribes

the Tang" 《唐紀》. [Heluochuan 合羅川 may be Etsin Gol. See Michael R. Drompp, *Tang China and the Collapse of the Uighur Empire*, (Brill, 2005), pp. 127-30. Translator's note.]

46 *New Tang History* 《新唐書》, ch. 217b, "Account of the Kirghiz" 《轄戛斯傳》. The *Comprehensive Mirror for Aid in Government* records that the last time the Kirghiz sent an envoy to the Tang court was in the seventh year of the Xiantong 咸通 reign period (866).

on their way back from the westward campaign. "Annals of Zhuangzong of the Latter Tang" 莊宗紀 in chapter 32 of the *Old History of the Five Dynasties* 舊五代史 records that in the third year of the Tongguang 同光 reign period (925) "on the guihai 癸亥 day of the sixth month, the official of Yunzhou 雲州 (present-day Datong 大同 in Shanxi 山西 Province) reported to the emperor: 'Last year when the Khitan retreated from the north of the Gobi Desert, the Tatars ambushed them. The clan of their chieftain *yuyue* 于越 (a Khitan title) came down from north of the Gobi Desert and surrendered, together with the clan's 30,000 goats and horses. They arrived at the southern border and now send envoys to the palace and issue memorials reporting events.'" The above quotations make it clear that from early on, before Yelü Abaoji's western expedition, the Zubu and Tatar tribes had already split apart in the area north of the Gobi Desert and spread out into many different places, including the region of the Uyghur capital, and had become important inhabitants of this region. It is clear that the power of the Kirghiz did not last long in the former Uyghur territory.[47] The vacuum left by the Uyghurs was quickly filled by the Zubu and Tatar people.

The name "Tatar" was first seen in Turkish in the *Kül Tegin Inscription* 闕特勤碑, which was set up in the 20th year of the Kaiyuan reign period in the Tang Dynasty (732). The inscription mentions Otuz Tatar (the Thirty Tatars), who were situated east of the Turks and north of the Khitan. In the Chinese records Otuz Tatar for the most part corresponds to Shiwei. Both were general names for the Mongolian-speaking tribes east and west of the Da Xing'an (Greater Khingan)

---

[47] After the Kirghiz *a're* 阿熱 (the title of a chieftain) attacked the Uyghur Qaghan, "he moved his camp to the area south of Lao Mountain 牢山, which was a 15-day journey by horse from the Uyghur generals' camp." In the second year of the Huichang reign period (842), their envoy Tabuhezu 踏布合祖 arrived at the Tang court and said that the Kirghiz "were about to move to Heluochuan, to settle in the former Uyghur territory"; in the fourth year, another envoy came to the Tang, and he too said, "they were going to move to the camp of the Uyghurs." This shows that they had not yet moved there. Whether they actually did move to the (former) Uyghur territory later on, history does not make clear. In the sixth year of the Huichang reign period, when the Tang were intending to send an envoy to crown the Kirghiz Qaghan, some officials were still arguing that the Kirghiz constituted "a small, remote country, and was not worth treating as an adversary." See *New Tang History*, ch. 217b, "Account of the Kirghiz"; *Comprehensive Mirror for Aid in Government*, chs. 246-8.

Mountain Range 大興安嶺. Tatar was originally the name of just one of these tribes. According to Rashīd al-Dīn, this tribe "for most of the distant past, conquered and ruled the majority of the Mongols and their territory…and because they were prominent and had a respected position, the other Turkish tribes, despite all belonging to different groups and all being called by different names, were all called Tatars."[48] Some scholars have deduced, based on Rashīd al-Dīn's words, that after the Uyghur Qaghanate was destroyed the Tatars rose on the Mongolian plain and ruled for a while – according to some, "they established an alliance uniting many tribes together" – and subsequently the other Mongolian and Turkic tribes on the Mongolian plain were also called Tatars, or claimed to be Tatars. For this reason, scholars tend to see any mention of Tatar or Zubu people in the Liao and Jin historical sources as a general reference to the nomadic tribes north and south of the desert, and not as specific references to Mongolian-speaking tribes. I believe that there is still room for debate on this question.

When the name Tatar 達靼 first appeared, it was already a collective name for a group of tribes, "the Thirty Tatars." Later there were also the "Tatars of the Nine Surnames" (Toquz Tatar) 九姓達靼, the "Black Cart Tatars" 黑車達怛, the "Yinshan Tatars" 陰山達靼 and other tribes that used this general name. We can see that the situation Rashīd al-Dīn described occurred at the latest at the beginning of the eighth century. Probably at that time the Tatar tribe was the strongest of the various Shiwei tribes. This is why the Turks used this name as a general term for the various Shiwei tribes, while the people of the Tang still used the old name of Shiwei, which had been in use since the Northern Wei. The *Jāmi' al-Tawārīkh* records six tribes of the Tatars. The first one of these was Tutuqliut-Tatar, of which it says: "The Tutuqliut tribe was the most respected of all the Tatar tribes (*wa qūm Tūtūqlīūt mo'tabar tarīn aqvam Tatarand*)."[49] Tutuqliut literally means "the people of the *tutuq*" ("Commander-in-chief" or "the tribe of the *tutuq*"), perhaps because the leaders of this tribe had previously been enfeoffed with the official title of Commander-in-chief 都督 (*tutuq*), and their descendants kept this title as their surname. This reminds us that in the Tang Dynasty the Shiwei

[48] *Jāmi' al-Tawārīkh*, Russian translation, vol. 1, part 1, p. 102.
[49] Ibid., p. 103.

tutuq,[50] and the chieftain of the strong tribe who received the title of *Commander-in-chief* from the Tang court, without a doubt possessed the position and power necessary to rule all the tribes in his clan. To summarize, during the Tang Dynasty, Tatar was the collective name of all the Mongolian-speaking tribes who had originally lived in the northern part of the Da Xing'an range and the Kölen na'ur-Buyur na'ur 呼倫貝爾 region.

According to the Turkish *Bilgä Qaghan Inscription* 毗伽可汗碑, at the beginning of the Kaiyuan reign period (713-741) of the Tang Dynasty the Wuhu of the Nine Surnames 烏紇九姓 (the Toquz Oghuz, also Tiele 鐵勒) had allied with the Tatars of the Nine Surnames for resisting and attacking the Later Turkish Qaghanate. They fought at Aghu (whose location is unknown, but it was probably within the region occupied by the Tiele tribe, near the present-day Tula River). Soon after the Uyghur Gele Qaghan 葛勒可汗 (Moyunčor 磨延啜, reigned 747-759) ascended the throne, the Tatars of the Nine Surnames, together with the Oghuz of the Eight Clans, attacked the Uyghurs, fighting at Bükeguk, Burghu, the Selenga River, and other places (see the Turkish *Moyunčor Inscription* 磨延啜碑). In the year 749 the Tatars advanced and attacked the Uyghurs, but were defeated, and half of the people surrendered to the Uyghurs. The next year Gele Qaghan again launched an expedition to the east against the Tatars. However, we know that from the beginning of the eighth century onward, the Tatars were more and more deeply involved in the struggle for the plateau north of the Gobi Desert. Moreover, one group of Tatar tribes (the Tatars of the Nine Surnames) entered the territory inhabited by the Tiele people in the region of the Tula River and the Selenga River.

Some Tatar tribes that submitted to the Uyghurs may have been moved to the region near the upper reaches Orkhon River and served the Uyghur nobility as their subordinates. Under the entry on the J̌alayir 札剌亦兒

---

[50] *Outstanding Models from the Storehouse of Literature* 《冊府元龜》, ch. 972, "Foreign Vassals Section" 《外臣部》, records that in the eighth year of the Zhenyuan 貞元 reign period (792), the Shiwei Commander-in-chief 都督 (the title of a tribal chieftain awarded by the Tang court and transliterated into Turkish as *tutuq*) Hejieresu 和解熱素 and others came to court; in the ninth year of the Taihe 太和 reign period (835), the Shiwei Great Commander-in-chief 大都督 Azhu 阿朱 and others came to court; and in the fourth year of the Kaicheng 開成 reign period (839), the Shiwei Great Commander-in-chief Zhichong 秩蟲 and others came to court.

tribe in the "Treatise on the Tribes" in the *Jāmi' al-Tawārīkh*, there is the following record: "It is said that their campground was in the Qara-Qorum 哈剌和林 region in the place that is called QDIMA; they were so blindly loyal that they gave their yoghurt to the Uyghur leader Gür Qaghan 古爾汗 for the camels to eat" (*wa mī gūīnd yurt īshān qadīmā dar Qarā-qūrum budeh ast wa īshān ra ta'sab ān ast keh shataran nar Gur khan ra keh pādshāh Ūīghūr budeh rūghan mī dadehand*).[51] J̌alayir was one of tribes of the Tatar group. The *Jāmi' al-Tawārīkh* records that its most important camp was in the region of the Onon River. The passage quoted here must refer to the J̌alayir tribe who were subordinate to the Uyghurs during the period of the Uyghur Qaghanate and had lived in the vicinity of the Uyghur Qaghan's court. Jia Dan's 賈耽 *Routes from the Border Districts into the Regions Inhabited by the Barbarians of the Four Directions* 邊州入四夷道里 records that on the road from Shoujiang City 受降城 to the Uyghur capital, there is a place named Tatar Lake 達旦泊, about which Wang Guowei wrote, "I suspect it has this name because it was a place inhabited by the Tatars, and it was probably the place where the Tatars of the Nine Surnames lived."[52] Although this is speculation, there is no doubt that under the Uyghur Qaghanate there was a group of Tatar tribes who moved west and entered Uyghur territory.

There are also portions of the Shiwei and Tatar tribes, which from the late eighth century to the early ninth century appeared in Zhenwu 振武, Youzhou 幽州, and even Tiande 天德 beyond the Tang border. In the fourth year of the Zhenyuan reign period (788) during the Tang there is a record of the Shiwei and Xi 奚 bandits together raiding Zhenwu.[53] In the Yuanhe reign period (806-820) the Shiwei tribe appeared on the frontier at Zhenwu and Tiande; they had been long-term residents there.[54] They were probably part of what were later on called the Yinshan Tatars. By the middle of the ninth century, even the region outside the frontier at

---

[51] *Jāmi' al-Tawārīkh*, Russian translation, vol. 1, part 1, p. 93.

[52] Wang Guowei 王國維, "A Study of the Tatars"《韃靼考》, in *Collected Works from the Hall of Observation*《觀堂集林》, ch. 14.

[53] *Comprehensive Mirror for Aid in Government*, ch. 233.

[54] *Important Documents of the Tang*《唐會要》, ch. 73, in the section on "Shanyu Protectorates"《單于都護府》; *Gazetteer of the Provinces and Counties in the Yuanhe Period, no. 4*《元和郡縣志四》, the section on "Tenduc [Tiande Base]"《天德軍》.

Youzhou (in the northern part of present-day Xilin Gol 錫林郭勒盟) had been settled by the "Black Cart Tatar tribe."[55] The decline of the Uyghurs and the scattering of their tribes also gave the Shiwei-Tatars a good opportunity to expand their pastureland. After the Kirghiz forces retreated to their homeland along the Yenisei River, the Tatars naturally became the masters of the extensive region both north and south of the desert. But the Tatars' move westward did not take the form of one strong nomadic political power conquering another and occupying a large territory all at once. Instead, it consisted of gradual movement and penetration. Therefore, when they became the most prominent inhabitants of the Mongolian plateau, they were still living in a scattered manner, in a state of disunion. They had not had time to establish a united nomadic power before the Khitan people came and conquered them.

The process described above, by which the Shiwei-Tatar tribes moved westward, shows clearly that after the tenth century the Tatar-Zubu tribes who inhabited the Mongolian plateau must have come from eastern Mongolian-speaking tribes. Even though remnants of the Turkish peoples might have been absorbed into the Tatar tribes, Tatar was still regarded as the common name for a particular ethnic group – all the Mongolian-speaking tribes – and this situation did not change. In fact, the tribes recorded in the *History of the Liao* (except for the Zubu, who are also called Shubugu 朮不姑), still included the Turks, Shatuo 沙陀, Tangut 黨項, Dalidi 達里底, Basmil 拔思母 (same as 拔悉密), Urianghat 斡朗改, Kirghiz, Naiman, and so forth. The name Zubu was certainly not used for all the tribes in the areas north and south of the desert.

The earliest Muslim work to record the tribal name Tatar was the *Hudūd al-'Ālam* (*The Regions of the World*), which was written in the year 982. The author clearly did not travel himself, but obtained all of his information from books. The contents of the work were mostly taken from other sources and were largely hearsay. Without a doubt he took his information from the ninth century work by Ibn Khurdādhbih and the tenth century works by Balkhī, Istakhrī, Jayhānī, and other such authors, as well

---

[55] See Wang Guowei 王國維, "A Study of the Black Cart Shiwei" 《黑車子室韋考》, in *Collected Works from the Hall of Observation* 《觀堂集林》, ch. 14. Wang Guowei determined that this "Black Cart Shiwei" is the Shiwei tribe called Hejie 和解, which originally lived southeast of Hulun Lake 呼倫湖.

as from ancient maps.[56] Section twelve of the work is called "Discourse on the Toghuzghuz and its Towns" ("Toghuzghuz" referring to the Uyghurs). It says, "This country is the largest of the Turkish countries and the Toghuzghuz were originally (*dar asl*) the most numerous tribe (*qaum*). The kings of the whole of Turkistan in the days of old were from the Toghuzghuz." It continues: "The Tātār too is a race (*jinsī*) of the Toghuzghuz."[57] This may reflect the period of the Uyghur Qaghanate in the north of the Gobi Desert, when the Tatars were subordinate tribes of the Uyghur Qaghanate and therefore were seen as one of the Uyghur tribes. We can say for certain that there were quite a few Tatars who penetrated into the territory of the Uyghur Qaghanate.

A work completed around 1050 by Gardīzī, entitled *Zayn al-Akhbār* (*The Ornament of Histories*), also mentions the Tatars, but says only that the Tatars were one of the seven *kimak* tribes.[58] They may have been a small Tatar tribe exiled to the upper reaches of the Irtysh River, but they were definitely not the major portion of the Tatar tribe.

The most detailed account of the eastern tribes is in Mahmūd al-Kāshgharī's Turkish dictionary, *Dīwān lughāt al-Turk*, which was completed in the 1070s. The author was a Kashgar Uyghur who understood the eastern tribes' languages, geography, and customs much better than Muslim writers of other ethnicities. He listed the Turkish tribes of the northern regions, from west to east in the following order: Pecheneg, Qïpčaq, Oghuz, Yimak, Bashghirt, Basmil, Qāy, Yabāqū, and Tātār. On the map that accompanies the text, the Qāy are shown on the left bank of the Yamar River (the present-day Ob River), and the Jumul tribe is found south of them. al-Kāshgharī says that the Jumul, Qāy, Yabāqū, Tātār, and Basmil tribes each had their own languages, but at the same time they spoke good "Turkish."[59] He also pointed out that the Ötüken (Ütüken, written here 於都斤) Mountains (the present-day Khangai Mountains)

---

[56] Vladimir Minorsky's (Владимир Минорский) "Translator's Preface" and V. V. Bartol'd's (Василий Владимирович Бартольд) "Preface" to Minorsky's English translation and annotated edition *Hudūd al-ʻĀlam, The Regions of the World: A Persian Geography, 372 A.H./982 A.D.*, 2nd edition, ed. by C. E. Bosworth, E. J. W. Gibb Memorial Series, New Series XI (London: Luzac, 1970).

[57] *Hudūd al-ʻĀlam*, p. 94.

[58] Ibid., p. 270, note 3; page 304.

[59] Ibid., p. 285.

were within the region where the Tatars lived.[60] This is completely consistent with the Chinese records from the Liao period, which talk about the regional distribution of the Zubu-Tatar tribes. The Tatars in al-Kāshgharī's book clearly refer to Mongols, who were different from other Turkish-speaking tribes. The Ötüken Mountains were formerly the sacred territory for the Turks and Uyghurs, but at that time became the region inhabited by Tatars. This truly reflects an enormous change in the composition of the peoples in the area north of the Gobi Desert.

The Zubu-Tatar tribes who lived in the Ötüken Mountains – the Khangai Mountains and the upper reaches of the Orkhon River – during the Liao Dynasty were none other than the Kerait tribe. Feng Chengjun 馮承鈞 in his *A Study of the Tribes in the Northern Area during the Liao and Jin Periods* 遼金北邊部族考[61] documented the fact that Ong Khan's grandfather Marcus Buyiruq Khan was the northern Zubu leader named Mogusi 磨古斯 (Marcus, a Christian name), who raised troops against the Liao at the end of 11th century as recorded in the *History of the Liao*. Marcus' tribe lived near Zhenzhou 鎮州 (its ruins are the ancient city of Chin-Tologhai 青托洛蓋, south of the present-day Qalqa River 喀魯哈河, a branch of the Tula River), and its chieftain also had a Christian name. Both the region of their residence and their religious orientation are consistent with their identification as Kerait. The *Jāmi' al-Tawārīkh* records that Marcus was captured during the war against the Tatar Na'ur Buyiruq Khan 納兀爾・不亦魯黑汗 and was handed over to the Jurchen emperor, who nailed him to a wooden donkey and killed him.[62] The *History of the Liao* records that Marcus was captured in 1100 by Yelü Wotela 耶律斡特剌, Pacification Commissioner of the Northwest Route 西北路招討使, and sent to the Liao court, where he was put to death.[63] Because Ong Khan was in the same generation as Chinggis Khan's father, his grandfather must have been active at the end of the Liao period. Thus when the *Jāmi' al-Tawārīkh* refers to the Jurchen emperor, it probably

[60] *Encyclopaedia of Islam*, vol. 4 (Leiden: Brill, 1936), entry on the Tatars by V. V. Bartol'd.

[61] Feng Chengjun 馮承鈞, *Assembled and Compiled Philological Essays on Historical Places in the Western Regions and Southern Seas* 《西域南海史地考證論著匯輯》 (Zhonghua Book Company, 1957), pp. 190-2.

[62] *Jāmi' al-Tawārīkh*, Russian translation, vol. 1, part 1, p. 129.

[63] *History of the Liao* 《遼史》, ch. 26, "Annals of Daozong" 《道宗紀》.

means the Khitan emperor. Feng Chengjun follows the *History of the Liao* and finds another Zubu leader earlier than Marcus, named Yugunan 余古赧, which is also the Christian name Yohanan. At that time the Kerait tribe was the only one of the various tribes north of the Gobi Desert who believed in Christianity. This is sufficient to show that the Kerait people were one of the Liao Dynasty's Zubu-Tatar tribes.

Finally, we can take one step further and try to understand even more clearly the origin of the Zubu-Tatar tribes that were distributed in the Khangai Mountains and the Orkhon River region. This will provide an even more solid basis for understanding the ethnic background of the Kerait tribe. Maeda Naonori's 前田直典 outstanding article, "The Nine Tatar Clans of the Tenth Century" 「十世紀時代の九族韃靼」[64] was the most important development in the study of this question. From the information about the Tatars of the Nine Surnames provided in the Turkish *Bilgä Qaghan* and *Moyunčor Inscriptions*, he inferred that this was an alliance of nine Tatar tribes who lived east of the Selenga River and were the earliest of all the Zubu-Tatar (Mongolian-speaking) tribes to become civilized, due to their frequent and multifarious contact with the Turks and the Tiele of the Nine Clans (the Toquz Oghuz referred to in the inscriptions). In the latter half of the ninth century, the Tatars, who had expelled the Kirghiz people and settled in the Orkhon River basin, must have constituted the nine Tatar tribes. These were called collectively the "Tatar kingdom" 達旦國 or the "nine tribes of the Tatar kingdom" 達旦國九部 (also called the Zubu 阻卜) living in the Zhenzhou region, as recorded in the *History of the Liao*. Maeda thought that the Zubu chieftain Alidu 阿里睹, or Zubu Alidi 阿離底 as recorded in the *History of the Liao,* must have actually been the name of a tribe, and he suspected that it was the subgroup of the Kerait tribe called the Aliat.[65] Maeda had planned to write *The Establishment of the Mongols in the Mongolian Territory*

[64] Maeda Naonori 前田直典, "Jyūseiki jidai no kyūzoku tatsutan" (The Nine Tatar Clans of the Tenth Century) 「十世紀時代の九族韃靼」in *Gencho shi no kenkyū* (*Research on Yuan Dynasty History*) 『元朝史の研究』 (Tokyo, 1973), pp. 232-63. This paper was originally published in *Tōyō Gakuhō* (*Journal of Oriental Studies*) 『東洋学報』, vol. 32, no. 1.

[65] The Persian collated edition writes it Albāt; the Paris and Soviet Union Academy manuscripts omit the diacritical mark on the third syllable. The London and Leningrad manuscripts write it Alīāt. See the Persian collated edition, p. 259.

(*Mōkonin no mōkochihō no seiritsu* 『蒙古人の蒙古地方の成立』), a series of articles covering 360 years, from the time of the fall of the Uyghur Qaghanate to Chinggis Khan's unification of the Mongols, and the process by which Turkish influence was replaced by Mongol influence; this was one of those articles. He had planned to write three additional articles, whose titles were to be: "Zubu and Dadan and Tatar" ("Sobōku to tatsutan to Tatar" 「阻卜と韃靼と Tatar」), "The Zubu (Tatar) Resistance Against the Khitan" ("Sobōku (tatsutan) to keitan to no kōsō" 「阻卜（韃靼）と契丹との抗争」), and "The Kerait Tribe and the Emergence of the Mongol Tribes" ("Mōkobu no taitō to kereito bu" 「蒙古部の台頭とケレイト部」), but unfortunately he passed away before he was able to complete them. He lived from 1915 to 1949.

By connecting the Zubu-Tatars of the Orkhon region in the Liao Dynasty with the Tatars of the Nine Surnames of the Tang Dynasty, Maeda made an outstanding breakthrough. Apart from the "Nine tribes of the Tatar Kingdom," pointed out by Wang Guowei and quoted by Maeda, there are additional sources that can be used. First, "Biography of Yelü Susa" 耶律速撒傳 in chapter 94 of the *History of the Liao* says that in the third year of the Baoning 保寧 reign period (971) of Emperor Jingzong 景宗, Yelü Susa was appointed General of the Nine Tribes 九部都詳穩 to guard the western border regions. The people he conquered and summoned to surrender were mostly from the Zubu tribes, and the region where he camped was in the Northwest Route 西北路. Thus we can see that the so-called "Nine Tribes" should be called the "Nine Zubu Tribes." Xiao Talin 蕭撻凜, who succeeded him in charge of the Northwest Route, had the official title Chief General of the Zubu 阻卜都詳穩.[66] After Xiao Talin pacified the various Zubu tribes, he established three towns in this region and sent troops to guard it. In the 22nd year of the Tonghe 統和 reign period (1004) the three towns of Zhenzhou 鎮州, Weizhou 維州, and Fangzhou 防州 were founded. From this time on, Zhenzhou became the seat of government for the Northwest Route.[67] Second, "Biography of

---

[66] *History of the Liao*, ch. 85, "Biography of Xiao Talin" 《蕭撻凜傳》. According to chapter 104 of this work, "Biography of Yelü Zhao" 《耶律昭傳》, Xiao Talin's official title was Pacification Commissioner 招討使 of the Northwest Route.

[67] See Chen Dezhi 陳得芝, "The Liao Dynasty Northwest Route Pacification Commission" 《遼代的西北路招討司》, in *Collected Papers of Research on Yuan*

Gouying" 斛英傳 in chapter 72 of the *History of the Jin Dynasty* 金史 records that "he accompanied the Left Army Supervisor 左監軍 Yila Yudu 移剌余睹 on an expedition to summon the various tribes of the northwestern regions to surrender. Gouying rode with 3,500 cavalry and pacified the nine tribes; he also captured 3,000 prisoners, as well as horses, oxen, and sheep numbering 150,000." This passage records the events of the eighth year of the Tianhui 天會 reign period in the Jin Dynasty (1130), when Yelü Yudu 耶律余睹 led troops northward to attack Qadun City 曷董城 (Kedun City 可敦城). This shows that the Tatar Kingdom of the Nine Tribes (or the Nine Tribes of the Zubu) were the tribes in the region of the Orkhon River, the Tula River, and Qadun City. The Tatars of the Nine Surnames were the first to enter the central region of the area north of the Gobi Desert. After the Uyghur Qaghanate was destroyed, they sensibly occupied the best pastureland that the Uyghurs had left behind and the area that had been the heartland of nomadic power throughout the ages: the Khangai Mountains and the upper reaches of the Orkhon River.

Because the Tatars of the Nine Surnames had had an intimate connection with the Turks from early on and had lived together with them, Turkish influence was deepest among this group. Thus we can use Yekemingghadai Irinchin's words, with slight modification, and conclude this section by saying that the Kerait people were probably the most Turkicized of all the proto-Mongols.

4. The Strength and Prosperity of the Kerait and the Region under their Control

After Yelü Abaoji went on his westward expedition, the Zubu-Tatar tribes in the region of the Uyghur cities submitted to the Khitan. The Khitan simply removed one part of the subject people "and formed three tribes from them…neither establishing cities, nor deploying guard troops" in this region.[68] The Zubu also submitted annual tribute. In the ninth year of the Huitong reign period (746) the Liao emperor Taizong 太宗 "appointed the Zubu chieftain Hela 曷刺 as the *yilijin* 夷離董 (tribal chief, Turkish *irkin*)

History and Northern Nationalities History 《元史及北方民族史研究集刊》, Nanjing University 南京大學, no. 2 (1978).

[68] *History of the Liao*, ch. 103, "Biography of Xiao Hanjianu" 《蕭韓家奴傳》.

of his own tribe."[69] This was the earliest instance of the Liao court granting a title of Great Tribal Chief 大部族张官 to a chieftain of the Zubu. Hela was probably the leader of the Zubu tribal union, because for about 30 years after this no other person was given this title. Only in the first year of the Qianheng 乾亨 reign period of Emperor Jingzong (979) was it seen again in the record, in the passage "The Zubu [written here 阻卜] *tiyin* 惕隱 Helu 曷魯, and the *yilijin* Alidu 阿里睹, and others came to court."[70] From this we can speculate that in the middle of the tenth century the Zubu tribe organized a rather large alliance among the tribes and also produced a great leader to head that alliance.

At the beginning of the Liao, when Emperor Shengzong 聖宗 ascended the throne (982), there was a great rebellion among the various Zubu tribes. After the successive suppressions and attacks carried out by the aforementioned Yelü Susa and Xiao Talin, the rebellion was for the most part put down by the 22nd year of the Tonghe reign period (1004). It was after this that Zhenzhou and the other fortifications were established in order to administer the territory, and it was then that Xiao Tuyu 蕭圖玉 went out to take up his post as Pacification Commissioner of the Northwest Route. He presented a memorial to the Emperor, saying: "Since the Zubu people have now submitted, they should be divided into separate tribal units, each governed by a Military Commissioner 節度使." Therefore in the 29th year of the Tonghe reign period (1011), posts of

---

[69] Ibid., ch. 4, "Annals of Taizong" 《太宗紀》. Note that the term *yilijin* 夷離堇 was the Liao Dynasty transliteration of *irkin*, a Turkish tribal leader. The Khitan had been ruled by the Turks, and this is why the Khitan also used this Turkish title. At the beginning of the Liao Dynasty, the title was given both to the Northern Administration Official 北面官 "in charge of the tribal army and the people" and also to the Northern Administration Official in Charge of Tribes 北面部族官 as the leader of the "Great Tribe." Later it was changed to "Grand Prince" 大王. The "Monograph on Official Posts" 《百官志》 in the *History of the Liao* says, "In the list of tribal titles, the leader of a large tribe is called 'Grand Prince' 大王, but in their own language the title was *yilijin*."

[70] *History of the Liao*, ch. 9, "Annals of Jingzong" 《景宗紀》. Note that *tiyin* 惕隱 was the Liao Dynasty transliteration of the Turkic official title *tegin*, which was originally the title of the children of the Turkish khan. In the Liao Dynasty it was used for officials in charge of tribal politics and religious affairs, and it was also used for officials of large tribes whose position was lower than the *yilijin*. The "Monograph on Official Posts" in the *History of the Liao* says, "For large tribes, a tribe's *situ* 司徒 [literally 'Minister of Education,' a prestigious title] was originally called *tiyin*."

Military Commissioner were established for the various Zubu tribes.[71] This shows that after the Zubu tribes in this region allied with each other they gradually grew in strength. Because they were able to raise troops to oppose the Liao, they were able to maintain their struggle against them for about 20 years. After it pacified the Zubu rebellion, the Liao court saw that when the Zubu tribes united they became a strong force. This is why the Liao adopted a policy of divide and rule. However, because the appointed Military Commissioners "were frequently not very capable, the people under their rule resented them and contemplated rebellion." In the first year of the Kaitai 開泰 reign period (1012) "The Sub-tribe Grand Preceptor 石烈太師 Alidi 阿里底 killed his Military Commissioner and fled westward to Ordubalïq 窩魯朵城 (which had been the capital of the Uyghur Qaghanate)." The Zubu revolted again. They surrounded and attacked Zhenzhou (Qadun City), but were shot at by arrows and forced to retreat by the Liao garrison, under the command of Xiao Tuyu, and then to camp in Ordubalïq.[72] Later on, the Liao court sent the Commissioner of the Northern Establishment Bureau of Military Affairs 北院樞密使 Yelü Huage 耶律化哥 to command a great army that would go to their aid. Xiao Tuyu again adopted a policy of pacification, and the rebellious tribes only then submitted to his authority.

The above-mentioned Zubu tribes used Ordubalïq as a center, distributing themselves in the region of the upper reaches of the Tula and Orkhon Rivers. This is the same place as the region inhabited by the Kerait tribe. The Syrian historian Bar-Hebraeus (1226-1286) in his *Chronicon Ecclesiasticum* recorded that the Kerait people were converted to Nestorian Christianity at the beginning of the 11th century. It is said that the Kerait Khan once lost his way on the steppe, when he was rescued by Saint Sergis, who fortunately appeared to him and pointed out the way. Having received the encouragement of a Christian merchant who was in the country at the time, he sent someone to invite the Nestorian bishop of

---

[71] *History of the Liao*, ch. 93, "Biography of Xiao Tuyu" 《蕭圖玉傳》; ch. 15, "Annals of Shengzong" 《聖宗紀》.

[72] *History of the Liao*. 'Ala-al-Dīn 'Ata-Malik Juwaīnī's *Ta'rīkh-i Jahān-Gushā* (*The History of the World-Conqueror*) records that the qaghan of the Bugu 卜古 Uyghurs established his capital on the banks of the Orkhon River and called it Ordubalïq (Ordo City). Boyle's English translation, vol. 1, p. 54; He Gaoji's 何高濟 Chinese translation, 《世界征服者史》, vol. 1, p. 62. *New Tang History* 《新唐書》, in "Biography of Huihe" 《回紇傳》, writes it as *Huihucheng* 回鶻城 (Uyghur City).

Merv, Ebedjesu, to come in person or send another priest in his stead in order to baptize him and his tribe. Bar-Hebraeus quoted the letters that Ebedjesu wrote in 1009 to the Pope John VI reporting this event. He also said that 200,000 Kerait people and their Khan received the rite of baptism:

> The Kerait Khan, who had gone astray in the steppes, is said to have been saved by the apparition of Saint Sergius. At the instigation of the Christian merchants who chanced to be in the country at the time, he asked Ebedjesu, the Nestorian metropolitan of Merv, in Khorasan, either to come himself or to send a priest to baptize him, together with his tribe. Ebedjesu's letter to the Nestorian patriarch (of Baghdad) John VI (d. 1011) – a letter dated from 1009 and quoted in Bar-Hebraeus – states that 200,000 Kerait Turks were baptized with their Khan.[73]

This shows that in the beginning of the 11th century the Kerait tribe was a large tribe of about 200,000 people, though the precise figure may be slightly exaggerated.

Having been attacked by a large Liao army, the Zubu tribal alliance probably collapsed. In the *History of the Liao* we read that various tribal chiefs separately approached the Liao court to surrender and pay tribute. By the 14th year of the Chongxi 重熙 reign period of Emperor Xingzong 興宗 (1045), the *History of the Liao* records that "The great king of the Zubu, Dun Tugusi 屯禿古斯 led the various tribal leaders to court"; and that in the 22nd year of the Chongxi reign period, "he once more led the various tribal leaders in presenting horses and camels [to the Chinese emperor]."[74] Dun Tugusi was probably appointed by the Liao court as the tribal Chief (*yilijin*, *irkin*) and commanded the various tribes as their great leader. In the fifth year of the Da'an 大安 reign period of Emperor

[73] "Le khan kérait, qui s'était égaré dans la steppe fut sauvé par l'apparition de saint Sergis (saint Serge). A l'instigation de marchands chrétiens qui se trouvaient dans le pays, il demanda alors au métropolite nestorien de Merv (au Khorassan), Ébedjésu, de venir ou d'envoyer un prêtre pour le baptiser avec sa tribu. La lettre d'Ébedjésu au patriarche nestorien (de Baghdad), Jean VI, lettre datée de 1009 et citée par Bar-Hebraeus, dit que 200,000 Turcs Kérait se firent baptiser avec leur khan." René Grousset, *L'empire des steppes*, p. 245. [English translation, slightly modified, from René Grousset, *The Empire of the Steppes*, trans. Naomi Walford (Rutgers University Press, 1970), p. 191.]

[74] *History of the Liao*, ch. 19-20, "Annals of Xingzong" 《興宗紀》.

Daozong 道宗 (1089), the northern Zubu leader Mogusi 磨古斯 (Marcus, Ong Khan's grandfather), on the recommendation of Yelü Tabuye 耶律撻不也, Pacification Commissioner of the Northwest Route, was appointed head of all the Zubu tribes.[75] In the eighth year, the Northwest Route Pacification Commissioner Yelü Helusaogu 耶律何魯掃古 was occupied with attacking the rebellious tribes and attacked Marcus by mistake, who also rebelled. This rebellion spread and reached the entire Northwest Route – the Merkit 梅里急 (蔑兒乞), Naiman 粘八葛 (乃蠻), and other great tribes all became involved in the rebellion. Although Marcus was not necessarily the leader of all the rebellious tribes, he had great influence and inflicted many defeats on the Liao army.

In the sixth year of the Shouchang 壽昌 reign period (1100) Marcus was captured and killed, and the disorder in the Northwest Route was gradually put down. The various tribes "each returned to their own homelands and presented local products as tribute." After this there were no more major troubles for the most part, and little else is said in the *History of the Liao* about the Zubu tribe. As the Liao Dynasty declined and the Jurchen arose, the Liao gradually relaxed its hold on the Northwest Route. In the fourth year of the Baoda 保大 reign period (1124) of the Tianzuo 天祚 Emperor, Yelü Dashi 耶律大石 led his troops to Zhenzhou (Qadun City) and established political power there. He used all of the tribal forces north of the Gobi Desert to resist and oppose the Jin. In the eighth year of the Tianhui reign period (1130), the Jin Emperor Taizong 太宗 sent out troops on an expedition northwards to Qadun City, making it difficult for Yelü Dashi to establish a foothold north of the Gobi Desert. He therefore enlisted troops from various tribes under his Khitan soldiers and went forth on an expedition to the Western regions. The Zubu-Tatar tribes in the regions north and south of the desert sooner or later all submitted to the Jin Dynasty.[76] However, most of the Jin strength was

---

[75] Ibid., ch. 25, "Annals of Daozong" 《道宗紀》; ch. 96, "Biography of Yelü Dabuye" 《耶律撻不也傳》.

[76] The Liao Dynasty Tianzuo 天祚 Emperor had taken refuge in the region of the Yinshan Tatars 陰山韃靼 and from there led an expedition southwards. After his forces were defeated, the Yinshan Tatars and other tribes south of the desert one by one submitted to the Jin Dynasty. "Annals of Taizong" 《太宗紀》 in the *History of the Jin Dynasty* 《金史》 records that in the third year of the Tianhui reign period Wolu 斡魯 "presented a memorial to the emperor recommending that since the Mogeshi 謨葛失 tribe had come to

applied in the south to advance the struggle for the central plain [China proper], so that its control of the tribes in the north was not consolidated as solidly as that of the Liao Dynasty. For example, the Jin Pacification Commissioner of the Northwest Route was first established in Yanzi City 燕子城 (present-day Zhangbei 張北 in Hebei 河北 Province) and later moved slightly north to Huanzhou 桓州 (present-day Zhenglan Banner 正藍旗 in Inner Mongolia), which was 2,000-3,000 *li* 里 away from the center of the Kerait and other tribes.

At the end of the Liao and the beginning of the Jin, the control over the region north of the Gobi Desert by both of the central dynasties was weakening. This situation encouraged the tribes in this region to seek opportunities for increasing their own power. Therefore, conflicts increased between the tribes that were involved in the power struggle. From this time onwards the records of the Mongol Yuan period become more detailed, and gradually a clearer picture of the history of the Mongolian plateau in the 12th century emerges in front of our eyes.

According to the *Jāmi' al-Tawārīkh*, after the ruler of the Kerait, Ong Khan's grandfather Marcus, was captured by the Tatar Khan Na'ur Buyiruq and sent to the Jurchen emperor (see above, this is an error for the Khitan emperor) and was put to death, his wife plotted revenge. She

---

submit to the court, an official seal with a ribbon should be granted to them." Mogeshi was a tribe based north of the Yinshan. The submission of the various tribes north of the Gobi Desert occurred after Yelü Dashi 耶律大石 moved westward. The *History of the Jin Dynasty* "Biography of Gouying" 《彀英傳》 records that he accompanied Yilayudu 移剌余睹, who went to summon the various tribes in the Northwest, and "pacified the nine tribes." This refers to the Qadun City 曷董城 military campaign in the eighth year of the Tianhui reign period (1130), but this campaign in fact accomplished nothing and they returned. The people of the nine tribes did not necessarily all submit at that time. *Record of the Great Jin State* 《大金國志》 in chapter 14 records that in the first year of the Zhenglong 正隆 reign period (1156), Polongdun 婆隆敦 was appointed as Commander Director-in-chief on the Left 左都監帥, and he was ordered to manage the cultivation of wasteland in Qadun City. It was at this time that a roving Western Liao cavalryman came to the front, shouted awhile, and then withdrew. This shows that at this time the Jin Dynasty's influence had already reached the region of Hedong City. However, the area not far to the west of that region was still under the rule of the Western Liao. By the time of the 15th year of the Dading reign period (1175), the Naiman 粘拔思 tribe west of the Khangai Mountains began turning away from the Western Liao and giving its allegiance to the Jin Dynasty. See *History of the Jin Dynasty*, "Biography of Niangehannu" 《粘割韓奴傳》.

pretended to go to Na'ur Khan and present tribute consisting of sheep, horses, and koumiss (a liquid made from mare's milk), and in the leather bags supposedly filled with koumiss she secretly hid 100 brave soldiers. They took advantage of the banquet that was being held by Na'ur Khan to present the koumiss. At that point the brave soldiers jumped out of the leather bags and killed Na'ur Khan and his many officials.[77]

The *Jāmi' al-Tawārīkh* also records another large struggle between the Kerait and Tatar tribes. The most important record of this struggle is in the "Treatise on the Tribes" under the heading "Tatar tribes." Its main point (according to the Russian translation) is that Qūrīdaī Tātīr[78] and Gūmūs Sinjāng[79] from the Alchi Tatar tribe (a branch of the Tatars) led troops in an attack on Sārīq Khan, the king of the Kerait tribe. Gūmūs, fighting as the vanguard, attacked and defeated Sārīq Khan, but the lone army went deeply into enemy territory and was taken prisoner by the Kerait. After Sārīq Khan killed Gūmūs, he took advantage of the opportunity, collected the troops together, and united the army on the banks of the Orkhon River, preparing to attack the Tatars. One of the warriors in his tribe rebelled and joined Qūrīdaī Tātīr, to whom he reported what had happened. Thereupon Qūrīdaī Tātīr sent troops up the Orkhon River against the current, who advanced and attacked the Kerait camp. Having underestimated his enemy, Sārīq Khan suffered a great defeat, and only 40 of the original 40,000 soldiers of his tribe escaped with their lives. He threw in his lot with Buyiruq Khan (Bītāktāī ōtōku qōrchī buīrūq khan).[80] "When [Sārīq Khan] presented himself for this tribe's protection, he married his daughter off to Qūrjāghūsh Buyiruq Khan.[81] This daughter was named Tūreh Qaīmishi; she was Qājīr Khan's sister" (*wa čun ū be hamāīt ān qūm dar āmadeh būd,*

---

[77] *Jāmi' al-Tawārīkh*, Russian translation, vol. 1, section 1, p. 129.

[78] In various editions the second character of this name is written Tāt?r, Bā?r, Bāīr, and in other ways. Pelliot thought that it should be Tāīr (Dāīr). See *Histoire des Campagnes de Gengis Khan*, p. 241.

[79] The second word of this name in the collated edition was originally written Sījānk. Pelliot thought that it should be Saījāng, which seems to be a name borrowed by the Khitan or Jurchen from Chinese; -jāng may be derived from *zhang* 長 (leader). *Histoire des Campagnes de Gengis Khan*, pp. 241-2.

[80] The first part of this name refers to the Beteki tribe, a sub-tribe of the Naimans. The name means a person from the Beteki tribes, called Old Qōrchī Buyiruq Khan. But Pelliot thought it should be Ōbā-kōtūrčī, a Turkic name. See *Histoire des Campagnes de Gengis Khan*, p. 246.

[81] This person is Ong Khan's father, Qurjaqus 忽兒札胡思.

dokhtar khud-ra beh Qūrjāqūs khān dād; wa ān dokhtar Tūreh Qaīmishi nām būd khwaher Qājīr khān). Later, Qājīr Khan and Sārīq Khan together attacked the Tatars and recovered the Kerait *ulus* [homeland, or hereditary territory] for Sārīq Khan. Ong Khan and his mother Yilma Qadun, who had previously been captured by the Tatars, were also released. Yūlā Māghūs, Tāī Tīmūur, and Tāīshī were Tūreh Qaīmishi's sons.[82] She had four other sons whose names are unknown.

This passage records a very important event in the history of the Kerait tribe. It also reveals that the heart of the Kerait tribe's territory was the upper reaches of the Orkhon River. However, some individuals and relationships between them mentioned in this passage are unclear or confused.

First, Sārīq Khan, whose name in Turkish means Yellow Khan, does not appear in the Kerait section of the "Treatise on the Tribes." Who was this person? Pelliot thought that he was Qūrjāghūsh's father, and that his Christian name was Marcus, but he was also known by the Turkish name Sārīq Khan:

> …finally there's the case of Sārīq Khan himself. Everything leads to the suggestion that he was the father of Qūrjāghūsh. But we know through the Kerait family that Qūrjāghūsh's father was Marγuz, Marcus. The only possible solution I can see, is that Prince Kerait, whose Christian name was Marγuz, was also known by the Turkish name Sārīq Khan.[83]

However, the *Jāmi' al-Tawārīkh* has a very clear record of Marcus, saying that he was captured by the Tatars and sent to the Jurchen sovereign (the Jin [actually the Liao] Dynasty), where he was put to death. Unfortunately, the time period in this record is not completely consistent

---

[82] "Tāīshī (Taiši)" is a title, which has its origin in the Chinese word "taizi" 太子 (heir apparent). Tai Temür Taiši 台・帖木兒・太石 is probably a person's title, referring to Ong Khan's brother, Tai Temür Taizi 台帖木兒太子, as recorded in *The Secret History of the Mongols*, section 177. Yūlā Māghūs 玉剌・馬忽思 is also a person's name. See the "Treatise on the Tribes" in the *Jāmi' al-Tawārīkh*, the section on the Kerait tribe.

[83] "…reste enfin le cas de Sariq-khan lui-même, Tout suggère qu'il ait été le père de Qurjaγus. Mais nous savons par la notice des Kerait que le père de celui-ci était Marγuz, Marc. La seul solution que j'entrevoie est que le prince Kerait qui portait le nom chrétien de Marγus était aussi connu sous la désignation turque de Sariq khan." *Histoire des Campagnes de Gengis Khan*, p. 247.

with the facts as we know them. Marcus (who was called Mogusi 磨古斯 in the *History of the Liao*) died in 1100, when Ong Khan was not yet born (Ong Khan died in 1203), but this passage of the *Jāmi' al-Tawārīkh* records that Sārīq Khan attacked the Tatar tribe together with Qājīr Khan 合只爾汗 and won a victory, rescuing Ong Khan and his mother. According to *The Secret History of the Mongols*, section 152, when Ong Khan and his mother were captured by the Tatar Ajai Khan 阿澤汗, he (Ong Khan) was already 13 years old. Pelliot followed a corresponding passage in *The Secret History of the Mongols*, which was copied into the *Altan Tobči* (*Golden Summary*), where in the corresponding paragraph Ajai Khan was written Ači Khan. He thought this was probably Alči Khan, referring to the khan of the Alči Tatar tribe.[84] The capture of Ong Khan and his mother must have occurred at the time when Qūrīdaī Tātīr attacked the Kerait camp on the Orkhon River. If we estimate that Ong Khan died at about 70 years old (the Naiman leader Tayang Khan 太陽汗 called him "Old Ong Khan," see section 189 of *The Secret History of the Mongols*), this event probably took place around 1140 at the latest. Sārīq Khan was probably Marcus' successor as khan of Kerait, or this may have been another khan who reigned before Ong Khan's father Qūrjāghūsh. It could also have been another name for Qūrjāghūsh.

Second, according to the *Jāmi' al-Tawārīkh*, lady Tūreh Qaīmishi, who was married to Qūrjāghūsh Buyiruq Khan, was the daughter of Sārīq Khan, but this text also says that she was Qājīr Khan's sister. This is impossible for two reasons: one is that Sārīq Khan and Qūrjāghūsh were both from Kerait, and there was a customary law that people from same clan could not become related by marriage. Moreover, even if Sārīq Khan was from another tribe in the Kerait alliance, and not from the same clan as Qūrjāghūsh, when Sārīq escaped and hid among the Beteki tribe they would not have needed to arrange the marriage. Here the records of this event become incomprehensible. The other reason is that if Tūreh Qaīmishi was Sārīq Khan's daughter, Qājīr Khan would have been his son. If this had been true, then it would be difficult to explain why it says later that Qājīr Khan helped Sārīq Khan recover the Kerait *ulus*. Actually Qājīr Khan was not a Kerait, but the leader of the Beteki Naiman tribe, Qadir 合迪爾汗 (Qadir in Turkish, Qājīr in Mongolian), as recorded in the Naiman section of the "Treatise on the Tribes." Pelliot thought that after

[84] *Histoire des Campagnes de Gengis Khan*, p. 245.

the Sārīq Khan of the Kerait tribe had been defeated by the Tatars, he fled westward to the Beteki tribe of the Naimans, and the leader of the Beteki Naiman tribe, who was Qājīr Khan's father, married off his daughter to Qūrjāghūsh of the Kerait tribe, thereupon uniting them both by marriage. It was for this reason alone that Qājīr Khan helped Sārīq Khan recover the Kerait *ulus*.[85] This explanation appears correct.

The *Jāmi' al-Tawārīkh* continues by saying that after Sārīq Khan had returned to the country, some Mongols attached themselves to him. Ötögü Qorči Buyiruq Khan of the Beteki tribe wanted them to become his subjects, but Sārīq Khan refused, and pointed out a way for them to escape by skirting along the Dālān-tābān Mountains. He also moved in that direction along that route, but returned from Tūi-Taghaču. These two place names also indicated territory where the Kerait tribe was active.

Dālān-tābān (Dalan-Daban) is the same as Dalan-Daba 達蘭達葩 or Dalan-Dabas 答蘭·答八思, as recorded in the "Annals of Emperor Taizong" in the *History of the Yuan*. The latter name in Mongolian means "70 mountain ridges." This is the precise location where Ögödei Khan held a great assembly (*quriltai*) of all the princes and officials and issued regulations (條令, or *jasaq* in Mongolian) in the fifth month of 1234. Later, Empress Naimajin 乃馬真 also met the princes and officials at this place to consult with them about the election of her son Güyüq as Khan. According to Carpini's account, the setting for the great meeting was at *Šira urdo*,[86] which was where Ögödei Khan had established his summer palace. This place was called Örmektü, which was probably over 100 *li* west of the Qara-Qorum, in the upper reaches of the Jirmatai River 吉爾馬泰河, a branch of the Orkhon River.[87] Dālān-tābān must be the name of the mountain ridges in the vicinity of this summer palace, probably the present-day Subarkhan Khairkhan Mountains 蘇巴爾漢海爾罕山. Yelü Zhu's 耶律鑄 poem entitled *Sound of Pines* 松聲 says:

岩聲何事韻錚錚
風入寒梢鳥自驚

[85] *Histoire des Campagnes de Gengis Khan*, p. 246.
[86] Christopher Dawson, ed., *The Mongol Mission*, p. 62.
[87] See Chen Dezhi 陳得芝, "Yuan Dynasty Helin City and its Surroundings" 《元和林城及其周圍》, *Collected Papers of Research on Yuan History and Northern Nationalities History*《元史及北方民族史研究集刊》, Nanjing University 南京大學, no. 3 (1979).

七嶺夜寒篩漢月
九霄霜冷奏秦箏

Why is there all this clanging in the cliffs?
The wind rushes into the wintry treetops, startling the birds.
The seven mountain ridges screen out the Han moonlight on
a cold night,
Somewhere in the nine layers of cloud, the chilling music of
the *zheng* of Qin.

He adds an annotation saying, "The 'Seven Mountain Ridges' is the name of the place where the summer palace was."[88] Note that Yelü Zhu lived in Qara-Qorum for a long time and often accompanied the Mongol great khan on his seasonal imperial tour. He knew that the name "Seven Mountain Ridges" was short for seventy mountains, and that the location of the summer palace was at Dālān-tābān.

The placc name "Tūi-Tāghājū" does not appear in the Yuan Dynasty Chinese historical records, but it became famous in the Ming Dynasty when Esen Khan 也先汗 occupied the area north of the Gobi Desert. He once in camped in Tūi-Tāghājū Qonghortan 推-塔出·晃忽爾壇. This was the land between the Tui River 推河 and the Tāghājū River 塔出河, south of the Khangai Mountains. The *Record of Later Travel beyond the Great Wall* 後出塞錄 by the Qing Dynasty writer Gong Zhiyue 龔之鑰 explains: "In the past, the Tui River was a park for the Yuan ruling house. It was warm there and the land was suitable for cultivation."[89] It was therefore an important place during the Yuan Dynasty.

Qūrjāghūsh Buyiruq Khan had many wives and concubines, and he had forty sons.[90] Ong Khan (To'oril) was the eldest and, as noted above, was born to the wife named Yilma Qadun. When the mother and son were captured and taken away by the Tatars, Qūrjāghūsh threw in his lot with

---

[88] Yelü Zhu 耶律鑄, *Anthology of the Drunken Hermit at the Twin Streams* 《雙溪醉隱集》, ch. 4 (Zhifu Studio Series 知服齋叢書 edition).

[89] Quoted by Zhang Mu 張穆 in his *Notes on the Mongolian Nomads* 《蒙古游牧記》, ch. 8, Shouyang 壽陽, Qi family 祁氏 block printing edition, the Qing Dynasty sixth year of the Tongzhi 同治 reign (1866).

[90] *Jāmi' al-Tawārīkh*, Russian translation, vol. 1, part 1, p. 130; *The Secret History of the Mongols*, section 177.

the Beteki Naiman tribe and took another wife, the daughter of Ötögü Qorci Buyiruq Khan, who was the leader of that tribe. That daughter, named Tūreh Qaīmishi, gave birth to the Tai Temür Taizi, Yūlā Māghūs, and several other sons. Those whose names we know are Erke Qara 也力可・合剌, Jaghagambo 劄阿紺孛, Buqa Temür 不花・帖木爾, and others. The brothers must have struggled fiercely among themselves for the succession to the khan throne. Moreover, Qūrjāghūsh had a younger brother called Gür Khan, who also coveted the khan throne. In order to avoid a power struggle among his sons, Qūrjāghūsh gave the territory of Yāgh-Yābghān 牙黑-牙不罕 to Gür Khan and Ong Khan as a fief, and he gave the territory of Qārāghās-Būrughūs 哈剌哈思-博羅兀思 to Tai Temür Taizi and Yūlā Māghūs. This separated them and gave them each their own fiefs. His own camp was in the region of Ordubalïq.[91]

When the historical records of the Mongol Yuan period record the place names in the area north of the Gobi Desert, they often combine the names of two nearby rivers together into a joint name usually referring to a rather large area. For example, the Onon-Kerulen 斡難-怯綠連, Tūi-Tāghājū, Alei-Salas 阿雷-撒剌思, and so forth.[92] The names Yāgh-Yābghān and Qārāghās-Būrughūs were probably created in this way. These two river systems are distinguished by being on two different sides of the Orkhon River – east and west – and are rather far apart. Thus Qūrjāghūsh's sons and brother could be kept apart to prevent a power struggle. West of the Orkhon River is the Jābqān River 劄不罕河, which has its origin on the southwest side of the Khangai Mountains and flows westward into Qara Lake 哈臘河. The *Jāmi' al-Tawārīkh* records that during the reign of Qubilai Khan, Möngke's 蒙哥 son Ürüng Tashi 玉龍答失 camped next to the Jābqān River beside the Altai Mountains. In the fifth year of the Dade reign period of Emperor Chengzong (1301), Qaidu 海都 crossed the Altai Mountains and headed eastwards to fight a great battle with the Yuan army in the Tekelgu 鐵堅古 Mountains near the Jābqān River.[93] When Uyghur script is used to write Mongolian, the two

[91] *Jāmi' al-Tawārīkh*, vol. 1, part 1, p. 129.

[92] Ālūī-Sīlās 阿雷-撒剌思 was the place where the Naiman tribe lived. See the *Jāmi' al-Tawārīkh*, vol. 1, part 1, p. 137. It is the present-day Alui Sharys River, a branch of the Ebi River in its upper reaches.

[93] John Andrew Boyle, *The Successors of Genghis Khan*, translated from the Persian of Rashīd al-Dīn *Jāmi' al-Tawārīkh*, vol. 2 (New York: Columbia University Press, 1971), p.

sounds "j" and "y" are represented by the same mark, and these can become confused in transliteration. For example, J̌alayir (Jalayir) 札剌亦兒 is also transliterated Yalayir 押剌伊而 (Yalayier), and Jābqān can also be read Yabqan. I suspect that the land granted to Ong Khan and Gür Khan, which was called Yabqan 牙不罕, was the area of the Jābqān River 劄不罕河. In the same way, Yaq 牙黑 was perhaps Jaq. East of the upper reaches of the Jābqān River was the Zhake River 劄克河 in the upper reaches of the Bayidaraq River 拜答里克河, and I suggest that this is the same as the Yaq River in the *Jāmi' al-Tawārīkh.* Yaq-Yabqan probably referred to the territory in the upper regions of the Zhake and Jābqān Rivers.

Furthermore, I suggest that the place called Qārāghās-Būrughūs may be the region of the Tula River on the eastern edge of the area inhabited by the Kerait tribe. The *Record of the Personal Campaigns of the Holy Warrior* records: "In the autumn of the next year, the emperor (Chinggis Khan) sent troops to the Qara 哈剌 River and attacked the leader of the Merkit 蔑兒乞 tribe, Toqto'a 脫脫. They fought at Monacha Mountain 莫那察山. They then plundered two tribes of the Uduyit-Merkit 兀都夷篾里乞 and absorbed their population, letting Ong Khan have all the booty." Rashīd al-Dīn's *Jāmi' al-Tawārīkh* also records this battle, but calls the Qala River the Qarās-Mūras (Būras?). He also says that the land is not very far from the Kerulen River and is close to the Selenga River.[94] Hong Jun 洪鈞 transliterates this name as Huolasibulasi 霍拉思布拉思.[95] Tu Ji changed it to Helasibulasi 合剌思不剌思 and said in a note: "There is a river called Qara gol 哈剌果勒 (*gol* in Mongolian means 'river') in the last banner of the left wing 左翼末旗 of the Tüsiyetü 土謝圖 [khan] tribe, which flows westward through the northern part of Kulun 庫倫 (the present-day Ulaanbaatar). The Boro River 博羅河 flows northwards into it. After the two rivers converge they flow further to the northwest where they meet the Orkhon River....This is what is called Helasibulasi, which is

260 and p. 27, note; *Jāmi' al-Tawārīkh*, vol. 2, Persian collated edition (Moscow, 1980), p. 32.

[94] *Jāmi' al-Tawārīkh*, Russian translation, vol. 1, part 2, p. 111.

[95] Hong Jun 洪鈞, *Yuan History Translated and Corrected* 《元史譯文證補》 [Hong Jun's introduction of the *Jāmi' al-Tawārīkh* to Chinese scholars, 1897], ch. 1a, "Basic Annals of Taizu Translated and Corrected" 《太祖本紀譯證》.

probably where the Qara and Boro Rivers converge."[96] Wang Guowei in his annotated and collated edition of the *Record of the Personal Campaigns of the Holy Warrior* quotes from Yao Sui's 姚燧 "Spirit Way Stele for the Industrious Executor of the Grand Secretariat Lord Mangwu" 平章政事忙兀公神道碑 (in *Categorized Literature from the Yuan Period* 元文類, chapter 59) where he says: "in the sixteenth year of the Zhiyuan reign period (1279), the Halasi 哈剌斯, Boluosi 博羅斯, Woluohan 斡羅罕, and Xueliangan 薛連斡 were all strong clans 宗. They were irreconcilable with each other, so they asked the court to send a prominent official there to serve as a supervisor. An imperial order was issued for Boroqul 博羅歡 to go there, and he stayed for two years." He thought that Halasi and Bolasi were Hong Jun's transliterations of the name Huolasibulasi (Qarās-Mūras [Būras]) in Rashīd al-Dīn's work, and this is correct. Wang Guowei agreed with Tu Ji that Halasi was derived from the Qara River, but he thought that Bulasi probably came from the Bula River (a small river south of present-day Qiaketu 恰克圖), which is in the Bu'ura ke'er 不兀剌川 region, where the Merkit tribe lived, as recorded in *The Secret History of the Mongols*. We note that the present Bula River is located rather far north and is quite far from the Qala River in the south. Between them lie the Yiluo 依羅 and Xila 席剌 Rivers. Therefore, their names should not be combined. As for their geographical location, probably Tu Ji's view is the best.

The place called Helasi-Bulasi 合剌思-布剌思 (Halasi-Buluosi 哈剌斯-博羅斯) is probably north of the upper reaches of the Tula River. Ong Khan once lived "in the Black Forest 黑林 of the Tula River."[97] Zhang Mu 張穆 thinks this is Ja'u Modo 昭莫多 (which means "100 trees"), southeast of Kulun (Ulaanbaatar),[98] which is presently called Nailanqa 納賴哈. This region in the upper reaches of the Tula River was the territory

[96] Tu Ji 屠寄, *Historical Record of the Mongols* 《蒙兀爾史記》, ch. 2, "Annals of Taizu" 《太祖紀》.

[97] See *The Secret History of the Mongols*, sections 96, 104, 164. Chinggis Khan also established a temporary camp (*ordo*) in the Black Forest of the Tula River after destroying the Kerait tribe, and when he came back from the westward expedition in the year 1225, he took up residence in this "Black Forest Ordo." See *The Secret History of the Mongols*, section 264.

[98] Zhang Mu 張穆, *Notes on the Mongolian Nomads* 《蒙古游牧記》, ch. 7.

of the Kerait tribe. I think that this is the Qarās-Mūras (Būras) which Qūrjāghūsh gave as a fief to his son Tai Temür Taizi, and that it must refer to a large region in the valley of the Qara and Boro Rivers, rather than being limited to the place where these two rivers come together.

Ong Khan probably lost favor with his father, and this was why, after Qūrjāghūsh died, the khan throne passed on to Tai Temür Taizi, while Ong Khan was sent to guard the frontier. Ong Khan plotted secretly to recapture the throne and sent troops to attack Tai Temür Taizi and Yūlā Māghūs. They fled to Toqto'a, leader of the Merkit tribe. However, Toqto'a was intimidated by Ong Khan's power, so he seized them and sent them to Ong Khan. Thereupon Ong Khan killed the two younger brothers and absorbed their fiefs into his own territory.[99]

5. The Kingdom of Kerait during Ong Khan's Rule

Ong Khan recaptured the Khan throne in the 1160s, at which time the Mongol tribes were under the control of Qutula Khan 忽圖剌汗. After Ong Khan had killed the two brothers, his uncle Gür Khan raised troops against him in retribution. Ong Khan was defeated and retreated along the Selenga River into Qala'un Qabčil 哈剌溫隘.[100] From there he took refuge with and lived among the Merkit tribe. He requested help from the Mongol tribe's Yisügei Ba'atur 也速該·把阿禿爾 (Chinggis Khan's father), but Qutula Khan scorned Ong Khan for killing his own brothers and urged Yisügei to have nothing to do with him. However, Yisügei did not listen to him, and he sent out troops to help Ong Khan defeat Gür Khan and recapture the Kerait *ulus*.

---

[99] In the *Jāmi' al-Tawārīkh*, in addition to the place where the Kerait entry in the "Treatise on the Tribes" says that the two younger brothers who Ong Khan killed were Tai Temür Taizi and Yūlā Māghūs, the event is mentioned in other places, and they all say that the brothers killed by Ong Khan were Tai Temür Taizi and Buqa Temür. Both the *Record of the Personal Campaigns of the Holy Warrior* and *The Secret History of the Mongols* (section 177) record that Ong Khan killed Tai Temür Taizi and Buqa Temür. I suspect that Yūlā Māghūs was the same person as Buqa Temür.

[100] This Qara'un Qabčil 哈剌溫隘 must be near the present-day Selenga River, south of the homeland of the Merkit tribe. Later, after the leader of the Merkit tribe had surrendered to Chinggis Khan, they then revolted and fled to this place. Between the present-day Selenga River and the lower reaches of the Orkhon River is Halong 哈隆 Mountain, which is located in exactly the right position to be identified as this place.

After Ong Khan returned to his own country, his power and influence increased day by day. His younger brother Erke Qara 也力可哈利 was intimidated by him, so he fled to the Naiman tribe. The Naiman ruler Inanča Bilge Khan 亦難赤汗 (father of Tayang Khan) sent troops to attack Ong Khan. He took his (Ong Khan's) *ulus* and gave it to Erke Qara to rule. The records of these events in *The Secret History of the Mongols*, the "History of Chinggis Khan" in the *Jāmi' al-Tawārīkh*, the *Record of the Personal Campaigns of the Holy Warrior*, and the "Annals of Emperor Taizu" in the *History of the Yuan* all say that Ong Khan suffered a serious defeat and was forced to flee to the Western Liao 西遼. They also recount that he later entered the Western Xia 西夏 Kingdom, where he experienced difficulty and hardship, before retracing his steps and heading back north of the Gobi Desert. By this time Yisügei had already died, and Temüjin (Chinggis Khan), remembering the former friendship between Ong Khan and Yisügei, welcomed him into his tribe. Temüjin obtained supplies and material resources for him by levying and collecting taxes from the people of his tribe and bestowed these on him. Later he also met Ong Khan in the Black Forest of the Tula River, treated him with the respect due to a father, and they observed the rituals of father and son. However, the Kerait section of the "Treatise on the Tribes" in the *Jāmi' al-Tawārīkh* says that it was Yisügei who helped Ong Khan flee from Erke Qara, and allowed Ong Khan to recapture the Kerait *ulus* once again.

Of course the consistency of the records mentioned above makes them more credible. However, exactly when these events took place is difficult to determine. Each source, while talking about Ong Khan's younger brother Ja'agambo's quest for shelter with Temüjin along with the "defeated and scattered people" of the Tübegen and Dongqayit 董合亦惕 Kerait tribes, returns to narrate the earlier history of Ong Khan, from the time the latter ascended the throne until he returned north of the Gobi Desert from the Western Xia. The aim of these historical records is clearly to show the honor and help that father and son, Yisügei and Temüjin, gave to Ong Khan. *The Secret History of the Mongols* looks back to this event and records it under the *takiya* year (1201), after Temüjin had attacked and destroyed the Tayiči'ut tribe. However, the *Jāmi' al-Tawārīkh* and the *Record of the Personal Campaigns of the Holy Warrior* say that Ong Khan and Temüjin aided the Jin Dynasty in attacking the Tatars, and that this was after Temüjin had toppled the J̌ürkin (Jürkin, Yürkin) 月爾斤 (also called the J̌ürki) tribe. Only the *Jāmi' al-Tawārīkh* dates this event. It records Ong Khan's return from the Western Xia to Küse' ür na'ur 曲薛兀爾澤 north of the Gobi Desert as taking place in the spring of the dragon year, which it identifies with the year 582 in the Islamic calendar.[101] However, the Islamic year 582 is 1186 in the Western calendar, and this was a horse year. If the *Jāmi' al-Tawārīkh* is right in saying that it was a dragon year, it must have been 1184 or 1196. According to the *Jāmi' al-Tawārīkh*, the Merkit people attacked Temüjin and captured Lady Börte 孛爾帖. Because the Merkit tribe was friendly with Ong Khan, they turned her over to Ong Khan. Ong Khan regarded her as his daughter-in-law and returned her to Temüjin. On the way back home she gave birth to her eldest son J̌oči (Jochi) 朮赤. Börte's third son was Ögödei, born in 1186. Therefore J̌oči must have been born in 1184, or 1183 at the latest. At this time, Ong Khan was still north of the Gobi Desert and had not yet taken flight. The year was 1196 when Ong Khan and Temüjin united to aid the Jin Dynasty in its attack on the rebellious Tatar tribes and fought at the Ulja River 斡里札河. That same year Ong Khan received the title of *Ong* (*wang* 王, king) from the Jin Dynasty for his service, and the exact date of this event is provided in the *History of the Jin Dynasty*. If Ong Khan had just returned from his desperate flight to the north of the Gobi Desert in the spring of that year and was dependent on Temüjin's help for his survival, it would have been unreasonable for him to have received the title of *Ong* from the Jin Dynasty after attacking the Tatars, while Temüjin only received the title of *J̌a'ut quri* (governor of the subordinate tribes), lower in position than *Ong*. According to "Biography of Buhumu" 不忽木傳 in the *History of the Yuan*, the leader of the Kangli tribe, Hailanbo 海藍伯, had once served Ong Khan. When Ong Khan was destroyed, Chinggis Khan sent an envoy to Hailanbo to persuade him to surrender. Hailanbo replied, "In the past I served Ong Khan 王可汗 together with your majesty. Now that Ong Khan is gone, I cannot bear to change my allegiance and serve another ruler." So he fled. "Biography of Yelü Ahai" 耶律阿海傳 in the *History of the Yuan* records that Ahai was sent by the Jin emperor to Ong Khan's court on a mission and that he saw Temüjin there at this time. It is clear that Ong Khan was the strongest leader north of the Gobi Desert at that time, and that Temüjin was just his minister. From the words used

[101] *Jāmi' al-Tawārīkh*, Russian translation, vol. 1, part 2, p. 110.

by Temüjin to reprimand Ong Khan, as recorded in the *Jāmi' al-Tawārīkh*, we can see that Temüjin referred to himself as Ong Khan's subordinate.

According to the above analysis, the attack on Ong Khan by the Naiman leader Inanča Bilge Khan probably occurred some years before 1196. After the Naiman Khan gave his support to Erke Qara, he may have taken advantage of the opportunity to occupy the western part of the Kerait *ulus*' territory. This is probably the reason why the *Jāmi' al-Tawārīkh* includes Qara-Qorum in its description of the land occupied by the Naimans. After Ong Khan returned north of the Gobi Desert, he received Temüjin's help, quickly expelled Erke Qara, and restored his original power base. To summarize, from the time when he ascended throne, despite the fact that the throne was stolen by his uncle Gür Khan and his brother Erke Qara, he achieved ultimate victory over all of them. After he received the title of *Ong* (king) from the Jin Dynasty, his power increased. In 1198 he attacked the Merkits, chased Toqto'a into Barqujin Töküm 八爾忽真隘, and captured his wife and children. In 1199 he and Temüjin together attacked the Naiman leader Buyiruq Khan, and they fought all the way to the hinterland of Heixinbashi 黑辛八石 (Kišil Baši Lake 乞則里八寺海, present-day Buluntuo Lake 布倫托海). Later, although he encountered the Naimans' attack and lost much territory and many followers, with Mongol help he was quickly able to recover what he had lost. In 1200 he also led an attack with Temüjin against the Tayiči'ut tribe, destroyed it, and captured the Qatagin 合答斤, Salji'ut 散只兀, and other tribes. In 1202 they also defeated the eastern tribal alliance that had been organized by J̌amuqa. In the Battle of Koyiten 闕奕壇 they routed the allied forces of the Naiman Buyiruq Khan and the Oyirat tribal leader Qutuqa Beki 忽都合別乞, as well as the Merkit tribe, J̌amuqa, and others. By this time, for Ong Khan the only remaining powerful enemy of the eastern Mongols was his unruly adopted son Temüjin. In 1203 in the battle of Qalaqaljit elet he [Ong Khan] inflicted a serious defeat on Temüjin, who was forced to flee into the Baljuna Marsh 班朱尼澤. Many nobles of the Mongol tribes, including J̌amuqa, Temüjin's uncles Dāritai Otčigin, and others, threw in their lot with Ong Khan's banner. Thereafter, satisfied with having achieved his goals, he raised the golden tent and held an enormous celebration banquet. Unexpectedly, the height of his success proved to be the day of his defeat. The inner tensions of his alliance erupted, and the senior nobles of each of the tribes that had sought refuge with him plotted a political takeover. This failed, and they scattered in great confusion, but in the end they were all destroyed by Temüjin.

Ong Khan was shocked and stunned by these events; it was if he had lost his whole family. He fled into Naiman territory and was killed by the Naiman border generals. In the words of the Tayang Khan:

> I hear that there are a few Mongols yonder in the east. These people with their quivers terrified the great old Ong Khan of former days, causing him to desert his own companions and perish. Do they now want to be rulers themselves? Even if there are two shining lights, the sun and the moon, in the sky above – both sun and moon are indeed there – yet how can there be two rulers on earth?
>
> *ene dorona jö'eket Mongghol bui ke'ekdemüi, tede irgen ötögü yeke erten-ü Ong qan-i qor-iyar-iyan ayu'ulju dayiji'ulju ükü'ülba. Edö'e mün qan bolsu ke'en aqun-u tede tenggeri de'ere naran sara qoyar gereten gege'en boltuqai ke'en naran sara qoyar büi-je, qajar de'ere qoyar qat ker bolqu.*[102]

Tayang Khan took Ong Khan's head and performed sacrifices to it. From this we can see how highly renowned Ong Khan was. He was probably recognized by all the tribes in the land north of the Gobi Desert as the most highly respected and honored king, a title imperially conferred by the Jin emperor.

Ong Khan's summer and winter camping places, and the places where the left and right wings of his army were stationed are recorded right at the beginning of the Kerait section of the "Treatise on the Tribes" in the *Jāmi' al-Tawārīkh*. This is the most important source material on the places that were ruled by the Kerait kingdom at the height of its rule. The Russian edition (translated by Khetagurov) renders the place names as follows:

> Wang Khan's summer camps: Талан-Гусэур, Дабан, and Наур;
>
> His right wing army's yurt: Тулсутан and Джалсутан;

[102] *The Secret History of the Mongols*, section 189. [The English translation follows Igor de Rachewiltz, *The Secret History of the Mongols*, volume 1 (Leiden: Brill, 2006), p. 111.]

His left wing army's yurt: Илат, Тарат, Айджиэ, Кутукэн, Урут, Йилет (?), and Тертит;

His winter camps: Утекин-Мурэн, Орон-Куркин, Тош, Еарау, Щирэ, Кулусун, Отку-Кулан, and Джелаур-Кулан.

Because the Russian translator was not very proficient in geography, he made many mistakes in the place names. Boyle corrected these mistakes by consulting the Persian original.[103] In the Persian original, these names (here transliterated) are written out in the following fashion:[104]

Wang Khan's summer camp:

Dālan	Kūsāūūr
Dabān	Nāūūr

The army's yurts:

Right wing		Left wing	
Tūlsūtān	Jālsūtān	Īlāt-Tarāt	
(Tūlūtān)	(Jālūtān)	Āijih	Kūtkan
		(Aījaeh)	(Kūtkar)
		(A?jieh)	
		Aūrūt	Aūkūrūt
		(Aūrū)	
		(Aūrū?)	
		Īilat	Tartat
			(Tar?t)
			(Tart?)

Winter camps:

Aūtkin	Aūrū'n	Tūsh	Bāraūū	
Mūrān	Kūrkïn			
Shireh	Qūlūsūn	Aūtkū	Qūlān	Jalāūr Qulan

(Alternative spellings found in other editions are given in parentheses. Between the two roots of each word there is no vowel, so I have used the letter 'a' to represent this.)

---

[103] John Andrew Boyle, "The Summer and Winter Camping Grounds of the Kereit," in *Central Asiatic Journal*, no. 17, nos. 2-4, 1973.

[104] *Jāmi' al-Tawārīkh*, vol. 1, part 1, Persian collated edition, p. 252.

Most of these place names occur either in the Chinese sources or in Rashīd al-Dīn's work, so they can be identified. Here I offer the following explanations, based on Boyle's interpretations.

Ong Khan's Summer Camps:

Dālān-Dābān is a single place, which is the same as the Dalan-Daba or Dalan-Dabasi in the *Record of the Personal Campaigns of the Holy Warrior* and the "Annals of Taizong" in the *History of the Yuan*. Its literal meaning is "seventy mountains." See the discussion of Dālān-tābān above.

Küseür-na'ur is a single place, which is written Quxuewuer ze 曲薛兀兒澤 (also written Quxiaoer ze 曲笑兒澤) in the *Record of the Personal Campaigns of the Holy Warrior*, and which is written Güse'ür na'ur (lake) in *The Secret History of the Mongols*. When Ong Khan, on his return from the Western Xia to the land north of the Gobi Desert, reached the shores of this lake, Temüjin sent someone to welcome him and also went there to receive him in person. The *Jāmi' al-Tawārīkh* says that this place was near Chinggis Khan's camp,[105] so it must not have been too far to the southwest of the upper reaches of the Kerulen River. Ong Khan was extremely tired, exhausted, hungry, and thirsty when he arrived here, so it must be on the northern side of the Gobi Desert. It is probably the lake north of the Mandal Gobi 曼達勒戈壁 on modern maps.

The Yurt of the Army's Right Wing:

Tūlsūtān and Jālsūtān must be the Tulietan-Tulinggu 禿烈壇・禿零古 and Zhansutan-Zhanlinggu 盞速壇・盞零古 of the *Record of the Personal Campaigns of the Holy Warrior*. In these names, the first name in each combination should be written Tūlūtān, as in other editions. When Yisügei helped Ong Khan attack Gür Khan, he is said to have "crossed over" these two places and then "reached the border (of the land of the Mongol tribe)." The *Jāmi' al-Tawārīkh* records that Ögödei stayed in Ōngin for the winter and hunted in the two mountains of Bülengü and Jelingü.[106] It may be referring to these places.

---

[105] *Jāmi' al-Tawārīkh*, Russian translation, vol. 1, part 2, p. 110.

[106] *Jāmi' al-Tawārīkh*, vol. 2, p. 41; Boyle, *The Successors of Genghis Khan*, p. 64. Additional note: These two place names are written Tūlūnkū and Jālīnkū in the Persian collated edition (Moscow, 1980), p. 145. I suspect they are the Tulinggu 禿零古 and Zhanlinggu 盞零古 in the *Record of the Personal Campaigns of the Holy Warrior*, which must be two mountains that are connected, possibly in the southern foot of the Khangai

The Yurt of the Army's Left Wing:

Boyle thought that the eight names listed in the Russian translation were really only four place names, and he was correct. The first place name should be 'Ilat-tarat; the second should be corrected to Ābjieh Küteger. This is the place where Chinggis Khan was stationed during the winter after he defeated Ong Khan. It is the same place described in Section 187 of *The Secret History of the Mongols*, where it is called Abji'a Ködeger 阿卜只合・闊帖格爾. According to the *Jāmi' al-Tawārīkh*, when Chinggis Khan and Ong Khan fought in the battle against the alliance of the Naiman's Buyiruq Khan and J̌amuqa, they hid inside the borders of Jin territory. After the Battle of Köyiten they went outside the borders, and spent the winter at Ābjieh Küteger: "This place was originally the winter camp of the Qonggirat 弘吉剌 (or Onggirat) tribe. Later Qubilai Khan and Ariq-Böke 阿里不哥 fought there. This is a vast wasteland which has no water."[107] The same work records that Qubilai Khan, while leading his army on his northern expedition

> …encountered Ariq-Böke on the edge of the desert (川勒, *chöl* in Mongolian). They joined battle in a place called Ābjieh Küteger, in front of a hill called Khucha Boldaq and a *na'ur* (lake) called Shimultai (Shimultu Lake 昔木土湖 in Chinese sources). Ariq Böke's army was defeated.[108]

This is the famous Battle of Shimultai. Looking generally at the above-quoted material, this place is probably outside the border walls of Linhuang Route 臨潢路 of the Jin Dynasty, which is probably north of Bayan Qurughai Mountain 巴楊呼爾赫山, which is north of present-day Ujumuchin 烏珠穆沁 banner in the eastern part of Inner Mongolia, on the southeast border of Mongolia's Dornod province. The third place name was Ūrūt-Ūkūrūt and the fourth was Īlat-tartat (?). Neither of these has been identified to date.

Mountains at the source of the Ongin River. The Russian and English translations write the former place name as Bulengu, but "B" is a mistake for "T" (due to a mistake in the Persian diacritical mark).

[107] *Jāmi' al-Tawārīkh*, Russian translation, vol. 1, part 2, p. 122.

[108] Ibid., Russian translation, vol. 2, part 2, p. 163; Boyle, *The Successors of Genghis Khan*, p. 256.

Ong Khan's Winter Camps:
The Russian translator was of the opinion that the first place name, Ūtkin, should be identified as the Ötüken 於都斤 Mountains, also written as 烏德鞬 (Wudejian), which are the Khangai Mountains, and that Ūtkin-Mūrān refers to a small river in the vicinity of these mountains. Note that the Ötüken Mountains were famous at the time of the Turkish Qaghanate, and this was not used as the name of a river at that time. However, the word *müren* in Mongolian refers to a large river. Boyle corrected this name to Ōngin müren (in Persian, the sounds 't' and 'n' differ only by a single diacritical mark), and he was right. This is where Ögödei's winter camp was located. The *History of the Yuan* calls it Wang Ji's 汪吉 territory. Luo Hongxian's 羅洪先 *Unfolded Terrestrial Atlas* 廣輿圖 [first edition about 1541] calls it Wangji River, which is today's Ongin River 翁金河 in Mongolia. The second place name seems to be Ōrōn-Kūrkin (Ōrōn meaning "many" in Mongolian); the third place name is probably Tush-bara'un (*bara'un*, means "right" or "west"); the fourth place name is probably Sira-qulusun, which means "yellow reeds." The fifth place name should be Ōtōgū-qūlān, which means "an old wild horse." The latter is the same as Etieguhulan Mountain 鈋鐵鈷胡蘭山 in "Annals of Taizong" of the *History of the Yuan* (written Yuetieguhulan 月帖古忽蘭 in "Annals of Xianzong" 憲宗紀). In 1241, Ögödei died after drinking all night following a hunt in this place; its location must have been near the Ongin River. The sixth place name can be corrected to Jālāwu-Qulan 劄剌兀忽蘭, which means "small wild horse." The location must have been near Ötegü Qulan 月帖古忽蘭.

According to the investigations described above, the territory ruled by Ong Khan extended east to Mongolia's eastern border and west to the Khangai Mountains. The western border for the most part kept its original integrity. The eastern border extended beyond what it had been at the time of his grandfather or his father.

A Study of Küšän Tarim (Quxiantalin 曲先塔林) in the Yuan Dynasty

Liu Yingsheng 劉迎勝

1. A History of the Quxian 曲先 Region from the Mid-Tang to the Early Yuan
2. The Meaning of the name "Talin" 塔林
3. The Vice Marshal of the Left 左副元帥 and the Küšän Tarim Chief Military Command 都元帥府 of the Yuan Period

The name Quxiantalin 曲先塔林 appears frequently in the *History of the Yuan* 元史. For example, the "Biography of Bayan Ba'atur" 拜延八都魯傳 records that in the 30th year of Zhiyuan 至元 reign period (1293) the Yuan government appointed the son of Wuhuncha (Uqunča) 兀渾察 to the post of Vice Marshal of the Left 左副元帥 of Quxiantalin.[1] The "Annals of Emperor Chengzong" 成宗紀 (Temür, reigned 1294-1307) record that in the first year of the Yuanzhen 元貞 reign period (1295), the Quxiantalin Chief Military Command 都元帥府 was established by the Yuan government.[2] The present-day location of this military outpost has never been clearly identified. According to Yan Congjian's 嚴從簡 *Informative Record on Countries Far Away* 殊域周咨錄 and other Ming Dynasty geographical works, the Quxiantalin Chief Military Command 都元帥府 (also written as 元帥府) was located at Quxian Guardstation 曲先衛, the Sari Uyghur region during the Ming Dynasty. One modern scholar, Cen Zhongmian 岑仲勉, thinks that Talin is the Tarim River.[3] Another scholar, Hsiao Ch'i-ch'ing (Xiao Qiqing) 蕭啟慶 of Taiwan, argued in a 1978

---

1 *History of the Yuan* 《元史》, punctuated edition (Beijing: Zhonghua Book Company 中華書局), p. 3024.

2 Ibid., p. 390.

3 Cen Zhongmian 岑仲勉, "A Study of the Four Guardstations of Quxian, Aduan, Anding, and Handong" 《明初曲先、阿端、安定、罕東四衛考》, *Nanking Journal* 《金陵學報》, vol. 6, no. 2 (1936), p. 2.

publication that Quxiantalin was a town west of Beshbalïq 北庭.[4] Since there are so many different identifications of Quxiantalin, it is evident that this question is far from settled. This article will examine the standard historical sources and conduct a further investigation into this and related questions.

1. A History of the Quxian Region from the Mid-Tang to the Early Yuan

The name "Quxiantalin" occurs in historical materials dating from the 13th and 14th centuries. It is probably a combination of the two names "Quxian" and "Talin." "Quxian" is a Yuan Dynasty Chinese transcription of Qiuci 龜茲 (Kuchā). This name has excited a lot of interest among orientalists of all countries in recent decades because of the discovery of the Tokharian language.[5] In the Yuan Dynasty, Quxian was also called Kuxian 苦先 or Kucha 苦叉 (Kuchā). During the Tang, from the mid-seventh century to the end of the eighth century – with the exception of the twenty-odd years from the Xianheng 咸亨 reign period (670-674) to the first year of the Changshou 長壽 reign period (692) – Qiuci was under the jurisdiction of the Anxi 安西 Protectorate 都護府. At the beginning of the Zhenyuan 貞元 reign period (785-805), in the last decade of the eighth century, its territory was included within Tibet 吐蕃. Later, the Chinese in the interior of China lost all knowledge of the place. Scholars now seeking to understand the history of the Qiuci region during this period need to study the entire range of historical materials.

At the beginning of the Tang period, the Arab empire was rising in the West. After 840, the Uyghur tribes moved from the Mongolian plateau to Gaochang 高昌, where they settled down. This migration had a deep and far-reaching influence on the later history of Qiuci. After the Arabs came

---

[4] Hsiao Ch'i-ch'ing 蕭啟慶, *The Military Establishment of the Yuan Dynasty* (Cambridge, Mass.: Harvard University Press, 1978), p. 59.

[5] Ma Yong 馬雍 thinks that the origin of the name Quxian (Kuche) may have something to do with woolen fabrics. In the Kharoshthi script, woolen fabric as *kośava*, which at the time in Chinese may have been *qusou* 氍毹. See "A Study of the Word *Kośva* as the Kharoshthi Word for *Qusou* in Xinjiang, Plus a Discussion of Qusou 渠搜, and Other Related Ancient Place Names" 《新疆佉盧文書的 *Kośva* 即"氍毹"考—兼論"渠搜"及其他有关的古地名》 in *Papers from the Founding Conference of the History of Central Asia Study Group* 《中亞史學會成立大會論文》, unpublished manuscript.

eastward, many geographical works were written by Muslim scholars, among which are abundant sources relating to the history of Central Asia. The geographical work entitled *Hudūd al-'Ālam* (*Regions of the World*, usually translated into Chinese as 世界境域志), completed in the tenth century by an anonymous Persian writer, mentions Qiuci under the name Kuchā. Although only a few words are recorded about it, it reflects the situation in Qiuci at the time:

> 5. KUCHĀN – a small town in which reside Tibetan and Chinese merchants…
> 10. KUCHĀ (*sic*) is situated on the frontier and belongs to China, but constantly (*har vaqt*) the Toghuzghuz raid (*tāzand*) the inhabitants and loot them. The town possesses many amenities.[6]

It is clear that during the time of the Tang's military campaigns in the "Western Regions" this area was not yet entirely occupied by Turkish-speaking peoples. After the Tang withdrew from Central Asia, the Qiuci region went through the two stages of Turkicization under Uyghur rule and then Islamicization.

The fact that Qiuci was ruled by the Gaochang Uyghurs is a point that is well-documented in a wide variety of sources. For instance, the *Record of Wang Yande's Embassy to Gaochang* 王延德使高昌記, dated 982, in its discussion of the area ruled by the Gaochang Uyghurs says that

---

[6] *Hudūd al-'Ālam, The Regions of the World: A Persian Geography, 372 A.H./982 A.D.*, translated and explained by Vladimir Minorsky (Владимир Минорский), 2nd edition, ed. by C. E. Bosworth, E. J. W. Gibb Memorial Series, New Series XI (London: Luzac, 1970), p. 85. The anonymous author takes Qiuci to be part of China, not realizing that that he was recording the situation after the Tang withdrew from the Western regions. Toghuzghuz is the same as Toquz Oghuz, which means the "Wuhu of the Nine Surnames" 烏護九姓. This name is recorded in both the Turkish *Bilgä Qaghan Inscription* and the Turkish *Bayan Čör Inscription*, and it is roughly equivalent to the Chinese word Tiele 鐵勒. In the Muslim historical sources, such as those by Qudāma, Mas'ūdī, Gardīzī, and even the above-mentioned *Hudūd al-'Ālam, The Regions of the World*, Toghuzghuz usually refers to the Gaochang Uyghurs. In the *Dīwān lughāt al-turk* (*Compendium of the Languages of the Turks*), Mahmūd al-Kāshgharī no longer used the word Toghuzghuz to refer to the Gaochang Uyghurs, but had changed it to Uyghur. In the Muslim sources of the Mongol period, the word Toghuzghuz is also no longer used to refer to the Gaochang Uyghurs. Minorsky discusses this point in detail in his translation of *The Regions of the World*, pp. 263-8. For V. V. Bartol'd's (Василий Владимирович Бартольд) discussion, see the *Encyclopaedia of Islam*, vol. 4 (1936), under Toghuzghuz.

"Gaochang is Xizhou 西州. This territory is several thousand *li* 里 from Khotan in the south, from Arabia 大食 and Persia in the southwest, and from Peshawar 西天步路涉, the Snowy Mountains 雪山 [the Tianshan mountain range], and the Pamirs 蔥嶺 in the west....The peoples they ruled included the Southern Turks, the Northern Turks, the Greater Dūmūda/Dūnuda/Jungul 大眾熨, the Lesser Dūmūda/Dūnuda/Jungul 小眾熨, Yaghma 樣磨 Qarluq 割祿, Kirghiz 黠戛斯, Moman 末蠻, the Geduo 格哆 people, the Yulong 預龍, and peoples called by numerous other such names."[7] In the Yuan Dynasty period the descendants of the former Uyghur Idi-qut (a Turkish term which means "lord of fortune," transcribed into Chinese as 亦都護), also said that their ancestors, having moved from the Mongolian plateau to settle in Jiaozhou 交州 (Yarkhoto, in Turfan), "governed the territory of Beshbalïq, extending north to the Azhu River 阿朮河, south to Jiuquan 酒泉, east to Wudun 兀敦 (Hami) and Jiashiha 甲石哈 (Kashgar), and west to the vicinity of Tibet 西蕃..."[8] In the fourth

[7] *History of the Song*《宋史》, ch. 490, p. 14,112. Investigating the names of these ethnic groups would be superfluous here.

[8] Yu Ji 虞集, *Record of Learning the Ancient Traditions*《道園學古錄》, ch. 24, "Stele of the Achievements of the Ancestors of the Qočo (Gaochang) Prince"《高昌王世勛之碑》, *Four Branches of Literature Collection*《四部叢刊》edition, p. 218; see also *History of the Yuan*, ch. 122, "Biography of Barčuq art Tegin"《巴而朮阿而忒的斤傳》, and Huang Wenbi 黃文弼, "Reconstructed and Edited Text of the Stele of the Achievements of the Ancestors of the Idi-qut, the Qočo Prince"《亦都護高昌王世勛碑復原並校記》, *Cultural Relics*《文物》, 1964, no. 2. Professor Yekemingghadai Irinchin 亦鄰真 has pointed out that this passage on the epitaph of the Qočo Prince was an example of the way the Uyghur people were influenced by the Turks. See "On the Origins of the Ethnic Groups of Northern China and the Mongols"《中國北方民族與蒙古族族源》, *Journal of Inner Mongolia University*《內蒙古大學學報》, 1979, nos. 3-4 (joint volume), pp. 1-23. The same article, in note 1 (p. 17), also talks about the mistaken direction with regard to Wudun 兀敦 (Hami) and Jiashiha 甲石哈 (Kashgar).

In the *Gazetteer of Wuwei*《武威志》, instead of saying "it extended east to Wudun and Jiashiha," it says, "to the east it connects to 通 Wudun and Shiha'er 失哈兒." The part above the fifth paragraph 欄 from the bottom of the Uyghur text on the funerary inscription for the Qočo Prince has already disappeared, therefore it is not possible to examine the spelling and location of Wudun and Jiashiha. For a Chinese translation and annotation of the Uyghur text on this funerary inscription, see Geng Shimin 耿世民, "A Study of the Text in the Old Uyghur Scripts of the Stele of the Achievements of the Ancestors of Idi-qut, the Qočo Prince"《回鶻文亦都護高昌王世勛碑研究》, *Acta*

year of the Xianping 咸平 reign period (1001) of the Song Dynasty, the Qiuci envoy to the Song, Cao Wantong 曹萬通, said to the Song officials, "Our country reaches east to the Yellow River and west to the Snowy Mountains (the Tianshan). It has several hundred small commanderies 郡..."[9] F. W. K. Müller's publication of the inscription on the wooden stake 杵 excavated at Huozhou 火州 (Gaochang, or Kočo in Uyghur) also makes clear that the information about the Gaochang Uyghur territory in the above-mentioned historical sources is not exaggerated. The inscription says:

> On the third day of the new moon, in the second month of the huoyang 火羊 year (a designation in the early Turkish calendar, equivalent to a dingwei 丁未 year), when our Qaghan, Kün Ay Tängridä Qaghan, qut bolmïsh alp bilgä ürüg qut Ornamïsh·Atpïn·ärdämin il tudunmïsh alp arslan qutluq Kül bilgä Tängri Qaghan...was on the throne, he ruled an area that extended eastward to Shazhou 沙州 (Sachiu, Dunhuang) and westward to Nuchi Basaigan 篏赤拔塞干 (Nuč Barsxan). When Il-ügäsi alp tutuq ügä ruled the imposing and magnificent country of Gaochang...[10]

Archaeologica Sinica 《考古學報》, 1980, no. 4, pp. 515-29. Tu Ji 屠寄 believes that Wudun and Jiashiha are near Lake Wunogesheng 烏諾格升, 600 *li* east of present-day Hami (Qamul). See Tu Ji 屠寄, *Historical Record of the Mongols* 《蒙兀爾史記》, ch. 36, p. 6. It is not known what the present-day location of the Azhu River 阿朮河 is.

[9] *Manuscript Compendium of Important Documents of the Song* 《宋會要輯稿》, vol. 197, "Foreigners 蕃夷 4," item 13, p. 7720.

[10] The Prussian investigation team in Turfan discovered this wooden post in a ruined wall of a broken rampart of a temple. See F. W. K. Müller, "Zwei Pfahlinschriften aus den Turfanfunden," *Abhandlungen der Königlich Preussischen Akademie der Wissenschaften zu Berlin*, 1915, Linguistics and History Section, no. 3, within which is included "Inscription on the Third Post Unearthed at Huozhou." Here I use the late Professor Han Rulin's 韓儒林 translation. See "On Several Western Liao Place Names" 《關於西遼的幾個地名》, *Collected Papers of Research on Yuan History and Northern Nationalities History* 《元史及北方民族史研究集刊》, Nanjing University 南京大學, no. 4, p. 49. Annemarie von Gabain tried to date this artifact. She thinks that the date given as the "year of fire and sheep" 火羊年 may be 1019, but it could also be 60 years before or after that year. See Annemarie von Gabain, *Das Leben im uigurischen Königreich von Qocho, 850-1250* (*The Lives of the Uyghur Kings of Gaochang, from 850 to 1250*),

The pastureland of the Yaghma is in the region of present-day Kashgar 喀什, and Gelu 割祿 is Qarluq 歌邏祿. These places are located in the region west of today's Kuche 庫車, all the way to the Chu River 楚河 valley. Barsxan is located on the shores of the "Hot Sea" 熱海 (Lake Issyk Kul). Qiuci is of course within this vast area.[11]

The rule of Qiuci by the Uyghurs, after their westward move, probably began soon after 840. According to the *New Tang History* 新唐書, "after the Zhide 至德 reign period (756-758), when Turkish power in the area weakened, the members of the Yellow and Black clans all set up Qaghanates and fought among themselves. China at that time was preoccupied with enemies on so many fronts that it could not exert control over the region. In the Qianyuan 乾元 reign period (758-759) the head of the Black Clan Qaghanate 黑姓可汗, surnamed Aduopeiluo 阿多裴羅 (Ata Boyla) was still able to send envoys to the Chinese court. After the Dali 大力 reign period (766-779), Qarluq became prosperous and its people moved to settle in Sūyāb 碎葉 in the Chu River valley. The 'People of the Two Surnames' declined, and soldiers were regularly stationed at Qarluq, and the remnants of the Huseluo 斛瑟羅 tribe attached themselves to the Uyghurs. When [the Uyghurs] were destroyed, some 'Tepangle' 特

Veröffentlichung der Societas Uralo-Altaica, vol. 6 (1973), p. 20. There are two points worthy of mention here. First, Gabain makes an error in speculating about the year. The year 1019 was not a fire and sheep year. It should be 1007. Second, it seems that the range of the dates proposed by Gabain can be shortened. Sixty years after 1007 was when al-Kāshgharī's dictionary was completed, and by this time the Uyghur area of influence in Gaochang had shrunk to the area east of present-day Luntai 輪臺. This will be discussed further below.

V. V. Bartol'd, in his *Zwölf Vorlesungen über die Geschichte der Türken Mittleasiens* (Berlin: 1935) writes the following on p. 94 concerning Barsghan: "According to the explanation by Gardīzī, Barsghan means 'Great Official of Persia,' which can explain the two syllables 'Pars' and 'chan.' Mahmūd al-Kāshgharī also mentioned two other different explanations. According to one, Bārs-chan was the name of the son of Afrāsijāb. According to the other, he was one of the Uyghur Khan's shepherds. The latter explanation is very interesting, and from this we can conclude that the territory of the Uyghurs extended westward all the way to Lake Issyk Kul, and that even as late as the 11th century this was still in people's memory."

[11] *Hudūd al-'Ālam, The Regions of the World* describes the territory inhabited by the "Wuhu of the Nine Surnames"烏護九姓. Minorsky investigates the place names in this book and enumerates them. See the English translation Vladimir Minorsky, *The Regions of the World*, pp. 94-95, 271-277. These await further investigation by Chinese scholars.

龐勒 people settled in the city of Yanqi 焉耆, and were called Yehu 葉護. The rest of the tribe were protected at Jinsha Mountain 金沙嶺, numbering up to 200,000."[12]

"Tepangle" may refer to Pangteqin (Pang Tigin) 龐特勤, who led fifteen Uyghur tribes in flight to Qarluq. According to the *Comprehensive Mirror for Aid in Government* 資治通鑑, the Pangtele 龐特勒 tribe lived in Anxi (Qiuci): "On the xinhai day in the third month of the tenth year of the Dazhong 大中 reign period (856), under the Emperor Xuanzong 宣宗, the Emperor proclaimed...that in the Huichang 會昌 reign period (841-846), during the disorder within the barbarian's court, the Qaghan fled.... Recently one of those who had surrendered said that Yipangli 已龐歷 was the Qaghan at that time, and still resided at Anxi" (Yipangli refers to the same person as Pangle; the words are sometimes rearranged in Chinese transliterations; for Pangle's enthronement as Qaghan, see the previous chapter of the *Comprehensive Mirror for Aid in Government*, under the second year).[13]

That the Uyghurs established themselves on the southern side of the Tianshan Mountains is documented by Arab geographers. For example, according to Mas'ūdī (d. 956), at the time when he was writing the country of the Uyghur of the Nine Surnames (Toghuzghuz) expanded from Khorasan all the way to China, with its capital at Kūshān (i.e., Quxian).[14]

Some Song records also reflect this point. The *Manuscript Compendium of Important Documents of the Song* 宋會要輯稿 says:

---

[12] *New Tang History* 《新唐書》, ch. 215, "Turks, second part" 《突厥下》, the punctuated edition (Beijing: Zhonghua Book Company 中華書局), pp. 60-9.

[13] Ibid., ch. 249, pp. 8059. The relationship between this branch of the Uyghurs and the Qarluq and the later Gaochang Uyghurs still awaits further study.

[14] Here I follow E. Bretschneider's *Mediaeval Researches from Eastern Asiatic Sources: Fragments towards the Knowledge of the Geography and History of Central and Western Asia from the 13th to the 17th Century* (London, 1910), vol. 1, p. 253. Barbier de Meynard takes Kushan as Gaochang, and his view is adopted in *A Brief History of the Uyghurs*, part 1, translated into Chinese as 《維吾爾族簡史(一)》 (China Ethnic Minorities Series 中國少數民族叢書), unpublished work, p. 50. Minorsky already suspected that Kūshān was the same as Kucha. See *Hudūd al-'Ālam, The Regions of the World*, English translation, p. 497. In fact, in Rashīd al-Dīn's *Jāmi' al-Tawārīkh* (*Compendium of Chronicles*), the Persian collated edition (Moscow, 1965) vol. 1, ch. 1, p. 277, the various transliterations of Quxian that it lists include Kūsān and Kūshān. In Persian, the difference between *kūsān* and *kūshān* is just three diacritical marks.

"[The people of] Qiuci were a particular group of Uyghurs. Their leader called himself Shiziwang 師子王 (Lion King, Arslan Qaghan). He wore a jeweled crown and a yellow robe, and had nine ministers, who together managed the country's affairs....Some people call them Xizhou 西州 Uyghurs; others call them Xizhou Qiuci; and still others call them the Qiuci Uyghurs, but they are all referring to the same people." Apart from this, the Qaghan of the Xizhou Uyghurs was also called by the following title in the Song: "the Qaghan King Shanyu Junkehan 軍剋韓 of the Great Uyghur country of Qiuci in the Great Protectorate of Anxi Prefecture."[15] We can see that at the beginning of the Northern Song, the Han people in the interior of China did not make a clear distinction between the Uyghurs and the people of Qiuci who had been "Uyghurized" or influenced by the Uyghurs – they were all called Uyghurs. It was only when the term "Uyghur" was used to modify a place name or to identify "a particular group of Uyghurs" that the distinction was clear. This reflects the level of understanding that people of the Song had of the peoples of that region.

With the rise and flourishing of the Qarakhanids, the Qiuci region in the 11th century underwent a profound change. The people of that region opposed the Uyghurs and in fact threw off Uyghur rule. According to the Persian writer Muhammad al-'Awfī, the stalwart Turkish Muslim ruler of Qiuci, whose name was Khidr Beg, won a victory over the Uyghur kingdom. Because he had aided the Qaghan of Kashgar in a struggle against his enemies, the Kashgar Qaghan bestowed the title of Qaghan on him (Khidr).[16] The *Dīwān lughāt al-turk*, by Mahmūd al-Kāshgharī,

[15] *Manuscript Compendium of Important Documents of the Song* 《宋會要輯稿》, vol. 197, "Foreigners" 《藩夷》, p. 7720. See also *History of the Song*, ch. 490, the section on Qiuci 龜茲 in "Account of Foreign Countries" 《外國傳》, punctuated edition (Beijing: Zhonghua Book Company), p. 14,123. Based on this passage in the *History of the Song*, Sylvain Lévi thinks that the region of Qiuci had already been Turkicized in the 11th century. See Sylvain Lévi, "'Tokharien B', langue de Koutcha," *Journal Asiatique*, 1913, translated in to Chinese by Feng Chengjun 馮承鈞 as "A Study of Khotanese" 《龜茲語考》 in Feng Chengjun 馮承鈞, ed., *Collected Essays on Historical Geography* 《史地叢考》 (Commercial Press 商務印書館, 1931), p. 36.

[16] See V. V. Bartol'd, *Turkestan Down to the Mongol Invasion* (*Туркестан в эпоху монгольскаго нашествия*), part 1, texts, 2nd edition, E. J. W. Gibb memorial series, New series, V (London: Luzac, 1928). Here I follow Bartol'd's *Zwölf Vorlesungen über die Geschichte der Türken Mittleasiens* (Berlin, 1935), p. 132.

Awfī's dates are not known. His work, *Jāmi' al-Hikāyāt* (*Collected Stories*), was written in India in about 1228. Before the Mongols invaded Central Asia, he lived in

composed in four different redactions between 1075 and 1094, lists the "five Uyghur cities" as Qočo, Beshbalïq, Sulmi (Suolimi 唆里迷), Jambalïq (Zhangbali 彰八里), and Yängi-balïq (Yangjibali 仰吉八里).[17] Qiuci is definitely not mentioned among them. This reflects the fact that Uyghur power and influence had by that time retreated eastward. As for Quxian, al-Kāshgharī called it Kusan, "the name of a fortified village called Kujā [Qiuci], on the border of Uyghur territory."[18] Not only did Qiuci not belong to Uyghur territory at that time, but even Bögör 布告爾 (Bugur, present-day Luntai 輪臺), east of Qiuci, did not belong to Uyghur territory. al-Kāshgharī called Bögör "the name of a castle on a high mountain between Kuça and Uyğur, one of the frontier posts."[19]

At that time the culture of Qiuci had already begun to differentiate itself from that in Gaochang. A proportion of the people in Qiuci were at the forefront in receiving Islam from the West. al-Kāshgharī said, "At that time the Muslim culture in the east extended northward to Qiuci and Bögör, and southward to Yuechang 約昌 (Cherchen, present-day Qiemo 且末)."[20] At the time of Wang Yande 王延德, Gaochang had "over fifty

---

Khorasan. His work is particularly valuable because it records many Qarakhanid anecdotes. Apart from this, he also included a section describing East Asia and Turkish tribes. The author was the earliest one to mention the Persian geographers who were Uyghur. See Edward Granville Browne, *A Literary History of Persia*, vol. 2, p. 477; V. V. Bartol'd, *Turkestan Down to the Mongol Invasion*, English version, 2nd edition, p. 36; and the *Encyclopaedia of Islam*, vol 1, p. 517.

[17] This is cited in *Hudūd al-'Ālam, The Regions of the World*, English translation, p. 272. See also V. V. Bartol'd's *Zwölf Vorlesungen über die Geschichte der Türken Mittleasiens*, p. 92. Geng Shimin and Zhang Guangda 張廣達, in "A Study of Suolimi" 《唆里迷考》, say that Suolimi can be identified with Yanqi 焉耆. See *Historical Research* 《歷史研究》, 1980, no. 2.

[18] Here I follow *Hudūd al-'Ālam, The Regions of the World*, English translation, p. 232.

[19] Mahmūd al-Kāshgharī, *Dīwān lughāt al-turk*, vol. I, p. 361. Here I follow Gerard Clauson, *An Etymological Dictionary of Pre-Thirteenth-Century Turkish* (Oxford: Clarendon, 1972), p. 328.

[20] Mahmūd al-Kāshgharī, *Dīwān lughāt al-turk* (*Compendium of the Languages of the Turks*), published edition, vol. I, pp. 239, 301, and 364, quoted in V. V. Bartol'd, *Zwölf Vorlesungen über die Geschichte der Türken Mittleasiens*, p. 90. Chinese historical sources still have records of Buddhism being worshipped in Qiuci at that time. For example, on the sixth day of the sixth month of the sixth year of the Xianping 咸平 reign period (1003), "The monk Yixiu 義修 from the country of Qiuci came to present palm-leaf scriptures 梵夾, Bodhisattva [images], printed leaves 印葉, prayer beads 念珠, and the like"; in the fourth month of the first year of the Tianxi 天禧 reign period (1017),

"The Qaghan King 剋韓, Zhihai 智海, sent the envoy Zhang Fu 張復 to present jade and other things as tribute." From the name Zhihai we can tell that the Qaghan King was a Buddhist devotee; in the first year of the Qianxing 乾興 reign period (1022), "A monk of the country of Qiuci, Huayan 華嚴, came from India 西天, and presented offerings including a bone of the Buddha, a *śarīra* 舍利, and palm-leaf scriptures." For the above, see *Manuscript Compendium of Important Documents of the Song* 《宋會要輯稿》, vol. 197, pp. 7720-1. The *History of the Song* also records that "from the Tiansheng 天聖 reign period (1023-1031) to the fourth year of the Jingyou 景祐 reign period (1037), five people came from Qiuci to bring tribute, and the last one presented a copy of the Buddhist sutra 佛經一藏." In the third year of the Shaosheng 紹聖 reign period (1096), an envoy from Qiuci "came to Tao Xi 洮西 with memorials to the throne and jade Buddhas" (*History of the Song*, ch. 490, "Account of Foreign Countries," p. 14,123).

Huang Wenbi 黃文弼, in his *Archaeological Records of the Tarim Basin* 《塔里木盆地考古記》 (Beijing: Science Press 科學出版社, 1958), p. 31, mentions that at the time when the Mongols came west to Qiuci, spreading Islam, the earliest pious men said:

"Northeast of Kuche 庫車, on Kuche River (庫車河 or 城上河), the place called Pilang 皮郎 was also called Haladun 哈拉墩 (Qara dun, literally 'Black Mound'). There was one large earth mound…and about one *li* north of it there were the Mazar 麻札 [people]. It is said that these were the earliest ancestors of the Uyghur 維 who came west….When Andijan (Anji 安集) occupied Kuche, he began repairing and building shrines, which were rather grand and imposing. Below the western corridor of the monastery, there was a wooden plaque on which were written in four large characters, 'Pious Men of Mecca' 天方列聖. On either side was written, 'At the time of Emperor Lizong 理宋 of the Song period, there was a pious man named Mawlana Eshiding 默拉納額什丁 in the ancient country of Qiuci, who journeyed 10,000 *li* from his ancestral country in the western regions to spread the holy way of Mecca 天方聖道. He converted several hundred thousand people of the Tuhulu kumu (qum) 土胡魯庫木 tribe and taught them Islamic law. I passed here while transporting the soldiers' payment and provisions and fortunately had the opportunity to see the shrines and tombs. I have written these four characters here to extol the achievements of this pious man. Written by Li Fan 李藩, who holds the rank of Associate Administrator 同知, belongs to the candidate group of Henan 河南, and was the former District Magistrate 知縣, Zhili Prefecture 直隸州, Lanna 蘭納. Early autumn of the seventh year of Emperor Guangxu 光緒 of the Great Qing Dynasty (1881).'

"According to the Mullah 毛拉 of this region, 'Molana' (Mawlana) means the descendants of Muhammad the Prophet, and Eshiding is the name of a Mazar. 'Tuhulu' is a place name, *kumu* (*qum* in Turkish) means sand….From this we know that Islam had spread to Qiuci at the time of Emperor Lizong 理宗 of the Song Dynasty (1225-1264)."

By the end of the former Qing Dynasty it was already unclear when the Uyghur people in that territory began to adopt Islam. Huang Wenbi's conclusion still leaves room for further discussion. Wang Zhilai 王治來 in his "The Development of Islam in

Buddhist temples…as well as Manichaean temples, and Persian monks (Nestorians), each choosing their own method of practice."[21] The differentiation of Qiuci culture from Gaochang culture continued right up to the rule of the Western Liao (1124-1211) and the Mongolian conquest. Rashīd al-Dīn, when narrating the story of the flight of the Kerait tribal leader Ong Khan's 王罕 son Sengün 桑昆, wrote:

> When his father was taken captive and killed, Sengün, Ong Khan's son, fled and went outwards and passed through a settlement village called Ishiq Balghasun (AYSHYK MLGHSWN) which was at the edge of the desert and at the frontiers of Mogholistan. Then he entered the Land of Böri Tübüd, that is to the land of Tibet, pillaged some of the people of that land and dwelled there for some time. He devastated the countryside, and the people of Tibet assembled and cornered him so that they would (*sic*) seize him, and he came out of that region and fled from the hands of those people, too. He arrived in the region of Khotan and Kashgar and came to a region called *Küchetü Sari Kesme (SARKASHMH). A ruler/commander from the rulers/commanders of the Khalaj people [whose name was] Qilij Qara, who was the ruler of that region, took him prisoner and killed him. It is told that that ruler had taken the wife and children of Sengün and sent them to Chinggis Khan as [a token] of his submission.[22]

Xinjiang" 《論伊斯蘭教在新疆的發展》 in *Collected Essays on Xinjiang History* 《新疆歷史論文集》 (1977), p. 263, adopts Huang Wenbi's view. As for the problem of the conversion to Islam of the rulers of the Chaghatay Khanate, the author plans to treat this separately elsewhere.

[21] *History of the Song*, ch. 490, "Account of Foreign Countries," p. 14,112.

[22] The English translation is from Isenbike Togan, *Flexibility and Limitation in Steppe Formations* (Brill, 1998), p. 107, slightly modified. Rashīd al-Dīn's *Jāmi' al-Tawārīkh* (*Compendium of Chronicles*), the Persian collated edition (Moscow, 1965) vol. 1, ch.1, p. 277, Russian translation vol. 1, ch. 1, p. 133. In the *History of the Yuan*, "Annals of Taizu" 《太祖紀》, p. 12, the ruler of Qiuci is called Sovereign 國主 of Qiuci. Whether Qilij was originally written QiLNJ awaits further investigation. The name Jahār-Kara in other Persian manuscripts is written KhaRFShRH. Perhaps it should be written JaRQShRH, because this would correspond to Qie'ergesi 徹兒哥思, but it is still impossible to decipher the last part. Paul Pelliot, in "About the Kuman (*kuman* 庫蠻)" in *Second Collection of Translations and Studies on Historical Places in the Western Regions and Southern Seas* 《西域南海史地考證譯叢二編》 (Commercial Press, 商務

In this source, the fact that Rashīd al-Dīn refers to Quxian as "the borderlands of Khotan and Kashgar" and also calls its leader "sultan," suggests the status of Quxian at the time.

2. The Meaning of the Name "Talin" 塔林

Reading through the *History of the Yuan*, one discovers that the name Talin always appears together with the name Quxian. Apart from the two references discussed at the beginning of this article, others can be pointed out as well: "On the xinsi 辛巳 day in the second month of the 29th of the Zhiyuan reign period (1292), at the request of the Bureau of Military Affairs 樞密院, an official named An Bo 暗伯 and others went to Xiangyang 襄陽 (on the Han River 漢水 in Hubei 湖北 Province) and gave to 637 households Quxiantalin and Qarluq 哈剌魯 farming implements to use in planting grain for their cultivation and consumption"[23]; "In the seventh month of the first year of Dade (1297), a *tümen* (a unit of 10,000 soldiers) 萬戶府 in the Mongol army was abolished and the territory was incorporated into the Quxiantalin Chief Military Command 都元帥府"[24]; "...three people from the Quxiantalin Chief Military Command..."[25]; and there are other such passages.

Hsiao Ch'i-ch'ing 蕭啟慶 has transcribed Talin as Daril, but, unfortunately, he bases it on section 263 of *The Secret History of the Mongols* 元朝秘史, which writes the name as Guxiandalinle 古先答鄰勒. Actually, Paul Pelliot, in his translation of *The Secret History of the*

印書館, 1962), pp. 36-44, discusses these names in a very detailed manner and the problem of deciphering them.

[23] *History of the Yuan*, ch. 17, "Annals of Shizu" 《世祖紀》, p. 360.

[24] *History of the Yuan*, ch. 19, "Annals of Chengzong" 《成宗紀》, p. 412.

[25] *History of the Yuan*, ch. 90, "Monograph on Official Posts" 《百官志》, p. 2309. At Kyoto University in Japan a *Collection of Vocabulary Used in the History of the Yuan* (*Genshi goi shūsei*) 『元史語彙集成』 has been compiled to make it convenient to understand the vocabulary used in the history (Tamura Jitsuzō 田村田村実造, editor, Kyoto: Kyoto Daigaku Bungakubu 京都大學文學部, 1961-1963). Unfortunately, there are some gaps in the work, such as the term "Quxiantalin Vice-Marshall of the Left" 曲先塔林左副元帥(see the first page of this essay), which is omitted from the vocabulary.

Mongols had already doubted that Daril should be Tarim.[26] It was correct of Hsiao Ch'i-ch'ing to take Guxiandalinle as the same place as Quxiantalin of the *History of the Yuan*. As noted above, Talin is always combined with Quxian in the *History of the Yuan*, and we see the same thing happening in *The Secret History of the Mongols*, which links the two together in a slightly different transcription, in the name Guxiandalinle. This shows that Quxiantalin was a common place name at the time. It also encourages us to think that there was a connection between the two places, Talin and Quxian.

Cen Zhongmian 岑仲勉 has also offered an explanation of the name Talin. Cen Zhongmian pointed out: "At the time of the Yuan, Quxian was very well-known. Talin is pronounced the same as the present-day Tarim (Talimu 塔里木)"; Dalin is another way of writing Talin, though the meaning of the name has not yet been explained. In fact, the word *lin* 林 combines the two sounds *li* 里 and *mu* 木.[27] Cen Zhongmian's conclusion was therefore reasonable.

---

[26] Paul Pelliot, trans., *Histoire Secrete des Mongols* (Paris: Adrien-Maisonneuve, 1949), p. 108, note 6. Here I have benefited from the instruction of Professor Han Rulin 韓儒林. In the Phags-Pa script, "m" is different from "l," and there is no possibility of mixing them up. In the Uyghur syllabary, these two sounds can be interchangeable if they appear at the end of a word. This point may add weight to the theory that *The Secret History of the Mongols* was originally written in Mongolian using the Uyghur script.

[27] Cen Zhongmian 岑仲勉, "A Study of the Four Guardstations of Quxian, Aduan, Anding, and Handong" 《明初曲先、阿端、安定、罕東四衛考》. However, Cen Zhongmian tries to prove that the territory under the jurisdiction of the Quxian Military Guard 衛 during the Ming Dynasty was the same as Quxian (present-day Kuche) in Xinjiang. According to the *Veritable Records of the Ming* 《明實錄》 (Jiangsu 江蘇 Library manuscript edition), in the "Veritable Records of Emperor Taizu" 《太祖實錄》, ch. 90, p. 4, it says: "On the renxu 壬戌 day (in the sixth month of the seventh year of Hongwu, 1374), the prince of Anding 安定, of the Sari Uyghurs in the Western Regions, Buyan Temür 卜煙帖木兒, sent his Mentor-commandant 府尉 of the Madar 麻答兒 battalion (千戶所, a unit of 1,000 men called a 'chiliarchy office' in Hsiao Ch'i-ch'ing, *The Military Establishment of the Yuan Dynasty*, Harvard East Asian Monographs 77 [Cambridge, Mass.: Harvard University Press, 1978], p. 96), whose name was Laerjia 剌爾嘉, to court to pay tribute, consisting of armor, swords and daggers, and so forth. The Sari Uyghurs are a separate group of Tatars 韃靼 whose territory is 1000 *li* across. It is 1500 *li* from Gansu. To the east it stretches to Handong 罕東, and to the west it reaches Tengri (Tiankeli 天可里, presently unknown). To the north it comes close to Guazhou 瓜州, and to the south it borders on Turfan....The emperor then decreed that their leader be

In the *Mongolian Letters Arranged by Rhyme* 蒙古字韻, completed in the first year of the Zhida 至大 reign period (1308), the character *lin* 林 belongs to the rime *qin* 侵. The Phags-Pa writing in the marginal notes to the rime words of this section and the many other examples of Chinese transliterations of other foreign words at the time help us realize that the Chinese language in the Yuan Dynasty still preserved many final nasal endings with an "m" sound. In the *Rhymes of the Central Plain* 中原音韻, completed in the first year of the Taiding 泰定 reign period (1324), *lin* is also categorized as a *čim-sim* 侵尋 rime.[28] From this we can work out that Talin in Yuan Dynasty Chinese was pronounced "talim." Because of these two points – that Talin and Quxian were always seen together, and that Talin was pronounced "talim" in Yuan Dynasty northern Chinese – we come to the natural conclusion that Talin is most likely the name of both the Tarim River and the valley near Quxian through which it flowed.

established as [leader of] the four tribes 四部 and that bronze seals be bestowed on Aduan 阿端, Azhen 阿真, Kuxian 苦先, and Tieli 帖里."

For Mīrzā Muhammad Haidar's *Tārīkh-i Rashīdī* (*History of Rashid*), here I follow the English translation, *Tarikh-i-Rashidi: A History of the Moghuls of Central Asia*, N. Elias, ed., Edward Denison Ross, trans. (London, 1895, reprinted 1972), p. 7. In the discussion of the region controlled by the Moghuls, it says their territory extended northward to Quxian and southward to the region of the Sari Uyghurs. This work also refers in several places to the Sari Uyghur period, while also mentioning Jurjan, Lob Katak, and other such places (pp. 52, 64). Pelliot explains these place names in his annotated edition of Marco Polo's text *Marco Polo: The Description of the World*, trans. and annotated by A. C. Moule and Paul Pelliot, 2 vols. (London: G. Routledge, 1938), so there is no need to repeat it here. These various historical materials make it clear that the influence of the Sari Uyghurs had definitely not reached the northern end of the Tarim basin, and that the Quxian guard established at the beginning of the Ming Dynasty was not located at present-day Kuche.

[28] Manuscript edition of *Mongolian Letters Arranged by Rhyme* 《蒙古字韻》, section 13, on *cīm* 侵, page 24. See Luo Changpei 羅常培 and Cai Meibiao 蔡美彪, *Phags-Pa Script and the Chinese Language in the Yuan Dynasty* 《八思巴字與元代漢語, 資料匯編》 (Beijing: Science Press, 1959), p. 124; Zhao Yintang 趙蔭棠, *Research on Rhymes of the Central Plain* [China] 《中原音韻研究》 (Shanghai: Commercial Press, 1936), pp. 254 and 284. As for the problem of the use of the word ending with a labial sound "m" to transliterate words in other languages, see Han Rulin, "Phonetic Analysis and Identification in the Studies of the History of the Northwestern Ethnic Minorities" 《關於西北民族史中的審音與勘同》, in *Collected Papers of Research on Yuan History and Northern Nationalities* 《元史及北方民族史研究集刊》, no. 3, p. 3.

al-Kāshgharī's dictionary, *Dīwān lughāt al-turk*, mentions a river (or a region) called Tarim. In Qarakhanid Turkish, "tarim" refers to the "branches (*a'dād*) of a river which flows into swamps and quicksands." It is also defined as "the name of a place on the frontier of Uyğur near Kuça: called Tarim [sic]; a river flows through it; the river is called by the same name." Although we don't know its original pronunciation, "Usmi: Tarim" is defined as "the name of a large river which flows from the Moslem country to Uyğur and there sinks into the sand."[29]

Clearly, the Tarim mentioned by al-Kāshgharī was the same as the Talin of the Yuan Dynasty. Just as in *The Secret History of the Mongols*, "Guxian" and "Dalinle" were combined into a single place name, so in the *History of the Yuan*, Quxian and Talin were linked. When al-Kāshgharī explained Tarim, he also linked Qiuci with it, saying that Tarim was the name of a place near Qiuci in the Uyghur region. This makes it quite clear that Guxiandalinle and Quxiantalin actually refer to the present-day Tarim River basin near Quxian.

After this, the name Talin (and the other forms of it) was seen frequently in historical documents. For example, in the *Zafar-nāma* (*Book of Victory*), a historical work from the time of the Timurid Empire

[29] Gerard Clauson, *An Etymological Dictionary of Pre-Thirteenth-Century Turkish* (Oxford: Clarendon, 1972), pp. 548-9; Mahmūd al-Kāshgharī, *Dīwān lughāt al-turk*, vol. I, p. 130, cited in Gerard Clauson, *An Etymological Dictionary of Pre-Thirteenth-Century Turkish*, p. 549, col. 1. Note that *Usmi* is probably the pre-Turkish name. Mahmūd al-Kāshgharī, *Dīwān lughāt al-turk* (*Compendium of the Languages of the Turks*), edited by Bessim Atalay (Ankara: Alâeddin Kiral Basimevi, 1939-1943), vol. I, p. 396; vol. II, p. 13. Here I follow Gerard Clauson, *An Etymological Dictionary of Pre-Thirteenth-Century Turkish*, pp. 548-549. See also V. V. Bartol'd, *Zwölf Vorlesungen über die Geschichte der Türken Mittleasiens*, pp. 89-90 and the *Encyclopedia of Islam*, vol. 4, p. 637, the entry on "Tarim." The entry for Tarim in *Geographic Names of the Western Regions* 《西域地名》, originally edited by Feng Chengjun 馮承鈞, and revised and enlarged by Lu Junling 陸峻嶺 (Beijing: Zhonghua Book Company, 1980), p. 93, does not point out that Tarim in the Yuan Dynasty was transliterated as Talin 塔林. After this article was completed, I found out that the Japanese scholar Abe Takeo 安部健夫 had already linked the Tarim defined by al-Kāshgharī together with Quxiantalin of the Yuan Dynasty, see his *Nishi Uiguru kokushi no kenkyū* (*Studies on the Western Uyghurs*) 『西ウイグル国史の研究』 (Kyoto: Ibundō Shoten, 1955), p. 481. Concerning the prefix "Usmi" before Tarim, this is to be a subject on which I plan to conduct separate research.

completed in 1425, it is said that there was a place called Tarim not far from Baikent 拜城 and Quxian.[30]

The anonymous work *A Brief Treatise on the Personages in the Lands of the Western Regions* 西域土地人物略 of the Ming Dynasty period mentions a river called Talin near Kuxian 苦先:

> Two hundred *li* west of Turfan is the city of Anshi 俺石…50 *li* west of that is Kunmishi 昆迷失…200 *li* west of Kunmishi is Alamu 阿剌木, another 100 *li* west is Chalishi 叉力失 (near present-day Yanqi 焉耆), south of Chalishi is the Tarim River, 100 *li* west of Chalishi is Hei River spring 黑水泉…100 *li* west of that spring is the city of Shuang Shaner 雙山兒…100 *li* west of that is the city of Dushu 獨樹 (Lonely Tree)…100 *li* west of Lonely Tree is Chalicha well 察力察井…200 *li* west of that is Yuni spring 淤泥泉…100 *li* west of that is the Chawude River 察兀的…100 *li* west of that is the Tazi River 榻子河…10 *li* west of that is the city of Gukewu 古克兀…another 100 *li* from that is Kuxian City.[31]

Clearly the Tarim River "south of Chalishi" is the Yuan place name Talin, which is the present-day Tarim River. In Haidar's book *Tārīkh-i Rashīdī* (*History of Rashid*), Tarim is also listed as a place name, along with Turfan, Lop Nor 羅卜, and Kadak 怯台.[32]

Although *Hūdud al-'Ālam* (*Regions of the World*) does not mention Tarim by name, it writes about the Tarim River and region as follows:

---

[30] Sharaf ad-Dīn 'Alī Yazdī, *Zafar-nāma*, English translation, Muhammad Ilahdad, ed. (Calcutta, 1887-1888), vol. II, p. 219. This follows V. V. Bartol'd's entry in the *Encyclopaedia of Islam* for "Tarim." See footnote 29.

[31] Gu Yanwu 顧炎武, "The Four Barbarians of the Nine Frontiers" 《九邊四夷》, in *The Characteristics of Each Province in the Empire* 《天下郡國利病書》 (Shanghai: Hanfenlou 涵芬樓 facsimile edition, in the collection of Kunshan 昆山 Library), vol. 34, p. 34. Concerning the revision of the historical materials in this work, see Cen Zhongmian 岑仲勉, "The Travel Diary of a Ming Man from Jiaguguan to the Western Part of Southern Xinjiang" 《從嘉峪關到南疆西部之明人紀程》, in *Textual Research on Historical Geography Outside of China* 《中外史地考證》 (Beijing: Zhonghua Book Company 1962), vol. 2.

[32] *Tarikh-i-Rashidi: A History of the Moghuls of Central Asia*, N. Elias, ed., Edward Denison Ross, trans., p. 67.

3. Another river, called WAJĀKH, rises on the eastern side of the said mountain Mānisā at the extreme limit (*ākhir-i hadd*) of the desert. It skirts (*karān*) the towns (areas) of Thajākh [*sic*], Barīha, and Kūskān, flows on through the province of Khotan, and while passing through the region of *Sha-chou (Sājū) forms a swamp. Thence it flows down to the limits of Kuchā, then passes through the province of Kūr.sh (?) and the province of F.rāj.klī and empties itself into the Eastern ocean....The breadth of this river is half a parasang, and this breadth can never be crossed. When the river reaches the limits of Kuchchā [*sic*] it is called the RIVER OF KUCHCHĀ and as such is known in the books.[33]

---

[33] The passage goes on to describe the three rivers that have their sources in this neighborhood; *Hudūd al-'Ālam, The Regions of the World*, English translation, p. 70. What excites interest here is that the anonymous author also mistakenly calls the Tarim River the source of the Yellow River. Before Zhang Qian 張騫 went on his embassy to Central Asia, it was not known that the Yellow River disappeared into the sand and resurfaced again some distance away, a phenomenon called "renewed source" 重源. For example, the "The Classic of Regions beyond the Seas: The West" 《海内西經》 section of the *Classic of Mountains and Seas* 《山海經》 says, "In the void of the Kunlun Mountains within the seas 海内昆侖之虛...the river emerges from the northeastern corner and flows to the north..." Also, the *Examples of Refined Usage* (the *Erya*) 爾雅 in its explanation of "water," says: "The river comes from the void in the Kunlun Mountains. It is white in color..." After Zhang Qian returned home from Central Asia, he brought with him the idea of this phenomenon in connection with the Yellow River. In the "Account of Ferghana" 《大宛傳》 of *The Records of the Grand Historian* 《史記》, ch. 123, it says, "West of Khotan, the waters all flow westward, pouring into the Western Sea, the eastern waters flow eastward and pour into the Salt Marsh 鹽澤. At the Salt Marsh it sinks into the ground and emerges south of it as the source of the river. There are many jade stones there, and the river pours into China..." (*Records of the Grand Historian* 《史記》, punctuated edition, p. 3160). The *History of the Former Han* 《漢書》 says, "In the Western Regions...there are great mountains to the north and south, and in the center is a river. This river has two sources. One is in the Pamirs 蔥嶺, and the other is in Khotan. Khotan is below the Southern Mountains. Its rivers flow north, and join with the river from the Pamirs 蔥嶺. In the east it pours into the Puchang Sea 蒲昌海 [Lake Puchang, Lop Nor]. The Puchang Sea is also called the Salt Marsh. It is more than three hundred *li* from the Jade Gate and Yangguan 陽關, and three hundred *li* from north to south. The water stands still and does not rise or fall in winter or summer. Everyone thinks it sinks into the ground and emerges in the south among the piles of stones, to become China's [Yellow] River" ("Account of the Western Regions" 《西域傳》, *History of the Former Han* 《漢書》, punctuated edition, p. 3871). Cen Zhongmian 岑仲

Minorsky has pointed out that the river WĀJĀKH (which is called the Qiuci River after it flows into Qiuci) is the Tarim River.[34]

To summarize what has been said above, the name Tarim first appeared in 11th-century documents, while the name Quxiantalin (or Guxiandalinle) appeared in the 12th and 13th centuries. As a place name, Quxiantalin (Guxiandalinle) refers to the region of present-day Kuche and its nearby Tarim River basin.

3. The Vice Marshal of the Left 左副元帥 *and the Küšän Tarim (Quxiantalin* 曲先塔林*) Chief Military Command* 都元帥府 *of the Yuan Period*

Now that the meaning of Quxiantalin has been clarified, we can provide an explanation for the appointment of the son of Wuhuncha (Uqunča) as Vice Marshal of the Left of Quxiantalin by the Yuan government and the subsequent establishment of the Quxiantalin Chief Military Command.

In the disorder involving Ariq-Böke 阿里不哥, Cha'adai's 察合台 successor Alghu 阿魯忽 (reigned 1260-1265) gradually occupied the large region that extended from Jinshan 金山 in the east to the Amu Darya in the west. After Ariq-Böke lost his influence, Qubilai Khan sent out an army to occupy all the places in Turkestan as part of his plan to control Central Asia. Not long after that, Baraq 八剌 (1266-c. 1271) seized the Chaghatay Khanate and began to push the great Khan's forces out, expelling his army from the southwestern part of the Tarim basin. After the conference [of Mongol leaders] at Talas 塔剌思, Baraq and Qaidu 海都 concluded an agreement to oppose Qubilai and the Il Khan Abagha 阿八哈. In 1271, Baraq's invasion of the Ilkhanate failed. Subsequently, the various kings of Central Asia experienced a weakening of their influence, and the Yuan forces used this opportunity to expand into Central Asia,

---

勉 once investigated this problem. See his *A History of Changes and Movements of the Yellow River* 《黃河變遷史》 (Beijing: People's Publishing House, 1957), p. 32. The explanations of the place names involved in the description of the Tarim River in *Hudūd al-'Ālam, The Regions of the World*, which I have quoted from above, will not be discussed further here, for lack of space.

[34] Note that Minorsky says, "This river (i.e. Wajākh) is an imaginary combination of the Tarim and Huang-ho [Yellow River] of which the latter is represented as a continuation of the former through the Lob-nor," *Hudūd al-'Ālam, The Regions of the World*, Vladimir Minorsky, trans., p. 2067.

with the Uyghur region as their base. After Qubilai completed his conquest of the Southern Song in 1279, the Yuan government was ready to deal with the rebellious princes in the northwest. The great Chinese army, combined with Mongol *tammachi* 探馬赤 [garrison army] forces, set up military camps at Beshbalïq, Quxian, Woduan 斡端 (Khotan), and Kashgar. At this time, Quxian served as a bridge between the Yuan Dynasty on the one hand and the Uyghur region and what is now the upper reaches of the Tarim River on the other.

Bayan Ba'atur's 拜延八都魯 son Wuhuncha 兀渾察, in the 16th year of the Zhiyuan reign period (1279), accompanied the great army on its expedition to Woduan. In the 21st year of the Zhiyuan reign period (1284), "the various princes of the Zhubo 術伯 tribe (the tribe of Chübei, son of Alghu, as recorded in Rashīd al-Dīn's *Jāmi' al-Tawārīkh* [*Compendium of Chronicles*]), ordered Wuhuncha to go to the land of Kashgar to join the raiding armies." At this time the Yuan Dynasty was active in its struggle against Qaidu and Du'a 都哇, who wanted to possess the region that is present-day Xinjiang. The result of this conflict was that Yuan Dynasty military forces began to withdraw from the southwestern part of the Tarim basin. In the ninth month of the 26th year of the Zhiyuan reign period (1289), the Yuan government "abolished the military command of the Pacification Commissioner 宣慰使 in Woduan."[35] The *History of the Yuan* describes what happened to Wuhuncha's army after the abandonment of Khotan as follows:

> In the first month of the 30th year of the Zhiyun reign period (1293), an official in the Bureau of Military Affairs 密院 sent in a memorial saying, "the Wumoluhan 兀末魯罕 army of Wuhuncha's tribe sent in 6,426 *shi* 石 of rice, which has an estimated value of

[35] *History of the Yuan*, ch. 15, "Annals of Shizu" 《世祖紀》. The American scholar John W. Dardess believes that after 1289 the Yuan Dynasty's influence began to be withdrawn from Central Asia. Dardess is rather vague about this "withdrawal" from Central Asia and fails to take into account all the events that transpired after this date between the Yuan Dynasty and the Chaghatay *ulus* [hereditary territory]. His view is therefore not worthy of adopting. See John W. Dardess, "From Mongol Empire to Yuan Dynasty: Changing Forms of Imperial Rule in Mongolia and Central Asia," *Monumenta Serica*, vol. 30 (1972-1973), pp. 117-65. Hsiao Ch'i-ch'ing, in *The Military Establishment of the Yuan Dynasty*, p. 162, n. 84, addressed Dardess' view and expressed opposition to it.

> 12,852 *ding* 錠 of paper money." The emperor proclaimed, "If there is no trouble on the border, let that army cultivate it as a military colony and grow its own food to support themselves."[36]

In the same year, Wuhuncha "became ill and died; his second son succeeded him, and was appointed to the post of Vice Marshal of the Left of Quxiantalin." We can see that the soldiers of this branch of the *tammachi* army, which was under the leadership of the Zhubo tribe, did not return to their country after the Yuan forces abandoned Khotan, but remained stationed at Quxian.

In the first month of the first year of the Yuanzhen reign period (1295), the Yuan government established the Chief Military Commands of Quxiantalin and Beiting (Beshbalïq). In the second month of the same year, the government ordered the Marshal and Vice Marshal of the Beiting Chief Military Command, by the names of He Bo 合伯 and Saliman 撒里蠻, to go out on an expedition to receive the military commissioners of the various princes of the Chubo 出伯 (that is, the Zhubo) tribe. The establishment of these two Chief Military Commands is related to the activities surrounding the Yuan Dynasty's withdrawal from the Uyghur region after Khotan was abandoned. As far as the Yuan Dynasty was concerned, it did not want to leave the region of Quxiantalin isolated at the frontier. The Uyghur region was the key route between the Chinese Central Plain and Quxiantalin. Therefore the Yuan Dynasty considered the control of Quxiantalin and the direct rule of the Uyghur region to be intimately related.

In his narration of the story of the first years of the Emperor Chengzong's 成宗 reign, Rashīd al-Dīn wrote the following about the situation in the frontier region involving the Yuan on the one hand and Qaidu and Du'a on the other:

> Beginning in the East, princes and emirs have been stationed with armies (all along the frontier). In the extreme East, Prince Kambala, the great-uncle of the Khan on the father's side, is stationed with an army. Next to him is Körgüz Küregen, the son-in-law of the Khan; next to him, Čonqur, the son of Tutugh, who is one of Qubilai Khan's great emirs; next to him, Nangjiadai, the son

[36] *History of the Yuan*, ch. 17, "Annals of Shizu" 《世祖紀》, p. 369.

of Nayan Küyükchi, who also is a great emir; next to him, Kököchü, the uncle of Temür Khan. Then comes the Tangqut country, which is administered by Prince Ananda, the son of Mangqala, who is stationed there with his army in the neighborhood of Chaghan-Na'ur. Next to him is the frontier of Qara-Qočo, which is a town of the Uyghurs. There is good wine there. It is between the frontiers of the Khan and Qaidu, and the people are on good terms with them both and render service to both sides. Next to them are stationed the princes Ajïqï, the grandson of Cha'adai, and Chübei, the son of Alghu. Then come the difficult mountains of Tibet, already mentioned.[37]

Rashīd al-Dīn also records: "Prince Ananda was sent by the Khan to the country of the Tangqut at the head of his army and *ulus*. Prince Kököchü and Körgüz, who is the Khan's son-in-law, were sent to the frontier with Qaidu and Du'a. He dispatched Toghan with an army to Manzi to guard that country. The Emir Ajïqï he sent at the head of an army to the frontier at Qara-Qočo."[38]

These records in Rashīd al-Dīn's *Jāmi' al-Tawārīkh* show that soon after Chengzong (Temür) ascended the throne, Gaochang was still within

---

[37] Rashīd al-Dīn, *Jāmi' al-Tawārīkh* (*Compendium of Chronicles*), translated as *The Successors of Genghis Khan* by John Andrew Boyle (New York: Columbia University Press, 1971), pp. 285-6 [here slightly modified]. Kamala was the elder brother of Emperor Chengzong, not his uncle. Rashīd al-Dīn is mistaken here. What is strange is that Boyle was never able to identify this name (see p. 285, n. 180). However, this name in the same work is called Kamala on pages 242, 321, 322, and 330. Nangjiadai is 囊家歹, according to chapter 131 of the *History of the Yuan*, whose father was named Macha 麻察, and he was a member of the Man 蠻 ethnic minority. Zhou Qingshu 周清澍, following the Russian translation of the *Jāmi' al-Tawārīkh* (*Compendium of Chronicles*), chapter 2, mistakes Nangjiadai's father's name as Kubukchi, reads Nayan 那顔 as Boyan 伯顔 (Bayan), and also suspects that he was the Bayan who was the Commander-in-chief who attacked the Song, because the latter's second son was named Nangjiadai (see Zhou Qingshu 周清澍, "The Önggüd Tribe's Controlling Clan" 《汪古部統治家族》, *Literature and History* 《文史》, vol. 9, 1980, p. 128).

[38] Rashīd al-Dīn, *Jāmi' al-Tawārīkh* , the English translation *The Successors of Genghis Khan*, by Boyle, p. 322, here slightly modified. See also Professor Chen Dezhi's 陳得芝 Chinese translation 《史記鐵穆耳合浑本紀》, in Nanjing University's *Collected Papers of Research on Yuan History and Northern Nationalities History* 《元史及北方民族史研究集刊》, vol. 4, p. 31.

the range of the influence of the Yuan princes who were guarding the frontier. As noted above, the people of Gaochang were friendly with both the Yuan Dynasty on one hand and Qaidu and Du'a on the other and, moreover, paid tribute to both of them. These records show that the Yuan Dynasty was not entirely in control of the Uyghur territory at this time. Correspondingly, the biography of Ghazan Khan in the *Jāmi' al-Tawārīkh*, when discussing these circumstances, also says that the Uyghur territory was a province between the territories of the Great Khan and Qaidu.[39]

After this, Qaidu and Du'a continued their expansion into Uyghur territory, apart from the time when they did battle with the Yuan in the region of Jinshan. In its narration of the events of the winter of the second year of the Dade 大德 reign period (1298), after Du'a attacked and defeated the Yuan army and captured Körgüz, the *Jāmi' al-Tawārīkh* says: "Meanwhile, Du'a, his mind set at rest with the defeat of the [Khan's] army, was moving at a slow pace, intending to proceed to his own *ordos* and then to send troops to the posts and areas of Ananda, Ajïqï, and Chübei, which are in the region of Qara-Qočo, and whom he hoped to attack, defeat, and put to flight."[40]

The Yuan Dynasty forces again withdrew under the pressure and advance of Du'a. In the seventh year of the Dade reign period (1303), before the Yuan Emperor Chengzong made an agreement with Du'a,

---

[39] *Jāmi' al-Tawārīkh*, vol. 3, A. K. Arend's (А. К. Аренд) translation into Russian, Рашид-ад-дин, *Сборник Летописей* (Moscow-Leningrad, 1946), p. 308. The American scholar Thomas T. Allsen quotes from this passage in his paper, "The Yuan Dynasty and the Uighurs of Turfan in the Thirteenth Century," p. 20 [p. 257 in *China Among Equals*], of which he kindly gave me a copy at the Conference on East Asian International Relations of the Tenth to the Thriteenth Centuries. It was published in Morris Rossabi, ed., *China Among Equals: The Middle Kingdom and its Neighbors, Tenth-Fourteenth Centuries* (Berkeley: University of California Press, 1983), pp. 243-80. His source was the biography of Ghazan Khan in the E. J. W. Gibb memorial volume, 1940, Persian edition, Rashīd al-Dīn, *Tarīkh-i Mubārak-i Ghāzāni: Dāstān-i Ghazan-Khān* (*The History of Ghazan*), p. 350.

The Uyghur peoples of Huozhou 火州 took a neutral position between the Yuan Dynasty on the one hand and Qaidu and Du'a on the other. This situation was noticed both by V. V. Bartol'd and Paul Pelliot. See V. V. Bartol'd , *Zwölf Vorlesungen über die Geschichte der Türken Mittleasiens*, p. 184, and Paul Pelliot, *Notes on Marco Polo*, (Paris: Adrien-Maisonneuve, 1959-63), p. 164.

[40] Rashīd al-Dīn, *Jāmi' al-Tawārīkh*, the English translation *The Successors of Genghis Khan*, by Boyle, p. 328. See also in footnote 38 the previously cited Chinese translation of Professor Chen Dezhi 陳得芝, p. 34.

Chabar 察八兒, and others, Du'a had already started seeing Qara-Qočo as his own territory. Du'a wrote in a letter to Chabar saying: "We should hold a *khuriltai* at the border of Beshbalïq between our country (*mulk*) and the pride (*khāsah*) of the *ulus*, Qara-Qočo, on the one hand, and center of the empire, the source of good fortune, Qara-Qorum on the other..."[41]

The last time that the Quxiantalin Chief Military Command appears in the *History of the Yuan* is in the first year of the Dade reign period (1297). If we combine the letter from Du'a with the record in the *History of the Yuan* mentioned above, we can speculate that the time when the Yuan regime was retreating from the Quxiantalin region was roughly when Du'a was in complete control of the Gaochang region, which was between the third and sixth years of the Dade reign period (1299 and 1302). Of course it may have been a little earlier.

[41] Abū al-Qāsim ibn 'Alī ibn Muhammad al-Qāshānī, *Tarikh-i Uljaytu* (*Chronicle of Uljaytu*), edited by Mahin Hambly (Tehran, 1969), p. 34. Here I follow the thesis of Thomas Allsen in "The Yuan Dynasty and the Uighurs of Turfan in the Thirteenth Century," p. 24 [in the manuscript, p. 261 in *China Among Equals*]. al-Qāshānī was a scholar of Persian history, who served under the Ilkhanids. His book is a valuable study of the history of Central Asia in the first half of the 14th century.

Liquor Still and Milk-Wine Distilling Technology in the Mongol-Yuan Period

Luo Feng 羅豐

1

At the exhibition "Genghis Khan—the Ancient Nomadic Culture of Northern China" 成吉思汗——中國古代北方草原游牧文化大展 jointly presented by the China Millennium Monument World Art Museum 中華世紀壇藝術管 and the Inner Mongolia Autonomous Region Museum 内蒙古自治區博物管 in the spring of 2004, a bronze liquor still (figure 1; labeled "Bronze Fermentation-of-Alcohol Pot" 銅釀酒鍋 in the exhibit caption) attracted the author's attention. Later, the author had the opportunity to study this still closely with the assistance of colleagues at the Inner Mongolia Museum.

Figure 1 The Bronze Liquor Still Unearthed from Bairin Left Banner, Inner Mongolia

Figure 2 A Cross-Section of the Bairin Left Banner Still and its Condenser (reversed view) and the Details of the Handle and Spout

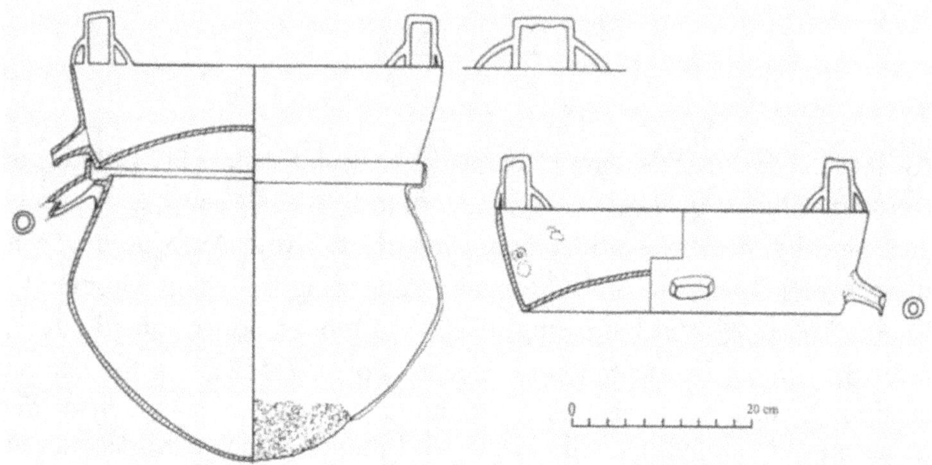

This bronze liquor still (figure 2) is 48.8 cm tall and consists of two parts: the bottom part is the boiler 釜 and the top part is a pan-shaped container (the condenser 甑). The boiler has a round bottom and a swelling belly; the steep shoulder atop it leads to the mouth, which has a circular gutter on its rim. The boiler is 33 cm tall and 42.4 cm wide at its largest diameter at the belly. The outer rim of the mouth is 3 cm in height and the inner rim 1.5 cm. The gutter between them, which leads to a spout attached to the outer rim, is 2.5 cm deep (figure 3-1). The spout (figure 3-4) is 6 cm in length and 2 cm in width. It is welded to the outer rim and the hole which links the gutter and the spout is rectangular, 2 cm in width and 0.5 cm in height. The boiler is cast of three pieces from a composite mold and the casting fins are not filed down. The bottom is slightly damaged: the inner and outer surfaces all show that the bottom has been burnt for a rather long time and damaged and mended with pig iron patches (figure 3-2). The very thick boiler body plus the patches make the remaining depth of the boiler only 32.4 cm. The pan-shaped container (condenser) is 17 cm in height and 41.6 cm in diameter. It has two rectangular handles, each 7.3 cm in width and 5.2 cm in height, with arc braces on both sides which are set symmetrically on the rim. On the outer wall near the bottom, two symmetric solid handles are attached (figure 3-3). The container body is only 11 cm tall, and its bottom, which is 38.4 cm in diameter, is convex (as seen from inside, figure 3-5) and in the shape of a dome, which at its

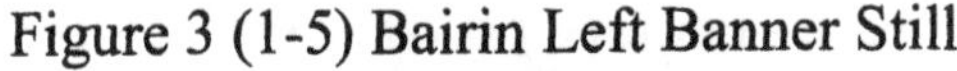
Figure 3 (1-5) Bairin Left Banner Still

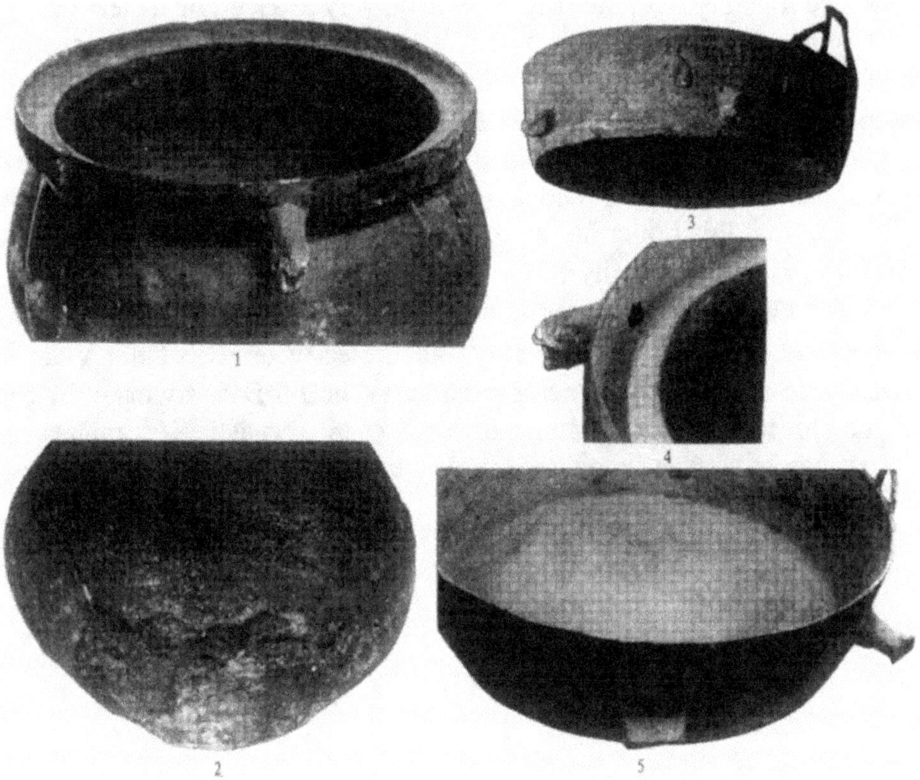

highest point is about 5 cm high. On the bottom rim is a spout leading outward, the length of which is 5 cm, with an outer diameter of 2.4 cm and an inner diameter of 1.9 cm. The edge of the dome-shaped bottom of the container fits tightly over the boiler. The container's body is thinner than that of the boiler. Some rust and a riveted crack can be seen on the outer surface.

According to the collection archive of the Inner Mongolia Museum, this still (the "Bronze Fermentation-of-Alcohol Pot") has been on loan from the Bairin Left Banner Museum 巴林左旗博物管, Chifeng City 赤峰市, since 1987. It was unearthed in 1983 at Shierduan Village 十二段村, Longchang Township 隆昌鎮, Bairin Left Banner 巴林左旗, Inner Mongolia, and dates roughly to the period of the Mongol Empire.[1]

[1] China Millennium Monument World Art Museum 中華世紀壇藝術館 and Inner Mongolia Autonomous Region Museum 内蒙古自治區博物館, editors, *Genghis Khan:*

However, because of the wide range in periods of the other objects unearthed together with the still, there is no way to ascertain a clear date.

Another discovery of this type is a set of bronze "stills" unearthed in Xishanzui Village 西山嘴村, Qinglong County 青龍县, Hebei 河北 Province in 1975 (figure 4), whose structure and composition are very similar to the one unearthed from Bairin Left Banner. The still in figure 4 also consists of a boiler and a pan-shaped condenser, with the slight difference that this boiler has an external flat ring around its belly and the condenser is taller. Initially this still was dated as an artifact of the Jin 金 Dynasty.[2] Later, through close comparisons, it was dated to between the later period of the Liao 遼 Dynasty and the early period of the Yuan 元 Dynasty. In other words, it belongs either to the Jin Dynasty or to the end of the Jin and the beginning of the Yuan Dynasties.[3] Enthusiastic discussions have been conducted in academic circles regarding the usage and mechanism of this still.

The Ancient Nomadic Culture of Northern China 《成吉思汗：中國古代北方草原遊牧文化》 (Beijing: Beijing Press 北京出版社, 2004), p. 298. In this book this "Bronze Fermentation-of-Alcohol Pot" is described as being unearthed from Bairin Right Banner, but without an exact location. Through the efforts of Ms. Su Dong 蘇東, my colleague working at the Inner Mongolia Museum, the author obtained reliable information that it was unearthed at Shierduan Village, Longchang Township, and that the old information was incorrect.

[2] Chengde City Bishushan Village Administration 承德市避暑山莊管理處, "A Jin Dynasty Bronze Liquor-Making Pot Unearthed in Qinglong County, Hebei" 《河北省青龍縣出土金代銅燒酒鍋》, *Cultural Relics* 《文物》, 1976, no. 9, pp. 98-9.

[3] Chengde City Bishushan Village Museum 承德市避暑山莊博物館, "A Brief Investigation of the Jin Dynasty Still" 《金代蒸餾器考略》, *Archaeology* 《考古》, 1980, no. 5, pp. 466-71 and 405, especially p. 468. Figure 4 here is reproduced from Chengde City Bishushan Village Museum, "A Brief Investigation of the Jin Dynasty Still," p. 468, figure 5-1.

Figure 4 A Cross-Section of the Bronze Liquor Still Unearthed in Qinglong County, Hebei Province

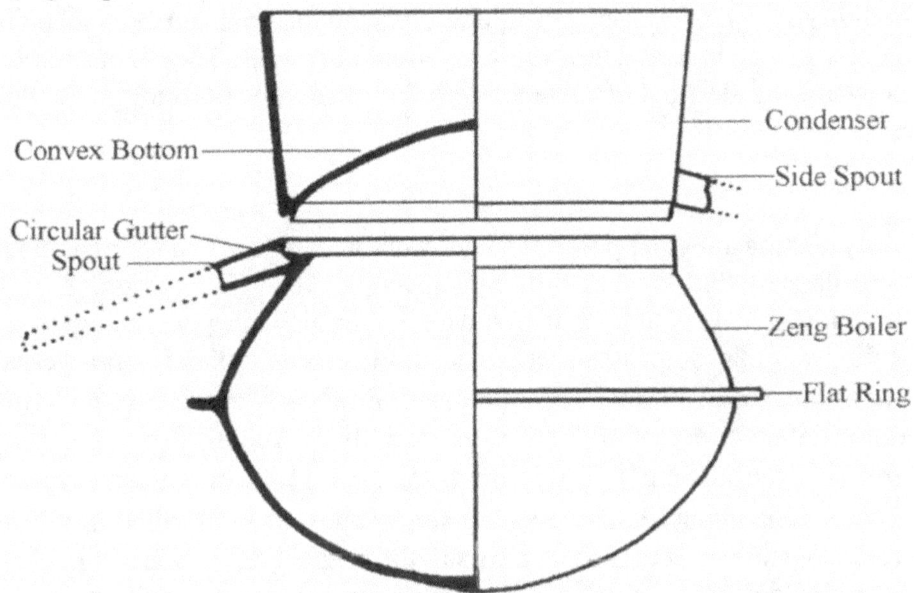

The majority opinion is that this still is important evidence showing the maturity of liquor distillation technology in China and can be regarded as the first formal apparatus for liquor distillation.[4] Of course, severe disagreement has taken place among scholars on the issue of whether liquor distillation was invented locally in China or was introduced from the Arabian region.[5] The purpose of this paper is not to settle these huge

---

[4] Li Huarui 李華瑞, "Debate on the Origin of Liquor Distillation in China" 《中國燒酒起始的論爭》, *Trends in Recent Research on the History of China* 《中國史研究動態》, 1990, no. 8, pp. 15-9.

[5] There have been many hypotheses on the origin of the alcohol distillation in China, and these can be classified into the following five types: 1) in the Eastern Han 東漢; 2) in the Tang Dynasty; 3) in the Song Dynasty; 4) in the Jin Dynasty (1115-1234); and 5) in the Yuan Dynasty. For type one see Sun Ji 孫機, "On the Origins of Grain Liquor and Distilled Liquor in China" 《我國穀物酒和蒸餾酒的起源》, in Yang Hong 楊泓 and Sun Ji 孫機, *The Exquisite in the Ordinary* 《尋常的精緻》 (Shenyang: Liaoning Education Press 遼寧教育出版社, 1996), p. 186; for type two see Zhou Jiahua 周嘉華, et al., *A History of Chinese Chemistry – Ancient Texts* 《中國化學史 – 古代卷》 (Nanning 南寧: Guangxi Education Press 廣西教育出版社, 2003), pp. 723-6. At the beginning stages (the 1950s-1960s), only general opinions about all of these hypotheses were published, without detailed discussions; cf. Yuan Hanqing 袁翰青, "The Origin and

and long-standing disputes, but to fill in a few gaps in the issues which have already been discussed. An in-depth discussion on some topics usually relies on new discoveries, and this new material can lead scholars to a new perspective and new thinking about old issues. The "Liquor Still" discovered in Bairin Left Banner may be positively meaningful in this sense.

2

From an archaeological point of view, what we are most concerned about is the date of this type of still. For example, the "liquor-making still" found in Qinglong County was first dated to the Jin Dynasty. The evidence for this was that porcelain sherds and bronze coins with 25 reign period titles of the Northern Song 北宋, Liao, and Jin Dynasties were found in the cultural layers where the "still" was unearthed. Among them the latest were from the Dading 大定 reign period (1161-1189) of the Jin Dynasty Emperor Shizong 世宗. The detailed stratigraphy was described in a later archaeological report and some errors in the original report were corrected. The report did not describe the excavation processes, but did explain the stratigraphy. According to my understanding, following the discovery of the still, a supplementary dig in the trench explained the piling up of the cultural layers. The trench measured three by two meters and 2.5 meters in depth. There were eight main types of artifacts found, divided into white-glazed porcelain sherds, pottery sherds and one drip-tile, other iron pots, a

---

Development of Wine Fermentation in China" 《釀酒在我國的起源和發展》, in Yuan Hanqing 袁翰青, *Collected Essays on the History of Chemistry in China* 《中國化學史論文集》 (Beijing: SDX Joint Publishing Company 生活・讀書・新知三聯書店, 1956), pp. 95-6. Recently, Li Huarui explained the origins of these hypotheses and supported the hypothesis that "(wine distillation was started in) the Song Dynasty"; cf. Li Huarui 李華瑞, *Song Dynasty Liquor Production and Tax Monopoly* 《宋代酒的生産和徵榷》 (Baoding 保定: Hebei University Press 河北大學出版社, 2001), pp. 43-71. The "Yuan Dynasty" hypothesis, although an old one, has recovered its prevailing influence because of the exceptional research by Huang Shijian 黃時鑑; see Huang Shijian 黃時鑑, "*Alaji* and the Origin of Liquor Distillation in China" 《阿剌吉與中國燒酒的起始》, *Literature and History* 《文史》, vol. 31 (1988), pp. 159-72, especially pp. 159-66. However, the above-mentioned text *A History of Chinese Chemistry – Ancient Texts* analyzed and disputed all of these hypotheses, and pointed out that it is unquestionable that liquor distillation had existed in the Yuan Dynasty, but the issue of whether liquor distillation was originated in the Yuan Dynasty or earlier is still awaiting further research (see *A History of Chinese Chemistry – Ancient Scrolls*, p. 733).

curve-handled iron hoe, a bronze Buddhist image, and more than one hundred *jin* 斤 [more than 100 pounds] of bronze coins. They were all said to have been unearthed from the same cultural layer. The opening of the pit was uncovered four meters from the trench of this cultural layer, and within the pit, 50 cm below the opening, the "liquor-making still" was discovered. These artifacts comprise the basic evidence for the dating: the porcelain reflects the period of the Liao or Jin Dynasties, the curve-handled iron hoe and pot are Jin Dynasty products, and the small bronze Buddha was a relic often seen during the Jin Dynasty, the *Bhikkhu* 比丘 image. The latest of the coins was minted in the Dading era. The shape of the drip-tile and the pattern of its surface decoration is very similar to that of ones unearthed from the Houyingfang 後英房 Yuan Dynasty residential remains in Beijing. However, the authors of the report argued that the drip-tile from the Qinglong site is large and coarse, and the decoration is crowded and awkward, differing from that of the Houyingfang site, whose tiles were slender and elegant. Therefore, the Qinglong drip-tile would have been earlier than the Houyingfang one, and thus it was a relic of the Jin Dynasty or the early period of the Yuan Dynasty. Having considered these factors, the authors of the report came to a comprehensive conclusion that this site was mainly a Jin one, whose *terminus post quem* would be the later period of the Liao Dynasty and *terminus ante quem* would be the early period of the Yuan Dynasty. Therefore the "liquor-making still" would be an artifact of the Jin Dynasty or the early period of the Yuan Dynasty. It must be said that this type of inference regarding the determination of the general period of archaeological remains appears to be without large error. However, the problem is that despite having made this inference (a Jin or early Yuan date), the report was entitled "Jin Still" and pointed out this dating as a special feature.[6] This led Mr. Huang Shijian 黃時鑒 to challenge the dating, as a key matter arose from this drip-tile. He believed that the Qinglong three-cornered drip-tile and the Yuan Dynasty drip-tiles unearthed from the sites of Qara-Qorum 哈拉和林, Daidu (Khanbalïq) 大都, Shangdu (Xanadu) 上都, and Daning Road 大寧路 were, in terms of design, obviously of the same type. As for the coarse manufacturing of the Qinglong drip-tile, the reason that it is

[6] The later research report still referred the date of this still as "Jin." See Chengde City Bishushan Village Museum 承德市避暑山莊博物館, "A Brief Investigation of the Jin Dynasty Still" 《金代蒸餾器考略》, *Archaeology* 《考古》, 1980, no. 5, p. 466.

different from the exquisite and elegant ones found in the other sites is absolutely because those were remains from high status architecture. In this way, the *terminus ante quem* of the Qinglong site should be the Yuan Dynasty.[7] Of course, from an even more perfectionist perspective, the original archaeological report had another flaw when it determined that there was a clear connection between the trench and the "liquor-making still": it was dug out of a cylindrical pit, but the trench did not open onto the cylindrical pit and was located four meters away from it. In other words, the dates of the relics unearthed from the trench can not be used to directly prove the date of the circular pit, let alone to infer the date of the making of the still. Therefore, even if the trench would make the dating of the site clear, the date of the "Qinglong liquor-making still" based on the site could still be as late as the Yuan Dynasty.

The shape and functions of the Bairin Left Banner still resemble those of the Qinglong still, and although there was no opportunity to closely examine the Qinglong still, via the archaeological report one can see that there are some differences in the details. The Qinglong still has an external flat ring around the center of its belly, but the Bairin Left Banner still does not; the condenser of the former is 16 cm tall, while that of the latter is only 11 cm tall; the condenser of the former has a ring foot with an inverted lip which fits tightly to the boiler, but that of the latter does not; no traces of casting can be seen on the former, but the latter clearly has casting fins showing that it was cast out of a three-piece composite mold; the body thickness of the former is even, but that of the boiler and steamer of the latter are very uneven. These differences mainly reflect a differing level of functional convenience and differing aspects of the manufacturing techniques. The flat ring on the belly makes the Qinglong still easy to carry and handle. The higher condenser contains more water for cooling, and contrary-wise for the smaller one. The ring foot of the condenser has an inverted lip making for a tight seal with the outer lip of the body and thus guaranteeing no leakage of steam. The multi-part casting and the uneven thickness of the Bairin Left Banner still show that the manufacturing technique was crude. Comparing all of these details, we can see that there is a chronological relationship between the Qinglong and the Bairin Left banner stills. The Qinglong still obviously is an advance in

[7] Huang, Shijian 黃時鑑, "The Origin of Liquor Distillation in China and Chinese Stills" 《中國燒酒的起始與中國蒸餾器》, *Literature and History* 《文史》 1996, no. 41, pp. 145-6.

both form and function over the Bairin Left Banner still, and it is not difficult to conclude that the Bairin Left Banner still is earlier, although they both could belong to the Mongol-Yuan period.

3

In the earliest report, the Qinglong still was considered to be a "liquor-making pot"[8] 燒酒鍋 [literally, a "burnt wine pot"], and later it was cautiously called a "still" 蒸馏器.[9] The Bairin Left Banner still has a similar shape, structure, and function. Their basic mechanism is this: the condenser (with a convex bottom) on the top is used to contain cold water. The side spout was corked when the cold water was poured in. The raw material (fermented mash) was put into the boiler, on top of which the condenser was mounted, and the assembled still was heated from the bottom. When the raw material was boiled, the vapor rising from it cooled down when it ran into the cold water-cooled convex bottom of the condenser (which forms a dome over the boiling raw material) and condensed into a liquid which flowed along the dome into the circular gutter and finally into a receiving container through the spout of the circular gutter. This is the workflow of distillation. The condenser on the top is a cooler into which cold water is added and out of which heated water is drained by unplugging the side spout (figure 5).[*]

---

[8] This object was called "a Jin bronze liquor-making still" in the earliest preliminary report and was used to conduct a liquor distilling experiment under the direction of technicians in the distillery workshop of the comprehensive processing plant of the Chengde Municipal Grain Bureau. See Chengde City Bishushan Village Administration, "A Jin Dynasty Bronze Liquor-Making Pot Unearthed in Qinglong County, Hebei", *Cultural Relics*, 1976, no. 9, p. 98.

[9] Chengde City Bishushan Village Museum, "A Brief Investigation of the Jin Dynasty Still," *Archaeology*, 1980, no. 5, p. 466.

[*] Figure 5 here is modified from Chengde City Bishushan Village Museum, "A Brief Investigation of the Jin Dynasty Still," p. 468, figure 5-2. Translator's note.

Figure 5 The Distillation Workflow of the Qinglong Still

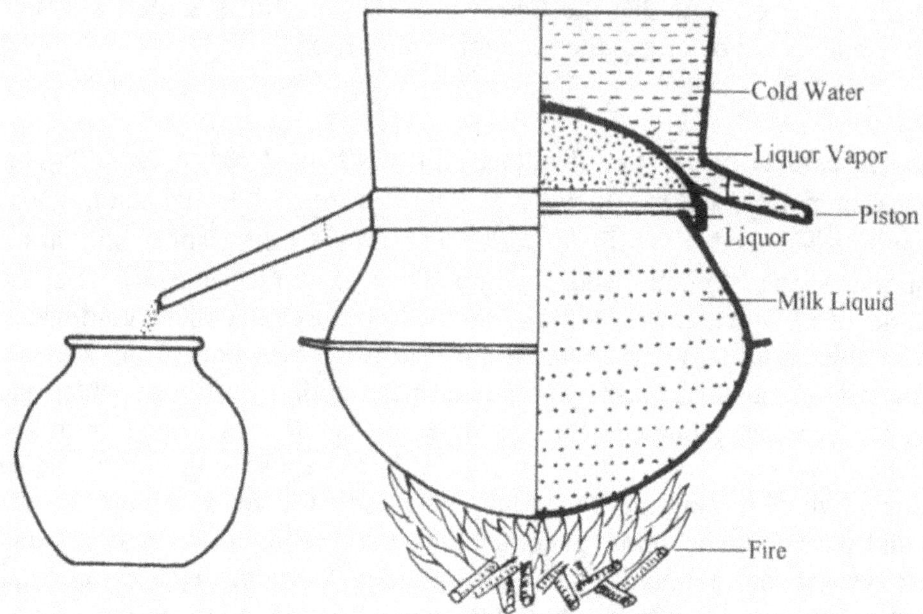

Under the impression that this was a distilling apparatus, the authors of the archaeological report conducted an experiment to distill liquor utilizing the Qinglong still. The experiment consisted of two trials. "In the first test, 8 *jin* 斤 of raw material (fermented rice husk) yielded 0.9 *jin* of liquor containing 9.4% alcohol; in the second test, 6 *jin* of raw material yielded 0.56 *jin* of liquor containing 9.7% alcohol." These results demonstrated that this "liquor-making still" could really make "liquor" in the strict sense, but the yield ratio and the alcohol percentage were low. Their explanation of these results had two parts. First, the mouth of the condenser had been broken, so it could only contain 4/5 of the cold water, which affected the cooling function; moreover, the spout conducting the liquor from the gutter into the outside container was leaking, so that some vaporized and liquefied liquor could have been lost. Second, the shape and structure of the boiler limited the volumes of raw material and water to a ratio of roughly one-to-one, which in comparison to the present-day ratio of alcohol-containing materials to water had much lower content of raw material. Therefore the yield ratio and the alcohol percentage were both very low. The authors of the report regretfully agreed that even if the broken places were repaired and the leaking was overcome, the still could not perform better.[10] However, was the unsatisfactory result caused by the imperfect still itself, or by the unsuitable operation and working procedure? First, let us examine their way of adding raw material to the still. A suitable quantity of water was poured into the boiler, and then a foldable grid woven of sorghum stalks or another similar material was set at one third of the height of the boiler. This acted as a permeable barrier holding the material in the boiler. During the distillation, the raw material (fermented mash) was gradually added according to the rising of the vapor until the still was filled up to its mouth with the correctly prepared steamed material. Second, the action of the foldable grid is the key to this method. As observed by the authors of the report, the traces on the inner wall of the boiler of the Qinglong still clearly divide it into three zones. The bottom zone, from the bottom to a height of 6 cm, is dark grey, which was formed by the boiling and immersing of the raw material in the water. The middle zone, about 10 cm in height, is light grey, formed by contact with the raw material. The top zone, also about 10 cm in height, has a layer of patina resulted from erosion caused by direct contact with the hot vapor and humid air.[11] Because the boiler's inner wall is plain and smooth without any preset struts or anything projecting for supporting a grid, therefore the authors of the report at the time of the experiment designed a foldable grid made of sorghum stalks to match the size of the boiler. Using a grid to hold the semi-finished product was a mistaken concept of the experimenters, and in reality at the time the still was in use, there fundamentally was no flexible grid of this kind holding the material. Just like Qinglong still, the Bairin Left Banner still also has a very dark zone near the bottom. Moreover, because of the frequent and long-lasting burning, the bottom had been damaged and mended several times. As for the traces of the two zones above the dark zone, this situation is often encountered by experienced archaeologists during their excavations of containers. If the vessel was completely or partly filled with silts, theses silts would have left clear marks on the inner wall when they are removed. Therefore, these marks are absolutely not necessarily traces of boiling or cooking, and the authors of the report did not even give any information indicating whether or not silt was found in the boiler when it was

---

[10] Chengde City Bishushan Village Administration, "A Jin Dynasty Bronze Liquor-Making Pot Unearthed in Qinglong County, Hebei", *Cultural Relics*, 1976, no. 9, p. 99.
[11] Chengde City Bishushan Village Museum, "A Brief Investigation of the Jin Dynasty Still," *Archaeology*, 1980, no. 5, p. 470.

excavated. The authors of the report also admitted that the raw material could have been placed directly into the boiler, but they believed that it was used in this way only for the distillation of medicinal elixirs from flowers, so they eliminated this possibility for distillation of liquor. Theoretically, the Qinglong still has the technical functions and structural features of a distilling apparatus, but, as shown by the experiment mentioned above conducted by the authors, it obviously cannot satisfactorily meet the demands of satisfactory production efficiency.

Hong Guangzhu 洪光住 also questioned the liquor-making capability of the Qinglong still. A still of this size (an overall height of 41.6 cm) could not be used in daily life. If it was used for the distilling of wine made by liquid fermentation, then this kind of wine would very likely have been koumiss, or mare's milk wine.[12] Huang Shijian used his profound knowledge of Mongolia to disprove Hong Guangzhu's supposition, and he said that the assumption that the Qinglong still was used to process koumiss seems not to match the actual situation. He explained that in the pastoral region the distillation of all of fermented material, including milk, is done with "Mongolian" stills (named by Joseph Needham, following Hommel), whose sizes are usually much larger than that of the Qinglong still. "Just acknowledging that this still could be used to distill liquor makes it possible that it represents the beginning of liquor distilling in China, although we cannot prove the validity of this yet."[13] Because Huang Shijian's view of the "Mongolian still" derives from Needham, it is necessary to have an in-depth discussion concerning the origin of this concept.

An achievement of modern research is that it gives people grounds to suppose that distillation technology originated in ancient India, the basis of which is understanding the phenomenon that similar techniques are widely diffused and distributed among Asian peoples. Of course, it is also easy for us to imagine that distillation technology was introduced into Central Asia and Mongolia following Buddhism. However, this question is difficult to answer at present, because there is no record in reliable

---

[12] Hong, Guangzhu 洪光住, *A Draft History of Chinese Food Products Science* 《中國食品科技史稿》 (Beijing: China Commercial Press 中國商業出版社, 1985), vol. 1, p. 144.

[13] Huang Shijian 黃時鑑, "The Origin of Chinese Liquor Distillation and Chinese Stills" 《中國燒酒的起始與中國蒸餾器》, *Literature and History* 《文史》, vol. 41 (1996), p. 145.

documents of the time of the invention of this technology.[14] The chronological reliability of Chinese historical documents provides favorable conditions for some useful exploration, especially regarding distillation apparatuses.

Figure 6 The Chinese or Mongolian Still; (1) Schematic Diagram; (2) Glass Model

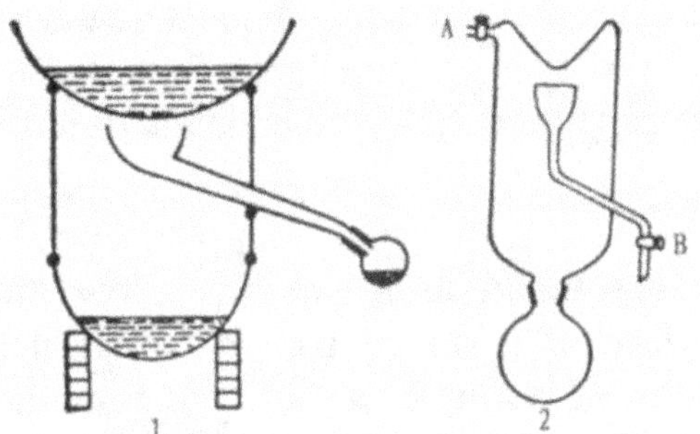

Dr. Needham conducted special investigations regarding the history and geographical distribution of all possible forms of distillation and extraction apparatuses, and among these East Asian types aroused his particular interest. Historians of chemistry had not fully realized that in this regard the two areas of China and Mongolia were important, especially the latter.[15] The route of Dr. Needham's exploration of ancient Chinese stills began with the examination of Daoist alchemists' devices for making elixirs and immortality drugs,[16] some methods and equipment of which had features in common with distillation apparatuses.[17] Even

---

[14] Gösta Montell, "Distilling in Mongolia," *Ethnos II* , 1937, no. 5, p. 321.

[15] Needham, Joseph and Ping-Yü Ho, *Science and Civilization in China, Volume 5: Chemistry and Chemical Technology, Part 4, Spagyrical Discovery and Invention: Apparatus, Theories and Gifts* (Cambridge: Cambridge University Press, 1980), pp. 103-7.

[16] Ho, Ping-Yü and Joseph Needham, "The Laboratory Equipment of the Early Mediaeval Chinese Alchemists," *Ambix*, no. 7 (1959), pp. 57-115; Ho, Peng-Yoke 何丙郁 and He Guanbiao 何冠彪, *Essays on the History of Chinese Technology* 《中國科技史概論》 (Hong Kong: China Book Company Hong Kong Branch 中華書局香港分局, 1983), pp. 250-9.

[17] A. R. Butler and Joseph Needham, "An Experimental Comparison of the East Asian, Hellenistic and Indian (Gandharan) Stills in Relation to the Distillation of Ethanol and Acetic Acid," *Ambix*, no. 27 (1980), pp. 69-76. Figure 6 here is taken from A. R. Butler and Joseph Needham, "An Experimental Comparison of the East Asian, Hellenistic and

though the objectives were the same, the still structures were different. Taking an understanding of the differences between distillation equipment among different civilizations as his objective, in addition to describing the four basic forms of stills, Dr. Needham created copies of these stills in glass for experimental purposes. Among these four forms two are related to China – the so-called Mongolian and the Chinese types (figure 6). Of course, the basis for Dr. Needham's copying of the "Chinese form" still was the elixir-making devices as recorded in ancient texts. The "Mongolian form" still was borrowed from Hommel's work written in the 1930s. This work had an illustration (figure 7), Dr. Needham's description of which is:

> The vapors from a boiling liquid in a pan 釜 below are condensed on the under surface of a similar pan of cold water placed above, and caught in a bowl resting on a shelf in the middle of the space formed by a wooden cylindrical barrel-like wall 桶. Such stills are used for preparing the spirit distilled from fermented mare's milk.[18]

Indian (Gandharan) Stills in Relation to the Distillation of Ethanol and Acetic Acid," p. 70, figure 1.

[18] Joseph Needham and Ping-Yü Ho, *Science and Civilization in China, Volume 5: Chemistry and Chemical Technology, Part 4, Spagyrical Discovery and Invention: Apparatus, Theories and Gifts*, p. 64 [the diagram is on p. 62]. See also Ping-Yü Ho and Joseph Needham, "The Laboratory Equipment of the Early Mediaeval Chinese Alchemists," *Ambix*, no. 7 (1959), pp. 57-115.

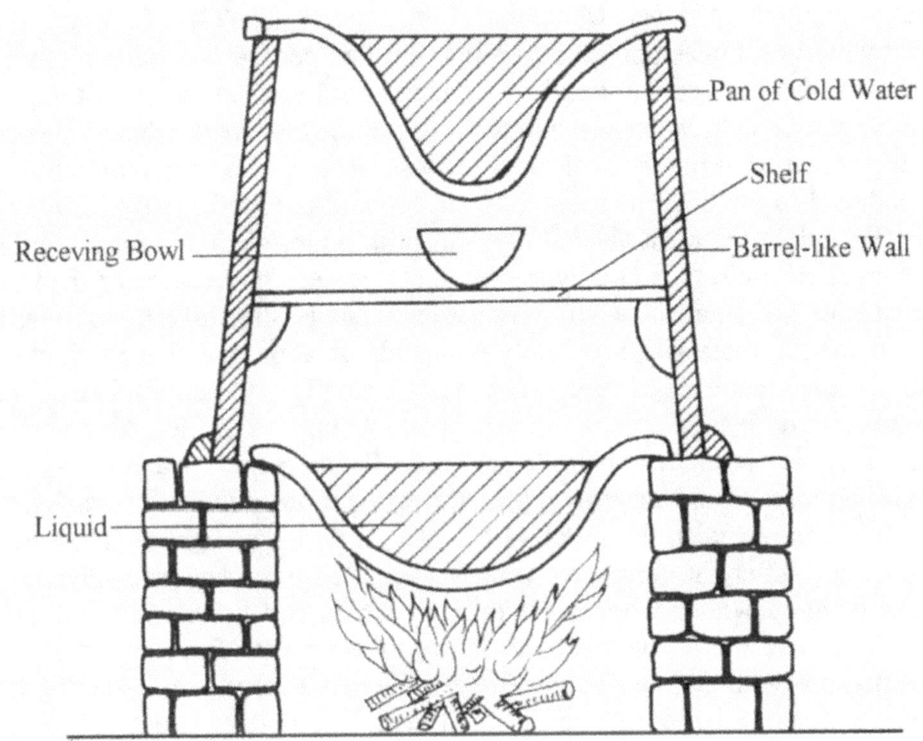

Although a bit convoluted, the core mechanism of this still is that when the raw material is heated, its steam rises to the cold bottom of the condenser above it, and then condenses and falls from the condenser bottom into a bowl on a shelf between the boiling material and the condenser bottom, successfully forming alcohol. Dr. Needham strongly recommends Montell's article on Mongolian distillation in which he described three types of still (*burchur*): "the Mongol one proper with the central catch-bowl, the Chinese one with the side-tube originating from a flat cup or shallow grooved rectangular wooden plate, and lastly one of retort type in which the heated pot is simply connected by an arched wooden leather covered tube with an iron receiver jug standing in a basin of cold water. Notable is the use of clay-daubed felt for making joints steam-tight, since felt was one of the most characteristic Mongol inventions."[19] The "central catch-bowl" system was the most common type seen in the Mongolian region. In the 1940s Dong Zhengjun 董正鈞 observed this distilling process when he was conducting sociological investigations in Inner Mongolia, Ejin Banner 額濟納旗. First, the fermented milk was poured into a pot and this pot was set into an empty bowl or basin. Then a bottomless wooden barrel was set on top of the pot, and a pot of cold water was mounted on top of the wooden barrel. When the fermented milk in the lower pot was heated, clear milk liquor was produced in the bowl or basin.[20] Gösta Montell used exhaustive efforts to try to outline the most general types of milk liquor distillation used in the Mongol steppe region and by the Mongol people. But because of the vast area and the small scale of production (usually the milk liquors were homemade), there was absolutely no standardization of either production or the manufacturing of equipment. So he actually could not find all of the types and derive the most basic principles. At the end of the 18th century, the famous German scholar Peter Simon Pallas observed and noted the milk liquor making technique of the Kalmyk people in the Volga valley. A tripod was set up in the middle of a yurt on which a large cauldron was mounted. After the fermented milk was poured in, a cauldron (*chaißun*) was covered with a wooden lid through which two holes were cut. The cauldron and the lid were sealed tightly together with fresh cow dung or sometimes with clay or dough. The distillate receiver was a kettle, the lid of which had a large hole and a small vent. The hole on the cauldron lid and that on the kettle were linked by a pipe named a Zooros (Zorgo in Mongolian), and the steam from the cauldron condensed into liquor in the kettle.[21] Based on accounts by Mongolians, Georg Soderbom drew a

---

[19] Gösta Montell, "Distilling in Mongolia," *Ethnos II* , 1937, no. 5, p. 324. Figure 8 here is taken from Gösta Montell, "Distilling in Mongolia," p. 328, figure 7. Needham, Joseph and Ping-Yü Ho, *Science and Civilization in China, Volume 5, Part 4*, p. 103.

[20] Dong Zhengjun 董正鈞, *Juyan Lake (Ejin Banner)* 《居延海 (額濟那旗)》 (1944), included in Chaogetu 朝格圖, ed., *Alxa League Historical Records* 《阿拉善盟旗志史料》 (Alxa League Political Consultative Literary and Historical Materials Research Committee 阿拉善盟政協文史資料研究委員會, 1987), p. 131.

[21] "Auf den Dreifuß in der Hütte wird ein grosser eiserner Kessel über ein kleines Feuer gesezt, mit etwas Wasser, welches man darinnen warm werden läst, ausgeschwenkt, und mit der wohl durchgearbeiteten, sauren Milch, bis etwan zwei Finger breit vom Hande, angefüllt. Solche Kessel halten ohngefähr drei rußische Eimer oder drüber. Auf den Kessel (*Chaißun*) wird ein paßlicher etwas ausgehöhlter Deckel (*Chapchak*) der entweder nur aus einem, oder aus zwei Stücken Holz gearbeitet ist und zwei viereckigte Oefnungen

diagram of a kind of distillation apparatus for making Mongolian milk-liquor (figure 8).

Figure 8 The Mongolian Koumiss Distillation Apparatus

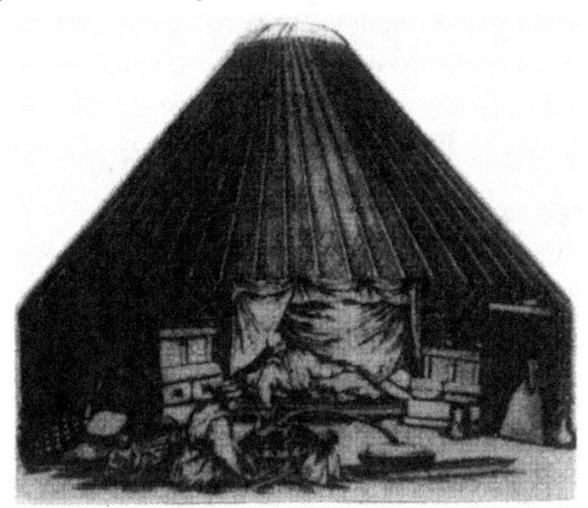

---

hat, gesezt. Den Rand und die Fugen pflegt man in der Steppe mit frischem Kuhmist zu verstreichen....Die Stawropolischen, getauften Kalmücken, welche das Meel reichlicher und wohlfeiler haben, nehmen zur Winterszeit, statt des Thons einen zäh geknäteten Teig von groben Meel.... — Statt des Recipieneinin kleineres Luftloch haben muß, und am Rande herum wohl verschmiben den Dreifuß in einen Kühltrog mit Schnee oder kaltem Wasser. Die Röhre (*Zorros*, mongol. *Zorgo*), welche den Milchbranntwein aus dem grossen Kessel in die Vorlage leiten soll, pflegt aus einem halbzirkelförmig gebognen Hälften ausgehöhlt, wieder aneinander gepast und mit rohem Leder oder Gedärm überzogen ist, zu bestehn und wird mit dem einen Ende auf die Oefnung der Vorlage, mit dem andern auf die eine Deckelöfnung des grossen Kettels gesezt und verschmiert....Sobald man mit den Vorbereitungen fertig ist, so wird frisch Feuer gegeben, wobei man durch die unbedeckte Oefnung des grossen Kessels acht giebt, bis die Milch in demselben aufsiedet, und ein starkriechender Dampf, der sich bei Destillation der besten Stutenmilch sogar entzünden läst, durch die Oefnung aufsteigt. Alsdenn wird einer der obgedachten Kegel auf diese Oefnung gesezt und angedrückt, das Feuer aber gemindert. Die kleine Oefnung der Vorlage bleibt allein unbedeckt, obgleich viele geistige Düste durch selbige verlohren gehn; denn ohne diese würde, nach dem Zeugniß der Kalmücken, die Destillation nicht gerathen. — Nach weniger als anderthalb Stunden vermindert sich der Dunst. Alsdenn ist aller Branntwein (Arr'ki) abgetrieben, und macht von Kuhmilch etwan den dreißgsten, höchstens einen fünf und zwanzigsten Theil, von Pferdemilch aber wohl ein Fünfzehntheil der ganzen Milchmasse aus. Er ist klar, sehr wäßrig und läst sich also nicht entzünden." Peter Simon Pallas, *Sammlungen historischer Nachrichten über die mongolischen Völkerschaften in einem ausführlichen Auszuge* (Frankfort and Leipzig: J. G. Fleischer, 1779), pp. 205-7.

The iron cauldron was covered by a lid and sealed tightly with mud. Two holes were drilled in the lid, through one of which the milk was added into the cauldron. The other was linked to an iron jar by a wooden pipe wrapped with animal hide. The iron jar rested on another iron cauldron filled with cold water. As the milk steam was conducted from the heated cauldron into the cold water-cooled iron jar it cooled down and condensed into milk liquor.[22] These two cases obviously have many details in common. The operating mechanism of this assemblage, named "Tungusic" by Pallas, is roughly similar to the milk liquor distilling pot popular in the Mongolian region. At present, the Mongol people in Subei 肅北, Gansu 甘肅 Province still make milk liquor with a specialized barrel-like steamer without a bottom at either end. When distillation is being done, this steamer is set on the cauldron containing the fermented milk. Another cauldron is rested on the top of this steamer, beneath which a catching-jar is hung with thin ropes. The steamer and the cauldron under it are sealed tightly together with clay and pieces of felt. The cauldron on the top of the steamer is used as condenser, which is filled with cold water. This water is kept from being heated up by repeatedly scooping it out and pouring it back, and when the temperature of the water surpasses 30 or 40 degrees centigrade it is changed.[23] The diversified distillation devices in the Mongolian region show us that the so-called "Mongolian form" of still actually has many varieties, which, however, should not create an obstacle to the correct understanding of this form. In order to study and understand the Bairin Left Banner and Qinglong stills, we will have to begin with the *alaji* 阿剌吉 liquor popular in the Mongol-Yuan period.

4

Although Chinese Daoist alchemists had a long history of using elixir and immortality drug making apparatuses, and they also used distillation methods when they were making these drugs, what they were doing was rather far removed from liquor distillation. The apparatuses for elixir and immortality drug making were usually very small and fundamentally had the objective of obtaining only a very small amount of elixir: they did not have the goal of the production of large quantities. Liquor making is, on

---

[22] Gösta Montell, "Distilling in Mongolia," *Ethnos II*, 1937, no. 5, p. 328.

[23] Cha Gankou 查干扣, ed., *The Mongolians of Subei* 《肅北蒙古人》 (Beijing: Nationalities Press 民族出版社, 2005), pp. 172-3.

the contrary, an activity for satisfying mass consumption and definitely requires large-scale production. Superficially, the distillation technique used by Daoist alchemists and that used in liquor making seem to have many very noticeable features and details in common, but a detailed investigation reveals that these "common" aspects are very problematic. They fundamentally cannot be supported by historical documents. Ye Ziqi 葉子奇, a philosopher living around the end of the Yuan and the beginning of the Ming Dynasties, noted in his *Master of Grasses and Trees* 草木子 that "The 'regulated wine' 法酒 (liquor) is obtained by heating wine and collecting its essence; it is called *halaji* 哈拉基 wine, very thick and strong and as clear as water. It is actually the dew of wine.…This is just the regulated wine of the Yuan Dynasty, and in ancient times they did not understand it."[24] Li Shizhen 李時珍 also wrote in his *Compendium of Materia Medica* 本草綱目[1578] that "burnt wine" 燒酒 (or "heated wine") was also called "fired wine" 火酒, which was *alaji* 阿剌吉 liquor and announced that "the making of burnt wine was not an ancient art. The technique was first developed in Yuan times. Strong wine is mixed with fermentation residues and put into a steamer. On steaming the vapor is made to rise and a vessel is used to collect the condensing drops."[25] Both Ye Ziqi and Li Shizhen noted that liquor distillation was not an ancient technique, but was invented in the Yuan Dynasty and was the so-called *halaji* or *alaji* liquor. Hu Sihui 忽思慧 in the Yuan Dynasty commented on this liquor in his *Principles of Correct Diet* 飲膳正要:

> *Alaji* liquor, sweet and pungent in flavor, is strongly heating and toxic. It relives cold obstructions and counteracts chilling

[24] "法酒, 用器燒酒之精液取之, 名曰哈拉基酒, 極醲烈, 其清如水, 蓋酒露也….此皆元朝之法酒,古無有也。" Ye Ziqi 葉子奇, *Master of Grass and Trees* 《草木子》, chapter three, "Miscellany" 《雜制篇》 (Beijing: Zhonghua Book Company 中華書局, 1997), p. 68.

[25] "燒酒非古法也. 自元時始創其法, 用濃酒和糟入甑, 蒸令氣上, 用器承取滴露。" Li Shizhen 李時珍, *Compendium of Materia Medica* 《本草綱目》 (Beijing: People's Health Press 人民衛生出版社, 1982), p. 1567, the entry "burnt wine" 《燒酒》. English translation by Dr. Joseph Needham.

vapors. Heat superior wine to its boiling point and collect the dew. This is *alaji* liquor.[26]

The term *alaji* is usually believed to be a transliteration of the Arabic term *'araq*, which had been thought to be a variation of "hollands" or alcohol. However, as Berthold Laufer's research has demonstrated, the term "alcohol" had not penetrated into China before modern times, therefore the Chinese term *alaji* could not represent alcohol.[27] In Tibetan the term representing distilled liquor is *ariki,* which is clearly derived from the Arabic term *'araq.*[28] It is said that the technique of distilling alcoholic beverages was a Western invention, and some historical documents say that the Arabian texts as early as the tenth century mention alcohol.[29] Of course, drinking alcoholic beverages is prohibited in Islam by the *Koran*, but alcohol is not forbidden to be used for medicinal purposes. Also, as Laufer's research indicates, in the Arabian and Persian literature from at least the tenth through the thirteenth centuries, nowhere is liquor distillation technology referenced.[30] However, some scholars have claimed that in the thirteenth century it was a completely common activity for the Arabs to make *'araq.*[31] Although, based upon the ancient texts, many non-

[26] "阿剌吉酒，味甘，辣，大熱，有大毒．主消冷堅積，去寒氣．用好酒蒸敖（熬），取露成阿剌吉." Hu Sihui 忽思慧, "The Categories and Products of Grains" 《米穀品》, in *Principles of Correct Diet* 《飲膳正要》 (Shanghai: The Commercial Press 商務印書館, 1934), vol. 3, p. 6, the entry "*Alaji* 阿剌吉 Liquor." English translation by Dr. Joseph Needham.

[27] Berthold Laufer, *Sino-Iranica: Chinese Contributions to the History of Civilization in Ancient Iran.* (Chicago: Field Museum of Natural History, 1919), pp. 236-7, especially footnote 6.

[28] Berthold Laufer, *Sino-Iranica*, pp. 236-7.

[29] Cf. Huang Shijian 黄時鑑, "*Alaji* and the Origin of Liquor Distillation in China" 《阿剌吉與中國燒酒的起始》, *Literature and History* 《文史》, vol. 31 (1988), p. 169.

[30] Berthold Laufer, *Sino-Iranica*, p. 238.

[31] John D. Bernal 貝爾納, *A Social History of Science* 《歷史上的科學》 (Chinese translation of *Sozialgeschichte der Wissenschaften* by Wu Kuangfu 伍況甫 , et al.) (Beijing: Science Press 科學出版社, 1959), p. 196; James R. Partington 柏廷頓, *A Short History of Chemistry* 《化學簡史》 (Chinese translation by Hu Zuoxuan 胡作玄) (Beijing: Commercial Press 商務印書館, 1979) pp. 46-7. Both works point out that distillation was applied to make alcoholic beverages in the 11th or 12th centuries in the West, and Huang Shijian states that the Persians learned distillation from the Arabs. See Huang Shijian 黄時鑑, "*Alaji* and the Origin of Liquor Distillation in China" 《阿剌吉與中國燒酒的起始》, *Literature and History* 《文史》, vol. 31 (1988), p. 166.

Chinese historians of science and technology have inferred the use of alcohol in formal accounts from the twelfth century, the Arabs could make alcohol for medicinal use not long after they began to make rosewater.[32] Yuasa Mitsutomo 湯浅光朝, a Japanese historian of science and technology, believed that at the end of the ninth century the Arabian doctor Muhammad ibn Zakariyā Rāzī (Rhazes, 865-925) already knew how to make sulfuric acid and alcohol.[33]

Regarding the meaning of the word *alaji*, in recent years there have been frequent discussions in academic circles. As noted by Liu Guangding 劉廣定, in Fairley's *Notes on the History of Distilled Spirits* (finished in 1905) the names of distilled spirits with similar pronunciation to *alaji* are *arrack* of India and Ceylon, *arika* of Mongolia, and *ava* of Tibet and the South Pacific Islands. Wu Deduo 吴德鐸 and Huang Shijian discovered that the terms used to represent "distilled liquor" in the Manchu and Uyghur languages were both pronounced similarly to *alaji*. Liu Guangding believes that ancient Chinese texts did not have records showing distilled liquor in the states around the South China Sea prior to the Yuan Dynasty, and that distilled liquor only emerged in the Yuan Dynasty. Therefore, in the Yuan Dynasty what the Chinese called distilled liquor, such as *halaji*, *aliqi* and so on, were all transliterations of *'araq* or *arrack*.[34] The Uyghur, Mongolian, and Manchu languages all belong to the Altaic system, so they had identical origins and their vocabulary has mutual borrowings. Mongolian also has a few Arabic terms which are not directly derived from Arabic, but come from Turkish. The Mongolian term *araki,* which is

---

[32] Liu Guangding 劉廣定, "The Problem of Chinese Liquor Distillation Prior to the Yuan Dynasty" 《元代以前中國蒸餾酒的問題》, in Collected Essays on the History of Chinese Science and Technology Editorial Group 中國科技史論文集編輯小組, ed., *Collected Essays on the History of Chinese Science and Technology* 《中國科技史論文集》 (Taipei: Linking Publishing Co. Ltd. 聯經出版事業公司, 1995), p. 212.

[33] Yuasa Mitsutomo 湯浅光朝, *A Chronological Table of Science and Cultural History Explained* (*Kaisetsu kagaku bunkashi nenpyō* [1966 nen zōhoban]) 『解説科学文化史年表 [1966 年増補版] 』. (Tokyo: Chūō kōron sha 中央公論社, 1966), p. 34. Another relatively reliable source shows that distilled alcoholic beverages became available around 1100 CE in Italy. Cf. Charles J. Singer, *A History of Technology*, vol. 2 of *The Mediterranean Civilizations and the Middle Ages, c. 700 B. C. to c. A. D . 1500* (Oxford: Clarendon Press, 1956), pp. 103-46.

[34] Liu Guangding 劉廣定, "The Problem of Chinese Liquor Distillation Prior to the Yuan Dynasty" 《元代以前中國蒸餾酒的問題》, pp. 198-9.

explained as "liquor, or alcoholic beverage made from milk" and the Turkish term araq were both derived from the Arabic term *'araq*.[35] The sequence of linguistic diffusion was from Arabic to Turkish to Mongolian. The ancient Chinese texts also seem to reflect and confirm this conjecture. After the Mongol Empire's campaign in Europe, distillation technology was introduced into China. This is supported by Xu Youren 許有壬, a Yuan official, in the prologue to his poem *Ode to the Wine Dew in Xie Shuzhai's Poem* 詠酒露次解恕齋韻, in which Xu Youren says that distillation came from the Western Regions.[36] The "Western Regions" as used here was a general term referring to all of the regions to the west of China, including Western Asia and even Europe. Distillation would have been first introduced to and spread through the northern area ruled by the Mongols. Based on the details provided in Yuan literature, the distillation of *alaji* was a very mature technology right from the beginning. The earliest such record of liquor distillation technology might be in the *Essential Arts and Assorted Techniques for Family Living* 居家必用事類全集 finished in the fifth year of the Dade 大德 reign period (1301). The entry "The Burnt-Wine Method of the Southern Tribal Folk" 南番燒酒法 reads as follows:

> The exotic name of this wine burning method is *aliqi* 阿裹乞. Take any kind of substandard wine, be it sweet, sour, insipid, or light. Pour it into a pot until it is about 80 percent full. Place another pot on top of the first one, with the two mouths facing each other at a slight angle. Bore a hole in the side of the empty pot and attach to it a hollow bamboo tube to act as a drain pipe. The other end of the tube is placed in the mouth of a second empty pot which acts as a receiver. Fill the space around the mouths of the two pots with pieces of porcelain or pottery and then seal it with a lute made

---

[35] Nikolaus N. Poppe, *Vergleichende Grammatik der altaischen Sprachen*, translated into Chinese by Zhou Jianqi 周建奇 as *An Introduction to Altaic Linguistics* 《阿爾泰語言學導論》 (Hohhot: Inner Mongolia Education Press 内蒙古教育出版社, 2004), p. 210. As the authors note, this opinion might have come from B. Ia. Vladimirtsov (Борис Яковлевич Владимирцов), a famous Mongolist of the former Soviet Union.

[36] "其法出西域, 由尚方達貴家, 今汗漫天下矣." Xu Youren 許有壬, chapter sixteen of "Collection of the Zhizheng Reign Period" 《至正集》, in *Beijing Library Ancient Books Rare Edition Series* 《北京圖書館古籍珍本叢刊》, vol. 95 (Beijing: Bibliography and Document Publishing House 書目文獻出版社, 1988), pp. 85-6.

> of a mixture of paper fiber and lime (so that the still will be airtight). Set the lower pot firmly on a large urn filled with the ashes of burnt paper. Place two to three *jin* 斤 of hot, burning charcoal in the ashes around the pot. The wine in the pot soon begins to boil. The vapor rises into the empty pot and condenses along its sides. The condensate flows into the bamboo tube and is collected in the receiver. The product is colorless, just like pure water. The distillate from sour wine is tangy and sweet, while that from weak wine tends to be sweet. About one third of the original volume can be recovered as good (distilled) wine. This method can be applied to any kind of wine.[37]

This technique of liquor distillation underwent modification to its method after being introduced into the Chinese proper. In another text, a distillation method with a similar mechanism, but different devices is recorded. Zhu Derun 朱德潤, who lived in the early fourteenth century, described the apparatus and workflow of distilling liquor in his *Rhapsody on Yalaiji Liquor* 軋賴機酒賦 as follows:

> The brewing ware is as precise as a lock and key, and the wine becomes warm or cool. The special steamer 殊甑 is a single vessel and has two rings. The pan 鐺 has a ring foot enclosing a concavity. The wine is filled in (the steamer), and it is closed seamlessly. Soon, when the flame is raging, the wine is boiling; the chaotic universe is filled with thick fog, and the primary vigor is ignited in the center. As the fog rises, it condenses. It is as spectacular as clouds rising and rain falling and as exquisite as mists vanishing

[37] "南番燒酒法 (番名阿裏乞). 右件不拘酸甜淡薄, 一切味不正之酒, 裝八分一甏, 上斜放一空甏, 二口相對. 先于空甏邊穴一竅, 安以竹管作嘴, 下再安一空甏, 其口盛住上竹嘴子. 向二甏口邊, 以白磁椀楪片, 遮掩令密, 或瓦片亦可. 以紙筋搗石灰, 厚封四指, 入新大缸内坐定. 以紙灰實滿. 灰内埋燒熟硬木炭火二三斤許, 下于甏邊. 令甏内酒沸, 其汗騰上空甏中, 就空甏中竹管内, 卻溜下所盛空甏内. 其色甚白, 與清水無異, 酸者味辛甘, 淡者味甘, 可得三分之一好酒. 此法臘煮等酒皆可燒." *Essential Arts and Assorted Techniques for Family Living* 《居家必用事類全集》 (Beijing: Bibliography and Document Publishing House 書目文獻出版社, 1988), p. 141. English translation by Dr. Joseph Needham, slightly modified.

> and dews dripping. The wine in the steamer is exhausted, and (the condensed spirit) flows from the top to the four sides.[38]

The apparatus was a "special steamer," the special feature of which was that it was divided into two sections, with two rim rings between which a circular gutter was formed, which fitted the pan tightly. When a fire underneath the cauldron 鼎 brought the wine to a boil, the steam rose and met the center of the pan bottom, and after encountering the cold the condensed distillate flowed along the pan bottom into the circular gutter around the sides of the steamer. The working principle and the form of the apparatus of the bronze pot that Zhu Derun describes here is identical to that of the Qinglong and Bairin Left Banner stills discussed above. Now let us look again at the raw material thrown into the pot. In the prologue of his rhapsody Zhu noted that "(*yalaiji*) is the transliteration of double-brewed wine." Hu Sihui also said, "heat superior wine to the boiling point and collect the dew, this is *alaji* liquor." Later it was also found that not only good wines could be used to boil into *alaji,* but that "soured wines could also be used."[39] Thus, we have made it clear that *alaji* is a kind of so-called "double-brewed" liquor made by a distillation technique using wine as a raw material. Xiong Mengxiang 熊夢祥, who lived at the end of the Yuan Dynasty, noted in his *Gazetteer of the Split Ford* 析津志 that grape wine and jujube wine were also "burnt (distilled) into *halaji* 哈剌吉 (*alaji*)."[40] Although *alaji* was a kind of wine made from "double-brewed" raw materials, the milk wine popular in the Mongolian region also could be a satisfactory factor of production. Therefore it may not be reckless to

---

[38] "觀其釀器扃鑰之機, 酒候温涼之殊. 甑一器而兩圈, 鐺外環而中窪. 中實以酒, 仍械合之無餘. 少焉, 火熾既盛, 鼎沸爲湯. 包混沌於鬱蒸, 鼓元氣於中央. 薰陶漸漬, 凝結爲煬. 滃渤若雲蒸而雨滴, 霏微如霧融而露瀼. 中涵既竭於連燒, 頂溜咸濡於四旁." Zhu Derun 朱德潤, "Rhapsody on Yalaiji Liquor" 《軋賴機酒賦》, in chapter three of his *Collected Works from the Studio for Self-Reflection* 《存復齋文集》, in Gu Tinglong 顧廷龍 , ed., *Continuation and Correction of the Complete Library of the Four Branches of Literature* 《續修四庫全書》 (Shanghai: Shanghai Ancient Books Press 上海古籍出版社, 1995-2002), ch. 1324, pp. 282-3.

[39] *Essential Arts and Assorted Techniques for Family Living* 《居家必用事類全集》, p. 141, the entry "The Way of Making Yeast" 《造麯法》.

[40] Xiong Mengxiang 熊夢祥, *Gazetteer of the Split Ford* [Beijing] *Compiled and Edited* 《析津志輯佚》 (Beijing: Beijing Ancient Books Publishers 北京古籍出版社, 1983), p. 239.

infer that the stills unearthed at Bairin Left Banner and Qinglong were this type of distillation apparatuses for turning milk wine into liquor.

5

The Ming Dynasty text *Interpretation* 譯語, written by Min'eshanren 岷峨山人, records the development of milk wine (koumiss) production methods in the Mongolian region:

> The Northern nomads used to pour animal milk into leather bags to brew it into wine, the taste of which was very thin. This was described by the Tang poet Gao Shi 高適 as "a thousand cups of 'prisoner's brew' can not make them drunk." In recent times they pour milk into a steamer 甑 (made of pewter or wood), just as the people in the Central Plains [China proper] distill liquor. The liquor made in this way is very fragrant and strong, very little of which may make people drunk. In the third or fourth month of every year, when mares are giving birth to foals, the nomads begin to make milk liquor (the way is to firmly tie foals somewhere, then the mares will come up to feed them; the nomads take this chance to get their milk to make koumiss; the dregs will be curdled and be made into cheese or used in other foods). At this time every household is making liquor and every person is drinking greedily.[41]

The method of making koumiss or other milk wine by putting animal milk in leather bags and accelerating the fermentation by punching (strongly churning) was invented by the nomadic people of the northern frontiers very early. In the *History of the Former Han* 漢書 there are records concerning this low-alcohol beverage.[42] Koumiss fermented by

---

[41] "虜素以獸乳置於皮袋中, 釀酒, 味極薄. 唐高適所謂'虜酒千鍾不醉人'者是也. 近則置於甑［或以錫或以木為之］, 如中國燒酒法, 得酒味極香洌, 飲少輒醉. 每歲三四月中, 牝馬生駒時［虜於此時, 率挐馬駒栓繫, 則牝馬皆來, 因而取乳造酒; 其凝結成滓者, 則作酪, 殫為食］, 家家造酒, 人人嗜飲." Min'eshanren 岷峨山人, *Interpretation* 《譯語》, in Wu Jian 吳堅, ed., *Collected Documents from Northwest China* 《中國西北文獻叢書》 (Lanzhou: Lanzhou Ancient Books Book Company 蘭州古籍書店, 1990), vol. 79, p. 507.

[42] It is recorded by Ban Gu 班固 in the *History of the Former Han* that "The Grand Keeper of Equipages 太僕 was a Qin office. [Its occupant] had charge of the [imperial]

being punched many times was handed down in the northern steppe region over a great many years, and later the nomad nobility made some improvements to it. Xu Ting 徐霆, an envoy of the Southern Song Dynasty to the Mongol Empire in the 1230s, saw black koumiss: "this is punched for seven or eight days; the more it is punched, the clearer it is; the clear koumiss does not smell nasty. I only drank it one time here, and never saw it elsewhere."[43] Black koumiss was a very rare and precious alcoholic beverage, which common people could not drink or even see. William of Rubruck, a European traveler in the 13th century, during his travels on the Mongolian steppe saw "*caracosmos*" (black koumiss) and

---

equipages and horses. He had two assistants 丞. Among his subordinate offices there were the three Directors 令 of the Great Stables, of the Inner Compound (Palace) Stables 未央[廄], and of the Household Mares 家馬. Each of them had five assistants and one Commandant 尉 <Yan Shigu 顏師古 glosses: '*Jiama* 家馬 were the horses used for private purposes by the emperor, not for sacrifice, military or other official affairs, so they were called Household Mares (*Jiama*) 家馬.'> ....In the first year of the Taichu 太初 reign period of Emperor Wu (104 BCE), the title [of the office of] Household Mares was changed to [that of] the Mare Milker 挏馬 and for the first time the Imperial Chariot Stables 路軨 were established. <Ru Chun 如淳 glosses: '[They] had charge of mares that give milk. They made double bags of leather which would hold several *dou* to contain the mare's milk. Tong 挏 is to take from [the mares'], nipples above [the bag], hence the office was named the Mare Milker 挏馬.' It was recorded in the *Monograph on Ritual and Music* 《禮樂志》 in the *History of the Former Han* 《漢書》 that the imperial chancellor, Kong Guang 孔光 memorialized that the office of music should be reduced by seventy-two persons 'to prepare the wine from milking mares for the Provisioner 大官.' At present in Liangzhou 梁州 [in present-day southern Shaanxi province] koumiss 馬酪 is likewise called mare's wine 馬酒.'>"

"太僕, 秦官, 掌輿馬, 有兩丞. 屬官有大廄、未央、家馬三令, 各五丞一尉<師古曰: '家馬者, 主供天子私用, 非大祀戎事軍國所須, 故謂之家馬也.'>...武帝太初元年更名家馬為挏馬, 初置路軨 <如淳曰: '主乳馬, 以韋革為夾兜, 受數斗, 盛馬乳, 挏取其上肥, 因名曰挏馬. 禮樂志丞相孔光奏省樂官七十二人, 給大官挏馬酒. 今梁州亦名馬酪為馬酒'>." See Ban, Gu 班固, *History of the Former Han* 《漢書》, "Tables of Official Posts of High Ranking Officials, First Part" 《百官公卿表上》 (Beijing: Zhonghua Book Company 中華書局, 1962), pp. 729-30. The English translation is by Homer Dubs (here modified) and as of this writing is available on-line at: http://libweb.uoregon.edu/ec/e-asia/read/Dubs_Vol_IV.pdf, pp. 60-2.

43 "此實撞之七, 八日; 撞多則愈清, 清則氣不膻. 祇此一次飲得, 他處更不曾見." Wang Guowei 王國維, *A Brief History of the Black Tatars Annotated* 《黑韃事略箋證》, in *Posthumous Papers of Wang Guowei* 《王國維遺書》 (Shanghai: Shanghai Ancient Books Book Company 上海古籍書店, 1983), vol. 13, ch. 57.

used a rather long piece of writing to record its production procedure.[44] However, the Mongolian people had not been using the method of distillation to get Koumiss for a very long time, and Rubruck also did not describe distillation — perhaps he only wrote about products that were rare in Europe. The description in *Interpretation* matches the diffusion history of liquor distillation, especially the device described as a steamer 甑 and the method "just as the people in the Central Plains [China proper] distill liquor." The top parts of the Bairin Left Banner and Qinglong stills are both in the shape of a steamer, the sizes of which are similar to the cauldrons popular in the steppe area during the Mongol-Yuan period with a diameter of approximately 40 cm.[45] Xiao Daheng 蕭大亨 methodically described the procedure for distilling koumiss in his *Customs of the Northern Barbarians* 北虜風俗:

> Just milked mare's milk is too sweet to drink; two or three days later it will be too sour to drink and can only be used to make liquor, the way of which is nothing different from our way of burning (distilling) wine. The first time it is milk which is being burnt; the second time it is wine (distilled from the milk); the end product after three or four times of burning is the strongest liquor, which is only presented to the lords as tribute or used to entertain guests, but not drunk on ordinary days.[46]

Drinking was an important component of traditional culture over the whole of the Mongolian steppe and the only means for people to associate.

---

[44] William of Rubruck, "The Journey of William of Rubruck," in Christopher Dawson, et al., *The Mongol Mission: Narratives and Letters of the Franciscan Missionaries in Mongolia and China in the Thirteenth and Fourteenth Centuries*. (New York: Sheed and Ward, 1955), pp. 98-9.

[45] China Millennium Monument World Art Museum 中華世纪壇藝術館 and Inner Mongolia Autonomous Region Museum 内蒙古自治區博物館, eds., *Genghis Khan: The Ancient Nomadic Culture of Northern China* 《成吉思汗: 中國古代北方草原遊牧文化》 (Beijing: Beijing Press 北京出版社 2004). The iron cauldrons listed on pp. 296-9 are all about 40 cm in diameter.

[46] "馬乳初取者, 太甘不可食; 越二三日, 則太酸不可食, 惟取之以造酒. 其酒與我燒酒無異. 始以乳燒之, 次以酒燒之, 如此三四次, 則酒味最厚; 非奉上敬賓, 不輕飲也." Xiao Daheng 蕭大亨, *Customs of the Northern Barbarians* 《北虜風俗》, the entry "Food and so on" 《食用》 (Taipei: Kuangwen Books 廣文書局, 1972), p. 13.

Many people were even deeply addicted to drink. Chinggis Khan repeatedly criticized drunkards in his last edicts and finally had no alternative but to say that if there was no way to entirely stop drinking, then in each month at most three bouts of drinking would be permitted. Drinking more than three times in a month would be considered a fault, two times would be better, and only one time would be best of all. And those who completely stopped drinking would be greatly rewarded.[47] The extraordinary consumption of liquor provided a powerful impetus for the development of liquor manufacturing. When distillation technology was introduced to the Mongols, the quality of the distilled alcoholic beverages rose rapidly. As Xu Youren of the Yuan Dynasty said, distillation skills were "diffused from the Imperial Manufactories 尚方 to the nobility and now spread everywhere under heaven."[48] At the very beginning distilled liquor was only popular among the nobility, and later it spread to the common people. Koumiss was a daily beverage of Mongolia, so the simple quantity of consumption could not act as a standard for social discrimination. So how many times liquor was distilled became a key choice for the Mongolian nobility. The quality of distilled koumiss rose according to the drinkers' position in the social hierarchy. Some have said that there were five ranks of distilled koumiss among the Mongol peoples: arkhi (αγχυ), arz (αγZ), khorz (XOγУ), sharz (щγΔZr), and dun (gүн), having differing alcohol content of between 9-11 and 30 or so percent.[49] Compared to non-distilled koumiss, the alcohol content of which was generally one to two percent, this was great progress. Similar koumiss grade titles given by the Kalmyk people were also found in Pallas' travels: their koumiss distilled from the raw material (Arr'ki) for the first time was called Dang, koumiss distilled for the second time was called Arsa, and

---

[47] Rashīd al-Dīn, *Jāmi' al-Tawārīkh* (*Compendium of Chronicles*), translated into Chinese by Yu Dajun 余大鈞, et al., as《史集》 (Beijing: The Commercial Press 商務印書館, 1997), vol. 1, pt. 2, p. 358.

[48] "由尚方達貴家，今汗漫天下矣." Xu Youren 許有壬, chapter sixteen of "Collection of the Zhizheng Reign Period"《至正集》, pp. 85-6.

[49] "Монголам известно пять степеней перегонки водка (*архи, арз, хорз, шарз, дун*), шкала крепости которых возрастает от 9-11 до 30°." Наталия Львовна Жуковская (N. L. Zhukovskaya), "Пища кочевников Центральной Азии: К вопросу об экологических основах формирования модели питания" ("The Food of the Nomads of Central Asia: On the Problem of the Ecological Basis of the Nutrient Model"), *Советская этнография* (*Soviet Ethnography*), 1979, no. 5, p. 72.

that for the third time Chorza. Further distillations were usually not done, but the Kalmyk people had terms referring to koumisses distilled for as many as six times, which were Schingza and Dingza.[50] The raw material for the Mongols to make this kind of liquor (*sayali-yinariqi*) was mainly cow's milk and mare's milk. The products were ranked from the first "pot" (time of distillation) through the sixth "pot." The sixth pot, "dungsugur," was the essence of koumiss and was paid as tribute to the emperor.[51] However, "dungsugur" seems not to have been the ultimate rank of koumiss. In the Mongol version of the Gesar Khan, Berthold Laufer found eight terms referring to koumiss, which were all supposed to be distilled from the first koumiss (*araki—alaji*). Their names are: *aradsa* (*araja*), *xoradsa* or *xuradsa*, *širadsa*, *boradsa*, *takpa*, *tikpa*, *marba,* and *mirba*.[52] *Xoradsa* or *xuradsa* and *širadsa* all have the same root and are derived from *aradsa*. *Širadsa* was "wine distilled for the fourth time (*esprit de vin quadruple*)."[53] Despite the fact that drinking simply-processed koumiss was a routine fact of life for the nomads, the ranking of food quality was a byproduct of the social hierarchy, for which the example of alcoholic beverages is especially outstanding. In nomadic society alcohol was one of the few luxury products of the nobility. The brewing of black koumiss mentioned above had been entrusted to a particular tribe since Chinggis Khan's reign.[54] When distillation technology was introduced, the people in each privileged social class

---

[50] "Der zum erstenmal vom *Arr'ki* übergetriebne Branntwein wird *Dang* genennt; nach der zweisten Verdoppelung heißt er *Arsa* und nach der dritten Chorza. Weiter pflegen sie nicht zu gehen, sie haben aber noch bis zur sechsten Rectification eigne Nahmen, wovon die ersten *Schingza* und *Dingza* sind." Peter Simon Pallas, *Sammlungen historischer Nachrichten über die mongolischen Völkerschaften in einem ausführlichen Auszuge* (Frankfort and Leipzig: J. G. Fleischer, 1779), p. 207.

[51] Cf. Kōkebuyan 呼和竇音, ed., *Monggol-un jang úile-yin mōrdel* 《蒙古風俗追溯》 (*Tracing Mongolian Customs*) ([Qaiilar]: Ōbōr Monggol-un Suyul-un Keblel- ún Qoriy-a (Inner Mongolia Cultural Press) 内蒙古文化出版社, 1988), pp. 89-91 (published in Mongolian); Rongsuhe 榮蘇赫, *A History of Literature of the Mongolian Nationality* 《蒙古族文學史》, vol. 1 (Hohhot: Inner Mongolia People's Press 内蒙古人民出版社, 2000), p. 553.

[52] Berthold Laufer, *Sino-Iranica*, p. 235.

[53] Ibid.

[54] A Qïpčaq tribe was in charge of making mare's milk wine for the Mongol chiefs. See Wang Guowei 王國維, *A Brief History of the Black Tatars Annotated* 《黑韃事略箋證》, in *Posthumous Papers of Wang Guowei* 《王國維遺書》 (Shanghai: Shanghai Ancient Books Book Company 上海古籍書店, 1983), vol. 13, ch. 57.

could each enjoy the koumiss whose quality matched their status.[55] Making every higher ranked koumiss required the use of lower ranked koumiss as raw material. Therefore, the koumisses of the fifth or sixth rank (let alone koumiss of the highest — the eighth rank) would consume surprisingly large quantities of koumiss of the first rank. As Xiao Daheng 蕭大亨 noted, the Mongol people "have wines of many titles and names, most of which are made from milk; several cups of the thickest one will get one deeply drunk."[56] The various titles and names of koumisses that are confusing to outsiders were actually names for koumisses distilled for different times and of different qualities. Efficient apparatuses, such as the Bairin Left Banner and Qinglong stills, could be used to produce a more purified koumiss.

In the feasts held by the Mongols, the offering of koumiss by the host signified the degree of importance they attached to their guests. By means of providing the best things, nomadic peoples expressed the respect of the host for his guests. When koumiss was being poured into a silver cup, all of the attendees at the feast first were silent; when this cup of koumiss was received by the most celebrated guest, this guest would ritually dip his finger into the koumiss and drip some drops into the hearth and onto the stove pan as offerings to the gods of fire and the hearth, and then would savor the koumiss. Then the host would perform the same ceremony with other guests in the order of their status. Each guest drank three silver-cups full of alcohol distributed by the host, and then the guests would do the same in the same order toward the host and others. Only when all of the traditional ceremonies were completely finished would the attendees be able to continue drinking without restraint.[57] This custom led to the situation that "every household makes liquor and every person drinks greedily — the Mongols drink like bulls without break. They get

---

[55] For example, in Mongolian folk songs lauding Chinggis Khan we can find this lyric: "Let us fill the re-heated milk-wine into our cups, celebrate and sing together." See D. Sambuu 達・桑布. *Monggol arad-un daġuu-yin cubural. Sili-yin Ġool Ayimaġ-un* (*A Collection of Mongolian Folk Songs from Xilin Gol League*) 《蒙古民歌叢書. 錫林郭勒盟集》 ([Kōkeqota]: Ōbōr Monggol-un Arad-un Keblel-ún Qoriy-a; Ōbōr Monggol-un Sinquva Bicig-ún Delgegúr tarqaġaba, 1988), p. 29 (published in Mongolian).

[56] Xiao Daheng 蕭大亨, *Customs of the Northern Barbarians* 《北虜風俗》, the entry "Food and so on" 《食用》 (Taipei: Kuangwen Books 廣文書局, 1972), p. 13.

[57] Gösta Montell, "Distilling in Mongolia," *Ethnos II*, 1937, no. 5, p. 321.

toweringly inebriated and sober up suddenly, no matter whether it is day or night."[58]

Figure 9 The Assemblage of the Bairin Left Banner Still and an Iron Tripod of the Mongol Empire Period

Although distillation technology had developed rapidly in different regions and civilizations, the critical technology was the important factor restricting progress. In the Bairin Left Banner and Qinglong stills we can see some of the key technical details. The cool water in the container (condenser) allows more of the steam to be condensed, and the spout allows the heated water be drained off easily; the assembly of the dome-shaped top (the convex bottom of the condenser) and the circular gutter

[58] "家家造酒，人人嗜飲［虜飲如牛不歇氣］. 兀然而醉，恍然而醒，無間晝夜." Min'eshanren, *Interpretation*, in Wu Jian, ed., *Collected Documents from Northwest China* (Lanzhou: Lanzhou Ancient Books Book Company, 1990), vol. 79, p. 507.

allow the distillate to be thoroughly collected; the direct addition of the fermented milk (primary koumiss) makes the operation of the apparatus simple and allows continuous distillation to be conducted. Furthermore, the tripod bracket which was cast and used during the Mongol Empire period[59] easily supported iron cauldrons 40 cm or so in diameter. This was the best stand for the still (figure 9), and under it the fuel could combust well.

Although this apparatus is easier to use and more effective than other methods, nonetheless it certainly did not spread especially widely, and the milk liquor distilling methods used across the vast Mongolian steppes up to today are not the technical offspring of the Bairin Left Banner and Qinglong stills, but rather are the "Mongolian type" stills mentioned by Hommel and Needham, discussed above. The reason may be that these stills have very limited volumes, which cannot satisfy the demands of mass consumption, unlike the so-called "Mongolian style" stills, which can make large amounts of low-quality koumiss in a short time and provide for many more consumers than the bronze stills can. In short, the Bairin Left Banner and Qinglong stills, which were made during the Mongol-Yuan period for the distilling of milk liquor, are the earliest alcoholic beverage distillation apparatuses seen in China to date. The discovery of the Bairin Left Banner still gives us a new opportunity to discuss liquor distillation technology and a route to obtaining a more in-depth understanding of this issue.

Postscript: During the writing of this paper the author received great assistance from Ms. Su Dong 蘇東 of the Inner Mongolia Museum, and the author takes the opportunity here to express his deep appreciation to her.

---

[59] China Millennium Monument World Art Museum and Inner Mongolia Autonomous Region Museum, eds., *Genghis Khan: The Ancient Nomadic Culture of Northern China* (Beijing: Beijing Press, 2004). On p. 296 an iron tripod "bracket" unearthed from Qingshui 清水 County, Inner Mongolia is listed with an iron cauldron it supported.

Reflections on the Appellations of Xiongnu Shanyu Titles

Luo Xin 羅新

As the highest position in the Xiongnu 匈奴 leadership, Shanyu is the earliest and most definite title found in Chinese sources for the supreme ruler of the polities formed by the Inner Asian peoples. After the evolution of the nomadic polities reached a new stage and the Xiongnu state emerged, political power struggles within the polities were mainly manifested as contests over the position of Shanyu.[1] Regardless of debates and explorations into the origin and etymology of the title Shanyu,[2] undoubtedly after the Xiongnu state was established Shanyu became the highest position within the political system in steppes, and, after this position solidified, it became an important part of Inner Asia's political system. Its influence reached far and wide and was a powerful force until around the fourth century CE, when it was replaced by the title of Qaghan.

The purpose of this paper is not to discuss the problems surrounding the title of Shanyu, or its etymology, semantics, political functions, or other issues concerning the political culture of the Inner Asian peoples, as these issues have either been extensively researched or are currently difficult to elaborate on.[3] Instead, this paper will focus on the appellations which always come before the title Shanyu and that are ornamental in nature. For example, among the Xiongnu Shanyu titles recorded in the *Records of the Grand Historian* 史記 and the *History of the Former Han* 漢書, some clearly have such appellations. The *History of the Former Han* records the death of Xulüquanqu 虛閭權渠 Shanyu and the plotting of Zhuanqu'e 顓渠閼 and Zuodaqiequdulongqi 左大且渠都隆奇, thus: "The Worthy King of the Right Tuqitang 屠耆堂 was established as Woyanqudi

---

[1] Owen Lattimore, *Inner Asian Frontiers of China* (Boston: Beacon Press, 1962), p. 452.

[2] Many scholars have delved deeply into the questions of the origin and etymology of the word Shanyu. Uchida Ginpu 内田吟風 gives a comprehensive introduction and discussion – see his 「単于の称号と「匈奴単于庭」の位置に就いて」 "On Shanyu Titles and the Position of the Xiongnu Shanyu Court" in 『北アジア史研究・匈奴篇』 *Studies on North Asian History: The Xiongnu* (Kyoto: 同朋舎出版, 1975), pp. 83-91.

[3] Peter B. Golden, *An Introduction to the History of the Turkic Peoples* (Wiesbaden: Otto Harrassowitz, 1992), pp. 57-60.

握衍朐鞮 Shanyu."[4] Here, Shanyu is an institutionalized political title with an office, Tuqitang is the given name, and Woyanqudi is the appellation for the Shanyu title. Later, King Guxi 故夕, "together with Wushanmu 烏禅幕 and the nobility of the left established Jihoushan 稽侯狦 as Huhanxie 呼韓邪 Shanyu."[5] Here, Jihoushan is the given name, and Huhanxie is the appellation for the Shanyu title. Woyanqudi and Huhanxie are ornamental words added before the title, and their inclusion is definitely not optional. After Tuqitang and Jihoushan became Shanyus, they received their respective appellations, which are Woyanqudi and Huhanxie. From then on they were referred to by their appellations and not by their given names. In the historical list of Shanyu titles, their own appellations for the Shanyu title gave them a unique identity.

This paper looks at the nature and structure of the political titulary of the Xiongnu, which includes both the Shanyu title and its appellations, from the perspective of Inner Asian political traditions, and attempts to restore the original features of the appellations for Xiongnu Shanyus during the Western Han. On this foundation we will investigate Huhanxie Shanyu and focus especially on the issue of the appellations of Southern Xiongnu Shanyus during the Eastern Han in order to seek out the great changes in Xiongnu political traditions that were caused by the strong influence of Chinese Han Dynasty culture.

I. Appellations of Western Han Xiongnu Shanyus

According to the *History of the Former Han*, after Huhanxie, Xiongnu Shanyus during the Western Han all had appellations for their Shanyu titles. For example, there were the so-called Five Shanyus during the Huhanxie period: apart from Huhanxie there was Tuqi 屠耆 Shanyu (whose given name was Boxutang 薄胥堂); the western King Hujie 呼揭, who named himself Hujie Shanyu; King Youaojian 右奥鞬, who named himself Cheli 車犁 Shanyu; and Commander Wuji 烏籍, who named himself Wuji Shanyu. Later, Tuqi Shanyu's younger cousin King Xiuxun 休旬 named himself Runzhen 閏振 Shanyu, and Huhanxie Shanyu's older brother Hutuwusi 呼屠吾斯 named himself Zhizhiguduhou 郅支骨都侯

[4] *History of the Former Han* 《漢書》, ch. 94, "Account of the Xiongnu" 《匈奴傳》 (Zhonghua Book Company punctuated edition, 1962), p. 3789.

[5] Ibid., p. 3790.

Shanyu. Once these Shanyus came to power they immediately obtained their own appellations for their Shanyu titles. During the late Western Han, Huhanxie's sons successively became Shanyus, and, following the rule, they each had their own appellations for their Shanyu titles. The practice of being given appellations for their Shanyu titles seems to have originated in the Xiongnu political culture, so does it follow that all Shanyus during the Western Han were given appellations for their Shanyu titles?

The earliest Xiongnu Shanyus mentioned in the *Records of the Grand Historian* are Touman 頭曼 (Tümen) and Modu 冒頓 (Baghatur):[6] "The Xiongnu Shanyu was called Touman…and the prince was named Modu."[7] From this account Touman and Modu seem to be their given names. After Modu died, "His son Jizhou 稽粥 became ruler, with the title Laoshang 老上 Shanyu."[8] Clearly, Jizhou was his name, and Laoshang (meaning "elder") was the appellation of his Shanyu title. However, the *Records of the Grand Historian* later says, "Laoshang Jizhou Shanyu first became ruler," which seems to imply that the appellation and the name can be used interchangeably.[9] According to the *Records of the Grand Historian*,

[6] The record of the Warring States battle between the Zhao 照 general Li Mu 李牧 and the Xiongnu in the *Records of the Grand Historian* 《史記》 (Zhonghua Book Company punctuated edition, 1959), ch. 81, "Biographies of Lian Po and Lin Xiangru" 《廉頗藺相如列傳》 mentions Xiongnu Shanyus; ch. 86, "Biographies of Assassins" 《刺客列傳》 records Ju Wu's 鞠武 admonition to Prince Dan of Yan 燕太子丹 as saying, "I ask you to make an agreement with the three Jins 晉 in the West, unite with Qi 齊 and Chu 楚 in the South, and pay off the Shanyu in the North" – see pp. 2450 and 2529. Therefore, in the Warring States period there already were Xiongnu Shanyus. However, these records do not state the names or appellations of these Shanyus, so there is no evidence from which to study the Xiongnu Shanyu lineage. Clear information on the Shanyu lineage and their names begins with Touman 頭曼 and Modu 冒頓.

[7] *Records of the Grand Historian* 《史記》, ch. 110, "Account of the Xiongnu" 《匈奴傳》, pp. 2887-8.

[8] Ibid., p. 2898.

[9] Pei Yin's 裴駰 *Records of the Grand Historian, Collected Annotations* 《史記集解》 cites Xu Guang 徐廣 as saying, "One version has 'Jizhou 稽粥 the second Shanyu,' and after this they are all distinguished as younger brothers." See *Records of the Grand Historian*, ch. 110, "Account of the Xiongnu," p. 2898. According to Xu Guang's understanding, after Modu 冒頓 the Xiongnu Shanyu succession was based on a genealogy, such as the one created by Qin Shihuang 秦始皇 which established the second, third, on down to the ten thousandth generation. However, apart from this sentence of Xu Guang's, there are no historical records that can prove that appellations of Han Xiongnu Shanyu titles had the function of showing genealogical order.

"After Laoshang Jizhou Shanyu died, his son Junchen 軍臣 became Shanyu." Junchen died, and "Junchen Shanyu's brother, Yizhixie 伊稚斜, the Left Guli King 左谷蠡王, named himself Shanyu." Yizhixie died, and "his son Wuwei 烏維 became Shanyu."[10] Junchen, Yizhixie, and Wuwei are read as personal names and not appellations of their Shanyu titles. After Wuwei died, "his son Wushilu 烏師盧 became Shanyu, and, as he was young, his title was Young 兒 Shanyu."[11] Wushilu is written as Zhanshilu 詹師盧 in the *History of the Former Han*.[12] If it were not for his young age, could he be directly given appellation of Wu(Zhan)shilu Shanyu? After Young Shanyu, the *Records of the Grand Historian* also mentions Xulihu 呴犁湖 Shanyu and Qiedihou 且鞮侯 Shanyu, and views Xulihu and Qiedihou as personal names, rather than the appellations for their Shanyu titles.[13]

According to the *Records of the Grand Historian*, most of the Xiongnu Shanyus put their personal names before the word Shanyu, and apart from Laoshang Shanyu and Young Shanyu, none of them had appellations for their Shanyu titles. Why did these two Shanyus become exceptions? Furthermore, according to the *History of the Former Han*, the Xiongnu Shanyus of the late Western Han all clearly had appellations for their Shanyu titles, which are different from their original personal names, and the Shanyu title had to have an appellation to be official. How did this distinction occur? Was it that Xiongnu Shanyus did not originally have appellations for their Shanyu titles, and that the appellations only appeared during the late Western Han? I believe that the appellations of Xiongnu Shanyu titles were a part of the Xiongnu political system and originated in the ancient traditions of the Inner Asian political culture, rather than during the late Western Han. Under this interpretation, Xiongnu Shanyus all had appellations for their Shanyu titles. These appellations were not the names of the individuals before they became Shanyu, but were special titles given to them afterwards.

---

[10] *Records of the Grand Historian*, ch. 110, "Account of the Xiongnu," pp. 2904-12.

[11] Ibid., p. 2914.

[12] *History of the Former Han* 《漢書》, ch. 94, "Account of the Xiongnu," p. 3774.

[13] Xulihu 呴犁湖 – the *History of the Former Han* uses Julihu 句犁湖; see *History of the Former Han*, ch. 94, "Account of the Xiongnu," p. 3775.

In my paper "A Study of Qaghan Appellations"[14] I come to the conclusion that "the form of early political organizations began with titles, which then split into official appellations and official positions." This conclusion was arrived at by examining the appellations of the Qaghan titles and official titles of the Rouran 柔然 and the Turkic 突厥 peoples from the Northern Dynasties to the Tang Dynasty in order to further examine the evolution of early forms of political organization. The appellations for the Qaghan titles, which developed from an earlier system of titles, are a type of official appellation. This type of system can be traced back to early Chinese peoples and is especially prominent in the historical records of the northern ethnic groups. Each Qaghan would receive his own personal appellation for his Qaghan title during his coronation ceremony, and from this moment on he could only be called by the appellation of his Qaghan title – his original personal name could not be mentioned. The function of the appellation of the Qaghan title was to give the person who bore the title of Qaghan an entirely new identity. The appellations both of Qaghan titles and other official titles should be understood in these terms. According to the *History of the Northern Dynasties*, "It is the custom of the Rouran for the ruler and ministers to have titles based on their conduct and abilities, as was the case with the posthumous titles of China. After death, the title cannot be used again."[15] This is an important insight into the appellations of the Qaghan titles of the northern peoples and the political titulary tradition. We can see that in the Rouran political system ornamental appellations were given based on "conduct and abilities" – not only those for Qaghan titles, but also those for other official titles. From the perspective of the development of early political organizations, titular titles precede official titles, and official titles are the result of the solidification of certain titularity. These kinds of titularity originated from the concept of "conduct and abilities," and their basic function was to give their bearers a new identity, thereby instilling them with new powers.[16]

The problem of appellations of Xiongnu Shanyu titles should be understood within the greater background of this political culture.

---

[14] Luo Xin 羅新: "A Study of Qaghan Appellations" 《可汗號研究》, in *China Social Sciences* 《中國社會科學》, 2005, no. 2.

[15] *History of the Northern Dynasties* 《北史》, ch. 98, "Account of the Ruru" 《蠕蠕傳》, punctuated edition (Zhonghua Book Company, 1974), p. 3251.

[16] Luo Xin: "A Study of Qaghan Appellations."

Therefore, as each Shanyu has his own appellation, he was also known by this appellation. It was already quite complicated to understand the sequential order of a distant rival regime's Shanyus and quite difficult to correctly record the changes in the names, appellations, or titles of the Shanyus before and after they assumed power. Especially for Chinese officials, by the time they began to collect information on the Xiongnu, there was a spatial, political, and cultural gulf between the two empires. The Chinese understanding of the Xiongnu political titulary system had to wait until they established close relations with the Xiongnu, which was not until Han Dynasty Emperor Xuan's 宣 reign (73 BCE – 49 BCE). Because of this, I believe that the Shanyus that preceded Xulüquanqu in the *Records of the Grand Historian* and *History of the Former Han* were records of the appellations of their Shanyu titles and not their personal names. That is to say, the list of names from Touman, Modu, and Junchen all the way up to Xulüquanqu are not personal names, but rather the appellations of their Shanyu titles. The long-term interpretation of Touman and Modu as personal names was a mistake, and built on top of this mistake was the Han Dynasty's lack of knowledge of the Shanyu title system. For example, the above quote from the *Records of the Grand Historian* record of Modu's death that "his son Jizhou became ruler, with the title Laoshang Shanyu," makes a clear distinction between the name Jizhou before he became Shanyu and the appellation of his Shanyu title he later assumed, but the later "Laoshang Jizhou Shanyu first became ruler" complicates the issue. Most likely, the Han Dynasty paid close attention to the news surrounding the death of Modu Shanyu so they could learn the name used by Laoshang Shanyu before he assumed power. And most likely they also learned that it was only after he assumed power that "he was called Laoshang Shanyu." The Han Dynasty was not clear as to the relationship between the appellation of his Shanyu title and his original personal name, however. Similarly, in the *Records of the Grand Historian* record of Wuwei Shanyu's death, "his son Wu(Zhan)shilu became Shanyu, and as he was young, his title was Young Shanyu." Actually, Wu(Zhan)shilu is not a given name, but a formal appellation of the Shanyu title, and it was only because he was young that he was called Young Shanyu – this was not a formal appellation. Most Shanyu names and appellations were transliterations of the Xiongnu language, but the

"Young" in Young Shanyu is clearly a translation of the meaning.[17]

As I have already explained that Touman and Modu were the appellations of Shanyu titles and not personal names, understanding their meanings can give us a new perspective. Friedrich Hirth was the first to discover that Touman is the same as the Turkic word "tümen," meaning ten thousand.[18] Shiratori Kurakichi 白鳥庫吉 approves of this association and points out that "tümen" is also the Mongol and Manchu word for "ten thousand." So Touman represents ten thousand people or households.[19] Using this kind of word for a name may seem unsuitable, but it may be more reasonable if we think of it as an appellation of a Xiongnu Shanyu who was not yet strong enough to unite the nomadic tribes. Hirth also determined that Modu was the transliteration of the Turkic and Mongolic word "bagatur," a view that E. H. Parker agrees with.[20] Shiratori Kurakichi believes this should be the Mongolic "bagdo," which means "saintly," and cites an example of the Qing Dynasty northern desert Tatars paying respects to the Qing prince as Bogdo Khan.[21] More research into this could be done,[22] but it would be a safer bet to understand these words as an appellation he received when he obtain the Shanyu title after killing

---

[17] Shiratori Kurakichi 白鳥庫吉, in his analysis of the origin of the Longxi Xianbei Qifu 隴西鮮卑乞伏 tribal titles from the Sixteen Kingdoms period believes that "Qifu" was the transliteration of the Mongolic word "köbun" or "köbung" and meant "son" or "child." Qifu Qaghan meant "child Qaghan," and Qifu was the Qaghan title – the Xiongnu "Young Shanyu" is used as an example. See Shiratori Kurakichi's 「東胡民族考」 "A Study of the Donghu Ethnic Group" in his *Research on Borderland Peoples* 『塞外民族研究』, vol. 1 (Tokyo: Iwanami Shoten 岩波書店, 1986 edition), pp. 145-6. Of course, I do not approve of Shiratori's analysis of the word "Qifu."

[18] Friedrich Hirth, *Sinologische Beiträge zur Geschichte der Türkvölker I: Die Ahnentafel Attila's nach Johannes von Thurócz* (St. Petersburg: Wissenschaften, 1900), p. 230.

[19] Shiratori Kurakichi 白鳥庫吉, "New Research on the History of the Western Regions" 「西域史上の新研究」 in his *Historical Research on the Western Regions* 『西域史研究』, vol. 1 (Tokyo: Iwanami Shoten 岩波書店, 1941 edition), pp. 223-4.

[20] E. H. Parker, *A Thousand Years of the Tartars* (London: 2002), p. 9.

[21] Shiratori Kurakichi 白鳥庫吉, *Historical Research on the Western Regions* 『西域史研究』, vol. 1, p. 224.

[22] Cen Zhongmian 岑仲勉: "The Etymology and Pronunciation of Modu" 《冒頓之語源及其音讀》, originally in *Northwest Newsletter* 《西北通訊》, vol. 3, no.1 (July, 1948), is included in Lin Gan 林幹, ed., *Collection of Selected Essays on the Xiongnu (1919-1979)* 《匈奴史論文選集（1919-1979）》 (Beijing: 1983), pp. 217-21.

his father and usurping the throne, rather than a personal name which he received when he was very young.

Now we turn to the problem of "Chengligutu 橕犁孤塗 Shanyu." According to the *History of the Former Han*: "The Shanyu had the surname Luandi 攣鞮, and he was called 'Chengligutu Shanyu' in his country. The Xiongnu call heaven 'chengli' 橕犁 and call a son 'gutu' 孤塗, and since the word Shanyu means great, he was called the Heavenly Shanyu."[23] Xun Yue's 荀悅 *Annals of the Han* 漢紀, chapter 11 says, "Since the Shang and Zhou Dynasty they (the Xiongnu and their ancestors) have troubled China a lot. When the Luandi family ruled the Xiongnu, people called them 'Chengliguturuo 橕犁孤塗若 Shanyu.' The Xiongnu call heaven 'chengli,' and call a son 'gutu,' as if to say the Son of Heaven. The Shanyu means great, so they were described in this way."[24] Clearly the latter passage was based on the former and some additions were made, such as "Ruo 若 Shanyu." Perhaps this refers to the posthumous Shanyu title "Ruodi" 若鞮 of the late Western Han and Eastern Han. If the *History of the Former Han* record is correct, then apart from the appellation of the Shanyu title, those who become Shanyu also had the title "Chengligutu Shanyu." The problem is that there is only one source for this, and records of Xiongnu emissaries and letters sent back and forth do not mention this title. In a letter from Modu Shanyu to Han Emperor Wen 文, he calls himself "The Great Xiongnu Shanyu Established by Heaven"; and in a letter from Laoshang Shanyu to Emperor Wen, he calls himself "The Great Xiongnu Shanyu Born of Heaven and Installed by the Sun and Moon."[25] The letter of Laoshang Shanyu was written by Zhonghang Yue 中行悅 of the Han, and Modu's letter was likely written by someone from the Han. Although they were "proud of their words," they could not avoid adopting some elements of the Chinese system, such as writing Great Shanyu instead of writing the appellation for the Shanyu title. Even though Modu and his son said they earned the praise of Heaven and believed that the Shanyu ruled by Heaven's grace, they did not claim the Shanyu was the "Son of Heaven." That is to say, that in Modu and his

---

[23] *History of the Former Han,* ch. 94, "Account of the Xiongnu," p. 3751.

[24] Xun Yue 荀悅, *Annals of the Han* 《漢紀》, ch. 11; see Zhang Lie's 張烈 annotated *Two Annals of the Han* 《兩漢紀》 (Zhonghua Book Company, 2002), p. 177.

[25] *Records of the Grand Historian*, ch. 110, "Xiongnu Biographies" 《匈奴列傳》, pp. 2896, 2899.

son's names for themselves we cannot find traces of "Chengligutu." Some scholars have recalled the letter sent by the Turk Qaghan [Shabolüe 沙鉢略] to Sui Emperor Wen, in which the he called himself "Great Turk Born of Heaven, Saintly Son of Heaven Sent to Earth, Yilijulushemoheshiboluo 伊利俱卢設莫何始波羅 [Ilig Külü Šad Bagha Išbara] Qaghan," and the Yuan Dynasty Mongolic style Chinese inscriptions which reads "Long Living Emperor with the Spirit of Heaven and Earth," and believe that this was an Inner Asian tradition.[26] However, the Turk Qaghan calling himself "Saintly Son of Heaven" was clearly just following the Sui system, and neither the word Qaghan nor the appellation "Yilijulushemoheshiboluo" of the Qaghan title have the meaning "Son of Heaven."

Therefore, I believe the *History of the Former Han* records on "Chengligutu" do not reflect the actual Xiongnu system of the appellations for Shanyu titles. This word was used by the Xiongnu when describing to the Chinese the position of Shanyu and follows the Chinese system, while originating from the Xiongnu language. Shiratori Kurakichi has found "chengli" to be the transliteration of the Mongolic "tängri," "tengeree," and "tangara," and the Turkic "tängri" means the "will of Heaven." "Gutu" is the transliteration of "hútta" of the Tungusic Apogir language and "gutó" of the Barguzin language, and both words mean "son."[27] Even though later scholars have had different opinions on the transliteration of "gutu,"[28] Shiratori's explanation of "chengli" as the transliteration of "tängri" has been widely accepted.[29] This research is, of course, of great use in understanding the relationship between the ancient Xiongnu language and the languages of the contemporary Altaic language family. However, it cannot help in clarifying the appellations of the Shanyu title system, because "Chengligutu" at the time was only an explanatory word and not a formal appellation or title. The *Collection of Literature Arranged by Categories* 藝文類聚 quotes Huangfu Mi's 皇甫謐 *Spring and Autumn of Xuanyan* 玄晏春秋, according to which a candle-carrying

[26] Feng Jiasheng 馮家昇, "The Xiongnu People and their Culture" 《匈奴民族及其文化》, in *Journal of Historical Geography* 《禹貢》, vol. 7, no. 5 (1937).

[27] Shiratori Kurakichi 白鳥庫吉, *Historical Research on the Western Regions* 『西域史研究』, vol. 1, p. 212.

[28] Edwin G. Pulleyblank, "The Consonantal System of Old Chinese: Part II," *Asia Major*, new series, vol. 9 (1963), pp. 206-65.

[29] Gerard Clauson, *An Etymological Dictionary of Pre-Thirteenth-Century Turkish* (Oxford: The Clarendon Press, 1972), pp. 523-4.

foreign slave explained "Tangligutu" 堂梨孤塗 as "Tangli, Son of Heaven, which the Xiongnu call their Shanyu, just as the Chinese have the Son of Heaven."[30] This foreign slave clearly regarded "Tangligutu" for the Shanyu as being modeled after the Chinese "Son of Heaven." Chen Sanping 陳三平 studied the heavy influence ancient Iranian culture had on the Altaic peoples by examining the ancient titles "Son of Heaven" and "Son of God."[31] When touching on the word "Chengligutu," he was inclined to disregard the foreign slave's words "Tangli Son of Heaven" and interpret "chengli" (tangli) directly as meaning Son of Heaven. I believe the foreign slave's response was an explanation of "Tangligutu," only, however, omitting the "gutu"; but based on this we cannot prove that "gutu" had no meaning. Overall, no matter how many comparative linguistic problems still exist, "Chengligutu" was a direct translation into the Xiongnu language of the Chinese "Son of Heaven." This was done so that the Shanyu would receive the protocol and position corresponding to that of the Chinese emperor, and a crude explanation was made to the Chinese. It was not an appellation of a Shanyu title that was stable or official in nature, or that was actually used within Xiongnu political life.[32]

To summarize, in the *Records of the Grand Historian* list of Shanyus from Touman to Qiedihou, apart from the entry giving Laoshang Shanyu's original name as Jizhou, all of the entries only give the appellations of the Shanyu title and not personal names. Due to the Chinese lack of understanding of the appellation system during Sima Qian's time, these appellations were seen as personal names. The *History of the Former Han* continues the *Records of the Grand Historian* account after Qiedihou Shanyu with Hulugu 狐鹿孤 Shanyu, Huyandi 壺衍鞮 Shanyu, and Xulüquanqu Shanyu, but changes the narrative. For example, when

---

[30] Ouyang Xun 歐陽詢, *Collection of Literature Arranged by Categories* 《藝文類聚》, ch. 80 (Shanghai: Shanghai Ancient Books Press 上海古籍出版社, 1982), p. 1371.

[31] Chen Sanping 陳三平, "Son of Heaven and Son of God: Interactions among Ancient Asiatic Cultures Regarding Sacral Kingship and Theophoric Names," *Journal of the Royal Asiatic Society*, series 3, vol. 12, no. 3 (2002), p. 308.

[32] Peter Boodberg had an article titled "Dayan, Činggis, and Shan-yü" in *Hu T'ien Han Yüeh Fang Chu* (*The Mirrorings of the Chinese Moon in a Barbarian Sky*) 《胡天漢月方諸》 (no. 2, April 1932) in which he discussed the titles of rulers in the ancient steppe empires of northern Asia and directly connects the meaning of "Chengligutu" with "said he was like a heavenly Shanyu." This is another result of the inflexible interpretations of the Han Dynasty. Reprinted in *Selected Works of Peter A. Boodberg*, compiled by Alvin P. Cohen (Berkeley: University of California Press, 1979), pp. 85-9.

Qiedihou Shanyu died, "his eldest son, the Left Wise King 左賢王, became Hulugu Shanyu"; when Hulugu Shanyu died, "his son, King Zuoguli 左谷蠡, became Huyandi Shanyu"; and when Huyandi Shanyu died, "his younger brother, Left Wise King 左賢王, became Xulüquanqu Shanyu."[33] This change in narrative does not allow for mistaking the appellation of the Shanyu title as a personal name and shows that the title was obtained only after rising to power. This shows that Ban Gu 班固 [author of the *History of the Former Han*] knew that before Hulugu Shanyu became Shanyu he was not called Hulugu, and it was only because his identity changed that he "became Hulugu Shanyu." According to our understanding of early political organizations, when Hulugu Shanyu was the Left Wise King, he should have had his own appellation for his title of Left Wise King that replaced his original personal name. During Han Emperor Xuan's 宣帝 reign the balance of power between the Chinese and the Xiongnu changed, and the previous state of tension for the most part dissipated. By this time the Chinese people already had quite a clear and deep understanding of Xiongnu society and its politics. Therefore, the *History of the Former Han* more accurately recorded the late Western Han Xiongnu Shanyu reigns, their names before and after assuming the title, and their appellations, and did not have the confusion and misunderstanding shown in the *Records of the Grand Historian*.

II. The Southern Xiongnu Shanyu lineage and the appellations of Shanyu titles

Before discussing the appellations of Southern Xiongnu Shanyus, let us take another look at the era of Huhanxie 呼韓邪 Shanyu and his descendants after the Xiongnu became a vassal state of the Western Han, and Chinese culture started to influence the Xiongnu Shanyu title system. According to the *History of the Former Han*: "The Xiongnu word for 'filial' was 'ruodi' 若鞮. After the reign of Huhanxie, the Xiongnu grew closer to the Chinese and saw Han Emperors that had been given a 'filial' title when they passed away and admired this, which is why they took the appellations 'ruodi.'"[34] Shiratori Kurakichi concludes that "ruodi" during

---

[33] *History of the Former Han*, ch. 94, "Xiongnu Biographies" 《匈奴列傳》, pp. 3778, 3782, 3787.

[34] *History of the Former Han*, ch. 94, "Account of the Xiongnu," p. 3828.

the Han was read "zak-tai," and both the Tungusic word "säksäti" and the Mongolic word "šuktai" mean "spread with blood," or in a broader sense are words for blood relations. Shiratori believes these have the same morphology as "ruodi," and that "ruodi" is equivalent to the Khitan "chishideben" or "deshideben."[35] Further study awaits as to the relation between the Xiongnu language and other Altaic languages. However, ancient texts have confirmed that "ruodi" is the Xiongnu translation of the Chinese word for "filial," and along with Shiratori's comparative historical linguistic evidence, this conclusion is indisputable.

After Huhanxie died, six of his sons became Shanyus in succession.[36] The *History of the Former Han* records the appellations of their Shanyu titles as: Fuzhulei 复株累 Ruodi Shanyu (personal name Diaotaomogao 雕陶莫皋), Souxie 搜諧 Ruodi Shanyu (personal name Qiemixu 且靡胥), Cheya 車牙 Ruodi Shanyu (personal name Qiemoche 且莫車), Wuzhuliu 烏珠留 Ruodi Shanyu (personal name Nangzhiyasi 囊知牙斯), Wulei 烏累 Ruodi Shanyu (personal name Xian 咸), and Huduershidaogao 呼都而尸道皋 Ruodi Shanyu (personal name Yu 輿). These six appellations of Shanyu titles all have "Ruodi" at their end, just as posthumous titles for the Han emperors included the word "filial." Tezuka Takayoshi 手塚隆義

[35] Shiratori Kurakichi 白鳥庫吉, *Historical Research on the Western Regions* 『西域史研究』, vol. 1, pp. 219-22.

[36] *History of the Later Han*, ch. 89, "Account of the Southern Xiongnu" 《南匈奴傳》 says that after Huduershidaogao Ruodi Shanyu died, "his son, Left Wise King Wudadihou 烏達鞮侯 became Shanyu. When he died, his younger brother Left Wise King Punu 蒲奴 became Shanyu," (Zhonghua Book Company punctuated edition, 1965), p. 2942. According to this account, Wudadihou's younger brother was the Left Wise King. Later studies have been clearer in this respect, such as Uchida Ginpu's 内田吟風 Shanyu lineage chart, which agrees with this view – see his *Studies on North Asian History: The Xiongnu* 『北アジア史研究・匈奴篇』, p. 212. Some scholars take Punu to be Huduershidaogao Ruodi Shanyu's younger brother and not the younger brother of Wudadihou, and therefore when calculating the Xiongnu lineage they mistakenly believe that Huhanxie had seven sons who were Shanyus. For example, see the "Xiongnu Shanyu Lineage Chart" 《匈奴單于世系表》 in Lin Gan's 林幹 *History of the Xiongnu* 《匈奴史》 (Inner Mongolia People's Press, 1979), pp. 193-4. The same mistake appears again in the "Xiongnu Shanyu Lineage Chart" in Lin Gan's *Chronological Table of Xiongnu History* 《匈奴歷史年表》 and *Collection of Selected Essays on the Xiongnu (1919-1979)* 《匈奴史論文選集（1919–1979）》.

says this is a pure imitation of the Chinese system.[37] The problem is that the Han emperors did not have posthumous titles during their reigns and only were called "filial" after they died. In contrast, for the Xiongnu, the above six Shanyu titles should have been granted only once upon assuming leadership. If this were not the case, it would be difficult to understand why, after Huduershidaogao Ruodi Shanyu broke the sequence of Shanyus established by Huhanxie, ultimately causing the split between Northern and Southern Xiongnu,[38] he would still be awarded the posthumous title of "ruodi" by the southern Xiongnu, who relied on the Chinese to gain control of the legitimacy of the Xiongnu Shanyus. The *History of the Later Han* even mentions that in the passage, "Bi's 比 uncle, Filial 孝 (Xiao) Shanyu Yu,"[39] "Filial Shanyu" refers to Huduershidaogao Ruodi Shanyu. Of course, there is no way of knowing who decided to use "ruodi" in imitation of the Chinese system. The principle of succession after Huhanxie was determined by Huhanxie himself, so was the use of "ruodi" also started by him? Considering that "ruodi" is included in his appellation of his Shanyu title, and that the Southern Xiongnu thereinafter respected this tradition (the Southern Xiongnu shortened "ruodi" to "di," perhaps to make the transliteration simpler), it is highly probably that Huhanxie started this tradition himself. Perhaps Huhanxie created the word "ruodi" for his descendants' Shanyu

---

[37] Tezuka Takayoshi 手塚隆義, "Further Studies on Xiongnu Shanyus – Hulugu Shanyu's Rise to Power"「匈奴単于相続考ーとくに狐鹿姑単于の登位について」in *History Garden* 『史苑』, vol. 20, no. 2 (1959), pp. 17-27.

[38] The most obvious reason for the split between the Northern and Southern Xiongnu is that Huduershidaogao Ruodi Shanyu broke the order of succession and insisted that his sons succeed him rather than his brothers or older sons of former Shanyus, thereby stirring up contention amongst those towards the top of the succession order. However, I believe that there may be deeper reasons that are closely related to the struggle during the post-Huhanxie Shanyu years between internal Xiongnu factions that were for or against the Han. Huduershidaogao Ruodi Shanyu's killing of Wang Zhaojun 王昭君 and Huhanxie's son, Youguli 右谷蠡 King Yituzhiyashi 伊屠知牙師, thereby removing Wuzhuliu Ruodi Shanyu's eldest son Bi 比 from contention, signals that the balance between the pro- and anti-Han factions had broken down. The anti-Han faction gained a great advantage from the deterioration of Xiongnu relations with the Xin 新 (Wang Mang) and the Eastern Han, thereby forcing the situation to come to a head, causing the split. For studies on the succession system of the Xiongnu Shanyus, see Uchida Ginpu's *Studies on North Asian History: The Xiongnu* 《北アジア史研究・匈奴篇》, pp. 211-7.

[39] *History of the Later Han*, ch. 89, "Account of the Southern Xiongnu," p. 2939.

title appellations and did not use it in his own appellation, not only to imitate the Chinese system, but also for his descendants to follow his state policies and to fix his unique position within the Shanyu lineage. If this conclusion is correct, then Huhanxie's prominent position in future Xiongnu society, especially the Xiongnu historical traditions of the Southern Xiongnu, is easier to understand.

Apart from adding "ruodi" to the appellations of the Shanyu titles, another important influence the Western Han government had on the Xiongnu was compelling the Xiongnu Shanyus to accept the Chinese monosyllabic naming system and no longer use multi-syllabic names. *History of the Former Han*: "At that time Wang Mang 王莽 decreed that China was not to use two-syllable names, then sent emissaries to ask the Xiongnu to report to the Han court on adopting Chinese customs, and that the Xiongnu would use the monosyllabic naming system. The Shanyu followed this order, and wrote a letter saying: 'Fortunate to be your guardian servants, elated at your peaceful, sagely system, your servant's old name Nangzhiyasi has been respectfully changed to Zhi 知.' Wang Mang was greatly pleased, and asked the empress to send an emissary to respond, and reward them greatly."[40] The so-called "Chinese censuring of two-syllable names" caused some people to "eliminate two-syllable names"[41] and was a part of Wang Mang's cultural reform movement. It is hard to believe the Xiongnu would give up their original naming traditions and learn the common Chinese use of monosyllabic names. Just in terms of linguistic traditions, this would be impossible. I believe Wuzhuliu Ruodi Shanyu simplified Nangzhiyasi to Zhi only in his letter to the Han, and this abbreviation was only reflected in official writings and in dialogues with emissaries, which would have been in Chinese language.[42] This temporary measure became a new tradition, and after the Xiongnu Shanyu Nangzhiyasi changed his name to Zhi, the majority of the Shanyus only used their simplified names in Chinese historical materials. For

[40] *History of the Former Han*, ch. 94, "Account of the Xiongnu," p. 3819.

[41] For the "Chinese censuring of two names" see *History of the Former Han*, ch. 99, "Biography of Wang Mang" 《王莽傳》, p. 4051; as an example of "eliminate two names because of the system," Wang Huizong 王會宗 changed his name to Zong 宗; see *History of the Former Han*, ch. 99, "Biography of Wang Mang," p. 4153.

[42] Wang Mang's order for "the surrendering slaves to submit to Zhi" takes Zhi to be Wuzhuliu Shanyu's name; see *History of the Former Han*, ch. 99, "Biography of Wang Mang," p. 4121.

example, Xiluoshizhudi 醯落尸逐鞮 Shanyu, who was later established in the Southern Xiongnu, is only referred to by his simplified name "Bi" 比 in the *History of the Later Han*. Where the *History of the Former Han* mentions that "Wuzhuliu Shanyu's son Sutuhu 蘇屠胡 was originally the Left Wise King,"[43] Hui Dong's 惠棟 *A Supplementary Gloss on the History of the Later Han* 後漢書補注 points out that Sutuhu should be the same person as Bi, and the *History of the Later Han* uses Bi, "or there may be other evidence for this."[44] Actually, the so-called "there may be other evidence for this" is based on official documents from the Eastern Han. After Nangzhiyasi simplified his name, whenever the names of Xiongnu rulers appeared in official documents they were already simplified to monosyllabic names. That the following ruler, Wulei Ruodi Shanyu, simplified his name to Xian 咸 and that Huduershidaogao Ruodi Shanyu simplified his name to Yu 與 reflects this change. Because the struggle between the two leaders, Wudadihou and Punu, who succeeded Yu led to the split of the Xiongnu and a loss of formal contact with the Han court, they kept their multi-syllabic names. When Xian was the Left Lihan King 左犁汗王, he sent his two sons to Wang Mang's Xin court, where they were namcd Deng 登 and Zhu 助.[45] Xian had another son named Jiao 角[46] – all of his sons had monosyllabic names. Ten of the twelve Southern Xiongnu Shanyus before Han Emperor Shun's 順 reign had monosyllabic names. We can see that these kinds of Sinicized monosyllabic names that only appeared in written Chinese documents and correspondence with the imperial court had already become a Southern Xiongnu tradition.

The above developments took place during the late Western Han and Wang Mang's Xin Dynasties, and because the Xiongnu state had established a close and unprecedented relationship with the dynasties in the sedentary south, some changes took place within the appellation system. These changes clearly originated in the great political effect and cultural influence of the Chinese imperial courts. When the Xiongnu split,

---

43 *History of the Former Han*, ch. 94, "Account of the Xiongnu," p. 3827.

44 Hui Dong's 惠棟 *A Supplementary Gloss on the History of the Later Han* 《後漢書補注》 is cited in Wang Xianqian 王先謙, *Collected Commentaries on the History of the Later Han* 《後漢書集解》, ch. 89 (Zhonghua Book Company, reprint of the 1915 Xushoutang 虛受堂 edition, 1984), p. 1035.

45 *History of the Former Han*, ch. 94, "Account of the Xiongnu, " p. 3823.

46 Ibid., p. 3826.

the Southern Xiongnu came to the south and accepted the military protection and political supervision of the Eastern Han, and the influence the Eastern Han had on Southern Xiongnu society could only have increased in strength, duration, and depth. Here we will focus our attention on the problem of the appellations of Shanyu titles.

There were 20 Southern Xiongnu Shanyus in total. Among these the ninth Shanyu, Anguo 安國, raised an army against the Han and was killed by his subordinates; the 17th Shanyu, Huzheng 呼徵, was killed by a Han official who was acting without orders; and the 18th Shanyu, Qiangqu 羌渠, was killed by rebellious subordinates. None of these three Shanyus, who did not meet good ends, left behind any appellation for their Shanyu titles. The final Shanyu, Huchuquan 呼厨泉, was kept at court in the 21st year of the Jian'an 建安 reign period (216 CE), and never returned to Southern Xiongnu territory – he as well did not leave behind an appellation. The remaining 16 Shanyus all had full appellations. The familial and genealogical relations between the Shanyus are mostly clearly recorded in the sources, and only the 14th Shanyu Doulouchu 兜樓儲, the 15th Shanyu Juche'er 居車儿, and the 18th Shanyu Qiangqu, came from unclear lineages. We can draw some conclusions about them, however. For example, the 14th Shanyu Doulouchu, after Quteruoshizhujiu 去特若尸逐就 Shanyu Xiuli 休利 and his younger brother Left Wise King were forced to commit suicide, returned to Bingzhou 并州 from the Han capital Luoyang 洛陽 and assumed leadership. Doulouchu "used to be in the capital"[47] and was called "King Guarding Righteousness" 守義王,[48] and he may have lived in Luoyang as a hostage. The Southern Xiongnu had the Shanyu's sons take turns acting as hostages, and Xiuli was Shanyu for thirty years, so the hostage in Luoyang must have been his own son and not the son of a former Shanyu. Therefore, it is likely that Doulouchu was the son of Xiuli. If he was not a hostage while in Luoyang, Doulouchu may have been Xiuli's nephew and the son of Tan 檀 or Ba 拔. The 15th

[47] *History of the Later Han*, ch. 89, "Account of the Southern Xiongnu" 《南匈奴傳》, p. 2962.

[48] Ibid., ch. 6, "Annals of Emperor Xiaoshun" 《孝順帝紀》. Yuan Hong 袁宏, *Annals of the Later Han* 《後漢紀》, ch. 19, "Annals of Emperor Xiaoshun" 《孝順皇帝紀》 has "King Establishing Righteousness" 立義王; see Zhang Lie's annotated *Two Annals of the Han*, p. 373.

Shanyu, Juche'er, was either the son or younger brother of Doulouchu. From looking at the state of the Southern Xiongnu at the time, the 18th Shanyu, Qiangqu, may have been the uncle or younger brother of the former Shanyu Huzheng.

Among the twenty Southern Xiongnu Shanyus, the first three were the Southern Xiongnu founder Bi 比 and his two younger brothers Mo 莫 and Han 汗. The remaining seventeen were the descendants of these three brothers. During the process of splitting with the Northern Xiongnu and allying himself with the Han to create the Southern Xiongnu, the support of Bi's brothers was crucial. Therefore, the succession of Southern Xiongnu Shanyus remained with the heirs of the three brothers and followed the tradition of the next youngest brother taking over once the older brother was gone. Bi took his grandfather Huhanxie Shanyu's appellation as his own appellation. By doing so he showed to outsiders that he wanted to continue Huhanxie's practice of working with the Han, and to his own people that he respected the Shanyu lineage principles that Huhanxie had established. Of course, the practice of a younger brother taking over from an older brother could not be completely followed over the long-term. In actuality, the succession from Bi to Mo to Han to later generations only reached the second generation before Anguo was killed. From the third generation to the last, the Shanyu all belonged to the Bi branch. Bi's son Chang 長 and Chang's son Tan 檀 ruled for 23 years and 27 years, respectively, and this may have had decisive significance for the monopoly of succession by Bi's family branch.

The sixteen appellations for Southern Xiongnu Shanyu titles that have been preserved are all Chinese transliterations from the Xiongnu language, and their original meanings cannot be possibly known. But this method of transliteration has preserved some information, no matter how faint or hard to distinguish. I believe that by analyzing the appellations available we can discover that some relationship exists between the appellations of the first generation of Shanyus – the three who founded the Southern Xiongnu – and those of later generations. The following is a list of the names of the Southern Xiongnu Shanyus, along with their appellations, lineage, and reign period, followed by a brief discussion.

1. Bi 比 (Xiluoshizhudi 醯落尸逐鞮 Shanyu), son of Wuzhuliu 烏珠留 Shanyu, 48-56 CE

2. Mo 莫 (Qiufuyoudi 丘浮尤鞮 Shanyu), younger brother of Bi, 56-57 CE

3. Han 汗 (Yifayulüdi 伊伐于虑鞮 Shanyu), younger brother of Mo, 57-59 CE

4. Shi 适 (Xitongshizhuhoudi 醯僮尸逐侯鞮 Shanyu), son of Bi, 59-63 CE

5. Su 蘇 (Qiuchuchelindi 丘除車林鞮 Shanyu), son of Mo, 63 CE

6. Chang 長 (Huxieshizhuhoudi 胡邪尸逐侯鞮 Shanyu), younger brother of Shi, 63-85 CE

7. Xuan 宣 (Yituyulüdi 伊屠于閭鞮 Shanyu), son of Han, 85-88 CE

8. Tuntuhe 屯屠何 (Xiulanshizhuhoudi 休蘭尸逐侯鞮 Shanyu), younger brother of Chang, 88-93 CE

9. Anguo 安國 (no appellation for his Shanyu title), younger brother of Xuan, 93-94 CE

10. Shizi 師子 (Tingdushizhuhoudi 亭独尸逐侯鞮 Shanyu), son of Shi, 94-98 CE

11. Tan 檀 (Wanshishizhudi 萬氏氏逐鞮 Shanyu), son of Chang, 98-124 CE

12. Ba 拔 (Wujihoushizhudi 烏稽侯尸逐鞮 Shanyu), younger brother of Tan, 124-128 CE

13. Xiuli 休利 (Quteruoshizhujiu 去特若尸逐就 Shanyu), younger brother of Ba, 128-140 CE

14. Doulouchu 兜樓儲 (Hulanruoshizhujiu 呼蘭若尸逐就 Shanyu), son or nephew of Xiuli, 143-147 CE

15. Juche'er 居車儿 (Yilingshizhujiu 伊陵尸逐就 Shanyu), younger brother or son of Doulouchu, 147-172 CE

16. Name unknown (Tuteruoshizhujiu 屠特若尸逐就 Shanyu), son of Juche'er, 172-178 CE

17. Huzheng 呼徵 (no appellation for his Shanyu title), son of Tuteruoshizhujiu Shanyu, 178-179 CE

18. Qiangqu 羌渠 (no appellation for his Shanyu title), uncle or brother of Huzheng, 179-188 CE

19. Yufuluo 於扶羅 (Chizhishizhuhou 持至尸逐侯 Shanyu), son of Qiangqu, 188-195 CE

20. Huchuquan 呼厨泉 (no appellation for his Shanyu title), younger brother of Yufuluo, 195-? CE

What information can we get from this list?

The first Shanyu, Bi, had the appellation Xiluoshizhudi; Bi's son Shi, the fourth Shanyu, had the appellation Xitongshizhuhoudi; Shi's younger brother Chang, the sixth Shanyu, had the appellation Huxieshizhuhoudi; Chang's younger brother Tuntuhe, the eighth Shanyu, had the appellation Xiulanshizhuhoudi. The appellations of these fathers and sons, apart from the "di" 鞮, meaning "filial" (i.e. the above-mentioned "ruodi"), all contain the word "shizhu" 尸逐. Shi's, Chang's, and Tuntuhe's appellations all contain the word "shizhuhou" 尸逐侯. Mo, the second Shanyu, had the appellation Qiufuyoudi; Mo's son Su, the fifth Shanyu, had the appellation Qiuchuchelindi. The "qiufu" 丘浮 and "qiuchu" 丘除 are linguistically close.[49] Han, the third Shanyu, had the appellation Yifayulüdi; Han's son Xuan, the seventh Shanyu, had the appellation Yituyulüdi. The "yulü" (于虑 and 于閭) in these two appellations from father and son were pronounced the same, even though they were written differently, and must have been different transliterations of the same Xiongnu word. From these two appellations we can see that these appellations for two generations of Shanyus seem to have had the function of marking their father-son blood relationship. From the third generation down to the final Shanyu, apart from the three unknown appellations, there are eight appellations that contain the word "shizhu." Just by looking at the appellations we can infer that they are the descendants of Bi.

What does this mean? We know that in immature political organizations, especially the political organizations of the Inner Asian nomadic peoples, the appellations of Shanyu titles, Qaghan titles, and ordinary official titles all acted to ornament and stress a certain political position, and it was not necessary for them to have the function of showing blood relations or lineages. In the Southern Xiongnu appellations we see that the appellations of the three founding Shanyus had a certain connection with those of their descendants. This clearly is not a historical tradition from the Western Han period, nor can such an example be found within the traditions of the Inner Asian peoples such as the Rouran or the Turks. This is a cultural phenomenon unique to the Southern Xiongnu.

---

[49] According to Pulleyblank's reconstruction of Early Middle Chinese pronunciation, "qiufu" 丘浮 was pronounced K^{h}uw buw, and "qiuchu" 丘除 was pronounced K^{h}uw driě. See Pulleyblank, *Lexicon of Reconstructed Pronunciation in Early Middle Chinese, Late Middle Chinese, and Early Mandarin* (Vancouver, 1991), pp. 59, 96, and 257.

The appearance of this phenomenon is both related to the internal political environment at the founding of the Southern Xiongnu and the influence that arose from the Southern Xiongnu's reliance on the Eastern Han court and acceptance of their culture and systems.

When the Southern Xiongnu state was first established, Bi (Xiluoshizhudi Shanyu) reaffirmed the Shanyu succession principle of older to younger brother set up by Huhanxie Shanyu. This was both the moral basis for Bi's open split and the establishment of another Shanyu court, and a result of the sum of various political forces within the Southern Xiongnu.[50] Under this principle, Bi's descendants and his younger brothers would successively become future Shanyus. Even though they all were descendants of Modu and Huhanxie, it would be very easy for the special position of these three brothers to become buried within the lineage. Bi and his brothers found a solution to this problem in the blood relationships we saw in the appellations of the Shanyu titles. That is, the appellation tradition embodied the different lineages of the three brothers within the appellations themselves. I believe this solution may very likely have been inspired by the ancestral temple and temple name system of the Han imperial family. This ancestral temple and temple name system originally had the function of showing blood relationships. As explained above, Huhanxie was very close to the Han court at first, and the Xiongnu people took note of the Han issue of posthumous titles and immediately adopted the posthumous title system within the appellation system. As the Han and Xiongnu grew even closer, the Han ancestral temple and temple name system was eventually understood and studied by the Xiongnu leaders. I believe that the appellation inclusion of information on blood relationships was very likely a result of studying the temple name system.

Based on the above list of Southern Xiongnu appellations, starting from the 13th Shanyu Xiuli (Quteruoshizhujiu Shanyu), the appellations no longer used the word "di" (i.e. "filial"). Does this mean that from then on the Xiongnu appellations no longer included posthumous titles? Of course, there still may be some problems remaining from the Chinese transliteration. For example, can "shizhuhou" be simplified to "shizhu"? Is "shizhujiu" the same as "shizhuhou"? To tackle this problem would require a wide range of knowledge and materials and would be beyond the

---

50 Rafe de Crespigny, *Northern Frontier, The Policies and Strategy of the Later Han Empire* (Canberra: Australian National University, 1984), pp. 227-8.

scope of this paper. Here we are only doing our utmost to find useful relevant historical information from within limited and difficult-to-use materials.

III. When were Southern Xiongnu appellations awarded and other questions

Han imperial temple names and posthumous names were both awarded posthumously, and there was no corresponding "emperor appellation"[51] awarded during the ruler's life similar to the appellations of titles of Shanyu and Qaghan. In early political organizations, appellations were awarded upon an assuming a political post – this is particularly true for the official titles, Shanyu titles, and Qaghan titles of the Inner Asian polities. Official titles and their appellations were inseparable – one case in point is appellations and Shanyu/Qaghan titles.[52] Prior to the Southern Xiongnu, appellations of Shanyu titles were naturally awarded upon becoming Shanyu. But we are still faced with the question of whether the new Southern Xiongnu appellations that had been influenced by the Han posthumous titles and temple titles were awarded during the Shanyu's life, or after death. There are no historical materials that can directly explain this, but after analyzing a scattering of related materials, I believe that the Southern Xiongnu appellations were awarded posthumously. Let me try to explain this.

When Bi decided to split the Xiongnu and become a Shanyu himself, the appellation of his Shanyu title was Huhanxie. The *History of the Later Han* says, "In the spring of the twenty-fourth year of the Jianwu 建武 reign period, the leaders of the eight tribes met, intending to establish Bi as Huhanxie Shanyu. As his grandfather had once relied upon the Han to maintain peace, he wanted to continue to use the appellation. Thereupon, he went to the Han fort at Wuyuan 五原 and expressed his willingness to

[51] This situation changed in the Tang, after the Tang emperors had the so-called honorific appellations 尊號. This was different from the influence that Han political culture had on the changes in the Xiongnu appellation system. The reverse happened in the case of the Tang imperial system and the Qaghan appellation system – the Chinese imperial honorific appellation system was influenced by Inner Asian political culture. See Luo Xin, "From Qaghans' Appellations to Emperors' Honorific Appellations" 《從可汗號到皇帝尊號》 in the *Journal of Tang Studies* 《唐研究》, vol. 10 (2004).

[52] Luo Xin: "A Study of Qaghan Appellations."

act as a screen to defend against the Northern Xiongnu. The emperor discussed this with the General of the Imperial House for All Purposes 五官中郎將 Geng Guo 耿國 and gave his approval. That winter Bi established himself as Huhanxie Shanyu."[53] This resolution formed at the springtime meeting of the leaders of the eight Southern Xiongnu tribes had to be approved by the Han court before Bi could formally become Shanyu and take Huhanxie as his appellation. According to Li Xian's 李賢 notes on the *Han Records of the Eastern Pavilion* 東觀漢紀, the Xiongnu split on the third day (the guichou 癸丑 day) of the twelfth month, when Huhanxie Shanyu should have formally assumed the leadership.[54] At this time the Han court already understood the appellation system and may have even used it. For example, Wang Mang once established the Left Lihan King Xian as Xiao Shanyu and established Xian's son Zhu as Shun Shanyu.[55] Xiao and Shun are both appellations of Shanyu titles, and Wang Mang used these appellations to make an example of the new relationship with the Xiongnu. Wang Mang also planned to divide the Xiongnu into fifteen parts, each with its own Shanyu. If his plan would have been implemented, he would likely have arranged appellations for each of the fifteen Shanyus in a way that politically benefited the Xin Dynasty. It was within this environment that Bi used the method of requesting the establishment of himself as Huhanxie Shanyu in order to evoke the Han court's sweet memories of their vision of stabilizing the Xiongnu during the reigns of emperors Xuan and Yuan, thereby obtaining Han support for their resistance to the Northern Xiongnu. To Bi the appellation Huhanxie was extremely important in both strengthening relations with the Han court and in solidifying the eight tribes of the Southern Xiongnu. It is worth noting that neither "ruodi" nor "di" was

---

53 *History of the Later Han*, ch. 89, "Account of the Southern Xiongnu," p. 2942.

54 Ibid., p. 2943. Ibid., ch. 1, "Annals of Emperor Guangwu" 《光武帝紀》 says "in the tenth month in the wintertime, the Xiongnu Yujianrizhu 薁鞬日逐 King Bi 王比 established himself as the Southern Shanyu, and the Xiongnu split into the southern and the northern," p.76. Now the first day of the tenth month that year was a renwu 壬午 day; see Chen Yuan's 陳垣 *A Table of First Days and Intercalary Months in the 20 Histories* 《二十史朔閏表》 (Zhonghùa Book Company, 1962), p. 26. Therefore, the tenth month had no guichou 癸丑 day, so taking the *Han Records of the Eastern Pavilion* 《東觀漢記》 to be correct, the "Annals of Emperor Guangwu" is missing the character for "two" [which would make "tenth month" into "twelfth month"].

55 *History of the Former Han*, ch. 94, "Account of the Xiongnu," p. 3823.

added to the end of this appellation. There are no materials that show that Bi ever changed his appellation during the nine years of his rule. However, when the *History of the Later Han* formally lists his appellation, he is clearly called "Xiluoshizhudi Shanyu." This formal appellation (including the posthumous title "di") was not then awarded during his life, but only after his death.

Four of the Southern Xiongnu Shanyus did not have appellations, and, given that appellations were awarded only upon death, this fact makes sense. Among these four, the ninth Shanyu, Anguo, would naturally not have been awarded an appellation, because he was killed in an armed rebellion. The seventeenth Shanyu, Huzheng, was killed by Zhang Xiu 张脩, the commander in charge of monitoring the Southern Xiongnu, and even though Zhang Xiu was punished for "killing without first obtaining permission," it seems that the Han court did not view Huzheng as innocent. Under these circumstances, Huzheng also would not have obtained an appellation. Qiangqu, who took over after Huzheng, died in a large-scale rebellion within the Southern Xiongnu. Qiangqu's family members were either killed by the rebels or fled away from the Shanyu court in the heart of the Southern Xiongnu state, thereby removing themselves from the control of the Han and Wei courts for quite a long time. Under these circumstances, even if Qiangqu's son Yufuluo had re-established the Shanyu court while fleeing, this would have been a government in exile, and it would have been very late in establishing stable relations with the Han government. Even if Yufuluo did give his father an appellation during this time, there are no official Han records of it. If appellations were not awarded posthumously, but upon assuming the Shanyu title, then Qiangqu's appellation should have been recorded. A reasonable explanation is that he did not have an appellation while living, and that after his death the Han and Southern Xiongnu were plunged into rebellion and could not complete the procedure of bestowing an appellation upon Qiangqu, or that the Han court did not receive the relevant news. This can explain why, even though Yufuluo was expelled from the center of the Southern Xiongnu and set up a government in exile, he established relations with the Han court then controlled by Cao Cao 曹操, and therefore only after his death was he actually awarded the appellation "Chizhishizhuhou." His successor Huchuquan stayed in Luoyang for over fifty years. Even though he appeared as the "Xiongnu Southern Shanyu" at important state ceremonies[56] as an embellishment to "a peaceful and prosperous age," historical materials make no reference to when or where he died, and naturally there is no record of the appellation given to him by the Jin 晉 court. If Huchuquan had had an appellation during his life, it would have been seen in all sorts of ceremonial occasions where he was present.

The obtaining of appellations posthumously would explain why four of the Southern Xiongnu Shanyus did not have appellations. Furthermore, another situation worth noting is that the thirteenth Shanyu, Xiuli, was driven to commit suicide by the Xiongnu General of the Imperial House 中郎將 Chen Gui 陳龜, which led to the Southern Xiongnu not having a Shanyu for three or four years. But Chen Gui did not openly kill Xiuli, and the Han court removed him from his position. Afterward Ma Xu 馬續 relaxed government policy toward the Southern Xiongnu rebels, so it seems that Xiuli was not repudiated, and his successor was likely his hostage son in Luoyang. Therefore, after his death he could obtain an appellation. In actuality, Xiuli's appellation for his Shanyu title was "Quteruoshizhujiu."

The posthumous awarding of appellations for Shanyu titles was an important change in the tradition of Xiongnu Shanyu titles and appellations. The force behind this change certainly came from the Eastern

---

[56] According to Wei 魏 and Jin 晉 historical materials Huchuquan was in Luoyang through the Han to Wei and the Wei to Jin successions. The name list in the *Petition of Wei Dynasty Senior Officials Urging the Claiming of the Throne* 《魏公卿上尊號奏》 includes "Xiongnu Southern Shanyu Subject Quan 泉." See Hong Kuo's 洪适 *Corpus of Clerical Script* 《隸釋》 (Zhonghua Book Company replica of the Hong family Huimuzhai 洪氏晦木斋 woodblock version, 1985), ch. 19 , p. 186. After Cao Pi 曹丕 became Emperor, "he bestowed the Wei seal upon the Xiongnu Southern Shanyu Huchuquan and awarded him with covered carts, chariots, precious swords, and jade." See *Record of the History of the Three Kingdoms* 《三國志》, ch. 2, "History of the Wei: Annals of Emperor Wen" 《魏書・文帝紀》 (Zhonghua Book Company punctuated edition, 1959), p. 76. By the winter of the first year of the Taishi 泰始 reign period (265 CE) when Jin Emperor Wu 武 succeeded to the throne, it seems that Huchuquan attended the ceremonies: "an altar was set up in the southern suburbs, and all the officials and the Xiongnu Southern Shanyu of the barbarian tribes attended – tens of thousands of people were present." See *History of the Jin* 《晉書》, ch. 3 "Annals of Emperor Wu" 《武帝紀》 (Zhonghua Book Company punctuated edition, 1974), p. 50. If the Xiongnu Southern Shanyu that attended Jin Emperor Wu's coronation ceremony was Huchuquan, he must have been around 70 years old at the time.

Han court. Clearly the two traditions were different, as the Han temple titles and posthumous titles were both awarded posthumously, and the Xiongnu appellations of Shanyu titles were awarded upon assuming the office. The cultural differences between the two traditions lay in political, economic, and cultural inequalities, and it was inevitable that the weaker side would be influenced by the stronger side. The problem of how to deal with Shanyus' appellations, both in Eastern Han official documents and in ceremonies when the Shanyu met the Han emperor, must have raised great difficulties. The elimination of the differences in these cultural forms likely was greatly furthered by the change to the posthumous awarding of appellations. Furthermore, it is interesting to consider how much influence the Eastern Han government and its organizations – the General of the Imperial House 中郎將 Military Command 軍府 guarding the Xiongnu – had when deciding what kind of appellation to give to the deceased Shanyu. That the Xiongnu guardian General of the Imperial House would bully and even kill a Southern Xiongnu Shanyu shows that the political power of the Southern Xiongnu was greatly controlled and restricted, and that the General of the Imperial House enjoyed great power. We have many reasons to believe that the decision of whether to award an appellation to a deceased Shanyu as well as what kind of appellation to award would have been made by Han officials, even though the related ceremonies would have been held by the Xiongnu themselves.

With posthumously awarded appellations the problem of showing the Shanyu lineage within the Southern Xiongnu appellations and the hypothesis that changes in the system came from learning the Han imperial temple title system become easier to understand. This momentous change in Southern Xiongnu appellations signifies deep changes within Southern Xiongnu society and culture. When Inner Asian governments interacted with the more culturally refined and systemically complex courts in China proper, it would have been normal for some systemic elements to be introduced and for cultural change to occur. For example, the Rouran established a reign title system in the fifth century, and they had five such reign titles – this must have been learned during the interactions between Rouran and the Southern Dynasties and the Northern Wei.[57] Another example is that among the noble families of the Western Han Xiongnu we have Luandi 攣鞮 as well as Huyan 呼延, Lan 蘭, and

[57] *History of the Northern Dynasties*, ch. 98, "Account of the Ruru," pp. 3255-7.

Xubu 須卜: "these three families are from the nobility."[58] But by the Eastern Han "the four families of Huyan, Xubu, Qiulin 丘林, and Lan were well-known and often married Shanyus."[59] This record may truly reflect changes within Southern Xiongnu social structure, but a more likely origin is the Southern Xiongnu imitation of the "four families" structure of the imperial family's maternal side within Luoyang society. This is something we must consider when working with Southern Xiongnu historical materials. Once passing within the Great Wall, the basic lifestyle of the Southern Xiongnu nobility and the daily upkeep of the Southern Xiongnu government basically depended upon year after year of strong economic support from the Eastern Han government.[60] Under these circumstances, the deep societal and cultural changes in favor of the Eastern Han that took place in the Southern Xiongnu were only a matter of time.

The change to the posthumous awarding of appellations of Shanyu titles left traces in the way the Wei and Jin Dynasties handled problems with the frontier tribes. During the late Han, Wei, and Jin, many frontier tribes came to the borders and some came deep within the territory of China proper. The central government bestowed upon some of the leaders the title "Shanyu," which was an important legacy of the nomadic political and cultural traditions established by the Xiongnu. According to the Shanyu system of the pre-Eastern Han Xiongnu traditions, it would be meaningless to be a Shanyu without an appellation, and all Shanyus had one. However, none of the tribal leaders that were bestowed with the Shanyu title by the late Han, Wei, and Jin governments had appellations for their Shanyu titles. Also, none of the tribal leaders who called themselves Shanyu during the Wei and Jin had appellations. This is because that for the nearly two hundred years that the Southern Xiongnu existed, none of the Shanyus had appellations during their lives. Both the Han and Southern Xiongnu people had grown accustomed to this change, and saw it as the normal state of affairs. Therefore, when giving other tribal leaders the title of Shanyu, it was not necessary to add an appellation. Awarding Shanyu titles was one method the Chinese government used to deal with frontier problems, and it thereby became a part of the Chinese

[58] *Records of the Grand Historian*, ch. 110, "Account of the Xiongnu," pp. 2890-1.
[59] *History of the Later Han*, ch. 89, "Account of the Southern Xiongnu," pp. 2944-5.
[60] Ying-shih Yü 余英時, *Trade and Expansion in Han China* (Berkeley and Los Angeles: University of California Press, 1967), pp. 49-51.

tradition, unrelated to the growth and development of the polities of the Inner Asian peoples. In this way Chinese culture finally completed the transformation and dissolution of the ancient Shanyu appellation tradition. Appellations of Qaghan titles then subsequently appeared among the Inner Asian peoples. Qaghan replaced Shanyu as the signifier of a leader of Inner Asian peoples. There were many reasons for this, among which may have been that Shanyu titles had long since been Sinicized and no longer represented the spirit of the nomad political culture. One important symbol of the Sinicization of Shanyu titles and appellations was the change from awarding the appellation during the ruler's life to after his death.

From Tribal Confederacy to Ethnic Community: On Historical Changes in Manchu Identity before the Mid-Qing

Yao Dali 姚大力

When did the Manchus become an ethnic community? There are currently three different views on this question. One response is to say that it was in the first half of the 17th century. The landmark event here has been claimed by some to be the founding of the state by Nurhaci, by some to be the naming of the Jurchen-speaking people as "Manchu" that was supposedly "invented" by Hong Taiji 皇太极, and by still others to be the creation of the Manchu script at the end of the 16th century. The premises behind these explanations all focus on some primordial "common elements" that define the existence of a nationality. The second response to the question is that the Manchu ethnicity was formed at the end of the Qing and in the early Republican era, as it was only at that time that the Eight Banners went from being a multi-ethnic military organization and hereditary hierarchical system to being seen by itself and by contemporary society as an ethnic group. Such a view was held by Edward J. M. Rhoads, mainly derived from his investigations of Manchu-Han relations from the 1860s to the 1930s.[1] During this period the distinction between Manchus and Han bannermen in the quickly dying banner organization began to fade, as tensions were rapidly growing in the relationship between the entire banner organization and ordinary Han Chinese people. It was precisely because of this that Rhoads took the premise that "the Manchus are best viewed as equivalent to the banner people" as the starting point of his research, and he had his own reasons for doing so. However, during the two hundred years or so from the early to mid-Qing, the vast majority of the people, especially the Qing rulers, did not simply take bannermen to be Manchus. Even though the historical character of pre-19th century Manchus does not fall within the scope of Rhoads's main investigation

---

[1] Edward J Rhoads writes that by the end of the 19th century the banner people as a whole came to be called "Manchu." In the eyes of the revolutionaries, the Manchus were identical to the banner people, and so it was in the eyes of the Manchus. See Edward J. M. Rhoads, *Manchus and Han: Ethnic Relations and Political Power in Late Qing and Early Republican China, 1861-1928* (Seattle: University of Washington Press, 2000), pp. 18, 67-9. During the last ten plus years it has become a quite popular view in Western scholarship on Qing studies that Manchu ethnicity was formed at the end of the Qing and in the early Republican period.

described above, when he defined the Manchu community as "an occupational caste," he hinted also that a "sense of descent from common ancestors" was "very much a part of Manchu identity in the late eighteenth and nineteenth centuries."[2] In this respect Rhoads's view is very close to the third view raised by Pamela Crossley, who believes that the Manchus went through a process starting from their earliest cultural community to becoming a race during the Qianlong 乾隆 period, and finally becoming an ethnic group in the late Qing.[3] Her view touches deeply upon the key points regarding the historical transformation of Manchu identity. Nevertheless, many of the materials from this period are not fully exploited and must be further discussed.

The main purpose of this paper is not to artificially determine the birth date of the Manchu ethnicity, but rather to answer the question of how the historical character of the Manchu community continually changed as its members constantly remolded the specific form of their self-identity in response to changes in the political and social environment. There is no

---

[2] Edward J Rhoads, *Manchus and Han*, p. 290. See also R. Kent Guy, "Who were the Manchus? A Review Essay," *Journal of Asian Studies*, vol. 61, no. 1 (Feb. 2002).

[3] Pamela Crossley, "Thinking about Ethnicity in the Early Modern China," *Late Imperial China*, vol. 11, no. 1 (June 1990). In *Orphan Warriors: Three Manchu Generations and the End of the Qing World* (Princeton: Princeton University Press, 1990) and in *A Translucent Mirror: History and Identity in Qing Imperial Ideology* (Berkeley, CA and London: University of California Press, 1999), she enunciates this important idea in much greater detail. In "Voices of Manchu Identity: 1635-1935" Shelley Rigger holds that Manchu was originally a political category, and that it was the emperor Qianlong who consciously attempted to "ethnicize" the Manchu identity. After the Qing Dynasty was overthrown, the ethnicity of the Manchus quickly dissolved except as a tale of their ancestry. The Manchus were not reconstituted into a nationality 民族 until the 1950s. Rigger believes that Hong Taiji included all the Han bannermen in the Manchu category. This seems like an important reason why she concluded that Manchu was a "political category" down to the Qianlong era. But as the discussion below will show, Manchu was actually a substitute designation for "Jushen" 諸申 under Hong Taiji's reign. Although at that time among the people called "Manchu" there were really many "jushenized" Han Chinese, there is no denying the fact that "Manchu" is a particular name for a people culturally different from the Han and the Mongols, even within the Eight Banner system. Maybe Rigger is not so correct when she says that at the very beginning the designation of "Manchu" included all the members of a political polity "being loyal" to the Aisin Gioro clan. See her "Voices of Manchu Identity" in Steven Harrell ed., *Cultural Encounters on China's Ethnic Frontiers* (Seattle and London: University of Washington Press, 1995). See also the introduction written by Stevan Harrell in this book, especially pp. 30-1.

need for me to emphasize the importance of Manchu language sources in tracing the historical changes in Manchu self-identity. As much solid work has been done by Japanese scholars in this field, it is now much easier than ever before to use early Qing Manchu sources.

1. The Jushen 諸申 *tribes before Nurhaci's time*

At the turn of the 16th century the "three Jianzhou Commanderies" 建州三衛, which lay beyond the Liaodong 遼東 border of the Ming Dynasty and would become the core tribes of the "Manchus" in the near future, started to become active again after undergoing decades of decline caused by the casualties from the combined forces of the Ming and the Yi Dynasty of the Chosen (hereafter Yi Korea). At the same time, within the Jianzhou Commanderies, along with the successive decaying of the authority of original nobles within each tribe, the power to govern fell into the hands of new, powerful "barbarian leaders" that took advantage of the disorder.[4] The complicated situation in Liaodong was also increasingly on the minds of the Ming and the Koreans.

To the Ming, who continued a long tradition of historical writing handed down from the preceding dynasties, these tribesmen included the members of Jianzhou Commanderies and the Haixi Commanderies 海西衛, who were undoubtedly descended from the Jurchens under the Jin and Yuan regimes. Based on the continuity of its own historical records on tribes beyond its "northeastern frontier" 東北面 and information coming from China, Yi Korea had always seen the three Jianzhou Commanderies as "Jurchens." As for the East Mongols at that time, they still followed the old Yuan custom of calling their eastern neighbors the "Jürched," which should be a Mongolian form of what the Jurchens called themselves during the Jin times. Letters from the Eastern Mongolian nobility to Hong Taiji addressed the recipient as "Jürüchid" (Jürchid).[5] The *Erdeni-yin*

[4] See Kawachi Yoshihiro 河内良弘, 「建州三衛の消滅と新勢力の擡頭」 "The Elimination of Three Jianzhou Commanderies and the Rise of a New Power," in Kawachi Yoshihiro, *Studies on Ming Dynasty Jurchen History* 『明代女真史の研究』, chapter 21 (Kyoto: Dōhōsha, 1992), pp. 716-43.

[5] "The Letter from Tümed Erdini Dügüreng Qong Baghatur Taiji to Hong Taiji Reporting the Chahar Situation"; see Dalizhabu 達力扎布, "A Study of Mongolian Script Archives: Translation and Interpretation of Documents Concerning East Tümed Tribes" 《蒙古文檔案研究——有關東土默特部資料譯釋》, in Zhu Chengru 朱誠如, ed., *Collected Essays*

Tobči (*Precious Summary*), published in 1660s, on the one hand projects into the past, calling the Jin Jurchen "Manchus"; on the other hand, it inadvertently uses Jürchid, a historical term then still preserved in Mongolian, to designate Nurhaci's tribe and the Yehe 葉赫 tribe: "three Jurchen [tümens by] the water's (edge)" (usun – u ghurban jürchid) and "the White Jurchen of Yehe Tribe" (yekege chaghan jürchid).[6] For these Mongols it appeared that Jürchid and Manchu were basically interchangeable names.

This view is of course not without its reasons. If the Four Hūlun Tribes 扈倫四部 during the Ming really did come from the Hulun River 呼倫河 valley, and the Jianzhou Commanderies from the Woduolian 斡朵憐 tümens and the Huligai 胡里改 tümens of the Yuan Dynasty, then it is very likely that among the members of these tribes must be included the descendants of the Jurchen garrisoned in those areas during the Jin times within an organization named the Meng'an Mouke 猛安謀克.[7] Based on the best text of *A Textbook for Translation between the Chinese and Jurchen Languages* 女真譯語, published by Wilhelm Grube, scholars now agree that this material is sufficient to prove the following conclusion:

---

on Qing History: A Festschrift in Honor of the 90th Birthday of Professor Wang Zhonghan 《清史論集: 慶賀王鍾翰教授九十華誕》 (Beijing: Zijincheng Press, 2003), p. 376.

[6] Sagang Sečen, *Erdeni-yin Tobči*『蒙古源流』, trans. and annot. Wakata Hidehiro 岡田英弘 (Tokyo: Tōsui Shobō, 2004), pp. 317-8. He holds that the "water" here refers to the Songhua River 松花江 and that "three" refers to the three tümens who by the early Ming Dynasty still retained their old names from the Yuan Dynasty, i.e., Taowen 桃溫, Woduolian 斡朵憐, and Huligai 胡里改 respectively. Manchu sources translated this Mongolian name as "*mukei ilan tumen manju[i]*." When the name was translated from Manchu back into Mongolian, it was still written as "Manchu." See *A Manchu-Japanese and Mongolian-Japanese Translation of the Manchu Veritable Records* 『滿和蒙和対訳滿洲実録』, trans. Imanishi Shunjū 今西春秋 (Tokyo: Tōsui Shobō, 1992), pp. 456, 457.

[7] See the sections on official grain price leveling granaries 常平倉 in "Monograph on Foods and Goods" 《食貨志》 in the *History of the Jin Dynasty* 《金史》, volume 50. In the Jin Dynasty there were over 176,000 Meng'an Mouke households that were garrisoned in the administrative region of the Supreme Capital Route 上京路 and its subordinate units: the Puyu Route 蒲與路, the Supin Route 速頻路, the Helan Route 曷懶路, and the Huligai Route 胡里改路. The five tümens of Taowen, Huligai, Woduolian, Bokujiang 孛苦江, and Tuowolian 脱斡憐, established by the Yuan court within the region of the Shuidada Route 水達達路 in Liaoyang Province 遼陽行省, seem to be a readjustment of Meng'an Mouke household system of the Jin Dynasty.

that the Jurchen language is very closely related to the Manchu language.[8] Furthermore, investigations into the Alchuge and the Bara dialects, which belong to dialect systems different from written Manchu, also provide some evidence which, though not found in written Manchu, demonstrates the close relationship between the Manchu and Jurchen languages.[9] From the "Received Documents from Jurchen Tribes" 來文 collected in *A Textbook for Translation between the Chinese and Jurchen Languages,* we can see that until at least the 1520s the so-called Jurchen small character script was still used for communication between the Ming government and the Jurchen-speaking tribes of Liaodong.

However, the historical continuity between the Jin/Yuan Jurchens and the Ming "Jurchen" societies, shown exclusively by the texts from "outsiders," can easily lead to two kinds of historical misconceptions. The first is simply taking the Jurchen-speaking tribes in the Ming Dynasty as direct descendants of the Jurchen organized under the Meng'an Mouke system in the Jin Dynasty, thereby completely overlooking the following

---

[8] Wilhelm Grube, *Die Sprache und Schrift der Jučen* (Leipzig: Kommissions-Verlag von O. Harrassowitz, 1896), p. 7. In his "New Materials for Jurchen Language Studies" 「女真語研究の新資料」 in *Collected Papers on Oriental History: A Festschrift in Honor of the 60th Birthday of Dr. Kuwabara* 『桑原博士還曆記念東洋史論叢』 (Kyoto: Kōbundō, 1931), Ishida Mikinosuke 石田幹之助 classifies the extant versions of *A Textbook for Translation between the Chinese and Barbarian Languages* 《華夷譯語》 into three categories, that is, the A, B, and C categories. A refers to the edition published during Hongwu Reign period (in reality only containing the Mongolian translation part), which only includes the Chinese transcription of barbarian (Mongolian) languages; B refers to various textbooks used by the Bureau of Translation 四夷館 from its initial establishment during the Yongle reign of the Ming Dynasty to the early Qing Dynasty, in which "Glossaries" 字彙 and "Received Documents" 來文 listing barbarian originals and Chinese translations are included. But the languages covered by textbooks in the B category are quite different from each other due to, first, changes in and the abolition of the relevant bureaus, e.g. the Bureau of Tartars 韃靼館, the Bureau of Jurchen 女直館, and the Bureau of Tibet 西番館, and, second, some of them do not have the part of "Received Documents"; C refers to the version compiled by Mao Ruizheng 茅瑞徵 in the late Ming Dynasty, which contains only the Chinese transcription, without any "Received Documents." The version published and annotated by Gruber belongs to the B category.

[9] Ikegami Jiro 池上二良, "Study of Manchu Dialect Based on Materials Gathered from Mu Yejun" 「満洲語方言研究における穆曄俊採集資料について」, in Ikegami Jiro 池上二良, ed., *Studies on the Manchu Language* 『満洲語研究』 (Tokyo: Kyuko Shoin, 1999).

fact: the main component of the "Ming Jurchens" was in actuality the descendants of the peripheral tribes, e.g. the Wudegai 兀的改 people, outside of the Meng'an Mouke Jurchens under the Jin regime. As for the main body of the Meng'an Mouke Jurchens themselves, they had almost melted into the Han Chinese people of the North China and Liao River regions during the mid-Yuan, and they had disappeared from the stage of history.[10] This then led to the second kind of misconception, which is directly related to the main topic of this paper: assuming as self-evident that the "Ming Jurchens" society certainly had a widespread collective memory of the Jin Jurchen, and that they placed themselves in that historical position. As the creation of the Manchu script and the era of Manchu writing came rather late, research into the pre-history of the Manchus must rely mainly upon the historical records of the Ming and Yi courts. The above mentioned misconceptions are further exacerbated due to this.

If the name "Jurchen" or "Jürched" came only from the external world, then what did this people call themselves? They naturally called each other by the names of their own tribes. At the same time, above the level of their respective tribal identity, they may also have had a name to designate a broader and a much looser community. On the 13th day of the tenth month of the ninth year of the Tiancong 天聰 reign period (1635), Hong Taiji issued the famous edict stipulating that:

> The original names of the people in our country include Manchu, Hada 哈達, Ula 烏拉, Yehe, and Hoifa 輝發. But the ignorant people always call us 'Jushen.' The people named Jushen are all descendants of the Sibei Coo Mergen 席北超墨爾根 – what do they have to do with us? From now on everyone should

[10] "The so-called 'Manchus of the late Ming Dynasty' were not descendents of the Jurchens that had remained in the North China and Liao River plains, who had already lost their original characteristics, but were the descendents of another group of Jurchens that stayed in the distant northeast frontier, who 'nevertheless further developed.'" See Wang Zhonghan 王鍾翰, "The Socioeconomic Pattern of the Manchus in Nurhaci's Time," 《滿族在努爾哈齊時代的社會經濟形態》 in Wang Zhonghan 王鍾翰, *Self-Selected Anthology of Scholarly Writings by Wang Zhonghan* 《王鍾翰學術論著自選集》 (Minzu University of China Press 中央民族大學出版社, 1999), p. 28.

use our original name of 'Manchu' when referring to us. Anyone calling us 'Jushen' again must be punished.[11]

Even though Hong Taiji affirms that the name Jushen was used by "ignorant people," this decree itself proves the undisputable historical fact that at the time Jushen was used by these tribes as the name for their community as a whole.

"Jushen" in early Manchu historical materials has two meanings. Even though scholars disagree on the specific explanations of how this word came to have the derivative meanings of "subordinate tribal group" and "slaves of Manchus," they nearly all agree that it was a general name used to distinguish the Jurchen-speaking tribes of Liaodong from the Han Chinese people and the Mongols.[12] Wilhelm Grube's edition of *A*

---

[11] The gengyin 庚寅 day of the tenth month of the ninth year of the Tiancong reign period (1635), *Manchu Archives: The Ninth Year of Tiancong Reign Period* 《天聰九年檔》, trans. Guan Jialu 關嘉祿 and Tong Yonggong 佟永功 (Tianjin: Tianjin Ancient Books Press, 1987), p. 129.

[12] From the mid-Ming onwards, due to social stratification within Jushen tribes, the majority of their population gradually became "subordinate jushen commoners" (harangga jushen irgen) or "subordinate jushen" (harangga jushen) under a few tribal noblemen. This new set of meanings derived from the proper noun "Jushen," which is equivalent to "subordinate jushen commoners" and should have been a linguistic reflection of the changed social status of its majority population. The edict of Hong Taiji specifies that thereafter the word could only be used as a common noun denoting "jushen of a beile's 貝勒 family within a certain banner." It was the derivative meaning of this word that Hong Taiji permitted to be retained. In addition, as the concept of a master-servant relationship was penetrating into the realm of the beile-jushen and khan-irgen relationship, "jushen" became defined as "Manchu servant" (manju aha). It did not denote a servant of the Manchus, however, but a tribal commoner among the Manchus. The Mongolian translators in the Qing Dynasty translated "jushen irgen" as "ulus irgen" (people, commoners), "jushen" as "albatu" (commoners who pay taxes and are subject to corvée). In the *Manchu Veritable Records* 《满洲實錄》 the sentence "Beiles cherish jushen, and jushen respect beiles" is rendered in Chinese as "Therefore rulers ought to cherish their people, and the people respect their rulers" 至于王宜受民，民宜尊王, another instance of interpreting "jushen" as "people" or "commoners." All of the above translations catch the essence of its meaning. See Ishibashi Hideo 石橋秀雄, "Jushen in the Early Qing Dynasty: Focusing Especially on the Tianming Reign Period" 「清初のジュシェン jushen: 特に天命期までを中心として」, and "A Study on Jushen" 「ジュシェン小考」, in Ishibashi Hideo 石橋秀雄, *Studies on Qing History* 『清代史研究』 (Tokyo: Ryokuin Shobo, 1989); see also Imanishi Shunjū, *A Manchu-Japanese and Mongolian-Japanese Translation of the Manchu Veritable Records*,

Textbook for Translation (see footnote eight) includes this word; its Chinese transcription is "Zhuxian" 朱先 and its translation is "Nüzhi" 女直.[13] Even though the early Manchu historical texts have been edited several times, they still retain many instances of Jushen being used as the common designation for all the tribes. Russian sources generally call the tribes living in the middle reaches of the Heilongjiang 黑隴江 River in the 16th and 17th centuries "jucher," which is a plural form of "juchen/jushen" in the Northern Tungusic language. One part of them that were forced to move south by the Qing regime were known as the ancestors of the Hūrha tribe 瑚爾喀部.[14]

A little contact with the outside world would have informed those who called themselves Jushen that they were called Jurchen or Jürchid by their neighbors. However, the historical memory of the Jin/Yuan Jurchens contained within these names was not intrinsic to the knowledge system within Jushen society. As was mentioned above, most of the "Ming Jurchens" were descendents of the border peoples who had separated from the Jin Meng'an Mouke Jurchens. The glory and splendor of the Jin Jurchen may have never entered their collective memory. Modern studies can trace the historical origins of some Ming Jushens to the Yuan/Ming Jurchens, or can conclude that the surnames or titles of some Jushen noble families, such as Wang (< Wang 王 < Wanyan 完顏), Kim (< Jin 金), and Gurun 古論, came from the legacy of the Jin Dynasty under the reign of the Wanyan family. However, these were not a part of the self-awareness of the Jushen at the time, even though they might have had a vague idea from generations of oral transmission that some surnames represented high status in their clan.

There are two points that should be emphasized here. First, the Jin-Yuan transition, and especially turmoil in Liaodong during the late Yuan and early Ming period, led to large scale migration induced conflicts and societal changes within the Jurchen-speaking peoples. "Jurchen" society therefore formed a certain "geological fault" between the complete

---

p. 502.

13 Wilhelm Grube, *Die Sprache*, p. 18. He transcribes it as "chū – siēn" (p. 91). By the way, however, the word "tartar" (Mongols) in this book does not take its Manchu form "monggo," but is written as "mongghol," which should be a "mongolianized" Jurchen word.

14 Juha Janhunen, *Manchuria: An Ethnic History* (Helsinki: Finno-Ugrian Society, 1996), p. 102.

disintegration of the old ways and the gradual rebuilding of a new political order, so that it was hard for them to remember what had previously happened. Mitamura Taisuke 三田村泰助 has already pointed out that, generally speaking, Ming "Jurchens" genealogies mostly only go back to the Yuan-Ming transition, which was "the result of the break that occurred during this period in Jurchen society in Manchuria."[15]

Second, this situation is also closely related to the Yuan-Ming "Jurchens" lack of a written culture, which led to the paucity of written historical materials. Jurchen small script was only used by Jurchen-speaking tribes for communication with the Ming government. Apart from that, it was neither generally employed by them in written communication with Yi Korea, nor used in Jushen society.[16] It was because its only function was in external written communications with the Ming that by the mid-15th century in many Jurchen-speaking tribes of Liaodong "nobody could read Jurchen script." This led to the request that the Ming court "from now on only use Tatar script (i.e., Mongolian script) for imperial edicts."[17] In the late Ming the Jurchen small script probably

---

[15] Mitamura Taisuke 三田村泰助, chapter 2, "Manchu Clans and Their Origins in the Late Ming and the Early Qing Period" 「明末清初の満洲氏族とその源流」, in Mitamura Taisuke 三田村泰助, *Studies on Pre-Qing History* 『清朝前史の研究』 (Kyoto: Dōshōsha, 1965), pp. 57-106. For a tribal group that lacked a written tradition, there probably existed certain difficulties in recalling precisely their orally transmitted collective genealogy back for ten generations or more, though they still could arrange important historical memories concerning their group into a compressed or discontinuous genealogical system. The latter scenario means that the genealogy would omit specific calculations of generations or names of ancestors during some "unimportant" period. In this sense, it seems that the "geologic faults" of memory of the Jushen peoples were not only shown in the number of generations recorded in their lineage, but also reflected in the following fact, i.e. that the experience of mass migrations and upheavals in Yuan-Ming transition hardly left any trace in suggesting separate ancestry myths of the Jushen tribes.

[16] *Veritable Records of the Taizong Reign of Yi Korea* 《李朝太宗實錄》, ch. 5, the xinwei 辛未 day of the sixth month of the third year of the Taizong reign. "The chiefs of the Three Ministries 三府 jointly discuss issues concerning the Jurchens. The Emperor (the Yongle 永樂 Emperor of the Ming Dynasty) sent an edict to the Jurchen tribes such as the Wuduli 吾都里, Wuliangha 兀良哈, and Wudiha 兀狄哈, ordering them to become his subjects and present tribute to the Ming. The Jurchens were originally our subordinates; therefore the issue was discussed by the three ministers together. Being unable to understand the edict as it was written in Jurchen small script, they demanded a Jurchen to interpret it and carried out their discussion on the basis of the interpretation."

[17] *Veritable Records of Yingzong of the Ming Dynasty* 《明英宗實錄》, ch. 113, the jiawu

died out, and the tribes, including the Jianzhou 建州 "Jurchens," gradually started using Mongolian script for written records.[18] It may have been that with their unbroken written record of "Jurchen" history that the outside world was able to cross the above mentioned "geological fault" and find the origin of "Jurchen" people, but the Ming Jushen could not rely on their own resources to do the same. The Manchu noun "jioji" designating Jin-Yuan Jurchens, was actually a transcription of the Chinese word "Nüzhi" 女直 or, more explicitly, the Chinese loanword. This shows that Ming Manchu society came to know the Jin Jurchen at first through Han Chinese culture. The investigation into "Manchu origins" organized in the late Qianlong period resulted in a 20 volume book, *Research on Manchu Origins* 滿洲源流考, which also relied heavily upon Chinese sources. There was not even a single entry coming from contemporary Manchu tribes that was directly related to the historical accounts of the Jin Jurchen.

This being the case, what did "Jushen" mean for the group itself that was encompassed by this name?

Nurhaci's letter to Ligdan Khan of the East Mongols [the Northern Yuan Dynasty] reads, "The Ming and Korea are different states; even though their languages are different, their dress is similar....Even though the languages of our two states are different, our dress and hairstyles are also similar."[19] The similar dress did not necessarily mean that they were of the same ethnic community, but it still gave rise to a feeling of

甲午 day of the second month of the ninth year of the Zhengtong 正統 reign period (1444). According to the record, there were as many as "forty commanderies" who admitted to the Ming court that they could not read the Jurchen small script.

[18] Early in the Tianming 天命 reign period a Korean named Li Minhuan 李民寏 recorded that "Barbarians (i.e., the 'Jurchen') can only use Mongolian script, recording everything in Mongolian letters. If they want to communicate with our state, they would first draft in Mongolian script, and then Chinese scribes would translate it into Chinese." See Li Minhuan, "Records of Observation on Jianzhou" 《建州聞見錄》, in *Historical Materials of the Early Qing* 《清初史料叢刊》, no. 9 (Shenyang: Liaoning University History Department, 1978), p. 43. When Nurhaci instructed his subordinates to formulate the Manchu script, he castigated them, "Why do you think it so difficult to create a script for our own spoken language, but easy to learn a foreign language (script)?" See *Manchu Veritable Records*, ch. 3, first month of the year jihai 己亥 (1599).

[19] China First Historical Archive Office 中國第一歷史檔案館編, ed., *Old Archives in Manchu* 《滿文老檔》, the 17th day of the first month of the fifth year of the Tianming reign period (1620) (Beijing: Zhonghua Book Company, 1990), p. 129.

familiarity. Within the Jushen community, this feeling was naturally much stronger. Even more important than any similarities in dress were similarities between languages. According to the *Manchu Veritable Records* 滿洲實錄, the Yehe tribal leader once said to Nurhaci, "Ula, Hada, Yehe, Hoifa, and Manzhu all belong to one people, so what reason is there for five khans?" "One people" is written in the original text in Manchu as "people who speak one language" (emu gisungge gürün). The same book also says that after the Yehe died out, "From the eastern sea to the north of the Liao border, and from the Mongols' Nen River 嫩江 to Korea's Yalu River 鴨綠江, the Manchu State conquered all those of the same tongue." "Those of the same tongue" is in Manchu "people of the same Manchu language" (emu manju gisun i gürün). In the first month of the sixth year of the Tianming 天命 reign period (1621), Nurhaci prayed to Heaven and Earth, saying, "the Hoifa, Ula, Hada, and Yehe, who are all of the same tongue, are all mine." "Who are all of the same tongue" is in Manchu "Manchu people of the same language" (manjui emu gisun i gürün).[20] Some explain "gürün" in the three excerpts above as "tribe" or "state." Even if this were the case, it must be the plural form of "tribe" or "state," so it encompasses a wider group of people that includes all Jurchen-speaking tribes and states. The Mongolian counterpart for this word is "ulus," which also denotes "people."

Of course, this recognition of a common language and dress requires an awareness of the existence of those outside the scope of one's own group. However, since they were caught in the fight between the Ming government and Yi Korea for control over them, which lasted up to two centuries, the transmission of this knowledge throughout Jushen society must have started well before Nurhaci's time. It may have been utilized and exaggerated along with the intensification of the struggle for supreme rule within Jushen society, but was not a whole new "invention" by the rulers of those tribes. Instead, it should be a common consciousness,

---

[20] *Manchu Veritable Records*, ch. 2, the year xinmao 辛卯 (1591); vol. 6, the 22nd day of eighth month of the fourth year of the Tianming reign period (1619), the 12th day of the first month of the sixth year of the Tianming reign period (1621). See Imanishi Shunjū's version, pp. 120, 456, 492. After checking *Old Archives in Manchu* 《滿文老檔》 (the later archive version), the author finds that the entries in these places are generally the same, the only exception being the entry in 1619, which retains "jushen gisun" instead of changing it into "manju." This is an apt proof that the consciousness of origins derived from a common language actually emerged relatively early in Jushen society.

greatly furnished with grassroots level characteristics, which had long existed within the Jushen tribes.

By the time of the rise of Nurhaci, the collective self-identity of the Jushens had already to a certain extent transcended the recognition of common cultural elements such as language and dress. Nurhaci once said, "Manchu and Yehe belong to one state." Translating verbatim from Manchu, this means "Yehe and us are all Manchu peoples different [from the Ming]" (yehe muse encu manju gürün kai). The Mongolian translation is: "The Yehe and us are peoples of the same obuk" (yehege bida hoyar nigen obuktu ulus bülüge).[21] In another place the *Manchu Veritable Records* mentions a person who after yielding to the Ming surrendered to his own country, calling him "our countryman Shi Tianzhu 石天柱, who surrendered to the Ming as a chiliarch 千總." "Our countryman" is in Manchu "jushen giran" ("…of the Jushen giran"). Imanishi Shunjū 今西春秋 believes that the "giran" here means "of the same ethnos." Therefore he translates this phrase as "of the Manchu ethnos." The corresponding Mongolian translation is "of the Manchu obuk" (manju obuktu).[22] It is

[21] *Manchu Veritable Records*, ch. 4, the sixth month of the year jimao 己卯 (1591). See also Imanishi Shunjū, pp. 261, 263.

[22] *Manchu Veritable Records*, ch. 7, the 23rd day of the first month of the seventh year of the Tianming reign period. See also Imanishi Shunjū's version, pp. 570, 571. Remark: the Chinese translation of the Manchu word "giran" is "corpse," an explanation also seen in dictionaries of the Qing as well as in the *Manchu Veritable Records*. Nevertheless, obviously the "giran" here does not denote "corpse." It is used as a counterpart for Chinese words such as "noble pedigree" 門第 or "aristocratic family" 士族 by Imanishi on the basis of usages found in Qing documents, and he infers that it carries the meaning of "of the same ethnicity," covering a larger or smaller range. He conjectures that this usage of "giran" may be influenced by the connotation of a Mongolian word "yasun" ([of the same] bone). However, the Manchu word for "bone" is "giranggi." Apart from that, in Mongolian-Manchu translation, Qing translators would choose "oboq," instead of "yasun," as the counterpart for "giran." It seems difficult to decide whether Imanishi's inference is correct. That being said, judging from the Mongolian translation, his explanation for "giran" in this context seems fair and reasonable. Similar usage of this word can also be seen in Anon., *A Supplemented Translation to the Manchu Encyclopaedic Reference Book* 《〈補譯〉滿洲類書》, manuscript, Library of the Institute for Ethnological and Anthropological Studies, Chinese Academy of Social Sciences (中国社会科学院民族学与人类学研究所图书馆). The book says that "Although another person passes himself as a Korean, his parents are alive, both of whom are Jushen." The "Korean" in the text is written as "solho giran" in Manchu, which probably could be translated as "Korean ethnos." See Imanishi Shunjū, p. 743, note 96; Hu Zengyi 胡增益, *A New Manchu-Chinese Dictionary* 《新滿漢大詞典》 (Urumqi: Xinjiang People's Press

worth noting that the Mongolian "obuq" refers to a group of people with blood relations. If there was no misunderstanding of the Manchu text by the Mongolian translator of the *Manchu Veritable Records*, then it can be said that there already was the concept of common ancestry within the Jushen collective self-consciousness at the time, even if it was relatively weak and vague.

Up until Nurhaci's time, compared with the Jianzhou 建州 "Jurchen," the four Hūlun tribes may have been influenced by Mongolian culture to a much greater degree. They had once allied with the East Mongols in attacking the Jianzhou tribe. The leading family of the Yehe tribe had always said its ancestors came from the Tümed (Tumet) Mongols. Perhaps it was due to such a background that Guluke 古魯克 and Hanggao 杭高, who came from this family, went over to the Mongols. After Ligdan Khan was defeated, and these two led the remnants of their tribe in returning to the Manchu, they received Hong Taiji's order to command the Tümed Mongols. No matter what, the Yehe and Hada undoubtedly belonged to the Jushen community. Pamela Crossley says, "From the late fifteenth century the Ula and Yehe were part of the large Hūlun federation, all of whom were called 'Mongols'...by the Jianzhou and regarded them as foreign [sic]."[23] However, she seems to have no intention of giving the bare minimum basis for proving this startling conclusion.

We have long known that in pre-Qing history the predominant consciousness of identity in late Ming Jushen society was derived from political division among the people into different "gürün," i.e. "tribe" or "state." Below this level the *mukūn*, the lineage group that came from the *hala* [clan name], and even the *uksun* were also fundamental yardsticks against which the Jushen people could confirm their own identity. This paper aims to discuss the specific form of the collective subjective consciousness of the Jushen people as a community above the level of tribe or state. The collective identity of this loose tribal conglomerate, which was full of oppositions and conflicts, seems to have arisen from their perception of their common cultural forms such as language and

---

新疆人民出版社, 1994), p. 339.

[23] Pamela Crossley, *A Translucent Mirror*, p. 205; see also Crossley, *The Manchus* (Cambridge, Mass.: Blackwell, 1997), p. 7. Remark: In her earlier book *Orphan Warriors*, Crossley points out that the four Hūlun tribes were heavily influenced by Mongolian culture. Compared with her later view, this statement obviously is more natural and clear. See *Orphan Warriors*, p. 16.

dress. At the same time, their self-identity also showed signs of surpassing such a perception. In any case, at this stage, the Jushen collective identity did not include historical memories of the Jin-Yuan Jurchen. This helps to explain why in Nurhaci's time the first attempts at connecting with Jurchen history basically did not touch upon "ethnic group identity" within the Jushen people.

2. *The first attempts at connecting with the Jin Dynasty lineage*

Before Hong Taiji prohibited the use of the word Jushen in the ninth year of the Tiancong reign period (1635), it had always been a self-designation used by the Jurchen community outside of the Liaodong border during the Ming. *Old Archives in Manchu* 滿文老檔 (the later version of the Manchu archives) refers to Nurhaci in the Tianming reign period as "Wise Khan of the Jushen people" (jushen gurun i genggiyen han).[24] The *Old Archives in Manchu* entry on the third day of the third month of the first year of the Tiancong reign period has "one Manchu missive," while the corresponding section of the previous edition *Original Manchu Archives* 舊滿洲檔 (the earlier version of the Manchu archives) has "Jushen" instead of "Manchu." The places where *Old Archives in Manchu* substitutes "Manchu" for the original "Jushen" of *Original Manchu Archives* are not at all limited to just this one case.[25] We can see the widespread use of this name during this period.

Apart from the name Jushen, each tribe originally had its own name, such as Ula, Hada, Yehe, and Hoifa. A more important message conveyed by Hong Taiji's words seems to be that during the Tianming and Tiancong

---

[24] See Chen Jiexian 陳捷先, "A Commentary on Manchu" 《說滿洲》, in Chen Jiexian 陳捷先, *Collected Research on the Manchu* 《滿洲叢考》 (Taipei: National Taiwan University College of Liberal Arts, 1964), p. 8. Remark: In 1616, Nurhaci accepted the Manchu honorific title of "Heavenly Bestowed Nurturing All Guruns Wise Khan" proposed by his ministers and generals. Some scholars regard this event as marking the official establishment of Nurhaci's state. The above mentioned title of "Wise Khan" was also derived from this incident.

[25] Kanda Nobuo 神田信夫, "A Study of the State Title of Manju" 「滿洲（Manju）国号考」, in *Collection of Papers on Oriental History: A Festschrift in Honor of the 60th Birthday of Dr. Yamamoto*『山本博士還暦記念東洋史論叢』 (Tokyo: Yamakawa Shuppansha, 1972), pp. 155-66, especially page 159 and note 9. The article is also included in Kanda's collected essays *Reviews and Studies on Qing History* 『清朝史論考』 (Tokyo: Yamakawa Shuppansha, 2005).

reign periods, as the annexation of the tribes reached its conclusion and the new governing order in the hierarchy of khan, beile 貝勒, amban 暗班 (officials), and Jushen commoners under the Eight Banners system gradually stabilized, the previously dominant tribal identity within Jushen society quickly disintegrated. Tribal names such as Hada and Yehe either gradually became historical concepts or were only used as nouns indicating geographical location. In other words, the entire Jurchen-speaking community started to develop a collective identity under the name of Jushen. We can say that the strengthening of this trend was closely related to Nurhaci's using "Aisin" (meaning gold 金 in Chinese) as the official name of the state.

Throughout history, some of the northern tribes did not declare a state title upon the founding of their state. The name of the most dominant tribe was naturally used as the state title, and this then further evolved into a common name for all of the members of the governed tribal society. "Mongol" also went from being a tribal name to a state title in this way, and it expanded even further to become the common name for a larger group of nomads. If Nurhaci also followed this pattern, then the name of his own tribe, which he used to unite all the tribes he governed outside of the borders of Liaodong, may very likely have gradually come to replace the name Jushen and become a common name for the Jurchen-speaking peoples, with which they could differentiate themselves from other peoples such as the Mongols and the Nikan 尼堪. However, the use of "Jin" as a state title does not seem to have come from the name of Nurhaci's old tribe.[26] To confirm this we have to answer an additional

[26] Some scholars maintain that the family surname "Aisin" of Nurhaci had already become the name of tribe he governed by the time of promulgating the state title, so that the state title "Jin" did come from a former tribal name. See Cai Meibiao 蔡美彪, "State Titles, Tribal Names, and Chronology Prior to the Foundation of the Great Qing" 《大清國建號前的國號、族名和紀年》, *Historical Research* 《歷史研究》, 1987, no. 3. Nevertheless, even if we put aside the complex question of exactly when "Aisin Gioro" was first used as the surname of Nurhaci family, there is no evidence whatsoever that could prove that "Aisin" was once used as a tribal name, just like the earlier "Wanyan" had functioned both as surname of Jin emperors and tribal name of their tribe. The facts quoted in his article that "Jin" and "Han" appeared side by side in memorials of Han ministers in the early Qing seems insufficient to justify the statement that "there is abundant evidence proving that 'Jin' was [Nurhaci's] tribal name." In most cases, the counterpart for Nikan actually used in early Manchu sources is "Jushen." The reason why some Chinese documents in the early Qing period used "Jin" to cover all

question: what did people within the tribe that was referred to by the Ming and Yi Korea as the "Jianzhou Jurchen" call themselves?

In Nurhaci's early letters written in Chinese to the Ming and the Yi courts he refers to himself as "Nüzhi State Jianzhou Commandery Head Guardian of the Barbarians Tong Nurhaci" 女直國建州衛管東夷人之主佟奴兒哈赤 (1596); "Nüzhi State Dragon and Tiger General" 女直國龍虎將軍 (1601); "I, Nurhaci, Administrator of the Jianzhou People" 有我奴兒哈赤收管建州國人 (1605); "King Tong Governing Jianzhou and Other Places" 建州等處地方國王佟 (1605); and "Barbarian King Tong Governing Jianzhou and Other Places" 建州等處地方夷王佟 (1607). These letters came from the hand of a few Han Chinese accompanying him with limited cultural knowledge, and although they tried to follow Ming customs, their choice of words was not very consistent. It is better to believe that at the time this tribe still did not have a formal "state title," rather than to forcefully search for Nurhaci's early "state title."[27] Nevertheless, these titles quite accurately and consistently reflected Nurhaci's view of himself in respect to the Ming court. During the more than 30 year period, starting from his uprising in 1583 with 13 sets of inherited armor and less than 100 soldiers, to his final break with the Ming, in one way or another, Nurhaci needed to borrow the Ming's authority in order to command his tribesmen and to interact with the other Jushen tribes and even Yi Korea. It is entirely possible that the name "Jianzhou" could have entered Jushen society during this period, if not earlier, and

---

Jurchen-speaking peoples should be understood as the same as using "Qing" as the counterpart of "Han," or designating the Manchu language and script as the "Qing" language and script after "Qing" was established as the state title. Such usages were derived from the state title itself, so my opinion is just the opposite of the above mentioned inference.

[27] Huang Zhangjian 黃彰健, "A Study of the State Title Established by Nurhaci" 《努爾哈赤所建國號考》, *Bulletin of the Institute of History and Philology, Academia Sinica* 《中央研究院史語所集刊》, vol. 37, part 2 (1967). He maintains that Nurhaci changed his state title four times altogether, from the very first name of Nüzhi, to Nüzhen 女真, then to Jianzhou 建州, then to Later Jin 後金, and then to its final form Jin 金. These five titles "were established at different occasions, each being used for a certain period, and even Later Jin and Jin were also different." The mistakes made in his article seem to lie in his over-reliance on the "first-handedness and credibility" of Chinese materials. The fact is that "the name of 'Later Jin' was transmitted to the Ming from Yi Korea, so it is not a state title established by Nurhaci." See Cai Meibiao, "State Titles, Tribal Names, and Chronology Prior to the Foundation of the Great Qing."

was used by Nurhaci himself, and perhaps even by other tribes, as a name of his tribe. Even so, it seems that the "Jianzhou Jurchen" should still have another even earlier original name, just like other tribes did.

This leads us to recall what the Mongols originally called them. If the latter really was the translation of the original Jurchen name like "ilan tuman," then it should also have been the source of the names of the "three tümens" established in the early Ming. Even if this were the case, then it would still have been quite different from the original names of other Jurchen tribes.

Is it possible that the original name for the "Jianzhou Jurchen" was "Manchu"?

Many scholars still believe today that the name "Manchu" was fabricated by Hong Taiji. However, as a result of research over the past forty to fifty years, along with our deeper understanding of *Original Manchu Archives*, which was discovered in 1930, this conclusion is not as unshakeable as it used to be. By comparing the corresponding passages of *Original Manchu Archives* with the slightly later *Old Archives in Manchu*, it is not hard to find that the word "Manchu" in *Old Archives in Manchu* was changed from original words such as "Jushen," "Aisin," and "we" in *Original Manchu Archives*. Furthermore, while "Manchu" does appear in some places in *Original Manchu Archives*, a portion of these were written in the empty space next to the line of original text, and in some cases the original words were scraped away and the new ones were written on top of them. These revisions must have been done after the ninth year of the Tiancong reign period (1635). However, apart from these instances, there still are many cases in which *Original Manchu Archives* uses the word "Manzhou" 满洲 without visible signs of later revision. Even though we have to further eliminate the suspicious cases in the later recopied or excerpted archives (e.g. the archives edited within the volumes titled by the characters Huang 荒, Ze 昃, and Shou 收), perhaps we should still admit that the word "Manchu" is already to be seen in *Original Manchu Archives* records.[28] *Original Manchu Archives* basically uses undiacritic

[28] Kanda Nobuo 神田信夫, "A Study of the State Title of Manju." In addition, according to an expert who personally checked the original manuscript of *Original Manchu Archives*, those written on the reverse side of the waste document issued from the Ming court are the original files; those written on new paper made in Korea during the Tiancong reign period are copies made for compiling *The Veritable Records of Taizu* 《太祖實錄》. The latter are not the real originals, and therefore we cannot exclude the

old Manchu script, and occasionally has some sections on interactions with the Mongols in present-day Inner Mongolia that leave the Mongolian text untranslated. These must have been written down before diacritic Manchu script was created in the sixth year of the Tiancong reign period (1632). In recent years two early Manchu manuscripts and a woodblock print in old Manchu script that were originally kept in the Musée National des Arts Asiatiques Guimet in Paris were published, and the name "Manchu" appears among them as well.[29] It appears that Hong Taiji's declaration in the ninth year of Tiancong reign period that the name Manchu was "our original name" was not completely without basis.

Even though it is extremely likely that the name "Manchu" existed before the ninth year of the Tiancong reign period, we presently still have no way of concluding that it was definitely the original name of Nurhaci's tribe. What does seem certain is that he did not use the name of his old tribe, whatever it was, and instead chose "Aisin" to be the title of his

---

possibility of certain words or sentences being revised in the copying process. See Huang Zhangjian 黃彰健, "A Study of the State Title of the Manchu State" 《滿洲國國號考》, *Bulletin of the Institute of History and Philology, Academia Sinica* 《中央研究院史語所集刊》, vol. 37, part 2 (1967).

[29] See Tatiana A. Pang and Giovanni Stary, *New Light on Manchu Historiography and Literature: The Discovery of Three Documents in Old Manchu Script* (Wiesbaden: Harrassowitz, 1998), pp. 4, 47, and passim. The three documents are numbered as Guimet 61625, Guimet 61624, and Guimet 61626 respectively. The first MS consists of 141 pages, seven lines per page, written in old Manchu script, occasionally interspersed with later added circles and dots, containing 26 didactic or historical stories. The second has 66 pages in total, nine lines per page, written in diacritic Manchu script. Apart from the 24 stories identical with the first MS, there are 16 additional stories. The third one is a woodblock print version in old Manchu script, consisting of 78 pages, seven lines per page, its main content being very close to the Chinese text of *Proclamation of the Later Jin to the Ming Emperor Wanli* 《後金檄明萬曆皇帝文》. According to its publishers, the first two MSS were written in between 1626 and 1632 and between 1632 and 1635 respectively; the third one was finished in 1623 and was very likely a Manchu translation of *Proclamation of the Later Jin to the Ming Emperor Wanli*. In Guimet 61625 the name Jushen is found over 20 times, and the name Manchu is found twice. One such incidence refers to Aguda 阿骨打, calling him "a person of the Manchu gürün named Aguda" (manju gurun i aguda gebungge niyalma). This wording coincides with that of the earliest extant old Manchu woodblock print, Guimet 61626, which refers the history of the Jin Dynasty as "the history records of our state," i.e., they all regard the Jin Dynasty as their ancestor. This makes us have more confidence in believing that these three documents were all written before Hong Taiji abolished the state title of Jin and changed it to the Great Qing in order to sever historical relations with the Wanyan Jurchens.

regime. We still do not know the exact year when "Jin" became the state title. Certainly it happened between the time when he accepted the Manchu honorary title "Wise Khan" in 1616 and when he cast the Manchu script "Seal of the Heavenly Appointed Jin Khan" in 1619. To date, as far as we know, "State of Jin" (aisin gürün) is the one and only formal Manchu title that was declared by Nurhaci.[30]

Nurhaci seems to have followed a different tradition within the Jianzhou "Jurchen." In the second year of the Yi Korea Yeonsangun 燕山君 period (1496), Jinshanchixia 金山赤下, a member of a clan within the Jianzhou Commandery Jurchens, plundered the Ping'an Circuit 平安道 area with several followers. The Yi court sent a "naturalized" Jurchen, Tong Qingli 童清禮, a grandson of Ahachu 阿哈出, who had been living in Korea to the Jianzhou Commandery to make inquiries. The leader of the Jianzhou Commandery Lidahan 李達罕, a grandson of Limanzhu 李滿住, gathered those who had been involved in front of him. According to Tong Qingli's report:

> Dahan said to those above mentioned people: "What resentments do you hold towards Korea that has caused you to become bandits? You had better describe them to this emissary." The bandits did not respond for a long time. Finally, Shanchixia's father said, "During the Great Jin 大金, Huolawen 火剌溫 and Wudiha 兀狄哈 once plundered your great state. Your great state mistakenly accused our ancestor of this action and killed him. This is our first resentment. In the year gengchen 庚辰 (1460) the military governor Yang Ting 楊汀 summoned my distant uncle Qicun Langpuyikan 浪甫乙看 and killed him. This is our second resentment. For this reason Shanchixia often burns with anger and occasionally goes hunting and raiding [in your country]." The emissary [Tong Qingli] said, "Many years have passed since the Great Jin. The affairs of that period are long forgotten. You'd better say no more about that."[31]

---

[30] See Cai Meibiao, "State Titles, Tribal Names, and Chronology Prior to the Foundation of the Great Qing."

[31] *Daily Records of Yeonsangun of Yi Korea* 《燕山君日記》, the jiachen 甲辰 day, the first day of the 11th month of the second year of the YanshanJūn reign (1496). See Kawachi Yoshihiro 河内良弘, "Limanzhu and Great Jin" 「李満住と大金」, in *Collection*

The first resentment mentioned by Jinshanchixia's father is the plunder by Huolawen and Wudiha in the 14th year of the Korean Shizong 世宗 period (1432), which Yi Korea mistook as the actions of Limanzhu 李滿住. They therefore sent 15,000 troops the next year to attack Limanzhu's tribe and killed many of his people. Limanzhu himself was injured by nine wounds and his wife died in this incident. The "Great Jin" mentioned in this excerpt refers to Limanzhu. The next year Tong Qingli once again went as an emissary to Jianzhou. When discussing the Limanzhu affair Lidahan again used the name "Great Jin." So "Great Jin" was the title used by the Jianzhou Commandery in the Limanzhu period. Sixty years later in the 24th year of the Chengzong period (1493) the Yi court received the *Letter from the Three Commanderies Wildmen* 三衛野人致書. The wording in this letter was far from elegant and fluent, but it mentioned a "Jin emperor" more than once.[32] It seems that during this period the three commanderies likely still used the name "Jin." Even though Jurchen Jin history was not continued down into the Jushen's own knowledge system, it is entirely possible that some members of the tribal nobility liked to show off their limited knowledge on this subject gained from their contact with the outside world. Their understanding of the "Great Jin" may have been at most hearsay, but this would not have prevented them from using it as a kind of political resource for themselves. Kawachi Yoshihiro 河内良弘 points out that there is no evidence that Nurhaci's use of "Jin" as a state title was a direct continuation of the Jin state name from Limanzhu's time, but at the time Jurchen-speaking people most likely still retained their memory of being the descendants of the "Jin kingdom." His appraisal may very well be correct. Nevertheless, most of those who still remembered the "Jin kingdom" perhaps had no idea of the earlier Jin Dynasty of the 12th and 13th centuries. The Jin Dynasty was at its best only a superficial symbol, even at the highest level of Jurchen society.

It seems that Nurhaci relied upon the support of this symbol mainly because he wanted to enhance his political legitimacy in his interaction with the three foreign states, especially with the Ming and Korea. *Old Archives in Manchu*, in the fourth year of the Tianming reign period (1619), says, "Formerly, in Dading 大定 Khan's reign of our Jin Dynasty, a

---

of Papers on Qing History: A Festschrift in Honor of the 70th Birthday of Matsumura Jūn 『松村潤先生古稀記念清代史論叢』 (Tokyo: Kyuko Shoin, 1994).

32 Kawachi Yoshihiro, "Limanzhu and Great Jin.".

Korean minister Zhao Weichong 趙位寵 led residents of over forty cities to abandon their state and come over to us." This was only two or three years after the establishment of the Jin state title. The use of the possessive pronoun "our" (meni) before the Jin Khan seems to have been a formula in *Old Archives in Manchu*. For example, *Old Archives in Manchu* says, "The Great Liao emperor once wanted to kill the loyal and law abiding people, so our Jin Khan led an army to conquer his dynasty." *Old Archives in Manchu* also says, "Formerly your Zhao Huizong 趙徽宗 and Zhao Qinzong 趙欽宗 emperors were captured by our Jin Khan." *Old Archives in Manchu* also records, "For no reason the Ming emperor assisted other people outside of their borders and killed kinsmen of the Jin Khan – our fathers and ancestors." This wording can be confirmed in a Chinese source – an official announcement declaring war against the Ming, in which Nurhaci claimed that "We are the descendants of the Great Jin."[33] In the fifth month of the sixth year of the Tianming reign period Nurhaci "went to Anshanbao 鞍山堡 and met a man from Gai Prefecture 蓋州 coming to offer a bell cast in the third year of the Tianhui 天會 Khan period in the Jin Dynasty. The inscription on the bell reads: 'Made in the third year of the Tianhui Khan period.' Tianhui Khan is the younger brother of my ancestor Aguda of the state of Jin. His name was Wuqimai 烏齊邁 or 吳乞買, and his title was Tianhui Khan. The man who offered the bell was rewarded with a promotion, because he offered an ancient bell from the dynasty of our ancestor."[34]

These records not only highlight the source of Nurhaci's use of Jin as a state title, but also show a most fundamental subjective motive for his plan to continue the Jin Dynasty lineage: enhancing his own political status and historical character within the practice of early 17th century northeast Asian international relations. This point is so clear that there are always scholars who would go so far as to believe that the Jin state title was established for purposes of relations with the Ming and Korea. As for the

[33] *Old Archives in Manchu Archives* 《滿文老檔》, the third month of the fourth year of the Tianming reign period, the third month of the sixth year of the Tianming reign period, the third to fourth months of the sixth year of the Tianming reign period; "Proclamation of the Later Jin to the Ming Emperor Wanli" 《後金檄明萬曆皇帝文》, in *Selected Historical Materials before the Qing Entered the Shanhai Pass* 《清入關前史料選輯》, vol. 1 (Beijing: China People's University Press, 1984), p. 295; cf. footnote 39.

[34] *Old Archives in Manchu* 《滿文老檔》, the fifth month of the sixth year of the Tianming reign period (Beijing: Zhonghua Book Company, 1990), pp. 206-7.

title used internally, some of them believe it to be "Jushen," and others maintain that it was "Manchu" itself. In fact, even though the title "Manchu State" did exist in the Tianming reign period, it was simply a customary practice of using the original tribal name to designate the Jin regime. It would not have disappeared overnight due to a royal decree declaring a new state title. However, it is likely that it really started to die out from everyday life under the impact of the legal state title of "Aisin." Otherwise there would be no need for Hong Taiji to reinstate the name "Manchu" in the ninth year of the Tiancong reign period.[35] Mitamura Taisuke says, "After the Yehe surrendered and the unification of the Jurchen people was completed in the late Wanli 萬曆 period, the state was called Later Jin by outsiders, Jushen by their own people, and [the name of] Manchu began to fade.…Therefore, even though *Old Archives in Manchu* uses 'Manchu' to describe the activities of their own people, from the very beginning of the Tianming reign period its usage gradually died out. The name Manchu in *Old Archives in Manchu* in the late Tianming reign period must have been used as a description of the past history of their state."[36] The details of this explanation depart from contemporary knowledge, but Mr. Mitamura's historical sense of the strengthening effect the establishment of the Jin title had on Jushen identity is very close to the situation at the time.

Even though the view of two state titles existing side by side lacks historical evidence, it is entirely correct for Mr. Mitamura to point out that the influence of the Jin state title within the state was much smaller than the effect outside of the state. Here the key point is that the historical value attached to the Jin title was a concept extremely foreign to Jushen society. Nurhaci himself and even a small number of other high level people could come into contact with Chinese historical works on the Liao and Jin through the help of their Chinese contemporaries, and they were eager to

[35] Manchu sources seem invariably to refer to the Jin itself as "Manchu gürün" in narrating the interactions between the Jin state and Mongol tribes, and this was also the name for the Jin used by the Mongols. Nevertheless, this has not been confirmed by contemporary sources in other languages. We need further materials and research to solve this problem, and for the present we can only leave it open.

[36] Mitamura Taisuke 三田村泰助, appendix 5, "A Study of the Establishment Process of the Manchu State" 「滿洲國成立過程之一考察」, in Mitamura Taisuke 三田村泰助, *Studies of Pre-Qing History* 『清朝前史の研究』 (Kyoto: Dōshōsha, 1965). The quotation is on p. 473.

transmit this new knowledge.[37] However, it took time for this knowledge to penetrate into Jushen society. In other words, the establishment of the Jin state title provided a symbol for developing a certain common political identity amongst the Jushen, Mongols, and Nikan that were governed by Nurhaci. On the other hand, within the short span of ten or twenty years it was hard to truly internalize the symbol as the Jushen's consciousness of their own historical origins. In this situation, the Jurchen-speaking people increasingly tended to choose Jushen, a term very familiar to themselves, as a common designation of their collective identity.

Compared with the previous situation, Jushen identity underwent certain changes within the ten or so years of the Tianming and Tiancong reign periods. Using the military-political organization of the Eight Banners to eliminate the differences between the former tribes undoubtedly promoted the development of the Jushen's consciousness of their common identity. However, this process did not cause the content of Jushen identity to change in any great way. If Nurhaci's political and cultural strategy of continuing the Jin Dynasty lineage was not abandoned midway, then the history of the Jin Jurchen may well have smoothly followed the passage of time and finally been accepted and treasured by the Jushen as an inseparable part of themselves. In the 17th and 18th centuries we may not have seen the birth of the Manchu ethnicity, but a true reemergence of the ancient Jurchen ethnicity. However, the political arrangements of Hong Taiji in the late Tiancong reign period interrupted the direct realization of this possibility.

3. *The evolution of the myth of Manchu origins*

Based on the records available today, Hong Taiji, starting in the fifth year of the Tiancong reign period (1631), publicly denied the direct relationship with the Jin Dynasty. He wrote a letter to the Ming general Zu Dashou 祖大壽, saying, "The Great Ming Emperor is not a descendant of the Song emperors, just as I am not descendent from the former Jin Khans."[38] Since the connection with the 'Former Jin' was cut, a new agenda had to be

---

[37] For example, on the 14th day of the fourth month of the third year of the Tianming reign period, "that night Nurhaci told his sons-in-law Sigedeer 思格德爾, and Sahaliyan 薩哈連 the history of the Jin Dynasty." See the *Manchu Veritable Records*, ch. 4.

[38] *Old Archives in Manchu* 《滿文老檔》, the 8th-12th months of the fifth year of the Tiancong reign period, p. 1140.

created to explain the dynasty's origins. In the *Original Manchu Archives* records from four years later we see the earliest version of the story of the Manchu's ancestors. This story is said to have come from the mouth of someone named Muksike of the Hūrha tribe, which had just surrendered to the Jin army. The story goes:

> Our ancestors have lived for generation after generation by the Lake Bulhori (bulhori omo) under Mount Bukūri (bukūri alin). We keep no local records, so stories about ancient times have been passed down verbally throughout our history. There were once three Heavenly Maidens of Lake Bulholi named Enggulen, Jenggulen, and Fekulen. They were taking a bath when along came a magpie with a red fruit in its mouth, and it gave the fruit to Fekulen, the youngest of the three. She put it in her mouth and swallowed and afterward was with child and gave birth to Bokori Yongshon. He was of the Manchu tribe. The lake is one hundred *li* 里 around, 120 to 130 *li* away from Helongkiyang. After our second ancestor was born, they set out from Lake Bulhori and settled in a place named Narhun near the Sahaliyan River (sahaliyan ula).[39]

This Muksike may have been an actual historical figure, and the *Old Archives in Manchu* version of this story may have been based at least in part on his narrative. However, we do know that the story had some external sinicized elements to it. The name "Helongkiyang" is clearly a Manchu transliteration of the Chinese pronunciation of Heilongjiang. Meng Sen 孟森 has long since pointed out that the second word in the name "Bokori Yongshon" was translated back to "Yingxiong" 英雄, meaning hero, in the *Veritable Records of the Martial Emperor* 武皇帝實錄, and therefore "Yongshon" was originally a transcription of a Chinese word.[40] It is suspicious that this phrase should have come from the mouth

[39] *Manchu Archives: The Ninth Year of the Tiancong Reign Period* 《天聰九年檔》, the sixth day of the fifth month, p. 55. The Romanized transliterations of the Manchu words in parentheses are copied from *Original Manchu Archives: The Ninth Year of Tiancong Reign Period* 『舊滿洲檔 · 天聰九年』, vol.1, trans., Kanda Nobuo 神田信夫, Matsumura Jūn 松村潤, and Wakata Hidehiro 岡田英弘 (Tokyo: Toyo Bunko 東洋文庫, 1972), pp. 124-5.

[40] Meng Sen 孟森, "Textual Research on Bokori Yongshon, the First Ancestor of the

of a Hūrha "Wildman" 野人 as the first part of the ancestor's name "bokori" does not seem to be the original words of that narrator. In *Original Manchu Archives* the characters used to write this word are different from those used in the name of the mountain "Bukūri" that is just a few lines away in the text. We know that even though the pronunciation of the two is similar, the writer of the *Original Manchu Archives* did not believe there was any etymological relationship between them. Mitamura Taisuke thought it was a different way of writing the "Baohuoli" 保活里 found in the *History of the Jin Dynasty* 金史. This person was the younger brother of the Jin primogenitor Puhan 普函, who followed his elder brother in their move west from Korea.[41] We can accept his inference.

It is a little strange that the story of the Manchu ancestor's origins came from the mouth of a Hūrha. Matsumura Jūn 松村潤 keenly points out that the entry of the 12th month of the eighth year of the Tiancong reign period (less than half a year before Muksike told his story) in the *Veritable Records of Taizong* 太宗實錄 includes a passage that took place before Hong Taiji attacked the Hūrha: "Compared with the Warkas we captured from other places before, the people from this place (the Hūrha by the east sea) speak the same language as we do. We can use them after bringing them back with us. When you attack them, you should tell them, 'We both are of the same nation. Our emperor has long wanted to take you in as subjects, but he just did not have the time. Your people have no written records [of your history], so you are ignorant of this till now.' You should instruct them in this way."[42] When comparing Muksike's "We have no local records" and "He was of the Manchu tribe" and Taizong's

---

Qing," 《清始祖布庫里雍順之考訂》, *Bulletin of the Institute of History and Philology, Academia Sinica* 《中央研究院史語所集刊》, vol. 3, pt. 3 (1932).

[41] Mitamura Taisuke 三田村泰助, chapter 1, "The Foundation Myth and the Imperial Lineage of the Qing Dynasty" 「清朝の开国傳說とその世系」, in Mitamura Taisuke 三田村泰助, *Studies of Pre-Qing History* 『清朝前史の研究』. Hong Taiji publicly denied himself as "a descendent of the former Jin khans," but he still covertly sought his own origins from collateral branches of the Jin royal house. This may show that Jianzhou "Jurchens" really lacked memories of their origins.

[42] *Veritable Records of Taizong* 《太宗實錄》, the renchen 壬辰 day of the 12th month of the eighth year of the Tiancong reign period (1634). See Matsumura Jūn 松村潤, "On the Foundation Legend of the Qing Dynasty" 「清朝の開国説話について」, in *A Festschrift in Honor of Dr. Yamamoto* 『山本博士還暦記念東洋史論叢』 (Tokyo: Yamakawa Shuppansha, 1972).

"Your people have no written records" and "We both are of the same nation," it seems like quite a coincidence that these accounts match so well. It is almost certain that Taizong's words had undergone later revision. The writer of the *Veritable Records* was just employing this "compositional method" for the purpose of later using the Hūrhas' words to tell the story of the Manchu ancestor.

Not long after "discovering" the ancestral legend, Hong Taiji issued an edict formally abandoning the original meaning of the name Jushen and using Manchu to refer to "our country." Less than half a year later, in the fourth month of the tenth year of the Tiancong reign period, he changed the state title of Jin 金 to Great Qing 大清, and he changed the reign title to Chongde 崇德, thereby completely severing the historical relationship between his government and Jurchen-speaking community on the one side and the Wanyan 完顏 Jin 金 Dynasty and Jurchens of that time on the other. *Original Manchu Archives* shows that after the fourth month of the tenth year of Tiancong reign period, the old Jin state title was still seen in use in state letters to Korea. However, this did not last for long.

The internal relationship between the intention of discarding the Jushen name and the act of changing the state title to Great Qing was actually already revealed in Hong Taiji's edict declaring "The people named Jushen are all descendents of the Sibei Coo Mergen" 席北超墨爾根, but had just gone unnoticed. Twelve years ago Okada Hidehiro 岡田英弘 showed that "Coo Mergen" is actually Jürchidei Chuu Mergen, one of Genghis Khan's "nine generals" (yisün örlüg) popular in Mongol legends in the Ming. This name means a good archer of the Jurchen tribe named Chuu. Some have guessed that the character in this legend was based on the Khitan Yelü Chucai 耶律楚材 in early Yuan Dynasty, but he also could be a character completely fabricated by the storyteller. Okada points out that in 1593, when the Hūlun tribal federation attacked Nurhaci, the Kharachin Mongols sent troops to assist, which included the army of its subordinate tribe Sibei (Sibe). It wasn't until the Kangxi period that the Sibei tribe was released from the Kharachin Mongols and returned to the Eight Manchu Banners. Later the Kharachin Mongols negotiated peace and forged a marriage alliance with Nurhaci. After Hong Taiji ascended the throne, three out of the five main empresses and consorts came from the Kharachin tribe, including the Empress Xiaozhuang 孝莊, mother of emperor Shunzhi 順治, and two other Mongols. Hong Taiji said the Sibei were the descendants of Coo Mergen, a view that must have come from the Mongols he kept company with, especially those Kharachin Mongols. It was only natural for the latter to say that the Tungusic tribes with which they had close relations were the descendants of the Jin and Yuan Jurchens in their oral tradition.[43] With this important discovery made by Okada Hidehiro we can confidently say that the reason why Hong Taiji forbade the name Jushen was because he was suspicious of the consciousness of the historical relationship between the Jushen and Jurchens in the Wanyan Jin that was gradually being accepted by the people. He wanted to draw a clear line demarcating himself from the Jin-Yuan Jurchens – especially from the Yuan Jurchens, who later were vassals of the Mongols.

We can see that in the late Tiancong reign period Hong Taiji spent a lot of time pondering how to create a collective image of his own state and his people. Unfortunately, there is little evidence that can demonstrate why he changed the policy of his "Khan father" on continuing the Jin Dynasty lineage. Perhaps the strength and self-confidence of the Jin state made him to feel he no longer needed to use the Wanyan Jin to maintain his political authority, and no matter whether he interacted peacefully with the Ming or prepared to replace the Ming Dynasty as the ruler of Han Chinese society, the historical memories of the Song-Jin antagonism would only produce a negative psychological influence. Perhaps it was his status as the highest ruler of the Mongol tribes in present-day Inner Mongolia that caused Hong Taiji to feel that it was no longer appropriate to characterize himself as a descendant of the Wanyan Jin, a dynasty overthrown by the Mongols. In any case, as the name of Jushen could not be established by political authority as a legitimate name for the collective identity of the contemporary Jurchen-speaking community, and the concept of historical continuity between them and the Jurchen Jin had not fully matured, it was relatively easy for Hong Taiji to use state authority to implement the decision of changing the community name to Manchu and the state title to Great Qing.

According to the ancestral legend in *Original Manchu Archives*, Bokori Yongshon was born by Lake Bulholi at the foot of Mount Bukūri, adjacent to the Heilongjiang River. He later moved to the bank of the Sahaliyan (Heilongjiang) River. Matsumura Jūn 松村潤 points out that the

---

[43] Okada Hidehiro 岡田英弘, "The Mongol Elements in the Manchu Culture of the Early Qing Dynasty" 「清初の満洲文化におけるモンゴル的要素」, in *A Festschrift in Honor of Matsumura Jūn* 『松村潤先生古稀記念清代史論叢』.

place where the story is said to have occurred does exist. In the two maps drawn on the basis of the *Map of Imperial Territory under a Comprehensive Gaze* 《皇輿全覽圖》, entitled *Secret Imperial Map from the Qing Palace* 《清内府一統輿地秘圖》 and *Map of Shengjing, Jilin, Heilongjiang, and other Areas Marked with Military Campaign Sites* 《盛京吉林黑龍江等處標注戰迹輿圖》 respectively, Jin Liang 金梁 names one mountain and one lake near Heilongjiang River, the pronunciations of which are very close to those of the mountain and the lake mentioned above. In the "Mountains and Rivers" 山川 section of chapter 14 of the *Comprehensive Records of Shengjing* 盛京通志, these locations are listed under the item "Heilongjiang" within the Heilongjiang General's jurisdiction, and are written as "Mount Bokeli 薄科里山, 75 *li* 里 south of [Aihui 愛琿] city" and "Lake Boheli 薄和力池, 60 *li* 里 southeast of the city." This is not far from where the Hūrha tribe resided. From this we know that Muksike's story was a folktale rich in local characteristics.

However, the location of the birthplace of the Manchu ancestor as recorded in the *Veritable Records of Taizu Emperor Wu* 太祖武皇帝實錄 changed from the specific description of "120 to 130 *li* 里 from the Heilongjiang River" to the vague "northeast of Changbai Mountain 長白山." Conversely, the course of Bokori Yongshon's founding of his state has become more concrete. He no longer moved northward along the Sahaliyan River, but instead took a boat southward to Aoduoli 鰲朵里 city in Aomohui 鰲莫惠, "southeast of Changbai Mountain," and was made leader by the local tribes of "three surnames." Meng Sen says, "the Japanese were correct in proving that the Womuhe 斡木河 within the jurisdiction of Jing City 鏡城 in Korea were actually the Emohui 俄莫惠 in the *Veritable Records of the Qing Dynasty* 清實錄."[44] Korean histories say that Huining 會寧 was "Womuhe 斡木河 in the barbarian language, and some say Wuyinhui 吾音會." Here Womuhe does not mean a river named Womu 斡木, but rather a three character transcription of the "barbarian language," so it could also be rendered as Wuyinhui. Aomohui, Womuhe, and Wuyinhui are different transcriptions of the same place name, and this was the place where the tribe of Möngke Temür, the primogenitor of the later Jianzhou Left Commandery in the Ming, was

[44] Meng Sen, "Textual Research on Bokori Yongshon."

located, and was also the location of the tribe of Nurhaci's paternal ancestor.[45] The earliest version of the account does not mention Changbai Mountain at all, but the *Veritable Records of Taizu* unfolds its story around Changbai Mountain. The story of Bokori Yongshon's moving to the Sahaliyan (Heilongjiang) River is no longer mentioned. Scholars still do not agree as to whether the extant *Veritable Records of Taizu Emperor Wu* has preserved the original text from the *Veritable Records of Taizu and the Empress Dowager* 太祖太后實錄 compiled in the Chongde period of Hong Taiji's reign, or it was a revised version completed at the same time as the *Veritable Records of Taizong* in the tenth year of the Shunzhi period. But we can say that at the latest, the story of Bokori Yongshon took its basic shape in the Shunzhi period.

There is another item worth noting in the *Veritable Records of Taizu*. It traces Nurhaci's surname Aisin Gioro back to Bokori Yongshon. That the Muksike version does not mention this does not seem to be due to negligence. As at that time Bokori Yongshon was also the ancestor of the Hūrha tribe, Hong Taiji was naturally unwilling to share this honorable surname with those he had conquered. The *Veritable Records of Taizu* essentially strips the Hūrha tribe of their identity as descendants of Bokori Yongshon. Therefore they could now set their minds at rest in tracing the surname Aisin Gioro back to Bokori Yongshon.

After the *Veritable Records of Taizu Emperor Wu* was written, certain details of the legends of Manchu origins continued to be revised along

---

45 *Survey of the Geography of the Eastern State* (Korea) 《東國輿地勝覽》, ch. 50, "Huining Military Commission" 《會寧都督府》. Womuhe, Aomohui, and Emohui are all Chinese transcriptions of the Manchu word "omohui." The Korean pronunciation of Wuyinhui is oe-um-hui; in spoken form it is possible to add a weak vowel between the two syllables of um- and -hoi. Therefore, the above variations are really different transliterations of the same place name. As for the description of the Woduoli tribe entering and leaving the place of Wuyinhui, see Ikeuchi Hiroshi 池内宏, "The Northeastern Korean Borderland and Jurchen Tribes as well as their Relations in Early Yi Korea" 「鮮初の東北境と女眞との関係」, in Ikeuchi Hiroshi 池内宏, *Research on the History of Manchuria and Korea: the Early Modern Period* 『満鮮史研究· 近世篇』 (Tokyo: Chūō Koron Bijutsu Shuppan, 1972). Although Pamela Crossley has noticed that this myth "would be elaborated and refined over the next century or more" in her discussion of the foundation legend of the Manchus, she does not pay enough attention to the evolution of the story text itself, even going so far as to directly move the Woduolian tümen in the Yuan Dynasty to the east of Changbai Mountain. See Pamela Crossley, *A Translucent Mirror*, p. 196 and after.

with the changes in historical knowledge of their transmitters. This is mainly seen in the three following aspects.

First, in the revised Kangxi 康熙 version of the *Veritable Records of Taizu* the geographical location of Mount Bukūri was changed from "northeast of Changbai Mountain" to "east of the mountain." The position of Bokori Yongshon's birthplace relative to Changbai Mountain changed by nearly 180 degrees, and, furthermore, it became closer to the mountain. We know that only seven or eight years before the revision the Kangxi Emperor had sent someone to investigate Changbai Mountain, and he then sent a special envoy to offer sacrifices to the mountain spirit. The above textual changes provided a more reasonable historical explanation for beginning to conduct state worship of Changbai Mountain as their ""place of origin" in the Kangxi period.[46]

Second, the descriptions of the Yalu 鴨綠, Huntong 混同, and Aihu 愛滹 Rivers that flow down from Changbai Mountain, and especially the descriptions of Changbai Mountain itself, went from factual accounts to those exaggerating their spiritual aura. The *Veritable Records of Taizu Emperor Wu* narrative is more straightforward:

> Pearls and gems come from these three rivers. Changbai Mountain is tall and cold, with incessant winds. In the summer wildlife from surrounding area rests on the mountain. Covered in pumice, this mountain is a famous mountain of the Northeast.

The *Veritable Records of Taizu Emperor Gao* 太祖高皇帝實錄 edition revised during the Kangxi reign makes a slight change to this passage: "Pearls and gems come from these three rivers. The mountain is windswept and cold. Every summer wildlife from surrounding areas inhabits the mountain." The edition of the *Veritable Records of Taizu Emperor Gao* revised during the Qianlong reign not only adds the description of "commanding towering majesty and concentrating spiraling spiritual aura 樹峻極之雄觀，萃扶輿之靈氣," but also changes the original passage to:

---

[46] For a discussion of the official worship of Changbai Mountain by the Qing government starting from the Kangxi period, see Mark C. Elliott, "The Limits of Tartary: Manchuria in Imperial and National Geographies," *Journal of Asian Studies*, vol. 59, no. 3 (Aug. 2000).

> The three rivers nurture mysterious and rare things, producing precious pearls and shells that are highly treasured throughout the world. The mountain is windswept and cold. Unique plants and miraculous herbs grow in appropriate seasons. Every summer wildlife from surrounding areas inhabits the mountain.[47]

The Qianlong edition shows that the worship of Changbai Mountain became a part of official ceremonies starting in the Kangxi period and by the Qianlong period the process of "constructing" this "sacred mountain" of the Manchus by the Qing government had already been completed.

Third, in the *Research on Manchu Origins* 满洲源流考 compiled in the late Qianlong period, Eduoli City 鄂多里城 (in the *Veritable Records of Taizu* cited above it is written as Aoduoli 鰲朵里), "where our dynasty's primogenitor resided" or "where our state first flourished," is moved to another location. Although the book retains the original historical record of "Our primogenitor resided in Eduoli City in Emohui, to the east of Changbai Mountain," immediately following this is: "The city is 1,500 *li* east of Xingjing 興京 (Hetu Ala), and 330 *li* southwest of Ningguta City 寧古塔城, lying along the west bank of the Lefushan River 勒福善河."[48] The compilers clearly moved the city to the northwest of Changbai Mountain, but still copied the old record, only changing "southeast" to "east." It is simply hard to believe that such a thing would happen in a work compiled by imperial order and undertaken during the heyday of textual criticism and investigation. However, ever since the Qing court had been established in Beijing, "from the Shunzhi down to the Kangxi period, no knowledgeable old tribal man from beyond the Great Wall remained." Judging by the Kangxi Emperor's words that "our dynasty's ancestors originated from Changbai Mountain, but today no one knows exactly about it," we know that at that time the Manchus knew little about the

[47] The quotations in three editions of the *Veritable Records* are all copied from Imanishi Shunjū 今西春秋, *Collation of the Veritable Records of Qing Taizu* 『対校清太祖実録』 (Tokyo: Kokusho Kankōkai, 1974), pp. 1-2. The descriptions of Changbai Mountain in "The Era of Origination" 《發祥世紀》 in the preface of *History of the State-Founding Campaigns of the Great Qing* 《皇清開國方略》 are based on the Qianlong edition of the *Veritable Records of Taizu*.

[48] *Research on Manchu Origins* 《满洲源流考》, ch. 13, "Territory, six" 《疆域六》; and ch. eight, "Territory, one" 《疆域一》.

remote edges of their borderlands beyond the Great Wall. More importantly, as Meng Sen put it, "the phrase 'Jianzhou Commandery' was taboo in the Qing," so Han Chinese scholars dared not include the origins of the Manchus within the scope of their textual criticisms and investigations. From this it is not hard to understand why imperial scholars in the Qianlong period "placed" Eduoli city to the "west of Changbai Mountain, locating it approximately based on Xingjing's location, consequently claiming that Emohui is situated in present-day Dunhua County 敦化縣."[49]

Starting in the Kangxi period, there were two changes in the method of defining the Manchu community that are worth noting. One is that the status of Bokori Yongshon, who went from being the original imperial primogenitor to being the ambiguous "original founder" in the Kangxi edition of the *Veritable Records of Taizu* and the primogenitor of the Great Qing, was decreed to be Nurhaci's seventh ancestor, the Commander-in-chief 都督 Mengtemu 孟特穆. From today's vantage point, Nurhaci's lineage seems to include true records of only two generations – that of his father Taksi (塔克世 or 塔失) and his grandfather Giocangga 覺昌安 or 叫場, whereas Giocangga's father, the Commander-in-chief Fuman 福滿, and his grandfather Xibaoshi Biangu 錫寶失編古 are not seen in records other than in *Veritable Records of Taizu*. From Biangu's elder brothers Tuoluo 妥羅 and Anyimo 安義謨, all the way to Mengtemu of the early Ming, these scholars seem to have borrowed the genealogy of

[49] See Meng Sen, "Textual Research on Bokori Yongshon"; "Examination of the Jianzhou Commandery in the *Draft History of the Qing*" 《清史稿中建州衛考辨》, *Bulletin of the Institute of History and Philology, Academia Sinica* 《中央研究院史語所集刊》, vol. 3, pt. 3 (1932). In the Qianlong edition of the *Manchu Veritable Records*, there is also a similarly incredible mistake that places "Huining Prefecture City the Old Capital" 故都會寧府 patrolled by Jin Shizong 金世宗 at "the east of the white mountain (that is, Changbai Mountain)." Remark: Aomohui 鰲莫惠 was called Huining in the Korean administrative geography system at that time. In their specialized textual criticism and research, Qing scholars clearly knew the following fact, i.e., "the name of Huining 會寧 Prefecture in northern Korea is a borrowed name, which has nothing to do with [the Huining of the Jin Dynasty]" (*Research on Manchu Origins*, ch. 12). But generally Manchus tended to confuse Shangjing 上京 (Huining) of the Jin Dynasty with Huining in Korea. This shows that although the experience of living in the Tumen River 圖們江 valley had long left only fragmentary memories, it still seemed to tenaciously reside in the mind of the descents of the Jianzhou Jurchens.

the Jianzhou 建州 Left Guard's 左衛 Tong Möngke Temür 佟猛哥帖木兒 and his descendants. For the Kangxi Emperor, the exactness of the imperial lineage from Mengtemu on down was undisputable, and those that came before Mengtemu belonged to a far off era from which details were hard to retrieve. In the view of people after the Kangxi period, the historical factuality of Bokori Yongshon had already started to differ from that of Möngke Temür and his descendants.[50]

The second change is even more important. If we say that from Nurhaci's time to the pre-Kangxi era the accounts of the origins of the Jushen-Manchu community were mainly focused on the historical origin of the Aisin Gioro clan, then during the Kangxi period the common historical memory of the Manchu banners started to become an important source for defining who the Manchus were. This groundbreaking consciousness is adequately expressed by the Manchu explanation for the entry "Manchu" in the *Imperially Sanctioned Manchu Dictionary* 御製清文鑑, prefaced in the 47th year of the Kangxi period (1708).

> The Taizu Emperor Gao 高 was surnamed Aisin Gioro, whose ancestors first flourished at Changbai Mountain. Changbai Mountain is 200 *li* high and 80 *li* in circumference. The three rivers flowing down from the mountain are called the Yalu, Huntong, and Aihu respectively. When [our ancestor] arrived at Odoli [Eduoli] city in the Omohui [Emohui] area to the sun rising direction (east) of Changbai Mountain, he calmed the turmoil there and named his state Manchu. From there they moved to Hetu Ala, which today is also regarded as their place of origin. At that time the [seventeen] local powers named Suksuhu Aiman…all came to the Taizu Emperor Gao and followed him in attacking the [forty nine] states and tribes including Zaugia…and made them submit to him. These all were part of what were called the Manchu.

The seventeen local powers listed under Suksuhu Aiman and the forty nine states and tribes listed under Zaugia are named one by one in the original text and therefore need not be repeated here.[51] These calculations

---

[50] Mitamura Taisuke, "The Foundation Myth and Imperial Lineage of the Qing Dynasty."

[51] For an Manchu-Japanese translation of this entry, see Ishibashi Hideo 石橋秀雄, "A Study of the Name of Manchu after the Qing Entered the Shanhai Pass" 「清朝入関後の

were very crudely made.[52] But they had "imperially sanctioned" authority, and therefore, after it was issued, "the sixty six states following the dragon (Emperor Gao) were all called Manchu after their submission 從龍六十六國歸順俱名滿洲" for a time became the standard discourse for answering the question "who are Manchus."[53] In the entry "Manchu" in the *Imperially Sanctioned Manchu Dictionary (Revised and Enlarged Edition)* 御製增订清文鑑 prefaced in the 33rd year of the Qianlong period (1768), this section of old text is repeated word for word.

Of course, the common historical memory of "following the dragon" in the state's early days had existed long before the Kangxi period. However, it was only in the Kangxi period that we see this kind of common historical consciousness being stressed and promoted, and employed to answer the question of "who are Manchus." It must be emphasized that the serious concern with the definition of Manchu identity expressed by a few people at the higher levels of government did not simply suggest that the Manchu community was maturing naturally on its

---

マンジユ（Manju）滿洲呼称をめぐって」, in *Problems on Qing China* 『清代中国の諸問題』, Ishibashi Hideo 石橋秀雄, ed. (Tokyo: Yamakawa Shuppansha, 1995).

52 The fact that the so-called "Andarki Aiman" was listed in tribes that "came and followed [Nurhaci]" confirms that the compilers of the *Imperially Sanctioned Manchu Dictionary* did make a mistake. According to volume two of the *Manchu Veritable Records*, in the seventh month of the year bingxu 丙戌 (1586), in order to attack Nikan Wailan, one night Nurhaci cut across "adjacent hostile tribes," which in Manchu is written as "andarki dain i aiman." From this it can be concluded that the so-called "Andarki" here is not a proper noun but an adjective in the general sense. See *A Manchu-Japanese and Mongolian-Japanese Translation of the Manchu Veritable Records*, trans. Imanishi Shunjū, p. 738, footnote 56. Although the *Manchu Dictionary* was finished earlier than the *Manchu Veritable Records*, the source of this entry should be the same as that of the *Veritable Records*. In addition, the size of the 66 states varied, showing that they were political units at different levels. For instance, Sarhū, Giyamuhū, Antu Gūwalgiya, and Mardun were branches of Suksuhu Aiman, but they were listed together as five states. Many tribes were left off the list. Therefore, in the imperially commissioned *Research on Manchu Origins*, compiled in the 43rd year of Qianlong period, the northeastern tribes "that were registered as households" need to be reordered and recounted. See *Research on Manchu Origins*, volume 8, "Territory, one" 《疆域一》. A thorough and in depth comparative study of these two lists of tribes that surrendered or were vanquished should be quite rewarding.

53 *Collected Records of the Qing* 《清事彙書》 (1751), cited from Ishibashi Hideo 石橋秀雄, "A Study of the Names of the Manchu after the Qing Entered Shanhai Pass" 「清朝入関後のマンジユ(Manju)滿洲呼称をめぐって」, in Ishibashi Hideo 石橋秀雄, editor, *Problems on Qing China* 『清代中国の諸問題』 (Tokyo: Yamakawa Shuppansha, 1995).

own. The opposite may have actually been the case. The question "who are Manchus," which seems to be self-evident and need no elucidation, now increasingly needed to be clearly defined. This development on the one hand directly promoted the large scale official "genealization" of the collective memory of the Manchus during the Qianlong period. On the other hand, to further pursue the historical origin of this "following the dragon" community, further investigations had to be made into the origins of the Manchus. At this stage the historical process by which the Manchu community's collective consciousness was transformed into a pre-modern ethnic identity was gradually coming to an end.

4. The redefinition of "Manchu origins"

If we say that around the time of Nurhaci's rise the community that named themselves Jushen was a tribal assembly composed of the descendants of Jin-Yuan Jurchen border peoples, then by the early Qing the historical character of the community called "Manchus" had already seen great changes. The responses made by peoples in the early Qing to the question "what are Manchus" should include the following points.

First, they were all hereditary members of the Eight Manchu Banners, a military-administrative organization. The banner system undoubtedly was of great use in maintaining the collective identity of the Manchus. However, inclusion in the Eight Manchu Banners can not be seen as the only reason for their becoming Manchus. The exact opposite seems to have been the case: it was precisely because they were Manchus that they were included in the Manchu Eight Banners, just as Mongols and Liaodong Han Chinese were later incorporated into the Mongol Eight Banners and the Han Army Eight Banners. Even though most of the time during the Tianming and Tiancong reign periods many Liaodong Han Chinese were absorbed into the banner system that included a mixture of Jushen, Nikan, and Mongol elements, and even though in the banner organization Nurhaci did "give the Nikans the same treatment as the Manchus,"[54] the differences between the Jushen and the Han Chinese always existed alongside the effort to "Jushenize" the Han Chinese within the early banner system. When Liaodong had been completely conquered, the number of Han soldiers that were incorporated sharply increased, leading the Jin regime to change the strategy previously put in place in the

---

[54] Pamela Crossley, *A Translucent Mirror*, p. 94.

early years of Nurhaci's reign and to create divisions between the three types of groups in the banner system.[55] This fact itself shows that even though Manchu identity had to rely on the organization of the Manchu Eight Banners, it cannot be understood as just being the historical product of the banner system.

Second, Manchus shared a common language, common hairstyles and dress, and common shamanistic beliefs. These were clearly inherited from the historical legacy of earlier Jushen identity.

Third, they were a group of conquerors of Han Chinese societies, both in areas beyond the Great Wall and especially in the vast territory within it. The strong consciousness of being conquerors and living in a foreign land highlighted the two Manchu cultural features of "riding and shooting" and "national language."

Finally, Manchus must have had an historical identity of belonging to this or that specific tribe. This point cannot be more vividly reflected than in the above mentioned standard discourse of "the sixty six states following the dragon." This gives us an important piece of information: after sharing a common history of almost a century of bloody warfare and the integration of the banner system, the Manchu community still more or less preserved its historical memory of the old tribal identities, even though these memories had to a large extent lost their original color. In this way, in addition to the most important component – a cultural sense of belonging – Manchu identity up to the early Qing clearly also included

---

[55] "Ujen Cooha," the Manchu name for the later Han Army Eight Banners, was originally a proper name for the group of "old Han troops" who submitted themselves prior to the Daling 大凌 River battle. This happened in the eighth year of the Tiancong reign period (1634). Within several years, based on this "Ujen Cooha," the Qing regime set up and successively increased the number of Han Army Banners, but it was not until the 17th year of the Shunzhi reign (1660) that the "Han Army" was officially adopted as the Chinese counterpart for "Ujen Cooha." Although the official use of "Han Army" for "Ujen Cooha" was later than generally thought, there was a phrase "Nikan Cooha" for Han troops who had early on submitted to the Jin-Qing regime. In establishing the Han Army Eight Banners, most of the Han Chinese initially organized in the mixed Eight Banners were allocated to the Han Army Banners. This shows that the early banner system was far from eliminating the differences between Manchus and Han Chinese, whereas the latter ultimately led ultimately in Hong Taiji's reign to the "final definition" of the Manchu-Han division within the Eight Banners system. See Hosoya Yoshio, "The Gūsa (Banner) of Ujen Cooha (Han Army Eight Banners)" 「烏真超哈（八旗漢軍）の固山（旗）」, in *A Festschrift in Honor of Matsumura Jūn* 『松村潤先生古稀記念清代史論叢』; Pamela Crossley, *A Translucent Mirror*, p. 180.

some kind of political identity, including an identity of occupational status within the Eight Banners and a remnant consciousness of former tribes.

The above pattern of collective identity consciousness was not entirely the result of the political maneuvering of the governing group. Even though the phrase "revere Manchu above all" first came from the mouth of the Shunzhi Emperor, it clearly was the basic national policy of the Qing court from at least the time when the banner system was divided into Manchu, Mongol, and Han Chinese components. Nevertheless, in the arduous process of conquering a Han Chinese society that far surpassed the Manchus in terms of area and population, in order to make use of the Han bannermen's innate superiority to the full extent, early Qing rulers were forced to intentionally avoid the special problems of Manchu identity and promote the concept that within the banner system "Manchus and Han all belong to one body" in their public ideological propaganda. In this way the highlighting of the differences between Manchus and Han Chinese within the banner system and the development of Manchu consciousness in the early Qing was postponed for the long term due to the highly sensitive and tense state of early relations between Manchus and Chinese after Qing troops had entered the Shanhai Pass 山海關 [China]. Around the mid-18th century, the changes in the situation of the Qing Empire's governance necessitated a complete adjustment of their political ideology.[56] It was against this general background that enhancing Manchu consciousness was placed on the agenda. However, this account is not free from overgeneralization. Here I enumerate three reasons explaining why the Qing government at this time launched a large scale cultural movement promoting Manchu identity.

First, once the Qing regime had finished the military conquest of Han Chinese society and tried to transform its rule into stable and legitimate governance, the Han bannermen gradually lost their once held superior position. Furthermore, the Three Feudatories Rebellion 三藩之亂 that broke out in the late 17th century further eroded the Manchu rulers' political trust in the Han banners. The Han bannermen were marginalized within the banner system, which led to an increasingly visible gap in status between them and the other bannermen. In the 1680s the Kangxi Emperor

[56] Pamela Crossley periodizes the Qing Dynasty into several phases based on transitions in imperial ideology: Nurhaci to the early Hong Taiji reign, the later Hong Taiji reign to the mid-18th century, the mid-18th century to 1860, etc. This view is worth referencing. See Pamela Crossley, *A Translucent Mirror*, p. 28.

fulminated that "the bad habits of the Han bannermen have simply gone too far,"[57] which might be regarded as a clear signal of a shift in the Qing court's official attitude towards them. During the Yongzheng 雍正 reign "bad habits of the Han bannermen," "evil habits of the Han bannermen," and "bastard Han bannermen" became phrases commonly used by him to denounce his subjects.[58] However, at this time the Han bannermen were not yet completely equivalent to the Han people.[59] The Qianlong reign finally saw their formal official definition: "Han bannermen were originally Han people."[60] The new status of the Han Army Eight Banners showed that strengthening the policy of "revere Manchu above all" had started to become an important part of the Qing government's reformation of the banner structure and adjustment of dynastic ideology. It was against this background that the Qianlong court annulled the membership of Han bannermen,[61] and against which the 18th century Qing court strived diligently to promote the consciousness of Manchu identity.

Second, almost simultaneous with the shift of attitude of the ruling authorities, the Manchu Eight Banners that came within the Great Wall were indeed sliding dangerously towards the emptying of their subjective consciousness. This reality caused the Qing court to see the increasingly urgent necessity of enhancing Manchu identity. These Manchus that had

---

[57] Imperial edict issued on the 26th day of the tenth month on the 26th year of the Kangxi period, in *Comprehensive Records of the Eight Banners*, preface 8, imperial edict 2 《八旗通志》，卷首 8，敕諭 2 .

[58] See Sun Jing 孫靜, ch. 4, section 2, "The Marginalization of the Han Army Eight Banners" 《八旗漢軍的邊緣化》, in *Rethinking Manchu Nationality Formation: Research on Manchu Identity in the Mid-Qing* 《滿族形成的再思考：清中期滿洲認同意識研究》, Doctoral dissertation (History Department of Fudan University, 2005), p. 71.

[59] In the Yongzheng period one memorial requested, "Should Manchus, Mongols, Han Bannermen, and any others formed in companies commit a crime punishable by banishment, they are to be punished as the Han commoners." The emperor's response reads, "Manchus, Mongols, and Han Bannermen lead their lives in ways vastly different [from the Han Chinese], and they would suffer more than the average Han in banishment. Therefore, for the present this proposal will not be put into practice, so as to observe the effect on the people." See imperial edict on the 16th day of the tenth month on the fourth year of the Yongzheng period, in *Comprehensive Records of the Eight Banners*, preface 9, imperial edict 3《八旗通志》，卷首 9，敕諭 3 .

[60] Pamela Crossley, *A Translucent Mirror*, pp. 90-1.

[61] Sun Jing 孫靜, "A Discussion of the Status Change of the Han Army Eight Banners during the Qianlong Era" 《乾隆朝八旗漢軍身份變化述論》, *Heilongjiang National Series* 《黑龍江民族叢刊》, 2005, no. 2.

moved within the Great Wall felt the irresistible influence of living for a long period within Han Chinese society and urban culture. After only two or three generations, their Manchu culture characterized by riding, shooting, Manchu linguistic aptitude, frugality, diligence, and shamanistic beliefs had sharply declined. The Kangxi Emperor (in his later years) and the Yongzheng Emperor made several critiques of the decay of Manchu culture, though these were often quite restrained.[62] From the Yongzheng to Qianlong reigns these rebukes became more and more severe. Due to the fading of the "old Manchu ways," apart from membership in the Eight Banners, the definition of "what are Manchus" seems to have become increasingly ambiguous and unable to be described.

This identity crisis did not mean that the Manchus would quickly "sinicize" and blend into the Chinese society that they governed. Whether it was in the capital or in "Manchu cities" of their garrison, within the Manchus there unquestionably existed a clear consciousness of the insuperable boundary between them and the Chinese. However, this consciousness alone could not stop the Manchu community from being increasingly divided into countless small groups that were aware of their place as outsiders within Chinese society.[63] Completely different was the

---

[62] For example, the imperial edict issued on the fifth day of the first month of the 59th year of the Kangxi reign says, "Our Manchu customs are different from the past." In the imperial edict issued on the 13th day of the sixth month on the fourth year of the Yongzheng period, the Yongzheng Emperor also commented in a similarly mild tone, "Recently the Manchu soldiers have gradually developed the bad habits of the Han bannermen." See *Comprehensive Records of the Eight Banners*, preface 8, imperial edict 2; preface 9, imperial edict 3 《八旗通志》，卷首 8，敕諭 2；卷首 9，敕諭 3.

[63] It is very difficult for us to agree with Pamela Crossley's view on this issue. She believes that by the early Qianlong reign "Long habitation in closed garrison communities had forged the Manchus into a people who clearly identified themselves in racial terms." See "Manzhou Yuanliu Kao and the Formalization of the Manchu Heritage," *Journal of Asian Studies*, vol. 46, no. 4 (Nov. 1987). In *A Translucent Mirror* she maintains that in the building of the state thesis of Manchu origins, its basic guidelines or principles had been established in Hong Taiji's reign. According to these principles, Manchus were the descendants of a culturally distinguished, genealogically coherent succession of peoples in the Northeast. Their language, social structure, and customs were also descendents of their Northeast predecessors. See *A Translucent Mirror*, p. 299. Nevertheless, she seems to have forgotten the need to substantiate these two extremely important conclusions. As will be discussed below, the definition of "race" made by Crossley is very close to the above mentioned Manchu identity that she claims had come into being under Hong Taiji. That is to say, the keynote of Manchu "race" building was founded in Hong Taiji's reign and completed by the Qianlong period. If so,

situation in the latter half of the 19th century, when the Qing court had basically abandoned its reliance upon the Manchu as the underpinning of the empire. Since the Qing court at that time firmly believed that "the Manchu army is the foundation of our state," it had to manage to give the disappearing Manchu consciousness a somewhat feasible and effective definition.

Third, the Qing court's concern over the problem of defining Manchu identity was not a consequence of promoting its own position. Due to the fact that Han Chinese accounted for the vast majority of the population governed by the Qing, its state organization and institutions absorbed many elements of Han Chinese institutions and laws. But in terms of the territorial structure of the 18th century Qing Empire, Chinese areas only made up one third of the imperial map. The Qing court did not try to impose a highly sinicized administrative system used in Chinese territory on non-Chinese areas. Furthermore, the Qing authority should not be seen as a "sinicized" central dynasty using a single governing system to cover all parts of its territory, but rather as an "empire" simultaneously ruling over peoples with different cultures and social structures. The *Pentaglot Dictionary of the Qing Dynasty* 五體清文鑑, compiled in the Qianlong era, may be the most typical example symbolizing this kind of imperial concept. As hinted at in the *Pentaglot Dictionary*, here the Manchus must be restored from being a hereditary military household under the control of the Manchu Eight Banners back to a kind of "people" of the same nature as the Tibetans, Mongols, or Han Chinese. The problem then was that when the Han bannermen were classified as "those who were originally Han," this identity was self-evident, at most a "discovery" rather than an "invention." However, the case for the Manchus was different.[64] Here we return to the question placed before the Qing court that must be answered: Apart from the identity of belonging to the Manchu Eight Banners, what really causes the Manchus to form a "people?"

Riding and shooting, and the Manchu script and language were undoubtedly important. Up until the late 19th century the Qing government

---

however, what is the significance of the genealogization movement for the collective Manchu experience and the redefinition of Manchu origins during the Qianlong reign which Crossley repeatedly brings forward into the discussion? The low credit given by *A Translucent Mirror* to the historical influence of Qianlong's series of movements tracing Manchu origins may have a logical relationship with her views cited above.

[64] See Pamela Crossley, "Manzhou Yuanliu Kao and the Formalization of the Manchu Heritage"; and *A Translucent Mirror*, p. 116.

continually strove to maintain these abilities in members of the Manchu Eight Banners. But as early as the Yongzheng period the authorities had already discovered that an unavoidable trend had appeared: "We Manchus have settled in Han territory and have grown distant from our original customs." [65] The organizational control of the banner system was undoubtedly very important as well, but it is difficult to change people's minds using rigid regulations. Because it was unable to afford the very large institutional costs, the government by the mid-Qing period had no choice but to abandon some of the old practices that had been established ever since the Manchu troops entered the Shanhai Pass [China].[66] Clearly, the task at the time was no longer how to rectify the available "Manchuness,"[67] but rather that a new Manchuness had to be "invented" to support "Manchu" as the collective identity consciousness of a certain group of people. It is only against this historical background that we at last can understand the deep meanings of the series of cultural movements instigated by Qianlong in order to redefine the origins of Manchu history.

These cultural movements began with Qianlong's order to compile the *Comprehensive Genealogies of the Eight Banners Manchu Clans* 八旗滿洲氏族通譜 in 1735, a project that saw sporadic progress all the way up to the completion of the revised *Comprehensive Records of the Eight Banners* 八旗通志 in 1786, lasting for over fifty years – almost as long as the reign of Qianlong himself. The project centered on two themes. One was to conduct an extensive review of the records concerning the origins of various the Companies 佐領 and the Manchu genealogies which were stored in the Eight Banners archives, and to further collect and screen all

---

[65] See the imperial edict issued on the 23rd day of the seventh month of the second year of the Yongzheng reign, *Imperial Edicts on the Eight Banners by Shizong Emperor Xian* 《世宗憲皇帝上諭八旗》, ch. 2; also included in the *Comprehensive Records of the Eight Banners* 《八旗通志》, preface 9, imperial edict 3.

[66] A typical illustration of this aspect may be the forced abolishment of the "Back to the Banner" stipulation for the garrison soldiers of the Eight Banners in the Qianlong period. See Sun Jing 孫靜, "A Discussion of the Implementation and Abolishment of 'Back to the Banner' Stipulation in the Qing Dynasty" 《清代歸旗制度行廢述論》, *Journal of the Minzu University of China* 《中央民族大學學報》, 2005, no. 5.

[67] According to Pamela Crossley, the Manchu word "*manjurarenggen*" is the perfect counterpart for this concept. See "Manzhou Yuanliu Kao and the Formalization of the Manchu Heritage." However, it seems that this word was not included in any Manchu dictionary during the Qing Dynasty.

sorts of Manchu clan genealogies and related materials.[68] This was done in order to compile the *Comprehensive Genealogies* on the basis of all these materials. In this form they established a clear yardstick for Manchu identity and in the process forcefully strengthened and highlighted the common historical memory of the Manchus who had following the early Qing emperors in the "great enterprise." The second theme was to cross the "geological fault" of memory of the Ming Jushen, and to trace the Manchu ancestry directly back to the Jin-Yuan Jurchen, thereby giving to all Manchus the character of having origins in a common lineage. This symbolized the fact that the Manchu community would eventually become a pre-modern ethnicity.

The effort to demarcate a boundary for the Manchus as a specific people, differing from the Mongols or the Han Chinese, began no later than the late Kangxi era. The reason why this problem was raised

---

[68] It seems worth investigating whether or not Manchus of that era all had genealogies. The introduction to the *Comprehensive Genealogies of the Eight Banners Manchu Clans* 《八旗滿洲氏族通譜》 mentions that humble Manchu families also had "family genealogies for tracing [their ancestors]," but there were still cases where "[a bannerman] himself forgot his surname, his ancestors' residence, and the process of 'following the dragon,' and lost any evidence to trace." According to Zhuang Jifa 莊吉發 in "Borrowing Han and Adopting Jin: A Study of Changes and Adaptations of Manchu Culture in the Qing Based on Genealogical Compilation" 《參漢酌金：从家譜的撰修論清代滿族文化的變遷与適應》, the Sibei used a traditional form to record family genealogy. On a thin rope measuring over two zhang 丈 in length (one zhang equals approximately 11 feet), they tied models of small a bow and arrow (for the birth of a boy), a small strip of red cloth (for the birth of a girl), a small cradle (for a marriage), and put knee joints of pig or sheep on it to mark off generations. Normally this rope was coiled into a small cloth bag and hung on the tablet of the "Sirin Mamma" in the northwestern corner of the house. It was taken out before the lunar New Year and hung in the courtyard until the second day of the second lunar month. The so-called "Sirin Mamma" was the "genealogical grandmother of continuous family descent." This ancient form of genealogy among the Sibei should also reflect the basic method that Manchu families used in recording their descent prior to their adoption of written genealogies. If this was an ancient tradition, then the Qing court must have utilized such materials in compiling the *Comprehensive Genealogies*. In addition, this kind of cultural movement might have impelled families without formal genealogies to write down their oral tradition, or to transform the above traditional genealogical form into a written one. In any case, this measure taken by the Qing court promoted the genealogical consciousness of the Manchus. Zhuang Jifa's paper is included in *Proceedings of a Seminar on Socio-Cultural Changes and Adaptations of Ethnic Minorities in Chinese Mainland* 《中國大陸少數民族社會文化的變遷與適應學術研討會論文集》 (Taipei: National Chengchi University Nationalities Department, 2004).

repeatedly was that since Hong Taiji's time there had been no clear explanation of the outer boundaries of the Manchus. The explanation of Manchu origins formed in the late Tiancong reign period actually only accounted for the origins of the Aisin Gioro imperial house. Even after dividing the peoples within the banner system into groups of Manchus, Mongols, and Han Chinese, the Manchu Eight Banners still had many Mongol Companies (niru in Manchu) and Liaodong Chinese, who had long since joined forces. In the Kangxi era the demarcation of Manchu identity was attempted by using "the sixty six states following the dragon." However, as the Manchu confederation had many years previously unified Liaodong, it was no longer either suitable or realistic to use the separate political entities of the "states" (gürün) and "tribes" (aiman) that had been conquered by the Manchus to define their identity. Nevertheless, there was another significant measure undertaken in the Kangxi era: based on certain Manchu surnames and genealogical materials, the brothers Tong Yangzheng 佟養正 and Tong Yangxing 佟養性, who had always been part of the Han banners, and who had long since adopted Chinese customs, were now said to have Manchu backgrounds. So Qianlong's genealogical projects only had the function of extending the principles upon which this case was based into a commonly practiced policy. Crossley has long since pointed out that long term consideration of the meaning of Manchu history started in the late Kangxi period. Her explanation is very insightful.[69]

Among the 18th century Manchus, the *hala* and *mukūn* had long ceased to function as basic social organizations. However, after the political identity consciousness of these tribes and states had essentially disintegrated, the identity of the *hala* and *mukūn* became an explanation of Manchu background, thereby becoming an important basis for differentiating people within this group. After coming to China proper and being influenced by the lineage system of Chinese society, the tendency of the Manchus to use the *hala* and *mukūn* as markers of their lineage may have strengthened. Qianlong had no intention of and no way of restoring the historical function the *hala* and *mukūn* once had. He wanted nothing more than to bind the diverse *hala* and *mukūn* names together, thereby transforming the entire *Comprehensive Genealogies* into a basic yardstick for differentiating Manchus from other groups. The *Comprehensive Genealogies* collected a total of over 640 Manchu surnames, including

[69] See Pamela Crossley, *Orphan Warriors*, p. 19.

quite a few "rare surnames." Like a network, it linked together all people with these surnames. The problem of who were the Manchus then became more concrete and easy to define.[70] The "states" and "tribes" of the former era all became "areas" in the *Comprehensive Genealogies*, e.g. the "Hada area" (hada – i ba) and the "Neyen area" (neyen – i ba). These once independent political entities that had opposed the Manchus had become geographical units included within Manchu society. This gives us a glimpse into the Qing court's painstaking intentions in "reconstructing" Manchu history.

The *Comprehensive Genealogies* is a "Who's Who" for generations of famous Manchus. According to the book's introduction, each surname has "the founder of the surname and the first to pledge allegiance." Actually, apart from the larger clans with more detailed records, the "founder of the surname" for many of the entries could not be traced, so under the heading "a certain generation of the clan lived in a certain place" what is written is: "the first to pledge allegiance" or "submitted in the early years of the state." Apart from "the first to pledge allegiance" under a surname, all of those who submitted in the early years of the state whose names could be found were "all included" in the genealogy. One important criterion here is that those persons whose names were listed needed to have performed meritorious deeds and have obtained official rank. Therefore, even though

[70] The introduction to the *Comprehensive Genealogies* gives the guidance that "For those Mongols, Solhos, Nikans, Tai i nikans, and Fusi i nikans who were long organized into the Manchu Eight Banners, their origins should be marked out and their surnames appended to that of Manchus." That is, although the above mentioned peoples had long been included in the Manchu banners, they were now excluded from the Manchu group. In addition, for the "hunting tribes" of the Solons (Evenks), the Dahurs (Daur), and the Oroncuns, as well as the Sibei (Sibe) who were later incorporated into the Eight Banners system, their surnames were listed as Manchu clans. But, due to their late entry and banner organizations which were generally independent from the Manchu Companies (excepting the Sibei), they would still retain their tribal identity right up to the end of the Qing, instead of blending into the Manchu community. The Manchus in late Qing claimed that, "the new residents in Beijing who have come from the Northeast…are all called Manchus, but they are not real Manchus. They come from their own tribes such as the Sibe or Solon….Their languages are vastly different. When they speak in their own tongues, the languages used are neither Manchu nor Mongolian, but their different dialects." This does not necessarily mean that the genealogical movement had failed, but rather that it reflected the natural limits in time and space of the Manchus envelopment of peripheral peoples. Quoted from Yi Geng 奕賡, *Works Written on the Sweet Dream Veranda: Addenda to Trivial Words of the Imperial Guards* 《佳夢軒叢著・侍衛瑣言補》.

they may have submitted in the early years of the state, if they and their descendants "did not have official ranks, then it is enough for them to be listed in their own genealogy, and they would not be included in the present record." Even though the details of their submission may not have been available, "those who performed remarkable service should be included in the record, and a brief biography written." The brief biographies under each surname included in the record must "start with those who performed the greatest meritorious service." For those with official rank but "without achievements to be recounted," they would be "appended at the end of each surname and area entry." These general principles were only relaxed for rare surnames. For those clans that did not have any members with official rank, "one or two people would be recorded to preserve the surname."

We cannot say that the *Comprehensive Genealogies* was not a collection of Manchu clans, but at the same time it was developed closely around a central narrative. Its focus was to forge a common Manchu memory of the momentous and eventful period when the state was founded. The *Comprehensive Genealogies* arranges the recorded figures into three categories of "those who submitted in the early years of the state," "those who submitted in the Tiancong reign period," and "those whose year of submission is unknown." This practice also demonstrates the key role of the timing of "following the dragon" in weaving the collective Manchu memory.

One needs only to browse the Manchu genealogies from later periods to see the huge influence that the *Comprehensive Genealogies* exerted on later Manchu consciousness. As a reserve of materials to be drawn from, it became the fundamental resource for each clan to confirm their own Manchu identity and trace the origin of their surname. The *hala* and *mukūn*, which formerly were symbols of the history of Manchu families, may have themselves possessed the potential to allow them to highlight the collective identity of the Manchu community. Nevertheless, if this kind of potential had not been consciously developed, then it would not have been realized on its own. "Invention" is not like a conjuring trick – it cannot make something out of nothing. However, simply on account of this we should deny neither the fact of that invention itself nor its historical meaning and value.

Just like a rope tying bundle of rice tightly together, from the perspective of Manchuness the new explanation for the common history of both the Manchu clans and the origin of "following the dragon," once being promoted as an ideology, greatly shortened the distance between members of the Manchu community. This was important compensation for the damage inflicted on the collective Manchu identity consciousness by the decline of common cultural symbols, by the widening of the gaps between the poor and the rich as well as between the humble and the noble, and by their geographic scattering. However, up to this point, there was still no reason to believe that the closer relationship within the community driven by the genealogy movement had changed the basic nature of Manchu identity, which dated back to the early Qing.

Here we encounter one vital problem. If we could call the historical memories of a certain group of people regarding what led directly up to their current living conditions "living memories," then it would be extremely difficult to directly remold living memories to change the basic nature of that group's collective identity. Therefore, it was necessary that certain key clues, which could shed light upon later conditions, be followed to an even earlier and therefore less distinct historical period than the time of the "living memories." The *Research on Manchu Origins* was created in response to this circumstance.

In accordance with Qianlong's views, *Research on Manchu Origins* overturned Hong Taiji's edict of the ninth year of the Tiancong reign period banning the original meaning of "Jushen." Nevertheless, to avoid explicitly rebuking the deceased emperor, the book employs the subtle expression of "Our dynasty formerly called its subjects 'Zhushen' (珠申, an alternative Chinese transcription for Jushen 諸申)," in order to tactfully declare that the definition was obsolete:

> Remark: The primogenitor of the Jin originally came from Silla…therefore the ancient roots of the Jin were in Silla. He lived in the White Mountain and the Black River, stretching two thousand *li* from south to north, and this is the same area that our dynasty originated from. *Record of the Great Jin State* 大金國志 says that the Jin was originally called the Zhulizhen 珠里真. This is similar to Zhushen 珠申, the old name of our dynasty's subjects, and is a different pronunciation of Sushen 肅慎.[71]

[71] *Research on Manchu Origins* 《满洲源流考》, ch. 7, "Tribes, seven: Wanyan" 《部族七・完顏》.

This section seems to have been copied almost verbatim from Qianlong's order to compile the *Research on Manchu Origins*. However, in that order Qianlong mentioned only that Zhushen and Sushen were variations of one another, while the *Research on Manchu Origins* asserts that the original name of the Jurchens, Zhulizhen, like Zhushen, was also a variation of Sushen. There is as of yet no satisfactory explanation for the phonetic similarity of the two proper names of Sushen and Jushen, or for the phonetic change from Zhulizhen to Jushen. However, to the authors of the *Research on Manchu Origins*, it was very important to persist with this explanation and especially to advocate that Jushen and Zhulizhen were actually different transcriptions of the same name. They regarded the connection between such appellations as the most direct evidence of the historical continuity between the relevant peoples. If the middle link of Jurchen was missing, it would have been very difficult to trace the history of the Jushen to an even earlier era, let alone to its historical origins.

Therefore, in the late Qianlong period, nearly 150 years after the early Qing investigations into the historical relationship between Jushen and Jurchen were forcefully terminated by Hong Taiji, these investigations were restarted in the imperial court. Purely biologically speaking, Meng'an Mouke Jurchen of the Jin Dynasty had long since blended with other groups, so their descendants were indistinguishable. The Yuan and Ming Liaodong tribes that were called Jurchens in Chinese sources could only be said to be descendants of Jin Dynasty Jurchens in terms of their culture. But at the time, this boundary was unclear. Therefore, the research results at the cultural level would often naturally be transformed on their own accord into a confirmation of lineage. When the *Research on Manchu Origins* mentions the Yuan Dynasty establishment of the Huligai 胡里改 and Woduolian 斡朵憐 tümens in the region of the Shuidada Route 水達達路 it only notices that "Odoli [Eduoli] was the place of residence of our dynasty's ancestors" from a geographical perspective, and it is not conscious of the problem of whether there was a direct lineage relationship between the tribes under these two tümens and the later Hūluns and Jianzhou Jurchens.[72] Its claim that the Manchus were the

[72] *Research on Manchu Origins* 《满洲源流考》, ch. 13, "Territory, 6: Hailan Prefecture, Shuodaleda, and other Routes" 《疆域六：海蘭府碩達勒達等路》. "Shuidada" 水達達 was a Chinese transcription of a Mongolian phrase for "water people" (usu irgen). The Manchus transliterated it as "Shuodaleda" 碩達勒達 and mistakenly translated it as "secret shelter." Note: The fact that Hong Taiji traced the legend of Manchu origins from

descendants of the Jurchen mainly revolved around aspects such as the "position of the terrain" 地形之方位 and the "preservation of old customs" 舊俗之流傳. The latter includes matching surnames, prowess in riding and shooting, and similarities in language.[73]

In addition, the above methods were also used to trace the historical connectivity of the northeastern tribes from the Jin Jurchen back to the Sushen. In the view of the compilers of this work, there were three periods of great cultural change and prosperity in the northeastern tribes starting with the Sushen. The first period coincided with the rise and fall of Bohai 渤海. The text reads:

> Note: The Sushen era roughly corresponded to the period of using knots as records. Then the rites and teachings began to flourish in Fuyu 夫餘 times, and they held sacrificial ceremonies just like the Three Dynasties in ancient North China did. The cultures of Paekche and Silla were indeed flourishing! The two

---

the Hūrha tribe in the remote Heilongjiang River valley showed that he seemed to still have some kind of vague awareness of his own tribe coming from there, but in the Qianlong period the Manchus seemed to have already lost that awareness.

[73] The Manchus emphasized that both the Jin Dynasty and the Qing originated from Changbai Mountain and the Heilongjiang River, to which the above quotations testify. This afterwards became the standard view in the various Manchu genealogies for tracing their ancestral residence. The *Research on Manchu Origins* says, "The surnames recorded in the *History of the Jin Dynasty* all coincide with Manchu ones." However, many of the "corrections" it made to the records of the old history based on the *Comprehensive Genealogies* are quite unreliable. For instance, it changes the two Jurchen surnames "Jiagu" 夾谷 and "Gulijia" 古里甲 into a Manchu surname "Gūlwalgiya," "Puxian" 蒲鮮 into "Buhi," and "Hesujia" 和速嘉 into "Hasara." The book also claims, "As for miraculous military maneuvers and each soldier fighting by himself, just as the *History of the Jin Dynasty* has described, brothers and cousins were all brave warriors; tribes and registered households all possessed great military skills; state level requisition and deployment were like matters within a single family. These points in particular resemble the customs of our dynasty." Furthermore, the Manchus "are masters in riding and shooting, even superior to that recorded in the *History of the Jin Dynasty*." As to language, it says, "The language of the Jin was the same as Manchu, so its official titles are especially traceable, and some of them are even identical to those of our dynasty." Therefore the Jurchen language of the Jin Dynasty is called the "old state language" by the book. Quoted from the *Research on Manchu Origins*, ch. 7, "Tribes, seven: Appendix, Notes on Surnames of the Jin" 《部族七・附金姓氏考》; ch. 16, "Customs, one: Dress" 《國俗一・冠服》; ch. 18, "Customs, three: Explanations of the Old State Language Recorded in the *History of the Jin Dynasty*" 《國俗三・金史舊國語解考》.

> states frequently exchanged envoys with the Sui and Tang Dynasties, and their scholars could write beautiful prose and poems. Once Bohai began to prosper, its cultural and literary reputation reached its height. After the Khitan army came and burned everything, the prominent families dwelling in those once prosperous capitals and cities fled to other prefectures, and then the simple and unsophisticated tradition prevailed in the Wanyan tribe. They were not distracted by outsiders, had a peaceful society, and remained like the old Sushen.[74]

With this return to the old ways, the Jin era Jurchen once again found themselves on the path to prosperity:

> Eight generations and ten rulers passed from the first ancestor down to Taizu. The latter then took the opportunity to found the state, overthrew the Liao, and made the Song his vassal state. Nevertheless, at first his [Jurchen] troops were less than one thousand. It was really the nurturing of local rivers and mountains and their mastery of riding and archery that made them invincible in their conquest, expanding their territory to all of North China.[75]

The third period of cultural prosperity was, of course, achieved by the Manchus.

Through a cultural history that "uses our dynasty as the major framework and describes the other dynasties in detail to trace our origins,"[76] the *Research on Manchu Origins* takes the many tribes that waxed and waned throughout the history of Liaodong and combines them into an immense group of people with an extended, continuous ancestry. This group had a succession of distinct cultural traditions, whose uniqueness was enough to clearly distinguish it from other large contemporary groups, from which Manchus were the sole group of descendants. It was with this method that the *Research on Manchu Origins* reveals where the historical roots of all Manchus were, thereby giving this

---

[74] *Research on Manchu Origins*, ch. 17, "Customs, two: Civilizing Practices" 《國俗二・政教》.

[75] Ibid., ch. 7, "Tribes, seven: Wanyan" 《部族七・完顏》.

[76] A brief abstract of the edition of *Research on Manchu Origins* contained in the *Complete Library of the Four Treasures* 《四庫全書》, following the table of contents.

community a kind of consciousness of "common lineage." When Manchu identity was promoted to the level of a feeling of "common lineage," the process by which the Manchu community became a pre-modern ethnicity came to an end.[77]

When tracing their ancestry to the Jin Jurchen, they were faced with an unavoidable problem: what was the relationship between the ancestors of the Aisin Gioro clan and the Wanyan house of the Jin Dynasty? Qianlong knew that his ministers dare not even comment on this problem and could only "follow verbatim of the imperial edict." Therefore his response was:

> Our dynasty is surnamed Aisin Gioro, and in our state language (Manchu) we call "Jin" Aisin, which is proof of our common origins with the Jin. In the Jin Dynasty the ancestors of our dynasty were subordinates of the Wanyan house, just like all members of the Wanyan clan today are our subjects. All under heaven are united under our administration, and this is the way it should be.

He went on to say that, as a rule, in the successive dynastic changes of Han, Tang, Song, and Ming, the subjects became the rulers. Therefore they should not be afraid of mentioning the fact that the Manchus were once subjects of the Wanyan house.[78] As a surname of the Manchu clans, Wanyan was initially listed in chapter 28 of the already completed *Comprehensive Genealogies*. Since its relationship to the Manchus had now been clarified, the treatment of the Wanyan in the newly added "clan record" 氏族志 in the *Comprehensive Records of the Eight Banners* revised in the 51st year of the Qianlong period "follows the example of *An Abridged Reader of the Comprehensive Mirror for Aid in Government* 通鑑輯覽, which retains the Ming reign title of Hongguang 宏光 even after

---

[77] Some scholars hold that the concept of common descent among the Manchus came into being before this. Pamela Crossley interprets the myth of Manchu origins as being that all Manchus believed that they were the descendents of Bokori Yongshon; see Pamela Crossley, *A Translucent Mirror,* pp. 196-8. This can only be her imagination. Mark Elliot also maintains that the primogenitor in the myth of the origins of the Qing royal house was also the ancestor to whom every ordinary Manchu traced their descent. See Mark C. Elliott, "The Limits of Tartary."

[78] Imperial edict issued on the 19th day of the eighth month of the 42nd year of the Qianlong reign, serving as the preface to the *Research on Manchu Origins*.

the Ming lost its throne, and still places Wanyan at the head of the Manchu banner clans."[79]

If the tribe of Aisin Gioro already existed in the Jin Dynasty, of course they would have had to push its origins back to pre-Jin times. Therefore, the above "clan record" asserts explicitly: "The grand foundations upon which our dynasty was built started in Changbai, where the Jin originated as well. Nevertheless, the imperial lines of the two came from different clans. It was really prior to the origin of the Jin that our ancestors had received the mandate of Heaven which forecasted their auspiciousness."[80] By this time the disparate explanations coming from different historical periods had been embedded in a generally stable manner in the same system of discourse. The Manchus' long term consideration of their own origins then moved on to a new era.

5 Conclusion: Ethnic consciousness and the formation of pre-modern ethnicities

Prior to the mid-20th century, some people believed that "nations" or "ethnicities" had existed since ancient times as some sort of universal and natural units of human assemblage. As a "given," these nations/ethnicities were just as "natural" as gender, religion, language, and even humanity itself. This seemingly unspoken consensus was typically expressed within the academic world as an inclination toward "primordialism." This theory holds that nations and ethnic communities are natural units and integral elements of the human experience formed on the basis of "primordial" ties such as language, religion, "race," kinship, customs, and territory.[81] Therefore, the political entities we call "nations" and the consciousness and concepts we call "nationalism" in modern times had always existed in their natural state before modernity, even though people at that time did not refer them in these terms. In addition, compared with their historical

---

[79] *Comprehensive Records of the Eight Banners*, ch. 55, "Clan Record, two: Wanyan Clan" 《氏族志二・完顏氏》.

[80] Ibid., ch. 54, "Clan Record, one: The Origin of the State Surname" 《氏族志一・國姓原始》.

[81] "Race" here denotes types of physical appearance classified by features such as complexion, facial form, and hair. This classification is an artificial cultural "construct" rather than a reflection of any certain "biological" reality. However, the key here is not whether this notion is scientific, but whether people believe it to be true.

predecessors, the scope and effectiveness of modern nations and nationalism have received unprecedented promotion.[82]

If so, then what caused such a range of human ties to possess such an enormous emotional power beyond considerations of interest and rational calculation, and thereby enabled them to coalesce such large groups of people? Primordialists had already realized that it is not the ties themselves, but peoples' views, perceptions, and faith that turned power and meaning into "primordial attachments" attributed to those ties. Following this logic, "the main object of analysis for historians and social scientists studying ethnicity and nationalism" should be these kinds of subjective "primordial attachments" and cannot be limited to the set of primordial ties themselves.[83]

However, the primordialists appear to be unconcerned about this critical question. They view primordial attachments as having a natural or innate "existence" within human nature. Finding them is to reach the source. Therefore, the primordialists are inclined towards taking the identification of "primordial" attachments as the proper and successful end point of their analysis. As for these attachments or identities, there is nothing further to be said about them. Many of them see primordial attachments as being ineffable, and therefore, for social scholars, incapable of being analyzed.[84] It follows that the focus of the primordialists turns away from particular manifestations of ethnic sentiments and attitudes in social interactions and political shifts, as well as their specific process of development and changes "to the more unchanging cultural dimensions that unite and mark off groups of human beings – religion, customs, language, and historical memories."[85] That is to say, that in the end primordialism is very close to the theoretical orientation that derives or specifies the definition of ethnicity from four or five common cultural characteristics.

It is precisely because of the overemphasis on the semi-innateness of spontaneous primordial attachments, the pre-determinedness attributed to given primordial ties and their fixed or stagnant nature, that primordialists

---

[82] Anthony D. Smith, *The Ethnic Origins of Nations* (Oxford: Basil Blackwell, 1986), pp. 11-2.

[83] Anthony D. Smith, *The Nation in History: Historiographical Debates about Ethnicity and Nationalism* (Hanover: University Press of New England, 2000), p. 21.

[84] Jack Eller and Reed Coughlan, "The Poverty of Primordialism: The Demystification of Ethnic Attachments," *Ethnic and Racial Studies*, vol. 16, no. 2, 1993.

[85] Anthony D. Smith, *The Ethnic Origins of Nations*, p. 210.

have greatly overlooked the necessity of exploring the formative process of the subjective consciousness of ethnic identity. This not only causes them to simply ahistorically trace a result that actually formed over a long period of historical changes back to the initial stage of that process, but it also has led them to a lack of proper understanding and assessment of the subjective initiative of human consciousness as it reflects the existence of primordial ties in society. This is because the activity of human consciousness does not only passively reflect different given primordial ties, but also often "remolds" their real form by selecting, amplifying, restructuring, and reinterpreting them.

These weaknesses in primordialism mean it cannot adequately explain the rapid, intense changes taking place today in the global ethnic map. Therefore, in the latter half of the twentieth century, a variety of modernist theories of ethnicity and nationalism have been formed. These theories have deeply influenced research on modern and contemporary Chinese ethnicities in Western Chinese studies, and they have, within the last ten plus years, brought refreshing new perspectives to the field. Even though western academic circles are still far from covering all of China's current ethnicities, this "ethnic map is currently being filled in."[86] These works have adequately shown what kind of important role the "construction" of subjective consciousness on ethnic identity by modern nation states can play in the process of the formation of ethnicities.[87]

---

[86] Susan Blum, "Margins and Centers: A Decade of Publishing on China's Ethnic Minorities," *Journal of Asian Studies*, 64.4 (2002). Blum says that the most remarkable "gap" in the current academic environment is the lack of a "full fledged" investigation into the formation of "Han Chinese." This view is quite noteworthy.

[87] In the ethnic identification practice of the 1950s, Chinese theorists and field practitioners found that the classification of nations had to take into account the factor of a "nations' own will" 民族意願. This perhaps reflected the earliest consciousness of their attempt to adjust the definition of the "five commons" 五共同 method. By the 1980s, the Chinese academic community seemed to intentionally include the subjective consciousness of ethnic identity into the traditional conceptual framework of a "common psychological constitution expressed by common culture." The artificially constructed nature of ethnic groups was also expressed by Fei Xiaotong 費孝通, an ethnic sociologist of the older generation. In his preface to *Yao Ethnicity of Pan Village* 《盤村瑤族》, he plainly and vividly points out that the term "branch of nationality" 民族支系 that had been used all along is not accurate enough, because many of such ethnic groups are more like a water system with multiple origins and one mainstream than a tree with the same root and multiple branches. See Hu Qiwang 胡起望 and Fan Honggui 范宏貴, *Yao Ethnicity of Pan Village* 《盤村瑤族》 (Beijing: Nationalities Press, 1983), preface, p. 4.

The most remarkable contribution of modern ethnic theory is that it keenly senses that ethnicity possesses the attribute of being artificially and subjectively constructed. On the other hand, however, even though modernists emphasize different aspects of how the modernization process stimulated ethnic identity, they all see that the trend toward nations and nationalism as the product of modernity and modern civilization therefore had hardly any pre-modern roots. This has led other scholars to try to "distance their analysis from the more sweeping claims on either side," whether primordialism or modernism. This is because they cannot agree that ethnic primordial attachments are natural and universal and can only passively reflect given primordial ties, and that modern nation and nationalism are nothing but the expansion or latest version of those primordial ties and consciousnesses that already existed in pre-modern times. Nor can they agree that there was a radical break between modern nations and nationalism and the corresponding historical units and sentiments within pre-modern society.[88]

Following this line of thinking, Anthony Smith proposes six main dimensions to the identification of pre-modern ethnicities: a collective name, a common myth of descent, a shared history, a distinctive shared culture, an association with a specific "homeland," and a sense of solidarity that existed among at least the elite.[89] Smith calls pre-modern ethnicities "ethnie," and points out that it is not necessary for a modern nation to have a former existence as an "ethnie," but there do exist many modern nations that were built around a core of a strong, internally unified ethnie. If those nations that lack such a core are to survive, they must

---

[88] Anthony D. Smith, *The Ethnic Origins of Nations*, p. 13. Remark: The focus of his argument here is the historical relations between pre-modern ethnicities and modern nations. In the introduction to *Ethnicity* (Oxford Readers), he classifies the existing approaches to ethnicity into two opposite categories: primordialist and instrumentalist. He points out that few scholars in practice would solely adhere to either one. In those "systematic attempts" to combine the two categories, he lists three main approaches, namely the "transactionalist" approach of F. Barth, the "social psychologist" approach of Horowitz, and the "ethnosymbolicist" approach of John Armstrong and himself. See J. Hutchinson and A. D. Smith, *Ethnicity* (Oxford: Oxford University Press, 1996), pp. 7-10. In the latter classification, the modernist viewpoint that an ethnic group is the indirect product of modernity (regarding ethnic consciousness as the response of marginalized people in a nation state towards the nationalist movement of the majority of the citizens) may have been included in Barth's approach of transaction analysis.

[89] Anthony D. Smith, *The Ethnic Origins of Nations*, pp. 22-30.

"reinvent" one. "That means discovering a suitable and convincing past which can be reconstructed and re-presented to members and outsiders."[90]

In this case, how can we distinguish between an ethnie and a modern nation? Smith answers, "While ethnies share with nations the elements of common name, myth and memory, their center of gravity is different: ethnies are defined largely by their ancestry myths and historical memories; nations are defined by the historic territory they occupy and by their mass, public cultures and common laws. A nation must possess its homeland, an ethnie need not."[91]

At first glance Smith's six dimensions of ethnie look very similar to the six proposed primordial ties outlined by Clifford Geertz, a well known advocate of primordialism – imagined lineage, race, language, territory, religion, and customs.[92] This may be related to the reason why Anthony Smith and John Armstrong were recognized by other scholars as the two most outstanding representative figures of primordialism.[93] However, after careful comparison of the two discussions it is not hard to see that Smith's investigation is concentrated on the formation and development of a subjective consciousness, i.e. the common identity within a group, while primordialists shift their focus to the "primordial" ties themselves, thereby, in effect, almost completely discarding the discussion of "primordial attachments."

Therefore the key to the problem is the question posed by anthropologists and ethnic sociologists regarding modern nation or ethnic groups, i.e., what kind of role has the subjective consciousness of group "self-ascription" played in the formation of ethnicities or ethnic groups. This question should be introduced into the field of history and answered using the methods of historical study. Of course, due to the limitations in materials, we are unable to make detailed investigations into the identity consciousness of many historical groups. However, the current situation is that many cases for which the historical materials are adequate have not up to now received our attention due to a lack of awareness of the issue. Apart from the Manchus, Hui, Tibetans, and Mongols, all mentioned in

---

90 Ibid., p. 212.

91 Anthony D. Smith, *The Nation in History,* p. 65.

92 Clifford Geertz, "The Integrative Revolution," in Clifford Geertz, ed., *Old Societies and New States* (New York: Free Press, 1963), pp. 108-13, quoted in J. Hutchinson and A. D. Smith, *Ethnicity*, pp. 43-5.

93 Sukumar Periwal, "Conclusion of Notions of Nationalism," in Sukumar Periwal, ed., *Notions of Nationalism* (Budapest: Central European University Press, 1995), p. 232.

this paper, the formation of Han ethnicity is, of course, one of the topics that we should first turn to.[94]

Smith points out that in the six dimensions that constitute the social culture or symbols of pre-modern ethnie, a myth of common descent is "the sine qua non of ethnicity, the key element of that complex of meanings which underlie the sense of ethnic ties and sentiments for the participants." Here "common descent" is not concerned with actual descent, but rather with a sense of subjectively imputed common origins. To the pre-modern way of thinking, the distinction between succession in the biological sense and that in the cultural sense is more vague and less significant than ours. Therefore, even though the common indicators of the group were mainly cultural, society has always seen them from the perspective of biological descent. A myth of common descent provides a kind of general response regarding the similarity and common belonging of the members of a group: Why are we all so alike? Why are we one community? Because we came from the same place, at a definite period of time, and are descended from the self-same ancestor, we necessarily belong together and share the same perceptions and interests.[95]

In this view, the consciousness of a common descent to a large extent may be seen as a combined reflection of the many common experiences and sentiments within a group, and may even be said to be a kind of upgrading. It is this kind of combination or upgrading that caused pre-modern ethnicities to evolve from their original community form. This is what Smith means when he defines the existence of a common myth and memory as the main difference between pre-modern ethnicity and Handelman's "ethnic category."[96]

---

[94] Some Mongolian scholars who have received anthropological training in the West believe that the Mongols did not become an ethnicity until the early 20th century. The process of the Mongolian community becoming a pre-modern ethnicity seems not to have been completed in the Yuan Dynasty, but I am afraid that it is hardly convincing that this process had not finished even by the end of the Qing. See Almaz Khan, "Chinggis Khan: From Imperial Ancestor to Ethnic Hero," in Stevan Harrell, *Cultural Encounters on China's Ethnic Frontiers* (University of Washington Press, 1994).

[95] Anthony D. Smith, *The Ethnic Origins of Nations*, pp. 24, 58; Pierre van den Berghe, "Does Race Matter?" *Nations and Nationalism*, vol. 1, no. 3 (1995).

[96] J. Hutchinson and A. D. Smith, *Ethnicity*, p. 5-7. Don Handelman divides the human cultural community into four levels, namely, ethnic category, ethnic network, ethnic association, and ethnic community. Smith holds that the second and third levels actually parallel his definition of "ethnie" (pre-modern ethnicity). The fourth level is generally known as the modern nation. As for the so-called "ethnic category," it denotes a certain

We know that Max Weber's key basis for determining an ethnic group was their subjective faith in their common descent. But over the past few decades, western sociologists, especially in their teaching practice in universities, have to a great extent abandoned Weber's definition, and they prefer to equate ethnicity with a common culture. The confusion caused by this new definition of "ethnicity" has been criticized by many scholars.[97] Walker Connor points out that if we follow this new definition made by "American sociologists," then "ethnic group" will become a synonym for "minority." The result would be the important differences between different forms of identity may be completely lost.[98] Furthermore, simply attaching a wider theoretical meaning to a given concept cannot change the factual conclusions of empirical research. Of course people can take "ethnic group" to be the equivalent of "minority," but if they do so, they must invent a different word to be used to indicate a minority that is conscious of its common descent. Therefore, a large portion of anthropologists and sociologists would rather continue to use this term in a way that is closer to Weber's point of view.

Two basic methods of showing common descent exist within pre-modern ethnicities. One is to trace all members of the group back to a common ancestor in ancient times. The myth of descent of the Kazakhs is the most typical example of this type of expression. The other method is not so straightforward. It traces the group to a group of people who possessed a certain unique culture, which was enough to differentiate it from other contemporary groups. This method of expression may not take the full form that a "myth" would have. Therefore, Smith's account probably should be slightly adjusted. It is very important for us to fully comprehend the consciousness of common descent expressed in this manner in order to understand the historical form of pre-modern ethnic identity.[99]

---

kind of the loosest cooperative relations, which only includes awareness of the cultural differences between the group and outsiders, as well as the consciousness of boundaries derived from this awareness. Perhaps "ethnic category" can be approximately understood as a kind of latent pre-modern ethnicity.

[97] Stephen Cornell and Douglas Hartmann, *Ethnicity and Race: Making Identities in a Changing World* (Thousand Oaks, CA: Pine Forge Press, 1998), pp. 16-8.

[98] Walker Connor, "A Nation Is a Nation, Is a State, Is an Ethnic Group, Is a ...," *Ethnic and Racial Studies*, 1.4 (1978).

[99] In her paper quoted above discussing the *Research on Manchu Origins*, Crossley writes that because the term "ethnicity" is more appropriate in the background of the 19th

The reason why I have used this last section to give a brief assessment of the concepts of common descent, ethnic consciousness, pre-modern ethnicity, and the modern nation, as well as the relations between them, is because an analysis of the historical changes in Manchu identity must be supported by an explanatory framework. The Manchu community began to exist the day Hong Taiji issued his edict changing the name to "Manchu." However the nature of this community underwent several profound changes. As this paper has already discussed in detail, Manchu identity became a pre-modern ethnic identity in nature only when the concept of a common Manchu descent was established in the Qianlong period. At the same time this also marked the fact that "Manchu" truly went from being a cultural-military community to a pre-modern ethnicity. Lasting roughly one and a half centuries, only when it was under attack from the anti-Qing revolution and the trend toward modern nationalism was it that this pre-modern ethnicity began to transform into a modern nation or ethnic group. The members of the Han Army Eight Banners were enveloped by the "Manchu" ethnicity due to the then dominant belief that "bannermen are Manchu." This was the historical root of including Han bannermen into the Manchu group when China's various nationalities 民族 were assigned in 1950s. However, the problem of how the Manchu were transformed into a modern nation is beyond the scope of this paper, and it should be the topic of another study.

---

and 20th centuries, she prefers to choose the word "race" to describe the Qing concept of descent and identity in the 18th century. She says that in its rather archaic sense "race" denotes a people sharing a common point of origin, whether a single individual in historical times, or an archetypical figure (an individual or a group) from pre-history. It is obvious that "race" as used by Crossley is in actuality the same as "ethnie" as used by Smith. Still other scholars believe that there is another, looser form for showing the consciousness of common descent. "The descendents from the same homeland are often loosely understood as carrying the implication of from a common ancestor. For instance, all Cubans coming to U.S. actually do not consider that they are from a common ancestor, but they do claim that they are the descents of the same homeland, which implies mutual consanguinity." See Stephen Cornell and Douglas Hartmann, *Ethnicity and Race,* p. 19. Nonetheless, in this example it is more probable that the consciousness of common descent derives from the existence of Cuban as a "nation." Whether the consciousness of common descent can be directly derived from belonging of a same homeland seems to remain a question that needs further investigation.

Maps

Note: All locations on the maps are listed in the Index.

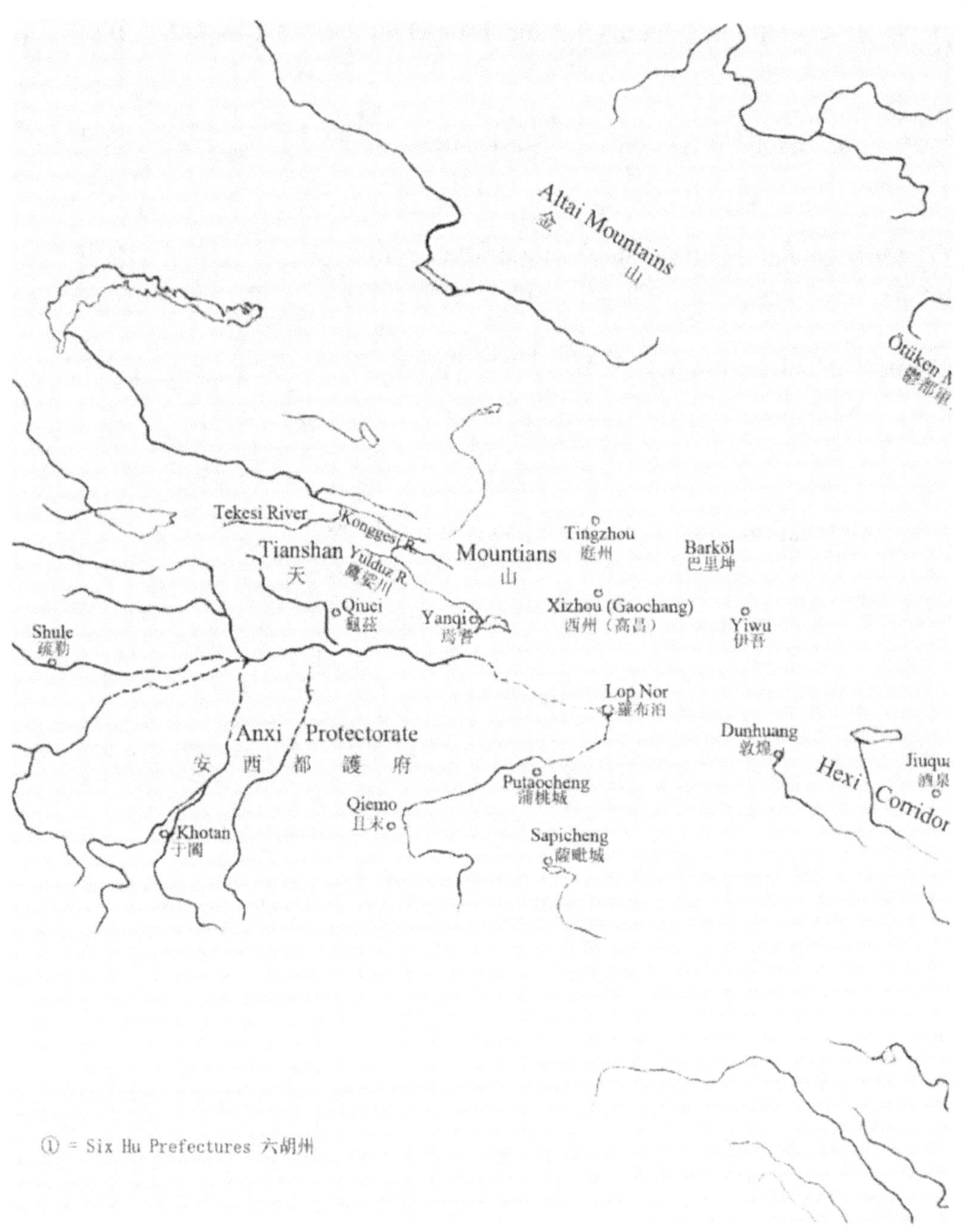

Map 1: The Western Regions in the

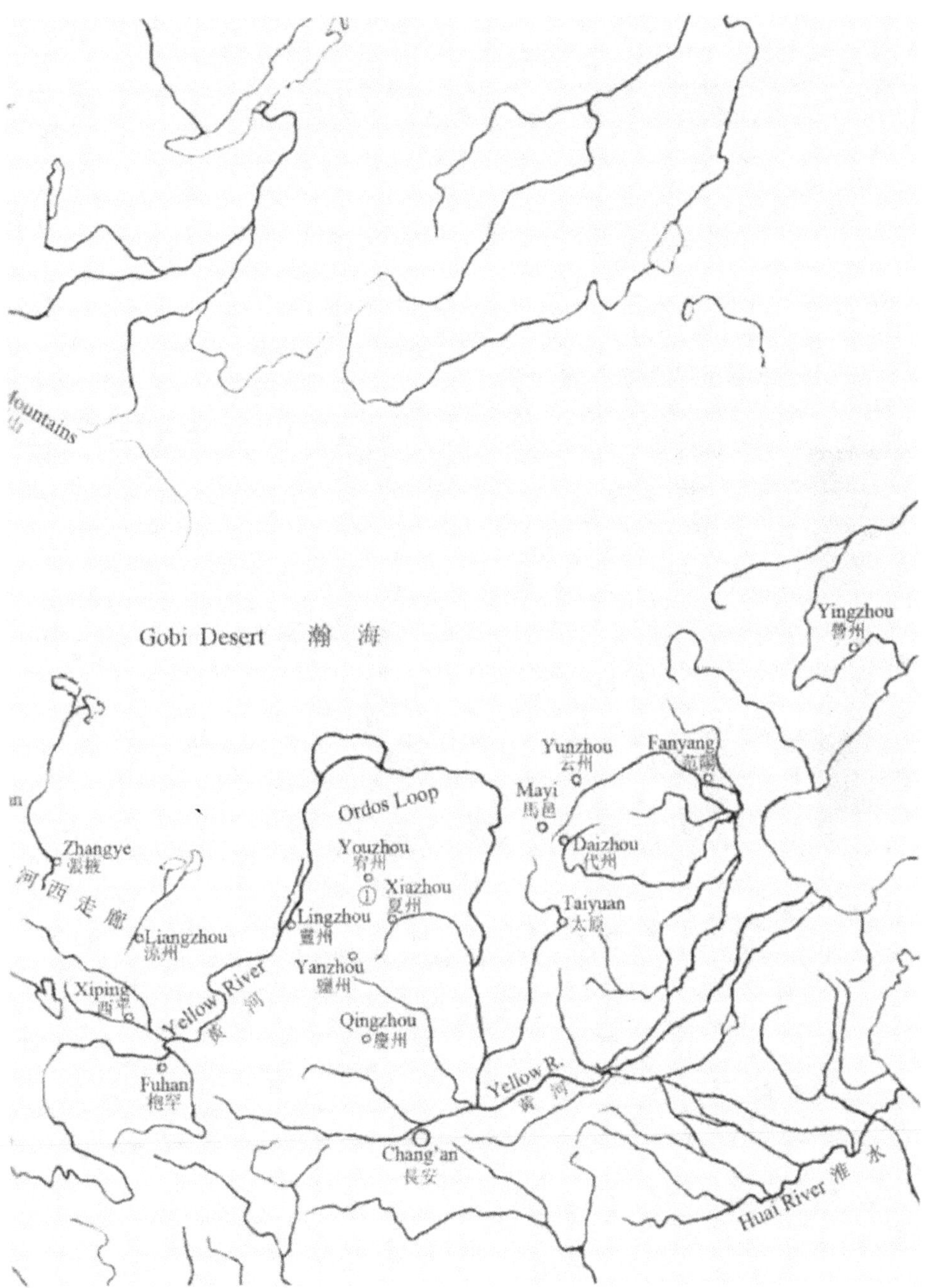

Sui and Tang Dynasties

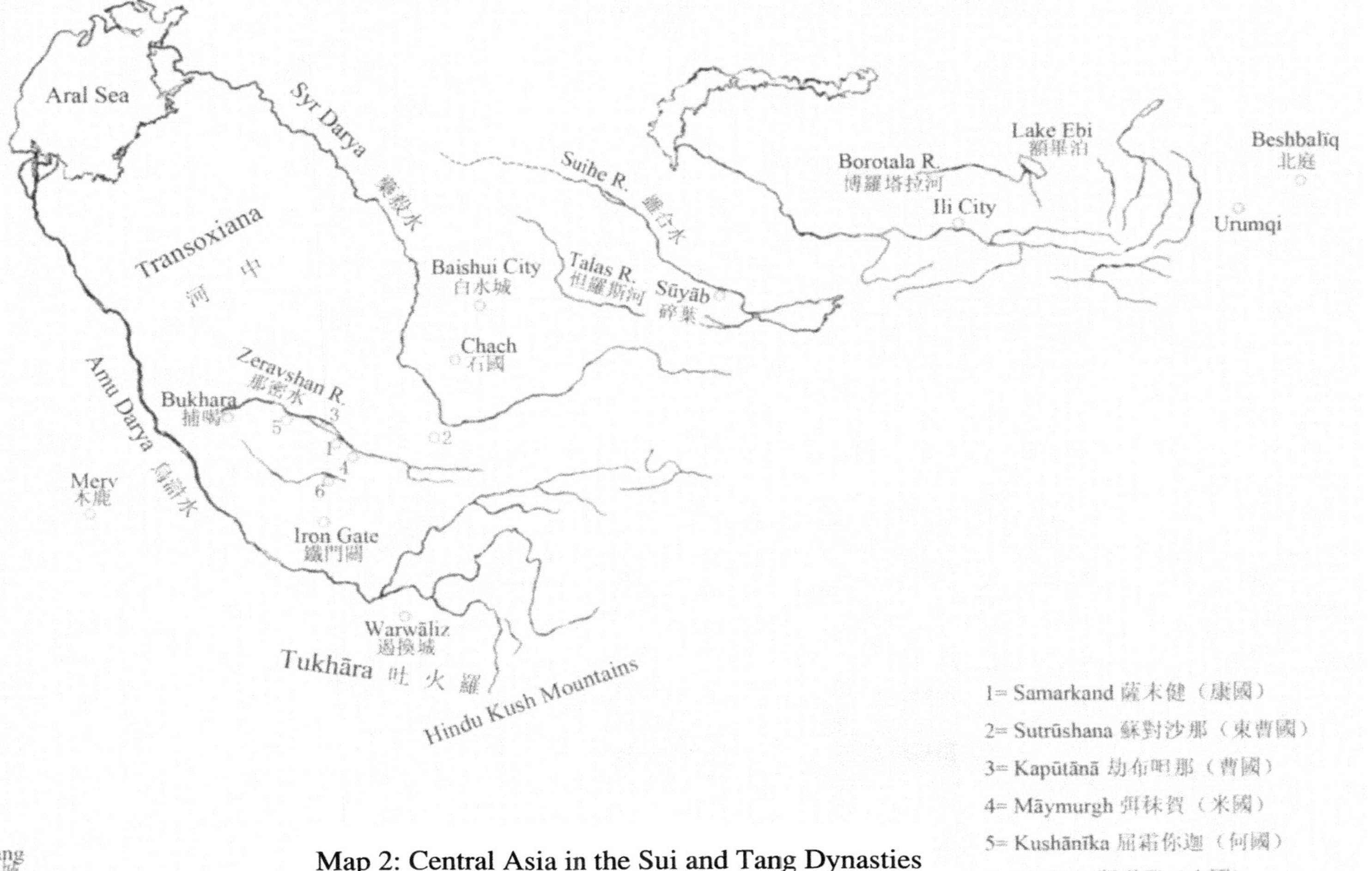

Map 2: Central Asia in the Sui and Tang Dynasties

Map 3: Mongolia and Siberia in the Mongol-Yuan Period

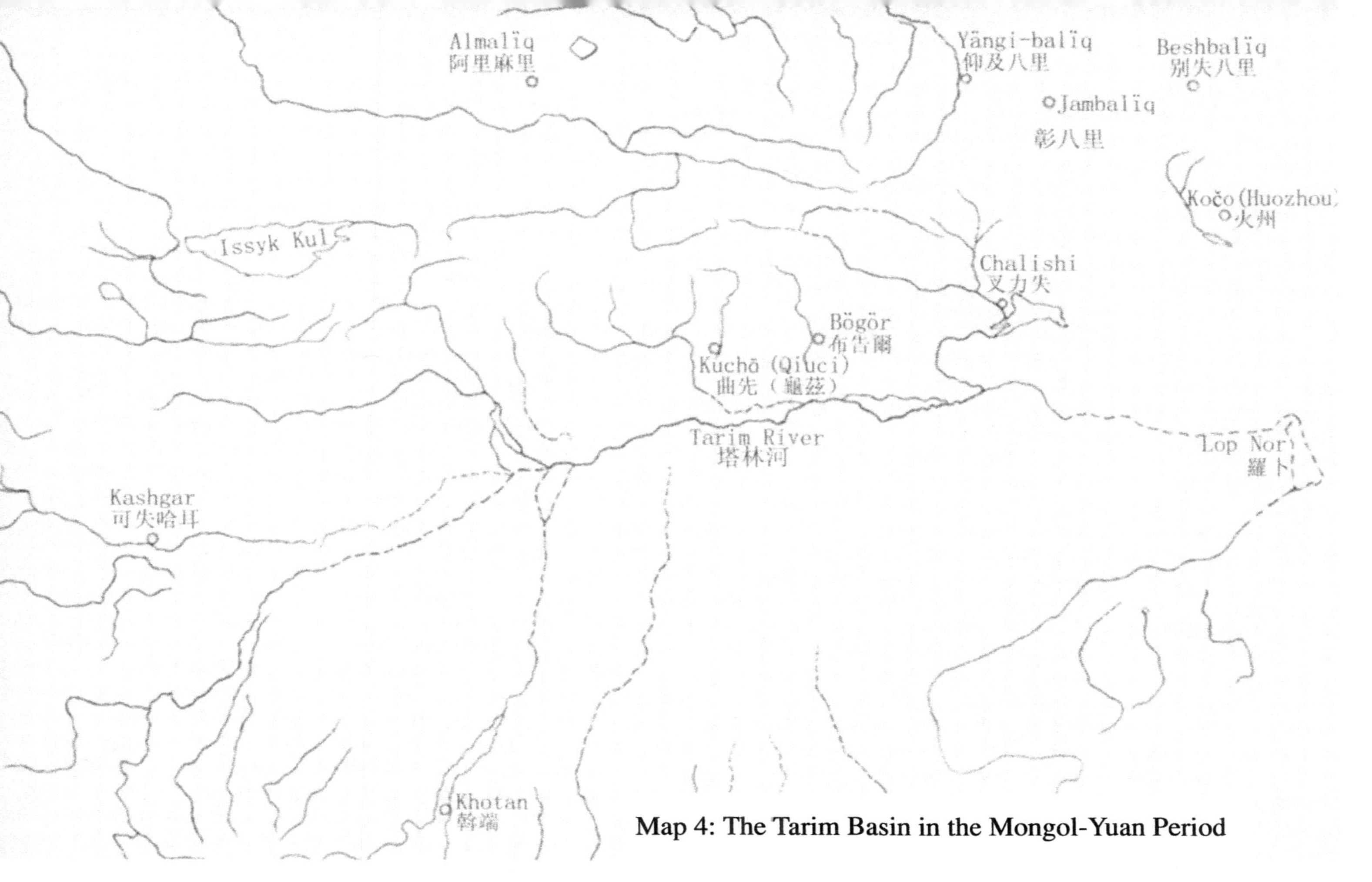

Map 4: The Tarim Basin in the Mongol-Yuan Period

CHINESE-LANGUAGE PRIMARY SOURCES CITED

Note: Any references in the original Chinese essays to specific editions of the sources listed here are indicated in the footnotes of the translations. Those unfamiliar with Chinese scholarship should recognize that essays written by scholars of older generations very seldom cite editions for Chinese-language primary sources.

An Abridged Reader of the Comprehensive Mirror for Aid in Government 《通鑑輯覽》 (*Tongjian jilan*).

Account of Family History of the Xie Clan of Gaochang 《高昌偰氏家傳》 (*Gaochang Xieshi jiazhuan*), Ouyang Gui 歐陽圭.

Annals of the Han 《漢紀》 (*Han ji*), Xun Yue 荀悅.

Annals of the Later Han 《後漢紀》 (*Hou Han ji*), Yuan Hong 袁宏.

Annotated Catalog of the Imperial Library by Command 《四庫全書總目提要》(*Siku quanshu zongmu tiyao*).

Anthology of the Drunken Hermit at the Twin Streams 《雙溪醉隱集》 (*Shuangxi zuiyin ji*), Yelü Zhu 耶律鑄.

Ast-III-4-093 [Dunhuang text, see Jiang Boqin's essay, footnote six].

Biographical Sketch of Master Guo, Administrator of the Astrological Commission Bureau 《知太史院事郭公行狀》 (*Zhitaishi yuanshi Guogong xingzhuang*).

Biographies of Eminent Monks Compiled in the Song Dynasty 《宋高僧傳》 (*Song gaoseng zhuan*), Shi Zanning 釋贊寧.

Biography of the Tripitaka Dharma-Master of the Great Compassion Monastery 《大慈恩寺三藏法師傳》 (*Dacien si sanzang fashi zhuan*).

Book of Documents 《商書》 (*Shang shu*).

A Brief History of the Black Tatars《黑韃事略》(*Heida shilüe*), Peng Daya 彭大雅 and Xu Ting 徐霆.

A Brief History of the Eastern Capital Era 《東都事略》 (*Dongdu shilüe*), Wang Cheng 王稱.

A Brief Treatise on the Personages in the Lands of the Western Regions 《西域土地人物略》 (*Xiyu tudi renwu lüe*).

Categorized Literature from the Yuan Period 《元文類》 (*Yuan wenlei*), Su Tianjue 蘇天爵.

The Characteristics of Each Province in the Empire 《天下郡國利病書》 (*Tianxia junguo libing shu*), Gu Yanwu 顧炎武.

Classic of Mountains and Seas 《山海經》 (*Shanhai jing*).

Collected Books in the House for Regal Writings《宸翰樓叢書》(*Chenhanlou congshu*).

Collected Gazetteer Records of Xijin 《析津志輯佚》 (*Xijin zhi jiyi*).

Collected Notes of an Aged Learner at the Commoner's Study 《庶齋老學叢談》 (*Shuzhai laoxue congtan*), Sheng Ruzi 盛如梓.

Collected Records of the Qing 《清事彙書》 (*Qing shi huishu*).

Collected Works by the Prime Minister during the Huichang Reign Period 《會昌一品集》 (*Huichang yipin ji*).

Collected Works from the Studio for Self-Reflection 《存復齋文集》 (*Cunfuzhai wenji*), Zhu Derun 朱德潤.

Collected Works of Chen Boyu《陳伯玉文集》 (*Chen Boyu wenji*), Chen Zi'ang 陳子昂.

Collected Works of Gaofeng 《高峰文集》 (*Gaofeng wenji*), Liao Gang 廖剛.

Collected Works of Guizhai 《圭齋文集》 (*Guizhai wenji*), Ouyang Xuan 歐陽玄; also *Collection of Guizhai* 《圭齋集》(*Guizhai ji*).

Collected Works of Huang Jinhua 《黃金華文集》 (*Huang Jinhua wenji*), Huang Jin 黄溍.

Collected Works of Yan Lugong 《顏魯公文集》 (*Yan Lugong wenji*) , Yan Zhenqing 顏真卿.

Collected Works of Zhang Jiuling 《曲江集》 (*Qujiang ji*) [literally, *Collection from Qujiang*], Zhang Jiuling 張九齡.

Collected Works of Zhang Yue《張說之集》(*Zhang Yue zhiji*), Zhang Yue 張說.

Collection from the Snowy Tower 《雪樓集》 (*Xuelou ji*), Cheng Jufu 程鉅夫.

Collection of Literature on Military Issues 《登壇必究》 (*Dengtan bijiu*), Wang Minghe 王鳴鶴.

Collection of Literature Arranged by Categories 《藝文類聚》 (*Yiwen leiju*), Ouyang Xun 歐陽詢.

Collection of the Best Bronze and Stone Inscriptions 《金石萃編》 (*Jinshi cuibian*).

Collection of the Zhizheng Reign Period 《至正集》 (*Zhizheng ji*), Xu Youren 許有壬.

Commentary on the Return of the Army 《班師議》 (*Banshi yi*), Hao Jing 郝經.

Compendium of Administrative Law of the Six Divisions of the Tang Bureaucracy 《唐六典》 (*Tang liudian*).

Compendium of Materia Medica 《本草綱目》 (*Bencao gangmu*), Li Shizhen 李時珍.

Compendium of the Doctrines and Styles of the Teaching of Mani, the Buddha of Light [Dunhuang text] 《摩尼光佛教法儀略》 (*Moni guangfo jiaofa yilüe*).

Compilation of Surnames in the Era of Yuanhe 《元和姓纂》 (*Yuanhe xing zuan*), Lin Bao 林寶.

Complete Prose Literature of the Tang 《全唐文》 (*Quan Tang wen*).

Complete Report on the Mongolian Tatars 《蒙韃備錄》 (*Mengda beilu*), Zhao Gong 趙珙.

Complete Stories of the Court and the People《朝野僉載》 (*Chao ye qianzai*), Zhang Zhuo 张鷟.

Complete Tang Poems《全唐詩》 (*Quan Tang shi*).

Comprehensive Genealogies of the Eight Banners Manchu Clans 《八旗滿洲氏族通譜》 (*Baqi manzhou shizu tongpu*).

Comprehensive Investigations based on Literary and Documentary Sources 《文獻通考》 (*Wenxian tongkao*), Ma Duanlin 馬端臨.

Comprehensive Mirror for Aid in Government 《資治通鑒》 (*Zizhi tongjian*); also *Comprehensive Mirror*《通鑑》(*Tongjian*), Sima Guang 司馬光.

Comprehensive Mirror for Aid in Government, Textual Analysis 《資治通鑒考異》 (*Zizhi tongjian kaoyi*).

Comprehensive Records of Shengjing 《盛京通志》 (*Shengjing tongzhi*).

Comprehensive Records of the Censorate 《憲臺通紀》 (*Xiantai tongji*).

Comprehensive Records of the Eight Banners 《八旗通志》 (*Baqi tongzhi*).

Continuation of Comprehensive Investigations based on Literary and Documentary Sources 《續文獻通考》 (*Xu Wenxian tongkao*), Wang Qi 王圻.

Continuation of the Comprehensive Mirror for Aid in Government 《續資治通鑒》 (*Xu zhi tongjian*).

Corpus of Clerical Script 《隸釋》 (*Lishi*), Hong Kuo 洪适.

Corrected Records of the Northern Routes 《北道刊誤志》 (*Beidao kanwu zhi*), Wang Guan 王瓘.

Customs of the Northern Barbarians 《北虜風俗》 (*Beilu fengsu*), Xiao Daheng 蕭大亨.

Daily Records of Yeonsangun of Yi Korea 《燕山君日記》 (*Yanshanjun riji*).

Debate on Orthodoxy《正統辨》 (*Zhengtong bian*), Yang Weizhen 楊維楨.

Discussing the Ten Tribes and the Four Frontier Defense Commands 《論十姓四鎮疏》 (*Lun shixing sizhen shu*), memorial by Guo Yuanzhen 郭元振.

Encyclopaedic History of Institutions 《通典》 (*Tongdian*).

Epitaph of Cao Runguo 《曹閏國墓誌》 (*Cao Runguo muzhi*).

Epitaph of Han Dechang 《韓德昌墓誌銘》 (*Han Dechang muzhiming*).

Epitaph of Han Kuangsi 《韓匡嗣墓誌銘》 (*Han Kuangsi muzhiming*).

Epitaph of He Shu 《何數墓誌》 (*He Shu muzhi*).

Epitaph of Lady Xiao, Princess of Jin Principality and Wife of Yelü Yuan 《耶律元妻晉國夫人蕭氏墓誌》 (*Yelü Yuan qi Jinguo shiren Xiaoshi muzhi*).

Epitaph of Lady Xiao, Princess of Qin Yue Principality and Wife of the Younger Brother of the Emperor 《皇弟秦越國妃蕭氏墓誌》 (*Huangdi Qinyueguo fei Xiaoshi muzhi*).

Epitaph of Lady Xiao, Wife of Han Kuangsi 《韓匡嗣妻蕭氏墓誌銘》 (*Han Kuangsi qi Xiaoshi muzhiming*).

Epitaph of Liu Yuanshang 《劉元尚墓誌》 (*Liu Yuanshang muzhi*).

Epitaph of Lord An, the Great Chief of the Tang Six Hu Prefectures 《唐故六胡州大首領安君墓誌》 (*Tang gu Liuhuzhou dashouling An jun muzhi*).

Epitaph of the Great Princess of Liang Principality《梁國太妃墓誌銘》(*Liangguo taifei muzhiming*).

Epitaph of the Great Princess of Qin Principality 《秦國太妃墓誌》 (*Qinguo taifei muzhi*).

Epitaph of the Princess of Song Wei Principality 《宋魏國妃墓誌銘》 (*Songweiguo fei muzhiming*) [also《宋魏國妃蕭氏墓誌銘》 (*Songweiguo fei Xiaoshi muzhiming*)].

Epitaph of the Wuwei Tang Dynasty Tuyuhun Murong Family 《武威唐代吐谷渾慕容墓誌》 (*Wuwei Tangdai Tuyuhun Murong muzhi*).

Epitaph of Xiao Dewen 《蕭德温墓誌》 (*Xiao Dewen muzhi*).
Epitaph of Xiao Jin 《蕭僅墓誌銘》 (*Xiao Jin muzhiming*).
Epitaph of Xiao Wuluben Niangzi 《蕭烏盧本娘子墓誌銘》 (*Xiao Wuluben Niangzi muzhi*).
Epitaph of Xiao Xiaozhong 《蕭孝忠墓誌》 (*Xiao Xiaozoing muzhi*)
Epitaph of Yelü Qingsi 《耶律慶嗣墓誌》 (*Yelü Qingsi muzhi*).
Epitaph of Yelü Renxian 《耶律仁先墓誌》 (*Yelü Renxian muzhi*).
Epitaph of Yelü Xinie 《耶律習涅墓誌銘》 (*Yelü Xinie muzhiming*).
Epitaph of Yelü Yuanning 《耶律元寧墓誌》 (*Yelü Yuanning muzhi*).
Epitaph of Yelü Yuanzuo 《耶律元佐墓誌銘》 (*Yelü Yuanzuo muzhiming*).
Epitaph of Yelü Zhixian 《耶律智先墓誌銘》 (*Yelü Zhixian muzhiming*).
Epitaph of Yelü Zongjiao《耶律宗教墓誌銘》 (*Yelü Zongjiao muzhiming*).
Epitaph of Zhao Kuangyu 《趙匡禹墓誌》 (*Zhao Kuangyu muzhi*).
Essential Arts and Assorted Techniques for Family Living《居家必用事類全集》 (*Jujia biyong shilei quanji*).
Essentials of Government of the Three Reigns in the Late Song《宋季三朝政要》(*Songji sanchao zhengyao*).
Essentials of Government of the Zhenguan Era 《貞觀政要》 (*Zhenguan zhengyao*), Wu Jing 吴競.
Examination on Political Questions 《策對》 (*Cedui*). In *Collection of the Jade Tablet Studio* 《圭齋集》 (*Guizhai ji*).
Examples of Refined Usage 《爾雅》 (*Erya*).
Extended Continuation of the Comprehensive Mirror for Aid in Government 《續資治通鑒長編》 (*Xu zizhi tongjian changbian*), Li Tao 李燾
Extended Rhymes《廣韵》 (*Guangyun*), Chen Pengnian 陳彭年.
Extensive Notes on the Comprehensive Mirror for Aid in Government 《資治通鑒廣注》 (*Zizhi tongjian guang zhu*), Hu Sanxing 胡三省.
Factual Traces of An Lushan 《安祿山事跡》 (*An Lushan shiji*), Yao Runeng 姚汝能.
Fan Deda's Official Certificate《氾德達告身》 (*Fan Deda gaoshen*).
Firewood Cart Text Fragment [Gaochang text] 《調薪車殘文書》 (*Diaoxinche can wenshu*).
Four Branches of Literature Collection 《四部叢刊》 (*Sibu congkan*).
Gaochang Duzi Provisioning Record 《高昌都子等傳供食帳》 (*Gaochang Duzi deng chuan gongshi zhang*).
Gaochang Huya Duzi Provisioning Record 《高昌虎牙都子等傳供食帳》 (*Gaochang Huya Duzi deng chuan gongshi zhang*).
Gaochang Huya Yuanzhi Provisioning Record 《高昌虎牙元治等傳供食帳》(*Gaochang Huya Yuanshi deng chuan gongshi zhang*).
Gaochang Linghu Provisioning Record 《高昌令狐等傳供食帳》 (*Gaochang Linghu deng chuan gongshi zhang*).

Gaochang 31st Year of Yanchang (591) Zhang Yi's Wife Meng Gravestone 《高昌延昌三十一年(591)張毅妻孟氏墓表》 (*Gaochang Yanchang sanshiyi nian (591) Zhang Yi qi Meng Shi mubiao*).

Gaochang 37th Year of Yanchang (597) Zhang Yi Epitaph 《高昌延昌三十七年(597)張毅墓志》 (*Gaochang Yanchang sanshiqi nian (597) Zhang Yi muzhi*).

Gaochang Xia Village Family Person's Wheat Field Contract 《高昌某人夏鎮家麥田券》(*Gaochang mouren Xia zhen jia maitian quan*).

Gaochang Yihe Fourth Year (unknown name) Burial Clothing and Objects Record 《高昌義和四年缺名隨葬衣物疏》 (*Gaochang Yihe si nian queming suizang yiwu shu*).

Gaochang Zhufotu Provisioning Record 《高昌竺佛圖等傳供食帳》(*Gaochang Zhufotu deng chuan gongshi zhang*).

Gaochang □shan Provisioning Record 《高昌□善等傳供食帳》 (*Gaochang □shan deng chuan gongshi zhang*).

Gazetteer of Liaodong 《遼東志》 (*Liaodong zhi*).

Gazetteer of Shazhou and Yizhou [Dunhuang text S. 367] 《沙州伊州地志》 (*Shazhou Yizhou dizhi*).

Gazetteer of the Split Ford 《析津志》 (*Zhejin zhi*), Xiong Mengxiang 熊夢祥.

Gazetteer of the Western Regions 《西域圖志》 (*Xiyu tuzhi*).

Gazetteer of Wuwei 《武威志》 (*Wuwei zhi*).

General Gazetteer of the Unity of the Yuan 《元一統志》 (*Yuan yitong zhi*).

Golden Light Sutra (*Suvarṇaprabhāsa*) [Turfan text] 《金光明經》(*Jin guangming jing*).

Great Tang Dynasty Record of the Western Regions 《大唐西域記》 (*Datang xiyu ji*).

Han Records of the Eastern Pavilion 《東觀漢記》 (*Dongguan Han ji*).

History of the Former Han 《漢書》 (*Han shu*).

History of the Jin 《晉書》 (*Jin shu*).

History of the Jin Dynasty 《金史》 (*Jin shi*).

History of the Later Han 《后漢書》 (*Hou Han shu*).

History of the Liao 《遼史》 (*Liao shi*).

History of the Northern Dynasties 《北史》 (*Bei shi*).

History of the Northern Qi 《北齊書》 (*Beiqi shu*).

History of the Song 《宋史》 (*Song shi*).

History of the State-Founding Campaigns of the Great Qing 《皇清開國方略》 (*Huang-Qing kaiguo fanglüe*).

History of the Sui 《隋書》 (*Sui shu*).

History of the Wei 《魏書》 (*Wei shu*).

History of the Yuan 《元史》 (*Yuan shi*).

History of the Zhou 《周書》 (*Zhou shu*)

Hymns for the Lower Section [Dunhuang text] 《下部贊》 (*Xiabu zan*).

Imperial Decree to King Julie, Officer Ketuyu, and Other People of the Khitan 《敕契丹王據埒可突于等書》 (*Chi Qidan Wang Julie Ketuyu deng shu*). In *Collected Works of Zhang Jiuling* 《曲江集》 (*Qujiang ji*).

Imperial Decree Dispatching Niu Xianke to Inside the Pass for Settling Down in Peace the Sogdians of the Six Prefectures 《遣牛仙客往關内諸州安輯六州胡敕》 (*Qian Niu Xianke wang guannei zhuzhou anji Liuzhouhu chi*).

Imperial Decree to the Military Commander (tutuq) Nieli of the Khitan 《勅契丹都督涅禮書》 (*Chi Qidan dudu Nieli shu*). In *Collected Works of Zhang Jiuling* 《曲江集》 (*Qujiang ji*).

Imperial Decree to Songmo Military Commander (tutuq) Nieli 《勅松漠都督涅禮書》 (*Chi Songmo dudu Nieli shu*). In *Collected Works of Zhang Jiuling* 《曲江集》 (*Qujiang ji*).

Imperial Edicts on the Eight Banners by Shizong Emperor Xian 《世宗憲皇帝上諭八旗》 (*Shizong Xian huangdi shangyu baqi*).

Imperially Sanctioned Manchu Dictionary 《御製清文鑑》 (*Yuzhi qingwen jian*).

Imperially Sanctioned Manchu Dictionary (Revised and Enlarged Edition) 《御製增订清文鑑》 (*Yuzhi zengding qingwen jian*).

Important Documents of the Tang 《唐會要》 (*Tang huiyao*), Wang Pu 王溥.

Informative Record on Countries Far Away 《殊域周咨錄》 (*Shuyuzhou zilu*), Yan Congjian 嚴從簡.

Inscription of the Great Tang Boling Commandery Dedicated at North Peak Antianwang Temple on Heng Mountain 《大唐博陵郡北嶽恒山封安天王之銘》 (*Datang Bolingjun beiwei Hengshanfeng Antianwang zhiming*).

Interpretation 《譯語》 (*Yiyu*), Min'eshanren 岷峨山人.

Laozi Converts the Buddhists Sutra 《老子化佛經》 (*Laozi huafo jing*); also *Laozi Converts the Foreigners Sutra* 《老子化胡經》 (*Laozi huahu jing*).

Law of Etiquette [Tang statute; see Jiang Boqin, footnote 13] 《儀制令》 (*Yizhiling*).

Letter from the Three Commanderies Wildmen 《三衛野人致書》(*Sanwei yeren zhi shu*).

Mahāmāyā Sutra 《觀佛三昧海經》 (*Guanfo sanmeihai jing*).

Manchu Veritable Records 《满洲實錄》 (*Manzhou shilu*).

Manichaean Sutra Fragment Number One [Dunhuang text] 《摩尼教殘經一》 (*Monijiao sanjingyi*).

Manuscript Compendium of Important Documents of the Song 《宋會要輯稿》 (*Song huiyao jigao*).

Map of Imperial Territory under a Comprehensive Gaze 《皇輿全覽圖》 (*Huangyu quanjian tu*).

Map of Shengjing, Jilin, Heilongjiang, and other Areas Marked with Military Campaign Sites 《盛京吉林黑龍江等處標注戰迹輿圖》(*Shengjing Jilin Heiongjiang dengchu biaozhu zhanji yutu*).

Maps and Gazetteer of the Provinces and Counties in the Yuanhe Period 《元和郡縣圖志》 (*Yuanhe junxian tuzhi*), Li Jifu 李吉甫.

Master of Grass and Trees 《草木子》 (*Caomu zi*), Ye Ziqi 葉子奇.

Memorandum for Money and Grain of Jiabi Tanhan and Others in an Unknown Year in Gaochang Kingdom 《高昌年次未詳迦匕貪旱等錢谷備忘》 (*Gaochang nianci Weixiang Jiabi Tanhan deng qiangu beiwang*).

Miscellanea in the Khitan Court 《虜廷雜記》 (*Luting zaji*), Zhao Zhizhong 趙志忠.

A Miscellaneous Collection of Sanskrit Terms 《梵語雜名》 (*Fanyu zaming*), Li Yan 利言.

Miscellaneous Records at Yin Mountain 《陰山雜錄》 (*Yinshan zalu*), Zhao Zhizhong 趙至忠.

Mongolian Letters Arranged by Rhyme《蒙古字韻》 (*Menggu zi yun*).

New History of the Five Dynasties《新五代史》 (*Xin Wudai shi*).

New Tales from the Mountain Dweller 《山居新話》 (*Shanju xinhua*), Yang Yu 陽瑀.

New Tang History 《新唐書》 (*Xin Tang shu*).

Notice for Sending Someone from the Military Bureau to Safeguard the Foreign Emissary at the Guesthouse in the 14th Year of the Yanshou Reign Period (637) in Gaochang Kingdom 《高昌延壽十四年（637）兵部差人看額館客使文書》 (*Gaochang Yanshou shisinian (637) bingbu chairen kan eguan keshi wenshu*).

Ode to the Wine Dew in Xie Shuzhai's Poem 《詠酒露次解恕齋韻》 (*Yong jiulu ci Xie Shuzhai yun*), Xu Youren 許有壬.

Old History of the Five Dynasties 《舊五代史》 (*Jiu Wudai shi*).

Old Tang History 《舊唐書》 (*Jiu Tang shu*).

One Thousand Character Sanskrit Glossary 《梵語千字文》 (*Fanyu qianziwen*).

Order from the Capital Administration Office to the Adjutant of Shichang County for Sending Master Bow Maker Hou Weixiang and Others to the Court in the Second Year of the Yihe Reign Period (615) in Gaochang Kingdom《高昌義和二年（615）都官下始昌縣司馬主者符為遣弓師侯尾相等詣府事》 (*Gaochang Yihe er nian (615) duguan xia shichang xian Sima zhuzhe fu wei qian gongshi Hou weixiang deng yi fushi*).

Order from Tuyou Battalion to Jianzhong Zhao Wuna for the Arrest of Zhang Shixuan, a Soldier from Jiaohe County in the 18th Year of the Tang Kaiyuan Reign Period (740) 《唐開元二十八年土右營下建忠趙伍那牒為訪捉配交河兵張式玄事》 (*Tang Kaiyuan ershiba nian tuyouying xiajianzfu zhao Wuna die wei fang zhuopei jiaohebing Zhang Shixuan shi*).

Order in the First Year of the Yonglong Reign Period from the Army Office for Recording the Yangren of Guardsmen on March and in Garrison, as well as Meritorious Service Conferees, Augerers, and Others [Gaochang text] 《唐永隆元年軍團牒為記注所屬衛士徵鎮樣人及勳官讖符諸色事》 (*Tang Yonglong yuannian juntuandie wei jizhu suoshu weishi zhengzhen yangren ji xunguan chenfu zhuseshi*).

Outline of the Waterways 《水道提綱》 (*Shuidao tigang*), Qi Zhaonan 齊召南.

Outstanding Models from the Storehouse of Literature 《冊府元龜》 (*Cefu yuangui*).

Pentaglot Dictionary of the Qing Dynasty 《五體清文鑑》 (*Wuti qingwen jian*).

Petition of Wei Dynasty Senior Officials Urging the Claiming of the Throne 《魏公卿上尊號奏》 (*Wei Gongqing shang zunhao zou*).

Poem on the Zoroastrian Temple in Ancheng [Dunhuang text] 《安城祆詠》 (*Ancheng Xian yong*).

Preface to Bashi's Poetry from the Veranda of the Four Recitations 《拔實彥卿四詠軒詩序》 (*Bashi Yanqing siyongxuan shi xu*), Xu Youren 許有壬.

Principles of Correct Diet 《飲膳正要》 (*Yinshan zhengyao*), Hu Sihui 忽思慧.

Proclamation of the Later Jin to the Ming Emperor Wanli 《後金檄明萬曆皇帝文》 (*Houjin chi Ming Wanli huangdi wen*).
P.t.1263 [Dunhuang text; a Chinese-Tibetan lexicon].
Qu Family Temple Construction Stele 《麴氏造寺碑》 (*Qushi zaosi bei*).
Record of an Embassy to the West 《西使記》 (*Xi shi ji*), Liu Yu 劉郁.
Record of an Embassy to the Liao 《使遼錄》 (*Shi Liao lu*), Zhang Shunmin 張舜民.
Record of Events from the Eastern Study 《東齋紀事》 (*Dongzhai jishi*), Fan Zhen 范鎮.
Record of Knowledge Gained Day by Day 《日知錄》 (*Ri zhi lu*), Gu Yanwu 顧炎武.
Record of Later Travel beyond the Great Wall 《後出塞錄》 (*Hou chu sai lu*), Gong Zhiyue 龔之鑰.
Record of Learning the Ancient Traditions 《道園學古錄》 (*Daoyuanxue gulu*), Yu Ji 虞集.
Record of the Contraction of an Illness by the Soldier Sun Haizang of the Tang Dynasty from Xizhou, Gaochang County, Taiping Township 《唐西州高昌縣下太平鄉符為檢兵孫海藏患狀事》 (*Tang xizhou Gaochangxian Xiataipingxiangfu wei jianbing Sun Haizang huanzhuang shi*).
Record of the Embassy to the North 《北使記》 (*Beishi ji*), Liu Qi 劉祁.
Record of the Facial Features of Zhao Xuzhang and Others [Turfan text] 《唐趙須章等貌定簿》 (*Tang Zhao Xuzhang deng maoding bu*).
Record of the Great Jin State 《大金國志》 (*Dajinguo zhi*).
Record of the History of the Three Kingdoms 《三國志》 (*Sanguo zhi*).
Record of the Journey to the West of the Daoist Monk Changchun 《長春真人西游記》 (*Changchun zhenren xiyouji*), Li Zhichang 李志常.
Record of the Khitan State 《契丹國志》 (*Qidan guo zhi*).
Record of the Lands North of Yan 《燕北錄》 (*Yanbei lu*), Wang Yi 王易.
Record of the Personal Campaigns of the Holy Warrior 《聖武親征錄》 (*Shengwu qinzheng lu*).
Record of the Water Routes of the Western Regions 《西域水道記》 (*Xiyu shuidao ji*), Xu Song 徐松.
Record of Wang Yande's Embassy to Gaochang 《王延德使高昌記》 (*Wang Yande shi Gaochang ji*).
Record of Yuanli and Others from Gaochang County Regarding their Provisioning in Turn 《高昌元禮等傳供食帳》 (*Gaochang Yuanli deng chuan gongshi zhang*).
Record of Zhongbao and Others from Gaochang County Regarding their Provisioning in Turn 《高昌衆保等傳供糧食帳》 (*Gaochang Zhongbao deng chuangong liangshi zhang*).
Records of Armaments and Military Provisions 《武備錄》 (*Wubei lu*).
Records of Observation on Jianzhou 《建州聞見錄》 (*Jianzhou weujian lu*), Li Minhuan 李民寏.
Records of the Grand Historian 《史記》 (*Shiji*), Sima Qian 司馬遷.
Records of the Grand Historian, Collected Annotations 《史記集解》 (*Shiji jijie*), Pei Yin 裴駰.

Register of Painting Masters, Master Gluers, and Other Workers Sent from Gaochang County 《高昌入作人畫師、主膠人等名籍》 (*Gaochang ruzuoren huashi, zhujiaoren deng mingji*).

Register of the Craftsman He Haoren and Others of the Tang Dynasty [Gaochang text] 《唐何好忍等匠人名籍》 (*Tang He haoren deng jiangren mingji*).

Register of the Escapee Shi Yanming and Others in Gaochang County 《高昌逋人史延明等名籍》 (*Gaochang buren Shi Yanming deng mingji*).

Report to the Court Asking for the Forbiddance of Cults and Heresy 《乞禁妖教扎子》 (*Qi jinyaojiao zhazi*). In *Collected Works of Gaofeng*《高峰文集》 (*Gao Feng wenji*).

Report to the Court of Eight Items on Classified and Important Military and State Issues 《上軍國機要事八條》 (*Shang junguo jiyaoshi batiao*). In *Collected Works of Chen Boyu*《陳伯玉文集》 (*Chen Boyu wenji*).

Research on Manchu Origins 《滿洲源流考》 (*Manzhou yuanliu kao*).

Rhapsody on Yalaiji Liquor 《軋賴機酒賦》 (*Yalaji jiu fu*), Zhu Derun 朱德潤.

Rhymes of the Central Plain《中原音韻》 (*Zhongyuan yinyun*).

Ritual Regulations Written in the Kaiyuan Reign Period 《開元禮》 (*Kaiyuan li zazhi*).

Routes from the Border Districts into the Regions Inhabited by the Barbarians of the Four Directions 《邊州入四夷道里》 (*Bianzhou ru siyi daoli*), Jia Dan 賈耽.

Secret History of the Mongols 《元朝秘史》 (*Yuanchao mishi*); literally *Secret History of the Yuan Dynasty*; also《蒙古秘史》 (*Menggu mishi*).

Secret Imperial Map from the Qing Palace 《清内府一統輿地秘圖》 (*Qing neifu yitong yudi mi tu*).

Selective Imposition Register [Dunhuang text P. 3559] 《差科簿》 (*Chaliao bu*).

Song of Yingzhou [poem]《營州歌》 (*Yingzhou ge*), Gao Shi 高適.

Sound of Pines [poem]《松聲》 (*Song sheng*), Yelü Zhu 耶律鑄.

South Village Records Compiled after Returning to the Farm 《南村輟耕錄》 (*Nancun chuogeng lu*), Tao Zongyi 陶宗儀.

Spirit Way Stele for Hexi Longyou Circuit Surveillance Commissioner Lord Kailie 《河西隴右道肅政廉訪使凱烈公神道碑》 (*Hexi Longyou dao suzheng lianfang shi Kailie gong shendaobei*).

Spirit Way Stele for Lord Wang from Taiyuan, the Commander-in-Chief of Tang Dynasty Xiazhou 《唐故夏州都督太原王公神道碑》 (*Tang gu Xiazhou dudu Taiyuan Wanggong shendaobei*).

Spirit Way Stele for the Honorable Kang, Lord Specially Advanced, Acting Left Guard of the Imperial Insignia, General-in-Chief, Supreme Pillar of the State, Qinghe Commandery Dynasty-Founding Duke, Posthumous Commander Unequalled in Honor, and Xiazhou Commander-in-Chief 《特進行左金吾衛大將軍上柱國清河郡開國公贈開府儀同三司兼夏州都督康公神道碑》 (*Tejinxing youjin wuwei dajiang shangzhuguo Qinghejun kaiguo gongzeng kaifu yitong sansijian Xiazhou dudu Kanggong shendaobei*), Yan Zhenqing 顏真卿 [cited as here in Rong Xinjiang's essay; cited Zhang Guangda's essay with a shorter title]. In *Collected Works of Zhang Yue*《張說之集》(*Zhang Yue zhiji*).

Spirit Way Stele for the Industrious Executor of the Grand Secretariat Lord Mangwu 《平章政事忙兀公神道碑》 (*Pingzheng zhengshi Mangwu gong shendaobei*).

Spirit Way Stele for the Marquis An, the Prefect of Weizhou 《唐維州刺史安侯神道碑》 (*Tang Weizhou cishi An hou shendaobei*).

Spirit Way Stele for Wen Zhengxu 《文正許先生神道碑》 (*Wen Zhengxu xiansheng shendaobei*).

Spirit Way Stele for Yelü Cong《耶律琮神道碑》 (*Yelü Cong shendaobei*).

Spirit Way Stele Inscription for Jigüntei, Late Overseer of the Bureau of All Classes of Artisans, Granted by Imperial Order under the Great Yuan 《大元敕賜故諸色人匠府達魯花赤竹公神道碑銘》 (*Dayuan chici gu zhese renjiangfu daluhuachi Fu gong shendao beiming*), Jie Xisi 揭傒斯.

Spring and Autumn of Xuanyan 《玄晏春秋》 (*Xuanyan chunqiu*), Huang Fumi 皇甫謐.

Stele at Xuansheng Confucian Temple in Zhending Route《真定路宣聖廟牌》 (*Zhending lu Xuansheng miao bei*).

Stele for Grand Councilor Dong Pingzhong Prince of Xian 《丞相東平忠憲王碑》 (*Chengxiang Dong Pingzhong Xianwang bei*).

Stele Inscription for Meritorious Service at Youzhou 《幽州紀功碑銘》 (*Youzhou jigong beiming*).

Stele Inscription for the Artillery Brigade Commander from the Kerait Clan 《炮手軍總管克烈君碑銘》 (*Paoshoujun zongguan Kelie jun beiming*).

Stele of Canonizing Kindness 《崇善碑》 (*Chongshan bei*).

Stele of the Achievements of the Ancestors of the Qočo (Gaochang) *Prince* 《高昌王世勛之碑》 (*Gaochang wangshi xun zhibei*).

Stele of the Śākya Temple 《釋迦院碑》 (*Shijia yuan bei*).

Stele Praising the Supervision of the Longyou Herds in the Thirteenth Year of the Kaiyuan Reign Period of the Great Tang Dynasty 《大唐開元十三年隴右監牧頌德碑》 (*Datang Kaiyuan shisan nian Longyou jianmu songde bei*), Zhang Yue 張説.

Stele Relating the Achievements of Čonqur's Family《句容郡王世續碑》 (*Jurong junwang shixu bei*).

Survey of the Geography of the Eastern State (Korea) 《東國輿地勝覽》 (*Dongguo yudi shengjian*) [*Dongguk Yeoji Seungram*].

Survey of the Geography of the Eastern State (Korea), *Revised and Augmented* 《(新增）東國輿地勝覽》(*(Xinzeng) Dongguo yudi shenglan*) [*Sinjeung Dongguk Yeoji Seungram*].

Synopsis and Detail Catalog of the Continuation of the Comprehensive Mirror for Aid in Government 《續通鑒綱目》 (*Xu tongjian gangmu*), Shang Lu 商輅.

Taiping Imperial Encyclopedia 《太平御覽》 (*Taiping yulan*).

Taisho Tripitaka《大正新修大藏經》 (*Dazheng xinxiu dazangjing*).

Tales of the Hierarchs Searching for Buddhist Scriptures in the Western Regions during the Tang Dynasty 《大唐西域求法高僧傳》 (*Datang xiyu qiufa gaoceng zhuan*), Yi Jing 義淨.

A Textbook for Translation between the Chinese and Barbarian Languages 《華夷譯語》 (*Hua yi yiyu*).

A Textbook for Translation between the Chinese and Jurchen Languages《女真譯語》 (*Nüzhen yiyu*).
A Thicket of Words by the Western Stream《西溪叢語》 (*Xixi congyu*), Yao Kuan 姚寬.
Topographical Classic of Shazhou [Dunhuang text] 《沙州圖經》 (*Shazhou tujing*).
Translated Words Written in the Zhiyuan Reign Period《至元譯語》(*Zhiyuan yiyu*); also *Mongol Translated Words* 《蒙古譯語》 (*Menggu yiyu*).
Unfolded Terrestrial Atlas 《廣輿圖》 (*Guang yutu*), Luo Hongxian 羅洪先.
Veritable Records of Chinggis Khan 《成吉思汗實錄》 (*Chengjisihan shilu*).
Veritable Records of Han Gaozu 《漢高祖實錄》 (*Han Gaozu shilu*).
Veritable Records of Renzong 《仁宗實錄》 (*Renzong shilu*).
Veritable Records of Taizong (Qing Dynasty) 《太宗實錄》 (*Taizong shilu*).
Veritable Records of Taizu (Qing Dynasty) 《太祖實錄》 (*Taizu shilu*).
Veritable Records of Taizu and the Empress Dowager (Qing Dynasty) 《太祖太后實錄》 (*Taizu Taihou shilu*).
Veritable Records of Taizu Emperor Gao (Qing Dynasty) 《太祖高皇帝實錄》 (*Taizu Gao huangdi shilu*).
Veritable Records of Taizu Emperor Wu (Qing Dynasty) 《太祖武皇帝實錄》 (*Taizu Wu huangdi shilu*).
Veritable Records of the August Ming 《皇明實錄》 (*Huangming shilu*); also *Veritable Records of the Ming* 《明實錄》 (*Ming shilu*).
Veritable Records of the Martial Emperor (Qing) 《武皇帝實錄》 (*Wu huangdi shilu*).
Veritable Records of the Qing Dynasty 《清實錄》 (*Qing shilu*).
Veritable Records of the Taizong Reign of Yi Korea 《李朝太宗實錄》 (*Lichao Taizong shilu*).
Veritable Records of Yingzong of the Ming Dynasty 《明英宗實錄》 (*Ming Yingzong shilu*).
Works Written on the Sweet Dream Veranda: Addenda to Trivial Words of the Imperial Guards 《佳夢軒叢著・侍衛瑣言補》 (*Jiameng xuancongzhu, shiwei suoyan bu*), Yi Geng 奕賡.
Yongle Encyclopedia《永樂大典》 (*Yongle dadian*).

BIBLIOGRAPHY

Abe Takeo 安部健夫. *Nishi Uiguru kokushi no kenkyū* (*Studies on the Western Uyghurs*) 『西ウイグル国史の研究』. Kyoto: Ibundō Shoten 彙文堂書店, 1955.

Aisin Gioro Ulhicun 愛新覺羅·烏拉熙春. "The Characteristics of the Khitan Names: with a Note about the Suffixes of the Derivative Adjectives in the Khitan Language" 「契丹人的命名特徵—兼論契丹語派生形容詞的後綴」. In *Studies of the Khitan Language and Scripts* 『契丹語言文字研究』. Kyoto: Research Institute for the History and Culture of East Asia 東亜歴史文化研究會, May 2004.

———. "A Comparative Study of the 'Epitaph of Yelü Renxian' and the 'Epitaph of Yelü Zhixian'" 「〈耶律仁先墓誌銘〉與〈耶律智先墓誌銘〉之比較研究」. *Ritsumeikan Bungaku* 『立命館文學』, no. 581 (Sep. 2003).

———. "An Examination of the Genealogies of the Tomb Owners Recorded in the 'Epitaph of Yelü Dilie' and the 'Epitaph of the Deceased Ms. Yelü': with a Note about the Khitan Forenames and Courtesy Names" 「〈耶律迪烈墓誌銘〉與〈故耶律氏銘石〉所載墓主人世系考—兼論契丹人的"名"與"字"」. *Journal of East Asian Literature and History* 『東亜文史論叢』, the premier issue, Festschrift in Memory of the 85th Anniversary of Mr. Jin Qicong's Birth (March 2003). Also published in *Ritsumeikan Bungaku* 『立命館文學』, no. 580 (June 2003).

———. "An Examination of the Genealogy of the Great King Gaojiu" 「高九大王世系考」. *Journal of East Asian Literature and History* 『東亜文史論叢』, the premier issue, Festschrift in Memory of the 85th Anniversary of Mr. Jin Qicong's Birth (March 2003).

———. "An Examination of Xiamage" 「匣馬葛考」. *Ritsumeikan Bungaku* 『立命館文學』, no. 582 (Sept. 2003).

———. *History of the Liao and Jin Dynasties and the Khitan and Jurchen Scripts* 『遼金史與契丹、女真文』. Kyoto: Research Institute for History and Culture of East Asia 東亜歴史文化研究會, 2004.

———. "Notes on the Khitan and Mongolian Histories" 「契丹蒙古剳記」, the entry "The Characteristics of the Northern Peoples' Names." *Ritsumeikan Bungaku* 『立命館文學』, no. 586 (Oct. 2004).

———. "An Overview of the Epitaphs in Khitan Small Script" 「契丹小字墓誌綜考」. In *Studies of the Khitan Language and Scripts* 『契丹語言文字研究』. Kyoto: Research Institute for History and Culture of East Asia 東亜歴史文化研究會, May 2004.

———. "The Phonetic Reconstruction of the Khitan Small Script" 「契丹小字的語音構擬」. *Ritsumeikan Bungaku* 『立命館文學』, no. 577 (Dec. 2002).

Allsen, Thomas T. "The Yuan Dynasty and the Uighurs of Turfan in the Thirteenth Century." In Morris Rossabi, editor, *China Among Equals: The Middle Kingdom and its Neighbors, Tenth-Fourteenth Centuries*. Berkeley: University of California Press, 1983.

Altan Tobči (*Golden Summary*). Translated into English by Charles Bawden as *The Mongol Chronicle Altan Tobči*. Göttinger asiatische Forschungen, Bd. 5. Wiesbaden:

O. Harrassowitz, 1955.

———.Translated into Japanese by Kobayashi Takashirō 小林高四郎 as *Mōko ōgonshi: Mōko minzoku no koten* 『蒙古黄金史:蒙古民族の古典』 (*The Golden Chronicle of Mongols—The Classic of Mongolian Nationality*). Tokyo: Seikatsusha 生活社, 1941.

———. New Mongolian translation. Ulaanbaatar: 1957.

Altan Tobči: *Erten-ü Qag-un Ündüsülegsen Törö Yosun-u J̌okiyal-i Tobčilan Quriyagsan Altan Tobči*. Ulaanbaatar: 1937.

Atago Matsuo 愛宕松男. *Studies of the Ancient History of the Khitan* 『契丹古代史の研究』 (*Kittan kodai shi no kenkyū*). Kyoto: The Society of Oriental Researches 東洋史研究会, 1959.

Atwood, Christopher P. *Encyclopedia of Mongolia and the Mongol Empire*. Facts on File, 2004.

al-'Awfī, Muhammad. *Jāmi' al-Hikāyāt* (*Collected Stories*).

Bacot, Jacques. "Reconnaissance en haute Asie septentrionale par cinq envoyés ouigours au VIIIe siècle." *Journal Asiatique*, no. 244 (1956).

Baddeley, John F. *Russia, Mongolia, China: Being Some Record of the Relations Between Them from the Beginning of the 17th Century to the Death of the Tsar Alexei Mikhailovich, A.D. 1602-1676*. London: Macmillan, 1919.

Bailey, H. W. "Ttaugara." *Bulletin of the School of Oriental and African Studies*, vol. 8, no. 4 (1937).

Bao Lianqun 包聯群. "A Supplementary Examination of the 'Epitaph of the Deceased Prince of Dilie of the Great Liao in Jambudvipa [the terrestrial world]' " 《〈南贍部洲大遼國故迪烈王墓誌文〉的補充考釋》("'Nanshanbuzhou daliaoguo guo gu wang muzhi wen' de bochong kaoshi"). *Journal of Inner Mongolia University* 《內蒙古大學學報》(*Neimenggu daxue xuebao*), 2002, no. 3.

Bartol'd (Barthold), V. V., (Василий Владимирович Бартольд). "Tarim." In the *Encyclopedia of Islam*, vol. 4. Leiden: Brill, 1936.

———. "Tatars." In the *Encyclopaedia of Islam*, vol. 4. Leiden: Brill, 1936.

———. "Toghuzghuz." In the *Encyclopaedia of Islam*, vol. 4. Leiden: Brill, 1936.

———. *Turkestan Down to the Mongol Invasion* (*Туркестан в эпоху монгольскаго нашествия*). Both the London: Luzac, 1928 edition and the London: E. J. W Gibb Memorial Trust, 1958 edition.

———. *Twelve Lectures on the History of the Turks of Central Asia*, translated into German by Theodor Menzel as *Zwölf Vorlesungen über die Geschichte der Türken Mittleasiens*. Berlin: Deutsche Gesellschaft für Islamkunde, 1935.

Bazin, L. "Turc et Sogdien." In *Mélanges linguistiques offerts à Émile Benveniste*. Paris: Peeters, 1975.

Beijing Library Epigraphy Group and China Buddhist Texts Library Stone Sutra Group 北京圖書館金石組、中國佛教圖書文物館石經組 (Beijing tushuguan jinshi zu, Zhongguo fojiao tushu wenwuguan shijing zu), editors. *Collected Fangshan Stone Sutra Inscriptions* 《房山石經題記彙編》(*Fangshan shijing tiji huibian*). Beijing: Bibliography and Document Publishing House 書目文獻出版社, 1987.

Beijing Youth Daily 《北京青年報》(*Beijing qingnian bao*) 12/13/1998. Archaeological report of a Tang grave at the Beijing Yanjing Automotive Factory 燕京汽車製造廠 (Yanjing qiche zhizaochang).

Belenitskii, A. M., and Marshak, B. I. "The Paintings of Sogdiana." In Guitty Azarpay, *Sogdian Painting, The Pictorial Epic in Oriental Art*. Berkeley: University of California Press, 1981.

van den Berghe, Pierre. "Does Race Matter?" *Nations and Nationalism*, vol. 1, no. 3 (1995).

Bernal, John D. *Sozialgeschichte der Wissenschaften*. Translated into Chinese by Wu Kuangfu 伍況甫, et al., as 貝爾納 (Bei'erna), *A Social History of Science* 《歷史上的科學》(*Lishishangde kexue*). Beijing: Science Press 科學出版社, 1959.

Blum, Susan. "Margins and Centers: A Decade of Publishing on China's Ethnic Minorities." *Journal of Asian Studies*, vol. 64, no. 4 (2002).

Boodberg, Peter. "Dayan, Činggis, and Shan-yü." *Hu T'ien Han Yüeh Fang Chu* (The Mirrorings of the Chinese Moon in a Barbarian Sky) 《胡天漢月方諸》, no. 2, April 1932. Reprinted in *Selected Works of Peter A. Boodberg*, compiled by Alvin P. Cohen. Berkeley: University of California Press, 1979.

Boyle, John A. "Chinggis Khan." In the *Encyclopedia of Islam,* second edition, vol. 2. Leiden: Brill, 1965.

———. "The Summer and Winter Camping Grounds of the Kereit." *Central Asiatic Journal*, vol. 17, nos. 2-4 (1973).

A Brief History of the Black Tatars 《黑韃事略》 (*Heida shilüe*). Translated into German as *Meng-ta pei-lu und Hei-ta shih-lüeh: chinesische Gesandten-berichte über die frühen Mongolen 1221 and 1237* by Erich Haenisch, Yao Ts'ung-wu, Peter Olbricht, and Elisabeth Pinks. Asiatische Forschungen series, 56. Wiesbaden: Otto Harrassowitz, 1980.

Bretschneider, E. *Mediaeval Researches from Eastern Asiatic Sources: Fragments towards the Knowledge of the Geography and History of Central and Western Asia from the 13th to the 17th Century*. London: 1910. Also published London: Kegan Paul, Trench, Trübner, 1888.

Brockelmann, Carl. *Mitteltürkischer Wortschatz nach Maḥmūd al-Kāšgarīs Dīvān luyāt al-Turk*. Budapest: Kőrösi Csoma-Gesellschaft, 1928.

Browne, Edward Granville. *A Literary History of Persia*. London: Fisher, Unwin, 1902-1924.

Budge, E. A. Wallace. *The Monks of Kublai Khan*. London: Religious Tract Society, 1928.

Bureau for the Administration of Cultural Relics at Zhaoling 昭陵文物管理所 (Zhaoling wenwu guanlisuo). "Record of the Investigation of Companion Burials at Zhaoling" 《昭陵陪葬墓調查記》 ("Zhaoling peizang mu diaocha ji"). *Cultural Relics* 《文物》 (*Wenwu*), 1977, no. 10.

Butler, A. R. and Needham, Joseph. "An Experimental Comparison of the East Asian, Hellenistic and Indian (Gandharan) Stills in Relation to the Distillation of Ethanol and Acetic Acid." *Ambix*, no. 27 (1980).

Cai Hongsheng 蔡鴻生. "Collected Studies of the Customs of Tang Dynasty Foreigners of the Nine Surnames" 《唐代九姓胡禮俗叢考》 ("Tangdai jiuxing lisu congkao"). *Literature and History* 《文史》 (*Wenshi*), no. 35 (1992).

———. *Tang Dynasty Foreigners of the Nine Surnames and Turkish Culture*《唐代九姓胡與突厥文化》(*Tangdai jiuxinghu yu tujue wenhua*). Beijing: Zhonghua Book Company 中華書局, 1998.

Cai Meibiao 蔡美彪. "State Titles, Tribal Names, and Chronology Prior to the Foundation of the Great Qing" 《大清國建號前的國號、族名和紀年》 ("Daqingguo jianhao qiande guohao, zuming he ji'nian"). *Historical Research*《歷史研究》(*Lishi yanjiu*), 1987, no. 3.

Carpini, Johann de Plano (Giovanni da Pian del Carpine). *Geschichte der Mongolen und Reisebericht 1245-1247*, translated and annotated by Friedrich Risch. Leipzig: E. Pfeiffer, 1930.

———. *The Journey of William of Rubruck to the Eastern Parts of the World 1253-55, As Narrated by Himself, with Two Accounts of the Earlier Journey of John of Pian de Carpine*, translated and annotated by William Woodville Rockhill. London: Hakluyt Society, 1900.

———. *Annotated Translation of Carpini's and William of Rubruck's Travels (Путешествие в восточные страны Плано Карпини и Гильома Рубрука)*, translated and annotated by N. P. Shastina (Н. П. Шастина). Москва: Государственное издательство географической литературы, 1957.

Carruthers, Douglas. *Unknown Mongolia: A Record of Travel and Exploration in North-west Mongolia and Dzungaria*. London: Hutchinson & Co, 1913; second edition, 1914.

Cen Zhongmian 岑仲勉. "Annotation and Translation of Turkish Stele Inscriptions"《突厥文碑注釋》("Tujue wenbei zhushi"). In *Collected Histories of the Turks* 《突厥集史》(*Tujue jishi*), vol. 2. Beijing: Zhonghua Book Company 中華書局, 1958.

———. *Collected Histories of the Turks* 《突厥集史》(*Tujue jishi*). Beijing: Zhonghua Book Company 中華書局, 1958.

———. "The Etymology and Pronunciation of Modu" 《冒頓之語源及其音讀》 ("Modu zhi yuyuan ji qi yindu"). Originally published in *Northwest Newsletter* 《西北通訊》 (*Xibei tongxun*), vol. 3, no. 1, July, 1948. Included in Lin Gan 林幹, editor, *Collection of Selected Essays on the Xiongnu (1919-1979)* 《匈奴史論文選集（1919-1979）》 (*Xiongnu shi lunwen xuanji, 1919-1979*). Beijing: Zhonghua Book Company 中華書局, 1983.

———. *Four Annotated Records of the Compilation of Surnames in the Era of Yuanhe* 《元和姓纂四校記》 (*Yuanhe xingzuan si xiaoji*) . Shanghai: Commercial Press 商務印書館, 1948.

———. *A History of Changes and Movements of the Yellow River* 《黃河變遷史》 (*Huanghe bianqian shi*). Beijing: People's Publishing House, 1957.

———. *Questions on Records of the Sui and Tang in the Comprehensive Mirror for Aid in Government* 《通鑒隋唐紀比事質疑》 (*Tongjian Sui Tang ji bishi zhiyi*). Beijing: Zhonghua Book Company 中華書局, 1964.

———. "A Study of the Four Guardstations of Quxian, Aduan, Anding, and Handong" 《明初曲先、阿端、安定、罕東四衛考》 ("Mingchu Quxian, Aduan, Anding, Handong siwei kao"). *Nanking Journal*《金陵學報》(*Jinling xuebao*), vol. 6, no. 2

(1936).

———. *Sui and Tang History* 《隋唐史》 (*Sui Tang shi*). Beijing: Zhonghua Book Company 中華書局, 1982.

———. *Supplementary Documents on the Western Turks and Related Textual Criticism* 《西突厥史料補闕及考證》(*Xi Tujue shiliao buque ji kaozheng*). Beijing: Zhonghua Book Company 中華書局, 1958.

———. "The Travel Diary of a Ming Man from Jiaguguan to the Western Part of Southern Xinjiang" 《從嘉峪關到南疆西部之明人紀程》 ("Cong Jiayuguan dao nanjiang xigu zhi mingren jicheng"). In *Textual Research on Historical Geography Outside of China* 《中外史地考證》 (*Zhongwai shidi kaozheng*), vol. 2. Beijing: Beijing: Zhonghua Book Company 中華書局, 1962.

Cha Gankou 查干扣, editor. *The Mongolians of Subei* 《肅北蒙古人》 (*Subei Menggu ren*). Beijing: Nationalities Press 民族出版社, 2005.

Chavannes, Édouard. *Documents sur les Tou-Kiue (Turcs) occidentaux*. St. Petersburg: 1903. Translated into Chinese as *Historical Documents of the Western Turks*《西突厥史料》 (*Xitujue shiliao*) by Feng Chengjun 馮承鈞. Beijing: Zhonghua Book Company 中華書局, 1958.

Chen Dezhi 陳得芝. "The Liao Dynasty Northwest Route Pacification Commission" 《遼代的西北路招討司》("Liaodaide Xibeilu zhaotaosi"). *Collected Papers of Research on Yuan History and Northern Nationalities History* 《元史及北方民族史研究集刊》 (*Yuanshi ji beifang minzu shi yanjiu jikan*), Nanjing University 南京大學, no. 2 (1978).

———. "A Study of the Postal Routes in Yuan Dynasty Lingbei Province" 《元嶺北行省諸驛道考》 ("Yuan Lingbei xingsheng zhu yidao kao"). *Collected Papers of Research on Yuan History and Northern Nationalities History* 《元史及北方民族史研究集刊》 (*Yuanshi ji beifang minzu shi yanjiu jikan*), Nanjing University 南京大學, no. 1 (1977).

———. "Yuan Dynasty Helin City and its Surroundings" 《元和林城及其周圍》 ("Yuan Helin cheng jiqi zhouwei"). *Collected Papers of Research on Yuan History and Northern Nationalities History* 《元史及北方民族史研究集刊》 (*Yuanshi ji beifang minzu shi yanjiu jikan*), Nanjing University 南京大學, no. 3 (1979).

Chen Guocan 陳國燦. "Research on the Stone Statues and their Name and Title Lists at the Tang Dynasty Qianling Mausoleum" 《唐乾陵石人像及其銜名的研究》 ("Tangchao lingshi renxiang jiqi xianmingde yanjiu"). In *Collected Works of Cultural Relics* 《文物集刊》(*Wenwu jikan*), vol. 2. Beijing: Cultural Relics Press 文物出版社, 1980.

Chen Haitao 陳海濤. "The Foreigner's Whirling Dance, the Foreigner's Leaping Dance, and the Cudrania Branch Dance – A Small Analysis of the Dances Belonging to the An Jia Tomb and the Yu Hong Tomb" 《胡旋舞、胡騰舞與柘枝舞——對安伽墓與虞弘墓中舞蹈歸屬的淺析》("Hu xuanwu, hu tengwu yu zhezhiwu – dui An Jia mu yu Yu Hong mu zhong wudao guishude qianxi"). *Archaeology and Cultural Relics* 《考古與文物》 (*Kaogu yu wenwu*), 2003, no. 3.

Chen Jiexian 陳捷先. "A Commentary on Manchu" 《說滿洲》("Shuo Manzhou"). In Chen Jiexian 陳捷先, *Collected Research on the Manchu* 《滿洲叢考》(*Manzhou congkao*). Taipei: National Taiwan University College of Liberal Arts, 1964.

Chen Naixiong 陳乃雄 and Yang Jie 楊傑. "An Examination of the Khitan Epitaph in Small Script Excavated from a Tomb of the Liao Dynasty in Wurigentala" 《烏日根塔拉遼墓出土的契丹小字墓誌銘考釋》("Wurigentala Liao mu chutude Qidan xiaozi muzhiming kaoshi"). *Northwest Journal of Ethnology* 《西北民族研究》(*Xibei minzu yanjiu*), 1999, no. 2.

Chen, Sanping 陳三平. "Son of Heaven and Son of God: Interactions among Ancient Asiatic Cultures Regarding Sacral Kingship and Theophoric Names." *Journal of the Royal Asiatic Society*, series 3, vol. 12, no. 3 (2002).

Chen Shu 陳述. *Khitan Government Historical Manuscripts* 《契丹政治史稿》(*Qidan zhengzhi shigao*). Beijing: People's Publishing House 人民出版社, 1986.

———. *A Study of Khitan Social and Economic History* 《契丹社會經濟史稿》(*Qidan shehui jingji shigao*). Shanghai: Sanlian Press 三聯出版社, 1963.

Chen Yinke 陳寅恪. *Manuscript of Discussions on the Political History of the Tang Dynasty* 《唐代政治史述論稿》(*Tangdai zhengzhi shi shulungao*). Shanghai: Commercial Press 商務印書館, 1947.

———. "The *Šes bya rab gsa* 《彰所知論》(*Clarification of What Should Be Known*) and the *Erdeni-yin Tobči* 《蒙古源流》." *Bulletin of the Institute of History and Philology, Academia Sinica*,《中央歷史語言研究所集刊》(*Zhongyang lishi yuyan yanjiusuo jikan*), vol. 2, no. 3 (1931).

Chen Yuan 陳垣. "A Study of the Entry of Manichaeism into China" 《摩尼教入中國考》("Monijiao ru Zhongguo kao"). In *Collected Academic Essays of Chen Yuan*《陳垣學術論文集》(*Chen Yuan xueshu lunwenji*), vol. 1. Beijing: Zhonghua Book Company 中華書局, 1980.

———. "A Study of the Entry of Zoroastrianism in to China"《火祆教入中國考》("Huoxianjiao ru Zhongguo kao"). *Journal of Sinological Studies*《國學季刊》(*Guoxue jikan*), vol. 1, no. 1, 1923. Corrected edition published in *Collected Academic Essays of Chen Yuan*《陳垣學術論文集》, vol. 1. Beijing: Zhonghua Book Company 中華書局, 1980.

———. *A Table of First Days and Intercalary Months in the 20 Histories*《二十史朔閏表》(*Ershi shi shuorun biao*). Beijing: Zhonghua Book Company 中華書局, 1962.

Chengde City Bishushan Village Administration 承德市避暑山莊管理處 (Chengdeshi Bishushan zhuang guanlichu). "A Jin Dynasty Bronze Liquor-Making Pot Unearthed in Qinglong County, Hebei" 《河北省青龍縣出土金代銅燒酒鍋》("Hebeisheng Qinglongxian chutu Jindai tong shaojiuguo"). *Cultural Relics* 《文物》(*Wenwu*), 1976, no. 9.

Chengde City Bishushan Village Museum 承德市避暑山莊博物館 (Chengdeshi Bishushan zhuang bowuguan). "A Brief Investigation of the Jin Dynasty Still" 《金代蒸餾器考略》("Jindai zhengliuqi kaolüe"). *Archaeology*《考古》(*Kaogu*), 1980, no. 5.

China Millennium Monument World Art Museum 中華世紀壇藝術館 (Zhonghua shiji tan yishuguan) and Inner Mongolia Autonomous Region Museum 内蒙古自治區博物館 (Neimenggu Zizhiqu bowuguan), editors. *Genghis Khan: The Ancient Nomadic Culture of Northern China* 《成吉思汗：中國古代北方草原遊牧文化》 (*Chengjisihan: Zhonghuo gudai beifang caoyuan youmu wenhua*). Beijing: Beijing Press 北京出版社, 2004.

Clauson, Gerard. *An Etymological Dictionary of Pre-Thirteenth-Century Turkish*. Oxford: The Clarendon Press, 1972.

Cleaves, Francis Woodman. "The Sino-Mongolian Inscription of 1338 in Memory of Jigüntei." *Harvard Journal of Asiatic Studies*, vol. 14, nos. 1-2 (June 1951).

Crespigny, Rafe de. *Northern Frontier, The Policies and Strategy of the Later Han Empire*. Canberra: Australian National University, 1984.

Crossley, Pamela. *The Manchus*. Cambridge, Mass.: Blackwell, 1997.

———. "Manzhou Yuanliu Kao and the Formalization of the Manchu Heritage." *Journal of Asian Studies*, vol. 46. no. 4 (Nov. 1987).

———. *Orphan Warriors: Three Manchu Generations and the End of the Qing World*. Princeton: Princeton University Press, 1990.

———. "Thinking about Ethnicity in the Early Modern China." *Late Imperial China*, vol. 11, no. 1 (June 1990).

———. *A Translucent Mirror: History and Identity in Qing Imperial Ideology*. Berkeley, CA and London: University of California Press, 1999.

Csongor, B. "Chinese in the Uighur Script of the T'ang-period." *Acta Orientalia Hungarica*, vol. 2 (1952).

Dalizhabu 達力扎布. "A Study of Mongolian Script Archives: Translation and Interpretation of Documents Concerning East Tümed Tribes" 《蒙古文檔案研究——有關東土默特部資料譯釋》("Mengguwen dang'an yanjiu – youguan dong Tumote bu ziliao yishi"). In Zhu Chengru 朱誠如, editor, *Collected Essays on Qing History: A Festschrift in Honor of the 90th Birthday of Professor Wang Zhonghan* 《清史論集: 慶賀王鍾翰教授九十華誕》(*Qingshi lunji: qinghe Wang Zhonghan jiaoshou jiushi huadan*). Beijing: Zijincheng Press 紫禁城出版社, 2003.

Damdinsürüng, Če. *Mongγol Uran J̌okiyal-un DegeJ̌i J̌ayun Bilig Orusibai* (*The Essence of Mongolian Literature*), vol. 14. Ulaanbaatar, 1959.

Dao Bu 道布, editor. *A Brief Survey of the Mongolian Language* 《蒙古語簡誌》 (*Menggu yu jianzhi*). Beijing: Nationalities Press 民族出版社, 1983.

Dardess, John W. "From Mongol Empire to Yuan Dynasty: Changing Forms of Imperial Rule in Mongolia and Central Asia." *Monumenta Serica*, vol. 30 (1972-1973).

D'Avezac, Armand. *Relation des Mongols ou Tartares par le frère Jean du Plan de Carpin*. Paris: Arthus-Bertrand, Don- dey-Dupré, 1839.

Dawson, Christopher, editor. *The Mongol Mission*. London and New York: Sheed and Ward, 1955.

Deng Guangming 鄧廣銘. "A Corrective Examination of the Two Entries of 'Yu Zhang Qin Jun' and 'Da Shou Ling Bu Zu Jun' of 'Monograph on the Army' in the *History of the Liao*" 《〈遼史·兵衛志〉"御帳親軍"、"大首領部族軍"兩事目考源辨誤》 ("'Liaoshi bingweizhi' 'Yu Zhang Qin Jun', 'Da Shou Ling Bu Zu Jun' liang shimu kaoyuan bianwu"). In *Academic Works of Deng Guangming Selected by Himself*《鄧廣銘學術論著自選集》(*Deng Guangming xueshu lunzhe zi xuanji*). Beijing: Capital Normal University Press 首都師範大學出版社, 1994.

Derevianko, Evgeniia Ivanova (Евгения Иванова Деревянко). *Amur Tribes of the First Millennium A.D.* (*Племена Приамурья. I тысячелетие нашей эры*). Original in Russian, translated into Chinese as [俄]E・I・傑烈維揚科 (E. I. Jielieweiyangke), *Tribes Along the Banks of the Heilongjiang* 《黑龍江沿岸的部落》 (*Heilongjiang yan'ande buluo*) by Lin Shushan 林樹山 and Yao Feng 姚鳳. Jilin Literature and History Press 吉林文史出版社, 1987.

Ding Qian 丁謙. *Textual Research on the Secret History of the Mongols* 《元秘史考証》(*Yuanmishi kaozheng*).

Ding Wenjiang 丁文江. *The Collected Yi Script Texts*《爨文叢刻》(*Cuanwen congke*). Shanghai: Commercial Press 商務印書館, 1936.

Documents Unearthed in Turfan《吐魯番出土文書》(*Tulufan chutu wenshu*). Beijing: Cultural Relics Press 文物出版社, 1981.

Dong Guodong 凍國棟 *The Tang Dynasty Commercial Economy and Business Management*《唐代的商品經濟與經營管理》 (*Tangdaide shangpin jingji yu jingying guanli*). Wuchang 武昌: Wuhan University Press 武漢大學出版社, 1990.

Dong Zhengjun 董正鈞. *Juyan Lake (Ejin Banner)* 《居延海（額濟那旗）》(*Juyanhai (Ejina qi)*). 1944. Included in Chaogetu 朝格圖, editor, *Alxa League Historical Records*《阿拉善盟旗志史料》(*Alashanmeng qi zhi shiliao*). Alxa League Political Consultative Literary and Historical Materials Research Committee 阿拉善盟政協文史資料研究委員會 (Alashanmeng zhengxie wenshi ziliao yanjiu weiyuanhui), 1987.

Drompp, Michael R. *Tang China and the Collapse of the Uighur Empire*. Leiden and Boston: Brill, 2005.

Du Xingzhi 都興智. "The Surnames and Forenames of the Khitans"《契丹族的姓氏和名稱》 ("Qidan zude xingshi he mingcheng"). *Journal of Liaoning Normal University* 《遼寧師範大學學報》 (*Liaoning shifan daxue xuebao*), 1990, no. 5.

Duan Lianqin 段連勤. "Several Problems Concerning the Early History of the Western Turks and the Western Turk Empire" 《關於西突厥與西突厥汗國早期歷史的幾個問題》 ("Guanyu Xitujue yu Xitujue hanguo zaoqi lishide jige wenti"). *Xinjiang Social Sciences*《新疆社會科學》(*Xinjiang shehui kexue*), 1984, no. 3.

Eller, Jack and Coughlan, Reed. "The Poverty of Primordialism: The Demystification of Ethnic Attachments." *Ethnic and Racial Studies*, vol. 16, no. 2 (1993).

Elliott, Mark C. "The Limits of Tartary: Manchuria in Imperial and National Geographies." *Journal of Asian Studies*, vol. 59, no. 3 (Aug. 2000).

Encyclopedia of Islam, new edition, vol. 3. Leiden: Brill, 1971.

Engels, Friedrich. *Der Ursprung-der Familie, des Privatei genthums und des Staats*. Translated into Chinese as *The Origin of the Family, Private Property, and the State* 《家庭、私有制和國家的起源》(*Jiating, siyouzhi he guojiade qiyuan*). People's Publishing House 人民出版社, 1954.

Essays on the History of the USSR in the 11th through 13th Centuries (*Очерки Истории

CCCP XI-XIII вв) . 1953. Translated into Chinese as *A Brief National History of Mongolia in the Feudal Period* 《蒙古統治时期的國史略》 (*Menggu Tongzhi shiqide guoshilüe*).

Fei Xiaotong 費孝通. "Preface." In Hu Qiwang 胡起望 and Fan Honggui 范宏貴, *Yao Ethnicity of Pan Village* 《盤村瑤族》(*Pancun Yaozu*). Beijing: Nationalities Press 民族出版社, 1983.

Feng Chengjun 馮承鈞. *Assembled and Compiled Philological Essays on Historical Places in the Western Regions and Southern Seas*《西域南海史地考證論著匯輯》(*Xiyu nanhai shidi kaozheng lunzhe huiji*). Beijing: Zhonghua Book Company 中華書局, 1957.

———. *Biography of Chinggis Khan* 《成吉思汗傳》 (*Chengjisihan zhuan*). Shanghai: Commercial Press 商務印書館, 1947

———. *Continued Collection of Translations and Studies on Historical Places in the Western Regions and Southern Seas*《西域南海史地考證譯叢續編》(*Xiyu nanhai shidi kaozheng shicong yicong xubian*). Shanghai: Commercial Press 商務印書館, 1933.

———. "A Study of the Tribes in the Northern Area during the Liao and Jin Periods"《遼金北邊部族考》("Liao Jin beibian buzu kao"), in *Assembled and Compiled Philological Essays on Historical Places in the Western Regions and Southern Seas* 《西域南海史地考證論著匯輯》(*Xiyu nanhai shidi kaozheng lunzhe huiji*). Beijing: Zhonghua Book Company 中華書局, 1957.

Feng Jiasheng 馮家昇. "An Interpretation of the Black Ox and White Horse as Khitan Worship" 《契丹祀天以青牛白馬之解釋》("Qidan sitian yi qingniu baima zhi jieshi"). In *A Compilation of the Best Works of Feng Jiasheng*《馮家昇論著輯粹》(*Feng Jiasheng lunzhe jicui*). Beijing: Zhonghua Book Company 中華書局, 1987.

———. "A Philological Study of the Sun and the Khitan" 《太陽契丹考釋》("Taiyang Qidan kaoshi"). In *A Compilation of the Best Works of Feng Jiasheng*《馮家昇論著輯粹》(*Feng Jiasheng lunzhe jicui*). Beijing: Zhonghua Book Company 中華書局, 1987.

———. "The Relationship between Khitan Conventions of Worship and other Religious Mythological Customs" 《契丹祀天之俗與其宗教神話風俗之關係》 ("Qidan sitian zhi su yuqi zongjiao shenhua fengsu zhi guanxi"). In *A Compilation of the Best Works of Feng Jiasheng* 《馮家昇論著輯粹》 (*Feng Jiasheng lunzhe jicui*). Beijing: Zhonghua Book Company 中華書局, 1987.

———. "The Xiongnu People and their Culture" 《匈奴民族及其文化》("Xiongnu minzu jiqi wenhua"). *Journal of Historical Geography* 《禹貢》 (*Yu Gong*) [literally, "Tribute of Yu"], vol. 7, no. 5 (1937).

Forte, Antonino. *The Hostage An Shigao and his Offspring*. Kyoto: Istituto Italiano di Cultura Scuola di Studi sull' Asia Orientale, 1995.

Frazer, James George. *Golden Bough*, the abridged edition. London: Macmillan, 1922.

von Gabain, Annemarie. *Alttürkische Grammatik*. Leipzig: Otto Harrassowitz, 1950.

———. *Das Leben im uigurischen Königreich von Qocho, 850-1250* (*The Lives of the Uyghur Kings of Gaochang, from 850 to 1250*), *Veröffentlichung der Societas*

Uralo-Altaica, vol. 6. Wiesbaden: Otto Harrassowitz, 1973.

Gai Zhiyong 蓋之庸. *A Study of the Stone Inscriptions of the Liao Dynasty in Inner Mongolia*《内蒙古遼代石刻文研究》(*Neimenggu Liaodai shikewen yanjiu*). Hohhot: Inner Mongolia University Press 内蒙古大学出版社, 2002.

Gardīzī, Maḥmūd. *Zayn al-Akhbār* (*The Ornament of Histories*).

Geertz, Clifford. "The Integrative Revolution." In Clifford Geertz, editor, *Old Societies and New States*. New York: Free Press, 1963.

Geng Shimin 耿世民. "A Study of the Text in the Old Uyghur Scripts of the Stele of the Achievements of the Ancestors of Idi-qut, the Qočo Prince" 《回鶻文亦都護高昌王世勛碑研究》 ("Huihuwen Yiduhu Gaochang Wang shixun bei yanjiu"). *Acta Archaeologica Sinica*《考古學報》 (*Kaogu xuebao*), 1980, no. 4.

Geng Shimin 耿世民 and Zhang Guangda 張廣達. "A Study of Suolimi" 《唆里迷考》 ("Suolimi kao"). *Historical Research*《歷史研究》(*Lishi yanjiu*), 1980, no. 2.

Gershevitch, I. *A Grammar of Manichean Sogdian*. Oxford: Blackwell, 1954; second edition, 1961.

Gexi Quzha Tibetan Dictionary 《格西曲札藏文辭典》 (*Gexi quzha zangwen cidian*) . Beijing: People's Publishing House 人民出版社, 1990. Chinese translation of the Tibetan *Chos kyi grags pa*.

al-Ghāzī Bahādur, Abū. *Šajara-yi Turk* (*Genealogical Tree of the Turkmen*). 1659.

———. *Šajara-yi Turk* (*Genealogical Tree of the Turkmen*). Translated into French and annotated by Le Baron Desmaisons as *Histoire des Mongols et des Tartares par Aboul-Ghâzi Bèhâdour Khan*. St. Petersburg: Imprimerie de l'Académie impériale des sciences, 1874.

Giles, Lionel. "A Chinese Geographical Text of the Ninth Century." *Bulletin of the School of Oriental Studies*, vol. 6, no. 4 (1932).

Golden, Peter B. *An Introduction to the History of the Turkic Peoples*. Wiesbaden: Otto Harrassowitz, 1992.

Gong Fangzhen 龔方震 and Yan Kejia 晏可佳. *History of Zoroastrianism*《祆教史》(*Xianjiao shi*). Shanghai Academy of Social Sciences Press 上海社會科學院出版社, 1998.

Grekov, B. D. and Iakubovskii, A. IU. (Б. Д. Греков and А. Ю. Якубовский). *Золотая Орда и её Падение* (*The Golden Horde and its Collapse*). Москва-Ленинград, 1950.

Grenet, F., Sims-Williams, N., and de la Vaissière, É. "The Sogdian Ancient Letter V." *Bulletin of the Asia Institute*, new series, vol. 12 (2001).

Grousset, René. *Le conquérant du monde: vie de Gengis-khan*. Paris: Éditions Albin Michel, 1944.

———. *L'empire des steppes: Attila, Gengis-Khan, Tamerlan*. Paris: Editions Payot, 1939.

———. *L'empire Mongol*. Paris: de Broccard, 1941.

———. *The Empire of the Steppes*. Translated by Naomi Walford. New Brunswick, New Jersey: Rutgers University Press, 1970.

Grube, Wilhelm. *Die Sprache und Schrift der Jučen*. Leipzig: Kommissions-Verlag von O. Harrassowitz, 1896.

Gu Yanwu 顧炎武. "The Four Barbarians of the Nine Frontiers"《九邊四夷》("Jiubian siyi"). In *The Characteristics of Each Province in the Empire* 《天下郡國利病書》(*Tianxia junguo libing shu*). Shanghai: Hanfenlou 涵芬樓 facsimile edition, in the collection of Kunshan 昆山 Library, vol. 34.

———. *Record of Knowledge Gained Day by Day* 《日知錄》(*Ri zhi lu*).

Guo Xiliang 郭錫良. *Handbook of Ancient Pronunciation of Chinese Characters* 《漢字古音手冊》(*Hanzi guyin shouce*). Beijing: Peking University Press 北京大學出版社, 1986.

Guy, R. Kent. "Who were the Manchus? A Review Essay." *Journal of Asian Studies*, vol. 61, no. 1 (Feb. 2002).

Haidar, Mīrzā Muhammad. *Tārīkh-i Rashīdī* (*History of Rashid*). Translated into English as *Tarikh-i-Rashidi: A History of the Moghuls of Central Asia*; N. Elias, editor, Edward Denison Ross, translator. London: Sampson Low, Marston and Company 1895; reprinted London: Curzon Press, 1972.

Haloun, G. and Henning, W. B. "The Compendium of the Doctrines and Styles of the Teaching of Mani, the Buddha of Light." *Asia Major*, new series, vol. 3 (1953).

Hambis, Louis. "Kaštim et Ges-dum." *Journal Asiatique*, no. 246 (1958).

———. "Notes sur Käm: Nom de L'Yénissei Supérieur." *Journal Asiatique*, no. 244 (1956).

Han Rulin 韓儒林, "Chinggis Khan's and Other Neighboring Tribes in the Yuan Dynasty"《元代的吉利吉思及其鄰近諸部》("Yuandaide Jilijisi jiqi linjin zhubu"). In Han Rulin 韓儒林, *Collection from the Yurt*《穹廬集》(*Qionglu ji*) [Han Rulin's papers]. Shanghai People's Press 上海人民出版社, 1982.

———. "A New Exploration of the Tang Dynasty Dubo" 《唐代都波新探》("Tangdai Dubo xintan"). In *Collection from the Yurt*《穹廬集》(*Qionglu ji*). Shanghai People's Press 上海人民出版社, 1982.

———. "A Philological Study of Turkish Official Position Titles" 《突厥官號考釋》("Tujue guanhao kaoshi"). In *Collection from the Yurt*《穹廬集》(*Qionglu ji*). Shanghai People's Press 上海人民出版社, 1982.

———. "Phonetic Analysis and Identification in the Studies of the History of the Northwestern Ethnic Minorities" 《關於西北民族史中的審音與勘同》("Guanyu xibei minzu shizhongde shenyin yu kantong"). In *Collected Papers of Research on Yuan History and Northern Nationalities History* 《元史及北方民族史研究集刊》(*Yuanshi ji beifang minzu shi yanjiu jikan*), Nanjing University 南京大學, no. 3 (1979).

———. "On Several Western Liao Place Names" 《關於西遼的幾個地名》("Guanyu Xiliaode jige diming"). *Collected Papers of Research on Yuan History and Northern Nationalities History*《元史及北方民族史研究集刊》(*Yuanshi ji beifang minzu shi yanjiu jikan*), Nanjing University 南京大學, no. 4 (1980).

———. "A Study of the Mongolian Dalahan" 《蒙古答刺罕考》. In *Collection from the Yurt*《穹廬集》(*Qionglu ji*). Shanghai People's Press 上海人民出版社, 1982.

———. "Tang Dynasty Dubo" 《唐代都波》("Tangdai Dubo"). *Social Science Front* 《社會科學戰綫》(*Shehui kexue zhanxian*), no. 3 (1978).

Haneda Tōru 羽田亨. *The Postal Stations of the Yuan Dynasty*『元朝駅傳雑考』(*Genchō ekiden zakkō*). Tokyo: Toyo Bunko 東洋文庫, 1930.

———. "The Region North of the Gobi Desert and the People from Samarkand" 「漠北之地和康國人」. In *Collected Historical Articles of Doctor Haneda*『羽田博士史學論文集』(*Haneda hakushi shigaku ronbunshū*), vol. 1. Kyoto: The Society of Oriental Researchs 東洋史研究會, 1957.

———. "The Tang First Year of the Guangqi Reign Period Manuscript Remnant of the Gazetteer of Shazhou and Yizhou"「唐光啟元年寫本沙州伊州地志殘卷」. In *Collected Essays on History and Geography Commemorating Doctor Ogawa*『小川博士還曆記念史學地理學論叢』. Tokyo: Kōbundō 弘文堂, 1930.

Harmatta, J. "A New Document in the History of the Silk Road." *Jahrbüch für Wissenschaftsgeschichte*, no. 11 (1971).

Harrell, Steven, editor. *Cultural Encounters on China's Ethnic Frontiers*. Seattle and London: University of Washington Press, 1995.

He Jiren 和即仁. "The Lahu People" 《拉祜族》 ("Lahu zu"). In Zhang Lianfang 張聯芳, editor, *Names of the Chinese People* 《中國人的姓名》 (*Zhongguo rende xingming*). Beijing: China Social Sciences Press 中國社會科學出版社, 1992.

———. "The Naxi People"《納西族》 ("Naxi zu"). In Zhang Lianfang 張聯芳, editor, *Names of the Chinese People* 《中國人的姓名》 (*Zhongguo rende xingming*). Beijing: China Social Sciences Press 中國社會科學出版社, 1992.

He Qiutao 何秋濤. *Complete Historical Record of the Northern Lands*《朔方備乘》(*Shuofang bei cheng*).

Henning, W. B., "Argi and the 'Tokharians'." *Bulletin of the School of Oriental Studies*, vol. 9, no. 3 (1938).

———. "The Date of the Sogdian Ancient Letters." *Bulletin of the School of Oriental and African Studies,* vol. 12, no. 3-4 (1948).

———. *Selected Papers I, Acta Iranica 14*. Leiden: Brill, 1977.

———. *Selected Papers II, Acta Iranica 15.* Leiden: Brill, 1977.

———. "The Sogdian Texts in Paris." *Bulletin of the School of Oriental and African Studies*, vol. 2, no. 4 (1946).

Hirth, Friedrich, "Nachwörte zur Inschrift des Tonjukuk." In Wilhelm Radloff, *Die alttürkischen Inschriften der Mongolei*. St. Petersburg: 1898.

———. *Sinologische Beiträge zur Geschichte der Türkvölker I: Die Ahnentafel Attila's nach Johannes von Thurócz* (*Sinological Contributions to the History of the Turks I: The Genealogical Table of Attila after Johannes von Thurócz*). St. Petersburg: Wissenschaften, 1900.

Historical Materials of the Early Qing《清初史料叢刊》(*Qingchu shiliao congkan*), no. 9. Shenyang 瀋陽: Liaoning University History Department, 1978.

Ho, Peng-Yoke 何丙郁 and He Guanbiao 何冠彪. *Essays on the History of Chinese Technology* 《中國科技史概論》 (*Zhongguo kejishi gailun*). Hong Kong: Zhonghua Book Company Hong Kong Branch 中華書局香港分局, 1983.

Ho, Ping-Yü and Needham, Joseph. "The Laboratory Equipment of the Early Mediaeval Chinese Alchemists." *Ambix*, no. 7 (1959).

Hong, Guangzhu 洪光住. *A Draft History of Chinese Food Products Science* 《中國食品科技史稿》 (*Zhongguo shipin keji shigao*), vol.1. Beijing: China Commercial Press 中國商業出版社, 1985.

Hong Jun 洪鈞. *Textual Analysis on the Age of Taizu* (Chinggis Khan) 《太祖年壽考異》 (*Taizu nianshou kaoyi*).

———. *Yuan History Translated and Corrected* 《元史譯文證補》 (*Yuanshi yiwen zhengbu*). Block printing by Lu Runxiang 陸潤庠, 1897.

Hose, Charles and McDougall, William. *The Pagan Tribes of Borneo*. London: Macmillan, 1912.

Hosoya Yoshio. "The Gūsa (Banner) of Ujen Cooha (Han Army Eight Banners)" 「烏真超哈（八旗漢軍）の固山（旗）」. In *A Festschrift in Honor of Matsumura Jūn* 『松村潤先生古稀記念清代史論叢』. Tokyo: Kyuko Shoin 汲古書院, 1994.

Howorth, Henry H. *History of the Mongols*. London: Longmans, Green, and Co., 1876-1880.

Hsiao Ch'i-ch'ing 蕭啟慶. *The Military Establishment of the Yuan Dynasty*. Cambridge, Mass.: Harvard University Press, 1978.

Hu Qiwang 胡起望 and Fan Honggui 范宏貴. *Yao Ethnicity of Pan Village* 《盤村瑤族》 (*Pancun Yaozu*). Beijing: Nationalities Press 民族出版社, 1983.

———. "The Yao People" 《瑤族》 ("Yao zu"). In Zhang Lianfang 張聯芳, editor, *Names of the Chinese People* 《中國人的姓名》 (*Zhongguo rende xingming*). Beijing: China Social Sciences Press 中國社會科學出版社, 1992.

Hu Zengyi 胡增益, *A New Manchu-Chinese Dictionary* 《新滿漢大詞典》. Urumqi: Xinjiang People's Press 新疆人民出版社, 1994.

Huang Huixian 黃惠賢. "The Change in the Political Situation in the Western Region during the Chuigong Reign Period according to the Military Name List of Gaochang County, Xizhou" 《從西州高昌縣徵鎮名籍看垂拱年間西域政局之變化》 ("Cong Xizhou Gaochangxian zhengzhen mingli kan Chuigong nianjian Xiyu zhengju zhi bianhua"). In *Preliminary Exploration of the Dunhuang and Turfan Documents* 《敦煌吐魯番文書初探》 (*Dunhuang Tulufan wenshu chutan*), Tang Zhangru 唐長孺, editor. Wuhan University Press 武漢大學出版社, 1983.

Huang Shijian 黃時鑑. "*Alaji* and the Origin of Liquor Distillation in China" 《阿剌吉與中國燒酒的起始》 ("Alaji yu Zhongguo haojiude qishi"). *Literature and History* 《文史》 (*Wenshi*), vol. 31 (1988).

———. "The Origin of Liquor Distillation in China and Chinese Stills" 《中國燒酒的起始與中國蒸餾器》 ("Zhongguo shaojiude qishi yu Zhongguo zhengliuqi"). *Literature and History* 《文史》 (*Wenshi*), vol. 41 (1996).

Huang Wenbi 黃文弼. *Archaeological Records of the Tarim Basin* 《塔里木盆地考古記》 (*Talimu pendi kaogu ji*). Beijing: Science Press 科學出版社, 1958.

———. "Chronological Record of the Qu Family of Gaochang" 《高昌麴氏紀年》 ("Gaochang Qushi jinian"). In *Northwest Science Field Study Group Series* 《西北科學考察團叢刊》 (*Xibei kexue kaochatuan congkan*) 2, *Archaeology* 《考古學》 (*Kaoguxue*), vol. 1, "Gaochang" part 1. 1930.

———. "Reconstructed and Edited Text of the Stele of the Achievements of the Ancestors of the Idi-qut, the Qočo Prince" 《亦都護高昌王世勛碑復原並校記》 ("Yiduhu Gaochang Wang shixun bei fuyuan bing xiaoji"). *Cultural Relics* 《文物》 (*Wenwu*), 1964, no. 2.

Huang Zhangjian 黃彰健. "A Study of the State Title Established by Nurhaci" 《努爾哈赤所建國號考》 ("Nuerhachi suojian guohao kao"). *Bulletin of the Institute of History and Philology, Academia Sinica* 《中央研究院史語所集刊》 (*Zhongyang yanjiuyuan shiyusuo jikan*), vol. 37, part 2 (1967).

———. "A Study of the State Title of the Manchu State" 《滿洲國國號考》 ("Manzhouguo guohao kao"). *Bulletin of the Institute of History and Philology, Academia Sinica* 《中央研究院史語所集刊》 (*Zhongyang yanjiuyuan shiyusuo jikan*), vol. 37, part 2 (1967).

Hucker, Charles O. *A Dictionary of Official Titles in Imperial China*. Stanford: Stanford University Press, 1985.

Hudūd al-'Ālam, The Regions of the World: A Persian Geography, 372 A.H./982 A.D. Translated and explained by Vladimir Minorsky (Владимир Минорский), second edition, edited by C. E. Bosworth, E. J. W. Gibb Memorial Series, New Series XI. London: Luzac, 1970.

Hui Dong 惠棟. *A Supplementary Gloss on the History of the Later Han* 《後漢書補注》 (*Houhanshu buzhu*).

Hung, William. "The Transmission of the Book Known as 'The Secret History of the Mongols'." *Harvard Journal of Asiatic Studies*, vol. 14, nos. 3-4 (Dec. 1951).

Hutchinson, J. and Smith, Anthony D. *Ethnicity*. Oxford: Oxford University Press, 1996.

Hutter, Manfred. *Manis kosmogonische Sābuhragān-Texte*. Wiesbaden: Harrassowitz, 1992.

Ikeda On 池田温. "A Concise Study of the Topographical Classic of Shazhou" 「沙州圖經略考」. In *A Festschrift of Articles on East Asian History on the Occasion of Dr. Enoki's 61st Birthday* 『榎博士還暦記念東洋史論叢』. Tokyo: Yamakawa Shuppansha 山川出版社, 1975.

———. "The Sogdian Settlements in Dunhuang in the Mid-Eighth Century" 「8 世紀中葉における敦煌のソグド人聚落」. *Eurasian Cultural Studies* 『歐亞大陸文化研究』 (*Yurashia Bunka-kenkyū*), no. 1 (1965).

Ikegami Jiro 池上二良. "Study of Manchu Dialect Based on Materials Gathered from Mu Yejun" 「満洲語方言研究における穆曄俊採集資料について」. In Ikegami Jiro 池上二良, editor, *Studies on the Manchu Language* 『満洲語研究』. Tokyo: Kyuko Shoin 汲古書院, 1999.

Ikeuchi Hiroshi 池内宏. "The Northeastern Korean Borderland and Jurchen Tribes as well as their Relations in Early Yi Korea" 「鮮初の東北境と女眞との関係」. In Ikeuchi Hiroshi 池内宏, *Research on the History of Manchuria and Korea: the Early Modern Period* 『満鮮史研究· 近世篇』. Tokyo: Chūō Koron Bijutsu Shuppan 中央公論美術出版, 1972.

Imanishi Shunjū 今西春秋. *Collation of the Veritable Records of Qing Taizu* 『対校清太祖実録』. Tokyo: Kokusho Kankōkai 國書刊行会, 1974.

Inner Mongolia Institute of Cultural and Historical Relics and Archaeology 内蒙古文物考古研究所 (Neimenggu wenwu kaogu yanjiusuo), "A Report on the Excavation of the Tomb of Yelü Yuzhi of the Liao Dynasty" 《遼耶律羽之墓發掘簡報》 ("Liao Yelü Yuzhi mu fajue jianbao"), *Cultural Relics*《文物》 (*Wenwu*), 1996, no. 1.

Investigative Team of the Orkhon River. *Catalog of the Ancient Objects of Mongolia* (*Каталог древних предметов Монголии*) . St. Petersburg: 1892.

Irinchin, Yekemingghadai 亦鄰真. "On the Origins of the Ethnic Groups of Northern China and the Mongols" 《中國北方民族與蒙古族族源》 ("Zhongguo beifang minzu yu Mengguzu zuyuan"). *Journal of Inner Mongolia University*《内蒙古大學學報》 (*Neimenggu daxue xuebao*), 1979, nos. 3-4 (joint volume).

Ishibashi Hideo 石橋秀雄. "Jushen in the Early Qing Dynasty: Focusing Especially on the Tianming Reign Period" 「清初のジュシェン jushen: 特に天命期までを中心として」. and "A Study on Jushen" 「ジュシェン小考」. In Ishibashi Hideo 石橋秀雄, *Studies on Qing History* 『清代史研究』. Tokyo: Ryokuin Shobō 绿荫書房, 1989.

———. "A Study of the Name of Manchu after the Qing Entered the Shanhai Pass" 「清朝入関後のマンジユ (Manju) 満洲呼称をめぐって」. In Ishibashi Hideo 石橋秀雄, editor, *Problems on Qing China* 『清代中国の諸問題』. Tokyo: Yamakawa Shuppansha 山川出版社, 1995.

———. "A Study on Jushen"「ジュシェン小考」. In Ishibashi Hideo 石橋秀雄, *Studies on Qing History* 『清代史研究』. Tokyo: Ryokuin Shobō 绿荫書房, 1989.

Ishida Mikinosuke 石田幹之助. "New Materials for Jurchen Language Studies" 「女真語研究の新資料」. In *Collected Papers on Oriental History: A Festschrift in Honor of the 60th Birthday of Dr. Kuwabara* 『桑原博士還曆記念東洋史論叢』. Kyoto: Kōbundō 弘文堂, 1931.

———. *Spring in Chang'an*『長安の春』. Tokyo: Sōgensha 創元社, 1941.

Itō Gikyō 伊藤義教. *An Introductory Study of Persian Culture*『波斯文化渡来考』 (*Perusha bunka torai kō: Shirukurodo kara Asuka e*). Tokyo: Iwanami Shoten 岩波書店, 1980.

Janhunen, Juha. *Manchuria: An Ethnic History.* Helsinki: Finno-Ugrian Society, 1996.

Ji Shi 即實. "The Decipherment of the 'Epitaph of Geyekun' "《〈戈也昆墓誌〉釋讀》 ("'Geyekun muzhi' shidu"). In Ji Shi 即實, *Seeking the Road out of the Forest of Enigmas: New Decipherments of the Khitan Small Script* 《謎林問徑——契丹小字解讀新程》 (*Milin wenjing – Qidan xiaozi jiedu xincheng*). Shenyang 瀋陽: Liaoning Nationalities Press 遼寧民族出版社, 1996.

———. "The Decipherment of the 'Epitaph of Jiulin' " 《〈糺鄰墓誌〉釋讀》 ("'Jiulin muzhi' shidu"). In *Seeking the Road out of the Forest of Enigmas: New Decipherments of the Khitan Small Script* 《謎林問徑——契丹小字解讀新程》 (*Milin wenjing – Qidan xiaozi jiedu xincheng*). Shenyang 瀋陽: Liaoning Nationalities Press 遼寧民族出版社, 1996.

———. "The Decipherment of the 'Epitaph of Sen Ne' "《〈森訥墓誌〉釋讀》 ("'Sen

Ne muzhi' shidu"). In *Seeking the Road out of the Forest of Enigmas: New Decipherments of the Khitan Small Script* 《謎林問徑——契丹小字解讀新程》 (*Milin wenjing – Qidan xiaozi jiedu xincheng*). Shenyang 瀋陽: Liaoning Nationalities Press 遼寧民族出版社, 1996.

———. "An Examination of the 'Epitaph of the Deceased Ms. Yelü'" 《〈銘石〉瑣解》 ("'Mingshi' suojie"). In *Seeking the Road out of the Forest of Enigmas: New Decipherments of the Khitan Small Script* 《謎林問徑——契丹小字解讀新程》 (*Milin wenjing – Qidan xiaozi jiedu xincheng*). Shenyang 瀋陽: Liaoning Nationalities Press 遼寧民族出版社, 1996.

Ji Xianlin 季羡林. *Collated and Annotated Edition of the Great Tang Dynasty Record of the Western Regions* 《大唐西域記校注》 (*Datang xiyuji xiaozhu*). Beijing: Zhonghua Book Company 中華書局, 1985.

Jia Jingyan 賈敬顏. *Collected Studies of Ancient Northeastern Nationalities Ancient Geography*《東北古代民族古代地理叢考》 (*Dongbei gudai minzu gudai dili congkao*). Beijing: China Social Sciences Press 中國社會科學出版社, 1994.

Jia Jingyan 賈敬顏 and Zhu Feng 朱鳳, co-editors. *Compilation of the Mongol Translated Words and the Nüzhen* (Jurchen) *Translated Words* 《蒙古譯語、女真譯語彙編》 (*Menggu yiyu, Nüzhen yiyu huibian*). Tianjin: Tianjin Ancient Books Press 天津古籍出版社, 1990. [*Mongol Translated Words* 《蒙古譯語》is another name for *Translated Words Written in the Zhiyuan Reign Period* 《至元譯語》]

———. "Khitan Script" 《契丹文》 ("Qidan wen"). In *Ancient Scripts of Chinese Nationalities* 《中國民族古文字》 (*Zhongguo minzu guwenzi*). China Nationalities Ancient Scripts Research Committee, 1982.

Jia Zhoujie 賈洲傑. "Research on the Khitan Funerary System" 《契丹喪葬制度研究》 ("Qidan sangzang zhidu yanjiu"). *Journal of Inner Mongolia University*《内蒙古大學學報》 (*Neimenggu daxue xuebao*), 1978, vol. 2. Also included in Sun Jinyi 孫進已, et al., editors. *Compilation of Works on Khitan History*《契丹史論著彙編》 (*Qidan shi lunzhe huibian*). Liaoning Province Social Sciences Academy History Research Institute 遼寧省社會科學院歷史研究所, 1988.

Jiang Boqin 姜伯勤. *Dunhuang and Turfan Documents and the Silk Road*《敦煌吐魯番文書與絲綢之路》 (*Dunhuang Tulufan wenshu yu sizhouzhilu*). Beijing: Cultural Relics Press 文物出版社, 1994.

———. "The Sogdians in Dunhuang, Turfan, and on the Silk Road" 「敦煌·吐魯番とシルクロ-ド上のソグド人」. *East and West Quarterly* 『季刊東西交涉』, vol. 5, nos. 1-3 (1986).

Jilin Provincial Museum 吉林省博物館 (Jilin sheng bowuguan). "A Brief Report on the Jilin Tahu City Survey" 《吉林他虎城調查簡記》 ("Jilin Tahu cheng diaocha jianji"). *Archaeology* 《考古》 (*Kaogu*), 1964, no. 1.

Jin Yongtian 金永田. "An Examination of the 'Epitaph of Yelü Xinie' in Khitan Large Script" 《契丹大字"耶律習涅墓誌"考釋》 ("Qidan dazi 'Yelü Xinie muzhi' kaoshi"). *Archaeology* 《考古》 (*Kaogu*), 1991, no. 4.

———. "An Examination of the Epitaphs of Han Dewei and Yelü Yuanzuo" 《韓德威和

耶律元佐墓誌銘考釋》 ("Han Dewei he Yelü Yuanzuo muzhiming kaoshi"). *Cultural Relics*《文物》 (*Wenwu*), 1998, no. 7.

Jin Zutong 金祖同, compiler. *Treasures Remaining in the Shifting Sands*《流沙遺珍》 (*Liusha yizhen*). 1940.

Juwaīnī (Juvaini), 'Ala-ad-Din 'Ata-Malik. *Ta'rīkh-i Jahān-Gushā* (*The History of the World-Conqueror*). J. A. Boyle, translator and editor. Cambridge: Harvard University Press, 1958.

———. *Ta'rīkh-i Jahān-Gushā* (*The History of the World-Conqueror*). Translated into Chinese by He Gaoji 何高濟 as《世界征服者史》(*Shijie zhengfuzhe shi*). Hohhot: Inner Mongolia People's Press 内蒙古人民出版社, 1981.

Kabo, Rafail Mikhaĭlovich (Рафаил Михайлович Кабо). *Очерки истории и экономики Тувы* (*Summary of Tuva's History and Economy*). Москва-Ленинград: Соцэкгиз, 1934.

Kanda Kiichirō 神田喜一郎. "Notes on Zoroastrianism"「祆教瑣記」. *Historical Review*『史林』 (*Shirin*), vol. 18, no. 1 (1933).

Kanda Nobuo 神田信夫. "A Study of the State Title of Manju"「滿洲 (Manju) 国号考」. In *Collection of Papers on Oriental History: A Festschrift in Honor of the 60th Birthday of Dr. Yamamoto*『山本博士還暦記念東洋史論叢』. Tokyo: Yamakawa Shuppansha 山川出版社, 1972. Also in *Reviews and Studies on Qing History*『清朝史論考』. Tokyo: Yamakawa Shuppansha 山川出版社, 2005.

al-Kāshgharī, Mahmūd. *Dīwān lughāt al-Turk* (*Compendium of the Languages of the Turks*). Bessim Atalay, editor. Ankara: Alâeddin Kiral Basimevi, 1939-1943.

———. *Compendium of the Turkic Dialects*. Robert Dankoff and James Kelly, editors and translators. Duxbury, Mass.: Tekin, 1982-1985 [different edition of the above, *Dīwān lughāt al-Turk*].

Kawachi Yoshihiro 河内良弘. "The Elimination of Three Jianzhou Commanderies and the Rise of a New Power" 「建州三衛の消灭と新勢力の擡頭」. In Kawachi Yoshihiro, *Studies on Ming Dynasty Jurchen History*『明代女真史の研究』. Kyoto: Dōhōsha Shuppan 同朋舎出版, 1992.

———. "Limanzhu and Great Jin" 「李滿住と大金」. In *Collection of Papers on Qing History: A Festschrift in Honor of the 70th Birthday of Matsumura Jūn*『松村潤先生古稀記念清代史論叢』. Tokyo: Kyuko Shoin 汲古書院, 1994.

Ke Shaomin 柯紹忞. *New History of the Yuan* 《新元史》 (*Xin Yuanshi*). Shanghai: Kaiming Book Company 開明書局, 1936.

———. *Textual Research on the New History of the Yuan* 《新元史考證》 (*Xin Yuanshi kaozheng*).

Khan, Almaz. "Chinggis Khan: From Imperial Ancestor to Ethnic Hero." In Stevan Harrell, *Cultural Encounters on China's Ethnic Frontiers*. Seattle, WA: University of Washington Press, 1994.

Kikuchi Hideo 菊池英夫. "The Development of the 'Army' prior to the Establishment of the Military Commissioner"「節度使制確立以前における「軍」制度の展開」 ("Setsudoshisei kakuritsuizenniokeru 'gun' seido no tenkai"). *Tōyō Gakuhō* (*Journal of Oriental Studies*)『東洋学報』 vol. 44, no. 2, (1961).

Kiselev, S. V. (С. В. Киселев). *Древняя история Южной Сибири* (*The Ancient History of South Siberia*). Москва: Академия наук СССР, 1951.

Kiselev, S. V. (С. В. Киселев), et al. *Древнемонгольские города* (*Ancient Mongolian Cities*). Москва: Академия наук СССР, 1965.

Kliashtornyĭ, S. G. (С. Г. Кляшторный). *Древнетюркские рунические памятники. как источник по истории Средней Азии* (*Ancient Turkish Runic Monuments as Sources for the History of Central Asia*). Москва: Наука, 1964.

———. "Согдийцы в Центральной Азии" ("Sogdians in Central Asia"), in *Эпиграфика Востока* (*Epigraphy of the East*), no. 14 (1961). French version in *Ural-Altaische Jahrbücher*, vol. 33, nos. 1-2 (1961).

Kljaštornyj (Kliashtornyĭ), S. G. and Livšic, V. A. "The Sogdian Inscription of Bugut Revised." *Acta Orientalia Hungaricae*, vol. 26, fasc. 1 (1972).

Klimkeit, Hans-Joachim. *Manichaean Art and Calligraphy*. Leiden: Brill, 1982.

———. *Manichaean Art and Calligraphy*. Translated into Chinese by Lin Wushu 林悟殊 as [德]克林凯特 (Kelinkaite), *Ancient Manichaean Art* 《古代摩尼教藝術》 (*Gudai monijiao yishu*). Guangzhou: Sun Yat-sen University Press 中山大学出版社, 1989.

Kōkebuyan 呼和賓音, editor. *Monggol-un jang úile-yin mōrdel* (*Tracing Mongolian Customs*) 《蒙古風俗追溯》 (*Menggu fengsu zhuisu*). [Qaiilar]: Ōbōr Monggol-un Suyul-un Keblel- ún Qoriy-a (Inner Mongolia Cultural Press) 内蒙古文化出版社 (Neimenggu wenhua chubanshe), 1988.

Kowalewski, Joseph Etienne, *Dictionnaire Mongol-Russe-Français*. Taipei: SMC Publishing, 1993; reprint of the first edition, Kazan: Imprimerie de l'Université 1844-1849.

Kuwabara Jitsuzō 桑原隲藏. *The Collected Works of Kuwabara Jitsuzō* (*Kuwabara Jitsuzō zenshū*) 『桑原隲藏全集』, vol. 2. Tokyo: Iwanami Shoten 岩波書店, 1968.

———. *On the People from the Western Regions who Came to Live in China during the Sui and Tang Periods* (Zui-Tō jidai ni Shina ni raijūshita Seiikijin ni tsuite) 『隋唐時代に支那に來住した西域人に就いて』. In *Festschrift of Articles on Sinology in Honor of Dr. Naitō's 61st Birthday* 『内藤博士還暦祝賀支那學論叢』. Kyoto: Kōbundō 弘文堂, 1934.

Kyzlasov, L. R. (Л. Р. Кызласов). "Городище Дён-терек" ("The Hillfort of Dën-Terek"). In С. В. Киселев (S. V. Kiselev), et al., *Древнемонгольские Города* (Ancient Mongolian Cities). Москва-Ленинград: Академия наук СССР, 1965.

———. "Средневековые города Тувы" ("The Medieval Cities of Tuva"). *Советская археология* (*Soviet Archaeology*), 1959, no. 3.

Lattimore, Owen. *Inner Asian Frontiers of China*. Boston: Beacon Press, 1962.

Laufer, Berthold. *Sino-Iranica: Chinese Contributions to the History of Civilization in Ancient Iran*. Chicago: Field Museum of Natural History, 1919.

Lei Wen 雷聞. "The Five Peaks Immortals Temple and Tang Dynasty National Sacrificial Ceremonies" 《五嶽真君祠與唐代國家祭祀》 ("Wuyue zhenjunci yu Tangdai guojia jisi"). In Lei Wen 雷聞, *Excluding the Jiaomiao Sacrifices – Sui Tang National Sacrificial Ceremonies and Religion* 《郊廟之外——隋唐國家祭祀與宗教》 (*Jiaomiao zhiwai – Sui Tang guojia jisi yu zongjiao*). Beijing: SDX Joint

Publishing Company 生活・讀書・新知三聯書店, 2009.

Lenin, V. I. *Nations and Revolution*, translated into Chinese as《國家與革命》("Guojia yu geming"). In Lenin, V. I, *The Collected Works of Lenin*, Chinese title《列寧全集》(*Liening quanji*).

Lévi, Sylvain. "'Tokharien B', langue de Koutcha." *Journal Asiatique*, 1913. Translated into Chinese by Feng Chengjun 馮承鈞 as "A Study of Khotanese"《龜茲語考》("Qiuci yu kao"). In Feng Chengjun 馮承鈞, editor, *Collected Essays on Historical Geography*《史地叢考》(*Shidi congkao*). Shanghai: Commercial Press 商務印書館, 1931.

Li Ciming 李慈銘. *Diary from the Studio of Unadorned Silk*《越縵堂日紀》(*Yuemantang riji*). Photolithographic edition, 1922.

Li Fang 李方. "Translators in the Turfan Documents"《吐魯番文書中的譯語人》("Tulufan wenshu zhongde yiyuren"). *Cultural Relics*《文物》(*Wenwu*), 1994, no. 2.

Li Futong 李符桐. "Connections Between the Uyghurs and the Foundation of the Liao Dynasty State"《回鶻與遼朝建國之關係》(*Huihu yu Liaochao jianguo zhi guanxi*). Taipei: Wen Feng Press 文風出版社, 1968. Included in Li Futong 李符桐, *The Complete Collected Essays of Li Futong*《李符桐論著全集》(*Li Futong lunzhe quanji*), vol. 2. Taipei: Student Book Company 學生書局, 1992.

Li Huarui 李華瑞. "Debate on the Origin of Liquor Distillation in China"《中國燒酒起始的論爭》("Zhongguo shaojiu qishide lunzheng"). *Trends in Recent Research on the History of China*《中國史研究動態》(*Zhongguo shi yanjiu dongtai*), 1990, no. 8.

———. *Song Dynasty Liquor Production and Tax Monopoly*《宋代酒的生產和徵榷》(*Songdai jiude shengchan he zhengque*). Baoding 保定: Hebei University Press 河北大學出版社, 2001.

Li Jianchao 李健超. *A Revised and Expanded Study of Wards of the Two Tang Capital Cities*《增訂唐兩京城坊考》(*Zengding Tang liang jingcheng fang kao*). Xi'an: San Qin Press 三秦出版社, 1996.

Li Wentian 李文田. *Notes on the Secret History of the Mongols*《元秘史注》(*Yuan mishi zhu*).

Li Yiyou 李逸友. "The Stone Inscriptions from the Tomb and the Spirit Way Stele of Yelü Cong of the Liao Dynasty"《遼耶律琮墓石刻及神道碑銘》("Liao Yelü Cong mu shike ji shendao beiming"). In *Archaeology and History in Northeast China*《東北考古與歷史》(*Dongbei kaogu yu lishi*), vol. 1. Beijing: Cultural Relics Press 文物出版社, 1982.

Li Zhichun 李志純. *A Study of the History of the Yuan*《元史學》(*Yuanshi xue*).

Liang Zhenjing 梁振晶. "The Excavation Report of the Liao Tomb in Sijiazi, Fuxin"《阜新四家子遼墓發掘簡報》("Fuxin Sijiazi Liao mu fajue jianbao"). In *Collected Writings of Liaoning Archaeology*《遼寧考古文集》(*Liaoning kaogu wenji*). Shenyang 瀋陽: Liaoning Nationalities Press 遼寧民族出版社, 2003.

Lin Gan 林幹. *Chronological Table of Xiongnu History*《匈奴歷史年表》(*Xiongnu lishi *nianbiao*). Beijing: Zhonghua Book Company 中華書局, 1984.

———. *Collection of Selected Essays on the Xiongnu (1919-1979)* 《匈奴史論文選集（1919-1979）》 (*Xiongnu shi lunwen xuanji, 1919-1979*). Beijing: Zhonghua Book Company 中華書局, 1983.

———. *History of the Turks* 《突厥史》 (*Tujue shi*), appendix, "Turkish Language Stele Inscriptions Translated (Geng Shimin, translator)" 《突厥文碑铭譯文（耿世民譯）》 ("Tujue wenbeiming yiwen, Geng Shimin yi"). Hohhot: Inner Mongolia People's Press 内蒙古人民出版社, 1988.

———. *History of the Xiongnu* 《匈奴史》 (*Xiongnu shi*). Hohhot: Inner Mongolia People's Press 内蒙古人民出版社, 1979.

Lin Wushu 林悟殊. *Manichaeism and its Spread Eastward* 《摩尼教及其東漸》 (*Monijiao jiqi dongjian*). Beijing: Zhonghua Book Company 中華書局, 1987.

———. *Persian Fire Worship and Ancient China* 《波斯拜火教與古代中國》 (*Bosi baihuojiao yu gudai Zhongguo*). Taipei: Xin Wen Feng Publishing Company 新文豐出版公司, 1995.

———. "Questioning When Manichaeism Entered China" 《摩尼教入華年代質疑》 ("Monijiao ru hua niandai zhiyi"). In Lin Wushu 林悟殊, *Manichaeism and its Spread Eastward* 《摩尼教及其東漸》(*Monijiao jiqi dongjian*). Beijing: Zhonghua Book Company 中華書局, 1987.

———. "The Social Historical Origins of Uyghur Belief in Manichaeism" 《回鶻奉摩尼教的社會歷史根源》 ("Huihu feng Monijiaode shehui lishi genyuan"). In Lin Wushu 林悟殊, *Manichaeism and its Spread Eastward* 《摩尼教及其東漸》 (*Monijiao jiqi dongjian*) . Beijing: Zhonghua Book Company 中華書局, 1987.

Ling Chunsheng 淩純聲. *Chinese Ethnic Minorities in the Frontier Regions and the Culture of the Pacific Rim* 《中國邊疆民族與環太平洋文化》 (*Zhongguo bianjiang minzu yu huan taipingyang wenhua*). Taipei: Linking Publishing Co. Ltd. 聯經出版事業公司, 1979.

———. "An Examination of the Wuman and the Baiman Peoples in Yunnan in the Tang Dynasty" 《唐代雲南的烏蠻與白蠻考》 ("Tangdai Yunnande Wuman yu Baiman kao"). In The Institute of History and Philology, Academia Sinica 中央研究院歷史語言研究所 (Zhongyang yanjiuyuan lishi yuyan yanjiusuo), *Anthropology Bulletin* 《人類學集刊》 (*Renleixue jikan*), vol. 1, no. 1 (Dec. 1938).

———. "The Father-Son Name Linkage System in the Southeast Asia" 《東南亞的父子連名制》. Originally published in *Special Issue of the Continent Magazine* 《大陸雜誌》 (*Dalu zazhi*), series 1, 1952.

———. "The Hezhe People on the Lower Reaches of the Songhua River" 《松花江下游的赫哲族》. *Bulletin of the Institute of History and Philology, Academia Sinica* 《中央研究院歷史語言研究所單刊》 (*Zhongyang yanjiuyuan Lishi yuyan yanjiusuo dankan*), offprint edition, the first series, no. 14, part 1 (1934).

Liu Fengzhu 劉鳳翥, "A Concise Commentary on the Phylum Identity and Characteristics of the Khitan Language" 《略論契丹語的語系歸屬與特點》

("Lüelun Qidan yude yuxi guishu yu tedian"). *The Continent Magazine* 《大陸雜誌》 (*Dalu zazhi*), vol. 84, no. 5 (May 1992).

———. "An Examination of the 'Epitaph of Han Gaoshi' in Khitan Small Script" 《契丹小字〈韓高十墓誌〉考釋》 ("Qidan xiaozi 'Han Gaoshi muzhi' kaoshi"). In *A Bow to Fragrance Collection: Festschrift in Memory of the Ninetieth Anniversary of Mr. Zhang Zhenglang's Birth* 《揖芬集——張政烺先生九十華誕紀念文集》 (*Yi fen ji – Zhang Zhenglang xiansheng jiushi huadan jinian wenji*). Beijing: China Social Sciences Press 中國社會科學出版社, 2002.

———. "A Fourth Decipherment of the Khitan Small Script" 《契丹小字解讀四探》 ("Qidan xiaozi jiedu si tan"). In *Proceedings of the 35th Permanent International Altaistic Conference*. Taipei: Center for Chinese Studies Materials, United Daily News Cultural Foundation, 1992.

———. *A New Study of the Khitan Scripts* 《契丹文字新研究》 (*Qidan wenzi xin yanjiu*). Unpublished.

———. "Remarks on the Source of the 'Amuer' and the Khitan Language 'Black River'" 《"阿穆爾"源於契丹語的"黑水"說》 ("'Amuer' yuanyu Qidan yude 'heishui' shuo"). In *Collected Writings on Heilongjiang Cultural Relics* 《黑龍江文物叢刊》 (*Heilongjiang Wenwu congkan*), 1984, no. 1. Included in Sun Jinyi 孫進已, et al., editors, *Compilation of Works on Khitan History* 《契丹史論著彙編》 (*Qidan shi lunzhe huibian*). Liaoning Province Social Sciences Academy History Research Institute 遼寧省社會科學院歷史研究所, 1988.

———. "A Study of Liao Taizu's Imperial Honorific Title and Posthumous Honorary Title" 《遼太祖尊號謚號考辨》 ("Liao Taizu zunhao shihao kaobian"). *Social Sciences Journal* 《社會科學輯刊》 (*Shehui kexue jikan*), 1979, no. 1. Included in Sun Jinyi 孫進已, et al., editors. *Compilation of Works on Khitan History* 《契丹史論著彙編》 (*Qidan shi lunzhe huibian*). Liaoning Province Social Sciences Academy History Research Institute 遼寧省社會科學院歷史研究所, 1988.

Liu Fengzhu 劉鳳翥 and Jin Yongtian 金永田. "An Examination of the Three Epitaphs of Han Kuangsi and his Family of the Liao Dynasty" 《遼代韓匡嗣與其家人三墓誌銘考釋》 ("Liaodai Han Kuangsi yu qi jiaren san muzhiming kaoshi"). *Journal of Chinese Studies* 《中國文化研究所學報》 (*Zhongguo wenhua ynajiusuo xuebao*). Hong Kong: Chinese University Press, new series, 2000, no. 9.

Liu Fengzhu 劉鳳翥 and Qing Gele 清格勒, "An Examination of the 'Epitaph of Han Dechang' and the 'Epitaph of Yelü (Han) Gaoshi' of the Liao Dynasty" 《遼代〈韓德昌墓誌銘〉和〈耶律(韓)高十墓誌銘〉考釋》 ("Liaodai 'Han Dechang muzhiming' he 'Yelü (Han) Gaoshi muzhiming' kaoshi"), *Studies in Sinology* 《國學研究》 (*Guoxue yanjiu*), vol. 15 (2005).

———. "An Examination of the 'Epitaph of the Princess of Song Wei Principality' and the 'Epitaph of Yelü Hongyong' in Khitan Small Script" 《契丹小字〈宋魏國妃墓誌銘〉和〈耶律弘用墓誌銘〉考釋》 ("Qidan xiaozi 'Song Weiguo fei muzhiming' he 'Yelü Hongyong muzhiming' kaoshi"). *Literature and History* 《文史》 (*Wenshi*), 2003, no. 4.

Liu Fengzhu 劉鳳翥, Tang Cailan 唐彩蘭, and Gaowa 高娃. "An Examination of the Epitaph of Xiao Wuluben and Two Others in the Liao Dynasty" 《遼代蕭烏盧本等三人的墓誌銘考釋》 ("Liaodai Xiao Wuluben dengsan rende muzhiming kaoshi"). *Literature and History* 《文史》 (*Wenshi*), 2004, no. 2.

Liu Fengzhu 劉鳳翥 and Wang Yunlong 王雲龍. "An Examination of the 'Epitaph of Yelü Changyun' in Khitan Large Script" 《契丹大字〈耶律昌允墓誌銘〉之研究》 ("Qidan dazi 'Yelü Changyun muzhiming' zhi yanjiu"). *Yenching Journal of Chinese Studies* 《燕京學報》 (*Yanjing xuebao*), Peking University Press, new series, vol. 17 (Nov. 2004).

Liu Fengzhu 劉鳳翥, Zhu Zhimin 朱志民, Zhou Hongshan 周洪山, and Zhao Jie 趙傑, "A Fifth Decipherment of the Khitan Small Script" 《契丹小字解讀五探》 ("Qidan xiaozi jiedu wu tan"). *Chinese Studies* 《漢學研究》 (*Hanxue yanjiu*), vol. 13, no. 2 (Dec. 1995).

Liu Guangding 劉廣定. "The Problem of Chinese Liquor Distillation Prior to the Yuan Dynasty" 《元代以前中國蒸餾酒的問題》 ("Yuandai yiqian Zhongguo zhengliujiude wenti"). In Collected Essays on the History of Chinese Science and Technology Editorial Group 中國科技史論文集編輯小組 (Zhongguo keji shi lunwenji bianji xiaozu), editors, *Collected Essays on the History of Chinese Science and Technology* 《中國科技史論文集》 (*Zhongguo keji shi lunwenji*). Taipei: Linking Publishing Co. Ltd. 聯經出版事業公司, 1995.

Liu Mau-tsai. *Die Chinesischen Nachrichten zur Geschichte der Ost-Türken (T'u-küe)*. Wiesbaden: Otto Harrassowitz, 1958.

Liu Pujiang 劉浦江. "The Historical Memory of the Khitan People—Taking the 'Black Ox and White Horse' Legend as its Center" 《契丹族的歷史記憶——以"青牛白馬"說為中心》 ("Qidan zud lishi jiyi – yi 'qingniu baima' shuo weo zhongxin"). In *Collection of Commemorative Essays for Mr. Qi Xia* 《漆俠先生紀念文集》 (*Qi Xia Xiansheng jinian wenji*). Hebei University Press, 2002.

Liu Shiheng 劉世珩, compiler. *Collectanea from the Studio of Accumulated Learning* 《聚學軒叢書》 (*Juxuexuan congshu*).

Lu Junling 陸峻嶺 (originally edited by Feng Chengjun 馮承鈞). "Tarim." In *Geographic Names of the Western Regions* 《西域地名》 (*Xiyu diming*). Beijing: Zhonghua Book Company 中華書局, 1980.

Lu Yinghong 盧迎紅 and Zhou Feng 周峰. "An Examination of the 'Epitaph of Yelü Dilie' in Khitan Small Script"《契丹小字〈耶律迪烈墓誌銘〉考釋》("Qidan xiaozi 'Yelü Dilie muzhiming' kaoshi"). In *Minority Languages of China* 《民族語文》 (*Minzu yuwen*), 2000, no. 1.

Lu Zengxiang 陸增祥, preparer. "The Eight Jades Hall Bronze and Stone Inscriptions Supplement and Correction"《八瓊室金石補正》 (*Baqiongshi jinshi buzheng*). Included in *A New Collection of Stone Carved Materials*《石刻史料新編》 (*Shike shiliao xinbian*) part 1, book 7. Taipei: Xin Wen Feng Publishing Company 新文豐出版公司, 1977.

Luo Bingliang 羅炳良, editor. *An Unofficial History of China: Liao, Xia, Jin, and Yuan*

Dynasties volume《中華野史·遼夏金元卷》(*Zhonghua yeshi: Liao, Xia, Jin, Yuan juan*). Ji'nan 济南: Taishan Press 泰山出版社, 2000.

Luo Changpei 羅常培 and Cai Meibiao 蔡美彪. *Phags-Pa Script and the Chinese Language in the Yuan Dynasty*《八思巴字與元代漢語, 資料匯編》(*Basibazi yu Yuandai hanyu, ziliao huibian*). Beijing: Science Press 科學出版社, 1959.

Luo Feng 羅豐. *Sui and Tang Tombs in the Southern Suburbs of Guyuan*《固原南郊隋唐墓地》(*Guyuan nanjiao Sui Tang mudi*). Beijing: Cultural Relics Press 文物出版社, 1996.

Luo Jizu 羅繼祖. *Collation Notes to the History of the Liao*《遼史校勘記》(*Liaoshi jiaokan ji*). Shanghai People's Press 上海人民出版社, 1958.

Luo Xin 羅新. "From Qaghans' Appellations to Emperors' Honorific Appellations"《從可汗號到皇帝尊號》("Cong kehanhao dao huangdi zunhao"). *Journal of Tang Studies*《唐研究》(*Tang yanjiu*), vol. 10 (2004).

———. "A Study of Qaghan Appellations"《可汗號研究》("Kehanhao yanjiu"). *China Social Sciences*《中國社會科學》(*Zhongguo shehui kexue*), 2005, no. 2.

Luo Zhiji 羅之基, et al. "A Report on the Surnames of the Wa People in Ximeng County"《西盟佤族姓氏調察報告》("Ximeng Wazu xingshi diaocha baogao"). In *The Reports of Society and History of the Wa People*《佤族社會歷史調察》(*Wazu shehui lishi diaocha*), vol. 4. Kunming 昆明: Yunnan People's Press 雲南人民出版社, 1987.

Ma Yong 馬雍. "A Study of the Establishment of Diplomatic Relations between the Turks and the Gaochang Qu Family Dynasty"《突厥與高昌麴氏王朝始建交考》("Tujue yu Gaochang Qushi wanhchao shijian jiao kao"). In Yan Wenru 閻文儒 and Chen Yuong 陳玉龍, eds., *A Collection of Essays in Commemoration of Mr. Xiang Da*《向達先生紀念論文集》(*Xiang Da Xiansheng jinian lunwenji*). Urumqi: Xinjiang People's Press 新疆人民出版社, 1986.

———. "A Study of the Word *Kośva* as the Kharoshthi Word for *Qusou* in Xinjiang, Plus a Discussion of Qusou 渠搜, and Other Related Ancient Place Names"《新疆佉盧文書的 *Kośva* 即"氍毹"考—兼論"渠搜"及其他有关的古地名》("Xinjiang qulu wenshude *Kośva* ji 'Qusou' kao – jianlun 'Qusou' ji qita youguande gudiming"). In *Papers from the Founding Conference of the History of Central Asia Study Group*《中亞史學會成立大會論文》(*Zhongya shi xuehui chengli dahui lunwen*). Unpublished.

Maeda Naonori 前田直典. "The Nine Tatar Clans of the Tenth Century"「十世紀時代の九族韃靼」("Jyūseiki jidai no kyūzoku tatsutan"). In *Gencho shi no kenkyū* (*Research on Yuan Dynasty History*)『元朝史の研究』. Tokyo: Tokyo University Press 東京大学出版会, 1973. Originally published in *Tōyō Gakuhō* (*Journal of Oriental Studies*)『東洋学報』, vol. 32, no. 1.

Maejima Shinji 前嶋信次. "Some Central Asian Words of the Time of the An Lu-shan and Shih Ssu-ming Rebellion"「安史之亂時的幾個中亞語詞」. *Memoirs of the Research Department of the Toyo Bunko*『東洋文庫研究部歐文紀要』, no. 35 (1977).

Malov, Sergeĭ Efimovich. (Сергей Ефимович Малов). *Памятники Древнетюркской Письменности* (*Ancient Turkic Stele Inscriptions*). Москва-Ленинград, 1959.

———. *Памятники древнетюрской письменности Монголии и Киргизии* (*Monuments of Ancient Turkish Writing of Mongolia and Kyrgyzia*). Москва-Ленинград: Издательство Академии наук СССР, 1959.

———. *Памятники древнетюркской письменности* (*Monuments of Ancient Turkic Writing: Texts and Research*). Москва-Ленинград : Издательство Академии наук СССР, 1951.

Manchu Archives: The Ninth Year of Tiancong Reign Period 《天聰九年檔》 (*Tiancong jiunian dang*). Translated by Guan Jialu 關嘉祿 and Tong Yonggong 佟永功. Tianjin: Tianjin Ancient Books Press 天津古籍出版社, 1987.

A Manchu-Japanese and Mongolian-Japanese Translation of the Manchu Veritable Records 『満和蒙和対訳満洲実録』. Translated by Imanishi Shunjū 今西春秋. Tokyo: Tōsui Shobō 刀水書房, 1992.

Manchu Veritable Records, see *A Manchu-Japanese and Mongolian-Japanese Translation of the Manchu Veritable Records.*

Mandel'shtam, A. M. (A. M. Мандельштам). "К вопросу о значении термина 'чакир'" ("Towards the Question of the Meaning of the Term 'čakir'"). *Известия Отделения общественных наук Академии наук Таджикской ССР* (*Bulletin of the Department of Social Sciences of the Academy of Sciences of the Tajik Soviet Socialist Republic*), vol. 5 (1954).

Marquart, Josef. *Die Chronologie des Alttürkischen Inschriften.* Leipzig: Dieterich, 1898.

Marx, Karl. *Capital.* Translated into Chinese as《資本論》 (*Ziben lun*). People's Publishing House 人民出版社.

Marx, Karl and Engels, Friedrich. *The Complete Works of Marx and Engels,* Chinese translation,《馬克思恩格斯全集》 (*Makesi Engesi quanji*).

Maspero, Henri. *Les documents chinois de la troisième expedition de Sir Aurel Stein en Asie Centrale.* London: Trustees of the British Museum, 1953.

Matsuda Toshio 松田寿男. *Research on the History and Geography of Ancient Tianshan* 《古代天山歷史地理學研究》 (*Gudai Tianshan lishi dilixue yanjiu*), part 3, "A Discussion of the Topography of Tianshan as Reported in Sui and Tang Historical Documents"《論隋唐史籍所載天山形勢》 ("Lun Sui Tang shili suozai Tianshan xingshi"), paper 1, "A History of the Rise of the Turks"《突厥勃興史論》 ("Tujue boxing shilun"). Translated into Chinese by Chen Junmou 陳俊謀. China Nationalities Academy Press 中央民族學院出版社, 1987.

Matsui Hitoshi 松井等. "History of the Rise of the Khitan" 「契丹勃興史」. In *Manchuria-Korea Geographical History Research Report*『満鮮地理歴史研究報告』Man-Sen chiri-rekishi kenkyu hokoku, no. 1. 1915.

Matsumura Jūn 松村潤. "On the Foundation Legend of the Qing Dynasty" 「清朝の開国説話について」. In *A Festschrift in Honor of Dr. Yamamoto* 『山本博士還暦記念東洋史論叢』. Tokyo: Yamakawa Shuppansha 山川出版社, 1972.

Meng Sen 孟森. "Examination of the Jianzhou Commandery in the *Draft History of the Qing*" 《清史稿中建州衛考辨》("Qing shigao zhong Jianzhou wei kaobian").

Bulletin of the Institute of History and Philology, Academia Sinica 《中央研究院史語所集刊》 (*Zhongyang yanjiuyuan shiyusuo jikan*), vol. 3, pt. 3 (1932).

———. "Textual Research on Bokori Yongshon, the First Ancestor of the Qing," 《清始祖布庫里雍順之考訂》. *Bulletin of the Institute of History and Philology, Academia Sinica* 《中央研究院史語所集刊》 (*Zhongyang yanjiuyuan shiyusuo jikan*), vol. 3, pt. 3 (1932).

Meynard, Barbier de. *A Brief History of the Uyghurs*, part 1. Translated into Chinese as 《維吾爾族簡史(一)》 (*Weiwuerzu jianshi (yi)*), China Ethnic Minorities Series 中國少數民族叢書. Unpublished.

Mitamura Taisuke 三田村泰助. "The Foundation Myth and the Imperial Lineage of the Qing Dynasty" 「清朝の开国傳說とその世系」. In Mitamura Taisuke 三田村泰助, *Studies of Pre-Qing History* 『清朝前史の研究』 (*Shinchō zenshi no kenkyū*). Kyoto: The Society of Oriental Researches 東洋史研究会, 1965.

———. "Manchu Clans and Their Origins in the Late Ming and the Early Qing Period" 「明末清初の满洲氏族とその源流」. In Mitamura Taisuke 三田村泰助, *Studies on Pre-Qing History* 『清朝前史の研究』 (*Shinchō zenshi no kenkyū*). Kyoto: The Society of Oriental Researches 東洋史研究会, 1965.

———. "A Study of the Establishment Process of the Manchu State" 「滿洲國成立過程之一考察」. In Mitamura Taisuke 三田村泰助, *Studies of Pre-Qing History* 『清朝前史の研究』 (*Shinchō zenshi no kenkyū*). Kyoto: The Society of Oriental Researches 東洋史研究会, 1965.

Montell, Gösta. "Distilling in Mongolia." *Ethnos II*, 1937, no. 5.

Mori Masao 護雅夫, "Chinggis Khan" in *Encyclopaedic Dictionary of the World* 『世界大百科事典』. Tokyo: Heibonsha 平凡社, 1955-1957.

———. "Sogdian Clan Settlements in the East Turkish Qaghanate" 「東突厥汗國内的粟特人部落」. In *Historical Studies of the Ancient Turkic Peoples* 『古代トルコ民族史研究』, I. Tokyo: Yamakawa Shuppansha 山川出版社, 1975.

Moriyasu Takao 森安孝夫. "The Chinese Silk Road and the Tang Empire" 「シルクロードと唐帝国」. In *What is Human History?*, no. 5 『興亡の世界史5』. Tokyo: Kodansha 講談社, 2007.

———. "The Hu (Sogdians) during the Tang Dynasty and Buddhist World Geography" 「唐代における胡と仏教的世界地理」. *Journal of Oriental Research* 『東洋史研究』, vol. 66, no. 3 (2007).

———. "The Northern Peoples DRU-GU and HOR in Tibetan Sources" 「チベット語史料中に現すれる北方民族——DRU-GU と HOR」. *Journal of African and Asian Studies* 『アジア·アフリカ言語文化研究』, no. 14 (Dec. 1977).

Moriyasu Takao 森安孝夫, editor. *Provisional Report of Researches on Historical Sites and Inscriptions in Mongolia from 1996 to 1998* 『モンゴル国現存遺迹·碑文調査研究報告』. Toyonaka-shi 豊中市: Chūō Yūrashiagaku Kenkyūkai 中央ユーラシア学研究会, 1999.

Mostaert, Antoine. "Ordosica." *Bulletin of the Catholic University of Peking* 《輔仁英文學志》, no. 9 (1934).

Moule, A. C. and Pelliot, Paul, translators and annotators. *Marco Polo: The Description of the World*. London: G. Routledge, 1938.

Müller, F. W. K. "Zwei Pfahlinschriften aus den Turfanfunden." *Abhandlungen der Königlich Preussischen Akademie der Wissenschaften zu Berlin*, 1915, no. 3.

Murakami Masatsugu 村上正二. "The Nomadic Tribes before the Emergence of the Mongol Empire" 「モンゴル帝国成立以前における遊牧民諸部族について」 ("Mongoru teikoku seiritsu izen ni okeru yūbokumin shobuzoku ni tsuite"). *Tōyōshi kenkyū* (*Journal of Oriental Research*) 『東洋史研究』 , vol. 23, no. 4 (1964).

———. "Yuan Taizu" 「元太祖」. In *Historical Dictionary of Asia* 『亞細亞歷史事典』 (*Ajia rekishi jiten*). Tokyo: Heibonsha 平凡社, 1959-1962.

Murzaev, E. M. (Э. М. Мурзаев). *Схема физико-географического районирования Средней Азии* (A Schema of the Physical-Geographic Division into Regions of Central Asia). Translated into Chinese by Yu Hao 郁浩 as 穆爾札也夫, 《中亞細亞（自然地理概要）》 (*Zhongya xiya (ziran dili gaiyao)*). Beijing: Commercial Press 商務印書館, 1959.

Naka Michiyo 那珂通世. "Textual Criticism and Annotation of the Yuan Dynasty 'Record of the Personal Campaigns of the Holy Warrior'" 「校正增注元親征錄」 (*Kōsei zōchū Gen shinsei roku*). In *The Posthumous Works of Naka Michiyo* 『那珂通世遺書』. Tokyo: Dai Nihon Tosho Kabushiki Kaisha 大日本圖書株式會社, 1915.

Namcarai 拿木四來. "The Genitive Suffixes of the Daur Nouns" 《達斡爾語名詞的領屬附加成分》 ("Dawoer yu mingcide lingshu fujia chengfen"). In *Collected Studies of Minority Languages of China* 《民族語文研究文集》 (*Minzu yuwen yanjiu wenji*). Xining 西寧: Qinghai Nationalities Press 青海民族出版社, 1982.

Naribilige 納日碧力戈. "An Analysis of Restrictive Lingual Factors in Ethnic Names" 《民族姓名的語言制約因素析要》 ("Minzu xingmingde yuyan Zhiyue yinsu xiyao"). *Minority Languages of China* 《民族語文》 (*Minzu yuwen*), 1990, no. 4.

———. *On the Surnames and Forenames* 《姓名論》 (*Xingming lun*). Beijing: Social Sciences Academic Press 社会科学文献出版社, 1997.

Needham, Joseph and Ho, Ping-Yü. *Science and Civilization in China, Volume 5: Chemistry and Chemical Technology, Part 4, Spagyrical Discovery and Invention: Apparatus, Theories and Gifts*. Cambridge: Cambridge University Press, 1980.

Nie Hongyin 聶鴻音. "The Substantive Suffixes of *-n and *-in in the Khitan Language" 《契丹語的名詞附加成分*-n 和 *-in》 ("Qidan yude mingci Fujia chengfen *-n he *-in"). *Minority Languages of China* 《民族語文》 (*Minzu yuwen*), 2001, no. 2

Niida Noboru 仁井田陸. *Collected Vestiges of the Tang Statutes* 『唐令拾遺』 (*Tōrei shui*). Tokyo: Tōhō Bunka Gakuin Kenkyūjo 東方文化学院東京研究所, 1933.

d'Ohsson, Constantin Mouradja. *Histoire des Mongols, depuis Tchinguiz Khan jusqu'à Timour Bey ou Tamerlan*. La Haye: Les frères Van Cleef, 1834-1835.

Okada Hidehiro 岡田英弘. "The Mongol Elements in the Manchu Culture of the Early Qing Dynasty" 「清初の満洲文化におけるモンゴル的要素」. In *A Festschrift in Honor of Matsumura Jūn* 『松村潤先生古稀記念清代史論叢』. Tokyo: Kyuko Shoin 汲古書院, 1994.

Old Archives in Manchu《滿文老檔》(*Manwen laodang*)

Onogawa Hidemi 小野川秀美. "The Evolution of the Six Hu Prefectures of the Ordos Loop"「河曲六州胡の沿革」. *Journal of East Asian Humanities*『東亞人文學報』, vol. 1, no. 4 (1942).

Original Manchu Archives《舊滿洲檔》 (*Jiu Manzhou dang*).

Original Manchu Archives: The Ninth Year of Tiancong Reign Period 『舊滿洲檔· 天聰九年』. Translated by Kanda Nobuo 神田信夫, Matsumura Jūn 松村潤, and Wakata Hidehiro 岡田英弘. Tokyo: Toyo Bunko 東洋文庫, 1972.

Pallas, Peter Simon. *Sammlungen historischer Nachrichten über die mongolischen Völkerschaften in einem ausführlichen Auszuge*. Frankfort and Leipzig: J. G. Fleischer, 1779.

Pang, Tatiana A. and Stary, Giovanni. *New Light on Manchu Historiography and Literature: The Discovery of Three Documents in Old Manchu Script*. Wiesbaden: Harrassowitz, 1998.

Parker, E. H. *A Thousand Years of the Tartars*. London & New York & Bahrain: Kegan Paul Limited, 2002.

Partington, James R. *A Short History of Chemistry*. Translated into Chinese by Hu Zuoxuan 胡作玄 as 柏廷頓 (Baitingdun),《化學簡史》(*Huaxue jianshi*). Beijing: Commercial Press 商務印書館, 1979.

Pelliot, Paul. "About the Kuman (*kuman* 庫蠻)." In *Second Collection of Translations and Studies on Historical Places in the Western Regions and Southern Seas*《西域南海史地考證譯叢二編》 (*Xiyu nanhai shidi kaozheng yicong erbian*). Commercial Press, 商務印書館, 1962.

———. "Le 'Cha tcheou tou tou fou t'ou king' et la colonie sogdienne de la région du Lob nor." *Journal Asiatique*, série 2, vol. 7 (1916).

———. *La Haute Asie*. Paris: L'édition artistique J. Goudard, 1931.

———. *Histoire ancienne du Tibet*. Paris: Librarie d'Amérique et d'Orient, Adrien-Maisonneuve, 1961.

———. *Notes critiques d'histoire Kalmouke*. In *Oeuvres Posthumes de Paul Pelliot*, vol. 6. Paris: Librarie d'Amérique et d'Orient, Adrien-Maisonneuve, 1960.

———. *Notes on Marco Polo*. Paris: Librarie d'Amérique et d'Orient, Adrien-Maisonneuve, 1959.

———. *Notes sur l'histoire de la Horde d'or*. Paris: Librarie d'Amérique et d'Orient, Adrien-Maisonneuve, 1950.

Periwal, Sukumar. "Conclusion of Notions of Nationalism." In Sukumar Periwal, editor, *Notions of Nationalism*. Budapest: Central European University Press, 1995.

Pėrlėė, Khodoogiĩn (Х. Пэрлээ). "К истории древних городов и поселений в Монголии" ("On Ancient Mongolian Cities and the History of their Settlements"). *Советская археология* (*Soviet Archaeology*), 1957, no. 3.

'Phags-pa Blo-gros-rgyal-mtshan, *Šes bya rab gsa*; Chinese title: *Clarification of What Should Be Known*《彰所知論》(*Zhangsuozhi lun*).

Poppe, Nikolaus N. *Vergleichende Grammatik der altaischen Sprachen*. Translated into Chinese by Zhou Jianqi 周建奇 as 鮑培 (Baopei), *An Introduction to Altaic Linguistics*《阿爾泰語言學導論》 (*Aertai yuyanxue daolun*). Hohhot: Inner

Mongolia Education Press 内蒙古教育出版社, 2004.

Pritsak, Omeljan. "Qara, Studie zur türkischen Rechtssymbolik." In *Zeki Velidi Togan'a Armağan*. Istanbul, 1955.

Pulleyblank, Edwin. "An Lu-Shan." In *Encyclopaedia Iranica*. London: Routledge & Kegan Paul, 1985.

———. *The Background of the Rebellion of An Lu-Shan*. London: Oxford University Press, 1955.

———. "The Consonantal System of Old Chinese: Part II." *Asia Major*, new series, vol. 9 (1963).

———. *Lexicon of Reconstructed Pronunciation in Early Middle Chinese, Late Middle Chinese, and Early Mandarin*. Vancouver: University of British Columbia Press, 1991.

———. "A Sogdian Colony in Inner Mongolia." *T'oung Pao*, vol. 41 (1952).

al-Qāshānī, Abū al-Qāsim ibn 'Alī ibn Muhammad. *Tarikh-i Uljaytu* (*Chronicle of Uljaytu*), edited by Mahīn Hambly. Tehran: Bungāh-i Tarjimah va Nashr-i Kitāb, Persian Texts Series, no. 40, 1969.

Qenggeltei 清格爾泰. *Questions on the Decipherment of the Khitan Small Script* 《契丹小字釋讀問題》 (*Qidan xiaozi shidu wenti*). Tokyo: Research Institute for Languages and Cultures of Asia and Africa at the Tokyo University of Foreign Studies 東京外國語大學亞非語言文化研究所, 2002.

———. *Mongolian Grammar* 《蒙古語語法》 (*Mengguyu yufa*). Huhhot: Inner Mongolia People's Press 内蒙古人民出版社, 1991.

Qenggeltei 清格爾泰 and Liu Fengzhu 劉鳳翥. *Research on the Khitan Small Script*《契丹小字研究》 (*Qidan xiaozi yanjiu*). Beijing: China Social Sciences Press 中國社會科學出版社, 1985.

Qian Daxin 錢大昕. "Postscript to the Imperial Edict for the Yichuan Academy Stele" 《敕賜伊川書院碑跋》 ("Chici Yichuan shuyuan beiba"). In *Postscript to Bronze and Stone Inscriptions from the Hall of Subtle Research*《潛研堂金石跋尾》 (*Qianyantang jinshi bawei*).

———. *Study of the Intercalary Months in the Four Histories of the Song, Liao, Jin, and Yuan Dynasties*《宋遼金元四史朔閏考》("Song Liao Jin Yuan sishi shuorun kao"). In *Textual Analysis in the 22 Histories*《廿二史考異》(*Nian'er shi kaoyi*). Shanghai: Kaiming Book Company 開明書局.

———. *Textual Analysis in the 22 Histories* 《廿二史考異》 (*Nian'er shi kaoyi*). Shanghai: Kaiming Book Company 開明書局.

Radloff, Wilhelm. *Die alttürkischen Inschriften der Mongolei*. St. Petersburg: 1895-1899.

———. *Aus Sibiren: Lose Blätter aus dem Tagebuche eines reisenden linguisten*. Leipzig: T. O. Weigel, 1884.

———. *Versuch eines Wörterbuch der Turk. Dialekte*. St. Petersburg: 1893-1911.

Radov, V., IAdrintsev, N., Vasiliev, V., et. al. (В. Радов, Н. Ядринцев, В. Васильев и др.). *Сборникъ трудовъ Орхонской Экспедиціи* (*Reports by the Investigative Team of the Orkhon River*). Vols. 1-5, St. Petersburg: 1892; vol. 6, St. Petersburg: 1903.

Rao Zongyi 饒宗頤. "A Study of the Song Muhu"《穆護歌考》 ("Muhu ge kao"). In *Collected Works of Xuantang* (Rao Zongyi)*: Works on History* 《選堂集林·史林》

(*Xuantang jilin: shilin*). Hong Kong: Zhonghua Book Company 中華書局, 1982.

Rashīd al-Dīn, *Jāmi' al-Tawārīkh* (*Compendium of Chronicles*). I. N. Berezin (И. Н. Березин) editor and translator, published as *Сборник Летописей. Труды Восточнаго Отдѣленія Императорскаго Археологическаго Общества* (*Transactions of the Eastern Department of the Imperial Archaeological Society*), vols. 5, 7, 13, 15. St. Petersburg: 1851, 1861, 1868, 1888.

———. *Jāmi' al-Tawārīkh* (*Compendium of Chronicles*). Edgar Blochet, editor, published as *Djami et-tévarikh. Histoire générale du monde par fadl Allah Rashid ed-Din*. Leiden: 1911.

———. *Jāmi' al-Tawārīkh* (*Compendium of Chronicles*). Translated by J. A. Boyle as *The Successors of Genghis Khan*. New York: Columbia University Press, 1971.

———. *Jāmi' al-Tawārīkh* (*Compendium of Chronicles*). Translated into Chinese by Chen Dezhi 陳得芝 as 《史記鐵穆耳合浑本紀》 (*Shiji Tiemuerhehan benji*). In Nanjing University's *Collected Papers of Research on Yuan History and Northern Nationalities History* 《元史及北方民族史研究集刊》, no. 4, 1980.

———. *Jāmi' al-Tawārīkh* (*Compendium of Chronicles*). The Persian collated edition. Москва: 1965; and Москва: 1980.

———. *Jāmi' al-Tawārīkh* (*Compendium of Chronicles*). Translated into Russian as Рашид-ад-Дин, *Сборник Летописей*. Volume 1 translated by L. A. Khetagurov (Л.А. Хетагуров) and edited by A. A. Semenova (A. A. Семенова), Москва-Ленинград: Издательство Академии Наук СССР, 1952. Volume 3 translated by A. K. Arend (A. K. Аренд) and edited by A. A. Romaskevich (A. A. Ромаскевич), et al., Москва-Ленинград: Издательство Академии Наук СССР, 1946.

———. *Jāmi' al-Tawārīkh* (*Compendium of Chronicles*). Translated into Chinese by Yu Dajun 余大鈞, et al., as《史集》 (*Shiji*). Beijing: Commercial Press 商務印書館, 1997.

———. *Tarīkh-i Mubārak-i Ghāzāni: Dāstān-i Ghazan-Khān* (*The History of Ghazan*, part of the *Jāmi' al-Tawārīkh*). Persian edition, E. J. W. Gibb memorial series. London: Luzac and Co., 1940.

Record of the Personal Campaigns of the Holy Warrior 《聖武親征錄》 (*Shengwu qingzhenlu*). Translated into French and edited by Paul Pelliot and Louis Hambis as *Histoire des campagnes de Gengis Khan: Cheng-wou ts'in-tcheng lou*. Leiden: Brill, 1951.

Record of the Personal Campaigns of the Holy Warrior, Collated and Annotated Edition 《聖武親征錄校注》 (*Shengwu qinzhenglu xiaozhu*). In *Posthumous Papers of Wang Guowei* 《王忠愨公遺書》 (*Wang Guowei yishu*). Shanghai Ancient Books Book Company 上海古籍書店, 1983.

Reichelt, H. *Die Soghdischen Handschriftenreste des Britischen Museums*, vol. II. Heidelberg: Carl Winter, 1931.

Rhoads, Edward J. M. *Manchus and Han: Ethnic Relations and Political Power in Late Qing and Early Republican China, 1861-1928*. Seattle: University of Washington Press, 2000.

Rigger, Shelley. "Voices of Manchu Identity." In Steven Harrell, editor, *Cultural Encounters on China's Ethnic Frontiers*. Seattle and London: University of Washington Press, 1995.

Rong Xinjiang 榮新江. "A Few Issues Concerning the Tomb of the Northern Zhou Tongzhou Sabao An Qie" 《有關北周同州薩保安伽墓的幾個問題》 ("Youguan Beizhou Tongzhou sabao An Jia mude jige wenti"). In *Northern China and the Eurasian Continent in the Fourth through Sixth Centuries*《4～6 世紀的北中國與歐亞大陸》 (*4-6 shijide bei Zhongguo yu Ouya dalu*), Zhang Qingjie 張慶捷, et al., editors. Beijing: Science Press 科學出版社, 2006.

———. "Foreigner Settlement Religious Beliefs and Social Function of Zoroastrian Temples in the Northern Dynasties, Sui, and Tang"《北朝隋唐胡人聚落的宗教信仰與祆祠的社會功能》 ("Beichao Sui Tang huren juluode zongjiao xinyang yu Xiancide shehui gongneng"). In Rong Xinjiang 榮新江, editor, *Tang Dynasty Religious Beliefs and Society*《唐代宗教信仰與社會》(*Tangdai zongjiao xinyang yu shehui*). Shanghai Lexicographical Publishing House 上海辭書出版社, 2003.

———. "Further Remarks on Sogdians in the Western Regions." In *Exegisti Monumenta. Festschrift in Honour of Nicholas Sims-Williams* (Iranica 17), edited by Werner Sundermann, Almut Hintze, and François de Blois. Wiesbaden: Harrassowitz Verlag, 2009.

———. "The Golden Light Sutra Unearthed at Turfan, the Manuscript Text and Issues of When Zoroastrianism First Spread to Gaochang"《吐魯番出土〈金光明經〉寫本題記與祆教初傳高昌問題》 ("Tulufan chutu 'Jinguang mingjing' xiebentiji yu Xianjiao chuchuan Gaochang wenti"). In Zhu Yuqi 朱玉麒, general editor, *Literature and History of the Western Regions* 《西域文史》 (*Xiyu wenshi*), vol. 2. Beijing: Science Press 科學出版社, 2007.

———. "The Migrations and Settlements of the Sogdians in the Northern Dynasties, Sui, and Tang" 《北朝隋唐粟特人之遷徙及其聚落》 ("Beichao Sui Tang Sute ren zhi qianxi jiqi juluo"). In Peking University Chinese Traditional Culture Research Center 北京大學中國傳統文化研究中心, editors, *Studies in Sinology*,《國學研究》 (*Guoxue yanjiu*), vol. 6 (1999). Translated and edited by Bruce Doar in *China Archaeology and Art Digest*, vol. 4, Zoroastrianism in China (Dec. 2000).

———. "Regarding Several Problems of the Influence of Tang-Song Period Central Plains Culture on Khotan"《關於唐宋時期中原文化對于闐影響的幾個問題》 ("Guanyu Tang Song shiqi zhongyuan wenhua dui Yutian yingxiangde jige wenti"). *Studies in Sinology*《國學研究》 (*Guoxue yanjiu*), vol. 1 (1993).

———. "Sogdian Foreigners Movements after the An Shi Rebellion" 《安史之亂後粟特胡人的動向》. In Ji Zongan 紀宗安 and Tang Kaijian 湯開建, editors-in-chief, *Ji'nan University Historical Studies*《暨南史學》, vol. 2. Guangzhou 廣州: Ji'nan University Press 暨南大學出版社, 2003.

———. "Sogdians around the Ancient Tarim Basin." In *Ērān ud Anērān, Studies Presented to Boris Il'ič Maršak on the Occasion of his 70th Birthday*, edited by M. Compareti, P. Raffetta and G. Scarcia. Venezia: Libreria Editrice Cafoscarina, 2006.

———. "Sogdians Seen in New Documents from Turfan" 《新出吐魯番文書所見的粟特人》 ("Xin chutu Tulufan wenshu suojiande Sute ren"). *Turfan Studies*《吐魯番學研究》 (*Tulufanxue yanjiu*), 2007, no. 1.

———. "A Study of the Longjias"《龍家考》 ("Longjia kao"). *Journal of Central Asia*

《中亞學刊》 (*Zhongya xuekan*), Peking University Press, vol. 4 (1995).

———. "A Study of Sogdian Migrations and Settlements in the Western Regions"《西域粟特移民聚落考》 ("Xiyu Sute yimin juluo kao"). In Ma Dazheng 馬大正 and Yang Qian 楊鐮, editors, *Investigations and Research into the Western Regions* 《西域考察與研究》 (*Xiyu kaocha yu yanjiu*). Urumqi: Xinjiang People's Press 新疆人民出版社, 1994.

———. "A Study of When Zoroastrianism was First Introduced to China"《祆教初傳中國年代考》 ("Xianjiao chuchuan Zhongguo niandai kao"). In *Medieval China and Foreign Civilizations*《中古中國與外來文明》 (*Zhonggu Zhongguo yu wailai wenming*). Beijing: Sanlian Press 三聯書店, 2001.

———. "Supplement to a Study of Sogdian Migrations and Settlements in the Western Regions" 《西域粟特移民聚落補》 ("Xiyu Sute yimin juluo bu"). *Studies of the Western Regions*《西域研究》 (*Xiyu yanjiu*), 2005, no. 2.

Rongsuhe 榮蘇赫. *A History of Literature of the Mongolian Nationality* 《蒙古族文學史》(*Menggu zu wenxue shi*), vol. 1. Hohhot: Inner Mongolia People's Press 内蒙古人民出版社, 2000.

Roth, Henry Ling. *The Natives of Sarawak and British North Borneo*. London: Truslove & Hanson, 1896.

van Ruysbroeck, Willem. *Reise zu den Mongolen 1253-1255*, translated and annotated by Friedrich Risch. Leipzig: A. Deichertsche verlags-buchhandlung D. Werner Scholl, 1934.

Rygdylon, E. R. (Э. Р. Рыгдылон). "О монгольском термине онгу-богол" ("About the Mongolian Term *ongqun bo'ol*"). In *Филология и история монгольских народов. Памяти академика Б.Я. Владимирцова* (*Philology and History of the Mongolian Peoples*). Москва: Издательство восточной литературы, 1958.

Sagang Sečen. *Erdeni-yin Tobči* (*Precious Summary*) 《蒙古源流箋證》 (*Menggu yuanliu jianzheng*). Chinese annotated edition reprint. Beijing: Zhonghua Book Company 中華書局, 1962.

———. *Erdeni-yin Tobči* (*Precious Summary*), annotated by Isaac Jacob Schmidt as *Geschichte der Ost-Mongolen und ihren Fürstenhauses, verfasst von Ssanang Ssetsen, Chungtaidschi der Ordus*. St. Petersburg: 1829.

———. *Erdeni-yin Tobči* (*Precious Summary*)『蒙古源流』. Translated and annotated by Wakata Hidehiro 岡田英弘 . Tokyo: Tōsui Shobō 刀水書房, 2004.

———. *Erdeni-yin Tobči* (*Precious Summary*). Harvard-Yenching Institute, Scripta Mongolica II. Harvard University Press, 1956.

Sakurai Masuo 桜井益雄. "A Study of the Kerait" 「怯烈考」("Kyō retsu kō"). *Tōhō Gakuhō* (*Journal of Oriental Studies*) 『東方学報』, vol. 7, Tokyo (1935).

Sambuu, D.達・桑布. *Monggol arad-un daguu-yin cubural. Sili-yin Ġool Ayimaġ-un* (*A Collection of Mongolian Folk Songs from Xilin Gol League*) 《蒙古民歌叢書. 錫林郭勒盟集》. [Kōkeqota]: Ōbōr Monggol-un Arad-un Keblel-ún Qoriy-a; Ōbōr Monggol-un Sinquva Bicig-ún Delgegúr tarqaġaba, 1988.

Schafer, Edward H. *The Golden Peaches of Samarkand. A Study of T'ang Exotics*. Berkeley, CA: University of California Press, 1963.

———. "Non-Translation and Functional Translation – Two Sinological Maladies." *The Far Eastern Quarterly*, vol. 13, no. 3 (May, 1954).

Schlegel, Gustav. *Chinesische Inschrift auf dem uigurischen Denkmal in Kara Balgassun*. Helsingfors: Société Finno-ougrienne, 1896.

The Secret History of the Mongols. Translated into English by Francis Woodman Cleaves. Cambridge, Mass.: Harvard University Press, 1982.

———. Translated into Japanese by Naka Michiyo 那珂通世 as *Chinggis Khan's Veritable Records* (*Jingis Kan jitsuroku*) 『成吉思汗実録』. Tokyo: Chikumi Shobō 筑摩書房, 1943.

———. Translated into French by Paul Pelliot as *Histoire Secrete des Mongols*. Paris: Adrien-Maisonneuve, 1949.

———. Translated into English by Igor de Rachewiltz as *The Secret History of the Mongols: A Mongolian Epic Chronicle of the Thirteenth Century*, 2 vols., Brill's Inner Asian Library, 7. Leiden: Brill, 2006.

Selected Historical Materials before the Qing Entered the Shanhai Pass 《清入關前史料選輯》 (*Qing ruguan qian shiliao xuanji*), vol. 1. Beijing: China People's University Press 中国人民大学出版社, 1984.

Shaanxi Provincial Archaeological Research Institute 陕西省考古研究所 (Shaanxisheng kaogu yanjiusuo). *The Northern Zhou Tomb in Xi'an of An Qie*《西安北周安伽墓》 (*Xi'an Beizhou An Qie mu*). Beijing: Cultural Relics Press 文物出版社, 2003.

Shao Jinhan 邵晉涵. *The South of the River Catalog* 《南江書錄》 ("Nanjiang shulu"), 42a, the entry "Yuan History" 《元史》 ("Yuanshi"). In Liu Shiheng 劉世珩, compiler, *Collectanea from the Studio of Accumulated Learning*《聚學軒叢書》 (*Juxuexuan congshu*).

Shao Yuanping 邵遠平. *History of the Yuan, Classified Compilation* 《元史類編》 (*Yuanshi leibian*). Block printing by Sao Ye Shan Fang 掃業山房, 1795.

Sharaf ad-Dīn ʻAlī Yazdī. *Zafar-nāma* (*Book of Victory*). English translation, edited by Muhammad Ilahdad. Calcutta: Bibliotheca Indica, 1887-1888.

Shen Hui 沈彙. "An Examination of the Authors of the Stone Inscriptions in Khitan Small Script" 《契丹小字石刻撰人考》("Qidan xiaozi shike zhuanren kao"). *Archaeology and Cultural Relics* 《考古與文物》 (*Kaogu yu wenwu*), 1982, no. 6.

Shi Jinmin 石金民 and Yu Zemin 于澤民. "An Examination of the 'Epitaph of Yelü Nu' in Khitan Small Script" 《契丹小字〈耶律奴墓誌銘〉考釋》 ("Qidan xiaozi 'Yelü Nu muzhiming' kaoshi"). *Minority Languages of China* 《民族語文》 (*Minzu yuwen*), 2001, no. 2.

Shi Shijie 施世傑. *A Study of the Toponyms of Mountains and Rivers in the Secret History of the Mongols*《元秘史山川地名考》.

Shiratori Kurakichi 白鳥庫吉. *Historical Research on the Western Regions* 『西域史研究』. Tokyo: Iwanami Shoten 岩波書店, 1941.

———. "New Research on the History of the Western Regions" 「西域史上の新研究」. In Shiratori Kurakichi 白鳥庫吉, *Historical Research on the Western Regions*『西域史研究』, vol. 1. Tokyo: Iwanami Shoten 岩波書店, 1941.

———. "A Study of the Donghu Ethnic Group"「東胡民族考」. In Shiratori Kurakichi 白鳥庫吉, *Research on Borderland Peoples*『塞外民族研究』, vol. 1. Tokyo: Iwanami Shoten 岩波書店, 1986.

Sims-Williams, N. "The Sogdian Ancient Letter II." In *Philologica et Linguistica: Historia, Pluralitas, Universitas. Festschrift für Helmut Humbach zum 80. Geburtstag am 4. Dezember 2001*, M. G. Schmidt and W. Bisang, editors. Trier: Wissenschaftlicher Verlag, 2001.

Singer, Charles J. *A History of Technology*, vol. 2 of *The Mediterranean Civilizations and the Middle Ages, c. 700 B. C. to c. A. D . 1500*. Oxford: Clarendon Press, 1956.

Sinor, Denis. *Inner Asia: History, Civilization, Languages; A Syllabus*, Uralic and Altaic Series, vol. 96. Bloomington, Indiana: Indiana University, 1969.

Šir-a Tu'uji (*Yellow Annals*); *Erten-ü Mongghol-un Qad-un Ündüsün-ü Yeke Šir-a Tu'uji* (*The Great Yellow Annals of the Origin of the Ancient Mongolian Khans*). In N. P. Shastina (Н. П. Шастина), editor and translator, *Шара Туджи. Монгольская Летопись XVII века* (*Shara Tudzhi. A Mongolian Chronicle of the 17th Century*). Москва-Ленинград: Наука, 1957.

Smith, Anthony D. *The Ethnic Origins of Nations*. Oxford: Basil Blackwell, 1986.

———. *The Nation in History: Historiographical Debates about Ethnicity and Nationalism*. Hanover: University Press of New England, 2000.

Société Asiatique. "Séance du 9 Décembre 1938." *Journal Asiatique*, no. 231 (1939).

Soviet Science Academy and Mongolian People's Republic Science Committee, editors. *История Монгольской Народной Республики* (*History of the Mongolian People's Republic*). Москва: 1954. Translated into Chinese as *A Comprehensive History of the Mongolian People's Republic*《蒙古人民共和國通史》(*Menggu renmin gongheguo tongshi*).

Spanien, A. and Imaeda, Y., editors. *Choix de documents tibétains, II*. Paris: Bibliotheque Nationale, 1979.

Su He 蘇赫. "An Examination of 'The Stele Inscription of Canonizing Kindness'"《崇善碑考述》("Chongshan bei kaoshu"). In *Collected Essays on Liao and Jin History*《遼金史論集》(*Liao Jin shi lunji*), vol. 3. Beijing: Bibliography and Literature Press 書目文獻出版社, 1987.

Sun Ji 孫機. "On the Origins of Grain Liquor and Distilled Liquor in China"《我國穀物酒和蒸餾酒的起源》("Woguo jiu he zhengliujiude qiyuan"). In Yang Hong 楊泓 and Sun Ji 孫機, *The Exquisite in the Ordinary*《尋常的精緻》(*Xunchangde jingzhi*). Shenyang 瀋陽: Liaoning Education Press 遼寧教育出版社, 1996.

Sun Jimin 孫繼民. "Identification and Explanation of the Document Fragment Unearthed at Turfan *Official Document of the Tang Department of State Affairs*"《吐魯番所出〈唐尚書省牒〉殘卷考釋》("Tulufan suochu 'Tang shangshusheng die' canjuan kaoshi"). *Dunhuang Research*《敦煌研究》(*Dunhuang yanjiu*), 1990, no. 1.

Sun Jing 孫靜. "A Discussion of the Implementation and Abolishment of 'Back to the Banner' Stipulation in the Qing Dynasty"《清代歸旗制度行廢述論》("Qingdai guiqi zhidu xingfei shulun"). *Journal of Minzu University of China*《中央民族大學學報》(*Zhongyang minzu daxue xuebao*), 2005, no. 5.

———. "A Discussion of the Status Change of the Han Army Eight Banners during the

Qianlong Era" 《乾隆朝八旗漢軍身份變化述論》, *Heilongjiang National Series* 《黑龍江民族叢刊》, 2005, no. 2.

———. "The Marginalization of the Han Army Eight Banners" 《八旗漢軍的邊緣化》 ("Baqi Hanjunde bianyuanhua"). In *Rethinking Manchu Nationality Formation: Research on Manchu Identity in the Mid-Qing* 《滿族形成的再思考：清中期滿洲認同意識研究》 (*Qingzu xingchengde zai sikao: Qing zhongqi Manzhou rentong Yishi yanjiu*), Doctoral dissertation. History Department of Fudan University, 2005.

A Supplemented Translation to the Manchu Encyclopaedic Reference Book 《〈補譯〉滿洲類書》 ('*Buyi*' *Manzhou leishu*). Manuscript, Library of the Institute for Ethnological and Anthropological Studies, Chinese Academy of Social Sciences (中国社会科学院民族学与人类学研究所图书馆).

Takikawa Masajirō 瀧川政次郎 and Shimada Masao 島田正郎. *Studies on Liao Law* 『遼律之研究』(*Ryōritsu no kenkyū*). Tokyo: Ōsaka Yagō Shoten 大坂屋号書店, 1944.

Tamura Jitsuzō 田村実造, editor. *Collection of Vocabulary Used in the History of the Yuan* 『元史語彙集成』 (*Genshi goi shūsei*). Kyoto: Kyoto University Literature Department 京都大學文學部, 1961-1963.

———. "Studies of the Khitan during the Tang Dynasty" 「唐代に於ける契丹族の研究」 ("Tōdai niokeru kittenzoku no kenkyū"). In *Collected Essays on Manchu and Mongolian History* 『満蒙史論叢』 (*Man-Mō shi ronsō*), vol. 1. Shinkyō 新京: Nichi-Man Bunka Kyōkai 日満文化協會, 1938.

Tan Qixiang 譚其驤, editor. *The Historical Atlas of China* 《中國歷史地圖集》 (*Zhongguo lishi dituji*), vol. 7. Beijing: China Cartographic Publishing House 中國地圖出版社, 1988.

Tang Cailan 唐彩蘭, et al. "An Examination of the 'Epitaph of Han Dilie'" 《契丹小字〈韓敵烈墓誌銘〉考釋》 ("Qidan xiaozi 'Han Dilie muzhiming' kaoshi"). In *Minority Languages of China* 《民族語文》 (*Minzu yuwen*), 2002, no. 6.

Tang Zhangru 唐長孺. *Annotations to the Monograph on the Army in the Tang Histories* 《唐書兵志箋正》(*Tangshu bingzhi jianzheng*). Beijing: Science Press 科學出版社, 1957.

———. "Notes on Turfan Documents Concerning the Impressment of Soldiers" 《唐西州差兵文書跋》("Tang Xizhou chabing wenshu ba"). In *Preliminary Exploration of the Dunhuang and Turfan Documents* 《敦煌吐魯番文書初探》(*Dunhuang Tulufan wenshu chutan*), Tang Zhangru 唐長孺, editor. Wuhan: Wuhan University Press 武漢大學出版社, 1983.

———. "A Study of Mixed Foreigners in the Wei and Jin" 《魏晉雜胡考》 ("Wei Jin zahu kao"). In *Commemorative Essays on Wei, Jin, and Northern and Southern Dynasties History*《魏晉南北朝史論叢》(*Wei Jin Nanbeichao shi luncong*). Beijing: Sanlian Press 三聯書店, 1978.

Tang Zhangru 唐長孺, editor. *Documents Unearthed at Turfan* 《吐魯番出土文書》 (*Tulufan chutu wenshu*), vol. 1. Beijing: Cultural Relics Press 文物出版社, 1992.

Tao Baolian 陶保廉. *Travel Diary of the Xinmao Year* (1891) 《辛卯侍行記》 (*Xinmao shixingji*).

Tao Ketao 陶克濤. *Outline of the Development of Inner Mongolia* 《内蒙古發展概述》 (*Neimenggu fazhan gaishu*). Hohhot: Inner Mongolia People's Press 内蒙古人民出版社, 1957.

Tekin, Talât. *A Grammar of Orkhon Turkic*. Bloomington, IN: Indiana University, 1968.

Tezuka Takayoshi 手塚隆義. "Further Studies on Xiongnu Shanyus – Hulugu Shanyu's Rise to Power" 「匈奴単于相続考－とくに狐鹿姑単于の登位について」. In *History Garden* 『史苑』, vol. 20, no. 2 (1959).

Thomsen, Vilhelm. "Alttürkische Inschriften aus der Mongolei." *Zeitschrift der Deutschen Morgenlandischen Gesellschaft*, New Series 3, cumulative vol. 78 (1924).

———. *Inscriptions de l'Orkhon déchiffrées*. Helsingfors: Société de la litterature finnoise, 1896.

———. *Turcica: études concernant l'interprétation des inscriptions turques de la Mongolie et de la Sibérie*. Helsingfors: Société Finno-ougrienne, 1916.

Tian Jizhou 田繼周, et al. "A Report of the Society and Economy of the Wa People in Yuesong, Ximeng County" 《西盟縣岳宋佤族社會經濟調查》 ("Ximengxian Yuesong Wazu jingji diaocha"). In *The Reports of Society and History of the Wa People* 《佤族社會歷史調查》 (*Wazu shehui lishi diaocha*), vol. II. Kunming 昆明: Yunnan People's Press 雲南人民出版社, 1983.

Tian Yuqing 田餘慶. "The Formation and Development of the Inner Palace Institution of the 'Mandatory Suicide of the Birth Mother of the Crown Prince' after the Northern Wei" 《北魏後宫子貴母死之制的形成和演變》 ("Beiwei hou gongzigui musi zhi zhide xingcheng he yanbian"). In *Studies in Sinology* 《國學研究》 (*Guoxue yanjiu*), vol. 5 (1998).

Togan, Isenbike. *Flexibility and Limitation in Steppe Formations*. Leiden: Brill, 1998.

Torii Ryūzō 鳥居龍藏. "A Study of the Khitan Black Mountain and Black Range" 《契丹黑山黑嶺考》 ("Qidan heishan heiling kao"). In *Yenching Journal of Chinese Studies* 《燕京學報》 (*Yanjing xuebao*), vol. 28, Dec. 1930. Included in Sun Jinyi 孫進已, et al., editors, *Compilation of Works on Khitan History* 《契丹史論著彙編》 (*Qidan shi lunzhe huibian*). Liaoning Province Social Sciences Academy History Research Institute 遼寧省社會科學院歷史研究所, 1988.

Tu Ji 屠寄. *Historical Records of the Mongols* 《蒙兀爾史記》 (*Mengwuer shiji*).

Treasures of Dunhuang 《敦煌寶藏》 (*Dunhuang baozang*). Taipei: Xin Wen Feng Publishing Company 新文豐出版公司, 1985.

Uchida Ginpu 内田吟風. "On Chanyu Titles and the Position of the Xiongnu Chanyu Court" 「単于の称号と「匈奴単于庭」の位置に就いて」. In *Studies on North Asian History: The Xiongnu* 『北アジア史研究· 匈奴篇』. Kyoto: Dōhōsha Shuppan 同朋舎出版, 1975.

———. *Studies on North Asian History: The Xiongnu* 『北アジア史研究· 匈奴篇』. Kyoto: Dōhōsha Shuppan 同朋舎出版, 1975.

al-'Umārī (1301-1349), *Masālik al-absār fī mamālik al-amsār* (*The Routes toward Insights of the Capital Kingdoms*).

Utsugawa Nenozō 移川子之蔵. *A Study of the Genealogy of the Gaosha People in*

Taiwan 『台湾高砂族系統所属の研究』. Research Institute of Folklore and Anthropology at Taipei Imperial University, 1935. Reprinted in photocopies, Tokyo: Gaifusha 凱風社, 1988.

de la Vaissiere, É. *Sogdian Traders. A History*. Translated by J. Ward, Handbook of Oriental Studies, Section 8: Central Asia, vol. 10. Leiden and Boston: Brill, 2005.

Vladimirtsov, Boris Iakovlevich (Борис Яковлевич Владимирцов). *Чингис-хан* (*Chinggis Khan*). Translated into Chinese by Yu Yuan'an 余元盦 as 《成吉思汗傳》 (*Chengjisihan zhuan*). Shanghai People's Press 上海人民出版社, 1955.

———. "Mongolica I." In *Записки. Восточного отделения Российского Археологического общества* (*Proceedings of the Eastern Department of the Russian Archaeological Society*). 1925.

———. *Отчет о командировке к баитам Кобдоского округа* (*A Report on the Bait People of the Khovd Region*). St. Petersburg, 1912.

———. *Общественный строй монголов. Монгольский кочевой феодализм* (*The Social System of the Mongols. Mongolian Nomadic Feudalism*). Translated into Chinese by Liu Rongjun 劉榮焌 as *A History of the Mongol Social System* 《蒙古社會制度史》(*Menggu shehui zhidu shi*). Beijing: China Social Sciences Press 中國社會科學出版社, 1980.

Wada Sei 和田清. "A Study of the Miekeli" 「乜克力考」 ("Bame koku riki kō"). In *Collected Papers on Oriental History: A Festschrift in Honor of the 60th Birthday of Dr. Kuwabara* 『桑原博士還暦記念東洋史論叢』(*Kuwabara hakase kanreki kinen tōyōshi ronsō*). Kyoto: Kōbundō 弘文堂, 1931.

Waley, Arthur. "Some References to Iranian Temples in the Tun-huang Region." In *Bulletin of the Institute of History and Philology, Academia Sinica*, vol. 28, part 1 (1956).

Wang Guowei 王國維. *A Brief History of the Black Tatars Annotated* 《黑韃事略箋證》 (*Heida shilüe jianzheng*). In *Posthumous Papers of Wang Guowei* 《王國維遺書》 (*Wang Guowei yishu*). Shanghai Ancient Books Book Company 上海古籍書店, 1983.

———. *Record of the Personal Campaigns of the Holy Warrior, Collated and Annotated* 《聖武親征錄校注》 (*Shengwu qinzhenglu xiaozhu*). In *Posthumous Papers of Wang Guowei* 《王忠愨公遺書》 (*Wang Guowei yishu*). Shanghai Ancient Books Book Company 上海古籍書店, 1983.

———. *Collected Works from the Hall of Observation* 《觀堂集林》 (*Guantang jilin*), new photocopy edition. Beijing: Zhonghua Book Company 中華書局, 1959.

———. *Complete Report on the Mongolian Tatars Annotated and Corrected* 《蒙韃備錄箋證》 (*Mengda beilu jianzheng*).

———. *Corrected Records of Ancient Travel Accounts* 《古行記校錄》 (*Gu xingji xiaolu*).

———. *Four Ancient Travel Diaries* 《古行記四種》 (Gu xingji sizhong). In *Posthumous Papers of Wang Guowei* 《王國維遺書》(*Wang Guowei yishu*), vol. 13. Shanghai Ancient Books Book Company 上海古籍書店.

———. "A Study of the Black Cart Shiwei" 《黑車子室韋考》 ("Heichezi Shiwei kao").

In *Collected Works from the Hall of Observation* 《觀堂集林》 (*Guantang jilin*).

———. "A Study of the Tatars"《韃靼考》 ("Dada kao"). In *Collected Works from the Hall of Observation* 《觀堂集林》 (*Guantang jilin*).

Wang Hongli 王弘力. "A Study of the Khitan Epitaphs in Small Script" 《契丹小字墓誌研究》 ("Qidan xiaozi muzhi yanjiu"). *Minority Languages of China*《民族語文》 (*Minzu yuwen*), 1986, no. 4.

Wang Li 王力. *Dictionary of Cognate Words* 《同源字典》 (*Tongyuan zidian*). Beijing: Commercial Press 商務印書館, 1982.

———. "Introductory Remarks" 《例言》 ("Liyan"). *China Social Sciences* 《中國社會科學》 (*Zhongguo shehui kexue*), 2004, no. 4.

Wang Mingsheng 王鳴盛. *Disputations on the 17 Histories* 《十七史商榷》 (*Shiqi shi shangque*).

Wang Minxin 王民信. "The Formation of the Community of Khitan Royal Relatives on the Distaff Side" 《契丹外戚集團的形成》 ("Qidan waiqi jituande xingcheng"). In *Commemorative Essays on Khitan History* 《契丹史論叢》 (*Qidan shi luncong*). Taipei: Xue Hai Press 學海出版社, 1973.

———. "The Khitan Firewood Investiture Ceremony and the Rebirth Ceremony" 《契丹的柴册儀與再生儀》 ("Qidande chaiceyi yu zaishengyi"). In *Commemorative Essays on Khitan History*《契丹史論叢》(*Qidan shi luncong*). Taipei: Xuehai Press 學海出版社, 1973.

———. "The Relationship between the Ancient Eight Tribes of the Khitan and the Dahe, Yaonian, and Diela Clans"《契丹古八部與大賀遥輦迭剌的關係》("Qidan gubabu yu Dahe Yaonian Dielade guanxi"). In *Commemorative Essays on Khitan History* 《契丹史論叢》 (*Qidan shi luncong*). Taipei: Xuehai Press 學海出版社, 1973.

———. "Who is the Mada Recorded in the *History of the Liao*?" 《〈遼史〉裏的麻答是誰？》 ("'Liaoshi' lide Mada shi shei?"). In *Studies of the Liao, Jin and Western Xia Histories* 《遼金西夏史研究》 (*Liao Jin Xixia shi yanjiu*). Tianjin: Tianjin Ancient Books Press 天津古籍出版社, 1997.

Wang Riwei 王日蔚. "Research on Connections Between the Khitan and the Uyghurs" 《契丹與回鶻關係考》 ("Qidan yu Huihu guanxi kao"). *Journal of Historical Geography* 《禹貢》 (*Yugong*), vol. 4, no. 8 (Dec. 1935).

Wang Su 王素. "'Documents Unearthed in Turfan,' Evaluation of the First Three Books" 《〈吐魯番出土文書〉前三冊評介》 ("'Tulufan chutu wenshu'qiansance pingjia"). *The Study of Chinese History*《中國史研究》 (*Zhongguo shi yanjiu*), 1983, no. 2.

Wang Xianqian 王先謙. *Collected Commentaries on the History of the Later Han*《後漢書集解》(*Houhanshu jijie*). Beijing: Zhonghua Book Company 中華書局, reprint of the 1915 Xushoutang 虛受堂 edition, 1984.

Wang Xiaofu 王小甫. "The Cult of Fire and the Rise and Decline of the Turks: A Case Study of the Ancient Turkic God of War"《拜火教與突厥興衰——以古代突厥鬥戰神研究爲中心》 ("Baihuojiao yu Tujue xingshuai – yi gudai Tujuemen zhanshen yanjiu wei zhongxin"). *Historical Research*《歷史研究》(*Lishi yanjiu*), 2007, no. 1.

———. *The History of Political Relations between the Tang, Tibet, and the Arabs in*

Central Asia (634-792 A.D.) 《唐、吐蕃、大食政治關係史》. Beijing: Peking University Press 北京大學出版社, 1995.

Wang Zhenghua 王正華 and He Shaoying 和少英. *A Cultural History of the Lahu People* 《拉祜族文化史》(*Lahuzu wenhua shi*). Kunming 昆明: Yunnan Nationalities Press 雲南民族出版社, 1999.

Wang Zhilai 王治來. "The Development of Islam in Xinjiang" 《論伊斯蘭教在新疆的發展》 ("Lun Yisilanjiao zai Xinjiangde fazhan"). In *Collected Essays on Xinjiang History* 《新疆歷史論文集》 (*Xinjiang Lishi lunwenji*). Urumqi: Xinjiang People's Press 新疆人民出版社, 1977.

Wang Zhonghan 王鍾翰. "The Socioeconomic Pattern of the Manchus in Nurhaci's Time" 《滿族在努爾哈齊時代的社會經濟形態》 ("Manzu zai Nuerhaqi shidaide shehui jingji xingtai"). In Wang Zhonghan 王鍾翰, *Self-Selected Anthology of Scholarly Writings by Wang Zhonghan* 《王鍾翰學術論著自選集》 (*Wang Zhonghan xueshu lunzhe zixuanji*). Beijing: Minzu University of China Press 中央民族大學出版社, 1999.

Weber, Dieter. "Zur sogdischen Personennamengebung." *Indogermanische Forschungen*, vol. 77 (1972).

Wei Deming 魏德明. *A Cultural History of the Wa People* 《佤族文化史》 (*Wazu wenhua shi*). Kunming 昆明: Yunnan Nationalities Press 雲南民族出版社, 2001.

Wei Yuan 魏源. *History of the Yuan, New Compilation* 《元史新編》 (*Yuanshi xin bian*). Shaoyang 邵陽: Block printing by Wei family 魏氏 Shen Wei Tang 慎微堂, 1905.

———. *Illustrated Treatise on the Maritime Kingdoms* 《海國圖志》 (*Haiguo tuzhi*).

Wen Tingshi 文廷式. *The Digressions of Chunchangzi* [Wen Tingshi] 《純常子枝語》 (*Chunchangzi zhiyu*).

William of Rubruck. "The Journey of William of Rubruck." In Christopher Dawson, et al., *The Mongol Mission: Narratives and Letters of the Franciscan Missionaries in Mongolia and China in the Thirteenth and Fourteenth Centuries*. New York: Sheed and Ward, 1955.

———. *The Journey of William of Rubruck to the Eastern Parts of the World 1253-55, As Narrated by Himself, with Two Accounts of the Earlier Journey of John of Pian de Carpine*, translated and annotated by William Woodville Rockhill. London: Hakluyt Society, 1900.

———. *Annotated Translation of Carpini's and William of Rubruck's Travels (Путешествие в восточные страны Плано Карпини и Гильома Рубрука)*, translated and annotated by N. P. Shastina (Н. П. Шастина). Москва: Государственное издательство географической литературы, 1957.

World History (*Всемирная История*). Translated into Chinese as *A Comprehensive History of the World* 《世界通史》 (*Shijie tongshi*).

Wu Jian 吳堅, editor. *Collected Documents from Northwest China* 《中國西北文獻叢書》 (*Zhongguo xibei wenxian congshu*). Lanzhou: Lanzhou Ancient Books Book Company 蘭州古籍書店, 1990.

Wu Yugui 吳玉貴. "A New Study of the Western Turks" 《西突厥新考》 ("Xitujue xin kao"). *Northwest Journal of Ethnology* 《西北民族研究》 (*Xibei minzu yanjiu*),

1988, no. 1.

———. "Two Gaochang Provisioning Texts" 《兩件高昌供食文書》 ("Liangjian Gaochang gongshi wenshu"). *The Study of Chinese History* 《中國史研究》 (*Zhongguo shi yanjiu*), 1990, no. 1.

Wu Yugui 吴玉貴, editor. *Chinese-language Historical Materials on the Second Turkish Qaghanate Chronologically Compiled and Researched*《突厥第二汗國漢文史料編年輯考》 (*Tujue dier hanguo hanwen shiliao biannian jikao*) . Shanghai: Zhonghua Book Company 中華書局, 2009.

Xi'an City Cultural Relics Preservation and Archaeology Institute 西安市文物保護考古所 (Xi'anshi Wenwu baohu kaogusuo). "A Brief Archaeological Report on the Excavation in Xi'an of the Tomb of the Northern Zhou Dynasty Liangzhou Sabao Shi Jun"《西安北周涼州薩保史君墓發掘簡報》 ("Xi'an Beizhou Liangzhou sabao Shi Jun mu fajue jianbao"), *Cultural Relics*《文物》 (*Wenwu*), 2005, no. 3.

Xia Nai 夏鼐. "Epitaph of the Wuwei Tang Dynasty Tuyuhun Murong"《武威唐代吐谷渾慕容氏墓誌》. Originally published in *Collected Essays of the Institute of History and Philology, Academia Sinica*《中央研究院歷史語言研究所集刊》 (*Zhongyang yanjiuyuan lishi yuyansuo jikan*), no. 20, 1948. Republished in *Collected Essays on Archaeology*《考古學論文集》 (*Kaoguxue lunwenji*). Beijing: Science Press 科學出版社, 1961.

Xiang Da 向達. *Tang Dynasty Chang'an and the Civilization of the Western Regions*《唐代長安與西域文明》 (*Tangdai Chang'an yu Xiyu wenming*). Beijing: Sanlian Press 三聯書店, 1957.

Xiang Nan 向南, editor. *The Stone Inscriptions of the Liao Dynasty* 《遼代石刻文編》 (*Liaodai shike wenbian*). Shijiazhuang 石家莊: Hebei Education Press, 1995.

Xie Haiping 謝海平. *A Study and Review of the Life of Foreigners Staying in Tang Dynasty China*《唐代留華外國人生活考述》 (*Tangdai liuhua waiguoren shenghuo kaoshu*). Taipei: The Taiwan Commercial Bookstore 臺灣商務印書館, 1978.

Yan Gengwang 嚴耕望. "A Study of the Aides and Staff of Commanders of Military Provinces in the Tang Period" 《唐代方鎮使府僚佐考》 ("Tangdai fangzhen shifu liaozuo"). In *Collected Manuscripts on Tang History Research* 《唐史研究叢稿》 (*Tang shi yanjiu conggao*). Hong Kong: New Asia Institute of Advanced Chinese Studies 新亞研究所, 1969.

Yan Wanzhang 閻萬章. "An Examination of the Khitan Epitaph Excavated from a Tomb of the Jin Dynasty in Xinglong, Hebei Province" 《河北興隆金墓出土契丹文墓誌銘考釋》 ("Hebei Xinglong Jin mu chutu Qidanwen muzhiming kaoshi"). In *Archaeology and History in Northeast China* 《東北考古與歷史》 (*Dongbei kaogu yu lishi*), vol. 1. Beijing: Cultural Relics Press 文物出版社, 1982.

———. "An Examination of the 'Epitaph of Yelü Zongjiao' in Khitan Small Script"《契丹小字〈耶律宗教墓誌銘〉考釋》 ("Qidan xiaozi 'Yelü Zongjiao muzhiming' kaoshi"). *Journal of Liaohai Cultural Relics* 《遼海文物學刊》 (*Liaohai wenwu xuekan*), 1993, no. 2.

Yanai Wataru 箭内亙. *Research on Mongolian History* 『蒙古史研究』 (*Mōkoshi *kenkyū*). Tokyo: Tōkō Shoin 刀江書院, 1930.

———. "A Study of the Names of the Three Guard-Stations in the Uriyangkhai Region" (Uryōgō san'ei Meishō kō) 「兀良哈三衛名称考」. *Tōyō Gakuhō* (*Journal of Oriental Studies*) 『東洋学報』, 1914.

Yang Debing 楊德炳. "A Preliminary Exploration of the Treatment of Soldier-Patients and the Provisions for their Return Journey Home"《關於唐代對患病士兵的處理與程糧等問題的初步探索》 ("Guanyu Tangdai dui huanbing shibingde chuli yu chengliang deng wentide chubu tansuo"). In *Preliminary Exploration of the Dunhuang and Turfan Documents*《敦煌吐魯番文書初探》(*Dunhuang Tulufan wenshu chutan*), Tang Zhangru 唐長孺, editor. Wuhan: Wuhan University Press 武漢大學出版社, 1983.

Yang Fuxue 楊富學. "A Discussion of the Origin Myth of the Khitan People Borrowed from the Uyghurs" 《契丹族源傳説借自回鶻論》 ("Qidan zuyuan chuanshuo jie zi huihu lun"). In *Essays on the Historical Culture of Chinese Northern Nationalities* 《中國北方民族歷史文化論稿》 (*Zhongguo beifang minzu lishi wenhua lungao*). Lanzhou 蘭州: Gansu People's Press 甘肅人民出版社, 2001.

Yang Liansheng. "An Inscribed Han Mirror Discovered in Siberia." *T'oung Pao*, vol. 42 (1954).

Yang Ximei 楊希枚. "The Evolution from the *Congming* System to the Parent-Child Name Linkage System" 《從名制與親子聯名制的演變關係》 ("Congming zhi yu qinzi lianming zhide yanbian guanxi"). In *Bulletin of the Institute of History and Philology, Academia Sinica*, the fourth supplementary issue: *Festschrift in Memory of the 65th Anniversary of Mr. Dong Zuobin's Birth* 《慶祝董作賓先生六十五歲論文集》 (*Qinghe Dong Zuobin Xiansheng liushiwu sui lunwenji*), part II, June 1961.

———. "The Personal Denomination System among the Saisiyat People in Taiwan" 《臺灣賽夏族的個人命名制》 ("Taiwan Saixiazude geren mingming zhi"). *Bulletin of Academia Sinica* 《中央研究院院刊》 (*Zhongyang yanjiuyuan yuankan*), vol. 3 (1956).

———. "A Study of the Name Linkage System and the Surname and Clan Name System"《聯名與姓氏制度的研究》 ("Congming yu xingshi zhidude yanjiu"). In *Bulletin of the Institute of History and Philology, Academia Sinica* 《中央研究院歷史語言研究所集刊》 (*Zhongyang yanjiuyuan lishi yuyan yanjiusuo jikan*), *Festschrift in Memory of the 65th Anniversary of Mr. Hu Shi's (胡適) Birth*, vol. 28, part 2 (May 1957).

Yang Zhijiu 楊志玖. "A Study of Abaoji's Ascent to the Throne" 《阿保機即位考辨》 ("Abaoji jiwei kaobian"). *Bulletin of the Institute of History and Philology, Academia Sinica* 《中央研究院歷史語言研究所集刊》 (*Zhongyang yanjiuyuan lishi yuyan yanjiusuo jikan*), vol. 17 (April 1948).

Yao Runeng 姚汝能. *Factual Traces of An Lushan* 《安祿山事跡》 (*An Lushan shiji*). Translated into French by Robert des Rotours as *Histoire de Ngan lou-chan* (Ngan lou-chan che tsi). Paris: Presses Universitaires de France, 1962.

Yoshida Yutaka 吉田豊. "Notes on the Sogdian Language" 「ソグド語雑録」, part 2. *Orient*『オリエント』, vol. 31, no. 2 (1989).

———. "Review of N. Sims-Williams, Sogdian and other Iranian Inscriptions of the Upper Indus II." *Bulletin of the School of Oriental and African Studies*, vol. 57, no. 2 (1994).

You Li 尤李. "A Philological Study of 'The Ode of the Treasure Pagoda of the Temple to Mourn the Loyal,' Also Discussing the Multi-Valent Nature of An Lushan's and Shi Siming's Religious Beliefs" 《〈憫忠寺寶塔頌〉考釋——兼論安祿山、史思明宗教信仰的多樣性》 ("'Minzhongsi baota song' kaoshi – jianlun An Lushan, Shi Siming zongjiao xinyangde duoyangxing"). *Literature and History* 《文史》 (*Wenshi*), 2009, no. 4.

Yu, Ying-shih 余英時. *Trade and Expansion in Han China*. Berkeley and Los Angeles: University of California Press, 1967.

Yu Yuan'an 余元盦. *Biography of Chinggis Khan*《成吉思汗傳》 (*Chengjisihan zhuan*). Shanghai People's Press 上海人民出版社, 1955.

———. *Outline of Inner Mongolian History*《内蒙古歷史概要》 (*Neimenggu lishi gaiyao*). Shanghai People's Press 上海人民出版社, 1958.

Yuan Haibo 袁海波. "Addenda of the Genealogy of the Xiao He Family, the Maternal Relatives of the Liao Emperor" 《遼外戚蕭和家族世系表新補》 ("Liao waiqi Xiao He jiazu shixibiao xin bu"). *Journal of Liaoning Technical University* (Social Sciences Edition) 《遼寧工程技術大學學報》(社科版) (*Liaoning gongcheng jishu daxue xuebao, sheke ban*), 2003, no. 3.

Yuan Hanqing 袁翰青. "The Origin and Development of Wine Fermentation in China" 《釀酒在我國的起源和發展》 ("Niangjiu zai woguod qiyuan he fazhan"). In Yuan Hanqing 袁翰青, *Collected Essays on the History of Chemistry in China* 《中國化學史論文集》 (*Zhongguo huaxueshi lunwenji*). Beijing: Sanlian Press 三聯書店, 1956.

Yuasa Mitsutomo 湯浅光朝. *A Chronological Table of Science and Cultural History Explained*『解説科学文化史年表 [1966 年増補版] 』(*Kaisetsu kagaku bunkashi nenpyō* [1966 nen zōhoban]). Tokyo: Chūō Kōronsha 中央公論社, 1966.

Zeng Lian 曾廉. *Yuan Documents* 《元書》 (*Yuanshu*). Zeng family 曾氏 Cengyi Tang 層漪堂 block printing edition, 1911.

Zhan Chengxu 詹承緒. "The Father-Son Name Linkage System"《父子連名制》("Fuzi lianming zhi"). In *Encyclopedia of China*, *Volume of Nationalities* 《中國大百科全書•民族卷》 (*Zhongguo dabaike quanshu, minzu juan*). Beijing: The Encyclopedia of China Publishing House 中國大百科全書出版社, 1986.

Zhang Zhenpei 張振佩. *A Critical Biography of Chinggis Khan*《成吉思汗評傳》 (*Chengjisihan pingzhuan*). Beijing: Zhonghua Book Company 中華書局, 1946.

Zhang Guangda 張廣達. "On the Chinese Manichaean Fragmentary Texts of the Tang Dynasty"《唐代漢譯摩尼教殘卷》 ("Tangdai Hanyi Monijiao canjuan"). *The Journal of Oriental Studies*《東方學報》, Kyoto, vol. 77, 2004. Reprinted in Zhang Guangda 張廣達, *The Transmission of Text, Image, and Culture* (*The Collected Works of Zhang Guangda*, volume 3) 《文本、圖像與文化流傳》 (張廣達文集 3) (*Wenben, tuxiang yu wenhua liuchuan; Zhang Guangda wenji 3*). Guilin 桂林: Guangxi Normal University Press 廣西師範大學出版社, 2008.

Zhang Guoqing 張國慶. "A Brief Discussion of the Naming Customs of the Khitans in the Liao Dynasty" 《略談遼代契丹人的命名習俗》 ("Lüetan Liaodai Qidan rende mingming xisu"). *Museum Research* 《博物館研究》 (*Bowuguan yanjiu*), 1991, no. 2.

Zhang Lianfang 張聯芳, editor. *Names of the Chinese People* 《中國人的姓名》 (*Zhongguo rende xingming*). Beijing: China Social Sciences Press 中國社會科學出版社, 1992.

Zhang Lie 張烈, annotator. *Two Annals of the Han* 《兩漢紀》 (*Liang Hanji*). Beijing: Zhonghua Book Company 中華書局, 2002.

Zhang Mu 張穆. *Notes on the Mongolian Nomads* 《蒙古游牧記》 (*Menggu youmu ji*). Shouyang 壽陽: Qi family 祁氏 block printing edition, 1866.

Zhang Qingjie 張慶捷. "The Sogdian 'Foreigner's Leaping Dance' in the Northern Dynasties, Sui, and Tang" 《北朝隋唐粟特的"胡騰舞"》 ("Beichao Sui Tang Sutede 'Hutengwu'"). In Rong Xinjiang, editor, *Sogdians in China – New Explorations in History, Archaeology, and Language* 《粟特人在中國——歷史、考古、語言的新探索》 (*Sute ren zai Zhongguo – lishi, kaogu, yuyande xin tansuo*). Beijing: Zhonghua Book Company 中華書局, 2005.

Zhang Xiangwen 張相文. *Collected Manuscripts from the South Garden* 《南園叢稿》.

Zhang Xinglang 張星烺. *Collection of Records on Sino-Western Relations* 《中西交通史料滙編》 (*Zhong Xi jiaotong shiliao huibian*), vol. 3. Beijing: Zhonghua Book Company 中華書局, 1978.

Zhang Xuecheng 章學誠. *Posthumous Papers of Zhang Xuecheng, Miscellaneous Notes* 《章氏遺書外編》 (*Zhang shi yishu waibian*). Wuxing 吳興: Liu family 劉氏 block printing edition.

Zhao Yi 趙翼. *Critical Notes on the 22 Histories* 《廿二史劄記》 (*Nian'er shi zhaji*).

Zhao Yintang 趙蔭棠. *Research on Rhymes of the Central Plain* 《中原音韻研究》 (*Zhongyuan yinyun yanjiu*). Shanghai: Commercial Press 商務印書館, 1936.

Zhao Zhenhua 趙振華 and Zhu Liang 朱亮. "A Preliminary Study of the An Pu Tomb Inscription" 《安菩墓誌初探》 ("An Pu muzhi chutan"). *Cultural Relics of the Central Plains* 《中原文物》 (*Zhongyuan wenwu*), 1982, no. 2.

Zhao Zhiwei 趙志偉 and Baoruijun 包瑞軍. "An Examination of the 'Epitaph of Yelü Zhixian'" 《契丹小字〈耶律智先墓誌銘〉考釋》 ("Qidan xiaozi 'Yelü Zhixian muzhiming' kaoshi"). *Minority Languages of China* 《民族語文》 (*Minzu yuwen*), 2001, no. 3.

Zhong Han 鍾焓. "The Inner Asian Cultural Background of An Lushan and Other Mixed-Race Foreigners" 《安祿山等雜胡的內亞文化背景》 ("An Lushan deng zahude neiya wenhua beijing"). *The Study of Chinese History* 《中國史研究》 (*Zhongguo shi yanjiu*), 2005, no. 1.

Zhou, Jiahua 周嘉華 et al. *A History of Chinese Chemistry – Ancient Texts* 《中國化學史 - 古代卷》 (*Zhongguo huaxue shi – gudai juan*). Nanning 南寧: Guangxi Education Press 廣西教育出版社, 2003.

Zhou Qingshu 周清澍. "The Ethnic Origin of the Önggüd" 《汪古部的族源》

("Wanggu bude zuyuan"). In *Collected Papers of the Memorial Conference for the Foundation of the China Mongolian History Institute* 《中國蒙古史學會成立大會紀念集刊》 (*Zhongguo Menggu shi xuehui chengli dahui jinian jikan*). Hohhot: China Association of Mongolian History 中國蒙古史學會, 1979.

———. "The Önggüd Tribe's Controlling Clan"《汪古部統治家族》 ("Wanggu bu tongzhi jiazu"). *Literature and History* 《文史》 (*Wenshi*), vol. 9, 1980.

Zhou Shaoliang 周紹良 editor-in-chief. *Collected Tang Dynasty Epitaphs*《唐代墓誌彙編》(*Tangdai muzhi huibian*). Shanghai Classics Publishing House 上海古籍出版社, 1992.

Zhuang Jifa 莊吉發. "Borrowing Han and Adopting Jin: A Study of Changes and Adaptations of Manchu Culture in the Qing Based on Genealogical Compilation" 《參漢酌金：从家譜的撰修論清代滿族文化的變遷与適應》 ("Can Han zhuo Jin: cong jiapude zhuanxiu lun Qingdai Manzu wenhuade bianqian yu shiying"). In *Proceedings of a Seminar on Socio-Cultural Changes and Adaptations of Ethnic Minorities in Chinese Mainland* 《中國大陸少數民族社會文化的變遷與適應學術研討會論文集》 (*Zhongguo dalu shaoshu minzu shehui wenhuade bianqian yu shiying xueshu yantaohui wenji*). Taipei: National Chengchi University Nationalities Department 國立政治大學民族學系, 2004.

Zhukovskaya, N. L. (Наталия Львовна Жуковская). "Пища кочевников Центральной Азии: К вопросу об экологических основах формирования модели питания" ("The Food of the Nomads of Central Asia: On the Problem of the Ecological Basis of the Nutrient Model"). *Советская этнография* (*Soviet Ethnography*), 1979, no. 5.

Zlatkin, I. Ia. (И. Я. Златкин). "Генезис крепостничества в средневековой Монголии" ("The Origination of the Medieval Mongolian Serf System"). *Народы Азии и Африки* (*Peoples of Asia and Africa*), 1977, no. 1.

Index

CONTRIBUTORS

Cai Meibiao 蔡美彪 is Professor in the Institute of Modern Chinese History, Chinese Academy of Social Sciences and an eminent member of the Academic Committee of the Chinese Academy of Social Sciences. He is the co-editor of the multi-volume *Comprehensive History of China* 《中國通史》 (1953-2008; with Fan Wenlan 范文瀾). He has been working on the history of the Liao and Jin Dynasties, and on Mongolic philology. *Phags-pa Script and the Chinese Language in the Yuan Dynasty* 《八思巴字與元代漢語》 (1959, rev. 2004; with Luo Changpei 羅常培) is one of his books.

Chen Dezhi 陳得芝 is Professor in the Department of History, Nanjing University. His research interests are primarily the history and language of the Mongols, on which he has published *Collected Papers of Mongol-Yuan Studies* 《蒙元史研究叢稿》 (2005). He made contributions to *The Historical Atlas of China* 《中國歷史地圖集》(vols. 6 and 7, 1982; edited by Tan Qixiang 譚其驤). Nearly half of the *History of the Yuan Dynasty* 《元朝史》(1986, revised 2008; edited by Han Rulin 韓儒林) was written by him.

Han Rulin 韓儒林（1903–1983）was Professor in the Department of History, Nanjing University. From 1933 to 1936 he studied in Belgium, Berlin, and Paris, where he became a student of Paul Pelliot and learned several European languages. He published a series of translations and annotations of the Orkhon Turkic inscriptions in the early years of his academic career. His achievements in the history and language of the Mongols were compiled in *Collection from the Yurt* 《穹廬集》(1982). He founded the influential journal *Studies on Mongol-Yuan and China's Border Areas* 《元史及民族與邊疆研究集刊》 (1977–). He was the editor of the *History of the Yuan Dynasty* 《元朝史》 (1986, rev. 2008).

Yekemingghadai Irinchin 亦鄰真（1931–1999）was Professor in the Department of History, University of Inner Mongolia. He was a native Mongolian. His research concerns were mainly the history and language of the Mongols. *The Secret History: Reconstruction of the Mongolian Language in Uyghur Script* 《元朝秘史（畏吾體蒙古文復原）》 (1987) is one of his most important academic achievements. *Irinchin's Collected*

Works on Mongolic Studies 《亦鄰真蒙古學文集》 (2001) was edited by his students in memory of him.

Jiang Boqin 姜伯勤 is Professor in the Department of History, Sun Yat-sen University. His academic concerns include the history of the Sui and Tang Dynasties, Dunhuang studies, the history of the Silk Road, and art history. He has published twelve monographs in those fields, among which are *Dunhuang and Turfan Documents and the Silk Road* 《敦煌吐魯番文書與絲綢之路》 (1994) and *The Monastery Serf System in Dunhuang in the Tang and Five Dynasties*《唐五代敦煌寺戶制度》 (1987).

Kang Peng 康鵬 received his doctoral degree from Peking University with his dissertation "Research on the Five-Capital System of the Liao Dynasty"《遼代五金體制研究》 (2007). He works in the Institute of History Studies, Chinese Academy of Social Sciences.

Liu Pujiang 劉浦江 is Professor in the Center for Research on Ancient Chinese History, Peking University. He has published primarily on the history of Jin, Liao, and Song Dynasties. His recent books are *Between Pine and Desert: Studies on History of the Liao, Jin, Khitan, and Jurchen* 《松漠之間——遼金契丹女真史研究》 (2008) and *Bibliography of 20th Century Studies on the History of Liao and Jin Dynasties*《二十世紀遼金史論著目錄》 (2003).

Liu Yingsheng 劉迎勝 is Professor in the Department of History, Nanjing University. He has been the president of the Society of Yuan History Research since 2003. His research interests are the history the Mongol-Yuan period and ethnic groups on China's borders, on which he has published *Studies on Chaghatay History* 《察合臺汗國史研究》 (2006) and *A Study of Two Medieval Sino-Persian Glossaries* 《〈回回館雜字〉與〈回回館譯語〉研究》 (2008). He has been the editor of the journal *Studies on the Mongol-Yuan and China's Border Areas*《元史及民族與邊疆研究集刊》since 2005.

Luo Feng 羅豐 is Professor and Director of the Institute of Archaeology and Antiquities, Ningxia. He is an archaeologist interested in the multi-cultural exchanges of the medieval period. *Between Han and Non-Han: The Silk Road and Historical Archaeology of China's Northwestern Regions* 《胡漢之間——"絲綢之路與西北歷史考古"》 (2004) and *Sui and Tang Tombs in the Southern Suburbs of Guyuan* 《固原南郊隋唐墓地》 (1996) are his representative books.

Luo Xin 羅新 is Professor in the Center for Research on Ancient Chinese History, Peking University. His academic interests are the history of the Chinese medieval period and Inner Asian peoples. He has recently published *Studies on the Titulary of Medieval Inner Asian Peoples* 《中古北族名號研究》 (2009), which deals with the political titulary and other proper names of the Altaic peoples. He was the editor of the Chinese translation *Selected Works of Denis Sinor on Inner Asia* 《丹尼斯・塞諾内亞研究文選》 (2006).

Rong Xinjiang 榮新江 is Professor in the Center for Research on Ancient Chinese History, Peking University. His research interests include the contacts between China and the West from the Han to Tang Dynasties, Dunhuang and Turfan documents, and the history of China's Western Regions. His representative publications are *Studies on the History of Khotan* 《于闐史叢考》 (1993, revised 2008; with Zhang Guangda 張廣達), *Eighteen Lectures on Dunhuang Studies* 《敦煌學十八講》 (2001), and *Studies on the History of Guiyijun: Research on the History of Dunhuang in the Tang and Song Dynasties* 《歸義軍史研究——唐宋時代敦煌歷史考索》 (1996). He has been the editor of the *Journal of Tang Studies* 《唐研究》 since 1995.

Wang Xiaofu 王小甫 is Professor in the Center for Research on Ancient Chinese History, Peking University. He did his post-doctoral research in the School of Oriental and Africa Studies, University of Cambridge (1994). His main research interests are the history of the Sui and Tang Dynasties and the relationships between China and its neighbours. *The History of Political Relations between the Tang, Tibet, and the Arabs in Central Asia (634-792 A.D.)* 《唐、吐蕃、大食政治關係史》 (1992) is his representative monograph. *History of the Sui, Tang, and Five Dynasties* 《隋唐五代史》 (2008) is one of his recent publications.

Wu Yugui 吴玉貴 is Professor in the Institute of History Studies, Chinese Academy of Social Sciences. His main research interests are the history of the Sui and Tang Dynasties and the ancient Turks. He was the Chinese translator of *The Golden Peaches of Samarkand: A Study of T'ang Exotics* by Edward H. Schafer and *Central Asia* edited by Gavin Hambly. *Historical Studies on the Relationships between the Turk Qaghanates and the Su and Tang Empires* 《突厥汗國與隋唐關係史研究》 (1998) is his representative monograph. He has recently published *Chinese-language Historical Materials on the Second Turkish Qaghanate Chronologically Compiled and Researched*《突厥第二汗國漢文史料編年輯考》 (2009), which is a landmark in the field of Turkish historical studies.

Yao Dali 姚大力 is Professor in the Center of Historical Geography Studies, Fudan University. He was a visiting scholar at the Harvard-Yenching Institute (1993) and the Department of East Asian Languages and Civilizations, Harvard University (1995). His main research interests are the history of the Yuan Dynasty, Mongolic studies, and the history of Inner Asian peoples, on which he has published *Ten Lectures on Inner Asian Peoples*《北方民族史十論》 (2007).

Zhang Guangda 張廣達 was formerly Professor in the Department of History, Peking University. He was a visiting scholar in the Department of East Asia, Princeton University (1999-2002), and is now a visiting Professor in the Department of History, National Chengchi University, Taiwan. His academic interests are the social transformation from the end of the Tang Dynasty to the beginning of the Song Dynasty, cultural exchanges in Medieval Inner Asia, and Sinology and Oriental studies in Europe over the last century. He has published *First Compilation of Collected Papers on the History and Geography of the Western Regions* 《西域史地叢稿初編》 (1995). Recently, a three-volume edition of his collected papers has been edited and published: *Documents, Classical Records, and the History and Geography of the Western Regions* 《文書、典籍與西域史地》 (2008); *Texts, Images, and Cultural Diffusion* 《文本、圖像與文化流傳》 (2008); *Historian, Historiography, and the Modern Academy* 《史家、史學與現代學術》 (2008).

Zhou Qingshu 周清澍 was Professor in the Department of History, University of Inner Mongolia. He is the co-editor of the *Comprehensive History of China* 《中國通史》, volume 6 (1979; with Cai Meibiao 蔡美彪). He was a member of the joint editorship of the punctuated edition of the *History of the Yuan* 《元史》 (1974). He was the editor of *Historical Geography of Inner Mongolia* 《内蒙古歷史地理》 (1993). He has published the *Bibliography of the Editions of the Collections by the Literati Living in the Yuan Dynasty* 《元人文集版本目錄》 (1983).

www.ingramcontent.com/pod-product-compliance
Lightning Source LLC
LaVergne TN
LVHW010347080826
844660LV00003B/210

* 9 7 8 0 9 3 3 0 7 0 5 8 5 *